ROAD ATLAS
ATLANTE STRADALE
ATLAS DE CARRETERAS
ATLAS ROUTIER
STRASSENATLAS

EUROPE
EUROPA

Contents

II-III Legend
IV-V Central-northern Europe 1: 8 000 000
VI-VII Central-southern Europe 1: 8 000 000
VIII Useful information
1-207 **Road atlas**
208-264 Index of names
Principal urban areas plans

Sommario

II-III Legenda
IV-V Europa centro-settentrionale 1: 8 000 000
VI-VII Europa centro-meridionale 1: 8 000 000
VIII Numeri utili
1-207 **Atlante stradale**
208-264 Indice dei nomi
Piante delle principali aree urbane

Sumario

II-III Leyenda
IV-V Europa centro-norte 1: 8 000 000
VI-VII Europa centro-sur 1: 8 000 000
VIII Direcciones útiles
1-207 **Atlas de carreteras**
208-264 Índice de topónimos
Planos de las principales áreas urbanas

Sommaire

II-III Légende
IV-V Europe centre-nord 1: 8 000 000
VI-VII Europe centre-sud 1: 8 000 000
VIII Informations utiles
1-207 **Atlas routier**
208-264 Index des noms
Plans des principales aires urbaines

Inhaltsverzeichnis

II-III Zeichenerklärung
IV-V Mittelnördliche Europa 1: 8 000 000
VI-VII Mittelsüdliche Europa 1: 8 000 000
VIII Nützliche Auskünfte
1-207 **Straßenatlas**
208-264 Namenverzeichnis
Wichtigste Stadtpläne

GB Legend	I Legenda
Toll motorway, dual carriageway	Autostrada a pedaggio a doppia carreggiata
Toll motorway, single carriageway	Autostrada a pedaggio a singola carreggiata
Non-toll motorway, dual carriageway	Autostrada senza pedaggio a doppia carreggiata
Non-toll motorway, single carriageway	Autostrada senza pedaggio a singola carreggiata
Interchange; restricted interchange; service area	Svincolo; svincolo con limitazione; area di servizio
Motorway under construction	Autostrada in costruzione
Motorway in tunnel	Autostrada in galleria
Number of motorway; european road; national road; regional or local road	Numero di autostrada; itinerario europeo; strada nazionale; strada regionale o locale
National road, dual carriageway	Strada nazionale a doppia carreggiata
National road, single carriageway	Strada nazionale a singola carreggiata
Regional road, dual carriageway	Strada regionale a doppia carreggiata
Regional road, single carriageway	Strada regionale a singola carreggiata
Local road, dual carriageway	Strada locale a doppia carreggiata
Local road, single carriageway	Strada locale a singola carreggiata
Secondary road	Strada secondaria
Road under construction	Strada in costruzione
Road in tunnel	Strada in galleria
Motorway distances in kilometres (miles in United Kingdom and Ireland)	Distanze in chilometri (miglia nel Regno Unito e Irlanda) sulle autostrade
Road distances in kilometres (miles in United Kingdom and Ireland)	Distanze in chilometri (miglia nel Regno Unito e Irlanda) sulle strade
Gradient 14% and over; gradient 6%–13%	Pendenza maggiore del 14%; pendenza dal 6% al 13%
Panoramic routes	Percorsi panoramici
Pass with height and winter closure	Passo di montagna, quota e periodo di chiusura invernale
Toll point	Barriera di pedaggio
Railway and tunnel	Ferrovia e tunnel ferroviario
Ferry route (with car transportation) and destination	Linea di traghetto (con trasporto auto) e destinazione
Transport of cars by rail	Trasporto auto per ferrovia
National park, natural reserve	Parco nazionale, riserva naturale
International boundaries	Confini internazionali
Internal boundary	Confine interno
International airport	Aeroporto internazionale
Religious building	Edificio religioso
Castle, fortress	Castello, fortezza
Isolated monument	Monumento isolato
Ruins, archaeological area	Rovine, area archeologica
Cave	Grotta
Natural curiosity	Curiosità naturale
Panoramic view	Punto panoramico
Other curiosities (botanical garden, zoo, amusement park etc.)	Altre curiosità (giardino botanico, zoo, parco divertimenti ecc.)
Town or place of great tourist interest	Città o luogo di grande interesse turistico
Interesting town or place	Città o luogo interessante

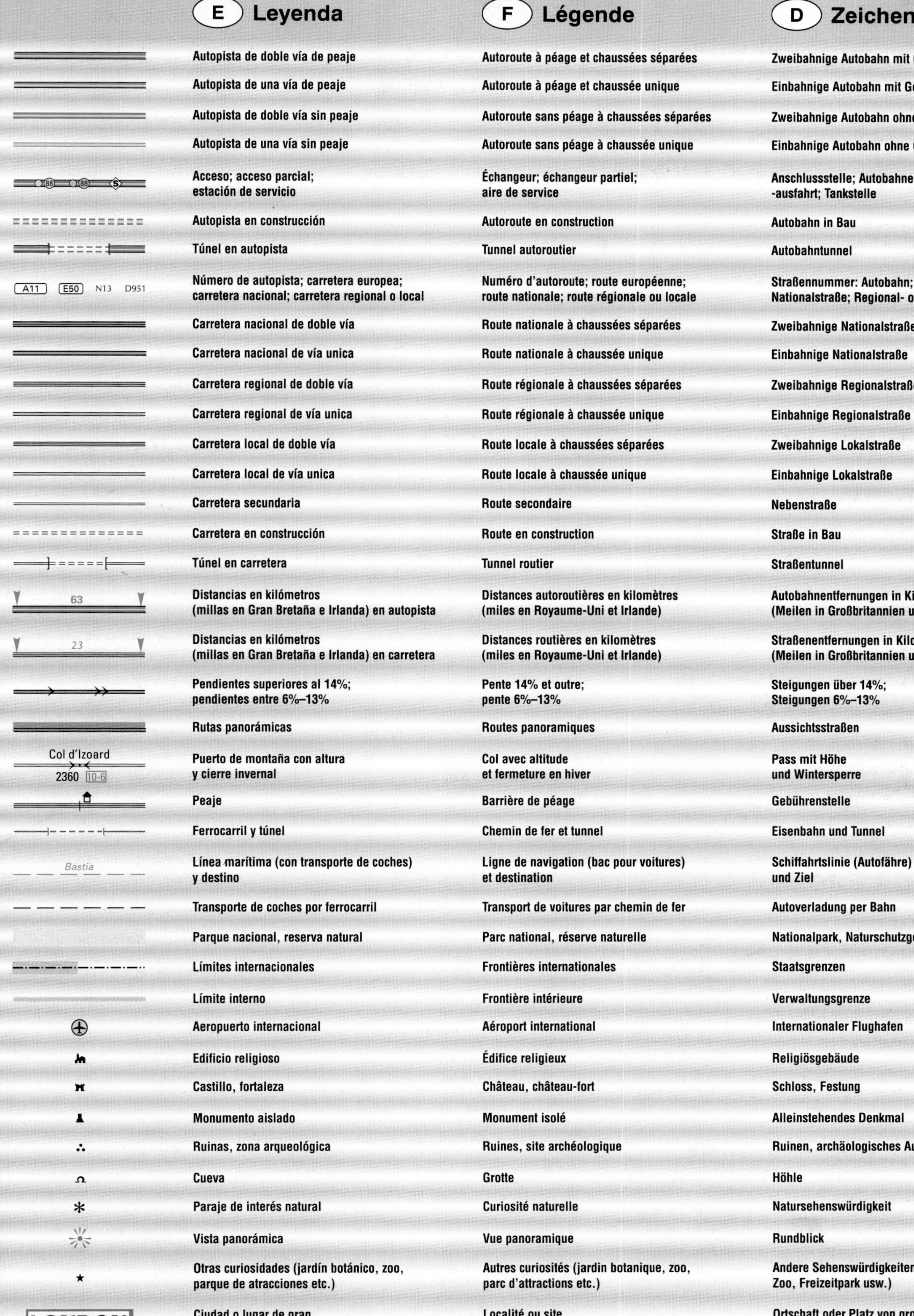

	E Leyenda	F Légende	D Zeichenerklärung
	Autopista de doble vía de peaje	Autoroute à péage et chaussées séparées	Zweibahnige Autobahn mit Gebühr
	Autopista de una vía de peaje	Autoroute à péage et chaussée unique	Einbahnige Autobahn mit Gebühr
	Autopista de doble vía sin peaje	Autoroute sans péage à chaussées séparées	Zweibahnige Autobahn ohne Gebühr
	Autopista de una vía sin peaje	Autoroute sans péage à chaussée unique	Einbahnige Autobahn ohne Gebühr
	Acceso; acceso parcial; estación de servicio	Échangeur; échangeur partiel; aire de service	Anschlussstelle; Autobahnein- und/oder -ausfahrt; Tankstelle
	Autopista en construcción	Autoroute en construction	Autobahn in Bau
	Túnel en autopista	Tunnel autoroutier	Autobahntunnel
A11 E50 N13 D951	Número de autopista; carretera europea; carretera nacional; carretera regional o local	Numéro d'autoroute; route européenne; route nationale; route régionale ou locale	Straßennummer: Autobahn; Europastraße; Nationalstraße; Regional- oder Lokalstraße
	Carretera nacional de doble vía	Route nationale à chaussées séparées	Zweibahnige Nationalstraße
	Carretera nacional de vía unica	Route nationale à chaussée unique	Einbahnige Nationalstraße
	Carretera regional de doble vía	Route régionale à chaussées séparées	Zweibahnige Regionalstraße
	Carretera regional de vía unica	Route régionale à chaussée unique	Einbahnige Regionalstraße
	Carretera local de doble vía	Route locale à chaussées séparées	Zweibahnige Lokalstraße
	Carretera local de vía unica	Route locale à chaussée unique	Einbahnige Lokalstraße
	Carretera secundaria	Route secondaire	Nebenstraße
	Carretera en construcción	Route en construction	Straße in Bau
	Túnel en carretera	Tunnel routier	Straßentunnel
63	Distancias en kilómetros (millas en Gran Bretaña e Irlanda) en autopista	Distances autoroutières en kilomètres (miles en Royaume-Uni et Irlande)	Autobahnentfernungen in Kilometern (Meilen in Großbritannien und Irland)
23	Distancias en kilómetros (millas en Gran Bretaña e Irlanda) en carretera	Distances routières en kilomètres (miles en Royaume-Uni et Irlande)	Straßenentfernungen in Kilometern (Meilen in Großbritannien und Irland)
	Pendientes superiores al 14%; pendientes entre 6%–13%	Pente 14% et outre; pente 6%–13%	Steigungen über 14%; Steigungen 6%–13%
	Rutas panorámicas	Routes panoramiques	Aussichtsstraßen
Col d'Izoard 2360 10-6	Puerto de montaña con altura y cierre invernal	Col avec altitude et fermeture en hiver	Pass mit Höhe und Wintersperre
	Peaje	Barrière de péage	Gebührenstelle
	Ferrocarril y túnel	Chemin de fer et tunnel	Eisenbahn und Tunnel
Bastia	Línea marítima (con transporte de coches) y destino	Ligne de navigation (bac pour voitures) et destination	Schiffahrtslinie (Autofähre) und Ziel
	Transporte de coches por ferrocarril	Transport de voitures par chemin de fer	Autoverladung per Bahn
	Parque nacional, reserva natural	Parc national, réserve naturelle	Nationalpark, Naturschutzgebiet
	Límites internacionales	Frontières internationales	Staatsgrenzen
	Límite interno	Frontière intérieure	Verwaltungsgrenze
⊕	Aeropuerto internacional	Aéroport international	Internationaler Flughafen
	Edificio religioso	Édifice religieux	Religiösgebäude
	Castillo, fortaleza	Château, château-fort	Schloss, Festung
	Monumento aislado	Monument isolé	Alleinstehendes Denkmal
∴	Ruinas, zona arqueológica	Ruines, site archéologique	Ruinen, archäologisches Ausgrabungsgebiet
∩	Cueva	Grotte	Höhle
✳	Paraje de interés natural	Curiosité naturelle	Natursehenswürdigkeit
☀	Vista panorámica	Vue panoramique	Rundblick
★	Otras curiosidades (jardín botánico, zoo, parque de atracciones etc.)	Autres curiosités (jardin botanique, zoo, parc d'attractions etc.)	Andere Sehenswürdigkeiten (Botanischer Garten, Zoo, Freizeitpark usw.)
LONDON	Ciudad o lugar de gran interés turístico	Localité ou site de grand intérêt touristique	Ortschaft oder Platz von großem touristischen Interesse
BIRMINGHAM	Ciudad o lugar interesante	Localité ou site remarquable	Sehenswerte Ortschaft oder Platz

LEGEND - SEGNI CONVENZIONALI - LEYENDA - LÉGENDE - ZEICHENERKLÄRUNG

Motorway and road with motorway characteristics
Autostrada e strada con caratteristiche autostradali
Autopista y autovía con calzadas separadas
Autoroute et route de type autoroutier
Autobahn und Schnellstraße mit getrennten Fahrbahnen

Other roads
Altre strade
Otras carreteras
Autres routes
Sonstige Straßen

E15 — European road number
Numero di strada europea
Número de carretera europea
Numéro de route européenne
Europastraßennummer

169 — Distances in kilometres
Distanze in chilometri
Distancias en kilómetros
Distances en kilomètres
Distanzen in Kilometern

Distances in Great Britain and Ireland are expressed in miles.
Nel Regno Unito e in Irlanda le distanze sono espresse in miglia.
Las distancias en Gran Bretaña e Irlanda son expresas en millas.
Les distances en Grande-Bretagne et Irlande sont exprimées en miles.
Entfernungsangaben in Großbritannien und Irland sind in Meilen wiedergegeben.

Scale - Scala - Escala - Échelle - Maßstab
1 : 8 000 000 (1 cm = 80 km)

0 100 200 300 400 500 km

FØROYAR/ FÆRØERNE
FR
SHETLAND ISLANDS
ORKNEY ISLANDS
HEBRIDES
Thurso
Inverness
Aberdeen
Edinburgh
Glasgow
Stranraer
Carlisle
Newcastle-upon-Tyne
ISLE OF MAN
GBM
GB
Londonderry
Sligo
Larne
Belfast
Galway/ Gaillimh
IRL
DUBLIN/ BAILE ÁTHA CLIATH
Limerick/ Luimneach
Cork/ Corcaigh
Waterford/ Port Lairge
Rosslare
Holyhead
Liverpool
Leeds
Kingston-upon-Hull
Manchester
Fishguard
Birmingham
Norwich
Cambridge
Ipswich
Harwich
Cardiff
Bristol
Oxford
LONDON
Penzance
Plymouth
Southampton
Portsmouth
Dover
Folkestone
CHANNEL ISLANDS
GBG
Cherbourg
Calais
Lille
Oostende
Antwerpen
BRUSSEL / BRUXELLES
B
Liège
AMSTERDAM
Den Haag
Rotterdam
NL
Groningen
Arnhem
Duisburg
Düsseldorf
Köln
Bonn
Dortmund
Kassel
Emden
Bremen
Osnabrück
Hannover
Cuxhaven
Wilhelmshaven
Hamburg
Esbjerg
DK
Ålborg
Kristiansund
Ålesund
Florø
N
Bergen
Haugesund
Stavanger
Kristiansand

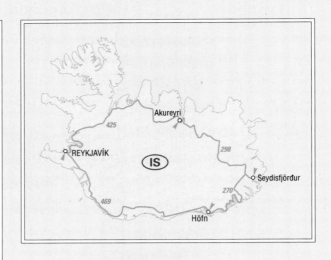

Hammerfest
Kirkenes
Murmansk
Tromsø
Ivalo
Narvik
Sørvågen
Kiruna
Kandalakša
Bodø
Rovaniemi
Mo-i-Rana
Kuusamo
Archangel'sk
Severodvinsk
Luleå
Kemi
Oulu/
Uleåborg
FIN
Storuman
Skellefteå
Umeå
Kokkola/
Karleby
Iisalmi
Trondheim
S
Östersund
Vaasa/
Vasa
Kuopio
Joensuu
Jyväskylä
Petrozavodsk
Sundsvall
Pori/
Björneborg
Tampere/
Tammerfors
Lappeenranta
Lillehammer
Mora
Lahti
Gävle
ÅLAND/
AHVENANMAA
Turku/
Åbo
Vologda
Borlänge
HELSINKI/
HELSINGFORS
Sankt-Peterburg
OSLO
Uppsala
Kappelskär
RUS
Karlstad
STOCKHOLM
TALLINN
Örebro
HIIUMAA
Novgorod
EST
Tartu
Norrköping
Pärnu
SAAREMAA
Pskov
Göteborg
Tver
Jönköping
MOSKVA
GOTLAND
RĪGA
LV
Velikije
Luki
Kalmar
Liepāja
ÖLAND
Daugavpils
Helsingborg
Helsingør
Kristianstad
KØBENHAVN
Klaipėda
Šiauliai
Panevėžys
Vitebsk
Kaluga
Tula
Malmö
LT
Smolensk
Ystad
BORNHOLM
DK
Kaunas
Orša
Kaliningrad
RUS
VILNIUS
Gedser
Saßnitz
Gdańsk
MINSK
Mogil'ov
Bryansk
Rostock
Koszalin
Świnoujście
Orel
Neubrandenburg
Augustów
Grodno
BY
Szczecin
Baranoviči
Bobrujsk
Bydgoszcz
Białystok
Gomel
BERLIN
PL
WARSZAWA
Poznań
Pinsk
Mozyr
Brest
Chernihiv
Łódź
Leipzig
Radom
Lublin
Dresden
KYÏV

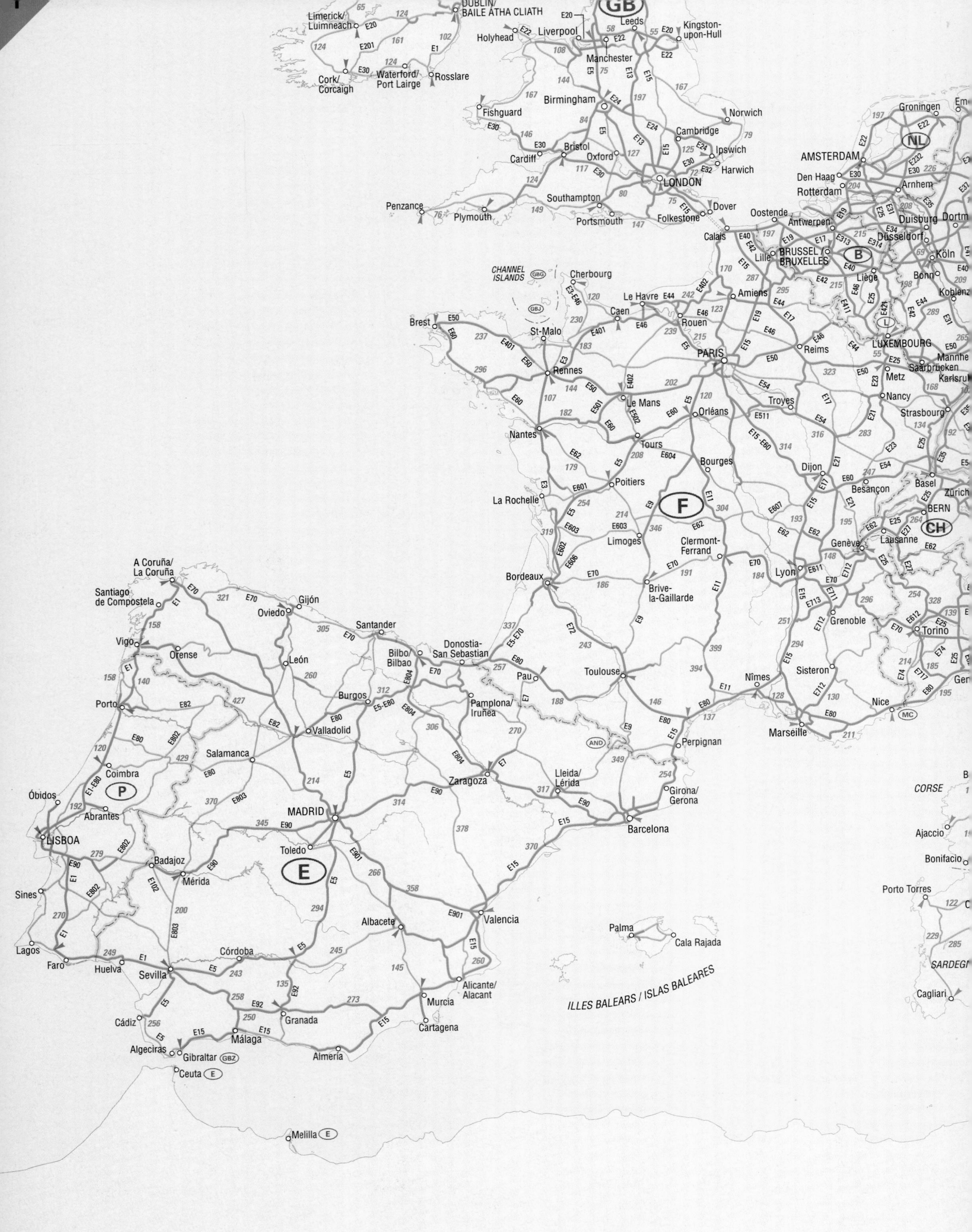

DUBLIN/
BAILE ATHA CLIATH
Limerick/
Luimneach
Cork/
Corcaigh
Waterford/
Port Lairge
Rosslare
Holyhead
Liverpool
Leeds
Kingston-
upon-Hull
Manchester
GB
Birmingham
Fishguard
Norwich
Cambridge
Ipswich
Harwich
Bristol
Oxford
Cardiff
LONDON
Southampton
Portsmouth
Penzance
Plymouth
Dover
Folkestone
Calais
Groningen
NL
AMSTERDAM
Den Haag
Rotterdam
Arnhem
Oostende
Antwerpen
Duisburg
Düsseldorf
Lille
BRUSSEL/
BRUXELLES
B
Köln
Liège
Bonn
Koblenz
CHANNEL
ISLANDS
Cherbourg
Le Havre
Amiens
Caen
Rouen
Brest
St-Malo
PARIS
Reims
LUXEMBOURG
Saarbrücken
Metz
Nancy
Rennes
Le Mans
Orléans
Troyes
Strasbourg
Nantes
Tours
Bourges
Dijon
Basel
Zürich
BERN
CH
Besançon
Poitiers
La Rochelle
F
Limoges
Clermont-
Ferrand
Genève
Lausanne
Bordeaux
Brive-
la-Gaillarde
Lyon
Grenoble
Torino
Toulouse
Nîmes
Sisteron
Nice
Marseille
Perpignan
A Coruña/
La Coruña
Santiago
de Compostela
Gijón
Oviedo
Santander
Vigo
Orense
León
Bilbo/
Bilbao
Donostia-
San Sebastian
Pau
Burgos
Pamplona/
Iruñea
Porto
Valladolid
Salamanca
Zaragoza
Lleida/
Lérida
Girona/
Gerona
Coimbra
P
Óbidos
Abrantes
MADRID
Barcelona
LISBOA
Toledo
Badajoz
Mérida
E
Sines
Valencia
Albacete
Palma
Cala Rajada
Lagos
Faro
Huelva
Córdoba
Sevilla
Alicante/
Alacant
Murcia
Granada
Cartagena
ILLES BALEARS / ISLAS BALEARES
Cádiz
Málaga
Almería
Algeciras
Gibraltar
Ceuta
Melilla
CORSE
Ajaccio
Bonifacio
Porto Torres
SARDEGNA
Cagliari

VII
Odense
Malmö
Ystad
BORNHOLM
DK
Rødbyhavn
Kiel
Puttgarten
Gedser
Saßnitz
Lübeck
Rostock
Hamburg
Świnoujście
Koszalin
Gdańsk
Kaliningrad
RUS
Kaunas
VILNIUS
Neubrandenburg
Szczecin
Augustów
Grodno
MINSK
Orša
Mogil'ov
Smolensk
Bryansk
Hannover
BERLIN
Bydgoszcz
Białystok
Baranoviči
BY
Bobrujsk
Gomel
PL
Poznań
WARSZAWA
Brest
Pinsk
Mozyr
Chernihiv
Magdeburg
Łódź
Radom
Lublin
Kassel
Halle
Leipzig
Erfurt
Dresden
Wrocław
Częstochowa
Luck
KYÏV
D
Zhytomyr
UA
Würzburg
PRAHA
CZ
Katowice
Kraków
Rzeszów
L'viv
Ternopol
Vinnytsia
Kirovohrad
Nürnberg
Plzeň
Ostrava
Stuttgart
Regensburg
Brno
SK
Košice
Uzhorod
Augsburg
München
Linz
WIEN
BRATISLAVA
Miskolc
Chernivtsi
MD
Mikolaiv
Bregenz
Salzburg
A
Győr
BUDAPEST
Satu Mare
Debrecen
CHIŞINĂU
Innsbruck
Graz
Székesfehérvár
Oradea
Cluj Napoca
Bacău
Odessa
Bolzano/
Bozen
H
RO
LJUBLJANA
Pécs
Szeged
Arad
Galaţi
SLO
ZAGREB
Timişoara
Braşov
Tulcea
Verona
Venezia
Trieste
Rijeka
Osijek
Novi Sad
HR
Bihać
Banja
Luka
BEOGRAD
Piteşti
Constanţa
BUCUREŞTI
Bologna
BiH
Zadar
Craiova
Vidin
Ruse
Firenze
RSM
Ancona
SARAJEVO
Užice
Varna
Perugia
Split
Mostar
YU
Niš
Šumen
Veliko
Tŭrnovo
I
Priština
SOFIYA
BG
Burgas
Pescara
Dubrovnik
Podgorica
Stara Zagora
Plovdiv
Shkodër
SKOPJE
Edirne
V
ROMA
İstanbul
MK
İzmit
Foggia
Durrës
TIRANË
Ohrid
Kavála
Bari
Napoli
Thessaloníki
Brindisi
Taranto
Lecce
AL
Çanakkale
Bursa
Balıkesir
Igoumenítsa
Ioánnina
Lárisa
Vólos
GR
TR
Catanzaro
Lamía
ÉVVOIA
Çeşme
İzmir
SICILIA
Trapani
Palermo
Messina
Reggio di Calabria
Pátra
ATHÍNA
Kórinthos
Denizli
Agrigento
Catania
Gela
Kalamáta
Areópoli
RÓDOS
MALTA
M
KRÍTI
Chaniá
Irakleío
Siteía

USEFUL INFORMATION
NUMERI UTILI
DIRECCIONES ÚTILES
INFORMATIONS UTILES
NÜTZLICHE AUSKÜNFTE

			☎	🚔	✚	🔥	ℹ	🚗
A	Österreich	0043	112	112	112	(43) 1 5872000	ÖAMTC (43) 1 711990
AL	Shqiperia	00355	24445*	22235*	23333*	(355) 42 4853	—
AND	Andorra, Andorre	00376	110	116	118	(376) 820214	ACA (376) 8 20890
B	België, Belgique	0032	112	112	112	(32) 2 5040390	TCB (32) 2 2332211
BG	Bǎlgarija	00359	166	150	160	(359) 2 84131	UAB (359) 2 86151
BiH	Bosna i Hercegovina	00387	92	94	93	(387) 71 532281	BIHAMK (387) 71 212772
BY	Belarus'	00375	02	03	01	(375) 17 2269840	ADAS (375) 17 2231055
CH	Schweiz, Suisse, Svizzera	0041	117	144	118	(41) 900 552000	TCS (41) 22 4172424
CZ	Česká Republika	00420	158	155	150	(420) 2 24197111	ÚAMK ČR (420) 2 61104242
D	Deutschland	0049	110	110	112	(49) 69974640	ADAC (49) 8976760
DK	Danmark	0045	112	112	112	(45) 33111325	FDM (45) 45270707
E	España	0034	112	112	112	(34) 91 3433710	RACE (34) 91 5947400
EST	Eesti	00372	110	112	112	(372) 6411420	EAK (372) 6969100
F	France	0033	112	112	112	(33) 1 42967000	ACN (33) 1 44515399
FIN	Suomi, Finland	00358	112	112	112	(358) 9 4176911	ATCF (358) 9 72584400
FL	Fürstentum Liechtenstein	0041	117	144	118	(41) 75 21443	ACFL (41) 75 2326767
GB	United Kingdom	0044	999	999	999	(44) 207 7303400	AA (44) 1256 320123
GR	Hellas	0030	100	104	199	(30) 1 3223111	ELPA (30) 1 6068800
H	Magyarország	0036	107	94	105	(36) 1 3179800	MAK (36) 1 2122938
HR	Hrvatska	00385	92	118	93	(385) 1 4556455	HAK (385) 1 4554433
I	Italia	0039	112	112	115	(39) 06 49711	ACI (39) 06 4477
IRL	Ireland, Éire	00353	112	112	112	(353) 1 6024000	AA (353) 316779950
IS	Ísland	00354	112	113	112	(354) 5 623045	FIB (354) 5 629999
L	Lëtzebuerg, Luxembourg	00352	113	112	113	(352) 222809	ACL (352) 4500451
LT	Lietuva	00370	112	112	112	(370) 2 622610	LAS (370) 2 250556
LV	Latvija	00371	112	196	112	(371) 7213652	LAMB (371) 7325111
M	Malta	00356	191	112	199	(356) 238282	TCM (356) 241665
MC	Principauté de Monaco	00377	112	903	112	(377) 93 92166116	ACM (377) 93152624
MD	Moldova	00373	902	94	901	(373) 2 540301	CTA (373) 2 255513
MK	Makedonija	00389	92	113	93	(389) 91 114359	AMSM (389) 91 116011
N	Norge	0047	112	112	110	(47) 82060100	NAF (47) 22 341400
NL	Nederland	0031	112	112	112	(31) 70 3705705	ANWB (31) 70 3147147
P	Portugal	00351	112	999	112	(351) 21 3575086	ACP (351) 21 3180100
PL	Polska	0048	997	961	998	(48) 22 8260271	PZM (48) 22 8499361
RO	România	0040	955	03	981	(40) 1 6145160	ACR (40) 1 6593910
RUS	Rossija	007	02	112	01	(7) 95 2921278	RAS (7) 95 2297540
S	Sverige	0046	112	155	112	(46) 8 7892490	M (46) 8 6903800
SK	Slovensko	00421	158	112	150	(421) 7 212828	NAMK ŠR (421) 7 43413915
SLO	Slovenija	00386	113	112	112	(386) 61 1891840	AMZS (386) 61 1890600
TR	Türkiye Cumhuriyeti	0090	155	03	110	(90) 312 2128300	TTOK (90) 212 2828140
UA	Ukrajina	00380	02	94	01	(380) 44 2943111	FAU (380) 322 743562
YU	Jugoslavija	00381	92		93	—	AMSJ (381) 11 401699

* Tiranë

ROAD ATLAS
ATLANTE STRADALE
ATLAS DE CARRETERAS
ATLAS ROUTIER
STRASSENATLAS

Legend
Legenda
Leyenda
Légende
Zeichenerklärung

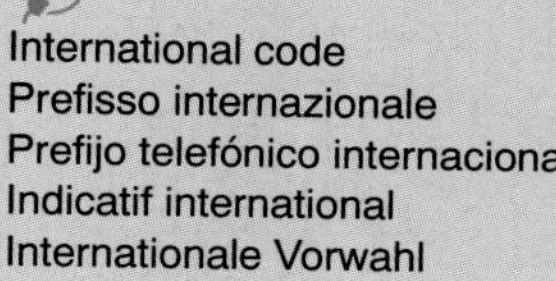

International code
Prefisso internazionale
Prefijo telefónico internacional
Indicatif international
Internationale Vorwahl

Police
Polizia
Policía
Police
Polizei

Ambulance
Ambulanza
Ambulancia
Ambulance
Ambulanz

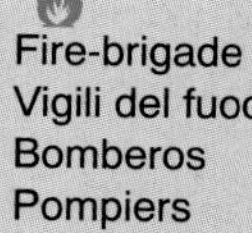

Fire-brigade
Vigili del fuoco
Bomberos
Pompiers
Feuerwehr

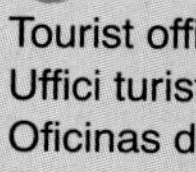

Tourist offices
Uffici turistici
Oficinas de turismo
Bureaux de tourisme
Touristenämter

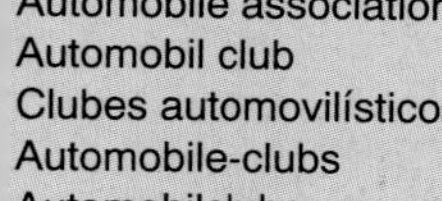

Automobile associations
Automobil club
Clubes automovilísticos
Automobile-clubs
Automobilclubs

A
B
C
D
1
2
3
4
5
6
Aran Is
Rossan Point
Malin More
Glencolumbkille
Gleann Cholm Cil
Carrick/
An Charraig
601
SLIEVE LEAGUE
Kilcar/
Cill Charthaigh
Killybegs
St John's Point
Donegal Bay
Erris Head
Broad Haven
Portacloy
Belmullet/
Béal an Mhuirhead
Knocknalina
Glenamoy
Downpatrick Head
Inishkea North
Inishkea South
Bunnahowen
Aghleam
Duvillaun More
Carrowmore Lough
Ballycastle
Bangor Erris
Creevagh
Killala
Killala Bay
FIRBIS CASTLE
Easky
Inishmurray
Bundoran
Cliffoney
Grange
Kinlough
525
BENBULBEN
Rosses Point
Blacksod Bay
Doohooma
RATHFRAN ABBEY
MOYNE ABBEY
ROSSERK ABBEY
Enniscrone
Dromore West
Sligo Bay
Strandhill
Achill Head
672
SLIEVE MORE
Keel
Shranamanragh Bridge
722
Crossmolina
Ballina
OX MTS
Sligo/
Sligeach
Ballysadare
Lough Gill
Dromahair
Achill Island
Srahmore
807
NEPHIN
Lough Conn
Bunnyconnellan
Collooney
Cloghmore
Lough Feeagh
Moy
Pontoon
Foxford
Tobercurry
Ballymote
Drumkeeran
Clare Island
Bolinglanna
Clew Bay
Newport
Lough Cullin
Swinford
Charlestown
Lough Arrow
Ballyfarnan
Inishturk
Roonah Quay
MURRISK ABBEY
Castlebar
Turlough
Knock International
Ballinafad
Keadue
Inishshark
Inishbofin
Caher Island
Louisburgh
765
CROAGH PATRICK
Westport
ABBEY BALLINTOBER
Kiltimagh
Lough Gara
Lough Key
Kinnadoohy
Balla
Ballaghaderreen
Boyle
KYLEMORE ABBEY
Knock
Letterfrack
682
Lough Carra
Partry
Ballyglass
CONNAUGHT
Grallagh
Mannin Bay
CONNEMARA NATIONAL PARK
730
Leenane
Lough Mask
Claremorris
Ballyhaunis
Loughglinn
Frenchpark
Clifden
Tourmakeady
Elphin
Doonloughan
Maumtrasna
Ballinrobe
Ballindine
CLONALIS HOUSE
Castlerea
RATHCROGHAN
Ballyconneely
Connemara
Castleplunkett
Tulsk
Strokestown
Clonbur
Neale
Kilmaine
Ballymoe
Roundstone
Cong
Lough Corrib
Shrule
Dunmore
Glinsk/
Glinsce
ROSS ABBEY
Glenamaddy
Screeb
Tuam/
Tuaim
Ard
Kilkieran/
Cill Ciaráin
Oughterard
Headford
Lanesborough
Roscommon
Athleague
Knockcroghery
Gorumna Island
Lettermullan
Carraroe
Mount Bellew
RINDOWN CASTLE
Lough Ree
North Sound
Spiddal/
An Spidéal
BALLINDOOLY CASTLE
Caltra
Ballymahon
DUNAENGUS
Inishmore
Monivea
Thomas Street
Galway/Gaillimh
Oranmore
Athenry
Ahascragh
ARAN ISLANDS
Galway Bay
Clarinbridge
Kilconnell
Athlone/
Baile Átha Luain
Ballykeeran
Inisheer
CORCOMROE ABBEY
Craughwell
South Sound
Ballyvaughan
Kinvarra
Loughrea
THE TUROE STONE
Ballinasloe
CLONMACNOISE
Shannon
Shannonbridge
Togher
CLIFFS OF MOHER
The Burren
Lisdoonvarna
KILMACDUAGH CATHEDRAL
Gort
SLIEVE AUGHTY MTS
368
Laurencetown
Ballycumber
Ferbane
Kilfenora
Lahinch
Ennistymon
Lough Cutra
Killimor
Clonfert
Banagher
Clogan
Grand
Mal Bay
Milltown Malbay
Corofin
Kilcormac
Crusheen
Lough Graney
Woodford
Portumna
Birr
Feakle
Doo Lough
Ennis/
Inis
Tulla
Lough Derg
Scarriff
Borrisokane
Kinnitty
Clonaslee
Doonbeg
Kilkee
Cahermurphy
Clarecastle
QUIN ABBEY
Mountshannon
Shinrone
Cooraclare
KNAPPOGUE CASTLE
Newmarket-on-Fergus
532
Portroe
Cloughjordan
529
SLIEVE BLOOM MTS
Loop Head
Kilbaha
Kilrush
Killadysert
Shannon
Broadford
Killaloe
462
MT. ST. JOSEPH ABBEY
Roscrea
Nenagh
Mountrath
Mouth of the Shannon
Killimer
Sixmilebridge
BUNRATTY CASTLE
Ballina
Kerry Head
Ballybunion
Tarbert
Foynes
Bunratty
Cloonlara
Moneygall
Borris-in-Ossory
Ballylongford
Glin
Askeaton
694
Silvermines
Toomyvara
4

E
F
G
H
8
Bridgend
Bowmore
Portnahaven
Loch Indaal
Islay
Laggan Bay
Glenegedale
Lower Killeyan
Mull of Oa
Port Ellen
Ardbeg
Rudha na Traille
Port Mor
Gigha
Tayinloan
Arnicle
Glenbarr
Carradale
Bellochantuy
Sound of Gigha
Machrihanish
Campbeltown
Ru Stafnish
Feochaig
Southend
Mull of Kintyre
Sanda
Tory Island
Tory Sound
Horn Head
Bloody Foreland
Gola Island
Dunfanaghy
Fanad Head
Malin Head
Inishtrahull Sound
Ballyhillin
Malin
Culdaff
Dunaff
Clonmany
Rosapenna
Carrigart
Portsalon
DOE CASTLE
Cresslough
Carndonagh
INISHOWEN
Crolly/
Croithlí
ERRIGAL
GLENVEAGH NATIONAL PARK
Dungloe/
Clochan Liath
Milford
Buncrana
Stroove
Inishowen Head
Rathmullan/
Rathmullen
Carrowkeel
Moville
Kilmacrenan
Lough Foyle
Rathmelton
Muff
City of Derry
GIANT'S CAUSEWAY
DUNLUCE CASTLE
White Park Bay
Rathlin Island
Portrush
Portstewart
Bushmills
Ballycastle
Fair Head
BONAMARGY FRIARY
Letterkenny
GRIANAN OF AILEACH
Carrigans
Eglinton
Limavady
Coleraine
Dervock
Armoy
Glenties
St Johnstown
LONDONDERRY
(DERRY)
ULSTER
Ballybofey
Stranorlar
Lifford
Claudy
Dungiven
Ballymoney
Kilrea
Garvagh
Dunloy
Cushendall
Red Bay
GB
Garron Point
Lough Eske
Donegal /
Dún na nGall
Mount Charles
Strabane
Sion Mills
Clady
Castlederg
SPERRIN MTS
Plumbridge
Swatragh
Rasharkin
Carnlough
Glenarm
NORTHERN
Ballintra
Killeter
Newtownstewart
Gortin
Maghera
Tobermore
Portglenone
Cullybackey
Broughshane
Carnalbanagh
Sheddings
Ballygalley Head
Ballyshannon
Belleek
Pettigo
Glenhull
Draperstown
Gulladuff
Ahoghill
Ballymena
Stranraer
Corsewall Point
Kirkcolm
Lower Lough Erne
Kesh
Drumquin
Omagh
Magherafelt
Bellaghy
IRELAND
Kells
Larne
Rosscor
Garrison
Dromore
Carrickmore
Moneymore
Randalstown
Island Magee
Millbay
Derrygonnelly
Irvinestown
Beragh
Kilderss
SPRINGHILL
Cookstown
Ballyronan
SHANE'S CASTLE
Antrim
Doagh
Ballynure
Ballyclare
Fintona
Seskinore
Pomeroy
Coagh
ARDBOE
Ballycarry
Whitehead
Stranraer
Templepatrick
Belfast International
COOLARKAN CAVE
Ballinamallard
ROUND TOWER
Enniskillen
Stewartstown
Coalisland
Lough Neagh
Crumlin
Portpatrick
Carrickfergus
Belcoo
Ballygawley
Dungannon
DUNSKEY CASTLE
Newtownabbey
Blacklion
MARBLE ARCH CAVE
Fivemiletown
Augher
Clogher
Glenavy
Holywood
Copeland
CASTLE COOLE
Lisbellaw
Aughnacloy
BELFAST
Bangor
FLORENCE COURT
Upper Lough Erne
Maguiresbridge
Moy
Dunmurry
Lisburn
Donaghadee
Swanlinbar
Lisnaskea
Emyvale
Benburb
Loughgall
Lurgan
Newtownards
IRON MTS
Derrylin
Caledon
Craigavon
Mazetown
MOUNT STEWART GARDENS
Newtown Butler
Rosslea
Armagh
Portadown
Hillsborough
Carryduff
Comber
Ballywalter
Drummore
Liverpool
Aghalan
Clones
Monaghan
Tandragee
Gilford
Ballygowan
Greyabbey
Ballinamore
Belturbet
Tyholland
Markethill
Dromore
GARDEN OF ROWALLANE
Saintfield
Kircubbin
Fenagh
Butler's Bridge
Newbliss
Keady
Poyntzpass
Banbridge
Ballynahinch
Killyleagh
Killashandra
Rockcorry
Loughbrickland
DUNDRUM CASTLE
INCH ABBEY
CASTLEWARD HOUSE
Portavogie
Carrigallen
Cootehill
Ballybay
Newtown-hamilton
Portaferry
Mohill
Lough Oughter
Cavan/An Cabhán
DERRYMORE HOUSE
Rathfriland
Strangford
NARROW WATER CASTLE
Newry
Castlewellan
Downpatrick
Castleblayney
Clough
Arvagh
Stradone
Hilltown
Ballinagh
ULSTER
Crossmaglen
MOURNE MTS
Newcastle
Ardglass
Drumlish
Warrenpoint
St John's Point
Shercock
Rostrevor
Lough Gowna
Kilnaleck
Bailieborough
Kilcurry
Longford
Granard
Carrickmacross
Carlingford
Annalong
Ballyjamesduff
Kilkeel
Greencastle
Virginia
Kingscourt
Dundalk /
Dún Dealgan
Isle of Man
Finnea
CASTLE PEEL
Edgeworthstown
Oldcastle
Lough Ramor
Dundalk Bay
Drumconrath
Castlebellingham
Coole
Moynalty
GBM
Ardee
Castlepollard
Lough Derravaragh
Dunany
Dunany Point
Crossakeel
Kells
Dunleer
Port Erin
MELLIFONT ABBEY
Lough Owel
Crookedwood
Kilberry
MONASTERBOICE
Calf of Man
St. Mary
MAN VILLAGE FOLK MUSEUM
Delvin
Clonmellon
Termonfeckin
Ballymore
Slane
Mullingar
Athboy
Navan/
An Uaimh
NEWGRANGE
Drogheda/
Droichead Átha
Raharney
Ballivor
Trim
Duleek
GORMANSTON CASTLE
Kilbeggan
Kinnegad
TARA
Balbriggan
Clonard
Tyrrellspass
Garristown
Naul
IRISH SEA
Rathmolyon
Dunshaughlin
IRL
Skerries
DURROW ABBEY
Tullamore
Enfield
Ashbourne
Daingean
Edenderry
Lusk
10
Rush
Kilcock
Dunboyne
Geashill
Swords
Lambay
Maynooth
Dublin
Malahide
CASTLETOWN HOUSE
Lucan
ST. DOULAGH'S CHURCH
Portmarnock
Rathangen
Celbridge
Kilmeage
Clane
Howth
Portarlington
Clondalkin
Rathcoole
DUBLIN /
BAILE ÁTHA CLIATH
Douglas
Liverpool
Newbridge/
Droichead Nua
Monasterevin
Naas/
An Nás
Tallaght
Kildare
Dun Laoghaire
Kilcullen
Blessington
Dalkey
Holyhead
Stradbally
Ballymore Eustace
5
BATH OF MULLAMAST
POWERSCOURT
Bray/Bré
1
2
3
4
5
6

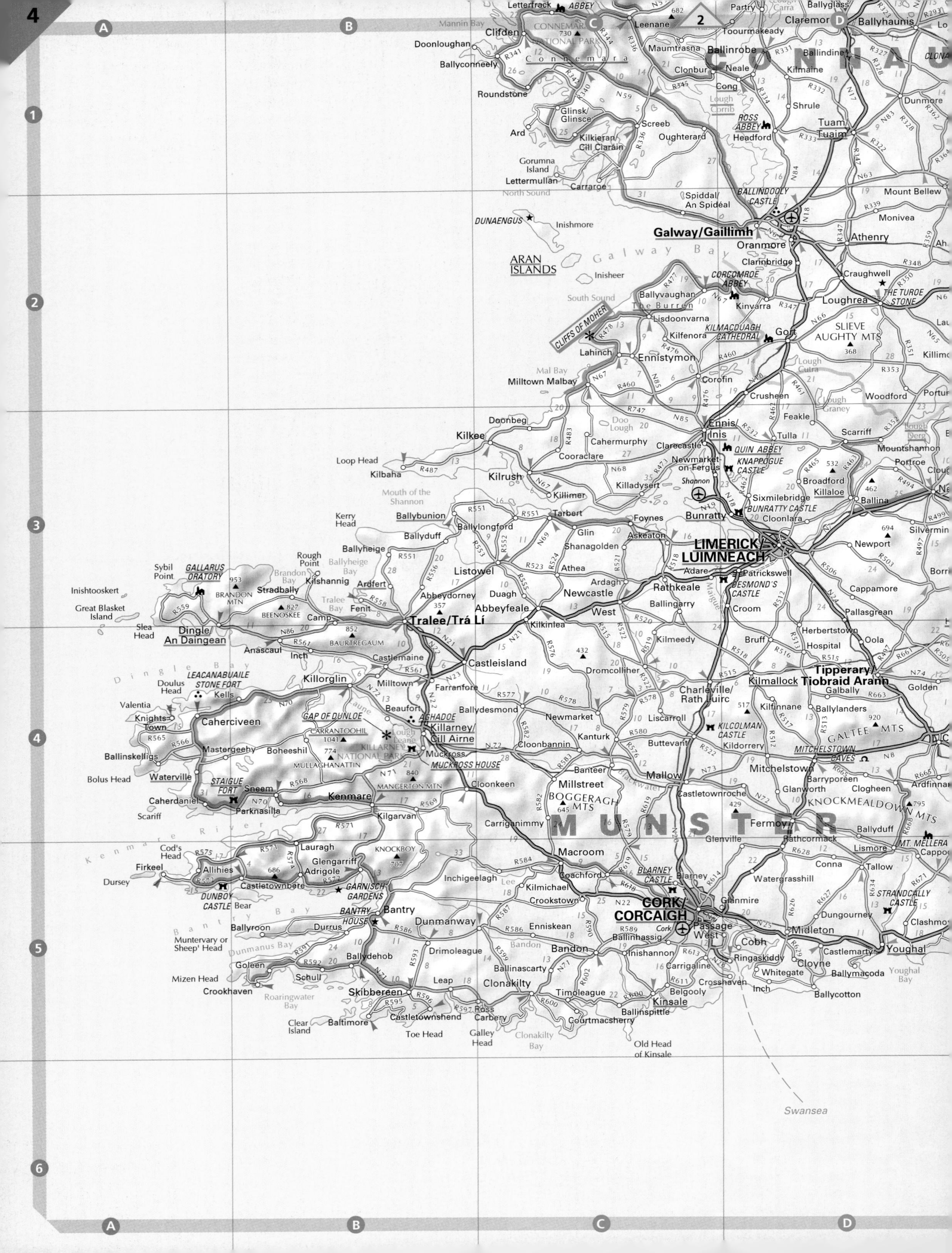
A
B
C
D
1
2
3
4
5
6
CONNAUGHT
MUNSTER
Letterfrack
Clifden
Doonloughan
Ballyconneely
Roundstone
Connemara
CONNEMARA NATIONAL PARK
Leenane
Partry
Claremorris
Ballyhaunis
Tourmakeady
Maumtrasna
Ballinrobe
Ballindine
Clonbur
Neale
Kilmaine
Cong
Lough Corrib
Shrule
Dunmore
Glinsk/Glinsce
Screeb
Oughterard
ROSS ABBEY
Headford
Tuam/Tuaim
Ard
Kilkieran/Cill Ciaráin
Gorumna Island
Lettermullan
Carraroe
North Sound
Spiddal/An Spidéal
BALLINDOOLY CASTLE
Mount Bellew
Monivea
DUNAENGUS
Inishmore
Galway/Gaillimh
Oranmore
Athenry
ARAN ISLANDS
Galway Bay
Inisheer
Clarinbridge
Craughwell
CORCOMROE ABBEY
South Sound
Ballyvaughan
The Burren
Kinvarra
Loughrea
THE TUROE STONE
CLIFFS OF MOHER
Lisdoonvarna
Kilfenora
KILMACDUAGH CATHEDRAL
Gort
SLIEVE AUGHTY MTS
Lahinch
Ennistymon
Mal Bay
Milltown Malbay
Corofin
Crusheen
Woodford
Doonbeg
Doo Lough
Ennis/Inis
Feakle
Kilkee
Cahermurphy
Clarecastle
Tulla
Scarriff
Loop Head
Cooraclare
QUIN ABBEY
Mountshannon
Kilbaha
Kilrush
Newmarket-on-Fergus
KNAPPOGUE CASTLE
Portroe
Killadysert
Shannon
Broadford
Killaloe
Mouth of the Shannon
Killimer
Sixmilebridge
BUNRATTY CASTLE
Ballina
Kerry Head
Ballybunion
Tarbert
Foynes
Bunratty
Cloonlara
Ballylongford
Glin
Askeaton
LIMERICK/LUIMNEACH
Silvermines
Ballyduff
Shanagolden
Newport
Ballyheige
Rough Point
Ballyheige Bay
Listowel
Athea
Adare
Patrickswell
Sybil Point
GALLARUS ORATORY
Brandon Bay
Kilshannig
Ardfert
Ardagh
Rathkeale
DESMOND'S CASTLE
Cappamore
Inishtooskert
BRANDON MTN
Stradbally
Abbeydorney
Duagh
Newcastle
Great Blasket Island
BEENOSKEE
Tralee Bay
Camp
Fenit
Abbeyfeale
West
Ballingarry
Croom
Pallasgreen
Slea Head
Dingle/An Daingean
Tralee/Trá Lí
Kilkinlea
Herbertstown
BAURTREGAUM
Oola
Anascaul
Inch
Kilmeedy
Bruff
Hospital
Dingle Bay
Castlemaine
Castleisland
Dromcolliher
Tipperary/Tiobraid Arann
Doulus Head
LEACANABUAILE STONE FORT
Killorglin
Milltown
Charleville/Rath Luirc
Kilmallock
Galbally
Golden
Kells
Farranfore
Valentia
Knights-Town
GAP OF DUNLOE
Beaufort
AGHADOE
Ballydesmond
Newmarket
Liscarroll
Kilfinnane
Ballylanders
Cahersiveen
CARRANTOOHIL
Killarney/Cill Airne
KILCOLMAN CASTLE
GALTEE MTS
Mastergeehy
Boheeshil
KILLARNEY NATIONAL PARK
Cloonbannin
Kanturk
Buttevant
Kildorrery
MITCHELSTOWN CAVES
Ballinskelligs
MULLAGHANATTIN
Muckross
MUCKROSS HOUSE
Banteer
Mallow
Mitchelstown
Bolus Head
Waterville
MANGERTON MTN
Millstreet
Barryporeen
Clogheen
Ardfinnan
STAIGUE FORT
Sneem
Kenmare
Cloonkeen
BOGGERAGH MTS
Castletownroche
Glanworth
KNOCKMEALDOWN MTS
Caherdaniel
Parknasilla
Kilgarvan
Carriganimmy
Fermoy
Ballyduff
Scariff
Kenmare River
Glenville
Rathcormack
MT. MELLERAY
Cod's Head
Lauragh
KNOCKBOY
Macroom
Lismore
Cappoquin
Firkeel
Allihies
Glengarriff
Adrigole
Inchigeelagh
Coachford
BLARNEY CASTLE
Blarney
Watergrasshill
Conna
Tallow
Dursey
DUNBOY CASTLE
Bear
Castletownbere
GARNISH GARDENS
Kilmichael
Crookstown
Glanmire
STRANCALLY CASTLE
BANTRY HOUSE
Bantry
Dunmanway
CORK/CORCAIGH
Dungourney
Bantry Bay
Ballyroon
Durrus
Enniskean
Passage West
Ballinhassig
Midleton
Clashmore
Muntervary or Sheep' Head
Dunmanus Bay
Drimoleague
Bandon
Cobh
Castlemartyr
Youghal
Ballydehob
Ballinascarty
Inishannon
Carrigaline
Ringaskiddy
Cloyne
Goleen
Schull
Whitegate
Ballymacoda
Youghal Bay
Mizen Head
Crookhaven
Roaringwater Bay
Leap
Clonakilty
Timoleague
Belgooly
Crosshaven
Inch
Ballycotton
Skibbereen
Kinsale
Castletownshend
Ross Carbery
Ballinspittle
Clear Island
Baltimore
Toe Head
Galley Head
Clonakilty Bay
Courtmacsherry
Old Head of Kinsale
Swansea

E
F
G
H
3
ULSTER
LEINSTER
IRL
GB
Frenchpark
Drumsna
Killashandra
Butler's Bridge
Rockcorry
Ballybay
Newtown-hamilton
Poyntzpass
Loughbrickland
DUNDRUM CASTLE
INCH ABBEY
Castlerea
Elphin
Mohill
Carrigallen
Lough Oughter
Cootehill
DERRYMORE HOUSE
Rathfriland
Downpatrick
RATHCROGHAN
Castleplunkett
Tulsk
Cavan/An Cabhán
Castleblayney
Newry
NARROW WATER CASTLE
Castlewellan
Clough
Ballymoe
Strokestown
Roosky
Arvagh
Stradone
Ballinagh
Hilltown
MOURNE MTS
Newcastle
Ardglass
Drumlish
Shercock
Crossmaglen
Warrenpoint
St John's Point
Lough Gowna
Kilnaleck
Bailieborough
Carrickmacross
Kilcurry
Rostrevor
CASTLE FORBES
Longford
Granard
Carlingford
Annalong
Roscommon
Lanesborough
Ballyjamesduff
Virginia
Kingscourt
Dundalk / Dún Dealgan
Kilkeel
Greencastle
Athleague
Killashee
Finnea
Knockcroghery
Oldcastle
Lough Ramor
Edgeworthstown
Drumconrath
Dundalk Bay
RINDOWN CASTLE
Keenagh
Lough Ree
Coole
Moynalty
Castlebellingham
Castlepollard
Lough Derravaragh
Ardee
Dunany
Dunany Point
Thomas Street
Ballymahon
Crossakeel
Kells
Dunleer
MELLIFONT ABBEY
Moyvore
Lough Owel
Crookedwood
Delvin
Clonmellon
Kilberry
MONASTERBOICE
Athlone/ Baile Átha Luain
Ballymore
Slane
Termonfeckin
Ballykeeran
Mullingar
NEWGRANGE
Athboy
Navan/ An Uaimh
Drogheda/ Droichead Átha
Ballinasloe
Moate
CLONMACNOISE
Raharney
Ballivor
Shannon
Trim
Duleek
Shannonbridge
Togher
Kinnegad
GORMANSTON CASTLE
Kilbeggan
Ballycumber
Clonard
Rathmolyon
TARA
Boyne
Garristown
Naul
Balbriggan
Ferbane
Clara
Tyrrellspass
Dunshaughlin
Clonfert
Grand Canal
DURROW ABBEY
Enfield
Ashbourne
Skerries
Banagher
Clogan
Tullamore
Daingean
Edenderry
Lusk
Kilcormac
Kilcock
Dunboyne
Rush
Birr
Killeigh
Geashill
Maynooth
Swords
Lambay
Dublin
Malahide
CASTLETOWN HOUSE
Lucan
ST.DOUGLAH'S CHURCH
Kinnitty
Clonaslee
Rathangen
Celbridge
Portmarnock
Howth
Portarlington
Kilmeage
Clane
Clondalkin
Shinrone
SLIEVE BLOOM MTS
Mountmellick
Rathcoole
DUBLIN / BAILE ÁTHA CLIATH
MT. ST. JOSEPH ABBEY
Newbridge/ Droichead Nua
Tallaght
Roscrea
Monasterevin
Portlaoise
Naas/ An Nás
Douglas
Liverpool
Mountrath
Kildare
Dun Laoghaire
Moneygall
Borris-in-Ossory
Kilcullen
Blessington
Dalkey
Stradbally
Ballymore Eustace
Poulaphouca Resr
Holyhead
Fontstown
Bray/Bré
Donaghmore
Abbeyleix
Timahoe
Athy
RATH OF MULLAMAST
Dunlavin
POWERSCOURT HOUSE
MULLAGHCLEEVAUN
Templetouhy
Durrow
Ballinakill
HIGH CROSS
Greystones
LOUGHMOE CASTLE
Ballylynan
GLENDALOUGH
WICKLOW
Roundwood
Kilcoole
Johnstown
Clogh
Castledermot
Newtownmountkennedy
Ballyragget
Baltinglass
LUGNAQUILLA MTS
Laragh
Urlingford
Castlecomer
Freshford
Carlow/ Ceatharlach
Rathvilly
Glenealy
Rathnew
Wicklow
KILCOOLEY ABBEY
DUNMORE CAVES
Rathdrum
Hacketstown
Wicklow Head
Kilkenny/ Cill Chainnigh
Tullow
Leighlinbridge
Killenaule
Paulstown
Aughrim
Bagenalstown/ Muine Bheag
CASTLE HOWARD
Brittas Bay
Ballingarry
Ballon
Tinahely
Callan
Gowran
Myshall
Shillelagh
Mizen Head
IRISH SEA
Fethard
Goresbridge
Borris
Carnew
SLIEVE NAMAN
MT LEINSTER
Arklow/ An Tinbhear Mór
Thomastown
Bunclody
Kilmaganny
JERPOINT ABBEY
Graiguenamanagh
Kilmichael Point
Gorey
Knocktopher
Clonmel / Cluain Meala
Kiltealy
Ferns
Courtown Harbour
Ballycanew
Carrick-on-Suir
Enniscorthy
Ballyedmund
Cahore Point
FAUSCOUM
Mullinavat
Clonroche
Glenmore
New Ross/ Ros Mhic Thriúin
CURRAGHMORE
WATERFORD/ PORT LÁIRGE
J.F.KENNEDY MEMORIAL FOREST PARK
Aberdaron
Blackwater
Bardsey Island
Kilmeaden
DUNBRODY ABBEY
Kill
Taghmon
Castlebridge
Bunmahon
Arthurstown
Passage East
Wexford/Loch Garman
Wexford Bay
Annestown
Tramore
TINTERN ABBEY
Dunmore East
Fethard
Duncormick
Churchtown
Ballyteige Bay
Rosslare Harbour
Hook Head
Kilmore Quay
Churchtown
Carnsore Point
ST GEORGE'S CHANNEL
Pembroke
Cherbourg
New Quay
Strumble Head
Cardigan
Fishguard
Newport
CILGERRAN CASTLE
PEMBROKESHIRE COAST
Ramsey
St. David's
Newcastle Emlyn
12
10
1
2
3
4
5
6

OUTER HEBRIDES
Isle of Lewis
Rudha Rhobhanais/ Butt of Lewis
Port Nis/ Port of Ness
Barabhas/ Barvas
Tolastadh/ Tolsta
Tolsta Head
Gallan Head
Tobson
Miabhig/ Miavag
DUM CARLOWAY BROCH
Breascleit/ Breasclete
Islivig/ Islibhig
STANDING STONES
Broad Bay
Tiumpan Head
Mealasta
Steornabhagh/ Stornoway
LEWS CASTLE
Portnaguran/ Portnan Giuran
Scarp
Baile Ailein/ Balallan
Tabhaidh Mhor
Hushinish
West Loch Tarbert
Leumrabhagh/ Lemreway
Taransay
Tairbeart/ Tarbert
Eilean Iubhard
Toe Head
Pabbay
Scalpay
Ensay
Shiant Islands
Berneray
Boreray
Port nan Long/ Newtonferry
Roghadal/ Rodel
Harris
Renish Point
Tigha Ghearraidh/ Tigharry
Sound of Harris
Loch nam Madadh/ Lochmaddy
Monach Island
Baleshare
Sidinish
Uibhist a Tuath/ North Uist
Baile a Mhanaich/ Bailivanich
Ronay
Beinn na Faoghla/ Benbecula
Ardivachar Point
Creagorry/ Creag Ghoraidh
Wiay
Stadhlaigearraidh/ Stilligarry
Uibhist a Deas/ South Uist
Loch Baghasdail/ Lochboisdale
Pollachar
Sgeir a' Mhill
Eriskay
Sound of Barra
Bagh a Chaisteil/ Castlebay
The Little Minch
The Minch
Rudha Hunish
Duntulm
Waternish Point
Loch Snizort
Loch Dunvegan
Stein
Quiraing
Staffin
Uig
Claigan
Milovaig
Neist Point
OLD MAN OF STORR
THE STORR
DUNVEGAN CASTLE
Dunvegan
Bernisdale
Sound of Raasay
PRINCE CHARLE'S CAVE
Portree
Bracadale
Idrigill Point
Wiay
Isle of Skye
Sligachan
Loch Eynon
Sconser
Raasay
Inner Sound
Rona
Applecross
Toscaig
Crowlin
Scalpay
Loch Brittle
SGURR ALASDAIR
BLAVEN
Rudh'an Dunain
Broadford
Elgol
Soay
Loch Scavaig
Loch Eishort
Canna
Sanday
Sound of Canna
Isle Ornsay
Tarskavaig
Rum
Kinloch
Ardvasar
Sound of Sleat
Point of Sleat
Sound of Rum
Mallaig
Cleadale
Eigg
Arisaig
Muck
Port Mór
Loch Morar
Lochailort
Sound of Arisaig
Rhudha Aird Druimnich
Point of Ardnamurchan
Ardnamurchan
Portuairk
Kilchoan
Acharacle
Salen
Polloch
Ardmore Point
Calliach Point
Tobermory
Drimnin
Strontian
Treshnish Point
Loch Frisa
Loch Tuath
Sound of Mull
ARDTORNISH CASTLE
Lochaline
Ulva
Staffa
FINGAL'S CAVE
Loch Na Keal
INNER HEBRIDES
Coll
Sorisdale
Arinagour
Arileod
Tiree
Scarinish
Balephuil
Skerryvore
Castlebay
Scurrival Point
Pollachar
Eriskay
Barra
KIESSIMUL CASTLE
Vatersay
Bagh a Chaisteil/ Castlebay
Sandray
Pabbay
Oban
Cape Wrath
Sandwood Loch
Balchrick
Kinlochbervie
Loch Inchard
Gualin House
Loch Laxford
Handa
OINAVEN
Scourie
Eddrachillis Bay
Alltnacai
Point of Stoer
Loch More
Stoer
QUINAG
Loch Glendhu
BEN HEE
Lochinver
Loch Glencoul
Loch Assynt
Rudha Coigeach
Reiff
Enard Bay
Inchnadamph
Summer Isles
Cam Loch
BEN MORE ASSYNT
Achiltibuie
Duchally
Priest Island
Knockan
Ledmore
Loch Lurgainn
Loch Shin
Greenstone Point
Horse Island
Loch Urigill
Opinan
Rudha Reidh
Gruinard
Cove
Laide
Ullapool
Melvaig
Loch Ewe
INVEREWE GARDENS
Longa
Dundonnell
AN TEALLACH
Croick
Loch Gairloch
Gairloch
Fionn Loch
Port Henderson
Braemore
Loch Maree
Lochan Fada
CORRIESHALLOCH GORGE
Talladale
Rudha na Fearn
Loch a' Bhraoin
SGURR MOR
Loch Glascamoch
Fearnmore
Loch Torridon
LAITHACH
Kinlochewe
Loch Fannich
Inchbae Lodge
Torridon
Shieldaig
BEN WYVIS
Loch Glass
Loch Damh
Achnasheen
Craig
GB
Contin
Dingwall
Loch Kishorn
Lochcarron
Orrin Resr
Muir of Ord
BEAULY PRIORY
Kyle of Lochalsh
Kyleakin
SGURR NA LAPAICH
Mullardoch House
EILEAN DONAN CASTLE
Cannich
Inverness
Loch Mullardoch
Affric Lodge
Shiel Bridge
Drumnadrochit
Dores
URQUHART CASTLE
Loch Affric
THE SADDLE
Cluanie
Loch Cluanie
Kinloch Hourn
Invermoriston
Errogie
Loch Nevis
Ceannacroc Lodge
Loch Ness
Loch Mhor
Fort Augustus
Loch Quoich
Tomdoun
Coignafearn
Murlaggan
Loch Garry
Invergarry
Loch Lochy
Brae Roy Lodge
Loch Arkaig
ACHNA CARRY HOUSE
Glenfinnan
Spey
Newtonmore
Loch Shiel
Spean Bridge
Cromra
Loch Eil
Fort William
INVERLOCHY CASTLE
BEN NEVIS
Moy
Ardgour
Loch Treig
Loch Ericht
Loch Leven
Kinlochleven
Pass of Drumochter
Glencoe
Blackwater Resr
Loch Linnhe
Ballachulish
Pass of Glencoe
Loch Garry
CASTLE STALKER
Portnacroish
Loch Laidon
Loch Errochty
Tummel
HIGHLANDS
NORTH WEST HIGHLANDS
GRAMPIAN MOUNTAINS
SCOTLAND

8

7
E
F
G
H
1
2
3
4
5
6
ORKNEY
ISLANDS
Lerwick
Mull Head
NOLTLAND CASTLE
KNAP OF HOWAR
Westray
Papa
Westray
Pierowall
Hollandstoun
North
Ronaldsay
Fair Isle
The North Sound
Rapness
Westray Firth
Rousay
Wasbister
Calfsound
Northwall
Eday
Sanday
Birsay
A966
ST. MAGNUS
CHURCH
Braeswick
Egilsay
Backaland
Mainland
Dounby
SKARA BRAE
Hackland
Stronsay Firth
Whitehall
RING OF BRODGAR
Stromness
Balfour
Stronsay
MAES
HOWE
Finstown
Stenness
Lamb Head
Shapinsay
OLD MAN OF HOY
DWARFIE
STONE
Rora Head
Kirkwall
Auskerry
Rackwick
Houton
Hoy
Cava
Scapa
Flow
Skaill
St Marys
Lyness
Burray
Copinsay
Melsetter
Flotta
HOWE OF HOXA
St Margaret's Hope
Tor Ness
South
Ronaldsay
Swona
Burwick
Brough Ness
Pentland Firth
Dunnet
Head
Stroma
Whiten Head
Strathy Point
Bettyhill
A838
A836
Melvich
Scrabster
Thurso
CASTLE OF MEY
Tongue
Reay
Duncansby Head
Lettermore
Achargary
Castletown
John O'Groats
Loch
Loyal
Loch
Calder
BRAAL CASTLE
Dalhavaig
Halkirk
Syre
B873
B871
A897
Sinclair's Bay
Westerdale
Walten
Noss Head
Loch
Naver
Badanloch
Lodge
Wick
961
BEN
KLIBRECK
Loch
Rimsdale
Loch
Choire
Achavanich
CASTLE OF
OLD WICK
Kinbrace
705
MORVEN
Latheron
STONE ROWS
Braemore
Lybster
Kildonan
Lodge
Dunbeath
Aberdeen
Loch
Brora
Helmsdale
DUNROBIN
CASTLE
Lothbeg Point
Golspie
Dornoch
Tarbat Ness
Tain
Portmahomack
Balintore
Invergordon
Cromarty
Moray Firth
SHETLAND
ISLANDS
Herma Ness
Unst
Burrafirth
North Neaps
Baltasound
Haroldswick
Cullivoe
Gutcher
Yell
Uyeasound
Uyea
The Faither
Isbister
Mid
Yell
West
Sandwick
Tresta
Fetlar
Yell
Sound
GATE OF GIANTS
Hillswick
Ollaberry
Funzie
Rams
Ness
Booth of Toft
Ulsta
Burravoe
St Magnus
Bay
Muckle
Roe
Lunna Ness
Papa Stour
Brae
Hamnavoe
Laxo
Out Skerries
Sandness
Voe
Vidlin
Whalsay
Symbister
418
Foula
Walls
Bixter
Brettabister
Vaila
Heglibister
Mainland
GB
Scalloway
Score Head
Lerwick
West Burra
Kirkabister
Isle of Noss
Bressay
ORKNEYMAN'S CAVE
Fladdabister
Sandwick
MOUSA BROCH
Fitful Head
Tolob
Grutness
Stromness
Aberdeen
Sumburgh Head
JARLSHOF
The Bar
Burghead
Hopeman
Lossiemouth
SUENO'S
STONE
DUFFUS CASTLE
SPYNIE
PALACE
Nairn
Spey Bay
Forres
Elgin
Kingston
Buckie
Cullen
Littlemill
PLUSCARDEN
ABBEY
CULLEN
HOUSE
Banff
Macduff
Troup Head
Rothes
CRAIGSTON
CASTLE
Aitnoch
Craigellachie
Keith
Fraserburgh
Lochindorb
Aberlour
Aberchirder
Loch of
Strathberg
BALVENIE CASTLE
DELGATE
CASTLE
New
Pitsligo
Grantown-
on-Spey
Dufftown
BEN RINNES
Huntly
Turriff
DEER ABBEY
Dulnain
Bridge
Shenval
AUCHINDOUN
CASTLE
Mintlaw
PICARDY
STONE
Peterhead
LEITH
HALL
HADDO
HOUSE
Methlick
Tomintoul
Rhynie
Stromness
LOCH EN EILEAN
THE BUCK
KILDRUMMY
CASTLE
Insch
TOLQUHON
CASTLE
Buchan Ness
CAIRNGORM
MOUNTAINS
STONE CIRCLE
BULLERS OF BUCHANS
Strathdon
Oldmeldrum
Ellon
Lerwick
Cruden
Bay
1309
BEN MACDHUI
CRAIGIEVAR
CASTLE
Alford
Inverurie
PITMEDDEN
HOUSE
SLAINS CASTLE
CRATHIE
CHURCH
873
MORVEN
CASTLE
FRASER
KINKELL
CHURCH
Newburgh
Crathie
STONE
CIRCLE
MIDMAR
CASTLE
Aberdeen
Dyce
Braemar
Aboyne
Inverey
BALMORAL
CASTLE
Ballater
CRATHES
CASTLE
DRUM
CASTLE
ABERDEEN
Loch
Muick
670
Cairnwell Pass
Banchory
Peterculter
Girdle Ness
9
Auchronie
Bridge
MUCHALLS CASTLE

6
10
INNER HEBRIDES
Isle of Mull
Skerryvore
Balephuil
Scarinish
Treshnish Point
Loch Tuath
Staffa
FINGAL'S CAVE
Ulva
Iona
Fionnphort
THE BURGH
Bunessan
Rudh' Ardalanish
BEN MORE
Loch Scridain
Loch Frisa
Salen
Drimnin
ARDTORNISH CASTLE
Lochaline
Craignure
Lismore
Firth of Lorne
DUNSTAFFNAGE CASTLE
Oban
ARDCHATTAN PRIORY
Loch Etive
CASTLE STALKER
Portnacroish
Achnacroish
Ballachulish
Glencoe
Kinlochleven
BEN NEVIS
Ardgour
Loch Leven
Blackwater Resr
Pass of Glencoe
Loch Laidon
Rannoch Station
Gualachulain
Bridge of Orchy
Bridge of Balgie
Cashlie
BEN DORAIN
BEN CRUACHAN
KILCHURN CASTLE
Tyndrum
BEN LUI
Crianlarich
Luib
Killin
BEN MORE
Lochearn
Seil
Easdale
Luing
Lunga
Scarba
Gulf of Corryvreckan
Loch Avich
Loch Awe
Kilmelford
Eilean Dubh
Kiloran
Colonsay
Scalasaig
Oronsay
CARNASSARIE CASTLE
Kilmartin
Ford
Inveraray
Cairndow
Ardlui
Furnace
MINARD CASTLE
Strachur
Lochgoilhead
THE COBBLER
Tarbet
Stronachlacher
BEN LEDI
BEN VENUE
THE TROSSACHS
Callander
QUEEN ELIZABETH FOREST PARK
Aberfoyle
INCHMAHOME PRIORY
ARGYLL FOREST PARK
STANDING STONE
Tayvallich
Lochgilphead
Ardlussa
Jura
Lagg
Sound of Jura
Rudha a' Mhail
Ardnave Point
Ardnave
Sanaigmore
Coul Point
Port Askaig
Feolin Ferry
Craighouse
Port Charlotte
Bridgend
Bowmore
Loch Indaal
Portnahaven
Islay
Laggan Bay
Glenegedale
Lower Killeyan
Port Ellen
Ardbeg
Mull of Oa
Rudha na Traille
Loch Coalisport
CASTLE SWEEN
Kilberry
Tighnabruaich
Otter Ferry
Glendaruel
Ardentinny
Garelochead
Luss
Loch Lomond
Balmaha
Coulport
Helensburgh
Colintraive
Dunoon
Innellan
Gourock
Greenock
Balloch
Alexandria
Dumbarton
Stirling
Port Lamont
Rothesay
Tarbert
Kennacraig
Skipness
Claonaig
Gigha
Port Mor
Sound of Gigha
Firth of Clyde
Skelmorlie
Kilmacolm
HILL OF STAKE
Glasgow
Clydebank
GLASGOW
Lennoxtown
Kilsyth
Largs
Millport
Johnstone
Paisley
Kilbirnie
Beith
Dalry
West Kilbride
East Kilbride
Motherwell
Hamilton
Bothwell
Sound of Bute
Lochranza
Kilchattan
Tayinloan
Arnicle
Glenbarr
Carradale
Bellochantuy
Kilbrannan Sound
Pirnmill
Dougarie
GOAT FELL
Brodick
Arran
Holy Island
Whiting Bay
Ardrossan
Saltcoats
Kilwinning
ROWALLAN CASTLE
Stewarton
Irvine
Kilmarnock
Galston
Strathaven
CRAIGNETHAN CASTLE
Kirkmuirhill
Darvel
Troon
Prestwick
Ayr
Dungavel
Mauchline
Machrihanish
Campbeltown
Southend
Mull of Kintyre
Sanda
Ru Stafnish
Feochaig
Inishowen Head
GIANT'S CAUSEWAY
DUNLUCE CASTLE
White Park Bay
Rathlin Island
Portrush
Portstewart
Bushmills
Ballycastle
Fair Head
BONAMARGY FRIARY
Coleraine
Dervock
Armoy
Ballymoney
Cushendall
Red Bay
Garron Point
Garvagh
Kilrea
Dunloy
Rasharkin
Carnlough
Glenarm
Portglenone
Cullybackey
Broughshane
Carnalbanagh
Sheddings
Ballygalley Head
Gulladuff
Ahoghill
Ballymena
Bellaghy
Kells
Larne
Randalstown
Ballyronan
Island Magee
Millbay
Ballynure
Doagh
SHANE'S CASTLE
Antrim
Ballyclare
Coagh
ARDBOE
Belfast International
Ballycarry
Whitehead
Templepatrick
Carrickfergus
Lough Neagh
Crumlin
Newtownabbey
Glenavy
Holywood
BELFAST
Bangor
Copeland
Donaghadee
Dunmurry
Lisburn
Lurgan
Newtownards
MOUNT STEWART GARDENS
Mazetown
Craigavon
Hillsborough
Carryduff
Comber
Ballygowan
Ballywalter
Greyabbey
Gilford
Dromore
GARDEN OF ROWALLANE
Saintfield
Kircubbin
Banbridge
Ballynahinch
Killyleagh
Portavogie
Loughbrickland
DUNDRUM CASTLE
INCH ABBEY
CASTLEWARD HOUSE
Portaferry
Rathfriland
NARROW WATER CASTLE
Downpatrick
Strangford
Castlewellan
Hilltown
Clough
MOURNE MTS
Newcastle
Ardglass
Warrenpoint
St John's Point
Rostrevor
Annalong
Kilkeel
Greencastle
NORTH CHANNEL
Liverpool
IRISH SEA
GBM
Point of Ayre
Cranstal
Andreas
Ballaugh
Isle of Man
Ramsey
Dunure
CULZEAN CASTLE
Turnberry
Maybole
Dalrymple
Ailsa Craig
CROSSRAGUEL ABBEY
Straiton
Dalmellington
Girvan
South Balloch
Loch Doon
Auchinleck
Cumnock
Muirkirk
Douglas
New Cumnock
Crawfordjohn
Dalleagles
Leadhills
Craigdarroch
CAIRNSMORE
Dalgonar
Sanquhar
GREEN LOWTHER
Carsphairn
DRUMLANRIG CASTLE
Pinwherry
Ballantrae
GALLOWAY FOREST PARK
MERRICK
Thornhill
Corsewall Point
Kirkcolm
Loch Ryan
Cairnryan
Bargrennan
Clatteringshaws Loch
St. John's Town of Dalry
Moniaive
CASTLE KENNEDY
Craigencallie
New Galloway
Dunscore
Stranraer
Glenluce
Newton Stewart
CAIRNSMORE OF FLEET
Lochanbriggs
Portpatrick
DUNSKEY CASTLE
TORHOUSE STONE CIRCLE
Wigtown
Creetown
Upper Ruskoe
Gatehouse of Fleet
THREAVE CASTLE
Castle Douglas
Crocketford
Loch Ken
Ardwell
Luce Bay
CAIRN HOLY
CARDONESS CASTLE
Dalbeattie
SWEETHEART ABBEY
MOTE OF DRUCHTAG
Sorbie
Drummore
Port William
Wigtown Bay
Kirkcudbright
Kirkbean
Whithorn
Dundrennan
Balcarry Point
Mull of Galloway
ST. NINIAN'S CAVE
Isle of Whithorn
Burrow Head
Abbey Head
Solway Firth
Silloth
Beckfoot
Maryport
Workington
Whitehaven
St Bees Head
Cleator Moor
Egremont
Buttermere
Ullock

7
11
E
F
G
H
1
2
3
4
5
6
SCOTLAND
Stromness
Lerwick
Pass of Drumochter
Braemar
Inverey
BALMORAL CASTLE
Ballater
CIRCLE
Aboyne
CRATHES CASTLE
DRUM CASTLE
Dyce
ABERDEEN
BLAIR CASTLE
Cairnwell Pass
Loch Muick
Banchory
Peterculter
Girdle Ness
Tummel Bridge
Blair Atholl
Glendoll
Auchronie
Bridge of Dye
Strachan
MUCHALLS CASTLE
SCHIEHALLION
Loch Tummel
Pitlochry
Spittal of Glenshee
Clova
North Esk
Stonehaven
DUNNOTTAR CASTLE
Aberfeldy
Fettercairn
EDZELL CASTLE
Laurencekirk
Inverbervie
Kenmore
GEORGE OF ERICHT
Kirriemuir
Tannadice
FINAVON CASTLE
Brechin
AIRLIE CASTLE
Dunkeld
Blairgowrie
GLAMIS CASTLE
Glamis
Forfar
GUTHRIE CASTLE
Montrose
Scurdie Ness
BEN CHONZIE
Coupar Angus
REDCASTLE
Inverkeilor
Lang Craig
KELLIE CASTLE
AFFLECK CASTLE
Crieff
Muirhead
Balbeggie
Arbroath
Perth
Dundee
Carnoustie
Tayport
Firth of Tay
Newport-on-Tay
Auchterarder
Newburgh
Gleneagles
LINDORES ABBEY
Leuchars
St Andrews Bay
Dunblane
CASTLE CAMPBELL
Auchtermuchty
Bridge of Allan
FALKLAND PALACE
Cupar
St Andrews
Tillicoultry
Kinross
Alloa
Fife Ness
Glenrothes
Largo
Clackmannan
Kincardine
Cowdenbeath
Leven
Crail
Culross
Buckhaven
Anstruther
Grangemouth
Dunfermline
Kirkcaldy
Isle of May
Aberdour
Burntisland
South Queensferry
Linlithgow
Firth of Forth
Bathgate
Broxburn
Edinburgh (Turnhouse)
EDINBURGH
North Berwick
TANTALLON CASTLE
Musselburgh
Livingston
EDINBURGH CASTLE
West Calder
Tranent
Haddington
Dunbar
Roslin
Dalkeith
Penicuik
Bonnyrigg
Gorebridge
FAST CASTLE
West Linton
Carnwath
LAMMERMUIR
GB
St Abb's Head
Grantshouse
DROCHIL CASTLE
HILLS
Eyemouth
Biggar
Eddleston
Broughton
Peebles
Lauder
THIRLESTANE CASTLE
NEIDPATH CASTLE
Stow
Duns
Chirnside
TINNIS CASTLE
Innerleithen
TRAQUAIR HOUSE
Galashiels
Gordon
Swinton
Berwick-upon-Tweed
MELLERSTAIN HOUSE
Tweedsmuir
Melrose
DRYBURGH ABBEY
Coldstream
ABBOTSFORD HOUSE
St Boswells
Selkirk
Kelso
Holy Island
GREY MARE'S TAIL
Birkhill
Tushielaw Inn
Lowick
Yetholm
Bamburgh
Moffat
Hawick
Jedburgh
Wooler
Davington
Bonchester Bridge
CHILLINGHAM CASTLE
Beadnell
Teviothead
Chatto
THE CHEVIOT
Eskdalemuir
CHEVIOT HILLS
Ingram
Eglingham
Embleton
CALDCLEUGH HEAD
NORTHUMBERLAND
DUNSTANBURGH CASTLE
Boreland
Fiddleton
Powburn
Alnwick
HERMITAGE CASTLE
Riccarton
Byrness
NATIONAL
CALLALY CASTLE
Longhoughton
Lockerbie
Langholm
Kielder
ALNWICK CASTLE
Alnmouth
THE BORDER
PARK
Rothbury
Warkworth
Newcastleton
Kielder Water
Otterburn
Amble
BRINKBURN PRIORY
Falstone
FOREST PARK
Netherwitton
Longtown
Bellingham
WALLINGTON HALL
Ashington
Gretna Green
Bewcastle
Morpeth
Newbiggin-by-the-Sea
LANERCOST PRIORY
HOUSESTEADS FORT
CARRAWBURGH
MANOR HOUSE
Bedlington
Stavanger
Bergen
Low Brunton
Carlisle
Brampton
Haltwhistle
CHESTERS FORT
Blyth
CHESTERHOLM
Ponteland
Newcastle (Woolsington)
Wetheral
Lambley
Hexham
Corbridge
Whitley Bay
Welton
HADRIAN'S WALL
CORBRIDGE
NEWCASTLE UPON TYNE
Tynemouth
Prudhoe
Tyne
South Shields
Caldbeck
Alston
Gateshead
Washington
Stanley
Consett
LAKE DISTRICT
Melmerby
Chester-le-Street
SUNDERLAND
Penrith
CROSS FELL
Lanchester
Amsterdam
Stanhope
FINCHALE PRIORY
BROUGHAM CASTLE
Durham
Houghton le Spring
Seaham
Appleby-in-Westmorland
Wolsingham
Brandon
Patterdale
Crook
Peterlee
Ullswater
DOVE COTTAGE
Middleton
Spennymoor

8
GBM
Isle of Man
Douglas
Ramsey
Peel
Castletown
IRISH
SEA
Dublin / Baile Átha Cliath
Belfast
Anglesey
Holyhead
Caernarfon
Bangor
Llandudno
Colwyn Bay
Rhyl
Conwy
Cardigan Bay
Aberystwyth
Barmouth
Dolgellau
Pwllheli
Porthmadog
Betws-y-Coed
Wrexham
Chester
LIVERPOOL
Birkenhead
Southport
PRESTON
BLACKPOOL
Fleetwood
Morecambe
Barrow-in-Furness
Workington
Keswick
LAKE DISTRICT
Shrewsbury
Telford
WOLVERHAMPTON
Oswestry
Welshpool
Newtown
Machynlleth
Llangollen
SNOWDONIA NAT. PARK
WALES
Lampeter
Ludlow
Crewe
Whitchurch
Market Drayton
Bridgnorth
Kidderminster
Stourbridge
Dudley
West Bromwich
5
13
14

11
E
F
G
H
9
15
1
2
3
4
5
6
Wetherall
Hexham
CORBRIDGE
Corbridge
NEWCASTLE UPON TYNE
Whitley Bay
Tynemouth
South Shields
HADRIAN'S WALL
Alston
Prudhoe
Gateshead
Washington
Consett
Stanley
Chester -le Street
SUNDERLAND
Stavanger
Bergen
Amsterdam
Melmerby
Penrith
CROSS FELL
Lanchester
FINCHALE PRIORY
Durham
Houghton le Spring
Seaham
Stanhope
BROUGHAM CASTLE
Appleby-in-Westmorland
Wolsingham
Brandon
Crook
Peterlee
Spennymoor
Middleton in Teesdale
Bishop Auckland
Ferryhill
SHAP ABBEY
Sedgefield
Hartlepool
RABY CASTLE
Brough
Staindrop
Barnard Castle
Stockton on Tees
Billingham
Redcar
Darlington
Middlesbrough
Kendal
EGGLESTONE ABBEY
TAN HILL
Whaw
Saltburn
Loftus
Garsdale Head
Keld
Yarm
Teesside
Sedbergh
Scotch Corner
Guisborough
BOUTBY CLIFFS
Hawes
Reeth
Richmond
Stokesley
Mickleby
YORKSHIRE
CASTLE BOLTON
Great Ayton
Kirkby Lonsdale
DALES
Aysgarth
Catterick
Westerdale
Whitby
Leyburn
NORTH YORK MOORS
Yockenthwaite
INGLEBOROUGH
MOUNT GRACE PRIORY
Ingleton
JERVAULX ABBEY
Bedale
Northallerton
NORTH YORK MOORS NAT. PARK
Buckden
Horton-in-Ribblesdale
NAT.
INGLEBOROUGH CAVE
Kettlewell
GREAT WHERNSIDE
RIEVAULX ABBEY
Thirsk
Saltergate
Settle
PARK
Lofthouse
Helmsley
Scalby
Threshfield
Ripon
GILLING CASTLE
Pickering
Scarborough
Long Preston
Ebberston
Slaidburn
Pateley Bridge
FOUNTAINS ABBEY
ISURIUM
BOLTON ABBEY
Easingwold
Gisburn
Malton
Wintringham
Filey
Clitheroe
Skipton
Stillington
CASTLE HOWARD
Norton
Barnoldswick
Knaresborough
Harrogate
BENINGBROUGH HALL
THE WOLDS
Filey Bay
Colne
Ilkley
KIRKHAM PRIORY
Sledmere
Nelson
Keighley
Otley
YORK MINSTER
Flamborough
Flamborough Head
Padiham
Burnley
Bingley
Yeadon
Harewood
Wetherby
YORK
Burton Agnes
Blackburn
Shipley
Leeds Bradford
Bridlington
Darwen
Rawtenstall
BRADFORD
LEEDS
Tadcaster
Pocklington
Kirkburn
Driffield
Halifax
Ripponden
Brighouse
Market Weighton
Rochdale
Selby
Bubwith
Hornsea
Bury
Dewsbury
BURTON CONSTABLE HALL
Oldham
HUDDERSFIELD
Wakefield
Knottingley
Carlton
Beverley
Holmfirth
CANNON HALL
NOSTELL PRIORY
Goole
Willerby
Aldbrough
MANCHESTER
KINGSTON-UPON-HULL
Ashton-under-Lyne
Barnsley
Eastoft
Barton-upon-Humber
Hedon
Glossop
Hyde
PEAK
Burton-upon-Stather
THORNTON ABBEY
Withernsea
STOCKPORT
Doncaster
Scunthorpe
Patrington
Hazel Grove
GB
Immingham
Manchester
DISTRICT
Rotherham
Humberside
Kilnsea
SHEFFIELD
Brigg
Keelby
Grimsby
Wilmslow
Maltby
Bawtry
Spurn Head
Castleton
Cleethorpes
Buxton
Dronfield
Gainsborough
Caistor
NAT. PARK
CHATSWORTH HOUSE
Staveley
Retford
Market Rasen
Congleton
Bakewell
Worksop
LITTLE MORETON HALL
HADDON HALL
Chesterfield
Rotterdam
Zeebrugge
Biddulph
Youlgreave
Clay Cross
Kidsgrove
Matlock
Warsop
Louth
Leek
HARDWICK HALL
Ollerton
STOKE-ON-TRENT
Wragby
Mablethorpe
Cheadle
Mansfield
LINCOLN
Ashbourne
Alfreton
ALTON TOWERS
NEWSTEAD ABBEY
Bardney
Alton
Belper
Ripley
Horncastle
Mumby
KEDLESTON HALL
Heanor
Hucknall
Southwell
Waddington
Ulceby Cross
Stone
Eastwood
Newark-on-Trent
Uttoxeter
Ilkeston
Ingoldmells
DERBY
Leadenham
Coningsby
Stafford
BLITHFIELD HALL
Stapleford
NOTTINGHAM
TATTERSHALL CASTLE
Stickney
GUNBY HALL
Skegness
SHUGBOROUGH
Long Eaton
West Bridgford
Radcliffe-on-Trent
Sleaford
Rugeley
Burton upon Trent
East Midlands
Wainfleet all Saints
Gibraltar Point
Grantham
BELTON HOUSE
Cannock
Ashby-de-la-Zouch
Wrangle
Lichfield
Shepshed
BELVOIR CASTLE
Boston
LETOCETUM
Loughborough
Brownhills
Coalville
Barrow-on-Soar
Colsterworth
Donington
The Wash
Walsall
Tamworth
Hunstanton
Brancaster
Sutton Coldfield
Anstey
Syston
Melton Mowbray
Spalding
Gedney Drove End
Wells-next-the-Sea
HOLKHAM HALL
Atherstone
Bourne
Holbeach
Docking
BIRMINGHAM
LEICESTER
Oakham
Dersingham
CASTLE RISING
SANDRINGHAM HOUSE
Little Walsingham
Market Deeping
Long Sutton
Wigston
Stamford
King's Lynn
Fakenham
Nuneaton
Bedworth
ARBURY HALL
BURGHLEY HOUSE
Crowland
Uppingham
Melton Constable
NORTH
YORKSHIRE AND HUMBERSIDE
EAST MIDLANDS
THE WOLDS

A
B
5
C
D
1
2
3
4
5
6
Strumble Head
Rosslare Harbour
Cardigan
Fishguard
Newport
CILGERRAN CASTLE
Ramsey
St. David's
PEMBROKESHIRE COAST
PENTRE IFAN
Rosslare Harbour
St. Brides Bay
NATIONAL
Pantymenyn
Llandissilio
Skomer
Haverfordwest
Milford Haven
Dale
Narberth
St Clears
Neyland
PARK
Pembroke
Pendine
Saundersfoot
Manorbier
Tenby
Caldey
Carmarthen Bay
WEOB
Worms H
Cork / Corcaigh
B R I S T
Lundy
Morte Point
Woolacombe
Baggy Point
Croyde
Barnstaple or Bideford Bay
Braunton
Hartland Point
Westward Ho!
Hartland
Clovelly
Bideford
Kilkhampton
Bude
Bude Bay
Holsworthy
Boscastle
KING ARTHUR'S CASTLE
Tintagel
Halwill
Trevose Head
Padstow
Camelford
Launceston
BROWN WILLY
Bridestowe
Wadebridge
PETER TAVY CO.
TAVY
Newquay
Bodmin
BODMIN MOOR
Colliford Lake
Perranporth
TRERICE MANOR
LANHYDROCK HOUSE
Callington
Tavistock
COTEHELE HOUSE
WISTMAN'S WOOD
Princetown
St Austell
Lostwithiel
Liskeard
BUCKLAND ABBEY
Yelverton
St Ives
Portreath
LANYON QUOIT
Hayle
St Just
ST MICHAEL'S MOUNT
Camborne
Redruth
Truro
Fowey
Polperro
Looe
Saltash
BUCKFAST AB
Buckfas
Sennen
Marazion
Torpoint
SHIPPLEY BRIDGE
Land's End
Penzance
Mevagissey
Penryn
PLYMOUTH
Plympton
Mounts Bay
Portloe
Gwennap Head
Helston
Falmouth
St Mawes
Dodman Point
Rame Head
Ivybr
Falmouth Bay
Wembury
Modbury
Bigbury Bay
Bigbury-on-Sea
St Keverne
KYNANCE COVE
Lizard
Lizard Point
Salcombe
ISLES OF SCILLY
Tresco
St Martin's
Bryher
St Mary's
Hugh Town
St Agnes
Bilbo / Bilbao
Santander (Summer only)
Roscoff
A
B
C
D

10
WALES
WEST MIDLANDS
SOUTH WEST
CHANNEL
ENGLISH CHANNEL
GB
Lyme Bay
Bridgwater Bay
Swansea Bay
Isle of Wight
BRECON BEACONS NAT. PARK
EXMOOR NAT. PARK
SALISBURY PLAIN
BLACK MTS
Forest of Dean
New Forest
New Quay
Tregaron
Lampeter
Carmarthen
Llandovery
Llandeilo
Ammanford
Llanelli
SWANSEA
Mumbles
Oxwich
Port Talbot
Neath
Bridgend
Porthcawl
Pontypridd
Merthyr Tydfil
Brecon
Builth Wells
Llandrindod Wells
Rhayader
Abergavenny
Monmouth
Pontypool
Cwmbran
Caerphilly
NEWPORT
CARDIFF
Penarth
Barry
Cowbridge
Llantwit Major
Chepstow
Lydney
Hereford
Leominster
Ludlow
Kington
Hay-on-Wye
Presteigne
Knighton
Clun
Bridgnorth
WOLVERHAMPTON
Walsall
West Bromwich
Dudley
Stourbridge
BIRMINGHAM
Solihull
Sutton Coldfield
COVENTRY
Kenilworth
Warwick
Leamington Spa
Stratford-upon-Avon
Redditch
Bromsgrove
Kidderminster
Droitwich
Worcester
Great Malvern
Bromyard
Ledbury
Evesham
Pershore
Tewkesbury
Cheltenham
Gloucester
Ross-on-Wye
Stroud
Cirencester
Tetbury
Chipping Campden
Moreton-in-Marsh
Stow-on-the-Wold
Chipping Norton
Banbury
Woodstock
Witney
OXFORD
Abingdon
Didcot
Wantage
Faringdon
Swindon
Chippenham
Malmesbury
Marlborough
Hungerford
Newbury
Reading
Basingstoke
Andover
Winchester
Alresford
Alton
Salisbury
Wilton
Amesbury
Devizes
Trowbridge
Frome
Warminster
Melksham
Calne
BATH
BRISTOL
Clevedon
Portishead
Weston-super-Mare
Burnham-on-Sea
Bridgwater
Cheddar
Wells
Glastonbury
Shepton Mallet
Taunton
Yeovil
Sherborne
Shaftesbury
Crewkerne
Chard
Ilminster
Honiton
Minehead
Dunster
Porlock
Lynton
Lynmouth
Tiverton
Wellington
Cullompton
EXETER
Exmouth
Sidmouth
Seaton
Lyme Regis
Bridport
Dorchester
Weymouth
Bill of Portland
Blandford Forum
Wimborne Minster
Ringwood
Poole
BOURNEMOUTH
Christchurch
Swanage
SOUTHAMPTON
Eastleigh
Romsey
Fareham
Gosport
PORTSMOUTH
Havant
Chichester
Hayling Island
Newport
Ryde
Cowes
Sandown
Shanklin
Ventnor
St Catherine's Point
The Needles
Teignmouth
Dawlish
Newton Abbot
Torquay
Paignton
Brixham
Dartmouth
Start Point
Crediton
Tiverton
Cherbourg
St-Peter Port
Cherbourg
St-Malo
Bilbo / Bilbao
Le Havre
Caen
E
F
G
H
1
2
3
4
5
6
14
26

10
13
WALES
MIDLANDS
SOUTH WEST
GB
ENGLISH CH
Newtown
Montgomery
Llanidloes
Ponterwyd
Llangurig
Rhayader
Llanbister
ABBEYCWMHIR
FLORIDA ABBEY
Claerwen Resr
Knighton
Llandrindod Wells
Builth Wells
Llyn Brianne
Llandovery Wells
Sennybridge
Brecon
BRECON BEACONS NAT. PARK
BLACK MTS
LLANTHONY PRIORY
LLANVIHANGEL COURT
Ystradgynlais
Pontardawe
Glyn Neath
Neath
Hirwaun
Treherbert
Merthyr Tydfil
Ebbw Vale
Brynmawr
Blaenavon
Abergavenny
Aberdare
Rhymney
Abertillery
Cymmer
Mountain Ash
MARGAM ABBEY
Tonypandy
Porth
Bargoed
Pontllanfraith
Pontypool
Pontypridd
Llantrisant
Caerphilly
Cwmbran
ROMAN AMPHIT
Bridgend
Cowbridge
Llantwit Major
CARDIFF
CARDIFF CASTLE
Penarth
Barry
NEWPORT
TREDEGAR PARK HOUSE
CALDICOT CASTLE
Chepstow
Usk
Raglan
Monmouth
Coleford
Lydney
TINTERN ABBEY
Forest of Dean
Church Stretton
Bishop's Castle
Clun
STOKESAY CASTLE
Craven Arms
Ludlow
CROFT CASTLE
Presteigne
Kington
CLIFFORD CASTLE
Hay-on-Wye
BURTON COURT
Dilwyn
Leominster
DINMORE MANOR
Peterchurch
ABBEY DORE COURT
Hereford
Fownhope
Pontrilas
WHITE CASTLE
GOODRICH CASTLE
Ross-on-Wye
Newent
Ledbury
Great Malvern
Bromyard
Tenbury Wells
Cleobury Mortimer
Cleobury North
Bridgnorth
Much Wenlock
SHIPTON HALL
BUILDWAS ABBEY
IRON BRIDGE
Telford
Shifnal
Dorrington
WOLVERHAMPTON
West Bromwich
Dudley
Stourbridge
Kidderminster
HARTLEBURY CASTLE
Bewdley
Stourport-on-Severn
Bromsgrove
Droitwich
Redditch
HANBURY HALL
Worcester
Halesowen
Solihull
BIRMINGHAM
ARBURY HALL
Walsall
Brownhills
Sutton Coldfield
Cannock
Lichfield
LETOCETUM
Tamworth
Atherstone
Nuneaton
Bedworth
COVENTRY
Kenilworth
Stoneleigh
Rugby
Lutterworth
Warwick
Leamington Spa
STANFORD HALL
Studley
COUGHTON COURT
Alcester
RAGLEY HALL
Stratford-upon-Avon
ANNE HATHAWAY'S COTTAGE
Bidford-on-Avon
Pershore
Evesham
Broadway
HIDCOTE MANOR
Chipping Campden
Shipston on Stour
UPTON HOUSE
COMPTON WYNYATES
Banbury
Wellesbourne
Southam
Daventry
Towcester
Ashby-de-la-Zouch
Coalville
Shepshed
Anstey
Tewkesbury
Bishop's Cleeve
Winchcombe
Cheltenham
Gloucester
Cinderford
Blakeney
Moreton-in-Marsh
ROLLRIGHT STONES
Stow-on-the-Wold
Bourton-on-the-Water
Chipping Norton
Brackley
STOWE
Buckingham
Bicester
Winslow
CLAYDON HOUSE
Leighton
BLENHEIM PALACE
Woodstock
Kidlington
WADDESDON MANOR
Aylesbury
Northleach
Bibury
Burford
ROMAN VILLA
Witney
OXFORD
Thame
Stroud
Nailsworth
Dursley
Berkeley
Thornbury
Tetbury
Cirencester
Lechlade
Faringdon
Abingdon
Princes Risborough
Wendover
Avonmouth
Portishead
Chipping Sodbury
Clevedon
Nailsea
BLAISE CASTLE
BRISTOL
Bristol
Malmesbury
Cricklade
Highworth
Lydiard Tregoze
Swindon
WHITE HORSE
Wantage
Stadhampton
Didcot
Dorchester
Wallingford
Ewelme
High Wycombe
Marlow
Henley-on-Thames
Weston-super-Mare
Congresbury
Bridgwater Bay
Castle Combe
Chippenham
Marshfield
Keynsham
Wootton Bassett
BATH
CLAVERTON MANOR
Corsham
Lacock
Calne
Melksham
Avebury
Marlborough
Lambourn
Pangbourne
READING
Twyford
Porlock
Minehead
Dunster
Watchet
Burnham-on-Sea
Cheddar
CHEDDAR GORGE
WOOKEY HOLE
Wells
Radstock
Bradford-on-Avon
Trowbridge
Devizes
Hungerford
Newbury
Thatcham
Wokingham
Wheddon Cross
CLEEVE ABBEY
Bridgwater
Meare
Glastonbury
Beckington
NUNNEY CASTLE
Frome
Westbury
Littleton Panell
Pewsey
Burbage
Highclere
STRATFIELD SAYE
Kingsclere
Camberley
Wiveliscombe
Bishop's Lydeard
Shepton Mallet
Street
Warminster
SALISBURY PLAIN
Upavon
Ludgershall
Bampton
Wellington
Taunton
Othery
Somerton
Bruton
LONGLEAT HOUSE
Shrewton
Bulford
STONEHENGE
Deptford
LYTE'S CARY
STOURHEAD
Stourton
Langport
BARRINGTON COURT
Stoke sub Hamdon
Ilchester
Wincanton
Chicklade
Amesbury
Andover
Overton
Basingstoke
THE VYNE
Hartley Wintney
Fleet
Odiham
Aldershot
Farnham
Cullompton
Ilminster
Montacute
MONTACUTE HOUSE
Gillingham
WARDOUR CASTLE
OLD SARUM
FIGSBURY RING
Stockbridge
Alton
Guildford
Yarcombe
Chard
Yeovil
Sherborne
Shaftesbury
Wilton
Salisbury
LONGFORD CASTLE
Winchester
Alresford
Honiton
FORDE ABBEY
Crewkerne
Sixpenny Handley
Coombe Bissett
Breamore
Romsey
Eastleigh
Southampton (Eastleigh)
Milford
Hindhead
Godalming
Axminster
Beaminster
Holywell
Sturminster Newton
Farnham
Cranborne
Fordingbridge
Verwood
RUFUS STONE
Lyndhurst
Totton
Bishop's Waltham
Liphook
Haslemere
Ottery St Mary
Exmouth
Budleigh Salterton
Sidmouth
Beer
Branscombe
Seaton
Lyme Regis
Bridport
Cerne Abbas
Blandford Forum
HARDY'S COTTAGE
Puddletown
Wimborne Minster
Ringwood
NETLEY ABBEY
SOUTHAMPTON
Petersfield
Midhurst
Winterbourne Abbas
HARDY MONUMENT
Lyme Bay
Abbotsbury
Dorchester
ATHELHAMPTON
Bovington Camp
Brockenhurst
Beaulieu
New Forest
Waterlooville
Petworth
Poole
BOURNEMOUTH
Christchurch
Fawley
Fareham
Portchester
Havant
Singleton
GOODWOOD HOUSE
Weymouth
CREECH GRANGE
Wareham
Sandbanks
Poole Bay
Lymington
Milford-on-Sea
Cowes
East Cowes
Gosport
Chichester
Arundel
ROMAN PALACE
Fortuneswell
West Lulworth
Corfe Castle
Studland
Swanage
Yarmouth
Freshwater
The Needles
OSBORNE HOUSE
Fishbourne
Ryde
PORTSMOUTH
Southsea
Hayling Island
West Wittering
Selsey
Bognor Regis
Middleton
Littlehampton
Bill of Portland
St Alban's Head
CARISBROOKE CASTLE
Newport
Bembridge
Godshill
Sandown
Shanklin
Ventnor
Isle of Wight
Chale
St Catherine's Point
Cherbourg
St-Peter Port
Cherbourg
St-Malo
Bilbo / Bilbao
Le Havre
Caen
A
B
C
D
1
2
3
4
5
6

11
E
F
G
H
1
2
3
4
5
6
Grantham
BELVOIR CASTLE
BELTON HOUSE
Wainfleet all Saints
Gibraltar Point
Wrangle
Boston
The Wash
Hunstanton
Brancaster
Wells-next-the-Sea
Blakeney
Sheringham
Cromer
HOLKHAM HALL
Docking
Colsterworth
Melton Mowbray
Donington
Spalding
Gedney Drove End
Holbeach
Bourne
Market Deeping
Oakham
Stamford
BURGHLEY HOUSE
Dersingham
CASTLE RISING
SANDRINGHAM HOUSE
Little Walsingham
Long Sutton
King's Lynn
Fakenham
Holt
Melton Constable
BLICKLING HALL
Mundesley
North Walsham
Aylsham
Uppingham
ROCKINGHAM CASTLE
KIRBY HALL
Corby
Crowland
Thorney
Peterborough
Wisbech
Castle Acre
Bawdeswell
Rothwell
Kettering
Oundle
Whittlesey
March
Downham Market
Swaffham
East Dereham
Norwich
NORWICH
Wroxham
Hemsby
Caister-on-Sea
Great Yarmouth
Oxborough
Watton
Sawtry
Ramsey
Chatteris
Wymondham
A1(M)
EAST ANGLIA
GRIME'S GRAVES
Mundford
Littleport
Brandon
Attleborough
Loddon
Hopton-on-Sea
Lowestoft
Rushden
Somersham
Ely
Thetford
Long Stratton
Bungay
Beccles
Kessingland
THAMPTON
Huntingdon
Buckden
St Ives
St Neots
Mildenhall
Kenninghall
Diss
Scole
Halesworth
Southwold
Walberswick
Clapham
Burwell
Bedford
Kempston
Cambridge
Newmarket
Ixworth
Gamlingay
Sandy
Ampthill
Biggleswade
Old Warden
WANDLEBURY
ICKWORTH HOUSE
Bury St Edmunds
Stowmarket
Stradbroke
Dennington
Framlingham
Woburn
WOBURN ABBEY
Shefford
Melbourn
Sawston
Stradishall
Royston
Linton
Haverhill
Clare
Lavenham
Wickham Market
Leiston
Letchworth
Hitchin
Baldock
AUDLEY END HO
Saffron Walden
Long Melford
KENTWELL HALL
Needham Market
Luton
Dunstable
Stevenage
KNEBWORTH HOUSE
LUTON HOO
Buntingford
Great Yeldham
Sudbury
Hadleigh
Woodbridge
Aldeburgh
Orford
Orford Ness
M11
Stansted
Thaxted
IPSWICH
Hollesley Bay
Hemel Hempstead
Harpenden
Welwyn Garden City
Bishop's Stortford
Great Dunmow
Halstead
Earl's Colne
Deben
Bawdsey
Felixstowe
Göteborg
Esbjerg
Hamburg
St Albans
Hertford
Ware
Braintree
Coggeshall
Parkeston Quay
Harwich
Hatfield
Harlow
Leaden Roding
CHURCH OF COPFORD
Colchester
The Naze
Watford
Potters Bar
WALTHAM ABBEY
Witham
Layer Marney
Walton-on-the-Naze
SALISBURY HALL
Enfield
ST OSYTH'S PRIORY
Frinton-on-Sea
Rotterdam
Gerrards Cross
Harrow
Chelmsford
Maldon
West Mersea
Clacton-on-Sea
Chigwell
Ingatestone
M25
Ealing
Brentwood
Billericay
Bradwell-on-Sea
ST PETER ON THE WALL
Colne Point
LONDON
Romford
Heathrow
Richmond
Basildon
Burnham-on-Crouch
Southminster
London City
Greenwich
Rayleigh
Foulness Island
HAMPTON COURT
Dartford
Grays
Southend-on-Sea
Tilbury
Canvey Island
Shoeburyness
Esher
Croydon
Epsom
Orpington
Cliffe
Gravesend
Grain
Sheerness
Minster
Leatherhead
Cobham
Rochester
Gillingham
Dorking
Caterham
Eynsford
M20
Chatham
Leysdown
Reigate
Westerham
M26
Sittingbourne
Herne Bay
REGULBIUM
Margate
North Foreland
M23
CHARTWELL
Sevenoaks
Whitstable
Gatwick
Edenbridge
HEVER CASTLE
Hadlow
Faversham
M2
Broadstairs
Ramsgate
Crawley
PENSHURST PLACE
Tonbridge
Maidstone
Lenham
Sturry
Canterbury
East Grinstead
Tunbridge Wells
Staplehurst
Headcorn
Charing
Chilham
RICHBOROUGH
Sandwich
Haywards Heath
Lamberhurst
Crowborough
Biddenden
Ashford
Deal
WALMER
Kingsdown
South Foreland
Cranbrook
Tenterden
Eythorne
SHEFFIELD PARK
Uckfield
Mayfield
Hawkinge
ROYAL PAVILION
BODIAM CASTLE
Dover
Folkestone
Heathfield
Northiam
LYMPNE CASTLE
Oostende
Hythe
Sandgate
Dymchurch
Lewes
Glynde
Herstmonceux
Battle
CAMBER CASTLE
Rye
New Romney
BRIGHTON
Hove
Hailsham
HERSTMONCEUX CASTLE
R. GREENWICH OBSERVATORY
Winchelsea
Lydd
Rye Bay
Dungeness
EUROTUNNEL
Strait of Dover
Pas de Calais
Polegate
CHARLESTON MANOR
Pevensey
Bexhill
St Leonards-on-Sea
Hastings
Shoreham-by-Sea
Rottingdean
Newhaven
Seaford
Beachy Head
Eastbourne
29
Middelkerke
Westende
Koksijde-Bad
De Panne
Dunkerque Ouest
Dunkerque
Malo-les-Bains
Blériot-Plage
Calais
Gravelines
Cap Gris Nez
Wissant
Framzelle
Bergues
Guînes
Bourbourg
Looberghe
Marquise
Audruicq
Ardres
Wimereux
Nordausques
Licques
Wormhout
Boulogne-sur-Mer
Watten
Le Portel
Pont-de-Briques
Quercamps
Cassel
Hardelot-Plage
Desvres
St-Omer
Steenvoorde
28
EL / LA MANCHE
Dieppe

A
B
C
D
1
2
3
4
5
6
Texel
De Koog
Göteborg
Den Helder
Newcastle-
-upon-Tyne
De Kooy
Schagen
Bergen aan Zee
Bergen
Alkmaar
Egmond aan Zee
Huizen
Castricum
Beverwijk
Wormerveer
IJmuiden
NATIONAAL PARK DE
KENNEMER DUINEN
HAARLEM
Zaandam
Zandvoort
Heemstede
AMSTERDAM
Hillegom
Kingston-
-upon-Hull
Noordwijk
aan Zee
Lisse
Schiphol
Sassenheim
Aalsmeer
Katwijk
aan Zee
Uithoorn
Wassenaar
Leiden
Scheveningen
Voorschoten
Alphen-
a/d Rijn
DEN HAAG
Zoetermeer
Bodegraven
Woerden
Harwich
Hoek van
Holland
Poeldijk
Boskoop
Delft
UTRECHT
Europoort
Rotterdam
Oudewater
Brielle
Gouda
Maassluis
ROTTERDAM
Goeree
Vlaardingen
Ouddorp
Hellevoetsluis
Schoonhoven
Stellendam
Spijkenisse
MOLENS VAN
KINDERDIJK
Schouwen
Grevelingen
ZUID-
-HOLLAND
Oud Beijerland
Leerdam
Burgh-Haamstede
Zwijndrecht
Sliedrecht
Brouwershaven
Middelharnis
DORDRECHT
Gorinchem
Goeree
NATIONAAL PARK DE BIESBOSCH
Zierikzee
Zaltbommel
Walcheren
Noord-
Beveland
Sluis
Willemstad
Oosterschelde
Hollands Diep
Domburg
Zijpe
Geertruidenberg
Krammer Volkerak
Westkapelle
Veere
Stavenisse
Steenbergen
Made
ZEELAND
Zevenbergen
Oosterhout
Waalwijk
Middelburg
Goes
Kaatsheuvel
Vlissingen
Halsteren
BREDA
Knokke-
Heist
Bergen
op Zoom
Zeebrugge
Breskens
Kruiningen
Roosendaal
Blankenberge
Hoedeken-
skerke
Westerschelde
TILBURG
De Haan
Sluis
Schoondijke
Perkpolder
Zundert
30
NOORD

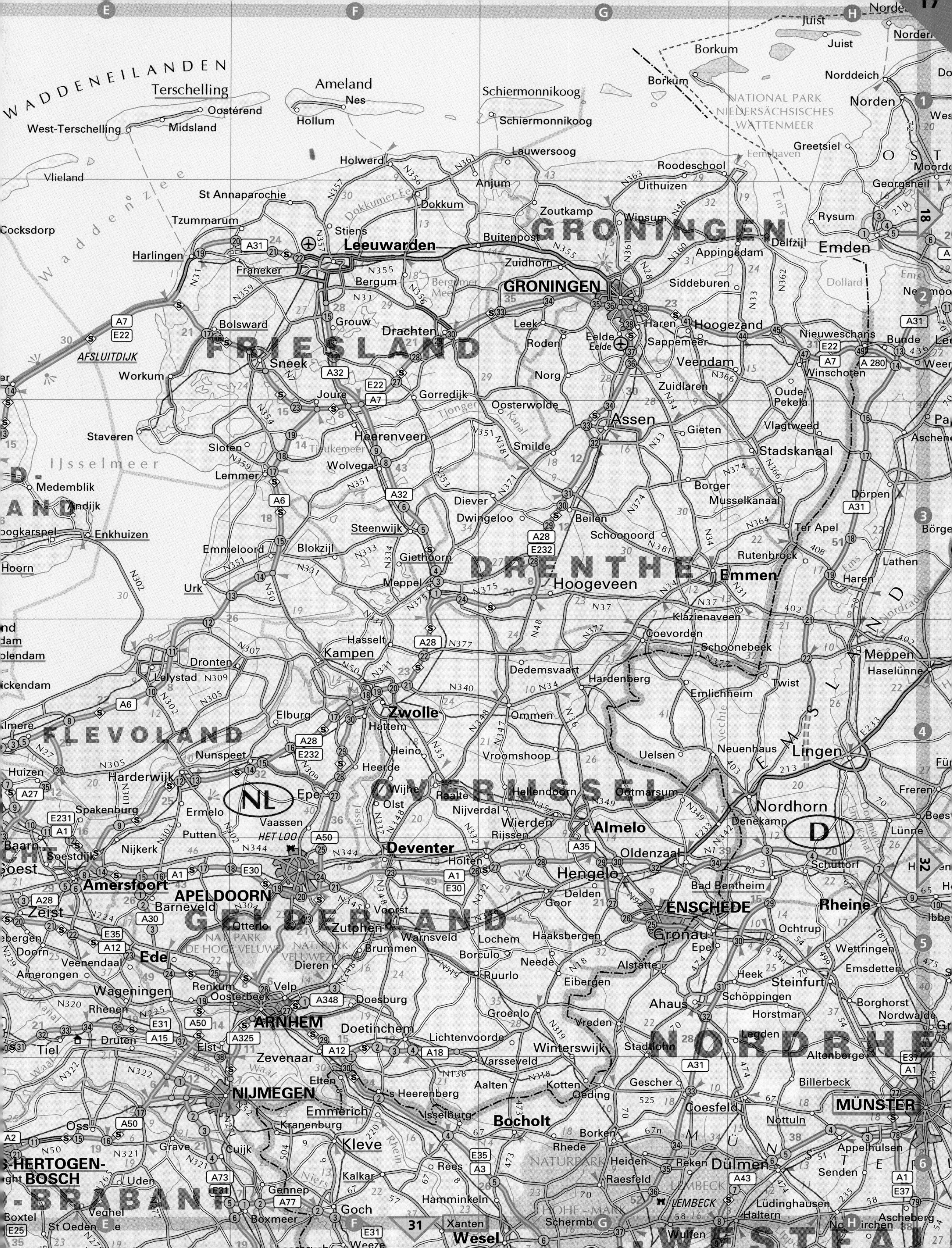

E
F
G
H
WADDENEILANDEN
Terschelling
West-Terschelling
Oostérend
Midsland
Ameland
Nes
Hollum
Schiermonnikoog
Borkum
Juist
Norderney
Norden
Norddeich
NATIONAL PARK NIEDERSÄCHSISCHES WATTENMEER
Greetsiel
Vlieland
Waddenzee
Holwerd
Lauwersoog
Roodeschool
Uithuizen
Eemshaven
Anjum
Dokkum
St Annaparochie
Tzummarum
Cocksdorp
Harlingen
Franeker
Stiens
Leeuwarden
Buitenpost
Zoutkamp
Winsum
GRONINGEN
Appingedam
Delfzijl
Emden
Rysum
Georgsheil
Zuidhorn
Bergum
Bergumer Meer
Siddeburen
Dollard
Bolsward
Grouw
Drachten
Leek
Haren
Hoogezand
Nieuweschans
Bunde
Weener
AFSLUITDIJK
FRIESLAND
Sneek
Roden
Eelde
Sappemeer
Veendam
Winschoten
Workum
Norg
Zuidlaren
Oude-Pekela
Joure
Gorredijk
Oosterwolde
Assen
Vlagtwedde
Staveren
Heerenveen
Tjonger
Smilde
Gieten
Stadskanaal
Sloten
Tjeukemeer
IJsselmeer
Lemmer
Wolvega
Aschendorf
Medemblik
Andijk
Diever
Dwingeloo
Beilen
Borger
Musselkanaal
Dörpen
Enkhuizen
Steenwijk
Schoonoord
Ter Apel
Emmeloord
Blokzijl
Giethoorn
DRENTHE
Rutenbrock
Lathen
Hoorn
Urk
Meppel
Hoogeveen
Emmen
Haren
Klazienaveen
Hasselt
Kampen
Coevorden
Schoonebeek
Meppen
Dronten
Lelystad
Dedemsvaart
Hardenberg
Twist
Haselünne
Emlichheim
Zwolle
Hattem
Ommen
FLEVOLAND
Elburg
Heino
Vroomshoop
Uelsen
Neuenhaus
Lingen
Nunspeet
Heerde
Huizen
Harderwijk
NL
Epe
OVERIJSSEL
Wijhe
Olst
Raalte
Hellendoorn
Ootmarsum
Nordhorn
Freren
Spakenburg
Ermelo
Vaassen
Nijverdal
Wierden
Almelo
Denekamp
D
Putten
HET LOO
Rijssen
Lünne
Baarn
Soestdijk
Nijkerk
Deventer
Holten
Oldenzaal
Schüttorf
Soest
Amersfoort
Hengelo
Bad Bentheim
APELDOORN
Barneveld
Delden
Goor
Zeist
GELDERLAND
Voorst
ENSCHEDE
Rheine
Otterlo
Zutphen
Haaksbergen
Gronau
Ochtrup
Doorn
NAT. PARK DE HOGE VELUWE
NAT. PARK VELUWEZOOM
Warnsveld
Lochem
Epe
Wettringen
Veenendaal
Ede
Brummen
Borculo
Emsdetten
Amerongen
Dieren
Neede
Alstätte
Wageningen
Renkum
Velp
Ruurlo
Eibergen
Heek
Steinfurt
Oosterbeek
Doesburg
Ahaus
Schöppingen
Rhenen
ARNHEM
Groenlo
Vreden
Horstmar
Borghorst
Nordwalde
Tiel
Druten
Elst
Doetinchem
Lichtenvoorde
Winterswijk
Stadtlohn
NORDRHEIN
Legden
Altenberge
Zevenaar
Varsseveld
Waal
NIJMEGEN
Elten
's Heerenberg
Aalten
Kotten
Oeding
Gescher
Billerbeck
Emmerich
Coesfeld
MÜNSTER
Oss
Kranenburg
Isselburg
Bocholt
Nottuln
Kleve
Borken
Grave
Cuijk
Rhede
Appelhülsen
'S-HERTOGEN-BOSCH
NATURPARK
Heiden
Reken
Dülmen
Senden
Uden
Kalkar
Rees
Raesfeld
MÜNSTERLAND
BRABANT
Gennep
Hamminkeln
LEMBECK
Lüdinghausen
Veghel
Goch
HOHE MARK
Haltern
Ascheberg
Boxtel
Boxmeer
Xanten
Schermbeck
Nordkirchen
St Oeden
Wesel
Wulfen
WESTFALEN
Weeze
Niers
Rhein
Ems
Vechte
EMSLAND
OST
Ijssel
31
32
18

NATIONALPARK SCHLESWIG-HOLSTEINISCHES WATTENMEER
Helgoland
Harwich
Deutsche Bucht
NATIONALPARK NIEDERSÄCHSISCHES WATTENMEER
OSTFRIESISCHE INSELN
Borkum
Juist
Norderney
Baltrum
Langeoog
Spiekeroog
Wangerooge
NATIONAL PARK NIEDERSÄCHSISCHES WATTENMEER
OSTFRIESLAND
Norden
Norddeich
Aurich
Emden
Wilhelmshaven
Jever
Leer
Papenburg
OLDENBURG
BREMEN
Delmenhorst
Bremerhaven
Nordenham
Cloppenburg
Meppen
Vechta
Quakenbrück
GRONINGEN
Assen
Emmen
Hoogeveen
Hoogezand
Veendam
Delfzijl
Cuxhaven
St Peter-Ording
Wittdün
Amrum
Scharhörn
Neuwerk
Wildeshausen
Sulingen
Diepholz
Lingen
Haselünne
Herzlake
Löningen
Friesoythe
Westerstede
Bad Zwischenahn
Varel
Brake
Küsten-Kanal
Ems-Jade Kanal
NATURPARK WILDESHAUSER GEEST
NIEDERSACHSEN
NL

17
32

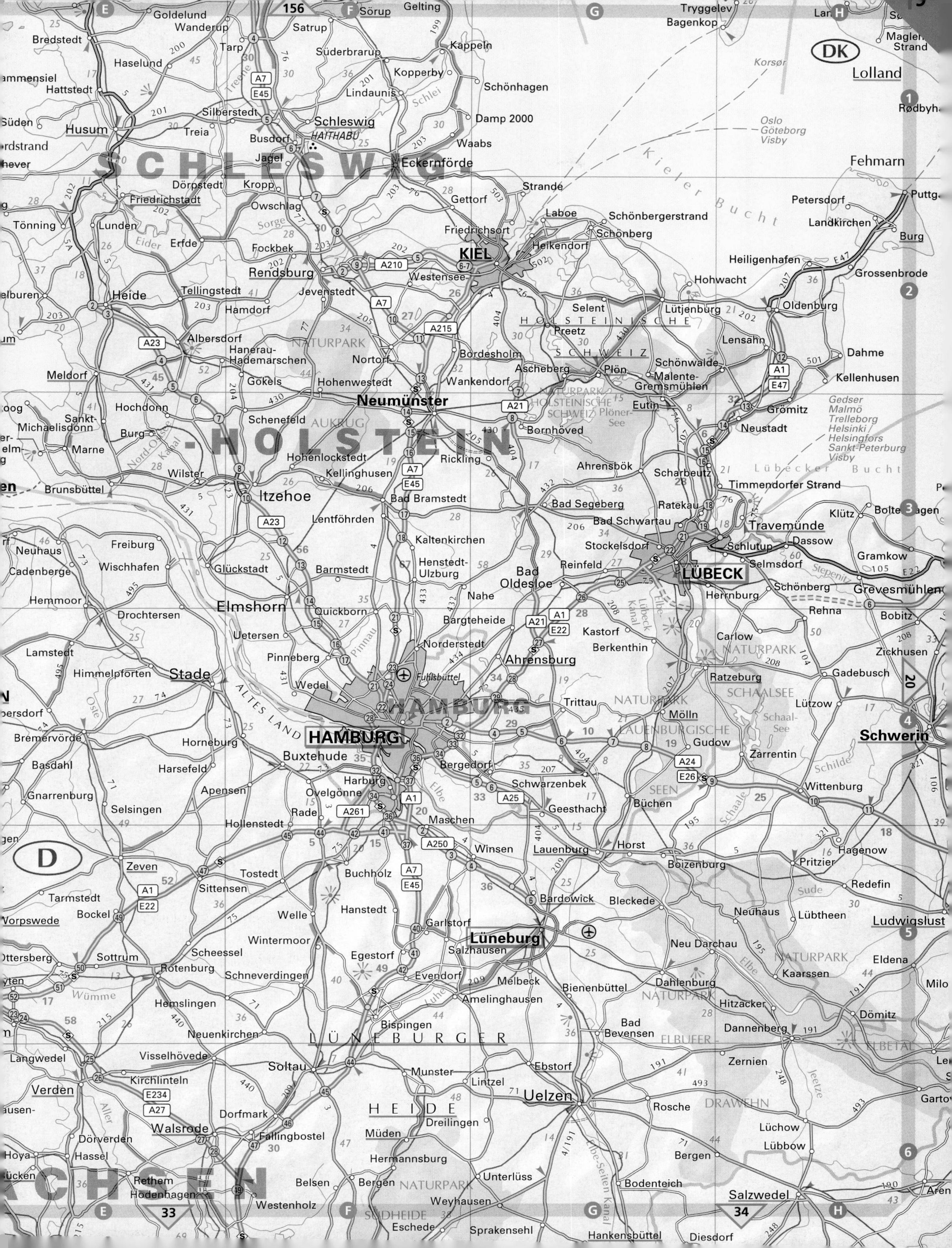

156
DK
Lolland
Fehmarn
SCHLESWIG-HOLSTEIN
Kieler Bucht
Lübecker Bucht
Goldelund
Wanderup
Sörup
Gelting
Tryggelev
Bagenkop
Maglen Strand
Bredstedt
Tarp
Satrup
Kappeln
Korsør
Haselund
Süderbrarup
Kopperby
Hattstedt
Lindaunis
Schönhagen
Rødbyhavn
Silberstedt
Schleswig
Damp 2000
Oslo
Göteborg
Visby
Husum
Treia
Busdorf
Haithabu
Waabs
Jagel
Eckernförde
Dörpstedt
Kropp
Strande
Friedrichstadt
Owschlag
Gettorf
Petersdorf
Tönning
Lunden
Laboe
Schönbergerstrand
Landkirchen
Friedrichsort
Schönberg
Burg
Erfde
Fockbek
Heikendorf
KIEL
Rendsburg
Westensee
Heiligenhafen
Hohwacht
Grossenbrode
Heide
Tellingstedt
Jevenstedt
Hamdorf
Selent
Lütjenburg
Oldenburg
Holsteinische Schweiz
Naturpark
Albersdorf
Preetz
Lensahn
Hanerau-Hademarschen
Nortorf
Bordesholm
Schönwalde
Dahme
Meldorf
Gokels
Hohenwestedt
Wankendorf
Ascheberg
Plön
Malente-Gremsmühlen
Kellenhusen
Neumünster
Eutin
Grömitz
Gedser
Malmö
Trelleborg
Helsinki
Helsingfors
Sankt-Peterburg
Hochdonn
Aukrug
Plöner See
Neustadt
Sankt-Michaelisdonn
Burg
Schenefeld
Bornhöved
Marne
Hohenlockstedt
Rickling
Ahrensbök
Scharbeutz
Wilster
Kellinghausen
Timmendorfer Strand
Brunsbüttel
Itzehoe
Bad Bramstedt
Bad Segeberg
Ratekau
Klütz
Boltenhagen
Lentföhrden
Bad Schwartau
Travemünde
Kaltenkirchen
Stockelsdorf
Schlutup
Dassow
Neuhaus
Freiburg
Henstedt-Ulzburg
Bad Oldesloe
Reinfeld
Gramkow
Cadenberge
Wischhafen
Glückstadt
Barmstedt
LÜBECK
Selmsdorf
Grevesmühlen
Hemmoor
Drochtersen
Elmshorn
Nahe
Schönberg
Herrnburg
Quickborn
Bargteheide
Rehna
Bobitz
Uetersen
Kastorf
Carlow
Norderstedt
Berkenthin
Zickhusen
Lamstedt
Pinneberg
Fuhlsbüttel
Ahrensburg
Ratzeburg
Gadebusch
Himmelpforten
Stade
Wedel
Schaalsee
Altes Land
HAMBURG
Trittau
Mölln
Lützow
Lauenburgische Seen
Schwerin
Bremervörde
Horneburg
Gudow
Zarrentin
Buxtehude
Bergedorf
Basdahl
Harsefeld
Harburg
Schwarzenbek
Wittenburg
Gnarrenburg
Apensen
Ovelgönne
Selsingen
Rade
Geesthacht
Büchen
Hollenstedt
Maschen
D
Winsen
Lauenburg
Horst
Hagenow
Zeven
Tostedt
Boizenburg
Pritzier
Buchholz
Sittensen
Redefin
Tarmstedt
Bardowick
Bleckede
Bockel
Welle
Hanstedt
Neuhaus
Lübtheen
Worpswede
Ludwigslust
Garlstorf
Lüneburg
Wintermoor
Neu Darchau
Scheessel
Salzhausen
Ottersberg
Sottrum
Egestorf
Eldena
Rotenburg
Schneverdingen
Evendorf
Karrenzin
Wümme
Melbeck
Dahlenburg
Hemslingen
Amelinghausen
Bienenbüttel
Hitzacker
Dömitz
Bispingen
Bad Bevensen
Dannenberg
Neuenkirchen
Lüneburger Heide
Elbufer-Drawehn
Elbetal
Langwedel
Visselhövede
Soltau
Zernien
Ebstorf
Kirchlinteln
Munster
Lintzel
Verden
Uelzen
Rosche
Dorfmark
Dreilingen
Walsrode
Lüchow
Dörverden
Fallingbostel
Müden
Lübbow
Hoya
Hassel
Hermannsburg
Bergen
Rethem
Unterlüss
Hodenhagen
Belsen
Bergen
Bodenteich
Salzwedel
Westenholz
Weyhausen
Südheide
Elbe-Seiten Kanal
Eschede
Sprakensehl
Hankensbüttel
Diesdorf
Arendsee
33
34
20

FALSTER
157
Sakskøbing
Maribo
Nykøbing
Falster
Lolland
Rødby
Holeby
Øster Ulslev
Nysted
Rødbyhavn
Væggerløse
Marielyst
Marrebæk
Hesnæs
KRENKERUP
ÅLHOLM SLOT
DK
Gedser
Fehmarn
Puttgarden
Burg
Grossenbrode
Dahme
Kellenhusen
Travemünde
Trelleborg
Mecklenburger Bucht
NATIONALPARK VORPOMMERSCHE BODDENLANDSCHAFT
Kap Arkona
Dranske
Wiek
Altenkirchen
Glowe
Hiddensee
Schaprode
Grosser Jasmunder Bodden
Darsser Ort
Prerow
Zingst
Barth
Wustrow
Saaler Bodden
Gross Mohrdorf
Rambin
Bergen
Binz
Samtens
Putbus
Garz
Stralsund
Löbnitz
Graal-Müritz
Ribnitz-Damgarten
Zudar
Greifswalder Bodden
Kühlungsborn
Nienhagen
Warnemünde
Rövershagen
Richtenberg
Reinberg
Rerik
Bad Doberan
Petersdorf
Marlow
Franzburg
Abtshagen
Kröpelin
ROSTOCK
Sanitz
Bad Sülze
Tribsees
Grimmen
Greifswald
Lubmin
Poel
Neubukow
Tessin
Glewitz
Poggendorf
Kemnitz
Boltenhagen
Klütz
Satow
Recknitz
Trebel
Loitz
Peene
Gramkow
Wismar
Züsow
Schwaan
Gnoien
Laage
Weitendorf
Jördenstorf
Dargun
Demmin
Jarmen
Gützkow
Grevesmühlen
Neukloster
Bützow
A20
E22
MECKLENBURG
Bobitz
Warin
Güstrow
A19
E55
Thürkow
Neukalen
Tollense
Ziethen
Zickhusen
Bad Kleinen
Kummerower-See
Golchen
Brüel
Teterow
Malchin
Gadebusch
Sternberg
Schweriner-See
Malchiner See
SCHLITZ
Krakow am See
Reuterstadt Stavenhagen
Schwanbeck
Friedland
Altentreptow
Schwerin
MECKLENBURGISCHE SEENPLATTE
Mestlin
Dahmen
VORPOMMERN
Goldberg
Crivitz
A241
Karow
Kl. Plasten
Neubrandenburg
Elde
Severin
Malchow
Waren
Tollense-See
Hagenow
Lübz
Klink
D
Penzlin
Parchim
Plau
Plauer-See
Müritz See
Burg Stargard
Woldegk
Redefin
Neustadt-Glewe
Röbel
MÜRITZ
Ludwigslust
Marnitz
Neustrelitz
Möllenbeck
Zierzow
Meyenburg
Fürstenwerder
Grabow
Freyenstein
Wredenhagen
Eldena
E26
A24
Putlitz
Mirow
NATIONALPARK
Feldberg
Carwitz
Boitzenburg
Milow
Wesenberg
Lychen
Dömitz
Karstädt
Pritzwalk
Ravensbrück
Hassleben
Wittstock
Fürstenberg
Mittenwalde
ELBETAL
Lenzen
Perleberg
Schnackenburg
Herzsprung
Tüchen
Templin
Gartow
Schönebeck
Fretzdorf
Rheinsberg
Dannenwalde
Köpernitz
Wittenberge
Bad Wilsnack
Katerbow
Gransee
Gumtow
Lindow
Zehdenick
Kyritz
Alt Ruppin
Joachimsthal
Glöwen
Neuruppin
Arendsee
Seehausen
JAGDSHL HUBERTUSSTOCK
Wusterhausen
BRAND
Werben
34
Herzberg
Löwenberg
Lückstedt
Havelberg
Neustadt
Gross
Dosse
Aland
Havel

159
E
F
G
H
Trelleborg
Rønne
TUHL
NATIONALPARK
JASMUND
ssnitz
Göhren
Rønne
Ystad
København
Thiessow
Łazy
Mielno
Sarbinowo
Ustronie Morskie
Jezioro Jamno
Kołobrzeg
Będzino
Koszalin
Mrzeżyno
Niechorze
Rewal
Pobierowo
Dziwnów
Peenemünde
Zinnowitz
Wolgast
Koserow
Usedom
Wolin
Kamień Pomorski
Trzebiatów
Gościno
Karlino
Niedalino
Biesiekierz
Białogard
Bansin
Heringsdorf
Ahlbeck
Lassan
NATURPARK
Wisełka
Kołczewo
Międzyzdroje
Świerzno
Rymań
Murchin
Świnoujście
Zirchow
Usedom
WOLIŃSKI PARK NARODOWY
Rzewnowo
Brojce
Podwilcze
Byszyno
Gryfice
Sławoborze
Mechowo
Wolin
Parłówko
Golczewo
USEDOM - ODERHAFF
Stettiner Haff
Zalew Szczeciński
Płoty
Resko
Świdwin
Starogard
Połczyn-Zdrój
Ueckermünde
Altwarp
Nowe Warpno
Przybiernów
Błotno
Eggesin
UECKERMÜNDER HEIDE
Ahlbeck
Trzebież
Babigoszcz
Stepnica
Nowogard
Radowo Wielkie
PL
Łobez
Łabędzie
DRAWSKI PARK KRAJOBRAZOWY
Torgelow
Hintersee
PUSZCZA WKRZAŃSKA
PUSZCZA GOLENIOWSKA
Ostrowice
Goleniów
Dobra
Police
Pasewalk
Buk
Nastazin
Węgorzyno
Zarańsko
Jezioro Dąbie
Maszewo
Drawsko Pomorskie
Złocieniec
Lubieszyn
SZCZECIN
Löcknitz
Göritz
Chociwel
Łęczyca
Jezioro Lubie
Konotop
Ińsko
Brüssow
Dąbie
Dobrzany
Morzycyn
Pomellen
Stargard-Szczeciński
Schmölln
Kołbaskowo
Kołbacz
Mirosławiec
Penkum
A6
E28
A11
E28
Jezioro Miedwie
Stare Czarnowo
NATIONALPARK
Gartz
Gryfino
Suchań
Kalisz Pomorski
Bronikowo
Recz
Gramzow
Casekow
Będgoszcz
Warnice
Kolin
Drawno
Tuczno
UNTERES ODERTAL
Nowe Czarnowo
Dolice
Lubiatowo
Choszczno
Widuchowa
Pyrzyce
DRAWIEŃSKI PARK NARODOWY
Greiffenberg
Schwedt
Banie
Ognica
Piaseczno
Jesionowo
Krzęcin
Łasko
Człopa
Angermünde
Krajnik Gorny
Trzcińsko Zdrój
Lipiany
Pełczyce
Bierzwnik
Breń
Radęcin
Otanów
Rów
Sowiniec
Stare Osieczno
Chojna
STOLPE
Barlinek
Dobiegniew
Dankow
KLOSTER CHORIN
Oderberg
Cedynia
Myślibórz
Strzelce
Trzcinna
35
36
22
POBRZEŻE
POJEZIERZE
Dar
We
Ty
Stare D
Czap
Ru

A
B
C
D
1
2
3
4
5
6
NADMORSKI PARK KRAJOBRAZOWY
SŁOWIŃSKI PARK NARODOWY
Jezioro Łebsko
Jezioro Gardno
Jezioro Wicko
Jezioro Jamno
Łeba
Ulinia
Wierzchucino
Krokowa
Żelazno
Choczewo
Mierzyno
Zamostne
Bolszewo
Reda
Wejherowo
Godętowo
Kluki
Rowy
Smołdzino
Wicko
Ustka
Objazda
Żelkowo
Główczyce
Jarosławiec
Lubuczewo
Damno
Lębork
Postomino
Słupsk
Mianowice
Osowo Leborskie
Darłówko
Darłowo
Staniewice
Dębnica Kaszubska
Oskowo
Kołeczkowo
Chwaszczyno
Łebno
Miszewo
Bukowo Morskie
Sławno
Czarna Dąbrówka
Sierakowice
Kartuzy
KASZUBSKI PARK KRAJOBRAZOWY
PARK KRAJOBRAZOWY DOLINA SŁUPI
Budowo
Łazy
Malechowo
Ostrowiec
Barcino
Suchorze
Unichowo
Jasień
Klukowa Huta
Sulęczyno
Egiertowo
Mielno
Kępice
Kołczygłowy
Pomysk Maly
WIEŻYCA
Krąg
Sianów
Koszalin
Bytów
Półczno
Nowa Karczma
Trzepowo
Lubno
Tuchomie
Kościerzyna
Skarszew
Biesiekierz
Polanów
Mostowo
Dretyń
Lipusz
Niedalino
Radew
Rosnowo
Piaszczyna
Białogard
Wdzydze Kiszewskie
Starogard Gdański
Głodowa
Miastko
Lipnica
Dziemiany
Weldkowo
Bobolice
ZABORSKI PARK KRAJOBRAZOWY
Jezioro Wdzydze
Tychowo
Wiele
Bytonia
Zblewo
Biały Bór
Koczała
Zielona Chocina
Brusy
Stare Dębno
Wierzchowo
Osowo Leśne
Parsęta
Brzezie
Grzmiąca
Mecikat
Czarna Woda
Przechlewo
PARK NAR. BORY TUCHOLSKIE
BORY TUCHOLSKIE
Wda
Kołacz
Barwice
Czersk
Rytel
DRAWSKI PARK KRAJOBRAZOWY
Rzeczenica
PL
Szczecinek
Legbąd
Śliwice
Czarne
Człuchów
Chojnice
Ostrowice
TUCHOLSKI PARK KRAJOBRAZOWY
Silno
Tleń
Jelenino
Barkowo
Zamarte
Tuchola
Osie
Łubowo
Jezioro Piłe
Czaplinek
Debrzno
Karmień Krajenskie
Ledyczek
Okonek
Złocieniec
Pamiętowo
Ostrowite
Machliny
Lipka
Gostycyn
Jezioro Lubie
Podgaje
Radawnica
Sępólno Krajenskie
Iłowiec
Jastrowie
Byszki
Górzna
Mąkowarsko
Złotów
Łowin
Mirosławiec
Kłebowiec
Więcbork
Chełmno
Szwecja
Pruszcz
Plytnica
Rudna
Krajenka
Wierzchucin Krolewski
Koronowo
Bronikowo
Wałcz
Łobżenica
Mrocza
Skórka
Tryszczyn
Tuczno
Gostomia
Wysoka
Kosztowo
Sadki
Rusinowo
Piła
Ślesin
Szydłowo
Wyrzysk
Nakło nad Notecią
Śmiłowo
DRAWIEŃSKI PARK KRAJOBRAZOWY
Człopa
BYDGOSZCZ
Trzcianka
Noteć
Smogulec
Rynarzewo
Ujście
Szamocin
Brzoza
Kcynia
Szubin
Stare Osieczno
Margonin
Siedlisko
Chodzież
Łabiszyn
Sarbia
Drawa
POJEZIERZE DRAWSKIE
POMORSKIE
SŁOWIŃSKIE
KASZUBY
21
36

KALININGRAD
Kaliningrad
Yantarnyy
Primorsk
Baltiysk
Ushakovo
Južnyj
RUS
Mamonovo
Bagrationovsk
Domnovo
Pravdinsk
Gvar
Karlskrona
Visby
Nynäshamn
Oxelösund
Hel
Zatoka Gdańska
Kaliningradskiy Zaliv
Prokhladnaya
Pregolya
GDYNIA
Sopot
GDAŃSK
Nowa Karczma
Krynica Morska
PARK KRAJOBR. MIERZEJA WIŚLANA
Zalew Wiślany
Frombork
Braniewo
Lelkowo
Górowo Iławeckie
Sępopol
Stegna
Tolkmicko
Pogrodzie
Płoskinia
Pluty
Bartoszyce
Pruszcz Gdański
Trutnowy
Nowy Dwór Gdański
Milejewo
Pakosze
Pieniężno
Galiny
Korsze
ELBLĄG
Młynary
Nowica
Orneta
STOCZEK KLASZTORNY
Lidzbark Warmiński
Bisztynek
Nowy Staw
Tczew
Jegłownik
Krosno
Pasłęk
Godkowo
Lubomino
Malbork
Str. Pole
Zwierzno
Kalnik
Wilczkowo
Radostowo
Dobre Miasto
Lutry
Jeziorany
Rychliki
Rudno
Sztum
Dzierzgoń
Małdyty
Morąg
Kalisty
Tuławki
Pelplin
Balewo
Przezmark
Spręcowo
Biskupiec
Gniew
Mikołajki Pomorskie
Stary Dzierzgoń
Zalewo
Barczewo
Kromerowo
Łukta
Jerzwałd
Jezioro Jeziorak
OLSZTYN
Mała Karczma
Prabuty
Susz
Siemiany
Ostróda
Gietrzwałd
Dźwierzuty
Kwidzyn
Mańki
Stawiguda
Pasym
Nowe
Szymbark
Gardeja
Kisielice
Lipowo
Rychnowo
Pietrzwałd
Iława
DYLEWSKA GORA
Olsztynek
Zgniłocha
Szcz
Dusocin
Lubawa
Marwałd
Frygnowo
Jedwabno
Łasin
Grunwald
Dolina Grupa
Biskupiec
Grudziądz
Nowe Miasto Lubawskie
Rączki
Dąbrówno
Okonin
Jabłonowo Pomorskie
Kurzętnik
Nidzica
Muszaki
Wielbark
Paparzyn
Radzyn Chełmiński
Brzozie Lubawskie
Uzdowo
Janowo
Płużnica
Kozłowo
Papowo Biskupie
Wąbrzeżno
Grzybno
Brodnica
Lidzbark
Działdowo
Chorzele
Bielczyny
Orzechowo
Górzno
Kuklin
Chełmża
Zieluń-Osada
Krzynowłoga Mała
Kowalewo Pomorskie
Lubowidz
Mława
Drazdze
Golub Dobrzyń
Rypin
Okalewo
Żuromin
Rzęgnowo
Radomin
Grudusk
Szreńsk
Przasnysz
Zbojno
Bieżuń
Szulmierz
Mdzewo
Czernikowo
Kikół
Grodzeń
Radzanów
Ciechanów
Opinogóra
Rościszewo
Mak Mazowie
POJEZIERZE
Wisła
Nogat
Pasłęka
Łyna
Drwęca
A192
A193
A194
A195
A196
A229
E77
E75
202
24
37
38
1
2
3
4
5
6
E
F
G
H

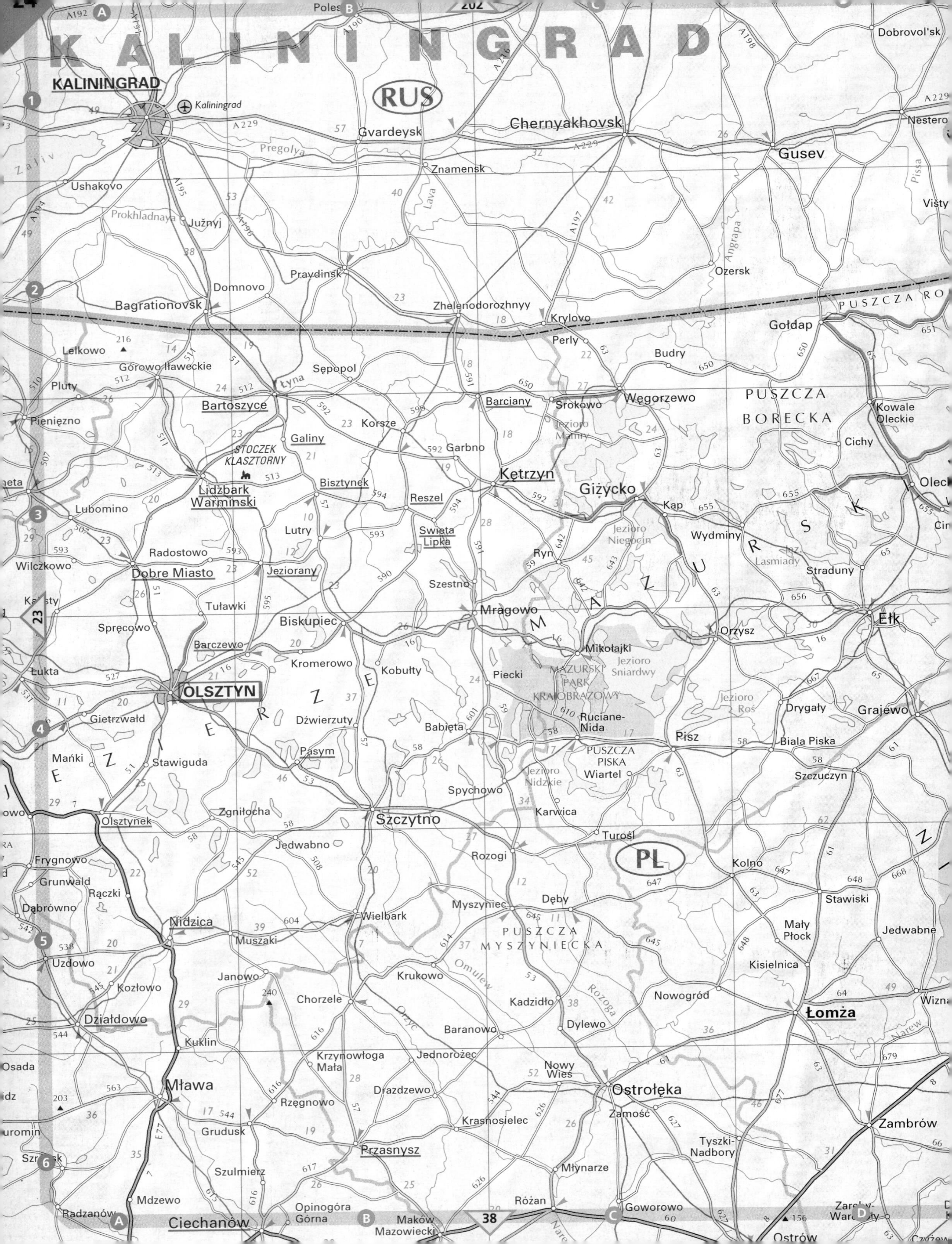

KALININGRAD
RUS
PL
Kaliningrad
Chernyakhovsk
Gvardeysk
Gusev
Znamensk
Dobrovol'sk
Nestero
Višty
Ushakovo
Južnyj
Prokhladnaya
Pregolya
Pravdinsk
Ozersk
Domnovo
Bagrationovsk
Zhelenodorozhnyy
Krylovo
Gołdap
PUSZCZA RO
Perly
Budry
Lelkowo
Górowo Iławeckie
Sępopol
Pluty
Bartoszyce
Barciany
Srokowo
Węgorzewo
PUSZCZA BORECKA
Kowale Oleckie
Pieniężno
Korsze
Galiny
Jezioro Mamry
Cichy
STOCZEK KLASZTORNY
Garbno
Kętrzyn
Giżycko
Olecko
Lidzbark Warmiński
Bisztynek
Reszel
Kap
Lubomino
Lutry
Święta Lipka
Jezioro Niegocin
Wydminy
Radostowo
Ryn
Jez. Łaśmiady
Straduny
Wilczkowo
Dobre Miasto
Jeziorany
Szestno
Tuławki
Mrągowo
Biskupiec
Orzysz
Ełk
Sprecowo
Barczewo
Kromerowo
Mikołajki
Jezioro Śniardwy
Łukta
Kobułty
Piecki
MAZURSKI PARK KRAJOBRAZOWY
OLSZTYN
Jezioro Roś
Drygały
Grajewo
Gietrzwałd
Dźwierzuty
Babięta
Ruciane-Nida
Pisz
Biała Piska
Mańki
Stawiguda
Pasym
PUSZCZA PISKA
Wiartel
Szczuczyn
Jezioro Nidzkie
Spychowo
Olsztynek
Zgniłocha
Szczytno
Karwica
Jedwabno
Turośl
Rozogi
Frygnowo
Grunwald
Kolno
Rączki
Dąbrówno
Stawiski
Dęby
Myszyniec
PUSZCZA MYSZYNIECKA
Nidzica
Wielbark
Muszaki
Mały Płock
Jedwabne
Uzdowo
Kisielnica
Kozłowo
Janowo
Krukowo
Omulew
Rozoga
Chorzele
Kadzidło
Nowogród
Łomża
Wizna
Działdowo
Baranowo
Dylewo
Narew
Kuklin
Krzynowłoga Mała
Jednorożec
Osada
Orzyc
Nowy Wieś
Mława
Drazdzewo
Ostrołęka
Rzęgnowo
Zamość
Zambrów
Grudusk
Krasnosielec
Tyszki-Nadbory
Przasnysz
Szulmierz
Młynarze
Mdzewo
Różan
Radzanów
Opinogóra Górna
Goworowo
Zaręby-Warchoły
Ciechanów
Maków Mazowiecki
Ostrów
E77
A229
A192
A190
A216
A198
A195
A196
A197
A194
MAZURY
WARMIA
POJEZIERZE

23
38
202

Kudirkos Naumiestis
Kazlu-Rūda
Pilviškiai
Vilkaviškis
Marijampolė
Prienai
Vilunai
Jieznas
Birštonas
Igliauka
TRAKU ISTORINIS NACIONALINIS PARKAS
Trakai
Lentvaris
Vilnius
Aukštadvaris
Rūdiškės
Alytus
LT
Valkininkai
Šalčinink
Girgantai
Kalvarija
Krosna
Wiżajny
Babriškes
Varena
Byenyako
Varanava
Eišiškės
Szypliski
Lazdijai
Seriaji
Merkine
Nemunas
Merkys
DZŪKIJOS NACIONALINIS PARKAS
Radun'
Suwałki
Sejny
WIGIERSKI PARK NARODOWY
Jez Wigry
Zelwa
Kapčiamiestis
Druskininkai
Matyli
Raczki
Rospuda
PUSZCZA
AUGUSTOWSKA
Rudawka
Parechcha
Myto
Vasilishki
Augustów
Sapotskin
Azyory
Astryna
Netta
Kurianka
Lipsk
HRODNO
ГРОДНО
Rajgród
Dąbrowa Białostocka
Zhaludok
Shchuchin
Nyoman
BIEBRZAŃSKI PARK
Debowo
Nowy Dwór
Skidal'
Sidra
Suchowola
Kuźnica
BY
Nowowola
Lunna
Indura
Masty
Goniądz
Korycin
Janów
Sokółka
Kazlow
Mońki
Jasionówka
PARK
Ros'
Dzyareck
Krasne Folwarczne
Gugny
Knyszyn
KRAJOBRAZOWY
Czarna Białostocka
Krynki
PUSZCZY KNYSZYŃSKIEJ
Supraśl
Vawkavysk
Zyel'va
Zal'vyan'ka
Wasilków
Jurowce
Tykocin
Żółki
Królowy Most
Bobrowniki
Pahranichny
Choroszcz
Jeżewo
BIAŁYSTOK
Grabówka
Svislach
NARWIAŃSKI PARK NARODOWY
Michałowo
Jałówka
Padarosk
Zabłudów
Porazava
Łapy
Sokoły
Suraż
Narew
Ruzhany
PODLASK
PUSZCZA
BIAŁOWIESKI PARK NARODOWY
Bielsk Podlaski
Hajnówka
Naraw
203
205
39
E
F
G
H
1
2
3
4
5
6

CHANNEL ISLANDS /
ILES NORMANDES
Golfe de St-Malo
Côte d'Émeraude
BRETAGNE
GBG
GBJ
Guernsey/
Guernesey
St-Peter Port
Vale
Forest
Sark/Sercq
Alderney /
Aurigny
Jersey
Grosnez Point
l'Etacq
St. John
la Pulente
Gorey
St-Helier
Poole
Rosslare Harbour
Portsmouth
Cap de
la Hague
Auderville
St-Germain-
des-Vaux
Nez de
Jobourg
Beaumont
Vauville
Cherbourg
Maupertus
Les Pieux
Bricquebec
Carteret
Barneville-
Carteret
Cap de Carteret
Portbail
St-Sauveur
le-Vicomte
La Haye-
du-Puits
St-Germain-
Plage
Lessay
Pirou-Plage
Périers
Agon-
Coutainville
Coutances
Hauteville
Plage
ILES
CHAUSEY
Bréhal
Gavray
Granville
Percy
Villedieu-
les-Poêles
Jullouville
Sartilly
St-Jean-
le-Thomas
Avranches
Brécey
Pontaubault
Ducey
Le Mont-
St-Michel
Baie du Mont St-Michel
Pontorson
St-James
Antrain
St-Brice-
en-Coglès
Fougères
Dompierre-
du-Chemin
St-Aubin-
du-Cormier
Liffré
Val-d'Izé
Châteaubourg
Vitré
CHÂT. DES ROCHERS
Châteaugiron
Janzé
La Guerche-de-
Bretagne
RENNES
Mordelles
Pont-Réan
Guichen
Bain-de-Bretagne
Ploumanac'h
Perros-Guirec
Sillon de Talbert
Ile de Bréhat
Pointe de l'Arcouest
Tréguier
Lézardrieux
Paimpol
Lannion
CHÂTEAU DE
TONQUÉDEC
TEMPLE DE LANLEFF
Pontrieux
Bégard
Plouha
Lanvollon
St-Quay-
Portrieux
Etables-sur-Mer
Binic
Guingamp
St-Brieuc
Le Val-André
Erquy
Sables-d'Or-
les-Pins
Cap Fréhel
FORT LA LATTE
St-Cast-le-Guildo
Matignon
St-Jacut
St-Lunaire
Dinard
St-Malo
Rothéneuf
Pointe du
Grouin
Cancale
Ploubalay
Plancoët
Lamballe
CHÂT. DE
HUNAUDAYE
MONT-DOL
Dol-de-
Bretagne
Dinan
Jugon-
les-Lacs
Moncontour
Quintin
St-Nicolas-
du-Pélem
Corlay
Gouarec
Uzel
Lac-de-
Guerlédan
Mur-de-
Bretagne
Plouguenast
Collinée
Broons
Evran
Combourg
Bécherel
St-Jouan-
de-l'Isle
Hédé
Sens-
de-Bretagne
St-Aubin-
d'Aubigné
Canal d'Ille et Rance
Loudéac
Merdrignac
St-Méen
Montauban
Bédée
Montfort
Gaël
Mauron
Pontivy
Rohan
La Trinité-
Porhoët
ST-NICODÈME
Baud
Locminé
Josselin
Ploërmel
Plélan-le-Grand
CHÂT. DE
TRECESSON
Guer
Maure
Lohéac
Pipriac
Malestroit
Sérent
TOUR
D'ELVEN
St-Jean-
Brévelay
Grand-
Champ
Pluvigner
Ste-Anne-
d'Auray
Auray
Rance
Oust
Yvel
Meu
Vilaine
Trieux
Couesnon
Sélune
Sienne
PARC N
RÉG. DES MA
A
B
C
D
1
2
3
4
5
6
40
41
E401
E50
N12
N24
N137
N164
N176
N175
A84
E03
N13

E
F
G
H
ENGLISH CHANNEL/
LA MANCHE
Portsmouth
Portsmouth
Pointe de Barfleur
Barfleur
St-Vaast-la-Hougue
Quinéville
Ste-Mère-Eglise
Grandcamp-Maisy
Isigny-sur-Mer
Côte du Calvados
St-Laurent
Port-en-Bessin
Arromanches-les-Bains
Baie de la Seine
Courseulles-sur-Mer
St-Aubin-sur-Mer
Luc-sur-Mer
CHÂTEAU DE FONTAINE HENRY
Bayeux
ABB.DE MONDAYE
St-Lô
Balleroy
Ouistreham
Riva-Bella
Cabourg
Côte Fleurie
Houlgate
Dives-sur-Mer
Villers
Deauville
Trouville
Villerville
Honfleur
CAEN
ST-CLAIR
Troarn
Dozulé
Caumont
Torigni-sur-Vire
Villers-Bocage
Aunay-sur-Odon
Cambremer
Pont-l'Evêque
Beuzeville
St-Maclou
Pont-Audemer
Cormeilles
Lisieux
LE HAVRE
Cap de la Hève
Octeville
Cauville
Montivilliers
Harfleur
Tancarville
POINTE DE LA ROQUE
Cap d'Antifer
FALAISE D'AVAL
Etretat
Yport
Fécamp
BAILLEUL
Goderville
Bolbec
Lillebonne
Caudebec-en-Caux
St-Wandrille
Barentin
Pavilly
Yvetot
Duclair
Jumièges
Fauville
Yerville
Doudeville
Bacqueville-en-Caux
Cany-Barville
Veulettes-sur-Mer
St-Valery-en-Caux
Veules-les-Roses
Fontaine-le-Dun
Bourneville
Bourg-Achard
Bourgtheroulde-Infreville
Elbeuf
ABB. DE BONPORT
Louviers
Lieurey
Brionne
CHÂT. DU CHAMP DU BATAILLE
Le Neubourg
Bernay
Beaumont-le-Roger
Beaumesnil
Thiberville
Orbec
Broglie
Livarot
St-Pierre-sur-Dives
Vimoutiers
Courteilles
BASSE-NORMANDIE
HAUTE-
Thury-Harcourt
Clécy
Vire
Vassy
Condé-sur-Noireau
ROCHE D'OËTRE
Falaise
Tinchebray
Sourdeval
Flers
Mortain
Putanges-Pont-Ecrepin
Trun
Fromental
Briouze
Argentan
HARAS DU PIN
Le Pin-au-Haras
Exmes
Gacé
Nonant-le-Pin
Le Merlerault
Ste-Gauburge-Ste-Colombe
L'Aigle
Rugles
La Neuve-Lyre
Conches-en-Ouche
Evreux
Damville
Breteuil
Verneuil-sur-Avre
Nonancourt
Barenton
Domfront
La Ferté-Macé
Rânes
Le Teilleul
PARC NATUREL RÉGIONAL NORMANDIE-MAINE
Bagnoles-de-l'Orne
Mortrée
CHÂT. D'O
Sées
Carrouges
Couterne
Couptrain
Moulins-la-Marche
Courtomer
Gorron
Lassay
Ambrières
Pré-en-Pail
MONT DES AVALOIRS
Javron
Bazoches-sur-Hoëne
Longny-au-Perche
La Ferté-Vidame
Brézolles
Mortagne-au-Perche
Alençon
Mayenne
Villaines-la-Juhel
Senonches
Châteauneuf-en-Thymerais
Bais
La Hutte
Fresnay-sur-Sarthe
Mamers
Bellême
Rémalard
MANOIR DE COURBOYER
La Loupe
Courville
CHÂT. DU ROCHER
Montsûrs
Evron
Champrond-en-Gâtine
Beaumont-sur-Sarthe
Sillé-le-Guillaume
Argentré
Nogent-le-Rotrou
Thivars

28
42

Hurstpierpoint
Steyning
ROYAL PAVILION
SHEFFIELD PARK
Uckfield
Mayfield
BODIAM CASTLE
Hawkinge
Kingsdown
South Foreland
LYMPNE CASTLE
GB
Dover
Folkestone
Heathfield
Northiam
Lewes
Glynde
Herstmonceux
Battle
CAMBER CASTLE
Rye
Hythe
Dymchurch
Sandgate
BRIGHTON
CISSBURY
Worthing
Lancing
Shoreham-by-Sea
Hove
Rottingdean
Hailsham
HERSTMONCEUX CASTLE (R. GREENWICH OBSERVATORY)
Winchelsea
Rye Bay
Lydd
New Romney
Dungeness
Polegate
CHARLESTON MANOR
Pevensey
Bexhill
St Leonards-on-Sea
Hastings
Newhaven
Seaford
Beachy Head
Eastbourne
EUROTUNNEL
Strait of Dover/
Pas de Calais
Blériot-Plage
Cap Gris Nez
Wissant
Framzelle
Marquise
Wimereux
Boulogne-sur-Mer
Le Portel
Pont-de-Briques
Hardelot-Plage
Desvres
Samer
ENGLISH CHANNEL/
LA MANCHE
Le Touquet-Paris-Plage
Etaples
Montreuil
Berck-Plage
ABBAYE DE VALLOIRES
Fort-Mahon-Plage
Hesdin
Portsmouth
Vron
Rue
Crécy-en-Ponthieu
Le Crotoy
Nouvion
St-Valery-sur-Somme
Somme
Ault
Le Tréport
Mesnil-Val
Eu
Abbeville
St-Riquier
Veulettes-sur-Mer
St-Valery-en-Caux
Varengeville-sur-Mer
Dieppe
Gamaches-en-Vexin
Veules-les-Roses
Cany-Barville
MANOIR D'ANGO
Blangy-sur-Bresle
Oisemont
Etretat
Yport
Fécamp
Fontaine-le-Dun
Airaines
Cap d'Antifer
FALAISE D'AVAL
BAILLEUL
Bacqueville-en-Caux
Londinières
Picquigny
Molliens
HAUTE-
Goderville
Doudeville
Foucarmont
Hornoy
Cauville
Octeville
Fauville
Yerville
Bellencombre
Neufchâtel-en-Bray
Aumale
Montivilliers
Tôtes
St-Saëns
Poix
de la Hève
Harfleur
Bolbec
Yvetot
Les Hayons
HAVRE
Lillebonne
Pavilly
Clères
Conty
Tancarville
Caudebec-en-Caux
St-Wandrille
Barentin
PARC ZOOL.
Buchy
Formerie
Grandvilliers
Villerville
Honfleur
POINTE DE LA ROQUE
Duclair
Forges-les-Eaux
Trouville
Beuzeville
St-Maclou
Marseille-en-Beauvaisis
Pont-l'Evêque
Bourneville
Jumièges
ROUEN
Crevecoeur
Pont-Audemer
Boos
Bourg-Achard
Gournay-en-Bray
Cormeilles
Bourgtheroulde-Infreville
Oissel
ABB. DE FONTAINE GUÉRARD
Lyons-la-Forêt
St-Germer-de-Fly
Beauvais
Cambremer
Lieurey
Fleury
Lisieux
Elbeuf
ABB. DE BONPORT
Pont-de-l'Arche
Ecouis
Auneuil
Brionne
Etrepagny
Thiberville
CHÂT. DU CHAMP DU BATAILLE
Louviers
Le Vaudreuil
Gisors
Les Andelys
Livarot
Bernay
Le Neubourg
Gaillon
Noailles
Mouy
NORMANDIE
Beaumont-le-Roger
Orbec
Broglie
Méru
Magny-en-Vexin
Clermont
PAS-
NO
27
42
15

Vlissingen
Knokke-Heist
Zeebrugge
Blankenberge
De Haan
Oostende (Ostende)
Breskens
Sluis
Oostburg
Terneuzen
Hoedekenskerke
Kruiningen
Perkpolder
Hoogerheide
NL
Middelkerke-Bad
Westende-Bad
Koksijde-Bad
De Panne
Nieuwpoort
Gistel
BRUGGE (BRUGES)
Damme
Maldegem
Axel
Hulst
Dunkerque Ouest
Dunkerque
Gravelines
Malo-les-Bains
Veurne (Furnes)
Eeklo
Zelzate
ANTWERPEN (ANVERS)
Bourbourg
Bergues
Diksmuide
Torhout
VLAANDEREN
Aalter
St-Niklaas (St-Nicolas)
Looberghe
Audruicq
Nordausques
GENT (Gand)
OOIDONK
Lokeren
Dendermonde (Termonde)
Roeselare (Roulers)
Wormhout
Watten
Tielt
Deinze
Ingelmunster
Poperinge
Cassel
Izegem
Wetteren
Willebroek
St-Omer
Steenvoorde
Ieper (Ypres)
Waregem
B
Aalst (Alost)
Méteren
Menen
Halluin
Kortrijk (Courtrai)
Oudenaarde (Audenarde)
Ninove
BRUSSEL/ BRUXELLES
Hazebrouck
Bailleul
Thérouanne
Nieppe
Armentières
Tourcoing
Roubaix
Brakel
Aire
Merville
Cuhom
Ronse (Renaix)
Geraardsbergen
GAASBEEK
Fruges
Lillers
Estaires
Lomme
LILLE
Lessines
Halle
Béthune
La Bassée
Seclin
Lesquin
Tournai (Doornik)
Enghien
Noeux
Carvin
Leuze
Ath
Houdain
CHÂTEAU FÉODAL D'OLHAIN
ATTRE
Braine-le-Comte
St-Pol-sur-Ternoise
Lens
Orchies
Belœil
Soignies
Nivelles
Hénin Beaumont
St-Amand-les-Eaux
Péruwelz
Casteau
RŒULX
Avesnes-le-Comte
Frévent
Douai
Valenciennes
Arras
Fresnes
Crespin
Onnaing
Denain
Mons (Bergen)
La Louvière
MARIEMONT
Gosselies
Beaumetz
Aniche
Binche
Doullens
Pas-en-Artois
Hordain
CHARLEROI
GROTTES DE NACOURS
Bucquoy
Marquion
Bavay
Givry
Thuin
Le Quesnoy
Maubeuge
Jeumont
Bapaume
Solesmes
Cambrai
Hautmont
Acheux-en-Amiénois
F
Englefontaine
Contay
Beaumont
Albert
ABB. DE VAUCELLES
Caudry
Landrecies
Walcourt
Le Cateau-Cambrésis
AMIENS
Corbie
Bray-sur-Somme
Longueau
Le Catelet
Avesnes-sur-Helpe
Péronne
Bohain-en-Vermandois
Villers-Bretonneux
Roisel
Le Nouvion-en-Thiérache
Fourmies
Chimay
La Capelle
Couvin
Moreuil
St-Quentin
Guise
Hirson
Canal de St-Quentin
Roye
Nesle
Ham
Ribemont
Rocroi
Sains
Vervins
Montdidier
Rumigny
Auvillers-les-Forges
Lassigny
Tergnier
La Fère
Crécy-sur-Serre
Marle
Cuvilly
Noyon
Chauny
Brunehamel
St-Just-en-Chaussée
Ressons
St-Gobain
Montcornet
Rozoy
Charleville-Mézières
ABB. D'OURSCAMPS
Ribécourt
Coucy-le-Château-Auffrique
Signy-l'Abbaye
Blérancourt
Laon
Estrées-St-Denis
Sissonne
Seraincourt
Arsy
Compiègne
Canal de l'Oise à l'Aisne
Novion-Porcien
Vic-sur-Aisne
Château-Porcien
CAVERNE DU DRAGON
Verberie
Pierrefonds
Vailly
Corbeny
Asfeld
Rethel
Ramsgate
PICARDIE
PAS-DE-CALAIS

16
44
29
Kingston-upon-Hull
Ramsgate
ROTTERDAM
Gouda
Brielle
Maassluis
Vlaardingen
Hellevoetsluis
Spijkenisse
Goeree
Ouddorp
Schoonhoven
MOLENS VAN KINDERDIJK
ZUID-HOLLAND
Oud Beijerland
Zwijndrecht
Sliedrecht
Middelharnis
Goeree
DORDRECHT
NATIONAAL PARK DE BIESBOSCH
Schouwen
Stellendam
Grevelingen
Haringvliet
Burgh-Haamstede
Brouwershaven
Zierikzee
Walcheren
Noord-Beveland
Sluis
Willemstad
Hollands Diep
Geertruidenberg
Domburg
Zijpe
Krammer Volkerak
Made
Stavenisse
Steenbergen
Westkapelle
Veere
ZEELAND
Oosterschelde
Zevenbergen
Oosterhout
Middelburg
Goes
BREDA
Vlissingen
Halsteren
Bergen op Zoom
Roosendaal
TILBURG
Knokke-Heist
Breskens
Hoedekenskerke
Kruiningen
Westerschelde
Zeebrugge
Blankenberge
De Haan
Schoondijke
Perkpolder
Zundert
Oostende (Ostende)
Sluis
Oostburg
Terneuzen
Hoogerheide
Baarle-Nassau
Damme
Wuustwezel
Hoogstraten
Middelkerke-Bad
BRUGGE (BRUGES)
Maldegem
Axel
Hulst
Brasschaat
Brecht
Nieuwpoort
Gistel
ANTWERPEN (ANVERS)
Turnhout
Oostmalle
Eeklo
Zelzate
Schilde
Veurne (Furnes)
Kanaal v. Brugge
Deurne
Kasterlee
Torhout
Aalter
St-Niklaas (St-Nicolas)
Diksmuide
VLAANDEREN
GENT (Gand)
Lokeren
Temse
Herentals
OOIDONK
Dendermonde (Termonde)
Lier
Roeselare (Roulers)
Tielt
Deinze
Boom
Geel
Ingelmunster
Willebroek
Mechelen (Malines)
Westerlo
Poperinge
Izegem
Wetteren
Waregem
Aalst (Alost)
Herselt
AVERBODE
Ieper (Ypres)
BRUSSEL BRUXELLES
Aarschot
Menen
Halluin
Kortrijk (Courtrai)
Oudenaarde (Audenarde)
Diest
BRUSSEL/ BRUXELLES
National
HORST
Brakel
Ninove
Armentières
Tourcoing
Roubaix
Escaut (Schelde)
Dender
GAASBEEK
Leuven (Louvain)
Lomme
Ronse (Renaix)
Geraardsbergen
BEERSEL
Tervuren
Tienen (Tirlemont)
Zoutleeuw
LILLE
Lessines
Halle
Enghien
St-Truiden (St-Trond)
Waterloo
Seclin
Lesquin
Tournai (Doornik)
Ath
Wavre (Waver)
Carvin
Leuze
Jodoigne
ATTRE
Braine-le-Comte
Beloeil
Soignies
Nivelles
Waremme
Orchies
St-Amand-les-Eaux
Péruwelz
Genappe
Hannut (Hannuit)
ROEULX
VILLERS
Eghezée
Douai
Casteau
Gembloux
Valenciennes
Crespin
Mons (Bergen)
La Louvière
MARIEMONT
Fleurus
Fresnes
Denain
Onnaing
Binche
Gosselies
Aniche
Namur (Namen)
Andenne
Hordain
CHARLEROI
Châtelet
Givry
Bavay
Maubeuge
Thuin
Fosses
Wépion
RÉGION WALLONNE
Marquion
Le Quesnoy
Profondeville
Solesmes
Jeumont
Cambrai
Hautmont
Mettet
Yvoir
Havelange
ABB. DE VAUCELLES
Englefontaine
Beaumont
Florennes
Bouvignes
Dinant
Ciney
Caudry
Landrecies
Walcourt
Hastière-Lavaux
Le Cateau-Cambrésis
Avesnes-sur-Helpe
Philippeville
Anseremme
Marche-en-Famenne
Le Catelet
Waulsort
Givet
Rochefort
Bohain-en-Vermandois
Le Nouvion-en-Thiérache
Fourmies
Chimay
Beauraing
Han-sur-Lesse
Roisel
La Capelle
Couvin
Wellin
St-Quentin
Guise
Hirson
Fumay
Revin
Gedinne
St-Hubert
Ribemont
Meuse
Dijle
F
B

17
NL
D
NORD-BRABANT
LIMBURG
NORDRHEIN-WESTFALEN
RHEINLAND-
ARDENNE
Ede
ARNHEM
NIJMEGEN
Doetinchem
Emmerich
Kleve
Bocholt
Wesel
Xanten
Dorsten
Marl
Recklinghausen
Gelsenkirchen
Herne
Castrop-Rauxel
Bottrop
Oberhausen
ESSEN
BOCHUM
Witten
Hagen
Moers
DUISBURG
Mülheim
KREFELD
Venlo
Roermond
MÖNCHENGLADBACH
Rheydt
Neuss
DÜSSELDORF
WUPPERTAL
Remscheid
SOLINGEN
Leverkusen
LEVERKUSEN
Bergisch Gladbach
Gummersbach
KÖLN
Brühl
BONN
Siegburg
Euskirchen
Düren
AACHEN
Heerlen
MAASTRICHT
Genk
LIEGE
(LUIK)
Verviers
Eupen
Malmedy
Spa
Stavelot
Bad Neuenahr
Ahrweiler
Andernach
Neuwied
Koblenz
Mayen
Nürburg
NÜRBURGRING
Prüm
Gerolstein
Daun
St Vith
EINDHOVEN
Helmond
Weert
'S-HERTOGEN-
BOSCH
Oss
Tiel
Gorinchem
Culemborg
Doorn
Wageningen
Zevenaar
Winterswijk
Gronau
Ahaus
Coesfeld
Dülmen
Haltern
Dinslaken
Gladbeck
Velbert
Ratingen
Hilden
Langenfeld
Kempen
Viersen
Erkelenz
Grevenbroich
Jülich
Eschweiler
Stolberg
Kerpen
Frechen
Bergheim
Zülpich
Mechernich
Schleiden
Monschau
Blankenheim
Adenau
Sinzig
Linz
Bad Honnef
Königswinter
Hennef
Lommel
Hasselt
Tongeren
(Tongres)
Valkenswaard
Venray
Geldern
Goch
Sittard
Geleen
Kerkrade
Wuppertal
45

17
18
46
31
Zwolle
Hattem
Dedemsvaart
Hardenberg
Twist
Emlichheim
Haselünne
Herzlake
Quakenbrück
Essen
Vechta
Lohne
Dinklage
Diepholz
Ommen
Vroomshoop
Uelsen
Neuenhaus
Lingen
NATURPARK NÖRDL.
Bersenbrück
Ankum
Fürstenau
Holdorf
Steinfeld
Dümmer See
Damme
OVERIJSSEL
Wijhe
Olst
Raalte
Nijverdal
Hellendoorn
Ootmarsum
Nordhorn
Denekamp
Freren
Beesten
Lünne
TEUTOBURGER
WALD
Vörden
NL
Deventer
Wierden
Rijssen
Almelo
Oldenzaal
Holten
Hengelo
Schüttorf
Hopsten
Recke
Bramsche
Bad Bentheim
Rheine
Hörstel
Ibbenbüren
Mettingen
WIEHENGEBIRGE
Bohmte
Goor
Delden
Voorst
ENSCHEDE
Gronau
Ochtrup
Lotte
Bad Essen
OSNABRÜCK
Warnsveld
Lochem
Haaksbergen
Epe
Wettringen
Emsdetten
Tecklenburg
Borculo
Neede
Alstätte
Heek
Steinfurt
Saerbeck
Lengerich
Melle
Ruurlo
Eibergen
Ahaus
Schöppingen
Borghorst
Nordwalde
NATURPARK
Bad Iburg
Doesburg
Groenlo
Vreden
Horstmar
Greven
Ladbergen
Bad Rothenfelde
Doetinchem
Lichtenvoorde
Winterswijk
Stadtlohn
Legden
NORDRHEIN-
Glandorf
Borgholzhausen
Varsseveld
Altenberge
Brock
Ostbevern
Versmold
Werther
Halle
Aalten
Kotten
Oeding
Gescher
Billerbeck
TEUTOBURGER WALD
's Heerenberg
Coesfeld
Nottuln
MÜNSTER
Telgte
Sassenberg
BIELEFELD
Isselburg
Bocholt
Warendorf
Harsewinkel
Brackwede
Kleve
Rhede
Borken
Dülmen
Appelhülsen
Freckenhorst
Gütersloh
Rees
NATURPARK
Heiden
Reken
Senden
Raesfeld
LEMBECK
Lüdinghausen
Sendenhorst
Rheda
Hamminkeln
HOHE MARK
Schermbeck
Haltern
Drensteinfurt
Oelde
Wiedenbrück
Goch
Xanten
Wesel
Wulfen
Ascheberg
Nordkirchen
Neubeckum
-WESTFALEN
Rietberg
Ahlen
D
Weeze
Sonsbeck
Alpen
Dorsten
Marl
Datteln
Selm
WASSERSCH. CAPPENBERG
Bockum-Hövel
Beckum
HAMM
Lippborg
Lippstadt
Kamp Lintfort
Rheinberg
Dinslaken
Gladbeck
Recklinghausen
Waltrop
Werne
Rhynern
Herzfeld
Salzkotten
Lünen
Bottrop
Gelsenkirchen
Castrop-Rauxel
Kamen
Erwitte
Geseke
Kerken
Moers
Oberhausen
Herne
Unna
Werl
Soest
ESSEN
BOCHUM
DORTMUND
Kempen
DUISBURG
Mülheim
Witten
Schwerte
Neheim-Hüsten
Menden
Rüthen
KREFELD
Süchteln
Viersen
Hattingen
HOHENSYBURG
NATURPARK ARNSBERGER WALD
Belecke
Kettwig
Wetter
Hemer
Arnsberg
Warstein
Ratingen
Velbert
Hagen
Iserlohn
Beckum
Brilon
Düsseldorf
Hohenlimburg
Letmathe
Mettmann
Schwelm
Sundern
Meschede
Nuttlar
Olsberg
Neuss
DÜSSELDORF
WUPPERTAL
Altena
Werdohl
BRUCHHSR. STEINE
Rheydt
Rheindahlen
DYCK
BENRATH
Radevormwald
Lüdenscheid
Eslohe
Hilden
Grevenbroich
SOLINGEN
Remscheid
Halver
Plettenberg
HOMERT
Finnentrop
Siedlinghausen
Erkelenz
Dormagen
Langenfeld
Opladen
Wermelskirchen
Wipperfürth
Meinerzhagen
Attendorn
Schmallenberg
KAHLER ASTEN
Winterberg
ALTENBERGER DOM
NATURPARK
Grevenbrück
Langewiese
Titz
Mersch
LEVERKUSEN
Bergisch Gladbach
Gummersbach
EBBEGEBIRGE
Altenhundem
Kirchundem
Hallenberg
Bergheim
Jülich
Elsdorf
Engelskirchen
Bensberg
Berg-Neustadt
Olpe
RHEIN-WESER-TURM
Hilchenbach
Bad Berleburg
Frechen
Kerpen
KÖLN
Overath
WIEHLER TROPFSTEINH.
BERGISCHES LAND
Erndtebrück
KELLERBERG
Battenberg
LÖRSFELD
Köln/Bonn
Kreuztal
ROTHAARGEBIRGE
Düren
Erftstadt
Brühl
Much
Waldbröl
Freudenberg
SIEGEN
Bad Laasphe
Biedenkopf
Siegburg
Windeck
Wilnsdorf
Zülpich
BONN
Beuel
Hennef
Eitorf
Wissen
Betzdorf
Eschenburg-Eibelshausen
Daaden
Burbach
Marburg
Euskirchen
Königswinter
MARIENTHAL
MARIENSTATT
Gladenbach
Bad Godesberg
DRACHENFELS
Altenkirchen
Dillenberg
Mechernich
Bad Honnef
Weimar

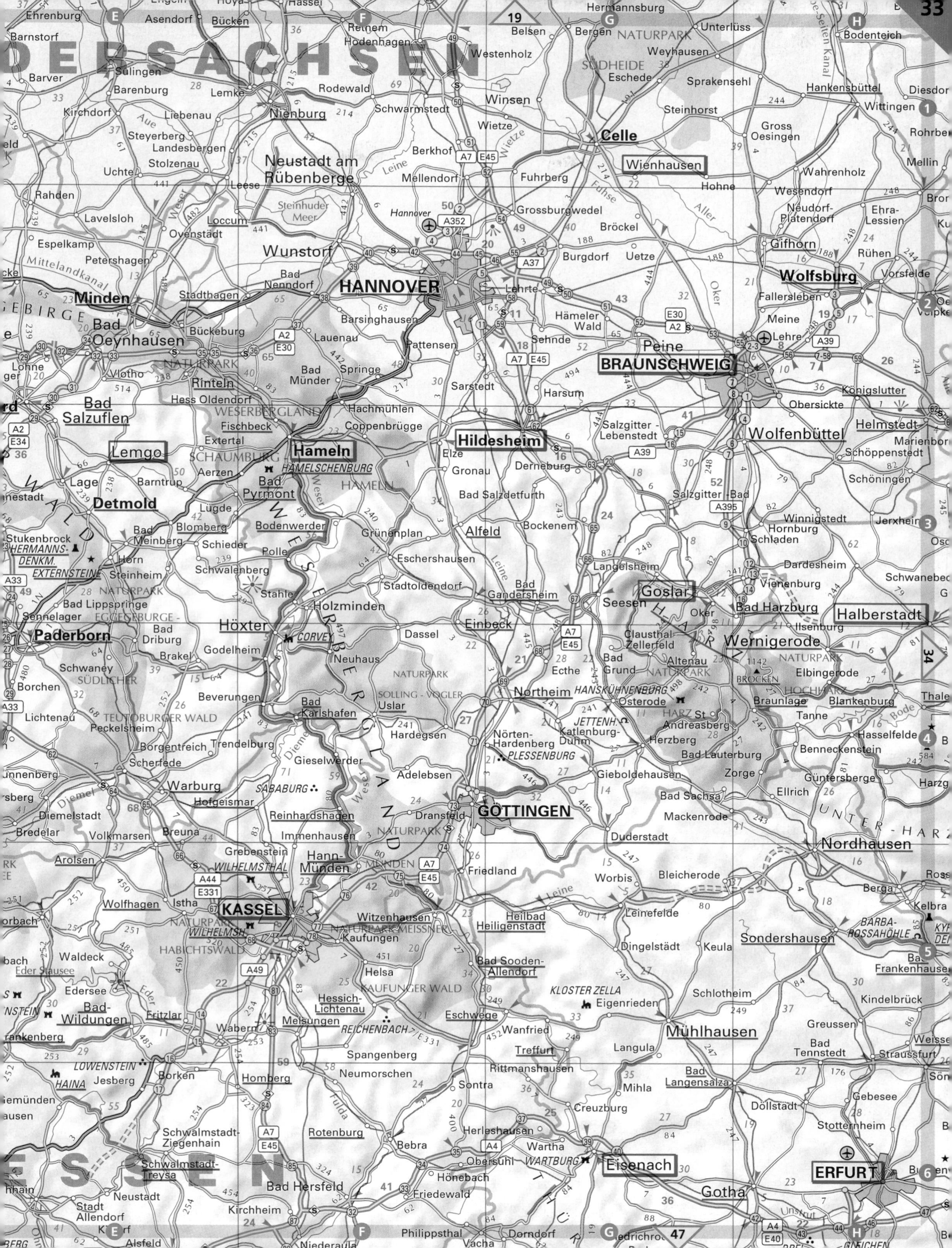

DERSACHSEN
HESSEN
Nienburg
Celle
Wienhausen
Neustadt am Rübenberge
Steinhuder Meer
Loccum
Wunstorf
HANNOVER
Minden
Bad Oeynhausen
Bückeburg
Rinteln
Bad Salzuflen
Lemgo
Detmold
Paderborn
Hameln
HAMELSCHENBURG
Bad Pyrmont
WESERBERGLAND
Hildesheim
Peine
BRAUNSCHWEIG
Wolfsburg
Gifhorn
Königslutter
Helmstedt
Wolfenbüttel
Salzgitter - Lebenstedt
Salzgitter -Bad
Goslar
Bad Harzburg
Halberstadt
Wernigerode
BROCKEN
HARZ
Alfeld
Bad Gandersheim
Einbeck
Holzminden
Höxter
CORVEY
Northeim
Osterode
Herzberg
GÖTTINGEN
Duderstadt
Nordhausen
Hann.-Münden
KASSEL
WILHELMSHÖHE
Warburg
Arolsen
Bad Wildungen
Fritzlar
Melsungen
Eschwege
Heilbad Heiligenstadt
Mühlhausen
Sondershausen
Bad Langensalza
Eisenach
WARTBURG
Gotha
ERFURT
Bad Hersfeld
Rotenburg
Homberg
Schwalmstadt-Treysa
TEUTOBURGER WALD
HABICHTSWALD
KAUFUNGER WALD
NATURPARK SÜDHEIDE
NATURPARK

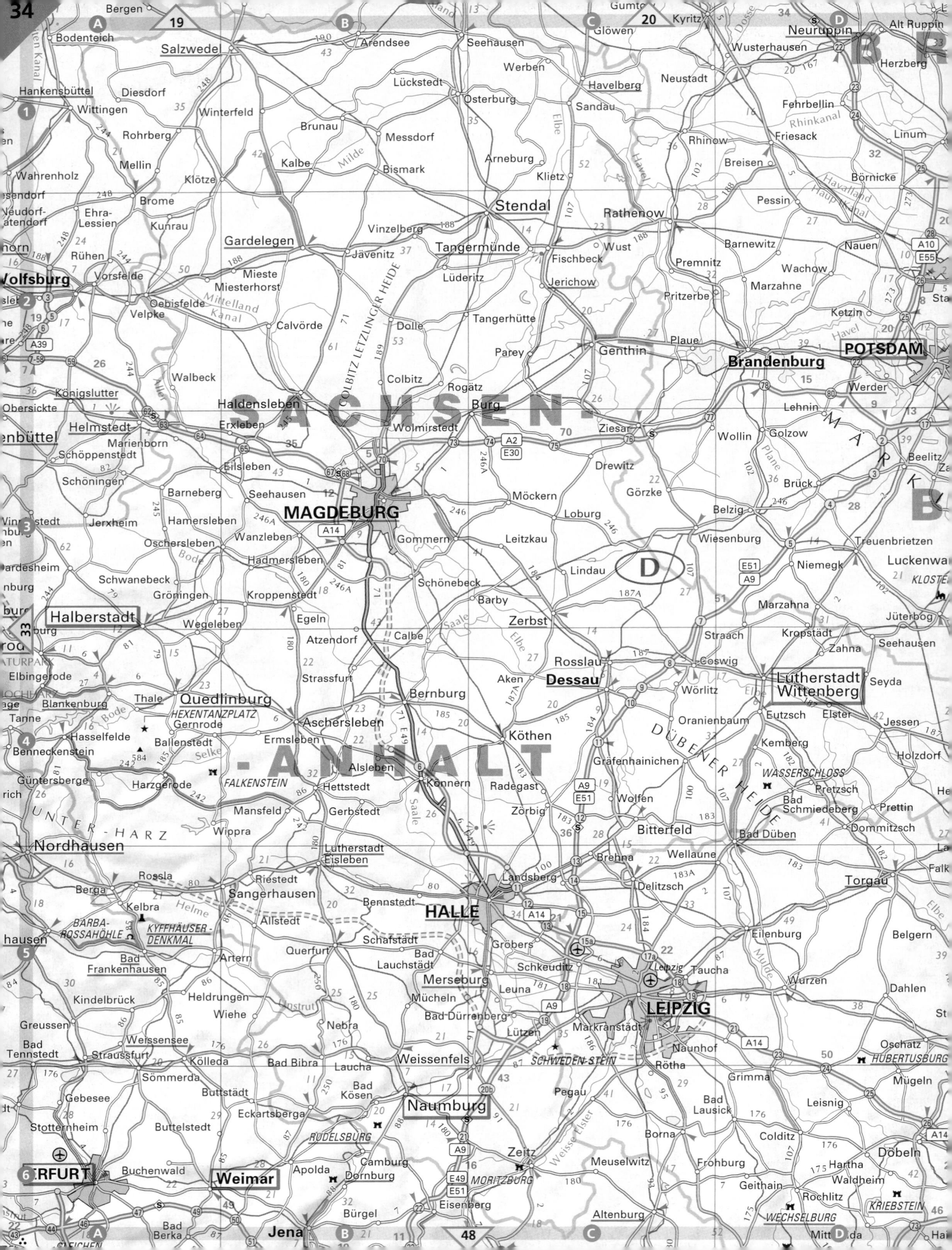

SACHSEN-ANHALT
MAGDEBURG
HALLE
LEIPZIG
POTSDAM
Brandenburg
Stendal
Salzwedel
Gardelegen
Tangermünde
Wolfsburg
Helmstedt
Halberstadt
Quedlinburg
Aschersleben
Bernburg
Dessau
Köthen
Zerbst
Lutherstadt Wittenberg
Bitterfeld
Merseburg
Weissenfels
Naumburg
Weimar
Erfurt
Jena
Zeitz
Torgau
Nordhausen
Sangerhausen
Lutherstadt Eisleben
Genthin
Rathenow
Burg
Schönebeck
Staßfurt
Wernigerode
DÜBENER HEIDE
COLBITZ LETZLINGER HEIDE
UNTER-HARZ

Joachimsthal
JAGDSHL HUBERTUSSTOCK
STOLPE
KLOSTER CHORIN
Oderberg
Löwenberg
Gross Schönebeck
Liebenwalde
Finow
Eberswalde
Oranienburg
Wandlitz
Biesenthal
Bad Freienwalde
Schönwalde
Bernau
Wriezen
Tiefensee
Werneuchen
Prötzel
Reichenberg
BERLIN
Tegel
Altlandsberg
Strausberg
Marxwalde
Letschin
Buckow
Seelow
Manschnow
Müncheberg
BERLIN
Tempelhof
Rudersdorf
Herzfelde
Köpenick
Grünheide
Fürstenwalde
Lebus
Grossbeeren
Schönefeld
Blankenfelde
Frankfurt (Oder)
Mittenwalde
Königs Wusterhausen
Friedersdorf
Bad Saarow-Pieskow
Storkow
Scharmützelsee
Müllrose
Nunsdorf
Trebbin
Zossen
Töpchin
Selchow
Beeskow
Dammendorf
Klausdorf
Neuhof
Teupitz
Märkisch Buchholz
Alt Schadow
Spree
Friedland
Trebatsch
Stülpe
Neu Lübbenau
Treppeln
Baruth
HEIDE
Petkus
SPREEWALD
Lieberose
Golssen
Lübben
Biebersdorf
Lamsfeld
Dahme
Straupitz
Lübbenau
Duben
Luckau
Burg
Peitz
Wüstermarke
Vetschau
Cottbus
SCHL.BRANITZ
Calau
Schlieben
Münchhausen
Drebkau
Doberlug Kirchhain
Finsterwalde
Spremberg
Gross Räschen
Kl Elster
Schwarze Elster
Bad Liebenwerda
Senftenberg
Schwarze Pumpe
Tschernitz
Weisswasser
Lauchhammer
Mühlberg
Ruhland
Gröditz
Elsterwerda
Hoyerswerda
MUSKAUER FORST
Uhyst
Ortrand
Bernsdorf
Wittichenau
Thiendorf
Grossenhain
Kamenz
Königsbrück
SACHSEN
Radeburg
SCHLOSS MORITZBURG
Moritzburg
Meissen
Pulsnitz
Bautzen
Radebeul
Radeberg
Bischofswerda
Löbau
DRESDEN
Neukirch
Oppach
Neustadt
Tharandt
Freital
Heidenau
Pirna
NATIONALPARK SÄCHSISCHE SCHWEIZ
Sebnitz
Herrnhut
Ostritz
Görlitz
Reichenbach
Niesky
Rothenburg
Krajnik Gorny
Trzcinsko Zdrój
Chojna
Rów
Lipiany
Barlinek
Danków
Cedynia
Myślibórz
Moryń
Trzcinna
Strzelce Krajeński
Siekierki
Warnice
Lubianka
Smolnica
Tarnów
Kłodawa
Mieszkowice
Różanki
Santok
Odra
ODERBRUCH
Boleszkowice
Dębno
Baczyna
Gorzów Wielkopolski
Witnica
Bogdaniec
Nowe
Sarbinowo
Bolemin
Warta
Kostrzyn
Krzeszyce
Waldowice
Skwierzyna
Słońsk
Górzyca
Ośno Lubuskie
Lubniewice
Sulęcin
Pieski
Lisów
PUSZCZA
Słubice
Rzepin
Łagów
Świecko
Torzym
Pożrzadło
RZEPIŃSKA
Brieskow-Finkenheerd
Sądów
Debrznica
Świebodzin
PL
Cybinka
Eisenhüttenstadt
Wegrzynice
Skąpe
Korczyców
NIZINA
Neuzelle
Maszecwo
Radnica
Krosno Odrzanskie
Chlebowo
Czerwieńsk
Guben
Gubin
Bobrowice
Lésniów Wielki
Świdnica
Lubsza
Bóbr
Nowogród Bobrzański
Brody
Lubsko
Jasień
Kożuchów
Zasieki
Forst
Tuplice
Lipinki Łużyckie
Olszyna
Döbern
Trzebiel
Żary
Żagań
Łeknica
Bad Muskau
Neisse
Iłowa
Rudawica
Kwisa
Gozdnica
BORY DOLOŚLA
Ruszów
Jagodzin
Kliczków
Węgliniec
Bolesławiec
Pieńsk
Żebrzydowa
Nowogrodziec
Zgorzelec
Lubań
Olszyna
Zawidów
Lésna
Habartice
Gryfów Śląsk

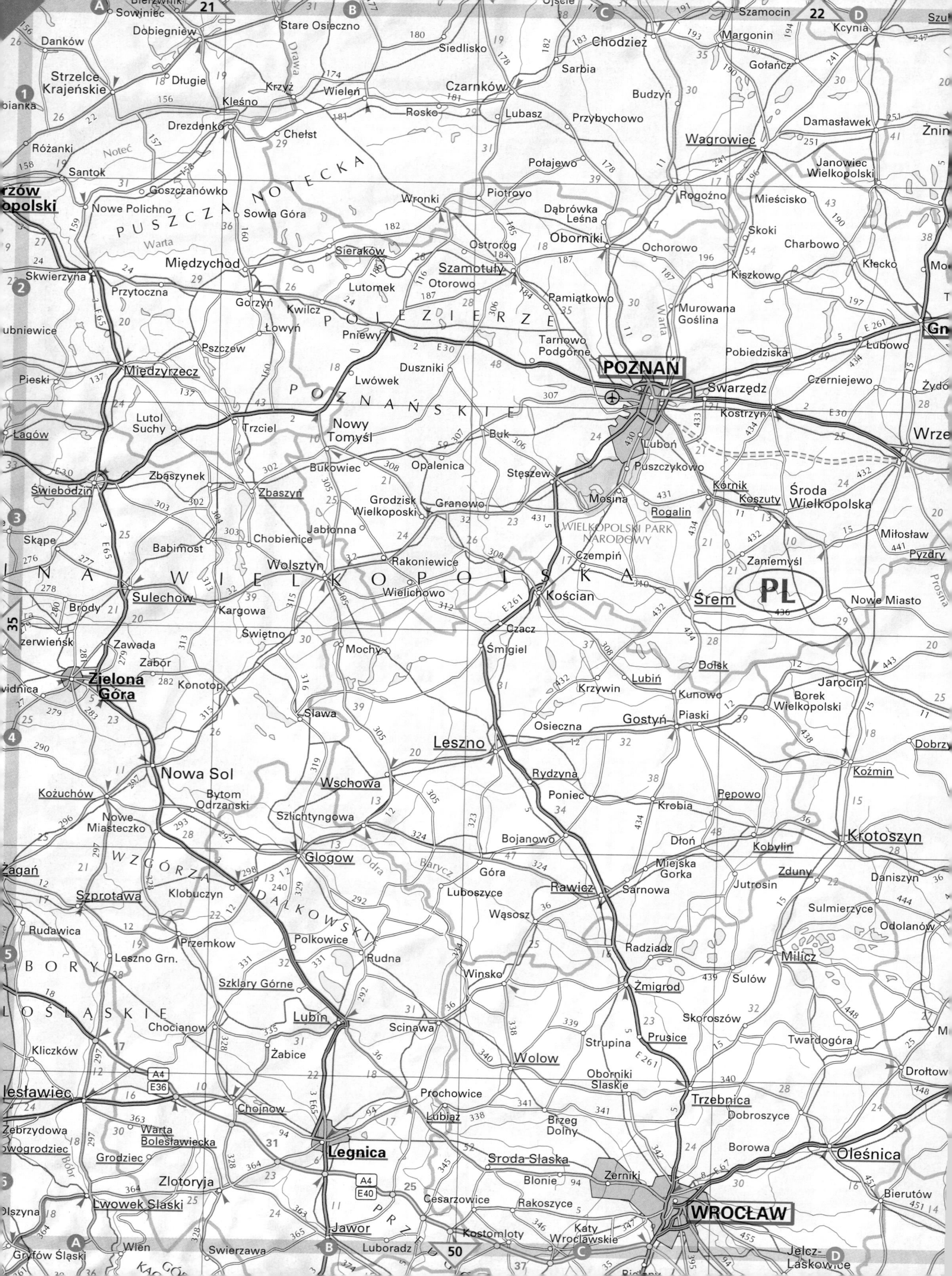

21
22
Sowiniec
Stare Osieczno
Szamocin
Kcynia
Dobiegniew
Siedlisko
Chodzież
Margonin
Danków
Sarbia
Gołańcz
Strzelce Krajeńskie
Długie
Krzyż
Wieleń
Czarnków
Budzyń
Kleśno
Rosko
Lubasz
Przybychowo
Damasławek
Żnin
Drezdenko
Chełst
Wągrowiec
Różanki
Noteć
Połajewo
Janowiec Wielkopolski
Santok
PUSZCZA NOTECKA
Goszczanówko
Piotrowo
Rogoźno
Mieścisko
Nowe Polichno
Sowia Góra
Wronki
Dąbrówka Leśna
Skoki
Warta
Oborniki
Charbowo
Ostroróg
Ochorowo
Sieraków
Kłecko
Międzychód
Szamotuły
Kiszkowo
Skwierzyna
Lutomek
Otorowo
Pamiątkowo
Przytoczna
Gorzyń
Kwilcz
Murowana Goślina
POJEZIERZE
Łowyń
Pniewy
Tarnowo Podgórne
Pszczew
Pobiedziska
Łubowo
Duszniki
POZNAŃ
Międzyrzecz
Lwówek
Czerniejewo
Pieski
POZNAŃSKIE
Swarzędz
Lutol Suchy
Trzciel
Nowy Tomyśl
Kostrzyn
Łagów
Buk
Luboń
Wrześ
Zbąszynek
Bukowiec
Opalenica
Stęszew
Puszczykowo
Świebodzin
Zbąszyń
Grodzisk Wielkopolski
Granowo
Mosina
Kórnik
Koszuty
Środa Wielkopolska
Rogalin
Jabłonna
WIELKOPOLSKI PARK NARODOWY
Skąpe
Babimost
Chobienice
Miłosław
Rakoniewice
Czempiń
Zaniemyśl
Pyzdry
Wolsztyn
WIELKOPOLSKA
Sulechów
Wielichowo
Kościan
Śrem
PL
Brody
Kargowa
Nowe Miasto
Czerwieńsk
Zawada
Świętno
Czacz
Mochy
Śmigiel
Zabór
Dolsk
Zielona Góra
Konotop
Lubiń
Krzywiń
Jarocin
Kunowo
Borek Wielkopolski
Sława
Osieczna
Gostyń
Piaski
Leszno
Nowa Sol
Rydzyna
Koźmin
Kożuchów
Wschowa
Bytom Odrzański
Poniec
Pępowo
Krobia
Nowe Miasteczko
Szlichtyngowa
Bojanowo
Dłoń
Kobylin
Krotoszyn
WZGÓRZA DALKOWSKIE
Głogów
Odra
Barycz
Góra
Miejska Górka
Żagań
Zduny
Rawicz
Sarnowa
Daniszyn
Jutrosin
Szprotawa
Klobuczyn
Luboszyce
Wąsosz
Sulmierzyce
Rudawica
Odolanów
Przemków
Polkowice
Radziądz
Leszno Grn.
Rudna
Milicz
BORY
Winsko
Żmigród
Sułów
Szklary Górne
DOLNOŚLĄSKIE
Lubin
Skoroszów
Chocianów
Ścinawa
Strupina
Prusice
Twardogóra
Kliczków
Żabice
Wołów
Oborniki Śląskie
Drołtowo
Bolesławiec
Prochowice
Trzebnica
Chojnów
Lubiąż
Brzeg Dolny
Dobroszyce
Zebrzydowa
Warta Bolesławiecka
Legnica
Borowa
Oleśnica
Nowogrodziec
Grodziec
Środa Śląska
Zerniki
Złotoryja
Blonie
Bierutów
Lwówek Śląski
Cesarzowice
Rakoszyce
WROCŁAW
Olszyna
Jawor
Kostomłoty
Kąty Wrocławskie
Gryfów Śląski
Wleń
Swierzawa
Luboradz
50
Jelcz-Laskowice
A4
E40
E36
E30
E261
E65
E67

TORUŃ
Zbojno
Bieżuń
Radzanów
Łabiszyn
Czernikowo
Kikół
Grodzeń
Rościszewo
Barcin
Złotniki
Gniewkowo
Aleksandrów Kujawski
Ciechocinek
Skępe
Sierpc
Nieszawa
Lipno
Pakość
Inowrocław
Raciążek
Jeżewo
Raciąż
Bobrowniki
Mochowo
Tłuchowo
Łochocin
Drobin
Zakrzewo
Tupadły
Lelice
Bądkowo
Brudzeń Duży
Kruszwica
Mogilno
WŁOCŁAWEK
Dobrzyń nad Wisłą
Bielsk
Góra
Sikórz
Strzelno
Radziejów
Brześć Kujawski
Staroźreby
Ciółkowo
Nowy Duninów
PŁOCK
Bulkowo
GOSTYNIŃSKO - WŁOCŁAWSKI PARK KRAJOBRAZOWY
Kowal
Radziwie
Lubraniec
Słupno
Piotrków Kujawski
Bodzanów
Choceń
Łąck
Skulsk
Gostynin
Noteć
Izbica Kujawski
Chodecz
Lubień Kujawski
Gąbin
Wisła
Witkowo
Wyszogród
Powidz
Kleczew
Sompolno
Sanniki
Kamion
Ślesin
Babiak
Przedecz
Strzałkowo
Kasimierz Biskupi
Luboniek
Strzelce
Pacyna
Słupca
Oporów
Kiernozia
Wrząca Wielka
Krośniewice
Sochaczew
Golina
Warta
Kłodawa
Kutno
Żychlin
Konin
Święte
Koło
Lad
Drzewce
Daszyna
Łowicz
Bzura
Szetlew
Wyszyna
Kościelec
Grabów
Łukom
Ner
Arkadia
Dąbie
Łęczyca
Tum
Piątek
Nieborów
Rychwał
Turek
Uniejów
Gostków
Powodów
Ozorków
Glowno
Pleszew
Stawiszyn
Dobra
Dąbrowa
Poddębice
Stryków
Byczki
Janków
Ceków Kolonia
Tokari
Porczyny
Aleksandrów Łódzki
Zgierz
Kurzeszyn
Gołuchów
Bratków Din
Brzeziny
Jeżów
Lutomiersk
ŁÓDŹ
KALISZ
Opatówek
Konstantynów Łódzki
Andrespol
Koluszki
Jezioro Jeziorsko
Wola Rakowa
Nowe Skalmierzyce
Warta
Szadek
Pabianice
Kurowice
Rzgów
Ostrów Wielkopolski
Błaszki
Zduńska Wola
Męka
Łask
Tuszyn
Ujazd
Wróblew
Sieradz
Brzeziny
Będków
Mikstat
Buczek
Wadlew
Tomaszów Mazowiecki
Czajków
Zelów
Wolbórz
Grabów n Prosną
Burzenin
Szydłów
Jezioro Sulejowskie
Widawa
Mzurki
Piotrków Trybunalski
Złoczew
Januszewice
Ostrzeszów
Lututów
Kluki
Bełchatów
Podklasztorze
Wielgie
Sulejów
Prosna
Wieruszów
Sokolniki
Rusiec
Szczerców
Chorzyna
Łękawa
Rozprza
Żarnów
Kępno
Mroczen
Opatów
Wieluń
Gorzkowice
Bolesławiec
Krzeczów
Sulmierzyce
Kamieńsk
Ręczno
Kostów
Skomlin
Pątnów
Pajęczno
Bogumiłowice
Fałków
Komorzno
Byczyna
Działoszyn
Nowa Brzeźnica
Kodrąb
Strzelce Małe
Przedbórz
Praszka
Ważne Młyny
Radomsko
Kobiele Wlk.
Namysłów
Wołczyn
Gorzów
Rudniki
Zawady
Wólka
A2
E30
A1
E75
E67
23
38
51

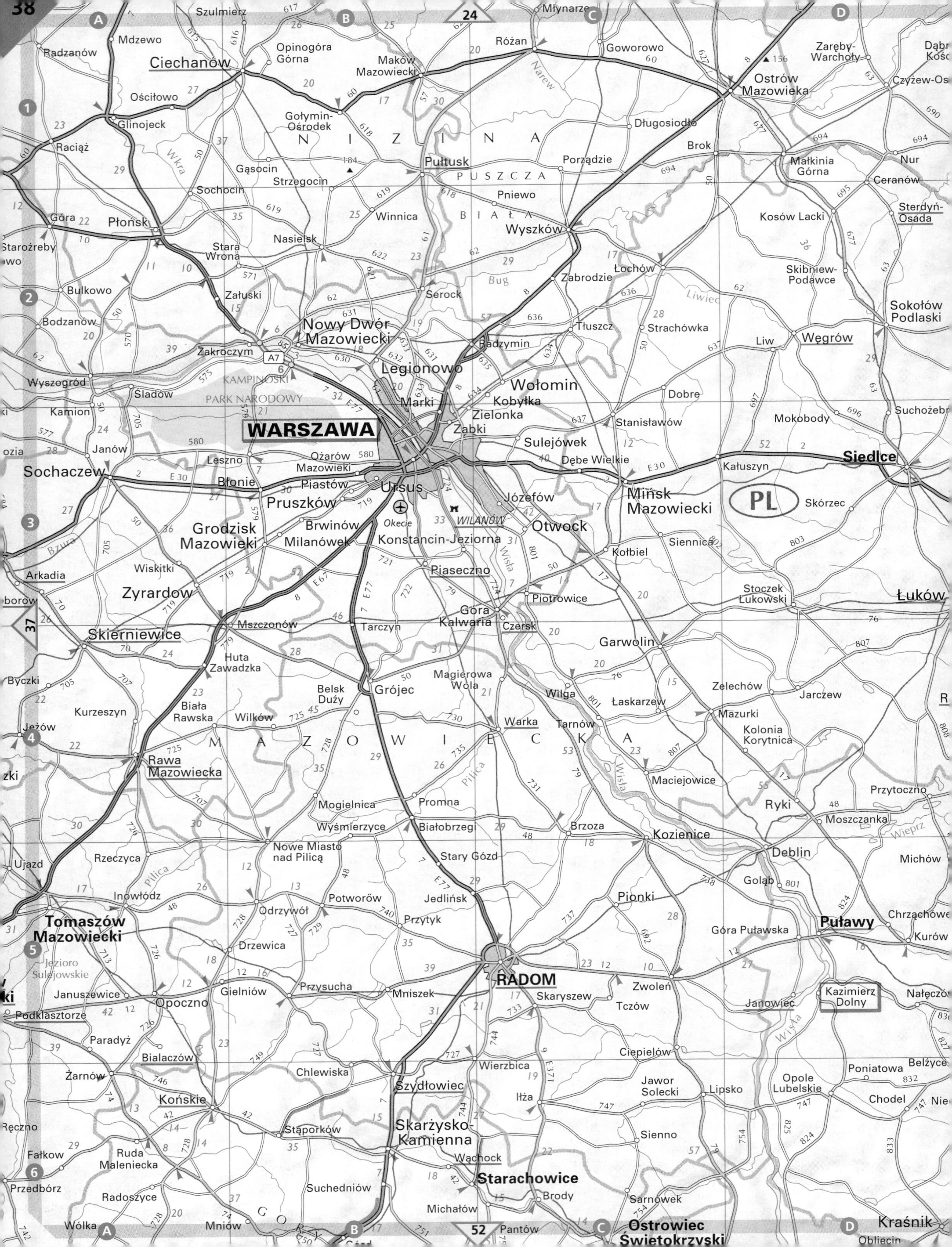
Szulmierz
Mdzewo
Radzanów
Ciechanów
Opinogóra Górna
Maków Mazowiecki
Różan
Mlynarze
Goworowo
Zaręby-Warchoły
Ostrów Mazowiecka
Ościłowo
Glinojeck
Gołymin-Ośrodek
Raciąż
N I Z I N A
Długosiodło
Brok
Gąsocin
Strzegocin
Pułtusk
P U S Z C Z A
Porządzie
Małkinia Górna
Nur
Ceranów
Sochocin
Pniewo
Winnica
B I A Ł A
Wyszków
Kosów Lacki
Sterdyń-Osada
Góra
Płońsk
Nasielsk
Stara Wrona
Zabrodzie
Łochów
Skibniew-Podawce
Bulkowo
Załuski
Serock
Bug
Liwiec
Sokołów Podlaski
Bodzanów
Nowy Dwór Mazowiecki
Tłuszcz
Strachówka
Liw
Węgrów
Zakroczym
Radzymin
Legionowo
Wyszogród
Ślądów
KAMPINOSKI PARK NARODOWY
Wołomin
Kobyłka
Dobre
Kamion
Marki
Zielonka
Ząbki
Stanisławów
Mokobody
Suchożebry
WARSZAWA
Sulejówek
Janów
Leszno
Ożarów Mazowiecki
Dębe Wielkie
Siedlce
Sochaczew
Błonie
Piastów
Ursus
Kałuszyn
Mińsk Mazowiecki
PL
Skórzec
Pruszków
Józefów
Grodzisk Mazowiecki
Brwinów
Okęcie
Wilanów
Otwock
Milanówek
Konstancin-Jeziorna
Bzura
Kołbiel
Siennica
Arkadia
Wiskitki
Piaseczno
Wisła
Żyrardów
Piotrowice
Stoczek Łukowski
Łuków
Skierniewice
Mszczonów
Tarczyn
Góra Kalwaria
Czersk
Garwolin
Huta Zawadzka
Magierowa Wola
Byczki
Belsk Duży
Grójec
Wilga
Żelechów
Jarczew
Kurzeszyn
Biała Rawska
Wilków
Warka
Tarnów
Łaskarzew
Mazurki
Kolonia Korytnica
Jeżów
M A Z O W I E C K A
Rawa Mazowiecka
Pilica
Maciejowice
Przytoczno
Mogielnica
Promna
Ryki
Moszczanka
Wyśmierzyce
Białobrzegi
Brzoza
Kozienice
Wieprz
Ujazd
Rzeczyca
Nowe Miasto nad Pilicą
Stary Gózd
Dęblin
Michów
Gołąb
Inowłódz
Odrzywół
Potworów
Jedlińsk
Pionki
Tomaszów Mazowiecki
Przytyk
Góra Puławska
Puławy
Chrząchowe
Kurów
Drzewica
Jezioro Sulejowskie
RADOM
Zwoleń
Januszewice
Opoczno
Gielniów
Przysucha
Mniszek
Skaryszew
Tczów
Janowiec
Kazimierz Dolny
Nałęczów
Podklasztorze
Paradyż
Bialaczów
Ciepielów
Wierzbica
Żarnów
Chlewiska
Szydłowiec
Jawor Solecki
Lipsko
Opole Lubelskie
Poniatowa
Bełżyce
Końskie
Iłża
Chodel
Ręczno
Stąporków
Skarżysko-Kamienna
Sienno
Fałkow
Ruda Maleniecka
Wąchock
Przedbórz
Suchedniów
Starachowice
Radoszyce
Brody
Sarnówek
Michałów
Wólka
Mniów
G Ó R Y
Pantów
Ostrowiec Świętokrzyski
Kraśnik
Obliecin

PUSZCZA
BIAŁOWIESKA
BIAŁOWIESKI PARK NARODOWY
NACYJANAL'NY PARK BELAVEŽSKAJA PUŠČA
БЕЛОВЕЖСКИЙ НАЦ. ПАРК
Bielsk Podlaski
Hajnówka
Białowieża
Grodek
Brańsk
Rudka
Bocki
Pobikry
Dziadkowice
Ostrożany
Milejczyce
Kamyanyuki
Kamyanyets
Siemiatycze
Drohiczyn
Sarnaki
Vysokaye
Vidamlya
Pruzhany
Linova
Byaroza
Tewli
Zaprudy
Kobryn
Кобрын
Antopal'
Kanal Dnyaprowska Buhski
BY
Platerów
Dąbrowa
Konstantynów
Łosice
Janów Podlaski
Błonie
BREST
БРЭСТ
Terespol
Wólka Dobryńska
Kobylany
Zauczyn
Biała Podlaska
Międzyrzec Podlaski
Koden
Charnyany
Dzivin
Rossosz
Turów
Żelizna
Ulan Majorat
Podlaski
Wisznice
Sławatycze
Malaryta
Ratne
Czemierniki
Parczew
Mosty
Pishcha
Arèhava
Zabolottia
Kock
Krymne
Włodawa
Shats'k
Sosnowica
POLESKI PARK NARODOWY
Okuninka
Sobibór
Kołacze
Firlej
Lubartów
Prypiat
Butsyn
Zarichchia
ŠAC'KYJ PRYRODNYJ NACIONAL'NYJ PARK
Holovne
UA
Łęczna
Cyców
Liuboml'
LUBLIN
Majdanek
Swidnik
Marynin
Stołpie
Okopy Nowe
Dorohucza
Rejowiec Fabryczny
Chełm
Piaski
Wola Idzikowska
Turiis'k
Piotrów
Krupe
Bychawa
Krasnystaw
Buśno
Teratyn
Uchanie
Volodymyr-Volyns'kyi
Володимир-Волинський
Ustyluh
Żołkiewka-osada
Stryjów
Strzyżów
Hrubieszów
Turiia
Yasyel'da
Naraw
Lyasnaya
Bug
25
53
205
206

A
B
C
D
Plymouth
Ile de Batz
Roscoff
Brignogan-Plage
L'Aber-Wrac'h
Lampaul
Ile d'Ouessant
Ploudalmézeau
Lannilis
Plouescat
St-Pol-de-Léon
Carantec
Trégastel
Ploumanac'h
Perros-Guirec
Trébeurden
Primel-Trégastel
Plougasnou
Locquirec
Lannion
Tréguier
Lézardrieux
Lampaul-Plouarzel
Ile de Molène
le Folgoet
Lesneven
CHÂTEAU DE KERJEAN
Lanmeur
St Michel-en-Grève
CHÂTEAU DE TONQUEDEC
Plabennec
Guipavas
Landivisiau
St-Thégonnec
Morlaix
Plestin-les Grèves
Plouaret
Pontrieux
Ile de Beniguet
St-Renan
Le Conquet
Landerneau
Guimiliau
Plouigneau
ROCHE DE KIRIOU
Bégard
POINTE DE ST-MATHIEU
BREST
Plougastel-Daoulas
Daoulas
Sizun
PARC NATUREL RÉGIONAL
D'ARRÉE
Lanvollon
Belle-Isle-en-Terre
Guingamp
PARC NATUREL RÉGIONAL D'ARMORIQUE
Pointe de Penhir
Camaret
Crozon
Morgat
Landévennec
Le Faou
MONTS
ROC TREVEZEL
MONTAGNE ST-MICHEL
D'ARMORIQUE
Huelgoat
Callac
Bourbriac
MÉNEZ HOM
Pentrez-Plage
Ile de Sein
Pointe du Van
Pointe du Raz
Ste-Anne-la-Palud
Châteaulin
Pleyben
Carhaix-Plouguer
St-Nicolas-du-Pélem
Quintin
Tréboul
Douarnenez
Locronan
ROCHE DU FEU
Châteauneuf-du-Faou
Audierne
Pont-Croix
Briec
MONTAGNES NOIRES
Rostrenen
Corlay
Gouarec
Uzel
Plozévet
Baie d'Audierne
CHAPELLE DE LANGUIDOU
Quimper
Gourin
Plouray
Lac-de-Guerlédan
Mur-de-Bretagne
Coray
Scaër
N.-D. DE KERDEVOT
VIRE COURT
Ploneour Lanvern
Rosporden
STE-BARBE
Le Faouët
Guémené-sur-Scorff
Loudéac
St-Guénolé
Pont-l'Abbé
Fouesnant
Bannalec
ST-FIACRE
Kernascléden
Pontivy
POINTE DE PENMARCH
Bénodet
Concarneau
Guilvinec
Loctudy
Beg-Meil
Pont-Aven
Quimperle
Plouay
Bubry
ST-NICODÈME
Port-Manech
ILES DE GLÉNAN
Pont-Scorff
Hennebont
Baud
Locminé
Le Pouldu
Lorient
Larmor
Port-Louis
Pluvigner
Ile de Groix
Groix
Belz
Ste-Anne-d'Auray
Grand-Champ
Auray
MENEC
Vannes
Carnac
La Trinité
TUMULUS DE GAVRINIS
St-Pierre-Quiberon
Locmariaquer
Port-Navalo
Quiberon
Sarzeau
CHÂT. DE SUSCINIO
Pointe des Poulains
Sauzon
GROTTE DE L'APOTHICAIRERIE
Le Palais
Ile de Houat
Bangor
Belle-Ile
Locmaria
Ile de Hoedic
Piriac-sur-Mer
Le Croisic
Pointe du Croisic
Batz-sur-Mer
KORRIGANS
Côte d'Amour
1
2
3
4
5
6

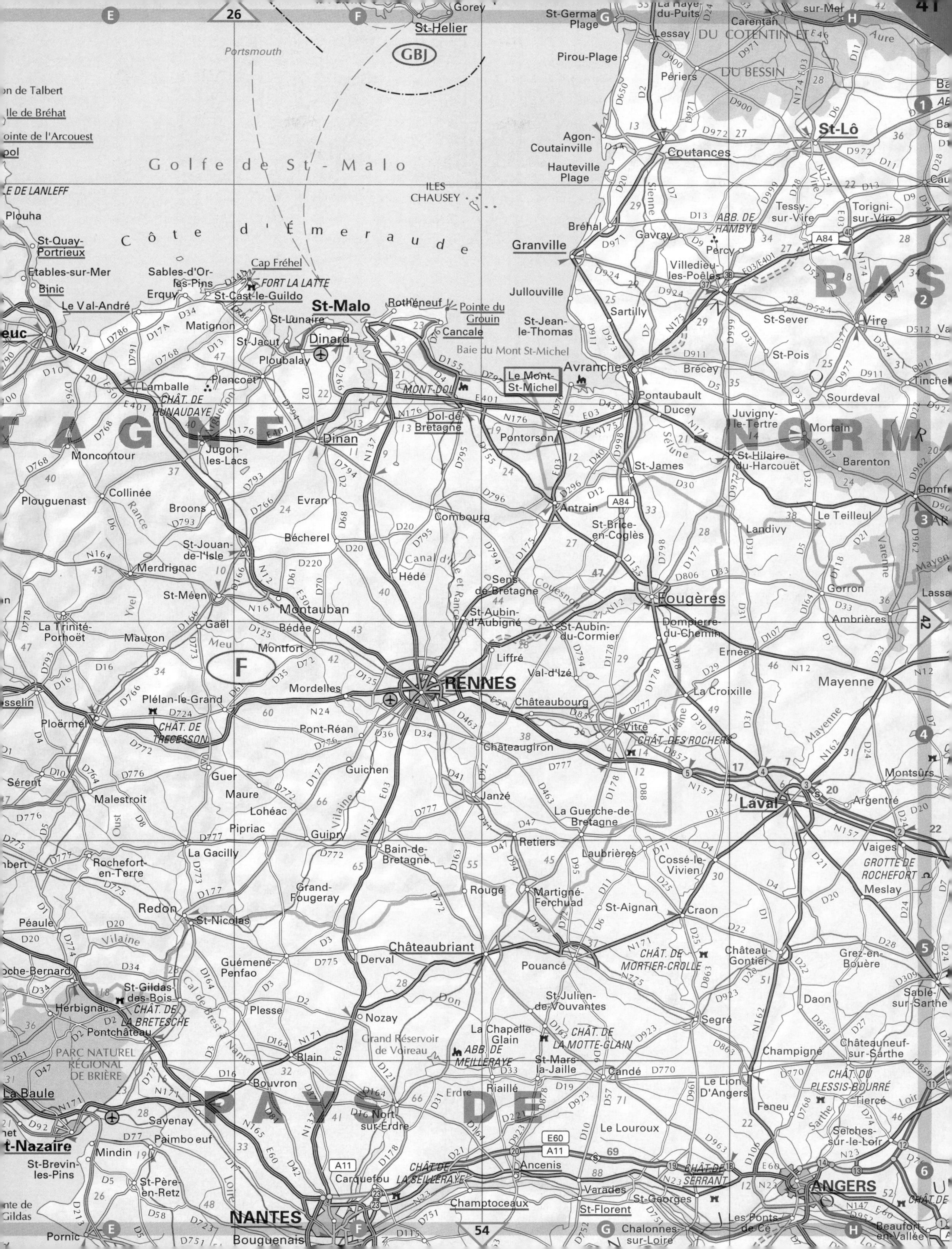
26
St-Helier
Gorey
GBJ
Portsmouth
Golfe de St-Malo
Côte d'Émeraude
ILES CHAUSEY
Ile de Bréhat
Pointe de l'Arcouest
Plouha
St-Quay-Portrieux
Etables-sur-Mer
Binic
Le Val-André
Cap Fréhel
FORT LA LATTE
Sables-d'Or-les-Pins
Erquy
St-Cast-le-Guildo
St-Malo
Dinard
Rothéneuf
Pointe du Grouin
Cancale
Baie du Mont St-Michel
Le Mont-St-Michel
MONT-DOL
Matignon
St-Jacut
St-Lunaire
Ploubalay
Plancoët
Lamballe
CHÂT. DE HUNAUDAYE
Dinan
Dol-de-Bretagne
Pontorson
Avranches
Granville
Bréhal
Jullouville
St-Jean-le-Thomas
Sartilly
Coutances
Agon-Coutainville
Hauteville Plage
Pirou-Plage
Lessay
Périers
St-Lô
Carentan
DU COTENTIN ET DU BESSIN
Gavray
Percy
Villedieu-les-Poêles
ABB. DE HAMBYE
Tessy-sur-Vire
Torigni-sur-Vire
St-Sever
Vire
St-Pois
Brecey
Sourdeval
Pontaubault
Ducey
Juvigny-le-Tertre
Mortain
St-Hilaire-du-Harcouët
Barenton
St-James
Antrain
St-Brice-en-Coglès
Landivy
Le Teilleul
Fougères
Gorron
Ambrières
Moncontour
Jugon-les-Lacs
Collinée
Plouguenast
Broons
Evran
Combourg
Bécherel
Hédé
Canal d'Ille et Rance
Sens-de-Bretagne
St-Jouan-de-l'Isle
Merdrignac
St-Méen
Montauban
St-Aubin-d'Aubigné
St-Aubin-du-Cormier
Dompierre-du-Chemin
Ernée
Mayenne
La Trinité-Porhoët
Mauron
Gaël
Bédée
Montfort
Liffré
Val-d'Izé
RENNES
Mordelles
Plélan-le-Grand
Ploërmel
CHÂT. DE TRECESSON
Châteaubourg
Vitré
CHÂT. DES ROCHERS
La Croixille
Pont-Réan
Châteaugiron
Guichen
Guer
Maure
Lohéac
Janzé
La Guerche-de-Bretagne
Laval
Montsûrs
Argentré
Vaiges
GROTTE DE ROCHEFORT
Meslay
Sérent
Malestroit
Pipriac
Guipry
Retiers
Laubrières
Cossé-le-Vivien
La Gacilly
Rochefort-en-Terre
Bain-de-Bretagne
Grand-Fougeray
Rougé
Martigné-Ferchaud
St-Aignan
Craon
Redon
St-Nicolas
Péaule
Vilaine
Châteaubriant
Derval
Guémené-Penfao
Pouancé
CHÂT. DE MORTIER-CROLLE
Château-Gontier
Grez-en-Bouère
Sablé-sur-Sarthe
Daon
St-Gildas-des-Bois
CHÂT. DE LA BRETESCHE
Herbignac
Pontchâteau
PARC NATUREL RÉGIONAL DE BRIÈRE
Plessé
Nozay
St-Julien-de-Vouvantes
Segré
La Chapelle-Glain
CHÂT. DE LA MOTTE-GLAIN
Grand Réservoir de Voireau
ABB. DE MEILLERAYE
St-Mars-la-Jaille
Candé
Champigné
Châteauneuf-sur-Sarthe
CHÂT. DU PLESSIS-BOURRÉ
Blain
Bouvron
La Baule
Riaillé
Le Lion-d'Angers
Feneu
Tiercé
Savenay
Nort-sur-Erdre
Le Louroux
Seiches-sur-le-Loir
St-Nazaire
Paimboeuf
Mindin
St-Brevin-les-Pins
St-Père-en-Retz
Carquefou
CHÂT. DE LA SEILLERAYE
Ancenis
Varades
CHÂT. DE SERRANT
ANGERS
Champtoceaux
St-Georges
St-Florent
NANTES
Bouguenais
Chalonnes-sur-Loire
Les Ponts-de-Cé
Beaufort-en-Vallée
Pornic
54
42
PAYS DE
BAS
NORMA
TAGNE
F

42
27
28
41
55
Baie de la Seine
Portsmouth
LE HAVRE
BASSE-NORMANDIE
HAUTE-NORMANDIE
F
St-Laurent
Port-en-Bessin
Arromanches-les-Bains
Courseulles-sur-Mer
St-Aubin-sur-Mer
Luc-sur-Mer
CHÂTEAU DE FONTAINE HENRY
Bayeux
ABB. DE MONDAYE
Balleroy
St-Lô
Cap de la Hève
Harfleur
Bolbec
Yvetot
Lillebonne
Pavilly
St-Wandrille
Barentin
Caudebec-en-Caux
Duclair
Tancarville
POINTE DE LA ROQUE
Honfleur
Villerville
Trouville
Deauville
Villers
Côte Fleurie
Riva-Bella
Cabourg
Ouistreham
Houlgate
Dives-sur-Mer
Pont-l'Evêque
Beuzeville
St-Maclou
Bourneville
Jumièges
Pont-Audemer
Bourg-Achard
Bourgtheroulde-Infreville
Elbeuf
ABB. DE BONPORT
CAEN
ST-CLAIR
Troarn
Dozulé
Cormeilles
Cambremer
Lisieux
Lieurey
Brionne
CHÂT. DU CHAMP DU BATAILLE
Louviers
Le Neubourg
Caumont
Torigni-sur-Vire
Tessy-sur-Vire
Villers-Bocage
Aunay-sur-Odon
Thury-Harcourt
Clécy
Vire
Vassy
Sever
Condé-sur-Noireau
Tinchebray
ROCHE D'OËTRE
Sourdeval
Flers
Mortain
Barenton
Domfront
Le Teilleul
PARC NATUREL RÉGIONAL NORMANDIE-MAINE
Bagnoles-de-l'Orne
La Ferté-Macé
Rânes
Carrouges
Couterne
Couptrain
Lassay
Gorron
Ambrières
Pré-en-Pail
MONT DES AVALOIRS
Javron
Villaines-la-Juhel
Mayenne
Alençon
Falaise
St-Pierre-sur-Dives
Livarot
Orbec
Thiberville
Bernay
Beaumont-le-Roger
Broglie
Beaumesnil
Courteilles
Vimoutiers
Trun
Putanges-Pont-Ecrepin
Briouze
Fromental
Argentan
HARAS DU PIN
Le Pin-au-Haras
Nonant-le-Pin
Exmes
Gacé
Mortrée
CHÂT. D'O
Sées
Le Merlerault
Ste-Gauburge-Ste-Colombe
L'Aigle
Rugles
La Neuve-Lyre
Conches-en-Ouche
Evreux
Damville
Breteuil
Verneuil-sur-Avre
Nonancourt
Moulins-la-Marche
Courtomer
Bazoches-sur-Hoëne
Mortagne-au-Perche
Longny-au-Perche
La Ferté-Vidame
Brézolles
Senonches
Château-en-Thymerais
La Loupe
Courville
Rémalard
MANOIR DE COURBOYER
Bellême
Mamers
La Hutte
Fresnay-sur-Sarthe
Bais
CHÂT. DU ROCHER
Montsûrs
Evron
Argentré
Sillé-le-Guillaume
Beaumont-sur-Sarthe
Ste-Suzanne
Vaiges
GROTTE DE ROCHEFORT
Meslay
St-Denis-d'Orques
Conlie
Ballon
Bonnétable
Champrond-en-Gâtine
Nogent-le-Rotrou
Illiers-Combray
Thivars
Luigny
La Ferté-Bernard
Authon-du-Perche
Brou
La Bazoche-Gouet
Tuffé
Connerré
Montmirail
Chapelle-Royale
Brûlon
Loué
CHÂT. DE VERDELLES
LE MANS
ABB. DE L'EPAU
Grez-en-Bouère
ABB. DE SOLESMES
Sablé-sur-Sarthe
Daon
Châteauneuf-sur-Sarthe
La Suze-sur-Sarthe
Arnage
Malicorne
Ecommoy
Vibraye
Bouloire
St-Calais
Mondoubleau
Cloyes-sur-le-Loir
Châteaudun
Bonneval
Le Grand-Lucé
Monplaisir
CHÂT. DE COURTANVAUX
Savigny-sur-Braye
Fréteval
CHÂT. DU PLESSIS-BOURRÉ
Tiercé
Durtal
La Flèche
Pontvallain
Mayet
Château-du-Loir
La Chartre-sur-le-Loir
Trôo
Lavardin
Montoire-sur-le-Loir
Vendôme
Binas
Oucques
Seiches-sur-le-Loir
Le Lude
Vaas
ANGERS
Baugé
CHÂT. DE MONTGEOFFROY
Noyant
Château-la-Vallière
Neuillé-Pont-Pierre
Mouliherne
Beaufort-en-Vallée
St-Amand-Longpré
TALCY
Beaugency
Château-Renault

PICARDIE
ÎLE-DE-FRANCE
St-Saëns
Les Hayons
Aumale
Poix
Bretonneux
Péronne
Roisel
St-Q
Buchy
Forges-les-Eaux
Formerie
Grandvilliers
Conty
Moreuil
Marseille-en-Beauvaisis
Crevecoeur
Breteuil
Montdidier
Roye
Nesle
Ham
Boos
Gournay-en-Bray
Lyons-la-Forêt
Froissy
Cuvilly
Lassigny
Tergnier
La Fère
ABB. DE FONTAINE GUÉRARD
Fleury
St-Germer-de-Fly
Beauvais
St-Just-en-Chaussée
Ressons
Noyon
Chauny
St-Gobain
Ecouis
Etrepagny
Auneuil
ABB. D'OURSCAMPS
Ribécourt
Blérancourt
Coucy-le-Château-Auffrique
Vaudreuil
Les Andelys
Gisors
Clermont
Estrées-St-Denis
Noailles
Mouy
Arsy
Compiègne
Vic-sur-Aisne
Gaillon
Méru
Verberie
FORÊT DE COMPIÈGNE
Pierrefonds
Soissons
Vernon
Magny-en-Vexin
Creil
St-Leu-d'Esserent
Senlis
Chantilly
Marines
ABB. DE LA VICTOIRE
ABB. DE LIEU-RESTAURÉ
Bonnières
L'Isle-Adam
ABB. DE ROYAUMONT
Luzarches
ABB. DE CHAALIS
Crépy-en-Valois
Longpont
Villers-Cotterêts
Chaufour-lès-Bonnières
Mantes-la-Jolie
Meulan
Auvers-s-Oise
Pontoise
Survilliers
Ermenonville
Nanteuil-le-Haudouin
Betz
La Ferté-Milon
Neuilly-St-Front
Dammartin-en-Goële
Anet
Epône
Flins
Orgeval
St-Denis
Bourget
Charles de Gaulle
Lizy
Château-Thierry
PARC ZOOL.
Houdan
St-Germain
Pontchartrain
Montfort l'Amaury
Meaux
Montreuil-aux-Lions
Dreux
Trappes
PARIS
Lagny
Couilly
Charly
DISNEYLAND
Jouarre
La Ferté-sous-Jouarre
Nogent-le-Roi
FORÊT DE RAMBOUILLET
Versailles
Dampierre
Chevreuse
Coutevroult
Crécy
Rambouillet
Palaiseau
Orly
Tournan
Coulommiers
Rebais
Montmirail
Maintenon
Epernon
Limours
Evry
Brie-Comte-Robert
Fontenay-Trésigny
Chartres
Arpajon
CHÂT. DU VIVIER
Rozay-en-Brie
La Ferté-Gaucher
Ablis
Dourdan
Corbeil-Essonnes
Guignes
CHÂT. DE LA GRANGE-BLENEAU
Auneau
Allainville
Mormant
Esternay
Sézanne
Voise
Étampes
Melun
VAUX-LE-VICOMTE
Villiers-St-Georges
Villenauxe-la-Grande
CHÂT. DE FARCHEVILLE
Nangis
Provins
Barbizon
FORÊT DE FONTAINEBLEAU
GORGES D'APREMONT
Voves
Angerville
Méréville
Fontainebleau
Dontilly
Nogent-sur-Seine
Montereau-Faut-Yonne
Allaines
Janville
Toury
Malesherbes
Ury
Moret-sur-Loing
Bray-sur-Seine
Nemours
Marcilly-le-Hayer
Pithiviers
Puiseaux
Artenay
Neuville-aux-Bois
Souppes-sur-Loing
Pont-sur-Yonne
Patay
CHÂT. DE CHEVILLY
Château-Landon
Chéroy
Sens
Beaune-la-Rolande
Dordives
Ferrières
Villeneuve-l'Archevêque
Cerisiers
Aix-en-Othe
ORLÉANS
Ladon
Canal d'Orléans
Meung-sur-Loire
Olivet
Bellegarde
Courtenay
Villeneuve-sur-Yonne
Cléry
Jargeau
Châteauneuf-sur-Loire
Montargis
Lorris
Douchy
Joigny
Migennes
Germigny-des-Prés
St-Benoît-sur-Loire
Châteaurenard
St-Florentin
Ervy-le-Châtel
Estissac
Champ
56
57
44

30
43
57
St-Quentin
Vermandois
Roisel
Le Nouvion-en-Thiérache
Fourmies
Chimay
Couvin
Beauraing
Han-sur-Lesse
Wellin
La Capelle
Guise
Hirson
Fumay
Gedinne
St-Hubert
Ham
Canal de St-Quentin
Ribemont
Sains
Vervins
Rocroi
Revin
ROCHES DE LAIFOUR
Monthermé
Vresse
Paliseul
Rumigny
Auvillers-les-Forges
Château-Regnault
ROCHE AUX 7 VILLAGES
Rochehaut
Tergnier
La Fère
Crécy-sur-Serre
Marle
Brunehamel
Bertrix
Chauny
St-Gobain
Montcornet
Rozoy
Charleville-Mézières
Bouillon
Neufchâteau
Oise
OURSCAMPS
Coucy-le-Château-Auffrique
Laon
Signy-l'Abbaye
Sedan
Herbeumont
Sissonne
Seraincourt
Flize
Poix-Terron
Florenville
Canal de l'Oise à l'Aisne
Novion-Porcien
Douzy
Carignan
ABBAYE D'ORVAL
Château-Porcien
Mouzon
CAVERNE DU DRAGON
Vailly
Corbeny
Asfeld
Canal des Ardennes
Rethel
Soissons
Bourg-et-Comin
Neufchâtel-sur-Aisne
Attigny
Le Chesne
Braine
Aisne
Stenay
Longpont
Bourgogne
Juniville
Machault
Vouziers
Buzancy
Fismes
Vesle
Grandpré
Dun
Neuilly-St-Front
CHATEAU DE FÈRE
Fère-en-Tardenois
REIMS
Monthois
Damvillers
Ville-en-Tardenois
Séchault
Château-Thierry
Châtillon-sur-Marne
Verzy
Sept-Saulx
Varennes-en-Argonne
Champillon
F
FORT DU DOUAUMONT
Dormans
Suippes
Bras-sur-Meuse
Condé-en-Brie
Épernay
Ay
Marne
Ste-Menehould
Verdun
CHAMPAGNE-ARDENNE
Clermont-en-Argonne
Montmort
Vertus
Montmirail
Champaubert
l'Epine
Châlons-en-Champagne
Triaucourt-en-Argonne
Givry-en-Argonne
Souilly
Ecury
Fère-Champenoise
Nettancourt
Chaumont-sur-Aire
Pierrefitte-sur-Aire
Esternay
Sézanne
Villiers-St-Georges
Sommesous
Pargny-sur-Saulx
Revigny-sur-Ornain
VOIE SACRÉE
Villenauxe-la-Grande
Mailly-le-Camp
Vitry-le-François
Thiéblemont-Farémont
Sermaize-les-Bains
Bar-le-Duc
Salon
Anglure
ABB. DES TROIS FONTAINES
Commercy
Ligny-en-Barrois
Romilly-sur-Seine
St-Dizier
Stainville
Ancerville
Méry
Arcis-sur-Aube
La Belle Etoile
Marigny-le-Châtel
Lac du Der-Chantecoq
Montier-en-Der
Wassy
Houdelaincourt
Canal de la Marne au Rhin
Marcilly-le-Hayer
Lesmont
Aube
Piney
Brienne-le-Château
Joinville
Gondrecourt
Troyes
PARC NAT. RÉGIONAL DE LA FORÊT D'ORIENT
Soulaines-Dhuys
Poissons
Estissac
Doulevant-le-Château
Germay
Villeneuve-l'Archevêque
Lusigny
Lac du Temple
Lac d'Orient
Maison-Neuve
Domrémy-la-Pucelle
Aix-en-Othe
Bouilly
Doulaincourt
Neufchâteau
Vendeuvre
Bar-sur-Aube
Vignory
St-Blin
Seine
Colombey-les-Deux-Églises
Andelot
Bologne
Canal de la Marne à la Saône
Ervy-le-Châtel
Chaource
Bar-sur-Seine
Juzennecourt
St-Thiébault
Bourmont
St-Florentin
Essoyes
Chaumont
Bulgnéville

31
RHEINLAND
PFALZ
SAARLAND
LORRAINE
ALSACE
EIFEL
HUNSRÜCK
B
L
D
La Roche-en-Ardenne
Nadrin
St Vith
Champlon
Houffalize
Wemperhaardt
Prüm
Gerolstein
Nürburg
Kelberg
Mayen
Bassenheim
Pronsfeld
Schönecken
Daun
Ulmen
Kaisersesch
Maria Martental
Brodenbach
Eltz
Boppard
Bastogne
(Bastenaken)
Clervaux
Dasburg
Waxweiler
Deutsch-Luxemburgischer Naturpark
Manderscheid
Bad Bertrich
Cochem
Treis
Falkenstein
Kyllburg
Alf
Burg Metternich
Oberwesel
St Goar
Kastellaun
Wiltz
Esch-sur-Sûre
Vianden
Bitburg
Wittlich
Marienburg
Zell
Bacharach
Martelange
Wikingerburg
Pauls-Kirche
Traben-Trarbach
Rheinböllen
Simmern
Ettelbruck
Diekirch
Mülheim
R. Landshut
Bernkastel-Kues
Kirchberg
Karlsberg
Habay
Larochette
Echternach
Schweich
Trittenheim
Stromberg
Gemünden
Arlon
(Aarlen)
Saeul
Mersch
Wasserbillig
Trier
Ruwer
Morbach
Wildenburg
Kirn
Bad Kreuznach
Thalfang
Rotenfels
Bad Münster
Ebernburg
LUXEMBOURG
Grevenmacher
Konz
Findel
Ehnen
Aubange
Pétange
Reinsfeld
Heiligenbösch-Kirche
Longwy
Saarburg
Trassem
Zerf
Hermeskeil
Birkenfeld
Idar-Oberstein
Meisenheim
Differdange
Esch-sur-Alzette
Remich
Baumholder
Lauterecken
Dudelange
Mondorf-les-Bains
Orscholz
Primstal
Nohfelden
Wolfstein
Kirchheim
Losheim
Mettlach
St. Gangolf
Altenglan
Rockenhausen
Aumetz
Audun-le-Roman
Hettange-Grande
Sierck-les-Bains
Merzig
Tholey
Kusel
Winnweiler
Spincourt
Thionville
Lohnsfeld
Hayange
Florange
Uckange
Metzervisse
Lebach
St Wendel
Otterbach
Bouligny
Piennes
Dillingen
Ramstein
Guenange
St. Oswald
Ottweiler
Neunkirchen
Landstuhl
Kaiserslautern
Briey
Rombas
Saarlouis
Bouzonville
Auboué
Hagondange
Völklingen
St Ingbert
Homburg
Conflans en Jarnisy
Jarny
Argancy
Boulay-Moselle
Creutzwald
Ensheim
Blieskastel
Zweibrücken
Waldfischbach
Les Boulay Lue
Carling
Forbach
SAARBRÜCKEN
Pfälzerwald
Chambley-Bussières
Ars-sur-Moselle
METZ
Freyming Merlebach
Farébersviller
Pirmasens
St-Avold
Park Archéol. de Bliesbruck-Reinheim
Hinterweidenthal
Annweiler
Pagny-sur-Moselle
Faulquemont
Sarreguemines
Dahn
Altdahn
Frescaty
Thiaucourt-Regniéville
Verny
Puttelange
Rohrbach-lès-Bitche
Parc Naturel Régional
Bitche
Fischbach
Bad Bergzabern
Pont-à-Mousson
Grostenquin
Château de Wasigenstein
Weintor
De Lorraine
Sarralbe
Château de Falkenstein
Château de Fleckenstein
De Pierrefort
Nomeny
Delme
Morhange
Lorentzen
Des Vosges du Nord
Lembach
Domèvre-en-Haye
Dieulouard
Sarre-Union
Niederbronn-les-Bains
Lichtenberg
Woerth
Château-Salins
La Petite-Pierre
Soultz
Fénétrange
Pompey
Dieuze
Ingwiller
Schlosspark
Toul
Parc Nat. Rég. de Lorraine
Bouxwiller
NANCY
Soufflenheim
Arracourt
Sarrebourg
Neuves-Maisons
St Nicolas-de-Port
Phalsbourg
Haguenau
Canal de la Marne au Rhin
Jardin Botan.
Hochfelden
Drusenheim
Dombasle
Hèming
Chât. du Haut-Barr
Saverne
Brumath
Pont-St-Vincent
Flavigny-sur-Moselle
Lunéville
Marmoutier
Dabo
Chap. St.-Léon
Truchtersheim
Rheinau
Blâmont
Abreschviller
Roch. de Dabo
Wangenbourg
Wasselonne
La Wantzenau
Vézelise
Gerbéviller
Cirey
Chât. du Nideck
Marlenheim
Sion
Haroué
Bayon
Badonviller
Col du Donon
Donon
Molsheim
Strasbourg International
STRASBOURG
Kehl
Baccarat
Charmes
Raon-l'Etape
Col du Hantz
Schirmeck
Obernai
Appenweier
Rouvres-en-Xaintois
Senones
Le Hohwald
Mont-Ste-Odile
Mirecourt
Rambervillers
Nomexy
Erstein
Offenburg
Vittel
58
St-Dié
Saales
Col de Saales
Champ du Feu
Villé
Barr
59
Gengenbach
Moselle
Meurthe
Sarre
Rhin
Mosel
Nahe
Glan
Kyll
Ourthe
Alzette
Sûre
Saar
46

32
Königswinter
DRACHENFELS
Altenkirchen
MARIENTHAL
Wissen
Betzdorf
Daaden
Burbach
MARIENSTATT
Marburg
Gladenbach
Dillenberg
Kirchhain
Neustadt
Stadt Allendorf
Kirtorf
Alsfeld
Weimar
FRAUENBERG
Homberg
Bad Honnef
Remagen
Linz
Hachenburg
Bad Marienberg
Herborn
Rennerod
Sinzig
Bad Breisig
Bad Hönningen
Brohl
Dierdorf
Langenhahn
WESTERWALD
HESSEN
JUGENDBURG
Giessen
Grünberg
EISENBACH
Wetzlar
VOGELSBERG
MARIA LAACH
Andernach
Neuwied
Wehr
Maria Laach
Montabaur
Hadamar
Weilburg
Braunfels
Lich
Schotten
Hungen
ARNSBURG
Münzenberg
KRISTALL HÖHLE
NATURPARK
Koblenz
Mayen
BASSENHEIM
Bad Ems
Limburg
Diez
Butzbach
Bad Nauheim
Gedern
Hartmann
Lahnstein
Nassau
KLOSTER ARNSTEIN
HOCHTAUNUS
Usingen
Kaisersesch
Brodenbach
MARIA MARTENTHAL
ELTZ
Rhens
Braubach
MARKSBURG
NASSAU
Camberg
Friedberg
Ortenberg
Treis
Cochem
Boppard
SAALBURG
Florstadt
Büdingen
HOHENSTEIN
NATURPARK RHEIN-TAUNUS
Idstein
Bad Homburg
Nieder-Wöllstadt
Wächtersbach
Nidderau
St Goarshausen
St Goar
BURG METTERNICH
Bad Schwalbach
Königstein
TAUNUS
Alf
Kastellaun
Oberwesel
LORELEY
Kaub
Taunusstein
Langenselbold
Bad
MARIENBURG
Schlangenbad
FRANKFURT AM MAIN
Hanau
Gelnhausen
Zell
Bacharach
Lorch
WIESBADEN
Bieber
Rheinböllen
EBERBACH
Eltville
Offenbach
Traben-Trarbach
Simmern
Assmannshausen
Rüdesheim
MAINZ
Frankfurt
Alzenall
Schöllkrippen
LANDSHUT
KARLSBERG
Kirchberg
Bingen
Neu-Isenburg
Seligenstadt
Stromberg
Ingelheim
Rüsselsheim
Goldbach
HUNSRÜCK
Gemünden
Mörfelden
Langen
Ober-Roden
Gross-Gerau
Aschaffenburg
Morbach
WILDENBURG
Bad Kreuznach
Wörrstadt
Nierstein
Dieburg
Babenhausen
Kirn
ROTENFELS
Bad Münster Ebernburg
Nahe
Oppenheim
DARMSTADT
Gross-Umstadt
Mespelbrunn
PFALZ
SPESSART
Idar-Oberstein
BÖLLERKIRCHE
Guntersblum
Pfungstadt
BREUBERG
Reinheim
Obernburg
Erlenbach
Birkenfeld
Alsenz
Alzey
Gernsheim
NATURPARK BERGSTRASSE-ODENWALD
Höchst
Meisenheim
Eich
Bad König
Wörth
Baumholder
Lauterecken
Osthofen
AUERBACHER SCHLOSS
Lindenfels
Wertheim
Wolfstein
Kirchheimbolanden
Freudenberg
Altenglan
Rockenhausen
Worms
Bensheim
Michelstadt
Winnweiler
HOHENFELS
Monsheim
Bürstadt
Heppenheim
ODENWALD
Miltenberg
Kusel
Grünstadt
Erbach
Amorbach
Lohnsfeld
WITTGENSTEIN
Otterbach
Frankenthal
Beerfelden
WILDENBURG
Ramstein
Weinheim
LUDWIGSHAFEN
MANNHEIM
Walldürn
Hochspeyer
Landstuhl
Kaiserslautern
Bad Dürkheim
Schriesheim
Hirschhorn
Mudau
NECKARTAL
Buchen
Homburg
Lambrecht
Deidesheim
Mutterstadt
HEIDELBERG
Eberbach
Zwingenberg
Osterburken
Neustadt an der Weinstrasse
Schifferstadt
Schwetzingen
Neckarsteinach
Neckargerach
Zweibrücken
Waldfischbach
SCHLOSS
Neckargemünd
PFÄLZERWALD
Speyer
Adelsheim
KALMIT
Mosbach
Pirmasens
Edenkoben
Hockenheim
Walldorf
HORNBERG
Möckmühl
Wiesloch
Gundelsheim
TRIFELS
Hinterweidenthal
Annweiler
Germersheim
Landau
Sinsheim
Jagst
Dahn
LINDELBRUNN
Bad Wimpfen
Bad Friedrichshall
ALTDAHN
Klingenmünster
Rülzheim
Bad Schönborn
STEINSBERG
NEUENSTEIN
PARC NATUREL REGIONAL
Fischbach
Bad Bergzabern
Neudorf
Wald-angelloch
HORNBERG
Neckarsulm
Bitche
CHÂT. DE WASIGENSTEIN
WEINTOR
CHÂTEAU DE FLECKENSTEIN
Rheinzabern
Bruchsal
Eppingen
Heilbronn
Öhringen
CHÂTEAU DE FALKENSTEIN
Kandel
Wörth
RAVENSBURG
Schwaigern
Weinsberg
WALDEN
DES VOSGES DU NORD
Lembach
Wissembourg
Brackenheim
Niederbronn-les-Bains
Güglingen
Lauffen
F
Woerth
Hunspach
KARLSRUHE
Bretten
Bonnigheim
WILDECK
LICHTENBERG
Petite-Pierre
Soultz
Lauterbourg
Maulbronn
Besigheim
Neckar
Oberstenfeld
Ingwiller
SCHLOSSPARK
Seltz
Ettlingen
Mühlacker
Illingen
Bietigheim
Bouxwiller
BADEN
Soufflenheim
Marxzell
Pforzheim
Vaihingen
Marbach
Backnang
Rastatt
Haguenau
FAVORITE
Ludwigsburg
JARDIN BOTAN.
Hochfelden
Drusenheim
Gaggenau
Neuenburg
Ditzingen
Kornwestheim
Winnenden
Saverne
Brumath
Bad Herrenalb
59
Tiefenbronn
Leonberg
Waiblingen
31
45

Bad Hersfeld
Hönebach
Friedewald
33
Gotha
Weimar
34
Jena
Kirchheim
Philippsthal
Dorndorf
Friedrichroda
Bad Berka
Bürgel
Niederaula
Vacha
Bad Liebenstein
Arnstadt
DREI GLEICHEN
HOHEN WEHRDA
Bad Salzungen
Barchfeld
Ohrdruf
Kranichfeld
Blankenhain
Stadtroda
Burghaun
Kahla
LEUCHTENBURG
Schlitz
Geisa
Dermbach
Stadtilm
Teichel
Hünfeld
Schmalkalden
THÜRINGER WALD
THÜRING
NATURPARK
Tann
Wasungen
Oberhof
Ilmenau
PAULINZELLA
Bad Blankenburg
Rudolstadt
Neustadt
Zella-Mehlis
HESSISCHE RHÖN
GR. BEERBERG
Kaltennordheim
Königsee
Pössneck
Fulda
Hilders
Meiningen
Suhl
Gehren
Schwarzburg
Hohenwarte Talsperre
MILSEBURG
SCHL. FASANERIE
Fladungen
Saalfeld
Ziegenrück
WASSERKUPPE
Werra
Grossbreitenbach
FEENGROTTEN
Henneberg
Themar
Schleusingen
Neuhaus
Leutenberg
Gersfeld
RHÖN
Döllbach
Ostheim
Eussenhausen
Probstzella
Bleiloch-Talsperre
Schlüchtern
Bischofsheim
Mellrichstadt
Hildburghausen
Eisfeld
Ludwigsstadt
HESSISCHER
Wurzbach
Lobenstein
Heustreu
STEINSBURG
SCHWARZENFELS
Bad Neustadt
Rottenbach
Rudolphstein
Bad Brückenau
BAYERISCHE RHÖN
SALZBURG
Bad Königshofen
Rodach
Neustadt
Sonneberg
FRANKENWALD
Nordhalben
Lichtenberg
Naila
A7
E45
Münnerstadt
Coburg
Stockheim
Hasslach
VESTE ROSENBERG
Bad Kissingen
Stadtlauringen
Mitwitz
Wallenfels
Hammelburg
TRIMBURG
Kronach
Hofheim
BETTENBURG
Pfaffendorf
Marktzeuln
Markleugast
Poppenhausen
HASSBERGE
Lichtenfels
BANZ
Stadtsteinach
Gemünden
Burgkunstadt
Kupferberg
D
Schweinfurt
Ebern
Vierzehnheiligen
PLASSENBURG
Gefrees
Staffelstein
Weismain
Kulmbach
Lohr
Arnstadt
Hassfurt
Bad Berneck
FICHTELGEBIRGE
Karlstadt
Werneck
A70
E48
Ebelsbach
Zapfendorf
Thurnau
Eltmann
Schesslitz
FELSENGARTEN
Warmensteinach
Birkenfeld
Gerolzhofen
Breitengüssbach
Hallstadt
Hollfeld
WÜRGAU
Marktheidenfeld
Veitshöchheim
Volkach
Bamberg
Bayreuth
EREMITAGE
Weidenberg
WÜRZBURG
Ebrach
FRÄNKISCHE SCHWEIZ
Dettelbach
Prichsenstadt
Wiesentheid
Burgebrach
Hirschaid
Waischenfeld
Kemnath
A3
E41
Höchberg
BINGHÖHLE
SOPHIENHÖHLE
Kitzingen
Schlüsselfeld
Streitberg
Muggendorf
Creussen
Pommersfelden
Ebermannstadt
Behringersmühle
Gerchsheim
Iphofen
WEISSENSTEIN
Gössweinstein
TEUFELSHÖHLE
SPEINSHART
Kirchenthumbach
Eschenbach
Höchstadt
Pottenstein
Marktbreit
Ochsenfurt
Pegnitz
STEIGERWALD
Forchheim
Markt Bibart
Scheinfeld
A73
WELDENSTEINER
Grafenwöhr
Gräfenberg
Auerbach
Königshofen
A9
E51
Plech
Neuhaus
Gollhofen
SPIELBG
Neustadt an der Aisch
Herzogenaurach
Erlangen
Röttingen
Uffenheim
Velden
Forth
Vilseck
Bad Mergentheim
Weikersheim
Creglingen
Bad Windsheim
Emskirchen
HOHENECK
Heroldsberg
MAXIMILIANSGROTTE
R. ROTHENBURG
HERRGOTTS KIRCHE
Markt Erlbach
Langenzenn
Hersbruck
Hahnbach
Fürth
Nürnberg
Lauf
Dörzbach
Rothenburg ob der Tauber
Burgbernheim
NÜRNBERG
Sulzbach-Rosenberg
Amberg
Grosshabersdorf
Alfeld
FRANKENHÖHE
E50
A6
Künzelsau
Blaufelden
Lehrberg
Heilsbronn
Feucht
Altdorf
Langenburg
Gerabronn
Ansbach
Schwabach
Lauterhofen
Kupferzell
Kastl
Kirchberg
Windsbach
Abenberg
KÖNIG-OTTO-HÖHLE
Aurach
Roth
Allersberg
Neumarkt
Ilshofen
Wolframs-Eschenbach
Merkendorf
Schmidmühlen
Velburg
Feuchtwangen
Freystadt
Crailsheim
Spalt
Hilpoltstein
COMBURG
Bechhofen
Gunzenhausen
Burglengenfeld
Obersontheim
Dinkelsbühl
Pleinfeld
Dasswang
Parsberg
FRÄNKISCHE ALB
Thalmässing
Berching
ST. MARIA
Ellenberg
Wassertrüdingen
Weissenburg
Ellingen
Greding
NATURPARK
REGENSBURG
Gschwend
Ellwangen
Oettingen
Beilngries
Dietfurt
Hemau
Kinding
Nittendorf
SCHLOSS PRUNN
Treuchtlingen
Wallerstein
60
61
Altmühl
Main
Regnitz
Saale
Tauber
Jagst
Kocher
Rezat
Aisch
Pegnitz
Donau-Kanal

THÜRINGEN
Weimar
Bürgel
Eisenberg
Altenburg
Geithain
Rochlitz
Waldheim
KRIEBSTEIN
WECHSELBURG
Mittweida
Bad Berka
Jena
GLEICHEN
Arnstadt
Kranichfeld
Blankenhain
Stadtroda
GERA
Schmölln
ROCHSBURG
Frankenberg
Flöha
Ronneburg
Meerane
Waldenburg
Stadtilm
Teichel
Kahla
LEUCHTENBURG
Crimmitschau
Glauchau
CHEMNITZ
PAULINZELLA
Bad Blankenburg
Rudolstadt
Neustadt
Weida
Werdau
ZWICKAU
Lichtenstein
Zschopau
Gehren
Königsee
Schwarzburg
Pössneck
Auma
Stollberg
Thalheim
Saalfeld
Hohenwarte Talsperre
Ziegenrück
Zeulenroda
Greiz
Thum
Grossbreitenbach
FEENGROTTEN
Reichenbach
Wolkenstein
Neuhaus
Leutenberg
Schleiz
Elsterberg
Schneeberg
Aue
Annaberg-Buchholz
Probstzella
Bleiloch Talsperre
Rodewisch
Schwarzenberg
Ludwigsstadt
Wurzbach
Lobenstein
Gefell
Plauen
Auerbach
Eibenstock
Falkenstein
Vejprty
Rudolphstein
Sonneberg
Nordhalben
Hirschberg
Oelsnitz
Johanngeorgenstadt
Oberwiesenthal
Klášterec nad Ohří
Neustadt
Lichtenberg
Naila
Klingenthal
KLÍNOVEC
Stockheim
NATURPARK
Hasslach
VESTE ROSENBERG
Hof
Adorf
Kraslice
Jáchymov
HIMSTEIN
Mitwitz
Wallenfels
Bad Elster
Markneukirchen
Nejdek
Ostrov
DOUPOV
Kronach
FRANKENWALD
Rehau
Aš
Bad Brambach
Lichtenfels
Marktzeuln
Markleugast
Schwarzenbach
HIRSCH-STEIN
Karlovy Vary
Stadtsteinach
Münchberg
Selb
ELSTERGEBIRGE
Schönberg
Burgkunstadt
Kirchenlamitz
Vojtanov
Sokolov
Loket
Vierzehnheiligen
PLASSENBURG
Kupferberg
Hazlov
Františkovy Lázně
HORY
Weismain
Kulmbach
Gefrees
Weissenstadt
NATURPARK Ohre
FICHTELGEBIRGE
Pomezí nad Ohří
Bochov
Bečov nad Teplou
Thurnau
Bad Berneck
FICHTEL
Schirnding
SLAVKOVSKÝ LES CHKO
Zapfendorf
Bischofsgrün
Wunsiedel
Arzberg
Cheb
Žlutice
FELSENGARTEN
Warmensteinach
Tröstau
Waldsassen
SLAVKOVSKÝ LES
Toužim
LUISENBURG
Marktredwitz
Lázně Kynžvart
WÜRGAU
Hollfeld
Bayreuth
EREMITAGE
Weidenberg
GEBIRGE
GRENZLAND-TURM
Mariánské Lázně
KLÁŠTER TEPLÁ
FRÄNKISCHE SCHWEIZ
Mitterteich
Velká Hleď'sebe
Teplá
TEPELSKÁ PLOŠINA
Hirschaid
Waischenfeld
Kemnath
Wiesau
BINGHÖHLE
SOPHIENHÖHLE
Tirschenreuth
Chodová Planá
Streitberg
Muggendorf
Creussen
STEINWALD
Erbendorf
Ebermannstadt
Behringersmühle
Bärnau
Planá
GUTŠTEJN
Úněšov
Gössweinstein
TEUFELSHÖHLE
SPEINSHART
NATURPARK
Windisch
Černošín
Pottenstein
Kirchenthumbach
Eschenbach
Pressath
Waldnaab
Mže
ST. QUIRIN
Tachov
VOLFŠTEJN
Forchheim
Pegnitz
HESSENREUTHER
Neustadt an der Waldnaab
Stříbro
WELDENSTEINER
Grafenwöhr
Auerbach
Kladruby
Kozolupy
Gräfenberg
Plech
MANTELER WALD
OBERPFÄLZER
Bor
Erlangen
Neuhaus
Weiden
Přimda
Forth
Velden
Waidhaus
Rozvadov
Vilseck
Vohenstrauss
MAXIMILIANS-GROTTE
Freihung
Stod
Dobřany
Heroldsberg
R.ROTHENBURG
Hirschau
NATURPARK
Bělá
Lauf
Hersbruck
Hahnbach
Eslarn
Nürnberg
Schnaittenbach
Wernberg
Staňkov
Přeštice
Sulzbach-Rosenberg
Pfreimd
Horšovský Týn
Alfeld
Amberg
Nabburg
Dražénov
Koloveč
Feucht
Altdorf
Oberviechtach
Domažlice
Lauterhofen
Schwarzenfeld
WALD
Kleneč
Waldmünchen
Babylon
RYZMBERK
Kastl
Neunburg
ČERCHOV
Kdyně
KÖNIG-OTTO-HÖHLE
Schwandorf
Schönthal
Janovice nad Úhlavou
Roth
Allersberg
Neumarkt
Wackersdorf
Rötz
Folmava
Freystadt
Schmidmühlen
Velburg
Bodenwöhr
Furth im Wald
Nýrsko
Hilpoltstein
Bruck
NATURPARK
Arnschwang
Burglengenfeld
Regen
Cham
Hojsova Stráž
Dasswang
Parsberg
Nittenau
Roding
Kötzting
Thalmässing
Berching
Kallmünz
PANCÍŘ
Lam
Greding
CHAMEREGG
BAYERISCHER
NATURPARK
Regenstauf
OBERER
Miltach
Lohberg
REGENSBURG
Falkenstein
Drachselsried
Beilngries
Dietfurt
Hemau
WALHALLA
Viechtach
Bodenmais
Kinding
Nittendorf
Donaustauf
Barbing
Wörth
Ascha
St Englmar
Bayerisch Eisenstein
ERZGEBIRGE
KRUŠNÉ
NATURPARK
47
34
61

DRESDEN
Freiberg
Tharandt
Freital
Heidenau
Pirna
NATIONALPARK SACHSISCHE SCHWEIZ
FESTUNG KÖNIGSTEIN
Bad Schandau
Königstein
Dippoldiswalde
Brand-Erbisdorf
Glashütte
Bad Gottleuba
Frauenstein
Lauenstein
Altenberg
Zinnwald-Georgenfeld
Cínovec
Olbernhau
Dubí
Hrob
Litvínov
Lom
Teplice
Duchcov
Bílina
Jirkov
Most
Neukirch
Löbau
Oppach
Neustadt
Sebnitz
Ebersbach
Neugersdorf
Rumburk
Schmilka
Hřensko
Krásná Lípa
Seifhennersdorf
Zittau
Varnsdorf
Herrnhut
Ostritz
Niederoderwitz
Lubań
Olszyna
Zawidów
Lésna
PL
Gryfów Śląski
Habartice
Mirsk
Pasiecznik
Frýdlant
Sieniawka
Bogatynia
Hejnice
Świeradów-Zdrój
Piechowice
Szklarska Poręba
Hrádek nad Nisou
Chrastava
JIZERSKÉ HORY
ELBSANDSTEINGEBIRGE
DĚČÍNSKÉ STĚNY
LUŽICKÉ HORY
Česká Kamenice
Děčín
Benešov nad Ploučnicí
Nový Bor
Cvikov
Jablonné v Podještědí
Liberec
Harrachov
Desná
Tanvald
Jablonec nad Nisou
Špindlerův Mlýn
Ústí nad Labem
Velké Březno
Česká Lípa
Zákupy
Mimoň
Hodkovice nad Mohelkou
Železný Brod
Kravaře
Úštěk
Litoměřice
Lovosice
Terezín
Třebenice
Doksy
Dubá
Bělá pod Bezdězem
Mnichovo Hradiště
Turnov
Semily
Jilemnice
Studenec
Libochovice
Roudnice n Labem
Štětí
Mšeno
Kokořín
Mladá Boleslav
Kosmonosy
Sobotka
Jičín
Nová Paka
Postoloprty
Žatec
Louny
Budyně nad Ohří
Liběchov
Mělník
Libáň
Zlonice
Velvary
Veltrusy
Kralupy nad Vltavou
Byšice
Benátky nad Jizerou
Neratovice
Kopidlno
Smidary
Křinec
Nový Bydžov
Městec Králové
Nechanice
Slaný
Řevničov
Krupá
Brandýsek
Kladno
Švermov
Roztoky
Brandýs nad Labem
Kostelec nad Labem
Lysá nad Labem
Čelákovice
Nymburk
Poděbrady
Chlumec nad Cidlinou
Rakovník
Nové Strašecí
PRAHA
Lidice
Zdiby
St.Vestec
Sadská
Jesenice
Ždár
Kyšice
Jeneč
Ruzyně
Unhošť
Úvaly
Český Brod
Křivoklát
Chyňava
Uhříněves
Kostelec nad Černými Lesy
Kolín
Pardubice
Kralovice
Beroun
Radotín
Zbraslav
Říčany
Přelouč
Heřmanův Městec
Plasy
Karlštejn
Zdice
Dobřichovice
Mnichovice
CZ
Kutná Hora
Čáslav
Žebrák
Mníšek pod Brdy
Davle
Jílové u Prahy
Pyšely
Uhlířské Janovice
Třemošná
Radnice
Břasy
Hořovice
Hostomice
Štěchovice
Sázava
Žleby
PLZEŇ
Mýto
Dobříš
Konopiště
Benešov
Zbraslavice
Golčův Jeníkov
Vilémov
Jince
Nový Knín
Kácov
Starý Plzenec
Rokycany
Příbram
Neveklov
Bystřice
Ledeč nad Sázavou
Mirošov
Obory
Vlašim
Chotěboř
Spálené Poříčí
Světlá nad Sázavou
Milín
Sedlčany
Blovice
Rožmitál pod Třemšínem
Votice
Čechtice
Lipnice nad Sázavou
Březnice
Havlíčkův Brod
Seč
Mladá Vožice
Petrovice
Košetice
Humpolec
Nepomuk
Mirovice
Orlík nad Vltavou
Jistebnice
Želiv
Kasejovice
Lnáře
Červená Řečice
Štoky
Blatná
Pacov
Milevsko
Tábor
Plánice
Sedlice
Opařany
Chýnov
Kámen
Pelhřimov
Horažďovice
Bernartice
Malšice
Sezimovo Ústí
Černovice
Jihlava
Rabí
Katovice
Písek
Bechyně
Planá nad Lužnicí
Horní Cerekev
Sušice
Strakonice
Putim
Mnich
Batelov
Soběslav
Kamenice nad Lipou
Počátky
Třešť
Stonařov
Kašperské Hory
Volyně
Drahonice
Protivín
Týn nad Vltavou
Veselí nad Lužnicí
Kardašova Řečice
Žirovnice
Rasná
Rejštejn
Stachy
Vodňany
Strmilov
Studená
Telč
Vlachovo Březí
Bavorov
Jindřichův Hradec
Kunžak
Vimperk
Hluboká
Lomnice nad Lužnicí
Modrava

A
B
C
D
36
49
63
WROCŁAW
Lwowek Slaski
Jawor
Cesarzowice
Rakoszyce
Katy Wroclawskie
Kostomloty
Luboradz
Swierzawa
Wlen
Gryfów Śląski
Pasiecznik
Jelenia Gora
GÓRY KACZAWSKI
Wojeieszow
Strzegom
Dobromierz
Bolkow
Kaczorow
Świeradów-Zdrój
Piechowice
Szklarska Poreba
Cieplice Slaskie-Zdrój
Marciszów
Sobieszów
KARKONOSKI PARK NAR.
Kowary
Karpacz
Kamienna Gora
Krzeszów
Boguszow-Gorce
KSIĄŻ
Swiebodzice
WAŁBRZYCH
Swidnica
Marcinowice
Zarów
Gniechowice
Sobotka
Bielany Wrocł.
Jordanow Slaski
PRZEDGORZE SUDECKIE
Jelcz-Laskowice
Oława
Brzeg
Odra
Lagiewniki
Strzelin
Kolnica
Przylesie
Lewin Brzeski
Grodków
GRODNO
Pieszyce
Dzierzoniów
Niemcza
Witostowice
Henryków
Bielawa
GÓRY SOWIE
1015 SOWA
Jedlina-Zdroj
Gluszyca
Mieroszow
Lubawka
Královec
KRKONOŠE
KRKONOŠSKÝ NÁRODNÍ PARK
Tanvald
Špindlerův Mlýn
Pec pod Sněžkou
Vrchlabí
Mladé Buky
Jilemnice
Janské Lázně
Semily
Studenec
Hostinné
Trutnov
Teplice nad Metují
Broumov
Świerki
Nowa Ruda
Slupiec
Zabkowice Slaskie
Ziębice
Jaszów
Kamieniec Zabkowicki
Sidzina
Korfantów
Nysa
Otmuchów
Paczków
Złoty Stok
Bardo
Radkow
Wambierzyce
Police nad Metují
Hronov
Úpice
Nová Paka
KUMBURK
Jičín
Dvůr Králové nad Labem
Červený Kostelec
Česká Skalice
Kudowa-Zdrój
PARK NARODOWY GÓR STOŁOWYCH
Náchod
Szczytna
Duszniki-Zdrój
Polanica-Zdroj
Klodzko
Javorník
Vidnava
Przelęk
Biała
Laka Prudnicka
Prudnik
Głuchołazy
Osoblaha
Kuks
Hořice
Jaroměř
JOSEFOV
Nové Město nad Metují
ORLICKÉ HORY
GÓRY BYSTRZYCKIE
ŚNIEŻNICKI
Gorzanów
Bystrzyca Kłodzka
Lądek-Zdrój
Stronie Slaskie
Mikulovice
NA ŠPIČÁKU
Smidary
Nový Bydžov
HRADEC KRÁLOVÉ
Nechanice
HRÁDEK
Dobruška
Opočno
1115 VELKÁ DEŠTNÁ
IGLICZNA
Bolesławów
NA POMEZÍ
Międzygorze
Zlaté Hory
Jeseník
HRUBÝ JESENÍK
Město Albrechtice
Třebechovice pod Orebem
Rychnov nad Kněžnou
Týniště nad Orlicí
Vamberk
Międzylesie
Staré Město
Červenohorské Sedlo
1013
Vrbno pod Pradědem
Krnov
Kostelec nad Orlicí
Holice
Pardubice
LITICE
Žamberk
Králíky
Hanušovice
CHKO JESENÍKY
Karlova Studánka
LANŠPERK
Červená Voda
Letohrad
Choceň
Dašice
Přelouč
Heřmanův Městec
JAKUB
Chrudim
SVATÝ MIKULÁŠ
Ústí nad Orlicí
Velké Losiny
Sobotín
Bruntál
Opava
Hrochův Týnec
Vysoké Mýto
Česká Třebová
Štíty
Šumperk
Rýmařov
RABŠTEJN
STRÁDOV
LICHTICE
Slatiňany
Chrast
Žleby
ŽELEZNÉ HORY
KOŠUMBERK
Litomyšl
Třebovice
Lanškroun
HOŠŤEJN
Zábřeh
LEŽÁKY
Seč
OHEB
Vilémov
Skuteč
RYCHMBURK
MENDRYKA
Šumvald
SOVINEC
Dvorce
Úsov
CHKO ŽELEZNÉ HORY
Doubrava
Krouna
Hlinsko
Svitavy
Moravská Třebová
Mohelnice
Uničov
Moravský Beroun
KARLŠTEJN
Chotěboř
Ždírec nad Doubravou
Polička
Křenov
CIMBURK
MLADEČSKÁ JESK.
Litovel
Šternberk
Město Libavá
Světlá nad Sázavou
CHKO ŽĎÁRSKÉ VRCHY
836 DEVĚT SKAL
STARKOV
Jimramov
Brněnec
PLANKENBURK
Jevíčko
Javoříčko
Morava
KOPEČEK
SV. ANNA
Havlíčkův Brod
Přibyslav
Nové Město na Moravě
Letovice
Konice
Drahanovice
Olomouc
Velký Újezd
Lipník nad Bečvou
Humpolec
ČESKOMORAVSKÁ VYSOČINA
Sázava
Žďár nad Sázavou
J. BLANICKÝCH RYTÍŘŮ
CZ
Kostelec na Hané
Štoky
Polná
Bystřice nad Pernštejnem
Kunštát
Boskovice
Prostějov
HELFŠTÝN
Přerov
Bohdalov
PERNŠTEJN
Černá Hora
SLOUPSKO - ŠOŠŮVSKÉ JESKYNĚ
Bystřice pod Hostýnem
Jihlava
Měřín
Křižanov
Blansko
MACOCHA
Kojetín
ROŠTEJN
Velké Meziříčí
KATEŘINSKÁ
Jedlovnice
Batelov
Brtnice
Tišnov
NOVÝ HRAD
Holešov
Třešť
Stonařov
STŘELIŠTĚ
Velká Bíteš
Kuřim
Svratka
Svitava
OCHOZSKÁ
Vyškov
Kroměříž
Hulín
Třebíč
Morkovice Slížany
Zdounky
Zlín
Telč
Náměšť nad Oslavou
Oslava
Otrokovice
Želetava
Rosice
BRNO
Slavkov u Brna (Austerlitz)
Brankovice
CHŘIBY
VELEHRAD
BABYLÓN
Jaroměřice nad Rokytnou
Hrotovice
Ivančice
Dolní Kounice
PRACKÝ
Bučovice
Koryčany
BUCHLOV
Staré Město
A4
E40
E50
E65
D1
D2
D47
E462
E442
E461
E67
E261
E59

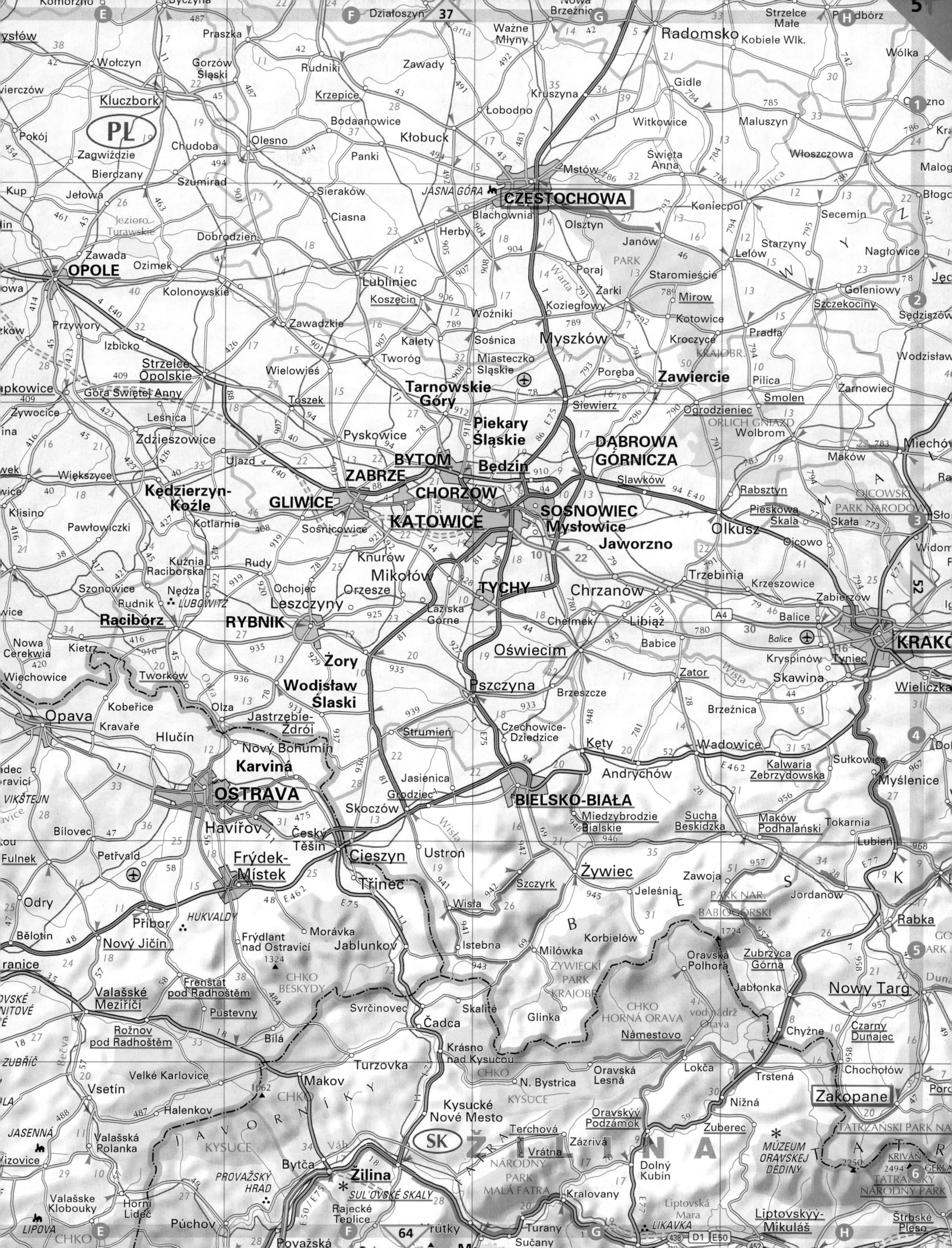

38
65
51
Starachowice
Przedbórz
Radoszyce
Suchedniów
Brody
Sarnówek
Małe
Kobiele Wlk.
Wólka
Mniów
Michałów
Pantów
Ostrowiec
Świętokrzyski
Annopol
GÓRY ŚWIĘTOKRZYSKIE
Gózd
Bodzentyn
ŚWIĘTOKRZYSKI
PARK NARODOWY
Ćmielów
Ożarów
Oleszno
Łopuszno
Maluszyn
KIELCE
Bidziny
Zawichost
Krasocin
JASKINIA RAJ
Nowa Słupia
Opatów
Zdzie
Włoszczowa
Górno
Malogoszcz
Daleszyce
Baćkowice
Chęciny
Łagów
Pilica
Błogoszów
Morawica
Lipnik
Tokarnia
Ociesęki
Ujazd
Secemin
Sobkow
Sandomierz
Raków
Starzyny
Lelów
Nagłowice
Mnichów
Piotrkowice
Chmielnik
Mostki
Jędrzejów
Goleniowy
Szydłów
Kurozwęki
Koprzywnica
Łoniów
Tarnobrzeg
Szczekociny
Kije
Staszów
Sędziszów
Pradła
Pińczów
Kargów
Osiek
Sandomierski
Busko-
Zdrój
Baranów
Sandomierski
Wodzisław
Bojanów
Stopnica
Połaniec
Nowa Dęba
Pilica
Żarnowiec
Smoleń
Wchadłów
Beszowa
Nuszów
Narodowy
PUSZCZA SANDOM
Książ
Wielki
Solec-
Zdrój
Słupia
LICH GNIAZD
Wolbrom
Działoszyce
Miechów
Mielec
Cmolas
Maków
Skalbmierz
Wiślica
Wisła
Racławice
Szczucin
Nowy
Korczyn
Kolbuszowa
Rabsztyn
Kazimierza
Wielka
Zgórsko
Pieskowa
Skała
OJCOWSKI
PARK NARODOWY
Opatowiec
Rzemień
Słomniki
Skała
Ojcowo
Klimontów
Radomyśl
Wielki
Widoma
Dąbrowa
Tarnowska
Pustków
Dunajec
Żabno
Krzeszowice
Proszowice
Koszyce
Brzeźnica
Sędziszów
Małopolski
Nowe
Brzesko
Wesoła
Zabierzów
Lisia
Góra
Dębica
Ropczyce
Balice
Igołomia
Szczurowa
PUSZCZA
NIEPOŁOMICKA
KRAKÓW
Niepołomice
Kryspinów
Tyniec
TARNÓW
Pilzno
Skawina
Bochnia
Brzesko
Leki
Górne
Bielowy
Wieliczka
Dębno
Wojnicz
Nowy
Wiśnicz
Tuchów
Strzyżów
Gdów
Joniny
Wiśniowa
Godowa
Brzostek
Frysztak
Dobczyce
Jurków
Zakliczyn
Kalwaria
Zebrzydowska
Sułkowice
Muchówka
Czchów
Gromnik
Wisłoka
Wisłok
Myślenice
Rożnów
Ciężkowice
Wiśniowa
Zborowice
Biecz
Jasło
Potok
Korczyn
Maków
Podhalański
Tokarnia
Łososina
Dolna
Gródek
nad Dunajcem
Krosno
Dobra
Lubień
Limanowa
Wielogłowy
Wilczyska
Bednarka
Mszana
Dolna
Grybów
Gorlice
Nowy
Żmigród
Iwonicz-
Zdrój
Jordanów
Przyszowa
Ropa
Rymanów
Rabka
Kamienica
Stary
Sącz
Nowy
Sącz
Dukla
GORCZAŃSKI
PARK NARODOWY
Uście
Gorlickie
MAGURSKI
PARK
NARODOWY
Zabrzeż
Berest
Tylawa
Poręba
Górna
POPRADZKI
PARK KRAJOBR.
Jabłonka
Nowy Targ
Dębno
Rytro
Konieczna
Łopuszna
Krościenko
nad Dunajcem
Piwniczna
Wysowa
500
Przełęcz
Dukielska
PRÍRODNÉ
MÚZEUM
Chyżne
Czarny
Dunajec
Szczawnica
Krynica
PIENIŃSKI
PARK NAR.
Żegiestów
Muszynka
Bukowina
Tatrzańska
ČERVENÝ
KLÁŠTOR
Muszyna
Bardejovské
Kúpele
Zborov
Svidník
Medzil
Trstená
Chochołów
Stará
Ľubovňa
Hniezdne
Bardejov
Zakopane
Poronin
SPIŠSKÁ MAGURA
ČERGOV
Nižná
1081
Sedlo
Prislop
Podolínec
Poprad
Jakubany
KAMENICHÝ
HRAD
Stropkov
TATRZAŃSKI PARK NAR.
Tatranská
Kotlina
MÚZEUM
ORAVSKEJ
DEDINY
KRIVÁŇ
2494
BELIANSKÁ
JASKYŇA
Spišská Belá
KAŠTIEĽ STRÁŽKY
Brezovica
Lipany
Marhaň
2250
GERLACHOVSKÝ
ŠTÍT
2663
Raslavice
TATRANSKÝ
NÁRODNÝ PARK
Tatranská
Lomnica
Kežmarok
PREŠOV
SK
Sabinov
Giraltovce
Domašská
Priehr
Nádrž
Liptovský
Mikuláš
Štrbské
Pleso
Starý
Smokovec
Poprad
ŠARIŠSKÝ HRAD
Veľký Šariš
Kapušany
Spišský
Dukovce

E
F
G
H
39
206
Uchanie
Teratyn
Ustyluh
Żołkiewka-osada
Stryjów
Strzyżów
Hrubieszów
Turobin
Chomęciska Małe
Novovolyns'k
Нововолинськ
Zamość
Miączyn
Terebiń
Modliborzyce
Bodaczów
Zaklików
Janów Lubelski
Szczebrzeszyn
Łabunie
Frampol
Przewale
Dolhobyczów
Zwierzyniec
Wólka Łabuńska
PARK KRAJOBR.
LASY JANOWSKIE
ROZTOCZAŃSKI PARK NARODOWY
Wożuczyn
Novoukraïnka
Łaszczów
Sokal'
Stalowa Wola
PUSZCZA
Biłgoraj
Tarnawatka
LUBELSKA
ROZTOCZE
Nowy Majdan
Józefów
Tomaszów Lubelski
Ulanów
Belz
Rudnik
SOLSKA
Bełzec
Krzeszów
Narol
Tarnogród
Hrebenne
Velyki Mosty
Dabrówka
Nowa Sarzyna
Rava-Rus'ka
Leżajsk
PL
Cieszanów
Dachnów
RADRUZ
Sokołów Małopolski
Oleszyce
Lubaczów
Maheriv
Zhovkva
Sieniawa
Tryńcza
Nemyriv
Budomierz
Zapałów
Łańcut
Kulykiv
Przeworsk
Jarosław
Buczyna
RZESZÓW
Kidałowice
Krakovets'
Yavoriv
Tyczyn
Kanczuga
Radymno
Ivano-Frankove
L'VIV
Львів
Rokietnica
Pruchnik
Szklary
Żurawica
Horodok
Mostys'ka
Sknyliv
Dynów
Sudova Vyshnia
Krasiczyn
Przemyśl
San
Blizne
Brzozów
Bircza
Komarno
Nyzhankovychi
Grabownica Starzeńska
Mrzygłód
Kuźmina
Dnister
Mykolaïv
Zarszyn
Sanok
Dobromyl'
Zagórz
Załuż
Khyriv
Sambir
Самбір
UA
Lesko
Uherse Mineralne
Staryi Sambir
Medenychi
Ustrzyki Dolne
Drohobych
Дрогобич
J Solińskie
Czarna
Komańcza
BIESZCZADY
Boryslav
БорисЛав
Truskavets'
Трускавець
Stryj
Стрий
Limna
Palota
Cisna
Turka
VÝCHODNÉ
BIESZCZADZKI PARK NARODOWY
Bolekhiv
Ustrzyki Górne
Skole
Hostov'ce
Borynia
Nová Sedlica
KARPATY
Dolyna
Koškovce
Uzhots'kyi Pereval
Stakčín
Snina
Vyhoda

41
66
PAYS DE LA LOIRE
CHAR
Pornichet
St-Nazaire
KORRIGANS
Savenay
Paimboeuf
Mindin
St-Brevin-les-Pins
St-Père-en-Retz
Pointe de St-Gildas
Côte de Jade
Pornic
NANTES
Bouguenais
Bouaye
Nantes Atlantique
Vertou
Carquefou
CHÂT DE LA SEILLERAYE
Nort-sur-Erdre
Ancenis
Le Louroux
Varades
St-Georges
CHÂT DE SERRANT
Champtoceaux
St-Florent
Chalonnes-sur-Loire
Les Ponts-de-Cé
Le Loroux-Bottereau
Montrevault
Vallet
Beaupréau
Chemillé
Thouarcé
Noirmoutier-en-l'Ile
Ile de Noirmoutier
Bourgneuf-en-Retz
Viais
St-Philbert
Clisson
Aigrefeuille-sur-Maine
Machecourt
Beauvoir-sur-Mer
Rocheservière
Montaigu
Cholet
Vihiers
CHÂT DE COUDRAY-MONTBAULT
Mortagne-sur-Sèvre
Challans
Legé
St-Jean-de-Monts
Port-Joinville
Ile d'Yeu
Maulévrier
Argenton-Château
St-Fulgent
ABB. DE LA GRAINETIÈRE
Commequiers
Le Poiré-sur-Vie
Mauléon
St-Gilles-Croix-de-Vie
Aizenay
Belleville-sur-Vie
Les Herbiers
Les Epesses
St-Michel-Mont-Mercure
Les Essarts
La Roche-sur-Yon
La Mothe-Achard
Pouzauges
Bressuire
Cerizay
Chantonnay
Bournezeau
Aubigny
Moncoutant
Les Sables-d'Olonne
La Caillère-St-Hilaire
La Châtaigneraie
Ste-Hermine
Moutiers
Mareuil
Talmont-St-Hilaire
Vouvant
GROTTE DU PÈRE DE MONTFORT
Parthenay
Secondigny
Jard-sur-Mer
Luçon
Fontenay-le-Comte
Triaize
Chaillé-les-Marais
Coulonges
Champdeniers
La Tranche-sur-Mer
L'Aiguillon
St-Michel-en-l'Herm
Maillezais
PHARE DES BALEINES
Ile de Ré
Pertuis Breton
Ars-en-Ré
St-Martin-de-Ré
Marans
PARC NATUREL RÉGIONAL DU MARAIS POITEVIN VAL DE SÈVRE ET VENDÉE
St-Maixent-l'Ecole
La Flotte
Coulon
Niort
Courçon
La Pallice
La Rochelle
Pertuis d'Antioche
Dompierre-sur-Mer
Epannes
Prahecq
St-Denis-d'Oléron
Aigrefeuille-d'Aunis
Mauzé-sur-le-Mignon
Beauvoir-sur-Niort
Châtelaillon-Plage
Ile d'Oléron
Ile d'Aix
Surgères
Melle
Fouras
Brioux-sur-Boutonne
St-Pierre-d'Oléron
Dampierre-sur-Boutonne
Rochefort
Tonnay-Boutonne
Loulay
Le Chateau-d'Oléron
Brouage
Tonnay-Charente
Aulnay
St-Agnant
St-Jean-d'Angély
Marennes
LA ROUCHE-COURBON
St-Porchaire
St-Hilaire-de-Villefranche
Le Tremblade
Matha
Le Palmyre
Pointe de la Coubre
Saintes
Burie
Siecq
St-Palais-sur-Mer
Saujon
Royan
St-Georges-de-Didonne
Cognac
ÉGLISE DE CHÂTRE
Pointe de Grave
Le Verdon
Jarnac
Cozes
Soulac-sur-Mere
Meschers-sur-Gironde
Gémozac
Segonzac
Hiersac
Talmont
Pons
Châteauneuf
St-Genis-de-
A
B
C
D
1
2
3
4
5
6
A11
A83
E03
E60
A10
E05
A837
N137
N160
N249
N11
N150
N141
N23
N148

Mayet
Château-du-Loir
La Chartre-sur-le-Loir
Trôo
Lavardin
Fréteval
Bin
Ouzouer-le-March
Le Lude
Vaas
Montoire-sur-le-Loir
Vendôme
Oucques
Baugé
CHÂT. DE MONTGEOFFROY
Noyant
Château-la-Vallière
Neuillé-Pont-Pierre
St-Amand-Longpré
TALCY
Beaugency
Beaufort-en-Vallée
Mouliherne
Château-Renault
Mer
Les Rosiers
Gennes
Longué
Rillé
Herbault
Blois
PARC DE CHAMBORD
Chambord
Cunault
Gizeux
TOURS
Vouvray
CHÂT. DE BOUMOIS
Allonnes
Saumur
Langeais
JARDIN
Chaumont-sur-Loire
Bracieux
Cour-Cheverny
Bourgueil
Villandry
Amboise
Fontevraud-l'Abbaye
Montsoreau
USSÉ
Azay-le-Rideau
Montbazon
Pontlevoy
Chenonceaux
Bléré
Montrichard
Contres
Montreuil-Bellay
Chinon
Cormery
MANOIR DE BEAUREGARD
Romorantin-Lanthenay
AIGUEVIVES
St-Aignan
Les Trois-Moutiers
Champigny-sur-Veude
L'Ile-Bouchard
Ste-Maure-de-Touraine
Genillé
Selles
Villefranche-sur-Cher
Loudun
Loches
CHAP. ST-JEAN-DU-LIGET
Chabris
Oiron
Richelieu
Montrésor
Nouans-les-Fontaines
Monts-s-Guesnes
Ligueil
Valençay
St-Jouin-de-Marnes
F
Airvault
Orches
Descartes
Ecueillé
Graçay
Dangé-St-Romain
Le Grand-Pressigny
Châtillon-sur-Indre
Lencloître
Vatan
BOUGES-LE-CHÂT.
Thénezay
Mirebeau
Preuilly-sur-Claise
Levroux
Châtellerault
Azay-le-Ferron
Neuville-de-Poitou
La Roche-Posay
Mézières-en-Brenne
Buzançais
Issoudun
Vasles
Vouillé
Pleumartin
Tournon-St-Martin
Châteauroux
Poitiers
TOUFFOU
Angles-sur-l'Anglin
Lureuil
FONTGOMBAULT
Sanxay
St-Julien-l'Ars
PARC NAT. RÉGIONAL DE LA BRENNE
Chauvigny
Le Blanc
ABB. DE LIGUGÉ
NOUVAILLÉ-MAUPERTUIS
St-Savin-sur-Gartempe
Ciron
St-Gaultier
Ardentes
St-Août
Lusignan
Fleuré
CHÂT. DE LA ROCHEROLLE
Vivonne
Bélâbre
Argenton-sur-Creuse
Bouesse
Neuvy
St-Sauvant
Gençay
Prissac
La Châtre
Thevet-St-Julien
Lussac-les-Châteaux
Montmorillon
La Trimouille
Lezay
Couhé
Gargilesse-Dampierre
Usson-du-Poitou
Moulismes
Lussac-les-Eglises
St-Benoît-du-Sault
Eguzon
Chaunay
Crozant
Aigurande
Ste-Sévère
l'Isle-Jourdain
Civray
ANC. ABB. DE LA RÉAU
Le Dorat
Magnac-Laval
La Celle-Dunoise
Charroux
Dun-le-Palestel
Pressac
Availles-Limouzine
La Souterraine
Bonnat
Boussac
Ruffec
Mézières
Châtelus-Malvaleix
Bellac
La Croisière
St-Vaury
Châteauponsac
Glénic
Champagne-Mouton
Confolens
Bessines-sur-Gartempe
Bénévent l'Abbaye
Le Grand-Bourg
Guéret
Jarnages
Chêne-Pignier
Laurière
Gouzon
St-Claud
Nieuil
Nantiat
la Péruse
Chabanais
Moutier-d'Ahun
St-Junien
Ambazac
La Rochefoucauld
Rochechouart
Bourganeuf
Pontarion
Ruelle-sur-Touvre
LIMOGES
St-Laurent
St-Léonard-
Aubusson
CENT
POITOU-
CHARENTES
LIMOUSIN
56
67
68
42

42
43
55
68
CENTRE
F
OUSIN
Fréteval
Binas
Ouzouer-le-Marché
ORLÉANS
Canal d'Orléans
Ladon
Bellegarde
Montargis
Courtenay
Vendôme
Oucques
Meung-sur-Loire
Olivet
TALCY
Beaugency
Cléry
St-Amand-Longpré
Jargeau
Châteauneuf-sur-Loire
Lorris
Châteaurenard
Douchy
Germigny-des-Prés
St-Benoît-sur-Loire
Château-Renault
Mer
La Ferté-St-Aubin
Sully-sur-Loire
Charny
Herbault
Blois
PARC DE CHAMBORD
Cosson
Châtillon-Coligny
Chambord
Le Rabot
Isdes
Gien
Bracieux
Neung-sur-Beuvron
Lamotte-Beuvron
Bléneau
Chaumont-sur-Loire
Cour-Cheverny
Briare
Canal de Briare
Pontlevoy
Nouan-le-Fuzelier
Argent-sur-Sauldre
St-Fargeau
Chenonceaux
Contres
Montrichard
Châtillon-sur-Loire
MANOIR DE BEAUREGARD
Souesmes
Aubigny-sur-Nère
Bonny-sur-Loire
Romorantin-Lanthenay
Salbris
St-Amand-en-Puisaye
AIGUEVIVES
St-Aignan
Vailly
Villefranche-sur-Cher
Selles
Genillé
CHAP. ST-JEAN-DU-LIGET
Chabris
La Chapelle-d'Angillon
Cosne-Cours-sur-Loire
Neuvy-sur-Barangeon
Nouans-les-Fontaines
Montrésor
Valençay
Henrichemont
St-Satur
Gde Sauldre
Vierzon
Sancerre
Donzy
Écueillé
Graçay
St-Martin-d'Auxigny
Pouilly
CHÂT. DE MAUPAS
Massay
Mehun-sur-Yèvre
Châtillon-sur-Indre
Vatan
BOUGES-LE-CHÂT.
Les Aix-d'Angillon
Reuilly
Yèvre
Levroux
Sancergues
La Charité-sur-Loire
Bourges
Chârost
Issoudun
Buzançais
Baugy
St-Florent
Pougues-les-Eaux
Guérigny
Mornay-Berry
Châteauroux
Cher
Canal du Berry
Airain
Nérondes
Levet
Nevers
Chézal-Benoît
Châteauneuf-sur-Cher
La Guerche-sur-l'Aubois
PARC NAT. RÉGIONAL DE LA BRENNE
Dun-sur-Auron
St-Benin
Magny-Cours
CHÂTEAU DE MEILLANT
Imphy
Ardentes
Thaumiers
St-Gaultier
St-Août
Lignières
Arnon
Bruère-Allichamps
CHÂT. DE LA ROCHEROLLE
Sancoins
CHÂT. DE ST-AUGUSTIN
St-Amand-Montrond
St-Pierre-le-Moûtier
Bouesse
Argenton-sur-Creuse
Neuvy
Indre
Decize
Prissac
Thevet-St-Julien
Charenton-du-Cher
Lurcy-Lévis
La Veurdre
La Châtre
Le Châtelet
Gargilesse-Dampierre
Allier
Urçay
Dornes
Châteaumeillant
Éguzon
Culan
Cérilly
Villeneuve-sur-Allier
Ste-Sévère
Crozant
Vallon-en-Sully
Bourbon-l'Archambault
Aigurande
Hérisson
Chevagnes
Préveranges
La Celle-Dunoise
Creuse
Cosne-d'Allier
Moulins
Dun-le-Palestel
Pont Cellier
Souvigny
Bonnat
Boussac
La Souterraine
Huriel
Châtelus-Malvaleix
Montluçon
Le Montet
La Croisière
St-Vaury
Glénic
Bessay-sur-Allier
Commentry
Néris-les-Bains
Bénévent l'Abbaye
Le Grand-Bourg
Guéret
Jarnages
Montmarault
Varennes-sur-Allier
Gouzon
St-Pourçain-sur-Sioule
Évaux-les-Bains
Chambon-sur-Voueize
Chénérailles
Marcillat-en-Combraille
Montaigut
Chantelle
Moutier-d'Ahun
St-Éloy-les-Mines
Bellenaves
Sioule
Bourganeuf
Pontarion
Pionsat
GORGES DE CHOUVIGNY
St-Germain-des-Fossés
Auzances
Menat
Tardes
Ebreuil
St-Léonard-de-Noblat
Aubusson
Bellegarde-en-Marche
St-Gervais-d'Auvergne
Gannat
Vichy
Cusset
MÉANDRE
A10
A71
A20
A77
A719
E05
E09
E11
E15
E60
E62
E604
N7
N20
N60
N76
N141
N144
N145
N151
N209
N1079

44
58
69
70
BOURGOGNE
PARC NATUREL RÉGIONAL DU MORVAN
MONTS DU MORVAN
MONTS DU CHAROLAIS
PLATEAU DE LANGRES
Villeneuve-sur-Yonne
Cerisiers
Aix-en-Othe
Bouilly
Lac d'Orient
Vendeuvre
Bar-sur-Aube
Doulaincourt
Vignory
Colombey-les-Deux-Églises
Andelot
Bologne
Joigny
Migennes
Ervy-le-Châtel
Chaource
Bar-sur-Seine
Juzennecourt
St-Florentin
Essoyes
Chaumont
Aillant-sur-Tholon
Pontigny
Flogny-la-Chapelle
Les Riceys
Châteauvillain
Foulain
Nogent
Clefmont
Auxerre
Tonnerre
Tanlay
Mussy
Montigny-sur-Aube
Montigny-le-Roi
Chablis
Châtillon-sur-Seine
Arc-en-Barrois
Coulanges-la-Vineuse
Ancy-le-Franc
Laignes
Leuglay
Recey-sur-Ource
Langres
Vermenton
Nitry
Noyers
Aisy-sur-Seine
Auberive
Courson-les-Carrières
Aisy-sur-Armançon
ABB. DE FONTENAY
Longeau
Montbard
Aignay-le-Duc
Grancey-le-Château
Chassigny
Clamecy
Vézelay
Avallon
Montréal
Baigneux-les-Juifs
Prauthoy
St-Père
Semur-en-Auxois
Les Laumes
Selongey
Champlitte
Bierre-Les-Semur
Moloy
Is-sur-Tille
Til-Châtel
Quarré-les-Tombes
St-Seine-l'Abbaye
Fontaine-Française
Brinon
Corbigny
Lormes
Précy-sous-Thil
Vitteaux
Val-Suzon
Saulieu
Mirebeau
Vauclaix
Pouilly-en-Auxois
Sombernon
Bazolles
Montsauche-les-Settons
DIJON
Liernais
Gevrey-Chambertin
Longvic
Pontailler-sur-Saône
Châtillon-en-Bazois
Château-Chinon
Arnay-le-Duc
Genlis
Pesmes
Lucenay
Nuits-St-Georges
Auxonne
Moulins-Engilbert
Montmirey
Bligny-sur-Ouche
ABB. DE CÎTEAUX
St-Jean-de-Losne
GROTTE DE L'ERMITAGE
Vandenesse
Autun
Sully
Beaune
Dole
Rochefort-s-Nenon
St-Honoré-les-Bains
St-Leger
Nolay
Seurre
Tavaux
Fours
Étang-sur-Arroux
Mesvres
Chagny
Demigny
Chemin
Chaussin
Luzy
Couches
Navilly
Mont-sous-Vaudrey
Le Creusot
Pierre-de-Bresse
Maltat
Chalon-sur-Saône
Toulon-sur-Arroux
Givry
Bellevesvre
Chaumergy
Montchanin
Bourbon-Lancy
Mervans
Sellières
Montceau-les-Mines
Buxy
St-Germain-du-Plain
St-Germain-du-Bois
CIRQUE DE LADOYE
Gueugnon
Bletterans
Génelard
Sennecey-le-Grand
Beaurepaire-en-Bresse
Lons-le-Saunier
ABBE LES M
Montret
Joncy
Digoin
Louhans
CIRQUE DE BAUME
Brancion
Tournus
Doucier
Paray-le-Monial
St-Bonnet-de-Joux
Cuisery
Taizé
Montpont-en-Bresse
St-Yan
Charolles
Clairvaux-les-La
Le Donjon
Brandon
Cluny
Pont-de-Vaux
St-Trivier-de-Courtes
Orgelet
Cuiseaux
Marcigny
Matour
St-Amour
Lac de Vouglans
Moirans-Montagne
La Clayette
MONT. DE DUN
ROCHE DE SOLUTRÉ
St-Julien
La Pacaudière
Mâcon
Coligny
Arinthod
Chauffailles
Montrevel-en-Bresse
Marboz
Crêches

44
45
57
70
FRANCHE-COMTÉ
VAUD
NEUCHÂTEL
JURA
LANGRES
Houdelaincourt
Vaucouleurs
Maisons
Dombasle
Lunéville
Hèming
CHÂT. DU HAUT-BARR
Dabo
Joinville
Gondrecourt
Colombey-les-Belles
Pont-St-Vincent
Flavigny-sur-Moselle
Blâmont
Abreschviller
ROCH. DE DABO
Wangenbourg
Poissons
Germay
Domrémy-la-Pucelle
Vézelise
Gerbéviller
Cirey
CHÂT. DU NIDECK
Doulaincourt
SION
Haroué
Bayon
Badonviller
Col du Donon
DONON
Neufchâteau
Baccarat
Vignory
St-Blin
Charmes
Raon-l'Etape
Col du Hantz
Andelot
Bologne
Rouvres-en-Xaintois
Châtenois
Senones
Mirecourt
Rambervillers
Chaumont
St-Thiébault
Bourmont
Nomexy
Saales
Col de Saales
Bulgnéville
Vittel
Dompaire
St-Dié
Contrexéville
Brouvelieures
Ste-Marie-aux-Mines
Foulain
Clefmont
Épinal
Bruyères
Col de Ste-Marie
Nogent
Dombrot-le-Sec
Fraize
CHÂT. ST.-ULRICH
Corcieux
Montigny-le-Roi
Lamarche
Darney
Dinozé
Arches
Granges-sur-Vologne
Col du Bonhomme
Lapoutroie
Riquewihr
Monthureux-sur-Saône
Xertigny
Orbey
Neuilly-l'Évêque
Bourbonne-les-Bains
Fresnes
Bains-les-Bains
Remiremont
St-Amé
Gérardmer
Les Trois-Epis
Langres
Plombières-les-Bains
Col de la Grosse Pierre
Col de la Schlucht
Hohrodberg
Turckheim
Corre
Vauvillers
HOHNECK
Munster
La Bresse
Laferté
St-Loup-sur-Semouse
Col du Mont de Fourche
Rupt
Saulxures
Cornimont
BALLONS DES CORNIMONT
Rouffach
Longeau
Jussey
Fougerolles
Le Markstein
Fayl-Billot
Amance
Le Thillot
Bussang
Col de Bussang
Guebwiller
Chassigny
Faucogney-et-la-Mer
St Maurice-sur-Moselle
Soultz
Luxeuil-les-Bains
Faverney
Col du Ballon d'Alsace
Prauthoy
Combeaufontaine
Mélisey
Cernay
Thann
Champlitte
N.-D.-DES VOSGES DU-HAUT
Giromagny
Masevaux
Port-sur-Saône
Saulx
Lure
Ronchamp
Rougemont
MULHOUSE
Vesoul
Dampierre-sur-Salon
Fontaine-Française
GROTTE DE LA BAUME
Belfort
ABB. DE LA CHARITÉ
Héricourt
ST.-MORAND
Villersexel
Dannemarie
Altkirch
Mirebeau
Gray
Fretigney-et-Velloreille
Hirsingue
Rougemont
Montbéliard
Sochaux
Bioz
Choye
Gy
L'Isle-sur-le-Doubs
Audincourt
Delle
Pontailler-sur-Saône
Valentigney
Mathay
Ferrette
Pesmes
Marnay
FORT DE CHAILLUZ
Clerval
ABB. D'ACEY
Recologne
Audeux
Marchaux
Baume-les-Dames
Pont-de-Roide
Porrentruy
VORBOURG
Auxonne
Montmirey
BESANÇON
Aïssey
Sancey-le-Grand
St-Hippolyte
St.-Ursanne
Delémont
GROTTE DE L'ERMITAGE
GORGES DE PICHOUX
Rochefort-s-Nenon
Dampierre
Goumois
Maîche
Saignelégier
Moutier
Dole
Quingey
Valdahon
NOTRE DAME DE CONSOLATION
Tramelan
Tavannes
Sonceboz
TAUBENLOCHSCHLUCHT
Ornans
Nods
Le Russey
St-Imier
Grenchen
Chaussin
Amancey
Mouthier
Villers-le-Lac
La Chaux-de-Fonds
Biel/Bienne
Mont-sous-Vaudrey
Mouchard
SOURCE DE LA LOUE
SOURCE DU LISON
Morteau
MT CHAUMONT
Vue des Alpes
TWANN-SCHLUCHT
St-Gorgon-Main
Le Locle
LE CHASSERAL
La Neuveville
Büren
Salins-les-Bains
Levier
Montbenoît
Neuchâtel
Lyss
Aarberg
Chaumergy
Arbois
CIRQUE DU FER À CHEVAL
Pontarlier
Ins
Sellières
Poligny
Travers
Boudry
GORGIER
Kerzers
La Cluse-et-Mijoux
Verrières-de-Joux
Couvet
Fleurier
CIRQUE DE LADOYE
Nozeroy
CHENAUX
Murten
Laupen
Lons-le-Saunier
ABBE DE BAUME-LES MESSIEURS
Malbuisson
Ste-Croix
Estavayer-le-Lac
Avenches
Köniz
Champagnole
Jougne
Grandson
Payerne
Belp
CIRQUE DE BAUME
Doucier
Metabief
CHAMPVENT
Düdingen
Mouthe
MONT D'OR
Yverdon-les-Bains
Les Planches-en-Montagne
Vallorbe
ABB. DE HAUTERIVE
Fribourg
PONT DE PEROLLES
Orbe
Bonlieu
BURGISTEIN
Clairvaux-les-Lacs
St-Laurent-en-Grandvaux
Pompaples
ST. BARTHÉLEMY
Romont
Orgelet
Le Sentier
Moudon
Echallens

ALSACE
BADEN-WÜRTTEMBERG
SCHWARZWALD
SCHWÄBISCHE
STRASBOURG
Baden-Baden
STUTTGART
Esslingen
Sindelfingen
Böblingen
Tübingen
Reutlingen
Offenburg
Freudenstadt
FREIBURG IM BREISGAU
Villingen
Schwenningen
Donaueschingen
Rottweil
Balingen
Tuttlingen
Sigmaringen
Singen
Konstanz
Friedrichshafen
Schaffhausen
Winterthur
Frauenfeld
ZÜRICH
St.Gallen
Bregenz
Lindau
Luzern
Zug
Schwyz
Glarus
Vaduz
Feldkirch
Aarau
Olten
Lörrach
Rheinfelden
Waldshut
Baden
CH
D
FL
46
71
59
60
72

Heilbronn
Neckarsulm
Öhringen
Kupferzell
Kirchberg
Aurach
Windsbach
Abenberg
Roth
Weinsberg
Schwaigern
WALDENBURG
Ilshofen
Feuchtwangen
Merkendorf
Wolframs-Eschenbach
Lauffen
Schwäbisch Hall
Crailsheim
Bechhofen
Spalt
Hilpoltstein
Bönnigheim
WILDECK
COMBURG
Gunzenhausen
Besigheim
Oberstenfeld
Obersontheim
Dinkelsbühl
Pleinfeld
Bietigheim
Sulzbach
Gaildorf
Thalmässing
Murrhardt
ST. MARIA
Wassertrüdingen
Weissenburg
Ellingen
Vaihingen
Marbach
Ellenberg
NATURPARK
Backnang
Ellwangen
Ludwigsburg
Gschwend
Oettingen
Kornwestheim
Winnenden
Welzheim
Kocher
Treuchtlingen
ALTMÜHLTAL
Waiblingen
Wasseralfingen
Wallerstein
Fellbach
Schorndorf
Aalen
Nördlingen
Wemding
Pappenheim
Solnhofen
STUTTGART
Bopfingen
WALLFAHRTSKIRCHE
Eichstätt
Lorch
Schwäbisch Gmünd
Esslingen
Monheim
(SÜDL. FRANKEN)
Oberkochen
Harburg
Plochingen
Göppingen
Neresheim
Böblingen
Eislingen
Kaisheim
Stuttgart
Böhmenkirch
Kirchheim unter Teck
Süssen
Donauwörth
Donau
Neuburg
BEBENHAUSEN
Heidenheim
Nürtingen
TECK
Geislingen
Giengen
Rain
Neuffen
Mühlhausen
HOHENNEUFFEN
Herbrechtingen
Lauingen
Höchstädt
Metzingen
Dillingen
Baar
Pöttmes
Weidenstetten
Reutlingen
Bad Urach
Merklingen
Langenau
Nieder Stotzingen
Gundelfingen
Wertingen
Pfullingen
Laichingen
NATURPARK
Meitingen
Schrobenhausen
SCHWÄBISCHE ALB
Leipheim
Günzburg
Welden
Langweid
SCHERNECK
LICHTENSTEIN
Engstingen
Münsingen
Blaubeuren
Burgau
Adelsried
Gersthofen
Aichach
Blaustein
Ulm
Nersingen
Zusmarshausen
MARIA BIRNBAUM
Ichenhausen
AUGSBURG
Dasing
WÜRTTEMBERG
Gammertingen
OBERMARCHTAL
Ehingen
WIBLINGEN
Weissenhorn
Friedberg
Vöhringen
Thannhausen
Odelzhausen
Zwiefalten
Donau
Laupheim
Krumbach
WESTLICHE
Bobingen
Mering
Riedlingen
Munderkingen
Dietenheim
Illertissen
Günz
Königsbrunn
Maisach
Altenstadt
Schwabmünchen
WÄLDER
Sigmaringen
HEILIGKREUZTAL
Scheer
Biberach an der Riss
Babenhausen
Pfaffenhausen
Fürstenfeldbruck
Mengen
Herbertingen
Bad Buchau
Ochsenhausen
Türkheim
Kaufering
ST. OTTILIEN
Grafrath
Messkirch
Saulgau
Steinhausen
Mindelheim
Berkheim
Heimertingen
Buchloe
Inning
Bad Schussenried
Landsberg
Wörthsee
Pfullendorf
Ostrach
Memmingen
Bad Wörishofen
Utting
Pilsensee
Aitrach
Starnberg
Altshausen
Bad Waldsee
Bad Wurzach
Ottobeuren
Herrsching
Ammersee
Heiligenberg
ZEIL
Iller
Diessen
ANDECHS
Rott
Weingarten
Leutkirch
STEILWÄNDE
Kaufbeuren
Feldafing
Überlingen
Wolfegg
Obergünzburg
Altenstadt
Wessobrunn
Tutzing
Salem
Birnau
Ravensburg
Kisslegg
Dietmannsried
Unteruhldingen
WALDBURG
Schongau
Weilheim
Meersburg
Markdorf
Meckenbeuren
Peiting
Seeshaupt
Konstanz
Tettnang
Wangen
Kempten
Marktoberdorf
Hohenpeissenberg
Peissenberg
Kreuzlingen
Isny
Friedrichshafen
Rottenbuch
Steingaden
ALTENKLINGEN
Weinfelden
Langenargen
Lindenberg
Mittelberg
Rosshaupten
WIESKIRCHE
Wies
Bodensee
Nonnenhorn
Murnau
Romanshorn
Nesselwang
Forggensee
Amriswil
Lindau
Simmerberg
Wertach
Oberstaufen
Pfronten
Füssen
Oberammergau
Eschenlohe
Arbon
PFÄNDER-TUNNEL
Immenstadt
PARADIES
Oberjoch
Hohenschwangau
NEUSCHWANSTEIN
CH
Rorschach
Bregenz
BREGENZERWALD
Sonthofen
Hindelang
Linderhof
Oberau
St.Gallen
Balderschwang
Haldensee
Reutte
Garmisch Partenkirchen
Gossau
Teufen
Lustenau
Dornbirn
Fischen
Tannheim
Plansee
Krün
Herisau
Altstätten
RAPPENLOCH-SCHLUCHT
Egg
Weissenbach
EHRENBURG
Heiterwang
Mittenwald
APPENZELL-INNER-RHODEN
Appenzell
Oberriet
Hohenems
Bezau
BREITACHKLAMM
Oberstdorf
KLEINWALSERTAL
Riezlern
Berwang
ALPENGARTEN
ZUGSPITZE
Urnäsch
Götzis
Schoppernau
Hirschegg
Lermoos
Ehrwald
Leutasch
Fern Pass 1209
VORARLBERG
Baad
HOHENBACHSCHLUCHT
Pfafflar
Holzleitensattel 1126
Seefeld in Tirol
Scharnitz
SÄNTIS 2502
Rankweil
Hochtannberg Pass
FERNSTEIN
Nassereith
Telfs
Schwägalp
Warth
Elbigenalp
Wildhaus
Gams
Feldkirch
Schröcken
Holzgau
ALPEN
Obsteig
Kranebitten
72
59

48
73
62
Kastl
KÖNIG-OTTO-HÖHLE
Neumarkt
Schwandorf
Wackersdorf
Neunburg
Schönthal
Rötz
Babylon
RYZMBERK
Kdyně
Janovice nad Úhlavou
Folmava
Furth im Wald
ČERCHOV
Plánice
Klatovy
Kolinec
Nýrsko
Schmidmühlen
Velburg
Bodenwöhr
Bruck
NATURPARK
Cham
Arnschwang
Burglengenfeld
Regen
Nittenau
Roding
Kötzting
CHAMEREGG
Lam
Hojsova Stráž
VELHARTICE
Sušice
CZ
KAŠPERK
Kašperské Hory
Dasswang
Parsberg
Berching
Kallmünz
Regenstauf
Greding
OBERER
BAYERISCHER
Miltach
Lohberg
Železná Ruda
Rejštejn
REGENSBURG
Falkenstein
Drachselsried
Beilngries
Kinding
Dietfurt
Hemau
Nittendorf
WALHALLA
Donaustauf
WALD
St Englmar
Viechtach
Bodenmais
Bayerisch Eisenstein
NÁRODNÍ
SCHLOß PRUNN
Prunn
Riedenburg
Barbing
Wörth
Ascha
Patersdorf
Zwiesel
NATURPARK BAYERISCHER WALD
Modrava
Bad Abbach
Pfatter
E56
A3
Regen
Frauenau
Kelheim
Weltenburg
Obertraubling
Donau
Ruhmannsfelden
GR.RACHEL
NATIONALPARK BAYER. WALD
PARK
B
A
Y
E
R
N
BEFREIUNGSHALLE
Saal
Abensberg
Schierling
Gr Laaber
Straubing
Bogen
Niederwinkling
Spiegelau
Grafenau
Neustadt
Vohburg
Langquaid
Geiselhöring
Aiterhofen
Metten
Deggendorf
Schönberg
A93
Siegenburg
Rohr i.Niederb.
Manching
Geisenfeld
Mallersdorf
Plattling
Hengersberg
Freyung
Aiglsbach
Rottenburg
Neufahrn
Weichshofen
Wallersdorf
Niederalteich
Pfeffenhausen
Ergoldsbach
Langenisarhofen
Wolnzach
Mainburg
E53
A92
Ganacker
Osterhofen
Tittling
Landau
Eichendorf
KLOSTERKIRCHE IN ALTENMARKT
Aussernbach
Essenbach
Arth
Dingolfing
Aicha
Au
Isar
Reisbach
Haunersdorf
Salzweg
Landshut
D
Frontenhausen
Vilshofen
Simbach
Aidenbach
Ortenburg
Passau
Moosburg
Allershausen
Geisenhausen
Vils
Fürstenzell
Freising
Vilsbiburg
Gangkofen
Neuburg
Münzkirchen
Berglern
Eggenfeld
Pfarrkirchen
Neuhaus
Griesbach
Schärding
Taufkirchen
Velden
Unterschleissheim
München
Erding
Neumarkt-St Veit
Pocking
St. Florian
Rotthalmünster
Moosinning
Dorfen
Reischach
Obernberg
Ismaning
Ampfing
Ort
Inn
E552
A94
Mühldorf
Neuötting
Marktl
Simbach
Braunau
Altheim
A8
E56
Hohenlinden
Waldkraiburg
Altötting
Haar
Zorneding
Haag
RANSHOFEN
Burghausen
Mauerkirchen
Ried im Innkreis
Uttendorf
MÜNCHEN
A99
E45
Garching
Alz
Hochburg
Eberschwang
Haag am Hausruck
Ebersberg
Mattighofen
HAUSRUCK
A995
Hohenbrunn
Grafing
Wasserburg
Trostberg
Schäftlarn
Höhenkirchen
Attel
Tittmoning
Frankenburg
BENEDIKTINER-ABTEI
Obing
Sauerlach
KLOSTER SCHÄFTLARN
Peiss
Assling
Rott
Altenmarkt
Seeon
SEEON
Lamprechtshausen
Wolfratshausen
MANGFALL BRÜCKE
Feldkirchen
Traunreut
Waginger See
Waging
Frankenmarkt
Vöcklabruck
Geretsried
Seebruck
Mattsee
Strasswalchen
Holzkirchen
Bad Aibling
Bad Endorf
Chiemsee
Gstadt
Chieming
Laufen
Oberndorf
Neumarkt
St Georgen
Seewalchen
Attersee
Kolbermoor
Prien
HERRENCHIEMSEE
Traunstein
Teisendorf
Freilassing
E55
E60
A1
Bad Tölz
Miesbach
Rosenheim
Raubling
Frasdorf
Bernau
Siegsdorf
E52
Mondsee
DRACHENWAND
Gmund
Tegernsee
Hausham
Schliersee
Aschau
Grassau
Reischenhart
Ruhpolding
SALZBURG
Traunkirchen
Bad Wiessee
Brannenburg
Marquartstein
Inzell
Unterach
Degerndorf
Schleching
GLETSCHER GARTEN
Bad Reichenhall
Salzburg
St Gilgen
SCHAFBERG
Lenggries
Rottach
Unterwössen
St Wolfgang
Strobl
Kreuth
Bayrischzell
Kössen
Stein Pass
SCHELLENBERGER EISHÖHLE
Hallein
HENNERHÖHLE
Bad Ischl
Oberaudorf
Reit im Winkl
Walchsee
CHIEMGAUER ALPEN
Achen Pass
Kiefersfelden
Kufstein
Berchtesgaden
Lofer
Kuchl
Bad Goisern
Thiersee
KAISERGEBIRGE
A
Pötschen Pass
MARIASTEIN
Waidring
Strub Pass
Königssee
Golling
Gschütt Pass
Achenkirch
Brandenberg
BARTHOLOMÄ
WATZMANN
Königssee
Lueg Pass
Abtenau
Gosau
Hallstatt
Hallstätter See
Achensee
Söll
St Johann in Tirol
LAMPRECHTSOFENLOCH
Annaberg
Pertisau
Rattenberg
Wörgl
Hopfgarten
Fieberbrunn
NATIONALPARK BERCHTESGADEN
Niederau
Westendorf
Kitzbühel
HOHENWERFEN
Werfen
EISRIESENWELT
Jenbach
Brixlegg
MATZEN
Kirchberg
Aurach
Saalfelden
HOHER DACHSTEIN
TRATZBERG
FREUNDSBERG
Auffach
Alpbach
Leogang
DACHSTEIN
Fügen
Schwaz
Saalbach
Bischofshofen
Eben im Pongau
Filzmoos
KITZBÜHELER ALPEN
Hinterthal
Mühlbach
Ramsau

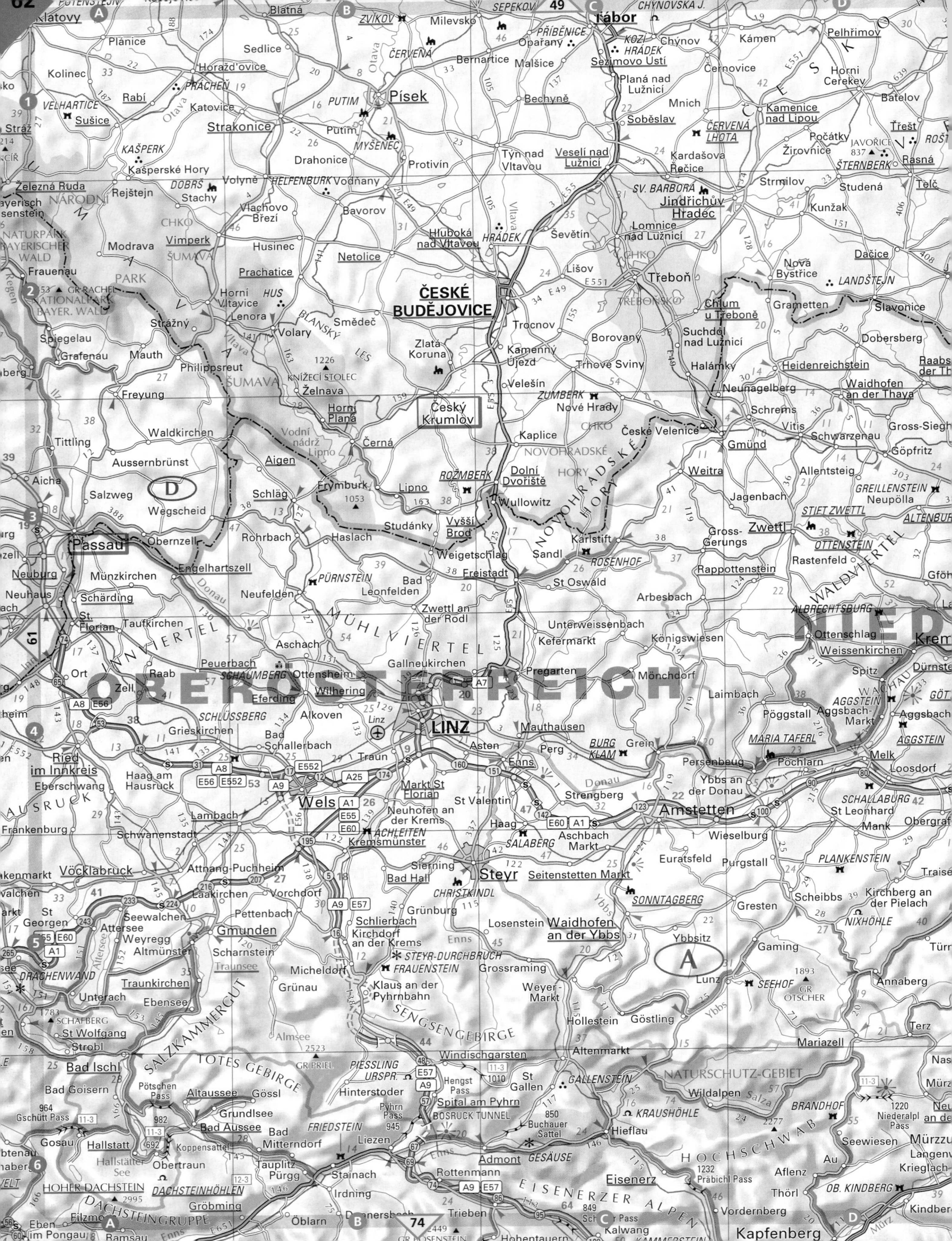

Klatovy
Blatná
Zvíkov
Milevsko
Sepekov
49
Tábor
Chýnovska J.
Plánice
Sedlice
Červená
Příběnice
Opařany
Kozí Hrádek
Chýnov
Kámen
Pelhřimov
Kolinec
Horažďovice
Bernartice
Malšice
Sezimovo Ústí
Planá nad Lužnicí
Černovice
Horní Cerekev
Prácheň
Písek
Putim
Velhartice
Rabí
Katovice
Bechyně
Mnich
Kamenice nad Lipou
Batelov
Sušice
Strakonice
Soběslav
Červená Lhota
Třešť
Stráž
Kašperk
Drahonice
Myšenec
Týn nad Vltavou
Veselí nad Lužnicí
Kardašova Řečice
Počátky
Javořice 837
Žirovnice
Rošť
Kašperské Hory
Protivín
Šternberk
Rasná
Železná Ruda
Dobrš
Volyně
Helfenburk
Vodňany
Sv. Barbora
Strmilov
Studená
Telč
Národní
Rejštejn
Stachy
Jindřichův Hradec
Kunžak
Bayerisch Eisenstein
Vlachovo Březí
Bavorov
Hluboká nad Vltavou
Hrádek
Ševětín
Lomnice nad Lužnicí
Naturpark Bayerischer Wald
CHKO
Modrava
Vimperk
Šumava
Husinec
Netolice
Dačice
Frauenau
Prachatice
Lišov
CHKO
Nová Bystřice
Park
Třeboň
Landštejn
Gr. Rachel
Nationalpark Bayer. Wald
Horní Vltavice
Hus
České Budějovice
Třeboňsko
Chlum u Třeboně
Gramatten
Slavonice
Lenora
Strážný
Smědeč
Blanský les
Trocnov
Borovany
Suchdol nad Lužnicí
Spiegelau
Volary
Zlatá Koruna
Kamenný Újezd
Dobersberg
Grafenau
Mauth
Philippsreut
Knížecí Stolec 1226
Trhové Sviny
Halámky
Heidenreichstein
Raabs an der Thaya
Šumava
Velešín
Freyung
Želnava
Zumberk
Nové Hrady
Neunagelberg
Waidhofen an der Thaya
Horní Planá
Český Krumlov
Schrems
Vitis
Gross-Siegharts
Tittling
Waldkirchen
Vodní nádrž Lipno
Kaplice
České Velenice
Gmünd
Schwarzenau
Černá
Novohradské hory
Göpfritz
Aussernbrünst
Aigen
Rožmberk
Dolní Dvořiště
Weitra
Allentsteig
Aicha
D
Frymburk
Lipno
Greillenstein
Neupölla
Salzweg
Schlägl
1053
Wullowitz
Jagenbach
Stift Zwettl
Altenburg
Wegscheid
Studánky
Vyšší Brod
Karlstift
Gross-Gerungs
Zwettl
Passau
Obernzell
Rohrbach
Haslach
Weigetschlag
Sandl
Ottenstein
Rastenfeld
Neuburg
Engelhartszell
Pürnstein
Bad Leonfelden
Freistadt
Rosenhof
Rappottenstein
Waldviertel
Münzkirchen
Neufelden
St Oswald
Gföhl
Neuhaus
Schärding
Donau
Mühlviertel
Zwettl an der Rodl
Arbesbach
St. Florian
Taufkirchen
Albrechtsburg
Unterweissenbach
Innviertel
Kefermarkt
Königswiesen
Ottenschlag
Niederösterreich
Aschach
Weissenkirchen
Krems
Peuerbach
Gallneukirchen
Dürnstein
Ort
Raab
Schaumberg
Ottensheim
Pregarten
Mönchdorf
Spitz
Oberösterreich
Zell
Wilhering
Eferding
Laimbach
Wachau
Aggstein
Göttweig
Schlüssberg
Alkoven
Linz
Pöggstall
Aggsbach-Markt
Aggsbach
Grieskirchen
Mauthausen
Bad Schallerbach
Asten
Burg Klam
Grein
Maria Taferl
Aggstein
Ried im Innkreis
Traun
Perg
Persenbeug
Pöchlarn
Melk
Haag am Hausruck
Enns
Loosdorf
Eberschwang
Markt St Florian
Strengberg
Ybbs an der Donau
Hausruck
Wels
Neuhofen an der Krems
St Valentin
Amstetten
Schallaburg
St Leonhard
Lambach
Haag
Achleiten
Mank
Obergrafendorf
Frankenburg
Schwanenstadt
Kremsmünster
Salaberg
Aschbach Markt
Wieselburg
Euratsfeld
Plankenstein
Vöcklabruck
Attnang-Puchheim
Sierning
Steyr
Seitenstetten Markt
Purgstall
Traisen
Bad Hall
Christkindl
Sonntagberg
Scheibbs
Kirchberg an der Pielach
Laakirchen
Vorchdorf
Grünburg
St Georgen
Seewalchen
Pettenbach
Schlierbach
Losenstein
Waidhofen an der Ybbs
Gresten
Nixhöhle
Attersee
Weyregg
Gmunden
Kirchdorf an der Krems
Ybbsitz
Steyr-Durchbruch
Gaming
Altmünster
Scharnstein
Traunsee
Frauenstein
Grossraming
A
Drachenwand
Micheldorf
Weyer-Markt
Lunz
Seehof
Gr. Ötscher 1893
Traunkirchen
Grünau
Klaus an der Pyhrnbahn
Annaberg
Unterach
Ebensee
Salzkammergut
Sengsengebirge
Hollenstein
Göstling
Schafberg 1783
St Wolfgang
Almsee
Terz
Strobl
Gr. Priel 2523
Altenmarkt
Mariazell
Windischgarsten
Bad Ischl
Totes Gebirge
Piessling Urspr.
Naturschutz-Gebiet
Hengst Pass
1010
St Gallen
Gallenstein
Bad Goisern
Pötschen Pass
Altaussee
Gössl
Hinterstoder
Wildalpen
Salza
Gschütt Pass 964
Grundlsee
Pyhrn Pass 945
Spital am Pyhrn
Bosruck Tunnel
850 Buchauer Sattel
Kraushöhle
Brandhof
1220 Niederalpl Pass
Neuberg an der Mürz
Bad Aussee
Bad Mitterndorf
Friedstein
2277
Gosau
Hallstatt
Koppensattel
Liezen
Hieflau
Hochschwab
Seewiesen
Mürzzuschlag
Hallstätter See
Obertraun
Admont
Gesäuse
Au
Langenwang
Tauplitz
Pürgg
Stainach
Rottenmann
Eisenerz
1232 Präbichl Pass
Aflenz
Krieglach
Hoher Dachstein
Dachsteinhöhlen
Irdning
Eisenerzer Alpen
Thörl
Ob. Kindberg
Dachsteingruppe 2995
Gröbming
Trieben
849 Schober Pass
Vordernberg
Kindberg
Eben im Pongau
Filzmoos
Ramsau
Öblarn
Donnersbach
74
Gr. Hösenstein
Hohentauern
Kalwang
Kammerstein
Kapfenberg
Mürz
64

Bohdalov
PERNŠTEJN
50
Prostějov
Přerov
HELFŠTÝN
ZBRAŠOV ARAGONITOVÁ JESKYNĚ
Černá Hora
SLOUPSKO - ŠOŠUVSKÉ JESKYNĚ
Bystřice pod Hostýnem
Jihlava
Měřín
Křižanov
Blansko
MACOCHA
ZUBŘÍČ
Velké Meziříčí
KATEŘINSKÁ
HOSTÝN
Tišnov
Jedovnice
Kojetín
Brtnice
NOVÝ HRAD
PRÁDLA
Holešov
Velká Bíteš
Hulín
STŘELIŠTĚ
Kuřim
Vyškov
Kroměříž
Fryšták
JASENNÁ
CZ
OCHOZSKÁ
Třebíč
Zdounky
Zlín
Vizovice
Morkovice
Slížany
Náměšť nad Oslavou
Otrokovice
MALENOVICE
Želetava
Rosice
BRNO
Slavkov u Brna (Austerlitz)
Brankovice
BABYLÓN
Jaroměřice nad Rokytnou
Ivančice
Bučovice
VELEHRAD
LIPOVÁ
Hrotovice
PRACKÝ KOPEC
Koryčany
Moravské Budějovice
Dolní Kounice
BUCHLOV
Staré Město
Luhačovice
IVANČICKÝ VIADUKT
Židlochovice
CIMBURK
Uherské Hradiště
Moravský Krumlov
Pravlov
Zarošice
Slavičín
Kunovice
Uherský Brod
Velké Němčice
Klobouky
Kyjov
Uh. Ostroh
Jevišovice
Bzenec
Hluk
Bánov
Dešov
Branišovice
Pohořelice
Veselí nad Moravou
Blatnice
KARPATY
Bítov
Hustopeče
Čejč
Strání
Štítary
NÁRODNÍ PARK PODYJÍ
DÍVČÍ HRADY
Hodonín
Strážnice
Velká nad Veličkou
Lechovice
Drnholec
REIGERSBURG
Hardegg
Znojmo
Moravské Lieskové
Podivín
Skalica
Hrušovany
Holíč
BÍLÉ KARPATY
Mikulov
TRENČIANSKE BOHUSLAVICE
Hátzelsdorf
Retz
Hatě
Hrádek
Lednice
Mikulčice
Drasenhofen
Radošovce
Myjava
Břeclav
Hevlín
Laa an der Thaya
FALKENSTEIN
Pulkau
Kleinhaugsdorf
Lanžhot
Sobotište
Cachtice
Haugsdorf
BRANČ
ŠTEFÁNIKOVA MOHYLA
Eggenburg
Bernhardsthal
Senica
Brezová
Staatz
Poysdorf
Kúty
Guntersdorf
Sitzendorf
WEINVIERTEL
Hohenau
Jablonica
Vrbové
Šaštín-Stráže
Piešťany
DOBROVODSKÝ HRAD
Maissau
Hollabrunn
Wilfersdorf
KORLÁTKA
Mistelbach
Zistersdorf
Ernstbrunn
CHKO
Drahovce
Veľké Leváre
Trstín
Ziersdorf
PLAVECKÝ HRAD
Dolná Krupá
Dürnkrut
Gajary
Sološnica
SCHÖNBORN
DRINY
ÖSTERREICH
TRNAVA
GRAFENEGG
HELDENBERG
Bad Pirawarth
Malacky
ČERVENÝ KAMEŇ
Bučany
Hlohovec
MALÉ KARPATY
Stockerau
KREUZENSTEIN
MATZEN
SK
Traismauer
Wolkersdorf
Trnava
HEILIGENKREUZ
Tulln
Korneuburg
Angern
Modra
Rišňovce
Herzogenburg
Gänserndorf
POTTENBRUNN
Klosterneuburg
SAFARI-PARK
Stupava
BRATISLAVA
Pezinok
Sereď
St. Pölten
WIEN
Deutsch-Wagram
Marchegg
BIELY KAMEŇ
Svätý Jur
Neulengbach
Purkersdorf
Leopoldsdorf
Rača
Senec
Sládkovičovo
Pressbaum
SCHLOSSHOF
Galanta
Grossenzersdorf
Petronell-Carnuntum
Ivanka
OCHSENBURG
Orth
Zlaté Klasy
WIENERWALD
Perchtoldsdorf
ECKARTSAU
Hainburg
Šaľa
Schwechat
Bad Deutsch Altenburg
Mödling
Fischamend
Kittsee
Lehnice
Heiligenkreuz
LANZENDORF
Alland
Hainfeld
Gumpoldskirchen
TRAUTMANNSDORF
Šamorín
Dunajská Streda
Baden
ARABURG
Traiskirchen
Bruck an der Leitha
Gattendorf
Rajka
Pottenstein
Bad Vöslau
Ebreichsdorf
Berndorf
Neusiedl am See
Nickelsdorf
Pernitz
HERNSTEIN
Sollenau
SCHARFENECK
Purbach
Hegyeshalom
Gabčíkovo
Gutenstein
Ebenfurth
Neusiedler See
Mönchhof
Wöllersdorf
Wiener Neustadt
Eisenstadt
Mosonmagyaróvár
Veľký Meder
EISENSTEINHÖHLE
Podersdorf am See
Puchberg
Rust
STIXENSTEIN
Jánossomorja
Medveďov
Mörbisch
Illmitz
H
Vámosszabadi
Neunkirchen
GYŐR-MOSON-SOPRON
Reichenau an der Rax
Ternitz
Klingenbach
Andau
Gloggnitz
Mattersburg
Fertőrákos
Öttevény
GYŐR
Gönyű
FORCHTENSTEIN
Bősárkány
Semmering
STEYERSBERG
THERNBERG
Sopron
Pamhagen
Siéggraben
FERTŐ TAVI NEMZETI PARK
Enese
Wiesmath
Kópháza
Ménfőcsanak
Semmering Pass
WARTENSTEIN
Deutschkreutz
Fertőd
Kapuvár
Csorna
Aspang Markt
Weppersdorf
Rábatamási
Pannonhalma
Pfaffen Sattel
THOMASBERG
Horitschon
Nagycenk
Fertőszentmiklós
Markt St Martin
Mönichkirchen
Bad Schönau
Kirchschlag
Szil
Tét
PANNONHALMA
Ratten
FESTENBURG
Csapod
Páli
KRUMBACH
Oberpullendorf
Lövő
75
Szany
Bőnypeterd
Friedberg
Lutzmannsburg
Gic

A
B
C
D
51
76
63
1
2
3
4
5
6
CZ
SK
Pustevny
Rožnov pod Radhoštěm
Bílá
Čadca
Skalité
Krásno nad Kysucou
Námestovo
HORNÁ ORAVA
Chyžne
Czarny Dunajec
Chochołów
Zakopane
ZUBŘÍČ
HOSTÝN
Velké Karlovice
Turzovka
Makov
Vsetín
Halenkov
JAVORNÍKY
KYSUCE
Kysucké Nové Mesto
N. Bystrica
Oravská Lesná
Lokča
Trstená
Nižná
Oravský Podzámok
Zuberec
MÚZEUM ORAVSKEJ DEDINY
Fryšták
JASENNÁ
Valašská Polanka
Vizovice
Bytča
Žilina
Terchová
Zázrivá
Vrátna
NÁRODNÝ PARK MALÁ FATRA
ŽILINA
Dolný Kubín
PROVAŽSKÝ HRAD
SUĽOVSKÉ SKALY
Kralovany
Liptovská Mara
LIKAVKA
Liptovský-Mikuláš
MALENOVICE
Valašske Klobouky
Horní Lideč
Púchov
Rajecké Teplice
Vrútky
Turany
Sučany
LIPOVÁ
Považská Bystrica
Rajec
Martin
Ružomberok
Vlkolinec
Demänová
Lazisko
VAŽECKÁ JA
DEMÄNOVSKÁ JASKYŇA
Slavičin
Bylnice
Beluša
SKALABIŇA
Uherský Brod
BÍLÉ
BIELE
Bánov
Nemšová
CHKO STRÁŽOVSKÉ
Kláštor
Príbovce
VEĽKÁ FATRA
Vyšná Revúca
Liptovská Osada
NÁRODNÝ PARK NÍZKE TATRY
Jasná
Nižná Boca
Starý Hrozenkov
Strání
KARPATY
Dubnica nad Váhom
Zliechov
Čičmany
ZNIEV
BLATNICKÝ HRAD
Srdiečko
Korytnica-Kúpele
Polomka
Trenčianske Teplice
Velaská Belá
Nitrianske Pravno
Harmanecký priesm
Trenčín
Moravské Lieskové
Trenčianska Turná
Nitrianske Rudno
Bojnice
Turčianske Teplice
Podbrezová
BYSTRIANSKA JASKYŇA
Slovenská Ľupča
Uľanka
Harmanes
Brezno
TRENCIANSKE BOHUSLAVICE
HRAD BECKOV
Prievidza
HARMANECKÁ J. IZBICA
Banská Bystrica
Čierny Balog
Nové Mesto nad Váhom
Bánovce n. Bebravou
UHROVSKÝ HRAD
Handlová
Poniky
Cachtice
Nováky
Kremnica
Čerín
TOPOĽČIANSKY HRAD
Partizánske
Osľany
VTÁČNIK
Sliač
BANSKÁ
Hriňová
Piešťany
Banka
Topoľčany
Bošany
Veľké Uherce
Žiar nad Hronom
ŠÁŠOVSKÝ HRAD
Zvolen
Detva
Kokava nad Rimavicou
Radošina
Kriváň
Drahovce
Veľké Ripňany
PONITRIE
Skýcov
REVIŠTE
Podkriváň
Mýtna
Málinec
Žarnovica
Banská Štiavnica
Dobrá Niva
BYSTRICA
DIVÍN
Poltár
Hlohovec
HRUŠOVSKÝ HRAD
Nová Baňa
Antol
Hor. Tisovník
Zlaté Moravce
ŠTIAVNICKÉ VRCHY
Krupina
Halič
Nové Sady
GÝMEŠ
Senohrad
Lučenec
Rišňovce
Čakajovce
Bátovce
Hontianske-Nemce
Bzovík
Fiľakovo
Sereď
Nitra
Tlmače
Žemberovce
Brusník
Cabaj-Čápor
Vráble
Branč
Kalná nad Hronom
Levice
Veľký Krtíš
Litke
Sládkovičovo
Karancslapujtő
Galanta
NITRA
KRUPINSKÁ PLANINA
Plášťovce
Šaľa
Tekovské Lužany
Šarovce
Šahy
Koláry
Kishartyán
Szécsény
Tvrdošovce
Šurany
Nagyoroszi
Balassagyarmat
Kolta
Želiezovce
Parassapuszta
Nagylóc
Kisterenye
Dunajská Streda
Neded
Mohora
Nové Zámky
Vámosmikola
NAGY-HIDEG-HEGY
Dvory n. Žit.
NÓGRÁD
Alsótold
Bíňa
TEMPLOM
Rétság
Becske
Pásztó
Kolárovo
Pribeta
BÖRZSÖNY
Bercel
Veľký Meder
Salka
Letkés
Galgaguta
Szurdokpüspöki
Hurbanovo
Gbelce
NASZALY
Jobbágyi
Kameničná
Štúrovo
Szob
Acsa
Vanyarc
Gyöngyöspata
Mužla
Nagymaros
Medveďov
Komárno
Moča
Esztergom
Visegrád
Vác
Vámosszabadi
Lőrinci
Komárom
Vachartyán
Kálló
Gönyű
Ács
Szőny
Nyerges-Ujfalu
Dorog
Szentendre
Göd
Galgamácsa
Aszód
Hort
GYŐR
PILIS
Bana
KOMÁROM-ESZTERGOM
Tata
Héreg
Bajna
Dunakeszi
Hatvan
Nagyigmánd
Pilisvörösvár
Tura
Mezőörs
Kőrnye
TATABÁNYA
Gödöllő
Jászfényszaru
Pannonhalma
Páty
ROMTEMPLOM
BUDAPEST
GÖDÖLLŐI-DOMBSÁG
PANNOHALMA
Kisbér
Oroszlány
Budaörs
Jászberény
Bakonypeterd
Bakonyszombathely
Bicske
Tápiószecső
Ferihegy
Gic
Bakonysárkány
Gyömrő
Sülysap
M1
M3
E60
E75
E71
E50
D1

65
52
77
Łopuszna
Szczawnica
Krynica
Żegiestów
Muszynka
Muszyna
Przełęcz Dukielska
PRÍRODNÉ MÚZEUM NA DUKLE
Komańcza
PIENIŃSKI PARK NAR.
PL
Bukowina Tatrzańska
Poronin
ČERVENÝ KLÁŠTOR
SPIŠSKÁ MAGURA
Hniezdne
Stará Ľubovňa
Bardejovské Kúpele
Zborov
Svidník
Medzilaborce
Palota
CHKO
Bardejov
ČERGOV
Podolínec
Tatranská Kotlina
Sedlo Prislop
BELIANSKA JASKYŇA
Spišská Belá
Jakubany
KAMENICHÝ HRAD
Stropkov
VÝCHODNÉ
Marhaň
Oľka
Hostov'ce
PREŠOV
KAŠTIEĽ STRÁŽKY
Brezovica
Lipany
Raslavice
Giraltovce
Domašská Priehr Nádrž
Hrubov
Tatranská Lomnica
Kežmarok
Starý Smokovec
Sabinov
Poprad
VRCHY
ŠARIŠSKÝ HRAD
Veľký Šariš
Hanušovce
Koškovce
Snina
Štrba
Spišský Štvrtok
Levoča
Kapušany
Spišská Nová Ves
Spišské Podhradie
SPIŠSKÝ HRAD
Široké
Prešov
Zlatá Baňa
Humenné
Krompachy
Kendice
Vranov
Strážske
Vernárske Sedlo
NÁRODNÝ PARK SLOVENSKÝ RAJ
Markušovce
Hornád
Margecany
Zemplínska Šírava
Podhorod'
Sedlo Besník
SLOVENSKÝ RAJ
Nálepkovo
Gelnica
Veľký Folkmar
Banské
DOBŠINSKÁ ĽADOVÁ J.
Hnilec
KOŠICE
Michalove
Tibava
Červená Skala
Prakovce
Bidovce
Sečovce
Nižná Slaná
Smolník
KOŠICE
Drahovský Priesm
Vojčice
Palín
Revúca
Gemerská Poloma
Jasov
JASOVSKÁ JASKYŇA
Uzhorod
Ужгород
RUDOHORIE
Betliar
Rožňava
KRÁSNA HORKA
Moldava n. Bodvou
Šaca
Trebišov
Ondava
CHKO SLOVENSKÝ KRAS
GOMBASECKA JASKYŇA
Turňa nad Bodvou
Seňa
Veľké Kapušany
Rybník
Slaná
Komjáti
AGGTELEKI NEMZETI PARK
Hidasnémeti
Plešivec
JASKYŇA DOMICA
Jósvafő
BARADLA
Krasznokvajda
Gönc
Kráľovský Chlmec
Slovenské Nové Mesto
Tornaľa
Aggtelek
Szalonna
Novajidrány
Regéc
Sátoraljaújhely
Záhony
Regaly
Gadna
Rimavská Sobota
Szendrő
BORSOD-ABAÚJ-ZEMPLÉN
Baktakék
Vizsoly
Ricse
Mándok
Felsőnyárád
CSERHÁT
Encs
Sárospatak
Putnok
Edelény
Csobád
Tolcsva
Bodrog
Cigánd
Bánréve
Hernád
Abaújszántó
Kisvárda
Kazincbarcika
Dombrád
Sajó
Ózd
Sajószentpéter
Szikszó
Boldva
Megyaszó
Mád
Gávavencsellő
Bodrogkeresztúr
Nagyhalász
Vásárosnamény
DIÓSGYŐR
Dédestapolcsány
Borsodnádasd
Szerencs
Tokaj
Rakamaz
Ibrány
Berkesz
Zabar
BÜKKI
Lillafüred
MISKOLC
Prügy
Székely
Szilvásvárad
Bélapátfalva
Miskolctapolca
Tiszalúc
Tiszalök
Nyírtelek
Nyírtura
Vaja
ISTÁLLÓSKŐ
NEMZETI PARK
Répáshuta
BÜKK
Nagycserkesz
Pétervására
Nyékládháza
NYÍREGYHÁZA
Ófehértó
Szarvaskő
Felsőtárkány
Tiszavasvári
Keleti főcsatorna
Emőd
Tisza
Recsk
Eger
Tiszaújváros
Nagykálló
Kállósemjén
Sirok
KÉKES
H
Polgár
Hajdúnánás
Nyírbogát
Mezőnyárád
Mezőkövesd
MÁTRA
Mátrafüred
Kerecsend
Mezőcsát
Hajdúdorog
Újfehértó
Mezőkeresztes
HEVES
Gyöngyös
Balkány
Téglás
Kápolna
Füzesabony
Egerlövő
Ároktő
Nyíradony
Kál
Dormánd
Tiszabábolna
Tiszacsege
Hajdúhadház
Hajdúböszörmény
Tarnaméra
Nyíracsád
Tenk
Poroszló
Tiszafüred
Balmazújváros
Hajdúsámson
Jászárokszállás
Tisza-tó
Egyek
HORTOBÁGYI NEMZETI PARK
Józsa
Nyírábrány
Heves
Kömlő
Hortobágy
Vámospércs
DEBRECEN
Jászapáti
Tiszaszőlős
Tiszaörs
Kisköre
Nagyiván
Hajdúszoboszló
Abádszalók
Bánk
Jászkisér
Kunmadaras
Nádudvar
Kösely
Sáránd

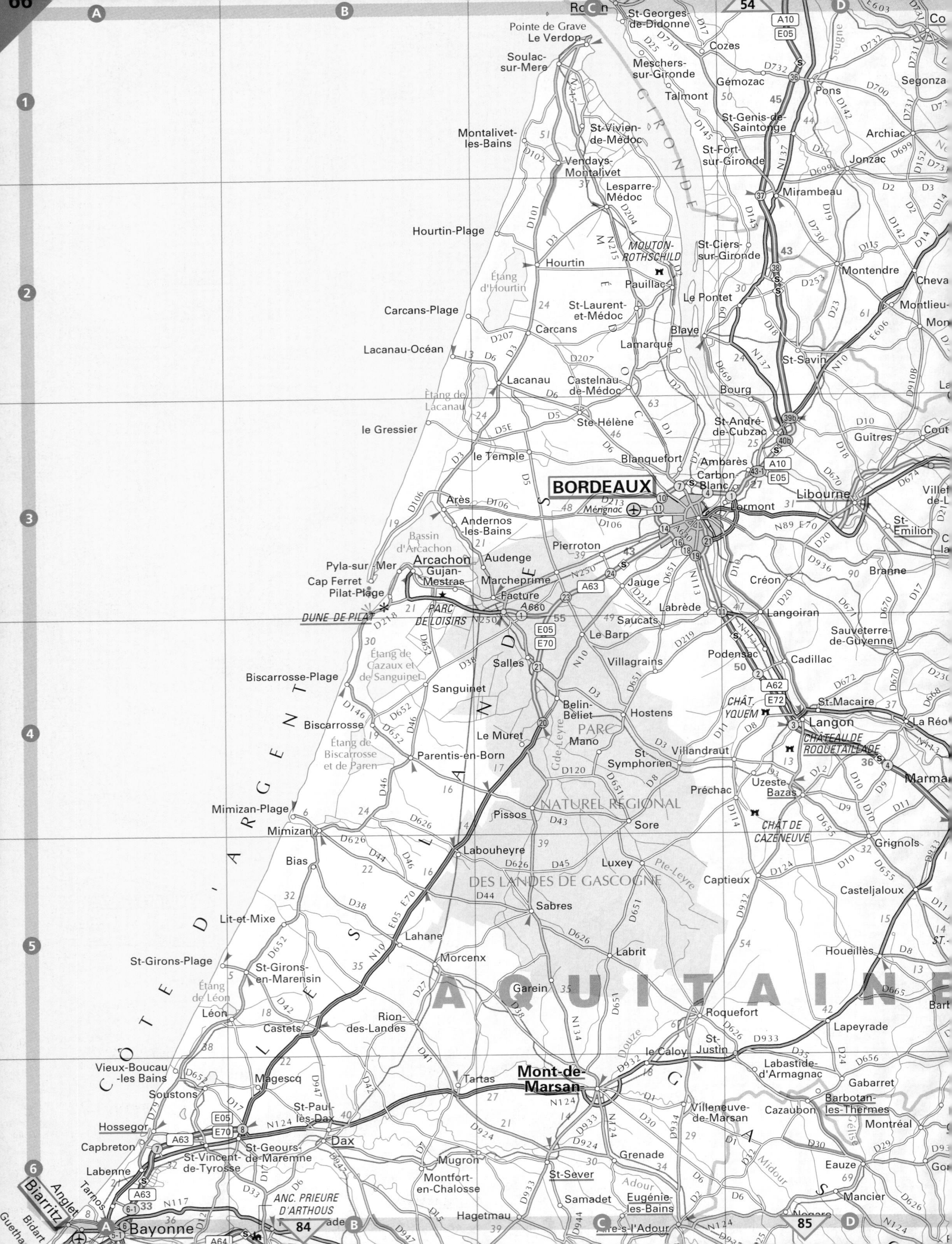

A
B
C
D
54
84
85
1
2
3
4
5
6
GIRONDE
Pointe de Grave
Le Verdon
Soulac-sur-Mere
St-Georges-de-Didonne
Meschers-sur-Gironde
Talmont
Cozes
Gémozac
Pons
Segonza
St-Genis-de-Saintonge
Archiac
St-Fort-sur-Gironde
Jonzac
Mirambeau
Montalivet-les-Bains
St-Vivien-de-Médoc
Vendays-Montalivet
Lesparre-Médoc
Hourtin-Plage
Hourtin
Étang d'Hourtin
MOUTON-ROTHSCHILD
Pauillac
St-Ciers-sur-Gironde
Montendre
Le Pontet
Carcans-Plage
St-Laurent-et-Médoc
Carcans
Blaye
Montlieu-
Lacanau-Océan
Lamarque
St-Savin
Lacanau
Castelnau-de-Médoc
Bourg
Étang de Lacanau
Ste-Hélène
St-André-de-Cubzac
le Gressier
Guîtres
le Temple
Blanquefort
Ambarès
Carbon-Blanc
BORDEAUX
Mérignac
Lormont
Libourne
Arès
Andernos-les-Bains
St-Emilion
Bassin d'Arcachon
Pierroton
Arcachon
Gujan-Mestras
Audenge
Pyla-sur-Mer
Cap Ferret
Pilat-Plage
Marcheprime
Facture
Jauge
Créon
Branne
DUNE DE PILAT
PARC DE LOISIRS
Labrède
Langoiran
Saucats
Le Barp
Sauveterre-de-Guyenne
Étang de Cazaux et de Sanguinet
Salles
Villagrains
Podensac
Cadillac
Biscarrosse-Plage
Sanguinet
Belin-Béliet
Hostens
CHÂT. YQUEM
St-Macaire
Langon
La Réole
Biscarrosse
Le Muret
PARC
Mano
Villandraut
CHÂTEAU DE ROQUETAILLADE
Étang de Biscarrosse et de Parentis
Parentis-en-Born
St-Symphorien
Uzeste
Bazas
Marmande
Préchac
NATUREL RÉGIONAL
Mimizan-Plage
Pissos
Sore
CHÂT DE CAZENEUVE
Mimizan
Grignols
Labouheyre
Bias
Luxey
Captieux
DES LANDES DE GASCOGNE
Casteljaloux
Sabres
Lit-et-Mixe
Lahane
Labrit
Houeillès
St-Girons-Plage
St-Girons-en-Marensin
Morcenx
Étang de Léon
Garein
AQUITAINE
Léon
Rion-des-Landes
Roquefort
Lapeyrade
Castets
le Caloy
St-Justin
Vieux-Boucau-les Bains
Magescq
Tartas
Mont-de-Marsan
Labastide-d'Armagnac
Gabarret
Soustons
St-Paul-lès-Dax
Villeneuve-de-Marsan
Barbotan-les-Thermes
Cazaubon
Montréal
Hossegor
Dax
Capbreton
St-Geours-de-Maremne
St-Vincent-de-Tyrosse
Mugron
Grenade
Eauze
Labenne
Montfort-en-Chalosse
St-Sever
Biarritz
Anglet
Tarnos
ANC. PRIEURE D'ARTHOUS
Samadet
Eugénie-les-Bains
Mancier
Bayonne
Hagetmau
Aire-s-l'Adour
Nogaro
Bidart
COTE D'ARGENT
LES LANDES
A10
E05
A62
E72
A63
E70
A64
A660
N10
N124
N134
N250
N215
N137
N89

LIMOUSIN
LIMOGES
Angoulême
Périgueux
Brive-la-Gaillarde
Tulle
Bergerac
Cahors
Agen
Montauban
Villeneuve-sur-Lot
Sarlat-la-Canéda
Figeac
Villefranche-de-Rouergue
Rochechouart
La Rochefoucauld
St-Junien
Chabanais
Aixe-sur-Vienne
St-Léonard-de-Noblat
Eymoutiers
Uzerche
St-Yrieix-la-Perche
Nontron
Brantôme
Ribérac
Mussidan
Thiviers
Excideuil
Montignac
Les Eyzies-de-Tayac
Souillac
Rocamadour
Gourdon
Fumel
Moissac
Castelsarrasin
Caussade
Decazeville
Marmande
Tonneins

56
Chénérailles
sur-Voueize
Moutier-d'Ahun
Marcillat-en-Combraille
Montaigut
St-Eloy-les-Mines
GORGES DE CHOUVIGNY
Chantelle
Bellenaves
Bourganeuf
Pontarion
Pionsat
Auzances
Menat
Ebreuil
Gannat
Vichy
Cusset
St-Germain-des-Fossés
St-Léonard-de-Noblat
Aubusson
Bellegarde-en-Marche
St-Gervais-d'Auvergne
MÉANDRE DE QUEUILLE
Aigueperse
Le Mayet
St-Yorre
Ferrières-sur-Sichon
Peyrat-le-Château
Royère-de-Vassivière
Felletin
St-Bard
Montel-de-Gelat
Combronde
Randan
Lac de Vassivière
Gentioux
Bunleix
Crocq
LA CHARTREUSE DE PORT-ST-MARIE
Manzat
Eymoutiers
PLATEAU DE MILLEVACHES
Pontaumur
Châtelguyon
CHÂTEAU DE TOURNOEL
Riom
Ennezat
Puy-Guillaume
Maringues
Volvic
Pontgibaud
Col des Goules
Aulnat
Herment
Sauvagnat
La Courtine
PUY DE DÔME
Lezoux
Thiers
Chamberet
Eygurande
Royat
Col de la Moreno
CLERMONT-FERRAND
Lempdes
Pont-de-Dore
Noirétable
Bugeat
Bourg-Lastic
Treignac
Laqueuille
Col de Guéry
MONTS DÔME
Col de la Ventouse
Vic-le-Comte
Billom
Courpière
SUC-AU-MAY
Meymac
Ussel
GORGE D'AVÈZE
La Bourboule
Le Mont-Doré
Col de la Croix Morand
St-Nectaire
AUVERGNE
Olliergues
Tauves
Chambon-sur-Lac
Champeix
CHÂT. DE BURON
Sugères
St-Amant-Roche-Savine
Seilhac
Egletons
CHÂTEAU DE VENTADOUR
PUY DE SANCY
GROTTES DE JONAS
Issoire
Sauxillanges
Lanobre
Besse-en-Chandesse
Col des Fourches
Neuvic
Bort-les-Orgues
Gimel-les-Cascades
Tulle
MONTS DORE
PARC NATUREL RÉGIONAL DES VOLCANS D'AUVERGNE
MONTS DU CÉZALLIER
St-Germain-Lembron
Brassac-les-Mines
St-Germain-l'Herm
PARC NATUREL RÉGIONAL DU LIVRADOIS FOREZ
Condat
Lempdes
Auzon
GORGES DE L'ALAGNON
Beynat
Mauriac
Riom-ès-Montagnes
Blesle
Arlanc
MASSIF CENTRAL
MONTS DU CANTAL
St-Privat
Argentat
67
Pleaux
Allanche
Massiac
Brioude
La Chaise-Dieu
TOURS DE MERLE
Salers
Pas de Peyrol
PUY MARY
Paulhaguet
Beaulieu-sur-Dordogne
St-Cernin
Murat
Col de la Fageole
Lavoûte-Chilhac
PLOMB DU CANTAL
St-Paulien
Bretenoux
Laroquebrou
Langeac
CASTELNAU
Vic-sur-Cère
ROCHER DES PENDUS
St-Flour
St-Céré
Sousceyrac
Aurillac
Loudes
CHÂTEAU D'ALLEUZE
MTS DE LA MARGERIDE
Pinols
Cayrols
Pierrefort
Latronquière
Mur-de-Barrez
Saugues
Lacapelle-Marival
Chaudes-Aigues
Monistrol-d'Allier
Maurs
PUY DE L'ARBRE
Fournels
Esplantas
Figeac
Montsalvy
Lacalm
St-Chély-d'Apcher
Capdenac-Gare
Entraygues-sur-Truyère
GORGES DU LOT
Laguiole
St-Alban
Grandrieu
Aumont-Aubrac
Decazeville
Conques
MONTS D'AUBRAC
Nasbinals
Pradelles
Langogne
Estaing
Aubrac
St-Amans
Villeneuve
Montbazens
Marcillac-Vallon
St-Chély-d'Aubrac
Châteauneuf-de-Randon
Espalion
St-Côme-d'Olt
MAILHEBIAU
Bozouls
Villefranche-de-Rouergue
Rignac
TROU DE BOZOULS
Marvejols
La Bastide-Puylaurent
CAUSSE DU COMTAL
St-Geniez-d'Olt
Mende
Bagnols-les-Bains
Rieupeyroux
Rodez
Laissac
La Canourgue
CAUSSE DE SAUVETERRE
La Salvetat
Baraqueville
Sévérac-le-Château
Ste-Enimie
MT LOZÈRE
Villefort
Laguépie
Pont-de-Salars
Bois-du-Four
POINT SUBLIME
La Malène
CASTELBOUC
Florac
le Pont-de-Montvert
Cassagnes-Bégonhès
106
Salles-Curan
St-Beauzély
Le Rozier
GORGES DU TARN
CAUSSE MÉJEAN
Génolhac
A75
A71
A72
A719
E11
E70
N141
N89
N120
N122
N88
N9
N102
N106
N140

Mâcon
Bourg-en-Bresse
Roanne
Villefranche-sur-Saône
LYON
ST-ÉTIENNE
Vienne
Chambéry
GRENOBLE
Valence
Romans-sur-Isère
Montélimar
Privas
Annonay
Voiron
Oyonnax
Nantua
Belley
Aubenas
Montbrison
Cluny
Bellegarde-sur-Valserine
Ambérieu-en-Bugey
Bourgoin-Jallieu
Die
Crest
Tournon
Yssingeaux
Firminy
Givors
Oullins
Tarare
Feurs
Meximieux
Pérouges
Trévoux
Anse
Ste-Julien-Chapteuil
Gap
Aspres-sur-Buëch
Veynes
Corps
La Mure
Vizille
Le Bourg-d'Oisans
Les Deux-Alpes
Aix-les-Bains
Le Bourget
Les Echelles
Viviers
Donzère
Dieulefit
Bourdeaux
Saillans
Luc-en-Diois
Châtillon-en-Diois
Clelles
Mens
BEAUJOLAIS
RHÔNE
ALPES
PARC NATUREL RÉGIONAL DU VERCORS
57
70
108

58
Bonlieu
Clairvaux-les-Lacs
St-Laurent-en-Grandvaux
Pompaples
Le Sentier
Cossonay
CHÂTEAU DE VUFFLENS
VAUD
ST. BARTHÉLEMY
Moudon
Echallens
CHARRIÈRES
Romont
FRIBOURG
Schwarzsee
Bulle
Jaun
Boltigen
BURGISTEIN
Orgelet
Lac de Vouglans
Morez
Moirans-en-Montagne
Les Rousses
La Cure
St-Cergue
Morges
Oron-la-Ville
Châtel-St-Denis
Gruyères
Jaunpass
SIMMENTAL
Zweisimmen
Frutigen
Arinthod
St-Claude
LAUSANNE
Rolle
Lac Léman
les Avants
Château d'Oex
Saanenmöser
Saanen
Gstaad
BERNER
Adelboden
Kandersteg
Col de la Faucille 1323
PARC RÉGIONAL DU HAUT-JURA
Divonne-les-Bains
Nyon
Yvoire
Amphion
Evian
Vevey
Montreux
CHILLON
Dortan
Mijoux
Gex
Oyonnax
MONT COLOMBY DE GEX
Thonon-les-Bains
St-Gingolph
ROCHERS DE NAYE
Col des Mosses
Col du Pillon
Leysin
Lenk
WILDSTRUBEL 3253
Versoix
Douvaine
Genève
GENÈVE
LES VOIRONS
Abondance
Aigle
Les Diablerets
Gsteig
Col de la Croix
WILDHORN
Leuk
Echallon
La Cluse
St-Germain-de-Joux
Nantua
Collonges
St-Julien-en-Genevois
Annemasse
Boëge
Pas de Morgins
Morgins
Châtel
Monthey
Bex
Villars
LES DIABLERETS
Montana
Crans
Sion
Sierre
Bellegarde-sur-Valserine
DÉFILÉ DE L'ÉCLUSE
Reignier
St-Jeoire
MT CHÉRY
Morzine
St-Maurice
Avoriaz
Champéry
PYRAMIDES
Val d'Anniviers
Hauteville-Lompnes
Frangy
MT SALÈVE
Cruseilles
Bonneville
La Roche-sur-Foron
Les Gets
Taninges
Plan-du-Lac
Samoëns
Cluses
LA BÂTIAZ
Martigny
Haute-Nendaz
Verbier
Evolène
Val d'Hérens
Zinal
GRAND COLOMBIER
Seyssel
Col de la Colombière 1618
CHÂTEAU DE THORENS-GLIÈRES
Flaine
Vallorcine
Col de la Forclaz 1527
Trient
Les Haudères
GORGES DU FIER
Rumilly
Artemare
Annecy
Veyrier
Sévrier
Thônes
CHAÎNE DES ARAVIS
MT BUET
Col des Montets
LE BRÉVENT
Argentière
Champex
Orsières
Val de Bagnes
Arolla
DENT BLANCHE
Culoz
Ruffieux
Menthon
Talloires
La Clusaz
Sallanches
Mauvoisin
ABB. DE HAUTECOMBE
Albens
St-Jorioz
Duingt
Col de Leschaux
Col des Aravis 1498
MT CHARVIN
Megève
le Fayet
St-Gervais-les-Bains
Les Houches
Chamonix-Mont-Blanc
TUNNEL DU MONT BLANC
Col du Grand-St-Bernard
Val d'Entremont
GRAND COMBIN
TUNNEL DU GRAND-ST-BERNARD
MATTERHORN/MONTE CERVINO
Belley
Yenne
Aix-les-Bains
Lac du Bourget
Faverges
Flumet
Les Contamines-Montjoie
MONT BLANC
Entrèves
Bionaz
Breuil-Cervinia
Valtournenche
Le Bourget
Le Châtelard
Col de Plainpalais
Ugine
Beaufort-sur-Doron
Courmayeur
Pré St-Didier
Morgex
Échevennoz
Aosta
Aoste
Ayas
69
Chambéry
Col du Frêne 950
St-Pierre-d'Albigny
Albertville
COFLANS
Cormet de Roselend
LANCE-BRANLETTE
La Thuile
Col du Petit St-Bernard
Nus
Châtillon
St-Vincent
Challes-les-Eaux
LE GRAND ARC
Bourg-St-Maurice
Valle d'Aosta
Pila
Fénis
USSEL
Col du Granier
Montmélian
Aiguebelle
Aime
Valgrisenche
VALLE D'AOSTA
Cogne
Verrès
Les Échelles
CHARTREUSE
La Rochette
Pontcharra
BAYARD
Les Arcs
LILLAZ
Issogne
GRANDE SASSIÈRE
Colle del Nivolet
PARCO NAZIONALE DEL GRAN PARADISO
Le Touvet
Allevard
Moûtiers
Valmorel
Col de la Madeleine
La Plagne
Bozel
Courchevel
Tignes
Val d'Isère
GRAN PARADISO
Pont
Campiglia Soana
St-Pierre-de-Chartreuse
Goncelin
CHAÎNE DE BELLEDONNE
Méribel-les-Allues
Val-Claret
ROCHER DE BELLEVARDE
MASSIF DE LA VANOISE
Ronco Canavese
Col de Porte
La Chambre
Pralognan-la-Vanoise
PARC NATIONAL DE LA VANOISE
Col de l'Iseran
Forno Alpi Graie
Ceresole Reale
Pont Canavese
Montbonnot
Brignoud
St-Jean-de-Maurienne
Les Menuires
Bonneval-sur-Arc
Locana
Col du Glandon
Val Thorens
CIAMARELLA
Ala di Stura
Cuorgnè
Castellamonte
GRENOBLE
Col de la Croix de Fer
St-Michel-de-Maurienne
Col du Télégraphe
Lanslebourg-Mont-Cenis
Col du Mont Cenis
Ceres
Uriage-les-Bains
Chamrousse
CRX DE CHAMROUSSE
PIC DU LAC BLANC
Allemont
Valloire
Modane
ST. PIERRE D'EXTRAVACHE
ABB. DI NOVALESA
Balme
Lanzo Torinese
Rivarolo Canavese
Usseglio
Viù
Ciriè
L'Alpe-d'Huez
CIME DES TORCHES
TUNNEL DE FRÉJUS
Le Bourg-d'Oisans
Col du Galibier
MT THABOR
Bardonècchia
Susa
Bussoleno
Condove
Città di Torino
Volpiano
Caselle
Col d'Ornon
La Grave
Col du Lautaret
Les Deux-Alpes
Avigliana
Venaria Reale
Leinì
Le Monêtier-les-Bains
Sauze d'Oulx
Oulx
FORTE
SACRA DI SAN MICHELE
Rivoli
Settimo Torinese
SUPERGA
La Bérarde
Colle di Sestriere
Fenestrelle
Valbonnais
PARC
MASSIF DES ÉCRINS
Col de Montgenèvre
Cesana Torinese
Sestriere
Collegno
TORINO
N.D. DE LA SALETTE
Corps
MT PELVOUX
Chantemerle
Briançon
Claviere
Montgenevre
Perosa Argentina
Orbassano
Piossasco
Moncalieri
Stupinigi
Chieri
Ailefroide
NATIONAL
Vallouise
la Chapelle-en-Valgaudemar
St-Firmin
Prali
Pinerolo
Airasca
PIEMONTE
Santena
Col d'Izoard
L'Argentière-la-Bessée
Aiguilles
Abriès
Bobbio Pellice
Torre Pellice
Carignano
Poirino
DES ÉCRINS
ROUTE NAPOLÉON
St-Bonnet-en-Champsaur
SOUMT. DROUVET
Arvieux
Château-Queyras
L'Echalp
Carmagnola
Cavour
Villafranca Piemonte
Col du Festre
Orcières
Col Bayard
Gap
108
St-Clément-sur-Durance
PARC NAT. REG.
Crissolo
Bagnolo Piemonte
109
Barge
Moretta
Racconigi
Sommariva del Bosco
La Bâtie-Neuve
Guillestre
St-Véran
BELVEDERE

59
110
72
CH
I
URI
GRAUBÜNDEN
TICINO
LOMBARDIA
BERNER OBERLAND
LICHTENSTEIN
Interlaken
Brienz
Meiringen
Lungern
Engelberg
Grindelwald
Wengen
Lauterbrunnen
Mürren
Kiental
Innertkirchen
Guttannen
Handegg
Göschenen
Wassen
Amsteg
Gurtnellen
Hospental
Andermatt
Realp
Gletsch
Oberwald
Münster
Airolo
Piotta
Faido
Fusio
Sedrun
Disentis/Mustér
Ilanz
Flims
Chur
Bonaduz
Thusis
Arosa
Lenzerheide
Tiefencastel
Bergün
Splügen
Hinterrhein
San Bernardino
Mesocco
Madésimo
Chiavenna
St Moritz
Silvaplana
Sils-Maria
Maloja
Biasca
Olivone
Giornico
Bellinzona
Locarno
Ascona
Brissago
Lugano
Gravedona
Colico
Sondrio
Morbegno
Bellano
Varenna
Menaggio
Bellagio
Lecco
Como
Chiasso
Varese
Luino
Verbania
Stresa
Baveno
Arona
Domodóssola
Crevoladossola
Formazza
Brig
Visp
Fiesch
Saas-Fee
Saas Grund
Saas Almagell
Macugnaga
Varallo
Orta San Giulio
Omegna
Biella
Borgomanero
Gallarate
Busto Arsizio
Legnano
Saronno
Seregno
Monza
Cantù
Erba
Merate
BERGAMO
MILANO
NOVARA
Vercelli
Vigévano
Abbiategrasso
Magenta
Rho
Melzo
Cassano d'Adda
Treviglio
Caravaggio
Crema
Lodi
Melegnano
Rozzano
Binasco
Pavia
Mortara
Casale Monferrato
Valenza
Voghera
Stradella
PIACENZA
Codogno
Casalpusterlengo
Pizzighettone
Cremona
Castelleone
Soresina
Asti
ALESSANDRIA
Tortona
Castelnuovo Scrivia
Salice Terme
Chiari
Rovato
Palazzolo sull'Oglio
Sárnico
Clusone
San Pellegrino Terme
Piazza Brembana
Orzinuovi

VORARLBERG
Rankweil
Hochtannberg Pass
HOHENBACHS
60
Pfafflar
Holzleitensattel
1126
Seefeld in Tirol
KARWENDELGEBIRGE
FERNSTEIN
Nassereith
Telfs
Hall in Tirol
Gams
Feldkirch
Schröcken
Warth
Elbigenalp
Holzgau
Obsteig
Zirl
Kranebitten
Nendeln
Lech
Steeg
LECHTALER ALPEN
Imst
Silz
Stams
Schaan
Vaduz
Bludenz
Klösterle
Langen
Stuben
Zürs
Flexen Pass
1784
PERJEN-TUNNEL
Arzl
PETERSBURG
Kühtai
INNSBRUCK
Igls
PATSCHERKOFEL
Patsch
FL
MONTAFON
St Anton
St Christoph
Landeck
Oetz
Gries in Sellrain
EUROPA-BRÜCKE
Brand
ARLBERG TUNNEL
Arlberg Pass
1802
WIESBERG
Wenns
STUBAIER ALPEN
Schönberg
Matrei am Brenner
Maienfeld
Schruns
St Gallenkirch
TRISANNA-BRÜCKE
Umhausen
STUIBENFALL
Lüsens
Mieders
Fulpmes
Neustift
Grüsch
Gaschurn
Ischgl
Kauns
BERNEK
Ried
Längenfeld
Steinach
Landquart
Gargellen
Partenen
Serfaus
MARSCHLINS
Zizers
Küblis
Bielerhöhe
2032
Galtür
PAZNAUNTAL
Pfunds
KAJETANS-BRÜCKE
Mittelberg
Gschnitz
Ranalt
Gries-am-Brenner
Brenner Pass/
Passo del Brennero
1374
Klosters
3403
FLUCHTHORN
Martina/
Martinsbruck
Sölden
Timmelsjoch/
Passo del Rombo
2509
Colle Isarco/
Gossensass
Chur
3312
PIZ BUIN
Nauders
ÖTZTALER ALPEN
3774
WILDSPITZE
Vent
Obergurgl
Passo di Monte Giovo/
Jaufen Pass
2094
Vipiteno/Sterzing
Arosa
Davos
Scuol
Reschen Pass/
Passo di Résia
1504
Curon Venosta/
Graun im Vinschgau
Moso in Passiria/
Moos in Passeier
Parpan
Lenzerheide
1549
Flüelapass
2383
Ardez
Tarasp
Lago di Résia/
Reschensee
San Valentino a. Muta/
Sankt Valentin a. d. Haide
San Leonardo in P./
Sankt Leonhard in P.
Riobianco/
Weissenbach
Passo di Pénnes
2215
Valbella
Lenzerheide
Susch
Zernez
ABB. DI M. MARIA/
KLOST. MARIENBERG
Ofen Pass/
Pass dal Fuorn
2149
Málles Venosta/Mals im Vinschgau
BÜNDEN
Tiefencastel
NATIONAL PARK
Tubre/
Taufers
Sluderno/
Schluderns
Madonna di Senales/
Unserfrau
ALTO ADIGE
SARNTALER ALPEN
Bergün
Albulapass
2315
Zuoz
MUNT LA SCHERA TUNNEL
Müstair
Naturno/
Naturns
Tirolo/
Tirol
Merano/
Meran
Savognin
CH
La Punt
Livigno
Passo d'Eira
Umbrailpass
2501
PARCO
Silandro/
Schlanders
Adige/Etsch
Avelengo/
Hafling
Sarentino/
Sarnthein
Chiusa/
Klausen
Celerina
Samedan
St Moritz
Pontresina
Trafoi
NAZIONALE
Lana
BOLZANO/
BOZEN
Cresta
Julierpass
2284
Silvaplana
Passo del Bernina
2330
Passo di Foscagno
2291
Bagni di Bormio
2757
Passo dello Stelvio/
Stilfser Joch
Solda/Sulden
Passo delle Palade
1518
Renon/
Ritten
Siusi/
Seis
Malojapass
1815
Sils-Maria
Maloja
Forcola di Livigno
2315
Bórmio
DELLO
STELVIO
Bagni di Rabbi
Santa Gertrude/
Sankt Gertraud
Appiano/
Eppan
4049
PIZ BERNINA
Santa Caterina
Valfurva
Fondo
Nova Levante/
Welschnofen
Passo di Costalunga
1753
Passo di Gávia
2621
Pejo
Carezza al Lago/
Karersee
Poschiavo
Sóndalo
Dimaro
Cles
Passo della Mendola
1363
3678
M DISGRAZIA
Chiesa in Valmalenco
Grósio
Passo del Tonale
1883
Vermiglio
Malé
Ora/Auer
DOLOMITI
Campocologno
Madonna di Tirano
Ponte di Legno
Folgarida
Egna/
Neumarkt
Predazzo
71
Sondrio
Teglio
Tirano
Campo Carlo Magno
1682
Lago di Tovel
Cavalese
Oglio
Berbenno di Valtellina
Adda
Tresenda
Édolo
CASCATA DI NARDIS
Madonna di Campiglio
Fai d. Paganella
Mezzolombardo
Sover
I
ALPI ORÓBIE
Aprica
Passo dell' Aprica
1181
3554
ADAMELLO
Pinzolo
CIMA BRENTA
3150
Molveno
Andalo
San Michele all' Adige
CIMA D'ASTA
2847
Fóppolo
Malonno
Baselga di Pinè
Lavis
TRENTINO
Passo del Vivione
1828
Valbondione
Saviore dell'Adamello
Vezzano
Piazzatorre
Schilpário
PARCO NAZIONALE DELLE INCISIONI RUPESTRI
Capo di Ponte
Tione di Trento
Trento
Pérgine Valsugana
Roncegno
Branzi
Gromo
Passo della Presolana
1297
Ponte Arche
Comano Terme
M. Bondone
Vetriolo Terme
Borgo Valsugana
Piazza Brembana
Levico Terme
Oltre il Colle
Boário Terme
Breno
Lardaro
Clusone
Castione della Presolana
Chiese
Lavarone
Passo di Vèzzena
1402
Primolano
Darfo
Condino
Riva del Garda
Arco
Lovere
Storo
Folgaria
Gandino
Limone sul Garda
Torbole
Mori
Rovereto
ALTOPIANO DEI SETTE COMUNI
Selvino
Bagolino
Pisogne
Cóllio
Asiago
Gaverina Terme
Lago d'Idro
Pian delle Fugazze
1159
Arsiero
Seriate
Trescore Balneario
Monte Isola
Malcesine
Avio
2218
M. BALDO
Bassano del Grappa
Vestone
Idro
Piovene-Rocchette
Sárnico
Iseo
Gardone Val Trómpia
Gargnano
Ala
Maróstica
Brenzone
MONTI LESSINI
Passo Xon
671
Toscolano Maderno
Lumezzane
Recoaro Terme
Schio
Thiene
LOMBARDIA
Palazzolo sull'Oglio
Concesio
Gardone Riviera
Bosco Chiesanuova
Malo
Sandrigo
Rovato
Gavardo
Lago di Garda
Torri del Benaco
Valdagno
Dueville
Cittadella
Treviglio
BRÉSCIA
Salò
Chiari
Manerba del Garda
Garda
Bolca
Caravaggio
Bardolino
Negrar
Chiampo
VICENZA
Antegnate
Sirmione
Lazise
VENETO
Lonato
Desenzano del Garda
Peschiera del Garda
Bussolengo
Arzignano
Soncino
Orzinuovi
Bagnolo Mella
Ghedi
Montichiari
Montecchio Maggiore
VERONA
Soave
Manérbio
San Martino d. Battaglia
San Martino Buon Albergo
S. MARIA DI BRESSANORO
Verolanuova
Leno
Castiglione d. Stiviere
Carpenédolo
Villafranca Veronese
Grisignano di Zocco
Barbarano Vicentino
Lonigo
110
Pontevico
Isorella
Valeggio S Mincio
Villafranca di Verona
111
San Giovanni Lupatoto
San Bonifácio
Albaredo
PADOVA
Abano Terme

61
112
74
A
SLO
KITZBÜHELER ALPEN
ZILLERTAL
Alpbach
Auffach
Fügen
Schwaz
Saalbach
Leogang
Saalfelden
Bischofshofen
Eben im Pongau
Filzmoos
DACHSTEINGRUPPE
Hinterthal
Filzen Sattel
Mühlbach
Altenmarkt
Ramsau
Radstadt
Schladming
Enns
PRELAU
Zell am See
Bruck an der Grossglocknerstrasse
Dienten
St Johann im Pongau
Wagrain
1274 Thurn Pass
WEYERBURG
Neukirchen
Uttendorf
Taxenbach
LIECHTENSTEINKLAMM
Zell am Ziller
Gerlos
Gerlos Pass 1628
Krimml
Mittersill
Kaprun
Saalach
KITZLOCH-KLAMM
Lend
GASTEINER KLAMM
Schwarzach
Obertauern
HOCHGOLLING
1739 Radstädter-Tauern Pass
Fusch
Rauris
Grossarl
GASTEINERTAL
TAUERN TUNNEL
Mayrhofen
KRIMMLER WASSERFÄLLE
NATIONALPARK
FELBER-TAUERN-TUNNEL
Ferleiten
Hüttschlag
Dornauberg
3674
VETTA D'ITALIA/ GLOCHKENKAR-K.
GROSSVENEDIGER
NATIONALPARK HOHE TAUERN
Bad Hofgastein
Badgastein
Rotgülden
Mur
Mauterndorf
MOOSHAM
Tamsweg
Grossglocknerstrasse 2503
GROSSGLOCKNER
3797
Böckstein
TAUERNTUNNEL
KATSCHBERG TUNNEL
St Michael i. Lungau
1641 Katschberg
Predoi/Prettau
Prägraten
Heiligenblut
Kals
Lutago/Luttach
Aurino/Ahrnbach
Virgen
WEIRENSTEIN
Matrei in Osttirol
Mallnitz
Rennweg
Lappago/Lappach
Campo Tures/Sand in Taufers
Döllach
Huben
HOHE TAUERN
WASSERFALL GROPPENSTN.
Obervellach
Malta
Turrach
AUTOBAHN
Erlsbach
Anterselva/Antholz
KIENBERG
TIROL
Möll
Gmünd
Staller Sattel/Passo Stalle
Winklern
Stall
NATIONALPARK NOCKBERGE
Brunico/Bruneck
Bagni di Salomone
Lienz
BRUCK
Iselsberg 1204
Möllbrücke
Seeboden
S.Maddalena Vallalta/Sankt Magdalena
Monguelfo/Welsberg
TEURNIA
Millstatt
Drau
Oberdrauburg
Greifenburg
Steinfeld
Spittal an der Drau
Radenthein
Bad Kleinkirchheim
Sillian
Mittewald
Dobbiaco/Toblach
San Cándido/Innichen
Sesto/Sexten
St Lorenzen
Gailbergsattel Pass 982
Techendorf
Weissensee
Döbriach
Feld
Marebbe/St Vigil
KARNISCHE DOLOMITENSTRASSE
Kötschach-Mauthen
Paternion
Annenheim
Plancios
Gardena/ Gröden
la Villa/Stern
Carbonin/Schluderbach
Passo Monte Croce di Comélico 1636
Weissbriach
Colfosco
Passo di Gardena 2121
Corvara in Badia
Passo di Falzarego 2117
Pso Tre Croci 1809
Misurina
Passo del Zovo 1482
Comelico Superiore
Plöcken Pass/Pso. di Monte Croce Carnico 1360
Hermagor
WASSERLEONBERG
Villach
Sappada
Forni Avoltri
Passo di Campolongo
Arabba
Cortina d'Ampezzo
Auronzo di Cadore
Santo Stéfano di Cadore
Paluzza
Nassfeld Pass 1530
DOBRATSCH
Arnoldstein
Warmbad
Faak
Passo Pordoi
Comeglians
Paularo
Pontebba
Lozzo di Cadore
San Vito di Cadore
Selva di Cadore
Passo della Mauria 1298
Arta Terme
Tarvisio
Rateče
1073 Wurzenpass
Piave
MARMOLADA
Pieve di Cadore
Podkoren
Kranjska Gora
Falcade
Alleghe
Forcella Staulanza 1773
Villa Santina
Cave del Predil
Passo del Predil 1156
Mojstrana
Tai di Cadore
Forni di Sopra
Ampezzo
Tolmezzo
Chiusaforte
Cencenighe
Passo Cibiana 1536
Forni di Sotto
Tagliamento
Predel
prelaz Vršič 1611
Passo di Rolle 1970
Passo Duran 1601
Forno di Zoldo
Passo di Sant' Osvaldo 827
Carnia
2864 TRIGLAV
Agordo
Venzone
1190 Passo di Nevea
Passo di Cereda 1369
Longarone
Tramonti di Sopra
Gemona del Friuli
Žaga
Bovec
TRIGLAVSKI NARODNI PARK
PARCO NAZ. D. DOLOMITI BELLUNESI
Cordévole
Cellina
Meduna
Arzino
Bohinjsko jezero
Fiera di Primiero
Ponte nelle Alpi
Bárcis
FRIULI-
Tarcento
Kobarid
Belluno
Maniago
Lago di S Croce
Montereale Valcellina
Drenchia
Tolmin
Sédico
Spilimbergo
San Daniele del Friuli
Tricesimo
Bača
Trichiana
CANSIGLIO
Aviano
Dignano
Feltre
Mel
NEVEGAL
VENEZIA GIULIA
Polcenigo
Cividale del Friuli
Kanal
Soča
Želin
S. Giorgio della Richinvelda
Campoformido
UDINE
Vittório Véneto
Cordenons
Follina
Pordenone
Sacile
Idrija
Valdobbiádene
Codróipo
Mortegliano
Nova Gorica
Lokve
Fener
Pederobba
Conegliano
San Vito al Tagliamento
Gorizia
Golak
Črni Vrh
Azzano Decimo
Palmanova
Maser
Cornuda
Fontanelle
Sesto al Reghena
Gradisca d'Isonzo
Vipava
Ajdovščina
Asolo
Nervesa della Battaglia
Motta di Livenza
Cervignano del Friuli
REDIPUGLIA
Montebelluna
Spresiano
Oderzo
Latisana
San Giórgio di Nogaro
Ronchi dei Legionari
Monfalcone
KRAS
Villorba
Ponte di Piave
Portogruaro
Marano Lagunare
Áusa Corno
Aquileia
Vedelago
Concordia Sagittaria
Duino
Sistiana
Treviso
Santo Stino di Livenza
Laguna di Marano
Resana
San Biagio di Callalta
Lignano Sabbiadoro
Grado
Golfo di Panzano
Sežana
CASTELLO DI MIRAMARE
Lipica
Villa Opicina
Roncade
San Donà di Piave
San Giorgio di Livenza
Livenza
Lignano Pineta
Bibione
TRIESTE
Scorzè
Mogliano Veneto
Eraclea
Cáorle
Golfo di Trieste
Noale
Múggia
Campodarsego
Mestre
Torcello
Eraclea Mare
Marco Polo
Jésolo
Ankaran
Mirano
Burano
Lido di Jésolo
Durrës
Piran
Izola
Koper
Murano
Cavallino
Savudrija
Portorož
Mira
VENÉZIA
Dolo
Strà
Lido di Venézia

62
DACHSTEINGRUPPE
Gröbming
Filzmoos
Eben im Pongau
Ramsau
Radstadt
Schladming
Öblarn
Donnersbach
Donnersbachwald
Trieben
GR BÖSENSTEIN
Hohentauern
Rottenmanner Tauern
ROTTENMANNER TAUERN
St Johann am Tauern
HOCHREICHART
Schober Pass
Kalwang
KAMMERSTEIN
Mautern
Vordernberg
Kapfenberg
Trofaiach
Leoben
Kindberg
Bruck an der Mur
St Michael
Seckau
WEYER
Frohnleiten
GLEINALM-TUNNEL
LURGROTTE
Peggau
SCHÖCKL
Gratkorn
ÖSTERR. FREILICHTMUSEUM
Kainach bei Voitsberg
REIN
GRAZ
STRASSENGEL
Voitsberg
Köflach
Gaberl
NATURPARK SÖLKTÄLER
St Nikolai
Sölk Pass
HOCHGOLLING
Obertauern
Radstädter-Tauern Pass
NIEDERE TAUERN
STEIERMARK
Oberzeiring
SAUERBRUNN
Oberwölzstadt
St Georgen
FRAUENBURG
Fohnsdorf
Knittelfeld
Judenburg
Zeltweg
Weisskirchen
EPPENSTEIN
Schöder
Mauterndorf
MOOSHAM
Tamsweg
St Michael i. Lungau
KATSCHBERG TUNNEL
Katschberg
Rennweg
Murau
Predlitz
Scheifling
Perchauer Sattel
Neumarkt
ZIRBITZKOGEL
St Lambrecht
NATURALPARK GREBENZEN
STUBALPE
Malta
AUTOBAHN
Turrach
Metnitz
Friesach
Gmünd
Flattnitz
Turracher Höhe
NATIONALPARK NOCKBERGE
Strassburg
DOM
Althofen
Bad St Leonhard
Lölling
SAUALPE
Twimberg
Packsattel
Stainz
Preding
Kalsdorf
Wildon
Seeboden
Millstatt
Patergassen
Bad Kleinkirchheim
Gurk
Eberstein
Glashütten
Wolfsberg
KORALPE
Deutschlandsberg
Spittal an der Drau
Döbriach
Radenthein
Feld
KÄRNTEN
St Veit
HOCHOSTERWITZ
TROPFSTEIN-HÖHLE
Brückl
St Andrä
HOLLENEGG
Leibnitz
SEGGAU
Ehrenhausen
Paternion
Feldkirchen
MAGDALENSBERG
Griffen
St Paul
Annenheim
Ossiacher See
Ossiach
Krumpendorf
Maria Saal
Klagenfurt
Völkermarkt
Lavamünd
Eibiswald
Spielfeld
WASSERLEONBERG
Villach
Pörtschach
Velden
Wörther See
Maria W.
KLAGENFURT
Eberndorf
Bleiburg
Vič
Radlje ob Dravi
Ožbalt
DOBRATSCH
Warmbad Villach
Arnoldstein
Faak
Rosegg
Viktring
Dravograd
Holmec
Lovrenc na Pohorju
MARIBOR
St Jakob im Rosental
Drau
Abtei
Sittersdorf
Tarvisio
Rateče
Wurzenpass
St. Peter
KARAWANKEN
Ferlach
WILDENSTEIN WASSERFALL
Mežica
Slovenj Gradec
POHORJE
Cave del Predil
Passo del Predil
Podkoren
Kranjska Gora
KARAVANŠKI PREDOR
Loiblpass
Eisenkappel
ČRNI VRH
Predel
prelaz Vršič
Mojstrana
Jesenice
Ljubelj
Solčava
Črna
Šentvid pri Zavodnju
Mislinja
Lukanja
TRIGLAV
VINTGAR
Bled
Jezersko
prelaz Jezersko
HUDA LUKNJA
Slovenska Bistrica
Nevea
TRIGLAVSKI NARODNI PARK
Bovec
Radovljica
Tržič
GRINTAVEC
Velenje
Dobrna
Stranice
Zreče
Slovenske Konjice
Bohinjsko jezero
Preddvor
KRVAVEC
Ljubno
Radmirje
Kobarid
Bohinjska Bistrica
Železniki
Sorica
Kranj
Kamnik
Vransko
Vojnik
Žalec
Drenchia
Tolmin
Škofja Loka
Brnik
Lukovica
Trojane
ŠEMPETER V SAVINJSKI DOLINI
Celje
Šentjur
Bača
Cerkno
Gorenja vas
Menges
Trbovlje
Laško
Cividale del Friuli
Kanal
Želin
Medvode
Domžale
Zagorje
Hrastnik
Rimske Toplice
Zidani Most
Planina pri Sevnici
Soča
LJUBLJANA
Dol pri Ljubljani
Litija
KUM
Radeče
Lokve
Idrija
Žiri
Nova Gorica
V. GOLAK
Vrhnika
Škofljica
Ivančna Gorica
Moravče pri Gabrovki
Sevnica
Senovo
Gorizia
Godovič
Črni Vrh
Logatec
Grosuplje
Krško
Gradisca d'Isonzo
Ajdovščina
Kalce
SLO
Trebnje
Mokronog
Raka
BREŽIŠKI GRAD
REDIPUGLIA
Monfalcone
KRAS
Planina
Velike Lašče
Krka
SAMOSTAN PLETERJE
POSTOJNSKA JAMA
Postojna
Cerknica
Žužemberk
Novo Mesto
Otočec
ŽUMBERAČKA GORA
Duino
Sistiana
Razdrto
Golfo di Panzano
Sežana
Bloška Polica
Sodražica
Ribnica
Dolenja vas
KOČEVSKI ROG
TRDINOV VRH
VILINSKA JAMA
Sošice
CASTELLO DI MIRAMARE
Villa Opicina
Lipica
Senožeče
Pivka
Lož
Kostanjevac
TRIESTE
ŠKOCJANSKE JAME
Kočevje
Jastrebarsko
Golfo di Trieste
Múggia
Kozina
Metlika
Ankaran
Izola
Piran
Ilirska Bistrica
SNEŽNIK
Črnomelj
Ozalj
Koper
Portorož
Podgrad
113
Gerovo
Rupa
SLAVNIK
A
I

BURGENLAND
VAS
VESZPRÉM
ZALA
SOMOGY
BAKONY
KESZTHELYI HEGYSÉG
MEDVEDNICA
BILOGORA
MOSLAVAČKA GORA
HR
H
Oberpullendorf
Kőszeg
Oberwart
SZOMBATHELY
Sárvár
Pápa
Ajka
Veszprém
Körmend
Zalaegerszeg
Keszthely
Hévíz
Tapolca
Sümeg
Nagykanizsa
Kaposvár
Lenti
Murska Sobota
Čakovec
Varaždin
Koprivnica
Bjelovar
Virovitica
Barcs
Szigetvár
ZAGREB
Sesvete
Güssing
Jennersdorf
Fürstenfeld
Hartberg
Ptuj
Ormož
Lendava
Daruvar
Križevci
Vrbovec
Čazma
Kutina
Nagyatád
Marcali
Balaton
Fonyód
Balatonboglár
Badacsonytomaj
Letenye
Csurgó
Durđevac
Ludbreg
Krapina
Zabok
Dugo Selo
Ivanić Grad
Garešnica
Popovača
Velika Gorica
Samobor
Stupnik

64
154
BUDAPEST
Ferihegy
Budaörs
Bicske
Biatorbágy
Tápiószecső
Gyömrő
Sülysáp
Vecsés
Üllő
Monor
Pilis
Tápiószele
Jászberény
Érd
Dunaharaszti
Ócsa
Sári
Dabas
Bugyi
Albertirsa
Cegléd
Hantháza
Martonvásár
Ercsi
Ráckeve
Kiskunlacháza
Gárdony
Seregélyes
Adony
Perkáta
Dömsöd
KISKUNSÁGI NEMZETI PARK
Örkény
Tatárszentgyörgy
Kunpeszér
Lajosmizse
Kunszentmiklós
Szalkszentmárton
Dunaújváros
Dunavecse
Szabadszállás
KECSKEMÉT
PANNONHALMA
Kisbér
Bakonyszombathely
Oroszlány
Bakonysárkány
Bakonypeterd
Gic
Veszprémvarsány
Csákvár
Mór
CSÓKAKŐI VARROM
Csesznek
Lovasberény
Söréd
Bakonygyimót
704 KÖRIS-HEGY
Zirc
SZÉKESFEHÉRVÁR
Csór
Várpalota
Farkasgyepü
Herend
Városlőd
VESZPRÉM
KAB-HEGY 600
Balatonfűzfő
Balatonkenese
Balatonalmádi
Polgárdi
Lepsény
Enying
Káloz
Sárkeresztúr
Aba
Sárviz
Sárbogárd
Balatonfüred
Aszófő
Tihany
Siófok
Balatonakali
Zamárdi
Révfülöp
Balaton
Balatonföldvár
Ságvár
Lajoskomárom
Balatonszemes
Balatonlelle
Pusztaszemes
Mezőszilas
Simontornya
Cece
Előszállás
Dunaföldvár
Solt
Fülöpszállás
Izsák
Orgovány
Jakabszállás
Kiskunfélegyháza
Visz
Tab
Magyarkeszi
Ozora
Németkér
Harta
Akasztó
Páhi
Iregszemcse
Pincehely
Lengyeltóti
Andocs
Tamási
Nagydorog
Paks
Dunapataj
Kiskőrös
Bócsa
Soltvadkert
Nagykónyi
Gyönk
Szakcs
Igal
Szakály
Kölesd
Kalocsa
Öregcsertő
Tázlár
Kecel
Kiskunmajsa
Mernye
Hőgyész
Fadd
Tolna
Dusnok
Hajós
Császártöltés
Kiskunhalas
Zsana
Kurd
Döbrököz
Zomba
Nagybajom
Baté
Dombóvár
Kapos
Kaposvár
Szekszárd
Bonyhád
Gödre
Sásd
Vardomb
Süksöd
Jánoshalma
Kadarkút
Bőszénfa
Oroszló
KELET-MECSEK TVT
682
Csávoly
Felsőszentiván
Mélykút
Tompa
Kelebia
Komló
Mánfa
Pécsvárad
Bátaszék
Baja
Tataháza
Kelebija
Szentlászló
Hetvehely
MECSEK
Bácsbokod
Bácsalmás
Subotica
Суботица
Lad
Bükkösd
PÉCS
Erzsébet
Dunaszekcső
Mala Bosna
Szigetvár
Szentlőrinc
Nagybaracska
Gara
Mohács
Ridjica
Bajmok
Žednik
Darány
Baksa
Sederkény
Bóly
Hercegszántó
Stanišić
Udvar
Bački Breg
Stara Moravica
Sellye
Túrony
Villány
Siklós
Batina
Bezdan
Svetozar Miletic
Bačka Topola
Vajszló
Harkány
Kneževo
Kapinci
Kémes
Moslavina
Drávaszabolcs
Beli Manastir
Sombor
Сомбор
Kljajićevo
Bajša
Knezevi Vinogradi
Cadjavica
Donji Miholjac
HR
Karašica
Pigrevica
Sivac
Lipar
Podravska Slatina
Milanovac
Belišće
Lug
Kopački rit
Apatin
Stapar
Crvenka
Veliki Kanal
Valpovo
Drava
Darda
Kula
Čačini
Beničanci
Bizovac
Bilje
Sonta
Srpski Miletić
Vrbas
Orahovica
Josipovac
Osijek
Ruski Krstur
Bogojevo
Dunav
Duna
FEJÉR
PEST
VESZPRÉM
BÁCS-KISKUN
TOLNA
SOMOGY
BARANYA
ÉSZAKI BAKONY
VÉRTES

JÁSZ-NAGYKUN
SZOLNOK
BÉKÉS
CSONGRÁD
SZOLNOK
Karcag
Kisújszállás
Törökszentmiklós
Mezőtúr
Gyoma
Endrőd
Szarvas
SZARVASI ARBORETUM
Kunszentmárton
Csongrád
Szentes
Orosháza
Békéscsaba
Békés
Gyula
Hódmezővásárhely
SZEGED
Mako
Hajdúszoboszló
Püspökladány
Berettyóújfalu
ORADEA
Salonta
Chișineu Criș
ARAD
Lipova
TIMIȘOARA
Timișoara
Sânnicolau Mare
Jimbolia
Kikinda
Кикинда
Senta
Bečej
Бечеј
Horgoš
Nădlac
Buziaș
Lugoj
YU
RO
HOGHIS
Mureșul
Canal Bega
65
155
206
E
F
G
H
1
2
3
4
5
6

A
B
C
D
1
2
3
4
5
6
Punta Candelaria
Cedeira
Cabo Prior
Valdoviño
Islas Sisargas
Cabo San Adrián
Malpica de Bergantiños
Punta del Roncudo
Cabo Prioriño
Ferrol
Xubia
Murgados
Neda
Fene
San Sadurniño
CAST. DE NARAIO
A CORUÑA / LA CORUÑA
Ria de Betanzos
Ares
Cabañas
Pontedeume
CAST. DE ANDRADE
El Real
Guisamo
As Pontes de García Rodríguez
Puentes de García Rodríguez
RÍAS GALLEGAS
Laxe
Ponteceso
Cabo Vilán
Camariñas
CEREIXO
Muxía
Cabo Touriñana
CASTRO DE BORNEIRO
Baio
San Roque
Arteixo
Cambre
Carballo
Laracha
Vimianzo
Zás
Silva
Carral
Betanzos
Coirós
Monfero
Embalse de Eume
Irixoa
Cerceda
Brandomil
Santa Comba
Mesón do Vento
Fisterra / Finisterre
Cee
Corcubión
Ponte Oliveras
Cabo Fisterra
Cabo Finisterre
Bembirre
Ordes
Lanzá
Lourdes
Guitiriz
Pino do Val
A Baña
Trazo
Oroso
Portomouro
Carnota
Embalse Barrié de la Maza
Negreira
Ru
Teixeiro
STA. MARIA DE MEZONZO
Baamonde
Muros
Ria de Muros
Santiago de Compostela
Sigüeiro
Pastor
SOBRADO DOS MONXES
Sobrado
Punta le Louro
Porto do Son
Noia
Noya
STA. MARIA DE CONXO
El Pino
Santiago
Arzúa
Friol
Toques
Padrón
Teo / Ramallosa
Fontedias
Melide
Pobra do Caramiñal / Puebla del Caramiñal
Cimadevilla
Catoira
Enfesta / Pontecesures
Ponte Ulla
Embalse de Portodemouros
Palas de Rei
Cabo Corrubedo
Oleiros
Vilagarcía de Arousa
Ulla
PAZO DE OCA
Santa Eugènia
Isla de Arousa
Cuntis
A Estrada
Cruces
Guntín
Punta de Couso
Vilanova de Arousa
Caldas de Reis
Silleda
Agolada
Monterroso
Isla Sálvora
Ría de Arousa
O Grove
Cambados
Umia
GALICIA
Narón
Portomarín
A Toxa
A Lagoa / Campo Lameiro
Lalín
Taboada
Forcarei
Isla Ons
O Convento
Poio
Rodeiro
Sanxenxo
Cerdedo
Soutelo
Dozón / Castro
Embalse de Belesar
725
Alto de Santo Domingo
1012
Marín
Pontevedra
SIERRA DEL FARO
Chantada
Ria de Pontevedra
Ponte-Caldelas
SIERRA DEL SUIDO
Beariz
STA. MARIA DA REAL
La Barrela
Escairón
Hío
Moaña
CAST. DE SOUTOMAIOR
Piñor
Islas Cíes
Cangas
Cea
Avión
O Carballiño
Embalse de los Peares
Pantón
VIGO
Redondela
Maside
Ria de Vigo
Leiro
Mondariz-Balneario
Cambeo
Monforte de Lemos
Punxín
Miño
Panxón
Nigrán
Mondariz
Sober
Cabo Silleiro
Baiona
Ramallosa
Ponteareas
Ribadavia
OURENSE / ORENSE
Parada del Sil
Embalse de San Esteban
O Porriño
A Cañiza
Cartelle
Castro Caldelas
Arrabal / Oia
Cortegada
Esgos
Valença do Minho
Tui
Salvaterra de Miño
Ramirás
A Merca
Maceda
A Guarda / La Guardia
Monção
Melgaço
São Gregório
Padrenda
950
Puerto de Alto del Rodicio
Paredes
M.TE DE STA. TEGRA
Vila Nova de Cerveira
Celanova
Allariz
Xunqueira de Ambía
Embalse de Chandreja
Caminha
Lanhelas
Extremo
SERRA DA PENEDA
Moledo
Paredes de Coura
PARQUE
Verea
Sandias
Vilar de Barrio
SIERRA DE
Vila Praia de Âncora
1416
NACIONAL
Bande
Afife
VIANA DO CASTELO
Arcos de Valdevez
Entrimo
Xinzo de Limia / Ginzo de Limia
Limia
STA. LUZIA
Ponte de Lima
Soajo
Muiños
Trasmiras
Laza
Viana do Castelo
Lima
Lindoso
Lobios
Puerto Estivadas
849
Campobecerros
Darque
Ponte da Barca
Portela do Home
Randín
Cualedro
Deão
Balugães
Baltar
Castelo do Neiva
P
SERRA DO GEREZ
PENEDA-GERÊS
Barragem de Paradela
Montalegre
Verín
Feitos
Vila Verde
N. S. D'ABADIA
Gerês
Paradela
Barragem de Venda Nova
Cávado
Ríos
Esposende
Oimbra
Barcelos
TIBAES
80
Gralhos
Vilardevós
BOM JESUS DO MONTE
Louredo
Barragem do
Estela

COSTA VERDE
ASTURIAS
CORDILLERA
SIERRA DE RAÑADOIRO
SIERRA DE ANCARES
SIERRA DEL CAUREL
SIERRA DE JISTREDO
MONTES DE LEÓN
SIERRA DE LA CABRERA
SIERRA DE LA CARBA
Cabo Ortegal
Cariño
Punta de la Estaca de Bares
Cabo de Bares
Vicedo
Ortigueira
Portocelo
Xove
Manon
Viveiro
Cervo
Cabo Burela
Burela
Ourol
720 La Gañadoira
Ferreira
Muras
XISTRAL 1036
Foz
San Cosme/ Barreiros
Mondoñedo
Lourenzá
Ribadeo
Cabo Cebes
Tapia de Casariego
Castropol
La Caridad
Trabada
Navia
POBLADO CELTICO
Coaña
Vegadeo
Villalba Alta
Abadín
590 Puerto de la Xesta
A Pontenova
Pastoriza
Taramundi
Boal
Luarca
Cabo Busto
Canero
Cabo Vidio
Brieves
Cadavedo
Cudillero
El Pito
Salinas
Cabo de Peñas
Luanco
Candás
575 Marco de Alvare
Castro de Rei
Meira
Illano
Embalse de Doiras
MINAS DE ORO (ROMANAS)
MONASTERIO DEL CRISTO
La Espina
Soto del Barco
Avilés
Pravia
CUEVA DE CANDAMO
Nubledo
Pol
Pesoz
Grandas de Salime
Tineo
Salas
Cornellana
Texeiro
Berducedo
Pola de Allande
La Florida
Grado
Posada
Lugones
Gijón
Lugo
A Fonsagrada
Castroverde
960 Alto de Cerredo
O Corgo
Baleira
Embalse de Grandas de Salime
Cangas del Narcea
Belmonte
S.M. DE NARANCO
OVIEDO
El Berrón
Pola de Siero
Santa Eulalia
Sama de Grado
Cecos
S. PEDRO DE TEVERGA
Caranga
Baralla
Puerto Campo de Arbol 794
A Pobra de Navia
Venta Nueva
Mieres
Riosa
La Plaza/ Teverga
Sotrondio/ San Martín del Rey Aurelio
Pola Lavia
Vallada
Pola de Somiedo
PARQUE NAT. DE SOMIEDO
Pola de Lena
Becerreá
MONASTERIO DE SAMOS
As Nogais
Samos
Puerto Leitariegos 1525
1486 Puerto Somiedo
1587 Puerto de Ventana
STA. CRISTINA
Cabañaquinta
1989 MIRAVALLES
Degaña
Pereda de Ancares
Villablino
Piedrafita de Babia
PARQUE NAT. DEL VALLE DE S. EMILIANO
Campomanes
Pino
Felechosa
Palacios del Sil
1109 Puerto Pedrafita do Cebreiro
Cebreiro
1270 Puerto de Piedrafita de Babia
San Emiliano
1379 Puerto de Pajares
1520 Puerto San Isidro
Pobra de Brollón/ A Pobra del Brollón
Balboa
Vega de Espinareda
Fabero
Páramo del Sil
Murias de Paredes
Sena de Luna
Villamanín/ de la Tercia
Folgoso
1616
Vega de Valcarce
Embalse de Barrios de Luna
Cármenes
Barjas
Trabadelo
Villafranca del Bierzo
Toreno
2111
Fasgar
Mirantes
Quiroga
Noceda
Igüeña
Valporquero de Torío
Embalse de Porma
Cacabelos
Toral de los Vados
Embalse de Bárcena
Riello
La Pola de Gordón
Vegacervera
La Magdalena
Embalse de Selga
Bembibre
Boñar
O Barco de Valdeorras
Ponferrada
San Miguel de las Dueñas
Embalse de Villameca
La Robla
La Vecilla
A Rúa
Priaranza del Bierzo
Torre del Bierzo
Quintana del Castillo
Cuadros
Garrafe de Torío
Manzaneda
Puente de Domingo Flórez
Riofrío
O Bolo
Embalse de Prada
1230 Puerto del Manzanal
Rodrigatos de la Obispalía
Carrizo
Villaquilambre
Vegas del Condado
1052 Alto de Covelo
Santa Colomba de Somoza
La Virgen del Camino
A Veiga
Astorga
Benavides
León
Pobladura de la Sierra
Onzonilla
Gradefes
Viana do Bolo
Villadangos del Páramo
La Baña
Hospital de Órbigo
Porto
Encinedo
Truchas
Destriana
Mansilla de las Mulas
S. MIGUEL DE ESCALADA
Portilla de la Canda 1262
Ribadelago
Morla
Santa María del Páramo
Puebla de Sanabria
La Bañeza
Santas Martas
1360 Portilla del Padornelo
Palacios de Sanabria
Castrocontrigo
Cebrones del Río
Donado
Ayoó de Vidriales
Villamañán
Valencia de Don Juan
81
82

A
B
C
D
1
2
3
4
5
6
VIGO
Cies
Ria de Vigo
Redondela
Mondariz-Balneario
Mondariz
Leiro
Panxón
Nigrán
Cabo Silleiro
Baiona
Ramallosa
O Porriño
Ponteareas
Ribadavia
A Cañiza
Cortegada
Arrabal/Oia
Salvaterra de Miño
Valença do Minho
Tui
Melgaço
Monção
São Gregório
Padrenda
Celanova
A Guarda
La Guardia
M.TE DE STA. TEGRA
Vila Nova de Cerveira
Caminha
Lanhelas
Extremo
Moledo
Vila Praia de Âncora
Paredes de Coura
SERRA DA PENEDA
PARQUE
NACIONAL
Afife
VIANA DO CASTELO
Arcos de Valdevez
Entrimo
STA. LUZIA
Ponte de Lima
Soajo
Viana do Castelo
Lindoso
Lobios
Ponte da Barca
Portela do Home
Darque
Deão
Balugães
Castelo do Neiva
SERRA DO GEREZ
PENEDA-GERÊS
Barragem de Paradela
Paradela
Gerês
Barragem de Venda
Feitos
Esposende
Vila Verde
N. S. D'ABADIA
Ofir
Barcelos
TIBAES
Caniçada
Louredo
BOM JESUS DO MONTE
Estela
Braga
Venda Nova
BRAGA
Póvoa de Lanhoso
Póvoa de Varzim
Rio Mau
Vila Nova de Famalicão
SERRA DO BA
Vila do Conde
BAGUNTE
Guimarães
Fafe
Arco de Baúlhe
Nespereira
Santo Tirso
Porto
Perafita
Caldas de Vizela
Felgueiras
N. SENHORA DA GRAÇA
Vila Pouca de Aguiar
Paços de Ferreira
Celorico de Basto
Mondim de Basto
Matosinhos
Maia
Alfena
Lousada
Lixa
PORTO
Valongo
Paredes
Amarante
Vila Real
Vila Nova de Gaia
Gondomar
Penafiel
Francelos
Aguda
Granja
Espinho
Entre Ambos-os-Rios
Baião
Mesão Frio
Penaguiao
Sabrosa
Peso da Régua
Santa Maria da Feira
Castelo de Paiva
SANTA MARIA MAYOR
Cinfães
SERRA DO MARÃO
Furadouro
São João da Madeira
SERRA
N. SENHORA DOS REMÉDIOS
SÃO PEDRO DE BALSEMÃO
Lamego
Ovar
Oliveira de Azeméis
Arouca
Rossas
Tabuaço
Válega
Bestida
Vale de Cambra
Tarouca
Estarreja
Torreira
Murtosa
SERRA GRALHEIRA
Castro Daire
Moimenta da Beira
São Jacinto
Praia da Barra
Angeja
Albergaria-a-Velha
Sever
São João da Serra
Costa Nova do Prado
Vila Nova de Paiva
Aveiro
Lamas do Vouga
São Pedro do Sul
Oliveira de Frades
VISEU
Ílhavo
Vagos
AVEIRO
Vouzela
Lordosa
Águeda
Oiã
Alcofra
Sátão
Praia de Mira
Aguiar da Beira
Oliveira do Bairro
Bolfiar
Caramulo
Viseu
Mira
Mamarrosa
Boialvo
SERRA DO CARAMULO
Penalva do Castelo
Anadia
Curia
Mangualde
Tondela
Fornos de Algodres
Cantanhede
Tocha
Mealhada
Luso
Canas de Senhorim
Nelas
Murtinheira
Arazede
Buçaco
Santa Comba Dão
Rio Torto
Cabo Mondego
SÃO MARCOS
Rojão Grande
Carregal do Sal
Seixo
Figueira da Foz
Tábua
Gouveia
Penacova
Oliveira do Hospital
Seia
NATURAL
COSTA VERDE
Miño
Lima
Douro
Tâmega
Vouga
Dão
Mondego

86
87

78
79
81
82
88
E
F
G
H
1
2
3
4
5
6
C
Pantón
A Pobra de Brollón/
Puebla del Brollón
Balboa
Vega de Espinareda
Páramo del Sil
Punxin
Cambeo
Monforte de Lemos
Folgoso
1616
SIERRA DEL CAUREL
Vega de Valcarce
SIERRA DE JISTREDO
Fasgar
Sober
Barjas
Trabadelo
Toreno
2111
Igüeña
OURENSE / ORENSE
Parada del Sil
Embalse de San Esteban
Quiroga
Villafranca del Bierzo
Noceda
Cacabelos
Embalse de Bárcena
Esgos
Castro Caldelas
Puerto de Alto de Cerdeira
890
Toral de los Vados
Maceda
950
Puerto de Alto del Rodicio
O Barco de Valdeorras
Ponferrada
San Miguel de las Dueñas
Bembibre
Embalse de Villameca
A Merca
Priaranza del Bierzo
Torre del Bierzo
Quintana del Castillo
Allariz
Xunqueira de Ambia
Paredes
A Pobra de Trives
A Rúa
Puente de Domingo Flórez
Embalse de Chandreja
Manzaneda
1778
MANZANEDA
O Bolo
Embalse de Prada
Cabrera
MONTES DE LEÓN
1230
Puerto del Manzanal
Rodrigatos de la Obispalía
Sandias
Vilar de Barrio
SIERRA DE QUEIJA
1052
Alto de Covelo
A Veiga
Embalse de Bao
Santa Colomba de Somoza
Astorga
Xinzo de Limia
Villariño de Conso
Pobladura de la Sierra
La Baña
Trasmiras
Laza
Viana do Bolo
Campobecerros
Puerto Estivadas
849
Encinedo
Porto
SIERRA DE LA CABRERA
Cualedro
Truchas
Destriana
Baltar
A Gudiña
Portilla de la Canda
1262
Morla
Verín
Ribadelago
La Bañeza
Ríos
A Mezquita
Puebla de Sanabria
Castrocontrigo
Oimbra
1360
Portilla del Padornelo
Palacios de Sanabria
Donado
Ayoó de Vidriales
Vilardevós
PARQUE NATURAL DE MONTEZINHO
N. SENHORA DA AZINHEIRA
Vila Verde da Raia
Landedo
Calabor
Chaves
Portelo
Embalse de Cernadilla
Montbuey
Santibáñez de Vidriales
Alija del Infantado
Boticas
Tronco
SIERRA DE LA CULEBRA
Rionegro del Puente
Vinhais
Villardeciervos
1243
Sitrama de Tera
Vilarandelo
Rebordelo
Bragança
Camarzana de Tera
Torre de D. Chama
SERRA DA NOGUEIRA
Otero de Bodas
Valpaços
MONTES
Mahide
Pueblica de Valverde
Benavente
Vila Mea
Carrazedo
1321
Santa Comba de Rossas
San Martín del Pedroso
Alfarela de Jales
Quintanilha
S.Vicente de la Cabeza
820
Portillo de Sazadón
Podence
Alcañices
Tábara
Mirandela
Macedo de Cavaleiros
SERRA DE BORNES
Izeda
Murça
Vimioso
Granja de Moreruela
1199
Peredo
Fonfría
Alijó
Trindade
BRAGANÇA
Malhadas
Carbajales de Alba
Brunheda
Vila Flor
Algoso
Miranda do Douro
Montamarta
Carrazeda de Ansiães
Alfândenga
Duas Igrejas
Embalse de Ricobayo
Junqueira
SERRA DE...
Torregamones
Mogadouro
Sendim
Muelas del Pan
São João da Pesqueira
Santiago
Barragem do Picote
Vilarouco
Castelo Branco
Bemposta
Zamora
Torre de Moncorvo
Fermoselle
Pereruela
Fresno de la Ribera
Carviçais
Aldeadávila de la Ribera
Vila Nova de Foz Côa
Embalse de Aldeadávila
PARQUE NATURAL ARRIBES DEL DUERO
Bermillo de Sayago
Freixo de Espada à Cinta
Embalse de Saucelle
Almeida de Sayago
Corrales
Meda
Trabanca
Peñausende
Almendra
Embalse de Almendra
El Piñero
La Fregeneda
Barruecopardo
El Cubo de Tierra del Vino
La Bóveda de Toro
Villaseco de los Reyes
Figueira de Castelo Rodrigo
CASTELO RODRIGO
Lumbrales
Ledesma
Fuentesaúco
Vitigudino
Y ÁGUEDA
Villanueva de Cañedo
Yecla de Yeltes
Villaseco de los Gamitos
Fuentelapeña
Pinhel
CASTILLO BUEN AMOR
S.Felices de los Gallegos
Villavieja
El Cubo de Don Sancho
Villarmayor
Almenara de Tormes
Cañizal
Freixedas
Sando
Golpejas
Pedrosillo el Ralo
Almeida
Villar de Ciervo
Cantalpino
Pinzio
La Fuente de San Esteban
SALAMANCA
Castillejo de Martín Viejo
Martín de Yeltes
Robliza de Cojos
Vilar Formoso
Santa Marta de Tormes
Villoria
Miño
Sil
Limia
Bibey
Tera
Tua
Sabor
Douro
Duero
Huebra
Tormes
Águeda
Côa
Esla
Aliste
Eria
Rabaçal
NVI
N120
N525
N536
N122
N630
N620
E80
E82
IP4
A52
C622
N103
N103-7
N218
N217
N216
N221
N220
N222
N213
N214
N215
N315
N212
N332
N102
E802
N2
C531
C532
C533
C536
C605
C612
C527
C525
C528
C517
C519
LE133
ZA321
ZA302
ZA301
ZA620
SA300
SA324

A
B
C
D
1
2
3
4
5
6
Luarca
Cabo Busto
Cabo Vidio
Cabo de Peñas
Canero
Cadavedo
Brieves
Cudillero
El Pito
Salinas
Luanco
Candás
MINAS DE ORO ROMANAS
MONASTERIO DEL CRISTO
Soto del Barco
Avilés
La Espina
Pravia
CUEVA DE CANDAMO
Nubledo
A8
GIJÓN
Tineo
Salas
Cornellana
Grado
Posada
A66
Tazones
Punta de Tazones
La Florida
S.M. DE NARANCO
Lugones
OVIEDO
El Berrón
Pola de Siero
Villaviciosa
Lastres
Cangas del Narcea
Belmonte
VALDEDIOS
Colunga
La Isla
Punta de Carreros
ASTURIAS
Santa Eulalia
Nava
MIRADOR DEL FITO
Ribadesella
CUEVA DE TITO BUSTILLO
S. PEDRO DE TEVERGA
Caranga
Sama de Grado
Infiesto
Arriondas
SAN PEDRO
Cangas de Onís
S. ANTOLÍN
Cabo Prieto
Riosa
Mieres
Posada
Llanes
Pola de Somiedo
La Plaza/ Teverga
Sotrondio/ San Martín del Rey Aurelio
Pola de Laviana
CUEVA DEL BUXU
SIERRA DE CUERA
PARQUE NAT. DE SOMIEDO
Pola de Lena
COVADONGA
Puerto Leitariegos 1525
1486 Puerto Somiedo
1587 Puerto de Ventana
STA. CRISTINA
Cabañaquinta
Campo de Caso/ Caso
Sarnes
PARQUE NACIONAL DE LA MONTAÑA DE COVADONGA
Arenas
Onguera
Villablino
Piedrafita de Babia
PARQUE NAT. DEL VALLE DE S. EMILIANO
Campomanes
Pino
Covadonga
Panes
1270 Puerto de Piedrafita de Babia
San Emiliano
1379 Puerto de Pajares
Felechosa
1490 Puerto de Tarna
Oseja de Sajambre
PICOS DE EUROPA
La Hermida
Murias de Paredes
Sena de Luna
1520 Puerto San Isidro
Posada de Valdeón
2648
Fuente Dé
STA. MARÍA DE LEBEÑA
Villamanín/ de la Tercia
Embalse de Barrios de Luna
Cármenes
Puebla de Lillo
1290 Puerto del Pontón
Espinama
Potes
Fasgar
Mirantes
Valporquero de Torío
Embalse de Porma
Burón
Portilla de la Reina
STO. TORIBIO DE LIÉBANA
Igüeña
La Pola de Gordón
Vegacervera
Embalse de Riaño
Riaño
1609 Puerto de San Glorio
Riello
La Magdalena
Embalse de Selga
Boñar
Boca de Huergano
1329 Puerto de Piedrasluengas
Embalse de Villameca
La Robla
La Vecilla
Prioro
1433 Puerto Monteviejo
Sabaro
Besande
Triollo
LEBANZA
Areños
Quintana del Castillo
Cuadros
Garrafe de Torío
Cistierna
Embalse de Requejada
Ríofrio
Puente Almuhey
Embalse de Camporredondo
1230 Puerto del Manzanal
Rodrigatos de la Obispalía
Carrizo
Brañosera
La Virgen del Camino
Villaquilambre
Vegas del Condado
Guardo
Cervera de Pisuerga
Astorga
Benavites
León
Santibáñez
Cantoral de la Peña
Onzonilla
Gradefes
Almanza
Villalba de Guardo
Hospital de Órbigo
Villadangos del Páramo
Valdepolo
Congosto de Valdavia
Embalse de Aguilar de Campoo
Destriana
Mansilla de las Mulas
S. MIGUEL DE ESCALADA
Vecilla de Valderaduey
La Puebla de Valdavia
Santa María del Páramo
La Bañeza
Santas Martas
N.S. DEL VALLE
Saldaña
Sotobañado y Priorato
Cebrones del Río
El Burgo Ranero
Cea
Villamañán
Valencia de Don Juan
E
Herrera de Pisuerga
Laguna de Negrillos
Matallana de Torío
Gordaliza del Pino
Sahagún
Terradillos de los Templarios
Bahillo
Ventosa de Pisuerga
Alija del Infantado
Ledigos
Osorno la Mayor
La Matanza
Melgar de Arriba
Calzadilla de la Cueza
Melgar de Fernamental
Villaquejida
Sitrama de Tera
Villada
Carrión de los Condes
Villalcázar de Sirga
Mayorga
Valderas
Becilla de Valderaduey
Villoldo
Frómista
Puebla de Valverde
Benavente
Fuentes de Ropel
Villalón de Campos
Frechilla
Paredes de Nava
Fuentes de Nava
Castrojeriz
Villanueva del Campo
Astudillo
Cerecinos de Campos
Villarramiel
Monzón de Campos
Granja de Moreruela
Villafrechós
Villalpando
Torremormojón
Villamartín de Campos
Torquemada
CASTILLA Y LEÓN
Medina de Rioseco
Palencia
Quintana del Puente
Castronuevo
Montealegre
Montamarta
Magaz de Pisuerga
Canal de Castilla
Canal de Campos
Canal del Esla
Esla
Cea
Carrión
Valderaduey
Porma
Torío
Luna
Omañas
Órbigo
Tuerto
Eria
Nalón
Sella
Cares
Trubia
Odra
Arlanzon

79
81
88
89

E
F
G
H
1
2
3
4
5
6
Plymouth
(Summer only)
Portsmouth
Plymouth
CORNISA CANTÁBRICA
San Vicente de la Barquera
Comillas
Santillana del Mar
Punta del Dichoso
Suances
Cabo Mayor
SANTANDER
CUEVAS DE ALTAMIRA
Cabezón de la Sal
Torrelavega
Las Caldas de Besaya
El Astillero
Valle de Cabuérniga
Puente Viesgo
Santa María de Cayón
Los Corrales de Buelna
Liérganes
Solares
Galizano
Isla
Cabo Quejo
Somo
Arnuera
Noja
Santoña
Colindres
Laredo
Puerto de Alisas
Ampuero
Islares
Castro-Urdiales
CANTABRIA
Molledo
CUEVAS EL CASTILLO PASIEGA LAS CHIMENAS
San Roque de Rio Miera
Rasines
Ramales de la Victoria
Bárcena de Pie de Concha
Vega de Pas
Molinar
Balmaseda
Zalla
Puerto del Escudo
VALNERA
Los Tornos
Corconte
Reinosa
Espinosa de los Monteros
Bercedo
Pozazal
Pantano del Ebro
HIJEDO
Soncillo
Puerto de Carrales
Villarcayo
La Cerca
Villasana de Mena
Angulo
Medina de Pomar
Valdenoceda
Puerto de la Mazorra
Escalada
Fuencaliente de Lucio
Basconcillos del Tozo
Tubilla del Agua
Pesadas de Burgos
Portillo del Fresno
Poza de la Sal
Oña
Trespaderne
S.Pantaleón de Losa
Berberana
San Millan
N. S. DE ANGOSTO
Frías
Puentelarra
Montorio
Villadiego
Cernégula
Quintanilla-Sobresierra
Terrazos
Cubo de Bureba
Pancorvo
STA. CASILDA
Santibañez Zarzaguda
Villanueva de Argaño
Quintanaortuño
Puerto de la Brújula
Briviesca
GARGANTA DE PANCORBO
Miranda de Ebro
Terminón
BURGOS
Villatoro
Rubena
LAS HUELGAS
MIRAFLORES
S. PEDRO DE CARDEÑA
Sarracín
Ibeas de Juarros
Villafranca Montes de Oca
Belorado
Santo Domingo de la Calzada
Tirgo
Casalarreina
Cogollos
Madrigalejo del Monte
Villahoz
Pradoluengo
Pineda de la Sierra
Ezcaray
San Millán de la Cogolla
MONASTERIO DE VALVANERA
Quintanilla
Santurtzi/Santurce
San Juan de Muskiz
Sestao
Barakaldo
Plentzia
Sopela
Getxo
Cabo Villano
Bakio
Cabo Matxitxako
Bermeo
Mungia
Puerto Sollube
Elantxobe
Lekeitio/Lequeitio
SANTIMAMIÑE
Gernika-Lumo
Bilbao
BILBO/BILBAO
Galdakao
Arene/Arrankudiaga
Llodio/Laudio
Ugao-Miraballes
Areatza
Amurrio
ARO
Orduña
Puerto de Orduña
Puerto de Altube
Alto de Barazar
Puerto de Urkiola
Durango
Markina-Xemein
Ondarroa
Mutriku
Deva
Zumaia
Zumaya
Puerto de Itziar
Eibar
Elizondo/Baztan
Zestoa
Azpeitia
SANTIGNA DE LOYOLA
EUSKADI
PAIS VASCO
Arrasate o Mondragón
Puerto de Elgeta
Bergara
Oñati
Aretxabaleta
Puerto de Descarga
Zumarraga
Puerto Bidania
Beasain
Leguatiano
Puerto de Arlaban
Murguía/Murgia
Vitoria
Embalse de Uribarri/Ganboa
AITZGORRI
Arantzazu
Puerto de Echegarate
Nanclares de la Oca
Langraiz Oka
Pobes
Fontecha
VITORIA-GASTEIZ
Argomaniz
Agurain/Salvatierra
Olazti/Olazagutia
Altsasu/Alsasua
Armiñon
CASTILLA LEÓN
KAPILDUI
Zambrana
Albaina
Maetzu
Eulate
Puerto Lizarraga
MONTE SANTO
SIERRA DE CANTABRIA
Santa Cruz de Campezo/Santi Kurutze Kanpezu
Peñacerrada
Haro
Briones
Bernedo
Acedo
Laguardia/Biasteri
San Asensio
Cenicero
Olon/Oyon
Fuenmayor
Viana
Murieta
Los Arcos
N. SEÑ. DE IRACHE
Allo
Nájera
Logroño
Navarrete
Baños de Rio Tobia
Villamediana de Iregua
Agoncillo
Mendavia
Sesma
Lodosa
Viguera
A8
E70
A67
N611
N623
N634
N629
C6210
C6318
C629
N232
N625
A68
E804
E05
E80
A1
N1
N120
C627
C6313
C6315
C6320
C6212
C6211
C6213
N111
C121
84
90

Golfe de Gascogne /
Bizkaiko Golkoa /
Golfo de Vizcaya
DONOSTIA-SAN SEBASTIÁN
Biarritz
Bayonne
Dax
PAMPLONA/IRUÑA
Tudela
Huesca
Lekeitio/Lequeitio
Ondarroa
Zumaia/Zumaya
Getaria
Zarautz
Eibar
Tolosa
Hernani
Pasaia
Errenteria/Rentería
Hondarribia/Fuenterrabía
Irun
Hendaye
Ciboure
St-Jean-de-Luz
Guethary
Bidart
Anglet
Hossegor
Capbreton
Labenne
Soustons
Vieux-Boucau-les Bains
St-Girons-en-Marensin
Léon
Castets
Rion-des-Landes
Magescq
St-Paul-lès-Dax
St-Vincent-de-Tyrosse
St-Geours-de-Maremne
Peyrehorade
Orthez
Salies-de-Béarn
Sauveterre-de-Béarn
Bidache
Hasparren
Ustaritz
Cambo-les-Bains
Espelette
Ainhoa
Ascain
St-Palais
Navarrenx
Mauléon-Licharre
St-Étienne-de-Baïgorry
St-Jean-Pied-de-Port
Elizondo
Roncesvalles
Auritz/Burguete
Zubiri
Lesaka
Vera de Bidasoa
Goizueta
Leitza
Lekunberri
Irurtzun
Altsasu/Alsasua
Estella/Lizarra
Puente la Reina/Gares
Tafalla
Olite
Sangüesa/Zangoza
Lumbier/Irunberri
Aoiz/Agoitz
Huarte
Noain/Elorz
Jaca
Sabiñánigo
Canfranc
Candanchú
Ansó
Isaba/Izaba
Ochagavía/Otsagi
Sos del Rey Católico
Uncastillo
Sádaba
Ejea de los Caballeros
Ayerbe
Calahorra
Alfaro
Corella
Cintruénigo
Tarazona
Ágreda
Borja
Cortes
Tauste
Lodosa
Los Arcos
Viana
Logroño
Arnedo
Zumarraga
Beasain
Bergara
Oñati
Azpeitia
Zestoa/Cestona
Deva
Mutriku
NAVARRA
NAFARROA
SIERRA DE LA PEÑA
SIERRA DE LEYRE
CÔTE
83
90
91
A
B
C
D
1
2
3
4
5
6

66
67
AQUITAINE
Roquefort
St-Justin
le Caloy
Mont-de-Marsan
Lapeyrade
Barbaste
Vianne
Lavardac
Nérac
Port-Ste-Marie
Agen
Beauville
Montcuq
Lauzerte
Calignac
Laplume
Labastide-d'Armagnac
Gabarret
Mézin
Astaffort
Fourquet
Valence
Molières
Villeneuve-de-Marsan
Cazaubon
Barbotan-les-Thermes
Fourcès
Montréal
Condom
Moissac
Lafrançaise
Grenade
Eauze
Gondrin
FLARAN
Valence
Lectoure
Castelsarrasin
Lavit
St-Sever
Samadet
Eugénie-les-Bains
Mancier
Aire-s-l'Adour
Nogaro
Vic-Fezensac
St-Clar
Fleurance
Beaumont-de-Lomagne
Montech
Gimat
Riscle
Sarron
Lupiac
MIDI-PYRÉNÉES
Grisolles
Fronton
Plaisance
Mauvezin
Cologne
Grenade
Theze
Marciac
Montesquiou
L'Isle-de-Noé
Auch
Gimont
St-Jory
Lembeye
Maubourguet
Mirande
L'Isle-Jourdain
Blagnac
Morlaàs
Vic-en-Bigorre
Miélan
Saramon
Léguevin
Colomiers
Pau
Rabastens-de-Bigorre
Masseube
Samatan
Lombez
Simorre
TOULOUSE
St-Lys
Gan
Soumoulou
Panassac
Seysses
Trie
Pontacq
Pouyastruc
Castelnau-Magnoac
L'Isle-en-Dodon
Boulogne-sur-Gesse
Rieumes
Muret
Castanet-Tolosan
Vernet
Tarbes
Lestelle Bétharram
Tarbes-Ossun-Lourdes
Tournay
GROTTES DE BÉTHARRAM
St-Pé
Lourdes
Col d'Aubisque
Argelès-Gazost
Bagnères-de-Bigorre
Lannemezan
Aurignac
Carbonne
Noé
Auterive
Nailloux
GROTTE DE MÉDOUS
Campan
Boussens
Rieux
St-Julien
Cazères
St-Martory
Montréjeau
Montesquieu-Volvestre
Saverdun
Col du Soulor
Arrens-Marsous
Pierrefitte-Nestalas
GROTTE DE GARGAS
Ste-Marie-de-Campan
St-Bertrand-de-Comminges
St-Gaudens
Salies-du-Salat
Ste-Croix-Volvestre
Le Fossat
Cauterets
PIC DU MIDI DE BIGORRE
Luz-St-Sauveur
Col d'Aspin 1489
Col des Ares
Aspet
Le Mas-d'Azil
Pailhès
Pamiers
Pont-d'Espagne
La Mongie
Col du Tourmalet
Arreau
Fronsac
GROTTE DU MAS D'AZIL
Baños de Panticosa
DES PYRÉNÉES
Cierp-Gaud
Col de Portet d'Aspet 1069
St-Lizier
VIGNEMALE 3298
PIC DE NEOUVILLE
Bordères
St-Béat
St-Girons
Varilhes
OCCIDENTALES
Gavarnie
St-Lary-Soulan
Col de Peyresourde 1563
Fos
Audressein
Lacourt
La Bastide-de-Sérou
MASSIF DE L'ARIZE
CIRQUE DE GAVARNIE
TUNNEL DE BIELSA
Les
Bagnères-de-Luchon
Foix
MONTE PERDIDO
CIRCO DE BARROSA
Bossòst
VALLE DE ARÁN
Eylie
Oust
Massat
Col de Port
Torla
Broto
PARQUE NACIONAL DE ORDESA
Bielsa
HOSPICE DE FRANCE
PIC DE MONTVALIER
PIC DES 3 SEIGNEURS
Tarascon-sur-Ariège
Gistaín
PICO POSETS
Viella
Salardú
Salau
Guzet-Neige
Aulus-les-Bains
GROTTE DE NIAUX
Lafortunada
Benasque
Arties
TÚNEL DE VIELLA
Port de la Bonaigua 2072
Vicdessos
GROTTE DE LOMBRIVES
Cinqueta
PICO DE ANETO
Sorpe
l'Artigue
Les Cabannes
Laguarta
Boltaña
COTIELLA
Castejón de Sos
Caldes de Boí
PARC NACIONAL D'AIGÜESTORTES I ESTANY DE ST MAURICI
Esterri d'Àneu
Tavascan
PIC D'ESTATS
Ax-les-Thermes
Ainsa
Seira
Taüll
Espot
El Serrat
Campo
TURBÓN
CORRUNCO
Ribera de Cardós
AND
Ordino
PIC DE CABAILLERE
Embalse de Mediano
el Pont de Suert
Capdella
Llavorsí
Soldeu
Port d'Envalira
Samitier
Roda de Isábena
Puerto de Viu
Sort
Andorra la Vella
Encamp
Pas de la Casa
Embalse de Escales
Puerto de Perves
STA. COLOMA
Les Escaldes
Sopeira
Vilamur
Sant Julià de Lòria
VIRGEN DE LA PEÑA
Senterada
Gerri de la Sal
Alquézar
Graus
92
106
Les de Cerdanya
Puigcerdà

A
B
C
D
1
2
3
4
5
6
Mira
Mamarrosa
Cantanhede
Tocha
Murtinheira
Arazede
SÃO MARCOS
Cabo Mondego
Figueira da Foz
Montemor-o-Velho
Mondego
Leirosa
Lavos
Condeixa-a-Nova
Soure
Ceira
CONIMBRIGA
Pedrógão
Carriço
Louriçal
Miranda do Corvo
Praia da Vieira
Vieira
Monte Redondo
Penela
Pombal
São Pedro de Muel
Marinha Grande
Pontão
LEIRIA
Abiúl
Leiria
Figueiró dos Vinhos
Alvaiázere
Farilhões
Nazaré
Batalha
Freixianda
Berlenga
São Martinho do Porto
Aljubarrota
Porto de Mós
Vila Nova de Ourém
Alfeizerão
Alcobaça
Fátima
Ferreira do Zêzere
Cabo Carvoeiro
Foz do Arelho
Peniche
Óbidos
Caldas da Rainha
ALCOBERTAS
SERRA DE AIRE
Tomar
Vila de Rei
Alcanede
Alcanena
Torres Novas
Barragem do Castelo de Bode
COSTA DE PRATA
Lourinhã
Bombarral
Tremês
Rio Maior
SANTARÉM
Pernes
Entroncamento
ALMOUROL
Porto Novo
Cadaval
Golegã
Abrantes
Praia de Santa Cruz
Cercal
Quebradas
Alcoentre
Chamusca
Rossio
São Pedro da Cadeira
Torres Vedras
Santarém
Ulme
Tejo
Bemposta
Aveiras de Cima
Almeirim
Vale do A
Ericeira
Sobral de Monte Agraço
Alenquer
Cartaxo
Chouto
LISBOA
Mafra
Arruda dos Vinhos
Carregado
Azambuja
Muge
Marianos
Pernacha de Cima
Domingão
Praia Grande
Malveira
Salvaterra de Magos
Raposa
CAST. DOS MOUROS
Montelavar
Colares
Lousa
Marinhais
Lamarosa
PORTALEGRE
Cabo de Roca
Sintra
Loures
Vila Franca de Xira
Alverca do Ribatejo
Benavente
GUINCHO
Cacemes
Montargil
Charneca
Sacavém
Porto Alto
Coruche
Barragem de Montargil
Cascais
Odivelas
Moscavide
Sorraia
Estoril
Queluz
LISBOA
Couço
Barragem do Maranhão
Carcavel
Trafaria
Amadora
Alcochete
Infantado
Cabação
Costa da Caparica
Almada
Montijo
Atalaia
Santana do Mato
Mora
Seixal
Barreiro
Arrentela
Moita
Taipadas
Canha
Pinhal Novo
Coina
Pavia
Lavre
Ciborro
Pegões
Poceirão
S. Geraldo
Palmela
QUINTA DA BACALHOA
Vendas Novas
Vila Nogueira de Azeitão
Nossa Senhora do Cabo
Vila Fresca de Azeitão
Setúbal
Cabrela
Arraiolos
Santa Justa
Cabo Espichel
Sesimbra
Portinho da Arrábida
Marateca
Tróia
Praias-Sado
CETÓBRIGA
Rio Sado
Montemor o-Novo
Barragem do Divor
São Romão
Santiago do Escoural
CONVENTO DE ESPINHEIRO
São Cristóvão
94

80
81
88
95
96
Viseu
Caramulo
SERRA DO CARAMULO
Bolfiar
Boialvo
Tondela
Mangualde
Penalva do Castelo
Fornos de Algodres
Trancoso
Figueira de Castelo Rodrigo
CASTELO RODRIGO
Lumbrales
Canas de Senhorim
Nelas
Celorico da Beira
Pinhel
Freixedas
S.Felices de los Gallegos
Villaviej
Santa Comba Dão
Rojão Grande
Carregal do Sal
Seixo
Rio Torto
Almeida
Villar de Ciervo
Tábua
Oliveira do Hospital
Gouveia
Seia
PARQUE NATURAL DA SERRA DA ESTRÊLA
SERRA DA ESTRÊLA
Pinzio
GUARDA
Guarda
Vilar Formoso
Castillejo de Martín Viejo
Gândara
São Martinho
SÃO PEDRO
Vendas de Galizes
Vide
Manteigas
Fuentes de Oñoro
Cerdeira
Vila Fernando
Arganil
Góis
Cepos
MALHÃO
1993
POÇO DO INFERNO
Belmonte
Pega
Ciudad Rodrigo
Covilhã
Caria
Aldeia da Ponte
Alfaites
Sabugal
El Bodón
Fuenteguinaldo
Embalse de Águeda
Barragem de Santa Luzia
Tortosendo
Silvares
Santo Estevão
Aldeia do Bispo
Embalse de Irueña
Robleda
Pampilhosa da Serra
Capinha
Fundão
Penamacor
Valverde del Fresno
Villasrubias
Robledillo de Gata
SIERRA DE GATA
Orvalho
SERRA DA GUARDUNHA
Alpedrinha
Barragem do Cabril
São Vicente da Beira
Orca
Foz Giraldo
Oleiros
São Miguel de Acha
Medelim
Hoyos
CASTELO BRANCO
Lardosa
Barragem da Idanha
Monsanto
Cilleros
Embalse de Borbollón
Villanueva de la Sierra
Sarzedas
Alcafores
Termas de Monfortinho
Pozuelo de Zarzón
Ahigal
Proença-a-Nova
Sobreira Formosa
Idanha-a-Nova
Moraleja
Montehermoso
Castelo Branco
Ladoeiro
Zebreira
Coria
de Codes
Perdigão
Carcaboso
Vila Velha de Ródão
Monforte da Beira
Segura
Zarza la Mayor
Pesqueza
Fratel
PORTAS DE RÓDÃO
Belver
Cedillo
Rosmaninhal
Piedras Albas
Ceclavín
Torrejoncillo
Galisteo
Riolobos
Montalvão
Santiago de Alcántara
Nisa
Alcántara
Portezuelo
Embalse de Alcántara
Tolosa
Carbajo
Barragem da Póvoa
Cañaveral
Puerto de los Castaños
493
Serradilla
Garrovillas
Alpalhão
Monte da Pedra
PARQUE NATURAL
Castelo de Vide
Membrío
Brozas
Navas del Madroño
Hinojal
Talaván
Marvão
Salorino
Santiago del Campo
Crato
Valencia de Alcántara
Herreruela
E
Monroy
PORTALEGRE
Portalegre
DA SERRA
1025
SERRA DE SÃO MAMEDE
Alter do Chão
DE S. MAMEDE
San Vicente de Alcántara
Arroyo de la Luz
Aliseda
624
Malpartida de Cáceres
Cáceres
VIRGEN DE LA MONTAÑA
PIEDRABUENA
La Codosera
SIERRA DE SAN PEDRO
Cabeço de Vide
Sierra de Fuentes
Fronteira
Arronches
Alburquerque
Torrequemada
Monforte
Embalse de la Peña de Águila
Puerto de Clavín
425
La Cumbre
MAYORALGO
Aldea del Cano
Torremocha
Veiros
Puebla de Obando
Villar del Rey
Santa Eulália
Campo Maior
Santo Aleixo
Barragem do Caia
Bótoa
Estremoz
La Roca de la Sierra
Cordobilla de Lácara
Puerto de Santa Cruz
Torre de Sta. María
Montánchez
Alcuéscar
Almoharín
Monte
Borba
ACUEDUCTO DE AMOREIRA
Elvas
La Nava de Santiago
Vila Viçosa
Badajoz
Talavera la Real
Aljucén
EXTREMADURA
Miajadas
Alandroal

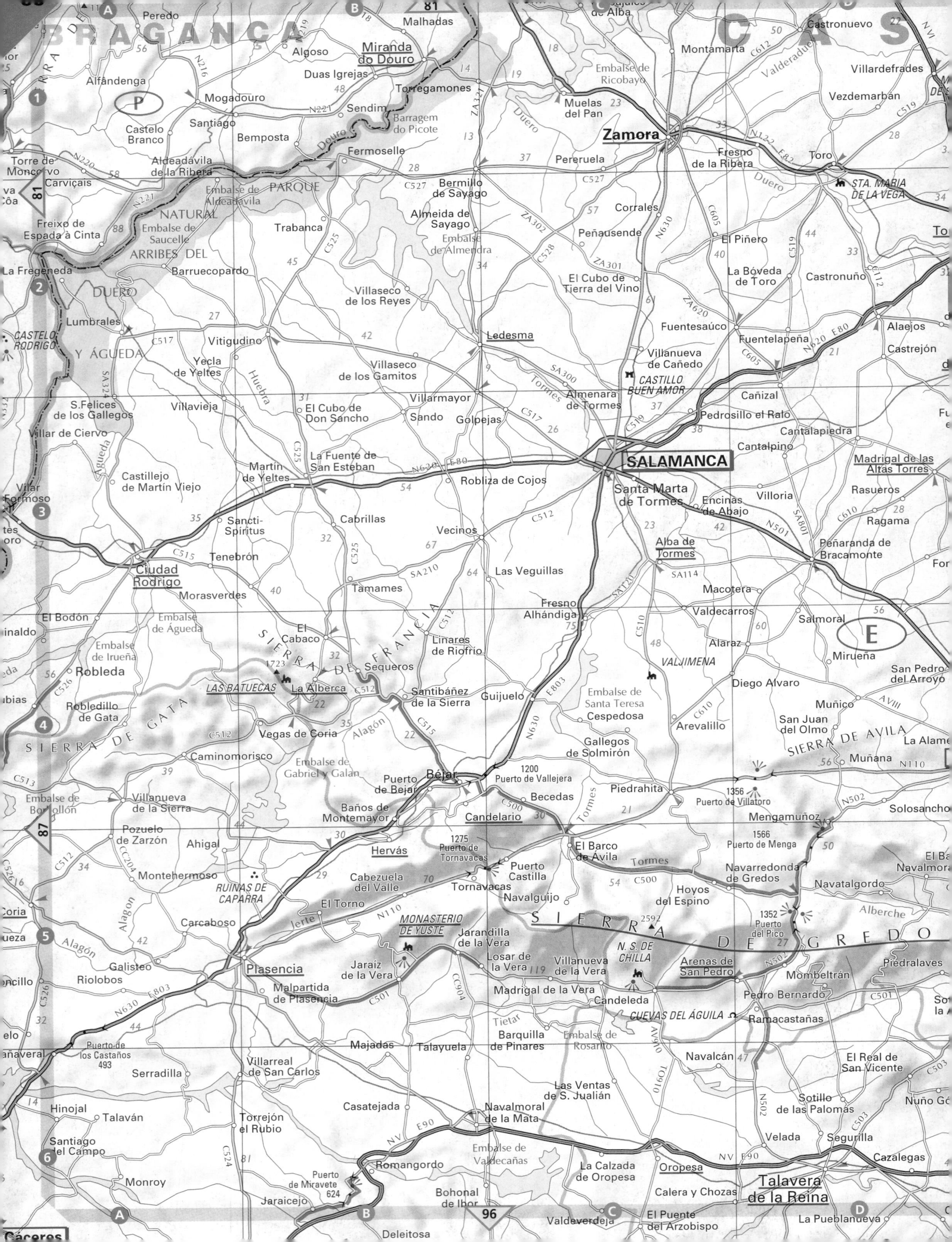

BRAGANÇA
CAS
81
Peredo
Malhadas
Algoso
Miranda do Douro
Duas Igrejas
Torregamones
Alfândenga
Mogadouro
Sendim
Castelo Branco
Santiago
Bemposta
Barragem do Picote
Fermoselle
Torre de Moncorvo
Carviçais
Aldeadávila de la Ribera
Embalse de Aldeadávila
PARQUE
NATURAL
ARRIBES DEL
DUERO
Y ÁGUEDA
Freixo de Espada à Cinta
Embalse de Saucelle
Trabanca
Barruecopardo
La Fregeneda
Lumbrales
CASTELO RODRIGO
Vitigudino
Yecla de Yeltes
Villavieja
S.Felices de los Gallegos
Villar de Ciervo
Castillejo de Martín Viejo
Vilar Formoso
Martín de Yeltes
La Fuente de San Esteban
El Cubo de Don Sancho
Villaseco de los Gamitos
Villaseco de los Reyes
Ledesma
Villarmayor
Sando
Golpejas
Bermillo de Sayago
Almeida de Sayago
Embalse de Almendra
Montamarta
Embalse de Ricobayo
Muelas del Pan
Zamora
Pereruela
Corrales
Peñausende
El Cubo de Tierra del Vino
Castronuevo
Valderaduey
Villardefrades
Vezdemarbán
Fresno de la Ribera
Toro
STA. MARIA DE LA VEGA
El Piñero
La Bóveda de Toro
Castronuño
Fuentesaúco
Fuentelapeña
Alaejos
Castrejón
Villanueva de Cañedo
CASTILLO BUEN AMOR
Almenara de Tormes
Cañizal
Pedrosillo el Ralo
Cantalapiedra
Cantalpino
SALAMANCA
Santa Marta de Tormes
Encinas de Abajo
Villoria
Madrigal de las Altas Torres
Rasueros
Ragama
Peñaranda de Bracamonte
Robliza de Cojos
Sancti-Spíritus
Cabrillas
Vecinos
Tenebrón
Ciudad Rodrigo
Morasverdes
Tamames
Las Veguillas
Alba de Tormes
Macotera
Fresno Alhándiga
Valdecarros
Salmoral
Alaraz
Mirueña
El Bodón
Embalse de Águeda
Embalse de Irueña
Robleda
Robledillo de Gata
El Cabaco
SIERRA DE FRANCIA
Linares de Riofrío
Sequeros
LAS BATUECAS
La Alberca
1723
Santibáñez de la Sierra
Guijuelo
VALJIMENA
Embalse de Santa Teresa
Cespedosa
Diego Alvaro
San Pedro del Arroyo
Muñico
San Juan del Olmo
Arevalillo
SIERRA DE GATA
Vegas de Coria
Caminomorisco
Gallegos de Solmirón
SIERRA DE AVILA
Muñana
La Alame
Embalse de Gabriel y Galán
Puerto de Béjar
Béjar
1200 Puerto de Vallejera
Piedrahita
1356 Puerto de Villatoro
Becedas
Solosancho
Villanueva de la Sierra
Embalse de Borbollón
Baños de Montemayor
Candelario
Mengamuñoz
Pozuelo de Zarzón
Ahigal
Hervás
1275 Puerto de Tornavacas
El Barco de Ávila
1566 Puerto de Menga
Montehermoso
RUINAS DE CAPARRA
Cabezuela del Valle
Puerto Castilla
Tornavacas
Navalguijo
Hoyos del Espino
Navarredonda de Gredos
Navatalgordo
Coria
El Torno
MONASTERIO DE YUSTE
Jarandilla de la Vera
2592
SIERRA DE GREDOS
1352 Puerto del Pico
Alberche
Carcaboso
Galisteo
Riolobos
Plasencia
Jaraiz de la Vera
Losar de la Vera
Villanueva de la Vera
N. S. DE CHILLA
Arenas de San Pedro
Mombeltrán
Piedralaves
Malpartida de Plasencia
Madrigal de la Vera
Candeleda
Pedro Bernardo
CUEVAS DEL ÁGUILA
Ramacastañas
Puerto de los Castaños 493
Majadas
Talayuela
Barquilla de Pinares
Embalse de Rosarito
Navalcán
El Real de San Vicente
Serradilla
Villarreal de San Carlos
Las Ventas de S. Julián
Sotillo de las Palomas
Nuño Gó
Hinojal
Talaván
Torrejón el Rubio
Casatejada
Navalmoral de la Mata
Velada
Segurilla
Santiago del Campo
Embalse de Valdecañas
Cazalegas
Monroy
Puerto de Miravete 624
Romangordo
La Calzada de Oropesa
Oropesa
Talavera de la Reina
Jaraicejo
Bohonal de Ibor
Calera y Chozas
96
Valdeverdeja
El Puente del Arzobispo
La Pueblanueva
Deleitosa
Cáceres
87
Tormes
Duero
Huebra
Águeda
Alagón
Jerte
Tiétar

82
83
97
98
90
E
F
G
H
1
2
3
4
5
6
CASTILLA Y LEÓN
MADRID
Medina de Rioseco
Montealegre
Palencia
Quintana del Puente
Cogollos
Madrigalejo del Monte
Villahoz
Quintanilla de las Viñas
Magaz de Pisuerga
Baños de Cerrato
Baltanás
Cuevas de San Clemente
Barbadillo de Herreros
La Mudarra
Dueñas
Lerma
Covarrubias
Hortigüela
Arlanza
Pisuerga
Cigales
Valoria la Buena
Cevico Navero
Villafruela
Retuerta
Villanubla
Tórtoles de Esgueva
Salas de los Infantes
Esguevillas de Esgueva
Castroverde de Cerrato
Santo Domingo de Silos
Simancas
VALLADOLID
Villafuerte
Esgueva
Castrillo de la Reina
Olmedillo de Roa
Caleruega
Laguna de Duero
Tudela de Duero
Quintanilla de Onésimo
La Horra
Gumiel de Hizán
CLUNIA
Huerta del Rey
Roa
Serrada
Peñafiel
Aranda de Duero
San Leonardo de Yagüe
Coruña del Conde
Rueda
Portillo
Coceges del Monte
Fuentecén
Peñaranda de Duero
Santa María de las Hoyas
Mojados
S.Miguel del Arroyo
Duraton
Moradillo de Roa
CAST. DE LA MOTA
Campaspero
Fuentelcésped
Íscar
Cuéllar
Olombrada
Valtiendas
Honrubia de la Cuesta
Langa de Duero
Olmedo
SIERRA DE PRADALES
Embalse de Linares
San Esteban de Gormaz
Eresma
Cega
San Miguel de Bernúy
1377 RUBIO
Maderuelo
El Burgo de Osma
CASTILLO DE FONSECA
Coca
Hontalbilla
Fuente de Santa Cruz
Pinarejos
Navas de Oro
Villanueva del Aceral
San Cristóbal de la Vega
Navalmanzano
Boceguillas
Ayllón
Nava de la Asunción
Aguilafuente
Cantalejo
Sepúlveda
Arévalo
N. S. DE HONTANARES
Montuenga
Carbonero el Mayor
Turégano
Riaza
Tiermas
Santa María la Real de Nieva
Santo Tomé del Puerto
2127
LA CEBOLLERA
RUINAS ROMANAS
Adanero
Pedraza
Prádena
SIERRA DE AYLLÓN
Matabuena
1404
Puerto de Somosierra
Campisábalos
Sanchidrián
Torrecaballeros
La Salceda
Somosierra
Sangarcía
SIERRA DE GUADARRAMA
Majaelrayo
Blascosancho
Abades
Segovia
Labajos
Embalse de Riosequillo
Embalse de Puentes Viejas
Fuentemilanos
Lozoya
Embalse del Vado
Sorbe
Mingorria
La Granja
Buitrago
Aldeavieja
Villacastín
Tamajón
Embalse de El Villar
Embalse de Palmaces
Puerto de Navacerrada 1860
2430
Rascafría
El Paular
Lozoyuela
La Cabrera
Embalse de El Atazar
Jarama
El Espinar
Cercedilla
1511
San Rafael
Puebla de Vallés
Cogolludo
Miraflores de la Sierra
Alto de los Leones de Castilla
Navacerrada
Torrelaguna
Jadraque
1416 Puerto de Malagón
Navalperal de Pinares
VALLE DE LOS CAÍDOS
Guadarrama
Soto del Real
Humanes
Las Navas del Marqués
San Lorenzo de El Escorial
Cerceda
Manzanares el Real
El Molar
Almadrones
Embalse de Santillana
Viñuelas
Yunquera de Henares
Hita
El Escorial
Villalba Baja
Colmenar Viejo
Cebreros
Robledo de Chavela
Torrelodones
El Casar de Talamanca
SILLA DE FELIPA
Circuito de Jarama
Galapagar
Tórtola de Henares
Embalse de San Juan
Valdemorillo
Torrejón del Rey
Torija
Fuente el Sauz
Brihuega
TOROS DE GUISANDO
El Pardo
Alcobendas
Guadalajara
Navas del Rey
Las Rozas
San Martín de Valdeiglesias
Majadahonda
Fuencarral
Azuqueca de Henares
LUPIANA
Aldea del Fresno
Brunete
Boadilla del Monte
Aravaca
Barajas
Torrejón de Ardoz
Durón
Almorox
Villa del Prado
Alcorcón
Alcalá de Henares
Horche
Armuña de Tajuña
Tendilla
Navalcarnero
Móstoles
MADRID
Alberche
Méntrida
Getafe
Loeches
Pezuela de las Torres
Embalse de Entrepeñas
Sacedón
El Álamo
Fuenlabrada
CERRO DE LOS ÁNGELES
Campo Real
Valmojado
Griñón
Pinto
San Martín de la Vega
Nuevo Baztán
Escariche
Arganda del Rey
Pastrana
Santa Cruz del Retamar
Casarrubios del Monte
Torrejón de la Calzada
Valdemoro
Mondéjar
Novés
Illescas
Ciempozuelos
Tajuña
Albares
Embalse de Buendía
Buendía
Fuensalida
Yuncos
Seseña Nuevo
Albalate de Zorita
Torrijos
Recas
Villarejo de Salvanés
Henares
Manzanares
N620 E80
N122
N I E05
N234
N110
N601
N VI
N403
N111
N603
N320
N II E90
N V E90
N III
N401
A6
A3
A10
A2
M40
M503
E901
C610
C611
C619
C112
C603
C114
C605
C606
C505
C501
C507
C101
C200
C201
C100
C300
CL601
CL601A
SG341
SG342
VA100
M604
M629
M611
M131
M608
M601
M607
M600
M505
M610
M103
M100
M501
M504
M506
M404
M311
M313
GU210

83
98
89
A
B
C
D
1
2
3
4
5
6
LA RIOJA
NAFAR
CORDILLERA IBERICA
SIERRA DE LA DEMANDA
SIERRA DE NEILA
SIERRA DE URBION
SIERRA DEL MONCAYO
SIERRA DE ALBA
E AYLLÓN
E
Ezcaray
Navarrete
Pineda de la Sierra
San Millán de la Cogolla
Baños de Rio Tobia
Villamediana de Iregua
Mendavia
Sesma
Lerín
Tafalla
San M de Un
Quintanilla de las Viñas
Arlanzon
2262
MONASTERIO DE VALVANERA
Viguera
Ribaflecha
Lodosa
Ebro
A68
Carcar
Miranda
Olite
Barbadillo de Herreros
Anguiano
N111
Ausejo
N232
San Adrián
Peralta
Santacara
Hortigüela
Embalse de Mansilla
Iregua
El Villar de Arnedo
Calahorra
Marcilla
Caparroso
Villavelayo
Viniegra de Abajo
Pradillo
San Roman de Cameros
Robres del Castillo
C123
A15
LA OLI
Salas de los Infantes
Arnedillo
Arnedo
Autol
Rincón de Soto
Castrillo de la Reina
Quintanar de la Sierra
2048
Montenegro de Cameros
Cidacos
VICO
Aldeanueva de Ebro
N121
Enciso
C115
NECROPOLIS ROMANA
2228
1710 Puerto de Piqueras
Yanguas
Alfaro
Valtierra
N234
Covaleda
Villarroja
Grávalos
Arguedas
Huerta del Rey
Hontoria del Pinar
Duruelo de la Sierra
Corella
STA. MARIA LA REAL
Huérteles
Vinuesa
N113
San Leonardo de Yagüe
Embalse de la Cuerda del Pozo
Almarza
Cervera del Río Alhama
Cintruénigo
Fitero
Coruña del Conde
Navaleno
El Royo
Canal de Lodesa
Tudela
Santa María de las Hoyas
Abejar
Cidones
1454 Puerto de Oncala
Magaña
Valverde de Cervera
Cascante
Duero
La Rubia
Ribaforada
Garray
NUMANCIA
Canal de Tauste
Calatañazor
Golmayo
Soria
Matalebreras
N122
Tarazona
San Esteban de Gormaz
Aldealpozo
Agreda
1140 Puerto del Madero
Cortes
El Burgo de Osma
Quintana Redonda
Lubia
Ólvega
MONCAYO
Borja
Almenar de Soria
2316
MONASTERIO DE VERUELA
Magallón
Gallur
Fuentepinilla
C101
Gómara
Beratón
Fuendejalón
A6
E80
Hortezuela
Berlanga de Duero
C116
Ciria
Tabuenca
Almazán
Torrelapaja
C220
ERMITA DE S. BAUDELIO
Serón de Nágima
Tierga
SANT. DE RODANAS
Tiermas
RUINAS ROMANAS
Retortillo de Soria
1140 Altos de Baraona
Morón de Almazán
Illueca
Campisábalos
Barcones
Adradas
Villarroya de la Sierra
Pozuel de Ariza
Ricla
Calatorao
Baraona
Atienza
Puerto de Morata 708
ANTIGUA BILBILIS
La Almunia de Doña Godina
Paredes de Sigüenza
Santa María de Huerta
Ariza
Jalón
CIUDAD IBERICA
Ateca
Calatayud
Puerto de Frasno 785
N II
E90
Embalse de Palmaces
Medinaceli
Arcos de Jalón
Alhama de Aragón
C114
Torralba
SO411
Embalse de la Tranquera
Jiloca
Cariñena
Sigüenza
Cogolludo
1150 Cuestas de Esteras
C204
Alcolea del Pinar
Sisamón
Nuévalos
MON. DE PIEDRA
C202
Fuentes de Jiloca
Codos
Paniza
Jadraque
C221
Miedes
La Torresaviñán
N211
Maranchón
Puerto de Paniza 925
Almadrones
Algora
Tajuña
Milmarcos
N330
Piedra
Daroca
Hita
CUEVA DE LOS CASARES
Anquela del Ducado
Cubel
Badules
Masegoso de Tajuña
N204
Puerto de Santed 1153
Abanades
Canales de Molina
Cillas
Báguena
Ferreruela de Huerva
Torija
Santed
C211
Brihuega
Cifuentes
Sacecorbo
Laguna de Gallocanta
Gargoles de Abajo
La Yunta
Trillo
Tajo
Gallo
Molina de Aragón
Bello
Fonfría
Durón
Zaorejas
Calamocha
Arbetera
Castellar de la Muela
Caminreal
Segura de los Baños
Tendilla
El Recuenco
Peñalén
El Pobo de Dueñas
Puerto Mínguez 1270
Embalse de Entrepeñas
Salmerón
Terzaga
Ojos Negros
Monreal del Campo
Cosa
Portalrubio
Sacedón
N. S. DE LA BIENVENIDA
GU210
Alcocer
Beteta
Tordesilos
Bueña
Cañizares
Peralejos de las Truchas
Rillo
Embalse de Buendía
Priego
S. MIGUEL DE LAS VICTORIAS
Orihuela del Tremedal
Visiedo
Buendia
Perales del Alfambra
Pozondón
1920
1498
TE902
Cañaveras
Albalate de las Nogueras
Poyatos

84
E
F
G
H
85
92
99
S. SALVADOR DE LEYRE
Aibar
Javier/ Xabier
Sangüesa/ Zangoza
Embalse de Yesa
Aragón
1062 PEÑA
Sos del Rey Católico
Berdún
Candanchú
Canfranc
Villanúa
Sallent de Gállego
Col du Pourtalet
Pont-d'Espagne
Baños de Panticosa
DES PYRÉNÉES
Col du Tourmalet
3091 PIC DE NEOUVILLE
Arreau
Bordères
St-Lary-Soulan
Col de Peyresourde 1563
Saqués
VIGNEMALE 3298
OCCIDENTALES
Gavarnie
TUNNEL DE BIELSA
Bagnères-de-Luchon
STA. ELENA
CIRQUE DE GAVARNIE
3355
MONTE PERDIDO
CIRCO DE BARROSA
PARQUE NACIONAL DE ORDESA
Puente la Reina de Jaca
Jaca
Biescas
SIERRA DE LA PEÑA
Santa Cruz de la Serós
Puerto de Santa Barbara 864
Puerto de Oroel 1080
1769
1132 CRUZ
1423 Puerto de Cotefablo
Torla
Broto
Bielsa
3371 PICO POSETS
Gistaín
Benasque
Castillo
Castilliscar
Uncastillo
1517
S. JUAN DE LA PEÑA
Sabiñánigo
Biel
Agüero
LOS MALLOS
Fiscal
Lafortunada
Cinqueta
Laguarta
Boltaña
2910 COTIELLA
Castejón de Sos
Embalse de la Peña
CAST. DE LOARRE
1262 Puerto de Monrepós
Arguís
Ayerbe
Embalse de Belsué
Nocito
SANTUARIO DE SAN URBEZ
SIERRA DE GUARA
2077
Aínsa
Campo
Seira
2492 TURBÓN
Pinsoro
Luna
Ardisa
Ejea de los Caballeros
Plasencia del Monte
Igriés
Embalse de Mediano
Samitier
Roda de Isábena
Erla
Sierra de Luna
Embalse de la Sotonera
Tormos
Huesca
Liesa
Ibieca
VIRGEN DE LA PEÑA
Graus
Gurrea de Gállego
Almudévar
Castejón de Valdejasa
Tauste
Angüés
Alquézar
Abiego
El Grado
Embalse de Barasona
Laguarres
Benabarre
Tardienta
Sesa
Pertusa
MONASTERIO DE PUEYO
Barbastro
Estada
Remolinos
Zuera
Grañén
Huerto
Embalse de Canelles
Alagón
Villanueva de Gállego
Robres
Azanúy
1677
Puerto de Àger
Leciñena
CARTUJA DE AULA DEI
Lalueza
El Tormillo
Monzón
Baells
SALDUBA
Utebo
Montañana
Alcubierre
822
SIERRA DE ALCUBIERRE
Lanaja
Sariñena
Pomar
Zaragoza
ZARAGOZA
Canal Imperial
Tamarite de Litera
Binéfar
les Avellanes
Alfajarín
Farlete
Pallaruelo de Monegros
Villanueva de Sigena
Albalate de Cinca
Embalse de Santa Ana
Alfarràs
El Burgo de Ebro
Monegrillo
Alcanadre
MONASTERIO DE SIGENA
Almenar
Balaguer
Muel
Osera de Ebro
Castejón de Monegros
Embalse de Mezalocha
Fuentes de Ebro
La Almolda
Ballobar
Almacelles
Vilanova de la Barca
Valmadrid
Villanueva de Huerva
Zaidín
Canal de Aragón y Cataluña
Pina de Ebro
ARAGÓN
Torrefarrera
Quinto
Gelsa
Bujaraloz
Candasnos
Lérida/ Lleida
Alcarràs
Mollerussa
CIUDAD ROMANA
Fraga
Belchite
Azuara
ACROPOLIS IBERICA
Azaila
Torrente de Cinca
Soses
Serós
Castelldans
Embalse de Moneva
Escatrón
MONASTERIO DE RUEDA
Embalse de Mequinenza
Mequinenza
l'Albagés
Lécera
Moyuela
Maials
L'Albi
Híjar
Caspe
Albalate del Arzobispo
la Granadella
Embalse de Flix
La Bisbal de Falset
Muniesa
Ulldemolins
Ariño
Nonaspe
Flix
Ascó
Embalse de Cueva Foradada
La Hoz de la Vieja
Maella
La Pobla de Massaluca
Batea
Garcia
Alcañiz
CUEVA DEL CHARCO DE AGUA AMARGA
Andorra
Falset
Castelserás
Calaceite
Gandesa
Miravet
Móra la Nova
Móra d'Ebre
Los Olmos
Montalbán
Calanda
Valdeltormo
Alcorisa
Mont-roig del Camp
Rasquera
POBLADO IBERICO
Escucha
Ejulve
Molinos
Mas de las Matas
Arnes
Prat de Compte
Cambrils
Valderrobres
Vandellós
Aliaga
CUEVA DE LAS GRADERAS
Castellote
Xerta
Miami Platja
L'Hospitalet de l'Infant

85
A
B
C
D
SAN URBEZ
SIERRA DE GUARA
2077
Campo
2492
TURBÓN
Embalse de Mediano
2742
CORRUNCO
el Pont de Suert
Capdella
Ribera de Cardós
Llavorsí
AND
Ordino
Andorra la Vella
Encamp
Les Escaldes
STA. COLOMA
Sant Julià de Lória
Samitier
Roda de Isábena
1325
Puerto di Viu
Puerto de Perves
1350
Sort
Vilamor
2437
Gerri de la Sal
Ibieca
VIRGEN DE LA PEÑA
Embalse de Escales
Sopeira
Senterada
Angüés
Alquézar
Graus
Laguarres
la Pobla de Segur
Abiego
El Grado
Embalse de Barasona
Noguera Ribagorzana
Noguera Pallaresa
Embalse de Talarn
Adrall
la Seu d'Urgell
Pertusa
Estada
Benabarre
Puente de Montañana
Tremp
PARC 2567 NAT.
SIERRA DEL CADÍ
MONASTERIO DE PUEYO
Barbastro
Embalse de Canelles
Embalse de Terradets
Huerto
Bóixols
Tuixén
SIERRA DEL MONTSECH
Coll de Nargó
Alinyá
Azanúy
1677
Cellers/ Castell de Mur
Isona
El Tormillo
Monzón
Baells
Puerto de Ager 912
Collado de Camiols 1102
Collado de Jou 1470
Oliana
Sant Llorenç de Morunys
Sariñena
Pomar
Tamarite de Litera
Embalse de Camarasa
Montargull/ Artesa de Segre
Binéfar
les Avellanes
Segre
Villanueva de Sigena
Embalse de Santa Ana
Albalate de Cinca
Alfarràs
Artesa de Segre
Ponts
Solsona
MONASTERIO DE SIGENA
Almenar
Canal de Zaidín
Canal de Aragón y Cataluña
Cinca
Balaguer
Cardona
Almacelles
Agramunt
Ballobar
Vilanova de la Barca
Bellcaire d'Urgell
Torà
M. D. DE PINÓS
Balsar
N
Zaidín
CATALUÑA
Torrefarrera
Guissona
Súria
E
Candasnos
Lérida/ Lleida
Alcarràs
Fraga
Mollerussa
Tàrrega
Cervera
Calaf
Sant Joan de Vilatorrada
Manresa
91
Torrente de Cinca
Soses
Bellpuig
Belianes
Castelldans
les Borges Blanques
Puerto Los Bruchs 620
Embalse de Mequinenza
Seròs
Mequinenza
l'Albagés
VALLBONA DE LES MONGES
Santa Coloma de Queralt
Igualada
MONTSERRAT
Santa Margarida de Montbui
Maials
L'Albi
Vinaixa
Sarral
Esparreguera
Caspe
la Granadella
l'Espluga de Francolí
POBLET
Montblanc
Embalse de Flix
La Bisbal de Falset
Esblada
Olesa de Montserrat
Nonaspe
Ulldemolins
Sant Martí Sarroca
Sant Sadurní d'Anoia
Martorell
Maella
Flix
Ascó
581 Puerto de Lilla
el Pla de Santa Maria
SANTES CREUS
Vila-rodona
Gelida
Batea
La Pobla de Massaluca
Valls
Vilafranca del Penedès
Garcia
Alcover
Sant Boi de Llobregat
EL CHARCO AMARGA
Matarraña
Falset
Ebro
ARC DE BERÀ
El Vendrell
Castelldefels
Valdeltormo
Calaceite
Gandesa
Mora la Nova
Móra d'Ebre
PUENTE DEL DIABLO
Miravet
Reus
Mont-roig del Camp
Altafulla
Coma-ruga
Calafell
Vilanova i la Geltrú
Sitges
Garraf
Rasquera
POBLADO IBERICO
Vila-seca
Torredembarra
Arnes
Prat de Compte
Cambrils
Tarragona
Valderrobres
Vandellós
Salou
TORRE DELS ESCIPIONS
Miami Platja
L'Hospitalet de l'Infant
1181
Xerta
L'ESPINA
Cabo del Término
Embalse de Pena
COSTA
El Perelló
Roquetes
L'Ametlla de Mar
Tortosa
Golfo de San Jorge
Mas de Barberans
L'Ampolla
L'Aldea
PARC NATURAL
99
Amposta
Cava
Riomar
la Sénia
Sant Jaume d'Enveja
Cabo de Tortosa
St. Carles de la Ràpita
DEL DELTA DE L' EBRE
Ulldecona
Traiguera
Puerto de los Alfaques
Alcanar
Playa del Trabucador
Càlig
Vinaròs
Santa Magdalena de Polpis
Benicarló
Peñíscola

106
Sournia
Estagel
Rivesaltes
Port-Barcarès
Baixas
PERPIGNAN
l'Hospitalet-l'Andorre
Col de Puymorens 1915
Formiguères
F
ST.-MICHEL-DE CUXA
Prades
Millas
Thuir
Canet-Plage
PIC CARLIT
BELVEDERE 2000
Font-Romeu
Col de la Quillane 1714
Olette
Villefranche-de-Conflent
Vinça
Vernet-les-Bains
Mont-Louis
St-Cyprien-Plage
Elne
Puigcerdà
Bourg-Madame
Saillagouse
ST.-MARTIN-DU-CANIGOU
PIC DU CANIGOU 2784
Le Boulou
Argelès-Plage
Argelès-sur-Mer
Collioure
Amélie-les-Bains
Céret
Valter-2000
Nuria
Alp
Collado de Toses 1800
La Molina
Prats-de-Mollo-la-Preste
Arles-sur-Tech
Le Perthus
Port-Vendres
Cap Béar
Banyuls-sur-Mere
Cap l'Abeille
Cerbère
Cap Cerbère
Portbou
Superespot
Setcases
Col d'Ares 1513
Ribes de Freser
Llobregat
la Jonquera
Darnius
la Pobla de Lillet
Sant Joan de les Abadesses
Camprodón
Sant Pau de Seguries
el Port de la Selva
Llançà
Ripoll
Vallfogona de Ripollès
Castellfollit de la Roca
Figueres/Figueras
QUERMANÇO
SANT PERE DE RODES
Cabo Creus
Borredà
Collado de Coubet 1010
Olot
Besalú
Castelló d'Empúries
Roses/Rosas
Cadaqués
Sant Agusti de Lluçanes
Sant Quirze de Besora
Empùriabrava
Cabo Norfeu
Fluvia
Sant Pere Pescador
Prats de Lluçanès
Sant Hipòlit de Voltregà
Torelló
Manlleu
M. D. DE LA SALUT
Banyoles/Bañolas
les Planes d'Hostoles
EMPÚRIES
Bahía de Roses
Olost
Viladamat
L'Escala
Embalse de Susqueda
Amer
Avinyó
Vic/Vich
Embalse de Sau
Salt
l'Estartit
Anglès
Gerona/Girona
POBLADO IBÉRICO
Torroella de Montgrí
Girona
la Bisbal d'Empordà
Tona
Cassà de la Selva
Begur
Moià
Sant Hilari Sacalm
Palafrugell
Centelles
Arbúcies
Santa Coloma de Farners
Aiguablava
Castellterçol
SIERRA DE MONSENY
1712
Sils
Caldes de Malavella
Llagostera
Calonge
Llafranc
ST. MIQUEL DEL FAI
Maçanet de la Selva
Calella de Palafrugell
Sant Feliu de Codines
Montseny
Palamós
Caldes de Montbui
La Garriga
Hostalric
Santa Cristina d'Aro
Platja d'Aro
S'Agaró
Sant Celoni
SANT GRAU
Sant Feliu de Guíxols
Cardedeu
Tordera
Granollers
Sabadell
La Roca del Vallès
Mollet del Vallès
Blanes
Lloret de Mar
Tossa de Mar
Santa Susanna
Pineda de Mar
Calella
Sant Pol de Mar
Canet de Mar
Arenys de Mar
Caldes d'Estrac
Mataró
Vilassar de Mar
Premià de Mar
El Masnou
Montgat
Badalona
BARCELONA
l'Hospitalet de Llobregat
el Prat de Llobregat
COSTA BRAVA
O R A D A
Palma - Mallorca
Eivissa/Ibiza
Maó/Mahón - Menorca

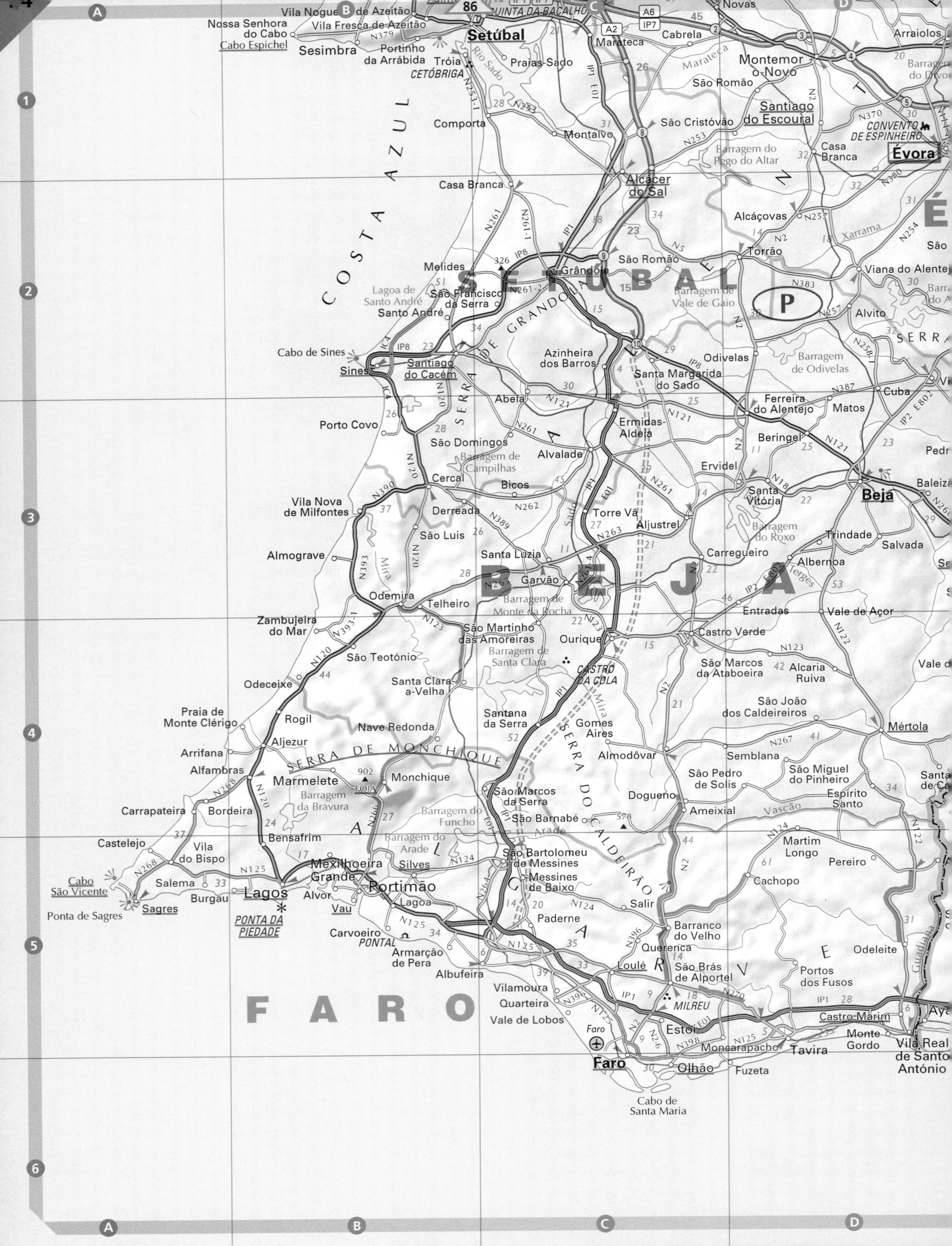
A
B
C
D
86
1
2
3
4
5
6
Vila Nogueira de Azeitão
Vila Fresca de Azeitão
Nossa Senhora do Cabo
Cabo Espichel
Sesimbra
Portinho da Arrábida
Setúbal
Tróia
CETÓBRIGA
Rio Sado
Praias-Sado
Marateca
Cabrela
Novas
Montemor o-Novo
Arraiolos
São Romão
Santiago do Escoural
São Cristóvão
Comporta
Montalvo
CONVENTO DE ESPINHEIRO
Évora
Barragem do Pego do Altar
Casa Branca
Alcácer do Sal
COSTA AZUL
Alcáçovas
Torrão
Xarrama
Viana do Alentejo
Melides
Grândola
São Romão
SETÚBAL
Lagoa de Santo André
São Francisco da Serra
Santo André
Barragem de Vale de Gaio
Alvito
SERRA DE GRANDOLA
Cabo de Sines
Sines
Santiago do Cacém
Azinheira dos Barros
Odivelas
Barragem de Odivelas
Santa Margarida do Sado
Abela
Ferreira do Alentejo
Cuba
Matos
Porto Covo
Ermidas-Aldeia
São Domingos
Barragem de Campilhas
Alvalade
Beringel
Ervidel
Cercal
Bicos
Santa Vitória
Beja
Vila Nova de Milfontes
Derreada
Torre Vã
Aljustrel
Barragem do Roxo
Trindade
Salvada
São Luis
Almograve
Santa Luzia
Carregueiro
Albernoa
Mira
Garvão
BEJA
Odemira
Telheiro
Barragem de Monte da Rocha
Entradas
Vale de Açor
Zambujeira do Mar
São Martinho das Amoreiras
Ourique
Castro Verde
São Teotónio
Barragem de Santa Clara
CASTRO DA COLA
São Marcos da Ataboeira
Alcaria Ruiva
Odeceixe
Santa Clara-a-Velha
São João dos Caldeireiros
Praia de Monte Clérigo
Rogil
Nave Redonda
Santana da Serra
Gomes Aires
Mértola
Aljezur
SERRA DE MONCHIQUE
Arrifana
Almodôvar
Semblana
Alfambras
Marmelete
902
FOIA
Monchique
SERRA DO CALDEIRÃO
São Pedro de Solis
São Miguel do Pinheiro
Barragem da Bravura
São Marcos da Serra
Dogueno
Espirito Santo
Carrapateira
Bordeira
Barragem do Funcho
Ameixial
São Barnabé
578
Vascão
Castelejo
Vila do Bispo
Bensafrim
Barragem do Arade
Martim Longo
Pereiro
Mexilhoeira Grande
Silves
São Bartolomeu de Messines
Messines de Baixo
Cachopo
Cabo São Vicente
Salema
Lagos
Portimão
Burgau
Alvor
Lagoa
Salir
Sagres
Vau
Paderne
Ponta de Sagres
PONTA DA PIEDADE
Carvoeiro
PONTAL
Barranco do Velho
Odeleite
Querença
Armação de Pera
Albufeira
Loulé
São Brás de Alportel
Portos dos Fusos
Vilamoura
Quarteira
MILREU
Vale de Lobos
Castro Marim
FARO
ALGARVE
Guadiana
Estói
Faro
Moncarapacho
Tavira
Monte Gordo
Vila Real de Santo António
Olhão
Fuzeta
Cabo de Santa Maria

87
96
102
101
E
F
G
H
1
2
3
4
5
6
EXTRE
ÉVORA
Vimieiro
Santa Justa
Estremoz
Évora Monte
Azaruja
Borba
Vila Viçosa
Elvas
ACUEDUCTO DE AMOREIRA
Santo Aleixo
Santa Eulália
Barragem do Caia
Botoa
Badajoz
Talavera la Real
Puebla de la Calzada
Montijo
La Roca de la Sierra
Cordobilla de Lácara
Alcuéscar
La Nava de Santiago
Aljucén
La Garrovilla
Calamonte
Mérida
Lobón
Arroyo de San Serván
Zarza de Alange
Alange
Torremejía
Guareña
Oliva de Mérida
São Miguel de Machede
Alandroal
Redondo
Olivenza
S.Benito de la Contienda
Valverde de Leganés
La Albuera
Solana de los Barros
Aceuchal
Almendralejo
Pias
Montoito
Reguengos de Monsaraz
Monsaraz
Cheles
Alconchel
Táliga
Almendral
Nogales
Santa Marta
Villalba de los Barros
Palomas
Embalse de Alange
Portel
Mourão
Barcarrota
Salvatierra de los Barros
Puebla de la Reina
Villanueva del Fresno
Higuera de Vargas
Villafranca de los Barros
Valle de la
Alqueva
Granja
Valle de Matamoros
Fuente del Maestre
Hornachos
Ribera del Fresno
Póvoa
Zahinos
Feria
Burguillos del Cerro
Los Santos de Maimona
Zafra
Jerez de los Caballeros
Hinojosa del Valle
Moura
Amareleja
Valencia de Mombuey
Oliva de la Frontera
Puerto de Sto Domingo 570
Llera
Safara
Pias
Barrancos
Usagre
Valencia de las Torres
Sobral da Adiça
Encinasola
Fregenal de la Sierra
Valencia del Ventoso
Fuente de Cantos
Bienvenida
Manguilla
Rosal de la Frontera
Vila Nova de São Bento
Vila Verde de Ficalho
Cumbres de S. Bartolomé
Higuera la Real
Puerto de la Loba
Segura de León
CIUDAD ROMANA
Llerena
Berlanga
Aroche
Cumbres Mayores
Fuentes de León
MON. DE TENTUDÍA
Montemolín
Casas de Reina
Monesterio
Pallarés
Paymogo
Santa Bárbara
Cortegana
Jabugo
Cañaveral de León
SIERRA DE TUDI
Fuente del Arco
Domingos
SIERRA DE ARACENA
Almonaster la Real
959
PARQUE NATURAL
Cala
Puebla del Maestre
CUEVAS DE SANTIAGO
Guadalcanal
San Telmo
Aracena
Embalse de Aracena
Puerto de las Marismas
Cabezas Rubias
El Cerro de Andévalo
CUEVA DE LAS MARAVILLAS
Santa Olalla del Cala
Embalse de El Pintado
Alanís
Puebla de Guzmán
Villanueva de las Cruces
Y PICOS DE AROCHE
Cazalla de la Sierra
Calañas
Minas de Riotinto
La Granada de Rio Tinto
Almadén de la Plata
Alosno
Zalamea la Real
Nerva
El Ronquillo
VIRGEN DEL MONTE
El Pedroso
Embalse de la Minilla
Embalse de Cala
El Madroño
Valverde del Camino
El Castillo de las Guardas
Berrocal
San Bartolomé de la Torre
El Garrobo
Venta El Alto
Castilblanco de los Arroyos
MULBA
Gibraleón
Beas
El Tumbalejo
Cartaya
Trigueros
Burguillos
Villanueva del Río y Minas
Lepe
Aljaraque
La Antilla
La Palma del Condado
Aznalcóllar
Villaverde del Río
Cantillana
Tocina
Huelva
San Juan del Puerto
Niebla
Bonares
Gerena
Guillena
Alcalá del Río
Brenes
Lora del Río
El Portil
Moguer
Palos de la Frontera
Manzanilla
ITALICA
La Rinconada
La Algaba
Punta Umbría
MONASTERIO DE LA RABIDA
Bollullos Par del Condado
Sanlúcar la Mayor
S. ISIDORO DEL CAMPO
NECRÓPOLIS ROMANA
Almonte
Pilas
SEVILLA
El Viso del Alcor
Carmona
Mazagón
NUESTRA SEÑORA DEL ROCIO
Villamanrique de la Condesa
Coria del Río
Alcalá de Guadaira
La Puebla del Río
El Rocío
Dos Hermanas
Mairena del Alcor
MARCHENILLA
MARISMAS
ASPERILLO 103
Villafranco del Guadalquivir
Guadiana
Ardila
Chanca
Odiel
Tinto
Huelva
Viar
Guadiamar
Bembézar
Huéznar
Matachel
Alcarrache
Corbones
A6
E90
E01
A49
N IV
E05
N4
N630
E803
N432
N435
N433
C436
C423
C437
C439
A431
A472
N431
H624
A495
A493
A470
H120
C421

Cáceres
VIRGEN DE LA MONTAÑA
Trujillo
Mérida
EXTREMADURA
SIERRA DE GUADALUPE
MONASTERIO DE GUADALUPE
Guadalupe
Talavera de la Reina
Medellín
Don Benito
Castuera
Cabeza del Buey
Almadén
SIERRA DEL PEDROSA
SIERRA DE ALCUDIA
SIERRA DE LOS SANTOS
Peñarroya-Pueblonuevo
Pozoblanco
Villanueva de Córdoba
PARQUE NATURAL SIERRA DE HORNACHUELOS
PARQUE NATURAL SIERRA DE CARDEÑA Y MONTORO
PARQUE NATURAL SIERRA NORTE
MEDINA AZAHARA
Montoro
Hornachuelos
Constantina
Cazalla de la Sierra
Guadalcanal
Azuaga
Llerena
Zafra
Alange
Miajadas
Logrosán
Zorita
Herrera del Duque
Fuenlabrada de los Montes
Puebla de Alcocer
Talarrubias
Siruela
Agudo
Saceruela
Hinojosa del Duque
Belalcázar
Fuente Obejuna
Cardeña
Fuencaliente
Espiel
Villaharta
Obejo
Cerro Muriano
Adamuz
87
88
95
102

89
Novés
Santa Olalla
Cebolla
Torrijos
Fuensalida
Illescas
Yuncos
Ciempozuelos
Seseña Nuevo
Tajuña
Mondéjar
Albares
Albalate de Zorita
El Carpio de Tajo
Recas
Chinchón
Villarejo de Salvanés
Estremera
Escalonilla
Bargas
Añover de Tajo
Aranjuez
Colmenar de Oreja
La Puebla de Montalbán
Mocejón
Fuentidueña de Tajo
Tajo
Jarama
Toledo
Ocaña
Villarubia de Santiago
Belinchón
Barajas de Melo
MONTALBÁN
GUADAMUR
CASTILLO DE SAN SERVANDO
STA. MARIA DE MELQUE
Argés
Nambroca
Huerta de Valdecarábanos
Dosbarrios
Santa Cruz de la Zarza
Tarancón
Polán
Gálvez
Villatobas
Carrascosa del Campo
Algodor
Escorchón
Riansares
UCLÉS
Menasalbas
Pulgar
Sonseca
Cuerva
A Guarda/ La Guardia
Saelices
Las Ventas con Peña Aguilera
Mora
Cabezamesada
Horcajo de Santiago
SEGÓBRIGA
Orgaz
Tembleque
Retuerta del Bullaque
Romeral
Lillo
Corral de Almaguer
Laguna de Hito
VIRGEN DE LA MUELA
Villarejo de Fuentes
Los Yébenes
Turleque
Villamayor de Santiago
El Molinillo
Embalse de Torre Abraham
Villacañas
La Puebla de Almoradiel
Villanueva de Alcardete
Fuentelespino de Haro
GUADALERZAS
Quintanar de la Orden
Pedrera
Consuegra
Madridejos
Cigüela
Miguel Esteban
Los Hinojosos
Zancara
Urda
MONTES DE TOLEDO
CASTILLA-LA MANCHA
Cortijos de Abajo
Villafranca de los Caballeros
El Toboso
La Toledana
SIERRA DE LA CALDERINA
ERMITA DE VILLAJOS
Belmonte
Herencia
Mota del Cuervo
CRISTO DEL ESPÍRITU-SANTO
Puerto Lápice
VIRGEN DE CRIPTANA
Puerto de los Majales
Fuente el Fresno
Alcázar de San Juan
El Pedernoso
Campo de Criptana
Las Pedroñeras
Porzuna
Villarrubia de los Ojos
Embalse de Gasset
Malagón
Pedro Muñoz
Las Mesas
Fernancaballero
Villarta de San Juan
PARQUE NACIONAL DE LAS TABLAS DE DAIMIEL
Vega de los Árboles
Luciana
Piedrabuena
El Minguillo
CALATRAVA LA VIEJA
Socuéllamos
Ciudad Real
Villarrobledo
Carrión de Calatrava
Torralba
Daimiel
Argamasilla de Alba
Tomelloso
Azuer
Manzanares
CASTILLO DE PEÑARROYA
Caracuel de Calatrava
Almagro
Bolaños de Calatrava
Membrilla
Embalse de Peñarroya
Granátula de Calatrava
La Solana
Argamasilla de Calatrava
Ruidera
Sotuélamos
Aldea del Rey
Moral de Calatrava
San Carlos del Valle
Munera
Jabalón
Alhambra
Lagunas de Ruidera
Ossa de Montiel
Puertollano
La Calzada de Calatrava
CUEVA DE MONTESINOS
El Bonillo
CONVENTO DE CALATRAVA
Valdepeñas
Carrizosas
SALVATIERRA
SIERRA MESTANZA
Mestanza
La Alameda
Salinas de Pinilla
Fresneda
CASTILLO DE MUDELA
Santa Cruz de Mudela
Villanueva de los Infantes
Villahermosa
Viveros
Cózar
Montiel
Villanueva de la Fuente
Viso del Marqués
Torre de Juan Abad
Almedina
Robledo
San Lorenzo de Calatrava
Almuradiel
Albaladejo
N. S. DE CORTÉS
Castellar de Santiago
Alcaraz
Peñascosa
Colonia Selladores
Villamanrique
Guadalmena
Villapalacios
El Centenillo
Pinto
Aldeaquemada
Embalse de Guadalmena
Embalse de Jándula
Guadalén
Santa Elena
Guarrizas
SIERRA DE ALCARAZ
Paterna del M
Embalse del Rumblar
La Carolina
Venta de los Santos
Riópar
Génave
Puente de Génave
Vilches
Baños de la Encina
Guarromán
Santisteban del Puerto
Guadalimar
103
Arquillinos
Siles
CUEVA DE LOS CHORROS
Molinicos
98

89
90
97
104
A
B
C
D
1
2
3
4
5
6
Mondéjar
Albares
Albalate de Zorita
Embalse de Buendía
Buendia
Priego
S. MIGUEL DE LAS VICTORIAS
Orihuela del Tremedal
Pozondón
Santa Eulalia
Villarquemado
Cella
Albarracín
SIERRA DE ALBARRACÍN
MONTES UNIVERSALES
SERRANÍA DE CUENCA
Poyatos
Albalate de las Nogueras
Cañaveras
Arcos de la Sierra
La Noguera
Tragacete
Estremera
Gascueña
La Peraleja
Torrecilla
Belinchón
Barajas de Melo
Huete
Villar de Domingo García
Villalba de la Sierra
Uña
CUEVAS DE ALBARRACÍN
Tarancón
Caracenilla
Sotos
LA CIUDAD ENCANTADA
Embalse de la Toba
Terriente
Embalse del Arquillo de San Blas
Carrascosa del Campo
Naharros
Chillarón de Cuenca
Valdecabras
Cuenca
UCLÉS
Saelices
Puerto de Cabrejas 1150
Villar de Olalla
Palomares del Campo
Valdemoro Sierra
Laguna del Marquesado
Toril
CUEVAS DE LA TAJADA
Villastar
Villel
SEGÓBRIGA
Horcajo de Santiago
LAS TORCAS
Montalbo
Altarejos
Arcas
Cañete
Salvacañete
Laguna de Hito
Villarejo de Fuentes
Villares del Saz
Fuentes
La Torre Baja
Ademuz
Villamayor de Santiago
San Lorenzo de la Parrilla
RUINAS ROMANE
Puerto de Tórdiga 1200
Puerto de Rocho 1150
Algarra
VALENCIA
Fuentelespino de Haro
Cervera del Llano
Olivares de Júcar
Valeria
Carboneras de Guadazaón
Fuentelespino de Moya
Santa Cruz de Moya
Villalgordo del Marquesado
Arguisuelas
Landete
Los Hinojonos
La Almarcha
Valverde de Júcar
Solera del Gabaldón
Embalse de Alarcón
Almodóvar del Pinar
Embalse de Villora
Talayuelas
Belmonte
Honrubia
Olmedilla de Alarcón
Cardenete
Garaballa
El Pedernoso
El Cañavate
Cañadajuncosa
Campillo de Altobuey
Mira
Las Pedroñeras
La Alberca de Záncara
Enguídanos
Sinarcas
Alarcón
Motilla del Palancar
SAN AGUSTÍN
Camporrobles
Embalse del Generalísimo
Las Mesas
Villar de Cantos
Embalse de Contreras
La Torre
N. S. DEL REMEDIO
San Clemente
Minglanilla
Villargordo del Cabriel
Utiel
Socuéllamos
Casas de Fernando Alonso
Sisante
Villalpardo
Villarrobledo
Villanueva de la Jara
Iniesta
Villarta
Requena
Casas de Benítez
Venta del Moro
Minaya
Quintanar del Rey
Ledaña
Villamalea
Los Isidros
Tarazona de la Mancha
La Roda
Villatoya
La Portera
Santa Marta
Cenizzate
Casas-Ibáñez
Mahora
Alborea
Sotuélamos
Munera
Ossa de Montiel
El Bonillo
La Gineta
Villar del Pozo
Valdeganga
Alcalá del Júcar
Villa de Ves
Embalse de Embarcaderos
Cofrentes
Barrax
Jorquera
Casas de Juan Núñez
Cortes de Pallás
Lezuza
Albacete
Alatoz
Jarafuel
Balazote
CUEVA DE LA VIEJA
CUEVA LA ARAÑA
Viveros
Chinchilla de Monte-Aragón
Ayora
San Pedro
El Salobral
Higueruela
Robledo
Pozuelo
Alpera
N. S. DE CORTÉS
CUEVA DEL REY MORO
Alcaraz
Peñascosa
Pozo-Cañada
Bonete
Pétrola
Villapalacios
Peñas de San Pedro
Pozohondo
Las Anorias
Montealegre del Castillo
Almansa
Navalón
SIERRA DE ALCARAZ
Paterna del Madera
Alcadozo
Bogarra
SANT. DE LA ENCARNACIÓN
Fuente Álamo
CUEVA DE EL ARABI
La Font de la Figuera
Riópar
Ayna
Liétor
Tobarra
Ontur
Caudete
CUEVA DE LOS CHORROS
Molinicos
Elche de la Sierra
Embalse de Talave
Hellín
Fuensanta
Caudete
MANCHA

91
92
105
E
F
G
H
1
2
3
4
5
6
Rill
Mezquita de Jarque
Escucha
Ejulve
Molinos
Mas de las Matas
Arnes
Prat de Compte
Rasquera
Visiedo
Perales del Alfambra
Aliaga
CUEVA DE LAS GRADERAS
Castellote
Valderrobres
Xerta
Embalse de Santolea
Monroyo
Embalse de Pena
1181
L'ESPINA
Alfambra
Aguilar del Alfambra
Guadaloupe
Sorita
El Perelló
Roquetes
Tortosa
Villarluengo
Forcall
Puerto Torre Miró 1250
Mas de Barberans
Villarroga de los Pinares
Cañada de Benatanduz
L'Ampolla
Allepuz
Cantavieja
Morella
MORELLA LA VELLA
L'Aldea
Amposta
Ebro
Camarles
Corbalán
La Iglesuela del Cid
Servol
la Sénia
Sant Jaume d'Enveja
Teruel
SIERRA DE GÚDAR
SIERRA DEL MAESTRAZGO
SIERRA DE CAMARENA
SIERRA PALOMERA
Vallivana
St. Carles de la Ràpita
Ares del Maestre/ Ares del Maestrat
Xerta
Ulldecona
DELTA DEL EBRE
Alcalá de la Selva
Traiguera
Puerto de los Alfaques
Puerto de Escandón 1242
NUESTRA SEÑORA DE LA VEGA
Villafranca del Cid/ Vilafranca del Maestrat
Alcanar
San Mateo de Gállego
Playa del Trabucador
Mosqueruela
Mora de Rubielos
Linares de Mora
Benassal
CUEVA DELS CIVILS
Càlig
La Puebla de Valverde
ST. JOAN DE PENYAGOLOSA
Vinaròs
Embalse de los Toranes
Albocácer/ Albocàsser
Santa Magdalena de Polpis
Benicarló
Camarena de la Sierra
Rubielos de Mora
Chodos/ Xodos
les Coves de Vinromà
Peñíscola/ Peníscola
Sarrión
Albentosa
Atzeneta del Maestrat
Castillo de Villamalefa
Vilanova d'Alcolea
Alcalá de Chivert/ Alcalà de Xivert
CASTELL DE XIVERT
Cabo de Irta
Olba
Lucena del Cid/ Llucena
La Pelechaneta/ Pelejaneta
Torreblanca
Manzanera
Cabanes
Alcocèber/ Alcossebre
Montanejos
Embalse Alcora
Barracas
la Pobla Tornesa
Torrenostra
Mijares
Viuda
Vilafamés
Alcora/ l'Alcora
Fuentes de Ayódar
Embalse María Cristina
Oropesa del Mar/ Orpesa
La Yesa
Borriol
Benicasim/ Benicàssim
Bejís
Viver
Onda
Andilla
Jérica
Castellón de la Plana/ Castelló de la Plana
Villanueva de los Infantes
Alcublas
Segorbe
Artana
Almazora/ Almassora
Altura
Villar del Arzobispo
Burriana/ Borriana
la Vall d' Uixó
Nules
Gátova
Casinos
GRUTA DE SANT JOSEP
Moncofa
VALÈNCIA
CARTOIXA DE PORTA COELI
Serra
Els Columbrets
Pedralba
Llíria
Turia
MON. ST. ESPERITU
la Pobla de Vallbona
Bétera
Sagunto/Sagunt
Puig
Puçol
Cheste
Riba-roja de Túria
Massamagrell
Chiva
Burjassot
Valencia
Paterna
Alboraya/Alboraia
Buñol
Torrent
VALENCIA
Turís/ Torís
Alfafar
Montroy/ Montroi
Catarroja
Golfo de Valencia
Picassent
El Saler
Silla
La Albufera
Xúquer
Benifaió
el Palmar
Sollana
Carlet
Alginet
El Perelló
L'Alcúdia
Palma-Mallorca
Navarrés
Algemesí
Sueca
Alberic
Cullera
Alzira
Sumacarcer
Carcaixent
Favara
Castelló de la Ribera
Eivissa/Ibiza
Tavernes de la Valldigna
Xàtiva
Xeraco
Xeresa
l'Olleria
Grao/el Grau
Benigànim
MONASTIR DE S. JERONIMO
Gandia
Ròtova
Albaida
Terrateig
Oliva
Puerto de Albaida 600
Muro de Alcoy/ Muro del Comtat
Pego
COSTA DEL AZAHAR
A7
E15
E6
V15
N420
N232
N234
N340
N225
N332
N330
N III
E901
C230
C235
C232
C223
C224
C225
C234
C3322
C3316
C320
C322
C3311
CS844
CS802
CS801
C2310
T331
N238

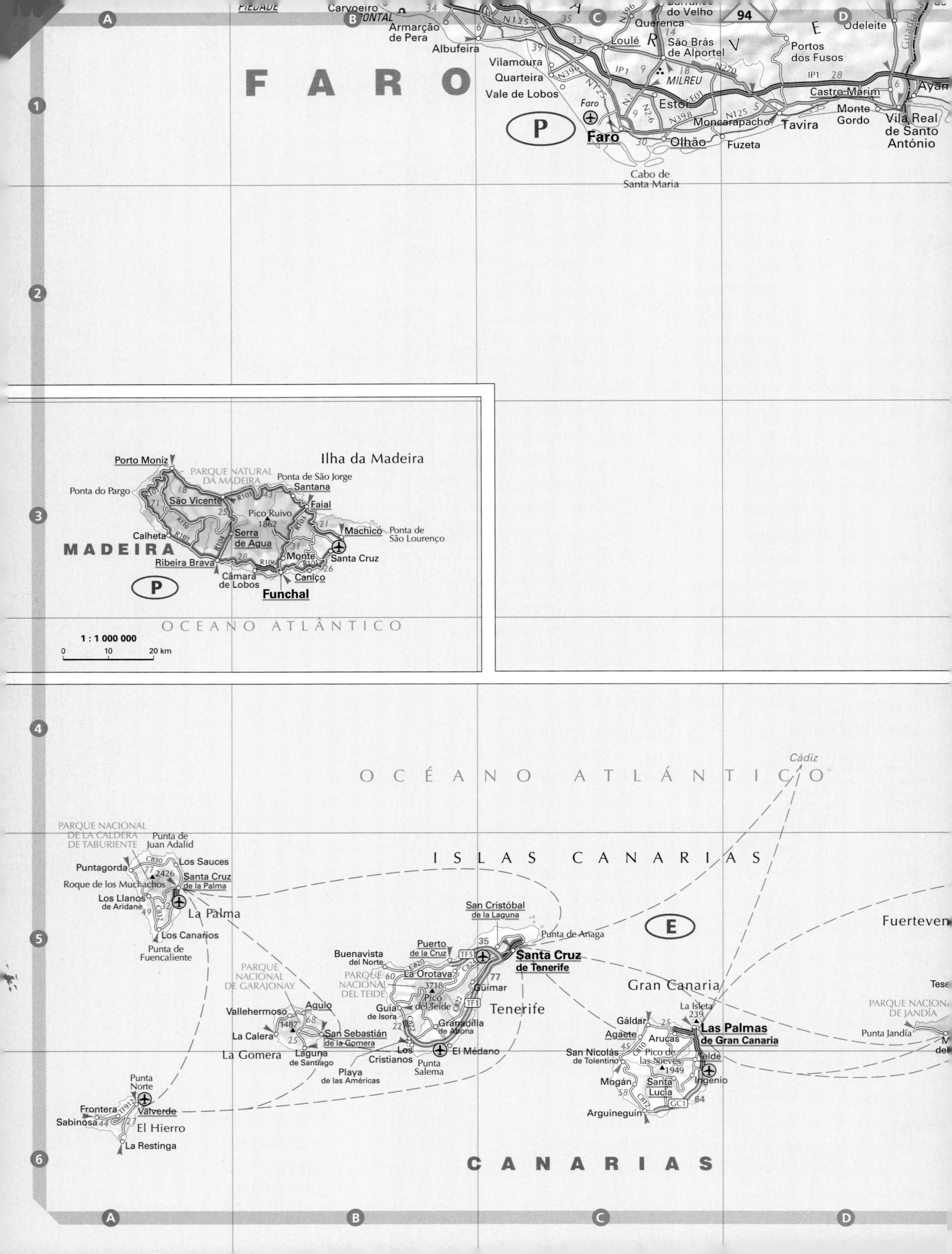
FARO
94
Armação de Pera
Albufeira
Vilamoura
Quarteira
Vale de Lobos
Loulé
Querença
São Brás de Alportel
MILREU
Estói
Faro
Olhão
Fuzeta
Moncarapacho
Tavira
Cabo de Santa Maria
Portos dos Fusos
Odeleite
Castro Marim
Monte Gordo
Vila Real de Santo António
P
Ilha da Madeira
Porto Moniz
PARQUE NATURAL DA MADEIRA
Ponta de São Jorge
Santana
Ponta do Pargo
São Vicente
Faial
Pico Ruivo 1862
Calheta
Serra de Agua
Machico
Ponta de São Lourenço
MADEIRA
Santa Cruz
Ribeira Brava
Monte
Câmara de Lobos
Caniço
Funchal
OCEANO ATLÂNTICO
1 : 1 000 000
0 10 20 km
OCÉANO ATLÁNTICO
Cádiz
ISLAS CANARIAS
PARQUE NACIONAL DE LA CALDERA DE TABURIENTE
Punta de Juan Adalid
Puntagorda
Los Sauces
Santa Cruz de la Palma
Roque de los Muchachos
Los Llanos de Aridane
La Palma
Los Canarios
Punta de Fuencaliente
San Cristóbal de la Laguna
Punta de Anaga
E
Fuerteventura
Puerto de la Cruz
Buenavista del Norte
Santa Cruz de Tenerife
La Orotava
PARQUE NACIONAL DEL TEIDE
Pico del Teide 3718
Güímar
PARQUE NACIONAL DE GARAJONAY
Tenerife
Gran Canaria
Vallehermoso
Agulo
Guía de Isora
La Calera
San Sebastián de la Gomera
Granadilla de Abona
La Gomera
Laguna de Santiago
Los Cristianos
El Médano
Playa de las Américas
Punta Salema
La Isleta
Gáldar
Agaete
Arucas
Las Palmas de Gran Canaria
San Nicolás de Tolentino
Pico de las Nieves 1949
Telde
Ingenio
Mogán
Santa Lucía
Arguineguín
PARQUE NACIONAL DE JANDÍA
Punta Jandía
Punta Norte
Frontera
Valverde
Sabinosa
El Hierro
La Restinga
CANARIAS

San Bartolomé de la Torre
Berrocal
95
El Garrobo
Venta El Alto
Castilblanco de los Arroyos
MULBA
Gibraleón
Beas
El Tumbalejo
Cartaya
Trigueros
Lepe
Aljaraque
La Antilla
Huelva
El Portil
San Juan del Puerto
Niebla
Bonares
Moguer
Palos de la Frontera
La Palma del Condado
Bollullos Par del Condado
Manzanilla
Aznalcóllar
Gerena
Burguillos
Guillena
Villaverde del Río
Cantillana
Villanueva del Río y Minas
Tocina
Alcalá del Río
La Rinconada
Brenes
Lora del Río
ITALICA
Sanlúcar la Mayor
La Algaba
S. ISIDORO DEL CAMPO
NECRÓPOLIS ROMANA
Punta Umbria
MONASTERIO DE LA RABIDA
Almonte
Pilas
SEVILLA
Sevilla
El Viso del Alcor
Carmona
Mazagón
NUESTRA SEÑORA DEL ROCIO
El Rocío
Villamanrique de la Condesa
Coria del Río
La Puebla del Río
Alcalá de Guadaira
Dos Hermanas
Mairena del Alcor
MARCHENILLA
M A R I S M A S
D E L
G U A D A L Q U I V I R
Villafranco del Guadalquivir
ASPERILLO 103
PARQUE NACIONAL DE DOÑANA
TORRE DE LA HIGUERA
LA HIGUERA
E
Los Palacios y Villafranca
Utrera
Paradas
Arahal
Los Molares
C O S T A D E L A L U Z
GOLFO DE CÁDIZ
Guadalquivir
Embalse de la Torre de Aguila
El Coronil
Morón de la Frontera
102
Lebrija
Las Cabezas de San Juan
AGUZADERA
La Encinilla y El Rubio
COTE
Montellano
Punta de Maladar
Trebujena
Sanlúcar de Barrameda
Chipiona
El Cuervo
Coripe
Espera
Puertoserrano
Bornos
Villamartín
JEREZ DE LA FRONTERA
Arcos de la Frontera
Rota
Santa Cruz de Tenerife
Las Palmas de Gran Canaria
Embalse de Bornos
Algodonales
Olvera
LA CARTUJA
MELGAREJO
La Barca de la Florida
Prado del Rey
Zahara
Embalse de Zahara
El Bosque
El Puerto de Santa María
Bahía de Cádiz
CÁDIZ
Embalse de Guadalcacín
SIERRA DE GRAZALEMA
Grazalema
ACINIPO
Algar
Puerto Real
Ubrique
FATIMA
Benaojón
BERROQUEJO
Embalse de Los Hurones
CUEVA DE LA PILETA
San Fernando
Paterna de Rivera
Medina-Sidonia
Chiclana de la Frontera
PARQUE
SERRANIA
Barrosa
La Sauceda
Alcalá de los Gazules
Gaucín
Igualeja
Roche
Embalse de Barbate
Cabo Roche
NATURAL
Conil de la Frontera
Benalup
Jimena de la Frontera
Casares
San Pedro de Alcántara
Vejer de la Frontera
CUEVA DEL TAJO DE LAS FIGURAS
DE LOS
Estepona
Guadalmina
Cabo de Trafalgar
Los Caños de Meca
Castellar de la Frontera
CASTILLO DE LA DUQUESA
Barbate
ALCORNOCALES
Punta de Chullera
Zahara de los Atunes
BAELO CLAUDIA
Los Barrios
San Roque
Torreguadiaro
Punta Mala
Punta Camarinal
North Front
La Línea de la Concepción
Algeciras
Gibraltar
GBZ
Bahía de Algeciras
Tarifa
Punta de Europa
Punta de la Tarifa
Estrecho de Gibraltar
Sète
TANGER
Ksar es-Seghir
Punta de la Almina
MA
Ceuta
E
Alegranza
Montaña Clara
Roque del Este
Graciosa
Orzola
Lanzarote
Haria
Tinajo
Teguise
PARQUE NACIONAL DE TIMANFAYA
San Bartolomé
Costa Teguise
Arrecife
Playa Blanca
Punta del Papagayo
Corralejo
Lobos
La Oliva
Puerto del Rosario
Antigua
Gran Tarajal
1 : 2 000 000
0 20 40 km

SIERRA NORTE
SIERRA DE HORNACHUELOS
96
MULBA
La Puebla de los Infantes
Hornachuelos
Embalse de la Breña
MEDINA AZAHARA
SANTO DOMINGO
Cerro Muriano
Adamuz
Montoro
Marmolejo
VIRGEN DE LA CABEZA
Villanueva del Río y Minas
ALMENARA
Embalse del Hornachuelo
Posadas
Almodóvar del Río
CÓRDOBA
El Carpio
Pedro Abad
Villa del Río
Lopera
Tocina
Lora del Río
Peñaflor
Palma del Río
Guadalcázar
Bujalance
Torres Cabrera
Fuente Palmera
Arjona
NECRÓPOLIS ROMANA
La Campana
La Carlota
Porcuna
Carmona
La Luisiana
Fernán Núñez
Santiago de Calatrava
MONCLOVA
Écija
La Rambla
Espejo
Castro del Río
Mairena del Alcor
Fuentes de Andalucía
Santaella
Montilla
Torredonjimeno
A N D A L U C
Aguilar de la Frontera
Nueva-Carteya
Baena
Embalse de Vadomojón
Paradas
La Lantejuela
Marchena
Doña Mencía
Arahal
El Rubio
Monturque
Luque
Alcaudete
CUEVA DE LOS MURCIÉLAGOS
Herrera
Cabra
La Puebla de Cazalla
Puente Genil
Castillo de Locubín
Carcabuey
Lucena del Cid/Llucena
Osuna
Estepa
Embalse de Cordobilla
ARACELI
Priego de Córdoba
El Coronil
Morón de la Frontera
Casariche
Alcalá la Real
LA MOTA
SIERRA DE YEGUAS
Alameda
Cuevas de San Marcos
Rute
Algarinejo
COTE
El Saucejo
La Roda de Andalucía
El Tejar
Embalse de Iznájar
Iznájar
Coripe
Sierra de Yeguas
Montefrío
Campillos
Puertoserrano
Mollina
Íllora
Pruna
CUEVA DE MENGA
Huétor Tájar
Algodonales
Olvera
Almargen
Cañete la Real
Embalse del Guadalteba-Guadalhorce
Loja
Salar
Moraleda de Zafayona
Pinos Puente
Embalse de Zahara
Alcalá del Valle
Antequera
Archidona
101
Cuevas del Becerro
El Bosque
SIERRA DE GRAZALEMA
ACINIPO
Valle de Abdalajís
1369
EL TORCAL
Embalse del Conde de Guadalhorce
GARGANTO DEL CHORRO
Castillo de Tajarja
Granada
Grazalema
Arriate
Ardales
Puerto de las Pedrizas 780
Ronda
Elburgo/Burgelu
Ventas de Zafarraya
Alhama de Granada
Ventas de Huelma
Benaojón
SERRANÍA DE RONDA
Casarabonela
Álora
Casabermeja
CUEVA DE LA PILETA
Puerto del Suspiro del Moro 860
Yunquera
Colmenar
Periana
Almogía
Tolox
Pizarra
Puerto del León 960
2065
Embalse de los Bermejales
Jayena
1918
Igualeja
LA CONCEPCIÓN
Gaucín
SIERRA DE ALMIJARA
Coín
Cártama
MÁLAGA
Albuñuelas
Embalse de la Concepción
Málaga
Rincón de la Victoria
Vélez-Málaga
Cómpeta
Ojén
Alhaurín el Grande
Alhaurín de la Torre
EL RETIRO
Bahía de Málaga
Torrox
Casares
San Pedro de Alcántara
Marbella
Benalmádena
Torremolinos
CUEVA DE NERJA
Torre del Mar
Estepona
Puerto Banús
Empúria-Brava
Mijas
Arroyo de la Miel-Benalmádena Costa
Torre
Nerja
Almuñécar
Guadalmina
Bahía de Marbella
Fuengirola
Punta de Torrox
BALCÓN DE EUROPA
CASTILLO DE LA DUQUESA
Calahonda-Chaparral
La Cala del Moral
Salobreña
Punta de Chullera
Torreguadiaro
Punta Mala
COSTA DEL SOL
Línea de la Concepción
Gibraltar
GBZ
Europa
Melilla
A B C D
1 2 3 4 5 6

E
F
G
H
97
104
1
2
3
4
5
6
Embalse del Rumblar
La Carolina
Santa Elena
Venta de los Santos
Génave
Riópar
Puente de Génave
Vilches
Baños de la Encina
Guarromán
Arquillinos
Santisteban del Puerto
Siles
CUEVA DE LOS CHORROS
Molinicos
Bailén
Linares
Navas de San Juan
Castellar
Sorihuela del Guadalimar
Beas de Segura
Orcera
Segura
Yeste
SANTUARIO DE GUADALUPE
N. S. DE LA ESTRELLA
Villanueva del Arzobispo
PARQUE NATURAL
Villanueva de la Reina
Embalse de la Fuensanta
Mengíbar
Rus
Sabiote
Villacarrillo
Hornos
Fuerte del Rey
Villagordo
Baeza
Úbeda
Torreperogil
Embalse del Tranco de Beas
DE LAS SIERRAS
SIERRA DE SEGURA
Embalse de la Novia
Mogón
Santiago de la Espada
Pontones
Nerpio
Santo Tomé
Embalse de Doña Aldonza
Pedro Andrés
CUEVAS DE NERPIO
SIERRA DE TAIBILLA
CUEVA DE LA GRAJA
Jaén
Jimena
Hornos de Peal
Peal de Becerro
SIERRA DE CAZORLA
SIERRA DE CAZORLA, SEGURA Y LAS VILLAS
Mancha Real
Jódar
Cazorla
La Guardia de Jaén
SIERRA MÁGINA
2167
Quesada
Puebla de Don Fadrique
El Moral
Archivel
E
1183 Puerto de Tiscar
PARQUE NATURAL DE LA SIERRA DE CASTRIL
Belmez de la Moraleda
Huesa
Valdepeñas de Jaén
Tiscar-Don Pedro
VIRGEN DE LA CABEZA
CUEVA DEL AGUA
Cabra del Santo Cristo
Castril
Topares
Campillo de Arenas
Huelma
Montejícar
Huéscar
Puerto de Carretero 1040
Guadahortuna
Alamedilla
Pozo Alcón
TÚTUGI
Galera
La Cañada de Cañepla
Campotejar
Villanueva de las Torres
Embalse del Negratín
Alcaide
Puerto de Onitar 1040
Pedro Martínez
Játar
María
Puerto el Zegri 1080
Piñar
Moreda
N. S. DE LA CABEZA
Baños de Alicún de las Torres
Vélez-Blanco
Iznalloz
Zújar
Cúllar
CUEVA DE LOS LETREROS
SIERRA HARANA
1931
Puerto Molinillo 1300
Darro
Vélez-Rubio
Baza
Chirivel
CASAS CUEVA
La Venta
SIERRA DE LAS ESTANCIAS
1390 Puerto de la Mora
Purullena
Caniles
Oria
GRANADA
Guadix
PARQUE NATURAL
2228 SANTA BÁRBARA
SIERRA DE BAZA
Güéjar Sierra
Jerez del Marquesado
Serón
Purchena
Olula del Río
Santa María de Nieva
La Zubia
Monachil
Sierra Nevada
Albox
PARQUE NATURAL
Padul
La Calahorra
Fiñana
Macael
Cantoria
Huércal-Overa
SIERRA NEVADA
3478
Mulhacén
3398
Pico Veleta
Puerto de la Ragua 2000
Escúllar
SIERRA DE LOS FILABRES
Albánchez
Abla
Velefique
Tahal
Cuevas del Almanzora
Lanjarón
Treveles
Lubrín
Vera
Órjiva
Cádiar
Gérgal
Uleila del Campo
Laujar de Andarax
Ugíjar
Canjáyar
Alcolea
Sorbas
Garrucha
CUEVA DE LOS MURCIÉLAGOS
SIERRA DE GÁDOR
Illar
CUEVA DE LOS MILLARES
Tabernas
Turre
Mojácar
Motril
2236
SIERRA DE ALHAMILLA
Lucainena de las Torres
Punta del Cabo
Albuñol
Berja
1359
Castell de Ferro
Gádor
Pechina
Níjar
Dalías
Venta del Pobre
Cabo Sacratif
Calahonda-Chaparral
La Rábita
Huércal de Almería
Viator
Campohermoso
Carboneras
Adra
El Ejido
Almería
PARQUE NATURAL DE CABO DE GATA-NÍJAR
Balanegra
Aguadulce
Agua Amarga
Guardias Viejas
Mojonera
Retamar
Roquetas de Mar
Golfo de Almería
Las Negras
Almerimar
Punta Polacra
Punta de los Baños
Cabo de Gata
Punta del Sabinal
SIERRA DE GATA
Los Escullos
San José
Cabo de Gata
Melilla

MURCIA
Murcia
Cartagena
Lorca
Elche/Elx
Alicante
Orihuela
Águilas
Mazarrón
Totana
Alhama de Murcia
Cieza
Jumilla
Yecla
Hellín
Caravaca
Cehegín
Mula
Molina de Segura
Torrevieja
San Javier
Mar Menor
La Manga del Mar Menor
Cabo de Palos
ISLAS HORMIGAS
Huércal-Overa
Vera
Mojácar
Carboneras
SIERRA DE ESPUÑA
SIERRA DE LA ALMENARA
SIERRA DE LA PILA
SIERRA DE TAIBILLA
COSTA BLANCA
BALEARS / BALEARES
Eivissa/Ibiza
Sant Antoni de Portmany
Santa Eulalia del Río/Santa Eulària des Riu
Sant Josep
Formentera
Sa Savina
Santa Ponça
Andraitx
Estellenchs
Banyalbufar

E
F
G
H
1
2
3
4
5
6
DE S. JERÓNIMO
Gandia
Rótova
Albaida
Terrateig
Oliva
Puerto de Albaida 600
Muro de Alcoy/ Muro del Comtat
Pego
Benimarfull
Ondara
Dénia
Cocentaina
les Rotes
Alcoy/ Alcoi
Benilloba
Orba
Cabo de San Antonio
Parcent
Collado de Rates
Puerto de Ares 966
Pedreguer
Xàbia
Guadalest
Gata de Gorgos
Puerto de la Carrasqueta 1020
Sella
Callosa d'en Sarrià
Teulada
Benissa
Cabo de la Nao
Punta de Moraira
Polop
CUEVA DE CANALOBRES
Finestrat
Altea
Calpe/Calp
Penyal d'Ifac
Alfàs
Busot
Benidorm
Villajoyosa/ la Vila Joiosa
el Campello
San Juan de Alicante/ Sant Joan d'Alacant
Playa de San Juán
ALICANTE/ALACANT
Cabo de las Huertas
B L A N C A
Eivissa/ Ibiza
Sa Conillera
Cala Tarida
Sant José/Sant Josep
Cala Vadella
Es Vedrá
Es Cubells
Cap Llentrisca
BALEARS / BALEARES
Punta de Sa Pe
Cap de Barbaría
Cap de Bajolí
Cala Morell
Cap de Cavalleria
Ciutadella de Menorca
Fornells
Cala Santandria
NAVETA DES TUDONS
COVA DE NA POLIDA
S'Arenal d'en Castell
Port d'Adaia
Cala Blanca
Ferreries
Es Mercadal
Cap de Favàritx
Son Xoriguer
Cala Galdana
MARE DE DÉU DEL TORO
Cap d'Artrutx
Sant Tomàs
Illa d'en Colom
Cala de Santa Galdana
Son Bou
Sant Lluís
Maó/ Mahón
Barcelona
Cala'n Porter
COVA D'EN XOROI
Menorca
Punta de S'Esperó
Villanueva de San Carlo
Cap d'En Font
Binibeca Vell
Algar
Punta Prima
Illa de l'Aire
Menorca
Punta Beca
El Port de Pollença
Cap de Formentor
cala Sa Calobra
MONESTIR DE LLUC
Pollença
Badia de Pollença
el Port/Sóller
PUIG MAJOR 1445
1348 MASSANELLA
COVES DE CAMPANET
Alcúdia
Cap des Pinar
Fornalutx
Deià
Sóller
1068 ALFABIA
Es Port d'Alcúdia
sa Pobla
Valldemossa
Badia d'Alcúdia
Inca
Can Picafort
Muro
Serra Nova
Santa Maria
Illa Ravena
Cap des Freu
Santa Margalida
PALMA DE MALLORCA
Sineu
Artà
Cala Ratjada
Petra
PARCO ZOOL.
COVES D'ARTA
Palma
Algaida
Vilafranca de Bonany
Costa de los Pins
Manacor
S'Arenal
Cala Millor
SANTUARI DE CURA
Punta de n'Amer
Llucmajor
Cala Moreia-Cala Morlanda
Cala Blava
COVES DETS HAMS
Porto Cristo
SANTUARI DE MONTI-SION
Felanitx
COVES DEL DRAC
Campos
SANT SALVADOR
Cales de Mallorca
Mallorca
Cala Pi
Porto Colom
Cap Blanc
Estanyol
Colònia de Sant Jordi
Cala d'Or
Santanyí
Cala Santanyí
Cap de Ses Salines
CUEVA AZUL
Illa des Conills
Cabrera
Cabrera
BALEARS / BALEARES
BALEARS / ISLAS BALEARES

67
68
St-Cirq-Lapopie
Cajarc
Montcuq
Lauzerte
Limogne-en-Quercy
Villeneuve
Montbazens
Marcillac-Vallon
Estaing
Espalion
Aubrac
St-Chély-d'Aubrac
St-Côme-d'Olt
Bozouls
TROU DE BOZOULS
CAUSSE DU COMTAL
Villefranche-de-Rouergue
Rignac
St-Geniez-d'O
Montpezat-de-Quercy
Molières
Caylus
Rieupeyroux
Aveyron
Rodez
Laissac
Moissac
Lafrançaise
Caussade
St-Antonin-Noble-Val
Najac
La Salvetat
Baraqueville
Pont-de-Salars
Sévérac-le-Château
Bois-du-Four
Montauban
Bruniquel
Laguépie
Cassagnes-Bégonhès
Salles-Curan
St-Beauzély
Montech
Cordes
Carmaux
Villefranche-de-Panat
Castelnau-de-Montmiral
Réquista
Millau
MONTPELLIER LE-VIE
Grisolles
Fronton
Villemur
Rabastens
Lisle-sur-Tarn
Gaillac
Albi
St-Juéry
Valence d'Albigeois
St-Rome-de-Tarn
MIDI-PYRÉNÉES
Grenade
Villefranche-d'Albigeois
Roquefort-sur-Soulzon
St-Jory
St-Sulpice
Alban
St-Sernin-sur-Rance
St-Affrique
Blagnac
Montastruc-la-Conseillère
Graulhet
Teillet
Colomiers
Lavaur
Réalmont
Montredon-Labessonnie
Belmont-sur-Rance
Camarès
Fondamente
TOULOUSE
Verfeil
Lautrec
Viane
Fayet
St-Paul-Cap-de-Joux
Lacaune
F
Castanet-Tolosan
Caraman
Puylaurens
Castres
MONTS DE LACAUNE
Brassac
Murat-sur-Vèbre
le Bousquet-d'Orb
Lunas
Muret
Vernet
Montgiscard
PARC NATUREL RÉGIONAL
DU HAUT LANGUEDOC
La Salvetat-sur-Agout
St-Gervais
85
Villefranche-de-Lauragais
Revel
Dourgne
Mazamet
MONTS DE L'ESPINOUSE
Bédarieux
Auterive
Nailloux
MONTAGNE NOIRE
Labastide-Rouairoux
Olargues
St-Pons-de-Thomières
Lamalou-les-Bains
Cintegabelle
PIC DE NOIRE
Salles-s.-l'Hers
Castelnaudary
Saissac
Saverdun
Mazères
St-Chinian
Cessenon-sur-Orb
Le Fossat
Cruzy
Bram
Alzonne
Caunes-Minervois
PROUILLE
OPPIDUM D'ENSERUNE
Fanjeaux
Béziers
Pailhès
Pamiers
Montréal
Carcassonne
Olonzac
Capestang
GROTTE DU MAS D'AZIL
Homps
Mirepoix
Capendu
Lézignan-Corbières
Coursan
Varilhes
Narbonne
Caudeval
Monze
Valras-P
Limoux
LANGUEDOC-ROUSSILLON
Foix
Laroque-d'Olmes
Lagrasse
Narbonne-Plage
Chalabre
Lavelanet
Villardebelle
ABB. DE FONTFROIDE
Gruissan
Nalzen
Puivert
Couiza
Durban-Corbières
Tarascon-sur-Ariège
Montségur
Sigean
Mouthoumet
GROTTE DE NIAUX
PIC DE BARTHÉLEMY
Quillan
CORBIÈRES
Port-la-Nouvelle
GROTTE DE LOMBRIVES
Les Cabannes
Belcaire
Tuchan
Col de Chioula
Axat
St-Paul-de-Fenouillet
CHÂT. DE QUÉRIBUS
Maury
Cap Leucate
Leucate
Ax-les-Thermes
PIC DE TARBEZOU
Usson-les-Bains
Aude
Salses-le-Château
Étang de Leucate
Port-Leucate
AND
PIC DE CABAILLERE
l'Hospitalet-l'Andorre
Sournia
Estagel
Rivesaltes
Port-Barcarès
Soldeu
Port d'Envalira
Col de Puymorens
Formiguères
Baixas
Canillo
Encamp
Les Escaldes
Pas de la Casa
PIC CARLIT
BELVÉDÈRE
Col de la Quillane
Prades
ST.-MICHEL-DE-CUXA
Millas
PERPIGNAN
Font-Romeu
Villefranche-de-Conflent
Vinça
Thuir
Canet-Plage
Olette
Vernet-les-Bains
Mont-Louis
Llivia
Puigcerdà
93
St-Cyprien-Plage
Elne
A
B
C
D
1
2
3
4
5
6

Mende
Privas
Aubenas
Montélimar
Alès
Orange
Carpentras
Avignon
NÎMES
MONTPELLIER
Arles
Sète
Salon-de-Provence
Martigues
MARSEILLE
Aigues-Mortes
Stes-Maries-de-la-Mer
Cavaillon
Nyons
Bagnols-sur-Cèze
Uzès
PONT DU GARD
PARC NATUREL RÉGIONAL DE CAMARGUE
GOLFE DU LION
CAUSSE MÉJEAN
CHAÎNE DES ALPILLES
LES CALANQUES
Cassis
La Ciotat

A
B
C
D
69
DU VERCORS
Sur-Drôme
Privas
789 Col de l'Escrinet
Baix
Cruas
Loriol-sur-Drôme
Crest
Die
Clelles
Mens
ROUTE
Corps
N.-D. DE LA SALETTE
Valbonnais
MASSIF DES ÉCRINS
3914 MT PELVOUX
Ailefroide
NATIONAL
Vallouise
la Chapelle-en-Valgaudemar
St-Firmin
L'Argentière-la-Bessée
Aubenas
1
Rochemaure
Le Teil
Villeneuve-de-Berg
Montélimar
Roubion
Saou
Saillans
Châtillon-en-Diois
1176 Col de la Croix Haute
1318 Col de Grimone
Lus-la-Croix-Haute
Col du Festre 1441
NAPOLÉON
St-Bonnet-en-Champsaur
DES ÉCRINS
3327 SOUMT. DROUVET
Orcières
la Bégude-de-Mazenc
Bourdeaux
Pradelle
Luc-en-Diois
Drôme
St-Julien-en-Beauchêne
Col Bayard 1248
St-Clément-sur-Durance
Viviers
Donzère
Dieulefit
MONASTÈRE DE LA TRAPPE D'AIGUEBELLE
AVEN DE MARZAL
Bourg-St-Andéol
Pierrelatte
Grignan
La Motte-Chalancon
1180 Col de Cabre
Aspres-sur-Buëch
Veynes
Gap
La Bâtie-Neuve
Chorges
Valréas
GROTTE DE ROCHECOURBIÈRE
Rémuzat
Eygues
Serres
Rosans
Embrun
BARRY
Nyons
Buëch
PROVENCE
Savines-le-Lac
St-Vincent-les-Forts
2
Pont-St-Esprit
Bollène
Aigues
Monêtier-Allemont
Tallard
Durance
Le Lauzet-Ubaye
St-Auban-sur-l'Ouvèze
Laragne-Montéglin
la Motte-du-Caire
ANC. BATTERIE
Ubaye
Seyne
Vaison-la-Romaine
Buis-les-Baronnies
Cèze
Bagnols-sur-Cèze
Orange
Ouvèze
Malaucène
Montbrun-les-Bains
MT VENTOUX
1909
Séderon
Col de Maure 1347
Le Vernet
Authon
Col d'Allos 2250
Rhône
Beaumes-de-Venise
Noyers-sur-Jabron
Sisteron
GROTTE DE ST-VINCENT
Col du Labouret 1240
107
Roquemaure
Châteauneuf-du-Pape
Carpentras
GORGES DE LA NESQUE
Sault
1826 MONTAGNE DE LURE
N.-D. DE LURE
ALPES-
La Javie
Bléone
Allos
Colmars
Sorgues
Villeneuve
Avignon
3
ABB. DE ST-ROMAN
Pernes-les-Fontaines
MONTS DE VAUCLUSE
Banon
St-Etienne-les-Orgues
Château-Arnoux
Beauvezer
2323 CHEVAL BLANC
Fontaine-de-Vaucluse
St-Saturnin-lès-Apt
PRIEURÉ GANAGOBIE
Peyruis
Digne-les-Bains
Noves
L'Isle-sur-la-Sorgue
Gordes
Forcalquier
F
Mézel
Tarascon
Roussillon
Coulon
Apt
La Brillanne
Bras-d'Asse
St-André-les-Alpes
LES ANTIQUES
St-Rémy-de-Provence
Cavaillon
CHAÎNE DES ALPILLES
Bonnieux
FORT DE BUOUX
Oraison
Voix
Barrême
Fontvieille
Arles
Les Baux-de-Provence
Orgon
Sénas
1125 MONTAGNE DU LUBERON
Manosque
CÔTE-D'AZUR
Valensole
Moustiers-Ste-Marie
Col des Leques 1146
Castellane
Eyguières
SILVACANE
Cadenet
Ste-Tulle
Gréoux-les-Bains
Riez
1931
Gorges du Verdon
ROUTE
Salon-de-Provence
Lambesc
Pertuis
Vinon-sur-Verdon
Verdon
Col d'Illoire 964
Lac de Ste-Croix
La Palud-sur-Verdon
Corniche Sublime
4
Mas Thibert
Miramas
St-Chamas
Durance
Peyrolles
Meyrargues
Montmeyan
Comps-sur-Artuby
Istres
Berre-l'Etang
ST. BLAISE
Rians
Aix-en-Provence
Vauvenargues
Tavernes
Aups
Montferrat
Fayence
Fos-sur-Mer
Port-de-Bouc
Marseille/Provence
Rognac
Barjols
Salernes
St-Louis-du-Rhône
Martigues
Marignane
Gardanne
Cotignac
Bagnols-en-Forêt
St-Maximin-la-Ste-Baume
Draguignan
Carro
Cap Couronne
Trets
Carcès
Lorgues
Les Arcs
Le Muy
Carry-le-Rouet
Allauch
Tourves
ABB. DU THORONET
Vidauban
CHÂTEAU D'IF
Aubagne
994 ST PILON
Nans-les-Pins
Brignoles
La Roquebrussanne
Le Luc
NOTRE-DAME DE-LA-ROQUETTE
Fréjus
5
MARSEILLE
Gémenos
Signes
Besse-sur-Issole
St-Aygulf
Cap Croisette
LES CALANQUES
Cassis
Puget-Ville
La Garde-Freinet
Ste-Maxime
Val d'Esc.
Ile de Riou
La Ciotat
Le Beausset
801 MT CAUME
Cuers
Grimaud
Beauvallon
Port-Grimaud
Les Lecques
Gapeau
MASSIF DES MAURES
Cogolin
St-Tropez
Bandol
MT FARON
Solliès-Pont
Sanary-sur-Mer
Bormes-les-Mimosas
La Croix-Valmer
Six-Fours-les-Plages
Ile des Embiez
La Seyne
TOULON
Hyères
Cap Camarat
N.-D. DU MAI
Carqueiranne
Cap Sicié
Cap Cépet
La Capte
Rayol
Cavalière
Aiguebelle
Le Lavandou
Cavalaire-sur-Mer
Tanger
Tunis
Bastia
L'Ile-Rousse
Calvi
Ajaccio
Propriano
Porto Torres
Giens
Cap Bénat
6
Porquerolles
Port-Cros
Ile de Porquerolles
Ile de Port-Cros
Ile du Levant
PARC NATIONAL DE PORT-CROS
ILES D'HYÈRES
A
B
C
D

PIEMONTE
TORINO
Moncalieri
Collegno
Orbassano
Piossasco
Perosa Argentina
Sestriere
Cesana Torinese
Claviere
Montgenèvre
Col de Montgenèvre 1850
Prali
Pinerolo
Airasca
Stupinigi
Chieri
Castelnuovo Don Bosco
VEZZOLANO
SANTUARIO DI CREA
Moncalvo
Vignale Monferrato
Carignano
Santena
Poirino
Villanova d'Asti
Carmagnola
Villafranca Piemonte
San Damiano d'Asti
Asti
ALESSANDRIA
Fubine
Col d'Izoard 2360
Aiguilles
Abriès
Bobbio Pellice
Torre Pellice
Arvieux
Château-Queyras
L'Echalp
Cavour
Bagnolo Piemonte
Barge
Moretta
Racconigi
Sommariva del Bosco
Canale
Castellazzo Bormida
PARC NAT. REG. DU QUEYRAS
Guillestre
St-Véran
Crissolo
BELVEDERE DEL CIRQUE
N. D. DE CLAUSIS
Pontechianale
M VISO 3841
Paesana
ABB. DI STAFFARDA
Saluzzo
Bra
Alba
Agliano
Santo Stefano Belbo
Nizza Monferrato
Cassine
Canelli
Vars
Casteldelfino
Savigliano
Cherasco
Col de Vars 2109
MT CHAMBEYRON 3389
Sampéyre
Verzuolo
Costigliole Saluzzo
Acqui Terme
St-Paul
Stroppo
Acceglio
Fossano
Busca
Roccaverano
Ovada
Larche
Col de Larche/Colle della Maddalena 1994
Centallo
Cortemilia
Molare
Dogliani
Barcelonnette
Argentera
Dronero
Caraglio
Carrù
Rossiglione
Castelmagno
Morozzo
Murazzano
Piana Crixia
Pian Castagna
Campo
Col de Restefond/La Bonette 2802
Cúneo
Mondovi
Ceva
Cairo Montenotte
Sassello
Col del Giovo 516
Pontinvrea
Col de la Cayolle 2326
Bagni di Vinadio
Vinádio
Boves
Borgo San Dalmazzo
SANTUARIO DI VICOFORTE
Voltri
Arenzano
St-Etienne-de-Tinée
SANTUARIO DI SANT'ANNA
Chiusa di Pesio
Terme di Lurisia
Millesimo
Carcare
Varazze
Auron
Isola
Colle della Lombarda/Col de la Lombarde 2350
CERTOSA DI PESIO
Frabosa Soprana
Colle dei Giovetti 912
Albissola Marina
Celle Lígure
Savona
PARC NATIONAL DU MERCANTOUR
Terme di Valdieri
ARGENTERA 3297
Limone Piemonte
Bossea
Vado Lígure
Col de la Couillole 1678
Isola 2000
Colle di Tenda/Col de Tende 1321
TRAFORO DEL COLLE DI TENDA
M MONGIOIE 2630
Garéssio
Colle San Bernardo 957
Valberg
Beuil
St-Sauveur-sur-Tinée
Le Boréon
Ormea
Noli
Spotorno
St-Martin-Vésubie
Tende
Col St-Martin 1500
Colle di Nava 941
GROTTE DI TOIRANO
Finale Lígure
Pietra Lígure
Loano
Gorges de Daluis
Gorges du Cians
Entrevaux
Puget-Théniers
Roquebillière
Monesi
NOTRE DAME DES FONTAINES
Pieve di Teco
Lantosque
Col de Turini 1607
Triora
Villars-sur-Var
N. D. DE MIRACLES
Saorge
Breil-sur-Roya
Montalto Ligure
Albenga
Alássio
Laiguéglia
Peïra-Cava
Col de Brouis 879
Pigna
Roquesteron
Col de Braus 1002
Levens
Sospel
Dolceácqua
Cervo
Diano Marina
L'Escarène
Gréolières
Taggia
Imperia
Col de Vence 970
Vence
Le Bar
NICE
La Turbie
Menton
Ventimíglia
Bordighera
Ospedaletti
San Remo
St-Paul
Grasse
Cagnes-sur-Mer
Cote d'Azur
Villefranche
Beaulieu-sur-Mer
St-Jean-Cap-Ferrat
Cap d'Ail
Monaco
Monte-Carlo
Roquebrune-Cap-Martin
MC
Mougins
Villeneuve-Loubet
Antibes
Juan-les-Pins
Cap d'Antibes
Golfe-Juan
Îles de Lérins
Cannes
La Napoule-Plage
Théoule
Le Trayas
Anthéor
RIVIERA DI PONENTE
CÔTE D'AZUR
Bastia
L'Ile-Rousse
Calvi
Ajaccio
Propriano
70
71
110
E
F
G
H
1
2
3
4
5
6

71
Trino
Casale Monferrato
Zeme
Tromello
Candia Lomellina
Garlasco
CERTOSA DI PAVIA
Sant'Angelo Lodigiano
Lodi
S. MARIA DI BRESSANORO
Verolanuova
Manérbio
Leno
Castelleone
Soresina
Pontevico
Isorella
Pavia
Lomello
Torre Beretti
Miradolo Terme
S. Colombano al Lambro
Casalpusterlengo
Castelverde
Gambara
Vignale Monferrato
Mede
Sannazzaro de' Burgondi
Codogno
Pizzighettone
Vescovato
Valenza
Stradella
Cremona
Canneto sull'Oglio
Fubine
S. Salvatore Monferrato
Sale
Broni
Castel San Giovanni
Piádena
Castelnuovo Scrivia
Casteggio
San Daniele Po
San Giovanni in Croce
ALESSANDRIA
Voghera
S. Maria della Versa
Borgonovo Val Tidone
PIACENZA
Caorso
Cortemaggiore
Roccabianca
Castellazzo Bormida
Tortona
Salice Terme
Pianello Val Tidone
Agazzano
Grazzano Visconti
Carpaneto Piacentino
Busseto
Casalmaggiore
Sissa
Fiorenzuola d'Arda
Soragna
Nizza Monferrato
SANT'ALBERTO DI BUTRIO
Rivergaro
Passo del Penice 1149
Ponte dell'Olio
Castell'Arquato
CHIARAVALLE DELLA COLOMBA
Colorno
Cassine
Garbagna
Varzi
Fontanellato
Fidenza
San Sebastiano Curone
Lugagnano Val d'Arda
Novi Ligure
VELLEIA
Salsomaggiore Terme
Acqui Terme
Caldirola
Bóbbio
Bettola
Noceto
Tabiano Bagni
PARMA
Castelletto d'Orba
Gavi
Farini
Ovada
Arquata Scrivia
Pellegrino Parmense
Mornese
Montaldo di Cosola
Sant'Andrea Bagni
Collécchio
Molare
CAST. DORIA
Monticelli Terme
Ronco Scrivia
Ottone
Ferriere
Fornovo di Taro
Rossiglione
Busalla
Carrega Ligure
Varsi
Pian Castagna
Campo Ligure
Bardi
CASTELLO DI TORRECHIARA
109
Sassello
Col del Giovo 516
Pontedecimo
Torriglia
Montebruno
1799
M. MAGGIORASCA
Langhirano
San Polo d'Enza
LIGURIA
Passo della Scoffera 674
S. Stefano d'Aveto
Bedonia
Borgo Val di Taro
CASTELLO DI CANOSSA
Voltri
Pegli
Passo della Cisa 1039
Berceto
Arenzano
ABB. DI BORZONE
EMILIA
Cristoforo Colombo
GÉNOVA
Passo di Cento Croci 1055
Albissola Marina
Varazze
Celle Ligure
Nervi
Passo di Bocco 956
Comiglio
Rapallo
Savona
Camogli
Pontremoli
PIETRA BISMANTOVA
Vado Ligure
Santa Margherita Ligure
BASILICA DEI FIESCHI
Varese Ligure
SAN FRUTTUOSO
Portofino
Zeri
Bagnone
Busana
Spotorno
Chiavari
Lavagna
Cavi
Licciana Nardi
Passo del Bracco 613
Brugnato
Sestri Levante
1261
1572
Passo di Pradarena
Finale Ligure
RIVIERA DI PONENTE
Monéglia
Fivizzano
Passo del Cerreto
2121
M. CUSNA
Bonassola
Aulla
Monterosso al Mare
SAN PELLEGRINO IN ALPE
Lévanto
Vernazza
Riomaggiore
Piazza al Serchio
RIVIERA DI LEVANTE
Sarzana
ALPI APUANE
LA SPÉZIA
Portovenere
Lerici
1946
Carrara
Castelnuovo di Garfagnana
Tūnis
Barcelona
Bastia
Calvi
Ajaccio
Porto Torres
Olbia
Arbatax
Cagliari
Palermo
Marina di Carrara
Massa
Fornaci di Barga
Marina di Massa
Seravezza
GROTTA DEL VENTO
Pietrasanta
Forte dei Marmi
Pescaglia
Marina di Pietrasanta
Camaiore
Lido di Camaiore
Viaréggio
Lucca
GOLFO DI GÉNOVA
Olbia
Torre del Lago Puccini
Lago di Massaciúccoli
Migliarino
Gombo
PISA
Marina di Pisa
Tirrénia
Galileo Galilei
LIVORNO
Capraia
Bastia
Collesalvetti
Olbia
Golfo Aranci
Cagliari
Palermo
Ísola di Gorgona
Quercianella
Rosignano
Castiglioncello
Rosignano Solvay
114

PADOVA
VENÉZIA
Mantova
Chióggia
Rovigo
FERRARA
Carpi
MODENA
BOLOGNA
RAVENNA
Imola
Faenza
FORLÌ
CESENA
RÍMINI
San Marino
Pistóia
Prato
FIRENZE
Empoli
Arezzo
TOSCANA
EMILIA-ROMAGNA
San Gimignano
Volterra

73
116
111
A
B
C
D
1
2
3
4
5
6
Mirano
Burano
Lido di Jésolo
Murano
Cavallino
VENÉZIA
Lido di Venézia
Strà
Dolo
Mira
Albignasego
Piove di Sacco
Bovolenta
Laguna Véneta
Bacchiglione
Pontelongo
Conselve
Chióggia
Sottomarina
Bagnoli di Sopra
Cavárzere
Anguillara Veneta
Rosolina Mare
Ádria
Loreo
Albarella
Contarina
Porto Levante
Táglio di Po
Porto Tolle
Pila
Bocche del Po della Pila
Ariano nel Polésine
DELTA DEL PO
Mésola
Scardovari
Codigoro
ABB. DI POMPOSA
Gnocchetta
Massa Fiscaglia
Gorino Veneto
Bocca del Po delle Tolle
Bocche del Po di Gnocca
Bocca del Po di Goro
Migliarino
Lagosanto
Lido delle Nazioni
Ostellato
Comácchio
Lido di Pompòsa
Porto Garibaldi
NECROPOLI DI SPINA
Lido degli Estensi
Lido di Spina
Reno
Alfonsine
Marina Romea
Porto Corsini
Marina di Ravenna
STRADA ROMEA
Bagnacavallo
Punta Marina
RAVENNA
Russi
SANT APOLLINARE IN CLASSE
Milano Marittima
Cérvia
FORLÌ
Forlimpopoli
Cesenático
Bertinoro
Bellária
I
Meldola
CESENA
Igea Marina
Savignano sul Rubicone
Santarcángelo di Romagna
RÍMINI
Civitella di Romagna
Miramare
Roncofreddo
Riccione
Mercato Saraceno
Verucchio
San Marino
RSM
Cattolica
Gabicce Mare
Sársina
San Leo
Pésaro
Novaféltria
Mercatino Conca
Morciano di Romagna
MONTEFELTRO
MONTE FUMAIOLO 1407
Pennabilli
Montécchio
Fano
Macerata Féltria
Madonna del Ponte
Carpegna
Fóglia
Torrette di Fano
Marotta
Badia Tedalda
Sassocorvaro
Mombaroccio
CONVENTO DI MONTEFIORENTINO
VIA FLAMINIA
Urbino
Senigállia
Passo di Viamaggio 983
Sant'Angelo in Vado
Fermignano
Fossombrone
Mondolfo
Urbánia
Metáuro
Marzocca
Corinaldo
Acqualagna
Falconara Marittima
San Lorenzo in Campo
Ostra
ANCONA
Chiaravalle
San Giustino
Apécchio
Piobbico
Cagli
Pergola
Serra dè Conti
SANTA MARIA DI PORTONOVO
BADIA DI SAN PIETRO
Arcévia
Jesi
Santa Maria
Sirolo
Peiraías
Al Iskandarīyah
İzmir
Kérkyra
Igoumenítsa
Pátra
Split
Durrës
Savudrija
Portorož
Koper
Umag
Buje
GROŽNJAN
Livade
Istarske Toplice
Mirna
Novigrad
Vižinada
Motovun
Poreč
Pazin
Baderna
Gračišće
Vrsar
Limski Kanal
Žminj
Kanfanar
Rovinj
Crveni Otok
Svetvinčenat
Barban
Bale
Vodnjan
NAC. PARK
Brijuni
Pula
Medulin
Rt Kamenjak

113
74
SLO
Karlovac
Rijeka
Opatija
Lovran
Matulji
Podgrad
Rupa
Gerovo
NAC. PARK RISNJAK
1528 RISNJAK
Banjaloka
Brod na Kupi
Delnice
Lokve
Skrad
Kupjak
Vrbovsko
Bosanci
Netretić
Duga Resa
Kupa (Kolpa)
Jamnička Kiselica
Pokupsko
Tušilović
Bović
Generalski Stol
Gvozd
Glina
Vojnić
PETROVA GORA
Ogulin
Veljun
Velika Kladuša
Mrežnica
Korana
Dobra
Bakar
Kraljevica
Bakarski Z.
Mrkopalj
1533 BIJELOLASICA
Jasenak
Mošćenička Draga
Mošćenice
Črišnjeva
Omišalj
Rijecki Zaljev
Voz
Crikvenica
Selce
Mosune
Novi Vinodolski
Josipdol
1396 UČKA
Vranja
Plomin
Labin
Rabac
Brestova
Porozina
Beli
Malinska
Šilo
Vrbnik
Krk
Baška
VELIKA KAPELA
MALA KAPELA
Plaški
Slunj
Jezerane
Koromačno
Cres
Valbiska
Senj
Žuta Lokva
HR
Saborsko
Rakovica
BiH
Lubarda
Jezersko
Cazin
Drežnik-Grad
NAC. PARK PLITVIČKA JEZERA
Plitvička jezera
Plitvice
Ostrožac
Pernat
Plavnik
Prvić
Jurjevo
LUBENICE
Vranski Jez
Cres
Vrana
Sv Grgur
Goli
Gusic Jezero
Otočac
Zalužnica
Babin Potok
Ličko Lešće
Plitvički Ljeskovac
Prijeboj
Bihać
SOKOLAC
Ripač
Gudavac
Zeča
Lopar
Starigrad
Devčići
Kampor
Rab
Osor
588
Jablanac
Lipovo Polie
KRBAVA
Vrelo
Korenica
Unije
Lun
Štirovača
Perušić
Bunić
154
Punta Križa
Ćunski
Lošinj
Stara Novalja
Prizna
Klanac
Lički Osik
Vrtoče
Susak
Mali Losinj
Veli Losinj
Novalja
Stara vrata 927
Baške Ostarije
Karlobag
Gospić
Udbina
Donji Lapac
Ilovik
Škrda
Maunski Kanal
Maun
Olib
Pag
Brušane
Lukovo Šugarje
Medak
Jadova
Lika
Gornji Lapac
Doljani
Silba
Tribanj Kruščica
NAC. PARK PAKLENICA
Gornja Ploča
Donja Suvaja
Bruvno
Premuda
Škarda
Ist
Virsko More
1758 VAGANSKI VRH
MANTIA PEĆ
Sveti Rok
Vir
Miletići
Starigrad Paklenica
Gračac
Mali Alan Prolaz 1045
Molat
Split
Privlaka
Nin
Donje Petrčane
Posedarje
Maslenica
Obrovac
CEROVAČKE SPILJE
Sučevici
Sestrunj
Novigrad
Kaštel Žegarski
Zrmanja
Božava
Ugljan
Zadar
Donji Zemunik
Medvida
Ervenik
Brbinj
Iž
Preko
Sukošan
ASSERIA
Benkovac
Padjene
Srednji Kanal
Zadarski Kanal
Knin
Dugi Otok
Zaglav
Sali
Pašman
Biograd
Vrana
Kistanje
Oklaj
Pakoštane
Tkon
Bribirske Mostine
1148 V. PROMINA
Vransko Jezero
NAC. PARK KRKA
Krka
Kornat
Žut
Murter
Pirovac
Skradin
Visovačko Jezero
NAC. PARK KORNATI
Tisno
Prukljansko Jezero
SKRADINSKI BUK
Lozovac
Lavsa
Vodice
Šibenik
Kakan
Zablaće
Vrpolje
Zlarin
Krapanj
Žirje
117
Primošten
Prapatnica

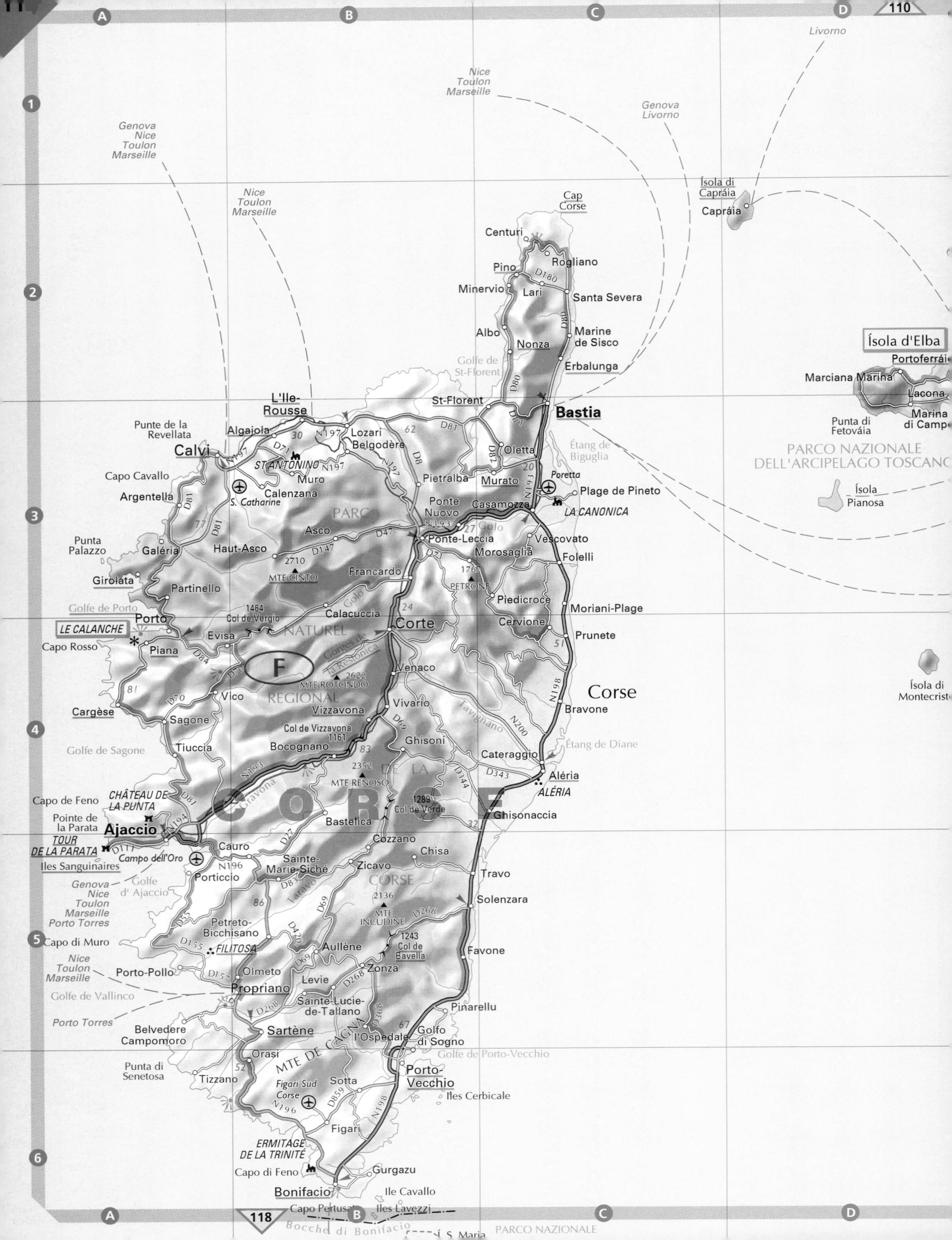
Livorno
Nice
Toulon
Marseille
Genova
Livorno
Genova
Nice
Toulon
Marseille
Nice
Toulon
Marseille
Ísola di Capráia
Capráia
Cap Corse
Centuri
Rogliano
Pino
Minervio
Lari
Santa Severa
Albo
Nonza
Marine de Sisco
Erbalunga
Golfe de St-Florent
Ísola d'Elba
Portoferraio
Marciana Marina
Lacona
Marina di Campo
Punta di Fetovàia
PARCO NAZIONALE DELL'ARCIPELAGO TOSCANO
Ísola Pianosa
St-Florent
Bastia
L'Ile-Rousse
Punte de la Revellata
Algajola
Calvi
Lozari
Belgodère
Oletta
Étang de Biguglia
ST ANTONINO
Muro
Calenzana
Capo Cavallo
Argentella
S. Catharine
Pietralba
Murato
Poretta
Plage de Pineto
Ponte Nuovo
Casamozza
LA CANONICA
PARC
Asco
Ponte-Leccia
Vescovato
Punta Palazzo
Galéria
Haut-Asco
Morosaglia
Folelli
2710
MTE CINTO
Francardo
1767
PETRONE
Girolata
Partinello
Piedicroce
Moriani-Plage
Golfe de Porto
1464
Col de Vergio
Calacuccia
Porto
Corte
Cervione
LE CALANCHE
Evisa
NATUREL
Prunete
Capo Rosso
Piana
Gorges de la Restonica
F
Venaco
2622
MTE ROTONDO
Vico
REGIONAL
Vivario
Corse
Cargèse
Vizzavona
Bravone
Sagone
Col de Vizzavona
1161
Ghisoni
Tiuccia
Bocognano
Golfe de Sagone
Étang de Diane
Cateraggio
2352
MTE RENOSO
DE LA
Aléria
ALÉRIA
Capo de Feno
CHÂTEAU DE LA PUNTA
1289
Col de Verde
CORSE
Ghisonaccia
Pointe de la Parata
Ajaccio
Bastelica
TOUR DE LA PARATA
Cauro
Cozzano
Chisa
Campo dell'Oro
Iles Sanguinaires
Sainte-Marie-Siché
Zicavo
Travo
Genova
Nice
Toulon
Marseille
Porto Torres
Golfe d' Ajaccio
Porticcio
CORSE
2136
MTE INCUDINE
Solenzara
Petreto-Bicchisano
1243
Col de Bavella
Capo di Muro
FILITOSA
Aullène
Favone
Nice
Toulon
Marseille
Porto-Pollo
Olmeto
Zonza
Levie
Propriano
Golfe de Valinco
Sainte-Lucie-de-Tallano
Pinarellu
Porto Torres
Belvedere Campomoro
Sartène
MTE DE CAGNA
L'Ospedale
Golfo di Sogno
Golfe de Porto-Vecchio
Punta di Senetosa
Orasi
Porto-Vecchio
Tizzano
Sotta
Figari Sud Corse
Iles Cerbicale
Figari
ERMITAGE DE LA TRINITÉ
Capo di Feno
Gurgazu
Bonifacio
Ile Cavallo
Capo Pertusato
Iles Lavezzi
Bocche di Bonifacio
Í. S. Maria
PARCO NAZIONALE
Ísola di Montecristo

Volterra
San Gimignano
Castellina in Chianti
111
Bucine
Arezzo
Anghiari
Città di Castello
Riparbella
Colle di Val d'Elsa
Cécina
Saline di Volterra
TORRE DI MONTEMICCIOLI
Monteriggioni
TOSCANA
Civitella in Val di Chiana
Morra
Forte di Bibbiona
Bibbiona
Pomarance
MUSEO DELLA GEOTERMIA
Siena
Pianella
Castelnuovo Berardenga
Monte San Savino
Lucignano
Castiglion Fiorentino
COLLINE METALLIFERE
Larderello
Bolgheri
Castagneto Carducci
Canneto
Castelnuovo di Val di Cecina
Monteroni d'Arbia
LE CRETE
Asciano
Foiano di Chiana
Cortona
Umbertide
Marina di Castagneto-Donorático
Sinalunga
Mercatale
Monterotondo Marittimo
ABBAZIA DI S. GALGANO
ABBAZIA DI MONTE OLIVETO MAGGIORE
Passignano sul Trasimeno
San Vincenzo
Suvereto
Monticiano
Murlo
Torrita di Siena
Buonconvento
Castiglione del Lago
Lago Trasimeno
Magione
Massa Marittima
VIA CASSIA
Montepulciano
PERUGIA
Montalcino
Pienza
NECROPOLI ETRUSCA
Corciano
TOMBE ETRUSCHE
Populónia
VIA AURELIA
Roccastrada
Civitella Paganico
San Quirico d'Orcia
Bagno Vignoni
Chianciano Terme
Chiusi
Piombino
Follónica
Golfo di Follónica
Ribolla
ABBAZIA DI SANT'ANTIMO
Castigliole d'Orcia
Sarteano
Cetona
UMBRIA
Tavernelle
Í. Palmaiola
Cavo
Í. Cerboli
Canale di Piombino
Cinigiano
Castel del Piano
Abbadia San Salvatore
Città della Pieve
Punta Ala
NECROPOLI ETRUSCHE
ROSELLE
Arcidosso
MT AMIATA
Marsciano
VOLTERRAIO
Porto Azzurro
Capolíveri
Punta dei Ripalti
Castiglione della Pescáia
Grosseto
Roccalbegna
San Casciano dei Bagni
San Venanzo
Ficulle
Marina di Grosseto
Acquapendente
Orvieto
Lago di Corbara
Marina di Alberese
TORRE DELL'UCCELLINA
Scansano
Sorano
San Lorenzo Nuovo
Magliano in Toscana
Saturnia
TERME DI SATURNIA
Bolsena
TOMBE ETRUSCHE
Acquaspar
Formiche di Grosseto
Manciano
Pitigliano
Bagnoregio
S. BRUZIO
Talamone
Valentano
Lago di Bolsena
Civita
116
Marsiliana
Farnese
CASTRO
Capodimonte
Marta
Montefiascone
Amélia
Orbetello
SPACCO DELLA REGINA
Capalbio
FERENTO
Bomarzo
Porto Santo Stéfano
Canino
TOMBE ETRUSCHE
BAGNI DI VITERBO
Orte
Gíglio Porto
Ísola del Gíglio
COSA
Ansedonia
VULCI
Tuscánia
Viterbo
MONTE CIMINO
Soriano nel Cimino
Monte Argentário
Porto Ércole
Montalto di Castro
Il Casalone
MONTI CIMINI
Vignanello
Lago di Vico
NORCHIA
Vetralla
Cívita Castellana
Ísola di Giannutri
Tarquínia
TARQUINIA
Blera
Ronciglione
FALERII NOVI
Capranica
Sutri
Tarquínia Lido
NECROPOLI ETRUSCA
PORTO CLEMENTINO
SAN GIOVENALE
Vejano
MONTI SABATINI
Nepi
Rignano Flaminio
Tolfa
Trevignano Romano
TERME TAURINE
Civitavécchia
BAGNI DI STIGLIANO
Bracciano
Lago di Bracciano
Lago di Martignano
Santa Marinella
NECROPOLI ETRUSCA
Anguillara Sabazia
Capo Linaro
Cerveteri
VEIO
Santa Severa
MADONNA DI BRACCIANO
Ladíspoli
Città del Vaticano
Olbia
Golfo Aranci
Arbatax
Cagliari
Fregene
Leonardo da Vinci
Fiumicíno
OSTIA
Lido di Óstia
Castel Porziano
Lido di Castel Fusano
Pomézia
Tor Vaiánica
VIA SEVERIANA
Marina di Ardea
E
F
G
H
1
2
3
4
5
6

112
120
115
MARCHE
UMBRIA
LAZIO
ABRUZZO
Città di Castello
Pietralunga
MONASTERO DI FONTE AVELLANA
Arcévia
Jesi
Santa Maria Nuova
Osimo
Sirolo
BADIA DI SAN PIETRO
Numana
Castelfidardo
Loreto
Porto Recanati
Recanati
Sassoferrato
Serra San Quirico
Cupramontana
Filottrano
Schéggia
GROTTE DI FRASASSI
Fabriano
San Vittore delle Chiuse
Cingoli
HELVIA RECINA
Potenza Picena
Porto Potenza Picena
Gúbbio
Umbertide
Villa Potenza
S. CLAUDIO AL CH.
Civitanova Marche
Colcerasa
S. MARIA DI RAMBONA
Macerata
Branca
Scritto
Gualdo Tadino
Matelica
San Severino Marche
SANTA MARIA A PIE DI CHIENTI
Porto Sant'Elpidio
Castelraimondo
Sforzacosta
Tolentino
Corridonia
Lido di Fermo
Magione
Valfábbrica
Pióraco
Terme S. Lucia
ABBADIA DI FIASTRA
S. Elpidio a Mare
Porto San Giorgio
PERÚGIA
Corciano
Bastia
Nocera Umbra
Camerino
Caldarola
Montegiorgio
Fermo
Marina Palmense
Assisi
SAN GIUSTO
Muccia
San Ginesio
Monterubbiano
EREMO DELLE CARCERI
Colfiorito
Servigliano
Pedaso
Torgiano
Sarnano
Spello
Deruta
Cupra Marittima
Cannara
Amandola
Ripatransone
Grottammare
Bevagna
Foligno
Marsciano
Visso
Comunanza
Montalto delle Marche
San Benedetto del Tronto
Montefalco
Offida
TEMPIO DEL CLITUNNO
Trevi
MONTI MARTANI
ABBAZIA DI S. EUTIZIO
MONTI SIBILLINI
PARCO NAZIONALE DEI MONTI SIBILLINI
Áscoli Piceno
Porto d'Áscoli
Martinsicuro
FONTI DEL CLITUNNO
Triponzo
Norcia
MONTE VETTORE 2476
Alba Adriatica
Nereto
Todi
Arquata del Tronto
Tortoreto Lido
Spoleto
Civitella del Tronto
Tortoreto
Lago di Corbara
Acquasanta Terme
Bellante
Giulianova
Acquasparta
SAN PIETRO IN VALLE
Cascia
MADONNA DELLA NEVE
Sambucheto
CARSULAE
Accumoli
Téramo
S. MARIA DI PROPEZZANO
Roseto degli Abruzzi
SAN GEMINI FONTE
Amatrice
Villa Vomano
San Gemini
MONTI DELLA LAGA
Montorio al Vomano
S. CLEMENTE AL VOMANO
Pineto
Amélia
Leonessa
Lago di Campotosto
TERNI
Narni
CASCATE DELLE MARMORE
Piediluco
Posta
Atri
Silvi Marina
S. MARIA DI RONZANO
Città Sant'Angelo
Orte
MONTE TERMINILLO 2213
Borbona
Montereale
Prati di Tivo
S. GIOVANNI AL MAVONE
Montesilvano
Soriano nel Cimino
CONVENTO LA FORESTA
Terminillo
Passo d. Capannelle
GRAN SASSO D'ITALIA
Isola del Gran Sasso d'Italia
PESCARA
Contigliano
Cittaducale
Pizzoli
AMITERNUM
CORNO GRANDE
Penne
Spoltore
Vignanello
CONVENTO DI FONTE COLOMBO
Rieti
Antrodoco
Assergi
Loreto Aprutino
Moscufo
Magliano Sabina
Civita Castellana
FALERII NOVI
MONTI SABINI
L'Aquila
PARCO NAZ. DEL GRAN SASSO E MONTI DELLA LAGA
Barisciano
Chieti
Rocca Sinibalda
San Paolo di Peltuino
Torre de' Passeri
Nepi
Fiamignano
Casamáina
Navelli
Rignano Flaminio
ABBAZIA DI FARFA
Lago di Turano
Lago del Salto
Rocca di Cambio
Bominaco
Capestrano
Scafa
S. MARIA ARABONA
Bucchianico
S. CLEMENTE A CASURIA
Orsogna
LUCUS FERONIAE
Castelnuovo di Porto
Borgorose
MONTE VELINO 2487
Rocca di Mezzo
Ovindoli
Popoli
PARCO NAZIONALE DELLA MAIELLA
Guardiagrele
Orvinio
S. MARIA IN VALLE PORCLANETA
Magliano dei Marsi
Castelvecchio Subequo
Palombara Sabina
Carsoli
Celano
Passo San Leonardo
MONTAGNA DELLA MAIELLA
Casoli
VEIO
Monterotondo
Tagliacozzo
ALBA FUCENS
Forca Caruso
Settebagni
ROMA
Vicovaro
Arsoli
Pescina
Sulmona
Città del Vaticano
Guidonia
Tivoli
Avezzano
San Benedetto dei Marsi
Pescina
Cansano
Lama dei Peligni
Capistrello
Luco dei Marsi
Palena
JUVANUM
VILLA ADRIANA
Subiaco
San Vito Romano
MONTI SIMBRUINI
Civitella Roveto
Rocca Pia
Arcinazzo Romano
Lago di Scanno
Scanno
Quadri
Pescocostanzo
Ciampino
Palestrina
Altipiani di Arcinazzo
Passo del Diavolo
PARCO NAZIONALE D'ABRUZZO
Roccaraso
Frascati
Valmontone
MONTI ERNICI
Balsorano
Pescasseroli
MONTE MARSICANO 2242
Lago Albano
Fiuggi
Guarcino
Opi
Villetta Barrea
Castel Porziano
Albano Laziale
Lago di Nemi
Lariano
Colleferro
Anagni
ABBAZIA DI TRISULTI
Forca d'Acero
Lago di Barrea
Castel di Sangro
Genzano di Roma
Alatri
Veroli
Sora
Pomézia
Velletri
Ferentino
Alvito
MONTI DELLA META
Civitella Alfedena
Tor Valánica
Cori
Carpineto Romano
ABBAZIA DI CASAMARI
Isola del Liri
Forlì del Sánnio
Ardea
Cisterna di Latina
Aprilia
Norma
Frosinone
ABBAZIA DI SAN VINCENZO
Marina di Ardea
NINFA
Supino
Atina
Isernia
Ceccano
Ceprano
MONTI LEPINI
Sant'Elia Fiumerapido

Primošten
Prapatnica
Rogoznica
Split
Marina
Rt
Ploča
Trogir
Kaštel
Stari
vo
1
Splitski
Kanal
HR
Drvenik
Maslinica
Šolta

154

Starigrad
Vela Luka
2
Viški Kanal
Jabuka
Svetac
Komiža
Vis
Vis

MODRA SPILJA
Biševo

3

Split

4
Palagruža

Ortona
San Vito Chietino
SAN GIOVANNI IN VENERE
E55
Torino di Sangro Marina
Torino di Sangro
Punta di Penna
Casalbordino
Vasto
Marina di Vasto
Cupello
Atessa
Gissi
San Salvo
Térmoli
Colledi-
mezzo
Maria
MADONNA DI
CANNETO
Montefalcone
nel Sannio
Castelmauro
Trivento
RUDERI ROMANI
ciano
Casalciprano
Petrella
Tifernina
Sant'Elia
a Pianisi

Í Pianosa

Í. Capráia
Í. S. Dómino ÍSOLE TRÉMITI
Í. S. Nicola

PARCO NAZIONALE
DEL GARGANO

5

Montenero
di Bisáccia
Guglionesi
Campomarino
Marina di Chiéuti
S.Martino
in Pensilis
Serracapriola
Larino
Ururi
Casacalenda
Bonefro
Colletorto
Santa Croce
di Magliano
Torremaggiore
San Paolo
di Civitate
Carlantino

Lido di
Torre Mileto
Lésina
Lago di Lésina
Lago di
Varano
PARCO
NAZIONALE
Sannicandro
Gargánico
Cagnano
Varano
Apricena
San Marco
in Lamis
San Severo
SANTA MARIA
DI SIPONTO

Rodi
Gargánico
Péschici
Vico del
Gargano
Carpino
PROMONTORIO DEL GARGANO
GARGANO
Monte
Sant'Angelo
San Giovanni
Rotondo
Vieste
Pugnochiuso
Baia
delle Zagare
Mattinata
Manfredónia

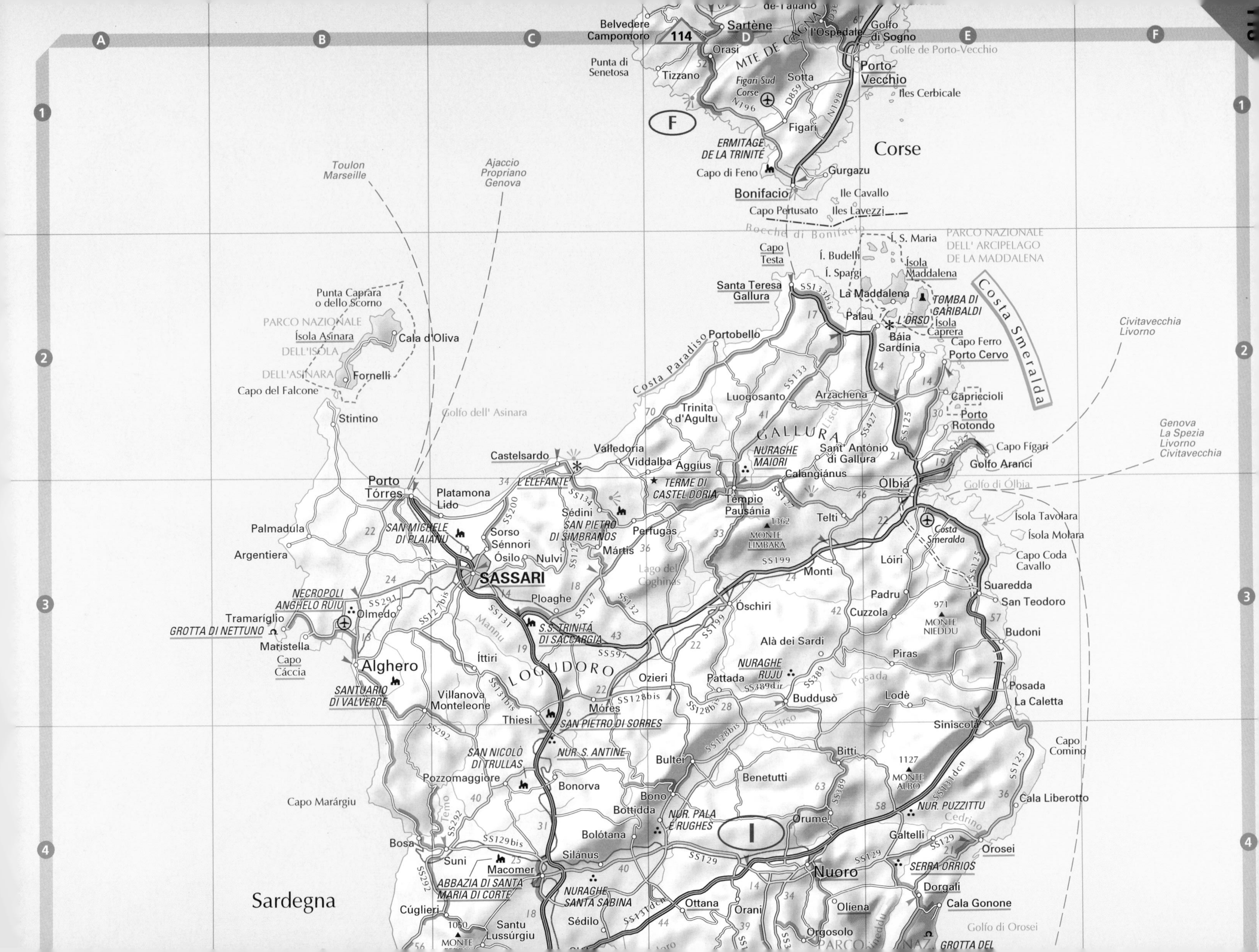

114
Corse
Sardegna
Sartène
Belvedere Campomoro
Punta di Senetosa
Tizzano
Orasi
MTE DE CAGNA
l'Ospedale
Golfo di Sogno
Golfe de Porto-Vecchio
Porto-Vecchio
Îles Cerbicale
Figari Sud Corse
Sotta
Figari
ERMITAGE DE LA TRINITÉ
Capo di Feno
Gurgazu
Bonifacio
Ile Cavallo
Capo Pertusato
Iles Lavezzi
Bocche di Bonifacio
Toulon Marseille
Ajaccio Propriano Genova
Civitavecchia Livorno
Genova La Spezia Livorno Civitavecchia
Capo Testa
Í. S. Maria
Í. Budelli
Í. Spargi
Ísola Maddalena
PARCO NAZIONALE DELL' ARCIPELAGO DE LA MADDALENA
Costa Smeralda
Santa Teresa Gallura
La Maddalena
TOMBA DI GARIBALDI
Palau
L'ORSO
Ísola Caprera
Báia Sardínia
Capo Ferro
Porto Cervo
Capriccioli
Porto Rotondo
Capo Fígari
Golfo Aranci
Golfo di Ólbia
Ólbia
Ísola Tavolara
Ísola Molara
Capo Coda Cavallo
Punta Caprara o dello Scorno
PARCO NAZIONALE DELL'ISOLA DELL'ASINARA
Ísola Asinara
Cala d'Oliva
Fornelli
Capo del Falcone
Stintino
Golfo dell' Asinara
Costa Paradiso
Portobello
Trinita d'Agultu
Luogosanto
Arzachena
GALLURA
NURAGHE MAIORI
Sant' António di Gallura
Calangiánus
Tempio Pausánia
Castelsardo
Valledoria
Viddalba
Aggius
TERME DI CASTEL DORIA
Porto Tórres
Platamona Lido
L'ELEFANTE
Sédini
SAN PIETRO DI SIMBRANOS
Perfugas
Palmadula
Argentiera
SAN MICHELE DI PLAIANU
Sorso
Sénnori
Ósilo
Nulvi
Mártis
Lago del Coghinas
MONTE LIMBARA
Telti
Monti
Lóiri
Costa Smeralda
SASSARI
Ploaghe
NECROPOLI ANGHELO RUIU
Olmedo
Tramaríglio
GROTTA DI NETTUNO
Maristella
Capo Cáccia
Alghero
SANTUARIO DI VALVERDE
S.S. TRINITÁ DI SACCARGIA
Íttiri
LOGUDORO
Óschiri
Padru
Cuzzola
MONTE NIEDDU
Suaredda
San Teodoro
Budoni
Alà dei Sardi
NURAGHE RUJU
Pattada
Ozieri
Budduso
Piras
Posada
La Caletta
Lodè
Siniscola
Villanova Monteleone
Thiesi
Móres
SAN PIETRO DI SORRES
NUR. S. ANTINE
SAN NICOLÒ DI TRULLAS
Pozzomaggiore
Bonorva
Bultei
Benetutti
Bitti
MONTE ALBO
Capo Comino
Cala Liberotto
NUR. PUZZITTU
Capo Marárgiu
Bono
Bottidda
NUR. PALA E RUGHES
Orune
Galtelli
Orosei
Bosa
Suni
Macomer
ABBAZIA DI SANTA MARIA DI CORTE
Bolótana
Silánus
NURAGHE SANTA SABINA
Nuoro
SERRA ORRIOS
Dorgali
Cala Gonone
Golfo di Orosei
Cúglieri
Santu Lussúrgiu
Sédilo
Ottana
Orani
Oliena
Orgosolo
GROTTA DEL

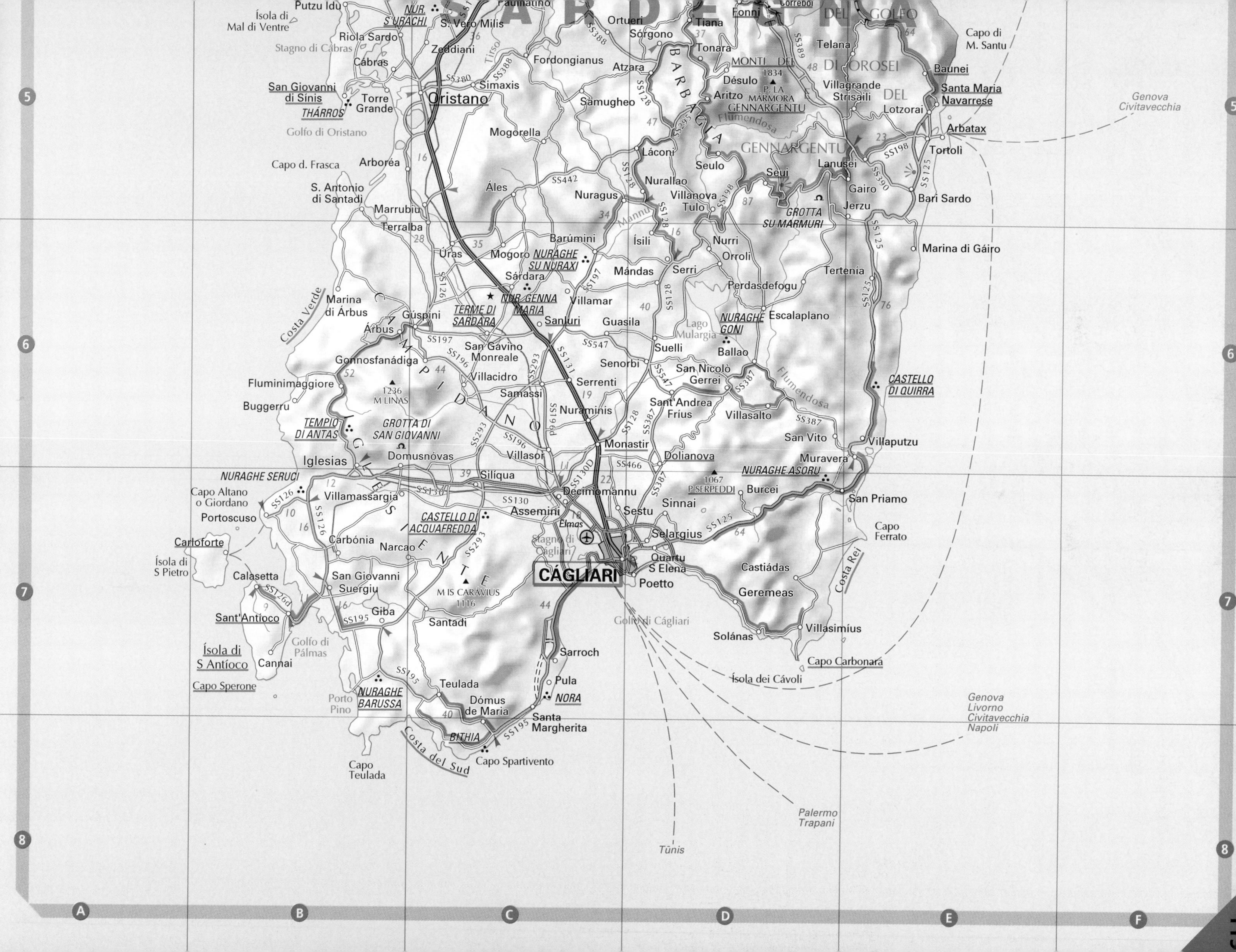
SARDEGNA
Putzu Idu
Ísola di Mal di Ventre
NUR. S'URACHI
S. Vero Milis
Riola Sardo
Stagno di Cábras
Cábras
Zeddiani
San Giovanni di Sínis
THÁRROS
Torre Grande
Oristano
Simaxis
Fordongianus
Golfo di Oristano
Capo d. Frasca
Arboréa
S. Antonio di Santadi
Marrubiu
Terralba
Úras
Mogoro
Mogorella
Áles
Ortueri
Sórgono
Atzara
Sámugheo
Tiana
Fonni
Tonara
Désulo
Aritzo
MONTI DEL GENNARGENTU
P. LA MÁRMORA
1834
BARBAGIA
Láconi
Seulo
Nurallao
Nuragus
Villanova Tulo
Ísili
Nurri
Orroli
Barúmini
NURAGHE SU NURAXI
Sárdara
NUR. GENNA MARIA
TERME DI SARDARA
Villamar
Mándas
Serri
Sanluri
Guasila
Suelli
Senorbì
San Gavino Monreale
Villacidro
Samassi
Serrenti
Nuraminis
Monastir
Gúspini
Árbus
Marina di Árbus
Costa Verde
Gonnosfanádiga
Fluminimaggiore
Buggerru
M LINAS 1236
TEMPIO DI ANTAS
GROTTA DI SAN GIOVANNI
Domusnóvas
Iglesias
Villasor
Sílíqua
Decimomannu
Assemini
Elmas
Stagno di Cágliari
CÁGLIARI
Sestu
Selargius
Quartu S Elena
Poetto
Golfo di Cágliari
CAMPIDANO
IGLESIENTE
NURAGHE SERUCI
Capo Altano o Giordano
Portoscuso
Villamassargia
Carbónia
Narcao
CASTELLO DI ACQUAFREDDA
M IS CARÁVIUS 1116
Carloforte
Ísola di S Pietro
Calasetta
Sant'Antíoco
Ísola di S Antíoco
Cannai
Capo Sperone
Golfo di Pálmas
San Giovanni Suergiu
Giba
Santadi
Porto Pino
NURAGHE BARUSSA
Teulada
Capo Teulada
Dómus de Maria
BITHIA
Costa del Sud
Capo Spartivento
Santa Margherita
Pula
NORA
Sarroch
Sinnai
Dolianova
Sant'Andrea Frius
San Nicolò Gerrei
Ballao
NURAGHE GONI
Lago Mulargia
Villasalto
Escalaplano
Perdasdefogu
Flumendosa
P SERPEDDI 1067
Burcei
NURAGHE ASORU
Muravera
San Vito
Villaputzu
CASTELLO DI QUIRRA
Tertenia
San Priamo
Capo Ferrato
Costa Rei
Castiádas
Geremeas
Solánas
Villasimíus
Capo Carbonara
Ísola dei Cávoli
Seui
Lanusei
GENNARGENTU
Gairo
Jerzu
GROTTA SU MARMURI
Marina di Gáiro
Bari Sardo
Tortolì
Arbatax
Lotzorai
Villagrande Strisaili
Telana
DI OROSEI
GOLFO
Baunei
Santa Maria Navarrese
Capo di M. Santu
Genova Civitavecchia
Genova Livorno Civitavecchia Napoli
Palermo Trapani
Túnis
5
6
7
8
A
B
C
D
E
F

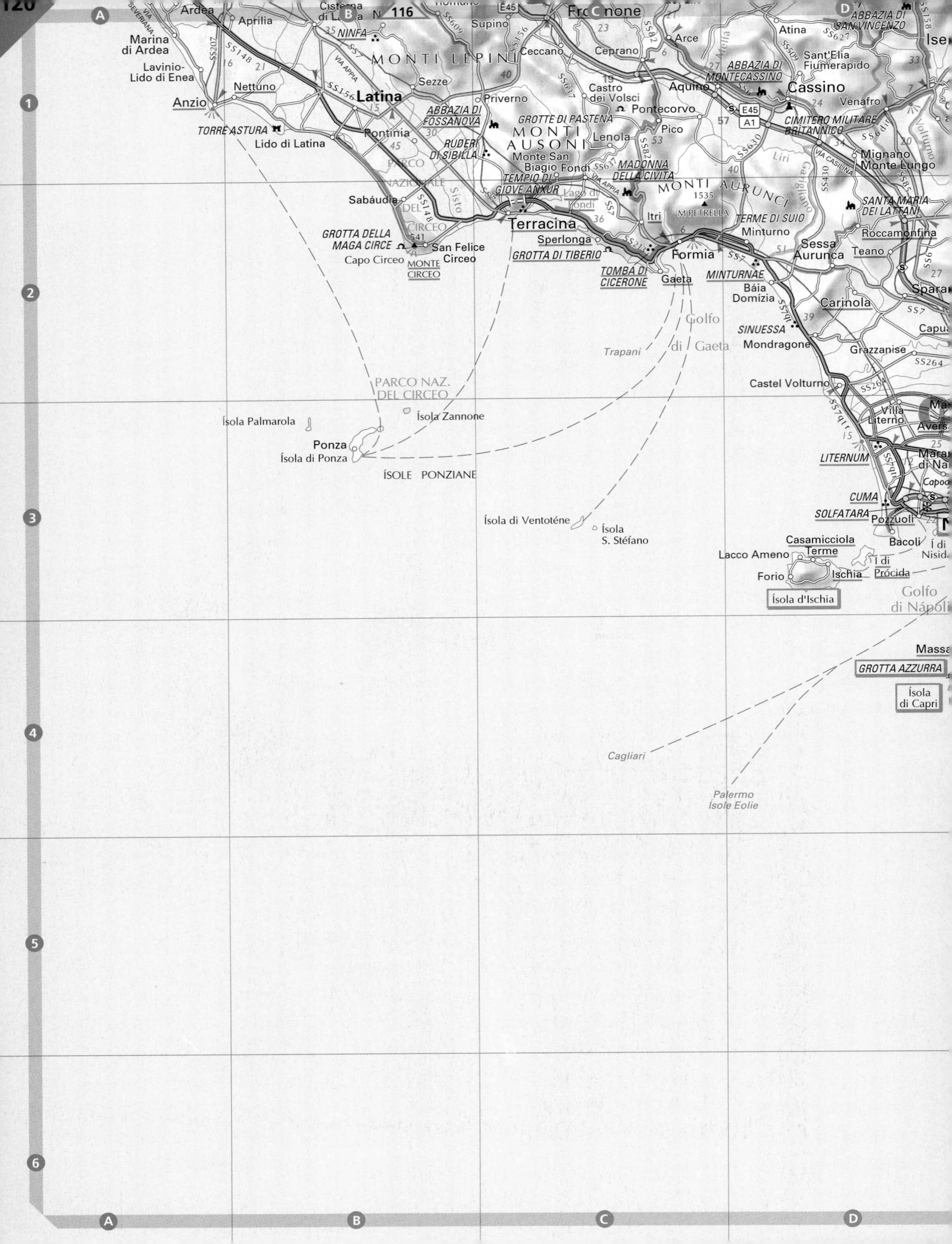
Ardea
Aprilia
Marina di Ardea
Lavinio-Lido di Enea
Anzio
Nettuno
TORRE ASTURA
Lido di Latina
Latina
NINFA
MONTI LEPINI
Sezze
Priverno
Pontinia
ABBAZIA DI FOSSANOVA
RUDERI DI SIBILLA
PARCO NAZIONALE DEL CIRCEO
Sabáudia
GROTTA DELLA MAGA CIRCE
San Felice Circeo
Capo Circeo
MONTE CIRCEO
Terracina
TEMPIO DI GIOVE ANXUR
Sperlonga
GROTTA DI TIBERIO
TOMBA DI CICERONE
Gaeta
Formia
MINTURNAE
Minturno
TERME DI SUIO
Supino
Ceccano
Ceprano
Castro dei Volsci
Pontecorvo
GROTTE DI PASTENA
MONTI AUSONI
Lenola
Pico
Monte San Biagio
Fondi
Lago di Fondi
MADONNA DELLA CIVITA
MONTI AURUNCI
M PETRELLA
1535
Itri
Arce
Aquino
ABBAZIA DI MONTECASSINO
Cassino
Atina
ABBAZIA DI SAN VINCENZO
Sant'Elia Fiumerapido
Venafro
CIMITERO MILITARE BRITANNICO
Mignano Monte Lungo
SANTA MARIA DEI LATTANI
Roccamonfina
Sessa Aurunca
Teano
Báia Domízia
Carinola
SINUESSA
Mondragone
Grazzanise
Castel Volturno
Villa Literno
LITERNUM
CUMA
SOLFATARA
Pozzuoli
Bacoli
Golfo di Gaeta
Trapani
PARCO NAZ. DEL CIRCEO
Ísola Palmarola
Ísola Zannone
Ponza
Ísola di Ponza
ÍSOLE PONZIANE
Ísola di Ventoténe
Ísola S. Stéfano
Casamicciola Terme
Lacco Ameno
Forio
Ischia
Ísola d'Ischia
Í di Prócida
Golfo di Nápoli
GROTTA AZZURRA
Ísola di Capri
Cagliari
Palermo
Ísole Eolie
1
2
3
4
5
6
A
B
C
D

MOLISE
Campobasso
Carpinone
Frosolone
Sant'Elia a Pianisi
Carlantino
Lago di Occhito
Castelnuovo della Dàunia
San Severo
Torremaggiore
San Marco in Lamis
117
San Giovanni Rotondo
SANTA MARIA DI SIPONTO
Manfredónia
SAN LEONARDO
Golfo di Manfredónia
Jelsi
Volturara Appula
Lucera
Gambatesa
MONTI DEL MATESE
M. MILETTO
Bojano
Vinchiaturo
Riccia
Castelvetere in Val Fortore
SAEPINUM
Lago del Matese
Sepino
Santa Croce del Sannio
Colle Sannita
Basilice
San Bartolomeo in Galdo
FOGGIA
Zapponeta
Piedimonte Matese
Morcone
Roseto Valfortore
Faeto
Troia
Castelluccio dei Sàuri
Orta Nova
SALINE
Margherita di Savoia
Trinitàpoli
San Ferdinando di Puglia
Pontelandolfo
Guardia Sanframondi
San Marco dei Cavoti
Castelfranco in Miscano
Orsara di Puglia
Giardinetto
HERDONIAE
Cerignola
CANNE
Canosa di Puglia
Andria
Caiazzo
Amorosi
Telese Terme
Buonalbergo
Bovino
Savignano Irpino
Ascoli Satriano
Benevento
Frasso
Sant'Agata dè Goti
Ariano Irpino
Accadia
Sant'Agata di Puglia
Lago di Capacciotti
CASTEL DEL MONTE
Santa Maria Capua Vetere
Caserta
Maddaloni
Montesarchio
Apice
Grottaminarda
Candela
Minervino Murge
Cervinara
S. Giorgio del Sannio
Flumeri
Vallata
Lacedonia
Lavello
CAMPANIA
SANTUARIO DI MONTE VERGINE
Cicciano
Acerra
Pomigliano d'Arco
Baiano
Casoria
Taurasi
Gesualdo
Bisaccia
Monteverde
Melfi
Guardia Lombardi
Paternopoli
Andretta
Aquilonia
VULTURE
Rapolla
Venosa
Spinazzola
Nola
Atripalda
Avellino
Lioni
Calitri
Rionero in Vùlture
Ripacandida
Palazzo San Gervasio
Monteforte Irpino
Ottaviano
Sarno
Forino
Serino
VESUVIO
POMPEI
Montella
Sant'Andrea di Conza
Pescopagano
Atella
Forenza
Genzano di Lucània
San Fele
Torre Annunziata
Castellammare di Stàbia
Pagani
Nocera
Mercato S. Severino
Calabritto
M. CERVIALTO
Acerenza
Gragnano
Cava de' Tirreni
Giffoni
MONTI PICENTINI
Muro Lucano
Avigliano
Pietragalla
Oppido Lucano
Vico Equense
Ravello
Maiori
SALERNO
Acerno
BAGNI CONTURSI
Ruoti
Vaglio Basilicata
Tolve
Positano
Vietri sul Mare
Montecorvino Rovella
S. Gregorio Magno
Amalfi
Praiano
Campagna
Contursi Terme
Picerno
Potenza
Tricàrico
122
Punta Campanella
Battipàglia
Éboli
Vietri di Potenza
Passo Croce di Scrivano
Albano di Lucania
Grassano
Spineta Nuova
Altavilla Silentina
Sicignano degli Alburni
M. ALBURNO
Auletta
Golfo di Salerno
GROTTA DI PERTOSA
BASILICATA
Anzi
Calvello
Accettura
Controne
Brienza
Laurenzana
Roccadàspide
PARCO NAZIONALE DEL CILENTO E VALLO DI DIANO
Marsico Nuovo
Paestum
PAESTUM
Capaccio
Castel San Lorenzo
San Rufo
Sala Consilina
Marsico Vetere
Corleto Perticara
Agropoli
Ogliastro Cilento
Piaggine
Viggiano
Prignano Cilento
Missanello
Castellabate
Montesano sulla Marcellana
GRUMENTUM
Perdifumo
Vallo di Lucania
M. CERVATI
Lago di Pietra del Pertusillo
Punta Licosa
Rofrano
Sanza
Casalbuono
Moliterno
Roccanova
Acciaroli
Alfano
Torre Orsaia
M. SIRINO
Castelsaraceno
Ascea
Pisciotta
Celle di Bulgheria
Lagonegro
Senise
Policastro Bussentino
Latronico
Palinuro
Sapri
Lauria
Episcopia
GROTTA AZZURRA
Capo Palinuro
San Giovanni a Piro
Maratea
Golfo di Policastro
Castelluccio Sup.
Marina di Camerota
Viggianello
Terranova di Pollino
Praia a Mare
Mormanno
SERRA DOLCEDORME
PARCO NAZIONALE DEL POLLINO
Papasidero
Morano Càlabro
Scalea
Orsomarso
Castrovillari
Cirella
Verbicaro
Lungro
Ì. di Cirella
124
Buonvicino
Altomonte
A1
A3
A16
A30
E45
E841
E842
E847

117
San Severo
San Marco in Lamis
San Giovanni Rotondo
SANTA MARIA DI SIPONTO
Manfredónia
SAN LEONARDO
Golfo di Manfredónia
Carlantino
Lago di Occhito
Castelnuovo della Dàunia
Volturara Appula
Gambatesa
Lucera
FOGGIA
Candelaro
Cervaro
Zapponeta
SALINE
Margherita di Savoia
Trinitápoli
Basilice
San Bartolomeo in Galdo
Celone
Roseto Valfortore
Faeto
Troia
Giardinetto
Castelluccio dei Sauri
Orta Nova
San Ferdinando di Puglia
Barletta
Trani
Bisceglie
Molfetta
Giovinazzo
San Marco dei Cavoti
Castelfranco in Miscano
Orsara di Puglia
HERDONIAE
Cerignola
CANNE
Canosa di Puglia
Ándria
DOLMEN DI CHIANCA
IL PULO
Buonalbergo
Bovino
Savignano Irpino
Ascoli Satriano
Ariano Irpino
Sant'Agata di Puglia
Accadia
Candela
Ófanto
Lago di Capacciotti
CASTEL DEL MONTE
Corato
Terlizzi
Ufita
Apice
Grottaminarda
Flumeri
Vallata
Bisaccia
Lacedónia
Lavello
Minervino Murge
Ruvo di Puglia
Bitonto
Modugno
Bitetto
Palo del Colle
Sannicandro di Bari
Giorgio del Sannio
Gesualdo
Taurasi
Guardia Lombardi
Paternopoli
Andretta
Monteverde
Aquilonia
Melfi
1326
VULTURE
Rapolla
Venosa
Spinazzola
PÚGLIA
Calitri
Lioni
Rionero in Vúlture
Ripacandida
Palazzo San Gervasio
Acquaviva delle Fonti
IL PULO
Cassano delle Murge
Montella
Sant'Andrea di Conza
Pescopagano
Atella
Forenza
Genzano di Lucánia
San Fele
Gravina in Puglia
Altamura
Calabritto
1809
M CERVIALTO
Acerenza
Bradano
MONTI PICENTINI
Muro Lucano
Avigliano
Pietragalla
Oppido Lucano
Irsina
Gravina di Picciano
Acerno
BAGNI CONTURSI
Ruoti
VIA APPIA
Vaglio Basilicata
Tolve
Matera
Montecorvino Rovella
Campagna
Contursi Terme
S. Gregorio Magno
Picerno
Potenza
Tricárico
Grassano
Lago di San Giuliano
Éboli
Vietri di Potenza
Calore
Platano
Albano di Lucánia
Miglionico
Altavilla Silentina
Sicignano degli Alburni
1742
M ALBURNO
Auletta
1143
Passo Croce di Scrivano
Melandro
Garaguso
Montescaglioso
Controne
GROTTA DI PERTOSA
Anzi
Accettura
BASILICATA
Pomarico
Brienza
Calvello
Laurenzana
Ferrandina
Roccadáspide
PARCO
Salandrella
Basento
Paestum
PAESTUM
Capaccio
Castel San Lorenzo
San Rufo
Marsico Nuovo
TAVOLE PALATINE
Bernalda
Agropoli
Ogliastro Cilento
NAZIONALE
Sala Consilina
Marsico Vetere
Corleto Perticara
Stigliano
Pisticci
Piaggine
Craco
Prignano Cilento
DEL CILENTO E
Agri
Viggiano
Missanello
Montalbano Jonico
Perdifumo
Vallo di Lucania
1899
M CERVATI
Montesano sulla Marcellana
GRUMENTUM
Lago di Pietra del Pertusillo
SANTA MARIA D'ANGLONA
Scanzano Jonico
ERACLEA
Policoro
Rofrano
Sanza
VALLO DI DIANO
Casalbuono
Moliterno
Roccanova
Sant'Arcangelo
Acciaroli
Alfano
Castelsaraceno
Senise
Rotondella
Ascea
Pisciotta
Torre Orsaia
Celle di Bulgheria
Lagonegro
M SIRINO
2005
Policastro Bussentino
Latronico
Rocca Imperiale
Palinuro
Sapri
Lauria
Episcopia
Noépoli
GROTTA AZZURRA
Capo Palinuro
San Giovanni a Piro
Oriolo
Montegiordano Marina
Marina di Camerota
Golfo di Policastro
Maratea
PARCO NAZIONALE
Castelluccio Sup.
Terranova di Pollino
Viggianello
Amendolara
Capo Spúlico
POLLINO
Alessandria del Carretto
SERRA DOLCEDORME
2267
Praia a Mare
Mormanno
Cerchiara di Calabria
Papasidero
Trebisacce
Morano Cálabro
DEL POLLINO
Scalea
Orsomarso
Castrovillari
Villapiana Scalo
Cassano allo Ionio
Verbicaro
Lungro
Sibari
Cirella
Í. di Cirella
Buonvicino
Altomonte
124
Spezzano
SYBARIS COPIA
Golfo di Corigliano
Diamante
121
ERNO
tipáglia
A
B
C
D
1
2
3
4
5
6

E
F
G
H
1
2
3
4
5
6
Kérkyra
Igoumenítsa
Pátra
Durrës
Bar
ARI
SS96
35
SS16
Mola
di Bari
Capurso
Rutigliano
E55
SS16
Polignano a Mare
SS634
Monopoli
Conversano
Turi
GROTTE DI CASTELLANA
Castellana
Grotte
SS379
Savelletri
SS172
Putignano
SS377
Torre Canne
GROTTA DI PUTIGNANO
SS172
Fasano
Gioia
del Colle
Alberobello
Noci
Rosa Marina
Villanova
SS379
SS604
SS377
ZONA
DEI TRULLI
SS172
Locorotondo
Cisternino
52
Torre S. Sabina
Ostuni
SS100
Martina Franca
A14
E843
San Vito
dei Normanni
SS379
E55
Papola Casale
Kérkyra
Igoumenítsa
Pátra
Ceglie
Messápica
SS581
SS16
Bríndisi
Móttola
Palagianello
Crispiano
San Michele
Salentino
GROTTA
S. GIOVANNI
VIA APPIA ANTICA
SS613
Massafra
Villa
Castelli
SS605
Palagiano
SS172
Grottaglie
SS7
Mesagne
SS16
VIA APPIA
Statte
Latiano
Francavilla
Fontana
E90
San Pietro
Vernotico
Oria
SS603
Torre
Santa Susanna
Casalabate
TÁRANTO
SS7
San Giorgio
Iónico
Carosino
San
Dónaci
Squinzano
Marina
di Ginosa
PONTIUM
Capo
San Vito
Lizzano
SS7ter
Sava
SS7ter
San Pancrazio
Salentino
Campi
Salentina
San Cataldo
Manduria
Torricella
LECCE
Lido
Silvana
Avetrana
SS174
Veglie
Monteroni
di Lecce
SS611
Campomarino
Rocca Vecchia
Cavallino
Porto
Cesareo
Copertino
SS16
SS101
SS476
SS664
SS16
Calimera
Durrës
Vlorë
Martano
Galatina
Nardo
Galatone
SS497
Otranto
SS497
SS16
Máglie
SS101
SS459
SS497
Capo d'Ótranto
Gallípoli
SS459
SS476
SS275
Parábita
Santa Cesarea
Terme
Casarano
Ruffano
GOLFO DI
Taviano
GROTTA ZINZULUSA
SS474
TÁRANTO
Ugento
Taurisano
AUSENTUM
Presicce
SS274
SS173
Gagliano
del Capo
Marina di
Léuca
Capo S Maria
di Léuca

SALERNO
Vietri sul Mare
Battipáglia
Spineta Nuova
Montecorvino Rovella
Campagna
Éboli
PICENTINI
BAGNI CONTURSI
Contursi Terme
S. Gregorio Magno
121
Ruoti
Potenza
Picerno
Vietri di Potenza
Vaglio Basilicata
Tolve
Tricárico
Grassano
Albano di Lucania
Passo Croce di Scrivano
Miglionico
Matera
122
Castellaneta
Laterza
Ginosa
Montescaglioso
Martina Franca
Móttola
Palagianello
Palagiano
Massafra
Crispiano
Statte
TÁRANTO
San Giorgio Ionico
Capo San Vito
Altavilla Silentina
Sicignano degli Alburni
M. ALBURNO
GROTTA DI PERTOSA
Auletta
Controne
Roccadáspide
Capaccio
Paestum
PAESTUM
Agropoli
Ogliastro Cilento
Castel San Lorenzo
San Rufo
Brienza
Marsico Nuovo
Sala Consilina
Marsico Vetere
BASILICATA
Anzi
Calvello
Accettura
Laurenzana
Garaguso
Ferrandina
Pomarico
Corleto Perticara
Stigliano
Pisticci
Bernalda
TAVOLE PALATINE
METAPONTIUM
Marina di Ginosa
Lido di Metaponto
Craco
Cavone
Montalbano Jonico
Missanello
Viggiano
GRUMENTUM
Lago di Pietra del Pertusillo
Moliterno
Roccanova
Sant'Arcangelo
SANTA MARIA D'ANGLONA
Lido di Scanzano
Scanzano Jónico
ERACLEA
Policoro
PARCO NAZIONALE DEL CILENTO E VALLO DI DIANO
Piaggine
M. CERVATI
Prignano Cilento
Vallo di Lucania
Castellabate
Perdifumo
Punta Licosa
Acciaroli
Rofrano
Sanza
Alfano
Torre Orsaia
Montesano sulla Marcellana
Casalbuono
Lagonegro
M. SIRINO
Castelsaraceno
Senise
Rotondella
Rocca Imperiale
Montegiordano Marina
Ascea
Pisciotta
Celle di Bulgheria
Policastro Bussentino
Sapri
Palinuro
GROTTA AZZURRA
Capo Palinuro
San Giovanni a Piro
Marina di Camerota
Golfo di Policastro
Lauria
Maratea
Latronico
Episcopia
Noépoli
Oriolo
PARCO NAZIONALE DEL POLLINO
Castelluccio Sup.
Terranova di Pollino
Viggianello
Amendolara
Capo Spúlico
GOLFO DI TÁRANTO
SERRA DOLCEDORME
Alessandria del Carretto
Mormanno
Praia a Mare
Papasidero
Cerchiara di Calabria
Trebisacce
Morano Cálabro
Castrovillari
Scalea
Orsomarso
Cassano allo Ionio
Villapiana Scalo
Sibari
SYBARIS-COPIA
Golfo di Corigliano
Verbicaro
Lungro
Cirella
Í. di Cirella
Buonvicino
Altomonte
Diamante
San Sosti
Spezzano Albanese
Belvedere Marittimo
Fagnano Castello
Tarsia
Corigliano Calabro
Capo Trionto
Mirto
Rossano
Crosia
Cariati
Torretta
Cetraro
San Marco Argentano
San Demetrio Corone
Bisignano
SILA GRECA
Cropalati
Terme Luigiane
Guárdia Piemontese
Luzzi
Acri
ABBAZIA DELLA SAMBUCINA
Montalto Uffugo
Longobucco
Crucoli
Campana
Punta Alice
TEMPIO DI APOLLO
Cirò Marina
Fuscaldo
Páola
Lago di Cecita
SILA GRANDE
PARCO NAZIONALE DELLA CALABRIA
Camigliatello
Rende
Celico
San Lúcido
M. BOTTE DONATO
Cosenza
Carolei
Lorica
Savelli
San Giovanni in Fiore
Torre Melissa
CASTELLO ARAGONESE

CALABRIA
ÍSOLE EÓLIE O LÍPARI
Í. Strómboli
SCIARA DEL FUOCO
Napoli
Í. Basiluzzo
Í. Panarea
Í. Filicudi
Pecorini a Mare
Alicudi
Alicudi Porto
Í. Salina
S. Marina Salina
Leni
Í. Lipari
Lipari
Porto di Levante
Í. Vulcano
Milazzo
Panarea
Crotone
TEMPIO DI HERA LACINIA
Ísola di Capo Rizzuto
Capo Rizzuto
Rocca di Neto
Cotronei
Cutro
Petilia Policastro
PARCO NAZIONALE D. CALABRIA
M GARIGLIONE
Villaggio Mancuso
Sersale
Cropani
Botricello
Rogliano
Colosimi
Soveria Mannelli
Cámpora San Giovanni
Falerna
Falerna Marina
Gizzeria
Serrastretta
Taverna
Nicastro
Sambiase
Lamezia Terme
Tiriolo
Sant'Eufémia Lamézia
CATANZARO
Máida
Girifalco
Golfo di S Eufémia
Catanzaro Marina
ROCCELLETTA DEL VESCOVO DI SQUILLACE
Golfo di Squillace
Squillace
Pizzo
Briatico
Olivadi
Soverato
S. Nicola da Crissa
Chiaravalle Centrale
Tropea
Vibo Valentia
Soriano Calabro
Capo Vaticano
Ricadi
Mileto
Serra San Bruno
Badolato
Badolato Marina
Nicotera
Acquaro
Dinami
Passo di Pietra Spada
Guardavalle
Rosarno
Laureana di Borrello
Stilo
CAULONIA
Gióia Táuro
Passo Croce Ferrata
Polistena
Cinquefrondi
Monasterace Marina
Punta Stilo
Palmi
Taurianova
Cittanova
Mammola
Grotteria
Caulonia
Stignano
Bagnara Calabra
Passo del Mercante
Roccella Iónica
Marina di Gioiosa Iónica
Spartà
Torre Faro
Scilla
Sinopoli
Oppido Mamertina
PARCO NAZIONALE DELL'ASPROMONTE
Gerace
Siderno
C. di Milazzo
Villafranca Tirrena
Delianuova
Platì
Ardore
Locri
LOCRI EPIZEFIRI
Gioiosa Marea
C. Calavà
TYNDARIS
Villa San Giovanni
ASPROMONTE
MESSINA
Terme Vigliatore
Santa Lucia del Mela
Patti
Falcone
Barcellona Pozzo di Gotto
Tremestieri
Gambárie
MONTALTO
San Luca
Bovalino
Castroreale
Galati Marina
RÉGGIO DI CALÁBRIA
Bianco
Ucria
Novara di Sicilia
Montalbano Elicona
MONTI PELORITANI
P.ZO DI VERNÀ
Stretto di Messina
Africo
Portella Mandrazzi
Portella dello Zoppo
Alì Terme
Roccalumera
Santa Teresa di Riva
San Lorenzo
Condofuri
Bruzzano Zeffirio
Bova
Francavilla di Sicilia
S. Alessio Siculo
Bova Marina
Brancaleone Marina
Melito di Porto Salvo
C Spartivento
Randazzo
Taormina
Mazzaró
Giardini-Naxos
NAXOS
Linguaglossa
Piedimonte Etneo
Bronte
M. ETNA
Fiumefreddo di Sicilia
Riposto
Giarre
Biancavilla
Zafferana Etnea
127

A
B
C
D
1
2
3
4
5
6
Cágliari
Gaeta
Valletta-Malta
Ústica
Cágliari
Génova
Livorno
Nápoli
Ísola delle Fémmine
Capo Gallo
Ísola delle Femmine
P Ráisi
Mondello
Punta Ráisi
Golfo di Palermo
MONTE PELLEGRINO
Capo S. Vito
San Vito lo Capo
Cínisi
Capaci
PALERMO
Castelluzzo
Golfo di Castellammare
Custonaci
SAN MARTINO DELLE SCALE
C. Zafferano
SOLUNTO
Balestrate
Monreale
Erice
Castellammare del Golfo
Partinico
Bagheria
686
Í. di Lévanzo
Trápani
Valderice
Misilmeri
Maréttimo
Levanzo
ÍSOLE ÉGADI
Paceco
Buseto Palizzolo
San Giuseppe Jato
Piana degli Albanesi
Términi Imerese
Favignana
Marineo
Birgi
A29dir
Álcamo
Trabia
Í. Favignana
SEGESTA
Calatafimi
San Cipirello
Cáccamo
MOZIA
MADONNA DEL ROSARIO
Buonfornello
Í. dello Stagnone
Camporeale
Villafrati
Cerda
1613
Marsala
Salemi
Gibellina
Corleone
R BUSAMBRA
Mezzojuso
Campofelice di Fitalia
Roccapalumba
Santa Ninfa
RUDERI DI GIBELLINA
Partanna
Campofiorito
Alia
Lago della Trinità
Lercara Friddi
Petrosino
Santa Margherita di Bélice
Castelvetrano
Bisacquino
Prizzi
Sambuca di Sicília
Mazara del Vallo
Palazzo Adriano
Pantelleria
Tūnis
Campobello di Mazara
Chiusa Scláfani
Cammarata
ROCCHE DI CUSA
Menfi
Bivona
SELINUNTE
Lago Aráncio
Santo Stéfano Quisquina
Marinella
C. Granítola
Caltabellotta
Búrgio
SAN CALOGERO
Alessándria della Rocca
Mussomeli
Casteltérmini
C. S. Marco
Sciacca
Ribera
Cianciana
San Biágio Plátani
Serradifalco
Pantelleria
Cattolica Eraclea
Milena
Aragona
Racalmuto
Raffadali
ERACLEA MINOA
Montallegro
Sicilia
Agrigento
Favara
VALLE DEI TEMPLI
Porto Empedocle
Naro
Campobello di Licata
CASTELLO DI MONTECHIARO
Palma di Montechiaro
Linosa
Trápani
Marsala
Pantelleria
Tracino
836
I
Ísola di Pantelleria
Porto Empedocle
Ísola di Linosa
Linosa
ÍSOLE PELÁGIE
I
Ísola di Lampione
Lampedusa
Ísola di Lampedusa
Gozo
Victoria
M
Palermo
Pozzallo
Mgarr
Mellieha
Sliema
Mosta
Valletta
Rabat
Vittoriosa
Dingli
Luqa
Żurrieq
Malta
Birżebbuga

Ísola di Ústica
Palermo
Lipari
Porto di Levante
Í. Vulcano
C. di Milazzo
Milazzo
Spartà
Torre Faro
Villafranca Tirrena
Gioiosa Marea
C. Calavà
Capo d'Orlando
Brolo
TYNDARIS
MESSINA
Terme Vigliatore
Santa Lucia del Mela
Barcellona Pozzo di Gotto
Castroreale
Patti
Falcone
Sant'Ágata di Militello
Naso
Cefalù
Marina di Caronía
Acquedolci
Santo Stefano di Camastra
Tortorici
Ucria
Novara di Sicilia
Montalbano Elicona
San Fratello
SANTUARIO DI GIBILMANNA
Collesano
Castelbuono
Mistretta
NÉBRODI
MONTI PELORITANI
P.ZO DI VERNÀ
Portella Mandrazzi
Portella dello Zoppo
M. SORO
Portella Femmina Morta
Capizzi
Lago d'Ancipa
Cesarò
Randazzo
Francavilla di Sicilia
Roccalumera
Santa Teresa di Riva
S. Alessio Siculo
Alì Terme
Galati Marina
Tremestieri
Taormina
Mazzaró
Giardini-Naxos
NAXOS
PZO CARBONARA
San Mauro Castelverde
Portella Madonnuzza
Colle del Contrasto
Castellana Sicula
Gangi
Cerami
Troina
Maletto
Linguaglossa
Piedimonte Etneo
Fiumefreddo di Sicilia
Riposto
Giarre
Petralia Soprana
Nicosia
Bronte
M. ETNA
Alimena
Gagliano Castelferrato
Lago di Pozzillo
Regalbuto
Adrano
Biancavilla
Zafferana Etnea
Trecastagni
Leonforte
Calascibetta
Agira
Centúripe
Assoro
Nicolosi
Acireale
Aci Trezza
ISOLE DEI CICLOPI
Aci Castello
Enna
Catenanuova
Paternò
Belpasso
SABBUCINA
Caltanissetta
Valguarnera Caropepe
Raddusa
Misterbianco
CATÁNIA
Fontana Rossa
Golfo di Catánia
Pietraperzia
MORGANTINA
Aidone
Piazza Armerina
Barrafranca
Ramacca
PIANA DI CATÁNIA
VILLA ROMANA DEL CASALE
Mirabella Imbáccari
Riesi
Mazzarino
Palagonia
Lentini
Ravanusa
Militello in Val di Catania
Mineo
Carlentini
Lago d. Disueri
Caltagirone
Grammichele
Francofonte
C. S. Croce
Augusta
Golfo di Augusta
MEGARA HYBLAEA
Melilli
Penisola Magnisi
Butera
Niscemi
Licodia Eubea
Vizzini
Buccheri
Sortino
NECROPOLI DI PANTALICA
Priolo Gargallo
CASTELLO DI FALCONARA
Gela
Mazzarrone
Ferla
Palazzolo Acréide
Giarratana
Floridia
CASTELLO EURIALO
SIRACUSA
C. S. Panagía
Acate
Chiaramonti Gulfi
AKRAI
Canicattini Bagni
Cassibile
Capo Murro di Porco
Cómiso
Vittoria
Ragusa
NOTO ANTICA
Noto
Scoglitti
Módica
Avola
Santa Croce Camerina
CAVA D'ISPICA
Rosolini
ELORO
Marina di Ragusa
Scicli
Íspica
I. Vendicari
Pozzallo
Pachino
Capo Pàssero
Portopalo di Capo Passero
P. d. Formiche
Capo delle Correnti
Valletta-Malta
Scilla
Villa San Giovanni
REGGIO CALABRIA
Stretto di Messina
Melito di Porto Salvo
A20
E90
A18
E45
A19
SS113
SS120
SS121
SS114
SS115
SS124
SS194
SS514
SS417
SS385
SS287
SS288
SS192
SS284
SS117
SS117bis
SS575
SS116
SS185
SS289
SS286
SS190
SS191
SS644
E931
125
3323
1847
1287
1264
1125
1524
1107
1147
1979
391

A
B
C
D
150
153
132
YU
AL
Muriquan
Vau i Dejës
Bicaj
MALI I GJALICËS
Brod
2748
TITOV VRH
Grupčin
Bushat
Gojani i Madh
Klos
1987
MAJE ZEBËS
Pirok
Ulcinj
Улцинj
Krajn
Bushtricë
Velipojë
Blinisht
Reç
Cegrane
Gostivar
Raste
1172
Rrëshen
Kurbnesh
2246
Shëngjin
Lezhë
MAL I DEJËS
Drin i Zi
Mavrovi Hanovi
Volkovija
2062
DOBRA VODA
Pellg i Drinit
Fushë Muhurr
Peshkopi
SVETI JOVAN BIGORSKI
СВ. ЈОВАН БИГОРСКИ
Mavrovsko Ezero
Mavrovo
Маврово
1200
Tuin
Ulëzë
Selishtë
Fushë-Kuqe
Magjellarë
Zajas
Gji i Rodonit
Laç
Burrel
NACIONALNI PARK MAVROVO
Kep i Rodonit
Debar
Дебар
Dolno Kosovrasti
Kičevo
Shetaj
Krujë
Bulqizë
Zerqan
Izvor
Celopeci
Gji i Lalzës
Fushë-Krujë
Klos
MAL I LÖPES
2020
2273
STOGOVO
СТОГОВО
Presek Prolaz
903
Rinas
Kep i Palit
Katundi i Ri
Crni Drim
Kraste
Mat
Klenjë
Lukovo
MAL I DAITIT
1612
1828
Kamëz
Vorë
Shëngjergj
Pesocani
Durrës
Shijak
TIRANË
Globočica Ezero
Belčišta
Botun
PLAĆENSKA PL
Ndroq
Petrelë
CERMENICA
Trieste Ancona Bari
Gji i Durrësit
2263
MAL I SHEBENIK
Librazhd
Veleštа
Ohrid
Mešeišta
1999
1190
Bukovo Prolaz
Kërrabë
Struga
Струга
Kosel
Kep i Lagit
Kavajë
Elbasan
Labinot Fushë
Ćafasan
Ohrid
Охрид
Resen
E65
Ohridsko Ezero
Охридско Езеро
NACIONALNI PARK GALIČICA
Rogozhinë
Prenjas
Lin
Carev Dvor
Çermë
Peqin
933
Pestani
Cërrik
Shtërmen
1840
MAL I SHPATIT
Stravaj
Otešovo
KURB
Shkumbin
Ballshi
Prespansko Ezero
Divjakë
Liqen i Ohrit
Ljubaništa
Kënet'e Karavastas
Lushnjë
2076
GURI I ZI
Podgradec
SVETI NAUM
Goricë
Kryekuq
Gramsh
Çërravë
Liqen i Prespes
Psa
ELBASAN-
Koklë
2376
VALAMARE
Podgorie
Pili
ARDENICËS
Kolonjë
Poshnjë
Kucovë
Grykë
Ura Vajgurore
Zvarisht
Seman
Moglicë
Zemblak
APOLLONIA
Fier
Berat
2416
Devoll
Maliq
KORÇË
Krist
Levan
Patos
BERAT
Gjerbës
Voskopojë
Korçë
Bilisht
HEKAL
Novoselë
Poliçan
Mifol
Vjosë
Ballsh
MALLAKASTRA
Terpan
2352
OSTROVICA
Vithkuq
1196
Dardhë
TOMORRIT
BYLLIS
Panajë
Kömni
903
Corovodë
1879
LOFKA
Selenicë
Gllavë
Nest
Vlorë
Aliákmonas
Kep i Gjuhëzës
Krahës
Çepan
Osum
Mollas
Pefkos
Gjol i Vlorës
Peshkëpija
Ballaban
GRAMMOS
Sevaster
Ersekë
AMANTIA
2253
Sinanaj
Kotë
GRIBES
Këlcyrë
Frashër
Vajza
Plikáti
Orikum
Tepelenë
TREMISHT
Barmash
Likórahi
2122
ANTIGONEA
Vjosë
NEMERCKES
Dukat
Brataj
Përmet
Pyrsógianni
Gusmar
133
1050
Shushicë
SHTËPËZ
1075
Amárandos
VLORË
Leskovik
Fourka
Kuç
Palokastër
Poliçan
Sam
Dhërmi
2486
Himarë
Dhrin
Çarshovë
2633
SMOLIKAS
Gjirokastër
1842
Konitsa
Melissópetra
Palermo
FARÁNGI VÍKOU
ФАРАГГІ ВІКОУ
Borsh
Piqeras
Libohovë
Kefalóvrisso
Pogoniani
2480

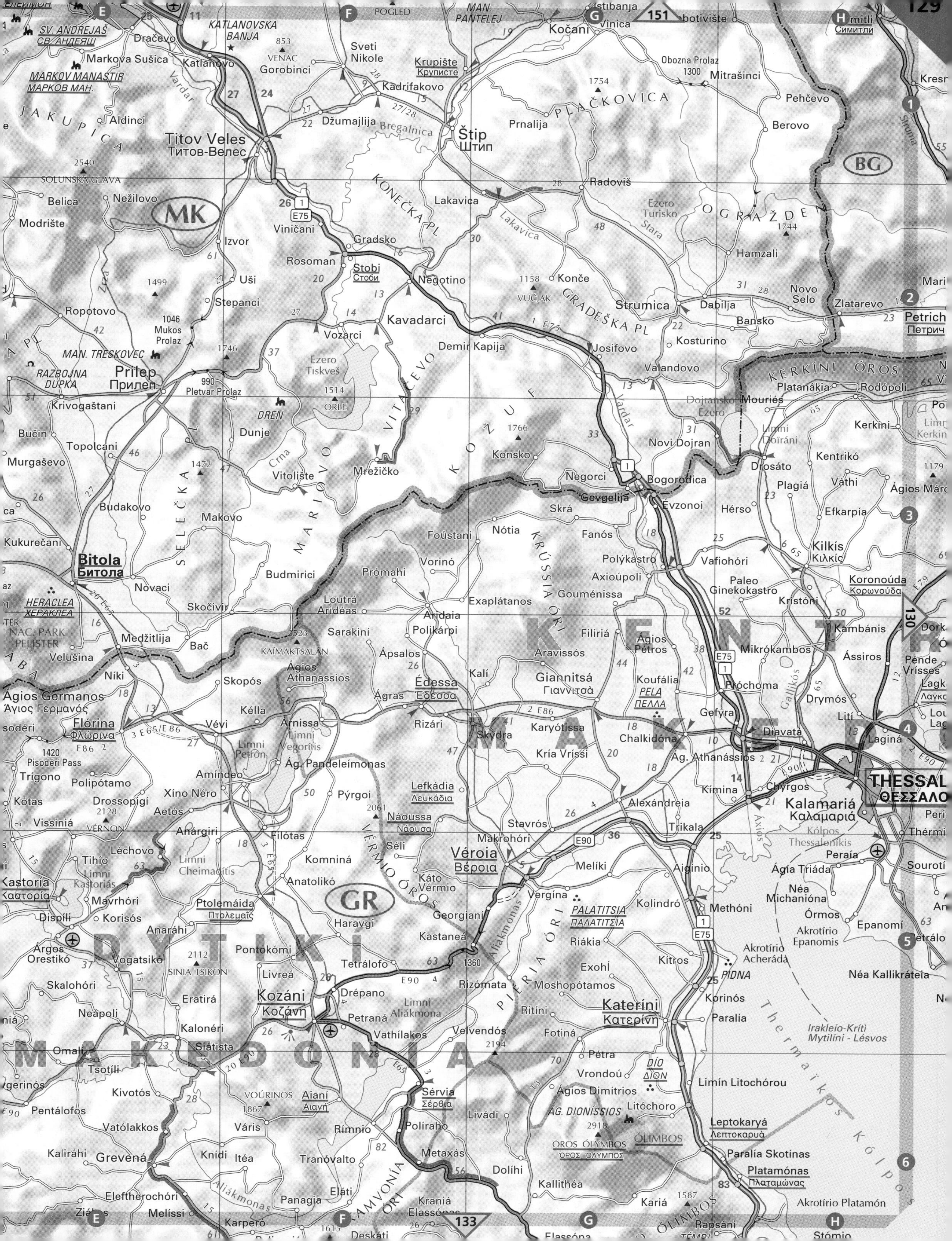

151
Simitli
Симитли
Gradevo
1140
Predel Pateka
Bansko
Банско
Dobrinishte
Добринище
2914
VIHREN
Vihren
Вихрен
PIRIN
ПИРИН
Kresna
1938
BESLET
Sŭrnitsa
Devin
Девин
Shiroka
Широка
868
Obozna Prolaz
1300
Mitrašinci
Pehčevo
Berovo
MK
OGRAŽDEN
1744
Hamzali
Kovachevica
Ковачевица
Dospat
Доспат
Satovcha
GOLYAN
Struma
Sandanski
Санданcки
Gotse Delchev
Гоце Делчев
Dŭbnitsa
1812
KAINCHAL
Pirin
ROŽENSKI MANASTIR
РОЖЕНСКИ МАН.
Popski Preslop
1380
Mesta
Melnik
Мелник
Skalotí
Dipót
Marikostinovo
Katuntsi
Exochí
Potamoí
Lefkógia
Sidirónero
Novo Selo
Dabilja
Zlatarevo
Petrich
Петрич
Kulata
2212
ALÍ BUTÚS
Katáfito
Káto Nevrokópi
Vólakas
Livaderó
Paranéstio
Bansko
Kosturino
Promachónas
Ahladohóri
Áno Vrondoú
Káto Vrondoú
2194
FALAKRÓ ÓROS
ANATO
Vathílakos
Makriplágio
Pteléa
alandovo
KERKÍNI ÓROS
Néon Petrítsi
Virónia
Sidirókastro
Σιδηρόκαστρον
Lailiás
Petroússa
Dráma
Δράμα
Lekáni
Platanákia
Rodópoli
Dojransko Ezero
Mouriés
Pontisméno
Orini
MENOÍKIO ÓROS
Mikrópoli
Prosotsáni
Nikifóros
Limní Kerkinítis
Kerkíni
Irákleia
Paleócastro
Ágios Pnevma
Kalithéa
Choristí
Limniá
Novi Dojran
Limní Doïráni
Doxáto
Drosáto
Kentrikó
1179
Skotoússa
Kalambáki
Krinídes
Bogorodica
Váthi
Plagiá
Ágios Márcos
Hímaros
Sérres
Σέρραι
Néa Zichni
Alistráti
Mavrolévki
FÍLIPI
ΦΙΛΙΠΠΟΙ
Amigdaleonas
Néa K
Kavála
Καβάλα
Évzonoi
Hérso
Efkarpía
Strimonikó
K. Kamila
Gázoros
St. Angístis
Skoútari
Nikíssiani
Pethelinós
Kilkís
Κιλκίς
Kalókastro
Vérgi
Anthí
Strimónas
Dravískos
1956
PANGAÍO
Próti
Eleftheroúpoli
Kólpos Ka
Vafiohóri
Ahínos
Terpní
Rodolívos
Akrovoúni
Paleo Ginekokastro
Koronoúda
Κορωνούδα
Lachanás
Nigríta
Mavrothálassa
Avlí
Néa Péramos
129
Kristóni
Xilópoli
Choumnikó
Ivira
Podochóri
Foleá
KENTRIKÍ
Kambánis
Dorkáda
VERTISKOS
AMFÍPOLI
Galipsós
Ormos
Όρμος
1107
Óssa
Sochós
Skepastó
Néa Kerdýlia
Akropótamos
Mikrókambos
Ássiros
Pénde Vrísses
Stefaniná
Kariani
E75
Próchoma
Lagkadás
Λαγκαδάς
Filadélfi
Akrogiáli
Asprovalta
Ασπροβάλτα
Loutrá Eleftherón
Λουτρά Ελευθερών
Gallikós
Drymós
Aretí
Askós
Megáli Vólvi
Aréthoussa
Strymonikós Kólpos
Gefýra
Liti
Loutrá Lagkadá
Profítis
Limni Vólvi
Stavrós
MAKEDONÍA
Diavatá
Lagina
Limni Koróneia
Loutrá Vólvis
Apollonía
Απολλωνία
Rentína
Ρεντίνα
GR
Ag. Athanássios
Olympías
Lagkadikia
Néa Mádytos
Varvará
Kímina
Chyrgos
THESSALONÍKI
ΘΕΣΣΑΛΟΝΙΚΗ
Melissourgós
Zangliveri
Akrotírio Marmari
Kalamariá
Καλαμαριά
Axios
Stanós
Stratoníki
Stratóni
Peristerá
Kólpos Thessaloníkis
Trikala
Thérmi
Livádi
Saná
Arnaía
Αρναία
Stágira
Akrotírio Arápis
Kólpos Ierissoú
Peraía
Vasiliká
Ágios Pródromos
1165
Palaiochóri
Aigínio
Ágia Triáda
Souroti
1020
Cholomón Monopati
Meg. Panagia
Néa Róda
Galátista
MONÍ HILIANDARÍOU
Μ. ΧΙΛΙΑΝΔΑΡΙΟΥ
Néa Michanióna
Ágios Andónios
Polýgyros
Ierissós
Methóni
Órmos
Vrástama
Trypití
HÁGION ÓROS
ΑΓΙΟ ΟΡΟΣ
MONÍ VATOPEDÍOU
Μ. ΒΑΤΟΠΕΔΙΟΥ
Akrotírio Epanomis
Epanomí
CHALKIDIKÍ
Pirgadíkia
Ouranópoli
Ουρανόπολις
Karyés
Καρυές
E75
Petrálona
Akrotírio Acherádа
Elaiochoria
ÓLINTHOS
ΌΛΥΝΘΟΣ
Gerakiní
Γερακινή
Metangítsi
Amolianí
MONÍ IVÍ
Μ. ΙΒΗΡΩ
Kitros
PIDNA
Néa Tríglia
Néa Kallikráteia
Órmos Panagías
Dáfni
Korinós
Nikítas
MONÍ SÍMONOS PÉTRAS
Μ. ΣΙΜΩΝΟΣ ΠΕΤΡΑΣ
Néa Plágia
2033
ÁTHOS
Paralía
Néa Moudaniá
Metamórfosi
Vourvouroú
MONÍ AG. DIONISSÍOU
Μ. ΑΓ. ΔΙΟΝΥΣΙΟΥ
Néa Poteídaia
Νέα Ποτείδαια
SITHONÍA
ΣΙΘΩΝΙΑ
Sárti
Akrotírio Pínnes
Irakleío-Kríti
Mytilíni - Lésvos
Néa Fókaia
Νέα Φώκαια
Néos Marmarás
Akrotírio Rigás
Kólpos Agíou Órous
Limín Litochórou
Sáni
Áfytos
Pórto Carras
Πόρτο Καρράς
Akrotírio Pírgos
Kallithéa
Sykeá
Akrotírio Adolo
Kólpos Kassándras
Thermaïkos
Kassándreia
Kriopigí
Chaniotis
Χανιώτης
Leptokaryá
Λεπτοκαρυά
Síviri
Kalándra
Καλάνδρα
KASSANDRA
ΚΑΣΣΑΝΔΡΕΙΑ
Toróni
Kalamítsi
Koufós
Paralía Skotínas
Paliouri
Παλιούριον
Possídi
Néa Skióni
Akrotírio Drépano
Platamónas
Πλαταμώνας
Akrotírio Posidion
Ágios Nikolaos
Akrotírio Paliouri
1587
Kariá
Akrotírio Platamón
ÓLIMBOS
133
134
Rapsáni
Stómio

148
BG
Kŭrdzhali
Кърджали
Yazovir Kŭrdzhali
Yazovir Studen Kladenec
Yazovir Ivaylovgrad
Progled
Pamporovo
Пампорово
Ardino
Kobilyane
Momchilgrad
Srednogortsi
Byal Izvor
Zvezdel
Madan
Rudozem
Krumovgrad
Popsko
Ivaylovgrad
Dobromirtsi
Podkova
Zlatograd
Kómara
Pláti
Rízia
Fyláki
Kavíli
Néa Vissa
Váltos
Orestiáda
Ambelákia
Zóni
Ládi
Thourio
Máni
Metaxádes
Didymóteicho
Διδυμότειχον
Mavroklíssio
Mikró Dérieio
Protoklíssio
Lávara
Mandra
Roússa
Sidiró
Gianoúli
Mega Dério
Orgáni
Souflí
Meriç
A. Drossiní
Nimféa
TSÍNGA
Livadítis
Melívia
Médoussa
Echínos
Sátres
ANATOLIKÍ RODÓPI
MAKEDONÍA
SÍLO
Dafnónas
Smínthi
Komotiní
Κομοτηνή
Fillira
Plagiá
Pessáni
Líkofos
Küplü
Kimméria
Íasmos
Sóstis
Néa Sánda
Aisými
İbriktepe
Komniná
Xánthi
Ξάνθη
Amvrosia
Sunion
Áratos
Thimariá
Paşayiğit
Parádissos
Vafaïka
Dialambí
Kósmio
Sápes
Koutsó
M. Doukáto
Limni Vistonída
Véna
Kírki
İpsala
Melissa
Pezoùla
Pórpi
Xylaganí
Mésti
Ávas
Lágos
Méssi
Ímeros
Loutrós
Féres
Chrysoúpoli
Fanári
Ávdira
AVDIRA
ΑΒΔΥΡΑ
Maróneia
Monastiráki
Yeni Karpuzlu
Ágios Charálampos
Messimvría
Mákri
Alexandroúpoli
Αλεξανδρούπολις
Orhaniye
Dassohóri
Keramotí
THRÁKI
Gala Gölü
Akrotírio Koén
Enez
TR
Thásos
Θάσος
Panagía
Παναγία
Makrýammos
Potamiá
Prínos
Theológos
Θεολόγος
Erikli
Abdürrahim
146
Akrotírio Stavrós
Alykí
ALYKÍ
Αλυκή
Palaiópoli
Thermá
Kamariótissa
Samothráki
Σαμοθράκη
Lákkoma
Akrotírio Kípos
Tayfur
Büyük Kemikli Burun
GELİBOLU
LİMNAE
Eceabat
YARIMADASİ
Kilitbahir
Kabaltepe
MİLLİ PARKI
Gökçeada
Kaleköy
İmroz
Aydıncık
Uğurlutepe
Ayagalip
Abide
İlyasbaba Burun
Kumkale
ACHILLEUM
Tevfikiye
Yeniköy
TRUVA
Límnos
Λήμνος
Akrotírio Pláka
Pláka
Akrotírio Moúrtzeflos
IFESTÍA
ΗΦΑΙΣΤΙΑ
Dáfni
Kontopoúli
Káspakos
Livadohóri
Moúdros
Kamínia
Mýrina
Μύρινα
Kontiás
Fissíni
Skandáli
Akrotírio Agía Eirínis
Ágios Efstrátios
Mytilíni - Lésvos
Bozca Adası
Geyikli
Ezine
Dalyan
ALEXANDRIA TROAS
NEANDRIA
135
Kösedere

128
Palermo
Borsh
Piqeras
Libohovë
Melissópetra
Kefalóvrisso
Pogoniani
Perivóli
Laísta
Venezia
Ancona
Bari
Brindisi
Dubrovnik
Lukovë
Kep
Kefali
Delvina
PHÖNIKE
Jergucati
Delvináki
Dolianá
Monodéndri
Vovoússa
AVGO
TYMFI ÓROS
Finiq
Kakavi
Ktismata
Kalpákio
Flambourári
Ereíkoussa
Saranda
AL
ZAGORIA
L. Pigon
Othoni
Vorion Stenón Kérkiras
Akrotírio Agios
Aikateríni
Róda
Ρόδα
Livadhja
Tsamandás
Kouklii
Asfáka
Votonósi
Kaminiá
Sidári
Kassiópi
Aetópetra
Mathráki
Avliótes
Karousádes
BUTHROTUM
Butrint
Zítsa
Pérama
Πέραμα
Afiónas
Ýpsos
Ύψος
Nisákio
Νησάκι
Soulópoulo
Mázia
PERISTÉRI
Palaiokastrítsa
Παλαιοκαστρίτσα
Gouniá
Konispol
Ágios Nikólaos
Keramitsa
Klimátia
Ioánnina
Ιωάννινα
Graméno
Liapádes
Kontokali
Sagiáda
Kourenda
Vrosína
Mouzakéi
Kérkyra
Κέρκυρα
Filiátes
Serviană
Prámanta
Pélekas
Parapótamos
Dodóni
Δωδώνη
Kaléntzi
Ágios Górdis
Άγ. Γόρδης
Benítses
Μπενίτσες
Ménina
Petoússio
TÓMAROS
Igoumenítsa
Ηγουμενίτσα
Ágnanta
Pérdika
Moraitika
Μοραΐτικα
Ágios
Mathéos
Akrotírio
Lefkímmi
Plataria
Paramythiá
Tsangário
Dafnoti
ATHAMÁNON ÓRI
Lefkímmi
Sivota
Karvounári
Dervíziana
Térovo
Kleisoúra
Argyrádes
Kávos
Pérdika
Kartéri
Margaríti
Paleohóri
Paleohori
Loúros
Pístiana
Akrotírio
Asprókavos
Glyki
Mórfi
Kerasóna
Amótopos
NEKROMANDÍO
ΝΕΚΡΟΜΑΝΤΕΙΟ
EFÍRAS
ΕΦΥΡΑΣ
Melátes
Párga
Πάργα
Kanaláki
Vrissoúla
Filippiáda
VLAHÉRNA
ΒΛΑΧΕΡΝΑ
Lákka
Paxoí
Mesopótamo
Stefáni
Loúros
Árta
Άρτα
KASSÓPI
ΚΑΣΣΩΠΗ
Archángelos
Psathotópi
Kompóti
Andípaxi
Kastrosykiá
Vigla
NIKÓPOLI
ΝΙΚΟΠΟΛΗ
Salaóra
Koméno
IÓNIA
NISSIÁ
Agía
Triáda
Ámvrakikos Kólpos
Bukka
Préveza
Πρέβεζα
Vónitsa
Βόνιτσα
Spárto
Ágios
Nikólaos
Monastiráki
Loutráki
Límni Voulkariá
Λ. Βουλκαριά
Lefkáda
Λευκάδα
Ágios
Nikitas
Pálairos
Katoúna
Brindisi
Karyá
Nydrí
Νυδρί
Lefkáda
Λευκάδα
Ágios
Pétros
Vlycho
Póros
Mýtikas
Aetós
Kálamos
Vasilikí
Meganísi
Ak. Doukáto
Ακ. Δουκάτον
Arcoúdi
Kastós
Akrotírio
Mélissa
Átokos
POLIS
ΠΟΛΙΣ
Fiskárdo
Kióni
Ithaki
Ιθάκη
Stavrós
Σταυρός
Petalás
Ehinádes Nissiá
Ásos
Άσος
Ithaki
Ιθάκη
Akrotírio Athéras
Athéras
Agia
Efimia
Oxéia
Kardakáta
MELISSÁNI
ΜΕΛΙΣΣΑΝΗ
Sámi
Σάμη
Lixoúri
Kefalloniá
Κεφαλλονιά
Póros
Πόρος
Argostoli
Αργοστόλιον
ÉNOS
Skála
Markópoulo
Akrotírio
A
B
C
D
1
2
3
4
5
6

129
Melíssi
Karperó
Paliouriá
1615
Deskáti
Kipoúrio
Ánixi
CHÁSIA ÓRI
1381
Kefalóvrisso
Agiófillo
Mavréli
Oxínia
Vlaháva
Koniskós
Korydallós
METÉORA
ΜΕΤΕΩΡΑ
Orthovoúni
Kalampáka
Καλαμπάκα
Kastaniá
Lióprasso
Rízoma
2204
TRINGÍA
Kraniá
Pertoúli
Eláti
Xilopáriko
Mesochóra
Paliomonastíri
Stournaréika
Pýli
Mouzáki
Μουζάκιον
Argithéa
Pigés
Elassóna
Ελασσών
Tsarítsani
Rodiá
Doméniko
Tírnavos
Messohóri
Longá
Verdikoússa
Agreliá
Sikiá
Diásselo
Damási
KÁTO ÓLIMBOS
Rapsáni
TÉMBI
ΤΕΜΠΗ
Góni
Γόννοι
Ampelákia
Evangelísmos
1978
ÓSSA
Anatoli
Sykoúri
Ambelónas
Pineiós
Kariá
Akrotírio Platamón
Stómio
Στόμιον
Kókino Neró
Akrotírio Dermatás
Agiá
Agiókampos
Dímitra
LÁRISA
ΛΑΡΙΣΑ
Elefthéri
Platýkampos
MAVROVOÚNI
1054
Sklíthro
Keramidi
Kalamáki
THESSALÍA
Trikala
Τρίκαλα
Paliópirgos
Neohóri
Grizáno
Zárkos
Farkadónas
Koutsóchero
Níkaia
Chálki
Ahílio
Megalochóri
Mavrovoúni
Vlochós
Ágios Anárgiri
Sofó
Arménio
Kanália
Zagorá
M. Kalívia
Agnanteró
Palamás
Itéa
Psihikó
Záppeio
Rizómylos
Makrinítsa
Μακρινίτσα
1547
PILIO
Fanári
Φανάρι
Mataranga
Ipéria
Chalkiádes
FÉRE
Velestínon
Βελεστίνον
Rigeo
Vólos
Βόλος
Portariá
Πορταριά
PAGASSÉS
Sésklo
Agriá
Miliés
Aereinó
Kalá Nerá
Oxiá
Mesenikólas
Tekhnití Límni Tavrópou
Mitrópoli
Μητρόπολη
Kardítsa
Καρδίτσα
Sofádes
Stavrós
Enipéfs
Vamvakoú
Nea Anchíalos
Νέα Άγχίαλος
Áfyssos
Neochóri
2154
VOUTISKAKI
Kastaniá
Gefýra
Fársala
Filáki
Mikrothíves
Pagasitikós Kólpos
Gramatikó
Néon Monastíri
Nartháki
Anthótopos
Amaliápoli
Achelóos
Kédros
Anavra
Almyrós
GR
Amárandos
Prassiá
Skopiá
Tríke
Loutrá Smokóvou
Λουτρά Σμοκόβου
Domokós
Δομοκός
Soúrpi
2128
PTÉRI
Loutrá Kaítsas
Anávra
Vrínena
Pigádi
Skoulikariá
Granítsa
Rentína
Kariés
ÓROS ÓTHRYS
Megdova
Agrafiótis
Mavromáta
1726
GERAKOVOÚNI
Ágios Theódori
Patiópoulo
Voúlpi
Fourná
Trílofo
Xiniáda
Pelasgía
Glýfa
Embessós
Kerassohóri
Platystomo
Dívri
Stylída
Agiókampos
Stènoma
Agios Geórgios
2316
TYMFRISTÓS
Makrakómi
Lamía
Λαμία
Ráches
Tekhnití Límni Kremastón
Τεχνητή Λίμνη Κρεμαστών
Frangísta
Spércheiós
Lianokládi
Ag. Marína
Kalívia
Karpenísi
Καρπενήσιον
Tymfristós
Spercheiáda
Loutrá Ypátis
Λουτρά Υπάτης
Maliakós Kólpos
Liháda
Giáltra
Gregolímano
Podogorá
Lutrá
Mikró Horió
THERMOPILES
ΘΕΡΜΟΠΥΛΕΣ
ÍTI
Iráklia
Mólos
Kámena Voúrla
Καμένα Βούρλα
Akrotírio Arkítsa
Gardíki
Meg Horió
Agios Vlásios
620
Kallidrómou Pass
Thermopiles
Agios Konstantínos
Bambalió
Krikelo
Domnitsa
Pávliani
Rengínio
Kastráki
Prousós
Grамméni Oxyá
VARDOÚSIA ÓRI
Artotína
Bralos
Kaloskopí
Zèlio
Potamoúla
PANAITOLIKÓ ÓROS
Arahova
2406
GKIÓNA ÓROS
Graviá
Amfíkleia
Módi
Elátia
Atalánti
Lepenoú
1924
Evinos
Ag. Dimítrios
Elatoú
Pendagí
2510
Lefkadíti
Eptálofos
PARNASSÓS
ΠΑΡΝΑΣΣΟΣ
Káto Tithoréa
Éxarhos
Stratos
Στράτος
Agrínio
Αγρίνιον
Paravóla
Panetólio
Límni Trichonída
Thérmo
Θέρμον
Limnitsa
Ámfissa
Άμφισσα
Elaiónas
DELFÍ
ΔΕΛΦΟΙ
2457
Dávlia
ORHOMENÓS
Chairóneia
Orhómeno
Ορχομενός
Zevgaráki
Stamna
Gavaloú
Rigáni
Paleópirgos
Mórnos
Lidoríki
Delfí
Itéa
Ιτέα
Aráchova
Αράχοβα
Dístomo
Leivádia
Káto Makrinoú
Kámbos
Malandrino
Desfína
M. ÓSSIOS LOUKÁS
Μ. ΟΣΙΟΣ ΛΟΥΚΑΣ
Altolikó
Αιτωλικόν
Agriliá
KALIDÓN
ΚΑΛΙΔΩΝ
Efpálio
Pigi
Amigdalía
Galaxídi
Antíkyra
Kiriáki
ELIKÓN ÓROS
Aliártos
Neochori
Mesolóngi
Μεσολόγγιον
Náfpaktos
Ναύπακτος
Marathiás
Glifáda
Erateiní
Akrotírio Andrómachi
Kólpos Antíkyras
Agía Ána
Evinochóri
Antírrio
Αντίρριον
Akrotírio Drepanon
Psathópyrgos
Akrotírio Psaromita
Akrotírio Agia Págkalos
Prodromós
Paralía
Thisví
Ag. Ioánis
Akrotírio Evinos
Patraïkós Kólpos
Río
Ρίον
Selianítika
Σελιανίτικα
Aígio
Αίγιον
Akrotírio Velanidia
PÁTRA
ΠΑΤΡΑΙ
Áno Kastrítsi
Valimítika
Βαλιμίτικα
Diakoftó
Korinthiakós Kólpos
Akrotírio Áraxos
Dáfnes
1926
PANACHAIKÓ ÓROS
Paralía Platanoú
Paralía Akrátas
Lakópetra
Λακκόπετρα
Paralía
Vrahnéika
Ftéri
Φτέρη
Dervéni
Kalogriá
Metóchi
Zahloroú
Xylókastro
Ξυλόκαστρο
Perachóra
Περαχώρα
Akrotírio Iraia
IRÉO
Loutrá Kounoupélli
Lápas
Káto Achaia
Chalandrítsa
Petsákoi
MÉGA SPILEO
ΜΕΓΑ ΣΠΗΛΑΙΟ
ELLÁDA
Kiáto
Κιάτον
Trikalon
Τρίκαλα
Loutráki
Λουτράκιον
Kalávryta
Καλάβρυτα
2341
36
Manolas
Várda
Kangádio
2224
AG. LAVRA
137
SIKIÓNA
Kórinthos
134
E65
E75
E92
E55
E952
8A
E
F
G
H
1
2
3
4
5
6

130
133
137
138
VÓRIES
SPORÁDES
GR
Psathoúra
Gioúra
570
Pipéri
Kyrá Panagía
299
Akrotírio
Gérakas
Alónnisos
Αλόννησος
456
Peristéra
Skíathos
Σκίαθος
KÁSTRO
ΚΑΣΤΡΟ
Glóssa
Skópelos
Σκόπελος
662
Patitíri
Koukounariés
Adelfí
Skantzoúra
Agnóntas
Akrotírio
Kártsino
Skýros
Σκύρος
Linariá
Skyropoúla
Valáxa
793
Sarakin
Vólos
Βόλος
AGASSES
Agriá
Sésklo
Néa Anchiálos
Νέα Αγχίαλος
Kalá Nerá
Áfyssos
Milies
Portariá
Πορταριά
Makrinítsa
Μακρινίτσα
1547
PILIO
Zagorá
Choreftó
Tsagkaráda
Τσαγκαράδα
Kalamáki
Neohóri
Argalastí
Metóhi
Milína
Plataniá
Tríkeri
Kanália
Keramidi
Sklíthro
Agiókampos
Pagasitikós Kólpos
Amaliápoli
Soúrpi
Pigádi
Artemísio
Αρτεμίσιο
Agriovótano
Istiaía
Ιστιαία
Vasiliká
Ágios Theódori
Glyfa
Agiókampos
Oreoí
Ωροί
Voutás
Kerassiá
Agía Ánna
Loutrá Aidipsoú
Λουτρά Αιδηψού
Giáltra
Lihåda
Gregolímano
Ília
Roviés
Strofyliá
Kimássi
Mantoudi
Límni
Λίμνη
M. GALATÁKI
Prokópi
Pílio
Akrotírio
Sarakíniko
Sarakíniko
Évvoia
Εύβοια
Liménas
Hiliadoú
Kými
Κύμη
Akrotírio Kýmis
Paralía Kýmis
DÍRFYS ÓROS
1743
Átali
Stravrós
Politiká
Psachná
Steni
Monódrio
Ochthoniá
Néa Artáki
Νέα Αρτάκη
Pissónas
Séta
Trahíli
Avlonári
Neohóri
Νεοχώρι
Akrotírio
Gadaros
Drossiá
Chalkída
Χαλκίς
Gimnó
Ag. Loukás
Alivéri
Lépoura
Kriezá
Vasilikó
Erétria
Ερέτρια
Amárynthos
Káravos
DÍSTOS
ΔΙΣΤΟΣ
Kóskina
Zárakes
Almyropótamos
Panagía
Akrotírio
Arkítsa
Arkítsa
Skála
Theológos
Malesína
Zèlio
Atalánti
Elátia
Éxarhos
Koláka
Lárymna
Pávlos
Martíno
ORHOMENÓS
Kástro
PTÓO
ΠΤΟΟ
Loukíssia
Orhómenos
Ορχομενός
GLA
ΓΛΑ
Akraifnio
AKRAIFIA
Paralimni
Chairóneia
M. ÓSSIOS LOUKÁS
M. ΟΣΙΟΣ ΛΟΥΚΑΣ
Aliartos
Vágia
Kiriáki
Agía Ána
ELIKON ÓROS
Prodromós
Paralia
Thisví
Ág. Ioánis
Léfktra
Thespiés
Thíva
Θήβα
Tanágra
Assopía
Vathý
Βαθύ
Dílessi
Skála Oropoú
Σκάλα Ωρωπού
Kálamos
AMFIARAIO
ΑΜΦΙΑΡΑΕΙΟ
RAMNOÚS
ΡΑΜΝΟΥΣ
Notios Evvoikós Kólpos
Avlóna
PÁRNITHA ÓROS
ΠΑΡΝΥΣ ΟΡΟΣ
1413
Kapandríti
Ag Marína
Néa Stýra
Νέα Στύρα
Vareleí
Kalérgo
Akrotírio
Kafiréa
Stýra
Marathónas
Μαραθώνας
Erythrés
Píli
ELEFTHERÉS
ΕΛΕΥΘΕΡΕΣ
Plataés
Πλαταιές
Pórto
Germenó
Vília
Βίλια
Oinói
EGÓSTHENA
ΑΙΓΟΣΘΕΝΑ
Ag.
Triáda
FILÍ
Filí
Φυλή
Ekáli
Kifisiá
Κηφισιά
Néa Mákri
Marmári
Μαρμάριον
1398
OCHI
Kato Alepochóri
Asprópirgos
Mándra
Acharnés
Rafína
Petalioí
Kárystos
Κάρυστος
Platanist
Perachóra
Περαχώρα
Akrotírio
Íraia
IRÉO
GERÁNEIA
1351
Spárta
Mégara
Μέγαρα
Elefsína
Ελευσίνα
DAFNÍ
Stavros
Pallíni
Loútsa
ATHÍNA
ΑΘΗΝΑ
Paiania
Spáta
VRAVRÓNA
ΒΡΑΥΡΩΝΑ
Kólpos Petalión
Kiáto
Κιάτον
Loutráki
Kinetá
Salamína
PEIRAIÁS
ΠΕΙΡΑΙΕΥΣ
Imitós
1026
Koropí
Κορωπίον
Pórto Ráfti
Kórinthos
Agioi Theodoroi
E75
E94
E962

131
Agía Eirínis
146
Kösedere
Tuzla
Ayvacık
Küçükkuyu
ANTANDRO
Gülpınar
ASSOS
Behramkale
Baba Burun
POLYMEDIUM
Edremit Körfezi
Alibey Adası
Ayvalık
ŞEYTAN SOFRASI
Altınova
Mýrina-Límnos
ÓREIO
AIGAÍO
Akrotírio Kalamáki
Ágios Efstrátios
Akrotírio Trypití
Mýrina-Límnos Thessaloníki
Akrotírio Skamnia
Míthymna
Μήθυμνα
Sikaminiá
Pétra
Πέτρα
Mantamádos
Stípsi
ÁNTISSA
Fília
Φιλια
Ántissa
Αντισσα
Agía Paraskeví
Mistegná
Thermís
Θερμή
Sígri
Σίγριον
Kalloní
Vatoúsa
Eresós
Ερεσός
Kólpos Kallonís
Keramía
Mytilíni
Μυτιληνη
Akrotírio Sígri
Parakilá
Skála Eresoú
Skála
Vassiliká
Agiássos
Αγιασος
Ambelikó
Polichnitos
Skópelos
Loutrá
Krátigos
Vaterá
Plomári
Lésvos
Λέσβος
Aslan Burun
Kara Burun
Hasseki
Karaburun
AK DAĞ
Küçükbahçe
Mordoğan
Psará
Antípsara
Agiásmata
Αγιάσματα
Kambiá
Kardámyla
Mármaro
Melaniós
Oinoússes
Volissós
Lagkáda
Vrontádos
Chíos
Χίος
Ildır
TR
NÉA MONÍ
ΝΕΑ ΜΟΝΗ
Çeşme
Uzunkuyu
Thimianá
Alaçatı
Kallimasiá
Passá Limáni
Véssa
Armólia
Mestá
Kalamotí
Pirgí
Πυργίον
Kómi
Emboriós
Εμπορειός
Akrotírio Masticho
Kora
Peiraías
Sámos
Lithári
Akrotírio Kampanós
Ándros
Άνδρος
Palivári
Gávrio
Γαύριον
Batsí
Μπατσί
Apoikía
Ándros
Άνδρος
Mesariá
Órmos
Tínos
139
Ikaría
Akrotírio Fanári

Póros
Πόρος
Igoumenitsa
Kérkyra
Dubrovnik
Bari
Ancona
Venezia
132
133
Metóchi
Lápas
Káto Achaïa
Chalandrítsa
ELLÁDA
Loutrá Kounoupélli
Manolas
Várda
Kangádio
Sandoméri
Killíni
Κυλλήνη
Lechainá
Bórsio
Káto Velitsés
HLEMOÚTSI
ΧΛΕΜΟΥΤΣΙ
Neochóri
Kástro
Andravída
Ανδραβίδα
Loutrá Kyllínis
Λουτρά Κυλλήνης
Gastoúni
Akrotírio Tripiti
Kendro
Ágia Triáda
Efýra
Amaliáda
Mouzáki
Koúmani
Kouroúta
Κουρούτα
Skafídia
Katákolo
Κατάκολον
Akrotírio Katákolo
Pýrgos
Πύργος
Plátanos
Lála
Olympía
Vasiláki
ARHÉA OLIMBÍA
ΑΡΧ. ΟΛΥΜΠΙΑ
Epitálio
Kréstena
Káto Samikó
Κάτω Σαμικόν
Kaïáfa
Καϊάφας
Platiána
Kallithéa
Zacháro
Kakóvatos
Tholó
Lépreo
Λέπρον
Platánia
FIGÁLIA
ΦΙΓΑΛΕΙΑ
MÍNTHI ÓROS
Kyparissiakós Kólpos
Kaló Nero
Kyparissía
Κυπαρισσία
Armenii
VARVÁRA
1218
Filiatrá
Φιλιατρά
Hristianó
Marathópoli
Gargaliánoi
Aristoménis
ANÁKTORA NESTOROS
ΑΝΑΚΤΟΡΑ ΝΕΣΤΟΡΟΣ
Chóra
Kazarmá
Koryfási
Chandrinós
959
Sfaktiría
Σφακτήρια
Pylos
Πύλος
Méthóni
Μεθώνη
Néa Koróni
Foinikoús
Sapiéntza
Vassilitsi
Schíza
Akrotírio Akrítas
Koróni
Κορώνη
Akrotírio Livada
Petalídi
Πεταλίδιον
Messiniakós Kólpos
Akrotírio Kitriés
Kalamáta
Καλαμάτα
Rizómylos
Aví́a
Messíni
Thouría
Artemisía
Androússa
Ανδρούσσα
Mavrommáti
PALEÁ MESSÍNI
ΠΑΛΕΑ ΜΕΣΣΗΝΗ
Meligalás
Arfará
Poliani
Dorio
PELOPÓ
Longaniko
Paradeísia
Leontário
Megalópoli
Μεγαλόπολις
LIKÓSSOURA
ΛΙΚΟΣΟΥΡΑ
VASSÉS
ΒΑΣΣΕΣ
Andrítsaina
Ανδρίτσαινα
Karítaina
Καρίταινα
Káto Ass
GÓRTIS
ΓΟΡΤΥΣ
Ypsous
GR
PELOPONNI
Loutrá
Stavrodrómi
Lagkádia
Λαγκάδια
Karkaloú
Vytina
Βυτίνα
Levid
Valtessiníko
Límni Ládon
Dáfni
Lámpeia
Tripótama
Aroanía
ERÝMANTHOS
2224
Kaléntzi
Káto Vlasiá
Kalávryta
Καλάβρυτα
AG. LAVRA
ΑΓ. ΛΑΥΡΑ
AROANÍA ÓRI
MEGA SPIL
ΜΕΓΑ ΣΠΗΛ
Petsakoi
2341
Káto Kleitoria
Kas
Alfeiós
Ládon
Erýmanthos
Vouraikós
Pineios
ÉNOS
1628
Skála
Markópoulo
Akrotírio Moúnta
Akrotírio Skinári
Koríthi
Volimés
Anafonítria
Alikanás
Katastári
756
Porthmós Zakýnthou
Zákynthos
Ζάκυνθος
Maherádo
Ágios Léon
Lithakiá
Argási
Laganás
Vasilikós
Agalas
Kólpos Lagana
Akrotírio Geráki
Kerí
Akrotírio Marathiá
Strofadés
Almi

137
ATHÍNA
ΑΘΗΝΑ
PEIRAIAS
ΠΕΙΡΑΙΕΥΣ
Perachóra
Περαχώρα
Akrotírio
Iraia
Kiáto
Κιάτον
IRÉO
Loutráki
Λουτράκιον
GERÁNEIA
Kinetá
Κινέτα
Μέγαρα
Ελευσίνα
Salamína
Σαλαμίς
Imitós
Υμηττός
Paiania
Spáta
Loútsa
VRAVRÓNA
ΒΡΑΥΡΩΝΑ
Pórto Ráfti
Koropí
Καρωπίον
Trikalon
Τρίκαλα
Mána
Kórinthos
Κόρινθος
SIKIÓNA
ΣΙΚΥΩΝΑ
Agioi Theódoroi
Αγ. Θεόδωροι
Diórуga Korínthou
Διώρυγα Κορίνθου
Selínia
Σελήνια
Ellinikó
Glyfáda
Γλυφάδα
Várkiza
Βάρκιζα
Markópoulo
Μαρκόπουλον
Kefalári
Isthmia
Ισθμία
Voúla
Βούλα
Keratéa
Kaliánoi
ARHÉA KÓRINTHOS
ΑΡΧ. ΚΟΡΙΝΘΟΣ
Loutró Elénis
SARONIKÓS KÓLPOS
Vouliagméni
Βουλιαγμένη
Lagonísi
Λαγονήσι
Saronída
Σαρωνίδα
Thorikó
Makrónisos
STYMFALÍA
ΣΤΥΜΦΑΛΙΑ
NEMÉA
Limni Stymfalía
Sofikó
Chiliomódi
Souvála
Σουβάλα
AFÉA
ΑΦΕΑ
Akrotírio Tourlos
Anávyssos
Ανάβυσσος
Lávrio
Nemea
Νεμέα
Kórfos
Aígina
Αίγινα
Agia Marina
Légrena
Soúnio
Σούνιον
Leóndio
MIKÍNES
ΜΥΚΗΝΕΣ
ONIA ÓRI
Angelókastro
Ankístri
Pórtes
Kandila
Fihtio
Límnes
Pérdika
Aígina
Αίγινα
Patróklou
Akrotírio Soúnio
ORHÓMENOS
ORHOMENOS
Dimena
Néa Epídavros
Νέα Επίδαυρος
ARHÉA EPÍDAVROS
ΑΡΧ. ΕΠΙΔΑΥΡΟΣ
Palaia Epídavros
Π. Επίδαυρος
Ágios Nikólaos
Koún
MANDÍNIA
ΜΑΝΤΙΝΕΙΑ
Midéa
IRÉO
Árgos
Άργος
Méthanon
Μεθάνων
Kapméni Chora
ATTIKÍ
Korissía-Kéa
TÍRINTHA
ΤΙΡΥΝΘΑ
Lygoúrio
Karía
Nestáni
Náfplio
Ναύπλιον
Dryópi
Kalloní
Póros
Póros
Πόρος
İstanbul
İzmir
Loukás
Mýloi
Trakheiá
Kándia
ASSÍNI
LÉRNI
ΛΕΡΝΗ
Kivéri
Toló
Τολός
Galatás
Γαλατάς
Ágios Geórgios
Achladókampos
Plati
Paralía Iríon
TRIZÍNA
Akrotírio Spáthi
Stemó
Parthéni
Dídyma
Thermisia
Paralía Ástrous
Παράλιον Άστρους
Kiláda
Plépi
Akrotírio Zoúrvas
138
Kato Doliana
TEGÉA
ΤΕΓΕΑ
Ástros
Kranídi
Ermióni
Ερμιόνη
Kólpos Ýdras
Chíos
Ermoúpolis-Sýros
Pátmos
Mérichas-Kýthnos
Páros
Ágios Andréas
Portochéli
Πορτοχέλιον
Argolikós Kólpos
Ýdra
Ύδρα
Ýdra
Vlachokerasiá
Kósta
Κόστα
Dokós
Akrotírio Kórax
Kariés
Ágios Pétros
Plátanos
Spétses
Spétses
Σπέτσαι
Kolínes
Tirós
Sambatikí
PELOPONNISOS
PÁRNON ÓROS
Akrotírio Savátaki
Paleohóri
Leonídio
Vassarás
Sellasía
Σελλασία
MONÍ ELONA
Ródos
Irakleío-Kríti
Réthymno-Kríti
Soúda-Kríti
Trýpi
Hrissafa
Kosmás
Akrotírio Tourkoviglia
Spárti
Σπάρτη
Peletá
Mistrás
Μυστράς
Gkoritsá
PÍRGOS GERAKÍOU
Amyklai
Skoúra
Paralía
Xirokámbi
Geráki
Γεράκιον
Kremasti
Velopoúla
Ágios Dimítrios
Falkonéra
Krokeés
Árna
Vlachiótis
Ríhea
Kastania
Ágios Nikólaos
Skála
Moláoi
Gérakas
Akrotírio Iérax
Gýtheio
Γύθειον
Asopós
Sykéa
KELEFÁ
Mavrovoúni
Elía
Papadiánika
Agéranos
Αγερανός
Liméni
Plýtra
Monemvasía
Μονεμβασία
Oítilon
Karioúpoli
Daimoniá
Akrotírio Xili
Areópoli
Αρεόπολις
Kótronas
Pantánassa
Ágios Apóstoli
Lakonikós Kólpos
Kastaniá
Mézapos
Kokála
MANI
ΜΑΝΗ
Kíta
Κοίτα
Neápoli
Νεάπολις
Elafónisos
Velanídia
Gerolimenas
Γερολιμήν
Akrotírio Maléas
Pórto Kágio
Akrotírio Spathí
Akrotírio Taínaro
Karavás
Agia Pelagía
Potamós
Kýthira
Κύθηρα
Mylopótamos
Livádi
Avlémonas
Kýthira
Kapsáli
Potamós-Andikýthira
140

ATHÍNA
ΑΘΗΝΑ
PEIRAIÁS
ΠΕΙΡΑΙΕΥΣ
Glyfáda
Γλυφάδα
Salamína
Σαλαμίς
Kinetá
Κινετά
Agioi Theódoroi
Αγ. Θεόδωροι
Selínia
Σελήνια
Imitós
Υμηττός
Paianía
Koropí
Κορωπίον
Spáta
Loútsa
VRAVRÓNA
ΒΡΑΥΡΩΝΑ
Pórto Ráfti
Markópoulo
Μαρκόπουλον
Várkiza
Βάρκιζα
Voúla
Βούλα
Vouliagméni
Βουλιαγμένη
Keratéa
Lagonísi
Λαγονήσι
Saronida
Σαρωνίδα
Thorikó
Anávyssos
Ανάβυσσος
Lávrio
Legrena
Soúnio
Σούνιον
Akrotírio Soúnio
Patróklou
Makrónisosi
Kólpos Petalión
Chíos
Istanbul
Izmir
SARONIKÓS KÓLPOS
Souvála
Σουβάλα
AFÉA
ΑΦΕΑ
Akrotírio Tourlos
Kórfos
Aígina
Αίγινα
Agía Marína
Pórtes
Ankístri
Pérdika
Néa Epídavros
Νέα Επίδαυρος
Palaía Epídavros
Π. Επίδαυρος
Ágios Nikólaos
Méthanon
Μεθάνων
Kapméni Chora
Dryópi
Kalloní
Póros
Πόρος
Galatás
Γαλατάς
TRIZÍNA
Dídyma
Thermisía
Plépi
Kranídi
Ermióni
Ερμιόνη
Akrotírio Spáthi
Akrotírio Zoúrvas
Kólpos Ýdras
Ýdra
Ύδρα
Kósta
Κόστα
Dokós
Spétses
ATIKÍ
Ágios Geórgios
Gávrio
Γαύριον
Batsí
Μπατσί
Apoikía
Messariá
Palaiópoli
Παλαιόπολις
Vourkári
Βουρκάρι
Korissía
Κορησσία
Kéa
Κέα
Pisses
Koúndouros
KARTHÉA
Akrotírio Tamélos
Stenó Kéas
Stenó Kýthnou
Gyáros
Akrotírio Trimeson
Sýros
Σύρος
Galissás
Poseidonía
Ποσειδωνία
Loutrá
Λουτρά
Akrotírio Kéfalos
Kýthnos
Mérichas
Dryopída
Kanála
Κύθνος
Akrotírio Agía Dimítrois
Serfopoúla
Stenó Sérifou
MONÍ TAXIARHÓN
Sérifos
Σέριφος
Livádi
Megálo Livádi
Akrotírio Kíklops
GR
Akrotírio Fílippos
Artemón
Kamáres
Apollonía
Απολλώνια
Sífnos
Σίφνος
Platýs Gialós
Πλατύς Γιαλός
Ródos
Irakleio-Kríti
Réthymno-Kríti
Soúda-Kríti
Velopoúla
Falkonéra
Andímilos
Kímolos
Κίμωλος
Psáthi
Polýaigos
Mílos
Μήλος
Apollonía
Adámas
Αδάμας
FILAKOPI
Zefyría
Akrotírio Psálidi
Foléga
Rihéa
Akrotírio Iérax
Monemvasía
Μονεμβασία
Ágios Apóstoli
Kastaniá
Velanídia
Akrotírio Maléas
Agia Pelagía
Kýthira
Κύθηρα
Avlémonas
Livádi
Kapsáli
NÓTIO
134
137
140

135
144
141
142
E
F
G
H
1
2
3
4
5
6
Marathókampos
Μαραθόκαμπος
1455
Sámos
Spatharé
Ag. Kiriakí
Sámos
Πόρος
Akrotírio Fanári
Ikaría
Ικαρία
Thérma
Θέρμα
Armenistís
Évdilos
Hristós
Ágios Kírykos
Thímena
Fournoi
Ág. Minás
Fournoi
984
Amálo
Akrotírio Pápas
Agath
Pátmos
Πάτμος
Arkoí
Kámpos
Skála
Pátmos
Πάτμος
Leipsoí
Leipsc
Parthéni
Léros
Λέρος
Xiróka
Kálymnos
Tínos
Τήνος
Kómi
Κώμη
Falatádos
EXÓMVOURGO
ΕΧΟΜΒΟΥΡΓΟ
Kiónia
Tínos
Τήνος
Ag. Stéfanos
Dragoníssi
Mýkonos
Μύκονος
Áno Merá
Platís
Mýkonos
Μύκονος
Ríneia
Ρήνεια
Dílos
DÍLOS
ΔΗΛΟΣ
Á D E S
Akrotírio Stavrós
Apóllon
Απόλλων
Koronós
Donoússa
Páros
Πάρος
Náousa
Νάουσα
Náxos
Νάξος
Moutsoúna
Kamáres
Filóti
Apeírados
Απείραθος
Levítha
Páros
Πάρος
Kóstos
Galanádo
745
Léfkes
Áno Sangkrí
Α. Σαγκρί
Náxos
Νάξος
Kínaros
Antíparos
Poúnda
Marpíssa
Μάρπησσα
Dryós
Δρυός
Pyrgakia
Koufonísi
Alyki
Aigiali
Αιγιάλη
Kéros
Akrotírio Petalída
HOZOVIÓTISSA
Amorgós
Αμοργός
Katápola
Κατάπολα
Amorgós
Αμοργός
Irákleia
Schoinoússa
Irákleia
MINÓA
Arkesíni
Αρκεσίνη
Íos
Ίος
Astypálaia
Αστυπάλαια
Síkinos
Σίκινος
Íos
713
Vathí
Síkinos
552
Manganari
Ánydro
Análipsi
Kálymnos
gandros
Akrotírio Achládes
Astypálaia
Αστυπάλαια
Ofidoússa
ostásis
Thíra/ Santorini
Θήρα/ Σαντορίνη
Oía
Oία
Thíra/Fira
Θήρα/Θήρα
Thirassia
24
Anáfi
Anáfi
THÍRA
ΘΙΡΑ
Akrotíri
Ακρωτήριον
Períssa
Makra
Pahiá
Christiáni
AIGAÍO
Zafóra
Irakleío-Kríti
Hamilí
Divoúnia

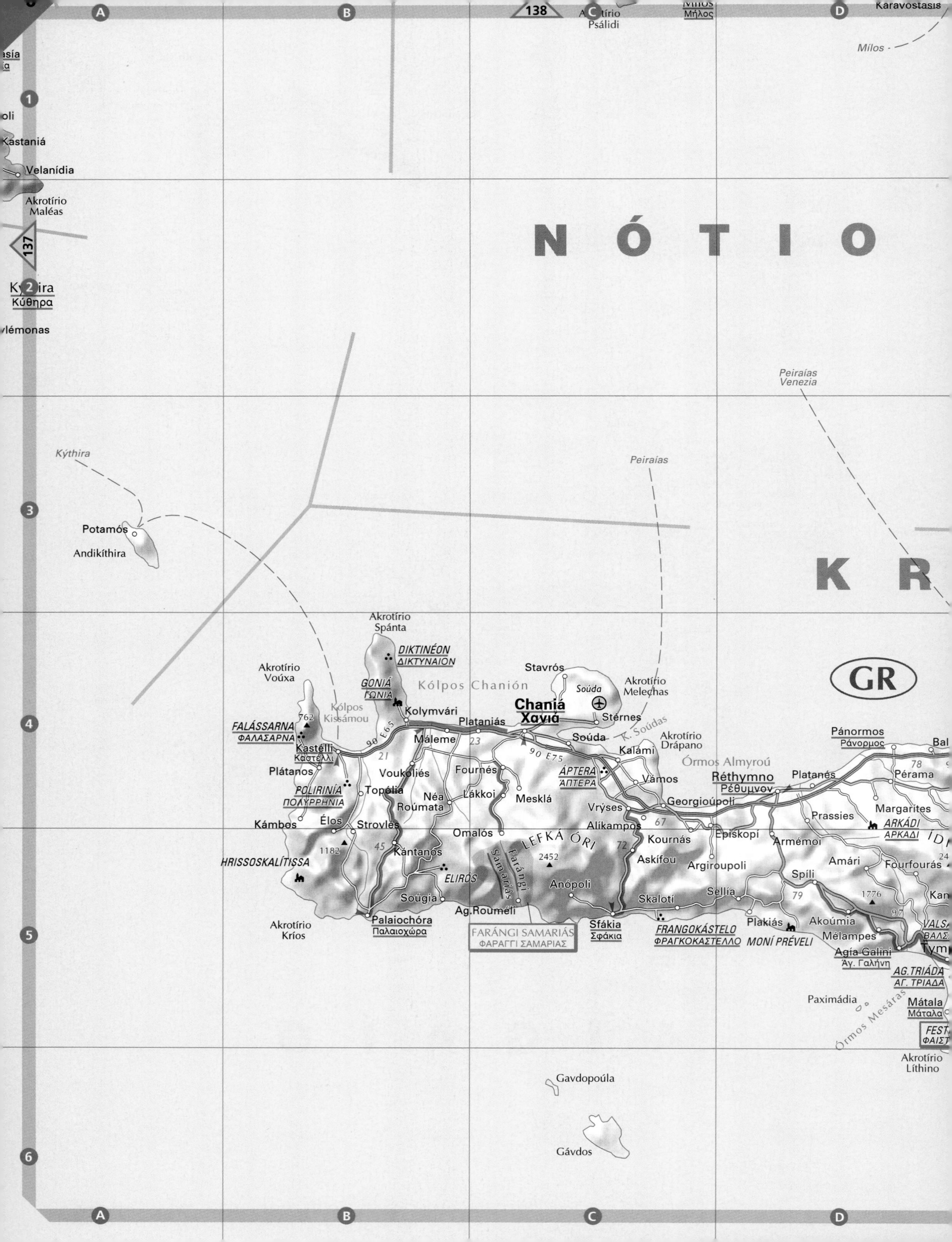

138

A. tírio
Psálidi

Karavostasis

Mílos
Μήλος

Mílos

N Ó T I O

Karavostasis

Peiraías
Venezia

Kýthira

Peiraías

K R

Potamós

Andikíthira

GR

Akrotírio
Spánta

Akrotírio
Voúxa

DIKTINÉON
ΔΙΚΤΥΝΑΙΟΝ

Stavrós

Akrotírio
Melechas

GONIÁ
ΓΩΝΙΑ

Kólpos Chanión

Soúda

FALÁSSARNA
ΦΑΛΑΣΑΡΝΑ

762

Kólpos
Kissámou

Kolymvári

Plataniás

Chaniá
Χανιά

Stérnes

Soúda

Akrotírio
Drápano

Pánormos
Πάνορμος

Bal

Kastélli
Καστέλλι

Máleme

23

90 E75

Kalámi

ÁPTERA
ΑΠΤΕΡΑ

Órmos Almyroú

Réthymno
Ρέθυμνον

Platanés

78
Pérama

Plátanos

90 E65

Voukoliés

21

Fournés

Vámos

POLIRINÍA
ΠΟΛΥΡΡΗΝΙΑ

Topólia

Néa
Roúmata

Lákkoi

Mesklá

Vrýses

Georgioúpoli

Prassies

Margarites

ARKÁDI
ΑΡΚΑΔΙ

Kámbos

Élos

Strovlés

Omalós

Alíkampos

67

Episkopí

Armémoi

Amári

ID

24

1182

45

Kántanos

LEFKÁ ÓRI

72

2452

Kournás

Askífou

Argiroupoli

Spíli

Fourfourás

HRISSOSKALÍTISSA

ELIRÓS

Farángi
Samariás

Anópoli

Skaloti

Sellía

79

1776

Kan

Soúgia

Ag. Rouméli

Sfákia
Σφάκια

FRANGOKÁSTELO
ΦΡΑΓΚΟΚΑΣΤΕΛΛΟ

Plakiás

Akoúmia

VALSA
ΒΑΛΣ

Akrotírio
Kríos

Palaiochóra
Παλαιοχώρα

FARÁNGI SAMARIÁS
ΦΑΡΑΓΓΙ ΣΑΜΑΡΙΑΣ

MONÍ PRÉVELI

Mélampes

Agía Galíni
Αγία Γαλήνη

Tym

AG. TRIÁDA
ΑΓ. ΤΡΙΑΔΑ

Paximádia

Mátala
Μάταλα

FEST
ΦΑΙΣΤ

Órmos Mesarás

Akrotírio
Líthino

Gavdopoúla

Gávdos

E F G H

Inset map (Karpáthos / Kásos)

Sýrna

Stenó Karpáthou

Ródos

Akrotírio Paraspóri

Saria
Σαρία
630

Diafáni

Ólimbos

Messohóri

Karpáthos
Καρπάθος

1215

Voláda

Pilés

Karpáthos
Καρπάθος

Arkása

Menetés

Armáthia

Fri

Ág. Marína

Síteia-
Kríti

Kásos
Κάσος

142

Oía
Οία

Thíra/ Santorini
Thíra/Σαντορίνη
Thíra/ Σαντορίνη

Thirassia

Thíra/Fira
Θήρα/Θήρα

24

THÍRA
ΘΗΡΑ

Akrotíri
Ακρωτήριον

Períssa

Anáfi
Anáfi

Makra

Pahiá

Christiáni

A I G A Í O

Thessaloníki

Í T I

Fri-Kásos

Día

Akrotírio
Stavrós

Ag.
Pelagía

IRAKLEÍO
ΗΡΑΚΛΕΙΟΝ

Iráklio

Gournés

Limín Chersonísou
Λιμάνι Χερσονήσου

Mílatos

Vrouhás

Akrotírio Agios
Ioánnis

SPINALÓNGA
ΣΠΙΝΑΛΟΓΚΑ

Dragonáda

Giannisáda

Akrotírio
Síderos

ITANÓS
ΙΤΑΝΟΣ

Elássa

Fodele
Φόδελε

Amoudára

Nirou
Khani

Goúves

Stalida
Σταλίδα

Mália
Μάλια

Eloúnta

Kólpos Mirampéllou

Vái
Βάι

Márathos

99

Mohos

68

Neápoli
Νεάπολις

Ágios Nikólaos
Αγ. Νικόλαος

TÓPLOU

Palaíkastro
Παλαίκαστρο

Tílisos
Τύλισος

KNOSSÓS
ΚΝΩΣΣΟΣ

Potamiés
Ποταμιαί

Síteia
Σητεί

Akrotírio Pláka

ia

Ágios Mýron
Αγ. Μύρων

Archánes
Αρχάνες

Kastéli

Tzermiádo
Τζερμιάδων

LATÓ
ΛΑΤΩ

90 E75

36

ÁNDRO
ΑΝΤΡΟ

45

109

Psihró

Kritsá
Κριτσά

Kaló
Chorió

Kavoúsi

Móchlos
Μόχλος

Sfáka

Skopi

Zákros

ZÁKROS
ΖΑΚΡΟΣ

VATHÍPETRO
ΒΑΘΥΠΕΤΡΟ

DIKTÉO ÁNDRO
ΔΙΚΤΑΙΟ ΑΝΤΡΟ

DÍKTI ÓRI

70

Sikea

Praisós

Káto Zákros

Ágios Myron

97

Arkalochóri
Αρκαλοχώριον

Panagía

2148

Máles

Pahiá Ámos

1237

GOURNIÁ
ΓΟΥΡΝΙΑ

Stavrohóri

Ζíros

Zarós

Ágia
Varvára

Agios
Thomas

Garipa

Áno
Viánnos

Koutsourás

58

Lithínes

GÓRTIS
ΓΟΡΤΥΣ

Teféli

99

Péfkos

Amoudára

Ag. Fotiá

Makrýgialos

Moíres

Agía Déka

114

Skiniás

Árvi

Ierápetra
Ιεράπετρα

17

Pómpia

Vagioniá

Chárakas

Pýrgos

Keradokampos

Mýrtos

Koufonísi

Léntas

1231

Tsoútsouros

Chrýsi

aloí Liménes

Kríti
Κρήτη

E F G H

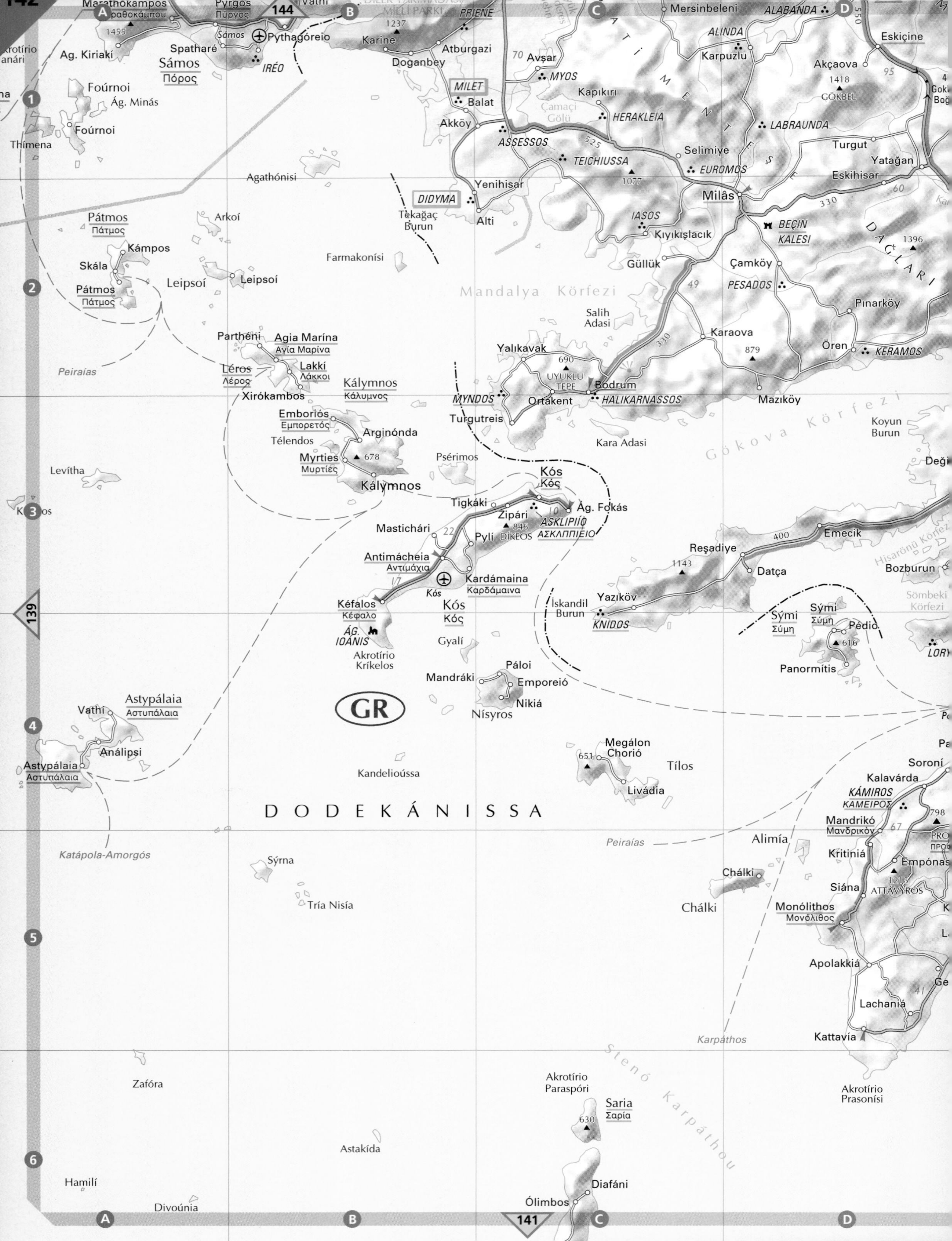

Marathokampos
Μαραθόκαμπος
Pyrgos
Πύργος
144
Sámos
Pythagóreio
Spatharé
Sámos
Πόρος
IRÉO
Ag. Kiriakí
Foúrnoi
Ág. Minás
Foúrnoi
Thímena
Karine
PRIENE
1237
Atburgazi
Doganbey
MILET
Balat
Akköy
ASSESSOS
Avşar
MYOS
Kapıkırı
HERAKLEIA
Çamaçi Gölü
TEICHIUSSA
1077
Mersinbeleni
ALABANDA
ALINDA
Karpuzlu
LABRAUNDA
Selimiye
EUROMOS
Milâs
Eskiçine
Akçaova
1418
GÖKBEL
Turgut
Yatağan
Eskihisar
Agathónisi
DIDYMA
Yenihisar
Alti
Tekağaç Burun
IASOS
Kıyıkışlacık
BEÇIN KALESI
1396
Güllük
Çamköy
PESADOS
Pınarköy
Pátmos
Πάτμος
Arkoí
Kámpos
Skála
Leipsoí
Leipsoí
Pátmos
Πάτμος
Farmakonísi
Mandalya Körfezi
Salih Adasi
Karaova
879
Ören
KERAMOS
Parthéni
Agia Marína
Αγία Μαρίνα
Lakkí
Λάκκοι
Léros
Λέρος
Xirókambos
Peiraías
Kálymnos
Κάλυμνος
Yalıkavak
690
UYUKLU TEPE
Bodrum
HALIKARNASSOS
MYNDOS
Ortakent
Turgutreis
Mazıköy
Emboriós
Εμπορετός
Arginónda
Télendos
Myrties
Μυρτίες
678
Kálymnos
Psérimos
Kara Adasi
Gökova Körfezi
Koyun Burun
Levítha
Kós
Κός
Tigkáki
Ág. Fokás
Zipári
846
DIKEOS
ASKLIPIÍO
ΑΣΚΛΗΠΙΕΙΟ
Mastichári
Pylí
Antimácheia
Αντιμάχεια
Kardámaina
Καρδάμαινα
Kós
Kéfalos
Κέφαλο
ÁG. IOÁNIS
Kós
Κός
Reşadiye
1143
Emecik
Datça
Bozburun
Hisarönü Körfezi
Sömbeki Körfezi
İskandil Burun
Yazıköv
KNIDOS
Sými
Σύμη
Sými
Σύμη
Pedio
616
Panormítis
139
Akrotírio Kríkelos
Gyalí
Páloi
Mandráki
Emporeió
Nikiá
Nísyros
GR
Astypálaia
Αστυπάλαια
Vathí
Análipsi
Astypálaia
Αστυπάλαια
Kandelioússa
Megálon Chorió
651
Tílos
Livádia
DODEKÁNISSA
Katápola-Amorgós
Peiraías
Alimía
Soroní
Kalavárda
KÁMIROS
ΚΑΜΕΙΡΟΣ
798
Mandrikó
Μανδρικό
Kritiniá
Empónas
1215
ATTÁVYROS
Siána
Monólithos
Μονόλιθος
Sýrna
Tría Nisía
Chálki
Chálki
Apolakkiá
Lachaniá
Kattavía
Karpáthos
Stenó Karpáthou
Akrotírio Prasonísi
Zafóra
Akrotírio Paraspóri
Saria
Σαρία
630
Astakída
Diafáni
Hamilí
Divoúnia
Ólimbos
141

Solmaz
Pınarlar
Acıpayam
Karamanlı
Kale
Kavaklıdere
Balkıca
Kumafşarı
Tefenni
Dedebağ
Çatak
Değirmenalanı
Kelekçi
Kınıkyeri
Muratlar
Beyağaç
Çavdır
Yemişendere
Gölhisar
Kızılcadağ
Muğla
TR
Çameli
Söğüt
Yerkesik
Ula
Golçük
GÖLGELİ DAĞ
Altınyayla
KOZAĞACI
Çiçeklibeli Boğaz
Bozyaka
Çubuklu
1580 Dirimli Boğaz
Bekçiler
IDYMA
Karabörtlen
Karabayır
İskele
Çıtlık
Kınık
Köyceğiz
Akköprü
Köyceğiz Gölü
Seki
Elmalı
ARDIÇ DAĞ
THERA
OINOANDA
Büyükkaraağaç
Akçakavak
İncirköy
KAUNOS
Ortaca
115 Göçek Boğaz
Marmaris
Çandır
Üzümlü
Girdev Gölü
İstuzu
Dalaman
Kargı
Adaköy
Kemer
AK DAĞLAR
Marmaris Limanı
Dalaman
KRYA
110 Metris Boğaz
Akçay
Turunç
KASTABOS
Sarsıla İskele
Fethiye Körfezi
TLOS
3024 UYLUK TEPE
Kadırga Burun
TELMESSOS
Fethiye
Kayaköy
Kurtoğlu Burun
Ölüdeniz
İblis Burun
Eşen
XANTHOS
1080 Belpınar Boğaz
Kasaba
Kınık
Yedi Burun
PYDNAY
TRYSA
Kalkan
PATARA
APOLLONIA
Kaş
Yalı Burun
Ulu Burun
Megísti
Μεγίστη
GR
Megísti (Kastelórizo)
Μεγίστη (Καστελλόριζον)
Ródos
Ρόδος
Triánta
Τριάντα
Ixia
Kremasti
Kallithéas
Καλλιθέα
IÁLISSOS
ΙΑΛΙΣΣΟΣ
Faliráki
Φαληράκι
Afántou
MONÍ TSAMBÍKA
Archángelos
FERAKLÓS
ΦΕΡΑΚΛΟΣ
Líndos
Λίνδος
Ródos
Ρόδος
E
F
G
H
1
2
3
4
5
6

A
B
C
D
146
139
142
135
1
2
3
4
5
6
Yeniköy
TRUVA
Yiğitler
Pazarköy
Kalkım
Gönen Çayı
Küçük Menderes
Bayramiç
Evciler
Serhat
KOCAKTRAN DAĞI
1767
KAZ DAĞI
MARMA
Balya
Kırıklar
BALIKESİR
Kepsut
Nusret
Ergama
Güngörmez
İvrindi
Çağış
Ertuğrul
Pamukçu
Konakpınar
Geyikli
Ezine
Bozca Adasi
Dalyan
ALEXANDRIA TROAS
NEANDRIA
Kısacık
776 DİKİLİ TEPE
Altınoluk
Akçay
Edremit
Havran
ADRAMITTIUM THEBE
Kösedere
672
Ayvacık
ANTANDROS
Küçükkuyu
Ören
Burhaniye
Kayapa
Korucu
Karacalar
BABAKÖY
Debeğur
Tuzla
Gülpınar
ASSOS
Behramkale
Baba Burun
POLYMEDIUM
Edremit Körfezi
PASSANDRA
Alibey Adasi
Armutova
1338 MADRA DAĞI
Madra Deresi
Duğla
Savaştepe
Karaçam
950
Gölcük
MANCINIK DAĞI
860
Thessaloníki Mýrina-Límnos
Míthymna
Sikaminiá
Akrotírio Skamnia
Ayvalık
Bağyüzü
CYTONIUM
Kozak
Turanlı
APOLLONIA
Gelembe
Pétra
Stipsi
Mantamádos
ŞEYTAN SOFRASI
Altınova
AKRAPOL
Bakır Çayı
Soma
Kırkağaç
ÁNTISSA
Fília
Agía Paraskeví
Mistegná
Nebiler
Bergama
ASKLEPİYON
Kınık
Sígri
Ántissa
Kalloni
Vatoúsa
Thermís
MELENE
E87
Kólpos Kallonís
Eresós
Keramía
Mytilíni
ATANNEUS
Palamut
Akrotírio Sígri
Parakilá
Dikili
TEUCHRANIA
Skála Eresoú
Skála
Vassiliká
Agiássos
CARENE
Bademli
Satırlar
Akhisar
Ambelikó
968
Loutrá
Krátigos
772
Zeytindağ
1084
KILIÇ DAĞI
Polichnitos
Skópelos
Yuntdağ
Kapaklı
Lésvos
Λέσβος
Vaterá
Plomári
Çandarlı
Çandarlı Körfezi
Yenişakran
MYRINA
Ilica Burun
Aliağa
Türkmen
Saruhanli
Gölmarmara
KYME
Halitpaşa
Peiraías
Yenifoça
1074
Muradiye
Yeniçöy
1034
Aslan Burun
KIYILA
GR
PHOKAIA
LARISSA
Gediz Nehri
Ahmetli
Manisa
SİPİL DAĞI MİLLİ PARKI
Kara Burun
Foça
Menemen
Emiralem
675 Cabuncubeli Boğaz
Hasseki
Karaburun
Turgutlu
1212 AK DAĞ
Uzon Adasi
İzmir Körfezi
İZMİR
Küçükbahçe
Çamaltı
Bornova
Kemalpaşa
Psará
Agiásmata
Kambiá
1297
Mármaro
Mordoğan
Armutlu
BOZ
Melaniós
Kardámyla
Oinoússes
İnciraltı
Buca
1506 NİFKARLIÇI TEPE
Volissós
Lagkáda
Balıklıova
Çeşmealti
KLAZOMENAI
Dağkızılca
Vrontádos
Chíos
Χίος
1042
Ildır
Urla
Güzelbahçe
Seydiköy
NÉA MONÍ
Bayındır
Çeşme
Uzunkuyu
Menderes
Thimianá
Alaçatı
Kallimasiá
Passá Liméni
Véssa
Armólia
Tahtalı Brj.
Seferihisar
Torbalı
Mahmutlar
Gökçen
Mestá
Kalamotí
Sığacık
TEOS
Değirmendere
Pamukyazı
Tire
Pirgí
Kómi
Emboriós
Sığacık Körfezi
COLOPHON
Gümüldür
Boğaziçi
Akrotírio Mastichó
Koraka Burun
Doğanbey
MYONNESOS
Doğanbey Burun
CLAROS
Belevi
AYDIN
BAYRAKÇI MAĞARASI
Peiraías
EPHESOS
Selçuk
Pamucak
Ortaklar
Germencik
MERYEMANA
MAGNESIA
1019
Kuşadasi
İncirliova
KARYAĞDI TEPE
Kuşadasi Körfezi
KADIKALESİ
Söke
Koçarlı
Agios Konstantinos
Avlákia
Kokkárion
Sámos
Σάμος
Davutlar
Bağarası
Karlovási
1153
Yenidoğan
Marathókampos
Pýrgos
Vathí
DİLEK YARIMADASI MİLLİ PARKI
Büyük Menderes Nehri
Mersinbeleni
1455
Sámos
Pythagóreio
1237
Karine
PRİENE
Spatharé
Sámos
Πόρος
IRÉO
Atburgazi
Doğanbey
Avşar
MYOS
Akrotírio Fanári
Ag. Kiriakí
Ikaría
Ικαρία
Foúrnoi
Ág. Minás
MİLET
Balat
Kapıkırı
Çamaçi Gölü
HERAKLEIA
Thérma
Armenistís
Évdilos
Ágios Kírykos
Foúrnoi
Akköy
ASSESSOS
Hristós
Thímena
984
Amálo
Mýkonos Páros
Pátmos
Agathónisi
TEICHIUSSA
1077
Yenihisar
DIDYMA
Akrotírio Pápas
Pátmos
Πάτμος
Arkoí
Tekağaç Burun
Altı
ASOS

147
E
F
G
H
A
Kavacık
Tavşanlı
Köprüören
Türkmendağı
Dursunbey
Gökçedağ
Balıköy
Tepecik
KÜTAHYA
1901
NALBANT TEPE
Kireç
Günlüce
Alçaşehir
Bayramşah
Kırka
1
Dağardı
2076
KOCAKIRDAĞ TEPE
ALAÇAM DAĞLARI
Yassiören
Emet
Yariş
1698
Gökbahçe
Yağcılar
Kocasu
Porsuk Çayı
Panayır
Hisarcık
Örencik
Aslanapa
ARSLANKAYA
Çamlık
1769
2089
AIZANOI
Çavdarhisar
Aykırıkçı
İhsaniye
Düvertepe
Yemişli
Efendiköprüsü
BATI
Ören
Altıntaş
Çaygören Barajı
Yeşilçay
Anıtkaya
SİMAV DAĞLARI
Simav
2120
ULUGEDİK TEPE
Eski Gediz
Çukurören
Yaylabayır
Yesilköy
Şaphane
Gediz
MURAT DAĞI
Çalköy
2
Haman
1676
2312
Demirci
Yarbasan
Abide
Dumlupınar
Kuşuköy
E
Hanya
Kulalar
Kerpiçlik
Ayrancı
Çamsu
Düzağac
Sinanpaşa
1535
Kizilkoltuk
Yeniköy
1201
1514
1915
Gördes
Banaz
Karabeyli
Gediz Nehri
Ahat
Şehirlioğlu
Saraycık
Uşak
Bozkuş
Hocalar
Köprübaşi
Borlu
Çalıklı
Selendi
Güre
Gördes Deresi
Akarca
Sandıklı
TR
Güre
3
Yenişehir
Çardak
Baştepe
Demirköprü Barajı
Sivaslı
1930
Poyrazdamları
Taşköy
Kişlaköy
Ağaçbeyli
ÇATMA DAĞI
AKDAĞ
Karataş
Kula
Banaz Çayı
KUMALAR DAĞI
Durasıllı
Ulubey
Isıklı
2445
SARDES
Kemaliye
1554
EUMENEIA
Salihli
Eşme
Hasköy
Karahallı
Çivril
Gümüşsu
Dereköy
Alaşehir Çayı
Tepeköy
UYSAL DAĞI
Sülümenli
Alaşehir
Yeşilyurt
Yeleğen
Bekilli
Yamanlar
Işıklı Barajı
Akçak
Azıtepe
Güllü
Büyük Menderes Nehri
2157
Akkent
Adigüzel Barajı
Karaköy
Süller
Dinar
Birgi
Sarıgöl
Güney
Kiraz
Sarıkaya
Kabalar
Kadıköy
Hadım
4
Derbent
Cindere
Çal
Karta
Kaymakçi
1840
İsabey
Baklan
Buldan
Ovakent
Beydağı
Denizler
Dazkırı
Başmakçı
1781
Tepeci
1827
Kayran
Köprübaşı
Hierapolis
1689
HACETDEDE TEPE
Samaılli
Sarayköy
Pamukkale
Çardak
Acıgöl
Burd
Horsunlu
Çubukdağı
Kaklik
SÖĞÜT DAĞI
Kuyucak
MASTAURA
LAODIKEIA
Burdur Gölü
Nazıllı
Atça
Sultanhisar
Babadağ
DENİZLİ
NYSA
Yenice
EŞLER DAĞI
Köşk
5
Umurlu
Yenipazar
Çukurköy
Karacasu
APHRODISIAS
1250
Kazıkbeli Boğaz
Dalama
Geyre
Serinhisar
Solda Gölü
Yeşilova
Akçay
Bozdoğan
NEAPOLIS
Vakıfköy
Tavas
1792
Çine Çayı
DOĞU MENTEŞE DAĞLARI
Yolüstü
Güney
2243
AKKAYA TEPE
Kemer
Çine
ALABANDA
Kemer Barajı
Solmaz
Medet
Pınarlar
Acıpayam
Kemer
Karamanlı
Eskiçine
Akçaova
Kale
Kumafşarı
Tefenni
1418
GÖKBEL
400
Gokbel Boğaz
Kavaklıdere
Balkıca
2421
Dedebağ
LABRAUNDA
Çatak
Değirmenalanı
Kelekçi
1892
OYUK DAĞ
Turgut
Kınıkyeri
6
Yatağan
Muratlar
Beyağaç
Dalaman Çayı
Çavdır
Eskihisar
Yemişendere
Ak Çayı
Gölhisar
Bayır
Kızılcadağ
143
Çameli

BG
GR
TRAKYA
MARMARA
ISTRANCA DAĞLARI
MARMARA DE
149
131
144
Knyazhevo
Topolovgrad
Ustrem
Bŭlgarska Polyana
Radovets
Lefka
Svilengrad
Свиленград
Kapitan Andreevo
EDIRNE
Petrotá
Dikea
Kastanies
Pláti
Rízia
Kómara
Fyláki
Kavíli
Néa Vissa
Váltos
Orestiáda
Ambelákia
Ivaylovgrad
Zóni
Ládi
Thourio
Máni
Metaxades
Didymóteicho
Διδυμότειχο
Mavroklissio
Mikró Dérieio
Protoklíssio
Lávara
Mándra
Roússa
Sidiró
Gianoúli
Souflí
Likófos
Thimariá
Loutrós
Féres
Monastirákí
Alexandroúpoli
Αλεξανδρούπολις
Yeni Karpuzlu
Orhaniye
Gala Gölü
Enez
Abdürrahim
Erikli
İbrikbaba
Saroz Körfezi
Kofçaz
Kayalıköy Barajı
Yoğuntas
Lalapaşa
Süloğlu
Demirhanlı
İnece
Hasköy
Teke Deresi
Havsa
Kuleli
Babaeski
Elçili
Kırcasalih
Pehlivanköy
Uzunköprü
Meriç
Küplü
İbriktepe
Paşayiğit
İpsala
Keşan
Kavacık
Hamidiye
Çöpköy
Şahin
Kozyürük
Malkara
Ergene Nehri
Meriç Nehri
Malko Tŭrnovo
Dereköy
Kırklareli
Kırklareli Barajı
Üsküp
Pınarhisar
Yancıklar
Karacaoğlan
Turgutbey
Ahmetbey
Lüleburgaz
Alpullu
Büyükkarıştıran
Hayrabolu
Dambaslar
Ceneköy
Muratlı
Banarli
NAPLES
İnecik
Kadıköy Barajı
Ballı
İshakı
GANOS DAĞI
KURU DAĞI
Kadıköy
Kocaçeşme
Kavak
Bolayır
Ocaklı
Gelibolu
Tayfur
GELİBOLU YARIMADASI
Büyük Kemikli Burun
GELİBOLU
LIMNAE
Eceabat
Kilitbahir
Kabaltepe
YARIMADASI MİLLİ PARKI
Çanakkale
Kepez
Abide
İlyasbaba Burun
Kumkale
ACHILLEUM
Tevfikiye
Yeniköy
TRUVA
Geyikli
Bozca Adası
Dalyan
ALEXANDRIA TROAS
NEANDRIA
Ezine
Kösedere
Kaleköy
İmroz
Aydıncık
Ayagalip
Iğneada
Iğneada Burnu
Demirköy
Kıyıköy
Poyralı
Vize
Saray
Istranca
Karacaköy
Gümüşpınar
Beyazköy
Çerkezköy
Sinekli
Kabakca
Vakiflar
Çorlu
Çorlu Suyu
Seymen
Silivri
Sultanköy
Yeniçiftlik
Liman Burun
Marmaraereğlisi
Tekirdağ
Barbaros
Kumbağ
Yeniköy
Mürefte
Şarköy
Marmara Adası
Marmara
Türkeli
Türkeli Adası
Paşalimanı Adası
Kara Burun
Erdek Körfezi
İlhan
KYZIKOS
Karşıyaka
Erdek
Bandırma Körfezi
Kurşunlu
Yenice
Bandırma
Edincik
Bezirci
KUŞCENNETİ MİLLİ PARKI
Kuş Gölü
Kemer
Aksaz
Karabiga
Şevketiye
Güreci
Çardak
Lapseki
Belıklıçeşme
Bayırköy
Umurbey Çayı
Umurbey
Bakacak
Biga
Sinekçi
Denizkent
Buğdayli
Sariköy
Aksakal
Ergili
Şevketiye
PEMANINOS
Manyas
Gönen
Göbel
Dondurma
KARA DAĞ
Maltepe
Aşağıinova
Çan
Ortaca
Kumarlar
Kirazlı
Etili
Ortaoba
Orhanlar
Ilıca
Ömerköy
Denizgören
Yenice
Danişment
Şamlı
Zeybekçayırı
Pazarköy
Yenikoy
Hamdibey
Gönen Çayı
Kalkım
Kepsut
Yiğitler
Küçük Menderes
Kırıklar
Balya
BALIKESİR
KOCAKTRAN DAĞI
Bayramiç
Evciler
Serhat
KAZ DAĞI
Ergama
Nusret
Güngörmez
İvrindi
Ertuğrul
Çağış
Pamukçu
Konakpınar
Kısacık
Akçay
Edremit
Altınoluk
Havran
Kavala
E80
E90
E84
E87
O-3
KARA

E
F
G
H
1
2
3
4
5
6
A
TR
Pazarbaşı Burun
Kefken
Karaağaç
Karasu
Kocaali
Darıçayırı
Karaburun
Terkoz
Ağaçlı
Kumköy
Çayağzi
Sahilköy
Şile
Ağva/Yeşilçay
Kandira
Kaynarca
Yassiören
Arnavutköy
Kemerburgaz
Sariyer
Rumelifeneri
Beykoz
Alacalı
Teke
Akçaova
Boyalık
İSTANBUL
Yeniköy
Mahmutşevketpaşa
Türas
Kocakaymaz
Kaymaz
Süğütlü
Soğuksu
Cumaova
Alemdağ
Cemke
Sangazi
Ömerli Barajı
Hendek
Esenyurt
Küçükçekmece
Samandıra
Akmeşe
Beşevlet
ADAPAZARI
Üsküdar
Bakirköy
Yeşilköy
Avcılar
Atatürk
Maltepe
Mollafeneri
Karayakuplu
Sapakpınar
Kazımpaşa
Kartal
Tepecik
İZMİT
Akyazı
ELMACIK
Pendik
Tuzla
Gebze
Hereke
Körfez
Yarımca
Uzuntarla
Sapanca Gölü
Ekinli
Karapürçek
Kuzuluk
Kızıl Adalar
Darıca
Tavşancil
Değirmendere
Gölcük
Kurtköy
Sapanca
Suadiye
Yeniköy
Bahçecik
İzmit Körfezi
Altınova
Karamürsel
DAĞLARI
KAPIORMAN DAĞI
Peiraías
Yalova
Yalakdere
Sarısu
SAMANLI
Kazkıran Geçit 800
Pamukova
Geyve
Göynük
Çınarcık
Termal
Yeniköy
Bayındır
Taraklı
Meyitler Geçit
Arnavutköy
Boyalıca
İznik
Beşevler
İznik Gölü
Orhangazi
NIKAIA
Osmaneli
İmralı Ad
Armutlu
Kapaklı
Gemlik
Sölöz
Gölpazarı
Gemlik Körfezi
Umurbey
Narlıca
Zeytinbaği
Mudanya
Ericek
Yenişehir
Köprühisar
Vezirhan
Yenipazar
Kurşunlu
Koyunhis
HISARTEPE DASCYLIUM
APAMEA
Esence
Demirtaş
Yunuseli
Nilüfer Çayı
Boğazköy
Bilecik
Sakarya Nehri
Sarıcakaya
Mihalgazi
Görükle
Gürsu
Turan
Küplü
Çalti
İnhisar
MILETOPOLIS
APOLLONIA
Hasanağa
BURSA
Söğüt
Uluabat
Gölyazi
Çali
Uludağ
ULUDAĞ MİLLİ PARKI
İnegöl
Hasanpaşa
Demirköy
Pazaryeri
SÜNDİKEN
Ulubat Gölü
ULUDAĞ
Çayyaka
Bozüyük
Muttalip
Sıncansarnıç
Poyra
ESKİŞEHİR
Söğütalan
TEPEL TEPE
Tahtaköprü
Kozpınar
Safa
Mustafa Kemalpaşa
Yürücekler
Keles
İnönü
Çaltılıbük
Orhaneli
Domaniç
Akpınar
Yeşiller
Cihangazi
Kümbet
Devecikonaği
Demirci
Böçen
Sobran
Porsuk Barajı
Kansız
Alacat
Gümüşyeni
Büyükorhan
Kınık
Harmancık
Yeniköy
Tunçbilek
Seyitömer
Tavşanlı
Kavacık
Köprüören
TÜRKMENDAĞI
Dursunbey
Gökçedağ
Balıköy
Tepecik
KÜTAHYA
NALBANT TEPE
Alçaşehir
Kireç
Günlüce
Bayramşah
Dağardı
KOCAKIRDAĞ TEPE
Yassiören
Yariş
Gökbahçe
Emet
145
ALAÇAM DAĞ
Örencik
Aslanapa
ARSLANKAYA

206
151
130
131
RO
BG
RUS
LOVECH
KHASKOVO
PLOVDIV
Brebeni
Şerbăneşti
Blejeşti
Videle
Ghimpaţi
Călugăreni
Herăşti
Curcani
Ulmeni
Dobroteşti
Văleni
Vârtoapele
Olteni
Botoroaga
Naipu
Schitu
Mihai Bravu
Prundu
Greaca
Căscioarele
Olteniţa
Brincoveni
Bălăneşti
Brebina
Drăgăneşti Vlaşca
Vlaşin
Teslui
Drăgăneşti Olt
Drăgăneşti de Vede
Băneasa
Ryakhovo
Staro Selo
Caracal
Dăneasa
Mihăeşti
Roşiori de Vede
Lăceni
Toporu
Daia
Băbiciu
Crângeni
Peretu
Buzescu
Vităneşti
Alexandria
Marten
Slivo Pole
Deveselu
Redea
Vlădila
Beciu
Călmăţuiu
Putineiu
Giurgiu
Plopii Slăviteşti
Vieru
Slobozia
Chervena Voda
Tetovo
Kubrat
Amărăştu de Jos
Smârdioasa
RUSE
РУСЕ
Novo Selo
Slobozia Mândra
Furculeşti
Vedea
Ocolna
Vişina Veche
Piatra
Vetovo
Vădastra
Izbiceni
Traian
Pisanets
Topchii
Corabia
Gârcov
Fântânele
Turnu Măgurele
Bujoru
Ivanovo Manastir
Иваново Ман.
Rusenski Lom
Kicher
Dăbuleni
Ianca
Grojdibodu
Cerkovitsa
Dunărea
Gigen
Гиген
Zimnicea
Khlebarovo
Osenets
Baykal
Somovit
Nikopol
Belene
Svishtov
Dve Mogili
Razgrad
Разград
Krushovene
Brest
Gulyantsi
Vardim
Tsarevets
Galovo
Debovo
Tsenovo
Volovo
Blagoevo
Stavertsi
Stezherovo
Dragomirovo
Borovo
Opaka
Trăstenik
Koilovtsi
Byala
Koprivets
Dolna Mitropoliya
Slavyanovo
Bŭlgarene
Gorna Studena
Polsko Kosovo
Popovo
Knezha
Yasen
Obnova
Kozar Belene
Polski Trŭmbesh
Voditsa
Pogoritsa
Pelovo
PLEVEN
Плевен
Grivitsa
Levski
Dolni Dŭbnik
Pordim
Sushitsa
Aprilovo
Letnitsa
Nicopolis ad Istrum
Никополис
Telish
Aleksandrovo
Dragomirovo
Tŭrgovishki Pateka
Sadovets
Pavlikeni
Polikrayshte
Arbanasi
Арбанаси
Antonovo
Bryag
Beglezh
Bjala Cherkva
Gorna Oryakhovitsa
Kesarevo
Omurtag
Devetaki
Vishovgrad
Samovodene
Lukovit
Preobrazhenski Man.
Преображенски Ман.
Lyaskovets
Lovech
Ловеч
Dermantsi
Dobromirka
Balvan
Debelets
Veliko Tŭrnovo
Велико Търново
Lisa Pl.
Zlatna Panega
Ugŭrchin
Dryanovo
Дряново
Kilifarevo
Bebrovo
Kotlenska Planina
Bŭlgarski Izvor
Ablanitsa
Bŭlgarene
Sennik
Sevlievo
Севлиево
Elena
Елена
Kotlenski Pateka
Yablanitsa
Mikre
Yavorets
Vŭglevtsi
Stara Reka
Zerevna
Жеравна
Glozhenski Manastir
Borima
Debnevo
Tryavna
Трявна
Republik Pateka
Gabrovo
Габрово
Bozhenci
Боженци
Vratnik Pateka
Teteven
Тетевен
Osikovitsa
Troyan
Троян
Oresak
Tvŭrdishki Pateka
Chumerna
Shipkovo
Troyanski Manastir
Троянски Ман.
Shipchenski Prokhad
Шипченски Проход
Sliven
Сливен
Ribaritsa
Troyanski Pateka
Eleno Tvardishka Pl.
Shivatsevo
Etropole
Етрополе
Zlatishko-Tetevenska Pl.
Vezhen
Вежен
Balkan
Botev
Shipka
Шипка
Tvŭrditsa
Zlatishki Pateka
Baba
Rosino
Kŭrnare
Kaloferska Pl.
Shipchenski Man.
Gurkovo
Silvenski bani
Силвенска бани
Zlatitsa
Pirdop
Klisura
Karlovo
Карлово
Kazanlŭk
Казанлък
Banya
Vetren
Kermen
Sopot
Kalofer
Mŭglizh
Korten
Koprivshtitsa
Копривщица
Rosova Dolina
Росова Долина
Pavel Banya
Yagoda
Nova Zagora
Нова Загора
Bogdan
Banya
Баня
Tundzha
Podslon
Gŭlŭbintsi
Khisariya
Хисаря
Bratan
STARA ZAGORA
Стара Загора
Poibrene
Oborishte
Strelcha
Стрелча
Sharnevo
Mlekarevo
Muhovo
Panagyurishte
Панагюрище
Krasnovo
Strelci
Rakitnica
Novoselets
Skalitsa
Popintsi
Kaloyanovo
Brezovo
Radnevo
Dolno Levski
Lyuben
Bratya Daskolovi
Sredets
Polski Gradets
Kalugerovo
Rakovski
Kostenets
Костенец
Trud
Stryama
Chirpan
Чирпан
Mŭdrets
Topolovgrad
Gŭlŭbovo
Septemvri
Pazardzhik
Пазарджик
Merichleri
Belovo
Lozen
Popovitsa
Pŭrvomay
Maritsa
Glavan
Bŭlgarska Polyana
Varvara
Novi Krichim
PLOVDIV
ПЛОВДИВ
Sadovo
Садово
Dimitrovgrad
Димировград
Simeonovgrad
Debŭr
Filevo
Dŭlbok Izvor
Peshtera
Пещера
Krichim
Кричим
Perushtica
Перущица
Asenovgrad
Асеновград
Podkrepa
Kharmanli
Bracigovo
Брацигово
Bachkovo
Бачково
Bachkovski Manastir
Бачковски Ман.
Mineralni Bani
Khaskovo
Хасково
Lyubimets
Lefka
Yazovir Batak
Rakitovo
Ракитово
Narechenski Bani
Нареченски бани
Topolovo
Yazovir Trakiec
Konush
Batak
Батак
Khrojna
Lŭki
Malko Gradishte
Svilengrad
Свиленград
Golyama Syutkya
Mikhalkovo
Михалково
Golyama
Komuniga
Tancovo
Kapitan Andreevo

149
Silistra
Силистра
Ostrov
Lipniţa
Adamclisi
Topraisar
Costineşti
23 August
Neptun
Jupiter
Venus
Saturn
Mangalia
Amzacea
Independenţa
Pecineaga
Albeşti
Dumbrăveni
Rosica
Popina
Srebărna
Сребърна
Zafirovo
Dobrotitsa
Glavinitsa
Alfatar
Sredishte
Krasen
Negru Vodă
Vama Veche
Krushari
Kardam
Durankulak
Alekovo
Dulovo
Tervel
Leskovo
General Toshevo
Spasovo
Preselentsi
Kochmar
Šhabla
Isperikh
Orlyak
Karapelit
Dobrich
Добрич
Vranino
Tyulenovo
Kaolinovo
Nikola Kozlevo
Senokos
Kavarna
Kamen Bryag
Kliment
Durach
Venets
VARNA
Sokolovo
Bŭlgarevo
Rusalka
Hŭrsovo
Stozher
Balchik
Балчик
Tuzlata
Nos Kaliakra
Obrochishte
Kaloyan
Vŭlchidol
Albena
Албена
Kranevo
Duran
Gara Khitrino
Stojan Mikhaylovski
ALADZHA MANASTIR
АЛАДЖА МАН.
Zlatni Pyasŭtsi
Златни Пясъци
Suvorovo
Kichevo
Novi Pazar
Pliska
Vetrino
Varna
Aksakovo
ZLATNI PYASŬTSI
Kaspichan
A2
E70
Druzhba
Дружба
Madara
Мадара
Devnya
A5
VARNA ВАРНА
SHUMENSKO PLATO
Shumen
Шумен
Provadiyska reka
Galata
Галата
Radko Dimitrievo
Provadiya
Провадия
Gebedzhensko ezero
Varnensko ezero
POBITI KAMŬNI
Priseltsi
Bliznak
Eliki Preslav
Преслав
Ivanski
Drumevo
Bozveliisko
Kamchiya
Камчия
Zlatar
Dŭlgopol
Goren Chiflik
Staro Oryakhovo
Ivanovo
Smyadovo
Grozd'ovo
Georgi Traykov
Shkorpilovtsi
Rudnik
Vŭrbitsa
KARNOBAYSKA PLANINA
Rish
Veselinovo
Asparukovo
Byala
AJTOSKA PLANNINA
Dyulino
800 Rishki Pateka
834
Dŭskotna
Obzor
Обзор
889 KALETO
390 Djulinski Pateka
Banya
Prosenik
Emona
Beronovo
Orizare
Nos Emine
Luda Kamchiya
414 Ajtoshi Pateka
Vlas
Lozarevo
Slŭnchev Bryag
Слънчев Бряг
Sungurlare
Aytos
Nesebŭr
Несебър
BURGAS
E773
Kableshkovo
Ravda
427 KRISTA
Bŭlgarovo
Vetren
Pomorie
Поморие
Karnobat
Venets
Kameno
Sarafovo
Troyanovo
Burgaski Zaliv
Straldzha
Ekzarh Antimovo
BURGAS
ВУРГАС
Chernomorets
Burgasko ezero
Kraymorie
Sozopol
Созопол
Yambol
Ямбол
Rusokastro
Meden Rudnik
Dyuni
Дюни
Rosen
Golyama reka
Zornitsa
Arkutino
Tamarino
Sredets
Primorsko
Приморско
Krushevets
Kiten
Yasna Polyana
Lozenets
Sredetska reka
Fakiyska reka
Tsarevo
Царево
Varvara
Golyalo Krushevo
Varovnik
Akhtopol
Izgrev
Zvezdets
Kondolovo
Sinemorets
Gramatikovo
Bolyarovo
Rezovo
Veleka
Knyazhevo
Malko Tŭrnovo
Rezovska reka
Kofçaz
Dereköy
Iğneada
Iğneada Burnu
Tundzha
Kayalıkoy Barajı
TR
ISTRANCA DAĞLARI
Demirköy
1030
Lalapaşa
Yoğuntas
Kırklareli Barajı
Süloğlu
Kırklareli
Üsküp
Kıyıköy
Demirhanlı
İnece
Pınarhisar
Poyralı
EDIRNE
Vize
146
Hasköy
Yancıklar
Karacaköy

155
128
153
SRBIJA
YU
AL
MK
SHKODËR
Draginje
Banjani
Stubline
Stepojevac
Sopot
Mladenovac Varoš
Selevac
Osipaonica
Lozovik
Aleksandrovac
Kučevo
RAJKOVA PEĆINA
Donji Milanovac
Majdanpek
Tamnava
Ub
Vreoci
Koceljevo
Venčane
Smederevska-Palanka
Veliko Orašje
Žabari
Petrovac
Melnica
CEREMOSNJA
Rudna Glava
Miloševa Kula
Lajkovac
Lazarevac
Osečina
Slovac
Partizani
Velika Plana
MAN. KOPORIN
Krepoljin
Donja Kamenica
Arandjelovac
Аранджеловац
Natalinci
Markovac
Svilajnac
MANASTIR GORNJAK
Žagubica
Valjevo
Mionica
Topola
Топола
Rača
Krupaja
Ljig
Donja Šatornja
MAN. OPLENAC
МАН. ОПЛЕНАЦ
Lapovo
MALJEN
Ugrinovci
Rudnik
Čumic
Batočina
MAN. MANASIJA
МАН. МАНАСЯ
BELJANICA
Krivelj
Bor
Poćuta
Bukovi
Divčibare
MAN. BLAGOVEŠTENJE
МАН. БЛАГОВЕШТЕНЕ
Mutanj
Desimirovac
Despotovac
RESAVSKA PEĆINA
Brestovačka Banja
POVLJEN
Bukovi Prolaz
RUDNIK
Vraćevšnica
RAVANIČKA PEĆINA
РАВАНИЧКА ПЕЦИНА
Ravna Reka
ZLOTSKA PEĆINA
Zlot
Pranjani
Kragujevac
Крагуевац
Jagodina
Светозарево
Rogačica
Kosjerić
Gornji Milanovac
MAN. JOŠANICA
MAN. RAVANICA
МАН. РАВАНИЦА
Podgorac
Šarbanovac
Dub
Zaglavak
Bajina Bašta
Brdjani
Vuckovica
Gornja Sabanta
Dragocvet
Ćuprija
SVETA PETKA
BOGOVINSKA PEĆINA
Bogovina
Kadinjača Prolaz
Čestobrodica
Kratovska Stena
Čačak
Чачак
Knić
Gruža
Izvor
Straža
Paraćin
Lukovo
Boljevac
Bioska
Ovčar Banja
Mrčajevci
Guberevac
Stolice Prolaz
Sevojno
Požega
GLEDIĆSKE PL.
Lasovo
Rtanj
Kremna
Užice
Ужице
Slatina
MAN. KALENIĆ
МАН. КАЛЕНИЧ
Belušić
Pojate
Čajetina
Guča
Viča
Kraljevo
Кралево
Vitanovac
Ćićevac
Moravica
Blendija
Partizanske Vode
Партизанске Воде
Arilje
Арилe
Booutovačka Banja
Mataruška Banja
Podunavci
MANASTIR LJUBOSTINJA
МАН. ЛЮБОСТИНЯ
Bačina
Stalać
Bovan
Soko Banja
Соко-Баня
Rožanstvo
ČEMERNA PL.
Velika Drenova
Jasika
TORNIK
Visoka
Prilike
Maglić
IBARSKA KLISURA
Vrnjačka Banja
Врнячка-Баня
Trstenik
Stopanja
Kruševac
Крушевац
Kaonik
Aleksinac
OZREN
DEVICA
Ivanjica
Jasenovo
Studenica
Студеница
VELUĆE
RUDENICAL
Veliki Šiljegovac
Priboj
Uvac
Zlatarsko Jezero
Kokin Brod
Pridvorica
Ušće
ŽELJIN
Grčak
Vitkovo
Gornja Toponica
Svrljig
Bistrica
Nova Varoš
ZLATAR NAC. PARK
Biljanovac
Zlatari
VELIKI JASTREBAC
Prijepolje
ZLATAR
Kladnica
MAN. GRADAC
МАН. ГРАДАЦ
Jošanička Banja
Brus
Džigolj
Niš
Ниш
Niška Banja
MANASTIR MILEŠEVA
МАН. МИЛЕШЕВА
HISARDŽIK
ХИСАДЖИК
JANKOV KAMEN
GOLIJA NAC. PARK
Brvenik
Razbojna
Blace
Prokuplje
Прокупле
JADOVIK
Postrman Prolaz
Duga Poljana
Raška
Rudnica
Brzeće
Merćez
Beloljin
Doljevac
Gadžin Han
Sjenica
Brodarevo
PANČIĆEV VRH
NAC. PARK KOPAONIK
Toplica
Žitoradja
Brestovac
CRNI VRH
DURDEVI STUPOVI
ДУРДЕВИ СТУПОВИ
Lešak
KOPAONIK
Dren
Kuršumlija
Južna Morava
MANASTIR SOPOĆANI
МАН. СОПОЧАНИ
Novi Pazar
Нови-Пазар
Sopoćani
Leposavić
RADAN
Rudare
GILJEVO
Sebečevo
Kašalj
ROGOZNA
Sočanica
Kuršumlijska Banja
Palatna
Bojnik
Leskovac
Лесковац
Bijelo Polje
Ugao
Tutin
Rača
CARIČIN GRAD
ЦАРИЧИН ГРАД
Bošnjace
Kristac Prolaz
Banjska
Lebane
Dobri Do
Mojkovac
NAC. PARK BIOGRADSKA GORA
Ribariće
Kosowska Mitrovica
Косовска-Митровица
Podujevo
Vina
Oraovica
Mehov Krš
Zubin Potok
Glavnik
Medvedja
Jablanica
Veternica
Batlava
Vučitrn
Predejane
MOKRA GORA
Berane
Rožaj
Klina Prolaz
Donje Ljupče
Batlavsko Jezero
Sijarinska Banja
Tulare
Rudnik
Gornja Klina
Kolašin
Kula Prolaz
Srbica
Kačikol
Lisca Prolaz
Golemo Selo
Vladičin Han
KUKAVICA
Mateševo
HAJLA
ČICA VIČA
Trstena
Andrijevica
Djurakovac
Priština
Приштина
KOZNICA
Drenovac
Trešnjevik Prolaz
Kućište
Vitomirica
Čakor Prolaz
Klina
Kosovo Polje
ULPIANA
Novo Brdo
Ново-Брдо
Ajnovce
MARKOVO KALE
Murino
Peć
Печ
Gračanica
Грачаница
Vranje
Вране
Vranjska Banja
Plava Rijeka
Vermosh
MAN. VISOKI DEČANI
МАН. ВИСОКИ ДЕЧАНИ
Kijevo
Komorane
K O S O V O
Plav
Dečanska Bistrica
Lipljan
Vel. Trnovac
Ristovac
Gusinje
Dečani
Mališevo
ŽEGOVAC
Gnjilane
Dobrčane
Tamarë
MAJE RADOHINËS
Valbonë
Tropojë
Skivjane
Ćaf Dulja Prolaz
Stimlje
Klenike
Okol
M I HEKURAVE
Bajram Curri
Đakovica
Джяковица
Orahovac
Suva Reka
Uroševac
Poženje
Binačka Morava
Prohor Pčinjski
Preševo
Zrze
Velika Kruša
ŠARA NAC. PARK
Doganović
Vitina
Nicaj-Shalë
Rajë
Zogaj
Prizren
Призрен
Brezovica
Брежовица
Kačanik
RAMNO
MANASTIR STARO NAGORIČANE
МАН. СТАРО НАГО
Dedaj
Liqeni i Fierzës
LJUBOTEN
Đeneral Janković
CRNA GORA
Kumanovo
Куманово
Mlado Nagoričane
Sredska
Liqeni i Komanit
Krumë
Vrbnica
Žur
Dragaš
Vratnica
SVETI NIKITA
СВ. НИКИТА
MAN. MATEJČE
Prekal
Gruemirë
MAJE CUKALIT
Shënmeri
Slatino
Aračinovo
Orašac
Koman
Kukës
Tetovo
Тетово
SCUPI
SKOPJE
СКОПЈЕ
SHKODËR
Fushë Arrëz
Pukë
Orgjost
Vau i Dejës
SVETI PANTELEJMON

206
CRAIOVA
RO
Negotin
Vidin
Видин
Calafat
Cetate
Maglavit
Băilești
Bistreț
Lacul Nedeia
Caracal
Corabia
Dunărea
Lom
Лом
Kozlodui
Oryakhovo
Оряхово
ZLATIYATA
MONTANA
Montana
Монтана
Belogradchik
Белоградчик
Berkovitsa
Берковица
Vratsa
Враца
LEDENIKA PEȘTERA
ЛЕДЕНИКА
Mezdra
Knezha
PLEVEN
Плевен
Lovech
Ловеч
Pirot
Пирот
STARA PLANINA
CHIPROVSKA PL.
Chiprovtsi
Чипровци
TEMNATA DUPKA
ТЕМНАТА ДУПКА
CHREPISHKI MAN.
ЧЕРЕПИШКИ МАН.
MAN. SEDEMTE PRESTOLA
МАН. СЕДЕМТЕ ПРЕСТОЛА
Botevgrad
Ботевград
Svoge
Своге
Kalotina
Калотина
Dimitrovgrad
Trŭn
Трън
GOLEMA PL.
Etropole
Етрополе
ZLATISHKO-TETEVENSKA PL.
Teteven
Тетевен
Troyan
Троян
GLOZHENSKI MANASTIR
Zlatitsa
Pirdop
SOFIYA
СОФИЯ
Bankja
Банкя
Dragalevci
Драгалевци
Pancharevo
Панчарево
BG
Pernik
Перник
VITOŠA
ВИТОША
Ikhtiman
Samokov
Самоков
Koprivshtitsa
Копривщица
Panagyurishte
Панагюрище
Strelcha
Стрелча
Pazardzhik
Пазарджик
Kyustendil
Кюстендил
Dupnitsa
Дупница
Rila
Рила
RILSKI MAN.
РИЛСКИ МАН.
Borovets
Боровец
Velingrad
Велинград
Peshtera
Пещера
Batak
Батак
Blagoevgrad
Благоевград
Yakoruda
Якоруда
Razlog
SOFIYA
PLOV
E80
A1
A2
129
130
148

154
HR
BiH
SARAJEVO
Split
SPLIT
Mostar
Dubrovnik
Livno
Sinj
Imotski
Makarska
Metković
Neum
Jablanica
Konjic
Nevesinje
Stolac
Trebinje
Bileća
Gacko
Foča
Čapljina
Međugorje
Ljubuški
Vrgorac
Posušje
Široki Brijeg
Prozor
Gornji Vakuf
Šuica
Tomislavgrad
Kupres
Kiseljak
Semizovac
Hadžići
Ilidža
Krupac
Pale
Trnovo
Kalinovik
Ulog
Tjentište
Čemerno
Plužine
Avtovac
Ljubinje
Ravno
Cavtat
Čilipi
Gruda
Herceg Novi
Igalo
Zelenika
Kamenari
Risan
Perast
Lepetane
Tivat
Kotor
Budva
Sveti Stefan
Ston
Slano
Trsteno
Lopud
Šipan
Mljet
Sobra
Korita
Govedjari
Korčula
Lumbarda
Vela Luka
Blato
Čara
Lastovo
Sušac
Kopište
Orebić
Trpanj
Janjina
Lovište
Pelješac
Hvar
Jelsa
Stari Grad
Vrboska
Vira
Sućuraj
Ščedro
Brač
Bol
Supetar
Sutivan
Milna
Nerežišća
Pučišća
Povlja
Sumartin
Omiš
Dugi Rat
Solin
Klis
Kaštel Stari
Trogir
Čiovo
SALONA
MOSOR
BIOKOVO
CANJON CETINE
Zadvarje
Šestanovac
Cista Provo
Blato
Trilj
Kamensko
Aržano
Budimir
Ugljane
Brnaze
Muć
Hrvace
Obrovac
Srdevići
Prisoje
Kolo
Lipa
Petrovići
Buško Jezero
Peručko Jezero
LIVANJSKO POLJE
CINCAR
LJUBUŠA
SVILAJA
ČVRSNICA
ČABULJA
PRENJ
VELEŽ
CRVANJ
BJELAŠNICA
TRESKAVICA
VISOČICA
ZELENGORA
GOLIJA
NJEGOŠ
ORJEN
NAC. PARK SUTJESKA
KLISURA SUTJESKA
NERETVA KANJON
BRUNA VRELO
MEGORJELO
PIVSKI MANASTIR
Blagaj
Buna
Žitomislići
Počitelj
Domanovići
Radimlje
Opuzen
Ploče
Gradac
Drvenik
Zaostrog
Živogošće
Igrane
Podgora
Tučepi
Baška Voda
Brela
Zagvozd
Slivno
Drinovci
Kozica
Vitina
Hamzići
Kočerin
Lištica
Bostan
Potoci
Pridvorci
Hutovo
Brijesta
Zavala
Dobromani
Veličani
Berkovići
Bijeljani
Korita
Plana
Gradac
Pocrnje
Tabaja
Fojnica
Lastva
Vilusi
Osječenica
Grahovo
Kuside
Grab
Han
Mlini
Lokrum
Bari
Dubrovnik
Sarajevo
Tivat
Ancona
Hvarski Kanal
Korčulanski Kanal
Lastovski Kanal
Mljetski Kanal
Brački Kanal
NAC. PARC MLJET
NAC. PARK BIOKOVO
NAC. PARK TREBEVIĆ
Jablaničko Jezero
Bilećko Jezero
Krupac Jezero
Jezero Šćit
Makljan Prolaz
Vitez Prolaz
Romanija
Sokolac
Podromanija
Pale
Prača
Dobro Polje
Ocrkavlje
Srbinje
Brod
E65
E73
E80
E71
E761
E762
A
B
C
D
1
2
3
4
5
6

155
150
150
129
128
E
F
G
H
YU
AL
MK
SR
A G O R A
SHKODËR
TIRANË
ZLATIBOR
ZLATAR
JADOVIK
GILJEVO
HAJLA
MOKRA GORA
ROGOZNA
KOPAONIK
ŽELJIN
ČEMERNA PL.
RADAN
VELIKI JASTREBAC
ŽEGOVAC
SUVA GORA
JAKUPICA
DUKAGJIN
MIRDITË
MI KRESHTES
SKANDERBEUT
DRINA KANJON
TARA
Kadinjača Prolaz
Kratovska Stena
Čačak
Чачак
Gruža
Paraćin
Ovčar Banja
Mrčajevci
Guberevac
Bioska
Sevojno
Požega
Užice
Ужице
Kremna
Mokra Gora
770 Šargan Prolaz
Pešurići
Višegrad
Dobrun
Ustiprača
Setihovo
765 Bjelo Brdo Prolaz
Uvac
1496 TORNIK
Cajetina
Partizanske Vode
Партизанске Воде
Rožanstvo
Arilje
Ариље
Guča
Slatina
Kraljevo
Краљево
Viča
Vitanovac
Podunavci
Bouotovačka Banja
Mataruška Banja
MAN. KALENIĆ
МАН. КАЛЕНИЋ
Belušić
Pojate
Ćićevac
Oparić
Bačina
MANASTIR LJUBOSTINJA
МАН. ЉУБОСТИЊА
Velika Drenova
Jasika
Stalać
Visoka
Prilike
Maglić
IBARSKA KLISURA
Vrnjačka Banja
Врњачка-Бања
Trstenik
Stopanja
Kruševac
Крушевац
VELUĆE
Kaonik
Priboj
Ustibar
Čajniče
Metaljka
Hercegovska Goleša
Banja
Баня
Jasenovo
Ivanjica
1579
Studenica
Студеница
RUDENICA
Veliki Šiljegovac
Kokin Brod
Zlatarsko Jezero
Pridvorica
Ušće
1785
Grčak
Vitkovo
Boljanići
Bistrica
Nova Varoš
ZLATAR NAC. PARK
Prijepolje
1627
Kladnica
Biljanovac
Zlatari
Brus
1492
Šula
Rudnica
Jabuka
MANASTIR MILEŠEVA
МАН. МИЛЕШЕВА
HISARDŽIK
ХИСАДЖИК
1833 JANKOV KAMEN
GOLIJA NAC. PARK
MAN. GRADAC
МАН. ГРАДАЦ
Brvenik
Jošanička Banja
Razbojna
Blace
Pljevlja
Плевља
Postrman Prolaz 1300
Duga Poljana
1788
Brzeće
Odžak
Ljutići
1734
Sjenica
Raška
Rudnica
2017 PANČIĆEV VRH
NAC. PARK KOPAONIK
Merćez
Beloljin
Prokuplje
Прокупље
1492 CRNI VRH
Brodarevo
ĐURĐEVI STUPOVI
ЂУРЂЕВИ СТУПОВИ
Kosanica
1499
MANASTIR SOPOĆANI
МАН. СОПОЋАНИ
Lešak
Dren
Kuršumlija
1409
LEDENIA PEĆINA
Žabljak
Djurdjevica Tara
Sopoćani
Novi Pazar
Нови-Пазар
Leposavić
2522
Crno Jezero
DURMITOR NAC. PARK
Tomaševo
Sebečevo
Kašalj
Kuršumlijska Banja
Rudare
Donja Bukovica
TARA KANJON
Bijelo Polje
Ugao
880
Sočanica
Palatna
Rača
1010 Kristac Prolaz
Brezna
Bistrica
Tutin
Ribariće
Banjska
Kosowska Mitrovica
Косовска-Митровица
CARIČ
Mojkovac
NAC. PARK BIOGRADSKA GORA
Šavnik
1440 Krnovo Prolaz
Mehov Krš
Zubin Potok
Ibar
Podujevo
Glavnik
Medve
Gvozd
2253
2137
Berane
Rožaj
Vučitrn
Batlava
730 Klina Prolaz
Donje Ljupče
Batlavsko Jezero
Kolašin
1781 Kula Prolaz
Rudnik
Gornja Klina
Kačikol
MAN. MORAČA
МАН. МОРАЧА
1064 Crkvina Prolaz
Mateševo
2400
Srbica
1091 ČIČA VIČA
1020 Lisca Prolaz
Rubeži
750 Stubička dola Prolaz
Kuta
Jasenovo
1598 Trešnjevik Prolaz
Andrijevica
Kućište
Djurakovac
Vitomirica
Priština
Приштина
1227 KOZNICA
MANASTIR OSTROG
Murino
1849 Čakor Prolaz
Peć
Печ
Klina
Kosovo Polje
ULPIANA
Novo Brdo
Ново-Брдо
Lijeva Rijeka
1260 Vjeternik Prolaz
Vermosh
Plav
MAN. VISOKI DEČANI
МАН. ВИСОКИ ДЕЧАНИ
Komorane
Gračanica
Грачаница
Kijevo
Dečanska Bistrica
1056
Danilovgrad
Даниловград
Gusinje
Dečani
Lipljan
Bioče
DOCLEA
ДОКЛЕА
Tamarë
MAJ'E RADOHINËS 2570
Valbonë
Okol
Tropojë
Skivjane
Mališevo
915 Čaf Dulja Prolaz
Štimlje
Sitnica
PODGORICA
ПОДГОРИЦА
Cetinje
Цетиње
Tuzi
Božaj
Golubovci
Podgorica
2561 M I HEKURAVE
Bajram Curri
Đakovica
Джяковица
Orahovac
Suva Reka
Uroševac
Požeranje
Binačka Morava
Vitina
Rijeka Crnojevića
Han i Hotit
Nicaj-Shalë
Zogaj
Zrze
Velika Kruša
ŠARA NAC. PARK
Doganović
Virpazar
Вирпазар
Bajzë
Dedaj
Rajë
Liqeni i Fierzës
Prizren
Призрен
Brezovica
Брежовица
1515
2499 LJUBOTEN
Kačanik
Skadarsko Jezero
Koplik
Prekal
Liqeni Komanit
Krumë
Sredska
Đeneral Janković
780
Liqen i Shkodrës
Gruemirë
1723 MAJ'E CUKALIT
Vrbnica
Žur
Vratnica
SVETI-NIKITA
СВ. НИКИТА
Tomore
Liqeni i Vaut të Dejës
Shënmëri
Dragaš
Slatino
Bar
Бар
Ostros
Shirokë
SHKODËR
Koman
Pukë
1284
849
Fushë Arrëz
Kukës
Orgjost
Tetovo
Тетово
SCUPI
Krute
Muriquan
Vau i Dejës
2487 MAL'I GJALICËS
Brod
2748 TITOV VRH
SVETI PANTELEJMON
СВ. ПАНТЕЛЕЈМОН
MAN. MATKA
Grupčin
SV. ANDREJA
СВ. АНДЕЈШ
Gojani i Madh
Bicaj
1987 MAJ'E ZEBES
Pirok
Vardar
Treska
MARKOV MAN.
МАРКОВ МАН.
Ulcinj
Улцињ
Bushat
Krajn
Klos
Bushtricë
Velipojë
Blinisht
Reç
1172
Cegrane
Zdunje
Shëngjin
Lezhë
Rrëshen
Kurbnesh
2246 MAL I DEJËS
Gostivar
Rasteš
Pellg i Drinit
Ulëzë
Fushë Muhurr
Selishtë
Peshkopi
Volkovija
Mavrovi Hanovi
SVETI JOVAN BIGORSKI
СВ. ЈОВАН БИГОРСКИ
Mavrovsko Ezero
Mavrovo
Маврово
NACIONALNI PARK MAVROVO
2062 DOBRA VODA
2540 SOLUNSKA GL.
Belica
Modrište
Fushë-Kuqe
Gji i Rodonit
Laç
Burrel
Magellarë
1200
Tuin
Zajas
Kep i Rodonit
Shetaj
Krujë
Debar
Дебар
Dolno Kosovrasti
Kičevo
Makedonski Brod
Izvor
Celopeci
Golema
Ropoto
Gji i Lalzës
Fushë-Krujë
Bulqizë
Zerqan
2273 STOGOVO
СТОГОВО
Presek Prolaz 903
1791
Kep i Palit
Katundi i Ri
Rinas
MAL I LOPES
Krastë
Klenjë
Crni Drim
MAN. TR
RAZBOJNA
BUSEVA PL.

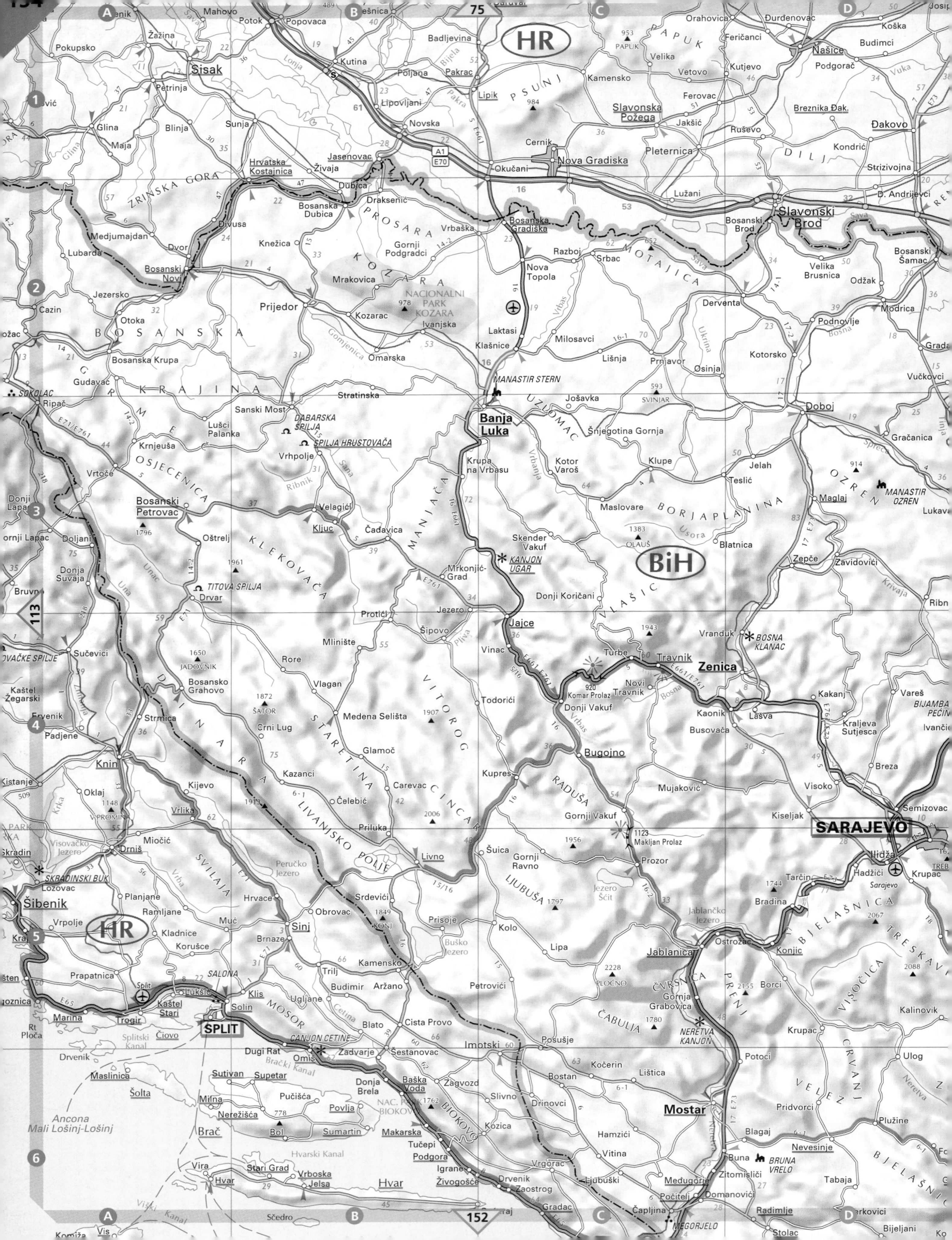

76
77
153
206
150
RO
YU
Osijek
Ruski Krstur
Srbobran
Bačko Gradište
Melenci
Foeni
Cruceni
Jaša Tomić
Bogojevo
Karavukovo
Odžaci
Оџаци
Savino Selo
Čurug
Žitište
Giera
Tenja
Dalj
Despotovo
Sirig
Zrenjanin
Зрењанин
Temerin
Lazarevo
Sutjeska
Bač
Bački Petrovac
Silbaš
Bodjani
Žabalj
Sečanj
Konak
Borovo
Vukovar
Mužlja
Ečka
Moravita
Nuštar
Bačko Novo Selo
NOVI SAD
НОВИ САД
Kać
Šajkaš
Jarkovac
Vatin
Vinkovci
Bačka Palanka
Бачка-Паланка
Gložan
Futog
Orlovat
Plandište
Sotin
Petrovaradin
Perlez
Farkaždin
Samoš
Orolik
Šarengrad
Ilok
Susek
Sremska Kamenica
Sremski Karlovci
Titel
Lokve
Vršac
Вршац
Privlaka
Tovarnik
NAC. PARK FRUŠKA GORA
Beočin
MAN. HOPOVO
МАН. ХОПОВО
Irški Venac
Stari Slankamen
Čenta
Padina
Otok
Šid
Erdevik
Vrdnik
Iriški Venac Prolaz
Beška
Kovačica
Alibunar
Uljma
Adaševci
Kukujevci
MAN. VELIKA REMETA
MAN. KRUŠEDOL
МАН. КРУШЕДОЛ
Irig
Mandelos
Surduk
Opovo
Banatsko Novo Selo
Županja
Bošnjaci
Morović
Kuzmin
Ruma
Inđija
Crepaja
Drašje
Vrbanja
Laćarak
Stara Pazova
Jabuka
Banatski Karlovac
Šušara
Sremska Mitrovica
Сремска-Митровица
Putinci
Nova Pazova
Dolovo
Lončari
Sremska Rača
Bosut
Batajnica
Pančevo
Панчево
Drenovci
Bosanska Rača
Glušci
Hrtkovci
Subotište
Vojlovica
Deliblato
Krnjača
Bavanište
Brčko
Brezovo Polje
Vršani
Bogatić
Šabac
Шабац
Dobanovci
Beograd
Surčin
BEOGRAD
БЕЛГРАД
Omoljica
Gaj
Dubovac
Kostolac
Pukiš
Badovinci
Dumača
Ašanja
Železnik
Kovin
Bijeljina
Čelić
Suho Polje
Petlovača
Varna
AVALA
АВАЛА
Smederevo
Смедерево
Janja
Prnjavor
Skela
Umka
Grocka
Vrčin
MANASTIR TAVNA
Lopare
Lešnica
RADOVAŠNICA
Obrenovac
Ripanj
Umčari
Kolari
Mala Krsna
Priboj
CER
Lojanice
Debrc
Ralja
Osipaonica
Gornja Tuzla
Glavičice
Tekeriš
Stubline
Beljina
Rastošnica
Loznica
Лозница
Draginje
Banjani
Stepojevac
Sopot
Mladenovac Varoš
Selevac
Tuzla
Banja Koviljača
Tršić
Tamnava
Tojšići
Kozluk
Zavlaka
Koceljevo
Vreoci
Ub
Kalesija
Radalj
Venčane
Smederevska Palanka
Veliko Orašje
Đurđevik
Caparde
Zvornik
Osečina
Lajkovac
Lazarevac
Žabari
Krupanj
Slovac
Partizani
Velika Plana
MAN. KOPORIN
Zvornik Jezero
Donja Kamenica
Arandjelovac
Аранђеловац
Natalinci
Markovac
Drinjača
Crnča
Pecka
Valjevo
Mionica
Topola
Топола
Rača
Ojsalići
Tišća
Gračanica
Ljig
Donja Šatornja
MAN. OPLENAC
МАН. ОПЛЕНАЦ
Lapovo
Nova Kassaba
MALJEN
Turalići
JAVOR
Vlasenica
Milići
Bratunac
Ljubovija
Počuta
Ugrinovci
Rudnik
Čumic
Batočina
Drlače
Bukovi
Divčibare
MAN. BLAGOVEŠTENJE
МАН. БЛАГОВЕШТЕЊЕ
Srebrenica
Bukovi Prolaz
Mutanj
RUDNIK
Desimirovac
Stupčanica
Olovo
Han Pijesak
POVLJEN
Vraćevšnica
Pranjani
Gornji Milanovac
Kragujevac
Крагујевац
Svetozarevo
Светозарево
Žep
Rogačica
Biostica
MAN. JOŠANICA
Kosjerić
Žljebovi
Brdjani
Vuckovica
Gornja Sabanta
Dub
Žepa
Zaglavak
Kadinjača Prolaz
Čestobrodica
Zapadna Morava
Knić
GLEDIĆSKE PL.
Sokolac
Bajina Bašta
Kratovska Stena
Čačak
Чачак
Gruža
Romanija
Podromanija
DRINA KANJON
NAC. PARK TARA
Stolac
DEVETAK
Bioska
Sevojno
Ovčar Banja
Mrčajevci
Guberevac
Pešurići
Užice
Ужице
Požega
Slatina
MAN. KALENIĆ
МАН. КАЛЕНИЋ
Kremna
Mokra Gora
Šargan Prolaz
Vitez Prolaz
Rogatica
Kraljevo
Краљево
Prača
Višegrad
ZLATIBOR
Cajetina
Arilje
Арилје
Guča
Viča
Vitanovac
NAC. PARK TREBEVIĆ
Dobrun
Partizanske Vode
Партизанске Воде
Booutovačka Banja
Podunavci
MANASTIR LJUBOSTINJA
МАН. ЉУБОСТИЊА
Jabuka
Ustiprača
Rožanstvo
ČEMERNA
Mataruška Banja
Goražde
Setihovo
Bjelo Brdo Prolaz
Tornik
Visoka
Prilike
Maglić
Vrnjačka Banja
Врњачка-Бања
Trstenik
Uvac
IBARSKA KLISURA
Polje
Priboj
Jasenovo
Ivanjica
ČEMERNA PL.
Čajniče
Ustibar
Banja
Бања
Studenica
Студеница
RUDENICAL
Metaljka Prolaz
Metaljka
Hercegovska Goleša
ŽELIN
Ocrkavlje
Srbinje
Straževnica
Kokin Brod
Zlatarsko Jezero
Pridvorica
Ušće
Grčak
Brod
Ćehotina
Boljanići
Bistrica
Nova Varoš
ZLATAR NAC. PARK
Biljanovac
Brus
NAC. PARK SUTJESKA
Šula
Prijepolje
Rudnica
Jabuka
MANASTIR MILEŠEVA
МАН. МИЛЕШЕВА
HISARDŽIK
ХИСАРЏИК
Kladnica
MAN. GRADAC
МАН. ГРАДАЦ
Brvenik
Jošanička Banja
Razbojna
Jankov Kamen
GOLIJA NAC. PARK
Tjentište
Šćepan Polje
Pljevlja
Плевља
Postrman Prolaz
Duga Poljana
Raška
Brzeće
Merćez
TARA KANJON
LJUBIŠNJA
Odžak
Ljutići
ZLATAR
JADOVIK
Sjenica
Vapa
Rudnica
Pančićev Vrh
NAC. PARK KOPAONIK
DURMITOR
ДУРМИТОР
LEDENIA PEĆINA
Crni Vrh
Brodarevo
DURDEVI STUPOVI
ЂУРЂЕВИ СТУПОВИ
Kosanica
Lešak
Dren
KOPAONIK
Plužine
PIVSKI MANASTIR
ПИВСКИ МАН.
Žabljak
Crno jezero
Djurdjevica Tara
Tara
MANASTIR SOPOĆANI
МАН. СОПОЧАНИ
Novi Pazar
Нови-Пазар
Sopoćani
Leposavić
Palatna
GILJEVO
Sebečevo
Kašalj
Pločanica
DURMITOR NAC. PARK
Donja Bukovica
TARA KANJON
Bijelo Polje
Ugao

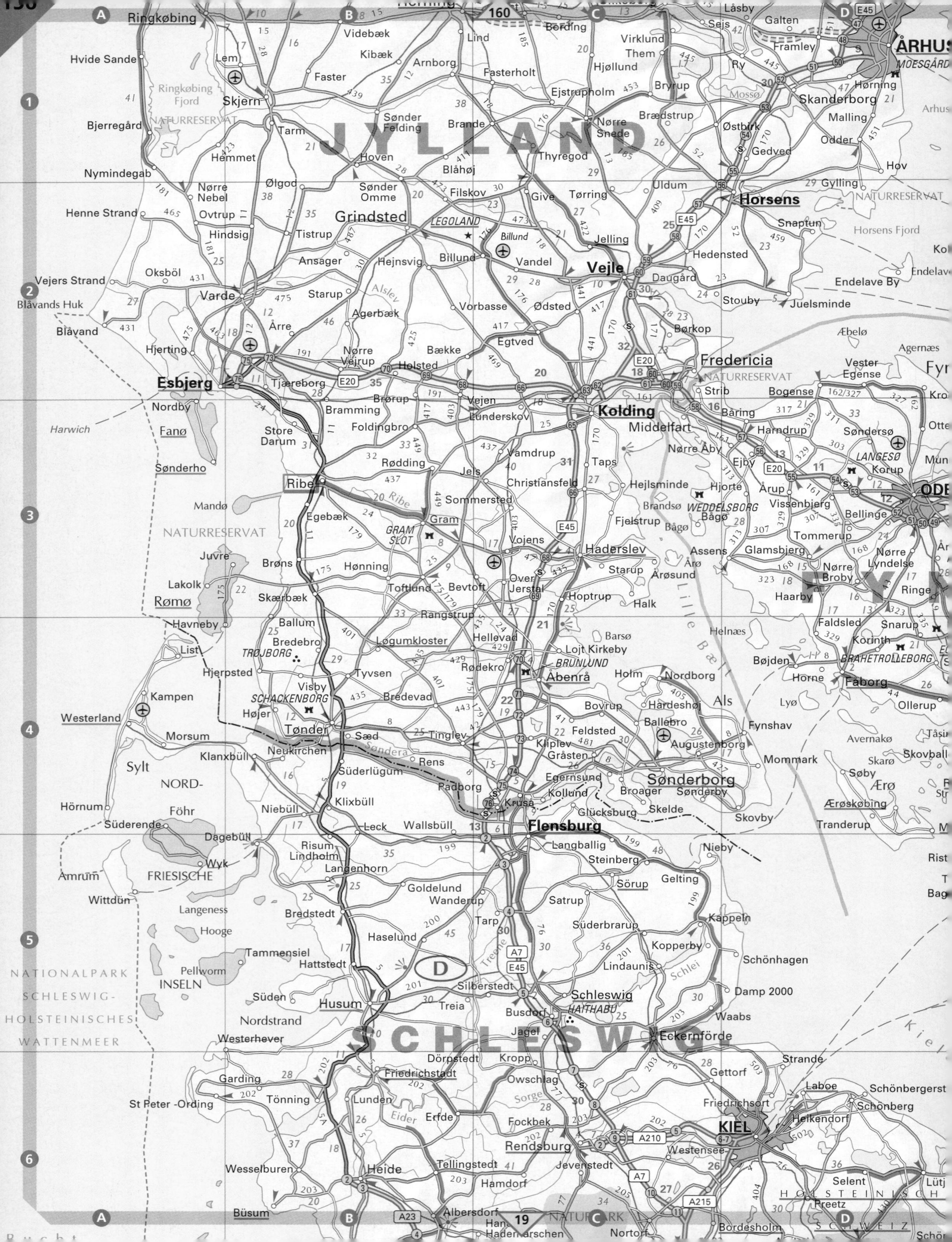

A
B
C
D
1
2
3
4
5
6
160
19
Ringkøbing
Videbæk
Lind
Bording
Låsby
Sejs
Galten
E45
ÅRHUS
MOESGÅRD
Hvide Sande
Lem
Kibæk
Arnborg
Virklund
Them
Hjøllund
Ry
Framley
Faster
Fasterholt
Bryrup
Ringkøbing Fjord
Skjern
Ejstrupholm
Mossø
Skanderborg
Hørning
Arhus
Bjerregård
NATURRESERVAT
Tarm
JYLLAND
Sønder Felding
Brande
Nørre Snede
Brædstrup
Østbirk
Malling
Odder
Gedved
Hemmet
Hoven
Thyregod
Blåhøj
Hov
Nymindegab
Nørre Nebel
Ølgod
Sønder Omme
Filskov
Give
Tørring
Uldum
Gylling
Horsens
Henne Strand
Ovtrup
Grindsted
LEGOLAND
Snaptun
Horsens Fjord
Hindsig
Tistrup
Billund
Jelling
Hedensted
Ansager
Hejnsvig
Vandel
Vejle
Daugård
Endelave
Endelave By
Oksbøl
Vejers Strand
Blåvands Huk
Varde
Starup
Alslev
Vorbasse
Ødsted
Stouby
Juelsminde
Agerbæk
Årre
Blåvand
Egtved
Børkop
Æbelø
Agernæs
Hjerting
Nørre Vejrup
Bække
Holsted
Fredericia
Vester Egense
Fyn
Esbjerg
Tjæreborg
E20
Strib
Bogense
Nordby
Brørup
Vejen
Kolding
Bramming
Lunderskov
Middelfart
Båring
Harndrup
Søndersø
Harwich
Fanø
Store Darum
Foldingbro
Nørre Åby
Ejby
LANGESØ
Korup
Vamdrup
Taps
Sønderho
Rødding
Jels
Ribe
Christiansfeld
Hejlsminde
Hjorte
Årup
ODE
Mandø
Sommersted
Brandsø
WEDDELSBORG
Bågø
Vissenbjerg
Bellinge
Egebæk
Gram
GRAM SLOT
Fjelstrup
Tommerup
NATURRESERVAT
Vojens
Haderslev
Assens
Glamsbjerg
Nørre Lyndelse
Juvre
Brøns
Hønning
Årø
Nørre Broby
Starup
Årøsund
Lakolk
Over Jerstal
Toftlund
Bevtoft
Hoptrup
Halk
Rømø
Skærbæk
Haarby
FYN
Ringe
Rangstrup
Lillebælt
Havneby
Ballum
Barsø
Helnæs
Faldsled
Snarup
Bredebro
Løgumkloster
Hellevad
Korinth
List
TRØJBORG
Lojt Kirkeby
Bøjden
BRAHETROLLEBORG
Hjerpsted
Tyvsen
Rødekro
BRUNLUND
Åbenrå
Holm
Nordborg
Horne
Fåborg
Kampen
Visby
SCHACKENBORG
Bredevad
Hardeshøj
Als
Lyø
Ollerup
Højer
Bovrup
Westerland
Tønder
Ballebro
Fynshav
Morsum
Sæd
Tinglev
Feldsted
Augustenborg
Avernakø
Tåsi
Sylt
Klanxbüll
Neukirchen
Søndera
Rens
Kliplev
Gråsten
Mommark
Skarø
Skovball
Süderlügum
Egernsund
Sønderborg
Søby
NORD-
Padborg
Kollund
Broager
Sønderby
Ærø
Hörnum
Föhr
Niebüll
Klixbüll
Kruså
Glücksburg
Skelde
Ærøskøbing
Süderende
Leck
Wallsbüll
Flensburg
Skovby
Tranderup
Dagebüll
Risum-Lindholm
Langballig
Nieby
Rist
Wyk
Steinberg
Amrum
FRIESISCHE
Langenhorn
Gelting
Sörup
Wittdün
Goldelund
Wanderup
Satrup
Langeness
Bredstedt
Tarp
Kappeln
Hooge
Haselund
Süderbrarup
Tammensiel
Treene
A7
E45
Kopperby
Schönhagen
NATIONALPARK SCHLESWIG-HOLSTEINISCHES WATTENMEER
Pellworm
Hattstedt
D
Lindaunis
INSELN
Silberstedt
Schlei
Süden
Husum
Treia
Schleswig
HAITHABU
Damp 2000
Nordstrand
Busdorf
Waabs
Westerhever
SCHLESWIG
Jagel
Eckernförde
Dörpstedt
Kropp
Strande
Garding
Friedrichstadt
Owschlag
Gettorf
Laboe
Schönbergerstr
Tönning
Sorge
St Peter-Ording
Lunden
Friedrichsort
Schönberg
Eider
Erfde
Heikendorf
Fockbek
KIEL
A210
Rendsburg
Westensee
Wesselburen
Heide
Tellingstedt
Jevenstedt
Selent
Hamdorf
A215
HOLSTEINISCH
Preetz
Büsum
Albersdorf
A23
Hanerau-Hademarschen
NATURPARK
Nortorf
Bordesholm
SCHWEIZ
Schön

161
20
158
157
Skovgårde
Ebeltoft
Ebeltoft Færge
Ørby
Hjelm
Grenå
Oslo
Göteborg
Mölle
Ängelholm
Tassjö
KRAPPERUP
BRUNNBY
Höganäs
Munka-Ljunby
Viken
KULLA GUNNARSTORP
Gilleleje
Rågeleje
Tisvilde
Hornbæk
SOFIERO
Græsted
Hittarp
Allerum
Åstorp
VRAMS GUNNARSTORP
Bjuv
ROSENDAL
Ljungby
Helsingør
HELSINGBORG
Nordby
Yderby
Havnebyen
Liseleje
Asserbo
Helsinge
NATURRESERVAT
Samsø
Ballen
Kolby
TINGSBORG
Samsø Bælt
Sejerø
Sejerby
Sejerø Bugt
Lumsås
Rørvig
Nykøbing
Hundested
Kulhuse
Frederiksværk
Fredensborg
Humlebæk
Råå
Vallåkra
Kågeröd
Hillerød
Nivå
Ven
ALABODARNA
Svalöv
Isefjord
Høve
Vig
Asnæs
Jægerspris
Frederikssund
Slangerup
Lillerød
Hørsholm
Vedbæk
Landskrona
Marieholm
Ulstrup
Saltbæk
Havnsø
DRAGSHOLM SLOT
Hørve
Orø
Bybjerg
Farum
Lille
Birkerød
Søllerød
Tårbæk
Værløse
Lyngby
Svinninge
Skibby
Jyllinge
SELSØ SLOT
Stenløse
BORGEBY
Kävlinge
Kalundborg
Asnæs
LERCHENBORG
Viskinge
Jyderup
Holbæk
Ballerup
Øresund
KØBENHAVN
Fyns Hoved
Nordskov
Mørkøv
Tølløse
Roskilde
LEDREBORG
Tåstrup
Glostrup
Bjärred
Lund
Lomma
Saltholm
Martofte
Romsø
DK
Tissø
Ruds-Vedby
Ugerløse
TERSLØSE
Hedehusene
Kirke Hvalsø
Tune
Kastrup
Arlöv
MALMÖ
Gørlev
Store Merløse
Greve Strand
Dragør
København
Amager
Limhamn
Oxie
Kerteminde
Drosselbjerg
Høng
Dianalund
Stenlille
Osted
Viby
Borup
Lille
Karlslunde Strand
Solrød Strand
SJÆLLAND
Ladby
Bovense
Store
Slagelse
Sorø
Køge Bugt
Køge
Svedala
Langeskov
TRÆLLEBORG
Frederiksberg
Ringsted
Gørslev
Herfølge
Strøby Egede
Vellinge
Ullerslev
FJENNESLEV
Sjælland
VALLØ SLOT
Höllviksnäs
Skanör
Falsterbo
Nyborg
Halsskov
Korsør
Vemmelv
Glumsø
Klippinge
Trelleborg
Ørbæk
Knudshoved
HOLCKENHAVN
Tårup
Fuglebjerg
Haslev
Hårlev
Store Heddinge
GISSELFELD
Dalby
Karise
Skælskør
Dalmose
Øksendrup
GLORUP
BORREBY
HERLUFSHOLM
Rønnede
Højerup
Bælt
Agersø
Næstved
SPARRESHOLM
Fakse
Rødvig
HESSELAGERGÅRD
Menstrup
Lohals
Omø
Karrebæksminde
GAVNØ SLOT
Fakse Ladeplads
Rønne
Świnoujście
Lundeborg
Vindbyholt
Fakse Bugt
Vester Egesborg
Præstø
Svendborg
Snøde
Knudshoved
Køng
Travemünde
Troense
Tranekær
Smålandsfarvandet
LOLLAND
Mern
Ulvshale
TRANEKÆR SLOT
Neder Vindinge
Vordingborg
Ørslev
KULSBJERGE
Tullebolle
Onsevig
Fejø
Sønderby
Kalvehave
Borre
Spodsbjerg
Vesterby
Femø
Storstrøm
LISELUND
Langeland
Horslunde
Orehoved
Stege
Sassnitz
KONG HUMBLES GRAV
Tårs
Kragenæs
Askø
Guldborg Sund
Nyby
Askeby
Møn
Klintholm
Humble
Nørre Alslev
Rostock
Travemünde
Møns Klint
Nakskov
Stokkemarke
Guldborg
FANEFJORD
Stubbekøbing
Bandholm
Sakskøbing
Horbelev
Langø
Søllested
FALSTER
Hesnæs
Maglehøj Strand
Maribo
KRENKERUP
Nykøbing
Falster
Lolland
Holeby
Rødby
Væggerløse
Øster Ulslev
Nysted
Rødbyhavn
Marielyst
ÅLHOLM SLOT
Oslo
Göteborg
Visby
Marrebæk
NATIONALPARK VORPOMMERSCHE BODDENLANDSCHAFT
Fehmarn
Gedser
Dranske
Wiek
Puttgarden
Petersdorf
Landkirchen
Burg
Hiddensee
Darsser Ort
Schaprode
D
Heiligenhafen
Prerow
Zingst
Grossenbrode
Oldenburg
Wustrow
Barth
Gross Mohrdorf
Rambin
Travemünde
Rostock
Saaler Bodden
Dahme
Mecklenburger Bucht
Graal-Müritz
Löbnitz
Stralsund

KØBENHAVN
MALMÖ
HELSINGBORG
Helsingør
Landskrona
Lund
Roskilde
Hillerød
Köge
Trelleborg
Ystad
Kristianstad
Hässleholm
Eslöv
Höganäs
Ängelholm
Stralsund
Rügen
Sassnitz
Bergen
Binz
Sellin
Göhren
Putbus
Barth
Zingst
Prerow
Falster
Møn
Stege
Sjælland
SKÅNE
S
DK
D
Öresund
Køge Bugt
Fakse Bugt
NATIONALPARK VORPOMMERSCHE BODDENLANDSCHAFT
NATIONALPARK JASMUND
Kap Arkona
Hiddensee
Oslo Göteborg
Rønne Świnoujście
Travemünde
Rostock Travemünde
Świnoujście
København
162
157
20

B L E K I N G E

Olofström
Svängsta
Asarum
Mörrum
Bräkne-Hoby
Ronneby
Karlshamn
Pukavik

Bökemåla
Tving
Kallinge
Hjortsberga
Nättraby
Rödeby
Sälleryd
Jämjö
Lyckeby
Karlskrona

163
Degerhamn
Kristianopel
Grönhögen
Ottenby
LÅNGE JAN
Ölands södra udde

Pukaviksbukten
Mjällby
Nogersund
Ivesborg

Torhamn

Utlängan

Gdynia

Hammerodde
Sandvig
HAMMERSHUS
Allinge
Tejn
Bornholm
Gudhjem
Hasle
Klemensker
Østerlars
Østermarie
Svaneke
DK
Rønne
Arnager
Aakirkeby
Neksø
Snogebæk
Dueodde

Helsinki /
Helsingfors

SŁOW
NA
Jezioro
Gardno
Rowy

PL
Ustka
Objazda
Jarosławiec
Jezioro
Wicko
Postomino
Słupsk
Darłówko
Staniewice
Darłowo
Wieprza
Sławno
22

FÆRØERNE
FØROYAR
FÆRØERNE / FØROYAR
FR
1 : 1 000 000
0 10 20 km
Kalsoy
Kunoy
Viðoy
Viðareiði
Tjørnuvík
Eiði
Gjóv
Oyntdartfjørður
Fugloy
Eysturoy
Streymoy
Fluglafjørður
Vestmanna
Mykines
Hvalvík
Leirvík
Klaksvík
Svínoy
Vágar
Sørvágur
Borðoy
Toftir
Tórshavn
Nólsoy
Kirkjubøur
Skopun
Sandoy
Sandur
Skálavík
Lerwich
Skúvoy
Suðuroyarfjørður
Hvalba
Tvøroyri
Fámjin
Suðuroy
Vágur
Sumba
Kristiansand
Egersund
Newcastle upon Tyne
Egersund
Bergen
Skallerup
Lønstrup
Løkken
BØRGLUMKLOSTER
Jammerbugten
Saltum
Blokhus
Brønderslev
Pandrup
Rødhus Klit
Kås
Tranum Strand
Lild Strand
Torup Strand
Vigsø Bugt
Hanstholm
Slettestrand
Åbybro
NATURRESERVAT
Klitmøller
Frøstrup
NATURRES.
Fjerritslev
Brovst
Korsø
Østerild
Vangså
Skinnerup
Øsløs
Aalborg
Lindholm
Attrup
Aggersund
ÅLBORG
Nørre Vorupør
Thisted
Løgstør
Nibe
Frejlev
Stenbjerg
Snedsted
Feggeklit
Sebbersund
Svenstrup
Vilsund
Sønder Dråby
Limfjorden
Ranum
VITSKØL KLOSTER
Vegger
Sørup
Solbjerg
Bedsted
Koldby
Hornum
Agger
Fur
Trend
Suldrup
Vestervig
Hurup
Karby
Nykøbing
Strandby
Aars
Thyborøn
Ør. Hvidbjerg
Mors
Glyngøre
Selde
BORREMOSE
Farsø
Roslev
Hvalpsund
Ålestrup
Nørager
Nissum Bredning
Hvidbjerg
SPØTTRUP
Sundsøre
Gedsted
Harboøre
Tambohuse
Rødding
HESSEL
Lovns Bredning
Hove
Oddesund
Sønder Balling
Ulbjerg
Lemvig
KRABBESHOLM
Øls
Hobro
Lihme
Skive
Møldrup
FYRKAT
Ferring
Humlum
Venø Bugt
Højslev Stby
LYNDERUPGÅRD
Skals
Fjaltring
Rom By
Struer
Vinderup
STUBBERGÅRD
DK
Bækmarksbro
Sevel
KALKGRUBER
Mønsted
TJELE
Råsted
Torsminde
Linde
Sjørup
Ørum
NATURRESERVAT
Nissum Fjord
Vemb
Skave
Viborg
Storå
Hagebro
Langå
Fjand Gårde
Holstebro
Haderup
Bjerringbro
Husby
Tvis
Rødkærsbro
Ulstrup
Vedersø Klit
Ulfborg
Karup
Frederiks
Gudenå
Sønderby
Avlum
Kjellerup
Ans
Hadsten
Ørnhøj
Vildbjerg
Ilskov
Fårvang
Hee
Storå
Gjern
Sunds
Hammel
Søndervig
Spjald
Engesvang
Herning
Ikast
Silkeborg
Låsby
Ringkøbing
Bording
Sejs
Galten
Videbæk
Lind
Virklund
Them
Framley
Hvide Sande
Lem
Kibæk
Arnborg
Hjøllund
Ry
Faster
Fasterholt
Brædstrup
Ringkøbing
Fjord
E45

156

Frederikshavn
Skagen
Grenen
Gammel Skagen
Læsø
Østerby Havn
Vesterø Havn
Byrum
Hornfiskrøn
GÖTEBORG
Mölndal
Kungälv
Kungsbacka
Varberg
Falkenberg
Anholt
Grenå
ÅRHUS
Ebeltoft
Ålborg Bugt
Laholmsbukten
Höganäs
Ängelholm
Torekov
Sæby
Hals
Dronninglund
Oslo
Oslo Moss Larvik
Amsterdam Harwich
København Kiel
Halmstad
Hundested
166
157
162

GÖTALAND
HALLAND
JÖNKÖ
KRONOE
166
167
161
158
Lilla Edet
Sollebrun
Floby
Tidaholm
Gräfsnäs
Faglavik
Madängsholm
St. Hoga
Lödöse
Herrljunga
Kinnarp
Brandstorp
Visingsö
Vårgårda
Tunnerstad
HOL
Utvängstorp
VISINGSBORG
Gränna
NÄS
Älvängen
Annelund
Öra
Trädet
Sandhem
Nol Alafors
Sjövik
Alingsås
Älmestad
Kungälv
Mjörn
V. Bodarna
Mullsjö
Brötjemark
NÄÄS
Surte
Dalum
Habo
Gråbo
Floda
Timmele
Bankervd
Kaxholmen
Lerum
Fristad
Ulricehamn
Partille
Bottnaryd
JÖNKÖPING
Huskvarna
NATURRESERVAT
Brämhult
Marbäck
Landvetter
Hindås
Sandared
Dalsjöfors
Axamo
Solb
Bollebygd
BORÅS
Tenhult
Mölnlycke
Dannike
Norrahammar
Forserum
Kållered
Viskafors
Aplared
TORPA STENHUS
Månsarp
Lindome
Hyssna
Mohärad
Bondstorp
Fritsla
Malmbäck
Kungsbacka
Skene
Kinna
Limmared
HOKS HERRGÅRD
Tranemo
Hok
Vickan
Fjäras
Svenljunga
Lygnern
Vaggeryd
Bodafors
Rydet
Tranhult
TJOLÖHOLM
Hestra
Svenarum
Skillingaryd
Åsa
Horred
Frillesås
Marieholm
Sävsjö
Överlida
Sjötofta
Gnosjö
Östra Frölunda
Vrigstad
Häcksvik
Gislaved
Klevshult
Hillerstorp
Veddige
Anderstorp
Stockaryd
Bua
Alvsered
STORE MOSSE NAT. PARK
Hjälmseryd
Tångaberg
Burseryd
Värnamo
Reftele
Varberg
Ullared
Smålandsstenar
Bredaryd
Forsheda
Ohs
Ätran
Skeppshult
Lammhult
Träslövsläge
Fegen
Tvååker
Landeryd
Dannäs
Hyltebruk
Horda
Torpsbruk
Vessingebro
Dörarp
Slätthog
Moheda
Torup
Flåren
Abild
Unnaryd
Rydaholm
Falkenberg
Lagan
Åby
Skrea
Femsjö
Växjö
Grenå
Bolmen
Alvesta
Oskarström
Lidhult
Odensjö
Ljungby
Bergunda
Harplinge
Åled
Annerstad
Vislanda
Haverdal
Simlångsdalen
Vrå
Halmstad
Torpa
Snöstorp
Tylösand
Söndrum
Trönninge
Möckeln
Hinneryd
V. Torsas
Pjätteryd
Dio
Mästocka
Laholmsbukten
Veinge
Traryd
Strömsnäsbruk
Mellbystrand
Laholm
Knäred
Älmhult
Häradsbäck
Torekov
Våxtorp
Markaryd
Ryd
Båstad
Emmaljunga
Osby
Lönsboda
Fridafors
Skålderviken
Skanes Fagerhult
Kullen
Vejbystrand
Mölle
Vittsjö
Kyrkhult
Ängelholm
KRAPPERUP
BRUNNBY
Tassjö
Asljunga
Hästveda
Glimåkra
Örkelljunga
Ängelholm
Bjärnum
Höganäs
Munka-Ljunby
Olofström
Bälinge
Broby
Sibbhult
Svängsta
Oderljunga
Jämshög
Viken
KULLA
Tyringe
VANÅS
Knislinge
Vånga
Mörrum
Lagan
Nissan
Helgeå

168
159
Boxholm
Sommen
Ulrika
Rimforsa
Falerum
Nora
Gryt
FÅGELVIK
Tranås
Blåvik
Örsebo
Björkefors
Edsbruk
Östra Ed
SABY
Hestra
Kisa
Dalhem
Överum
Åsunden
Sundhultsbrunn
Horn
Björnsholm
Loftahammar
Liden
N. Vi
Odensvi
Gamleby
Kälvik
Osterbymo
Ydrefors
Gullringen
Höghult
Blackstad
Almvik
Västervik
Anneberg
Svinhult
NORRA KVILLS NAT. PARK
Södra Vi
Frödinge
Gunnebo
SKURUGATA
Eksjö
Hult
Bruzaholm
Vimmerby
Ankarsrum
Totebo
HELGERUM
Mariannelund
Storebro
Tuna
Blankaholm
Bellö
Silverdalen
Vena
Björkö
Ekenässjön
Hultsfred
Visby
Paulistrom
Misterhult
Vetlanda
Järnforsen
Kvillsfors
Målilla
Kristdala
Landsbro
Fårbo
Figeholm
Nabbelund
Ölands norra udde
Nye
KALMAR
Virserum
Mörlunda
STENSJÖ
Byxelkrok
Grankullavik
Korsberga
Lemnhult
Oskarshamn
Böda
Döderhult
Byrum
BLÅ JUNGFRUN NATIONALPARK
Berga
Ramkvilla
Hultanäs
Fågelfors
Åseda
Fagerhult
Högsby
Finsjö
Påskallavik
Norrhult
Löttorp-Högby
Emsfors
Tolg
Böcksholm
Braås
Ruda
Fliseryd
Grönskåra
Sandvik
Dädesjö
Älghult
Mönsterås
Kråksmåla
Föra
Lenhovda
Sävsjöström
Blomstermåla
Alstermo
Ålem
Timmernabben
Öland
Fröseke
STRÖMSRUM
Furuby
Växjö
Gullaskruv
Bäckebo
Köpingsvik
Kosta
SOLLIDEN
Borgholm
Orrefors
Rockneby
KAPELLUDDEN
Hovmantorp
Åby
Gärdslösa
Lessebo
Eriksmåla
Boda glasbruk
Nybro
Linsdal
Rottnen
Långlöt
ISMANTORP
Örsjö
Johansfors
Trekanten
Kalmar
Glömminge
Algutsrum
Linneryd
KLÄCKEBERGA
GRÅBORG
Väckelsång
Emmaboda
Färjestaden
Skogsby
Lindås
Oskar
Ljungbyholm
Vassmolösa
KARLEVISTENEN
Gårdby
Hagby
Tingsryd
Rävemåla
Påryd
Resmo
Vissefjärda
Halltorp
Mörbylånga
Konga
BÅRBYBORG
Alby
Stora Alvaret
Gullabo
Söderåkra
Kastlösa
Holmsjö
Torsås
Eringsboda
Bidalite
Bergkvara
Hallabro
BLEKINGE
GETTLINGE
Segerstad
Degerhamn
Bökemåla
Flymen
Tving
Kallinge
Sälleryd
Grönhögen
Bräkne-Hoby
Hjortsberga
Rödeby
Kristianopel
Ottenby
Nättraby
Ronneby
Jämjö
LÅNGE JAN
E22

A
B
C
D
1
2
3
4
5
6
Utbjoa
170
Lono
Vågslid
Haukeligrend
Langevåg
Buavåg
Førde
Etne
Bergen
Bømlafjorden
Saudasjøen
Sauda
Nesflaten
Ølen
Sandeid
1540
SKAULEN
Bjerga
Bråtveit
Bjåen
Skjold
Vikedal
Ropeid
Vanvik
Sand
Suldalseid
Suldalsvatn
Våge
Haugesund
Grinde
Kårhus
Skjoldastraumen
Suldalsosen
1606
SNONUTEN
Hovden
1530
BRANDSNUTEN
Avaldsnes
ROGALAND
Øvre Moen
Slåttevik
Nedstrand
Vedavågen
Kopervik
Karmøy
Åkrehamn
Hervik
Karstø
Jelsa
SKARJENFOSSEN
Blåsjø
Vindsvik
Ombo
Nesvik
Tøtlandsvik
Bykle
Bjørnevasshytta
Arsvågen
Boknafjorden
Skudeneshavn
Hjelmeland
Finnøy
Rennesøy
Judaberg
Sørbø
UTSTEIN
Mosterøy
Årdalsosen
Rotemo
Eide
1304
LYSEKAMMEN
1434
URDALSNUTEN
Valle
Newcastle upon Tyne
Randaberg
Tau
Jørpeland
PREKESTOL
HALLANDSFOSSEN
Lysebotn
Roskreppfjorden
Hylestad
STAVANGER
Lysefjorden
Søngesand
Ådneram
Myklestøyl
Hommersåk
Sola
Eiane
Oanes
Øvre Espedal
N
Otra
SETESDALEN
E39
Vatne
Lauvvik
Austad
Gandal
Sandnes
Sinnes
Figgjo
Olteddal
Tjørhom
Ose
Klepp
Ålgård
811
Sira
Bryne
Åneb jør
Byrkjedal
Ljosland
Søyland
VEST - AGDER
1041
SKORE
Kvina
Bjordal
Espeli
Nærbø
Bue
Byglandsfjorden
Varhaug
Vassbø
Tonstad
Vikeså
Knaben
Vigrestad
Bjerkreim
Gya
Risnes
Gravdal
Haughom
Brusand
Helleland
Rusdal
Åseral
Sirevåg
Sirdalsvatn
Flystveit
Evje
Kvinlog
Egersund
Ystebrød
Eide
Moi
Hornnes
Sandvatn
Eiken
BLÅBERGET
681
Sveindal
Stapnes
Åpåsdal
Sira
Hauge
Råna
Tjørnhom
Skeie
Birkeland
Åvedal
Bjelland
Sogndalstrand
Loga
Hægeland
Åna-Sira
Kvinesdal
Lygna
Flekkefjord
Feda
Skarpengland
Kirkehamn
Abelnes
Rørvik
Førland
Kvås
Konsmo
Hidra
Listafjorden
Laudal
Listeid
Lyngdal
Nodeland
Øyslebø
Vestbygd
Vanse
Farsund
Alleen
Vigeland
Søgne
Spangereid
Høllen
Lindesnes
Mandal
Våge
Hanstholm
Harwich Hirtshals

TELEMARK
VESTFOLD
AUST-AGDER
Rjukan
Bondal
Hovin
Tuddal
Flesberg
Lampeland
Skotselv
Geithus
Åmot
Sylling
Sandvika
Asker
Tranby
Lierbyen
Nesoddtangen
Slemmestad
DRAMMEN
Hokksund
Vestfossen
Mjøndalen
Røyken
Fagerstrand
Hyggen
Åros
Sætre
Konnerud
Kongsberg
KONGENSGRUVE
Skollenberg
Eikeren
Vå
Rauland
Høyfjellshotell
Bossbøen
Berge
Sudbø
Vinje
Straume
Åmot
Nutheim
Sauland
Ørvella
STAVKIRKE
Heddal
Notodden
Gransherad
Bolkesjø
Ormemyr
BLETOPPEN
MAELEFJELL
EIDSBORG
Ofte
Høydalsmo
Seljord
Dalen
Morgedal
Lårdal
Brunkeberg
Bandak
Kviteseid
Vråliosen
Vrådal
Hauggrend
STORROAN
LIFJELL
Sanden
Stokkland
Klevar
Sanda
Bø
Kilen
Gvarv
Østenå
Åmnes
Lunde
Steane
Ulefoss
Valebø
MIKAELSHULEN
Siljan
Steinsholt
Dammen
Hvittingfoss
Svarstad
Lågen
Eidsfoss
Skoger
Svelvik
Sande
Verket
Drøbak
Berger
Tofte
Gullhaug
Holmestrand
Moss
Horten
Borre
Åsgårdstrand
Larkollen
Rygge
Sem
Tønsberg
Stokke
Nøtterøy
FREDR
Vikane
Arøysund
Sandefjord
Torp
Tjøme
Verdens Ende
Melsomvik
Kvelde
Fyresdal
Fjone
Grovo
Singusdal
Høydalen
Norsjø
Afoss
Skien
Porsgrunn
Eidanger
Herøya
Herre
Langangen
Brevik
Stathelle
Bamble
Langesund
Larvik
Stavern
Nevlunghavn
Åmli
Skomdal
Kile
Nisser
Bostrak
Prestestranda
Fyresvatn
Tveitsund
Smeland
Tjønnefoss
Straume
Sandnes
Heiland
Øy
Gjerstad
Kil
Helle
Kragerø
Stabbestad
Portør
Strömstad
Åmli
Dølemo
Vegårshei
Søndeled
Akland
Risør
Ubergsmoen
Gjeving
Lyngør
Svenes
Hynnekleiv
Mjåland
Bøylefoss
Tvedestrand
Fidje
Borås
Eydehavn
Kongshavn
Søre Herefoss
Blakstad
Arendal
Øyestad
TROMØY
Vatnstraum
Tovdalselva
Fevik
Vik
Birkeland
NØRHOLM
Grimstad
Ryen
Lillesand
Hamre
NSAND
Hirtshals Frederikshavn København Kiel
København Kiel
Frederikshavn
171
166

OSLO
DRAMMEN
Lillestrøm
Asker
Sandvika
Drøbak
Moss
Horten
Tønsberg
Sandefjord
Larvik
Stavern
FREDRIKSTAD
Sarpsborg
Halden
Askim
Mysen
ØSTFOLD
VESTFOLD
Strömstad
Uddevalla
Vänersborg
Trollhättan
Mellerud
Lysekil
Orust
Tjörn
Svinesund
Årjäng
Bengtsfors
København Kiel
Hirtshals Frederikshavn København Kiel
Frederikshavn
GLASKOGENS NATURRESERVAT
NATUR-RESERVAT
NATURVÅRDS-OMRÅDE
FREDRIKSTEN
BLOMSHOLMS-SKEPPET
HÄLLRISTNINGAR
KROPPEFJÄLL
165
161
172

Lysvik
Hagfors
173
Rammen
Lesjöfors
Nittkvarn
Grängesberg
Söderbärke
Norra Råda
KARNÄSENS HEMBYGDSGÅRD
Uddheden
Motjärnshyttan
Sunnemo
Högfors
NATURVÅRDSOMRÅDE
Malingsbo
Västerrottna
Sunne
Rottneros
MÅRBACKA
Munkfors
Bosjön
Nordmark
Sävsjön
Gåsborn
Långban
Ställdalen
Kopparberg
Bredsjö
Kloten
Skinnskatteberg
ÄRMLAND
Ämtervik
Olsätter
Paradisgård
Filipstad
Persberg
Hällefors
Riddarhytt
Ramsberg
Storå
Bonäs
Grythyttan
NATURVÅRDS-OMRÅDE
Yngen
Edane
Mellan Fryken
Molkom
Blombacka
Nykroppa
BRUNSORT FRÅN
Lindesberg
Boda
Deje
Klässbol
Fagerås
Forshaga
Kil
Värmeln
Värmskog
Storfors
Lungsund
Östra Kärne
Gyttorp
Nora
Grava
Skåre
Edsvalla
ALKVETTERN
Frøvik
Borgvik
Vålberg
Karlstad
Väse
Ölmbrotorp
Ödeby
Felli
Grums
Karlskoga
Hovsta
GARPHYTTANS NATIONALPARK
KILSBERGEN
ÖREBRO
E18
E20
E18/E20
Segmon
Kristinehamn
Latorpsbruk
NATURRESERVAT
Degerfors
Vintrosa
Värmlandsbro
NATUR-RESERVAT
Hult
Björneborg
Lannabruk
Mosås
Fjugesta
RISEBERGA KLOSTER
Säffle
Bäckhammar
Kumla
Odensba
Råglanda
Mo
Svartå
Hasselfors
BÅLBY
Sköllersta
168
Pålsboda
Ölserud
Hallsberg
Gullspång
Östansjö
Vretstorp
Laxå
Brevens bruk
Skagern
Sottern
Snavlunda
Asbro
Ekenäs
Delebäck
Lerbäck
Bo
TIVEDEN
Åmmeberg
NATURRESERVAT
Hova
Askersund
Mariedamm
Hjortkvarn
DJURÖ NATIONALPARK
Sjötorp
Älgarås
STJÄRNSUND
Grytgöl
Torsö
Hassle
Hammar
Unden
Tived
Ljusfallsham
Hallerud
Mariestad
Olshammar
Borggård
Hällest
Kållandsö
NATURVÅRDS-OMRÅDE
LÄCKÖ
Leksberg
Töreboda
Godegard
Tjällmo
Medevi
Finspå
Forshem
RÅBÄCK
KINNEKULLE
Lugnås
Moholm
Undenäs
STOLA
ÖVRALID
HUSABY
Tidan
Grytstorp
Örslösa
Götene
Borensberg
Lidköping
Timmersdala
Karlsborg
Motala
ULVÅSA
Mölltorp
Boren
Ljungsbro
MARIEDAL
VRETA KLOSTER
Roxen
Berg slussa
Tibro
Fagersanna
NÄSSJA
Vadstena
KAGA
Malmslätt
Saleby
Varnhem
Borghamn
Skara
Skövde
Skänninge
Linköping
Jung
Skultorp
Mantorp
STRA
Stenstorp
Hjo
OMBERG
Väderstad
N. Vånga
EKORNAVALLEN
Alvastra
Mjölby
Nikil
Blikstorp
Rök
SVANEHOLM
ÖSTER
Hästholmen
Ödeshög
Strålsnäs
Vedum
Falköping
Floby
Ekedalen
Tidaholm
TALAND
Boxholm
162
Sommen
163
Ulrika
Rimforsa
Kinnarp
Brandstorp
Sten

174
163
167
A
B
C
D
1
2
3
4
5
6
VÄSTMANLAND
SÖDERMANLAND
ÖSTERGÖTLAND
UPPSALA
STOCKHOLM
Västerås
Eskilstuna
Örebro
Norrköping
Linköping
Nyköping
Södertälje
Sigtuna
Skokloster
Strängnäs
Mariefred
Trosa
Söderbärke
Norberg
Fagersta
Västansfors
Malingsbo
Kloten
Skinnskatteberg
Riddarhyttan
Ramsberg
Storå
Lindesberg
Frövik
Ölmbrotorp
Ödeby
Hovsta
Mosås
Kumla
Sköllersta
Pålsboda
Hallsberg
Mariedamm
Godegard
Tjällmo
Borensberg
Boren
Vreta Kloster
Kåga
Malmslätt
Mantorp
Mjölby
Vanehölm
Ulrika
Rimforsa
Nykrogen
Ruhällen
Granlunda
Skyttorp
Salsta
Björkling
Gamla Grånome
Storvreta
Bälinge
Gamla Uppsala
Sala
Heby
Morgongåva
Järlåsa
Altuna
Fjärdhundra
Österunda
Ransta
Satra brunn
Salbohed
Virsbo
Virsbo bruk
Ramnäs
Färna
Surahammar
Skultuna
Hökåsen
Tilberga
Hed
Kolsva
Hallstahammar
Odensvi
Anundshögen
Hasslo
Köping
Strömsholm
Kolbäck
Gäddeholm
Ängsö
Tidö
Kvicksund
Naturreservat
Fellingsbro
Arboga
Kungsör
Torshälla
Sundbyholm
Fiholm
Kungshället
Enköping
Litslena
Ekolsund
Grillby
Bålsta
Örsundsbro
Venngarn
Märsta
Steninge
Rosersberg
Upplands Väsby
Bro
Kungsängen
Munsö
Sundbyberg
Ekerö
Sturehov
Tynnelsö
Ytterselö
Grönsö
Målsåker
Stallarholmen
Toresund
Lånna
Åkers-krutbruk
Tumba
Tullinge
Nykvarn
Pershagen
Järna
Gnesta
Sorunda
Ösmo
Tullgarn
Vagnhärad
Lästringe
Tystberga
Krabbfjärden
Naturreservat
Sävja
Sunnersta
Vik
Knivsta
Långhundra
Linnés Hammarby
Mora stenar
Arlanda
Skogstorp
Alberga
St. Sundby
Göksholm
Hjälmaren
Odensbacken
Julita
Äsköping
Läppe
Vingåker
Brevens bruk
Sottern
Hälleforsnäs
Malmköping
Sparreholm
Björnlunda
Stenhammar
Flen
Kantorp
Bie
Katrineholm
Tisnaren
Båven
Eriksberg
Bettna
Yngaren
Vrena
Aspa
Stigtomta
Björkvik
Strångsjö
Hävla
Bo
Hjortkvarn
Grytgöl
Igelfors
Rejmyre
Simonstorp
Ljusfallshammar
Hällestad
Borggård
Lotorp
Finspång
Stromsfors
Åby
Kolmården
Kvarsebo
Jönåker
Oxelösund
Tunaberg
Navekvaren
Svärtinge
Ringstad
Bråviken
Kungsängen
Ållonö
Grytstorp
Skärblacka
Lövstad
Norsholm
Ljungsbro
Roxen
Göta Kanal
Berg slussar
Söderköping
Stegeborg
Rönö
Arkösund
Helsinki /Helsingfors
Gdańsk
Linghem
Örtomta
Ost Ryd
Vårdsberg
Hjulsbro
Björsäter
Borrum
Ringarum
S. Anna
Tyrislöt
Nikil
Yxnerum
Gusum
Valdemarsvik
Bestorp
Brokind
Åtvidaberg
Nora
Gryt
Valerum
Fågelvik
E4
E18
E20
E22
E04
E18/E20

E

F

G

H

38 Hallstavik

22

Knutby 32

Skebobruk 280

282

Edsbro

25

Erken

Roslags-Bro

Björkö

Älmsta-Väddö

30

283

Vätö

Ålandshav

Lemland

Degerby

Håstersboda

Föglö

Herröskkatan

FIN

Kökar

Karlby

Hellsö

1

Visby

Turku/Åbo

EKEBYHOLM

FINSTA

76

Norrtälje

Gräddö

260

20

77

21

Rimbo 11

Husby Sjuhundra

24

9

PENNINGBY

E18 24

Kappelskär

Furusund

18

Bottniska viken /

Pohjanlahti

2

Bergshamra

E18

ÄNGSÖ NATIONALPARK

Blidö

268

Brottby

48

65

Roslags kulla

276

Ö. Lagnö

Ljusterö

Åkersberga

Tranvik

Möja

KHOLM

38

Vaxholm

Lidingö

Värmdö

Gustavsberg

222

26

Värmdölandet

Tallinn

Helsinki / Helsingfors

Sankt -Peterburg

3

19

228

Nacka

229

Saltsjöbaden

73 Vendelsö

Tyresö

Brevik

227

Dalarö

Runmarö

Nämdö

NATUR-RESERVAT

Mariehamn /
Maarianhamina
Nynäshamn

Lauter

Fårö

Holmudden

Hallshuk

Lickershamn

Kappelshamn

Fårösund

48

Lärbro

20

Kyllaj

LUMMELUNDAGROTTORNA

149

148

35

Tingstäde

Slite

24

Ornö

Muskö

NATURRESERVAT

Ulö

Helsinki /
Helsingfors

Bro

45

4

Visby

Travemünde
Gdańsk
Oskarshamn

Högklint

147

Gothem

Barlingbo

51

146

S

Gnisvärd

35

143

Roma

amn

Eskelhem

Isums

44

Ala

Katthammarsvik

48

142

Gdańsk

Västergärn

Hejde

Buttle

TORSBURGEN

Klintehamn

143

5

L. Karslö

22

Lojsta

Lye

144

Ljugarn

Visby

141

Sproge

30

Burs

Gotland

St. Karslö

DJAUVIK

Hemse

142

140

Hablingbo

Ronehamn

47

Havdhem

25

6

Burgsvik

Sallmunds

Sundre

Hoburgen

E

F

G

H

180
164
HORDALAND
BERGEN
Voss
Odda
Sognefjorden
Sognesjøen
Fensfjorden
Osterfjorden
Hjeltefjorden
Hardangerfjorden
Sørfjorden
Eidfjorden
Bjørnafjorden
Bømlafjorden
VIKAFJELL
FOLGEFONNI
HARDANGERVIDDA NASJONALPARK
HARDANGERJÖKULEN
Askvoll
Dale
Fure
Vaerlandet
Hellevik
Flekke
Bygstad
Sande
Guddal
Vadheim
Høyanger
Sula
Krakhella
Leirvik
Lavik
Daløy
Solund
Ytre Sula
Rutledal
Oppedal
Brekke
Solheim
Risnes
Mongstad
Duesund
Masfiordnes
Hoplandsjøen
Rossnes
Radøy
Hellesøy
Sævrasvåg
Vikanes
Manger
Seløy
Herdla
Bjørsvik
Rossland
Alversund
Skråmestø
Knarvik
Steinestø
Salhus
Lonevåg
Breistein
Solsvik
Ask
Florvåg
Kleppestø
Ytre Arna
Arna
Vaksdal
Trengereid
Espeland
Nesttun
Florø
Telavåg
Flesland
Fana
Sotra
Hjellestad
Klokkarvik
Stavanger
Lerwick
Newcastle upon Tyne
Hanstholm
Osøyro
Hatvik
Halhjem
Fusa
Eikelandsosen
Hufthamar
Huftarøy
Reksteren
Sævareid
Mundheim
Lygre
Kvalvåg
Våge
Gjermundshamn
Sandvikvåg
Tysnesøy
Husa
Fitjar
Flatråker
Stord
Jektevik
Rubbestadneset
Uskedal
Sunde
Husnes
Siggjarvåg
Leirvik
Sagvåg
Sæbøvik
Utåker
Mosterhamn
Bomlo
Valevåg
Skånevik
Utbjoa
Buavåg
Langevåg
Førde
Etne
Ølen
Skjold
Våge
Sandeid
Vikedal
Ropeid
Kårhus
Grinde
Skjoldastraumen
Haugesund
Moskog
Haukedal
Gaularfjell Pass
Eldalsosen
748
Fjærland
Ulvestad
Dragsvik
Nordeide
Balestrand
Kongsnes
Hella
Leikanger
Sogndal
SOGN FOLKEMUSEUM
Hermansverk
Vangsnes
Kaupanger
KVAMSØY GML. KIRKE
HOPPERSTAD STAVKIRKE
Vik
Soreide
Ortnevik
Feios
Revsnes
Fresvik
Arnafjord
1660
FRESVIKBREEN
Skar
986 Vikafjell Pass
Nygård
OMBYGGET STAVKIRKE
SYRDALSBREEN 1761
Mo
Gullbrå
STALHEIMSKLEIVENE MUSEUM
Gudvangen
KJELFOSSEN
Aurland
Stalheim
Vinje
Nesheim
Oppheim
Flåm
Eidslandet
1434 KVITANOSA
Brekkhus
Straume
Myrdal
Tyssebotn
Evanger
Bulken
Mjølfjell
Dale
Stanghelle
SKJERVEFOSSEN
VASSFJORA 1633
Hamlagrøosen
Ulvik
1351 SKJEMMENE
Rong
Granvin
Kvanndal
Bruravik
Ålvik
1862
Tysse
Norheimsund
Utne
Brimnes
Eidfjord
VØRINGSFOSSEN
TOKAGJELET
Øystese
Garen
Sæbø
Tveita
Kinsarvik
1649
Strandebarm
Tørvikbygd
Lofthus
Brattabø
Jondal
Hardangervidda Pa
Nå
Hovland
Hessvik
Flatabø
1690 HÅRTEIGEN
Tyssedal
1660 FONNANUTEN
Løfallstrand
Rosendal
Hildal
ESPELANDSFOSS
Steinaberg bru
Fjæra
Seljestad
Solfonn
1719 SANDFLOT
1602 KYRKJENUTEN
Breifonn
Røldal
Haukeliseter
Åkra
Kyrping
Lono
Vågslid
Saudasjøen
Sauda
Nesflaten
Haukeligrend
1540 SKAULEN
Bjåen
Bjerga
Bråtveit
Vanvik
Suldalseid
Suldalsvatn
Suldalsosen
1606
Hovden

181
OPPLAND
JOTUNHEIMEN NASJONALPARK
JOTUN
Skjolden
Fortun
Turtagrø
2405
SKAGASTOLSTINDANE
Lusterfjorden
FEIGUMFOSS
VETTISFOSSEN
Eidsbugarden
STAVKIRKE
Øvre Årdal
Årdalstangen
Årdalsfjorden
FILLEFJELL
Tyin
Nystova
1013
Fillefjell Pass
Lærdalsøyri
SVATEGJEL
Borgund
Borlaug
1836
STORRE HÅNOSA
1920
JUKLEGGA
Grindaheim
SLETTEFJELL
Bygdin
Gjende
1389
Valderesflya Pass
Haugsten
Bessheim
1783
SIKKILSDALSHO
Vinstervatn
1686
SKAGET
Beitostølen
Heggenes
Lomen
Skåbu
Vinstra
Harpefoss
Venabu
Hundorp
Ringebu
Golå
Dalseter
Espedal
Fåvang
Tretten
Svingvoll
Liomseter
Segalstad bru
Vestre Gausdal
Fåberg
Lenningen
1414
SPÅTIND
SYNNFJELL
Vingnes
Ulnes
Fagernes
Leira
Flatøydegard
Åmot
Svingstad
Nøsen
Hovda
Aurdal
VALDRES
Bagn
Dokka
Fluberg
Raufoss
Hov
Reinsvoll
Østerbø
Tuv
Hemsedal
1789
REINESKARVET
Storestølen
NYSTOLSVARDEN
1295
Gol
Torpo
Ål
Hovet
FOLARSKARNUTEN
1933
SKARVET
Hagafoss
Haugastøl
FAGERHEIM FJELLSTUE
Geilo
Ustaoset
Ustevatn
1212
Nesbyen
HALLINGDAL
Åsli
Hedal
Begndal
Engelia
Nes
Lindlia
Sperillen
Horn
172
Einavoll
Lisleset
Bromma
Tunhovd
Dagali
Tunhovdfjorden
Ossjøen
1315
HALLINGNATTEN
1280
SORBOLFJELL
BUSKERUD
Bergsjøstøl
Brøstrud
Flå
Gulsvik
Åmot
NOREFJELL
Haglebu
Tingelstad
Brandbu
Finsand
Granvollen
Onsaker
Bjørkflåta
Rødberg
1429
STORE SKREKKEN
1344
NONSHOVD
Eggedal
1466
GRÅFJELL
Ringnes
Orgenvika
Hallingby
Sokna
Krøderen
Noresund
Hen
Jevnaker
Hønefoss
VIDDA
NUMEDAL
Karlsrud
Stegaros
Krøderen
Tyristrand
Gøvstdal
Austbygdi
Veggli
Båsheim
Prestfoss
Sundvollen
704
OPPKUVEN
Tyrifjorden
KLEIVSTUA
Miland
Tinnsjø
Møsvatn
1630
FLISEGGA
Rjukan
Alfstad
Vikersund
Geithus
Åmot
Flesberg
Lampeland
Sylling
Sandvika
Asker
Bondal
Hovin
Vå
Rauland Høyfjellshotell
Bossbøen
1341
BLETOPPEN
Tuddal
Skotselv
Tranby
Lierbyen
Nesoddtangen
Slemmestad
Berge
Sudbø
Ormemyr
Hokksund
DRAMMEN
TELEMARK
Vinje
Bolkesjø
Gransherad
Vestfossen
Mjøndalen
Røyken
Straume
Kongsberg
165
Hagerstrand
KONGENSGRUVE
Sauland
Konnerud
Hyggen
Åros

A
B
C
D
182
166
171
HEDMARK
AKERSHUS
OSLO
ØSTERDALEN
SYNNFJELL
N
Vinstra
Venabu
Harpefoss
Ringebu
Hundorp
Golå
Lågen
Espedal
Fåvang
Åsheim
Koppang
Elvdal
Stai
Sjøli
Bekken
Engerneset
Storsjøen
Evenstad
TVERRFJELLET
1189
LYNGKEMPEN
Tretten
Nyskolla
Svingvoll
Øyer
Deset
Jordet
Trysilelva
Nordre Osen
Innbygda
1132
TRYSILFJELLET
Nybergsund
Rena
Segalstad bru
Vestre Gausdal
Nordseter
Sjusjøen
Fåberg
Lillehammer
Mesnalien
Vingnes
Lenningen
1414
SPÅTIND
Osensjøen
Midtskogberget
Linnerud
746
SKALBERGET
Ulvålia
826
BRUMUNDKAMPEN
Glomma
Flatøydegard
Åmot
Svingstad
Mjøsa
Biri
Moelv
Brumunddal
Elverum
Dokka
Redalen
Bagn
Fluberg
Gjøvik
Raufoss
Stavsjø
Hamar
Løten
Heradsbygd
Hov
Engelia
Begndal
Hedal
Reinsvoll
Bøverbru
Kapp
Stange
Vallset
Gata
Braskereidfoss
Lena
Eina
Skreia
Våler
Åsnes
Holtet
Flisbrua
Nes
Lindlia
Flisa
Tangen
Espa
Mjørlund
636
EIDSFJELLET
Malungen
Dulpetorpet
Breisjøberget
Sperillen
Horn
Einavoll
Feiring
Brandbu
Tingelstad
Jaren
Åmot
Finsand
Granvollen
Hurdal
Bruvoll
Mo
Sandstad
Kirkenær
Svullrya
Onsaker
Gran
Minnesund
Sand
Kuggerud
Storsjøen
Skasen
Orgenvika
Sokna
Hallingby
Rustad
Eidsvoll
Eidsvoll verk
Styri
Fallet
Roa
Vorma
Hen
Jevnaker
Grua
Maura
Råholt
Dal
Korsmo
Brandval
576
RAFJELLET
Lunderseter
Berg
Hønefoss
Nannestad
Gardermoen
Skarnes
Roverud
Øyermoen
Krøderen
Harestua
Jessheim
Nordkisa
Oppaker
Vormsund
Kongsvinger
Jammerdal
Vittjärn
Tyristrand
Prestfoss
Sundvollen
704
OPPKUVEN
Tyrifjorden
KLEIVSTUA
Nittedal
Kløfta
Årnes
Austmarka
Vikersund
Skedsmokorset
Bjørknes
Slattum
Geithus
Hvam
Glomma
Sørumsand
Mangen
414
Kjerret
Åmot
Sylling
Sandvika
Lillestrøm
Lørenskog
Strømmen
Fetsund
Aursmoen
Vestmarka
Skotterud
Magnor
Asker
Tranby
Lierbyen
Nesoddtangen
Fjellsrud
Øyeren
Bjørkelangen
Eda glasbruk
Skotselv
DRAMMEN
Slemmestad
Kolbotn
Charlottenberg
Tangen
Vestfossen
Mjøndalen
Røyken
Oppegård
Flateby
Løken
Enebakk
Krokebol
Fagerstrand
Hyggen
Åros
Ski
Konnerud
Hemnes
Flogned
Åmotfors
Hölj
Meds
E06
E16
E18
E134

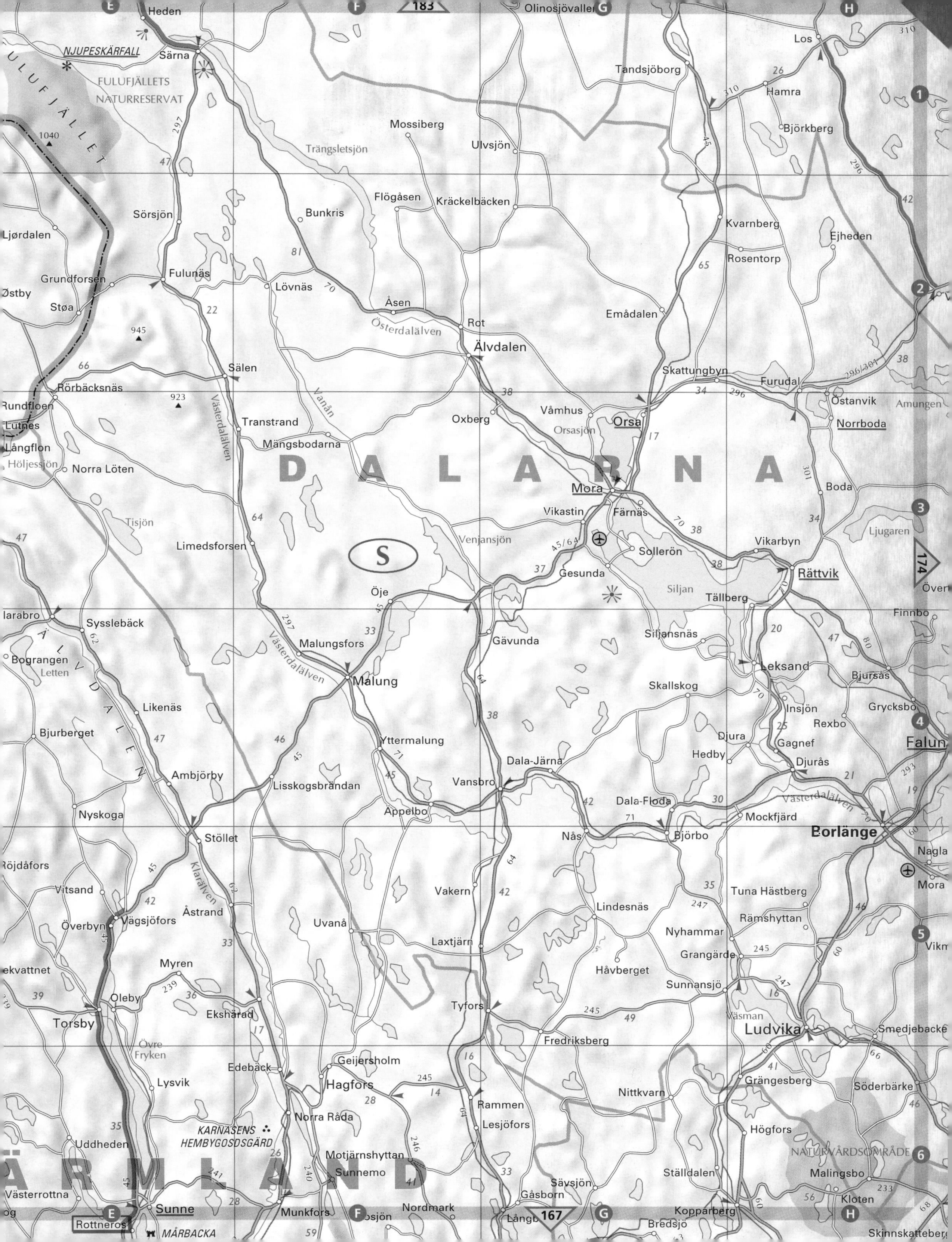
183
167
174
DALARNA
VÄRMLAND
Särna
Heden
NJUPESKÄRFALL
FULUFJÄLLETS NATURRESERVAT
FULUFJÄLLET
Trängsletsjön
Mossiberg
Ulvsjön
Olinosjövallen
Tandsjöborg
Los
Hamra
Björkberg
Flögåsen
Kräckelbäcken
Bunkris
Sörsjön
Ljørdalen
Kvarnberg
Ejheden
Rosentorp
Grundforsen
Fulunäs
Lövnäs
Østby
Støa
Åsen
Emådalen
Rot
Österdalälven
Älvdalen
Sälen
Rörbäcksnäs
Skattungbyn
Furudal
Östanvik
Amungen
Norrboda
Rundfloen
Lutnes
Transtrand
Vanån
Oxberg
Våmhus
Orsa
Orsasjön
Mångsbodarna
Långflon
Höljessjön
Norra Löten
Västerdalälven
Mora
Boda
Vikastin
Färnäs
Tisjön
Venjansjön
Sollerön
Ljugaren
Limedsforsen
Vikarbyn
Gesunda
Rättvik
Siljan
Tällberg
Öje
Finnbo
Överl
Sysslebäck
Siljansnäs
Bograngen
Letten
Malungsfors
Gävunda
Malung
Leksand
Bjursås
Skallskog
KLARÄLVDALEN
Likenäs
Insjön
Grycksbo
Rexbo
Bjurberget
Djura
Gagnef
Falun
Yttermalung
Hedby
Djurås
Dala-Järna
Ambjörby
Lisskogsbrändan
Vansbro
Dala-Floda
Mockfjärd
Äppelbo
Nyskoga
Nås
Björbo
Borlänge
Nagla
Stöllet
Röjdåfors
Mora
Klarälven
Vakern
Tuna Hästberg
Vitsand
Lindesnäs
Åstrand
Vägsjöfors
Rämshyttan
Överbyn
Uvanå
Nyhammar
Vikm
Laxtjärn
Grangärde
Myren
Håvberget
Sunnansjö
Oleby
Tyfors
Väsman
Torsby
Ekshärad
Ludvika
Smedjebacke
Fredriksberg
Övre Fryken
Geijersholm
Edebäck
Lysvik
Hagfors
Grängesberg
Nittkvarn
Söderbärke
Rammen
Norra Råda
Lesjöfors
KARNÄSENS HEMBYGDSGÅRD
Uddheden
Högfors
NATURVÅRDSOMRÅDE
Motjärnshyttan
Sunnemo
Ställdalen
Malingsbo
Sävsjön
Gåsborn
Västerrottna
Kloten
Sunne
Munkfors
Nordmark
Kopparberg
Rottneros
MÅRBACKA
Bredsjö
Skinnskatteberg

184
167
173
DALARNA
GÄVLEBO
Olinosjövallen
Delsbo
Färila
Los
Järvsö
Tandsjöborg
Hamra
Björkberg
Mossiberg
Ulvsjön
Nordsjö
Vallsta
Arbrå
Flögåsen
Kräckelbäcken
Kvarnberg
Ejheden
Rosentorp
Edsbyn
Bollnäs
Voxna
Alfta
Åsen
Rot
Emådalen
Österdalälven
Älvdalen
Annefors
Skattungbyn
Furudal
Kilafors
Östanvik
Amungen
Oxberg
Våmhus
Orsa
Orsasjön
Norrboda
Skålsjön
Holmsveden
HÄLSINGSKOGEN
Mora
Boda
Vikastin
Färnäs
Ljugaren
Åmot
Venjansjön
Sollerön
Vikarbyn
Svartnäs
Gesunda
Rättvik
Öje
Siljan
Tällberg
Övertänger
Finnbo
Enviken
Vintjärn
Siljansnäs
Linghed
Gävunda
Svärdsjö
Kungsberg
Malung
Leksand
Bjursås
Skallskog
Järbo
Insjön
Grycksbo
Rexbo
Sundborn
Yttermalung
Djura
Gagnef
Falun
Storvik
Hedby
Djurås
Dala-Järna
Runn
Vansbro
Vika
Hofors
Äppelbo
Dala-Floda
Mockfjärd
Västerdalälven
Torsåker
Nås
Björbo
Borlänge
Naglarby
Långshyttan
Lövåsen
Stjärnsund
Mora
Fäggeby
Dala-Husby
Vakern
Tuna Hästberg
KLOSTER
Säter
Lindesnäs
Rämshyttan
Garpenberg
Nyhammar
Vikmanshyttan
Horndal
Grangärde
Hedemora
Laxtjärn
Håvberget
Sunnansjö
Ingolsbenning
Fors
Tyfors
Väsman
Ludvika
Smedjebacken
Fredriksberg
Avesta
Folkärna
Geijersholm
Krylbo
Hagfors
Grängesberg
Söderbärke
Norberg
Nittkvarn
Rammen
Fagersta
Nykrogen
Lesjöfors
Högfors
Västansfors
NATURVÅRDSOMRÅDE
Sunnemo
Ställdalen
Malingsbo
Åmänningen
Sävsjön
Gåsborn
Kloten
Virsbo
Salbohed
Bosjön
Nordmark
Kopparberg
Långban
Bredsjö
Skinnskatteberg
Virsbo bruk
Sätra

185
E
F
G
H
1
2
3
4
5
6
168
169
176
Näsviken
Hudiksvall
Iggesund
Hornslandet
Enånger
Söderhamn
Sandarne
Ljusne
Bottniska viken/
Pohjanlahti
Norrsundet
Bergby
Hamrångefjärden
Trodje
Utvalnäs
GÄVLE
Gävlebukten
Furuvik
Skutskär
Gårdskär
Forsbacka
Storsjön
Fågelsundet
Älvkarleby
Årsunda
Karlholmsbruk
Marma
Skärplinge
Öregrundsgrepen
Norrboda
Västland
Hedesunda
Lövstabruk
Söderfors
Forsmark
Gräsö
Tierp
Öregrund
Södra Kvarken
Gysinge
Norrskedika
Östhammar
Börstil
Storby
Eckerö
Månkarbo
Örbyhus
ÖRBYHUS
Östervåla
Österbybruk
Gimo
Hargshamn
Singö
UPPSALA
Vendel
FIN
Tärnsjö
Tämnaren
Grisslehamn
Skyttorp
SALSTA
Alunda
Hallstavik
Granlunda
Skoby
Björkling
Ålandshav
GAMLA GRÄNOME
Älmsta-Väddö
Morgongåva
Storvreta
Skebobruk
Bälinge
Heby
Gamla Uppsala
Knutby
Järlåsa
Almunge
Sodderby Karl
Edsbro
Erken
Roslags-Bro
LINNÉS HAMMARBY
Mar
Marian
E04
E04
E04
80

Bottniska viken/

Pohjanlahti

PORI/ BJÖRNEBORG

Ahlainen
Pomarkku
Kairila
Reposaari
Noormarkku
Karhijärvi
Mäntyluoto
Pihlava
Kullaa
Kiikoir
Luvia
Ulvila
Sääksjärvi
Lievikoski
Nakkila
Harjavalta
Kokemäenjoki
Eurajoki
Koke

Rauma
Eura
Köyliö
Kauttua
Lappi
Säkylä
Reila
Vermuntila
Pyhäjärvi
Pyhämaa
Pyhäranta
Hinnerjoki
Laajoki
Laitila
Karjala
Kalanti
Uusikaupunki/ Nystad
Mynämäki
Tortinm
Lokalahti
Vehmaa
Rautila
Mietoinen
Paatinen
Kustavi
Askainen
Masku
Taivassalo
Raisio
Turku
Hakkenpää
KULTARANTA
Jurmo
Merimasku
Näantali
Velkua
Avå
TURKU/ ÅBO
Fiskö
Rymättylä
Brändö
Iniö
Pargas/ Parainen
Enklinge
Björkö
Houtsala
Lappo
Houtskär/ Houtskari
Lof
Kumlinge
Storlandet
Saltvik
Skiftet Kihti
Nagu/ Nauvo
Sund
Vårdö
Storby
Finström
KASTELHOLMS
Korpo/ Korppoo
Seglinge
Eckerö
Godby
Dele Teili
Jomala
Bomarsund
Sottunga
Korpoström

Åland/Ahvenanmaa

ÅLAND/
AHVENANMAA

Geta
BOLSTAHOLM
Hammarland

Mariehamn/ Maarianhamina
Lumparland
Långnäs
Överö
Lemland
Hastersboda
Degerby
Gullkrona Fjärd
Herröskkatan
Föglö
Nötö
Hellsö
Kökar
Karlby
SKÄRGÅRDSHAVETS NATIONALPARK / SAARISTOMEREN KANSALLISPUISTO

17
187
178
E
F
G
H
1
2
3
4
5
6
Viljakkala
Orivesi
Kylämä
Savi
Kyröskoski
Hämeenkyrö
Längelmävesi
Eräjärvi
Kuhmoinen
Päijänne
Näsijärvi
Ponsa
Sappee
Suopelto
Suodenniemi
TAMPERE
Ruutana
Kuhmalahti
Vehkajärvi
Ylöjärvi
Mouhijärvi
Kangasala
Sahalahti
Pohja
Putaja
Nokia
Pirkkala
Kuru
Rautajärvi
Arrakoski
Karkku
Roine
Pälkänevesi
Luopioinen
Porasa
Padasjoki
Tottijärvi
Tampere-Pirkkala
Pyhäjärvi
Pälkäne
Auttoinen
Stormi
Mallasvesi
Kiikka
Vammala
Valkeakoski
Laitikkala
Asikkala
Lempäälä
Kuohijärvi
Iso-Äiniö
Sääksmäki
Iso-Evo
Vääksy
Rautaniemi
Hauho
Tuulos
Vesijärvi
Illo
Savikoski
Viiala
Toijala
Vanajavesi
Huittinen
Kylmäkoski
Lammi
Eteläinen
Punkalaidun
Kalvola
Hattula
Koski
Urjala
LAH
Vampula
Hämeenlinna
Turenki
Kärkölä
Alastaro
Luhtikylä
Virttaa
Janakkala
Jokimaa
Järvelä
FIN
Humppila
Renko
ETELÄ-S
Teuro
Oripää
Tervakoski
Oitti
Forssa
Levanto
Tammela
Vojakkala
Hausjärvi
Loimaa
Jokioinen
Riihimäki
Kaukalam
Sälinkää
Pyhäjärvi
Loppi
Mellillä
Riihivalkama
Pöytyä
Hyvinkää
Mä
Pu
LIESJÄARVEN
K. PUISTO
Pitkäjärvi
Kyrö
Koski
Somero
Läyliäinen
Monninkylä
Aura
Marttila
Karkkila
Tarvasjoki
Somerniemi
Vihtijärvi
Rajamäki
Järvenpää
Por
Kikala
Pusula
Nurmijärvi
Tuusula
Lieto
Vaskio
Vihti
Otalampi
Kerava
Sibbo/
Sippo
Paimio
Pertteli
Klaukkala
Helsinki-Vantaa
Halikko
Salo
Kitula
Nummi
Saukkola
Vantaa/
Vanda
Kallbäck
Nummela
Sauvo
Suomusjärvi
Kauniainen/
Grankulla
Östersundom
Muurla
Tuohittu
Kisko
Lohja
Espoo/Esbo
Lohjanjärvi
Virkkala/
Virkby
Kaukuri
Mathildedal
Perniö
SUOMENLINNA/
SVEABORG
HELSINKI/
HELSINGFORS
Kirkkonummi/
Kyrkslätt
Kimito/
Kemiö
Pohja/
Pojo
Degerby
Sankt-Peterburg
Särkisalo/
Finby
Karis/
Karjaa
Ingå/
Inkoo
Tenala/
Tenhola
Porkkala/Porkkala
Dalsbruk /
Taalintehdas
Skata
Ekenäs/
Tammisaari
Porkkalanselkä
Bromarv
Nitlax
Skaldö
Kasnäs
Lappvik/
Lappohja
Hitis/
Hiitinen
Stockholm
Nynäshamn
Oxelösund
Travemünde
Rønne
Rosala
Hangö/
Hanko
Tallinn
Prangli
E12
E63
E18
E75

188
A
B
C
D
Särkilahti
Hartola
Ristiina
Hirvissalo
Päijänne
Pertunmaa
Toivola
Pellosniemi
Suopelto
Sysmä
Vihantasalmi
Mäntyharju
Suomenniemi
Onkiniemi
Varpanen
Kinni
Partakoski
Arrakoski
Padasjoki
Nikkaroinen
Nurmaa
Kiesilä
Voikoski
Savitaipale
Lusi
Vuohijärvi
Heinola
Huhdasjärvi
Heituinlahti
Lappee
Asikkala
Iso-Äiniö
Iso-Evo
Vääksy
Vesivehmaa
Tuohikotti
FIN
Lemi
Vesijärvi
Vierumäki
Vuolenkoski
Inkilä
Pyhäntaka
Jaala
Lammi
Jurvala
Taavetti
Luumäki
Koski
Valkeala
LAHTI
Iittin
Nastola
Uusikylä
Kuusankoski
Kaipiainen
Utti
Kausala
Kouvola
Koria
Kärkölä
Kuivanto
Muurola
Luhtikylä
Heinämaa
Jokimaa
Järvelä
Orimattila
Myllykoski
Sippola
Pyhältö
A - SUOMI
Elimäki
Anjalankoski
Miehikkälä
Oitti
Artjärvi
Anjala
Metsäkylä
Hausjärvi
Levanto
Paijärvi
Vaalimaa
Kaukalampi
Vastila
Virojoki
Sälinkää
Lapinjärvi/
Lappträsk
Myrskylä/
Mörskom
Hamina
Summa
Lindkoski
Klamila
Virolahti
177
Pukkila
Mäntsälä
Liljendal
Karhula
Journaankylä
Pyhtää/
Pyttis
Kotka
Koskenkylä/
Forsby
Mussalo
Monninkylä
Järvenpää
Lovisa/
Loviisa
Illby/
Ilbla
Pernå
Tuuski
Porvoo/Borgå
Isnäs
Kirkonmaanselkä
Valko/
Valkom
Haapasaari
Tuusula
Kerava
Sibbo/
Sippo
Ebbo/
Epoo
Söderby
Helsinki-
Vantaa
ÖSTRA FINSKA VIKENS
NATIONALPARK
Kabböle
Tolkis/
Tolkkinen
Kallbäck
Vantaa/
Vanda
Tirmo
Spjutsund
Sondby
Östersundom
Pellinge/
Pellinki
Gogland
HELSINKI/
HELSINGFORS
Suur Tütarsaar
Väike Tütarsaar
Tallinn
Stockholm
Nynäshamn
Oxelösund
Travemünde
Rønne
Viinistu
EST
Vergi
Loksa
Käsmu
Vainupea
Prangli

179
189
Kurkiyeki
Syyspohja
Laikko
Virmutjoki
Ruokolahti
Rautjärvi
Il'me
Khiytola
Ladozhskoye
Ozero
Saimaa
Imatra
Priozersk
Svetogorsk
Joutseno
Borodinskoye
Ravattila
Lesogorskiy
Sinevo
Kamennogorsk
Mel'nikovo
Nuijamaa
Hytti
Petrovka
Vainikkala
Sapernoje
Brusnichnoye
Barysevo
Vyborg
Veščevo
Vuoksa
Zaporozhskoye
Chulkovo
Iskra
Pchelino
Sosnovo
M10 E18
Sovetskiy
Kirovskoye
RUS
Vaskelovo
Kl'ucevoje
Kamenka
Vuolojarvi
Pervomajskoje
Termolovo
Ostrov Severnyy
Berezovyy
Verch. Oselki
Primorsk
Polyany
Lintula
Roščine
204
Ostrov Zapanyy
Berezovyy
Toksovo
Repino
Pesočnyj
Zelenogorsk
Железногорск
Ostrov Bol'shoy
Berezovyy
Ozerki
Pargolovo
Sestroretsk
Сестрорецк
Ostrov
Kotlin
Kronshtadt
SANKT-PETERBURG
САНКТ-ПЕТЕРБУРГ
Lomonosov
Ostrov
Lesnoy
Ostrov
Malyy
Stockholm
Travemünde
Petrodvorets
Петродворец
Strel'na
Pontonnyy
Pulkovo
Sosnovyy Bor
Krasnoye Selo
Красное Село
Puškin
Пускин
Kernovo
Gostilicy
Pavlovsk
Павловск
Logi
Gorki
Tajcy
Kipen'
Kurgolovo
Kopor'ye
Begunitsy
Gatchina
Гатчина
Koskolovo
Čirkovicy
Ust'-Luga
Kikerino
Ropsha
Kotly
Pružicy
Vyritsa
Volosovo
Siverskiy
Krikkevo
Vyra
Moloskovitsy
201
Narva-Jõesuu

A
B
C
D
1
2
3
4
5
6
Gossen
Hollings
Otrøy
Roald
Skjelten
Brattvåg
Vatne
Tomra
Søvik
Valderøy
Ålesund
Skodje
Langevåg
Spjelkavik
Sjøholt
Brandal
Hareidlandet
Magerholm
Nerlandsøy
Hareid
Sulesund
Solevåg
Aursnes
Ulsteinvik
Festøy
Sykkylven
Gurskøy
Storfjorden
Vartdal
Hjørundfjorden
Eiksund
1463
KOLÅSTIND
Stranda
Honningsvåg
Rjånes
Storestandal
Ervik
Larsnes
Årvik
Overåne
Ørsta
Sæbø
Koparnes
Leikanger
Lauvstad
BÅTMUSEUM
Volda
Leknes
Folkestad
Voldafjorden
Selje
Viddal
KLOSTERRUINER
Syvde
Raudeberg
Åheim
SØSTREFOSS
Vågsøy
Hellesylt
Kalvatn
Geirange
Måløy
Maurstad
HELLERISTNINGER
Nordfjord
Stårheim
SVORMUSEET
Oldeide
Hjelle
Hornindal
Bremangerlandt
Leirgulen
Isane
Nordfjordeid
Hornindalsvatn
Stryn
Lote
Frøya
Kalvåg
Smørhamn
Ålfoten
Hestenesøyri
Loen
Anda
1670
GJEGNALUNDSBREEN
Midtgulen
Svelgen
GRAVHAUG
Olden
Sandane
Utvik
1717
CECILIEKRUNA
Grøndal
Hyen
Haukå
Byrkjelo
Giengedal
NONSFOSSEN
1572
Florø
Nes
Birksdal
Storebru
SOGN OG
JOSTEDALSBREEN
Gjerd
Stavang
JOSTEDALSBREEN
NASJONALPARK
Aksla
Skei
Førdefjorden
Naustdal
Stavfjorden
Ålhus
Stongfjorden
Lunde
Selvik
1636
Førde
Vassenden
GROVEBREEN
Eikenes
FJORDANE
Bergen
Moskog
Nes
Askvoll
Dale
170
Haukedal
Vaerlandet
Fure
Bygstad
Gaularfjell
Fjærland

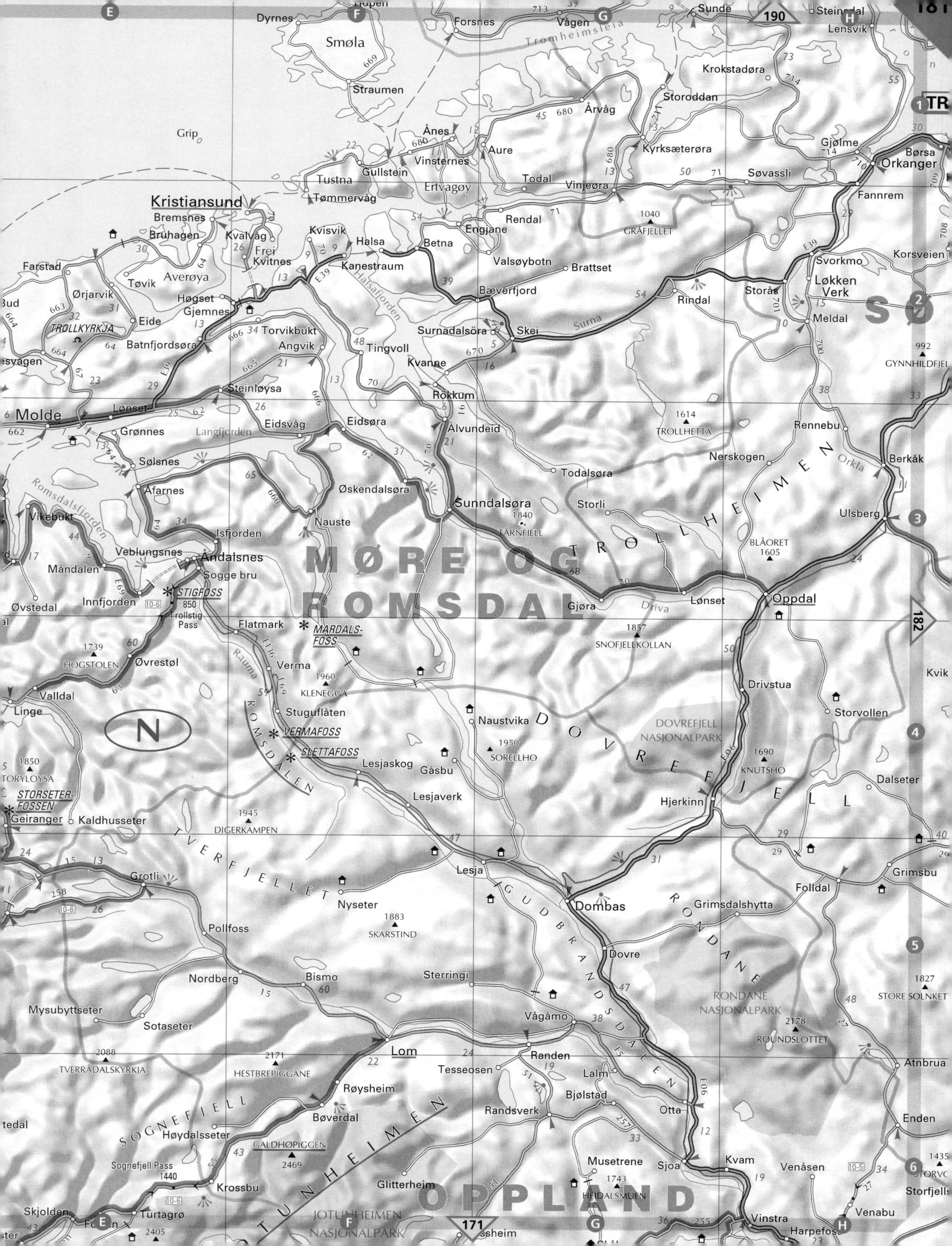

Dyrnes
Smøla
Straumen
Forsnes
Vågen
Tromheimsleia
Sunde
190
Lensvik
Krokstadøra
Storoddan
Årvåg
Grip
Ånes
Aure
Kyrksæterøra
Gjølme
Børsa
Orkanger
Vinsternes
Gullstein
Tustna
Tømmervåg
Ertvågøy
Todal
Vinjeøra
Søvassli
Fannrem
Kristiansund
Bremsnes
Bruhagen
Kvalvåg
Frei
Kvitnes
Kvisvik
Halsa
Betna
Engjane
Rendal
1040
GRÅFJELLET
Korsveien
Farstad
Averøya
Tøvik
Ørjarvik
Kanestraum
Halsafjorden
Valsøybotn
Brattset
Svorkmo
Løkken Verk
Bud
Høgset
Gjemnes
Eide
TROLLKYRKJA
Bæverfjord
Rindal
Storås
Meldal
Torvikbukt
Angvik
Batnfjordsøra
Tingvoll
Surnadalsöra
Skei
Surna
Kvanne
992
GYNNHILDFJEL
Steinløysa
Molde
Lønset
Rokkum
Grønnes
Langfjorden
Eidsvåg
Eidsøra
Ålvundeid
1614
TROLLHETTA
Rennebu
Sølsnes
Romsdalsfjorden
Åfarnes
Øskendalsøra
Todalsøra
Nerskogen
Orkla
Berkåk
Sunndalsøra
Storli
Vikebukt
Nauste
1840
TÅRNFJELL
Ulsberg
Isfjorden
Veblungsnes
Åndalsnes
Sogge bru
TROLLHEIMEN
BLÅORET
1605
Måndalen
MØRE OG ROMSDAL
Innfjorden
Øvstedal
STIGFOSS
850
Trollstig Pass
Gjøra
Driva
Lønset
Oppdal
182
Flatmark
MARDALSFOSS
1857
SNOFJELLKOLLAN
1739
HOGSTOLEN
Øvrestøl
Rauma
Verma
1960
KLENEGGA
Drivstua
Kvik
Valldal
Linge
Stugufläten
ROMSDALEN
N
VERMAFOSS
SLETTAFOSS
Naustvika
DOVREFJELL NASJONALPARK
Storvollen
1950
SORELLHO
1690
KNUTSHO
1850
TORYLOYSA
STORSETERFOSSEN
Geiranger
Kaldhusseter
Lesjaskog
Gåsbu
Lesjaverk
DOVREFJELL
Hjerkinn
Dalseter
1945
DIGERKAMPEN
TVERFJELLET
Grotli
Lesja
Nyseter
Dombas
Grimsdalshytta
Folldal
Grimsbu
1883
SKARSTIND
GUDBRANDSDALEN
RONDANE
Pollfoss
Dovre
Nordberg
Bismo
Sterringi
1827
STORE SOLNKET
Mysubyttseter
Sotaseter
Vågåmo
RONDANE NASJONALPARK
2178
ROUNDSLOTTET
2088
TVERRÅDALSKYRKJA
2171
HESTBREPIGGANE
Lom
Randen
Tesseosen
Lalm
Atnbrua
Røysheim
Bøverdal
SOGNEFJELL
Bjølstad
Otta
Randsverk
Enden
Høydalsseter
GALDHØPIGGEN
2469
JOTUNHEIMEN
Musetrene
Sjoa
Kvam
Venåsen
Sognefjell Pass
1440
Krossbu
Glitterheim
1743
HEIDALSMUEN
OPPLAND
Storfjell
Skjolden
Turtagrø
2405
JOTUNHEIMEN NASJONALPARK
171
Vinstra
Harpefoss
Venabu

TRONDHEIM
SØR-TRØNDELAG
Stjørdal
Orkanger
Løkken Verk
Oppdal
Røros
Melhus
Malvik
Hommelvik
Heimdal
Børsa
Buvik
Fannrem
Støren
Rognes
Singsås
Budal
Haltdalen
Ålen
Reitan
Glåmos
Brekken
Vauldalen
Hitterdal
Feragen
Os
Tolga
Vingelen
Hodalen
Narbuvollen
Tynset
Alvdal
Folldal
Grimsbu
Hjerkinn
Dovre
Otta
Sjoa
Kvam
Vinstra
Harpefoss
Venabu
Atnbrua
Enden
Atnosen
Storfjellseter
Barkald
Hanestad
Øvre Rendal
Otnes
Åsheim
Elvdal
Elvbrua
Galten
Drevsjø
Engerdal
Femundsenden
Buvika
Elgå
Valdalen
Seter
Holøydal
Spekedalssetra
Tylldal
Selbu
Fuglem
Okstad
Brøttem
Lundamo
Kråklivollen
Hilmo
Ås
Stugudal
Meråker
Kopperå
Hegra
Ytterås
Vaernes
Hell
Øvre Jervan
Flakk
Rørvik
Vanvikan
Haugan
Asen
Sulåmo
KJOLHAUGE
Steinsdal
Lensvik
Krokstadøra
Storoddan
Kyrksæterøra
Gjølme
Søvassli
Rindal
Storås
Svorkmo
Meldal
Korsveien
Rennebu
Berkåk
Nerskogen
Ulsberg
Lønset
Drivstua
Storvollen
Kvikne
Yset
Nytrøa
Dalseter
MONTRØEN
Enmo
Meiåvollen
Kjerrengvoll
Såtåhaugvoll
Søndervika
Fiskevollen
Grimsdalshytta
Venåsen
Flötningen
STJØRDALEN
GAULDALEN
TROLLHEIMEN
DOVREFJELL
DOVREFJELL NASJONALPARK
RONDANE
RONDANE NASJONALPARK
FEMUNDSMARKA NASJONALPARK
GUTULIA NASJONALPARK
Selbusjøen
Essandsjøen
Nesjøen
Storsjøen
Aursunden
Femunden
Sølnsjøen
Orkla
Glomma
1040 GRÅFJELLET
1614 TROLLHETTA
1605 BLÅORET
1690 KNUTSHO
992 GYNNHILDFJELL
941 REINSFJELL
1332 FORELSHOGNA
1441 FONGEN
1321 BLÅSTOTEN
1543 GRAHOGDA
1604 ELGEPIGGEN
1827 STORE SOLNKETTEN
2178 ROUNDSLOTTET
1435 STORVOLA
1743
1249
190
181
172
A
B
C
D
1
2
3
4
5
6
N

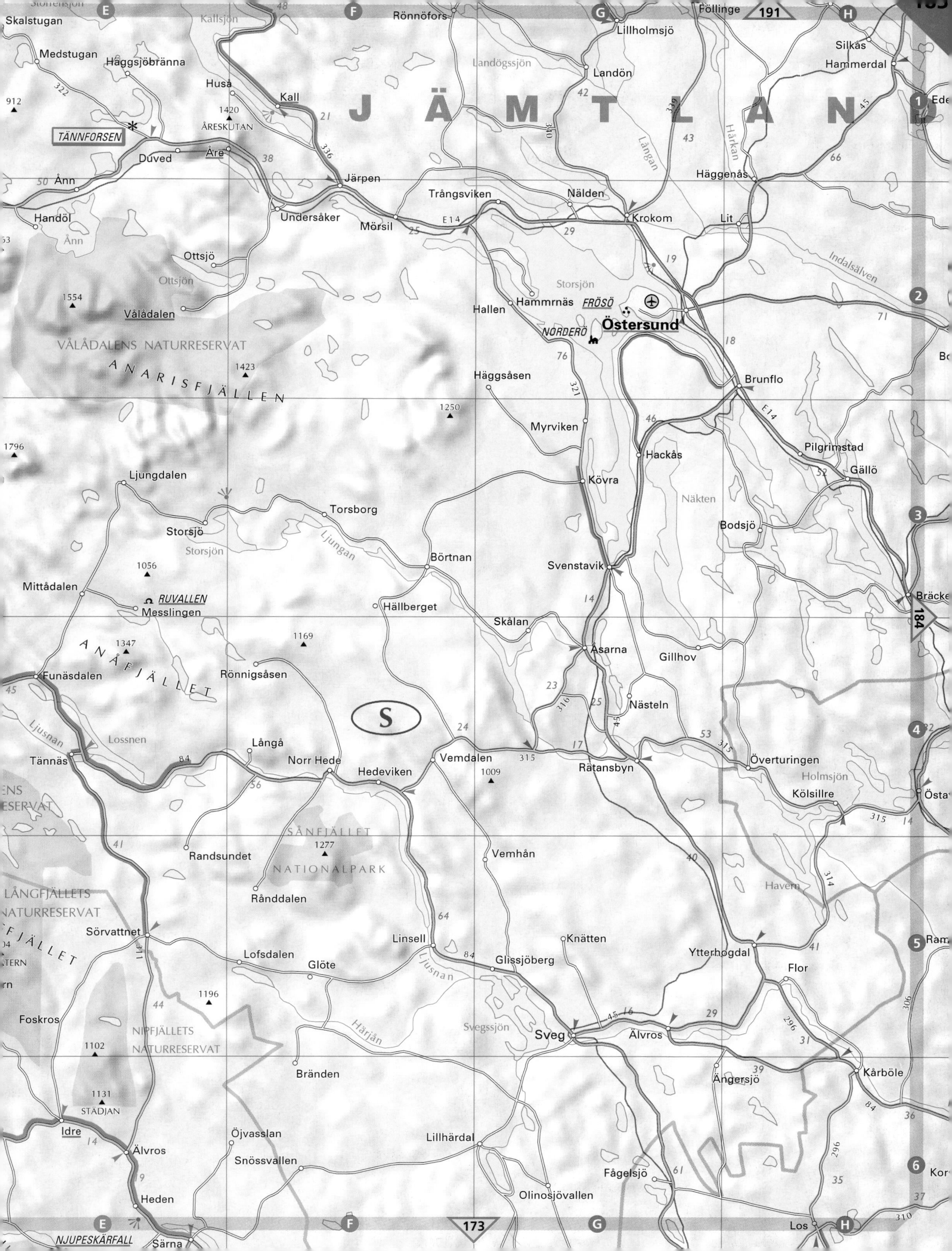
JÄMTLAND
Östersund
Skalstugan
Medstugan
Häggsjöbränna
Huså
Kall
Åreskutan
Tännforsen
Duved
Åre
Ånn
Järpen
Handöl
Undersåker
Mörsil
Ottsjö
Vålådalen
Vålådalens Naturreservat
Anarisfjällen
Rönnöfors
Föllinge
Lillholmsjö
Landön
Silkås
Hammerdal
Häggenås
Trångsviken
Nälden
Krokom
Lit
Indalsälven
Storsjön
Hallen
Hammrnäs
Frösö
Norderö
Brunflo
Häggsåsen
Myrviken
Hackås
Pilgrimstad
Gällö
Kövra
Näkten
Bodsjö
Svenstavik
Bräcke
Ljungdalen
Torsborg
Storsjö
Ljungan
Börtnan
Mittådalen
Ruvallen
Messlingen
Hällberget
Skålan
Åsarna
Gillhov
Anåfjället
Funäsdalen
Rönnigsåsen
Nästeln
Ljusnan
Lossnen
Tännäs
Långå
Norr Hede
Hedeviken
Vemdalen
Rätansbyn
Överturingen
Holmsjön
Kölsillre
Sånfjället Nationalpark
Randsundet
Vemhån
Rånddalen
Havern
Långfjällets Naturreservat
Sörvattnet
Lofsdalen
Glöte
Linsell
Knätten
Glissjöberg
Ytterhogdal
Flor
Foskros
Nipfjällets Naturreservat
Härjån
Svegssjön
Sveg
Älvros
Ängersjö
Kårböle
Bränden
Städjan
Idre
Öjvasslan
Snössvallen
Lillhärdal
Fågelsjö
Olinosjövallen
Heden
Njupeskärfall
Särna
Los
191
184
173

A
B
C
D
190
Föllinge
Lillholmsjö
Landögssjön
Landön
Silkås
Hammerdal
Görvikssjön
Edefors
Vallen
Ramsel
JÄMTLAND
Långan
Hårkan
Skyttmon
Edsele
Järpen
Trångsviken
Nälden
Häggenås
Björkhöjden
Mörsil
E14
Krokom
Lit
Mårdsjö
Lövasen
Indalsälven
Ammerån
Faxälven
Storsjön
FRÖSÖ
Hammrnäs
Hallen
Östersund
NORDERÖ
Stugun
Bomsund
Gesunden
Indalsälven
Hammarstrand
Häggsåsen
Brunflo
1250
Myrviken
Pilgrimstad
Kälarne
DÖDAFALLET
Hackås
Gällö
Kövra
Näkten
Nyhem
S
Bodsjö
Börtnan
Svenstavik
Sörbygden
Albacken
Järkvis
Ljungan
Bräcke
Hällberget
183
Skålan
Sandnäset
Åsarna
Gillhov
Marktjärn
Holmsjön
Nästeln
Ånge
Borgsjö
Hullsjö
Hede
Vemdalen
Rätansbyn
Överturingen
Erikslund
Fränsta
Stöde
Hedeviken
1009
Holmsjön
Kölsillre
Östavall
1277
Vemhån
Havern
Gässåsen
Linsell
Knätten
Ytterhogdal
Ramsjö
Kolsjö
Glöte
Ljusnan
Glissjöberg
Flor
Svegssjön
Härjån
Sveg
Älvros
Gåda
Hennan
Brändbo
Storsjön
Ängersjö
Kårböle
Ljusnan
Lillhärdal
Ljusdal
Bjuråker
Fågelsjö
Korskrogen
Olinosjövallen
Färila
Delsbo
174
Järvsö

STERNORRLAND
Hemling
Björna
Flärke
Lögdeå
Nordmaling
Rundvik
Grundtjärn
Storsjön
Kubbe
Häll Vatnet
Näsåker
Bredbyn
Mellansel
Degerfjärden
Moliden
Husum
Ålsjön
Sidensjö
Örnsköldsvik
Forsmo
Bjästa
Köpmanholmen
Långsele
Sollefteå
Helgum
Ångermanälven
Storsjön
Västansjö
Nyland
Sundbron
Bollstabruk
Lungvik
Kramfors
Herrskog
Lunde
SANDÖ BRO
Ramvik
Liden
Bredsjön
Älandsbro
Hemsö
Härnösand
Indalsälven
Stigsjö
Åsäng
Indal
Härnön
Vaasa/Vasa
Midlanda
Bergeforsen
Söråker
Kovland
Timrå
Huljen
Sundsvall
Bottniska viken/
Alnön
Matfors
Kvissleby
Sundsvallsbukten
Njurunda
Pohjanlahti
Svedje
Gnarp
Älgered
Bergsjö
Harmånger
Stocka
Norra Dellen
Strömsbruk
Södra Dellen
Näsviken
Hudiksvall

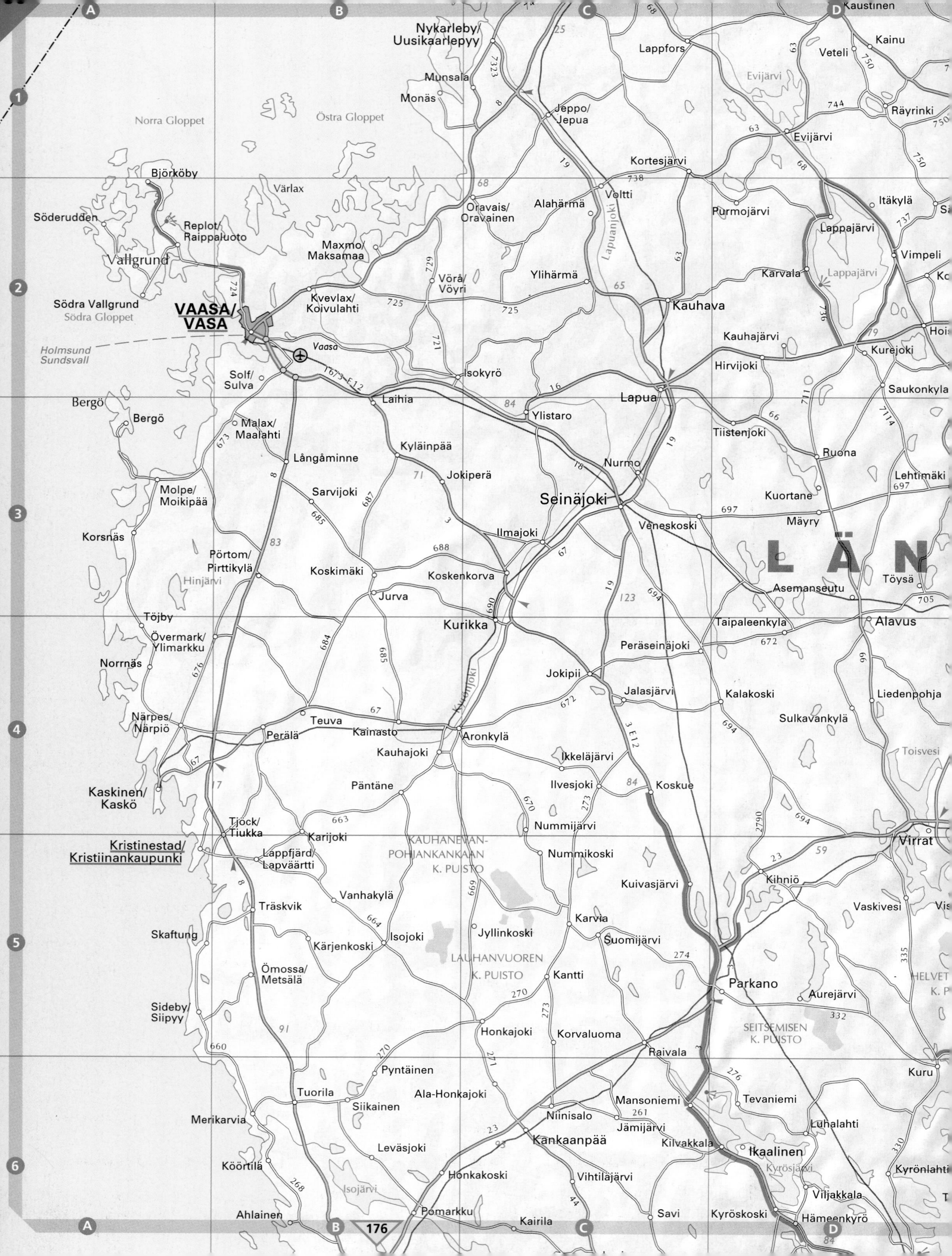
A
B
C
D
1
2
3
4
5
6
Nykarleby/
Uusikaarlepyy
Munsala
Monäs
Jeppo/
Jepua
Lappfors
Kaustinen
Veteli
Kainu
Evijärvi
Räyrinki
Norra Gloppet
Östra Gloppet
Björköby
Värlax
Söderudden
Replot/
Raippaluoto
Vallgrund
Södra Vallgrund
Södra Gloppet
Oravais/
Oravainen
Alahärmä
Voltti
Kortesjärvi
Purmojärvi
Itäkylä
Lappajärvi
Vimpeli
Maxmo/
Maksamaa
Vörå/
Vöyri
Ylihärmä
Lapuanjoki
Karvala
Kauhava
VAASA/
VASA
Kvevlax/
Koivulahti
Holmsund
Sundsvall
Vaasa
Kauhajärvi
Hirvijoki
Kurejoki
Solf/
Sulva
Isokyrö
Lapua
Saukonkyla
Bergö
Laihia
Ylistaro
Tiistenjoki
Malax/
Maalahti
Kyläinpää
Ruona
Långåminne
Nurmo
Jokiperä
Lehtimäki
Molpe/
Moikipää
Sarvijoki
Seinäjoki
Kuortane
Veneskoski
Mäyry
Korsnäs
Ilmajoki
LÄN
Pörtom/
Pirttikylä
Hinjärvi
Koskimäki
Koskenkorva
Töysä
Jurva
Asemanseutu
Töjby
Övermark/
Ylimarkku
Kurikka
Taipaleenkyla
Alavus
Peräseinäjoki
Norrnäs
Jokipii
Jalasjärvi
Kalakoski
Liedenpohja
Kurunjoki
Närpes/
Närpiö
Teuva
Kainasto
Aronkylä
Sulkavankylä
Perälä
Kauhajoki
Ikkeläjärvi
Toisvesi
Kaskinen/
Kaskö
Päntäne
Ilvesjoki
Koskue
Tjöck/
Tiukka
Karijoki
Nummijärvi
Virrat
Kristinestad/
Kristiinankaupunki
Lappfjärd/
Lapväärtti
KAUHANEVAN-
POHJANKANKAAN
K. PUISTO
Nummikoski
Kihniö
Vanhakylä
Kuivasjärvi
Träskvik
Vaskivesi
Skaftung
Kärjenkoski
Isojoki
Jyllinkoski
Karvia
Suomijärvi
Ömossa/
Metsälä
LAUHANVUOREN
K. PUISTO
Kantti
Parkano
Aurejärvi
Sideby/
Siipyy
SEITSEMISEN
K. PUISTO
Honkajoki
Korvaluoma
Raivala
Pyntäinen
Kuru
Tuorila
Ala-Honkajoki
Mansoniemi
Tevaniemi
Siikainen
Niinisalo
Merikarvia
Jämijärvi
Luhalahti
Leväsjoki
Kankaanpää
Kilvakkala
Ikaalinen
Köörtilä
Kyrösjärvi
Kyrönlahti
Honkakoski
Vihtilänjärvi
Isojärvi
Viljakkala
Ahlainen
Pomarkku
Kairila
Savi
Kyrösskoski
Hämeenkyrö
176

198
177
178
188
FIN
SUOMI
Halsua
Kanala
Yli-Lesti
Alvajärvi
Pihtipudas
Kärväskylä
Sulkavanjärvi
Lampaanjärvi
Kinnula
Salamajärvi
Muhola
Pielavesi
Maaninka
Oksakoski
Perho
Möttönen
SALAMAJÄRVEN K. PUISTO
Viitajärvi
Keitele
Kymönkoski
Hallapuro
Lahdenperä
Kivijärvi
Viitasaari
Jokijärvi
Hamula
Lokakylä
Huopanankoski
Suovanlahti
Niinivesi
Kyyjärvi
Möksy
Tervo
Vesanto
Karttula
Kimінki
Kannonkoski
Keisala
Humppi
PYHÄ-HÄKIN K. PUISTO
Karstula
Soini
Vahanka
Kalmari
Konginkangas
Kangasaho
Pääjärvi
Istunmäki
Kukko
Rautalampi
Saarijärvi
Pyhäjärvi
Konnevesi
Parantala
Äänekoski
Pylkönmäki
Vehu
Mahlu
Lannevesi
Suolahti
Väätäiskylä
Äijälä
Säkinmäki
Nikaranperä
Uurainen
Myllymäki
Kuusaa
Sahrajärvi
Liesjärvi
Laukaa
Hankasalmi
Tikkakoski
Multia
Vertaala
Leppävesi
Niemisjärvi
Lievestuore
Kintaus
Vesanka
Vaajakoski
Kylmämäki
Petäjävesi
Keuruu
JYVÄSKYLÄ
Haapamäki
Kotala
Pohjoislahti
Häppälä
Säynätsalo
Tikkala
Muurame
Toivakka
Kutemajärvi
Pohjaslahti
Kolho
Koskenpää
Kangasniemi
Korpilahti
Rutalahti
Vilppula
Mänttä
Läsänkoski
Leivonmäki
Hokka
Ruovesi
Jämsänkoski
Jokslahti
Kälä
Väärinmaja
Vanhamäki
Jämsä
Tammijärvi
Jäminkipohja
Luhanka
Tuukkala
Juupajoki
Joutsa
Judinsalo
Hirvensalmi
Kaanaa
Länkipohja
Harjunsalmi
Hirsilä
Enokunta
Ruorasmäki
Längelmäki
ISOJÄRVEN K. PUISTO
Orivesi
Kylämä
Särkilahti
Hartola
Kuhmoinen
Pertunmaa
Toivola
Eräjärvi
Päijänne
Ponsa
Sappee
Sysmä
Vihantasalmi

Pihtipudas
Kärväskylä
Sulkavanjärvi
Lampaanjärvi
Lapinlahti
Heinäaho
Varpaisjärvi
Palonurmi
Mäntylahti
Onkivesi
Syväri
Nilsiä
Kolima
Pielavesi
Alapitkä
Vuotjärvi
Pielavesi
Maaninka
Haluna
Juankoski
Viitajärvi
Keitele
Siilinjärvi
Nilakka
Kymönkoski
Jokijärvi
Viitasaari
Hamula
Kallavesi
Lokakylä
Huopanankoski
Suovanlahti
Niinivesi
Riistavesi
Tuusjärvi
Tervo
KUOPIO
Vesanto
Karttula
Pitkälahti
Tuusniemi
Kannonkoski
Syvänniemi
Virmasvesi
Keitele
Pellesmäki
Vehmasmäki
ITÄ-S
Suvasvesi
Konginkangas
Istunmäki
Pyhäjärvi
Rautalampi
Suonenjoki
Oravikoski
Konnevesi
FIN
Parantala
Äänekoski
Konnevesi
Suolahti
Leppävirta
Lannevesi
Äijälä
Säkinmäki
Unnukka
Uurainen
Kuusaa
Jäppilä
Varkaus
Kangaslampi
Kynsivesi
Laukaa
Hankasalmi
Tikkakoski
Pieksämäki
Vertaala
Leppävesi
Tiemassa
Lievestuore
Niemisjärvi
Joroinen
Kintaus
Vesanka
Vaajakoski
Kylmämäki
JYVÄSKYLÄ
Virtasalmi
Kantala
Rantasa
Häppälä
Säynätsalo
Tikkala
Muurame
Toivakka
Kutemajärvi
Narila
Haukivuori
Koskenpää
Kangasniemi
Korpilahti
Kaivomäki
Rutalahti
Kyyvesi
Juva
Kalvitsa
Läsänkoski
Leivonmäki
Hokka
Harjunmaa
Kaskii
Juokslahti
Kälä
Hiirola
Puula
Vanhamäki
Jämsä
Tammijärvi
Koikkala
Luhanka
Tuukkala
Mikkeli
Joutsa
Suontee
Luonteri
Judinsalo
Otava
Hirvensalmi
Anttola
Harjunsalmi
Ruorasmäki
Puu
Hietanen
Ristiina
Jääsjärvi
Särkilahti
Hurissalo
Hartola
Pertunmaa
Toivola
Pellosniemi
Päijänne
Sappee
Sysmä
187
178
E63
E75

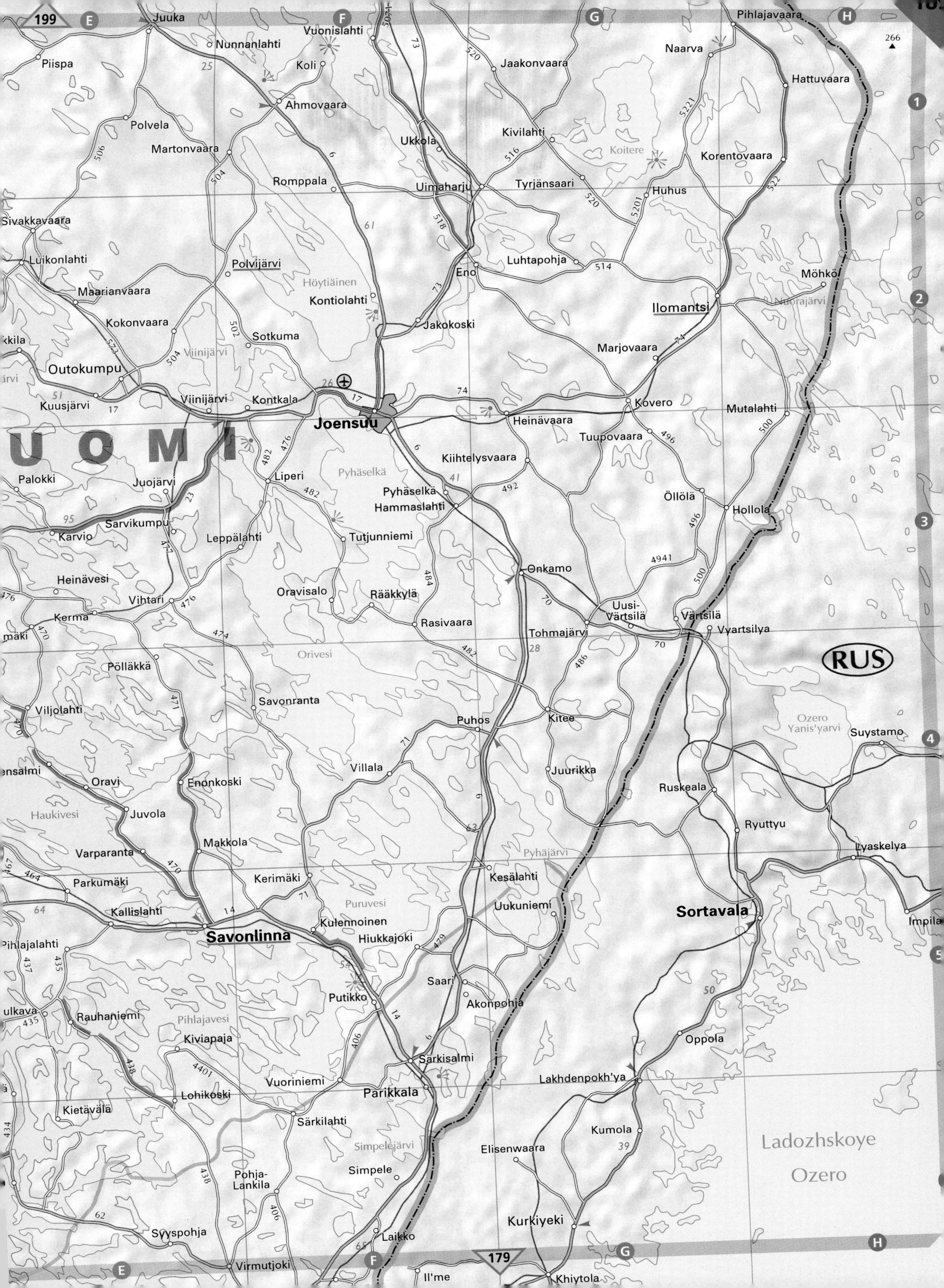
199
E
F
G
H
Juuka
Nunnanlahti
Vuonislahti
Koli
Piispa
Pihlajavaara
Naarva
Hattuvaara
Jaakonvaara
Ahmovaara
Polvela
Martonvaara
Ukkola
Kivilahti
Koitere
Korentovaara
Romppala
Uimaharju
Tyrjänsaari
Huhus
Sivakkavaara
Luikonlahti
Polvijärvi
Luhtapohja
Eno
Möhkö
Höytiäinen
Maarianvaara
Kontiolahti
Ilomantsi
Nuorajärvi
Kokonvaara
Jakokoski
Sotkuma
Marjovaara
Viinijärvi
Outokumpu
Kovero
Mutalahti
Kuusjärvi
Viinijärvi
Kontkala
Heinävaara
Joensuu
Tuupovaara
SUOMI
Kiihtelysvaara
Palokki
Juojärvi
Liperi
Pyhäselkä
Pyhäselkä
Hammaslahti
Öllölä
Hollola
Sarvikumpu
Karvio
Leppälahti
Tutjunniemi
Onkamo
Heinävesi
Oravisalo
Rääkkylä
Uusi-Värtsilä
Värtsilä
Vihtari
Kerma
Rasivaara
Tohmajärvi
Vyartsilya
RUS
Orivesi
Pölläkkä
Savonranta
Viljolahti
Kitee
Puhos
Ozero Yanis'yarvi
Suystamo
Villala
Juurikka
Oravi
Enonkoski
Ruskeala
Haukivesi
Juvola
Ryuttyu
Makkola
Varparanta
Pyhäjärvi
Lyaskelya
Parkumäki
Kerimäki
Kesälahti
Puruvesi
Uukuniemi
Kallislahti
Savonlinna
Kulennoinen
Sortavala
Impila
Pihlajalahti
Hiukkajoki
Saari
Akonpohja
Putikko
Rauhaniemi
Pihlajavesi
Oppola
Kiviapaja
Särkisalmi
Lakhdenpokh'ya
Vuoriniemi
Parikkala
Lohikoski
Kietävälä
Särkilahti
Kumola
Ladozhskoye Ozero
Simpelejärvi
Elisenwaara
Simpele
Pohja-Lankila
Kurkiyeki
Syyspohja
Laikko
179
Virmutjoki
Il'me
Khiytola
266
1
2
3
4

A
B
C
D
1
2
3
4
Tennholmf
Meløya
Amøya
Tjong
Nesøya
Jektvik
Trænfjorden
Kilboghamn
Tomma
Nesna
Lavong
991
Donna
Leinesodden
Sandnessjøen
Alstahaug
Tjøtta
Mosjøen
Kilværfjorden
1158
FINNKNEET
Forvik
Vega
Annadalsvagen
Horn
Vegafjorden
Brønnøysund
Trofors
Hommelstø
Gimsefjorden
1280
BLÅFJELLET
Tosbotn
Vennesund
Hortafjorden
Holm
1096
KVANNLITINDEN
Majavatn
Leka
Skei
Sørgutvik
Tørråk
Vikna
Naustbukta
Årsandøy
Smalåsen
Gardstad
Rørvik
Kolvereid
Foldereid
NONSFJELLET
927
Hofles
Indre Folda
806
Nesaseter
Namsskogan
Gøisnes
KJØRINGVASSFJELLET
Røyrvik
Salsbruket
Brekkvasselv
Gjersvik
FOLDA
Abelvær
Foldfjorden
Haraneset
Strompdalen
Salsvatnet
Aglen
Utvorda
Furutangvik
Duna
Høylandet
Tunnsjøen
Skorovatn
Statland
Eidsvatnet
Lauvsnes
Sør - Flatanger
Overhalla
Harran
1022
HAVDALSFJELLET
Namsos
NAMDALEN
Oksdøl
Grong
Sandøla
Nordli
Holand
Bagsund
Namsen
872
GEITFJELLET
Formofoss
1072
VESTRA BRANNFJELLET
Laksjøen
Osen
NYNESFJELLA
Sjøåsen
NORD-TRØNDELAG
FROHAVET
Skjørafjorden
Hofstad
Namdalseid
Snåsa
Lenglingen
Sørli
GRESSÅMOEN NASJONALPARK
Berglia
Stokkøya
Harsvik
676
FINNVOLLHEIA
Kvam
Snåsavatnet
Revsnes
Veldelen
Linesøya
Malm
Åsa
Årnes
763
Follafoss
762
Storbergvika
Selnes
Steinkjer
Gaulstad
Lysøysund
Beitstadfjorden
Bodom
Svellingen
Mære
SKJÆKERFJELLA
1266
MARKENE
Frøya
Tarvefjorden
Verrabotn
Verran
1118
Leksdalsvatnet
Torröjen
Titran
Flatval
Strømmen
Botngård
Frøyfjorden
Kjerringvåg
Verdalsøra
Stiklestad
1246
1229
Fillan
Brekstad
Levanger
Vera
KÄKERFJÄLLEN
Strøm
Valset
Fevåg
Leksvik
Skansen
Jänsmässh
Hitra
Sandstad
Moen
Vågen
Storvatnet
Rissa
Skogn
Kolåsen
Sunde
Trondheimsfjorden
Åbo
Forsnes
Trondheimsleia
Steinsdal
Vanvikan
Markabygd
Ådalsvollen
Kallsedet
Frankrike
Sul
Lensvik
Frosta
Åsen
Sandvika
Krokstadøra
Haugan
Skalstugan
Storrensjön
Storoddan
Sulåmo
1249
KJOLHAUGEN
Feren
Kallsjön
Rönnöfors
Flakk
Malvik
Stjørdal
Ånes
181
TRONDHEIM
Hegra
Værnes
Medstugan
Aure
Heimdal
Hell
182
Håggsjöbränna
Kyrksæterøra
Gjølme
Ytte
Meråker
Kopperå
912
Husåo
1420
ÅRESKUTAN
Kall
JÄ
Landögå
Ertvågøy
Todal
Vinjeøra
Børsa
Øvre Jervan
TÄNNFORSEN
183

192
193
184
185
198
E
F
G
H
1
2
3
4
5
6
NORDLAND
NORRBOTTEN
VÄSTERBO
VÄSTERNORRLAND
S
Storjord
Røkland
HOGTINDEN
SATERTIND
Balvatnet
Mavasjaure
TARREKAISE
Kvikkjokk
Tjaktjajaure
Porjus
MUDDAS NATIONALPARK
Harsprange
KRAFTVERK HARSPRANGET
Tjåmotis
Stalka
FARFORITA
Peuraure
Randijaure
Stora Luleälven
Karats
Karatjaure
Jokkmokk
Lille Luleälven
Vuollerim
SALTFJELLET-SVARTISEN NASJONALPARK
Graddis
Lønsdal
BREDEKFJELLET
BARTURTE
TJIDTJAK
Tjeggelvas
Riebnes
Stenudden
FIERRAS
NASAFJALL
Sädvaluspen
Sädvajaure
Labbas
PIELJEKAISE NATIONALPARK
Storforshei
Mo-i-Rana
Vuolvojaure
Lövnäs
Norre Bergnäss
Hornavan
Gittun
Adolfsström
BJÖRKFJÄLLET
Umbukta
VINDELFJÄLLENS NATURRESERVAT
Laisvall
Jäknajaure
Kitajaur
Kåbdalis
Strimasund
OKSSKOLTEN
Arjeplog
Abraur
Uddjaure
Ammarnäs
Laisälven
Östansjö
Moskosel
Piteälven
Klippen
NORRA STORFJÄLLET
Björkfors
Røssvatnet
Joesjö
Tärnaby
SÖDRA STORFJÄLLET
RYIVEGAISE
Storvindeln
Storavan
Arvidsjaur
Grundsel
Slagnäs
Avaviken
Ajaureforsen
Sorsele
Gardiken
Abborrträsk
Kroken
Storjuktan
Blattniksele
Fättjaur
Gargnäs
Glommersträsk
Kittelfjäll
Henriksfjäll
Ullisjaur
Blaiken
Gaskeluokta
Dikanäs
Juktån
Gubbträsk
Tväråträsk
Malå
FJÄLLFJÄLLEN
Grundfors
Daikanvik
Brattäker
Storuman
Stensele
Vindelgransele
Nicknoret
Petikträsk
Jörn
Klimpfjäll
Kristineborg
Skellefteälven
Marsliden
Blaikliden
Eriksberg
Liden
Gunnarn
NORRA BORGAFJÄLLEN
Vojmsjön
Skarvsjö
Björksele
Saxnäs
Stalon
Gråtanliden
Jovan
Grundfors
Norsjövallen
Norsjö
Ankarvattnet
Norra Tresund
Norrby
Boliden
Ankarede
S. Tresund
Malgomaj
Borgafjäll
SELKENTJAKKE
Pauträsk
Ruskträsk
Rusksele
Risliden
Bastuträsk
Nästansjö
Strömnäs
Kattisavan
Falträsk
Husbondliden
Brännåker
Risbäck
Rusfors
Skansholm
Nordansjö
Latikberg
Björkberg
Sjoutnäset
Storsjouten
Vilhelmina
Vinliden
Lycksele
Äträsk
Långsele
Amsele
Gäddede
Ekträsk
Vägsele
Norraker
Ormsjö
Ormsjön
Torvsjö
Västemyrriset
LLINGSÅFALLET
Bågede
Häggås
Lillögda
MUNSFJÄLLET
Lidsjöberg
Avaträsk
Ångermanälven
Nordanas
Vänjaurträsk
Hälinäs
Botsmark
Svaningen
Tasjön
Bellvik
Dorotea
Umeälven
Tåsjö
Älgsjö
Granö
Vindeln
Alanäs
Lövvik
Åsele
Örträsk
Sundö
Dragan
Hoting
Öreälven
Tvärålund
Hillsand
Havnäs
Granåsen
Fredrika
Renålandet
Öjarn
Häggsjömon
Lövberga
Bjurholm
Vännäs
Rossön
Brännland
Ålåsen
Strömsund
Ulriksfors
STORNORRFORS
Laxviken
Laxsjö
Näsviken
Aspsele
Mjösjöby
Gulsele
Solberg
Backe
Betarsjön
Nyåker
Knåsjö
Gräsmyr
Vängel
Gåxsjö
Junsele
Storborgaren
Hemling
Hörnefors
Föllinge
Lillholmsjö
Fjällsjöälven
Silkås
Görviksjön
Flärke
Lögdeå
Nordmaling
Landön
Hammerdal
Vallen
Björna
Rundvik
Edefors
Ramsele
Grundtjärn
Kubbe
Hall
Bredbyn
Mellansel
Näsåker
E12
E6
E4

Andenes
Andøya
Dverberg
Risøyhamn
Vesteralen
Skogsøya
Myre
Langøya
Sortland
Straumsnes
Vesterålsfjorden
Stokmarknes
Hadseløya
Melbu
Hadsel-fjorden
Harstad
Mybotn
Refnes
Hinnøya
Lødingen
Kongselva
Fiskebøl
Austvågøy
Digermulen
Svolvær
Gimsøya
Eggum
Vestvågøy
Lofoten
Leknes
Stamsund
Henningsværstraumen
Ramberg
Flakstadøya
Moskenesøya
Reine
Sørvågen
Moskenstraumen
Værøy
Røsthavet
Røst
Landegode
Vestfjorden
Bognes
Skarberget
Ulvsvåg
Skutvik
Steigen
Ålstad
Bogen
Tømmernes
Nordfold
Mørsvikbotn
Folda
SJUNKHATTEN
Rosvik
Festvåg
Bodø
Straumen
Saltfjorden
Fauske
Finneid
BLÅMANNSISEN
Sulitjelma
SULITELMA
Sandhornøya
Misvær
Rognan
Storjord
Inndyr
Tennholmfjorden
HOGTINDEN
Røkland
SATERTI
Ørnes
Meløya
Balvatnet
Pieskehaure
Mavasjaure
Narvik
Ofotfjorden
Riksgränsen
Bjerkvik
Bogen
SKITTENDAL-STINDEN
Grovfjord
Fossbakken
ISTIND
Ballangen
STORSTEINFJELLET
BJORNTOPPEN
Sjøvegan
Andørja
Sørvik
Ibestad
Rolla
Astafjorden
Vågsfjorden
Grytøya
Dyrøya
Mikkelbostad
HJERTTIND
Stonglandseidet
Andse
Vaggsvik
Sørr
Finnsnes
Senja
Gibostad
Straumsnes
Gryllefjord
Selfjorden
Andfjorden
Hillesøy
MØYSALEN
Akkajaure
KALLAKTJÅKKÅ
STORA STÖFA NATION
AKKAVARE
STORA SJÖFALL
RAGO NASJONALPARK
Vastenjaure
PADJELANTA
PADJELANTA NATIONALPARK
Virihaure
SAREKS NATIONALPARK
PÅRTEFJALLEN
TARREKAISE
Kvikkjokk

190
191

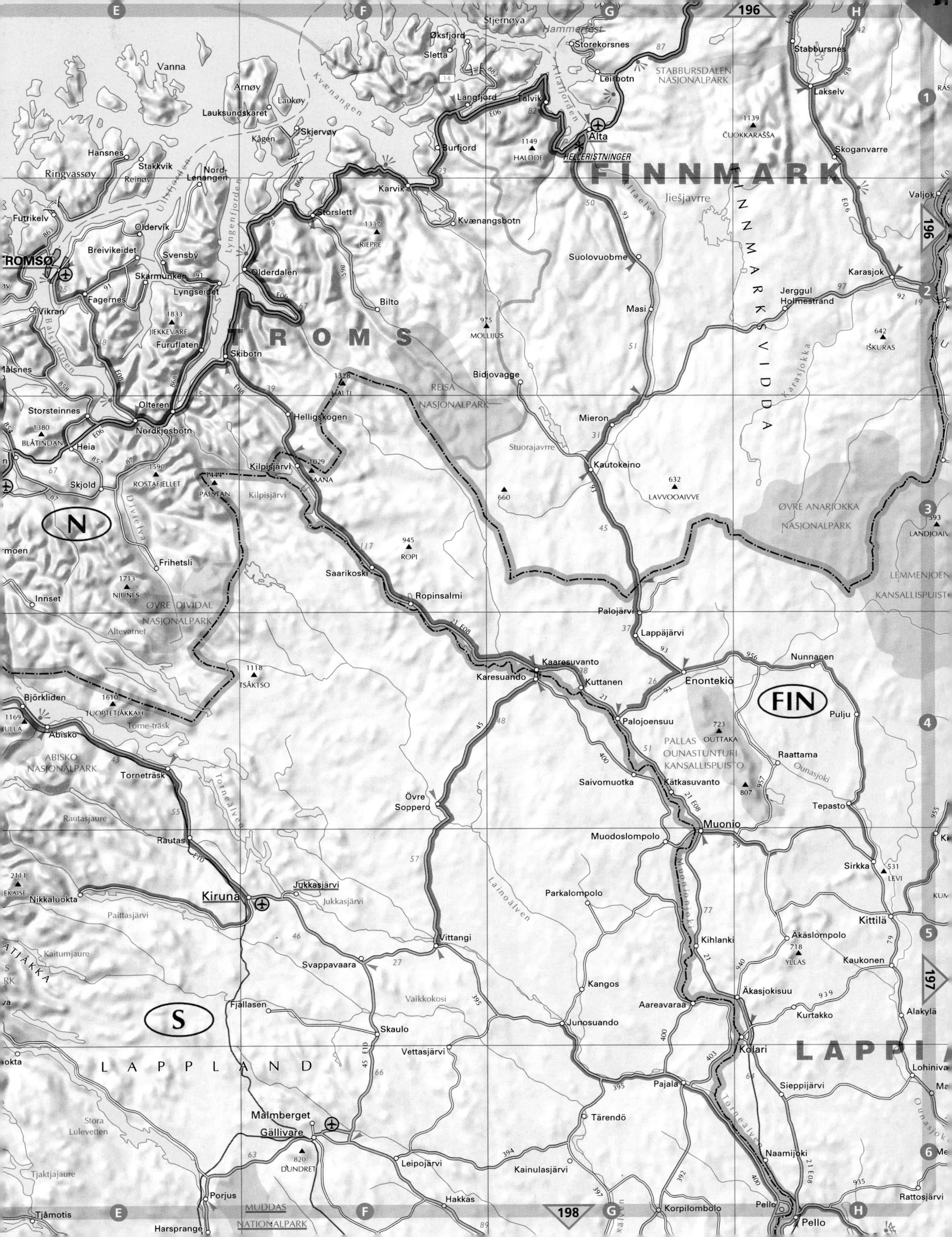

196
197
198
FINNMARK
TROMS
FINNMARKSVIDDA
LAPPLAND
LAPPI
N
S
FIN
Tromsø
Alta
Hammerfest
Storekorsnes
Stjernøya
Øksfjord
Sletta
Leirbotn
Stabbursnes
Lakselv
STABBURSDALEN NASJONALPARK
Langfjord
Talvik
Burfjord
Skjervøy
Arnøy
Laukøy
Lauksundskaret
Kågen
Vanna
Hansnes
Ringvassøy
Stakkvik
Reinøy
Nord-Lenangen
Karvik
Kvænangsbotn
Storslett
Olderdalen
Bilto
Skiboth
HELLERISTNINGER
HALDDE
ČUOKKARAŠŠA
Skoganvarre
Valjok
Karasjok
Jerggul
Holmestrand
Suolovuobme
Masi
Jiešjavrre
Futrikelv
Oldervik
Breivikeidet
Svensby
Skarmunken
Lyngseidet
Fagernes
Vikran
JIEKKEVARE
Furuflaten
Målsnes
Storsteinnes
Olteren
Nordkjosbotn
BLÅTINDAN
Heia
Skjold
ROSTAFJELLET
Helligskogen
HALTI
REISA NASJONALPARK
Bidjovagge
MOLLIJUS
RIEPPE
Mieron
Stuorajavrre
Kautokeino
LAVVOAIVVE
IŠKURAS
ØVRE ANARJOKKA NASJONALPARK
LANDJOAIV
LEMMENJOEN KANSALLISPUISTO
Kilpisjärvi
SAANA
PALSTAN
ROPI
Saarikoski
Ropinsalmi
Palojärvi
Lappäjärvi
Frihetsli
Innset
NJUNES
ØVRE DIVIDAL NASJONALPARK
Altevatnet
TSÅKTSO
Kaaresuvanto
Karesuando
Kuttanen
Enontekiö
Nunnanen
Björkliden
TUOPTETJÅKKAH
Torne-träsk
Abisko
ABISKO NASJONALPARK
Torneträsk
Palojoensuu
Pulju
PALLAS OUNASTUNTURI KANSALLISPUISTO
OUTTAKA
Raattama
Saivomuotka
Kätkasuvanto
Övre Soppero
Tepasto
Muonio
Muodoslompolo
Rautasjaure
Rautas
Sirkka
LEVI
Parkalompolo
Nikkaluokta
Kiruna
Jukkasjärvi
Paittasjärvi
Kittilä
Kihlanki
Äkäslompolo
YLLÄS
Vittangi
Svappavaara
Kaitumjaure
Kaukonen
Kangos
Äkasjokisuu
Fjällasen
Vaikkokosi
Aareavaara
Alakylä
Kurtakko
Skaulo
Junosuando
Kolari
Vettasjärvi
Lohiniva
Pajala
Sieppijärvi
Stora Luleveten
Malmberget
Gällivare
Tärendö
DUNDRET
Leipojärvi
Kainulasjärvi
Naamijoki
Tjaktjajaure
Porjus
Hakkas
Korpilombolo
Rattosjärvi
Tjåmotis
MUDDAS NATIONALPARK
Harsprånge
Pello

A
B
C
D
1
2
3
4
5
6
HORNSTRANDIR
Suðureyri
Bolungarvík
Flateyri
Ísafjörður
Ísafjarðardjúp
Unaðsdalur
DRANGAJÖKULL
Arnarfjörður
Thingeyri
Bjargtangar
Patreksfjörður
Tálkafjörður
957
GLÁMA
Brjanslækur
Hólmavík
Drangsness
Flatey
Breiðafjörður
Reykhólar
Húnaflói
Skagaströnd
Helissandur
Ólafsvík
SNÆFELLNESS
Grundarfjörður
Stykkishólmur
Blönduós
Hvammstangi
Sauðárkrókur
Búðardalur
Laugarbakki
Borðeyri
Blanda
Faxaflói
Borgarnes
Reykholt
HRAUNFOSSAR
Akranes
Kjölur
IS
LANGJÖKULL
1355
Keflavík
REYKJAVÍK
Mosfellsbær
THINGVELLIR NASJONALPARK
1763
HOFSJÖKULL
Hafnarfjörður
Kópavogur
Thingvellir
BLÁA LÓNIA
1204
Hvítárvatn
Grindavík
Thingvallavatn
GEYSER
BLÁFELL
Kleifarvatn
REYKJANES
Laugarvatn
GULLFOSS
Hveragerði
Thorlákshöfn
Selfoss
Eyrarbakki
Thjórsá
Skarð
Thórisvatn
Hella
1491
HEKLA
Hvolsvöllur
Landmannalaugur
LAKAGIGAR
THORSMÖRK
VESTMANNAEYJAR
Heimaey
Surtsey
MÝRDALSJÖKULL
SKÓGAFOSS
Kirkjubæjarklaustur
Skeiðflötur
Vík

E
F
G
H
1
2
3
4
5
6
Grímsey
Siglufjörður
Eyjafjörður
Ólafsfjörður
Hofsós
Flatey
Dalvík
Grenivík
Skjálfandi
Húsavík
Öxarfjörður
Rifstangi
Raufarhöfn
Kópasker
Thistilfjörður
Skinnastaðir
Fontur
Akureyri
Hrafnagill
GOÐAFOSS
Laugar
JÖKULSÁRGLJÚFUR NASJONALPARK
Thórshöfn
Bakkaflói
DETTIFOSS
Reykjahlið
Bakkafjörður
Myvatn
Grímsstaðir
Vopnafjörður
Vopnafjörður
Héraðsflói
Skjálfandafljót
1682
HERÐUBREIÐ
Jökulsá á Fjöllum
Öskjuvatn
1510
ASKJA
TUNGNAFELLSJÖKULL
1520
Jökulsá Brú
Borgarfjörður
DYNGJUJÖKKUL
Egilsstaðir
Lagarfljót
Seyðisfjörður
KVERKFJÖLL
1920
1833
SNÆFELL
Reyðarfjörðer
Neskaupstaður
Eskifjörður
1719
GRIMSFJALL
VATNAJÖKULL
BRÚARJÖKULL
Tórshavn
Fáskruðsfjörður
SKAFTAFELL NASJONALPARK
Stöðvarfjörður
Djúpivogur
ÖRÆFAJÖKULL
Hof
Papey
Skaftafell
2119
HVANNADALSHNJUKUR
JÖKULSARLON
Höfn
Fagurhólsmyri
ÍSLAND

FINNMARK
FINNMARKSVIDDA
VARANGERHALVØYA
Nordkapp
Honningsvåg
Magerøya
Skipsfjordfjell Pass
Kåfjord
Repvåg
SKARVBERG-TUNNELEN
Smørfjord
Olderfjord
Hammerfest
Kvaløya
Rypefjord
Kvalsund
Skaidi
Neverfjord
Havøysund
Valen
Rolvsøya
Skavik
Revsbotn
Sørvær
Sørøya
Breivikbotn
Hasvik
Seiland
Tromsø
Lerresfjord
Stjernøya
Øksfjord
Sletta
Storekorsnes
Leirbotn
Langfjord
Talvik
Alta
HELLERISTNINGER
Burfjord
Karvik
Kvænangsbotn
Bilto
STABBURSDALEN NASJONALPARK
Stabbursnes
Lakselv
Børselv
Porsangen
Indre Brenna
Veidnesklubben
Laksefjorden
Kalak
Kjøllefjord
Kifjord
Mehamn
Gamvik
Hopseldet
FLATTIND
Ifjord
Ifjordfjell Pass
Tanafjorden
Berlevåg
Kongsfjord
Båtsfjord
Syltefjordfjellet
Leirpollskogen
Rustefjelbma
Tana
Tanabru
Skiippagurra
Varangerbotn
Nesseby
Vadsø
Skallelv
Kiberg
Svartnes
Vardø
Varangerfjorden
Bugøynes
Grense-Jakobselv
Kirkenes
Bjørnevatn
Linachamari
Neiden
Polmak
Nuorgam
Sirma
KORGÅSEN
RÁSTTIGÁISÁ
ČUOKKARAŠŠA
HALDDE
Levajok
Utsjoki
Kevo
KALDDOAIVI
KEVON LUONNONPUISTO
Mieraslompolo
PAISTUNTURI
Valjok
Skoganvarre
Jiešjavrre
Altaelva
Suolovuobme
Karasjok
Jerggul Holmestrand
Karigasniemi
ŠKURAS
RUOHTIR
MUOTKATUNTURIT
Kaamanen
Masi
MOLLIJUS
Bidjovagge
REISA NASJONALPARK
Mieron
Stuorajavrre
Kautokeino
LAVVOAIVVE
ØVRE ANARJOKKA NASJONALPARK
Karasjokka
Angeli
Lemmenjoki
Menesjärvi
Sikovuono
Inari
Veskoniemi
Inarijärvi
Partakko
Supru
Sevettijärvi
Näätämöjoki
Iijärvi
Virtaniemi
Niskakoski
Nellim
Nautsi
ØVRE PASVIK NASJONALPARK
Nyrud
Skogly
Svanvik
Nikel'
Zapolyarnyy
Prirečnyj
RIEPPE
RUS
N
193

LAPPI / LAPPLAND
FIN
S
Rovaniemi
Kemijärvi
Sodankylä
Salla
Kuusamo
Muonio
Kittilä
Pello
Kolari
Enontekiö
Karesuando
Kaaresuvanto
Övertorneå
Aavasaksa
Ylitornio
Pajala
Savukoski
Posio
Tervola
Sinettä
Saarenkylä
Vikajärvi
Vuotso
Repojoki
Kuttura
Laanila
Kakslauttanen
Purnumukka
Pokka
Kiistala
Sirkka
LEVI
Tepsa
Vaalajärvi
Petkula
Tanhua
Lokka
Martti
Tulppio
Kuosku
Saija
Kotola
Kuoloyarvi
Kelloselkä
Ahvenselkä
Pelkosenniemi
Aapajärvi
Vuojärvi
Vuotsino
Javarus
Korvala
Yli-Nampa
Hyypiö
Isokylä
Joutsijärvi
Kallunki
Hautajärvi
Maaninkavaara
Luusua
Jumisko
Vanttauskoski
Pekkala
Autti
Perä-Posio
Pohjaslahti
Narkaus
Konteenperä
Portimo
Mäntyjärvi
Vasarapera
Ruka
Kuolio
Kuloharju
Nuupas
Muurola
Koivu
Peura
Sihtuuna
Juoksenki
Turtola
Svanstein
Raanujärvi
Rattosjärvi
Meltaus
Maijanen
Lohiniva
Unari
Kierinki
Syväjärvi
Alakylä
Kurtakko
Kaukonen
Äkäslompolo
Äkäsjokisuu
Kihlanki
Sieppijärvi
Naamijoki
Aareavaara
Junosuando
Kangos
Parkalompolo
Muodoslompolo
Saivomuotka
Kätkasuvanto
Palojoensuu
Kuttanen
Nunnanen
Pulju
Raattama
Tepasto
Lappäjärvi
Palojärvi
Ropinsalmi
Övre Soppero
Vittangi
Skaulo
Vettasjärvi
Tärendö
Leipojärvi
Kainulasjärvi
Hakkas
Korpilombolo
Lansjärv
Ansvar
Överkalix
Hedenäset
Vitträsk
Raja-Jooseppi
URHO KEKKOSEN KANSALLISPUISTO
SAARISELKÄ
SOKOSTI
TALKKUNAPÄÄ
LEMMENJOEN KANSALLISPUISTO
PALLAS OUNASTUNTURI KANSALLISPUISTO
OUTTAKA
YLLÄS
KUMPUTUNTURI
SORSATUNTURI
RUKATUNTURI
ISO PYHÄTUNTURI
PYHÄTUNTURIN K.PUISTO
RIISITUNTURIN K.PUISTO
VÄRRIÖN L.PUISTO
SOMPION L.PUISTO
KIUTAKÖNGÄS
Ala-Kitka
Yli-Kitka
Muonionjoki
Torneälven
Ounasjoki
Kemijoki
Kitinen
Luirojoki
Ivalojoki
Kalixälven
Lainioälven
Lokan tekojärvi
Porttipahdan tekojärvi
Simojärvi
Vaikkokosi
T E N
198
199
191

193
197
191
186
187
MUDDAS NATIONALPARK
Kainulasjärvi
Hakkas
Korpilombolo
Pello
Rattosjärvi
Yli-Nampa
Nattavaara
Raanujärvi
Sinettä
Vikajärvi
Rovaniemi
Saarenkylä
Turtola
Svanstein
Lansjärv
Juoksenki
Ansvar
Kalixälven
OTTEN
Vuollerim
Vitträsk
Övertorneå
Aavasaksa
Ylitornio
Muurola
Narkaus
Överkalix
Hedenäset
Sihtuuna
Koivu
Peura
Portimo
Edefors
Tervola
Nuupas
Karunki
Morjärv
Lappträsk
Karungi
Harads
KUKKOLANKOSKI
Ranua
Luleälven
Niemisel
Maula
Töre
Kalix
Haparanda
Tornio
Yli-Kärppä
Råneå
Vidsel
Boden
Kemi
Simo
Seskarön
Bergön
Pukkofjärden
Oijärvi
Piteälven
Rånön
Harufjärden
Vistheden
Gammelstaden
Kuivaniemi
Luleå
Grundsel
Älvsbyn
Tannila
Antnäs
Ohlava
Sandön
Yli-Ii
S
Iijoki
Germandön
Långträsk
Kallfjärden
Öjebyn
Piteå
Bergsviken
Haukipudas
Kiiminki
Grönbo
Hemmingsmark
Hailuoto
Marjaniemi
OULU/ ULEÅBORG
Oulujoki
Jävre
Madekoski
Fällfors
Åbyälven
Oulunsalo
Kempele
Laukka
Jörn
Åbyn
Karinkanta
Luodonselkä
Lumijoenselkä
Byske
Siikajoki
Lumijoki
Keskikylä
Muhos
Strömfors
Liminka
Tyrnävä
Boliden
Kåge
Revonlahti
Temmes
Skellefteå
Raahe
Ruukki
Skelleftestrand
Kylmä
Medle
Skelleftehamn
Paavola
Kärsämä
Skelleftebukten
Haapajoki
Rantsila
Rankinen
Bureå
Åtrask
Pyhäjoki
Vihanti
Kopisto
Alpua
Lampinsaari
Burträsk
Lappvattnet
Yppäri
Polusperä
Karhukangas
Uljuan tekojärvi
RBOTTEN
Bygdeträsket
Lövånger
Merijärvi
Vasankari
Oulainen
Pulkkila
KYRKSTAD
Kalajoki
Bygdsiljum
Mieluskylä
Leskelä
Ånäset
Botsmark
Rytkynkylä
Haapavesi
Typpö
Ylivieska
Robertsfors
Pankala
Rautio
Himanka
Raudaskylä
Alajoki
Sikeå
Lohtaja
Karsikas
Kärsämäki
Nivala
Maliskylä
Bygdeå
Marinkainen
Bullmark
Sievi
Kannus
Jokikylä
Kokkola/ Karleby
Parkkila
Ersmark
Sävar
Kälviä
Kiiskilä
Haapajärvi
Parkkima
Kuona
Pyhäsalmi
Välikylä
Toholampi
Holmön
Umeå
Holm
Larsmo/ Luoto
Nedervetil/ Alaveteli
Kangaskylä
Reisjärvi
Kalaja
Jakobstad/ Pietarsaari
Kronoby/ Kruunupy
Ullava
Ängesön
Holmsund
Pirttiniemi
Obbola
Västra Kvarken
Torsön
Esse/ Ähtävä
Sykäräinen
Muurasjärvi
Pitkäjärvi
Lestijärvi
Kaustinen
Yli-Lesti
Alvajärvi
Mjölefjärden
Nykarleby/ Uusikaarlepyy
Kainu
Kanala
Lappfors
Veteli
Halsua
Pihtipudas
Vaasa/Vasa
Munsala
Kinnula
Monäs
Räyrinki
Norra Gloppet
Östra Gloppet
Evijärvi
Salamajärvi
Muhola
A
B
C
D
1
2
3
4
5
6

E
F
G
H
1
2
3
4
5
6
Kemijärvi
Isokylä
Joutsijärvi
Kallunki
Zasheyek
Hautajärvi
Ozero
Tikshozero
Loukhi
Kemijärvi
452
Maaninkavaara
KIUTAKÖNGÄS
Luusua
Jumisko
Ala-Kitka
RIISITUNTURIN
K.PUISTO
Ozero
Pyaozero
Autti
494
RUKATUNTURI
Ruka
Perä-Posio
Yli-Kitka
Pohjaslahti
Vasarapera
Posio
Kesten'ga
Ozero
Keret'
Simojärvi
Kuusamo
Muojärvi
Sofporog
Mäntyjärvi
Lämsänkylä
Ozero
Topozero
469
IIVAARA
Kuolio
Kuloharju
Tungozero
Livojoki
Kostonjärvi
RUS
Kelankylä
ISO-SYÖTE
431
Syötekylä
Taivalkoski
Peranka
Chajkola
Kepa
Kalevala
Ozero
Srednyeye Kuyto
Voynitsa
Lonka
Metsäkylä
Pudasjärvi
Juntusranta
Näljänkä
Ozero
Verkhneye
Kuyto
Siivikko
Jongunjärvi
Ozero
Nizhneye Kuyto
Voknavolok
Yushkozero
Viinikoski
FIN
Joukokylä
Suomussalmi
Ämmänsaari
Särkijärvi
Puolanka
Juorkuna
KALLIUSKOSKI
Kytömäki
HEPOKÖNGÄS
Hyrynjärvi
Vuokkijärvi
Ala-Vuokki
Kuivajärvi
Sanginkylä
Hakokylä
Saarivaara
Kostomuksha
Ozero Nyuk
Paljakka
Puokio
Kalpio
Hyrynsalmi
Kumuu
Vartius
Otermajärvi
OULU/ULEÅBORG
Luvozero
Ojakylä
Oulujoki
Tormänmäki
Uva
Jokikylä
Matkavaara
Kongasmäki
Andronova
Gora
Rokua
Jaalanka
Liminpuro
Ristijärvi
Lentiira
Härmänkylä
Nuojua
Vaala
Kivesjärvi
Neittävä
Säräisniemi
Paltamo
Härmänmäki
Niva
Sumsa
Viiksimo
Veneheitto
Kaivanto
Kontiomäki
Lentua
Manamansalo
Hannusranta
Kellojärvi
Paltaniemi
Lemetinvaara
Hietaperä
Nirmiskylä
Kestilä
Oulujärvi
Anttila
Soidinvaara
Kajaani
Nuasjärvi
Ontojärvi
Kuhmo
Käkilahti
Vuolijoki
Ounas
Kontinjoki
Vuokatti
Sotkamo
Ontojoki
Tipasjoki
Yemel'yanovka
Tavastkenka
Vuottolahti
Mainua
Tuhkakylä
Rasktinkylä
Riihivaara
Otanmäki
Lehtovaara
Reboly
Pyhäntä
Sivakka
Lauvuskylä
Saarela
Ozero
Leksozero
Ahokylä
Kamula
Maanselkä
Mujejärvi
Teljo
Nissilä
Lahnasjärvi
Verkhnyaya
Tulivaara
Sukeva
Sivakka
Laakajärvi
Savijärvi
Salahmi
Petäiskylä
Remeskylä
Valtimo
Pajukoski
Ronkeli
Hattuselkonen
Vieremä
Nurmijärvi
Lendery
Sonkajärvi
Aittojärvi
Porokylä
Nurmes
Soinlahti
Koirakoski
Vieki
Kiuruvesi
Savikylä
Rautavaara
Iisalmi
Pyhäjärvi
Kalliokylä
Runni
Palomäki
Pankakoski
Hattuvaara
Inari
Ruutana
Lieksa
Kitsi
Peltosalmi
Juminen
Haapamäki
Vihtasuo
Koivujärvi
Sulkava
Pielinen
Heinäaho
Hankamäki
Vuonislahti
Lampaanjärvi
Varpaisjärvi
Pihlajavaara
Juuka
Nunnanlahti
Lapinlahti
Palonurmi
Naarva
Mäntylahti
Piispa
Sulkavanjärvi
Koli
Jaakonvaara
Hattuvaara
Sayneinen
Polvela
Ahmovaara
Pielavesi
Nilsiä
Viitaniemi
Martonvaara
Haluna
Maaninka
Korentovaara
Koitere
188
189

176
177
169
202
A
B
C
D
1
2
3
4
5
6
FIN
Jurmo
Hangö västra
fjärd
Helsinki/Helsingfors
Naissaar
Aegna
Stockholm
Tallinna Laht
TALLINN
Keila-Joa
Paldiski
Saue
Keila
Vasalemma
Kohila
Nova
Kirikküla
Hara
Valgeristi
Nissi
Varbola
Vormsi
Norbi
Risti
Haapsalu
Rohuküla
Märjamaa
Hiiumaa
Kärdla
Luidja
Ristna
Hellermaa
Suuremõisa
Käina
Martna
Puise
Väinameri
Lihula
Kirbla
Kivi-Vigala
Enge
Vijterna
Muhu
Liiva
Karuse
Koonga
Leisi
Virtsu
Vijküla
Kalli
Tagaranna
Metsküla
Orissaare
Undva
Vohma
Pöide
Varabla
Mustjala
Kurevere
Pärnu
Kihelkonna
Saaremaa
Köljala
Murru
Sandla
Karala
Kogula
Kipi
Kingissepp
Võiske
Lõmala
Salme
Siare
Kihnu
Häädemeeste
RIIA LAHT
Jamaja
Maebe
Ainaži
Sõrve
Ruhnu
Salacgrīva
Holmudden
SANDON
ALPARK
Sandön
Irbeni väin/
Irves Šaurums
Kolka
Mazirbe
Ezermuiža
RĪGAS JŪRAS
LĪCIS
Tūja
Laži
Dundaga
Roja
Ance
Skulte
Mērsrags
Valdemārpils
Ventspils
Pope
Nogale
Saulkrasti
Ciruli
Talsi
Lilaste
Ugāle
Nurmulža
Leči
Spāre
Usma
Piltene
Engure
Stende
Garkaln
Ragaciems
Kandava
RĪGA
Samate
Renda
Kupli
Kāpas
Sabile
Jūrmala
Tukums
Ēdole
Rīga
Labrags
Zemite
Alsunga
Kuldīga
Kalnciems
Vāne
Pavilosta
Apšupe
Olaine
Basi
Zante
Venta
Abava
Jaunpils
Lutrini
Lankas
Jelgava
Garoza
Ziemupe
Aizpute
Broceni
Skrunda
Saldus
Dobele
Gluda
Medze
Mazilmaja
Durbe
Jaunniumuiža
Ezernijeki
Bauska
Kuršiši
Liepāja
Krote
Embute
Grobina
Auce
Eleja
PILSRUNDALE
Priekule
Ezere
Ruba
Zāgare
Naujoji
Akmenė
Kiburi
Gramzda
Mažeikiai
Bernati
Joniškis
LT
Skuodas
Ylakiai
Viekšniai
Papile
Rucava
Barstyčiai
Pape
Varduva
Gruzdžiai
A1
A8
A9
A10
A11
A12

178
179
203
204
EST
LV
RUS
BY
Kohtla-Järve
Narva
Ivangorod
Kingisepp
Rakvere
Slantsy
Сланцы
Luga
Луга
Peipsi Järv
Chudskoye Ozero
Tartu
Viljandi
Pskovskoje Ozero
PSKOV
ПСКОВ
Porkhov
Valga
Valka
Võru
Valmiera
Cēsis
Ostrov
Остров
Sigulda
Gulbene
Madona
Opochka
Ogre
Rēzekne
Jēkabpils
Aizkraukle
Sebezh
Daugavpils
Krāslava

A
B
C
D
200
163
23
24
1
2
3
4
5
6
Holmudden
Fårö
Fårösund
Hallshuk
Kappelshamn
Lickershamn
Lärbro
Kyllaj
LUMMELUNDAGROTTORNA
Tingstäde
Slite
Visby
Bro
S
Högklint
Gothem
Barlingbo
Gnisvärd
Roma
Eskelhem
Isums
Ala
Katthammarsvik
TORSBURGEN
Klintehamn
Buttle
Ljugarn
L. Karlsö
St. Karlsö
Lye
DJAUVIK
Sproge
Burs
Gotland
Hemse
Hablingbo
Ronehamn
Havdhem
Burgsvik
Sallmunds
Sundre
Hoburgen
Nynäshamn
Mariehamn /
Maarianhamina
Ölands norra udde
Grankullavik
Oskarshamn
Travemünde
Kiel
Gdańsk
Karlskrona
Sõrve
Irbeni väin
Irves šaurums
Mazirbe
Laži
Dundaga
Ance
Ventspils
Pope
Ugāle
Leci
Piltene
Usma
Samate
Kapas
Ēdole
Labrags
Alsunga
Kuldīga
Pavilosta
Basi
Venta
Lankas
Ziemupe
Aizpute
Skrunda
Medze
Durbe
Mazilmaja
Liepāja
Grobina
Krote
Embute
Priekule
Gramzda
Kiburi
Bernati
Skuodas
Ylakiai
Rucava
Mosėdis
Barstyčiai
Pape
Varduva
Salantai
Darbėnai
Palanga
Kartena
Plungė
Kretinga
Kuliai
Rietavas
KLAIPEDA
Gargždai
Veivirženai
Kvedarna
Kuršių Nerija
Priekulė
Švėkšna
Saugos
Kintai
Vainuta
Neringa
Ventė
Šilutė
Žemaičių Naumiestis
Neringa-Nida
Kuršių marios
Rusnė
Juknaičiai
Katyčiai
Nemunas
Pagėgiai
Kurshskaya Kosa
Kurshskiy Zaliv
Sovetsk
RUS
Pionerskiy
Zelenogradsk
Bol'shakovo
Polessk
Yantarnyy
KALININGRAD
Primorsk
Kaliningrad
Gvardeysk
Chernyakhovsk
Baltiysk
Ushakovo
Znamensk
Kaliningradskiy Zaliv
Južnyj
Mamonovo
Bagrationovsk
Domnovo
Pravdinsk
Zhelenodorozhnyy
Krylovo
Nowa Karczma
Braniewo
Frombork
Lelkowo
Górowo
Pogrodzie
Pakosze
Bartoszyce
Węgorzewo
Pieniężno
Galiny
Nowica
Zalew Wiślany
PARK KRAJOBR. MIERZEJA WIŚLANA
Stegna
Nowy Dwór Gdański
GDAŃSK
Pruszcz-Gdański
Sopot
GDYNIA
Rumia
Zatoka Gdańska
Visby
Nynäshamn
Oxelösund
PL
NADMORSKI PARK KRAJOBRAZOWY
Władysławowo
Łeba
Krokowa
Puck
Zatoka Pucka
Hel
Żelazno
Kluki
Wicko
Wejherowo
Główczyce
Damno
Lębork
Osowo Lęborskie
Łebno
Chwaszczyno
Rebiechowo
Kartuzy
Żukowo
Sierakowice
Oskowo
Czarna Dąbrówka
Dębnica Kaszubska
Suchorze

RĪGAS JŪRAS LĪCIS
LV
LT
BY
RĪGA
Jūrmala
Valmiera
Cēsis
Sigulda
Ogre
Salaspils
Kekava
Olaine
Jelgava
Tukums
Dobele
Bauska
Aizkraukle
Jēkabpils
Madona
Gulbene
Alūksne
Balvi
Daugavpils
Krāslava
Rēzekne
Līvāni
Preiļi
Ainaži
Salacgrīva
Limbaži
Saulkrasti
Skulte
Lilaste
Garkalne
Ropaži
Kandava
Ragaciems
Engure
Mērsrags
Roja
Valdemārpils
Nogale
Saldus
Broceni
Auce
Kuldīga
Pilsrundāle
Skrīveri
Koknese
Pļaviņas
Lielvārde
Baldone
Iecava
Vecumnieki
Ērgļi
Cesvaine
Lubāna
Varakļāni
Viļāni
Ilūkste
Subate
Akniste
Nereta
Viesīte
Zasa
Šiauliai
Panevėžys
Pasvalys
Biržai
Joniškis
Pakruojis
Radviliškis
Kuršėnai
Rokiškis
Obeliai
Kupiškis
Zarasai
Visaginas
Dūkštas
Utena
Anykščiai
Ignalina
Švenčionėliai
Švenčionys
Molėtai
Ukmergė
Kėdainiai
Jonava
Kaunas
Vilnius
Trakai
Lentvaris
Širvintos
Pabradė
Nemenčinė
Šalčininkai
Eišiškės
Varėna
Alytus
Prienai
Birštonas
Marijampolė
Kalvarija
Vilkaviškis
Kybartai
Jurbarkas
Raseiniai
Tauragė
Kelmė
Ariogala
Šeduva
Kaltinėnai
Šakiai
Kazlų Rūda
Lazdijai
Seirijai
Merkinė
Druskininkai
Suwałki
Sejny
Gusev
Krasnoznamensk
Dobrovol'sk
Nesterov
Vištytis
Ashmyany
Smarhon'
Maladzyechna
Маладзечна
Kreva
Hal'shany
Zhuprany
Vishnyeva
Valozhyn
Psarshai
Naroch
Myadzyel
Svir
Kobyl'nik
Pastavy
Braslaw
Opsa
Vidzy
Kaz'yany
Varnyany
Medininkai
Turgeliai
Dieveniškės
Byenyakoni
Varanava
Yuratsishki
Lipnishki
AUKŠTAITIJOS NACIONALINIS PARKAS
TRAKŲ ISTORINIS NACIONALINIS PARKAS
DZŪKIJOS NACIONALINIS PARKAS
SUWALSKI PARK KRAJOBRAZOWY
Gauja
Daugava
Lielupe
Venta
Nemunas
Neris
Šventoji
Nevėžis
Merkys
Viliya
Vozyera Narach
Vozyera Drysvyaty
Vozyera Svir
201
204
205
25
E
F
G
H
1
2
3
4
5
6

HELSINKI/
HELSINGFORS
Espoo/
Esbo
Karkkila
Lohja
Järvenpää
Kerava
Porvoo
Anjalankoski
Hamina
Kotka
178
Vyborg
Solovjevka
179
Ladozhskoye
Ozero
Lodejnoje
Pole
Ustinski
Pogost
Alehovščina
Beloje Ozero
Belozersk
Kirillov
Primorsk
Zelenogorsk
Sestroretsk
Kronshtadt
Toksovo
SANKT-
PETERBURG
Novaja
Ladoga
Sjasstroj
Ostrov
Gogland
Ostrov
Moshchnyy
Sosnovyy
Bor
Petrodvorets
Krasnoye Selo
Kirovsk
Kolpino
Puškin
Volkhov
Gankovo
Stockholm
Stockholm
Travemünde
TALLINN
Narvski zaliv /
Narva laht
Koskolovo
Ivangorod
Gatchina
Tosno
Čvylevo
Tikhvin
Pikalevo
Somino
Kohtla-
Järve
Narva
Kingisepp
Volosovo
Siverskiy
Kukuj
Suda
CHEREPOVETS
Tapa
Rakvere
Ivangorod
Slantsy
Jashchera
Chudovo
Sazonovo
Märjamaa
Paide
EST
Lohusuu
Mustvee
Jõgeva
Ustyuzha
Ves'yegonsk
Pärnu-
Jaagupi
Vändra
Põltsamaa
Peipsi
Järv
Chudskoye
Ozero
Gdov
Luga
Batetskiy
Malaya
Vishera
Ljubytino
Pestovo
Rybinskoye
Vodokhranilishche
Viljandi
Lyady
Novgorod
Yamm
Tartu
Borovichi
Uulu
Kilingi-Nõmme
Võrtsjärv
Elva
Nikolayevo
Ozero
Il'men'
Kresttsy
Pskovskoje
Ozero
Krasnyy Kholm
RYBINSK
200
Rūjiena
Valka
Valga
Võru
Sol'tsy
Staraya Russa
Valdaj
Bezhetsk
Dno
Pskov
Porkhov
Uglich
Misso
Valmiera
Smiltene
Vireši
Demjansk
Vyshniy Volochek
Kashin
Alūksne
Kalyazin
Cēsis
Ostrov
VALDAYSKAYA
343
Ozero
Seliger
Sigulda
LV
Gulbene
Kholm
Ostashkov
Kuvshinovo
Torzhok
Ogre
Ērgli
Madona
Pytalovo
Novorzhev
VOZVYSHENNOST'
TVER'
Kimry
Kārsava
Krasnogorodskoye
Loknya
Seližarovo
Dubna
Plavinas
Opochka
Jelcy
RUS
Aizkraukle
Jēkabpils
Vilāni
Ludza
Rēzekne
Staritsa
Dmitrov
Sergiyev
Posad
Līvāni
Biržai
Malta
Velikiye Luki
Nelidovo
Rzhev
Zubtsov
Klin
Solnechnogorsk
Sebezh
Pustoshka
Novosokol'niki
Volokolamsk
MOSKVA
Puškino
Mytishchi
Rokiškis
Ilūkste
203
Krāslava
Daugavpils
Nevel'
Kupiškis
Panevėžys
Vyerkhnyadzvinsk
Zarasai
Braslaw
Belyy
Sychevka
Lyubertsy
Yezyaryshcha
LT
Velizh
Gagarin
Mozhaysk
Podol'sk
Domodedovo
Utena
Polatsk
Naro-
Fominsk
Vidzy
Haradok
Surazh
Chekhov
Širvintos
Pastavy
Ula
VITSYEBSK
Dukhovshchina
Vyaz'ma
Obninsk
Daugava
Gauja
Zakhodnyaya Dzvina
Volga
Moskva
Mologa
Msta
Mezha
Lovat'
Neva
Svir
Volchov

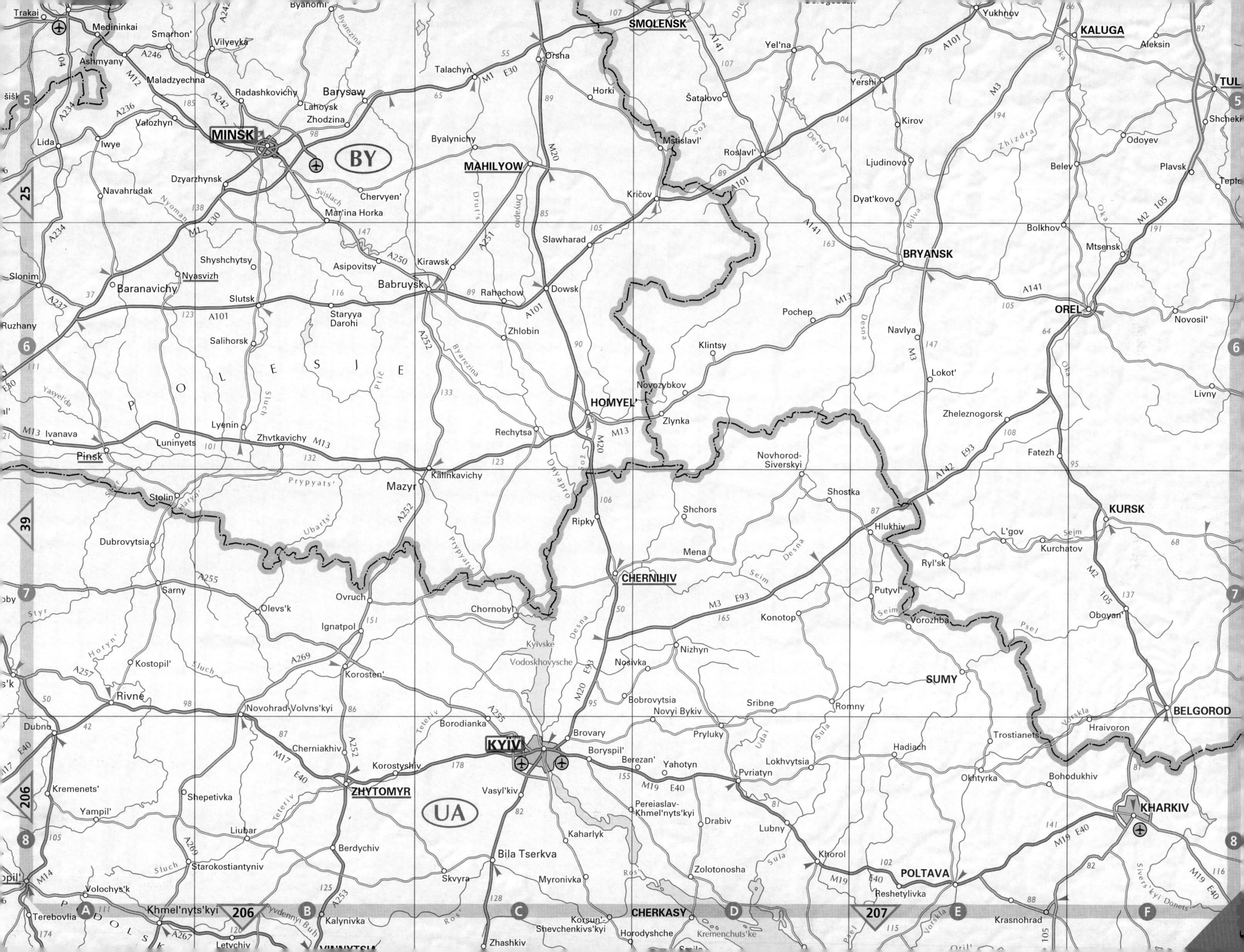

MINSK
BY
Trakai
Medininkai
Ashmyany
Smarhon'
Vilyeyka
Maladzyechna
Radashkovichy
Barysaw
Lahoysk
Zhodzina
Valozhyn
Lida
Iwye
Navahrudak
Dzyarzhynsk
Chervyen'
Mar'ina Horka
Shyshchytsy
Nyasvizh
Baranavichy
Slonim
Ruzhany
Slutsk
Starya Darohi
Salihorsk
Asipovitsy
Babruysk
Kirawsk
Byalynichy
MAHILYOW
Talachyn
Orsha
Horki
SMOLENSK
Mstislavl'
Kričov
Slawharad
Dowsk
Rahachow
Zhlobin
HOMYEL'
Rechytsa
Kalinkavichy
Mazyr
Zhytkavichy
Luninyets
Lyenin
Ivanava
Pinsk
Stolin
P O L E S J E
Yel'na
Yershi
Šatalovo
Roslavl'
Kirov
Ljudinovo
Dyat'kovo
BRYANSK
Yukhnov
KALUGA
Aleksin
TUL
Shcheki
Odoyev
Belev
Plavsk
Bolkhov
Mtsensk
OREL
Novosil'
Livny
Pochep
Klintsy
Novozybkov
Zlynka
Navlya
Lokot'
Zheleznogorsk
Fatezh
KURSK
Kurchatov
L'gov
Ryl'sk
Oboyan'
BELGOROD
Hraivoron
KHARKIV
Bohodukhiv
Krasnohrad
Novhorod-Siverskyi
Shostka
Hlukhiv
Putyvl'
Vorozhba
Konotop
SUMY
Trostianets'
Okhtyrka
Hadiach
Romny
Lokhvytsia
Lubny
Khorol
POLTAVA
Reshetylivka
Shchors
Mena
Ripky
CHERNIHIV
Nizhyn
Nosivka
Bobrovytsia
Novyi Bykiv
Pryluky
Sribne
Yahotyn
Berezan'
Pyriatyn
Pereiaslav-Khmel'nyts'kyi
Drabiv
Zolotonosha
CHERKASY
Horodyshche
Korsun'-Shevchenkivs'kyi
Kaharlyk
Myronivka
Bila Tserkva
Zhashkiv
Vasyl'kiv
KYIV
Brovary
Boryspil'
Borodianka
Chornobyl'
Kyivske Vodoskhovysche
Ovruch
Ignatpol
Korosten'
Olevs'k
Sarny
Dubrovytsia
Kostopil'
Rivne
Dubno
Novohrad-Volyns'kyi
Cherniakhiv
Korostyshiv
ZHYTOMYR
Berdychiv
Liubar
Shepetivka
Starokostiantyniv
Kremenets'
Yampil'
Volochys'k
Terebovlia
Khmel'nyts'kyi
Letychiv
Kalynivka
Skvyra
UA
Desna
Dnyapro
Prypyats'
Byarezina
Sluch
Teteriv
Horyn'
Styr
Seim
Psel
Sula
Vorskla
Oka
Zhizdra
Bolva
Sož
Drut's
Svislach
Nyoman
Ubarts'
Ptič
Udai
Ros'
Sivers'kyi Donets'
Yasyel'da
M1 E30
M2
M3
M13
M20
M19 E40
M17 E40
M14
M12
E93
A101
A141
A142
A250
A251
A252
A253
A255
A257
A267
A269
A234
A236
A237
A242
A246
A B C D E F
5 6 7 8
25
39
206
207

RADOM
38
39
Opoczno
Końskie
Radomsko
Puławy
Zwoleń
Kurów
Lubartów
Włodawa
LUBLIN
Kazimierz Dolny
Skarżysko-Kamienna
Starachowice
STOCHOWA
Kielce
PL
Ostrowiec Świętokrzyski
Koniecpol
Opatów
Kraśnik
Piaski
Chełm
Krasnystaw
Kovel'
Turiis'k
Holoby
Dubrovytsia
Sarny
Olevs'k
Zawiercie
Jędrzejów
Sandomierz
Janów Lubelski
Zamość
Hrubieszów
Volodymyr-Volyns'kyi
Luts'k
Kostopil'
Wolbrom
Staszów
Tarnobrzeg
Stalowa Wola
Biłgoraj
Miechów
Busko-Zdrój
Olkusz
Nisko
Tomaszów Lubelski
Rivne
Novohrad-Volyn
Mielec
Leżajsk
Cieszanów
Chervonohrad
Dubno
KRAKÓW
Tarnów
Dębica
Wieliczka
Przeworsk
Rava-Rus'ka
Myślenice
Pilzno
Rzeszów
Jarosław
Zhovkva
Brody
Kremenets'
Shepetivka
Rabka
Grybów
Gorlice
Jasło
Krosno
Przemyśl
Horodok
Bus'k
Yampil'
Liubar
Nowy Targ
Nowy Sącz
Krynica
Dukla
Sanok
Lesko
L'VIV
Starokostiantyniv
Przełęcz Dukielska
Sambir
Mykolaïv
Ternopil'
Volochys'k
Bardejov
Svidník
Ustrzyki Dolne
Khodoriv
Stará L'ubovňa
Kežmarok
SK
Drohobych
Rohatyn
Terebovlia
Khmel'nyts'kyi
Poprad
Levoča
Turka
Stryj
Spišská Nová Ves
Prešov
Snina
Uzhots'kyi Pereval
Letychiv
Humenné
Vranov
Velykyi Bereznyi
Skole
Kalush
Buchach
Yarmolyntsi
Rožňava
Košice
Michalove
Dolyna
Ivano-Frankivs'k
Chortkiv
Zhmer
Rimavská Sobota
Trebišov
Uzhorod
Seredni Verets'kyi Pereval
Tovste
Dunaïvtsi
Sátoraljaújhely
Chop
Mukacheve
Mizhiria
Zalishchyky
Dzhuryn
Ózd
Kazincbarcika
Encs
Sárospatak
Deliatyn
Kolomyia
Kamianets'-Podil's'kyi
Salgótarján
Tokaj
Kisvárda
Berehove
Yablunyts'kyi Pereval
Snjatyn
Khotyn
Mohyliv-Podilis'kyi
Miskolc
Vásárosnamény
Khust
Briceni
Eger
Nyíregyháza
Vynohradiv
CHERNIVTSI
Lipcani
Edinița
Gyöngyös
Mezőkövesd
Mátészalka
Darabani
Füzesabony
Újfehértó
Rakhiv
Soroca
Heves
Balmazújváros
Nyírbátor
Sighetu Marmației
MD
Tiszafüred
Hajdúböszörmény
Satu Mare
Baia Mare
Rădăuți
Siret
Dorohoi
Florești
Carei
Borșa
MĂNĂSTIREA SUCEVIȚA
Bălți
H
Debrecen
Valea lui Mihai
Vîrful Pietrosu
Pasul Prislop
MĂNĂSTIREA MOLDOVIȚA
Botoșani
Karcag
Hajdúszoboszló
Tîrgu Lăpuș
Cîmpulung Moldovenesc
Suceava
Szolnok
Püspökladány
Törökszentmiklós
Kisújszállás
Berettyóújfalu
Șimleu Silvaniei
MĂNĂSTIREA VORONEȚ
Fălticeni
Mezőtúr
Szeghalom
Oradea
Zălau
Năsăud
Vatra Dornei
Pasul Tihuța
MĂNĂSTIREA NEAMȚ
Pașcani
Tîrgu Frumos
Aleșd
Beclean
Dej
Bistrița
Tîrgu Neamț
Szarvas
Mezőberény
Békés
Salonta
Huedin
CLUJ NAPOCA
IAȘI
Ungheni
Békéscsaba
Gyula
Beiuș
Toplița
Piatra Neamț
Orosháza
Reghin
Gheorghieni
Bicaz
Roman
Hódmezővásárhely
Chișineu Criș
Turda
Cîmpia Turzii
Bahuși
Huși
Vîrful Curcubăta
Sovata
Tîrgu Mureș
Vaslui
Makó
Nădlac
Arad
Cîmpeni
Aiud
Tîrnăveni
Miercurea Ciuc
Comănești
Bacău
Sânnicolau Mare
Lipova
Brad
Blaj
Mediaș
Sighișoara
Odorheiu Secuiesc
Slănic Moldova
Onești
Bîrlad
Kikinda
Jimbolia
Ilia
Alba Iulia
Sebeș
Băile Tușnad
Deva
Agnita
Rupea
Sfîntu Gheorghe
Pasul Oituz
Adjud
TIMIȘOARA
Hunedoara
Orăștie
Sibiu
Făgăraș
Tîrgu Secuiesc
Tecuci
Lugoj
Poarta de Fier a Transilvaniei
Hațeg
RO
Cisnădie
Vîrful Moldoveanu
Zrenjanin
Sarmizegetuza
Pasul Turnu Roșu
Poiana Brașov
BRAȘOV
Focșani
Deta
Caransebeș
ULPIA TRAIANA
Petroșani
Petrila
Zărnești
Vulcănești
Reșița
Lupeni
MĂNĂSTIREA COZIA
Predeal
GALAȚI
Vršac
Alibunar
Oravița
Anina
MĂNĂSTIREA HUREZ
Sinaia
Nehoiu
Rîmnicu Sărat
Brăila
Pančevo
Bela Crkva
MĂNĂSTIREA TISMANA
Tîrgu Jiu
Călimănești
Cîmpulung
Curtea de Argeș
Vălenii de Munte
Buzău
BEOGRAD
Moldova Nouă
Mehadia
Ponoarele
Rîmnicu Vîlcea
Cîmpina
Smederevo
Orșova
PORȚILE DE FIER
Tîrgoviște
Pitești
Ploiești
Mizil
Însurăței
Požarevac
Kladovo
Strehaia
Găești
Drobeta-Turnu Severin
Filiași
Drăgășani
Costești
Urziceni
Hîrșova
Petrovac
Majdanpek
Slatina
Slobozia
YU
Negotin
CRAIOVA
BUCUREȘTI
Cernavodă
Kragujevac
Bor
Videle
150
151
148
149
Rgotina
Vidin
Roșiori de Vede
Budești
Călărași
Caracal
CARPAȚII MERIDIONALI
TRANSILVANIA
MARAMUREȘ
OLTENIA
CARPAȚI ORIENTALI
CARPATY

205
E
F
G
H
BY
RUS
UA
Mena
CHERNIHIV
Kurchatov
Ryl'sk
Gubkin
Oboyan'
Putyvl'
Vorozhba
Konotop
Chornobyl'
Nizhyn
Nosivka
SUMY
Kyïvske
Vodoskhovysche
BELGOROD
Bobrovytsia
Sribne
Romny
Hraivoron
Trostianets'
Borodianka
Brovary
Novyi Bykiv
Pryluky
Hadiach
KYÏV
Boryspil'
Berezan'
Yahotyn
Lokhvytsia
Okhtyrka
Bohodukhiv
Korostyshiv
Pvriatyn
KHARKIV
Vasyl'kiv
Pereiaslav-Khmel'nyts'kyi
Drabiv
Lubny
Kupians'k
Kaharlyk
Khorol
Bila Tserkva
Zolotonosha
Reshetylivka
POLTAVA
Krasnohrad
Skvyra
Myronivka
CHERKASY
Korsun'-Shevchenkivs'kyi
Horodyshche
Kremenchuts'ke
Izium
Smila
Hradvz'k
Vodoskhovyshche
Zhashkiv
Svitlovods'k
Kremenchuk
Pereshchepyne
Slovians'
Kamianka
Myshuryn Rih
Kramators'
Novomoskovs'k
Kostiantynivk
Oleksandriia
Verkhn'odniprovs'k
Znamianka
DNIPROPETROVS'K
Uman'
Novoarkhanhel's'k
KIROVOHRAD
DNIPRODZERZHYNS'K
Tul'chyn
Pjatihatki
Novoukraïnka
Pokrovs'ke
ZAPORIZHZHIA
Pervomais'k
KRYVYI RIH
Kryve Ozero
Marhanets'
Balta
Nikopol'
Polohy
Kotovs'k
Novyi Buh
Ribnita
Kamianka-Dniprovs'ka
Vasylivka
Troïts'ke
Vossijatskoje
Novovorontsovka
Voznesens'k
Tokmak
Kakhovs'ke
Veselynove
Vodoskhovyshche
Zhovten'
Snihurivka
Velyka Lepetykha
Melitopol'
MYKOLAÏV
Beryslav
Kakhovka
Berdians'k
Tiraspol
Tighina
Novaja Kakhovka
Tsiurupyns'k
KHERSON
Ochakiv
Hola Prystan'
Căusanii
ODESA
Heniches'k
AZOVSKE
Illichivs'k
Tarutino
Bilhorod Dnistrovs'kyi
Skadovs'k
Krasnoperekops'k
MORE
Karkinits'ka Zatoka
Voïnka
Artsyz
Sarata
Tatarbunary
Ozero Sasyk (Kunduk)
Dzhankoï
KRYMS'KYI
PIVOSTRIV
Chornomors'ke
KERCH
mys Tarhankut
Kyliia
Saky
Yevpatoria
Theodosiia
SIMFEROPOL'
Sudak
Sulina
mys Meganom
Murighiol
SEVASTOPOL'
Belokamensk
Alushta
mys Hersonesski
DELTA DUNĂRII
Yalta
mys Saryž
Alupka
67

INDEX OF NAMES
INDICE DEI NOMI
ÍNDICE DE TOPÓNIMOS
INDEX DES NOMS
NAMENVERZEICHNIS

How to use the index • Avvertenze per la ricerca
Instrucciones para la consulta • Notices pour la recherche
Erläuterungen des Suchsystems

The index lists the place names and the main tunnels and passes contained in the map, followed by the abbreviation of the country name to which they belong.
For easiness all names contained in two adjoining pages are referred to the even page number.

L'indice elenca i toponimi dei centri abitati e dei principali tunnel e passi presenti in cartografia accompagnati dalla sigla della nazione di appartenenza.
Per semplicità tutti i nomi contenuti in due pagine affiancate sono riferiti alla pagina di numero pari.

El índice presenta los topónimos de las localidades y de los principales túneles y puertos de montaña que figuran en el mapa, seguidos de la sigla que indica el País de pertenencia. Para simplicidad todos los nombres contenidos en dos páginas juntas éstan referidos a la página de número par.

L'index récense les noms des localités et des principales tunnels et cols contenus dans la carte, suivis par le sigle qui indique le Pays d'appartenance. Pour simplicité tous les noms contenus dans deux pages l'une à côté de l'autre sont rapportés à la page avec nombre pair.

Der Index enthält die in der Karte vorhandenen Namen von Ortschaften und wichtigsten Tunneln und Pässe, von dem zugehörigen Staatskennzeichen gefolgt. Zur Einfachheit sind alle in zwei anliegenden Seiten enthaltenen Namen auf die Seite mit gerader Zahl bezogen.

PRINCIPAL URBAN AREAS PLANS
PIANTE DELLE PRINCIPALI AREE URBANE
PLANOS DE LAS PRINCIPALES ÁREAS URBANAS
PLANS DES PRINCIPALES AIRES URBAINES
WICHTIGSTE STADTPLÄNE

Amsterdam	Frankfurt am Main	Milano
Athína	Genève	Moskva
Barcelona	Göteborg	München
Beograd	Helsinki/Helsingfors	Oslo
Berlin	İstanbul	Paris
Bern	København	Praha
Birmingham	Köln	Roma
Bratislava	Lisboa	Rotterdam
Brussel/Bruxelles	Liverpool-Manchester	Sofiya
Bucureşti	London	Stockholm
Budapest	Madrid	Warszawa
Edinburgh	Marseille	Wien

A

Ágios Geórgios [GR] 132 F4
Ágios Germanos [GR] 128 E4
Ágios Górdis [GR] 132 B2
Ágios Kírykos [GR] 138 G1
Agios Konstantinos [GR] 144 C5
Ágios Konstantínos [GR] 132 H4
Ágios Léon [GR] 136 A2
Ágios Márcos [GR] 128 H3
Ágios Mathéos [GR] 132 B2
Ágios Mýron [GR] 140 E5
Ágios Nikítas [GR] 132 C4
Ágios Nikólaos [GR] 132 C2
Ágios Nikólaos [GR] 136 G2
Ágios Nikólaos [GR] 136 E4
Ágios Nikólaos [GR] 140 F4
Ágios Nikólaos [GR] 132 D4
Ágios Nikolaos [GR] 130 C6
Ágios Pétros [GR] 136 E3
Ágios Pétros [GR] 132 C5
Ágios Pétros [GR] 128 G4
Ágios Pnevma [GR] 130 C3
Ágios Pródromos [GR] 130 B5
Ágios Theódori [GR] 132 H3
Agios Vlásios [GR] 132 E4
Agira [I] 126 F3
Ag. Kiriakí [GR] 138 H1
Aglen [N] 190 C4
Agliano [I] 108 H2
Agliate [I] 70 G4
Ag. Loukás [GR] 134 C5
Ag. Marina [GR] 132 G4
Ag. Marína [GR] 134 C5
Ágnanta [GR] 132 D2
Agnanteró [GR] 132 F2
Agnita [RO] 206 C5
Agnone [I] 116 E6
Agnóntas [GR] 134 B3
Agoitz / Aoitz [E] 78 C3
Agolada [E] 84 C4
Agoncillo [E] 82 H6
Agon-Coutainville [F] 26 D3
Agordo [I] 72 E4
Agost [E] 104 D2
Ág. Pandeleímonas [GR] 128 F4
Ag. Pelagía [GR] 140 E4
Agramunt [E] 92 C3
Ágras [GR] 128 F4
Agreda [E] 84 A6
Agreliá [GR] 132 F1
Agriá [GR] 132 H2
Agrigento [I] 126 D4
Agriliá [GR] 132 E5
Agrínio [GR] 132 E5
Agriovótano [GR] 134 B3
Agropoli [I] 120 F4
Ag.Rouméli [GR] 140 C5
Ågskaret [N] 190 D1
Ag. Stéfanos [GR] 138 E2
Ag. Triáda [GR] 134 C6
Agua Amarga [E] 102 H5
Aguadulce [E] 102 G5
A Guarda / La Guardia [E] 78 A5
A Guarda / La Guardia [E] 96 G2
Aguda [P] 80 B4
A Gudiña [E] 78 D6
Agudo [E] 96 C3
Águeda [P] 80 B5
Agüero [E] 84 C5
Aguiar da Beira [P] 80 D5
Aguilafuente [E] 88 F3
Aguilar de Campoo [E] 82 D4
Aguilar de la Frontera [E] 102 C2
Aguilar del Alfambra [E] 98 E1
Águilas [E] 104 B4
Agulo [E] 100 B5
Agurain / Salvatierra [E] 82 H5
Ağva / Yeşilçay [TR] 146 G2
Ag. Varvára [GR] 140 E5
Ahascragh [IRL] 2 D5
Ahat [TR] 144 G3
Ahaus [D] 16 G5
Åheim [N] 180 C4
Ahigal [E] 88 A5
Ahílio [GR] 132 G2
Ahínos [GR] 130 C3
Ahladohóri [GR] 130 B2
Ahlainen [FIN] 176 C1
Ahlbeck [D] 20 E4
Ahlbeck [D] 20 E3
Ahlen [D] 32 C3
Ahlhorn [D] 18 C6
Ahmetbey [TR] 146 C2
Ahmetli [TR] 144 D3
Ahmovaara [FIN] 188 F1
Ahoghill [GB] 2 G3
Ahokylä [FIN] 198 E5
Ahrensbök [D] 18 G3
Ahrensburg [D] 18 G4
Ahrweiler [D] 30 G5
Ähtäri [FIN] 186 E4
Ähtävä / Esse [FIN] 198 C6
Ahun [F] 54 H6
Åhus [S] 158 D2
Ahvensalmi [FIN] 188 E4
Ahvenselkä [FIN] 196 E7
Aianí [GR] 128 F6
Aibar [E] 84 C4
Aicha [D] 60 H3
Aichach [D] 60 D3
Aiddejavrre [N] 192 G3
Aidenbach [D] 60 G3
Aidone [I] 126 F4
Aigen [A] 62 B3
Aigiali [GR] 138 G3
Aígina [GR] 136 G2
Aigínio [GR] 128 G5
Aígio [GR] 132 F6
Aigle [CH] 70 C2
Aiglsbach [D] 60 E3
Aignay-le-Duc [F] 56 G2
Aigre [F] 54 D6
Aigrefeuille [F] 54 C5
Aigrefeuille-sur-Maine [F] 54 C2
Aiguablava [E] 92 G3
Aiguebelle [F] 108 D6
Aiguebelle [F] 70 B4
Aigueperse [F] 68 D1
Aigues-Mortes [F] 106 F4
Aiguilles [F] 70 B6
Aiguillon [F] 66 E5
Aigurande [F] 54 H5
Äijälä [FIN] 186 G3
Ailefroide [F] 70 B6
Aillant-sur-Tholon [F] 56 E1
Aime [F] 70 B4
Ainaži [LV] 200 D4
Ainhoa [F] 84 C2
Ainsa [E] 84 E6
Airaines [F] 28 D4
Airasca [I] 70 D6
Airdrie [GB] 8 D3
Aire [F] 28 E3
Aire-sur-l'Adour [F] 84 E2
Airolo [CH] 70 F2
Airvault [F] 54 E3
Aisey-sur-Seine [F] 56 G2
Aïssey [F] 58 B5
Aisými [GR] 130 G3
Aisy-sur-Armançon [F] 56 F2
Aiterhofen [D] 60 G2
Aitnoch [GB] 6 E5
Aitolikó [GR] 132 E5
Aitrach [D] 60 B4
Aittojärvi [FIN] 198 E6
Aittojärvi [FIN] 198 E3
Aiud [RO] 206 B5
Aix-en-Othe [F] 42 H6
Aix-en-Provence [F] 108 B4
Aixe-sur-Vienne [F] 66 G1
Aix-les-Bains [F] 68 H3
Aizenay [F] 54 B3
Aizkraukle [LV] 200 E5
Aizpute [LV] 200 B5
Ajaccio [F] 114 A5
Ajaureforsen [S] 190 F3
Ajdovščina [SLO] 74 A5
Ajka [H] 74 H2
Ajnovce [YU] 150 D5
Ajos [FIN] 198 C3
Akalan [TR] 146 D2
Akarca [TR] 144 G3
Akarp [S] 158 C3
Äkasjokisuu [FIN] 192 H5
Äkäslompolo [FIN] 192 H5
Akasztó [H] 76 C3
Akçakavak [TR] 142 F3
Akçaova [TR] 142 D1
Akçaova [TR] 146 G2
Akçay [TR] 142 H3
Akçay [TR] 144 C1
Aken [D] 34 C4
Åker [S] 168 C3
Åkersberga [S] 168 E2
Åkers krutbruk [S] 168 C3
Akhisar [TR] 144 D3
Akhtopol [BG] 148 G5
Akkent [TR] 144 G4
Akköprü [TR] 142 F2
Akköy [TR] 142 C1
Akland [N] 164 F4
Akmeşe [TR] 146 G3
Aknīste [LV] 200 F6
Akonpohja [FIN] 188 F5
Akoúmia [GR] 140 D5
Akpınar [TR] 146 H5
Åkra [N] 170 B5
Akraífnio [GR] 134 B5
Akranes [IS] 194 B4
Åkrehamn [N] 164 A2
Akrogiáli [GR] 130 C4
Akropótamos [GR] 130 C4
Akrotíri [GR] 138 F5
Akrovoúni [GR] 130 D3
Aksakal [TR] 146 D5
Aksakovo [BG] 148 F2
Aksaz [TR] 146 C4
Akujärvi [FIN] 196 D4
Akureyri [IS] 194 E3
Akyazı [TR] 146 H3
Ål [N] 170 F3
Ala [I] 72 C5
Ala [S] 168 G5
Alacalı [TR] 146 F2
Alacant / Alicante [E] 104 E2
Alacat [TR] 146 E5
Alaçatı [TR] 134 H5
Alà dei Sardi [I] 118 D3
Ala di Stura [I] 70 C5
Alaejos [E] 88 D2
Alagna-Valsésia [I] 70 E3
A Lagoa / Campo Lameiro [E] 78 B4
Alagón [E] 90 E3
Alahärmä [FIN] 186 C2
Ala-Honkajoki [FIN] 186 C6
Alajoki [FIN] 198 D5
Alakylä [FIN] 192 H5
Alameda [E] 102 C3
Alamedilla [E] 102 F3
Alamilla [E] 96 C4
Ala-Nampa [FIN] 196 D7
Alanäs [S] 190 E5
Alandroal [P] 94 E1
Ålandsbro [S] 184 F4
Alange [E] 94 H2
Alaniemi [FIN] 198 D2
Alanís [E] 94 H4
Alanta [LT] 202 G4
Ala-Paakkola [FIN] 198 C2
Alapitkä [FIN] 188 C1
Alaraz [E] 88 D4
Alarcón [E] 98 B3
Alaşehir [TR] 144 E4
Ålåsen [S] 190 E6
Alássio [I] 108 G4
Alastaro [FIN] 176 E3
Alatoz [E] 98 C5
Alatri [I] 116 C6
Alaveteli / Nedervetil [FIN] 198 C6
Alavieska [FIN] 198 C5
Ala-Vuokki [FIN] 198 F4
Alavus [FIN] 186 D4
Alba [I] 108 G2
Alba Adriatica [I] 116 D3
Albacete [E] 98 B5
Albacken [S] 184 D3
Alba de Tormes [E] 88 C3
Ålbæk [DK] 160 E2
Albaida [E] 98 E6
Albaina [E] 82 G5
Alba Iulia [RO] 206 B5
Albaladejo [E] 96 G5
Albalate de Cinca [E] 90 G4
Albalate del Arzobispo [E] 90 E5
Albalate de las Nogueras [E] 98 B1
Albalate de Zorita [E] 98 A1
Alban [F] 106 C3
Albánchez [E] 102 H4
Albano di Lucania [I] 120 H4
Albano Laziale [I] 116 A6
Albaredo d'Adige [I] 110 F1
Albarella [I] 110 H2
Albares [E] 88 H6
Albarracín [E] 98 D1
Albatana [E] 104 C1
Albena [BG] 148 G2
Albenga [I] 108 G4
Albens [F] 70 A3
Albentosa [E] 98 E3
Alberga [S] 168 B3
Albergaria-a-Velha [P] 80 B5
Alberic [E] 98 E5
Albernoa [P] 94 D3
Alberobello [I] 122 E3
Albersdorf [D] 18 E2
Albert [F] 28 E4
Albertirsa [H] 76 D1
Albertville [F] 70 B3
Albeşti [RO] 148 G1
Albi [F] 106 B2
Albignasego [I] 110 G1
Albisola Marina [I] 108 H3
Albo [F] 114 C2
Albocácer / Albocàsser [E] 98 G2
Albocàsser / Albocácer [E] 98 G2
Alboraia / Alboraya [E] 98 E4
Alboraya / Alboraia [E] 98 E4
Alborea [E] 98 C4
Albox [E] 102 H4
Albufeira [P] 94 C5
Albujón [E] 104 C4
Albuñol [E] 102 E5
Albuñuelas [E] 102 D4
Alburquerque [E] 86 F5
Alby [S] 162 G6
Alcácer do Sal [P] 94 C1
Alcáçovas [P] 94 D2
Alcadozo [E] 98 B6
Alcafores [P] 86 G3
Alcaide [E] 102 H3
Alcalá de Chivert / Alcalà de Xivert [E] 98 G2
Alcalá de Guadaira [E] 94 G6
Alcalá de Henares [E] 88 G6
Alcalá de la Selva [E] 98 E2
Alcalá del Júcar [E] 98 C5
Alcalá de los Gazules [E] 100 G4
Alcalá del Río [E] 94 G6
Alcalá del Valle [E] 102 A3
Alcalà de Xivert / Alcalá de Chivert [E] 98 G2
Alcalá la Real [E] 102 D3
Álcamo [I] 126 C2
Alcanar [E] 92 A6
Alcanede [P] 86 C4
Alcanena [P] 86 C4
Alcañices [E] 80 G4
Alcañiz [E] 90 F6
Alcántara [E] 86 G4
Alcantarilla [E] 104 C3
Alcaracejos [E] 96 C5
Alcaraz [E] 96 H6
Alcaria Ruiva [P] 94 D4
Alcarràs [E] 90 H5
Alcaşehir [TR] 144 G1
Alcaudete [E] 102 D2
Alcaudete de la Jara [E] 96 D1
Alcázar de San Juan [E] 96 G3
Alcester [GB] 12 H2
Alcobaça [P] 86 C3
Alcoba de los Montes [E] 96 D3
Alcobendas [E] 88 F5
Alcocèber / Alcossebre [E] 98 G3
Alcocer [E] 90 A6
Alcochete [P] 86 B5
Alcoentre [P] 86 B4
Alcofra [P] 80 C5
Alcoi / Alcoy [E] 104 E1
Alcolea [E] 102 F5
Alcolea del Pinar [E] 90 B4
Alconchel [E] 94 F2
Alcora / l'Alcora [E] 98 F3
Alcorcón [E] 88 F6
Alcorisa [E] 90 F6
Alcossebre / Alcocèber [E] 98 G3
Alcoutim [P] 94 D5
Alcover [E] 92 C4
Alcoy / Alcoi [E] 104 E1
Alcubierre [E] 90 F3
Alcublas [E] 98 E3
Alcúdia [E] 104 F4
Alcuéscar [E] 86 H6
Aldbrough [GB] 10 G4
Aldeacentenera [E] 96 B1
Aldeadávila de la Ribera [E] 80 F5
Aldea del Cano [E] 86 H6
Aldea del Fresno [E] 88 E5
Aldea del Rey [E] 96 E5
Aldealpozo [E] 90 C3
Aldeanueva de Ebro [E] 84 A5
Aldeaquemada [E] 96 F6
Aldeavieja [E] 88 E4
Aldeburgh [GB] 14 G3
Aldeia da Ponte [P] 86 G2
Aldeia do Bispo [P] 86 G2
Aldenhoven [D] 30 F4
Aldershot [GB] 14 D4
Aldinci [MK] 128 E1
Åled [S] 162 B5
Aledo [E] 104 B3
Alehovščina [RUS] 204 D1
Alekovo [BG] 148 E1
Aleksandrovac [YU] 150 C1
Aleksandrovo [BG] 148 B3
Aleksandrów Kujawski [PL] 36 F1
Aleksandrów Łódzki [PL] 36 G4
Aleksin [RUS] 204 F5
Aleksinac [YU] 150 D3
Ålem [S] 162 G4
Alemdağ [TR] 146 F2
Ålen [N] 182 C3
Alençon [F] 26 F6
Alenquer [P] 86 B4
Aléria [F] 114 C4
Alès [F] 106 F3
Áles [I] 118 C5
Aleşd [RO] 206 B4
Alessándria [I] 70 F6
Alessandria del Carretto [I] 122 D6
Alessándria della Rocca [I] 126 D3
Ålestrup [DK] 160 D4
Ålesund [N] 180 C3
Alexándreia [GR] 128 G4
Alexandria [GB] 8 D3
Alexandria [RO] 148 B1
Alexandroúpoli [GR] 130 G3
Alf [D] 44 G2
Alfafar [E] 98 E5
Alfaites [P] 86 G2
Alfajarín [E] 90 E4
Alfambra [E] 98 E1
Alfambras [P] 94 B4
Alfândenga [P] 80 F4
Alfano [I] 120 G5
Alfarela de Jales [P] 80 E4
Alfaro [E] 84 B5
Alfarràs [E] 90 H4
Alfas [E] 104 F2
Alfatar [BG] 148 E1
Alfedena [I] 116 D6
Alfeizerão [P] 86 B3
Alfeld [D] 46 H5
Alfeld [D] 32 F3
Alfena [P] 80 C4
Alfonsine [I] 110 G3
Alford [GB] 6 F6
Ålfoten [N] 180 C5
Alfreton [GB] 10 F5
Alfstad [N] 170 G5
Alfta [S] 174 D2
Algaida [E] 104 E5
Algajola [F] 114 B3
Algar [E] 100 G4
Algar [E] 104 H5
Ålgarås [S] 166 F4
Ålgård [N] 164 B3
Algarinejo [E] 102 D3
Algarra [E] 98 D3
Algeciras [E] 100 G5
Algemesí [E] 98 E5
Ålgered [S] 184 E5
Alghero [I] 118 B3
Älghult [S] 162 F4
Alginet [E] 98 E5
Algodonales [E] 100 H3
Algora [E] 90 A5
Algoso [P] 80 F4
Älgsjö [S] 190 G5
Alguazas [E] 104 C3
Algutsrum [S] 162 G5
Algyő [H] 76 E4
Alhama de Aragón [E] 90 C4
Alhama de Granada [E] 102 D4
Alhama de Murcia [E] 104 B3
Alhambra [E] 96 G5
Alhaurín de la Torre [E] 102 B5
Alhaurín el Grande [E] 102 B4
Ålhus [N] 180 C6
Alía [E] 96 C2
Ália [I] 126 D3
Aliaga [E] 98 F1
Aliağa [TR] 144 C3
Alíartos [GR] 134 A5
Alibunar [YU] 154 H2
Alicante / Alacant [E] 104 E2
Alicudi Porto [I] 124 A5
Alija del Infantado [E] 80 H3
Alijó [P] 80 E4
Alíkampos [GR] 140 C4
Alikanás [GR] 136 A2
Alimena [I] 126 E3
Alingsås [S] 162 B1
Alinyá [E] 92 D2
Aliseda [E] 86 G5
Alistráti [GR] 130 C3
Ali Terme [I] 124 B7
Alivéri [GR] 134 C5
Aljaraque [E] 94 E5
Aljezur [P] 94 B4
Aljubarrota [P] 86 C3
Aljucén [E] 86 G6
Aljustrel [P] 94 C3
Alkmaar [NL] 16 D3
Alkotz [E] 84 B3
Alkoven [A] 62 B4
Alksniupiai [LT] 202 F4
Allaines [F] 42 E5
Allainville [F] 42 E4
Allanche [F] 68 C3
Alland [A] 62 E5
Allariz [E] 78 C5
Allauch [F] 108 B5
Alleen [N] 164 C5
Álleghe [I] 72 E4
Allemont [F] 70 A5
Allensbach [D] 58 G4
Allentsteig [A] 62 D3
Allepuz [E] 98 E1
Allersberg [D] 46 G6
Allershausen [D] 60 E3
Allerum [S] 156 H1
Allevard [F] 70 A4
Allihies [IRL] 4 A5
Allingåbro [DK] 160 E5
Allinge [DK] 158 E4
Allo [E] 84 A4
Alloa [GB] 8 E3
Allonnes [F] 54 E2
Allos [F] 108 D3
Ållsjön [S] 184 E2
Allstedt [D] 34 B5
Alltnacaillich [GB] 6 D3
Almacelles [E] 90 H4
Almada [P] 86 B5
Almadén [E] 96 C4
Almadén de la Plata [E] 94 G5
Almadenojos [E] 96 D4
Almadrones [E] 90 A5
Almagro [E] 96 F4
Almandoz [E] 84 B3
Almansa [E] 98 D6
Almanza [E] 82 C4
Almargen [E] 102 B3
Almarza [E] 90 B2
Almassora / Almazora [E] 98 F3
Almazán [E] 90 B3
Almazora / Almassora [E] 98 F3
Almedina [E] 96 G5
Almeida [P] 80 E6
Almeida de Sayago [E] 80 G5
Almeirim [P] 86 C4
Almelo [NL] 16 G4
Almenar [E] 90 H4
Almenara de Tormes [E] 80 G6
Almenar de Soria [E] 90 C3
Almendra [P] 80 E5
Almendral [E] 94 G2
Almendralejo [E] 94 G2
Almenno S. Salvatore [I] 70 H4
Almere [NL] 16 E4
Almería [E] 102 G5
Almerimar [E] 102 F6
Ålmestad [S] 162 C1
Älmhult [S] 162 D5
Almirón [GR] 136 D4
Almodôvar [P] 94 C4
Almodóvar del Campo [E] 96 E4
Almodóvar del Pinar [E] 98 C3
Almodóvar del Río [E] 102 B1
Almogía [E] 102 C4
Almograve [P] 94 B3
Almoharín [E] 86 H6
Almonaster la Real [E] 94 F4
Almonte [E] 94 F6
Almoradí [E] 104 D3
Almorox [E] 88 E6
Älmsta [S] 168 E1
Älmsta-Väddö [S] 168 E1
Almudévar [E] 90 F3
Almuñécar [E] 102 D5
Almunge [S] 168 D1
Almuradiel [E] 96 F5
Almvik [S] 162 G2
Almyropótamos [GR] 134 D5
Almyrós [GR] 132 H3
Alness [GB] 6 E4
Alnmouth [GB] 8 G5
Alnwick [GB] 8 G5
Aloja [LV] 200 E4
Alol' [RUS] 200 H5
Alónnisos [GR] 134 C3
Álora [E] 102 B4
Alosno [E] 94 E5
Alost (Aalst) [B] 28 H2
Alp [E] 92 E2
Alpalhão [P] 86 E4
Alpbach [A] 60 E6
Alpedrinha [P] 86 F3
Alpen [D] 30 G2
Alpera [E] 98 C5
Alphen-aan den Rijn [NL] 16 D5
Alpirsbach [D] 58 F2
Alpua [FIN] 198 D5
Alpuente [E] 98 D3
Alpullu [TR] 146 B2
Alqueva [P] 94 E3
Alquézar [E] 90 G3
Alresford [GB] 12 H4
Als [DK] 160 E4
Alsager [GB] 10 D5
Alsasua / Altsasu [E] 82 H5
Alsenz [D] 46 B4
Alsfeld [D] 46 D1
Alsleben [D] 34 B4
Alsótold [H] 64 D5
Ålstad [N] 192 C5
Alstad [S] 158 C3
Alstahaug [N] 190 D2
Alstätte [D] 16 G5
Alstermo [S] 162 F4
Alston [GB] 8 F6
Alta [N] 192 G1
Altafulla [E] 92 C5
Altamura [I] 122 D3
Altarejos [E] 98 B2
Altaussee [A] 62 A6
Altavilla Silentina [I] 120 F4
Altdorf [CH] 58 F6
Altdorf [D] 46 G5
Altea [E] 104 F2
Altedo [I] 110 F3
Alteidet [N] 192 F1
Altena [D] 32 C5
Altenahr [D] 30 G5
Altenau [D] 32 G4
Altenberg [D] 48 E2
Altenberge [D] 16 H5
Altenburg [D] 34 C6
Altenglan [D] 44 H3
Altenhundem [D] 32 C5
Altenkirchen [D] 32 C6
Altenkirchen [D] 20 D1
Altenmarkt [A] 62 C6
Altenmarkt [D] 60 F5
Altenmarkt im Pongau [A] 72 H1
Altenstadt [D] 60 B4
Altenstadt [D] 60 D5
Altensteig [D] 58 G1
Altentreptow [D] 20 D4
Altenwalde [D] 18 D3
Alter do Chão [P] 86 E5
Altheim [A] 60 H4
Althofen [A] 74 B2
Altimir [BG] 150 G3
Altinkum [TR] 142 C2
Altınoluk [TR] 144 B1
Altınova [TR] 144 B2
Altınova [TR] 146 F3
Altıntaş [TR] 144 H2
Altınyayla [TR] 142 G2
Altipiani di Arcinazzo [I] 116 B6
Altkirch [F] 58 D4
Altlandsberg [D] 34 E2
Altmünster [A] 62 A5
Altnaharra [GB] 6 E3
Alto de los Leones de Castilla [E] 88 F4
Altomonte [I] 124 D3
Alton [GB] 10 E5
Alton [GB] 14 D4
Altopascio [I] 110 E5
Altötting [D] 60 G4
Altrincham [GB] 10 E4
Alt Ruppin [D] 20 C6
Altsasu / Alsasua [E] 82 H5
Alt Schadow [D] 34 F3
Altshausen [D] 58 H3
Altstätten [CH] 58 H5
Altuna [S] 168 C1
Altura [E] 98 E3
Altwarp [D] 20 E4
Alūksne [LV] 200 F4
Alunda [S] 168 D1
Alupka [UA] 206 G6
Alushta [UA] 206 G6
Alvaiázere [P] 86 D3
Alvajärvi [FIN] 186 F1
Alvalade [P] 94 C3
Älvängen [S] 160 H1
Alvastra [S] 166 G6
Alvdal [N] 182 B5
Älvdalen [S] 172 F2
Alverca do Ribatejo [P] 86 B5
Alversund [N] 170 B3
Alvesta [S] 162 D4
Alvignac [F] 66 G4
Ålvik [N] 170 C4
Alvito [I] 116 C6
Alvito [P] 94 D2
Älvkarleby [S] 174 E4
Alvor [P] 94 B5
Älvros [S] 182 E6
Älvros [S] 182 G5
Älvsbyn [S] 198 A3
Älvsered [S] 162 B3
Ålvundeid [N] 180 F3
Alykí [GR] 138 E3
Alykí [GR] 130 E4
Alytus [LT] 24 G2
Alzenau [D] 46 D3
Alzey [D] 46 B4
Alzira [E] 98 E5
Alzon [F] 106 E3
Alzonne [F] 106 B4
Amadora [P] 86 B5
Åmål [S] 166 D4
Amalfi [I] 120 E4
Amaliáda [GR] 136 C2
Amaliápoli [GR] 132 H3
Amálo [GR] 138 G1
Amance [F] 58 B3
Amancey [F] 58 B5
Amandola [I] 116 C2

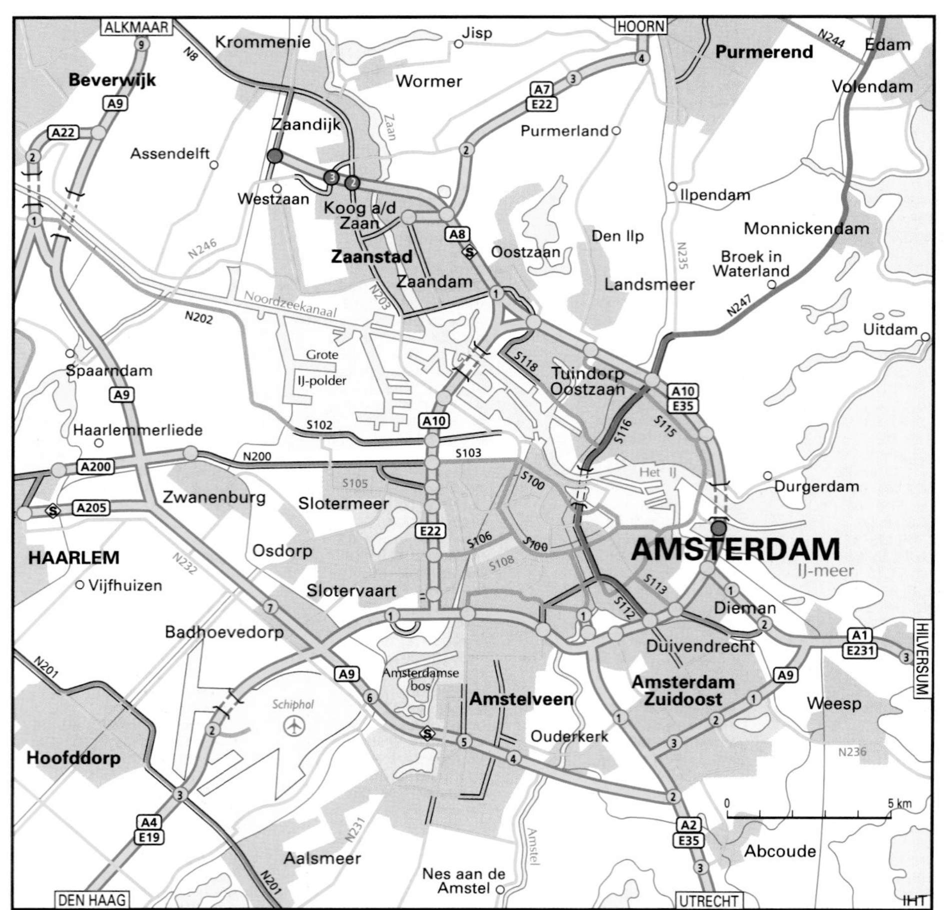

Amsterdam area map

Armémoi [GR] 140 D5
Arménio [GR] 132 G2
Armenistís [GR] 138 G1
Armentières [F] 28 F3
Armilla [E] 102 E4
Armiñon [E] 82 G5
Armólia [GR] 134 G5
Armoy [GB] 2 G2
Armuña de Tajuña [E] 88 H6
Armutlu [TR] 144 D4
Armutlu [TR] 146 E4
Armutova [TR] 144 B2
Árna [GR] 136 E4
Arna [N] 170 B4
Arnafjord [N] 170 C2
Arnage [F] 42 B5
Arnager [DK] 158 E4
Arnaía [GR] 130 C5
Arnavutköy [TR] 146 E2
Arnavutköy [TR] 146 E4
Arnay-le-Duc [F] 56 F4
Arnborg [DK] 156 B1
Arneburg [D] 34 C1
Arnedillo [E] 90 C1
Arnedo [E] 84 A5
Arnes [E] 90 G6
Årnes [N] 172 C5
Årnes [N] 190 B5
Arnhem [NL] 16 F5
Arnicle [GB] 2 H1
Árnissa [GR] 128 F4
Arnoldstein [A] 72 H3
Arnøyhamn [N] 192 F1
Arnprior [GB] 8 D2
Arnsberg [D] 32 C4
Arnschwang [D] 48 D6
Arnstadt [D] 46 G1
Arnstein [D] 46 E3
Arnuera [E] 82 F3
Aroanía [GR] 136 D1
Aroche [E] 94 F4
Ároktő [H] 64 F5
Arolla [CH] 70 D3
Arolsen [D] 32 E5
Arona [I] 70 F4
Aronkylä [FIN] 186 B4
Åros [N] 164 H1
Arosa [CH] 70 H1
Årøsund [DK] 156 C3
Arouca [P] 80 C5
Arøysund [N] 164 H3
Arpajon [F] 42 F4
Arpela [FIN] 198 C2
Arquà Petrarca [I] 110 G1
Arquata del Tronto [I] 116 C3
Arquata Scrivia [I] 110 B2
Arquillinos [E] 102 F1
Arrabal / Oia [E] 78 A5
Arracourt [F] 44 F5
Arraiolos [P] 86 D6
Arrakoski [FIN] 176 H1
Arras [F] 28 F4
Arrasate o Mondragón [E] 82 H4
Årre [DK] 156 B2
Arreau [F] 84 F4
Arrecife [E] 100 E4
Årrenjarka [S] 190 G1
Arrens-Marsous [F] 84 E4
Arrentela [P] 86 B5
Arriate [E] 102 A4
Arrifana [P] 94 B4
Arriondas [E] 82 C2
Arroba de los Montes [E] 96 D3
Arromanches-les-Bains [F] 26 F3
Arronches [P] 86 F5
Arroyo de la Luz [E] 86 G5
Arroyo de la Miel-Benalmádena Costa [E] 102 B5
Arroyo de San Serván [E] 94 G2
Arruda dos Vinhos [P] 86 B4
ÅrsandØy [N] 190 C4
Ars-en-Ré [F] 54 B4
Arsiè [I] 72 D5
Arsiero [I] 72 D5
Årslev [DK] 156 D3
Arsoli [I] 116 B5
Ars-sur-Moselle [F] 44 E4
Årsunda [S] 174 E4
Arsvågen [N] 164 A2
Arsy [F] 28 E6
Artà [E] 104 F5
Árta [GR] 132 D3
Artajona [E] 84 B4
Artana [E] 98 F3
Ártánd [H] 76 H2
Arta Terme [I] 72 G3
Arteixo [E] 78 C2
Artemare [F] 68 H3
Artemisía [GR] 136 D4
Artemísio [GR] 134 A3
Artemón [GR] 138 D3
Artenay [F] 42 E5
Artern [D] 34 A5
Artesa de Segre [E] 92 C3
Arth [CH] 58 F6
Arth [D] 60 F3
Arthog [GB] 10 B5
Arthurstown [IRL] 4 E5
Arties [E] 84 G5
Artix [F] 84 E3
Artjarvi [FIN] 178 B3
Artotína [GR] 132 F4
Artsyz [UA] 206 E5
A Rúa [E] 78 E5
Arucas [E] 100 C5
Arudy [F] 84 D3
Arundel [GB] 14 D5
Årup [DK] 156 D3
Årvåg [N] 180 G1
Arvagh [IRL] 2 E4
Árvi [GR] 140 F5
Arvidsjaur [S] 190 H3
Arvieux [F] 70 B6
Årvik [N] 180 C4
Arvika [S] 166 D2
Årviksand [N] 192 F1
Arzachena [I] 118 E2
Arzacq-Arraziguet [F] 84 E2
Aržano [HR] 152 B2
Arzberg [D] 48 C3
Arzignano [I] 72 D6
Arzl [A] 72 C1
Arzúa [E] 78 C3
As [B] 30 E4
Aš [CZ] 48 C3
Ås [N] 166 B2
Ås [N] 182 D2
Aså [DK] 160 E3
Åsa [N] 190 C5
Åsa [S] 160 H3
Aşağıinova [TR] 146 C5
Aşağıtefen [TR] 144 F3
Asäng [S] 184 E4
Ašanja [YU] 154 G2
Åsarna [S] 182 G4
Åsarum [S] 158 E1
Åsbro [S] 166 H4
Ascain [F] 84 C2
Ascea [I] 120 F5
Ascha [D] 60 G2
Aschach [A] 62 B4
Aschaffenburg [D] 46 D3
Aschau [D] 60 F5
Aschbach Markt [A] 62 C5
Ascheberg [D] 16 H6
Ascheberg [D] 18 G2
Aschendorf [D] 16 H3
Aschersleben [D] 34 B4
Asciano [I] 114 G1
Ascó [E] 90 H6
Asco [F] 114 B3
Áscoli Piceno [I] 116 C3
Ascoli Satriano [I] 120 G2
Ascona [CH] 70 F3
Åseda [S] 162 E4
Åsele [S] 190 G5
Asemanseutu [FIN] 186 D3
Åsen [N] 190 C6
Åsen [S] 172 F2
Asendorf [D] 18 E6
Asenovgrad [BG] 148 B6
Åsensbruk [S] 166 D4
Åseral [N] 164 D4
Asfáka [GR] 132 C1
Asfeld [F] 44 B2
Åsgårdstrand [N] 164 H2
Ashbourne [GB] 10 E5
Ashbourne [IRL] 2 F6
Ashburton [GB] 12 E5
Ashby-de-la-Zouch [GB] 10 E6
Åsheim [N] 182 C6
Ashford [GB] 14 F5
Ashington [GB] 8 G5
Ashmyany [BY] 202 H6
Ashton-under-Lyne [GB] 10 E4
Asiago [I] 72 D5
Asikkala [FIN] 176 H2
Asíni [GR] 136 F2
Asipovitsy [BY] 204 B6
Ask [N] 170 B3
Aska [FIN] 196 D6
Askainen [FIN] 176 D4
Askeaton [IRL] 4 C3
Askeby [DK] 156 G4
Asker [N] 164 H1
Askersund [S] 166 G4
Askífou [GR] 140 C5
Askim [N] 166 C2
Askim [S] 160 G2
Asköping [S] 168 B3
Askós [GR] 130 B4
Askvoll [N] 170 B1
Aslanapa [TR] 144 G1
Aslestad [N] 164 E2
Åsli [N] 170 G4
Åsljunga [S] 162 B6
Asmunti [FIN] 198 E2
Asnæs [DK] 156 F2
Åsnes [N] 172 D4
As Nogais [E] 78 E4
Asola [I] 110 E1
Asolo [I] 72 E5
Asopós [GR] 136 F4
Ásos [GR] 132 C5
Aspa [S] 168 C4
Aspang Markt [A] 62 E6
Asparukovo [BG] 148 F3
Aspe [E] 104 D2
Aspet [F] 84 G4
As Pontes de García Rodríguez / Puentes de Garcá Rodríguez [E] 78 D2
Aspres-sur-Buëch [F] 108 C2
Asprópirgos [GR] 134 B6
Asprόvalta [GR] 130 C4
Aspsele [S] 190 G6
Assebakte [N] 192 H2
Assemini [I] 118 C7
Assen [NL] 16 G3
Assens [DK] 156 D3
Assens [DK] 160 E5
Asserbo [DK] 156 G1
Assergi [I] 116 C4
Ássiros [GR] 128 H4
Assisi [I] 116 A2
Assling [D] 60 F5
Assmannshausen [D] 46 B3
Assopía [GR] 134 B5
Assoro [I] 126 F3
Astaffort [F] 66 E6
Astakós [GR] 132 D5
Asten [A] 62 B4
Asten [NL] 30 F3
Asti [I] 70 E6
Astorga [E] 78 G6
Åstorp [S] 156 H1
Åstrand [S] 172 E5
Ástros [GR] 136 E3
Astryna [BY] 24 G3
Astudillo [E] 82 D6
Astypálaia [GR] 138 H4
Asvyeya [BY] 200 G6
Aszód [H] 64 D6
Aszófő [H] 76 A2
Atalaia [P] 86 B5
Atalánti [GR] 132 H4
Atáli [GR] 134 C4
Atarfe [E] 102 E4
Atašiene [LV] 200 F5
Atburgazi [TR] 142 B1
Atça [TR] 144 E5
Ateca [E] 90 C4
Atella [I] 120 G3
Atessa [I] 116 E5
Ath [B] 28 G3
Athboy [IRL] 2 E5
Athea [IRL] 4 C3
Athenry [IRL] 2 C5
Athéras [GR] 132 C6
Atherstone [GB] 10 E6
Athína [GR] 134 C6
Athleague [IRL] 2 D5
Athlone / Baile Átha Luain [IRL] 2 D5
Athy [IRL] 4 F3
Atienza [E] 90 A4
Atina [I] 116 C6
Atkár [H] 64 E6
Atnbrua [N] 180 H6
Atnosen [N] 182 B6
Atostugan [S] 190 E3
A Toxa [E] 78 B4
Ätran [S] 162 B4
Åträsk [S] 190 H5
Atri [I] 116 D3
Atripalda [I] 120 F3
Atsalama [EST] 200 F1
Attel [D] 60 F4
Attendorn [D] 32 C5
Attersee [A] 60 H5
Attigny [F] 44 C2
Attleborough [GB] 14 G2
Attnang-Puchheim [A] 62 A5
Attrup [DK] 160 D3
Åtvidaberg [S] 168 B6
Atzara [I] 118 D5
Atzendorf [D] 34 B4
Atzeneta del Maestrat [E] 98 F3
Au [A] 62 D6
Au [D] 60 E3
Aubagne [F] 108 B5
Aubange [B] 44 E3
Aubenas [F] 68 E6
Auberive [F] 56 H2
Aubeterre-sur-Dronne [F] 66 E2
Aubigny [F] 54 B3
Aubigny-sur-Nere [F] 56 C2
Auboué [F] 44 E4
Aubrac [F] 68 C5
Aubusson [F] 68 B1
Auce [LV] 200 C6
Auch [F] 84 G2
Auchinleck [GB] 8 D4
Auchronie [GB] 8 F1
Auchterarder [GB] 8 E2
Auchtermuchty [GB] 8 E2
Audenge [F] 66 C3
Auderville [F] 26 D1
Audeux [F] 58 B4
Audierne [F] 40 A3
Audincourt [F] 58 C4
Audlem [GB] 10 D5
Audressein [F] 84 G5
Audruicq [F] 14 H6
Audun-le-Roman [F] 44 E3
Aue [D] 48 D2
Auer / Ora [I] 72 D4
Auerbach [D] 46 H4
Auerbach [D] 48 C2
Auffach [A] 60 F6
Augher [GB] 2 F3
Aughnacloy [GB] 2 F3
Aughrim [IRL] 4 G4
Augsburg [D] 60 D3
August [RO] 148 G1
Augusta [I] 126 G4
Augustenborg [DK] 156 C4
Augustów [PL] 24 E3
Augustusburg [D] 48 D1
Aukštadvaris [LT] 24 G1
Auktsjaur [S] 190 H3
Auletta [I] 120 G4
Aulla [I] 110 C4
Aullène [F] 114 B5
Aulnay [F] 54 D5
Ault [F] 28 C4
Aulus-les-Bains [F] 84 H5
Auma [D] 48 B2
Aumale [F] 28 D5
Aumetz [F] 44 E3
Aumont-Aubrac [F] 68 C5
Aunay-sur-Odon [F] 26 E4
Auneau [F] 42 E4
Auneuil [F] 28 D6
Auning [DK] 160 E5
Aups [F] 108 D4
Aura [FIN] 176 E4
Aurach [A] 60 F6
Aurach [D] 46 F5
Auray [F] 40 D4
Aurdal [N] 170 G3
Aure [N] 180 G1
Aurejärvi [FIN] 186 D5
Aurich [D] 18 B4
Aurignac [F] 84 G4
Aurillac [F] 68 B4
Auritz / Burguete [E] 84 C3
Aurland [N] 170 D2
Auron [F] 108 E3
Auronzo di Cadore [I] 72 F3
Aursmoen [N] 166 C1
Aursnes [N] 180 D3
Áusa Corno [I] 72 G5
Ausejo [E] 90 C1
Aussernbrünst [D] 60 H3
Austad [N] 164 D3
Austbygdi [N] 170 F5
Austertana [N] 196 D2
Austmarka [N] 172 D5
Auterive [F] 84 H4
Authon [F] 108 D3
Authon-du-Perche [F] 42 C5
Autol [E] 84 A5
Autti [FIN] 196 E8
Auttoinen [FIN] 176 H2
Autun [F] 56 F4
Auvers-s-Oise [F] 42 F3
Auvillers-les-Forges [F] 28 H5
Auxerre [F] 56 E2
Auxi-le-Château [F] 28 D4
Auxonne [F] 56 H4
Auzances [F] 56 B6
Auzon [F] 68 D3
Avå [FIN] 176 C4
Availles-Limouzine [F] 54 F5
Avaldsnes [N] 164 A2
Avallon [F] 56 E3
Ávas [GR] 130 G3
Avaträsk [S] 190 F5
Avaviken [S] 190 G3
Avcılar [TR] 146 E3
Ávdira [GR] 130 E3
Avebury [GB] 12 G3
Åvedal [N] 164 B5
A Veiga [E] 78 E6
Aveiras de Cima [P] 86 C4
Aveiro [P] 80 B5
Avelengo / Hafling [I] 72 D3
Avellino [I] 120 F3
Avenches [CH] 58 C6
Aversa [I] 120 D3
Avesnes-le-Comte [F] 28 E4
Avesnes-sur-Helpe [F] 28 G4
Avesta [S] 174 D5
Avetrana [I] 122 F4
Avezzano [I] 116 C5
Avgerinós [GR] 128 E6
Avía [GR] 136 D4
Aviano [I] 72 F5
Aviemore [GB] 6 E5
Avigliana [I] 70 D5
Avigliano [I] 120 G3
Avignon [F] 106 G3
Ávila [E] 88 E4
Avilés [E] 78 H3
Avinurme [EST] 200 F2
Avinyó [E] 92 E3
Avio [I] 72 C5
Avión [E] 78 C4
Avis [P] 86 D5
Avlákia [GR] 144 C5
Avlémonas [GR] 136 F6
Avlí [GR] 130 D3
Avliótes [GR] 132 A2
Avlóna [GR] 134 C5
Avlonári [GR] 134 C5
Avlum [DK] 160 C6
Avola [I] 126 G5
Avonmouth [GB] 12 F3
Avoriaz [F] 70 C2
Avramov [BG] 148 E4
Avranches [F] 26 D4
Avşar [TR] 142 C1
Avtovac [BIH] 152 D3
Axat [F] 106 B5
Axel [NL] 28 H1
Axioúpoli [GR] 128 G3
Ax-les-Thermes [F] 106 A6
Axminster [GB] 12 F4
Axós [GR] 140 E4
Ay [F] 44 B3
Ayagalip [TR] 130 G5
Ayamonte [E] 94 D5
Ayas [I] 70 D3
Aydın [TR] 144 D5
Aydıncık [TR] 130 G5
Ayerbe [E] 84 D6
Aykırıkçı [TR] 144 H2
Aylesbury [GB] 14 D3
Ayllón [E] 88 H3
Aylsham [GB] 14 G2
Ayna [E] 98 B6
Ayoó de Vidriales [E] 80 H3
Ayora [E] 98 D5
Ayr [GB] 8 C4
Ayrancı [TR] 144 G2
Aysgarth [GB] 10 E2
Aytos [BG] 148 F4
Ayvacık [TR] 134 H1
Ayvalık [TR] 144 B2
Azaila [E] 90 F5
Azambuja [P] 86 C4
Azanúy [E] 90 H3
Azaruja [P] 86 D6
Azay-le-Ferron [F] 54 G3
Azay-le-Rideau [F] 54 F2
Azinheira dos Barros [P] 94 C2
Azıtepe [TR] 144 E4
Aznalcóllar [E] 94 G5
Azpeitia [E] 82 H4
Azuaga [E] 96 A5
Azuara [E] 90 E5
Azuel [E] 96 D5
Azuqueca de Henares [E] 88 G5
Azyory [BY] 24 G4
Azzano Decimo [I] 72 F5

B

Baad [A] 60 B6
Baamonde [E] 78 D3
Baar [D] 60 D3
Baarle Nassau [NL] 30 D2
Baarn [NL] 16 E4
Babadag [RO] 206 E6
Babadağ [TR] 144 F5
Babaeski [TR] 146 B2
Babenhausen [D] 60 C4
Babenhausen [D] 46 D3
Babiak [PL] 36 F3
Babica [PL] 52 D4
Babice [PL] 50 G4
Băbiciu [RO] 148 A1
Babięta [PL] 24 B4
Babigoszcz [PL] 20 F4
Babimost [PL] 36 A3
Babin Potok [HR] 112 G3
Babócsa [H] 74 G5
Babriškes [LT] 24 G2
Babruysk [BY] 204 C6
Babušnica [YU] 150 E4
Babylon [CZ] 48 D5
Bač [MK] 128 E4
Bač [YU] 154 E1
Bača [SLO] 72 H4
Bacău [RO] 206 D5
Baccarat [F] 44 F6
Baceno [I] 70 F2
Bacharach [D] 46 B3
Bachkovo [BG] 148 B6
Bačina [YU] 150 C3
Backaland [GB] 6 G1
Bačka Palanka [YU] 154 F1
Bačka Topola [YU] 76 D5
Backe [S] 190 F6
Bäckebo [S] 162 F4
Bäckefors [S] 166 D4
Bäckhammar [S] 166 F3
Bački Breg [YU] 76 C5
Bački Petrovac [YU] 154 F1
Backnang [D] 46 D6
Bačko Gradište [YU] 154 G1
Bačko Novo Selo [YU] 154 E1
Bačko Petrovo Selo [YU] 76 E6
Bačkowice [PL] 52 C1
Bacoli [I] 120 D3
Bacqueville-en-Caux [F] 28 B4
Bácsalmás [H] 76 D5
Bácsbokod [H] 76 C5
Baczyna [PL] 34 H1
Bad Abbach [D] 60 F2
Badacsonytomaj [H] 74 H3
Bad Aibling [D] 60 F5
Badajoz [E] 86 F6
Badalona [E] 92 E4
Badanloch Lodge [GB] 6 E3
Bad Aussee [A] 62 A6
Bad Bentheim [D] 16 H5
Bad Bergzabern [D] 46 B5
Bad Berka [D] 46 H1
Bad Berleburg [D] 32 D5
Bad Berneck [D] 46 H3
Bad Bertrich [D] 44 G1
Bad Bevensen [D] 18 G5
Bad Bibra [D] 34 B5
Bad Blankenburg [D] 46 H2
Bad Brambach [D] 48 C3
Bad Bramstedt [D] 18 F3
Bad Breisig [D] 30 H5
Bad Brückenau [D] 46 E2
Bad Buchau [D] 60 A4
Bad Deutsch-Altenburg [A] 62 G5
Bad Doberan [D] 20 B3
Bad Driburg [D] 32 E4
Bad Düben [D] 34 D4
Bad Dürkheim [D] 46 B4
Bad Dürrenberg [D] 34 C5
Bad Dürrheim [D] 58 F3
Bad Elster [D] 48 C3
Bademli [TR] 144 C3
Bad Ems [D] 46 B2
Baden [A] 62 F5
Baden [CH] 58 F4
Baden-Baden [D] 58 F1
Bad Endorf [D] 60 F5
Badenweiler [D] 58 E3
Baderna [HR] 112 D2
Bad Essen [D] 32 D2
Bad Frankenhausen [D] 34 A5
Bad Freienwalde [D] 34 F1

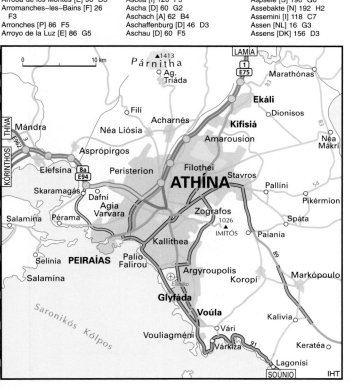

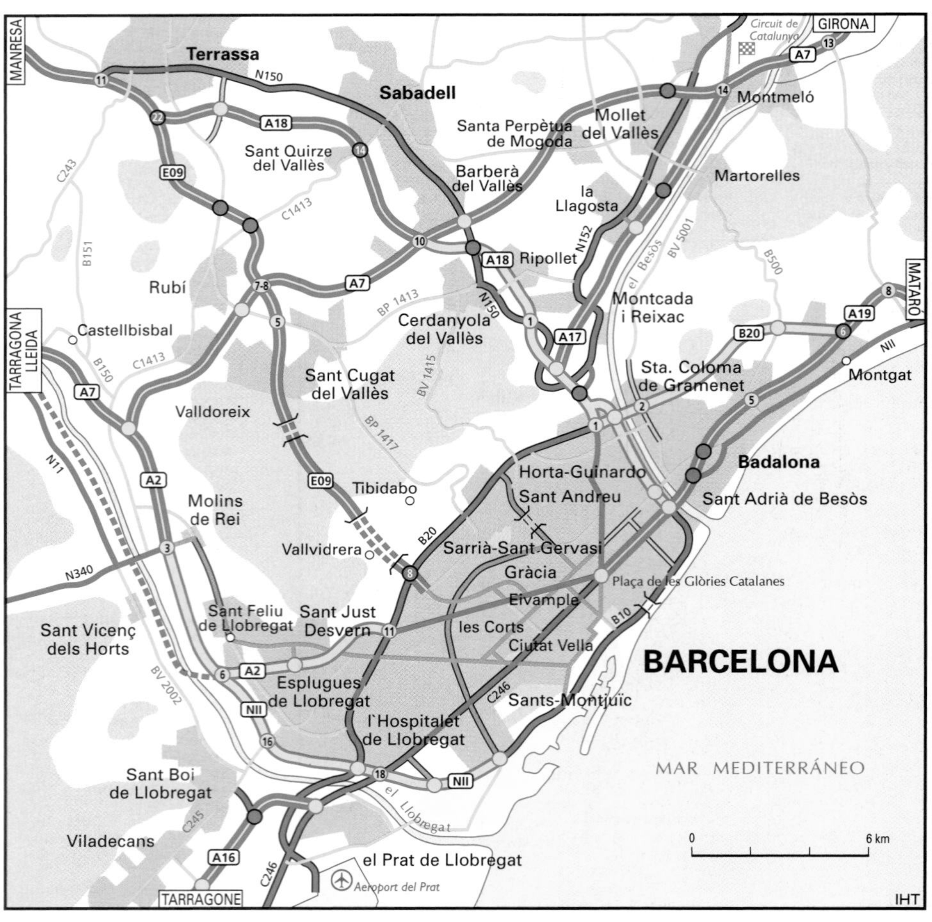

MANRESA
Circuit de Catalunya
GIRONA
Terrassa
N150
Sabadell
A7
Montmeló
A18
Santa Perpètua de Mogoda
Mollet del Vallès
Sant Quirze del Vallès
C243
E09
Barberà del Vallès
Martorelles
la Llagosta
C1413
N152
B151
A18
Ripollet
el Besòs
BV 5001
B500
Rubí
A7
BP 1413
N150
Montcada i Reixac
MATARÓ
A19
TARRAGONA LLEIDA
Castellbisbal
Cerdanyola del Vallès
B20
A17
C1413
B150
Sant Cugat del Vallès
BV 1415
Sta. Coloma de Gramenet
NII
Montgat
A7
Valldoreix
BP 1417
N11
A2
E09
Tibidabo
Horta-Guinardó
Badalona
Molins de Rei
Sant Andreu
Sant Adrià de Besòs
B20
Vallvidrera
Sarrià-Sant Gervasi
N340
Gràcia
Plaça de les Glòries Catalanes
Eixample
Sant Feliu de Llobregat
Sant Just Desvern
B10
Sant Vicenç dels Horts
les Corts
Ciutat Vella
BARCELONA
A2
BV 2002
Esplugues de Llobregat
C246
Sants-Montjuïc
NII
l'Hospitalet de Llobregat
Sant Boi de Llobregat
NII
MAR MEDITERRÁNEO
el Llobregat
C245
0
6 km
Viladecans
A16
el Prat de Llobregat
C246
Aeroport del Prat
TARRAGONE
IHT

NOVI SAD
TIMIŞOARA
ZAGREB
PODGORICA
SOFIYA
BEOGRAD
Zemun
Pančevo
Kačarevo
Jabuka
Nova Pazova
Batajnica
Krnjača
Vojlovica
Dobanovci
Beograd
Surčin
M Mokri Lug
Omoljica
Kneževac
Železnik
Umka
Vrčin
Grocka
Obrenovac
Ripanj
Dunav
Tamiš
Sava
0
10 km
IHT

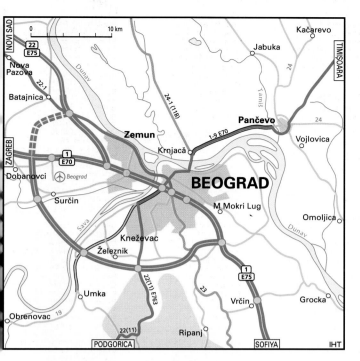

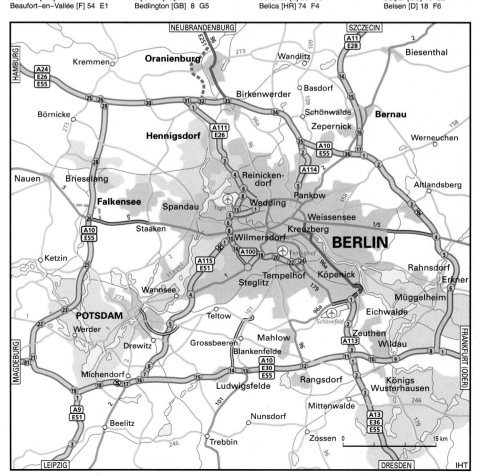

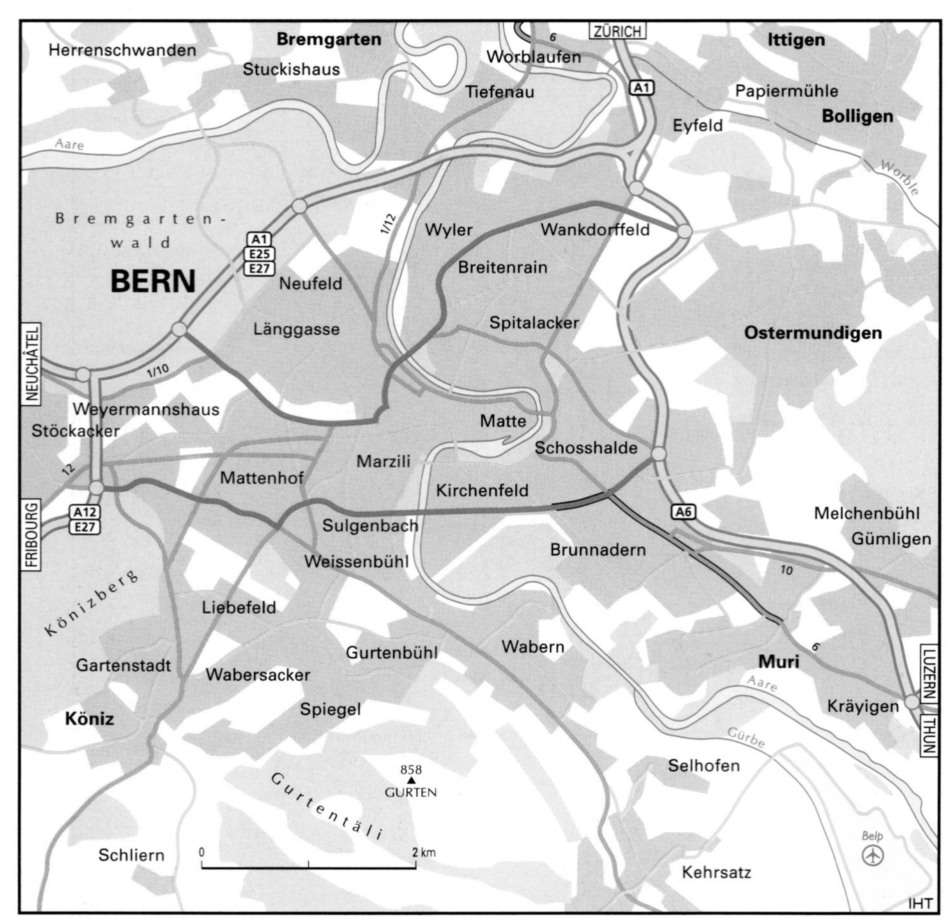
Herrenschwanden
Bremgarten
Stuckishaus
ZÜRICH
Worblaufen
Ittigen
Tiefenau
A1
Papiermühle
Bolligen
Eyfeld
Aare
Worble
Bremgarten-wald
A1
E25
E27
1/12
Wyler
Wankdorffeld
Breitenrain
BERN
Neufeld
Länggasse
Spitalacker
Ostermundigen
NEUCHÂTEL
1/10
Weyermannshaus
Stöckacker
Matte
Schosshalde
12
Marzili
Mattenhof
Kirchenfeld
FRIBOURG
A12
E27
Sulgenbach
A6
Melchenbühl
Gümligen
Brunnadern
Weissenbühl
10
Könizberg
Liebefeld
Gurtenbühl
Wabern
6
Muri
Gartenstadt
Wabersacker
Aare
Kräyigen
LUZERN
THUN
Köniz
Spiegel
Gürbe
858
GURTEN
Selhofen
Gurtentäli
Belp
Schliern
0
2 km
Kehrsatz
IHT

Blaenau Ffestiniog [GB] 10 B4
Blaenavon [GB] 12 F2
Blagaj [BIH] 152 C2
Blagoevgrad [BG] 150 F6
Blagoevo [BG] 148 D2
Blåhøj [DK] 156 B1
Blaiken [S] 190 F4
Blaikliden [S] 190 F4
Blain [F] 40 F5
Blair Atholl [GB] 8 E1
Blairgowrie [GB] 8 E2
Blaj [RO] 206 B5
Blakeney [GB] 14 G1
Blakeney [GB] 12 G2
Blakstad [N] 164 E5
Blâmont [F] 44 F6
Blanca [E] 104 C2
Blandford Forum [GB] 12 G4
Blanes [E] 92 F4
Blangy–sur–Bresle [F] 28 D4
Blankaholm [S] 162 G2
Blankenberge [B] 28 G1
Blankenburg [D] 32 H4
Blankenfelde [D] 34 E2
Blankenhain [D] 46 H1
Blankenheim [D] 30 G6
Blanquefort [F] 66 C3
Blansko [CZ] 50 C6
Blanzac [F] 66 E2
Blarney [IRL] 4 C5
Blascosancho [E] 88 E4
Błaszki [PL] 36 F5
Blatná [CZ] 48 E5
Blatnica [BIH] 154 C3
Blatnice [CZ] 62 H2
Blato [HR] 152 A2
Blato [HR] 152 A3
Blattniksele [S] 190 G3
Blaubeuren [D] 60 B3
Blaufelden [D] 46 E5
Blaustein [D] 60 B3
Blåvand [DK] 156 A2
Blåvik [S] 162 E1
Blaye [F] 66 C2
Blazquez [E] 96 B5
Bleckede [D] 18 G5
Bled [SLO] 74 B4
Bleiburg [A] 74 C3
Bleicherode [D] 32 G5
Bleik [N] 192 C3
Blendija [YU] 150 D3
Bléneau [F] 56 D2
Blera [I] 114 H4
Blérancourt [F] 28 F6
Bléré [F] 54 G2
Blériot–Plage [F] 14 G6
Blesle [F] 68 C3
Blessington [IRL] 2 F6
Bletchley [GB] 14 E3
Bletterans [F] 56 H5
Blexen [D] 18 D4
Blieskastel [D] 44 G4
Bligny–sur–Ouche [F] 56 G4
Blikstorp [S] 166 F6
Blinisht [AL] 128 B1
Blinja [HR] 154 A1
Bliznak [BG] 148 F3
Blizne [PL] 52 E4
Błogoszów [PL] 52 A2
Blois [F] 54 H1
Blokhus [DK] 160 D3
Blokzijl [NL] 16 F3
Blombacka [S] 166 F2
Blomberg [D] 32 E3
Blomstermåla [S] 162 G4
Blönduós [IS] 194 D3
Błonie [PL] 36 C6
Błonie [PL] 38 B3
Błonie [PL] 38 F3
Błoška Polica [SLO] 74 B6
Błotno [PL] 20 F4
Blovice [CZ] 48 E5
Bludenz [A] 72 A1
Blumberg [D] 58 F3
Blyth [GB] 8 G5
Bø [N] 164 F2
Bo [S] 166 H4
Boadilla del Monte [E] 88 F5
Boal [E] 78 F2
Boário Terme [I] 72 B5
Bobbio [I] 110 C2
Bobbio Pellice [I] 70 C6
Bobingen [D] 60 D4
Bobitz [D] 20 A4
Böblingen [D] 58 G1
Bobolice [PL] 22 B3
Boboshevo [BG] 150 F6
Bobovdol [BG] 150 F5
Bobrovytsia [UA] 206 F1
Bobrowice [PL] 34 H4
Bobrowniki [PL] 24 F5
Bobrowniki [PL] 36 F1
Boca de Huergano [E] 82 C3
Bocairent [E] 104 E1
Boceguillas [E] 88 G3
Boçen [TR] 146 F5
Bochnia [PL] 52 B4
Bocholt [D] 16 G6
Bochov [CZ] 48 D3
Bochum [D] 30 H3
Bockel [D] 18 E5
Bockenem [D] 32 G3
Bočki [PL] 38 E1
Böcksholm [S] 162 E4
Böckstein [A] 72 G2
Bockum–Hovel [D] 32 C3
Bocognano [F] 114 B4
Bócsa [H] 76 D3
Bocsig [RO] 76 H4
Böda [S] 162 H3
Boda [S] 172 H3
Boda [S] 166 E2
Bodaanowice [PL] 50 F1
Bodaczów [PL] 52 F1
Bodafors [S] 162 D3
Boda glasbruk [S] 162 F5
Bodegraven [NL] 16 D5
Boden [S] 198 B3
Bodenmais [D] 48 D6
Bodenteich [D] 18 G6
Bodenwerder [D] 32 F3
Bodenwöhr [D] 48 C6
Bodjani [YU] 154 E1
Bodman [D] 58 G4
Bodmin [GB] 12 C4
Bodø [N] 192 B6
Bodom [N] 190 C5
Bodrogkeresztúr [H] 64 G4
Bodrum [TR] 142 C2
Bodsjö [S] 182 H3
Bodträskfors [S] 198 A2
Bodzanów [PL] 36 H2
Bodzentyn [PL] 52 C1
Boëge [F] 70 B2
Boën [F] 68 E2
Bogarra [E] 98 A6
Bogatic [YU] 154 F2
Bogatynia [PL] 48 G1
Boğaziçi [TR] 144 D5
Boğazköy [TR] 146 F4
Bogda [RO] 76 H5
Bogdaniec [PL] 34 H2
Bogen [D] 60 G2
Bogen [N] 192 D4
Bogen [N] 192 C5
Bogen [S] 172 D6
Bogense [DK] 156 D2
Bogetiči [YU] 152 E4
Bognanco [I] 70 E3
Bognelv [N] 192 F1
Bognes [N] 192 C4
Bognor Regis [GB] 14 D5
Bogojevo [YU] 154 E1
Bogorodica [MK] 128 G3
Bogoroditsk [RUS] 204 F5
Bogovina [YU] 150 D2
Bogøy [N] 192 C5
Bograngen [S] 172 E4
Bogumiłowice [PL] 36 G6
Boguszow–Gorce [PL] 50 B2
Bohain–en–Vermandois [F] 28 F5
Bohdalov [CZ] 50 A5
Boheeshil [IRL] 4 B4
Bohinjska Bistrica [SLO] 74 A4
Böhmenkirch [D] 60 B2
Bohmte [D] 32 D2
Bohodukhiv [UA] 206 G2
Bohonal [E] 96 C2
Bohonal de Ibor [E] 88 B6
Böhönye [H] 74 H4
Boialvo [P] 80 B6
Boichinovtsi [BG] 150 F3
Bois–du–Four [F] 68 B6
Boitzenburg [D] 20 D5
Bóixols [E] 92 C2
Boizenburg [D] 18 G5
Bojano [I] 120 E1
Bojanów [PL] 52 D2
Bojanowo [PL] 36 C4
Bøjden [DK] 156 D4
Bojnica [BG] 150 E2
Bojnik [YU] 150 D4
Bökemåla [S] 162 E6
Bol [HR] 152 A2
Bolaños de Calatrava [E] 96 F4
Bolayır [TR] 146 B4
Bolbec [F] 26 H3
Bolca [I] 72 C6
Boldva [H] 64 F4
Bolekhiv [UA] 52 H6
Bolemin [PL] 34 H2
Bolesławiec [PL] 36 A6
Bolesławiec [PL] 36 E6
Bolesławów [PL] 50 C3
Boleszkowice [PL] 34 G2
Bolfiar [P] 80 B5
Bolgheri [I] 114 E1
Bolhrad [UA] 206 D5
Boliden [S] 198 A4
Bolinglanna [IRL] 2 B3
Boljaniči [YU] 152 E2
Boljevac [YU] 150 D2
BolkesjØ [N] 164 G1
Bolkhov [RUS] 204 E5
Bolków [PL] 50 B1
Bollebygd [S] 162 B2
Bollène [F] 106 G2
Bollnäs [S] 174 D2
Bollstabruk [S] 184 F3
Bollullos Par del Condado [E] 94 F6
Bologna [I] 110 F3
Bologne [F] 44 C6
Bolótana [I] 118 C4
Bolotovo [RUS] 200 H4
Bolsena [I] 114 H3
Bol'shakovo [RUS] 202 D5
Bol'shoy Sabsk [RUS] 200 G1
Bolstad [S] 166 D5
Bolsward [NL] 16 E2
Bolszewo [PL] 22 D2
Boltaña [E] 84 E5
Boltenhagen [D] 18 H3
Boltigen [CH] 70 D1
Bolton [GB] 10 E4
Bolungarvík [IS] 194 C1
Bóly [H] 76 B5
Bolyarovo [BG] 148 E5
Bolzano / Bozen [I] 72 D3
Bomarsund [FIN] 176 B5
Bomarzo [I] 114 H4
Bombarral [P] 86 B4
Bominago [I] 116 C4
Bomsund [S] 184 C2
Bonaduz [CH] 70 H1
Boñar [E] 82 C3
Bonar Bridge [GB] 6 E4
Bonares [E] 94 F6
Bonäs [S] 166 E2
Bonassola [I] 110 C4
Bonchester Bridge [GB] 8 F5
Bondal [N] 164 F1
Bondemon [S] 166 C4
Bondeno [I] 110 F2
Bondstorp [S] 162 C2
Bonefro [I] 116 F6
Bonete [E] 98 C6
Bonhomme, Col du– [F] 58 D2
Bonifacio [F] 114 B6
Bonlieu [F] 70 A1
Bonn [D] 30 G5
BonnåsjØen [N] 192 C5
Bonnat [F] 54 H5
Bonndorf [D] 58 F4
Bønnerup Strand [DK] 160 F5
Bonnétable [F] 42 C5
Bonneval [F] 42 D5
Bonneval–sur–Arc [F] 70 C4
Bonneville [F] 70 B2
Bonnières [F] 42 E3
Bonnieux [F] 106 H4
Bonnigheim [D] 46 D6
Bonnyrigg [GB] 8 E3
Bonny–sur–Loire [F] 56 D2
Bono [I] 118 D4
Bonorva [I] 118 C4
Bonyhád [H] 76 B4
Boom [B] 30 C3
Boos [F] 28 C5
Boot [GB] 10 D2
Booth of Toft [GB] 6 H3
Bootle [GB] 10 D4
Bootle [GB] 10 D2
Booutovačka Banja [YU] 150 B3
Bopfingen [D] 60 C2
Boppard [D] 44 H1
Bor [CZ] 48 D4
Bor [YU] 150 D2
Borås [N] 164 F4
Borås [S] 162 B2
Borba [P] 86 E6
Borbona [I] 116 B4
Borchen [D] 32 E4
Borci [BIH] 152 C2
Borculo [NL] 16 G5
Bordány [H] 76 E4
Bordeaux [F] 66 C3
Bordeira [P] 94 A4
Bordères [F] 84 F4
Bordesholm [D] 18 F2
Borðeyri [IS] 194 C3
Bordighera [I] 108 F4
Bording [DK] 160 C6
Borek Wielkopolski [PL] 36 D4
Boreland [GB] 8 E5
Borensberg [S] 166 H5
Borgå / Porvoo [FIN] 178 B4
Borgafjäll [S] 190 E4
Borgarfjörður [IS] 194 G5
Borgarnes [IS] 194 B4
Borgen [N] 164 E3
Borgentreich [D] 32 E4
Börger [D] 18 B5
Borger [NL] 16 G3
Borggård [S] 166 H5
Borghamn [S] 166 G6
Borgholm [S] 162 G4
Borgholzhausen [D] 32 D2
Borghorst [D] 16 H5
Borgoforte [I] 110 E2
Borgomanero [I] 70 F4
Borgonovo Val Tidone [I] 70 G6
Borgorose [I] 116 B5
Borgo San Dalmazzo [I] 108 F3
Borgo San Lorenzo [I] 110 F5
Borgosésia [I] 70 E4
Borgo Ticino [I] 70 F4
Borgo Tossignano [I] 110 F4
Borgo Val di Taro [I] 110 C3
Borgo Valsugana [I] 72 D4
Borgo Vercelli [I] 70 F5
Borgsjö [S] 184 D4
Borgund [N] 170 E2
Borgvik [S] 166 E3
Borima [BG] 148 B4
Borja [E] 90 D3
Börjelslandet [S] 198 B3
Borken [D] 32 E6
Borken [D] 16 G6
Borkenes [N] 192 C3
Børkop [DK] 156 C2
Borkum [D] 16 G1
Borlänge [S] 172 H4
Borlaug [N] 170 E2
Borlu [TR] 144 E3
Bormes–les–Mimosas [F] 108 D6
Bórmio [I] 72 B3
Borna [D] 34 C6
Bornhöved [D] 18 G3
Börnicke [D] 34 D1
Bornos [E] 100 G3
Bornova [TR] 144 C4
Borodianka [UA] 206 E2
Borodinskoye [RUS] 178 F2
Borovan [BG] 150 G3
Borovany [CZ] 62 C2
Borovets [BG] 150 G5
Borovichi [RUS] 200 H3
Borovichi [RUS] 204 D2
Borovik [RUS] 200 G3
Borovo [HR] 154 E1
Borovtsi [BG] 150 F3
Borowa [PL] 36 D6
Borrby [S] 158 D3
Borre [DK] 156 G4
Borre [N] 164 H2
Borredà [E] 92 E2
Borriana / Burriana [E] 98 F3
Börringe [S] 158 C3
Borriol [E] 98 F3
Borris [IRL] 4 F4
Borris–in–Ossory [IRL] 2 D6
Borrisokane [IRL] 2 D6
Borrisoleigh [IRL] 4 E3
Borrum [S] 168 C6
Borş [RO] 76 H2
Børsa [N] 182 B1
Borşa [RO] 206 C4
Børselv [N] 196 C2
Borsfa [H] 74 F4
Borsh [AL] 132 B1
Bórsio [GR] 136 C1
Borsodnádasd [H] 64 E4
Börstil [S] 174 G5
Borth [GB] 10 B5
Bort–les–Orgues [F] 68 B3
Börtnan [S] 182 F3
Borup [DK] 156 G3
Borynia [UA] 52 F6
Boryslav [UA] 52 G5
Boryspil' [UA] 206 F2
Borzechowo [PL] 22 D4
Bosa [I] 118 B4
Bosanci [HR] 112 G1
Bosanska Dubica [BIH] 154 B2
Bosanska Gradiška [BIH] 154 C2
Bosanska Krupa [BIH] 154 A2
Bosanska Rača [BIH] 154 F2
Bosanski Brod [BIH] 154 D2
Bosanski Novi [HR] 154 A2
Bosanski Petrovac [BIH] 154 A3
Bosanski Šamac [BIH] 154 D2
Bosansko Grahovo [BIH] 154 A4
Bošany [SK] 64 B3
Bősárkány [H] 62 G6
Boscastle [GB] 12 D4
Bosco Chiesanuova [I] 72 C5
Bösel [D] 18 C5
Bosilegrad [YU] 150 E5
Bosjön [S] 166 F1
Boskoop [NL] 16 D5
Boskovice [CZ] 50 C5
Bosna [HR] 74 F5
Bošnjace [YU] 150 D4
Bošnjaci [HR] 154 E2
Bosruck Tunnel [A] 62 B6
Bossbøen [N] 164 E1
Bossea [I] 108 G3
Bossòst [E] 84 F5
Bostan [BIH] 152 B2
Böste [S] 158 C3
Boston [GB] 10 G6
Bostrak [N] 164 F3
Bosut [YU] 154 F2
Bőszénfa [H] 76 A4
Botevgrad [BG] 150 G4
Bothel [GB] 8 D6
Bothwell [GB] 8 D3
Boticas [P] 80 E3
Botinec [HR] 74 E6
Botngård [N] 190 B6
Bótoa [E] 86 F6
Botoroaga [RO] 148 C1
Botoşani [RO] 206 D4
Botricello [I] 124 E5
Botsmark [S] 198 A5
Bottidda [I] 118 D4
Bottnaryd [S] 162 C2
Bottrop [D] 30 G3
Botun [MK] 128 D3
Botunets [BG] 150 G4
Bouaye [F] 54 B1
Boudry [CH] 58 C6
Bouesse [F] 54 H4
Bouguenais [F] 54 B1
Bouillon [B] 44 D2
Bouilly [F] 44 A6
Boulay–Moselle [F] 44 F4
Bouligny [F] 44 E3
Boulogne [F] 14 G6
Boulogne–sur–Gesse [F] 84 G3
Bouloire [F] 42 C5
Bouniagues [F] 66 E4
Bourbon–Lancy [F] 56 E5
Bourbon–l'Archambault [F] 56 D5
Bourbonne–les–Bains [F] 58 B2
Bourbourg [F] 14 H6
Bourbriac [F] 40 D2
Bourdeaux [F] 68 F6
Bourg [F] 66 D3
Bourg–Achard [F] 26 H3
Bourganeuf [F] 54 H6
Bourg–Argental [F] 68 F4
Bourg–de–Péage [F] 68 F5
Bourg–en–Bresse [F] 68 G2
Bourges [F] 56 C3
Bourg–et–Comin [F] 44 A2
Bourg–Lastic [F] 68 B2
Bourg–Madame [F] 92 E1
Bourgneuf–en–Retz [F] 54 B2
Bourgogne [F] 44 B3
Bourgoin–Jallieu [F] 68 G3
Bourg–St–Andéol [F] 106 G2
Bourg–St–Maurice [F] 70 C4
Bourgtheroulde–Infreville [F] 26 H4
Bourgueil [F] 54 E2
Bourmont [F] 58 B2
Bourne [GB] 10 G6
Bournemouth [GB] 12 G5
Bourneville [F] 26 H3
Bournezeau [F] 54 C3
Bourton–on–the–Water [GB] 12 H2
Boussac [F] 56 B5
Boussens [F] 84 G4
Bouvignes [B] 30 D5
Bouvron [F] 40 F6
Bouxwiller [F] 44 G5
Bouzonville [F] 44 F3
Bova [I] 124 C8
Bovalino [I] 124 D7
Bovallstrand [S] 166 C5
Bova Marina [I] 124 C8
Bovan [YU] 150 D3
Bovec [SLO] 72 H4
Bóveda [E] 78 D4
Bovense [DK] 156 E3
Bøverbru [N] 172 B4
Bøverdal [N] 180 F6
Boves [I] 108 F3
Bovey Tracey [GB] 12 E4
Bović [HR] 112 H1
Bovington Camp [GB] 12 G5
Bovino [I] 120 G2
Bovolenta [I] 110 G1
Bovolone [I] 110 F1
Bovrup [DK] 156 C4
Bowmore [GB] 2 H1
Boxberg [D] 46 E5
Boxholm [S] 166 G6
Boxmeer [NL] 16 F6
Boxtel [NL] 30 E2
Boyalı [TR] 144 E3
Boyalıca [TR] 146 F4
Boyalık [TR] 146 E2
Boyle [IRL] 2 D4
Bøylefoss [N] 164 F4
Božaj [YU] 152 E4
Božava [HR] 112 F5
Bozburun [TR] 142 D3
Bozdoğan [TR] 144 E5
Bozel [F] 70 B4
Bozen / Bolzano [I] 72 D3
Bozhenci [BG] 148 C4
Bozhurishte [BG] 150 F4
Božica [YU] 150 E5
Bozkuş [TR] 144 G3
Bozouls [F] 68 B5
Bozüyük [TR] 146 G5
Bozveliisko [BG] 148 F3
Bozyaka [TR] 142 G2
Bózzolo [I] 110 E1
Bra [I] 108 G2
Braås [S] 162 E4
Brabova [RO] 150 F1
Bracadale [GB] 6 B4
Bracciano [I] 114 H5
Bracieux [F] 54 H2
Bracigovo [BG] 148 A6
Bräcke [S] 182 H3
Brackenheim [D] 46 C6
Brackley [GB] 14 D3
Bracknell [GB] 14 D4
Brackwede [D] 32 D3
Braco [GB] 8 E2
Brad [RO] 206 B5
Bradford [GB] 10 E3
Bradford–on–Avon [GB] 12 G3
Bradina [BIH] 152 C1
Bradwell–on–Sea [GB] 14 F4
Brae [GB] 6 G3
Brædstrup [DK] 156 C1
Braemar [GB] 6 E6
Braemore [GB] 6 D4
Braemore [GB] 6 F3
Brae Roy Lodge [GB] 6 D6
Braeswick [GB] 6 G1
Braga [P] 80 C3
Bragança [P] 80 F3
Brăila [RO] 206 D6
Braine [F] 44 A2
Braine–le–Comte [B] 28 H3
Braintree [GB] 14 F3
Brake [D] 18 D4
Brakel [B] 28 G3
Brakel [D] 32 E4
Bräkne–Hoby [S] 158 F1
Brålanda [S] 166 D5
Brálos [GR] 132 G4
Bram [F] 106 B4
Brämhult [S] 162 B2
Bramming [DK] 156 B2
Brampton [GB] 8 E5
Bramsche [D] 32 D2
Branč [SK] 64 A4
Branca [I] 116 B1
Brancaleone Marina [I] 124 D8
Brancaster [GB] 10 H6
Brancion [F] 56 G6
Brand [A] 72 A1

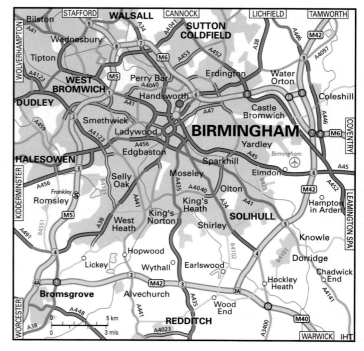

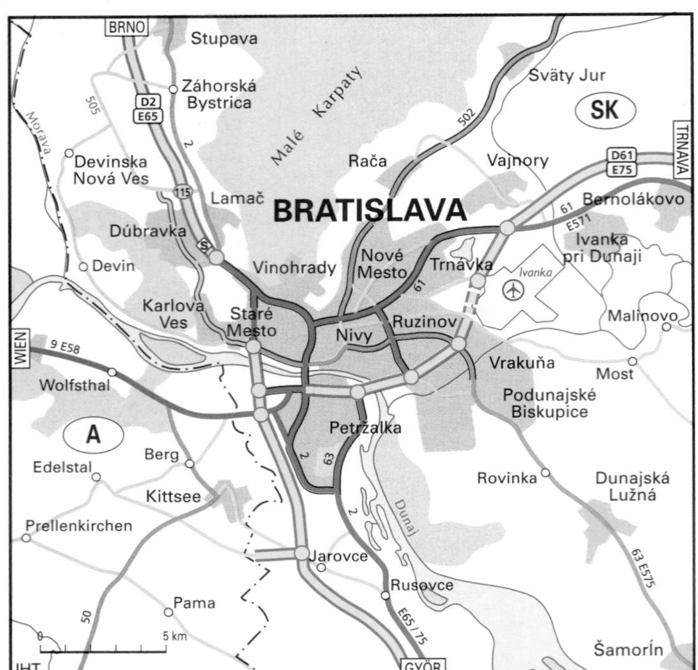
BRNO
Stupava
Záhorská Bystrica
Svätý Jur
SK
Malé Karpaty
Devinska Nová Ves
Rača
Vajnory
TRNAVA
Lamač
BRATISLAVA
Bernolákovo
Dúbravka
Ivanka pri Dunaji
Devin
Vinohrady
Nové Mesto
Trnávka
Ivanka
Karlova Ves
Staré Mesto
Ruzinov
Malinovo
WIEN
Nivy
Wolfsthal
Vrakuňa
Most
Podunajské Biskupice
A
Petržalka
Berg
Edelstal
Kittsee
Rovinka
Dunajská Lužná
Prellenkirchen
Dunaj
Jarovce
Rusovce
Pama
5 km
Šamorín
IHT
GYÖR

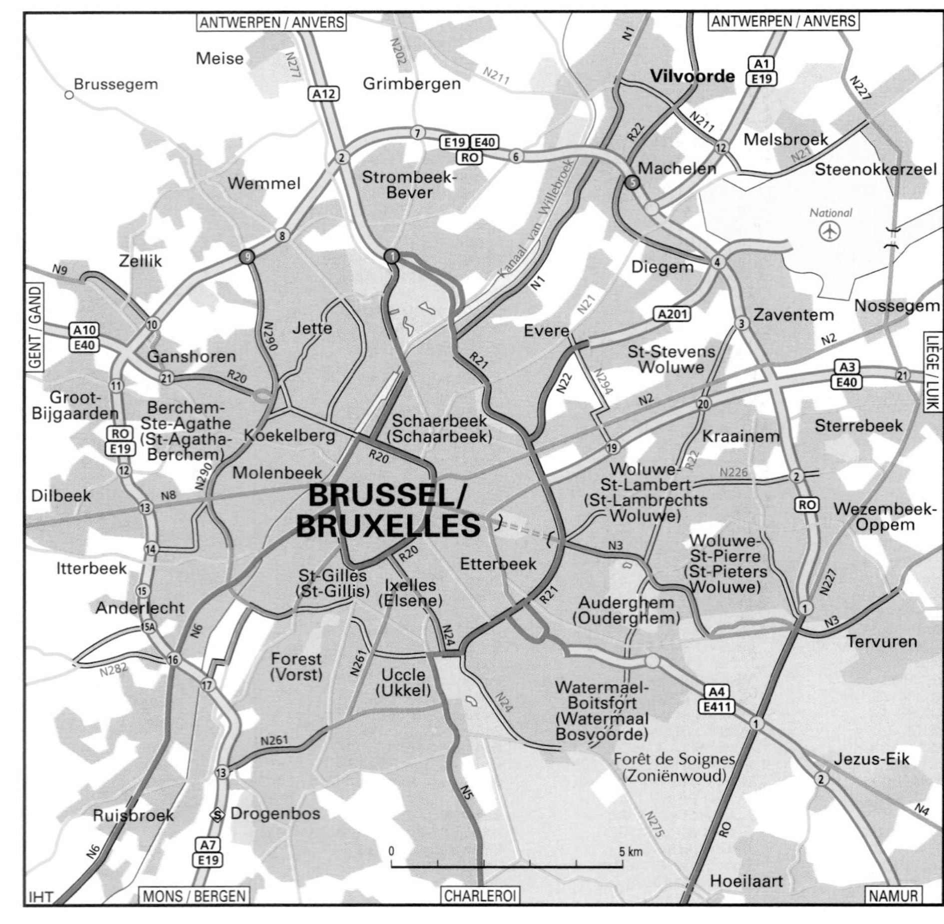
ANTWERPEN / ANVERS
Meise
Grimbergen
Vilvoorde
Brussegem
Melsbroek
Wemmel
Strombeek-Bever
Machelen
Steenokkerzeel
National
Zellik
Diegem
GENT / GAND
Jette
Evere
Zaventem
Nossegem
Ganshoren
St-Stevens Woluwe
LIÈGE / LUIK
Groot-Bijgaarden
Berchem-Ste-Agathe (St-Agatha-Berchem)
Koekelberg
Schaerbeek (Schaarbeek)
Kraainem
Sterrebeek
Molenbeek
Woluwe-St-Lambert (St-Lambrechts Woluwe)
Dilbeek
BRUSSEL/ BRUXELLES
Wezembeek-Oppem
Itterbeek
Etterbeek
Woluwe-St-Pierre (St-Pieters Woluwe)
St-Gilles (St-Gillis)
Ixelles (Elsene)
Anderlecht
Auderghem (Oudergem)
Tervuren
Forest (Vorst)
Uccle (Ukkel)
Watermael-Boitsfort (Watermaal Bosvoorde)
Forêt de Soignes (Zoniënwoud)
Jezus-Eik
Ruisbroek
Drogenbos
5 km
Hoeilaart
IHT
MONS / BERGEN
CHARLEROI
NAMUR

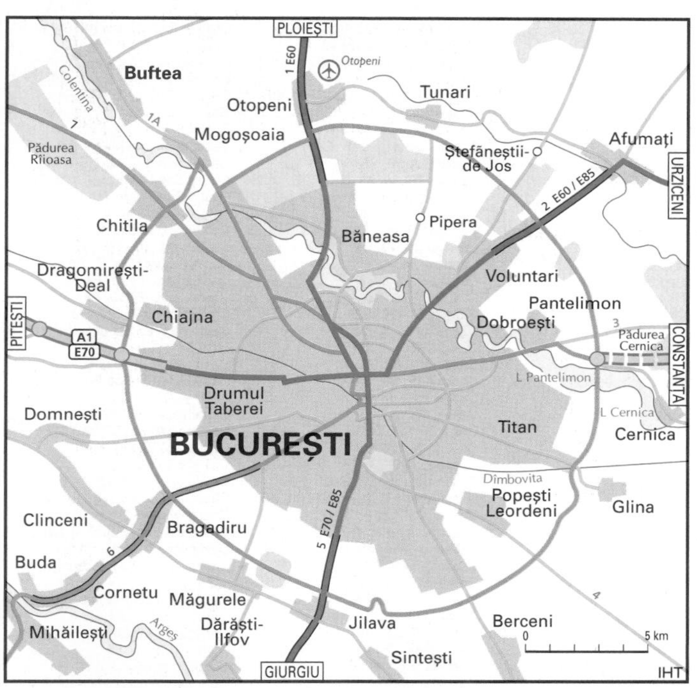

Buftea · PLOIEŞTI · Otopeni · Tunari · Mogoşoaia · Ştefăneştii-de Jos · Afumaţi · Chitila · Băneasa · Pipera · Dragomireşti-Deal · Voluntari · Chiajna · Pantelimon · Dobroeşti · Pădurea Cernica · CONSTANŢA · Drumul Taberei · **BUCUREŞTI** · Titan · Cernica · L. Pantelimon · L. Cernica · Domneşti · Popeşti Leordeni · Glina · Clinceni · Bragadiru · Buda · Corneţu · Măgurele · Dărăşti-Ilfov · Jilava · Berceni · Mihăileşti · Sinteşti · GIURGIU · IHT

Buçaco [P] 80 B6	Buk [PL] 36 C3	Burgsinn [D] 46 E3	Burry Port [GB] 12 E2
Bučany [SK] 62 H4	Buk [PL] 20 E5	Burg Stargard [D] 20 D5	Burs [S] 168 G5
Buccheri [I] 126 F4	Bukka [GR] 132 D4	Burgsvik [S] 168 G6	Bursa [TR] 146 F4
Bucchianico [I] 116 D4	Bükkösd [H] 76 A5	Burguete / Auritz [E] 84 C3	Burseryd [S] 162 B3
Buchach [UA] 206 C3	Bukovi [YU] 150 A2	Burguillos [E] 94 G5	Bürstadt [D] 46 C4
Buchen [D] 46 D4	Bukowiec [PL] 36 B3	Burguillos del Cerro [E] 94 G3	Burton Agnes [GB] 10 G3
Buchen [D] 18 E4	Bukowina Tatrzańska [PL] 52 B6	Burg Vetschau [D] 34 F4	Burton-upon-Stather [GB] 10 G4
Buchenwald [D] 34 A6	Bukowo Morskie [PL] 22 A2	Burhaniye [TR] 144 C2	Burton upon Trent [GB] 10 E6
Buchholz [D] 18 F5	Bukowsko [PL] 52 E5	Burie [F] 54 D6	Burträsk [S] 198 A5
Buchin Prohod [BG] 150 F4	Bülach [CH] 58 F4	Burila Mare [RO] 150 E1	Burwell [GB] 14 F2
Buchloe [D] 60 C4	Buldan [TR] 144 F4	Burjassot [E] 98 E4	Burwick [GB] 6 F2
Buchs [CH] 58 H6	Bulford [GB] 12 G4	Burladingen [D] 58 G2	Bury [GB] 10 E4
Buchy [F] 28 C5	Bülgarene [BG] 148 B3	Burnham-on-Crouch [GB] 14 F4	Bury St Edmunds [GB] 14 F3
Bučin [MK] 128 E3	Bülgarene [BG] 148 B4	Burnham-on-Sea [GB] 12 F3	Burzenin [PL] 36 F5
Búcine [I] 110 F6	Bülgarevo [BG] 148 G2	Burnley [GB] 10 E3	Busalla [I] 110 B3
Bučje [YU] 150 D2	Bülgarovo [BG] 148 F4	Burntisland [GB] 8 E3	Busana [I] 110 D4
Buckden [GB] 14 E2	Bülgarska Polyana [BG] 146 A1	Burón [E] 82 C3	Busca [I] 108 F2
Buckden [GB] 10 E2	Bülgarski Izvor [BG] 148 A4	Buronzo [I] 70 E4	Busdorf [D] 18 F1
Bückeburg [D] 32 E2	Bulgnéville [F] 58 B2	Burrafirth [GB] 6 H3	Buseto Palizzolo [I] 126 B2
Bücken [D] 18 E6	Bulken [N] 170 C3	Burravoe [GB] 6 H3	Bushat [AL] 128 A1
Buckfastleigh [GB] 12 E5	Bulkowo [PL] 36 H2	Burrel [AL] 128 B2	Bushmills [GB] 2 G2
Buckhaven [GB] 8 F3	Bullas [E] 104 B2	Burriana / Borriana [E] 98 F3	Bushtricë [AL] 128 C1
Buckie [GB] 6 F5	Bulle [CH] 70 C1		Bus'k [UA] 206 C2
Buckingham [GB] 14 D3	Bulqizë [AL] 128 C2		Busko–Zdrój [PL] 52 B2
Buckow [D] 34 F2	Bultei [I] 118 D4		Bušno [PL] 38 G6
Bučovice [CZ] 50 C6	Buna [BIH] 152 C2		Busot [E] 104 E2
Bucquoy [F] 28 E4	Bunclody [IRL] 4 F4		Busovača [BIH] 154 D4
Bucsa [H] 76 F1	Buncrana [IRL] 2 F2		Bussang [F] 58 D3
Bucureşti [RO] 206 C6	Bunde [D] 16 H2		Bussang, Col de– [F] 58 D3
Buczek [PL] 36 G5	Bünde [D] 32 D3		Busseto [I] 110 D2
Buczyna [PL] 52 F3	Bundoran [IRL] 2 D3		Bussolengo [I] 72 C6
Bud [N] 180 E2	Bunessan [GB] 8 B1		Bussoleno [I] 70 C5
Budakovo [MK] 128 E3	Bungay [GB] 14 G2		Bussum [NL] 16 E4
Budaörs [H] 64 C6	Bunič [HR] 112 G3		Busto Arsízio [I] 70 F4
Budapest [H] 64 C6	Bunkris [S] 172 F2		Busto Garolfo [I] 70 F4
Búðardalur [IS] 194 C3	Bunleix [F] 68 B2		Büsum [D] 18 E2
Buddusò [I] 118 D3	Bunmahon [IRL] 4 E5		Butan [BG] 150 G3
Bude [GB] 12 D4	Bunnahowen [IRL] 2 B3		Butera [I] 126 E4
Budeşti [RO] 206 C6	Bunnyconnellan [IRL] 2 C3		Bütgenbach [B] 30 F5
Budilovo [RUS] 200 G2	Buñol [E] 98 E4		Butler's Bridge [IRL] 2 E4
Budimci [HR] 154 D1	Bunratty [IRL] 2 C6		Butrint [AL] 132 B2
Budimir [HR] 152 A2	Buntingford [GB] 14 E3		Buttelstedt [D] 34 A6
Büdingen [D] 46 D2	Buonalbergo [I] 120 F2		Buttermere [GB] 8 D6
Budišov nad Budišovkou [CZ] 50 D4	Buonconvento [I] 114 G2		Buttevant [IRL] 4 C4
Budleigh Salterton [GB] 12 E5	Buonfornello [I] 126 D2		Buttle [S] 168 G5
Budmirici [MK] 128 E3	Buonvicino [I] 124 C3		Buttstädt [D] 34 B6
Budomierz [PL] 52 G3	Burano [I] 72 F6		Butzbach [D] 46 C2
Budoni [I] 118 E3	Burbach [D] 32 C6		Bützow [D] 20 B3
Budowo [PL] 22 C2	Burbage [GB] 12 H4		Buvik [N] 182 B1
Budrio [I] 110 F3	Burcei [I] 118 D7		Buvika [N] 182 D5
Budry [PL] 24 C2	Bureå [S] 198 A4		Buxtehude [D] 18 F4
Budva [YU] 152 D4	Burela [E] 78 E2		Buxton [GB] 10 E5
Budyně nad Ohří [CZ] 48 F3	Büren [CH] 58 D5		Buxy [F] 56 F5
Budzyń [PL] 36 C1	Büren [D] 32 D4		Büyükçekmece [TR] 146 E3
Bue [N] 164 B4	Burfjord [N] 192 F1		Büyükkaraağaç [TR] 142 E3
Bueña [E] 90 D6	Burford [GB] 12 H3		Büyükkarıştıran [TR] 146 C2
Buenavista del Norte [E] 100 B5	Burg [D] 34 C3		Büyükkorhan [TR] 146 F5
Buendia [E] 88 H6	Burg [D] 18 H2		Buzançais [F] 54 G3
Buğdayli [TR] 146 D5	Burg [D] 18 E3		Buzancy [F] 44 D3
Bugeat [F] 68 A2	Burgas [BG] 148 F4		Buzău [RO] 206 D6
Buggerru [I] 118 B6	Burgau [D] 60 C3		Buzescu [RO] 148 B1
Bühl [D] 58 F1	Burgau [P] 94 B5		
Büileşti [RO] 150 F2	Burgbernheim [D] 46 F5		
Builth Wells [GB] 12 F1	Burgdorf [CH] 58 E5		
Buis-les-Baronnies [F] 108 B2	Burgdorf [D] 32 G2		
Buitenpost [NL] 16 F2	Burgebrach [D] 46 F4		
Buitrago [E] 88 G4	Burgelu / Elburgo [E] 102 B4		
Bujalance [E] 102 D1	Burghaun [D] 46 E1		
Bujanovac [YU] 150 D5	Burghausen [D] 60 G4		
Bujaraloz [E] 90 F4	Burghead [GB] 6 E4		
Buje [HR] 112 D1	Burgh-Haamstede [NL] 16 B5		
Bujoru [RO] 148 C2	Búrgio [I] 126 C3		
	Burgjoss [D] 46 E3		
	Burgkunstadt [D] 46 G3		
	Burglengenfeld [D] 48 B6		

Buzet [HR] 112 D1	Cabezuela del Valle [E] 88 B5
Buziaş [RO] 76 H6	Cabo de Gata [E] 102 G6
Bwlch [GB] 12 F2	Cabo de Palos [E] 104 D4
Byahoml' [BY] 204 B5	Cabo São Vicente [P] 94 A5
Byala [BG] 148 C2	Cabourg [F] 26 F3
Byala [BG] 148 F3	Cabra [E] 102 C2
Byala Slatina [BG] 150 G3	Cabra del Santo Cristo [E] 102 F2
Byal Izvor [BG] 130 E1	Cábras [I] 118 B5
Byalynichy [BY] 204 C5	Cabreiros [E] 78 D2
Byczki [PL] 36 H4	Cabrela [P] 86 C6
Byczyna [PL] 36 E6	Cabrera [E] 104 E6
Bydgoszcz [PL] 22 D6	Cabrerets [F] 66 G5
Byenyakoni [BY] 202 G6	Cabrillas [E] 88 B3
Bygdeå [S] 198 A5	Cabuelos [E] 78 F5
Bygdin [N] 170 F2	Čačak [YU] 150 B2
Bygdsiljum [S] 198 A5	Cáccamo [I] 126 D2
Bygland [N] 164 D4	Cacemes [P] 86 A5
Byglandsfjord [N] 164 D4	Cáceres [E] 86 H5
Bygstad [N] 170 B1	Cachopo [P] 94 D5
Bykle [N] 164 D2	Čačini [HR] 76 A6
Bylnice [CZ] 64 A2	Cadaqués [E] 92 G2
Byrkjedal [N] 164 B3	Cadaval [P] 86 B4
Byrkjelo [N] 180 D5	Cadavedo [E] 78 G2
Byrness [GB] 8 F5	Čadavica [BIH] 154 B3
Byrum [DK] 160 F3	Čadca [SK] 50 F5
Byrum [S] 162 H3	Cadelbosco di Sopra [I] 110 E2
Byšice [CZ] 48 G3	Cadenábbia [I] 70 G3
Byske [S] 198 A4	Cadenberge [D] 18 E3
Bystřice [CZ] 48 G4	Cadenet [F] 108 B4
Bystřice nad Pernštejnem [CZ] 50 B5	Cádiar [E] 102 E5
Bystřice pod Hostýnem [CZ] 50 D6	Cadillac [F] 66 D4
Bystrzyca Kłodzka [PL] 50 C3	Cádiz [E] 100 F4
Byszki [PL] 22 B5	Cadjavica [HR] 76 A6
Byszyno [PL] 20 H4	Caen [F] 26 F3
Bytča [SK] 50 F6	Caernarfon [GB] 10 B4
Bytom [PL] 50 F3	Caerphilly [GB] 12 F3
Bytom Odrzański [PL] 36 A4	Caersws [GB] 10 C6
Bytonia [PL] 22 D4	Čafasan [MK] 128 C3
Bytów [PL] 22 C3	Cagli [I] 112 B6
Byxelkrok [S] 162 H3	Cágliari [I] 118 C7
Bzenec [CZ] 62 G2	Cagnano Varano [I] 116 G6
Bzovík [SK] 64 C4	Cagnes-sur-Mer [F] 108 E4
	Caherdaniel [IRL] 4 A4
	Cahermurphy [IRL] 2 B6
	Cahersiveen [IRL] 4 A4
	Cahir [IRL] 4 D4
	Cahors [F] 66 G5
	Cahul [MD] 206 D5
	Caiazzo [I] 120 E2
	Cairndow [GB] 8 D2
	Cairnryan [GB] 8 C5
	Cairo Montenotte [I] 108 G3
	Caister-on-Sea [GB] 14 H2
	Caistor [GB] 10 G4
	Caivano [I] 120 E3
	Cajarc [F] 66 G5
	Čajetina [YU] 150 A3
	Čajniče [BIH] 152 E2
	Çakırbeyli [TR] 144 E5
	Cakovec [HR] 74 F4

C

Cabação [P] 86 D5
Cabaj–Čápor [SK] 64 A4
Cabañaquinta [E] 78 H4
Cabañas [E] 78 D2
Cabanes [E] 98 G3
Cabeço de Vide [P] 86 E5
Cabeza del Buey [E] 96 C4
Cabezamesada [E] 96 G2
Cabezarados [E] 96 E4
Cabezas Rubias [E] 94 E4
Cabezón de la Sal [E] 82 E3

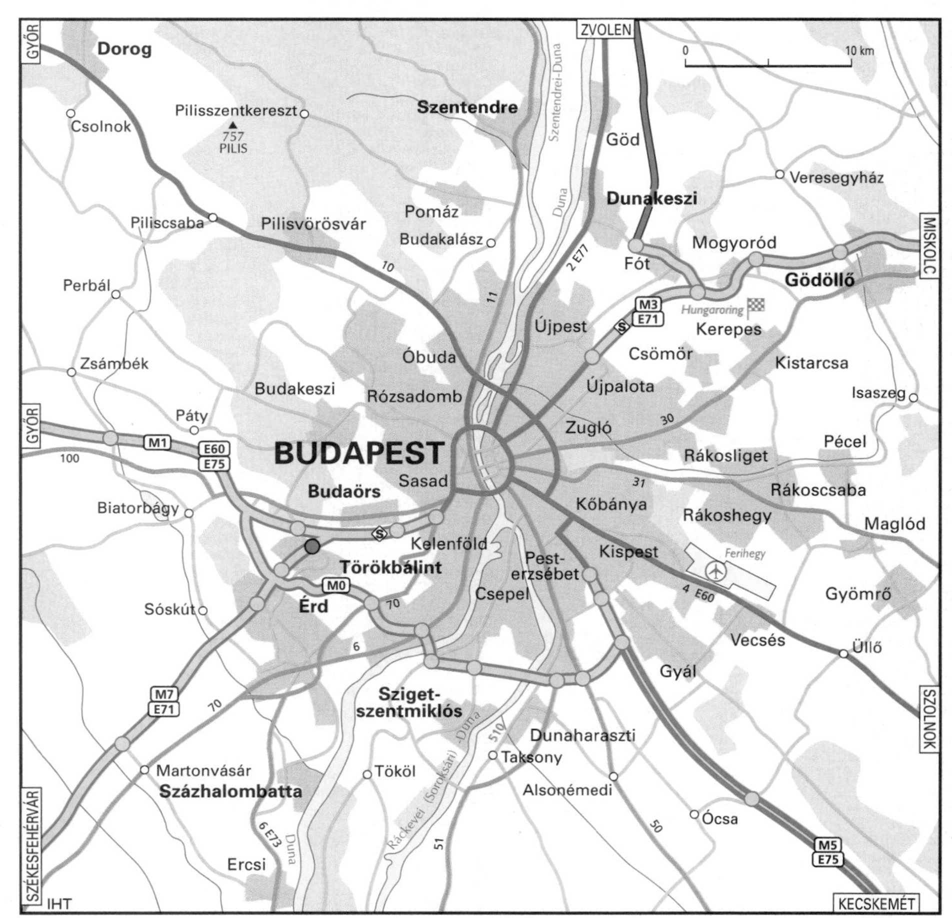

GYŐR · ZVOLEN · **Dorog** · Pilisszentkereszt · **Szentendre** · Csolnok · 757 PILIS · Göd · Veresegyház · **Dunakeszi** · Pomáz · Mogyoród · Piliscsaba · Pilisvörösvár · Budakalász · Fót · **Gödöllő** · MISKOLC · Perbál · M3 · E71 · Hungaroring · Kerepes · Zsámbék · Óbuda · Újpest · Csömör · Kistarcsa · Budakeszi · Rózsadomb · Újpalota · Isaszeg · **BUDAPEST** · Páty · M1 · E60 · E75 · Zugló · 30 · Pécel · GYŐR · Sasad · **Budaörs** · 31 · Rákosliget · Biatorbágy · Kőbánya · Rákoscsaba · **Törökbálint** · Kelenföld · Pester-zsébet · Rákoshegy · Maglód · Érd · M0 · Kispest · Ferihegy · Sóskút · Csepel · 4 E60 · Gyömrő · Szigetszentmiklós · Vecsés · Üllő · SZOLNOK · Dunaharaszti · Gyál · 50 · **Százhalombatta** · Martonvásár · Tököl · Taksony · Alsónémedi · Ócsa · SZÉKESFEHÉRVÁR · IHT · Ercsi · Ráckevei (Soroksári)-Duna · M5 · E75 · KECSKEMÉT

Çal [TR] 144 G4
Cala [E] 94 G4
Cala Blanca [E] 104 G4
Cala Blava [E] 104 E5
Calabor [E] 80 F3
Calabritto [I] 120 F3
Calaceite [E] 90 G6
Calacuccia [F] 114 B3
Cala del Moral, La- [E] 102 B5
Cala d'Oliva [I] 118 B2
Cala d'Or [E] 104 F6
Calaf [E] 92 D3
Calafat [RO] 150 F2
Calafell [E] 92 D5
Cala Galdana [E] 104 G4
Cala Gonone [I] 118 E4
Calahonda [E] 102 B5
Calahonda-Chaparral [E] 102 E5
Calahorra [E] 84 A5
Calais [F] 14 G6
Cala Liberotto [I] 118 E4
Cala Millor [E] 104 F5
Calamocha [E] 90 D5
Calamonte [E] 94 H2
Cala Moreia-Cala Morlanda [E] 104 F5
Cala Morell [E] 104 G4
Calañas [E] 94 F5
Calanda [E] 90 F6
Calangiánus [I] 118 D3
Cala'n Porter [E] 104 H5
Cala Pi [E] 104 E5
Călăraşi [MD] 206 D4
Călăraşi [RO] 206 D6
Cala Ratjada [E] 104 F5
cala Sa Calobra [E] 104 E4
Cala Santanyí [E] 104 E6
Calascibetta [I] 126 E3
Calasetta [I] 118 B7
Calasparra [E] 104 B2
Calatafimi Segesta [I] 126 B2
Calatañazor [E] 90 B3
Cala Tarida [E] 104 B5
Calatayud [E] 90 D4
Calatorao [E] 90 D4
Calau [D] 34 F4
Cala Vadella [E] 104 B5
Calbe [D] 34 B4
Caldarola [I] 116 C2
Caldas da Rainha [P] 86 B3
Caldas de Reis [E] 78 B3
Caldas de Vizela [P] 80 C3
Caldbeck [GB] 8 E6
Caldes de Boí [E] 84 F6
Caldes de Malavella [E] 92 F3
Caldes de Montbui [E] 92 E4
Caldes d'Estrac [E] 92 F4
Caldirola [I] 110 B2
Caledon [GB] 2 F4
Calella [E] 92 F4
Calella de Palafrugell [E] 92 G3
Calenzana [F] 114 B3
Calera y Chozas [E] 88 C6
Caleruega [E] 88 H2
Cales de Mallorca [E] 104 F5
Calfsound [GB] 6 G1
Calheta [P] 100 A3
Çali [TR] 146 F5
Càlig [E] 92 A6
Calignac [F] 66 E5
Çalıklı [TR] 144 F3
Călimăneşti [RO] 206 B6
Calimera [I] 122 G5
Calitri [I] 120 G3
Çalköy [TR] 144 H2
Callac [F] 40 D2
Callan [IRL] 4 E4
Callander [GB] 8 D2
Callington [GB] 12 D4
Callosa d'en Sarrià [E] 104 E2
Callosa de Segura [E] 104 D3
Călmăţuiu [RO] 148 B2
Calne [GB] 12 G3
Calnegre, Puntas de- [E] 104 B4
Calolziocorte [I] 70 G4
Calonge [E] 92 G3
Calpe / Calp [E] 104 F2
Caltabellotta [I] 126 C3
Caltagirone [I] 126 F4
Caltanissetta [I] 126 E3
Caltavuturo [I] 126 E2
Çaltı [TR] 146 H4
Çaltılıbük [TR] 146 E5
Caltra [IRL] 2 D5
Călugăreni [RO] 148 C1
Caluso [I] 70 D5
Calvello [I] 120 H4
Calvi [F] 114 A3
Calvörde [D] 34 B2
Calw [D] 58 G1
Calzadilla de la Cueza [E] 82 C5
Camaiore [I] 110 D5
Camaldoli [I] 110 G5
Çamaltı [TR] 144 C4
Câmara de Lobos [P] 100 B3
Camarena de la Sierra [E] 98 E2
Camarès [F] 106 D3
Camaret [F] 40 B2
Camariñas [E] 78 B2
Camarzana de Tera [E] 80 H3
Cambados [E] 78 B4
Cambeo [E] 78 C5
Camberg [D] 46 C2
Camberley [GB] 14 D4
Cambo-les-Bains [F] 84 C2
Camborne [GB] 12 C5
Cambrai [F] 28 F4
Cambre [E] 78 C2
Cambremer [F] 26 G4
Cambridge [GB] 14 F3
Cambrils [E] 92 C5
Camburg [D] 34 B6
Camelford [GB] 12 C4
Çameli [TR] 142 G2
Camenca [MD] 206 E3
Camerino [I] 116 B2
Camigliatello [I] 124 D4
Caminha [P] 78 A5
Caminomorisco [E] 88 A4
Caminreal [E] 90 D6
Çamköy [TR] 142 D2
Çamlık [TR] 144 F2
Cammarata [I] 126 D3
Camogli [I] 110 B3
Camp [IRL] 4 B3
Campagna [I] 120 F4
Campan [F] 84 F4
Campana [I] 124 E4
Campanario [E] 96 B3
Campanas / Kanpaneta [E] 84 B4
Campaspero [E] 88 F2
Campbeltown [GB] 2 H2
Campi Bisenzio [I] 110 E5
Campiglia Soana [I] 70 D4
Campillo de Altobuey [E] 98 C3
Campillo de Arenas [E] 102 E3
Campillo de Llerena [E] 96 A4
Campillos [E] 102 B3
Campione d'Italia [I] 70 G3
Campisábalos [E] 88 H4
Campi Salentina [I] 122 G4
Campo [E] 84 F6
Campobasso [I] 120 E1
Campobecerros [E] 78 D6
Campobello di Licata [I] 126 E4
Campobello di Mazara [I] 126 B3
Campocologno [CH] 72 B4
Campodarsego [I] 72 E6
Campo de Caso / Caso [E] 82 C2
Campo de Criptana [E] 96 G3
Campodón [E] 92 F2
Campofelice di Fitalia [I] 126 D2
Campofiorito [I] 126 C3
Campoformido [I] 72 G5
Campogalliano [I] 110 E3
Campohermoso [E] 102 G5
Campo Ligure [I] 110 A3
Campo Maior [P] 86 F6
Campomanes [E] 78 H4
Campomarino [I] 122 F5
Campomarino [I] 116 F5
Campora San Giovanni [I] 124 D5
Campo Real [E] 88 G6
Camporeale [I] 126 C2
Camporrobles [E] 98 D3
Campos [E] 104 E5
Camposampiero [I] 72 E6
Camposanto [I] 110 F2
Campotejar [E] 102 E3
Campo Tures / Sand in Taufers [I] 72 E2
Çamsu [TR] 144 G2
Çan [TR] 146 C5
Cañada de Benatanduz [E] 98 F1
Cañadajuncosa [E] 98 B3
Çanakkale [TR] 146 B5
Canale [I] 108 G1
Canales de Molina [E] 90 C5
Canal S. Bovo [I] 72 E4
Canas de Senhorim [P] 80 C6
Cañaveral [E] 86 H4
Cañaveral de León [E] 94 G4
Cañaveras [E] 98 B1
Canazei [I] 72 E3
Cancale [F] 26 C4
Cancon [F] 66 E4
Candanchú [E] 84 D4
Çandarlı [TR] 144 C3
Candás [E] 78 H3
Candasnos [E] 90 G4
Candé [F] 40 G6
Candela [I] 120 G2
Candelario [E] 88 B4
Candeleda [E] 88 C5
Candia Lomellina [I] 70 F5
Çandır [TR] 142 F3
Canelli [I] 108 H2
Canero [E] 78 G2
Canet [F] 106 E4
Canet de Mar [E] 92 F4
Cañete [E] 98 C2
Cañete la Real [E] 102 B3
Canet-Plage [F] 92 G1
Canfranc [E] 84 D4
Cangas [E] 78 B4
Cangas del Narcea [E] 78 F3
Cangas de Onís [E] 82 C2
Canha [P] 86 C5
Caniçada [P] 80 D3
Canicattini Bagni [I] 126 G5
Caniço [P] 100 B3
Caniles [E] 102 G4
Canino [I] 114 G4
Cañizal [E] 88 D2
Cañizares [E] 90 B6
Canjáyar [E] 102 F5
Cannai [I] 118 B7
Cannara [I] 116 A2
Cànnero Riviera [I] 70 F3
Cannes [F] 108 E5
Canneto [I] 114 E1
Canneto sull'Óglio [I] 110 D1
Cannich [GB] 6 D5
Cannóbio [I] 70 F3
Cannock [GB] 10 E6
Canosa di Puglia [I] 120 H2
Canossa [I] 110 D3
Can Pastilla [E] 104 E5
Can Picafort [E] 104 F4
Cansano [I] 116 D5
Cantalapiedra [E] 88 D3
Cantalejo [E] 88 F3
Cantalpino [E] 88 D3
Cantanhede [P] 80 B6
Cantavieja [E] 98 F2
Čantavir [YU] 76 D5
Canterbury [GB] 14 F5
Cantillana [E] 94 H5
Cantoral de la Peña [E] 82 D4
Cantoria [E] 102 H4
Cantù [I] 70 G4
Canvey Island [GB] 14 F4
Cany-Barville [F] 26 H2
Caorle [I] 72 D4
Cáorle [I] 72 F6
Caorso [I] 70 H6
Capaccio [I] 120 F4
Capaci [I] 126 C1
Capalbio [I] 114 F4
Capannoli [I] 110 E6
Caparde [BIH] 154 E3
Caparroso [E] 84 B5
Capbreton [F] 66 A6
Cap-d'Ail [F] 108 F4
Capdella [E] 84 G6
Capdenac-Gare [F] 66 H5
Cap d'En Font [E] 104 H5
Capendu [F] 106 C5
Capestang [F] 106 D4
Capestrano [I] 116 C4
Cap Ferret [F] 66 B3
Cap Gris Nez [F] 14 G6
Capinha [P] 86 F2
Capistrello [I] 116 C5
Capizzi [I] 126 F2
Čapljina [BIH] 152 C3
Capo Cavallo [F] 114 A3
Capodimonte [I] 114 G3
Capo di Ponte [I] 72 B4
Capo d'Orlando [I] 124 B6
Capolíveri [I] 114 E3
Capo Rizzuto [I] 124 F5
Cappamore [IRL] 4 D3
Cappoquin [IRL] 4 D5
Capracotta [I] 116 D6
Capráia [I] 114 D2
Capranica [I] 114 H4
Capri [I] 120 D4
Capriati a Volturno [I] 120 D1
Capriccioli [I] 118 E2
Captieux [F] 66 D5
Capua [I] 120 D2
Capurso [I] 122 E3
Caracal [RO] 148 A1
Caracenilla [E] 98 B2
Caracuel de Calatrava [E] 96 E4
Caraglio [I] 108 F2
Caraman [F] 106 B3
Caramulo [P] 80 C6
Caranga [E] 78 G4
Caransebeş [RO] 206 A5
Carantec [F] 40 C1
Caravaca [E] 104 B2
Caravaggio [I] 70 H5
Carbajales de Alba [E] 80 H4
Carbajo [E] 86 F4
Carballo [E] 78 C2
Carbon-Blanc [F] 66 D3
Carboneras [E] 102 H5
Carboneras de Guadazaón [E] 98 C3
Carbonero el Mayor [E] 88 F3
Carbónia [I] 118 B7
Carbonin / Schluderbach [I] 72 E3
Carbonne [F] 84 H4
Carcaboso [E] 88 A5
Carcabuey [E] 102 C3
Carcaixent [E] 98 E5
Carcans [F] 66 C2
Carcans-Plage [F] 66 B2
Carcar [E] 84 A5
Carcare [I] 108 H3
Carcassonne [F] 106 B4
Carcastillo [E] 84 B5
Carcavelos [P] 86 A5
Carcès [F] 108 C5
Carcoforo [I] 70 E3
Çardak [TR] 144 G3
Çardak [TR] 146 B5
Çardak [TR] 144 G5
Cardedeu [E] 92 E4
Cardeña [E] 96 D6
Cardenete [E] 98 C3
Cardiff [GB] 12 F3
Cardigan [GB] 4 H6
Cardona [E] 92 D3
Carei [RO] 206 B4
Carennac [F] 66 H4
Carentan [F] 26 E3
Carevac [BIH] 154 B4
Carev Dvor [MK] 128 D3
Carezza al Lago / Karersee [I] 72 D3
Cargèse [F] 114 A4
Carhaix-Plouguer [F] 40 C2
Caria [P] 86 F2
Cariati [I] 124 E4
Carignan [F] 44 D2
Carignano [I] 70 D6
Cariñena [E] 90 D4
Cariño [E] 78 E1
Carinola [I] 120 D2
Carisbrooke [GB] 12 H5
Carlantino [I] 120 F1
Carlentini [I] 126 G4
Carlet [E] 98 E5
Carling [F] 44 F4
Carlingford [IRL] 2 G4
Carlisle [GB] 8 E6
Carloforte [I] 118 B7
Carlow [D] 18 H4
Carlow / Ceatharlach [IRL] 4 F4
Carlton [GB] 10 F4
Carluke [GB] 8 D3
Carmagnola [I] 70 D6
Carmarthen [GB] 12 E2
Carmaux [F] 106 C2
Cármenes [E] 78 H4
Carmona [E] 94 H6
Carnac [F] 40 D5
Carnalbanagh Sheddings [GB] 2 G3
Carndonagh [IRL] 2 F1
Carnew [IRL] 4 F4
Carnia [I] 72 G4
Carnlough [GB] 2 G3
Carnota [E] 78 B3
Carnoustie [GB] 8 F2
Carnwath [GB] 8 E4
Carolei [I] 124 D4
Carolinensiel [D] 18 C3
Carosino [I] 122 F4
Carpaneto Piacentino [I] 110 C2
Carpegna [I] 110 H5
Carpenédolo [I] 72 B6
Carpentras [F] 106 H3
Carpi [I] 110 E2
Carpignano Sesia [I] 70 E4
Carpineti [I] 110 E3
Carpineto Romano [I] 116 B6
Cărpiniş [RO] 76 G5
Carpino [I] 116 G6
Carpinone [I] 120 E1
Carquefou [F] 40 F6
Carqueiranne [F] 108 C6
Carradale [GB] 8 C3
Carral [E] 78 C2
Carrapateira [P] 94 A4
Carrara [I] 110 D4
Carraroe [IRL] 2 B5
Carrascalejo [E] 96 C1
Carrascosa del Campo [E] 98 A2
Carrazeda de Ansiães [P] 80 E4
Carrazedo [P] 80 E3
Carrbridge [GB] 6 E5
Carregado [P] 86 B4
Carregal do Sal [P] 80 C6
Carrega Ligure [I] 110 B3
Carregueiro [P] 94 C3
Carrick / An Charraig [IRL] 2 D2
Carrickfergus [GB] 2 G3
Carrickmacross [IRL] 2 F4
Carrickmore [GB] 2 F3
Carrick-on-Shannon [IRL] 2 D4
Carrick-on-Suir [IRL] 4 E4
Carriço [P] 86 C2
Carrigaline [IRL] 4 C5
Carrigallen [IRL] 2 E4
Carriganimmy [IRL] 4 C4
Carrigans [IRL] 2 F2
Carrigart [IRL] 2 F1
Carrión de Calatrava [E] 96 F4
Carrión de los Condes [E] 82 C5
Carrizo [E] 78 G5
Carrizosas [E] 96 G5
Carro [F] 106 G5
Carrouges [F] 26 F5
Carrowkeel [IRL] 2 F2
Carrù [I] 108 G2
Carryduff [GB] 2 G4
Carry-le-Rouet [F] 106 H5
Çarshovë [AL] 128 C6
Carsoli [I] 116 B5
Carsphairn [GB] 8 D4
Cartagena [E] 104 C4
Cártama [E] 102 B4
Cartaxo [P] 86 C4
Cartaya [E] 94 E5
Cartelle [E] 78 C5
Carteret [F] 26 D2
Carviçais [P] 80 F5
Carvin [F] 28 F3
Carvoeiro [P] 94 B5
Carwitz [D] 20 D5
Casabermeja [E] 102 C4
Casabona [I] 124 E4
Casa Branca [P] 86 D5
Casa Branca [P] 94 C2
Casa Branca [P] 94 D1
Casacalenda [I] 116 E6
Casalabate [I] 122 G4
Casalarreina [E] 82 G6
Casalbordino [I] 116 E5
Casalbuono [I] 120 G5
Casalciprano [I] 116 E6
Casalecchio di Reno [I] 110 F3
Casale Monferrato [I] 70 E5
Casalmaggiore [I] 110 D2
Casalpusterlengo [I] 70 H6
Casamáina [I] 116 C4
Casamássima [I] 122 E3
Casamicciola Terme [I] 120 D3
Casamozza [F] 114 C3
Casarabonela [E] 102 B4
Casarano [I] 122 G5
Casares [E] 100 H5
Casariche [E] 102 B3
Casarubios del Monte [E] 88 F6
Casas de Benitez [E] 98 B4
Casas de Fernando Alonso [E] 98 B4
Casas de Juan Núñez [E] 98 C5
Casas del Puerto [E] 104 C2
Casas de Reina [E] 94 H4
Casas-Ibáñez [E] 98 C4
Casatejada [E] 88 B6
Cascais [P] 86 A5
Cascante [E] 84 B6
Cascia [I] 116 B3
Casciana Terme [I] 110 E6
Cáscina [I] 110 D5
Căscioarele [RO] 148 D1
Casekow [D] 20 E5
Caselle [I] 70 D5
Caserta [I] 120 E2
Cashel [IRL] 4 D4
Cashlie [GB] 8 D1
Casina [I] 110 E3
Casinos [E] 98 E4
Čáslav [CZ] 48 H4
Casola Valsenio [I] 110 G4
Casoli [I] 116 D5
Casoria [I] 120 E3
Caspe [E] 90 F5
Cassà de la Selva [E] 92 F3
Cassagnes-Bégonhès [F] 68 B6
Cassano allo Ionio [I] 122 C6
Cassano d'Adda [I] 70 G5
Cassano delle Murge [I] 122 D3
Cassel [F] 28 E2
Cassibile [I] 126 G5
Cassine [I] 108 H2
Cassino [I] 120 D1
Cassis [F] 108 B5
Castagneto Carducci [I] 114 E1
Castalla [E] 104 D2
Castañar de Ibor [E] 96 C1
Castanet-Tolosan [F] 106 A3
Castanheira de Pera [P] 86 E2
Casteau [B] 28 H3
Casteggio [I] 70 G6
Castejón de Monegros [E] 90 F4
Castejón de Sos [E] 84 F5
Castejón de Valdejasa [E] 90 E3
Castel Bolognese [I] 110 G4
Castelbuono [I] 126 E2
Casteldelfino [I] 108 E2
Castel del Piano [I] 114 G2
Castel del Rio [I] 110 F4
Castel di Sangro [I] 116 D6
Castelejo [P] 94 A5
Castelfidardo [I] 116 C1
Castelfiorentino [I] 110 E6
Castelfranco Emilia [I] 110 F3
Castelfranco in Miscano [I] 120 F2
Castelfranco Véneto [I] 72 E6
Castel Goffredo [I] 110 E1
Casteljaloux [F] 66 D5
Castellabate [I] 120 F5
Castellammare del Golfo [I] 126 C2
Castellammare di Stábia [I] 120 E3
Castellamonte [I] 70 D5
Castellana Grotte [I] 122 E3
Castellana Sícula [I] 126 E3
Castellane [F] 108 D4
Castellaneta [I] 122 E4
Castellar [E] 102 F1
Castellar de la Frontera [E] 100 G5
Castellar de la Muela [E] 90 C5
Castellar de Santiago [E] 96 F5
Castell' Arquato [I] 110 C2
Castellazzo Bormida [I] 108 H2
Castelldans [E] 90 H5
Castelldefels [E] 92 D5
Castell de Ferro [E] 102 E5
Castelleone [I] 70 H5
Castelletto d'Orba [I] 110 A2
Castellfollit de la Roca [E] 92 F2
Castellina in Chianti [I] 114 G1
Castelló de la Plana / Castellón de la Plana [E] 98 F3
Castelló de la Ribera [E] 98 E6
Castelló d'Empúries [E] 92 G2
Castellón de la Plana / Castelló de la Plana [E] 98 F3
Castellote [E] 90 F6
Castello Tesino [I] 72 D4
Castellterçol [E] 92 E3
Castellúccio dei Sáuri [I] 120 G2
Castelluccio Sup. [I] 120 H5
Castelluzzo [I] 126 B2
Castelmagno [I] 108 F2
Castelmassa [I] 110 F2
Castelmauro [I] 116 E6
Castelmoron [F] 66 E5
Castelnaudary [F] 106 B4
Castelnau-de-Médoc [F] 66 C2
Castelnau-de-Montmiral [F] 106 B2
Castelnau-Magnoac [F] 84 F3
Castelnovo ne' Monti [I] 110 D3
Castelnuovo Berardenga [I] 114 G1
Castelnuovo della Dáunia [I] 120 F1
Castelnuovo di Garfagnana [I] 110 D4
Castelnuovo di Porto [I] 116 A5
Castelnuovo di Val di Cecina [I] 114 F1
Castelnuovo Don Bosco [I] 70 E6
Castelnuovo Scrívia [I] 70 F6
Castelo Branco [P] 86 F3
Castelo Branco [P] 80 F5
Castelo de Paiva [P] 80 C4
Castelo de Vide [P] 86 F4
Castelo do Neiva [P] 78 A6
Castel Porziano [I] 114 H6
Castelraimondo [I] 116 B2
Castel San Giovanni [I] 70 G6
Castel San Lorenzo [I] 120 F4
Castel San Pietro Terme [I] 110 F4
Castelsaraceno [I] 120 H5
Castelsardo [I] 118 C2
Castelsarrasin [F] 66 F6
Castelseprio [I] 70 F4
Castelserás [E] 90 F6
Casteltérmini [I] 126 D3
Castelvecchio Subequo [I] 116 C5
Castelverde [I] 70 H6
Castelvetere in Val Fortore [I] 120 F1
Castelvetrano [I] 126 B3
Castel Volturno [I] 120 D2
Castenaso [I] 110 F3
Castets [F] 66 B5
Castiádas [I] 118 D7
Castigliole d'Orcia [I] 114 G2
Castiglioncello [I] 114 E1
Castiglione dei Pepoli [I] 110 F4
Castiglione del Lago [I] 114 H2
Castiglione della Pescáia [I] 114 E3
Càstiglione delle Stiviere [I] 72 B6
Castiglione Messer Marino [I] 116 E6
Castiglione Olona [I] 70 F4
Castiglion Fibocchi [I] 110 G6
Castiglion Fiorentino [I] 114 H1
Castilblanco [E] 96 C2
Castilblanco de los Arroyos [E] 94 G5
Castillejo de Martín Viejo [E] 86 H2
Castilliscar [E] 84 C5
Castillo de Locubín [E] 102 D3
Castillo de Tajarja [E] 102 D4
Castillo de Villamalefa [E] 98 F3
Castillon-la-Bataille [F] 66 D3
Castillonnès [F] 66 E4
Castione della Presolana [I] 72 A5
Castle Acre [GB] 14 G2
Castlebar [IRL] 2 C4
Castlebay [GB] 6 A5
Castlebellingham [IRL] 2 F5
Castleblayney [IRL] 2 F4
Castlebridge [IRL] 4 F5
Castle Combe [GB] 12 G3
Castlecomer [IRL] 4 E3
Castlederg [GB] 2 E2
Castledermot [IRL] 4 F3
Castle Douglas [GB] 8 D5
Castleisland [IRL] 4 B4
Castlemaine [IRL] 4 B4
Castlemartyr [IRL] 4 D5
Castleplunkett [IRL] 2 D4
Castlepollard [IRL] 2 E5
Castlerea [IRL] 2 D4
Castleton [GB] 10 E4
Castletown [GB] 6 F3
Castletown [GBM] 10 B2
Castletownbere [IRL] 4 B5
Castletownroche [IRL] 4 D4
Castletownsend [IRL] 4 B5
Castlewellan [GB] 2 G4
Castrejón [E] 88 D2
Castres [F] 106 B3
Castricum [NL] 16 D3
Castries [F] 106 F4
Castril [E] 102 G3
Castrillo de la Reina [E] 88 H2
Castro [E] 78 C4
Castro Caldelas [E] 78 D5
Castrocaro Terme [I] 110 G4
Castrocontrigo [E] 78 F6
Castro Daire [P] 80 C5
Castro dei Volsci [I] 120 C1
Castro del Río [E] 102 C2
Castro de Rei [E] 78 E3
Castrojeriz [E] 82 D6
Castro Marim [P] 94 D5
Castromonte [E] 88 E1
Castronuevo [E] 88 D1
Castronuño [E] 88 D2
Castropol [E] 78 F2
Castrop-Rauxal [D] 30 H3
Castroreale [I] 124 B7
Castroreale Terme [I] 124 A7
Castro-Urdiales [E] 82 G3
Castroverde [E] 78 E3
Castro Verde [P] 94 C4
Castroverde de Cerrato [E] 88 F2
Castrovillari [I] 122 C6
Castuera [E] 96 B4
Çatak [TR] 142 E1
Çatalca [TR] 146 D2
Catane [RO] 150 F2
Catánia [I] 126 G3
Catanzaro [I] 124 E5
Catanzaro Marina [I] 124 E5
Catarroja [E] 98 E5
Catenanuova [I] 126 F3
Cateraggio [F] 114 C4
Caterham [GB] 14 E5
Catoira [E] 78 B3

Catterick [GB] 10 F2
Cattolica [I] 112 B5
Cattolica Eraclea [I] 126 C3
Catus [F] 66 G5
Caudebec [F] 26 H3
Caudete [E] 104 D1
Caudeval [F] 106 B5
Caudry [F] 28 F4
Caulonia [I] 124 D7
Caumont [F] 26 E3
Caunes-Minervois [F] 106 C4
Cauro [F] 114 B5
Căusanii [MD] 206 E5
Caussade [F] 66 G6
Cauterets [F] 84 E4
Cauville [F] 26 G2
Cava [E] 92 B6
Cava de' Tirreni [I] 120 E3
Cavaglià [I] 70 E5
Cavaillon [F] 106 H4
Cavalaire-sur-Mer [F] 108 D6
Cavalese [I] 72 D4
Cavalière [F] 108 D6
Cavallino [I] 122 G5
Cavallino [I] 72 F6
Cavan / An Cabhán [IRL] 2 E4
Cavárzere [I] 110 G2
Çavdarhisar [TR] 144 G2
Çavdır [TR] 142 H1
Cave del Predil [I] 72 H4
Cavo [I] 114 E2
Cavour [I] 70 C6
Cavriglia [I] 110 F6
Cavtat [HR] 152 C4
Çayağzi [TR] 146 F2
Caylus [F] 66 G6
Cayrols [F] 68 A4
Çayyaka [TR] 146 F5
Cazalegas [E] 88 D6
Cazalla de la Sierra [E] 94 H5
Cazals [F] 66 F4
Cazaubon [F] 66 D6
Cazères [F] 84 G4
Cazin [BIH] 112 H2
Čazma [HR] 74 F6
Cazorla [E] 102 F2
Cea [E] 82 C5
Cea [E] 78 C4
Ceannacroc Lodge [GB] 6 C5
Ceatharlach / Carlow [IRL] 4 F4
Cebolla [E] 96 E1
Cebreiro [E] 78 E4
Cebreros [E] 88 E5
Cebrones del Rio [E] 78 G6
Ceccano [I] 120 C1
Cece [H] 76 B3
Čechtice [CZ] 48 G5
Cécina [I] 114 E1
Ceclavín [E] 86 G4
Cecos [E] 78 F4
Cedeira [E] 78 D1
Cedillo [E] 86 F4
Cedynia [PL] 34 F1
Cee [E] 78 B2
Cefalù [I] 126 E2
Cegléd [H] 76 D2
Céglie Messápica [I] 122 F4
Cegrane [MK] 128 D1
Cehegín [E] 104 B2
Ceira [P] 86 D2
Čejč [CZ] 62 G2
Ceków Kolonia [PL] 36 E4
Čelákovice [CZ] 48 G3
Celano [I] 116 C5
Celanova [E] 78 C5
Celaru [RO] 150 G1
Celbridge [IRL] 2 F6
Čelebić [BIH] 154 B4
Celerina [CH] 70 H2
Čelić [BIH] 154 E3
Celico [I] 124 D4
Celje [SLO] 74 D4
Cella [E] 98 D1
Celldömölk [H] 74 G1
Celle [D] 32 G1
Celle di Bulgheria [I] 120 G5
Celle Ligure [I] 108 H3
Cellers / Castell de Mur [E] 92 C2
Celles-sur-Belle [F] 54 D4
Celopeci [MK] 128 D2
Celorico da Beira [P] 80 D6
Celorico de Basto [P] 80 D4
Čemerno [BIH] 152 D2
Cemke [TR] 146 F2
Cencenighe [I] 72 E4
Ceneköy [TR] 146 C3
Cenicentos [E] 88 E5
Cenicero [E] 82 G6
Cenizzate [E] 98 C4
Čenta [YU] 154 G2
Centallo [I] 108 F2
Centelles [E] 92 E3
Cento [I] 110 F3
Centuri [F] 114 C2
Centúripe [I] 126 F3
Çepan [AL] 128 C5
Čepin [HR] 154 D1
Cepos [P] 86 E2
Ceprano [I] 120 C1
Cerami [I] 126 F2
Ceranów [PL] 38 D2
Cerbère [F] 92 G2
Cercal [P] 94 B3
Cercal [P] 86 B4
Cerceda [E] 78 C2
Cerceda [E] 88 F5
Cercedilla [E] 88 F4
Cerchiara di Calabria [I] 122 D6
Cerda [I] 126 D2
Cerdedo [E] 78 C4
Cerdeira [P] 86 G2
Cerea [I] 110 F1
Cerecinos de Campos [E] 82 B6
Cered [H] 64 E4
Ceres [I] 70 D5
Ceresole Reale [I] 70 C4
Céret [F] 92 F2
Cerignola [I] 120 H2
Cérilly [F] 56 C5
Čerín [SK] 64 C3
Cerisiers [F] 42 H6
Cerizay [F] 54 D3
Cerkezköy [TR] 146 D2
Cerknica [SLO] 74 B6
Cerkno [SLO] 74 B5
Cerkovitsa [BG] 148 B2
Cerkvenjak [SLO] 74 E3
Çermë [AL] 128 B3
Cermei [RO] 76 H3
Černá [CZ] 62 B3
Cerna [HR] 154 E2
Cernache do Bom Jardim [P] 86 D3
Černá Hora [CZ] 50 C5
Cernavoda [RO] 206 D6
Cernay [F] 58 D3
Cerne Abbas [GB] 12 F4
Cernégula [E] 82 E5
Cernihiv [UA] 204 C7
Cernik [HR] 154 C1
Cernóbbio [I] 70 G4
Černošín [CZ] 48 D4
Černovice [CZ] 48 G6
Çërravë [AL] 128 D4
Çërrik [AL] 128 B4
Cerro Muriano [E] 96 C6
Certaldo [I] 110 E6
Cervatos [E] 82 E4
Červená Řečice [CZ] 48 H5
Červená Skala [SK] 64 E2
Červená Voda [CZ] 50 C4
Červený Kostelec [CZ] 50 B2
Cervera [E] 92 C3
Cervera del Llano [E] 98 B3
Cervera del Río Alhama [E] 84 A6
Cervera de Pisuerga [E] 82 D4
Cerveteri [I] 114 H5
Cérvia [I] 110 H4
Cervignano del Friuli [I] 72 G5
Cervinara [I] 120 E3
Cervione [F] 114 C4
Cervo [E] 78 E1
Cervo [I] 108 G4
Cesana Torinese [I] 70 B6
Cesarò [I] 126 F2
Cesarzowice [PL] 36 C6
Cesena [I] 110 H4
Cesenático [I] 110 H4
Cēsis [LV] 200 E4
Česká Kamenice [CZ] 48 F2
Česká Lípa [CZ] 48 G2
Česká Skalice [CZ] 50 B3
Česká Třebová [CZ] 50 B4
České Budějovice [CZ] 62 C2
České Velenice [CZ] 62 C3
Český Brod [CZ] 48 G4
Český Krumlov [CZ] 62 B2
Český Těšín [CZ] 50 F5
Çeşme [TR] 134 H5
Çeşmealti [TR] 144 C4
Cespedosa [E] 88 C4
Cessenon-sur-Orb [F] 106 D4
Čestobrodica [YU] 150 A2
Cestona / Zestoa [E] 84 A2
Cesvaine [LV] 200 F5
Cetate [RO] 150 F1
Cetinje [YU] 152 E4
Cetona [I] 114 G2
Cetraro [I] 124 C4
Ceuta [E] 100 G6
Ceutí [E] 104 C3
Ceva [I] 108 G3
Cevico Navero [E] 88 F1
Čevo [YU] 152 E4
Ceyzériat [F] 68 G2
Chabanais [F] 54 F6
Chabeuil [F] 68 F5
Chablis [F] 56 E2
Chabreloche [F] 68 D2
Chabris [F] 54 H3
Chagny [F] 56 G5
Chaillé-les-Marais [F] 54 C4
Chairóneia [GR] 132 H5
Chajkola [RUS] 198 H3
Chalabre [F] 106 B5
Chalais [F] 66 E2
Chalamont [F] 68 G2
Chalampé [F] 58 E3
Chalandrítsa [GR] 132 F6
Chale [GB] 12 H5
Chálki [GR] 142 D5
Chálki [GR] 132 G2
Chalkiádes [GR] 132 G2
Chalkída [GR] 134 B5
Chalkidóna [GR] 128 G4
Challans [F] 54 B2
Challes-les-Eaux [F] 70 A4
Chalonnes [F] 54 D1
Chalonnes-sur-Loire [F] 54 D1
Châlons-en-Champagne [F] 44 B4
Chalon-sur-Saône [F] 56 G5
Châlus [F] 66 G2
Cham [CH] 58 F5
Cham [D] 48 C6
Chamberet [F] 66 H2
Chambéry [F] 68 H3
Chambley-Bussières [F] 44 E4
Chambon-sur-Lac [F] 68 C2
Chambon-sur-Voueize [F] 56 B6
Chambord [F] 54 H2
Chamonix-Mont-Blanc [F] 70 C3
Champagne-Mouton [F] 54 E5
Champagnole [F] 58 B6
Champaubert [F] 44 A4
Champdeniers [F] 54 D4
Champeix [F] 68 C3
Champéry [CH] 70 C2
Champex [CH] 70 C3
Champier [F] 68 G4
Champigné [F] 40 H6
Champigny-sur-Veude [F] 54 F2
Champillon [F] 44 B3
Champlitte [F] 58 A3
Champlon [B] 30 E6
Champoluc [I] 70 D3
Champrond-en-Gâtine [F] 26 H6
Champtoceaux [F] 40 F6
Chamrousse [F] 68 H5
Chamusca [P] 86 C4
Chanas [F] 68 F4
Chandrinós [GR] 136 C4
Chaniá [GR] 140 C4
Chaniotis [GR] 130 C6
Chantada [E] 78 D4
Chantelle [F] 56 D6
Chantemerle [F] 70 B6
Chantilly [F] 42 G3
Chantonnay [F] 54 C3
Chão de Codes [P] 86 D4
Chaource [F] 44 B6
Chapelle-Royale [F] 42 D5
Chárakas [GR] 140 E5
Charavines [F] 68 G4
Charbonnières-les-Bains [F] 68 F3
Charbowo [PL] 36 D2
Chard [GB] 12 F4
Charenton-du-Cher [F] 56 C4
Charing [GB] 14 F5
Charleroi [B] 30 C5
Charlestown [IRL] 2 D4
Charleville / Rath Luirc [IRL] 4 C4
Charleville-Mézières [F] 44 C2
Charlieu [F] 68 E1
Charlottenberg [S] 166 D1
Charly [F] 42 H3
Charmes [F] 44 E6
Charneca [P] 86 A5
Charny [F] 56 D1
Charnyany [BY] 38 G3
Charolles [F] 56 F6
Chârost [F] 56 B3
Charroux [F] 54 E5
Chartres [F] 42 E4
Chassigny [F] 56 H3
Château-Arnoux [F] 108 C3
Châteaubourg [F] 26 D6
Châteaubriant [F] 40 F5
Château-Chinon [F] 56 E4
Château d'Oex [CH] 70 D1
Château-du-Loir [F] 42 B6
Châteaudun [F] 42 D5
Châteaugiron [F] 26 C6
Château-Gontier [F] 40 H5
Château-la-Vallière [F] 42 B6
Châteaulin [F] 40 B2
Châteaumeillant [F] 56 B5
Châteauneuf [F] 66 E1
Châteauneuf-de-Randon [F] 68 D5
Châteauneuf-du-Faou [F] 40 C3
Châteauneuf-du-Pape [F] 106 G3
Châteauneuf-en-Thymerais [F] 26 H6
Chateauneuf-sur-Cher [F] 56 C4
Châteauneuf-sur-Loire [F] 42 F6
Châteauneuf-sur-Sarthe [F] 40 H6
Châteauponsac [F] 54 G5
Château-Porcien [F] 28 H6
Château-Queyras [F] 70 B6
Château-Regnault [F] 44 C1
Châteaurenard [F] 42 G6
Château-Renault [F] 54 G1
Châteauroux [F] 54 H4
Château-Salins [F] 44 F5
Château-Thierry [F] 42 H3
Châteauvillain [F] 56 G2
Châtel [F] 70 C2
Châtelaillon-Plage [F] 54 C5
Châtelet [B] 30 C5
Châtelguyon [F] 68 C2
Châtellerault [F] 54 F3
Châtel-Montagne [F] 68 E1
Châtel-St-Denis [CH] 70 C1
Châtelus-Malvaleix [F] 54 H5
Châtenois [F] 44 E6
Chatham [GB] 14 F4
Châtillon [I] 70 D4
Châtillon-Coligny [F] 56 D1
Châtillon-en-Bazois [F] 56 E4
Châtillon-en-Diois [F] 68 G6
Châtillon-sur-Chalaronne [F] 68 G2
Châtillon-sur-Indre [F] 54 G3
Châtillon-sur-Loire [F] 56 D2
Châtillon-sur-Marne [F] 44 A3
Châtillon-sur-Seine [F] 56 G2
Chatteris [GB] 14 F2
Chatto [GB] 8 F4
Chaudes-Aigues [F] 68 C5
Chauffailles [F] 68 F1
Chaufour-lès-Bonnières [F] 42 E3
Chaumergy [F] 56 H5
Chaumont [F] 54 G2
Chaumont [F] 56 H1
Chaumont-sur-Aire [F] 44 D4
Chaumont-sur-Loire [F] 54 G2
Chaunay [F] 54 E5
Chauny [F] 28 F6
Chaussin [F] 56 H5
Chauvigny [F] 54 F4
Chaves [P] 80 E3
Chazelles [F] 68 F3
Chazelles-sur-Lyon [F] 68 F3
Cheadle [GB] 10 E5
Cheb [CZ] 48 C3
Chęciny [PL] 52 B1
Cheddar [GB] 12 F3
Chef-Boutonne [F] 54 D5
Chekhov [RUS] 204 F4
Cheles [E] 94 F2
Chelm [PL] 38 F6
Chełmek [PL] 50 G3
Chełmno [PL] 22 D5
Chelmsford [GB] 14 F4
Chełmża [PL] 22 E6
Chełst [PL] 36 B1
Cheltenham [GB] 12 G2
Chelva [E] 98 D3
Chemillé [F] 54 D2
Chemin [F] 56 H5
Chemnitz [D] 48 D1
Chêne-Pignier [F] 54 F6
Chénérailles [F] 56 B6
Chenonceaux [F] 54 G2
Chepelare [BG] 130 E1
Chepstow [GB] 12 G3
Chera [E] 98 D4
Cherasco [I] 108 G2
Cherbourg [F] 26 D2
Cherepovets [RUS] 204 F2
Cherkasy [UA] 206 F2
Chernaya Rechka [RUS] 200 G3
Chernevo [RUS] 200 G2
Cherniakhiv [UA] 206 E2
Chernivtsi [UA] 206 C3
Cherno [RUS] 200 G1
Chernomorets [BG] 148 F4
Chernyakhovsk [RUS] 24 C1
Chéroy [F] 42 G5
Cherveix-Cubas [F] 66 G3
Chervena Voda [BG] 148 D2
Cherven Bryag [BG] 150 G3
Chervonohrad [UA] 52 H2
Chervyen' [BY] 204 B5
Chesham [GB] 14 E3
Cheste [E] 98 E4
Chester [GB] 10 D4
Chesterfield [GB] 10 F5
Chester-le-Street [GB] 8 F6
Chevagnes [F] 56 D5
Chevanceaux [F] 66 D2
Chevreuse [F] 42 F4
Chézal-Benoît [F] 56 B4
Chiampo [I] 72 D6
Chianciano Terme [I] 114 G2
Chiaramonti Gulfi [I] 126 F5
Chiaravalle [I] 112 C6
Chiaravalle Centrale [I] 124 D6
Chiari [I] 70 H5
Chiasso [CH] 70 G4
Chiavari [I] 110 B3
Chiavenna [I] 70 G2
Chichester [GB] 14 D5
Chicklade [GB] 12 G4
Chiclana de la Frontera [E] 100 F4
Chieming [D] 60 F5
Chieri [I] 70 D6
Chiesa in Valmalenco [I] 70 H3
Chieti [I] 116 D4
Chigwell [GB] 14 E4
Chilham [GB] 14 F5
Chiliomódi [GR] 136 F1
Chillarón de Cuenca [E] 98 B2
Chillón [E] 96 C4
Chimay [B] 28 H5
Chinchilla de Monte-Aragón [E] 98 C5
Chinchón [E] 96 G1
Chinon [F] 54 F2
Chióggia [I] 110 H1
Chíos [GR] 134 G4
Chipiona [E] 100 F3
Chippenham [GB] 12 G3
Chipping Campden [GB] 12 H2
Chipping Norton [GB] 12 H2
Chipping Sodbury [GB] 12 G3
Chiprovtsi [BG] 150 F3
Chirivel [E] 102 H3
Chirk [GB] 10 C5
Chirnside [GB] 8 F4
Chirpan [BG] 148 C5
Chisa [F] 114 B5
Chişinău [MD] 206 E4
Chişineu Criş [RO] 76 G3
Chiusa / Klausen [I] 72 D3
Chiusa di Pesio [I] 108 F3
Chiusaforte [I] 72 G4
Chiusa Scláfani [I] 126 C3
Chiusi [I] 114 H2
Chiva [E] 98 E4
Chivasso [I] 70 D5
Chlebowo [PL] 34 G3
Chlewiska [PL] 38 B6
Chlumec nad Cidlinou [CZ] 48 H3
Chlum u Třeboně [CZ] 62 C2
Chmielnik [PL] 52 B2
Chobham [GB] 14 D4
Chobienice [PL] 36 B3
Choceň [CZ] 50 B4
Choceń [PL] 36 F2
Chochołów [PL] 50 H5
Chocianów [PL] 36 B5
Chociwel [PL] 20 G5
Choczewo [PL] 22 D1
Chodecz [PL] 36 F2
Chodel [PL] 38 D6
Chodos / Xodos [E] 98 F2
Chodová Planá [CZ] 48 D4
Chodzież [PL] 22 B6
Chojna [PL] 20 F6
Chojnice [PL] 22 C4
Chojnów [PL] 36 B6
Cholet [F] 54 D2
Chomakovtsi [BG] 150 G3
Chomęciska Małe [PL] 52 F1
Chomutov [CZ] 48 E2
Chop [UA] 206 B2
Chóra [GR] 136 C4
Choreftó [GR] 134 A2
Chorges [F] 108 D2
Choristí [GR] 130 D3
Chorley [GB] 10 D3
Chornobyl [UA] 204 C7
Chornomors'ke [UA] 206 F5
Choroszcz [PL] 24 E5
Chortkiv [UA] 206 C3
Chorzele [PL] 22 H5
Chorzów [PL] 50 G3
Chorzyna [PL] 36 F5
Choszczno [PL] 20 G6
Chotěboř [CZ] 50 A5
Choumnikó [GR] 130 C3
Chouto [P] 86 D4
Choye [F] 58 A4
Chrast [CZ] 50 B4
Chrastava [CZ] 48 G1
Christchurch [GB] 12 G5
Christiansfeld [DK] 156 C3
Chrudim [CZ] 50 A4
Chrysochóri [GR] 130 E3
Chrysoúpoli [GR] 130 E3
Chrząchówek [PL] 38 D5
Chrzanów [PL] 50 G3
Chudoba [PL] 50 E1
Chudovo [RUS] 204 D2
Chulkovo [RUS] 178 E3
Chulmleigh [GB] 12 E4
Chuprene [BG] 150 E3
Chur [CH] 70 H1
Church Stretton [GB] 10 D6
Churchtown [IRL] 4 F5
Churchtown [IRL] 4 E5
Churek [BG] 150 G4
Chwaszczyno [PL] 22 D2
Chyňava [CZ] 48 F4
Chýnov [CZ] 48 G5
Chýrgos [GR] 128 H4
Chyżne [PL] 50 H5
Cianciana [I] 126 D3
Ciasna [PL] 50 F2
Ciąże [PL] 36 E3
Ciborro [P] 86 D6
Ciboure [F] 84 B2
Cicciano [I] 120 E3
Čičevac [YU] 150 C3
Cichy [PL] 24 D3
Cidones [E] 90 B2
Ciechanów [PL] 38 B1
Ciechanowiec [PL] 38 D1
Ciechocinek [PL] 36 F1
Ciempozuelos [E] 96 G1
Ciepielów [PL] 38 C5
Cieplice Śląskie-Zdrój [PL] 50 A1
Cierp-Gaud [F] 84 F4
Cieszanów [PL] 52 F3
Cieszyn [PL] 50 F4
Cieza [E] 104 C2
Ciężkowice [PL] 52 C4
Cifuentes [E] 90 A5
Cigales [E] 88 E1
Cigánd [H] 64 H4
Cigliano [I] 70 E5
Cihangazi [TR] 146 G5
Cilipi [HR] 152 D4
Cill Airne / Killarney [IRL] 4 B4
Cillas [E] 90 C5
Cill Chainnigh / Kilkenny [IRL] 4 E4
Cill Charthaigh / Kilcar [IRL] 2 D2
Cill Ciaráin / Kilkieran [IRL] 2 B4
Cilleros [E] 86 G3
Cimadevilla [E] 78 B3
Cimoszki [PL] 24 E3
Cîmpeni [RO] 206 B5
Cîmpia Turzii [RO] 206 B5
Cîmpina [RO] 206 C6
Cîmpulung [RO] 206 C6
Cîmpulung Moldovenesc [RO] 206 C4
Çınarcık [TR] 146 F3
Cindere [TR] 144 F4
Cinderford [GB] 12 G2
Çine [TR] 144 E6
Ciney [B] 30 D5
Cinfães [P] 80 C4
Cingoli [I] 116 C1
Cinigiano [I] 114 F2
Cínisi [I] 126 C1
Cínovec [CZ] 48 E2
Cinquefrondi [I] 124 D6
Cintegabelle [F] 106 A4
Cintruénigo [E] 84 A6
Ciółkowo [PL] 36 H2
Cirella [I] 124 C3
Cirencester [GB] 12 G3
Cirey [F] 44 G6
Ciria [E] 90 C3
Ciriè [I] 70 D5
Čirkovicy [RUS] 178 G6
Cirò Marina [I] 124 F4
Ciron [F] 54 G4
Ciruli [LV] 200 C4
Cisa, Passo della- [I] 110 C3
Cisna [PL] 52 E6
Cisnădie [RO] 206 B5
Cista Provo [HR] 152 B2
Cisterna di Latina [I] 116 B6
Cisternino [I] 122 F3
Cistierna [E] 82 C4
Çıtlık [TR] 142 E2
Cittadella [I] 72 D6
Città della Pieve [I] 114 H2
Città del Vaticano [V] 116 A5
Città di Castello [I] 116 A1
Cittaducale [I] 116 B4
Cittanova [I] 124 D7
Città Sant'Angelo [I] 116 D4
Ciudad Real [E] 96 E4
Ciudad Rodrigo [E] 88 A3
Ciumeghiu [RO] 76 H3
Ciutadella de Menorca [E] 104 G4
Cividale del Friuli [I] 72 G5
Civita [I] 114 H3
Cívita Castellana [I] 116 A4
Civitanova Marche [I] 116 C1
Civitavécchia [I] 114 G5
Civitella del Tronto [I] 116 C3
Civitella di Romagna [I] 110 G5
Civitella in Val di Chiana [I] 114 G1
Civitella Paganico [I] 114 F2
Civitella Roveto [I] 116 C5
Civray [F] 54 E5
Civrieux-d'Azergues [F] 68 F2
Çivril [TR] 144 G4
Clackmannan [GB] 8 E3
Clacton-on-Sea [GB] 14 G4
Clady [GB] 2 F2
Clairvaux-les-Lacs [F] 70 A1
Clamecy [F] 56 E3
Clane [IRL] 2 F6
Claonaig [GB] 8 C3
Clapham [GB] 14 E2
Clara [IRL] 2 D5
Clare [GB] 14 F3
Clarecastle [IRL] 2 C6
Claremorris [IRL] 2 C4
Clarinbridge [IRL] 2 C5
Clashmore [IRL] 4 D5
Claudy [GB] 2 F2
Clausthal-Zellerfeld [D] 32 G4
Clavière [I] 70 B6
Clay Cross [GB] 10 F5
Cleadale [GB] 6 B5
Cleanovu [RO] 150 F1
Cleator Moor [GB] 8 D6
Clécy [F] 26 F4
Cleethorpes [GB] 10 G4
Clefmont [F] 58 A2
Clelles [F] 68 G5
Cleobury Mortimer [GB] 10 D6
Cleobury North [GB] 10 D6
Clères [F] 28 C5
Clermont [F] 28 E6
Clermont-en-Argonne [F] 44 D4
Clermont-Ferrand [F] 68 C2
Clermont-l'Hérault [F] 106 E4
Clerval [CH] 58 C4
Clervaux [L] 44 F1
Cléry [F] 42 E6
Cles [I] 72 C3
Clevedon [GB] 12 F3
Clifden [IRL] 2 B4
Cliffe [GB] 14 F4
Cliffony [IRL] 2 D3
Clisson [F] 54 C2
Clitheroe [GB] 10 E3
Clogan [IRL] 2 D6
Clogh [IRL] 4 F3
Clogheen [IRL] 4 D4
Clogher [GB] 2 F3
Cloghmore [IRL] 2 B3
Clonakilty [IRL] 4 C5
Clonard [IRL] 2 E5
Clonaslee [IRL] 2 D6
Clonbur [IRL] 2 C4
Clondalkin [IRL] 2 F6
Clones [IRL] 2 E4
Clonfert [IRL] 2 D5
Clonmany [IRL] 2 F1
Clonmel / Cluain Meala [IRL] 4 E4
Clonmellon [IRL] 2 E5
Clonroche [IRL] 4 F4
Cloonbannin [IRL] 4 C4
Cloonkeen [IRL] 4 B4
Cloonlara [IRL] 4 D3
Cloppenburg [D] 18 C6
Clough [GB] 2 G4
Cloughjordan [IRL] 2 D6
Clova [GB] 8 F1
Clovelly [GB] 12 D3
Cloyes-sur-le-Loir [F] 42 D5

Daszyna [PL] 36 G3
Datça [TR] 142 D3
Datteln [D] 30 H2
Daugård [DK] 156 C2
Daugavpils [LV] 202 H3
Dauguli [LV] 200 E4
Daun [D] 30 G6
Daventry [GB] 14 D2
Daviá [GR] 136 D2
Davington [GB] 8 E4
Daviot [GB] 6 D5
Davle [CZ] 48 F4
Dávlia [GR] 132 H5
Davos [CH] 72 A2
Davutlar [TR] 144 D5
Dawlish [GB] 12 E5
Dax [F] 66 B6
Deal [GB] 14 G5
Deão [P] 78 A6
Deauville [F] 26 G3
Debar [MK] 128 C2
Debeburnu [TR] 144 D2
Debelets [BG] 148 C3
Dębe Wielkie [PL] 38 C3
Dębica [PL] 52 D3
Dębina [PL] 50 E3
Deblin [PL] 38 D5
Debnevo [BG] 148 B4
Dębnica Kaszubska [PL] 22 B2
Dębno [PL] 34 G1
Debno [PL] 52 B5
Dębno [PL] 52 B4
Debovo [BG] 148 B2
Debowo [PL] 24 E4
Debrc [YU] 154 F3
Debrecen [H] 64 G6
Debrznica [PL] 34 H3
Debrzno [PL] 22 C5
Debür [BG] 148 C6
Dęby [PL] 24 C5
Dečani [YU] 150 B5
Decazeville [F] 68 A5
Decimomannu [I] 118 C7
Děčín [CZ] 48 F2
Decize [F] 56 D4
De Cocksdorp [NL] 16 D2
Dedaj [AL] 152 E4
Dedebağ [TR] 142 G1
Dedemsvaart [NL] 16 G4
Dédestapolcsány [H] 64 E4
Degaña [E] 78 F4
Degebüll [D] 156 B5
Degerby [FIN] 168 G1
Degerby [FIN] 176 G5
Degerfors [S] 166 G3
Degerhamn [S] 162 G6
Degerndorf [D] 60 F5
Degernes [N] 166 C3
Deggendorf [D] 60 G2
Değirmenalanı [TR] 142 F1
Değirmendere [TR] 144 C5
Değirmendere [TR] 146 G3
De Haan [B] 28 F1
Dehesa de Campoamor [E] 104 D3
Deià / Deyá [E] 104 E4
Deidesheim [D] 46 B5
Deinze [B] 28 G2
Dej [RO] 206 B4
Deje [S] 166 F2
De Koog [NL] 16 D2
De Kooy [NL] 16 D2
Delbrück [D] 32 D3
Delčevo [MK] 128 G1
Delden [NL] 16 G5
Delebäck [S] 166 F4
Deleitosa [E] 96 C1
Delémont [CH] 58 D5
Delfí [GR] 132 G5
Delft [NL] 16 C5
Delfzijl [NL] 16 H2
Délia [I] 126 E4
Delianuova [I] 124 C7
Deliatyn [UA] 206 C3
Deliblato [YU] 154 H2
Delitzsch [D] 34 C5
Delle [F] 58 D4
Delme [F] 44 F5
Delmenhorst [D] 18 D5
Delnice [HR] 112 F1
Delsbo [S] 184 D6
Delvin [IRL] 2 E5
Delvina [AL] 132 B1
Delvináki [GR] 132 C1
Demandice [SK] 64 C4
Demigny [F] 56 G5
Demirci [TR] 144 E2
Demirci [TR] 146 F5
Demirhanlı [TR] 146 B2
Demir Kapija [MK] 128 G2
Demirköy [TR] 146 C1
Demirköy [TR] 146 G5
Demirtaş [TR] 146 F4
Demjansk [RUS] 204 D3
Demmin [D] 20 C3
Denain [F] 28 G4
Denbigh [GB] 10 C4
Den Burg [NL] 16 D2
Dendermonde [B] 28 H2
Denekamp [NL] 16 G4
Đeneral Jankovič [YU] 150 C6
Den Haag [NL] 16 C5
Den Helder [NL] 16 D2
Dénia [E] 104 F1
Denizgören [TR] 146 B5
Denizkent [TR] 146 C5
Denizler [TR] 144 G4
Denizli [TR] 144 G5
Denkendorf [D] 60 E2
Dennington [GB] 14 G3
Denny [GB] 8 D3
Den Oever [NL] 16 E2
Denzlingen [D] 58 E3
De Panne [B] 28 F1
Deptford [GB] 12 G4
Derbent [TR] 144 E4
Derby [GB] 10 E5
Derecske [H] 76 G1
Dereköy [TR] 146 C1
Dereköy [TR] 144 E4
Dermantsi [BG] 148 A3
Dermbach [D] 46 F1
Derneburg [D] 32 G3
Derreada [P] 94 B3
Derrygonnelly [GB] 2 E3
Derrylin [GB] 2 E4
Dersingham [GB] 10 H6
Deruta [I] 116 A2
Derval [F] 40 F5
Dervéni [GR] 132 G6
Derventa [BIH] 154 D2
Dervock [GB] 2 G2
Descartes [F] 54 F3
Desenzano del Garda [I] 72 B6
Desfína [GR] 132 G5
Desimirovac [YU] 150 C2
Desio [I] 70 G4
Desná [CZ] 48 H2
Dešov [CZ] 62 E2
Despotovac [YU] 150 C2
Despotovo [YU] 154 F1
Dessau [D] 34 C4
Destriana [E] 78 G6
Désulo [I] 118 D5
Desvres [F] 28 D2
Deszk [H] 76 E4
Deta [RO] 206 A5
Detmold [D] 32 E3
Dettelbach [D] 46 F4
Deurne [NL] 30 F2
Deutschkreutz [A] 62 F6
Deutschlandsberg [A] 74 D3
Deutsch-Wagram [A] 62 F4
Deva [E] 82 H4
Deva [RO] 206 B5
Dévaványa [H] 76 F2
Devčiči [HR] 112 F3
Devecikonağı [TR] 146 E5
Devecser [H] 74 H2
Devene [BG] 150 G3
Deventer [NL] 16 F5
Deveselu [RO] 148 A1
Devetaki [BG] 148 B3
Devin [BG] 130 D1
Devizes [GB] 12 G3
Devnya [BG] 148 F3
Dewsbury [GB] 10 F4
Deyá / Deià [E] 104 E4
Dhërmi [AL] 128 B6
Dheskáti [GR] 132 F1
Diafáni [GR] 140 H2
Diagučiai [LT] 202 G4
Diakoftó [GR] 132 G6
Dialambí [GR] 130 F3
Diamante [I] 124 C3
Dianalund [DK] 156 F3
Diano Marina [I] 108 G4
Diásselo [GR] 132 F1
Diavatá [GR] 128 H4
Dicomano [I] 110 F5
Didcot [GB] 14 D3
Dídyma [GR] 136 F2
Didymóteicho [GR] 130 H1
Die [F] 68 G6
Dieburg [D] 46 C3
Diego Alvaro [E] 88 D4
Diekirch [L] 44 F2
Diemelstadt [D] 32 E4
Dienten [A] 72 G1
Diepholz [D] 32 D1
Dieppe [F] 28 C4
Dierdorf [D] 46 B1
Dieren [NL] 16 F5
Diesdorf [D] 32 H1
Diessen [D] 60 D5
Diest [B] 30 D4
Dietenheim [D] 60 B4
Dietfurt [D] 46 H6
Dietikon [CH] 58 F5
Dietmannsried [D] 60 C5
Dieulefit [F] 68 F6
Dieulouard [F] 44 E5
Dieuze [F] 44 F5
Dieveniškės [LT] 202 G6
Diever [NL] 16 G3
Diez [D] 46 B2
Differdange [L] 44 E3
Digermulen [N] 192 C4
Dignano [I] 72 G4
Digne-les-Bains [F] 108 D3
Digoin [F] 56 E5
Dijon [F] 56 G4
Dikanäs [S] 190 F4
Díkea [GR] 146 A2
Dikili [TR] 144 C3
Diksmuide [B] 28 F2
Dílessi [GR] 134 C5
Dillenberg [D] 32 D6
Dillingen [D] 60 C3
Dillingen [D] 44 F3
Dilwyn [GB] 12 G1
Dimaro [I] 72 C4
Dimena [GR] 136 F2
Dímitra [GR] 132 G1
Dimitrovgrad [BG] 148 C6
Dimitrovgrad [YU] 150 E4
Dimovo [BG] 150 E2
Dinami [I] 124 D6
Dinan [F] 26 C5
Dinant [B] 30 D6
Dinar [TR] 144 H4
Dinard [F] 26 C4
Dingelstädt [D] 32 G5
Dingle [S] 166 C5
Dingle / An Daingean [IRL] 4 A3
Dingli [M] 126 C6
Dingolfing [D] 60 F3
Dingwall [GB] 6 D4
Dinkelsbühl [D] 46 F6
Dinklage [D] 32 D1
Dinozé [F] 58 C2
Dinslaken [D] 30 G2
Dio [S] 162 D5
Dipótama [GR] 130 D2
Dippoldiswalde [D] 48 E1
Dirráchi [GR] 136 D3
Disentis / Mustér [CH] 70 G1
Dispíli [GR] 128 E5
Diss [GB] 14 G2
Dístomo [GR] 132 H5
Dístrato [GR] 128 D6
Ditzingen [D] 58 G1
Diva Slatina [BG] 150 F3
Divčibare [YU] 150 A2
Dives-sur-Mer [F] 26 F3
Divjakë [AL] 128 A4
Divonne-les-Bains [F] 70 B2
Dívri [GR] 132 G4
Divusa [HR] 154 A2
Djúpivogur [IS] 194 G6
Djupvik [N] 192 F2
Djura [S] 172 H4
Djurakovac [YU] 150 B5
Djurås [S] 172 H4
Djurdjevica Tara [YU] 152 E2
Dłoń [PL] 36 C4
Długie [PL] 36 A1
Długosiodło [PL] 38 C1
Dmitrov [RUS] 204 F3
Dniprodzerzhyns'k [UA] 206 G3
Dnipropetrovs'k [UA] 206 G3
Dno [RUS] 204 C3
Doagh [GB] 2 G3
Dobanovci [YU] 154 G2
Dobbiaco / Toblach [I] 72 E3
Dobczyce [PL] 52 A4
Dobel [D] 58 G1
Dobele [LV] 200 D5
Döbeln [D] 34 D6
Doberlug Kirchhain [D] 34 E4
Döbern [D] 34 G5
Dobersberg [A] 62 D2
Dobiegniew [PL] 20 H6
Doboj [BIH] 154 D3
Doboz [H] 76 G3
Dobra [PL] 52 B4
Dobra [PL] 36 F4
Dobra [PL] 20 G4
Dobra [RO] 150 F1
Dobrá Niva [SK] 64 C3
Dobřany [CZ] 48 D5
Dobrčane [YU] 150 D5
Dobre [PL] 38 C2
Dobre Miasto [PL] 22 G3
Döbriach [A] 72 H3
Dobrich [BG] 148 F2
Dobřichovice [CZ] 48 F4
Dobri Do [YU] 150 C4
Dobrinishte [BG] 130 B1
Dobříš [CZ] 48 F4
Dobrodzień [PL] 50 F2
Döbrököz [H] 76 B4
Dobromani [BIH] 152 C3
Dobromierz [PL] 50 B1
Dobromirka [BG] 148 C3
Dobromirtsi [BG] 130 F2
Dobromyl' [UA] 52 F5
Dobro Polje [BIH] 152 D2
Dobrosloveni [RO] 150 H1
Dobroszyce [PL] 36 D6
Dobroteşti [RO] 148 B1
Dobrotitsa [BG] 148 E1
Dobrovol'sk [RUS] 24 D1
Dobruchi [RUS] 200 G2
Dobrun [BIH] 152 E1
Dobruška [CZ] 50 B3
Dobrzany [PL] 20 G5
Dobrzyca [PL] 36 D4
Dobrzyń nad Wisła [PL] 36 G2
Docking [GB] 10 H6
Döderhult [S] 162 G3
Dodóni [GR] 132 D2
Doesburg [NL] 16 F5
Doetinchem [NL] 16 F5
Doganbey [TR] 142 B1
Doganbey [TR] 144 C5
Doganovič [YU] 150 C6
Dogliani [I] 108 G2
Dogueno [P] 94 C4
Dokka [N] 170 H3
Dokkas [S] 192 F6
Dokkum [NL] 16 F2
Doksy [CZ] 48 G2
Dolceácqua [I] 108 F4
Dol-de-Bretagne [F] 26 C4
Dole [F] 56 H4
Dølemo [N] 164 E4
Dolenci [MK] 128 D3
Dolenja Vas [SLO] 74 C6
Dolga Vas [SLO] 74 F3
Dolgellau [GB] 10 B5
Dolhobyczów [PL] 52 H2
Dolianá [GR] 132 C1
Dolianova [I] 118 D6
Dolice [PL] 20 G6
Dolíhi [GR] 128 G6
Dolina Grupa [PL] 22 E5
Doljani [HR] 112 H4
Doljevac [YU] 150 D4
Döllach [A] 72 G2
Döllbach [D] 46 E2
Dolle [D] 34 B2
Döllstädt [D] 32 H6
Dolna Banya [BG] 150 G5
Dolna Dikanya [BG] 150 F5
Dolna Mitropoliya [BG] 148 A3
Dolni Dŭbnik [BG] 148 A3
Dolní Dvonste [CZ] 62 C3
Dolní Kounice [CZ] 62 F2
Dolni Lom [BG] 150 E3
Dolno Kamartsi [BG] 150 G4
Dolno Kosovrasti [MK] 128 C2
Dolno Levski [BG] 148 A5
Dolno Novkovo [BG] 148 D3
Dolno Tserovene [BG] 150 F3
Dolno Ujno [BG] 150 E5
Dolný Kubín [SK] 50 G6
Dolo [I] 110 H1
Dolores [E] 104 D3
Dolovo [YU] 154 H2
Dolsk [PL] 36 C4
Dolyna [UA] 52 H6
Domaniç [TR] 146 G5
Domanoviči [BIH] 152 C3
Domažlice [CZ] 48 D5
Dombås [N] 180 G5
Dombasle [F] 44 F5
Dombegyház [H] 76 G4
Dombóvár [H] 76 B4
Dombrád [H] 64 H4
Dombrot-le-Sec [F] 58 B2
Domburg [NL] 16 B6
Doméniko [GR] 132 F1
Domèvre-en-Haye [F] 44 E5
Domfront [F] 26 E5
Domingão [P] 86 D4
Dömitz [D] 18 H5
Domme [F] 66 G4
Dommitzsch [D] 34 D4
Domnítsa [GR] 132 F4
Domnovo [RUS] 22 H2
Domodedovo [RUS] 204 F4
Domodóssola [I] 70 E3
Domokós [GR] 132 G3
Dompaire [F] 58 C2
Dompierre [F] 56 E5
Dompierre-du-Chemin [F] 26 D5
Dompierre-sur-Besbre [F] 56 E5
Dompierre-sur-Mer [F] 54 C4
Domrémy-la-Pucelle [F] 44 D6
Dömsöd [H] 76 C2
Dómus de Maria [I] 118 C8
Domusnóvas [I] 118 B6
Domžale [SLO] 74 C5
Donado [E] 80 G3
Donaghadee [GB] 2 H3
Donaghmore [IRL] 4 E3
Doña Mencía [E] 102 C2
Donaueschingen [D] 58 F3
Donaustauf [D] 60 F2
Donauwörth [D] 60 D2
Don Benito [E] 96 B3
Doncaster [GB] 10 F4
Dondurma [TR] 146 B5
Donegal / Dún na nGall [IRL] 2 E2
Donington [GB] 10 G6
Donja Brela [HR] 152 B2
Donja Brezna [YU] 152 D3
Donja Bukovica [YU] 152 E3
Donja Kamenica [YU] 150 A1
Donja Ljubata [YU] 150 E5
Donja Šatornja [YU] 150 B2
Donja Suvaja [HR] 112 H4
Donje Ljupče [YU] 150 C5
Donje Petrčane [HR] 112 F5
Donji Koričani [BIH] 154 C3
Donji Lapac [HR] 112 H4
Donji Miholjac [HR] 76 B6
Donji Milanovac [YU] 150 D1
Donji Vakuf [BIH] 154 C4
Donji Zemunik [HR] 112 G5
Donnersbach [A] 62 B6
Donnersbachwald [A] 74 B1
Dønnes [N] 190 D2
Donostia-San Sebastián [E] 84 B2
Dontilly [F] 42 G5
Donzenac [F] 66 G3
Donzère [F] 68 F6
Donzy [F] 56 D3
Doohooma [IRL] 2 B3
Doonbeg [IRL] 2 B6
Doonloughan [IRL] 2 B4
Doorn [NL] 16 E5
Doornik (Tournai) [B] 28 G3
Dörarp [S] 162 C4
Dorchester [GB] 14 D3
Dorchester [GB] 12 F5
Dordives [F] 42 G5
Dordrecht [NL] 16 D5
Dores [GB] 6 D5
Dorfen [D] 60 F4
Dorfmark [D] 18 F6
Dorgali [I] 118 E4
Dório [GR] 136 D3
Dorkáda [GR] 130 B4
Dorking [GB] 14 E5
Dormagen [D] 30 G4
Dormánd [H] 64 E6
Dormans [F] 44 A3
Dornauberg [A] 72 E2
Dornbirn [A] 60 B6
Dornburg [D] 34 B6
Dorndorf [D] 46 F1
Dornes [F] 56 D5
Dornoch [GB] 6 E4
Dornstetten [D] 58 G2
Dornum [D] 18 B3
Dorog [H] 64 C6
Dorogobuzh [RUS] 204 D5
Dorohoi [RO] 206 D4
Dorohucza [PL] 38 F6
Dorotea [S] 190 F5
Dörpen [D] 16 H3
Dörpstedt [D] 18 E2
Dorrington [GB] 10 D6
Dorsten [D] 30 H2
Dortan [F] 68 H1
Dortmund [D] 32 C4
Dorum [D] 18 D3
Dörverden [D] 18 E6
Dörzbach [D] 46 E5
Dosbarrios [E] 96 G2
Dos Hermanas [E] 94 G6
Dospat [BG] 130 D1
Douai [F] 28 F4
Douarnenez [F] 40 B3
Douchy [F] 42 G6
Doucier [F] 58 A6
Doudeville [F] 26 H2
Doué-la-Fontaine [F] 54 E2
Dougarie [GB] 8 C3
Douglas [GB] 8 D4
Douglas [GBM] 10 B2
Doulaincourt [F] 44 D6
Doulevant-le-Château [F] 44 C6
Doullens [F] 28 E4
Dounby [GB] 6 F2
Dourdan [F] 42 F4
Dourgne [F] 106 B4
Douvaine [F] 70 B2
Douzy [F] 44 D2
Dover [GB] 14 G5
Dovre [N] 180 G5
Downham Market [GB] 14 F2
Downpatrick [GB] 2 G4
Dowra [IRL] 2 E3
Dowsk [BY] 204 C6
Doxáto [GR] 130 D3
Dozulé [F] 26 G3
Drabiv [UA] 206 F2
Dračevo [MK] 128 E1
Drachselsried [D] 48 D6
Drachten [NL] 16 F2
Dragalevci [BG] 150 F5
Drăgăneşti de Vede [RO] 148 B1
Drăgăneşti Olt [RO] 148 A1
Drăgăneşti Vlaşca [RO] 148 C1
Dragaš [YU] 150 B6
Drăgăşani [RO] 206 B6
Draginje [YU] 150 A1
Dragocvet [YU] 150 C2
Dragoman [BG] 150 F4
Dragomirovo [BG] 148 C3
Dragomirovo [BG] 148 B2
Dragør [DK] 156 H3
Dragovishtitsa [BG] 150 E5
Dragsfjärd [FIN] 176 E5
Dragsvik [N] 170 C1
Draguignan [F] 108 D5
Drahanovice [CZ] 50 C5
Drahonice [CZ] 48 F6
Drahovce [SK] 62 H3
Dráma [GR] 130 D3
Drammen [N] 164 H1
Drangsness [IS] 194 C2
Drânic [RO] 150 G1
Dransfeld [D] 32 F4
Dranske [D] 20 D1
Draperstown [GB] 2 F3
Drasenhofen [A] 62 F3
Drávaszabolcs [H] 76 B6
Dravískos [GR] 130 C3
Dravograd [SLO] 74 C3
Drawno [PL] 20 H6
Drawsko Pomorskie [PL] 20 H5
Drazdzewo [PL] 24 B6
Draženov [CZ] 48 D5
Drebkau [D] 34 F4
Dreilingen [D] 18 G6
Dren [YU] 150 B4
Drenchia [I] 72 H4
Drenovac [YU] 150 D5
Drenovci [HR] 154 E2
Drenovets [BG] 150 F2
Drensteinfurt [D] 32 C3
Drépano [GR] 128 F5
Dresden [D] 34 E6
Dretyń [PL] 22 B3
Dreux [F] 42 E3
DrevsjØ [N] 182 D6
Drewitz [D] 34 C3
Drewitz [D] 34 E2
Drezdenko [PL] 36 B1
Dreznik-Grad [HR] 112 G2
Driebergen [NL] 16 E5
Driffield [GB] 10 G3
Drimnin [GB] 6 B6
Drimoleague [IRL] 4 B5
Drinjača [BIH] 154 E4
Drinovci [BIH] 152 B2
Drionville [F] 28 E2
Drivstua [N] 180 H4
Drlače [YU] 154 F4
Drnholec [CZ] 62 F2
Drniš [HR] 154 A5
Drøbak [N] 166 B2
Drobeta-Turnu Severin [RO] 206 B6
Drobin [PL] 36 H1
Drochtersen [D] 18 E3
Drogheda / Droichead Átha [IRL] 2 F5
Drohiczyn [PL] 38 E2
Drohobych [UA] 52 G5
Droichead Átha / Drogheda [IRL] 2 F5
Droichead Nua / Newbridge [IRL] 2 E6
Droitwich [GB] 12 G1
Drołtowice [PL] 36 D5
Dromahair [IRL] 2 D3
Dromcolliher [IRL] 4 C4
Dromore [GB] 2 G4
Dromore [GB] 2 E3
Dromore West [IRL] 2 D3
Dronero [I] 108 F2
Dronfield [GB] 10 F5
Dronninglund [DK] 160 E3
Dronten [NL] 16 F4
Drosáto [GR] 128 H3
Drosendorf Stadt [A] 62 E2
Drosselbjerg [DK] 156 E3
Drossiá [GR] 134 B5
Drossopigí [GR] 128 E4
Drossopigí [GR] 132 D3
Drumconrath [IRL] 2 F5
Drumevo [BG] 148 E3
Drumkeeran [IRL] 2 D3
Drumlish [IRL] 2 E4
Drummore [GB] 8 C5
Drumnadrochit [GB] 6 D5
Drumquin [GB] 2 E3
Drumshanbo [IRL] 2 D4
Drumsna [IRL] 2 D4
Drusenheim [F] 44 H5
Druskininkai [LT] 24 F3
Drusti [LV] 200 F4
Druten [NL] 16 E5
Druzhba [BG] 148 G3
Drvar [BIH] 154 A3
Drvenik [HR] 152 B3
Dryanovo [BG] 148 C4
Drygały [PL] 24 D4
Drymós [GR] 128 H4
Dryópi [GR] 136 F2
Dryopída [GR] 138 C2
Dryós [GR] 138 E3
Drzewce [PL] 36 F3
Drzewica [PL] 38 B5
Duagh [IRL] 4 C3
Duas Igrejas [P] 80 G4
Dub [YU] 150 A2
Dubá [CZ] 48 G2
Dubăsari [MD] 206 E4
Duben [D] 34 E4
Dubí [CZ] 48 E2
Dubica [HR] 154 B2
Dublin / Baile Átha Cliath [IRL] 2 F6
Dubna [RUS] 204 F3
Dubnica nad Váhom [SK] 64 A2
Dŭbnitsa [BG] 130 C1
Dubno [UA] 206 C2
Dubrovnik [HR] 152 C4
Dubrovytsia [UA] 204 A7
Ducey [F] 26 D4
Duchally [GB] 6 D3
Duchcov [CZ] 48 E2
Ducherow [D] 20 E4
Duclair [F] 26 H3
Dudelange [L] 44 E3
Duderstadt [D] 32 G4
Dudeştii Vechi [RO] 76 F5
Düdingen [CH] 58 D6
Dudley [GB] 10 D6
Dueñas [E] 88 F1
Duesund [N] 170 B2
Dueville [I] 72 D6
Duffield [GB] 10 E5
Dufftown [GB] 6 F5
Duga Poljana [YU] 150 B4
Duga Resa [HR] 112 G1
Dugi Rat [HR] 152 A2
Duğla [TR] 144 C2
Dugo Selo [HR] 74 F6
Duhnen [D] 18 D3
Duingt [F] 70 B3
Duino [I] 72 H5
Duisburg [D] 30 G3
Dukat [AL] 128 A6
Dukat [YU] 150 E5
Dukhovshchina [RUS] 204 D4
Dukielska, Przełecz- [Eur.] 206 A2
Dukla [PL] 52 D5
Dūkštas [LT] 202 H4
Dŭlbok Izvor [BG] 148 C6
Duleek [IRL] 2 F5
Dŭlgopol [BG] 148 F3
Dülken [D] 30 F3
Dülmen [D] 16 H6
Dulnain Bridge [GB] 6 E5
Dulovka [RUS] 200 G4
Dulovo [BG] 148 E1
Dulpetorpet [N] 172 D4
Dumaca [YU] 154 F3
Dumbarton [GB] 8 D3
Dumbrăveni [RO] 148 F1
Dumfries [GB] 8 D5
Dumlupınar [TR] 144 H2
Dun [F] 44 D3
Duna [N] 190 C4
Dunaff [IRL] 2 F1
Dunaföldvár [H] 76 C3
Dunaharaszti [H] 76 C1
Dunaïvtsi [UA] 206 D3

Dunajská Streda [SK] 62 H5
Dunakeszi [H] 64 C6
Dunany [IRL] 2 F5
Dunapataj [H] 76 C3
Dunaszekcső [H] 76 C5
Dunaújváros [H] 76 C2
Dunavecse [H] 76 C2
Dunavtsi [BG] 150 E2
Dunbar [GB] 8 F3
Dunbeath [GB] 6 F3
Dunblane [GB] 8 E2
Dunboyne [IRL] 2 F6
Duncormick [IRL] 4 F5
Dundaga [LV] 200 C4
Dundalk / Dún Dealgan [IRL] 2 F4
Dún Dealgan / Dundalk [IRL] 2 F4
Dundee [GB] 8 F2
Dundonnell [GB] 6 D4
Dundrennan [GB] 8 D5
Dunfanaghy [IRL] 2 E1
Dunfermline [GB] 8 E3
Dungannon [GB] 2 F3
Dungarvan [IRL] 4 E5
Dungavel [GB] 8 D4
Dungiven [GB] 2 F2
Dungloe [IRL] 2 E2
Dungourney [IRL] 4 D5
Dunje [MK] 128 F3
Dunkeld [GB] 8 E2
Dunkerque [F] 14 H6
Dunkerque Ouest [F] 14 H6
Dunkineely [IRL] 2 D2
Dun Laoghaire [IRL] 2 F6
Dunlavin [IRL] 4 F3
Dunleer [IRL] 2 F5
Dun–le–Palestel [F] 54 H5
Dunloy [GB] 2 G2
Dunmanway [IRL] 4 C5
Dunmore [IRL] 2 C4
Dunmore East [IRL] 4 E5
Dunmurry [GB] 2 G3
Dún na nGall / Donegal [IRL] 2 E2
Dunoon [GB] 8 C3
Duns [GB] 8 F4
Dunscore [GB] 8 D5
Dunshaughlin [IRL] 2 F5
Dunstable [GB] 14 E3
Dunster [GB] 12 E3
Dun–sur–Auron [F] 56 C4
Duntulm [GB] 6 B4
Dunure [GB] 8 C4
Dunvegan [GB] 6 B4
Dupnitsa [BG] 150 F6
Durach [BG] 148 E2
Duran [BG] 148 E2
Durango [E] 82 H4
Durankulak [BG] 148 G1
Duras [F] 66 E4
Durasıllı [TR] 144 E3
Durban–Corbières [F] 106 C5
Durbe [LV] 200 B6
Durbuy [B] 30 E5
Dúrcal [E] 102 E4
Đurđenovac [HR] 154 D1
Đurđevac [HR] 74 G5
Düren [D] 30 G4
Đurěvik [BIH] 154 E3
Durham [GB] 8 F6
Durlas / Thurles [IRL] 4 E3
Durness [GB] 6 D2
Dürnkrut [A] 62 G4
Dürnstein [A] 62 D4
Durón [E] 90 A5
Durrës [AL] 128 A3
Durrow [IRL] 4 E3
Durrus [IRL] 4 B5
Dursley [GB] 12 G3
Dursunbey [TR] 144 E1
Durtal [F] 42 A6
Duruelo de la Sierra [E] 90 A2
Dusetos [LT] 202 G4
Düskotna [BG] 148 E3
Dusnok [H] 76 C4
Dusocin [PL] 22 E5
Düsseldorf [D] 30 G3
Duszniki [PL] 36 B2
Duszniki–Zdrój [PL] 50 B3
Duved [S] 182 E1
Düvertepe [TR] 144 E2
Düzağac [TR] 144 H2
Dve Mogili [BG] 148 C2
Dverberg [N] 192 C3
Dvor [HR] 154 A2
Dvorce [CZ] 50 D4
Dvory n. Žit. [SK] 64 B5
Dvůr Králové nad Labem [CZ] 50 A3
Dwingeloo [NL] 16 G3
Dyat'kovo [RUS] 204 E5
Dyce [GB] 6 F6
Dylewo [PL] 24 C5
Dymchurch [GB] 14 F5
Dynów [PL] 52 E4
Dyrnesvågen [N] 180 F1
Dyulino [BG] 148 F3
Dyuni [BG] 148 F4
Dzhankoï [UA] 206 G5
Dzhurovo [BG] 150 G4
Dzhuryn [UA] 206 D3
Dziadkowice [PL] 38 E2
Działdowo [PL] 22 G5
Działoszyce [PL] 52 B3
Działoszyn [PL] 36 F6
Dziemiany [PL] 22 C3
Dzierzgoń [PL] 22 F4
Dzierżoniów [PL] 50 C2
Džigolj [YU] 150 D3
Dzivin [BY] 38 H3
Dziwnów [PL] 20 F3
Džumajlija [MK] 128 F1
Dźwierzuty [PL] 22 H4
Dzyarechyn [BY] 24 H5
Dzyarzhynsk [BY] 204 B5

E

Ealing [GB] 14 E4
Earl's Colne [GB] 14 F3
Easdale [GB] 8 C2
Easingwold [GB] 10 F3
Easky [IRL] 2 D3
Eastbourne [GB] 14 E6
East Cowes [GB] 12 H5
East Dereham [GB] 14 G2
East Grinstead [GB] 14 E5
East Kilbride [GB] 8 D3
Eastleigh [GB] 12 H5
Eastoft [GB] 10 G4
Eastwood [GB] 10 F5
Eaux–Bonnes [F] 84 D4
Eaux–Chaudes [F] 84 D4
Eauze [F] 66 D6
Ebberston [GB] 10 G3
Ebbo / Epoo [FIN] 178 B4
Ebbw Vale [GB] 12 F2
Ebelsbach [D] 46 F3
Ebeltoft [DK] 156 E1
Ebenfurth [A] 62 F5
Eben im Pongau [A] 72 H1
Ebensee [A] 62 A5
Eberbach [D] 46 D5
Ebermannstadt [D] 46 G4
Ebern [D] 46 G3
Eberndorf [A] 74 C3
Ebersbach [D] 48 G1
Ebersberg [D] 60 E4
Eberschwang [A] 60 H4
Ebersdorf [D] 18 E4
Eberstein [A] 74 C3
Eberswalde [D] 34 F1
Ebingen [D] 58 G3
Éboli [I] 120 F4
Ebrach [D] 46 F4
Ebreichsdorf [A] 62 F5
Ebreuil [F] 56 C6
Ebstorf [D] 18 G6
Eccleshall [GB] 10 D5
Eceabat [TR] 130 H5
Echallens [CH] 70 C1
Echallon [F] 68 H2
Echarri / Etxarri [E] 84 A3
Échevennoz [I] 70 D3
Echínos [GR] 130 E2
Échourgnac [F] 66 E3
Echternach [L] 44 F2
Écija [E] 102 B2
Ečka [YU] 154 G1
Eckartsberga [D] 34 B6
Eckernförde [D] 18 F1
Eckerö [FIN] 176 A5
Ecommoy [F] 42 B5
Ecouis [F] 28 C6
Ecsegfalva [H] 76 F2
Ecthe [D] 32 G4
Ecueillé [F] 54 G3
Ecury [F] 44 B4
Ed [S] 166 C4
Eda glasbruk [S] 166 D1
Edam [NL] 16 E4
Edane [S] 166 E2
Edderton [GB] 6 E4
Eddleston [GB] 8 E4
Ede [NL] 16 E5
Edebäck [S] 172 F6
Edefors [S] 184 C1
Edefors [S] 198 A2
Edelény [H] 64 F4
Edenbridge [GB] 14 E5
Edenderry [IRL] 2 E6
Edenkoben [D] 46 B5
Edersee [D] 32 E5
Édessa [GR] 128 F4
Edewecht [D] 18 C5
Edgeworthstown [IRL] 2 E5
Edinburgh [GB] 8 E3
Edincik [TR] 146 D4
Ediniţa [MD] 206 D3
Edirne [TR] 146 A2
Edland [N] 164 D1
Édolo [I] 72 B4
Edremit [TR] 144 C1
Edsbro [S] 168 E1
Edsbruk [S] 162 G1
Edsbyn [S] 174 C2
Edsele [S] 184 D1
Edsleskog [S] 166 D4
Edsvalla [S] 166 E2
Eeklo [B] 28 G1
Efendiköprüsü [TR] 144 G2
Eferding [A] 62 B4
Efkarpia [GR] 128 H3
Eforie [RO] 206 E6
Efpálio [GR] 132 F5
Efýra [GR] 136 C2
Egebæk [DK] 156 B3
Egeln [D] 34 B3
Egense [DK] 160 E4
Eger [H] 64 E5
Egerlövő [H] 64 F5
Egernsund [DK] 156 C4
Egersund [N] 164 B4
Egervár [H] 74 G2
Egestorf [D] 18 F5
Egg [A] 60 B6
Eggedal [N] 170 G5
Eggenburg [A] 62 E3
Eggenfelden [D] 60 G3
Eggesin [D] 20 E4
Eggum [N] 192 B4
Eghezée [B] 30 D5
Egiertowo [PL] 22 D3
Egilsstaðir [IS] 194 G5
Egletons [F] 68 A3
Eglingham [GB] 8 G5
Eglinton [GB] 2 F2
Egmond aan Zee [NL] 16 D3
Egna / Neumarkt [I] 72 D4
Egremont [GB] 8 D6
Egtved [DK] 156 C2
Eguzon [F] 54 G5
Egyek [H] 64 F6
Ehingen [D] 60 B3
Ehnen [L] 44 F3
Ehra–Lessien [D] 32 H2
Ehrenburg [D] 18 D6
Ehrenhausen [A] 74 D3
Ehrwald [A] 60 D6
Eiane [N] 164 B3
Eibar [E] 82 H4
Eibenstock [D] 48 C2
Eibergen [NL] 16 G5
Eibiswald [A] 74 D3
Eich [D] 46 C4
Eichendorf [D] 60 G3
Eichstätt [D] 60 D2
Eidanger [N] 164 G3
Eide [N] 164 C3
Eide [N] 164 B4
Eide [N] 180 E2
Eidfjord [N] 170 D4
Eiði [FR] 160 B1
Eidsbugarden [N] 170 F1
Eidsdal [N] 180 E4
Eidsfoss [N] 164 G2
Eidslandet [N] 170 B3
Eidsøra [N] 180 F3
Eidsvåg [N] 180 F3
Eidsvoll [N] 172 C5
Eidsvoll verk [N] 172 C5
Eigenrieden [D] 32 G5
Eikelandsosen [N] 170 B4
Eiken [N] 164 C4
Eikenes [N] 180 B6
Eiksund [N] 180 C4
Eilenburg [D] 34 D5
Eilsleben [D] 34 A3
Eina [N] 172 B4
Einavoll [N] 172 B4
Einbeck [D] 32 F3
Eindhoven [NL] 30 E2
Einsiedeln [CH] 58 G6
Eisenach [D] 32 G6
Eisenberg [D] 34 B6
Eisenerz [A] 62 C6
Eisenhüttenstadt [D] 34 G3
Eisenkappel [A] 74 C4
Eisenstadt [A] 62 F5
Eisfeld [D] 46 G2
Eišiškės [LT] 24 H2
Eislingen [D] 60 B2
Eitorf [D] 30 H5
Eivissa / Ibiza [E] 104 C5
Ejby [DK] 156 D3
Ejea de los Caballeros [E] 84 C6
Ejheden [S] 172 H2
Ejstrupholm [DK] 156 C1
Ejulve [E] 90 E6
Ekáli [GR] 134 C6
Ekedalen [S] 166 F6
Ekenäs [S] 166 E4
Ekenäs / Tammisaari [FIN] 176 F6
Ekenässjön [S] 162 E3
Ekerö [S] 168 D3
Ekinli [TR] 146 H3
Ekshärad [S] 172 F5
Eksjö [S] 162 E2
Ekträsk [S] 190 H5
Ekzarh Antimovo [BG] 148 E4
Elaiochoria [GR] 130 B5
Elaiónas [GR] 132 G5
El Alamo [E] 88 F6
El Alcornocal [E] 96 B5
El Aljunzarejo [E] 104 C2
Elämäjärvi [FIN] 198 D6
Elantxobe [E] 82 H3
Elassóna [GR] 132 F1
El Astillero [E] 82 F3
Eláti [GR] 128 F6
Eláti [GR] 132 E2
Elátia [GR] 132 H4
Elatoú [GR] 132 F5
El Barraco [E] 88 E5
Elbasan [AL] 128 B3
El Berrón [E] 78 H3
Elbeuf [F] 26 H4
Elbigenalp [A] 72 B1
Elbingerode [D] 32 H4
Elbląg [PL] 22 F3
El Bodón [E] 86 H2
El Bonillo [E] 96 H5
El Bosque [E] 100 H4
Elburg [NL] 16 F4
Elburgo / Burgelu [E] 102 B4
El Burgo de Ebro [E] 90 E4
El Burgo de Osma [E] 90 A3
El Burgo Ranero [E] 82 B5
El Cabaco [E] 88 B4
el Campello [E] 104 E2
El Canal [E] 104 C6
El Cañavate [E] 98 B3
El Carpio [E] 102 C1
El Carpio de Tajo [E] 96 E1
El Casar de Talamanca [E] 88 G5
El Castillo de las Guardas [E] 94 G5
El Centenillo [E] 96 E6
El Cerro de Andévalo [E] 94 F4
Elche / Elx [E] 104 D2
Elche de la Sierra [E] 104 B1
Elçili [TR] 146 B2
El Coronil [E] 100 H3
El Cubo de Don Sancho [E] 80 F6
El Cubo de Tierra del Vino [E] 80 H5
El Cuervo [E] 100 G3
Elda [E] 104 D2
Eldalsosen [N] 170 C1
Eldena [D] 20 A5
Elefsína [GR] 134 B6
Elefthéri [GR] 132 G2
Eleftherochóri [GR] 128 E6
Eleftheroúpoli [GR] 130 D3
Eleja [LV] 200 D6
El Ejido [E] 102 F5
Elek [H] 76 G3
Elena [BG] 148 C4
El Escorial [E] 88 F5
El Espinar [E] 88 E4
el Fondó dels Frares [E] 104 D2
Elgå [N] 182 D5
El Gargantón [E] 96 E3
El Garrobo [E] 94 G5
Elgg [CH] 58 G5
Elgin [GB] 6 E5
Elgol [GB] 6 B5
El Grado [E] 90 G3
el Grau / Grao [E] 98 F6
El Guijo [E] 96 C5
Elimäki [FIN] 178 C3
Elin Pelin [BG] 150 G5
Elisenwaara [RUS] 188 G6
Eliseyna [BG] 150 G4
Elizondo [E] 84 C3
Elizondo / Baztan [E] 82 H4
Ełk [PL] 24 D4
Elkhovo [BG] 148 E5
Ellenberg [D] 46 E6
Ellesmere [GB] 10 D5
Elling [DK] 160 E2
Ellingen [D] 46 G6
Ellon [GB] 6 G6
Ellös [S] 166 C6
Ellrich [D] 32 H4
Ellwangen [D] 46 E6
Elm [CH] 58 G6
El Madroño [E] 94 F5
Elmalı [TR] 142 H2
El Masnou [E] 92 E4
El Médano [E] 100 B5
El Minguillo [E] 96 G4
El Molar [E] 88 G5
El Molinillo [E] 96 E2
El Moral [E] 102 H2
Elmpt [D] 30 F3
Elmshorn [D] 18 F3
Elne [F] 92 G1
Elnesvågen [N] 180 E2
Élos [GR] 140 B5
Előszállás [H] 76 C3
Eloúnta [GR] 140 F4
el Palmar [E] 98 F5
El Pardo [E] 88 F5
El Paular [E] 88 F4
El Pedernoso [E] 96 H3
El Pedroso [E] 94 H5
El Perelló [E] 98 F5
El Perelló [E] 92 B5
Elphin [IRL] 2 D4
El Piñero [E] 80 H5
El Pino [E] 78 C3
el Pinós / Pinoso [E] 104 D2
El Pito [E] 78 G3
el Pla de Santa Maria [E] 92 C4
El Pobo de Dueñas [E] 90 C6
el Pont de Suert [E] 84 F6
el Port / Sóller [E] 104 E4
el Port de la Selva [E] 92 G2
El Portil [E] 94 E6
el Prat de Llobregat [E] 92 E5
El Puente del Arzobispo [E] 96 D1
El Puerto de Santa Maria [E] 100 F4
El Real [E] 78 C2
El Real de San Vicente [E] 88 D6
El Recuenco [E] 90 B6
El Rocío [E] 94 F6
El Ronquillo [E] 94 G5
El Royo [E] 90 B2
El Rubio [E] 102 B2
El Sabinar [E] 102 H2
El Saler [E] 98 E5
El Salobral [E] 98 B5
El Saucejo [E] 102 B3
Elsdorf [D] 30 G4
El Serrat [AND] 84 H6
Elsfleth [D] 18 D5
Elst [NL] 16 E5
Elsten [D] 18 C6
Elster [D] 34 D4
Elsterberg [D] 48 C2
Elsterwerda [D] 34 E5
El Tejar [E] 102 C3
Elten [D] 16 F6
El Tiemblo [E] 88 E5
Eltmann [D] 46 F3
El Toboso [E] 96 G3
El Tormillo [E] 90 G3
El Torno [E] 88 B5
El Tumbalejo [E] 94 F5
Eltville [D] 46 B3
Elva [EST] 200 F3
Elvas [P] 86 F6
Elvbrua [N] 182 D6
El Vendrell [E] 92 D5
Elverum [N] 172 C3
Elvestad [N] 166 B2
El Villar de Arnedo [E] 84 A5
El Viso [E] 96 C5
El Viso del Alcor [E] 94 H6
Elx / Elche [E] 104 D2
Ely [GB] 14 F2
Elzach [D] 58 F2
Elze [D] 32 F3
Emådalen [S] 172 G2
Embessós [GR] 132 E3
Embleton [GB] 8 G5
Emboriós [GR] 142 B3
Emboriós [GR] 134 G5
Embrun [F] 108 D2
Embute [LV] 200 C6
Emden [D] 16 H2
Emecik [TR] 142 D3
Emet [TR] 144 F1
Emiralem [TR] 144 C3
Emlichheim [D] 16 G4
Emmaboda [S] 162 F5
Emmaljunga [S] 162 C6
Emmeloord [NL] 16 F3
Emmen [NL] 16 G3
Emmendingen [D] 58 E3
Emmerich [D] 16 F6
Emőd [H] 64 F5
Emona [BG] 148 G4
Empoli [I] 110 E5
Empónas [GR] 142 D5
Emporeió [GR] 142 C4
Empúriabrava [E] 92 G2
Empúria–Brava [E] 102 B5
Emsdetten [D] 16 H5
Emsfors [S] 162 G4
Emskirchen [D] 46 F5
Emstek [D] 18 C6
Emyvale [IRL] 2 F4
Enånger [S] 174 E1
Encamp [AND] 84 H6
Encinas de Abajo [E] 88 C3
Encinasola [E] 94 F3
Encinedo [E] 78 F6
Enciso [E] 90 C2
Encs [H] 64 F4
Endelave By [DK] 156 D2
Enden [N] 180 H6
Endingen [D] 58 E2
Endrőd [H] 76 F2
Enebakk [N] 166 C1
Enese [H] 62 H6
Enez [TR] 130 H3
Enfesta / Pontecesures [E] 78 B3
Enfield [GB] 14 E4
Enfield [IRL] 2 E6
Engelberg [CH] 70 F1
Engelhartszell [A] 62 A3
Engelia [N] 170 H4
Engeln [D] 18 D6
Engelskirchen [D] 30 H4
Engelsviken [N] 166 B3
Engen [D] 58 G3
Enger [D] 32 D2
Engerdal [N] 182 D6
Engerneset [N] 172 D1
Engesvang [DK] 160 C6
Enghien [B] 28 H3
Engjane [N] 180 F2
Englefontaine [F] 28 G4
Engstingen [D] 58 H2
Énguera [E] 98 E6
Enguídanos [E] 98 C3
Engure [LV] 200 D5
Enkhuizen [NL] 16 E3
Enklinge [FIN] 176 B5
Enköping [S] 168 C2
Enna [I] 126 E3
Ennezat [F] 68 D2
Ennis / Inis [IRL] 2 C6
Enniscorthy [IRL] 4 F4
Enniscrone [IRL] 2 C3
Enniskean [IRL] 4 C5
Enniskillen [GB] 2 E3
Ennistymon [IRL] 2 B5
Enns [A] 62 C4
Eno [FIN] 188 G2
Enokunta [FIN] 186 E6
Enonkoski [FIN] 188 E4
Enontekiö [FIN] 192 G4
Enschede [NL] 16 G5
Ensisheim [F] 58 D3
Entlebuch [CH] 58 E6
Entradas [P] 94 D3
Entraygues–sur–Truyère [F] 68 B5
Entre Ambos–os–Rios [P] 80 C4
Entrevaux [F] 108 E4
Entrèves [I] 70 C3
Entrimo [E] 78 C6
Entroncamento [P] 86 D4

EDINBURGH

0 5 km
0 3 mls

Cramond Island
Granton
Cramond
Davidson's Mains
Warriston
Portobello
Musselburgh
Duddingston
Corstorphine
Gogar
Craiglockhart
Newcraighall
Morningside
Millerhill
Colinton
Liberton
Juniper Green
Danderhall
Currie
Newmills
Dalkeith
Boghall
Loanhead
Bonnyrigg
Easter Howgate
Roslin
Newtongrange
Milton Bridge
Rosewell
Gorebridge
Penicuik
DUNFERMLINE
GLASGOW
BERWICK
COLDSTREAM
CARLISLE
PEEBLES
GALASHIELS
IHT

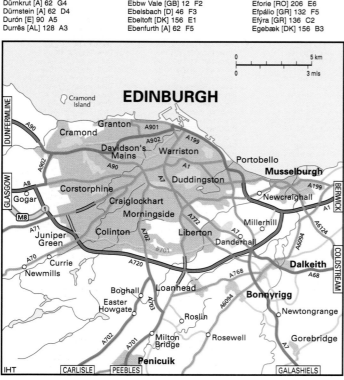

Enviken [S] 174 C4
Enying [H] 76 B2
Epannes [F] 54 D4
Epanomí [GR] 128 H5
Epe [D] 16 G5
Epe [NL] 16 F4
Épernay [F] 44 B3
Epernon [F] 42 E4
Épila [E] 90 D4
Épinal [F] 58 C2
Episcopia [I] 120 H5
Episkopí [GR] 140 C4
Epitálio [GR] 136 C2
Epône [F] 42 E3
Epoo / Ebbo [FIN] 178 B4
Eppan / Appiano [I] 72 D3
Eppingen [D] 46 C5
Epsom [GB] 14 E4
Eptachóri [GR] 128 D6
Eptálofos [GR] 132 G5
Eraclea [I] 72 F6
Eraclea Mare [I] 72 F6
Eräjärvi [FIN] 176 G1
Erateiní [GR] 132 G5
Eratirá [GR] 128 E5
Erba [I] 70 G4
Erbach [D] 46 D4
Erbalunga [F] 114 C2
Erbendorf [D] 48 B4
Ercolano [I] 120 E3
Ercsi [H] 76 C2
Érd [H] 76 C1
Erdek [TR] 146 D4
Erdevik [YU] 154 F2
Erding [D] 60 E4
Eresós [GR] 134 G2
Erétria [GR] 134 C5
Erfde [D] 18 E2
Erftstadt [D] 30 G5
Erfurt [D] 32 H6
Ergama [TR] 144 D1
Ergili [TR] 146 D5
Ērgli [LV] 200 E5
Ergoldsbach [D] 60 F3
Erice [I] 126 B2
Ericeira [P] 86 A4
Ericek [TR] 146 F4
Erikli [TR] 146 B4
Eriksberg [S] 190 F4
Erikslund [S] 184 D4
Eriksmåla [S] 162 E5
Eringsboda [S] 162 E6
Erkelenz [D] 30 F4
Erla [E] 84 C6
Erlangen [D] 46 G4
Erlenbach [D] 46 D4
Erlsbach [A] 72 E2
Ermelo [NL] 16 E4
Ermenonville [F] 42 G3
Ermidas-Aldeia [P] 94 C3
Ermióni [GR] 136 F3
Ermoúpolis [GR] 138 D2
Ermsleben [D] 34 B4
Erndtebrück [D] 32 D6
Ernée [F] 26 D6
Ernstbrunn [A] 62 F3
Erquy [F] 26 B4
Erratzu [E] 84 C3
Erro [E] 84 C3
Errogie [GB] 6 D5
Erronkari / Roncal [E] 84 C4
Ersekë [AL] 128 D5
Ersmark [S] 198 A6
Erstein [F] 44 H6
Ertenvåg [N] 192 B6
Ertuğrul [TR] 144 D1
Ervedosa [P] 80 D4
Ervenik [HR] 112 H5
Ervidel [P] 94 D3
Ervik [N] 180 B4
Ervy-le-Châtel [F] 44 A6
Erwitte [D] 32 D4
Erxleben [D] 34 B3
Erythrés [GR] 134 B6
Erzsébet [H] 76 B5
Eržvilkas [LT] 202 E5
Esa / Yesa [E] 84 C4
Esbjerg [DK] 156 A2
Esblada [E] 92 C4
Esbo / Espoo [FIN] 176 G5
Escairón [E] 78 D4
Escalada [E] 82 E4
Escalaplano [I] 118 D6
Escalona [E] 88 E6
Escalonilla [E] 96 E1
Escandón, Puerto de- [E] 98 E2
Escariche [E] 88 G6
Escároz / Ezkaroze [E] 84 C4
Escatrón [E] 90 F5
Eschede [D] 32 G1
Eschenbach [D] 46 H4
Eschenburg-Eibelshausen [D] 32 D6
Eschenlohe [D] 60 D6
Eschershausen [D] 32 F3
Esch-sur-Alzette [L] 44 E3
Esch-sur-Sûre [L] 44 E2
Eschwege [D] 32 G5
Eschweiler [D] 30 F4
Escombreras [E] 104 C4
Escos [F] 84 D2
Es Cubells [E] 104 C5
Escucha [E] 90 E6
Escúllar [E] 102 F4
Eşen [TR] 142 G4
Esence [TR] 146 E4
Esens [D] 18 C3
Esenyurt [TR] 146 E3
es Figueral [E] 104 C5
Esgos [E] 78 D5
Esguevillas de Esgueva [E] 88 F1
Esher [GB] 14 E4
Eskdalemuir [GB] 8 E5
Eskelhem [S] 168 F4
Eski [TR] 144 G2
Eskiçine [TR] 142 D1
Eskifjörður [IS] 194 G5
Eskihisar [TR] 142 D2
Eskilstuna [S] 168 B3
Eskin [TR] 144 F3
Eskişehir [TR] 146 H5
Eslarn [F] 48 C5
Eslohe [D] 32 D5
Eslöv [S] 158 C2
Eşme [TR] 144 F4
Es Mercadal [E] 104 H4
Espa [N] 172 C4
Espalion [F] 68 B5
Esparreguera [E] 92 D4
Espedal [N] 170 G1
Espejo [E] 102 C2
Espeland [N] 170 B4
Espelette [F] 84 C2
Espeli [N] 164 D4
Espelkamp [D] 32 E2
Espera [E] 100 G3
Espiel [E] 96 C5
Espinama [E] 82 D3
Espinho [P] 80 B4
Espinilla [E] 82 E4
Espinosa de los Monteros [E] 82 F4
Espírito Santo [P] 94 D4
Esplantas [F] 68 D5
Espoo / Esbo [FIN] 176 G5
Es Port d'Alcúdia [E] 104 F4
es Port d'Andraitx [E] 104 D5
Esposende [P] 78 A6
Espot [E] 84 G6
Esse / Ähtävä [FIN] 198 C6
Essen [D] 30 H3
Essen [D] 18 C6
Essenbach [D] 60 F3
Esslingen [D] 58 H1
Essoyes [F] 56 G1
Essunga [S] 166 D6
Estada [E] 90 G3
Estagel [F] 106 C6
Estaing [F] 68 B5
Estaires [F] 28 F3
Estanyol [E] 104 E5
Estarreja [P] 80 B5
Estavayer-le-Lac [CH] 58 C6
Este [I] 110 G1
Estela [P] 80 B3
Estella / Lizarra [E] 84 A4
Estellenchs [E] 104 D5
Estepa [E] 102 B3
Estepar [E] 82 E6
Estepona [E] 100 H5
Esternay [F] 42 H4
Esterri d'Àneu [E] 84 G5
Esterwegen [D] 18 C5
Estissac [F] 44 A6
Estói [P] 94 C5
Estoril [P] 86 A5
Estrées-St-Denis [F] 28 E6
Estremera [E] 96 H1
Estremoz [P] 86 E6
Esztergom [H] 64 C5
Étables-sur-Mer [F] 26 B4
Etain [F] 44 E3
Etalle [B] 44 E2
Étampes [F] 42 F4
Étang-sur-Arroux [F] 56 F4
Etaples [F] 28 D3
Eteläinen [FIN] 176 G2
Etili [TR] 146 B5
Etne [N] 164 B1
Etrepagny [F] 28 C6
Etretat [F] 26 G2
Etropole [BG] 150 G4
Ettelbruck [L] 44 F2
Ettenheim [D] 58 E2
Ettlingen [D] 46 B6
Etxarri / Echarri [E] 84 A3
Eu [F] 28 C4
Eugénie-les-Bains [F] 66 C6
Eulate [E] 82 H5
Eupen [B] 30 F5
Eura [FIN] 176 D2
Eurajoki [FIN] 176 C2
Euratsfeld [A] 62 C5
Europoort [NL] 16 C5
Euskirchen [D] 30 G5
Eussenhausen [D] 46 F2
Eutin [D] 18 G3
Eutzsch [D] 34 D4
Evangelísmos [GR] 132 G1
Evanger [N] 170 C3
Evaux-les-Bains [F] 56 B6
Evciler [TR] 144 B1
Évdilos [GR] 138 G1
Evendorf [D] 18 F5
Evenskjoer [N] 192 D4
Everöd [S] 158 D2
Evesham [GB] 12 H2
Evian-les-Bains [F] 70 C2
Evijärvi [FIN] 186 D1
Evinochóri [GR] 132 E5
Evisa [F] 114 A4
Evje [N] 164 D4
Evolène [CH] 70 D3
Évora [P] 94 D1
Évora Monte [P] 86 D6
Evran [F] 26 C5
Evreux [F] 42 D2
Evron [F] 26 E6
Evry [F] 42 F4
Évzonoi [GR] 128 G3
Ewelme [GB] 14 D3
Exaplátanos [GR] 128 F3
Éxarhos [GR] 132 H5
Excideuil [F] 66 G2
Exeter [GB] 12 E4
Exford [GB] 12 E3
Exmes [F] 26 G5
Exmouth [GB] 12 E5
Exochí [GR] 130 C2
Exohí [GR] 128 G5
Extertal [D] 32 E3
Extremo [P] 78 B5
Eydehavn [N] 164 F5
Eyemouth [GB] 8 F4
Eyguières [F] 106 H4
Eygurande [F] 68 B2
Eylie [F] 84 G5
Eymet [F] 66 E4
Eymoutiers [F] 66 H2
Eynsford [GB] 14 E4
Eyrarbakki [IS] 194 B5
Eythorne [GB] 14 G5
Ezcaray [E] 82 F6
Ezere [LV] 200 C6
Ezermuiža [LV] 200 C4
Ezernieki [LV] 200 G6
Ezernijeki [LV] 200 D6
Ezine [TR] 130 H6
Ezkaroze / Escároz [E] 84 C4

F

Faaborg [DK] 156 D4
Faak [A] 74 A3
Fåberg [N] 172 B2
Fabero [E] 78 F4
Fabriano [I] 116 B1
Facture [F] 66 C3
Fadd [H] 76 C4
Faenza [I] 110 G4
Faeto [I] 120 F2
Fafe [P] 80 C3
Făgăraş [RO] 206 C5
Fågelfors [S] 162 F4
Fågelsjö [S] 182 G6
Fågelsundet [S] 174 F4
Fageole, Col de la- [F] 68 C4
Fagerås [S] 166 E2
Fagerhult [S] 162 F4
Fagernes [N] 170 G3
Fagernes [N] 192 E2
Fagersanna [S] 166 F5
Fagersta [S] 168 A1
Fagerstrand [N] 166 B1
Fäggeby [S] 174 D5
Faglavik [S] 162 B1
Fagnano Castello [I] 124 D4
Fagurhólsmyri [IS] 194 E6
Faial [P] 100 B3
Fai della Paganella [I] 72 C4
Faido [CH] 70 F4
Fair Head [GB] 2 G2
Fakenham [GB] 14 G1
Fakse [DK] 156 G4
Fakse Ladeplads [DK] 156 G4
Falaise [F] 26 F4
Falatádos [GR] 138 E2
Falcade [I] 72 E4
Falconara Marittima [I] 112 C6
Falcone [I] 124 A7
Faldsled [DK] 156 D4
Falerna [I] 124 D5
Falerna Marina [I] 124 D5
Falerum [S] 162 G1
Faliráki [GR] 142 E4
Falkenberg [D] 34 E5
Falkenberg [S] 160 H4
Falkenstein [D] 48 C2
Falkenstein [D] 48 C6
Falkirk [GB] 8 E3
Falköping [S] 166 E6
Fałkow [PL] 36 H6
Fallersleben [D] 32 H2
Fallet [N] 172 C5
Fällfors [S] 198 A4
Fallingbostel [D] 18 F6
Falmouth [GB] 12 C5
Falset [E] 90 H6
Falsterbo [S] 156 H3
Falstone [GB] 8 F5
Fălticeni [RO] 206 C4
Falträsk [S] 190 G4
Falun [S] 174 C4
Fámjin [FR] 160 A3
Fana [N] 170 B4
Fanano [I] 110 E4
Fanári [GR] 132 F2
Fanári [GR] 130 F3
Fanbyn [S] 184 D4
Fanjeaux [F] 106 B4
Fannrem [N] 180 H1
Fano [I] 112 C5
Fanós [GR] 128 G3
Fântânele [RO] 148 B2
Fara Novarese [I] 70 F4
Fårbo [S] 162 G3
Farébersviller [F] 44 G4
Fareham [GB] 12 H5
Färgelanda [S] 166 C5
Färila [S] 184 C6
Faringdon [GB] 12 H3
Farini [I] 110 C2
Färjestaden [S] 162 G5
Farkadhónas [GR] 132 F2
Farkasgyepü [H] 74 H2
Farkaždin [YU] 154 G1
Farlete [E] 90 F4
Fârliug [RO] 76 H6
Färlöv [S] 158 D1
Färna [S] 168 B2
Färnäs [S] 172 G3
Farnborough [GB] 14 D4
Farnese [I] 114 G3
Farnham [GB] 14 D4
Faro [P] 94 C6
Fårösund [S] 168 H3
Farranfore [IRL] 4 B4
Fársala [GR] 132 G3
Farsø [DK] 160 D4
Farstad [N] 180 E2
Farsund [N] 164 C5
Farum [DK] 156 G2
Fårvang [DK] 160 D6
Fasano [I] 122 E3
Fasgar [E] 78 G5
Fáskrúðsfjörður [IS] 194 G5
Faster [DK] 156 B1
Fasterholt [DK] 156 C1
Fatezh [RUS] 204 E6
Fátima [P] 86 C3
Fättjaur [S] 190 E3
Faucille, Col de la- [F] 70 B1
Faucogney-et-la-Mer [F] 58 C3
Faulensee [CH] 70 E1
Faulquemont [F] 44 F4
Fauske [N] 192 C6
Fauville [F] 26 H2
Fåvang [N] 170 H1
Favara [E] 98 E5
Favara [I] 126 D4
Faverges [F] 70 B3
Faverney [F] 58 B3
Faversham [GB] 14 F5
Favignana [I] 126 A2
Favone [F] 114 B5
Fawley [GB] 12 H5
Fayence [F] 108 D4
Fayet [F] 106 D3
Fayl-Billot [F] 58 A3
Feakle [IRL] 2 C6
Fearnan [GB] 8 E1
Fearnmore [GB] 6 C4
Fécamp [F] 26 G2
Feda [N] 164 C5
Fegen [S] 162 B4
Feggeklit [DK] 160 C4
Fegyvernek [H] 76 F1
Fehrbellin [D] 34 D1
Fehring [A] 74 E2
Feios [N] 170 D2
Feiring [N] 172 C4
Feitos [P] 78 A6
Feketič [YU] 76 D6
Felanitx [E] 104 F5
Felber-tauern Tunnel [A] 72 F2
Feld [A] 72 H3
Feldafing [D] 60 D5
Feldbach [A] 74 E2
Feldberg [D] 58 F3
Feldberg [D] 20 D5
Feldkirch [A] 58 H5
Feldkirchen [A] 74 B3
Feldkirchen [D] 60 E5
Feldsted [DK] 156 C4
Felechosa [E] 82 B3
Felgueiras [P] 80 C3
Felixstowe [GB] 14 G3
Fellbach [D] 58 H1
Felletin [F] 68 B1
Fellingsbro [S] 168 A3
Felnac [RO] 76 G4
Felonica [I] 110 F2
Felsőnyárád [H] 64 F4
Felsőszentiván [H] 76 C4
Felsőtárkány [H] 64 E5
Feltre [I] 72 E5
Femsjö [S] 162 B4
Femundsenden [N] 182 D6
Fenagh [IRL] 2 E4
Fene [E] 78 D2
Fenékpuszta [H] 74 G3
Fener [I] 72 E5
Fenestrelle [I] 70 C5
Fénétrange [F] 44 G5
Feneu [F] 40 H6
Fénis [I] 70 D4
Fenit [IRL] 4 B3
Feochaig [GB] 2 H2
Feolin Ferry [GB] 8 B2
Feragen [N] 182 D4
Ferbane [IRL] 2 D5
Ferdinandshof [D] 20 E4
Fère-Champenoise [F] 44 B4
Fère-en-Tardenois [F] 44 A3
Ferentino [I] 116 B6
Féres [GR] 130 H3
Ferez [E] 104 B1
Feria [E] 94 G3
Feričanci [HR] 154 D1
Ferla [I] 126 G5
Ferlach [A] 74 B3
Ferleiten [A] 72 G1
Fermignano [I] 110 H6
Fermo [I] 116 C2
Fermoselle [E] 80 G5
Fermoy [IRL] 4 D4
Fernancaballero [E] 96 E4
Fernán Núñez [E] 102 C2
Ferns [IRL] 4 F4
Ferovac [HR] 154 C1
Ferrandina [I] 122 D4
Ferrara [I] 110 G2
Ferreira [E] 78 E2
Ferreira do Alentejo [P] 94 D3
Ferreira do Zêzere [P] 86 D3
Ferreries [E] 104 G4
Ferreruela de Huerva [E] 90 D5
Ferrette [F] 58 D4
Ferriere [I] 110 C3
Ferrières [F] 42 G6
Ferrières-sur-Sichon [F] 68 D2
Ferring [DK] 160 B5
Ferrol [E] 78 D1
Ferryhill [GB] 10 F2
Fertöd [H] 62 G6
Fertőrákos [H] 62 F6
Fertőszentmiklós [H] 62 G6
Festøy [N] 180 D4
Festvåg [N] 192 B6
Fethard [IRL] 4 E4
Fethard [IRL] 4 F5
Fethiye [TR] 142 G3
Fetsund [N] 166 C1
Fettercairn [GB] 8 F1
Feucht [D] 46 G5
Feuchtwangen [D] 46 F6
Feurs [F] 68 E2
Fevåg [N] 190 B6
Fevik [N] 164 E5
Fiamignano [I] 116 B4
Fibiş [RO] 76 G5
Ficulle [I] 114 H3
Fiddleton [GB] 8 E5
Fidenza [I] 110 D2
Fidje [N] 164 E4
Fieberbrunn [A] 60 F6
Fier [AL] 128 A4
Fiera di Primiero [I] 72 E4
Fiesch [CH] 70 E2
Fiésole [I] 110 F5
Fiesso Umbertiano [I] 110 G2
Figari [F] 114 B6
Figeac [F] 66 H5
Figeholm [S] 162 G3
Figgjo [N] 164 B3
Figline Valdarno [I] 110 F6
Figueira da Foz [P] 80 A6
Figueira de Castelo Rodrigo [P] 80 E6
Figueiró dos Vinhos [P] 86 D3
Figueras / Figueres [E] 92 G2
Figueres / Figueras [E] 92 G2
Filadélfi [GR] 130 B4
Filáki [GR] 132 G3
Fil'akovo [SK] 64 D4
Filevo [BG] 148 C6
Filey [GB] 10 G3
Filí [GR] 134 C6
Fília [GR] 134 G2
Filiaşi [RO] 206 B6
Filiátes [GR] 132 C2
Filiatrá [GR] 136 C3
Filippiáda [GR] 132 D3
Filipstad [S] 166 F2
Filíra [GR] 130 G2
Filiriá [GR] 128 G4
Fillan [N] 190 A6
Fillefjell Pass [N] 170 E2
Filótas [GR] 128 F4
Filóti [GR] 138 F3
Filottrano [I] 116 C1
Filskov [DK] 156 B2
Filzmoos [A] 72 H1
Finale Emília [I] 110 F2
Finale Ligure [I] 108 H3
Fiñana [E] 102 F4
Finby / Särkisalo [FIN] 176 E5
Finestrat [E] 104 E2
Finiq [AL] 132 B1
Finisterre / Fisterra [E] 78 A2
Finja [S] 158 C1
Finnbo [S] 174 C4
Finnbyen [N] 192 B4
Finnea [IRL] 2 E5
Finneid [N] 192 C6
Finneidfjord [N] 190 D2
Finnentrop [D] 32 C5
Finnsnes [N] 192 D3
Finntorp [S] 166 D3
Finow [D] 34 E1
Finsand [N] 170 H4
Finsjö [S] 162 G4
Finspång [S] 168 A5
Finsterwalde [D] 34 E5
Finstown [GB] 6 F2
Finström [FIN] 176 A5
Fintona [GB] 2 F3
Fionnphort [GB] 8 B1
Fiorenzuola d'Arda [I] 110 C2
Fira / Thíra [GR] 138 F5
Firenze [I] 110 F5
Firenzuola [I] 110 F4
Firkeel [IRL] 4 A5
Firlej [PL] 38 E4
Firminy [F] 68 E3
Fiscal [E] 84 E5
Fischamend [A] 62 F5
Fischbach [D] 44 H4
Fischbeck [D] 34 C2
Fischbeck [D] 32 F3
Fischen [D] 60 B6
Fishbourne [GB] 12 H5
Fishguard [GB] 4 H6
Fiskárdo [GR] 132 C5
Fiskebäckskil [S] 166 C6
Fiskebøl [N] 192 C4
Fiskö [FIN] 176 C4
Fismes [F] 44 A3
Fissíni [GR] 130 F6
Fisterra / Finisterre [E] 78 A2
Fitero [E] 84 A6
Fitíes [GR] 132 E4
Fitjar [N] 170 A5
Fiuggi [I] 116 B6
Fiumefreddo Bruzio [I] 124 D4
Fiumefreddo di Sicilia [I] 124 B8
Fiumicíno [I] 114 H6
Fivemiletown [GB] 2 F3
Fivizzano [I] 110 D4
Fjæra [N] 170 C5
Fjærland [N] 170 D1
Fjälkinge [S] 158 D2
Fjällasen [S] 192 F5
Fjällbacka [S] 166 C5
Fjällnäs [S] 182 D4
Fjaltring [DK] 160 B5
Fjand Gårde [DK] 160 B5
Fjäras [S] 160 H3
Fjellerup [DK] 160 E5
Fjellsrud [N] 166 C1
Fjelstrup [DK] 156 C3
Fjerritslev [DK] 160 D3
Fjone [N] 164 E3
Fjugesta [S] 166 G3
Flå [N] 170 G4
Fladdabister [GB] 6 G4
Fladungen [D] 46 F2
Flaine [F] 70 C3
Flakk [N] 182 B1
Flåm [N] 170 D3
Flamborough [GB] 10 H3
Flambourári [GR] 132 D1
Flärke [S] 184 G1
Flatabø [N] 170 C4
Flateby [N] 166 C1
Flåten [N] 192 F1
Flateyri [IS] 194 C1
Flatmark [N] 180 F4
Flatråker [N] 170 B5
Flattnitz [A] 74 B2
Flatval [N] 190 A6
Flavenskjold [DK] 160 E3
Flavigny-sur-Moselle [F] 44 E5
Fleet [GB] 14 D4
Fleetwood [GB] 10 D3
Flekke [N] 170 B1
Flekkefjord [N] 164 C5
Flen [S] 168 C4
Flensburg [D] 156 C5
Flers [F] 26 E4
Flesberg [N] 164 G1
Flesnes [N] 192 C3
Fleurance [F] 84 G2
Fleuré [F] 54 F4
Fleurier [CH] 58 C6
Fleurus [B] 30 C5
Fleury [F] 28 C6
Flims [CH] 70 G1
Flims Waldhaus [CH] 70 G1
Flins [F] 42 F3
Flint [GB] 10 D4
Flisa [N] 172 D4
Flisbrua [N] 172 D4
Fliseryd [S] 162 G4
Flix [E] 90 H5
Flize [F] 44 C2
Floby [S] 162 C1
Floda [S] 160 H2
Flögåsen [S] 172 F2
Flogned [S] 166 D1
Flogny-la-Chapelle [F] 56 F1
Flöha [D] 48 D1
Flor [S] 182 H5
Florac [F] 68 D6
Florange [F] 44 E3
Florennes [B] 30 C5
Florenville [B] 44 D2
Floreşti [MD] 206 D4
Florídia [I] 126 G5
Flórina [GR] 128 E4
Florø [N] 180 B5
Florstadt [D] 46 D2
Florvåg [N] 170 A3
Flötningen [S] 182 D6
Fluberg [N] 170 H3
Flüelen [CH] 58 F6
Fluglafjørður [DK] 160 B1
Flumeri [I] 120 F2
Flumet [F] 70 B3
Fluminimaggiore [I] 118 B6
Flums [CH] 58 H6
Flymen [S] 162 F6
Flystveit [N] 164 D4
Foça [TR] 144 B4
Fockbek [D] 18 F2
Focşani [RO] 206 D5
Fódele [GR] 140 E4
Foggia [I] 120 G1
Föglö [FIN] 168 H1
Fohnsdorf [A] 74 C2
Foiano di Chiana [I] 114 G1
Foinikoús [GR] 136 D4
Foix [F] 84 H5
Fojnica [BIH] 152 D2
Földeák [H] 76 F4
Foldereid [N] 190 C4
Földes [H] 76 G1
Foldingbro [DK] 156 B3
Foleá [GR] 130 D4
Folégandros [GR] 138 E4
Folelli [F] 114 C3
Folgaria [I] 72 C5
Folgarida [I] 72 C4
Folgoso [E] 78 E4

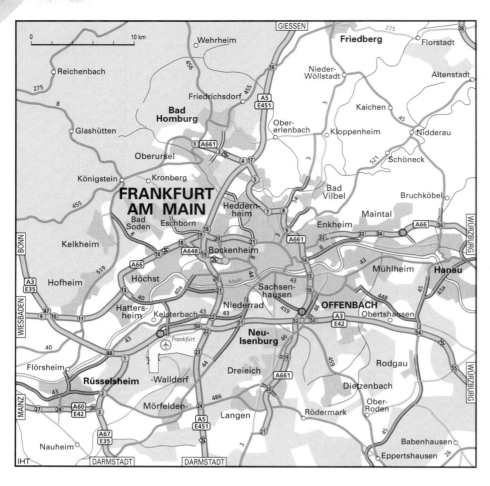

Foligno [I] 116 A2
Folkärna [S] 174 D5
Folkestad [N] 180 C4
Folkestone [GB] 14 F5
Follafoss [N] 190 C5
Folldal [N] 180 H5
Follina [I] 72 E5
Föllinge [S] 190 E6
Follónica [I] 114 E2
Folmava [CZ] 48 D5
Fölsbyn [S] 166 D2
Fondamente [F] 106 D3
Fondi [I] 120 C1
Fondo [I] 72 C3
Fonfría [E] 80 G4
Fonfría [E] 90 D5
Fonni [I] 118 D5
Fontainebleau [F] 42 G5
Fontaine-de-Vaucluse [F] 106 H3
Fontaine-Française [F] 56 H3
Fontaine-le-Dun [F] 26 H2
Fontanellato [I] 110 D2
Fontanelle [I] 72 F5
Fontanosas [E] 96 D4
Fontecha [E] 82 G5
Fontedias [E] 78 C3
Fontenay-le-Comte [F] 54 C4
Fontenay-Trésigny [F] 42 G4
Fontevraud-l'Abbaye [F] 54 E2
Fontiveros [E] 88 D3
Font-Romeu [F] 92 E1
Fontstown [IRL] 4 F3
Fontvieille [F] 106 G4
Fonyód [H] 74 H3
Fonzaso [I] 72 E5
Fóppolo [I] 70 H3
Föra [S] 162 G5
Forbach [D] 58 F1
Forbach [F] 44 G4
Forcall [E] 98 F1
Forcalquier [F] 108 C3
Forcarei [E] 78 C4
Forchheim [D] 46 G4
Ford [GB] 8 C2
Førde [N] 164 B1
Førde [N] 180 C6
Fordingbridge [GB] 12 G4
Fordongianus [I] 118 C5
Forenza [I] 120 H3
Forest [GBG] 18 C2
Forfar [GB] 8 F2
Forges-les-Eaux [F] 28 C5
Forino [I] 120 E3
Forio [I] 120 D3
Førland [N] 164 C5
Forlì [I] 110 G4
Forlì del Sánnio [I] 116 D6
Forlimpopoli [I] 110 G4
Formazza [I] 70 F2
Formby [GB] 10 D3
Formerie [F] 28 D5
Formia [I] 120 C2
Formigine [I] 110 E3
Formiguères [F] 92 E1
Formofoss [N] 190 C5
Fornaci di Barga [I] 110 D4
Fornalutx [E] 104 E4
Fornelli [I] 118 B2
Fornells [E] 104 H4
Forni Avoltri [I] 72 F3
Forni di Sopra [I] 72 F4
Forni di Sotto [I] 72 F4
Forno Alpi Graie [I] 70 C5
Forno di Zoldo [I] 72 E4
Fornos de Algodres [P] 80 D6
Fornovo di Taro [I] 110 D3
Forøy [N] 190 D1
Forráskút [H] 76 E4
Forres [GB] 6 E5
Fors [S] 174 D5
Fors [S] 166 D6
Forsbacka [S] 174 E4
Forsby / Koskenkylä [FIN] 178 B4
Forserum [S] 162 D2
Forshaga [S] 166 F2
Forsheda [S] 162 C4
Forshem [S] 166 E5
Forsmark [S] 174 F5
Forsmark [S] 190 F3
Forsmo [S] 184 E2
Forsnäs [S] 190 G2
Forsnes [N] 180 F1
Forssa [FIN] 176 F3
Forst [D] 34 G4
Fort Augustus [GB] 6 D5
Forte dei Marmi [I] 110 D5
Forte di Bibbiona [I] 114 E1
Forth [D] 46 G5
Fort-Mahon-Plage [F] 28 D3
Fortrose [GB] 6 E4
Fortun [N] 170 E1
Fortuna [E] 104 C2
Fortuneswell [GB] 12 F5
Fort William [GB] 6 C6
Forvik [N] 190 D3
Fos [F] 84 F5
Fossano [I] 108 G2
Fossbakken [N] 192 D3
Fosses [B] 30 C5
Fossombrone [I] 112 B6
Fos-sur-Mer [F] 106 G5
Fotiná [GR] 128 G5
Foucarmont [F] 28 C4
Fouesnant [F] 40 B3
Fougères [F] 26 D5
Fougerolles [F] 58 C3
Foulain [F] 56 H2
Fouras [F] 54 C5
Fourcès [F] 66 D6
Fourfourás [GR] 140 D5
Foúrka [GR] 128 D6
Fourmies [F] 28 G5
Fourná [GR] 132 F3
Fournels [F] 68 C5
Fournés [GR] 140 C4
Foúrnoi [GR] 138 H1
Fourquet [F] 66 F6
Fours [F] 56 E4
Foústani [GR] 128 G3
Fowey [GB] 12 C5
Fownhope [GB] 12 G2
Foxford [IRL] 2 C3
Foynes [IRL] 4 C3
Foz [E] 78 E2
Foz do Arelho [P] 86 B3
Foz Giraldo [P] 86 E3
Frabosa Soprana [I] 108 G3
Fraga [E] 90 G5
Fraize [F] 58 D2
Framley [DK] 156 D1
Framlingham [GB] 14 G3
Frammersbach [D] 46 D3
Frammestad [S] 166 D6
Frampol [PL] 52 F2
Francardo [F] 114 B3
Francavilla al Mare [I] 116 D4
Francavilla di Sicilia [I] 124 A8
Francavilla Fontana [I] 122 F4
Francelos [P] 80 B4
Francofonte [I] 126 G4
Frändefors [S] 166 D5
Franeker [NL] 16 F2
Frangísta [GR] 132 E4
Frangkokástelo [GR] 140 C5
Frangy [F] 70 A2
Frankenberg [D] 32 E5
Frankenberg [D] 48 D1
Frankenburg [A] 60 H4
Frankenmarkt [A] 60 H5
Frankenthal [D] 46 B4
Frankfurt (Oder) [D] 34 G3
Frankfurt am Main [D] 46 C3
Frankrike [S] 190 D6
Fränsta [S] 184 D4
Františkovy Lázně [CZ] 48 C3
Franzburg [D] 20 C3
Franz Josephs-Höhe [A] 72 F2
Frascati [I] 116 A6
Frasdorf [D] 60 F5
Fraserburgh [GB] 6 G5
Frashër [AL] 128 C5
Frasno, Puerto de- [E] 90 D4
Frasso [I] 120 E2
Fratel [P] 86 E4
Fratte Polesine [I] 110 G2
Frauenau [D] 60 H2
Frauenfeld [CH] 58 G4
Frauenstein [D] 48 E1
Frayssinet [F] 66 G4
Frechen [D] 30 G4
Frechilla [E] 82 C6
Freckenhorst [D] 32 C3
Fredensborg [DK] 156 G2
Fredericia [DK] 156 C2
Frederiks [DK] 160 C5
Frederiksberg [DK] 156 F3
Frederikshavn [DK] 160 E3
Frederikssund [DK] 156 G2
Frederiksværk [DK] 156 G2
Fredrika [S] 190 G5
Fredriksberg [S] 172 G5
Fredrikstad [N] 166 B3
Fregenal de la Sierra [E] 94 G3
Fregene [I] 114 H5
Freiberg [D] 48 E1
Freiburg [D] 18 E3
Freiburg im Breisgau [D] 58 E3
Freiensteinau [D] 46 D2
Freihung [D] 48 B5
Freilassing [D] 60 G5
Freising [D] 60 E3
Freistadt [A] 62 C3
Freital [D] 48 E1
Freixedas [P] 80 E6
Freixianda [P] 86 D3
Freixo de Espada à Cinta [P] 80 F5
Frejev [DK] 160 D4
Fréjus [F] 108 D5
Fréjus, Tunnel de- [Eur.] 70 B5
Frenchpark [IRL] 2 D4
Frenštát pod Radhoštěm [CZ] 50 E5
Freren [D] 32 C1
Freshford [IRL] 4 E4
Freshwater [GB] 12 H5
Fresnay-sur-Sarthe [F] 26 F6
Fresnes [F] 28 F4
Fresnes [F] 58 B3
Fresnes-en-Woëvre [F] 44 E4
Fresno Alhándiga [E] 88 C4
Fresno de la Ribera [E] 88 D1
Fréteval [F] 42 D6
Fretigney-et-Velloreille [F] 58 B4
Fretzdorf [D] 20 C6
Freudenberg [D] 46 D4
Freudenberg [D] 32 C6
Freudenstadt [D] 58 F2
Frévent [F] 28 E3
Freyenstein [D] 20 B5
Freyming Merlebach [F] 44 F4
Freystadt [D] 46 G6
Freyung [D] 60 H2
Fri [GR] 140 G3
Frías [E] 82 F5
Fribourg [CH] 58 D6
Frick [CH] 58 E4
Fridafors [S] 162 D6
Fridingen [D] 58 G3
Friedberg [A] 74 E1
Friedberg [D] 60 D3
Friedberg [D] 46 C2
Friedeburg [D] 18 C4
Friedersdorf [D] 34 F3
Friedewald [D] 32 F6
Friedland [D] 32 F5
Friedland [D] 20 D4
Friedland [D] 34 F3
Friedrichroda [D] 46 F1
Friedrichshafen [D] 58 H4
Friedrichskoog [D] 18 E3
Friedrichsort [D] 18 G2
Friedrichstadt [D] 18 E2
Friedrichswalde [D] 20 D6
Friesach [A] 74 B2
Friesack [D] 34 D1
Friesoythe [D] 18 C5
Friggesund [S] 184 D6
Frihetsli [N] 192 E3
Frillesås [S] 160 H3
Frinton-on-Sea [GB] 14 G4
Friol [E] 78 D3
Fristad [S] 162 B2
Fritsla [S] 162 B2
Fritzlar [D] 32 E5
Frödinge [S] 162 F2
Frodsham [GB] 10 D4
Frohburg [D] 34 C6
Frohnleiten [A] 74 D1
Froissy [F] 28 D5
Frombork [PL] 22 F2
Frome [GB] 12 G4
Fromental [F] 26 F5
Frómista [E] 82 D5
Fronsac [F] 84 F4
Fronteira [P] 86 E5
Frontenhausen [D] 60 F3
Frontera [E] 100 A6
Frontignan [F] 106 E4
Fronton [F] 84 H2
Fröseke [S] 162 F4
Frosinone [I] 116 C6
Fröskog [S] 166 D4
Frosolone [I] 120 E1
Frøstrup [DK] 160 C3
Frövik [S] 166 H2
Fruges [F] 28 E3
Frutigen [CH] 70 D1
Frýdek-Místek [CZ] 50 F5
Frýdlant [CZ] 48 G1
Frýdlant nad Ostravicí [CZ] 50 F5
Frygnowo [PL] 22 G5
Frymburk [CZ] 62 B3
Fryšták [CZ] 50 D6
Frysztak [PL] 52 D4
Frýýdlant [CZ] 48 G1
Ftéri [GR] 132 F6
Fubine [I] 70 E6
Fucécchio [I] 110 E5
Fuencaliente [E] 96 D5
Fuencaliente de Lucio [E] 82 E4
Fuencarral [E] 88 F5
Fuendejalón [E] 90 D3
Fuendetodos [E] 90 E4
Fuengirola [E] 102 B5
Fuenlabrada [E] 88 F6
Fuenlabrada de los Montes [E] 96 C3
Fuenmayor [E] 82 G6
Fuensalida [E] 96 E1
Fuente Álamo [E] 98 C6
Fuente Álamo de Murcia [E] 104 C4
Fuentecén [E] 88 G2
Fuente Dé [E] 82 D3
Fuente de Cantos [E] 94 G3
Fuente del Arco [E] 94 H4
Fuente del Maestre [E] 94 G3
Fuente de Santa Cruz [E] 88 E3
Fuente el Fresno [E] 96 F3
Fuente el Sauz [E] 88 G5
Fuente el Sol [E] 88 D3
Fuenteguinaldo [E] 86 H2
Fuentelapeña [E] 88 D2
Fuentelcésped [E] 88 G2
Fuentelespino de Haro [E] 96 H3
Fuentelespino de Moya [E] 98 D3
Fuentemilanos [E] 88 F4
Fuente Obejuna [E] 96 B5
Fuente Palmera [E] 102 B1
Fuentepinilla [E] 90 B3
Fuenterrabía / Hondarribia [E] 84 B2
Fuentes [E] 98 C2
Fuentesaúco [E] 80 H6
Fuentes de Andalucía [E] 102 A2
Fuentes de Ayódar [E] 98 F3
Fuentes de Ebro [E] 90 E4
Fuentes de Jiloca [E] 90 D4
Fuentes de León [E] 94 G4
Fuentes de Nava [E] 82 C6
Fuentes de Oñoro [E] 86 H2
Fuentes de Ropel [E] 82 A5
Fuentidueña de Tajo [E] 96 H1
Fuerte del Rey [E] 102 E2
Fügen [A] 72 E1
Fuglebjerg [DK] 156 F3
Fuhrberg [D] 32 G1
Fulda [D] 46 E2
Fulnek [CZ] 50 E5
Fülöpszállás [H] 76 C3
Fulpmes [A] 72 D1
Fulunäs [S] 172 E2
Fumay [F] 30 C6
Fumel [F] 66 F5
Funäsdalen [S] 182 E4
Funchal [P] 100 B3
Fundão [P] 86 F2
Fundres / Pfundres [I] 72 E2
Funzie [GB] 6 H3
Furadouro [P] 80 B4
Furculeşti [RO] 148 B2
Furnace [GB] 8 C2
Furnes (Veurne) [B] 28 F1
Fürstenau [D] 32 C1
Fürstenberg [D] 20 D5
Fürstenfeld [A] 74 E2
Fürstenfeldbruck [D] 60 D4
Fürstenwalde [D] 34 F2
Fürstenwerder [D] 20 D5
Fürstenzell [D] 60 H3
Furta [H] 76 G2
Fürth [D] 46 G5
Furth im Wald [D] 48 D6
Furtwangen [D] 58 F3
Furuby [S] 162 E4
Furudal [S] 172 H2
Furuflaten [N] 192 E2
Furusund [S] 168 F2
Furutangvik [N] 190 D4
Furuvik [S] 174 E4
Fusa [N] 170 B4
Fuscaldo [I] 124 D4
Fusch [A] 72 G1
Fushë Arrëz [AL] 128 B1
Fushë-Krujë [AL] 128 B2
Fushë-Kuqe [AL] 128 B2
Fushë Muhurr [AL] 128 C2
Fusio [CH] 70 F2
Füssen [D] 60 C6
Futog [YU] 154 F1
Futrikelv [N] 192 E2
Füzesabony [H] 64 E5
Füzesgyarmat [H] 76 G2
Fuzeta [P] 94 D6
Fyláki [GR] 130 H1
Fynshav [DK] 156 D4
Fyresdal [N] 164 E3

G

Gabarret [F] 66 D6
Gabčíkovo [SK] 62 H5
Gabicce Mare [I] 112 B5
Gąbin [PL] 36 H2
Gabrovo [BG] 148 C4
Gacé [F] 26 G5
Gacko [BIH] 152 D3
Gåda [S] 184 C5
Gäddede [S] 190 E5
Gadebusch [D] 18 H4
Gadna [H] 64 F4
Gádor [E] 102 G5
Gádoros [H] 76 F3
Gadžin Han [YU] 150 D4
Gaël [F] 26 B5
Găeşti [RO] 206 C6
Gaeta [I] 120 C2
Gagarin [RUS] 204 E4
Gaggenau [D] 46 B6
Gagliano Castelferrato [I] 126 F3
Gagliano del Capo [I] 122 G6
Gagnef [S] 172 H4
Gaildorf [D] 46 E6
Gaillac [F] 106 B2
Gaillimh / Galway [IRL] 2 C5
Gaillon [F] 28 C6
Gainsborough [GB] 10 F5
Gäïo [GR] 132 B3
Gairloch [GB] 6 C4
Gairo [I] 118 E5
Gaj [YU] 154 H2
Gajary [SK] 62 G4
Gakovo [HR] 74 G6
Galanádo [GR] 138 F3
Galanta [SK] 62 H4
Galapagar [E] 88 F5
Galashiels [GB] 8 E4
Galata [BG] 148 F3
Galatás [GR] 136 G2
Galaţi [RO] 206 D5
Galati Marina [I] 124 B7
Galatina [I] 122 G5
Galátista [GR] 130 B5
Galatone [I] 122 G5
Galaxídi [GR] 132 G5
Galbally [IRL] 4 D4
Galdakao [E] 82 G4
Gáldar [E] 100 C5
Galeata [I] 110 G5
Galera [E] 102 G3
Galéria [F] 114 A3
Galgaguta [H] 64 D5
Galgamácsa [H] 64 D6
Galicea Mare [RO] 150 F1
Galiny [PL] 22 H3
Galissás [GR] 138 D2
Galisteo [E] 86 H4
Galizano [E] 82 F3
Gallarate [I] 70 F4
Gallargues [F] 106 F4
Gallegos de Solmirón [E] 88 C4
Galliate [I] 70 F5
Gallípoli [I] 122 G5
Gällivare [S] 192 F6
Gallneukirchen [A] 62 B4
Gällö [S] 182 H3
Gallur [E] 90 D3
Galovo [BG] 150 G2
Galston [GB] 8 D3
Galtelli [I] 118 E4
Galten [N] 182 D6
Galton [DK] 156 D1
Galtür [A] 72 B2
Galveias [P] 86 D5
Gálvez [E] 96 E2
Galway / Gaillimh [IRL] 2 C5
Gamaches-en-Vexin [F] 28 C4

Gambara [I] 110 D1
Gambárie [I] 124 C7
Gambatesa [I] 120 F1
Gaming [A] 62 D5
Gamla Uppsala [S] 168 D1
Gamleby [S] 162 G2
Gamlingay [GB] 14 E3
Gammel Skagen [DK] 160 E2
Gammelstaden [S] 198 B3
Gammertingen [D] 58 H3
Gams [CH] 58 H5
Gamvik [N] 196 D1
Gamzigrad [YU] 150 D2
Gan [F] 84 E3
Ganacker [D] 60 G3
Gand (Gent) [B] 28 G2
Gandal [N] 164 B3
Gândara [P] 86 E2
Ganderkesee [D] 18 D5
Gandesa [E] 90 G6
Gandia [E] 98 F6
Gandino [I] 70 H4
Gandria [CH] 70 G3
Gandrup [DK] 160 E4
Gandvik [N] 196 E2
Ganges [F] 106 E3
Gangi [I] 126 F3
Gângiova [RO] 150 G2
Gangkofen [D] 60 G3
Gankovo [RUS] 204 D1
Gannat [F] 68 D1
Gänserndorf [A] 62 F4
Gap [F] 108 D2
Gara [H] 76 C5
Garaballa [E] 98 D3
Garaguso [I] 122 C4
Gara Khitrino [BG] 148 E2
Garbagna [I] 110 B2
Garbno [PL] 24 B3
Garbów [PL] 38 D5
Garching [D] 60 G4
Garcia [E] 90 H6
Garciaz [E] 96 B2
Gârcov [RO] 148 A2
Garda [I] 72 C6
Gardanne [F] 108 B5
Gårdby [S] 162 G5
Gardeja [PL] 22 E4
Gardelegen [D] 34 B2
Gardíki [GR] 132 F4
Garding [D] 18 E2
Gardone Riviera [I] 72 B5
Gardone Val Trompia [I] 72 B5
Gárdony [H] 76 B2
Gårdskär [S] 174 F4
Gärdslösa [S] 162 G5
Gardstad [N] 190 C4
Gårdstånga [S] 158 C2
Garein [F] 66 C5
Garelochead [GB] 8 D2
Garen [N] 170 D4
Garešnica [HR] 74 G6
Garéssio [I] 108 G3
Gargaliánoi [GR] 136 C4
Gargellen [A] 72 A2
Gargilesse-Dampierre [F] 54 H5
Gargnano [I] 72 C5
Gargnäs [S] 190 G3
Gargoles de Abajo [E] 90 A5
Gargždai [LT] 202 D4
Garípa [GR] 140 E5
Garkalne [LV] 200 D5
Garlasco [I] 70 F5
Garlstorf [D] 18 F5
Garmisch Partenkirchen [D] 60 D6
Garoza [LV] 200 D5
Garpenberg [S] 174 D5
Garraf [E] 92 D5
Garrafe de Torío [E] 78 H5
Garray [E] 90 B2
Garrel [D] 18 C5
Garrison [GB] 2 E3
Garristown [IRL] 2 F5
Garrovillas [E] 86 G4
Garrucha [E] 102 H5
Gars am Kamp [A] 62 E3
Garsdale Head [GB] 10 E2
Garsnas [S] 158 D3
Garstang [GB] 10 D3
Gartow [D] 20 A6
Gartringen [D] 58 G1
Gartz [D] 20 E5
Garvagh [GB] 2 G2
Garvão [P] 94 C3
Garwolin [PL] 38 C4
Garz [D] 20 D2
Gåsborn [S] 166 G1
Gaschurn [A] 72 B2
Gascueña [E] 98 B1
Gasen [A] 74 D1
Gaskeluokta [S] 190 F4
Gąsocin [PL] 38 B1
Gässåsen [S] 184 D5
Gastoúni [GR] 136 B2
Gasztony [H] 74 F2
Gata [N] 172 C4
Gata de Gorgos [E] 104 F1
Gatchina [RUS] 178 H6
Gatehouse of Fleet [GB] 8 D5
Gátér [H] 76 E3
Gateshead [GB] 8 G6
Gátova [E] 98 E4
Gattendorf [A] 62 G5
Gattinara [I] 70 E4
Gaucín [E] 100 H4
Gaulstad [N] 190 C5
Gaupne [N] 170 D1
Gautestad [N] 164 D4
Gavaloú [GR] 132 E5
Gavardo [I] 72 B6
Gavarnie [F] 84 E5
Gávavencsellő [H] 64 G4
Gaverina Terme [I] 72 A5
Gavi [I] 110 A2
Gavião [P] 86 E4
Gavirate [I] 70 F4
Gävle [S] 174 E4
Gavoi [I] 118 D4
Gavray [F] 26 D4
Gávrio [GR] 134 E6
Gávros [GR] 128 E5
Gavry [RUS] 200 G5
Gävunda [S] 172 G4
Gåxsjö [S] 190 E6
Gazoldo degli Ippoliti [I] 110 E1
Gázoros [GR] 130 C3
Gbelce [SK] 64 B5
Gdańsk [PL] 22 E2
Gdov [RUS] 200 G2
Gdów [PL] 52 B4
Gdynia [PL] 22 E2
Geashill [IRL] 2 E6
Gebesee [D] 32 H6
Gebze [TR] 146 F3
Gedem [D] 46 D2
Gedinne [B] 44 D1
Gediz [TR] 144 G2
Gedney Drove End [GB] 10 G6
Gedser [DK] 20 B1
Gedsted [DK] 160 D4
Gedved [DK] 156 D1
Geel [B] 30 D3
Geertruidenberg [NL] 16 D6
Geesthacht [D] 18 G4
Gefell [D] 48 B2
Gefrees [D] 46 H3
Gefýra [GR] 132 G3
Gefýra [GR] 128 H4
Gehren [D] 46 G2
Geijersholm [S] 172 F6
Geilenkirchen [D] 30 F4
Geilo [N] 170 E4
Geilo [N] 196 D2
Geiranger [N] 180 E4
Geisa [D] 46 E1
Geiselhöring [D] 60 F2
Geisenfeld [D] 60 E3
Geisenhausen [D] 60 F3
Geisingen [D] 58 G3
Geislingen [D] 60 B3
Geisnes [N] 190 C4
Geithain [D] 34 D6
Geithus [N] 170 G6
Geitvågen [N] 192 B6
Gela [I] 126 E5
Geldern [D] 30 G2
Geldrop [NL] 30 E2
Geleen [NL] 30 F4
Gelembe [TR] 144 D2
Gelgaudiškis [LT] 202 E5
Gelibolu [TR] 146 B5
Gelida [E] 92 D4
Gelnhausen [D] 46 D3
Gelnica [SK] 64 F2
Gelsa [E] 90 F4
Gelsenkirchen [D] 30 H3
Gelting [D] 156 C5
Gelu [RO] 76 G5
Gembloux [B] 30 D5
Gémenos [F] 108 B5
Gemerská Poloma [SK] 64 E3
Gemert [NL] 30 F2
Gemlik [TR] 146 F4
Gemona del Friuli [I] 72 G4
Gémozac [F] 54 C6
Gemünd [D] 30 F5
Gemunden [D] 46 E3
Gemünden [D] 32 E6
Gemünden [D] 44 H2
Genappe [B] 30 C4
Génave [E] 96 G6
Gençay [F] 54 E4
Génelard [F] 56 F5
Generalski Stol [HR] 112 G1
General Toshevo [BG] 148 F1
Genève [CH] 70 B2
Gengenbach [D] 58 F2
Genillé [F] 54 G3
Genk [B] 30 E4
Genlis [F] 56 H4
Gennádio [GR] 142 D5
Gennep [NL] 16 F6
Gennes [F] 54 E2
Génolhac [F] 68 D6
Génova [I] 110 B3
Gent (Gand) [B] 28 G2
Genthin [D] 34 C2
Gentioux [F] 68 A2
Genzano di Lucánia [I] 120 H3
Genzano di Roma [I] 116 A6
Georgianí [GR] 128 G5
Georgioúpoli [GR] 140 C4
Georgi Traykov [BG] 148 F3
Georgsheil [D] 18 B4
Gera [D] 48 C1
Geraardsbergen [B] 28 H3
Gerabronn [D] 46 E5
Gerace [I] 124 D7
Gérakas [GR] 136 F4
Geráki [GR] 136 E4
Gerakiní [GR] 130 B5
Gérardmer [F] 58 D2
Geras [A] 62 E3
Gerbéviller [F] 44 F6
Gerbstedt [D] 34 B4
Gerchsheim [D] 46 E4
Geremeas [I] 118 D7
Gerena [E] 94 G5
Gerês [P] 78 B6
Geretsried [D] 60 E5
Gérgal [E] 102 G5
Gerlos [A] 72 E1
Germay [F] 44 D6
Germencik [TR] 144 D5
Germersheim [D] 46 B5
Gernika-Lumo [E] 82 H4
Gernrode [D] 34 A4
Gernsbach [D] 58 F1
Gernsheim [D] 46 C4
Gerola Alta [I] 70 H3
Gerolimenas [GR] 136 E5
Gerolstein [D] 30 G6
Gerolzhofen [D] 46 F4
Gerona / Girona [E] 92 F3
Gerovo [HR] 112 F1
Gerrards Cross [GB] 14 E4
Gerri de la Sal [E] 92 C1
Gersfeld [D] 46 E2
Gersthofen [D] 60 D3
Gesäter [S] 166 C4
Gescher [D] 16 G6
Geseke [D] 32 D4
Gesualdo [I] 120 F3
Gesunda [S] 172 G3
Geta [FIN] 176 A5
Getafe [E] 88 F6
Getaria [E] 84 A2
Gettorf [D] 18 F2
Getxo [E] 82 G3
Gevgelija [MK] 128 G3
Gevrey-Chambertin [F] 56 G4
Gex [F] 70 B2
Geyikli [TR] 130 H6
Geyre [TR] 144 F5
Geyve [TR] 146 G3
Gföhl [A] 62 D3
Ghalipsós [GR] 130 C4
Ghedi [I] 72 B6
Gheorghieni [RO] 206 C4
Ghilarza [I] 118 C4
Ghimpaţi [RO] 148 C1
Ghisonaccia [F] 114 C4
Ghisoni [F] 114 B4
Giáltra [GR] 132 H4
Giannitsá [GR] 128 G4
Gianoúli [GR] 130 H2
Giardinetto [I] 120 G2
Giardini-Naxos [I] 124 B8
Giarmata [RO] 76 G5
Giarratana [I] 126 F5
Giarre [I] 124 A8
Giba [I] 118 B7
Gibellina [I] 126 B2
Gibellina Vecchia [I] 126 C2
Gibostad [N] 192 D2
Gibraleón [E] 94 E5
Gibraltar [GBZ] 100 G5
Gic [H] 74 H1
Gidle [PL] 50 G1
Gieboldehausen [D] 32 G4
Giedraičiai [LT] 202 G5
Gielniów [PL] 38 A5
Gien [F] 56 C2
Giengen [D] 60 C3
Giens [F] 108 C6
Gieselwerder [D] 32 F4
Giessen [D] 46 C1
Gieten [NL] 16 G3
Giethoorn [NL] 16 F3
Gietrzwałd [PL] 22 G4
Giffoni [I] 120 F3
Gifhorn [D] 32 H2
Gigen [BG] 148 A2
Giglio Porto [I] 114 E4
Gignac [F] 106 E4
Gijón [E] 82 B1
Giksi [LV] 200 E4
Gilford [GB] 2 G4
Gilleleje [DK] 156 G1
Gillhov [S] 182 G4
Gillingham [GB] 14 F4
Gillingham [GB] 12 G4
Gimat [F] 84 G2
Gimel-les-Cascades [F] 66 H3
Gimnó [GR] 134 C5
Gimo [S] 174 F5
Gimont [F] 84 G3
Ginosa [I] 122 D4
Gióia del Colle [I] 122 E3
Gióia Táuro [I] 124 C6
Gioiosa Marea [I] 126 G1
Giornico [CH] 70 G2
Giovinazzo [I] 122 D2
Giraltovce [SK] 52 D6
Girgantai [LT] 24 E2
Girifalco [I] 124 D5
Girolata [F] 114 A3
Giromagny [F] 58 C3
Girona / Gerona [E] 92 F3
Gironella [E] 92 E2
Girvan [GB] 8 C4
Gisburn [GB] 10 E3
Gislaved [S] 162 C3
Gislev [DK] 156 E3
Gisors [F] 28 C6
Gissi [I] 116 E5
Gistaín [E] 84 F5
Gistel [B] 28 F1
Gistrup [DK] 160 E4
Gittun [S] 190 G2
Giulianova [I] 116 D3
Giurgiţa [RO] 150 G2
Giurgiu [RO] 148 C1
Give [DK] 156 C2
Givet [F] 30 D6
Givors [F] 68 F3
Givry [B] 28 H4
Givry [F] 56 G5
Givry-en-Argonne [F] 44 C4
Giżalki [PL] 36 E3
Gizeux [F] 54 F2
Giżycko [PL] 24 C3
Gizzeria [I] 124 D5
Gjemnes [N] 180 F2
Gjerbës [AL] 128 C5
Gjerde [N] 180 D6
Gjermundshamn [N] 170 B5
Gjern [DK] 160 D6
Gjerrild [DK] 160 F5
Gjerstad [N] 164 F4
Gjersvik [N] 190 D4
Gjeving [N] 164 F4
Gjirokastër [AL] 128 C6
Gjølme [N] 180 H1
Gjøra [N] 180 G3
Gjóv [FR] 160 B1
Gjøvik [N] 172 B3
Gkoritsá [GR] 136 E4
Gkoúra [GR] 136 D1
Gladbeck [D] 30 H2
Gladenbach [D] 32 D6
Glamis [GB] 8 F2
Glamoč [BIH] 154 B4
Glåmos [N] 182 C3
Glamsbjerg [DK] 156 D3
Glandore [IRL] 4 B5
Glandorf [D] 32 D2
Glanmire [IRL] 4 C5
Glanworth [IRL] 4 D4
Glarus [CH] 58 G6
Glasgow [GB] 8 D3
Glashütte [D] 48 E1
Glashütten [A] 74 C3
Glastonbury [GB] 12 F4
Glauchau [D] 48 C1
Glava [S] 166 D2
Glavan [BG] 148 D5
Glavanovtsi [BG] 150 E4
Glavičice [BIH] 154 E3
Glavinitsa [BG] 148 E1
Glavnik [YU] 150 C4
Gleann Cholm Cille / Glencolumbkille [IRL] 2 D2
Gleinalm Tunnel [A] 74 D1
Gleisdorf [A] 74 E2
Glenamaddy [IRL] 2 D4
Glenamoy [IRL] 2 C3
Glenarm [GB] 2 G3
Glenavy [GB] 2 G3
Glenbarr [GB] 2 H1
Glencoe [GB] 6 C6
Glencolumbkille / Gleann Cholm Cille [IRL] 2 D2
Glendaruel [GB] 8 C2
Glendoll [GB] 8 F1
Gleneagles [GB] 8 E2
Glenealy [IRL] 4 G4
Glenegedale [GB] 2 G1
Glenfinnan [GB] 6 C6
Glengarriff [IRL] 4 B5
Glenhull [GB] 2 F3
Glénic [F] 54 H5
Glenluce [GB] 8 C5
Glenmore [IRL] 4 E4
Glenrothes [GB] 8 E3
Glenties [IRL] 2 E2
Glenville [IRL] 4 D5
Gletsch [CH] 70 F2
Glewitz [D] 20 C3
Glifáda [GR] 132 F5
Glifádha [GR] 136 G1
Glimåkra [S] 158 D1
Glin [IRL] 4 C3
Glina [HR] 112 H1
Glinka [PL] 50 G5
Glinojeck [PL] 38 A1
Glinsce / Glinsk [IRL] 2 B4
Glinsk / Glinsce [IRL] 2 B4
Glissjöberg [S] 182 G5
Gliwice [PL] 50 F3
Gllavë [AL] 128 B5
Głodowa [PL] 22 B3
Gloggnitz [A] 62 E6
Głogów [PL] 36 B5
Głogówek [PL] 50 E3
Głogów Malopolski [PL] 52 E3
Glomfjord [N] 190 E1
Glommersträsk [S] 190 H4
Glömminge [S] 162 G5
Glóssa [GR] 134 B3
Glossop [GB] 10 E4
Glostrup [DK] 156 G2
Glöte [S] 182 F5
Gloucester [GB] 12 G2
Główczyce [PL] 22 C2
Glowe [D] 20 D2
Glöwen [D] 20 B6
Glowno [PL] 36 H4
Gložan [YU] 154 F1
Glozhene [BG] 150 G2
Glozhene [BG] 148 A4
Głubczyce [PL] 50 E3
Głuchołazy [PL] 50 D3
Glücksburg [D] 156 C4
Glückstadt [D] 18 E3
Gluda [LV] 200 D5
Glumsø [DK] 156 F3
Glušci [YU] 154 F2
Głuszyca [PL] 50 B2
Glýfa [GR] 132 H3
Glykí [GR] 132 C3
Glynde [GB] 14 E5
Glyngøre [DK] 160 C4
Glyn Neath [GB] 12 E2
Gmünd [A] 72 H2
Gmünd [A] 62 C3
Gmund [D] 60 E5
Gmunden [A] 62 A5
Gnarp [S] 184 E5
Gnarrenburg [D] 18 E4
Gnesta [S] 168 D4
Gniechowice [PL] 50 C1
Gniew [PL] 22 E4
Gniewkowo [PL] 36 E1
Gniezno [PL] 36 D2
Gnisvärd [S] 168 F4
Gnjilane [YU] 150 D5

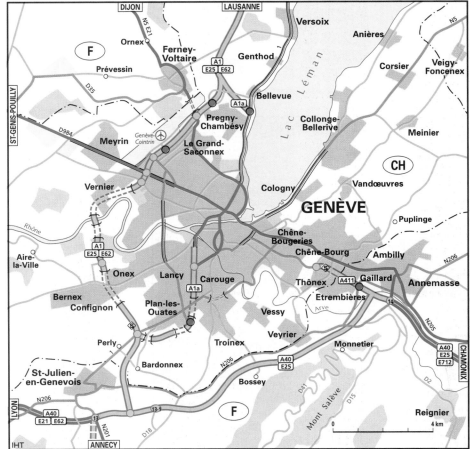

Göteborg area map (Uddevalla / Alingsås / Varberg / Borås): Harestad, Surte, Gunnesby, Vråkärr, Säve, Ranneberger, Kärra, Björlanda, Agnesberg, Angered, Olofstorp, Tuve, Backa, Kortedala, Kåhög, Torslanda, Biskopsgården, Tolered, Sävedalen, Partille, Hjuvik, Sandvik, Örgryte, Öjersjö, Landvetter, GÖTEBORG, Eckebäck, Älvsborg, Krokslätt, Hultet, Brännö, MÖLNDAL, Mölnlycke, Askim, Bolås, Näset, Styrsö, Kållered, Donsö, Skintebo, Billdal, Hallesåker, Vrångö, Lindome

Guémené-sur-Scorff [F] 40 D3
Guenange [F] 44 F3
Guer [F] 26 B6
Guérande [F] 40 D6
Guéret [F] 54 H6
Guérigny [F] 56 D4
Guethary [F] 84 C2
Gueugnon [F] 56 E5
Güglingen [D] 46 C6
Guglionesi [I] 116 F5
Gugny [PL] 24 E5
Guía de Isora [E] 100 B5
Guichen [F] 26 C6
Guidonia [I] 116 A5
Guignes [F] 42 G4
Guijuelo [E] 88 C4
Guildford [GB] 14 D4
Guillaumes [F] 108 E3
Guillena [E] 94 G5
Guillestre [F] 108 E2
Guilvinec [F] 40 B3
Güímar [E] 100 B5
Guimarães [P] 80 C3
Guimiliau [F] 40 C2
Guînes [F] 14 G6
Guingamp [F] 26 A4
Guipry [F] 40 F4
Guísamo [E] 78 D2
Guisborough [GB] 10 G2
Guise [F] 28 G5
Guissona [E] 92 C3
Guitiriz [E] 78 D2
Guîtres [F] 66 D3
Gujan-Mestras [F] 66 B3
Gulbene [LV] 200 F4
Guldborg [DK] 156 F5
Gullabo [S] 162 F6
Gulladuff [GB] 2 G3
Gullaskruv [S] 162 F4
Gullhaug [N] 164 H2
Gullringen [S] 162 F2
Gullspång [S] 166 F4
Gullstein [N] 180 F1
Güllü [TR] 144 F4
Güllüce [TR] 146 E5
Güllük [TR] 142 C2
Gülpınar [TR] 134 G1
Gulsele [S] 190 F6
Gulsvik [N] 170 G4
Gülübintsi [BG] 148 D5
Gülübovo [BG] 148 D5
Gulyantsi [BG] 148 B2
Gumiel de Hizán [E] 88 G2
Gummersbach [D] 32 C5
Gumpoldskirchen [A] 62 F5
Gumtow [D] 20 B6
Gümüldür [TR] 144 C5
Gümüşpınar [TR] 146 D2
Gümüşsu [TR] 144 H4
Gümüşyeni [TR] 146 G5
Gümzovo [BG] 150 E2
Gundelfingen [D] 60 C3
Gundelsheim [D] 46 D5
Güney [TR] 144 G5
Güney [TR] 144 F4
Güngörmez [TR] 144 D1
Günlüce [TR] 144 F1
Gunnarn [S] 190 G4
Gunnarskog [S] 166 D1
Gunnebo [S] 162 G2
Gunten [CH] 70 E1
Güntersberge [D] 32 H4
Guntersblum [D] 46 C4
Guntersdorf [A] 62 E3
Guntín [E] 78 D3
Günzburg [D] 60 C3
Gunzenhausen [D] 46 F6
Güre [TR] 144 H3
Güre [TR] 144 F3
Güreci [TR] 146 B5
Gurgazu [F] 114 B6
Gurk [A] 74 B2
Gurkovo [BG] 148 C4
Gürpinar [TR] 146 E3
Gurrea de Gállego [E] 90 F3
Gürsu [TR] 146 F4
Gurtnellen [CH] 70 F1
Gusev [RUS] 24 D1
Gusinje [YU] 150 A5
Gusmar [AL] 128 B6
Gúspini [I] 118 C6
Güssing [A] 74 F2
Gustavsberg [S] 168 E3
Gustavsfors [S] 166 D3
Güstrow [D] 20 B4
Gusum [S] 168 B6
Gutcher [GB] 6 H3
Gutenstein [A] 62 E5
Gütersloh [D] 32 D3
Guttannen [CH] 70 F1
Gützkow [D] 20 D3
Güzelbahçe [TR] 144 C4
Guzet-Neige [F] 84 H5
Gvardeysk [RUS] 24 B1
Gvarv [N] 164 F2
Gvodz [HR] 112 H1
Gvozd [YU] 152 E3
Gwatt [CH] 70 D1
Gwyddgrug [GB] 12 E1
Gy [F] 58 B4
Gya [N] 164 B4
Gylling [DK] 156 D2
Gyoma [H] 76 F2
Gyömrő [H] 76 D1
Gyöngyös [H] 64 E5
Gyöngyöspata [H] 64 D5
Gyönk [H] 76 B3
Győr [H] 62 H6
Gysinge [S] 174 E5
Gýtheio [GR] 136 E4
Gyttorp [S] 166 G2
Gyueshevo [BG] 150 E6
Gyula [H] 76 G3

H

Häädemeeste [EST] 200 D3
Haag [A] 62 C4
Haag [D] 60 F4
Haag am Hausruck [A] 62 A4
Haaksbergen [NL] 16 G5
Haapajärvi [FIN] 198 D6
Haapajoki [FIN] 198 C4
Haapamäki [FIN] 186 E4
Haapamäki [FIN] 198 E6
Haapavesi [FIN] 198 D5
Haapsalu [EST] 200 D2
Haar [D] 60 E4
Haarby [DK] 156 D3
Haaren [D] 32 E4
Haarlem [NL] 16 D4
Habartice [CZ] 48 G1
Habay [B] 44 E2
Hablingbo [S] 168 F5
Habo [S] 162 D2
Hachenburg [D] 46 B1
Hachmühlen [D] 32 F2
Hackås [S] 182 G3
Hacketstown [IRL] 4 F4
Hackland [GB] 6 G2
Håcksvik [S] 162 B3
Hadamar [D] 46 B2
Haddington [GB] 8 F3
Haderslev [DK] 156 C3
Haderup [DK] 160 C5
Hadiach [UA] 206 G2
Hadım [TR] 144 G4
Hadleigh [GB] 14 G3
Hadlow [GB] 14 F5
Hadmersleben [D] 34 B3
Hadsten [DK] 160 D6
Hadsund [DK] 160 E4
Hadžići [BIH] 152 C1
Hægeland [N] 164 D5
Hafnarfjörður [IS] 194 B4
Hagafoss [N] 170 F3
Hagby [S] 162 F5
Hagebro [DK] 160 C5
Hagen [D] 32 C4
Hagen [D] 18 D4
Hagenow [D] 18 H5
Hagetmau [F] 84 E2
Hagfors [S] 172 F6
Häggås [S] 190 F5
Häggenås [S] 182 H1
Häggsjöbränna [S] 182 E1
Häggsjömon [S] 190 G5
Haglebu [N] 170 G4
Hagondange [F] 44 E4
Haguenau [F] 44 H5
Hahn [D] 18 C4
Hahnbach [D] 46 H5
Hahót [H] 74 G3
Haigerloch [D] 58 G2
Hailsham [GB] 14 E6
Hailuoto [FIN] 198 D4
Hainburg [A] 62 G4
Hainfeld [A] 62 E5
Hainichen [D] 48 D1
Hajdúböszörmény [H] 64 G6
Hajdúdorog [H] 64 G5
Hajdúhadház [H] 64 H5
Hajdúnánás [H] 64 G5
Hajdúsámson [H] 64 H6
Hajdúszoboszló [H] 64 G6
Hajdúszovát [H] 76 G1
Hajnówka [PL] 38 F1
Hajós [H] 76 C4
Håkenby [N] 166 C3
Hakkas [S] 196 A7
Hakkenpää [FIN] 176 D4
Hakokylä [FIN] 198 F4
Halámky [CZ] 62 C2
Halberstadt [D] 34 A3
Hald [DK] 160 E5
Halden [N] 166 C3
Haldensee [A] 60 C6
Haldensleben [D] 34 B2
Halenkov [CZ] 50 E6
Halesowen [GB] 10 D6
Halesworth [GB] 14 G3
Halhjem [N] 170 B4
Halič [SK] 64 D4
Halifax [GB] 10 E4
Halikko [FIN] 176 E4
Halitpaşa [TR] 144 D3
Haljala [EST] 200 E1
Halk [DK] 156 C3
Halkirk [GB] 6 F3
Hallabro [S] 162 E6
Hallapuro [FIN] 186 E2
Hällberget [S] 182 F3
Halle [B] 28 H3
Halle [D] 34 C5
Halle [D] 32 D3
Hällefors [S] 166 G2
Hälleforsnäs [S] 168 B3
Hallein [A] 60 G6
Hallen [S] 182 G2
Hallenberg [D] 32 D5
Hallerud [S] 166 G4
Hällestad [S] 166 H5
Hällevadsholm [S] 166 C5
Hälleviksstrand [S] 166 C6
Hallingby [N] 170 H5
Hall in Tirol [A] 72 D1
Hällnäs [S] 190 H5
Hallsberg [S] 166 H4
Hallshuk [S] 168 G3
Hallstahammar [S] 168 B2
Hallstatt [A] 62 A6
Hallstavik [S] 168 E1
Halltorp [S] 162 F6
Halluin [B] 28 F2
Halmstad [S] 162 B5
Hals [DK] 160 E4
Halsa [N] 180 F2
Hal'shany [BY] 202 H6
Halsskov [DK] 156 E3
Halstead [GB] 14 F3
Halsteren [NL] 16 C6
Halsua [FIN] 186 E1
Haltdalen [N] 182 C3
Haltern [D] 30 H2
Haltwhistle [GB] 8 F5
Haluna [FIN] 188 D1
Halver [D] 32 C5
Halwill [GB] 12 D4
Ham [F] 28 F5
Hamamköy [TR] 144 E5
Hamar [N] 172 C3
Hambergen [D] 18 D5
Hamburg [D] 18 F4
Hamburgsund [S] 166 B5
Hamdibey [TR] 146 C6
Hamdorf [D] 18 F2
Hämeenkyrö [FIN] 176 E1
Hämeenlinna [FIN] 176 G3
Hämeler Wald [D] 32 G2
Hameln [D] 32 F3
Hamersleben [D] 34 A3
Hamidiye [TR] 146 B3
Hamilton [GB] 8 D3
Hamina [FIN] 178 D3
Hamlagrøosen [N] 170 C3
Hamm [D] 32 C3
Hammar [S] 166 G4
Hammarland [FIN] 176 A5
Hammarstrand [S] 184 D2
Hammaslahti [FIN] 188 F3
Hammel [DK] 160 D6
Hammelburg [D] 46 E3
Hammer [N] 190 C5
Hammerdal [S] 182 H1
Hammerfest [N] 196 B2
Hamminkeln [D] 16 G6
Hammrnäs [S] 182 G2
Hamnavoe [GB] 6 H3
Hamnbukt [N] 192 H1
Hamneidet [N] 192 F1
Hamningberg [N] 196 F1
Hamoir [B] 30 E5
Hamra [S] 172 H1
Hamrångefjärden [S] 174 E3
Hamre [N] 164 E5
Hamula [FIN] 186 G2
Hamzali [MK] 128 H2
Hamziči [BIH] 152 C2
Hån [S] 166 C2
Han [YU] 152 D4
Hanau [D] 46 D3
Hânceşti [MD] 206 D4
Handegg [CH] 70 F1
Handen [S] 168 E3
Handlová [SK] 64 B3
Handöl [S] 182 E2
Hanerau-Hademarschen [D] 18 E2
Hanestad [N] 182 C6
Hangö / Hanko [FIN] 176 E6
Han i Hotit [AL] 152 E4
Hankamäki [FIN] 198 F6
Hankasalmi [FIN] 186 H4
Hankensbüttel [D] 32 H1
Hanko / Hangö [FIN] 176 E6
Hann-Münden [D] 32 F5
Hannover [D] 32 F2
Hannuit (Hannut) [B] 30 D4
Hannusranta [FIN] 198 F5
Hannut (Hannuit) [B] 30 D4
Han Pijesak [BIH] 154 E4
Hansnes [N] 192 E1
Hanstedt [D] 18 F5
Hanstholm [DK] 160 C3
Han-sur-Lesse [B] 30 D6
Hantháza [H] 76 D2
Hanušovce [SK] 64 G2
Hanušovice [CZ] 50 C4
Hanya [TR] 144 E2
Haparanda [S] 198 C2
Häppälä [FIN] 186 H4
Hara [EST] 200 D2
Haradok [BY] 204 C4
Harads [S] 198 A2
Häradsbäck [S] 162 D5
Haraneset [N] 190 C4
Haravgi [GR] 128 F5
HarboØre [DK] 160 B4
Harburg [D] 60 C2
Harburg [D] 18 F4
Hardegg [A] 62 E3
Hardegsen [D] 32 F4
Hardelot-Plage [F] 28 D2
Hardenberg [NL] 16 G4
Harderwijk [NL] 16 E4
Hardeshøj [DK] 156 C4
Hardheim [D] 46 D4
Hareid [N] 180 C3
Haren [D] 16 H3
Haren [NL] 16 G2
Harestua [N] 172 B5
Harewood [GB] 10 F3
Harfleur [F] 26 G3
Hargla [EST] 200 F4
Hargshamn [S] 174 G5
Haría [E] 100 E4
Harjavalta [FIN] 176 D2
Harjunmaa [FIN] 188 C5
Harjunsalmi [FIN] 186 F6
Harkány [H] 76 B5
Harlech [GB] 10 B5
Hårlev [DK] 156 G3
Harlingen [NL] 16 E2
Harlösa [S] 158 C2
Harlow [GB] 14 E4
Harmancık [TR] 146 F6
Harmånger [S] 184 E6
Härmänkylä [FIN] 198 F4
Härmänmäki [FIN] 198 F4
Harndrup [DK] 156 D3
Härnosänd [S] 184 F4
Haro [E] 82 G5
Harodz'ki [BY] 202 H6
Haroldswick [GB] 6 H3
Haroué [F] 44 E6
Harpefoss [N] 170 H1
Harpenden [GB] 14 E3
Harplinge [S] 162 B5
Harpstedt [D] 18 D6
Harrachov [CZ] 48 H2
Harran [N] 190 D5
Harrogate [GB] 10 F3
Harrow [GB] 14 E4
Harsefeld [D] 18 E4
Harsewinkel [D] 32 D3
Harsprange [S] 190 H1
Harstad [N] 192 D3
Harstad [N] 166 D1
Harsum [D] 32 G2
Harsvik [N] 190 B5
Harta [H] 76 C3
Hartberg [A] 74 E1
Hartha [D] 34 D6
Hartland [GB] 12 D3
Hartlepool [GB] 10 G2
Hartley Wintney [GB] 14 D4
Hartmannshain [D] 46 D2
Hartola [FIN] 186 G6
Harwich [GB] 14 G3
Harzgerode [D] 34 A4
Hasanağa [TR] 146 E5
Hasanpaşa [TR] 146 G5
Haselund [D] 18 E1
Haselünne [D] 18 B6
Hasköy [TR] 146 B2
Hasköy [TR] 144 G3
Haslach [A] 62 B3
Haslach [D] 58 F2
Hasle [DK] 158 E4
Haslemere [GB] 14 D5
Haslev [DK] 156 G3
Hasparren [F] 84 C2
Hasseki [TR] 134 H4
Hassel [D] 18 E6
Hassela [S] 184 E5
Hasselfelde [D] 32 H4
Hasselfors [S] 166 G4
Hasselt [B] 30 E4
Hasselt [NL] 16 F4
Hassfurt [D] 46 F3
Hasslach [D] 46 H3
Hassle [S] 166 F4
Hassleben [D] 20 D5
Hässleholm [S] 158 D1
Hastersboda [FIN] 168 H1
Hästholmen [S] 166 G6
Hastiere-Lavaux [B] 30 D6
Hastings [GB] 14 F6
Hästveda [S] 158 D1
Hasvik [N] 196 A2
Hatě [CZ] 62 E3
Haţeg [RO] 206 B5
Hatfield [GB] 14 E3
Hatfjelldal [N] 190 E3
Hatherleigh [GB] 12 D4
Hattem [NL] 16 F4
Hatten [N] 190 D2
Hattingen [D] 30 H3
Hattstedt [D] 18 E1
Hattula [FIN] 176 G2
Hattuselkonen [FIN] 198 G5
Hattuvaara [FIN] 188 H1
Hattuvaara [FIN] 198 G6
Hatvan [H] 64 D6
Hatvik [N] 170 B4
Haugan [N] 190 B6
Haugastøl [N] 170 E4
Hauge [N] 164 B5
Haugesund [N] 164 A1
Hauggrend [N] 164 E2
Haughom [N] 164 C4
Haugsdorf [A] 62 E3
Haugsten [N] 170 G1
Hauho [FIN] 176 G2
Haukå [N] 180 B5
Haukeligrend [N] 164 D1
Haukeliseter [N] 170 D5
Haukipudas [FIN] 198 D3
Haukivuori [FIN] 188 C5
Haunersdorf [D] 60 G3
Hausach [D] 58 F2
Häusern [D] 58 F4
Hausham [D] 60 E5
Hausjärvi [FIN] 176 H3
Hautajärvi [FIN] 196 F7
Haut-Asco [F] 114 B3
Haute-Nendaz [CH] 70 D2
Hauteville-Lompnes [F] 68 H2
Hauteville Plage [F] 26 D3
Hautmont [F] 28 G4
Havant [GB] 14 D5
Håvberget [S] 172 G5
Havdhem [S] 168 G5
Håvedalen [S] 166 C4
Havelange [B] 30 D5
Havelberg [D] 34 C1
Haverdal [S] 162 B5
Haverfordwest [GB] 12 D1
Haverhill [GB] 14 F3
Håverud [S] 166 D4
Havířov [CZ] 50 F4
Håvla [S] 168 B4
Havlęíčkův Brod [CZ] 48 D4
Havlíčkův Brod [CZ] 48 H5
Havnäs [S] 190 F5

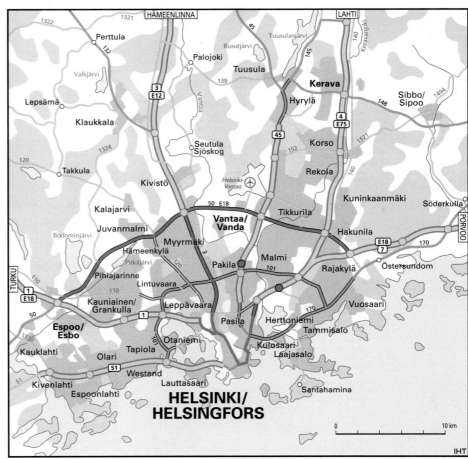

0
5 km
Belgrat Ormani
Rumeli Kavağı
Bahçeköy
Sarıyer
Büyükdere
Anadolu Kavağı
Kemerburgaz
Kefeliköy
Alibey Barajı
Tarabya
Yeniköy
Beykoz
Ayazağa
İstinye
Paşabahçe
Boyaciköy
Kanlica
E80 O-2
Alibeyköy
Kâğıthane
Rumeli Hisari
Anadolu Hisari
Gaziosmanpaşa
Kandilli
EDIRNE
O-1
Şişli
O-3
Eyüp
Mahmutbey
Boğaziçi
Çengelköy
E80 O-2
Beşiktaş
Beylerbeyi
Bağeilar
Beyoğlu
ŞILE
Bayrampaşa
Üsküdar
Güneşli
Ümraniye
Fatih
Eminönü
Harem
Sirinevler
Kadıköy
TEKIRDAĞ
Zeytinburnu
İSTANBUL
E80 O-4
İZMIT
Bakirköy
Erenköy
Atatürk
Fenerbahçe
Yeşilköy
Marmara Denizi
Suadige
IHT
GEBZE

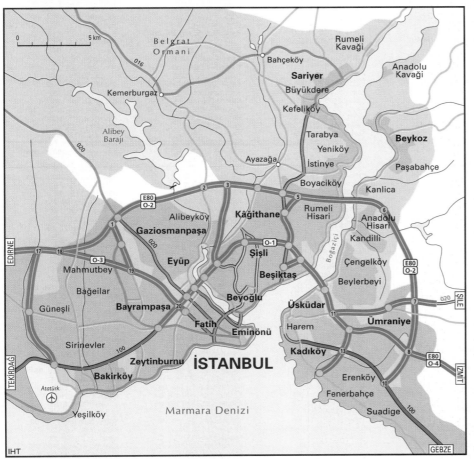

Jämshög [S] 158 E1
Janakkala [FIN] 176 G3
Jänese [EST] 200 F1
Janja [BIH] 154 F3
Janjina [HR] 152 B3
Janków [PL] 36 E4
Jánoshalma [H] 76 D4
Jánosháza [H] 74 G2
Jánossomorja [H] 62 G5
Janovice nad Úhlavou [CZ] 48 D5
Janów [PL] 50 G2
Janów [PL] 24 E4
Janów [PL] 38 A3
Janowiec [PL] 38 D5
Janowiec Wielkopolski [PL] 36 D1
Janów Lubelski [PL] 52 E2
Janowo [PL] 22 H5
Janów Podlaski [PL] 38 F3
Janské Lazně [CZ] 50 A2
Jänsmässholmen [S] 190 D6
Januszewice [PL] 38 A5
Janville [F] 42 E5
Janzé [F] 26 C6
Jäppilä [FIN] 188 C4
Jarafuel [E] 98 D5
Jaraicejo [E] 96 B1
Jaraíz de la Vera [E] 88 B5
Jarandilla de la Vera [E] 88 B5
Järbo [S] 174 D4
Jarcevo [RUS] 204 D4
Jarczew [PL] 38 D4
Jard-sur-Mer [F] 54 B3
Jaren [N] 172 B4
Jaren [S] 166 C3
Jargeau [F] 42 E6
Jarkovac [YU] 154 H1
Järkvissle [S] 184 E3
Järlåsa [S] 168 C1
Jarmen [D] 20 D3
Järna [S] 168 D4
Jarnac [F] 54 D6
Jarnages [F] 54 H6
Järnforsen [S] 162 F3
Jarny [F] 44 E4
Jarocin [PL] 36 D4
Jaroměř [CZ] 50 B3
Jaroměřice nad Rokytnou [CZ] 62 E2
Jarosław [PL] 52 F3
Jarosławiec [PL] 22 B2
Järpen [S] 182 F2
Järva-Jaani [EST] 200 E2
Järvakandi [EST] 200 E2
Järvelä [FIN] 176 H3
Järvenpää [FIN] 176 H4
Järvsö [S] 174 D1
Jaša Tomić [YU] 154 H1
Jaseń [PL] 22 C3
Jasenak [HR] 112 F2
Jasenovac [HR] 154 B1
Jasenovets [BG] 148 D2
Jasenovo [YU] 152 E3
Jasenovo [YU] 150 A3
Jashchera [RUS] 200 H1
Jasień [PL] 34 G4
Jasienica [PL] 50 F4
Jasienica Rosielna [PL] 52 E4
Jasika [YU] 150 C3
Jasionówka [PL] 24 E5
Jašiūnai [LT] 202 G6
Jasło [PL] 52 D4
Jasov [SK] 64 F3
Jastrebarsko [HR] 74 D6
Jastrowie [PL] 22 B5
Jastrzębie-Zdrói [PL] 50 F4
Jászágó [H] 64 D6
Jászapáti [H] 64 E6
Jászárokszállás [H] 64 E6
Jászberény [H] 64 E6
Jászfelsöszentgyörgy [H] 76 E1
Jászfényszaru [H] 64 D6
Jászkisér [H] 76 E1
Jászladány [H] 76 E1
Jaszów [PL] 50 D2
Jät [S] 162 E5
Játar [E] 102 G3
Jauge [F] 66 C3
Jaun [CH] 70 D1
Jaungulbene [LV] 200 F4
Jauniniumuiža [LV] 200 C6
Jaunjelgava [LV] 200 E5
Jaunpils [LV] 200 C5
Jauntsaras [E] 84 B3
Jauranna [LV] 200 F4
Jaurplebalga [LV] 200 F4
Jausiers [F] 108 E2
Jävall [N] 166 C2
Javarus [FIN] 196 D7
Jávea / Xàbia [E] 104 F1
Jävenitz [D] 34 B2
Javier / Xabier [E] 84 C4
Javořičko [CZ] 50 C5
Javorník [CZ] 50 C3
Jävre [S] 198 B4
Javron [F] 26 F5
Jawor [PL] 36 B6
Jawor Solecki [PL] 38 C6
Jaworzno [PL] 50 G3
Jayena [E] 102 D4
Jebel [RO] 76 G6
Jedburgh [GB] 8 F4
Jedlina-Zdrój [PL] 50 B2
Jedlińsk [PL] 38 B5
Jednorożec [PL] 24 B6
Jedovnice [CZ] 50 C6
Jędrzejów [PL] 52 B2
Jedwabne [PL] 24 D5
Jedwabno [PL] 22 H5
Jeesiö [FIN] 196 D6
Jegłownik [PL] 22 F3
Jēkabpils [LV] 200 F5
Jektevik [N] 170 B5
Jektvik [N] 190 D1
Jelah [BIH] 154 D3
Jelcy [RUS] 204 D3
Jelcz-Laskowice [PL] 50 D1
Jelenia Góra [PL] 50 A1
Jelenino [PL] 22 B4
Jeleśnia [PL] 50 G5
Jelgava [LV] 200 D5
Jelizarovo [RUS] 200 G3
Jelling [DK] 156 C2
Jelnja [RUS] 204 D5
Jełowa [PL] 50 E2
Jels [DK] 156 C3
Jelsa [HR] 152 A3
Jelsa [N] 164 B2
Jelsi [I] 120 F1
Jemnice [CZ] 62 D2
Jena [D] 46 H1
Jenbach [A] 60 E6
Jeneč [CZ] 48 F3
Jennersdorf [A] 74 E2
Jeppo / Jepua [FIN] 186 C1
Jepua / Jeppo [FIN] 186 C1
Jerez de la Frontera [E] 100 F3
Jerez del Marquesado [E] 102 F4
Jerez de los Caballeros [E] 94 F3
Jerggul Holmestrand [N] 192 H2
Jergucati [AL] 132 B1
Jérica [E] 98 E3
Jerichow [D] 34 C2
Jerup [DK] 160 E2
Jerxheim [D] 34 A3
Jerzu [I] 118 E5
Jerzwałd [PL] 22 F4
Jesberg [D] 32 E6
Jesenice [A] 74 B4
Jesenice [CZ] 48 E3
Jeseník [CZ] 50 D3
Jesenské [SK] 64 E4
Jesi [I] 116 C1
Jesionowo [PL] 20 G6
Jésolo [I] 72 F6
Jessen [D] 34 D4
Jessheim [N] 172 C5
Jeumont [F] 28 H4
Jevenstedt [D] 18 F2
Jever [D] 18 C4
Jevíčko [CZ] 50 C5
Jevišovice [CZ] 62 E2
Jevnaker [N] 170 H5
Jezerane [HR] 112 G2
Jezero [BIH] 154 B3
Jezersko [BIH] 112 H2
Jezersko [SLO] 74 B4
Jeżewo [PL] 36 H1
Jeżewo [PL] 24 E5
Jeziorany [PL] 22 H3
Jeżów [PL] 36 H4
Jičín [CZ] 48 H3
Jieznas [LT] 24 G1
Jihlava [CZ] 48 H5
Jijona / Xixona [E] 104 E2
Jilava [RO] 140 D6
Jilemnice [CZ] 48 H2
Jílové u Prahy [CZ] 48 F4
Jiltjaur [S] 190 F3
Jimbolia [RO] 76 F5
Jimena [E] 102 E2
Jimena de la Frontera [E] 100 H5
Jimramov [CZ] 50 B5
Jince [CZ] 48 F4
Jindřichův Hradec [CZ] 48 G6
Jirkov [CZ] 48 E2
Jistebnice [CZ] 48 F5
Joachimsthal [D] 20 D6
Jobbágyi [H] 64 D5
Jock [S] 196 B8
Jódar [E] 102 F2
Jodoigne [B] 30 D4
Joensuu [FIN] 188 F2
Joesjö [S] 190 E3
Jõgeva [EST] 200 F2
Johanngeorgenstadt [D] 48 D2
Johansfors [S] 162 F5
John O'Groats [GB] 6 F3
Johnstone [GB] 8 D3
Johnstown [IRL] 4 E3
Jõhvi [EST] 200 F1
Joigny [F] 42 H6
Joinville [F] 44 C5
Jokijärvi [FIN] 186 H2
Jokikylä [FIN] 198 D5
Jokikylä [FIN] 198 D6
Jokikylä [FIN] 198 F4
Jokimaa [FIN] 176 H3
Jokioinen [FIN] 176 F3
Jokiperä [FIN] 186 B3
Jokipii [FIN] 186 C4
Jokkmokk [S] 190 H1
Jolanda di Savóia [I] 110 G2
Joloskylä [FIN] 198 D3
Jomala [FIN] 176 A5
Jönåker [S] 168 C5
Jonava [LT] 202 F5
Joncy [F] 56 F5
Jondal [N] 170 C4
Joniny [PL] 52 C4
Joniškis [LT] 200 D6
Jönköping [S] 162 D2
Jonzac [F] 66 D1
Jordanów [PL] 50 H5
Jordanów Śląski [PL] 50 C1
Jördenstorf [D] 20 C3
Jordet [N] 172 D2
Jörlanda [S] 160 G1
Jormvattnet [S] 190 E4
Jörn [S] 190 H4
Joroinen [FIN] 188 D4
Jørpeland [N] 164 B3
Jorquera [E] 98 C5
Jošanička Banja [YU] 150 B3
Jošavka [BIH] 154 C3
Josipdol [HR] 112 G2
Josipovac [HR] 76 B6
Jössefors [S] 166 D2
Josselin [F] 26 B6
Jostedal [N] 180 D6
Jósvafő [H] 64 F3
Jouarre [F] 42 H4
Jougne [F] 58 B6
Joukokylä [FIN] 198 F3
Joure [NL] 16 F3
Journaankylä [FIN] 178 B4
Joutsa [FIN] 186 G6
Joutseno [FIN] 178 E2
Joutsijärvi [FIN] 196 E7
Jovan [S] 190 G4
Joyeuse [F] 68 E6
Józefów [PL] 52 F2
Józefów [PL] 38 C3
Józsa [H] 64 G6
Juankoski [FIN] 188 D1
Juan-les-Pins [F] 108 E5
Judaberg [N] 164 B2
Judenburg [A] 74 C2
Judinsalo [FIN] 186 G6
Juelsminde [DK] 156 D2
Jugon-les-Lacs [F] 26 B5
Juillac [F] 66 G3
Juist [D] 16 H1
Jukkasjärvi [S] 192 F5
Juknaičiai [LT] 202 D5
Jule [N] 190 D5
Jülich [D] 30 F4
Julierpass [CH] 70 H2
Jullouville [F] 26 D4
Jumeaux [F] 68 D3
Jumièges [F] 26 H3
Jumilla [E] 104 C1
Juminen [FIN] 198 F6
Jumisko [FIN] 196 E8
Jumurda [LV] 200 E5
Jung [S] 166 E6
Juniville [F] 44 C3
Junkerdal [N] 190 F1
Junosuando [S] 192 G5
Junqueira [P] 80 E4
Junsele [S] 190 F6
Juntusranta [FIN] 198 F3
Juodupė [LT] 200 F6
Juojärvi [FIN] 188 E3
Juoksenki [FIN] 196 C8
Juokslahti [FIN] 186 F5
Juorkuna [FIN] 198 E4
Jupiter [RO] 148 G1
Jurbarkas [LT] 202 E5
Jurjevo [HR] 112 F2
Jurków [PL] 52 B4
Jūrmala [LV] 200 D5
Jurmo [FIN] 176 D6
Jurmo [FIN] 176 C4
Jurmu [FIN] 198 E3
Jurowce [PL] 24 E5
Jurva [FIN] 186 B3
Jurvala [FIN] 178 D2
Jussey [F] 58 B3
Jüterbog [D] 34 D3
Jutrosin [PL] 36 D5
Juuka [FIN] 188 E1
Juupajoki [FIN] 186 E6
Juurikka [FIN] 188 G4
Juva [FIN] 188 D5
Juvigny-le-Tertre [F] 26 E4
Juvola [FIN] 188 E4
Juvre [DK] 156 B3
Juzennecourt [F] 44 C6
Južnyj [RUS] 22 H2
Jyderup [DK] 156 F2
Jyllinge [DK] 156 G2
Jyllinkoski [FIN] 186 C5
Jyväskylä [FIN] 186 G4

Kaamanen [FIN] 196 D4
Kaamasmukka [FIN] 196 D4
Kaanaa [FIN] 186 E6
Kaaresuvanto [FIN] 192 G4
Kaarssen [D] 18 H5
Kaatsheuvel [NL] 16 D6
Kaavi [FIN] 188 D2
Kaba [H] 76 G1
Kabakca [TR] 146 D2
Kabalar [TR] 144 G4
Kabaltepe [TR] 130 H5
Kabböle [FIN] 178 B4
Kåbdalis [S] 190 H2
Kabelvåg [N] 192 B4
Kableshkovo [BG] 148 F4
Kač [YU] 154 F1
Kačanik [YU] 150 C6
Kachanovo [RUS] 200 G4
Kačikol [YU] 150 C5
Kácov [CZ] 48 G4
Kaczorów [PL] 50 B1
Kadaň [CZ] 48 E3
Kadarkút [H] 74 H4
Kadıköy [TR] 146 B4
Kadıköy [TR] 144 F4
Kadrifakovo [MK] 128 F1
Kadzidło [PL] 24 C5
Kåfjord [N] 196 C1
Kåge [S] 198 A4
Kågeröd [S] 158 C2
Kaharlyk [UA] 206 E2
Kahla [D] 46 H1
Kaïáfa [GR] 136 C2
Käina [EST] 200 C2
Kainach bei Voitsberg [A] 74 D2
Kainasto [FIN] 186 B4
Kaindorf [A] 74 E2
Kainu [FIN] 186 D1
Kainulasjärvi [S] 192 G6
Kainuunkylä [FIN] 196 B8
Kaipiainen [FIN] 178 C2
Kairala [FIN] 196 E7
Kairila [FIN] 176 D1
Kaisersesch [D] 30 G6
Kaiserslautern [D] 44 H3
Kaiser-Wilhelm-Koog [D] 18 E3
Kaisheim [D] 60 D2
Kaišiadoris [LT] 202 F5
Kaivanto [FIN] 198 E4
Kaivomäki [FIN] 188 D5
Kajaani [FIN] 198 E5
Kakanj [BIH] 154 D4
Kakavi [AL] 132 C1
Kakhovka [UA] 206 G4
Käkilahti [FIN] 198 E5
Kaklik [TR] 144 G5
Kakóvatos [GR] 136 C3
Kakslauttanen [FIN] 196 D5
Kaktyni [LV] 200 E5
Kál [H] 64 E6
Kälä [FIN] 186 H5
Kalaja [FIN] 198 D6
Kalajoki [FIN] 198 C5
Kalak [N] 190 D5
Kalakoski [FIN] 186 D4
Kalamáki [GR] 132 H2
Kalamariá [GR] 128 H4
Kalamáta [GR] 136 D4
Kalambáki [GR] 130 D3
Kalámi [GR] 140 C4
Kalamítsi [GR] 130 D6
Kálamos [GR] 134 C5
Kalamotí [GR] 134 G5
Kalampáka [GR] 132 E2
Kalándra [GR] 130 B6
Kalá Nerá [GR] 132 H2
Kalanti [FIN] 176 C3
Kälarne [S] 184 D3
Kálathos [GR] 142 E5
Kalavárda [GR] 142 D4
Kalávryta [GR] 136 D1
Kalbe [D] 34 B1
Kalce [SLO] 74 B5
Kale [TR] 142 F1
Kaleköy [TR] 130 G5
Kaléntzi [GR] 136 C1
Kaléntzi [GR] 132 D2
Kalérgo [GR] 134 D5
Kalesija [BIH] 154 E3
Kalety [PL] 50 F2
Kalevala [RUS] 198 G3
Kálfafell [IS] 194 D6
Kalí [GR] 128 G4
Kaliánoi [GR] 136 E1
Kaliningrad [RUS] 22 G1
Kalinkavichy [BY] 204 C7
Kalinovik [BIH] 152 D2
Kalirráhi [GR] 128 E6
Kalisty [PL] 22 G3
Kalisz [PL] 36 E4
Kalisz Pomorski [PL] 20 H5
Kalithéa [GR] 130 C3
Kalivári [GR] 134 E6
Kalívia [GR] 132 E4
Kalix [S] 198 C2
Kalkan [TR] 142 G4
Kalkar [D] 16 F6
Kalkım [TR] 144 C1
Kall [S] 182 F1
Kallaste [EST] 200 F2
Kallbäck [FIN] 178 A4
Källered [S] 160 H2
Kalli [EST] 200 D3
Kallimasiá [GR] 134 G5
Kallinge [S] 158 F1
Kalliokylä [FIN] 198 E6
Kallislahti [FIN] 188 E5
Kallithéa [GR] 136 D2
Kallithéa [GR] 128 G6
Kallithéa [GR] 130 C6
Kallithéas [GR] 142 E4
Kallmünz [D] 48 B6
Kallo [FIN] 192 H5
Kálló [H] 64 D5
Kalloní [GR] 136 F2
Kalloní [GR] 134 G2
Kállósemjén [H] 64 H5
Kallsedet [S] 190 D6
Kallunki [FIN] 196 F7
Kalmar [S] 162 G5
Kalmari [FIN] 186 F3
Kalna [YU] 150 E3
Kalná nad Hronom [SK] 64 B4
Kalnciems [LV] 200 D5
Kalnik [PL] 22 G3
Kalochóri [GR] 128 E5
Kaló Chorió [GR] 140 F5
Kalocsa [H] 76 C4
Kalofer [BG] 148 B5
Kalogriá [GR] 132 E6
Kaloí Liménes [GR] 140 E5
Kalókastro [GR] 130 B3
Kalonéri [GR] 128 E5
Kaló Nero [GR] 136 C3
Kaloskopí [GR] 132 G4
Kalotina [BG] 150 F4
Kaloyan [BG] 148 F2
Kaloyanovo [BG] 148 B5
Káloz [H] 76 B2
Kalpákio [GR] 132 C1
Kalpio [FIN] 198 E4
Kals [A] 72 F2
Kalsdorf [A] 74 D2
Kaltanenai [LT] 202 G4
Kaltenkirchen [D] 18 F3
Kaltennordheim [D] 46 F2
Kaltinėnai [LT] 202 E4
Kaluga [RUS] 204 F5
Kalugerovo [BG] 148 A5
Kalundborg [DK] 156 E2
Kalush [UA] 206 C3
Kałuszyn [PL] 38 C3
Kalvåg [N] 180 B5
Kalvarija [LT] 24 E2
Kalvatn [N] 180 D4
Kalvehave [DK] 156 G4
Kälviä [FIN] 198 C6
Kälvik [S] 162 G2
Kalvitsa [FIN] 188 C5
Kalvola [FIN] 176 G2
Kalwang [A] 74 C1
Kalwaria Zebrzydowska [PL] 50 H4
Kalyazin [RUS] 204 F3
Kálymnos [GR] 142 B3
Kalynivka [UA] 206 D2
Kám [H] 74 G2
Kamáres [GR] 138 D3
Kamáres [GR] 140 D5
Kamáres [GR] 138 E3
Kamarína [GR] 132 C3
Kamário [GR] 142 B3
Kamariótissa [GR] 130 F4
Kambánis [GR] 128 H4
Kambiá [GR] 134 G4
Kámbos [GR] 132 F5
Kámbos [GR] 140 B4
Kamchiya [BG] 148 F3
Kámen [CZ] 48 G5
Kamen [D] 32 C4
Kamenari [YU] 152 D4
Kámena Voúrla [GR] 132 H4
Kamen Bryag [BG] 148 G2
Kamenica [MK] 150 E6
Kamenice nad Lipou [CZ] 48 G6
Kameničná [SK] 64 A5
Kamenka [RUS] 178 F3
Kamennogorsk [RUS] 178 F2
Kamenný Újezd [CZ] 62 C2
Kameno [BG] 148 F4
Kamensko [HR] 152 B2
Kamensko [HR] 154 C1
Kamenz [D] 34 F6
Kamëz [AL] 128 B2
Kamianets'-Podil's'kyi [UA] 206 D3
Kamianka [UA] 206 F3
Kamianka-Dniprovs'ka [UA] 206 G4
Kamień [PL] 52 E3
Kamienica [PL] 52 B5
Kamieniec Ząbkowicki [PL] 50 C2
Kamień Krajenskie [PL] 22 C5
Kamienna Góra [PL] 50 B2
Kamień Pomorski [PL] 20 F3
Kamieńsk [PL] 36 G6
Kamínia [GR] 130 F6
Kaminiá [GR] 132 D1
Kamion [PL] 38 A2
Kamnik [SLO] 74 C4
Kampen [D] 156 A4
Kampen [NL] 16 F4
Kamp Lintfort [D] 30 G3
Kampor [HR] 112 F3
Kámpos [GR] 136 D4
Kámpos [GR] 138 H2
Kamula [FIN] 198 E5
Kamyanyets [BY] 38 G2
Kamyanyuki [BY] 38 G2
Kanal [SLO] 72 H5
Kanala [FIN] 186 E1
Kanála [GR] 138 C2
Kanaláki [GR] 132 C3
Kanália [GR] 132 H2
Kańczuga [PL] 52 E3
Kandava [LV] 200 C5
Kandel [D] 46 B5
Kandern [D] 58 E4
Kandersteg [CH] 70 D2
Kandestederne [DK] 160 E2
Kándia [GR] 136 F2
Kandíla [GR] 136 E2
Kandira [TR] 146 G2
Kanestraum [N] 180 F2
Kanfanar [HR] 112 D2
Kangádio [GR] 136 C1
Kangasaho [FIN] 186 E3
Kangasala [FIN] 176 F1
Kangaskylä [FIN] 198 D6
Kangaslampi [FIN] 188 D4
Kangasniemi [FIN] 186 H5
Kangos [S] 192 G5
Kangosjärvi [FIN] 192 G5
Kanjiža [YU] 76 E5
Kankaanpää [FIN] 186 C6
Kannonkoski [FIN] 186 F2
Kannus [FIN] 198 C5
Kanpaneta / Campanas [E] 84 B4
Kansız [TR] 146 E5
Kantala [FIN] 188 C4
Kántanos [GR] 140 B5
Kantomaanpää [FIN] 196 C8
Kantorp [S] 168 B4
Kantti [FIN] 186 C5
Kanturk [IRL] 4 C4
Kányavár [H] 74 F3
Kaolinovo [BG] 148 E2
Kaonik [BIH] 154 D4
Kaonik [YU] 150 C3
Kap [PL] 24 C3
Kapaklı [TR] 146 E4
Kapaklı [TR] 144 D3
Kapandríti [GR] 134 C5
Kāpas [LV] 200 C5
Kapčiamiestis [LT] 24 F3
Kapfenberg [A] 74 D1
Kapıkırı [TR] 142 C1
Kapinci [HR] 74 H6
Kapitan Andreevo [BG] 146 A2
Kaplice [CZ] 62 C3
Kapméni Chora [GR] 136 G2
Kápolna [H] 64 E5
Kaposvár [H] 76 A4
Kapp [N] 172 B4
Kappeln [D] 18 F1
Kappelshamn [S] 168 G3
Kappelskär [S] 168 F2
Kaprun [A] 72 F1
Kapsáli [GR] 136 F6
Kápsas [GR] 136 E2
Kapušany [SK] 64 G2
Kapuvar [H] 62 G6
Karaağaç [TR] 146 G2
Karabayır [TR] 142 G2
Karabeylı [TR] 144 G3
Karabiga [TR] 146 C4
Karabörtlen [TR] 142 E2
Karaburun [TR] 144 B4
Karaburun [TR] 146 E2
Karacabey [TR] 146 E5
Karacaköy [TR] 146 D2
Karacalar [TR] 144 D2
Karaçam [TR] 144 D2
Karacaoğlan [TR] 146 B2
Karacasu [TR] 144 F5
Karahallı [TR] 144 G4
Karaköy [TR] 144 F4
Karamanlı [TR] 144 H6
Karamürsel [TR] 146 F3
Karamyshevo [RUS] 200 H3
Karancslapujtő [H] 64 D4
Karaova [TR] 142 C2
Karapelit [BG] 148 F2
Karapürçek [TR] 146 H3
Karasjok [N] 192 H2
Karasu [TR] 146 H2
Karataş [TR] 144 E3
Karats [S] 190 G1
Karavás [GR] 136 F6
Karávos [GR] 134 C5
Karavostásis [GR] 138 E4
Karavukovo [YU] 154 E1
Karawanken Tunnel [Eur.] 74 B4
Karayakuplu [TR] 146 G3
Kårböle [S] 182 H6
Karby [DK] 160 C4
Karcag [H] 76 F1
Kardakáta [GR] 132 C6
Kardam [BG] 148 G1
Kardámaina [GR] 142 B3
Kardámyla [GR] 134 G4
Kardamýli [GR] 136 D4
Kardašova-Řečice [CZ] 48 G6
Kardeljevo [HR] 152 B3
Kardítsa [GR] 132 F2
Kärdla [EST] 200 C2
Kardoskút [H] 76 F4
Karersee / Carezza al Lago [I] 72 D3
Karesuando [S] 192 G4
Kärevere [EST] 200 F2
Kargı [TR] 142 F3
Kargów [PL] 52 C2
Kargowa [PL] 36 B3
Karhujärvi [FIN] 196 E7
Karhukangas [FIN] 198 D5
Karhula [FIN] 178 C4
Kårhus [N] 164 B1
Kariá [GR] 128 G6
Kariá [GR] 136 E2
Kariani [GR] 130 C4
Kariés [GR] 136 E3
Kariés [GR] 132 G3
Karigasniemi [FIN] 196 C3
Karijoki [FIN] 186 B4
Karine [TR] 142 B1
Karinkanta [FIN] 198 D4
Karioúpoli [GR] 136 E5
Karis / Karjaa [FIN] 176 F5
Karise [DK] 156 G3
Karítaina [GR] 136 D2
Karjaa / Karis [FIN] 176 F5
Karjala [FIN] 176 D3
Kärjenkoski [FIN] 186 B5
Karkaloú [GR] 136 D2
Kärki [LV] 200 E4
Karkkila [FIN] 176 G4
Karkku [FIN] 176 E1
Kärkölä [FIN] 176 H3
Karksi-Nuia [EST] 200 E3
Karlby [FIN] 168 H1
Karlebotn [N] 196 E2
Karleby / Kokkola [FIN] 198 C6
Karlholmsbruk [S] 174 F4

Klina [YU] 150 B5
Klinča Selo [HR] 74 E6
Klingenbach [A] 62 F6
Klingenmunster [D] 46 B5
Klingenthal [D] 48 C3
Klink [D] 20 C5
Klintehamn [S] 168 F5
Klintholm [DK] 156 G4
Klintsy [RUS] 204 D6
Kliplev [DK] 156 C4
Klippan [S] 158 C1
Klippen [S] 190 E3
Klippinge [DK] 156 G3
Klis [HR] 152 A2
Klisino [PL] 50 E3
Klisura [BG] 148 A4
Klisura [YU] 150 E5
Klitmøller [DK] 160 C3
Klixbüll [D] 156 B4
Kljajićevo [YU] 76 D6
Kljuc [BIH] 154 B3
Klobouky [CZ] 62 G2
Kłobuck [PL] 50 F1
Kłobuczyn [PL] 36 B5
Kłodawa [PL] 34 H1
Kłodawa [PL] 36 F3
Kłodzko [PL] 50 C3
Kløfta [N] 172 B5
Klokkarvik [N] 170 A4
Klokočevac [YU] 150 D1
Klos [AL] 128 B2
Klos [AL] 128 B1
Kloštar [HR] 74 G5
Klösterle [A] 72 B1
Klosterneuburg [A] 62 F4
Klosters [CH] 72 A2
Kloten [S] 166 H1
Klötze [D] 34 A1
Kl. Plasten [D] 20 C4
Klubbukt [N] 196 B2
Kl'ucevoje [RUS] 178 F3
Kluczbork [PL] 50 E1
Kluki [PL] 36 G5
Kluki [PL] 22 C1
Klukowa Huta [PL] 22 D3
Klupe [BIH] 154 C3
Klütz [D] 18 H3
Klyastsitsy [BY] 200 H6
Knaben [N] 164 C4
Knäred [S] 162 B5
Knaresborough [GB] 10 F3
Knarvik [N] 170 B3
Knäsjö [S] 190 G6
Knätten [S] 182 G5
Knebel [DK] 160 E6
Knezevi Vinogradi [HR] 76 C6
Kneževo [HR] 76 B5
Knezha [BG] 150 G3
Knežica [BIH] 154 B2
Knič [YU] 150 B2
Knidas [TR] 142 C4
Knidi [GR] 128 F6
Kniebis [D] 58 F2
Knighton [GB] 10 C6
Knights Town [IRL] 4 A4
Knin [HR] 154 A4
Knislinge [S] 158 D1
Knittelfeld [A] 74 C2
Knivsta [S] 168 D2
Knjaževac [YU] 150 E3
Knock [IRL] 2 C4
Knockan [GB] 6 D3
Knockcroghery [IRL] 2 D5
Knocknalina [IRL] 2 C2
Knocktopher [IRL] 4 E4
Knokke-Heist [B] 28 G1
Knottingley [GB] 10 F4
Knudshoved [DK] 156 E3
Knurów [PL] 50 F3
Knutby [S] 168 E1
Knutsford [GB] 10 D4
Knyazevo [RUS] 200 H5
Knyazhevo [BG] 148 E5
Knyszyn [PL] 24 E5
Kobarid [SLO] 72 H4
Kobbfoss [N] 196 E3
København [DK] 156 H2
Kobeřice [CZ] 50 E4
Kobiele Wlk. [PL] 36 H6
Kobilyane [BG] 130 F1
Kobišnica [YU] 150 E1
Koblenz [D] 30 H6
Kobryn [BY] 38 G2
Kobułty [PL] 24 B4
Kobylany [PL] 38 F3
Kobylin [PL] 36 D4
Kobyłka [PL] 38 C2
Kobyl'nik [BY] 202 H5
Kocaali [TR] 146 H2
Kocaçeşme [TR] 146 B4
Kocakaymaz [TR] 146 G2
Kočani [MK] 128 G1
Koçarlı [TR] 144 D5
Koceljevo [YU] 150 A1
Kočerin [BIH] 152 B2
Kočevje [SLO] 74 C6
Kochel [D] 60 D5
Kocherinovo [BG] 150 F6
Kochmar [BG] 148 F2
Kock [PL] 38 E4
Koczała [PL] 22 B4
Kodeń [PL] 38 F3
Kodrąb [PL] 36 H6
Kofçaz [TR] 146 B1
Köflach [A] 74 D2
Køge [DK] 156 G3
Kohila [EST] 200 D2
Kohtla-Järve [EST] 200 F1
Koigi [EST] 200 E2
Koikkala [FIN] 188 D5
Koilovtsi [BG] 148 B3
Koirakoski [FIN] 198 F6
Koivu [FIN] 196 C8
Koivulahti / Kvevlax [FIN] 186 B2
Koivumäki [FIN] 188 E3
Kojetín [CZ] 50 D6
Kokála [GR] 136 E5
Kökar [FIN] 168 H1
Kokava nad Rimavicou [SK] 64 D3
Kokemäki [FIN] 176 D2
Kokin Brod [YU] 150 A3
Kókino Neró [GR] 132 H1
Kokkárion [GR] 144 C5
Kokkokylä [FIN] 198 E2
Kokkola / Karleby [FIN] 198 C6
Koklë [AL] 128 C4
Koknese [LV] 200 E5
Kokonvaara [FIN] 188 E2
Kokořín [CZ] 48 G3
Koksijde-Bad [B] 28 F1
Kołacz [PL] 20 H4
Kołacze [PL] 38 F5
Koláka [GR] 134 A5
Kolari [FIN] 192 H5
Kolari [YU] 154 H3
Kolárovo [SK] 64 A5
Koláry [SK] 64 C5
Kolasen [S] 190 D6
Kolašin [YU] 152 E3
Kolbäck [S] 168 B2
Kołbacz [PL] 20 F5
Kołbaskowo [PL] 20 F5
Kolbermoor [D] 60 F5
Kołbiel [PL] 38 C3
Kolbotn [N] 166 B1
Kolbuszowa [PL] 52 D3
Kolby [DK] 156 E2
Kolby Kås [DK] 156 E2
Kołczewo [PL] 20 F3
Kołczygłowy [PL] 22 C3
Koldby [DK] 160 B4
Kolding [DK] 156 C3
Koleczkowo [PL] 22 D2
Kölesd [H] 76 B4
Kolho [FIN] 186 E5
Koli [FIN] 188 F1
Kolín [CZ] 48 H4
Kolin [PL] 20 G5
Kolind [DK] 160 E6
Kolindrós [GR] 128 G5
Kolinec [CZ] 48 E6
Kolínes [GR] 136 E3
Köljala [EST] 200 C3
Kolka [LV] 200 C4
Kölleda [D] 34 A5
Kollund [DK] 156 C4
Kolmården [S] 168 B5
Köln [D] 30 G4
Kolnica [PL] 50 D2
Kolno [PL] 24 C5
Kolo [BIH] 152 B1
Koło [PL] 36 F3
Kołobrzeg [PL] 20 G3
Kolokolovo [RUS] 200 G2
Kolomyia [UA] 206 C3
Kolonia Korytnica [PL] 38 D4
Kolonjë [AL] 128 B4
Kolonowskie [PL] 50 F2
Koloveč [CZ] 48 D5
Kolpino [RUS] 204 C1
Kölsillre [S] 182 H4
Kolsjön [S] 184 D5
Kolsva [S] 168 B2
Kolta [SK] 64 B5
Koluszki [PL] 36 H4
Kolvereid [N] 190 C4
Kolymvári [GR] 140 B4
Komádi [H] 76 G2
Koman [AL] 128 B1
Komańcza [PL] 52 E5
Kómara [GR] 130 H1
Komárno [SK] 64 B5
Komarno [UA] 52 G4
Komárom [H] 64 A6
Komar Prolaz [BIH] 154 C4
Koméno [GR] 132 D3
Kómi [GR] 138 E1
Kómi [GR] 134 G5
Komito [GR] 134 D6
Komiža [HR] 116 H2
Komjáti [H] 64 F3
Komló [H] 76 B4
Kömlő [H] 64 E6
Komniná [GR] 128 F5
Komniná [GR] 130 E2
Kómninádes [GR] 128 D5
Komorane [YU] 150 C5
Komorzno [PL] 36 E6
Komotiní [GR] 130 F2
Kömpöc [H] 76 E4
Kompóti [GR] 132 D3
Konak [YU] 154 H1
Konakpınar [TR] 144 D1
Končanica [HR] 74 G6
Konče [MK] 128 G2
Kondolovo [BG] 148 F5
Kondoros [H] 76 F3
Kondrič [HR] 154 D1
Køng [DK] 156 F4
Konga [S] 162 E6
Köngäs [FIN] 192 H5
Kongasmäki [FIN] 198 E4
Kongerslev [DK] 160 E4
Konginkangas [FIN] 186 G3
Kongsberg [N] 164 G1
Kongselva [N] 192 C4
Kongsfjord [N] 196 E1
Kongshavn [N] 164 F5
Kongsnes [N] 170 C2
Kongsvinger [N] 172 D5
Konice [CZ] 50 C5
Koniecpol [PL] 50 H2
Konieczna [PL] 52 D5
Königsbrück [D] 34 F6
Königsbrunn [D] 60 D4
Königsee [D] 46 G2
Königsfeld [D] 58 F3
Königshofen [D] 46 E4
Königslutter [D] 32 H2
Königssee [D] 60 G6
Königstein [D] 46 C2
Königstein [D] 48 F1
Königswiesen [A] 62 C4
Königswinter [D] 30 H5
Königs-Wusterhausen [D] 34 E3
Konin [PL] 36 E3
Koniskós [GR] 132 F1
Konispol [AL] 132 B2
Kónitsa [GR] 128 D6
Köniz [CH] 58 D6
Konjic [BIH] 152 C1
Könnern [D] 34 B4
Konnerud [N] 164 H1
Konnevesi [FIN] 186 G3
Kõnnu [EST] 200 E1
Konopiště [CZ] 48 G4
Konotop [PL] 36 B4
Konotop [PL] 20 H5
Konotop [UA] 204 D7
Końskie [PL] 38 A6
Konsko [MK] 128 G3
Konsmo [N] 164 D5
Konstancin-Jeziorna [PL] 38 B3
Konstantynów [PL] 38 E3
Konstantynów Łodzki [PL] 36 G4
Konstanz [D] 58 G4
Konteenperä [FIN] 196 E8
Kontiás [GR] 130 F6
Kontinjoki [FIN] 198 F5
Kontiolahti [FIN] 188 F2
Kontiomäki [FIN] 198 F4
Kontkala [FIN] 188 F2
Kontokali [GR] 132 B2
Kontopoúli [GR] 130 F6
Konttajärvi [FIN] 192 H6
Konush [BG] 148 C6
Konyavo [BG] 150 F5
Konz [D] 44 F2
Kööritilä [FIN] 186 B6
Koosa [EST] 200 F2
Koparnes [N] 180 C4
Kópasker [IS] 194 F3
Kópavogur [IS] 194 B4
Köpenick [D] 34 E2
Koper [SLO] 72 H6
Köpernitz [D] 20 C6
Kopervik [N] 164 A2
Kópháza [H] 62 F6
Kopidlno [CZ] 48 H3
Köping [S] 168 B2
Köpingsvik [S] 162 G4
Kopisto [FIN] 198 C5
Koplik [AL] 152 E5
Köpmanholmen [S] 184 G2
Köpmannebro [S] 166 D4
Kopor'ye [RUS] 178 F5
Koppang [N] 172 C1
Kopparberg [S] 166 H1
Kopperå [N] 182 D1
Kopperby [D] 18 F1
Koppom [S] 166 D2
Koprivets [BG] 148 C3
Koprivnica [HR] 74 G5
Koprivshtitsa [BG] 148 A5
Köprübaşı [TR] 144 F5
Köprübaşı [TR] 144 E3
Köprühisar [TR] 146 G4
Köprüören [TR] 144 G1
Koprzywnica [PL] 52 D2
Köpu [EST] 200 E3
Korbach [D] 32 E5
Korbevac [YU] 150 D5
Korbielów [PL] 50 G5
Korçë [AL] 128 D5
Korcula [HR] 152 B3
Korczyców [PL] 34 G3
Korczyna [PL] 52 D4
Korenica [HR] 112 H3
Korentovaara [FIN] 188 H1
Korfantów [PL] 50 D2
Körfez [TR] 146 G3
Kórfos [GR] 136 F2
Korgen [N] 190 D2
Koria [FIN] 178 C3
Korinós [GR] 128 G5
Korinth [DK] 156 D4
Kórinthos [GR] 136 F1
Korisós [GR] 128 E5
Korissía [GR] 138 C2
Korita [BIH] 152 D3
Korita [HR] 152 C4
Koríthi [GR] 136 A1
Körmend [H] 74 F2
Korneuburg [A] 62 F4
Kórnik [PL] 36 C3
Kornsjø [N] 166 C4
Kornwestheim [D] 58 H1
Kőrnye [H] 64 B6
Koromačno [HR] 112 E2
Koróni [GR] 136 D4
Koronós [GR] 138 F3
Koronoúda [GR] 128 H3
Koronowo [PL] 22 D5
Koropí [GR] 136 H1
Körösladány [H] 76 G2
Köröstarcsa [H] 76 G2
Korosten' [UA] 206 E1
Korostyshiv [UA] 206 E2
Korpavár [H] 74 G4
Korpilahti [FIN] 186 G5
Korpilombolo [S] 196 B7
Korpo / Korppoo [FIN] 176 C5
Korpoström [FIN] 176 C5
Korppoo / Korpo [FIN] 176 C5

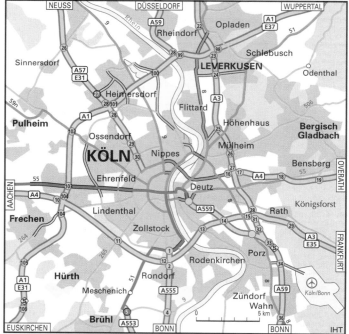

Korsberga [S] 162 E3
Korsholm [S] 158 C2
Korskrogen [S] 184 C6
Korsmo [N] 172 C5
Korsnäs [FIN] 186 A3
Korsø [DK] 160 C3
Korsør [DK] 156 E3
Korsun'-Shevchenkivs'kyi [UA] 206 F2
Korsveien [N] 182 B2
Korsze [PL] 24 B3
Korten [BG] 148 D4
Kortesjärvi [FIN] 186 C1
Korthí [GR] 138 D1
Kortrijk (Courtrai) [B] 28 G2
Korucu [TR] 144 C2
Korup [DK] 156 D3
Korušce [HR] 154 A5
Korvala [FIN] 196 D7
Korvaluoma [FIN] 186 C5
Koryčany [CZ] 62 G2
Korycin [PL] 24 E4
Korydallós [GR] 132 E1
Koryfási [GR] 136 C4
Kos [GR] 142 C3
Kosanica [YU] 152 E2
Kościan [PL] 36 C3
Kościelec [PL] 36 F3
Kościerzyna [PL] 22 D3
Kose [EST] 200 E1
Kösedere [TR] 134 G1
Kosel [MK] 128 D3
Koserow [D] 20 E3
Košetice [CZ] 48 G5
Košice [SK] 64 G3
Kosjerič [YU] 150 A2
Kösk [TR] 144 E5
Koška [HR] 154 D1
Koskela [FIN] 186 D2
Koskenkorva [FIN] 186 C3
Koskenkylä / Forsby [FIN] 178 B4
Koskenpää [FIN] 186 F5
Koski [FIN] 176 E4
Koski [FIN] 176 H2
Koskimäki [FIN] 186 B3
Kóskina [GR] 134 D5
Koskolovo [RUS] 178 F6
Koškovce [SK] 52 E6
Koskue [FIN] 186 C4
Kosmás [GR] 136 E3
Kósmio [GR] 130 F3
Kosmonosy [CZ] 48 G3
Kosovo Polje [YU] 150 C5
Kosovska Mitrovica [YU] 150 C4
Kosów Lacki [PL] 38 D2
Kössen [A] 60 F5
Kósta [GR] 136 F3
Kosta [S] 162 E5
Kostanjevac [HR] 74 D6
Kostelec nad Černími Lesy [CZ] 48 G4
Kostelec nad Labem [CZ] 48 G3
Kostelec nad Orlicí [CZ] 50 B3
Kostelec na Hané [CZ] 50 C5
Kostenets [BG] 150 G5
Kostiantynivka [UA] 206 H3
Kostinbrod [BG] 150 F4
Kostomłoty [PL] 36 C6
Kostomuksha [RUS] 198 G4
Kostopil' [UA] 206 D1
Kóstos [GR] 138 E3
Kostów [PL] 36 E6
Kostrzyn [PL] 36 D2
Kostrzyn [PL] 34 G2
Kosturino [MK] 128 G2
Koszalin [PL] 20 H3
Koszęcin [PL] 50 F2
Kőszeg [H] 74 F1
Kosztowo [PL] 22 C6
Koszuty [PL] 36 D3
Koszyce [PL] 52 B3
Kotala [FIN] 186 E4
Kotala [FIN] 196 F7
Kótas [GR] 128 E4
Kotë [AL] 128 B5
Kotel [BG] 148 D4
Kőtelec [H] 76 E1
Köthen [D] 34 C4
Kotka [FIN] 178 C4
Kotlarnia [PL] 50 F3
Kotly [RUS] 178 F6
Kotola [FIN] 196 F7
Kotor [YU] 152 D4
Kotorsko [BIH] 154 D2
Kotor Varoš [BIH] 154 C3
Kotovs'k [UA] 206 E4
Kotowice [PL] 50 G2
Kótronas [GR] 136 E5
Kötschach-Mauthen [A] 72 G3
Kotten [NL] 16 G6
Kötzting [D] 48 D6
Koufália [GR] 128 G4
Koufós [GR] 130 C6
Kouklií [GR] 132 C1
Koukounariés [GR] 134 B3
Koúmani [GR] 136 C2
Koúndouros [GR] 138 C2
Kourenda [GR] 132 C2
Kournás [GR] 140 C5
Kouroúta [GR] 136 B2
Koutsó [GR] 130 E3
Koutsóchero [GR] 132 G2
Koutsourás [GR] 140 G5
Kouvola [FIN] 178 C3
Kovachevica [BG] 130 C1
Kovachevtsi [BG] 150 F5
Kovačica [YU] 154 G2
Kovarskas [LT] 202 G4
Kovero [FIN] 188 G2
Kovin [YU] 154 H2
Kovland [S] 184 E4
Kövra [S] 182 G3
Kowal [PL] 36 G2
Kowale Oleckie [PL] 24 D3
Kowalewo Pomorskie [PL] 22 E6
Kowary [PL] 50 A2
Köyceğiz [TR] 142 F2
Köyliö [FIN] 176 D2
Koyunhis [TR] 146 F4
Kozak [TR] 144 C2
Kozáni [GR] 128 F5
Kozarac [BIH] 154 B2
Kozar Belene [BG] 148 B3
Kozica [HR] 152 B2
Koziegłowy [PL] 50 G2
Kozienice [PL] 38 C4
Kozina [SLO] 74 A6
Kozlodui [BG] 150 G2
Kozłowo [PL] 22 G5
Kozluk [BIH] 154 E3
Koźmin [PL] 36 D4
Kozolupy [CZ] 48 D4
Kozpınar [TR] 146 G5
Kożuchów [PL] 36 A4
Kozyürük [TR] 146 B3
Kräckelbäcken [S] 172 G2
Krąg [PL] 22 B3
Kragenæs [DK] 156 F4
Kragerø [N] 164 F4
Kragujevac [YU] 150 C2
Krahës [AL] 128 B5
Krajenka [PL] 22 B5
Krajn [AL] 128 B1
Krajnik Gorny [PL] 20 E6
Kråkberget [N] 192 C3
Krakës [LT] 202 F4
Krakhella [N] 170 B1
Krakovets' [UA] 52 F3
Kraków [PL] 52 A4
Krakow am See [D] 20 B4
Kråksmåla [S] 162 F4
Králíky [CZ] 50 C4
Kraljeva Sutjesca [BIH] 154 D4
Kraljevica [HR] 112 E2
Kraljevo [YU] 150 B3
Kralovany [SK] 50 G6
Královec [CZ] 50 B2
Kralovice [CZ] 48 E4
Kralovsky Chlmec [SLO] 64 H3
Kralupy nad Vltavou [CZ] 48 F3
Kramators'k [UA] 206 H3
Kramfors [S] 184 F3
Kranenburg [D] 16 F6
Kranevo [BG] 148 G2
Krani [MK] 128 D4
Kraniá [GR] 132 E2
Kraniá Elassónas [GR] 132 F1
Kranichfeld [D] 46 G1
Kranídi [GR] 136 F3
Kranj [SLO] 74 B4
Kranjá [GR] 132 E1
Kranjska Gora [SLO] 72 H3
Krapanj [HR] 112 H6
Krapina [HR] 74 E5
Krapinske Toplice [HR] 74 E5
Krapkowice [PL] 50 E2
Krasen [BG] 148 F1
Krasiczyn [PL] 52 F4
Krāslava [LV] 200 G6
Kraslice [CZ] 48 C3
Krásná Lípa [CZ] 48 G1
Krasne Folwarczne [PL] 24 E5
Krašnik [PL] 52 E1
Krasnogorodskoye [RUS] 200 G5
Krasnohrad [UA] 206 G2
Krásno nad Kysucou [SK] 50 F5
Krasnoperekops'k [UA] 206 G5
Krasnosielec [PL] 24 B6
Krasnovo [BG] 148 A5
Krasnoye Selo [RUS] 178 H5
Krasnoznamensk [RUS] 202 E5
Krasnyje Gory [RUS] 200 H1
Krasnystaw [PL] 38 F6
Krasnyy Kholm [RUS] 204 F2
Krasocin [PL] 52 A1
Krastë [AL] 128 C2
Krasznokvajda [H] 64 F3
Krátigos [GR] 134 H2
Kratovo [MK] 150 E6
Kratovska Stena [YU] 150 A2
Krauchenwies [D] 58 H3
Kravaře [CZ] 48 F2
Kravaře [CZ] 50 E4
Kravarsko [HR] 74 E6
Kraymorie [BG] 148 F4
Krefeld [D] 30 G3
Kremastí [GR] 142 E4
Kremasti [GR] 136 F4
Kremenchuk [UA] 206 G3
Kremenets' [UA] 206 C2
Kremmen [D] 34 D1
Kremna [YU] 152 E1
Kremnica [SK] 64 C3
Krems [A] 62 E4
Kremsmünster [A] 62 B5
Křenov [CZ] 50 C5
Krepoljin [YU] 150 D1
Kresna [BG] 130 B1
Kréstena [GR] 136 C2
Kresttsy [RUS] 204 D2
Kretinga [LT] 202 D4
Kreuth [D] 60 E5
Kreuzlingen [CH] 58 G4
Kreuztal [D] 32 C6
Kreva [BY] 202 H6
Kriakėnava [LT] 202 F4
Kría Vríssi [GR] 128 G4
Krichim [BG] 148 B6
Kričov [BY] 204 D5
Krieglach [A] 62 D6
Kriezá [GR] 134 C5
Krïkelo [GR] 132 F4
Krikkovo [RUS] 178 F6
Krimml [A] 72 E1
Krimpen aan den IJssel [NL] 16 D5
Křinec [CZ] 48 H3
Krinídes [GR] 130 D3
Kriopigí [GR] 130 C6
Kristalopig [GR] 128 E5
Kristdala [S] 162 G3
Kristianopel [S] 158 G1
Kristiansand [N] 164 D5
Kristianstad [S] 158 D2
Kristiansund [N] 180 F2
Kristiinankaupunki / Kristinestad [FIN] 186 A5
Kristineberg [S] 190 G4
Kristinehamn [S] 166 F3
Kristinehov [S] 158 D2
Kristinestad / Kristiinankaupunki [FIN] 186 A5
Kristóni [GR] 128 H3
Kritiniá [GR] 142 D5
Kritsá [GR] 140 F5
Kriva Feja [YU] 150 E5
Kriváň [SK] 64 D3
Kriva Palanka [MK] 150 E6
Krivelj [YU] 150 D2
Krivodol [BG] 150 F3
Krivogaštani [MK] 128 E3
Křivoklát [CZ] 48 E4
Křižanov [CZ] 50 B6
Križevci [HR] 74 F5
Krk [HR] 112 E2
Krka [SLO] 74 C5
Krnjača [YU] 154 G2
Krnjeuša [BIH] 154 A3
Krnov [CZ] 50 D4
Krobia [PL] 36 C4
Kroczyce [PL] 50 G2
Krøderen [N] 170 G5
Krokebol [N] 166 C1
Krokeés [GR] 136 E4
Kroken [N] 190 E3
Krokom [S] 182 G2
Krokowa [PL] 22 D1
Krokstad [S] 166 C5
KrokstadØra [N] 180 H1
Krokstrand [N] 190 E2
Królowy Most [PL] 24 F5
Kroměříž [CZ] 50 D6
Kromerowo [PL] 22 H4
Krompachy [SK] 64 F2
Kronach [D] 46 H3
Kronoby / Kruunupyy [FIN] 198 C6
Kronshtadt [RUS] 178 G4
Kröpelin [D] 20 B3
Kropp [D] 18 F2
Kroppenstedt [D] 34 B3
Kropstädt [D] 34 D3
Krościenko nad Dunajcem [PL] 52 B5
Krosna [LT] 24 F2
Krośniewice [PL] 36 G3
Krosno [PL] 52 D4
Krosno [PL] 22 F3
Krosno Odrzanskie [PL] 34 H3
Krossbu [N] 180 E6
Krotoszyn [PL] 36 D4
Krouna [CZ] 50 B4
Krško [SLO] 74 D5
Kruiningen [NL] 28 H1
Krujë [AL] 128 B2
Krukowo [PL] 24 B5
Krumbach [D] 60 C4
Krumë [AL] 150 B6
Krumovgrad [BG] 130 F1
Krumpendorf [A] 74 B3
Krün [D] 60 D6
Krupá [CZ] 48 E3
Krupac [BIH] 152 D1
Krupac [BIH] 152 C2
Krupaja [YU] 150 C1
Krupa na Vrbasu [BIH] 154 B3
Krupanj [YU] 154 F3
Krupe [PL] 38 F6
Krupina [SK] 64 C4
Krupište [MK] 128 F1
Krupp [RUS] 200 G3
Kruså [DK] 156 C4
Kruševac [YU] 150 C3
Kruševo [MK] 128 E2
Krushari [BG] 148 F1
Krushevets [BG] 148 F5
Krushovene [BG] 148 A2
Kruszwica [PL] 36 E2
Kruszyna [PL] 50 G1
Krute [YU] 152 E5
Krutvatn [N] 190 E3
Kruunupyy / Kronoby [FIN] 198 C6
Kryekuq [AL] 128 A4
Kryksæterøra [N] 180 G1
Krylbo [S] 174 D6
Krylovo [RUS] 24 C2
Krymne [UA] 38 H4
Krynica [PL] 52 C5
Krynica Morska [PL] 22 F2
Krynki [PL] 24 F5
Kryspinów [PL] 50 H4
Kryve Ozero [UA] 206 E4
Kryvyi Rih [UA] 206 G3
Krzęcin [PL] 20 G6
Krzeczów [PL] 36 F6
Krzepice [PL] 50 F1
Krzeszów [PL] 52 E2
Krzeszów [PL] 50 B2
Krzeszowice [PL] 50 H3
Krzeszyce [PL] 34 G2
Krzynowłoga Mała [PL] 22 H6
Krzywiń [PL] 36 C4
Krzyż [PL] 36 B1
Ksar es-Seghir [Eur.] 100 G6
Książ Wielki [PL] 52 A2
Ktísmata [GR] 132 C1
Kubbe [S] 184 F1
Küblis [CH] 72 A2
Kubrat [BG] 148 D2
Kuç [AL] 128 B6
Kučevo [YU] 150 D1
Kuchl [A] 60 G6
Kučište [YU] 150 A5
Kucovë [AL] 128 B4
Küçükbahçe [TR] 134 H4
Küçükçekmece [TR] 146 E3
Küçükkuyu [TR] 134 H1
Kudever' [RUS] 200 H5
Kudirkos Naumiestis [LT] 24 E1
Kudowa-Zdrój [PL] 50 B3
Kufstein [A] 60 F6
Kuggerud [N] 172 C5
Kuha [FIN] 198 E2
Kühlungsborn [D] 20 B3
Kuhmalahti [FIN] 176 G1
Kuhmo [FIN] 198 G5
Kuhmoinen [FIN] 176 H1
Kuhstedt [D] 18 E4
Kühtai [A] 72 C1
Kuivajärvi [FIN] 198 G4
Kuivaniemi [FIN] 198 D3
Kuivanto [FIN] 178 B3
Kuivasjärvi [FIN] 186 C5
Kukës [AL] 128 C1
Kukko [FIN] 186 E3
Kuklin [PL] 22 H5
Kuks [CZ] 50 B3
Kukuj [RUS] 204 D2
Kukujevci [YU] 154 F2
Kukurečani [MK] 128 E3
Kula [BG] 150 E2
Kula [TR] 144 F3
Kula [YU] 76 D6
Kulalar [TR] 144 E2
Kulata [BG] 130 B2
Kuldīga [LV] 200 C5
Kuleli [TR] 146 B2
Kulennoinen [FIN] 188 F5
Kulhuse [DK] 156 G2
Kuliai [LT] 202 D4
Kullaa [FIN] 176 D1
Kulmbach [D] 46 H3
Kuloharju [FIN] 198 E2
Kulykiv [UA] 52 H3
Kumafşarı [TR] 142 G1
Kumane [YU] 76 E6
Kumanovo [MK] 150 D6
Kumarlar [TR] 146 B5
Kumbağ [TR] 146 C3
Kümbet [TR] 146 H5
Kumkale [TR] 130 H5
Kumköy [TR] 146 E2
Kumla [S] 166 H3
Kumlinge [FIN] 176 B5
Kumola [RUS] 188 G6
Kumrovec [HR] 74 E5
Kumuu [FIN] 198 G4
Kunda [EST] 200 F1
Kunes [N] 196 C2
Kungälv [S] 160 G1
Kungsängen [S] 168 D2
Kungsbacka [S] 160 H3
Kungsberg [S] 174 D4
Kungsfors [S] 174 C4
Kungshamn [S] 166 B5
Kungsör [S] 168 B3
Kunhegyes [H] 76 F1
Kunmadaras [H] 76 F1
Kunovice [CZ] 62 H2
Kunowo [PL] 36 C4
Kunpeszér [H] 76 C2
Kunrau [D] 34 A2
Kunštát [CZ] 50 C5
Kunszentmárton [H] 76 E3
Kunszentmiklós [H] 76 C2
Kunžak [CZ] 48 H6
Künzelsau [D] 46 E5
Kuolio [FIN] 198 F2
Kuoloyarvi [RUS] 196 F7
Kuona [FIN] 198 D6
Kuopio [FIN] 188 D2
Kuortane [FIN] 186 D3
Kuosku [FIN] 196 E6
Kup [PL] 50 E2
Kupferberg [D] 46 H3
Kupferzell [D] 46 E5
Kupians'k [UA] 206 H2
Kupiškis [LT] 202 G4
Kupjak [HR] 112 F1
Kupkovo [RUS] 200 G2
Kupli [LV] 200 D5
Küplü [TR] 130 H2
Küplü [TR] 146 G4
Kuprava [LV] 200 G4
Kupres [BIH] 154 C4
Kurbnesh [AL] 128 B1
Kurchatov [RUS] 204 E7
Kurd [H] 76 B4
Kürdzhali [BG] 130 F1
Kurejoki [FIN] 186 D2
Kuremäe [EST] 200 F1
Kurevere [EST] 200 C3
Kurgolovo [RUS] 178 E5
Kurianka [PL] 24 F4
Kurikka [FIN] 186 C4
Kurilo [BG] 150 F4
Kuřim [CZ] 50 B6
Kurkiyeki [RUS] 188 G6
Kŭrnare [BG] 148 B4
Kurów [PL] 38 D5
Kurowice [PL] 36 H4
Kurozweki [PL] 52 C2
Kuršėnai [LT] 202 E4
Kuršiši [LV] 200 C6
Kursk [RUS] 204 F7
Kursu [FIN] 196 E7
Kuršumlija [YU] 150 C4
Kuršumlijska Banja [YU] 150 C4
Kurşunlu [TR] 146 F4
Kurşunlu [TR] 146 D4
Kurtakko [FIN] 192 H5
Kurtköy [TR] 146 G3
Kuru [FIN] 186 D6
Kuru [FIN] 176 F1
Kurvinen [FIN] 198 F2
Kurzeszyn [PL] 38 A4
Kurzętnik [PL] 22 F5
Kuşadası [TR] 144 D5
Kusel [D] 44 H3
Kuside [YU] 152 D3
Küssnacht [CH] 58 F6
Kustavi [FIN] 176 C4
Kuşuköy [TR] 144 F2
Kuta [YU] 152 E3
Kütahya [TR] 144 G1
Kutemajärvi [FIN] 186 H5
Kutina [HR] 154 B1
Kutjevo [HR] 154 D1
Kutná Hora [CZ] 48 H4
Kutno [PL] 36 G3
Kuttanen [FIN] 192 G4
Kuttura [FIN] 196 D5
Kúty [SK] 62 G3
Kuusaa [FIN] 186 G4
Kuusaa [FIN] 198 D5
Kuusajoki [FIN] 196 C6
Kuusalu [EST] 200 E1
Kuusamo [FIN] 196 F8
Kuusankoski [FIN] 178 C3
Kuusjärvi [FIN] 188 E2
Kuvshinovo [RUS] 204 E3
Kuyucak [TR] 144 E5
Kuzmin [YU] 154 F2
Kuzmina [PL] 52 E5
Kuźnia Raciborska [PL] 50 E3
Kuźnica [PL] 24 F4
Kuzovo [RUS] 200 H3
Kuzuluk [TR] 146 H3
Kvænangsbotn [N] 192 F2
Kværndrup [DK] 156 D4
Kvaløyseter [N] 190 B5
Kvalsund [N] 196 B2
Kvalvåg [N] 180 F2
Kvalvåg [N] 170 A5
Kvam [N] 180 H6
Kvam [N] 190 C5
Kvanndal [N] 170 C4
Kvanne [N] 180 F2
Kvarnberg [S] 172 G2
Kvarsebo [S] 168 C5
Kvås [N] 164 C5
Kvėdarna [LT] 202 D4
Kvelde [N] 164 G3
Kvenvær [N] 190 A6
Kvetkai [LT] 200 E6
Kvevlax / Koivulahti [FIN] 186 B2
Kvicksund [S] 168 B2
Kvikkjokk [S] 190 G1
Kvikne [N] 182 B4
Kvillsfors [S] 162 F3
Kvinesdal [N] 164 C5
Kvinlog [N] 164 C4
Kvissleby [S] 184 E5
Kvisvik [N] 180 F2
Kviteseid [N] 164 E2
Kvitnes [N] 180 F2
Kwidzyn [PL] 22 E4
Kwilcz [PL] 36 B2
Kybartai [LT] 24 E1
Kyïv [UA] 206 E2
Kyjov [CZ] 62 G2
Kyläinpää [FIN] 186 B3
Kylämä [FIN] 186 F6
Kyleakin [GB] 6 C5
Kyle of Lochalsh [GB] 6 C5
Kyliia [UA] 206 E5
Kyllaj [S] 168 G4
Kyllburg [D] 44 F1
Kyllíni [GR] 136 B1
Kylmäkoski [FIN] 176 F2
Kylmälä [FIN] 198 E4
Kylmämäki [FIN] 186 H4
Kými [GR] 134 C4
Kymönkoski [FIN] 186 G2
Kyparissía [GR] 136 C3
Kyritz [D] 20 B6
Kyrkhult [S] 162 D6
Kyrkslätt / Kirkkonummi [FIN] 176 G5
Kyrö [FIN] 176 E4
Kyrönlahti [FIN] 186 D6
Kyröskoski [FIN] 176 E1
Kyrping [N] 170 B6
Kyšice [CZ] 48 F3
Kysucké Nové Mesto [SK] 50 F6
Kýthira [GR] 136 F6
Kýthnos [GR] 138 C2
Kytömäki [FIN] 198 F4
Kyustendil [BG] 150 E6
Kyyjärvi [FIN] 186 E2

L

Laa an der Thaya [A] 62 F3
Laage [D] 20 B3
Laajoki [FIN] 176 D3
Laakajärvi [FIN] 198 F5
Laakirchen [A] 62 A5
La Alameda [E] 96 E5
La Alamedilla [E] 88 E4
La Alberca [E] 88 B4
La Alberca de Záncara [E] 98 A3
La Albuera [E] 94 G2
La Algaba [E] 94 G6
La Almarcha [E] 98 B3
La Almolda [E] 90 F4
La Almudena [E] 104 B2
La Almunia de Doña Godina [E] 90 D4
Laanila [FIN] 196 D5
La Antilla [E] 94 E6
Laarbruch [D] 30 F2
La Azohía [E] 104 C4
Labajos [E] 88 E4
la Balme [F] 68 G5
La Baña [E] 78 F6
La Bañeza [E] 78 G6
La Barca de la Florida [E] 100 G4
La Barrela [E] 78 D4
La Bassée [F] 28 F3
Labastide-d'Armagnac [F] 66 D6
La Bastide de-Sérou [F] 84 H5
Labastide-Murat [F] 66 G4
La Bastide-Puylaurent [F] 68 D6
Labastide-Rouairoux [F] 106 C4
La Bâtie-Neuve [F] 108 D2
La Baule [F] 40 E6
La Bazoche-Gouet [F] 42 D5
Łabędzie [PL] 20 H4
la Bégude-de-Mazenc [F] 68 F6
La Belle Etoile [F] 44 A5
Labenne [F] 66 A6
La Bérarde [F] 70 A5
L'Aber-Wrac'h [F] 40 B1
Labin [HR] 112 E2
Labinot Fushë [AL] 128 C3
La Bisbal de Falset [E] 90 H5
Łabiszyn [PL] 36 E1
Lábod [H] 74 H4
Laboe [D] 18 G2
Labouheyre [F] 66 B5
La Bourboule [F] 68 C2
La Bóveda de Toro [E] 88 D2
Labrags [LV] 200 B5
Labrède [F] 66 C3
La Bresse [F] 58 D3
La Brillanne [F] 108 C3
Labrit [F] 66 C5
Łabunie [PL] 52 G1
Laç [AL] 128 B2
La Cabrera [E] 88 G4
La Caillere-St-Hilaire [F] 54 C3
La Calahorra [E] 102 F4
La Calera [E] 100 B5
La Caletta [I] 118 E3
Lacalm [F] 68 C5
La Calzada de Calatrava [E] 96 E5
La Calzada de Oropesa [E] 88 C6
La Campana [E] 102 A2
La Cañada de Cañepla [E] 102 H3
Lacanau [F] 66 C2
Lacanau-Océan [F] 66 B2
La Canourgue [F] 68 C6
La Capelle [F] 28 G5
Lacapelle-Marival [F] 66 H4
La Capte [F] 108 C6
Lačarak [YU] 154 F2
La Caridad [E] 78 F2
La Carlota [E] 102 B2
La Carolina [E] 96 E6
Lacaune [F] 106 C3
La Cavalerie [F] 106 D3
Lacave [F] 66 G4
Lacco Ameno [I] 120 D3
Lacedonia [I] 120 G2
La Celle-Dunoise [F] 54 H5
Lăceni [RO] 148 B1
La Cerca [E] 82 F4
La Chaise-Dieu [F] 68 D3
La Chambre [F] 70 B4
Lachanás [GR] 130 B3
Lachaniá [GR] 142 D5
La Chapelle [F] 68 F1
La Chapelle-d'Angillon [F] 56 C3
la Chapelle-en-Valgaudemar [F] 70 A6
La Chapelle-en-Vercors [F] 68 G5
La Chapelle-Glain [F] 40 G5
La Charité-sur-Loire [F] 56 D3
La Chartre [F] 42 C6
La Châtaigneraie [F] 54 D3
La Châtre [F] 54 H5
La Chaux-de-Fonds [CH] 58 C5
La Ciotat [F] 108 B5
Łąck [PL] 36 G2
Läckö [S] 166 E5
La Clayette [F] 56 F6

La Clusaz [F] 70 B3
La Cluse [F] 68 H2
La Cluse-et-Mijoux [F] 58 B6
Lacock [GB] 12 G3
La Codosera [E] 86 F5
Lacona [I] 114 D3
Láconi [I] 118 D5
La Coquille [F] 66 G2
La Coronada [E] 96 B3
La Coruña / A Coruña [E] 78 C2
La Côte-St-André [F] 68 G4
Lacourt [F] 84 G5
La Courtine [F] 68 B2
la Couvertoirade [F] 106 E3
Lacq [F] 84 D3
La Croisière [F] 54 G5
La Croixille [F] 26 D6
La Croix-Valmer [F] 108 D6
La Cumbre [E] 96 B1
La Cure [F] 70 B1
Lad [H] 74 H5
Ląd [PL] 36 E3
Ladbergen [D] 32 C2
Ladby [DK] 156 E3
Lądek-Zdrój [PL] 50 C3
Ládi [GR] 130 H1
Ladíspoli [I] 114 H5
Ladoeiro [P] 86 F3
Ladon [F] 42 F6
La Encinilla y El Rubio [E] 100 G3
LærdalsØyri [N] 170 E2
La Espina [E] 78 G3
La Estrella [E] 96 D1
La Fère [F] 28 F6
La Ferrière-en-Parthenay [F] 54 E3
Laferté [F] 58 B3
La Ferté-Bernard [F] 42 C5
La Ferté-Gaucher [F] 42 H4
La Ferté-Macé [F] 26 F5
La Ferté-Milon [F] 42 H3
La Ferté-sous-Jouarre [F] 42 H3
La Ferté-St-Aubin [F] 56 B1
La Ferté-Vidame [F] 26 H5
Laffrey [F] 68 H5
Láfka [GR] 136 E1
La Flèche [F] 42 B6
La Florida [E] 78 G3
La Flotte [F] 54 B4
La Font de la Figuera [E] 98 D6
Lafortunada [E] 84 E5
Lafrançaise [F] 66 F6
La Fregeneda [E] 80 E5
La Frua [I] 70 F2
La Fuente de San Esteban [E] 80 F6
La Gacilly [F] 40 E5
Lagan [S] 162 C4
Laganás [GR] 136 B2
La Garde-Freinet [F] 108 D5
La Garriga [E] 92 E4
La Garrovilla [E] 94 G1
Lage [D] 32 E3
Lagg [GB] 8 B2
Łagiewniki [PL] 50 C2
Laginá [GR] 128 H4
La Gineta [E] 98 B5
Lagkáda [GR] 136 E4
Lagkáda [GR] 134 G4
Lagkadás [GR] 130 B4
Lagkádia [GR] 136 D2
Lagkadíkia [GR] 130 B4
Lagnieu [F] 68 G2
Lagny [F] 42 G3
Lagoa [P] 94 B5
Lagonegro [I] 120 G5
Lagonísi [GR] 136 H1
Lágos [GR] 130 F3
Lagos [P] 94 B5
Lagosanto [I] 110 H3
Łagów [PL] 52 C1
Łagów [PL] 34 H3
La Granada de Rio Tinto [E] 94 F4
la Granadella [E] 90 H5
La Grand-Combe [F] 106 F2
La Grande-Motte [F] 106 F4
La Granja [E] 88 F4
La Granjuela [E] 96 B5
Lagrasse [F] 106 C5
La Grave [F] 70 B5
La Guardia / A Guarda [E] 78 A5
La Guardia / A Guarda [E] 96 G2
Laguardia / Biasteri [E] 82 G6
La Guardia de Jaén [E] 102 E2
Laguarres [E] 90 H3
Laguarta [E] 84 E5
Laguépie [F] 66 H6
La Guerche [F] 56 D4
La Guerche-de-Bretagne [F] 40 G4
Laguiole [F] 68 B5
Laguna de Duero [E] 88 E2
Laguna del Marquesado [E] 98 C2
Laguna de Negrillos [E] 82 B5
Laguna de Santiago [E] 100 B5
La Haba [E] 96 B3
Lahane [F] 66 B5
La Haye-du-Puits [F] 26 D2
Lahdenperä [FIN] 186 F2
Lahemmaa [EST] 200 D1
La Hermida [E] 82 D3
Lahinch [IRL] 2 B5
Lahnasjärvi [FIN] 198 F5
Lahnstein [D] 30 H6
Laholm [S] 162 B5
La Horra [E] 88 G2
Lahoysk [BY] 204 B5
La Hoz de la Vieja [E] 90 E6
Lahr [D] 58 E2
Lahti [FIN] 178 B2
La Hutte [F] 26 F6
Laibgaliai [LT] 202 G3
Laichingen [D] 60 B3
Laide [GB] 6 C3
L'Aigle [F] 26 G5
La Iglesuela del Cid [E] 98 F2
Laignes [F] 56 F2
Laiguéglia [I] 108 G4
L'Aiguillon [F] 54 B4
Laihia [FIN] 186 B3
Laikko [FIN] 188 F6
Lailiás [GR] 130 C2
Laimbach [A] 62 D4
Lainate [I] 70 G4
Lairg [GB] 6 E3
La Isla [E] 82 C2
Laissac [F] 68 B6
Laísta [GR] 132 D1
Laisvall [S] 190 F2
Laitikkala [FIN] 176 G2
Laitila [FIN] 176 D3
La Javie [F] 108 D3
Lajkovac [YU] 150 A1
la Jonquera [E] 92 G2
Lajoskomárom [H] 76 B3
Lajosmizse [H] 76 D2
Łaka Prudnicka [PL] 50 D3
Lakatnik [BG] 150 F4
Lakaträsk [S] 196 A8
Lakavica [MK] 128 G2
Lakhdenpokh'ya [RUS] 188 G6
Lakitelek [H] 76 E3
Lákka [GR] 132 B3
Lakkí [GR] 142 B2
Lákkoi [GR] 140 C4
Lákkoma [GR] 130 G4
Lakolk [DK] 156 A3
Lakópetra [GR] 132 E6
Lakselv [N] 192 H1
Laktasi [BIH] 154 C2
Lála [GR] 136 C2
La Lantejuela [E] 102 B2
Lalapaşa [TR] 146 B1
l'Albagés [E] 90 H5
L'Albi [E] 92 B4
L'Alcïdia [E] 98 E5
l'Alcora / Alcora [E] 98 F3
L'Alcúdia de Crespins [E] 98 E6
L'Aldea [E] 92 B5
l'Alguenya [E] 104 D2
La Lima [I] 110 E4
Lalín [E] 78 C4
Lalinde [F] 66 F4
La Línea de la Concepción [E] 100 H5
Lalm [N] 180 G6
La Loupe [F] 26 H6
Lalouvesc [F] 68 F4
La Louvière [B] 28 H4
L'Alpe-d'Huez [F] 70 A5
Lalueza [E] 90 F3
La Luisiana [E] 102 B2
Lam [D] 48 D6
La Machine [F] 56 D4
La Maddalena [I] 118 E2
Lama dei Peligni [I] 116 D5
La Magdalena [E] 78 G5
La Malène [F] 68 C6
Lamalou-les-Bains [F] 106 D4
La Manga del Mar Menor [E] 104 D4
Lamarche [F] 58 B2
Lamarosa [P] 86 C5
Lamarque [F] 66 C2
Lamas do Vouga [P] 80 B5
Lamastre [F] 68 F5
La Matanza [E] 82 B5
La Maucarrière [F] 54 E3
Lambach [A] 62 B4
Lamballe [F] 26 B4
Lamberhurst [GB] 14 F5
Lambesc [F] 106 H4
Lambley [GB] 8 E6
Lambourn [GB] 12 H3
Lambrecht [D] 46 B5
Lamego [P] 80 D4
L'Ametlla de Mar [E] 92 B5
Lamezia Terme [I] 124 D5
Lamía [GR] 132 G4
Lammhult [S] 162 D4
Lammi [FIN] 176 H2
La Molina [E] 92 E2
La Mongie [F] 84 F4
La Mothe-Achard [F] 54 B3
Lamotte-Beuvron [F] 56 B2
La Motte-Chalancon [F] 108 B2
la Motte-du-Caire [F] 108 C2
Lampaanjärvi [FIN] 186 H1
Lampaul [F] 40 A1
Lampaul-Plouarzel [F] 40 A1
Lámpeia [GR] 136 C1
Lampeland [N] 164 G1
Lampeter [GB] 10 B6
Lampinsaari [FIN] 198 D5
L'Ampolla [E] 92 B5
Lamprechtshausen [A] 60 G5
Lamsänkylä [FIN] 198 F2
Lamsfeld [D] 34 F4
Lamstedt [D] 18 E4
La Mudarra [E] 88 E1
La Muela [E] 90 E4
La Mure [F] 68 H5
Lamure-sur-Azergues [F] 68 F2
Lana [I] 72 C3
Lanaja [E] 90 F4
La Napoule-Plage [F] 108 E5
Lanark [GB] 8 D4
La Nava de Ricomalillo [E] 96 D1
La Nava de Santiago [E] 86 G6
Lancaster [GB] 10 D2
Lanchester [GB] 8 F6
Lanciano [I] 116 E5
Lancing [GB] 14 E5
Łańcut [PL] 52 E3
Landau [D] 60 G3
Landau [D] 46 B5
Landeck [A] 72 C1
Landedo [P] 80 F3
Landerneau [F] 40 B2
Landeryd [S] 162 B4
Landesbergen [D] 32 E1
Landete [E] 98 D3
Landévennec [F] 40 B2
Landivisiau [F] 40 C2
Landivy [F] 26 D5
Landkirchen [D] 18 H2
Landmannalaugur [IS] 194 D5
Landön [S] 182 G1
Landquart [CH] 58 H6
Landrecies [F] 28 G4
Landsberg [D] 60 D4
Landsberg [D] 34 C5
Landsbro [S] 162 E3
Landshut [D] 60 F3
Landskrona [S] 156 H2
Landstuhl [D] 44 H3
Landvetter [S] 160 H2
Lanesborough [IRL] 2 D5
La Neuve-Lyre [F] 26 H5
La Neuveville [CH] 58 D5
Langa [DK] 160 D5
Långå [S] 182 F4
Langa de Duero [E] 88 H2
Långåminne [FIN] 186 B3
Langangen [N] 164 G3
Langballig [D] 156 C5
Långban [S] 166 G1
Langeac [F] 68 D4
Langeais [F] 54 F2
Längelmäki [FIN] 186 F6
Langelsheim [D] 32 G3
Langen [A] 72 B1
Langen [D] 46 C3
Langen [D] 18 D4
Langenargen [D] 58 H4
Langenau [D] 60 B3
Langenburg [D] 46 E5
Längenfeld [A] 72 C2
Langenfeld [D] 30 G4
Langenhahn [D] 46 B1
Langenhorn [D] 156 B5
Langenisarhofen [D] 60 G3
Langenlois [A] 62 E4
Langennaundorf [D] 34 E5
Langenselbold [D] 46 D3
Langenthal [CH] 58 E5
Langenwang [A] 62 E6
Langenzenn [D] 46 F5
Langeoog [D] 18 B3
Langeskov [DK] 156 E3
Langesund [N] 164 G3
Langevåg [N] 164 A1
Langevåg [N] 180 C3
Langewiese [D] 32 D5
Langfjord [N] 192 F1
Långflon [S] 172 E3
Langhirano [I] 110 D3
Langholm [GB] 8 E5
Långlöt [S] 162 G5
Långnäs [FIN] 176 B5
Langnau im Emmental [CH] 58 E6
Langø [DK] 156 E5
Langogne [F] 68 D5
Langoiran [F] 66 D3
Langon [F] 66 D4
Langport [GB] 12 F4
Langquaid [D] 60 F2
Langres [F] 56 H2
Långsele [S] 184 E2
Långsele [S] 190 F5
Långserud [S] 166 D3
Långshyttan [S] 174 D5
Långträsk [S] 198 A3
Langula [D] 32 G5
Langwarden [D] 18 D4
Langwedel [D] 18 E6
Langweid [D] 60 D3
Lanhelas [P] 78 A5
Lanjarón [E] 102 E5
Lankas [LV] 200 B5
Länkipohja [FIN] 186 F6
Lanmeur [F] 40 C1
Länna [S] 168 C3
Lannabruk [S] 166 G3
Lannemezan [F] 84 F4
Lannevesi [FIN] 186 F3
Lannilis [F] 40 B1
Lannion [F] 40 D1
Lanobre [F] 68 B3
La Noguera [E] 98 D1
Lanouaille [F] 66 G2
Lansjärv [S] 196 A8
Lanškroun [CZ] 50 C4
Lanslebourg-Mont-Cenis [F] 70 C5
Lantosque [F] 108 F4
Lanusei [I] 118 E5
Lanvollon [F] 26 A4
Lanzá [E] 78 C2
Lanžhot [CZ] 62 G3
Lanzo d'Intelvi [I] 70 G3
Lanzo Torinese [I] 70 D5
La Oliva [E] 100 E5
Laon [F] 28 G6
La Orotava [E] 100 B5
La Paca [E] 104 B3
La Pacaudière [F] 68 E1
Lapalisse [F] 56 D6
La Pallice [F] 54 B4
La Palma del Condado [E] 94 F6
La Palmyre [F] 54 B6
La Palud-sur-Verdon [F] 108 D4
Lápas [GR] 132 E6
La Pelechaneta / Pelejaneta [E] 98 F3
La Peraleja [E] 98 B1
la Péruse [F] 54 E6
La Petite-Pierre [F] 44 G5
Lapeyrade [F] 66 D5
Lapinjärvi / Lappträsk [FIN] 178 B3
Lapinlahti [FIN] 188 C1
La Plagne [F] 70 B4
La Plaza / Teverga [E] 78 G4
Laplume [F] 66 E5
la Pobla de Lillet [E] 92 E2
La Pobla de Massaluca [E] 90 G6
la Pobla de Segur [E] 92 C1
la Pobla de Vallbona [E] 98 E4
la Pobla Tornesa [E] 98 G3
La Pola de Gordón [E] 78 H5
La Portera [E] 98 D4
Lapoutroie [F] 58 D2
Lapovo [YU] 150 C2
Lappach / Lappago [I] 72 E2
Lappago / Lappach [I] 72 E2
Lappäjärvi [FIN] 192 G4
Lappajärvi [FIN] 186 D2
Läppe [S] 168 B3
Lappeenranta [FIN] 178 E2
Lappfjärd / Lapväärtti [FIN] 186 B5
Lappfors [FIN] 186 C1
Lappi [FIN] 176 D3
Lappo [FIN] 176 C5
Lappohja / Lappvik [FIN] 176 F6
Lappoluobbal [N] 192 G2
Lappträsk [S] 198 C2
Lappträsk / Lapinjärvi [FIN] 178 B3
Lappvattnet [S] 198 A5
Lappvik / Lappohja [FIN] 176 F6
Lapseki [TR] 146 B5
Laptevo [RUS] 200 H5
Lapua [FIN] 186 C2
La Puebla de Almoradiel [E] 96 G3
La Puebla de Cazalla [E] 102 A3
La Puebla de los Infantes [E] 96 B6
La Puebla del Río [E] 94 G6
La Puebla de Montalbán [E] 96 E1
La Puebla de Valdavia [E] 82 D4
La Puebla de Valverde [E] 98 E2
La Pueblanueva [E] 96 D1
la Pulente [GBJ] 18 C3
La Punt [CH] 72 A3
Lapväärtti / Lappfjärd [FIN] 186 B5
Łapy [PL] 24 E6
Laqueuille [F] 68 C2
L'Aquila [I] 116 C4
La Rábita [E] 102 E5
Laracha [E] 78 C2
Laragh [IRL] 4 G3
Laragne-Montéglin [F] 108 C2
La Rambla [E] 102 C2
L'Arbresle [F] 68 F2
Lärbro [S] 168 G4
Larche [F] 66 G3
Larche [F] 108 E2
Lårdal [N] 164 E2
Lardaro [I] 72 C4
Larderello [I] 114 F1
Lárdos [GR] 142 E5
Lardosa [P] 86 F3
Laredo [E] 82 F3
La Réole [F] 66 D4
La Restinga [E] 100 A6
Largentière [F] 68 E6
L'Argentière-la-Bessée [F] 70 B6
Largo [GB] 8 F3
Largs [GB] 8 C3
Lari [F] 114 C2
Lariano [I] 116 B6
La Rinconada [E] 94 G6
Larino [I] 116 F6
Lárisa [GR] 132 G2
Larkollen [N] 166 B3
Larmor [F] 40 C4
Larne [GB] 2 G3
La Robla [E] 78 H5
La Roca de la Sierra [E] 86 G6
la Roca del Vallès [E] 92 E4
La Roche-Bernard [F] 40 E5
La Roche-Chalais [F] 66 E2
La Roche-en-Ardenne [B] 30 E6
La Rochefoucauld [F] 54 E6
La Rochelle [F] 54 C4
La Roche-Posay [F] 54 F3
La Roche-sur-Foron [F] 70 B2
La Roche-sur-Yon [F] 54 B3
La Rochette [F] 70 A4
Larochette [L] 44 F2
La Roda [E] 98 B4
La Roda de Andalucía [E] 102 B3
Laroquebrou [F] 68 A4
La Roquebrussanne [F] 108 C5
Laroque-des-Arcs [F] 66 G5
Laroque-d'Olmes [F] 106 A5
La Roque-Gageac [F] 66 G4
Larraga [E] 84 B4
Larrau [F] 84 D3
Larseng [N] 192 E2
Larsmo / Luoto [FIN] 198 C6
Larsnes [N] 180 C4
l'Artigue [F] 84 H5
La Rubia [E] 90 B2
Laruns [F] 84 D4
Larvik [N] 164 G3
Lárymna [GR] 134 B5
La Salceda [E] 88 F4
La Salvetat [F] 66 H6
La Salvetat-sur-Agout [F] 106 C3
Läsänkoski [FIN] 188 C5
Las Anorias [E] 98 C6
Lasarte-Oria [E] 84 B2
La Sauceda [E] 100 G4
Låsby [DK] 160 D6
Las Cabezas de San Juan [E] 100 G3
Las Caldas de Besaya [E] 82 E3
la Sénia [E] 92 A6
la Seu d'Urgell [E] 92 D1
La Seyne [F] 108 C6
Łasin [PL] 22 E5
Łask [PL] 36 G5
Łaskarzew [PL] 38 C4
Laško [SLO] 74 D5
Laskowice [PL] 50 D3
Las Mesas [E] 96 H3
Las Navas de la Concepción [E] 96 B6
Las Navas del Marqués [E] 88 E5
Las Negras [E] 102 H5
La Solana [E] 96 G4
La Souterraine [F] 54 G5
Lasovo [YU] 150 D2
Las Palmas de Gran Canaria [E] 100 C5
Las Pedroñeras [E] 96 H3
La Spézia [I] 110 C4
Las Rozas [E] 88 F5
Lassan [D] 20 E3
Lassay [F] 26 E5
Lassigny [F] 28 E6
Las Torres de Cotillas [E] 104 C3
Lastovo [HR] 152 A3
Lastra a Signa [I] 110 E5
Lastres [E] 82 C2
Lästringe [S] 168 D4
Lastrup [D] 18 C6
Lastva [BIH] 152 D4
La Suze-sur-Sarthe [F] 42 B5
Lašva [BIH] 154 D4
Las Veguillas [E] 88 C3
Las Ventas con Peña Aguilera [E] 96 E2
Las Ventas de S. Julián [E] 88 C6
Łaszczów [PL] 52 G2
Laterza [I] 122 D4
Lathen [D] 16 H3
Latheron [GB] 6 F3
La Thuile [I] 70 C4
Latiano [I] 122 F4
Latikberg [S] 190 F5
Latina [I] 120 B1
Latisana [I] 72 G5
La Toledana [E] 96 E3
Latorpsbruk [S] 166 H3
La Torre [E] 98 D4
la Torre Baixa [E] 98 D2
La Torresaviñán [E] 90 A5
La Tour-du-Pin [F] 68 G3
La Tranche-sur-Mer [F] 54 B4
La Tremblade [F] 54 B5
La Trimouille [F] 54 G4
La Trinité [F] 40 D5
La Trinité-Porhoët [F] 26 B5
Latronico [I] 120 H5
Latronquière [F] 66 H4
La Turbie [F] 108 F4
Laubrières [F] 40 G5
Laucha [D] 34 B5
Lauchhammer [D] 34 E5
Laudal [N] 164 D5
Lauder [GB] 8 F4
Laudio / Llodio [E] 82 G6
Laudona [LV] 200 F5
Lauenau [D] 32 F2
Lauenburg [D] 18 G5
Lauenstein [D] 48 E2
Lauf [D] 46 G5
Laufen [CH] 58 D4
Laufen [D] 60 G5
Laufenburg [CH] 58 F4
Laufenburg [D] 58 F4
Lauffen [D] 46 D6
Laugar [IS] 194 F3
Laugarbakki [IS] 194 C3
Laugarvatn [IS] 194 C4
Laugharne [GB] 12 D2
Lauingen [D] 60 C3
Laujar de Andarax [E] 102 F5
Laukaa [FIN] 186 G4
Laukka [FIN] 198 D4
Lauksundskaret [N] 192 F1
Laukuva [LT] 202 E4
Laukvik [N] 192 C5
Laukvik [N] 192 B4
Laukvik [N] 192 D2
Launceston [GB] 12 D4
La Unión [E] 104 C4
Laupen [CH] 58 D6
Laupheim [D] 60 B4
Lauragh [IRL] 4 B5
Laureana di Borrello [I] 124 D6
Laurencetown [IRL] 2 D5
Laurenzana [I] 120 H4
Lauria [I] 120 H5
Laurière [F] 54 G6
Lausanne [CH] 70 C1
Lauter [S] 168 H3
Lauterbach [D] 46 E1
Lauterbourg [F] 46 B6
Lauterbrunnen [CH] 70 E1
Lautere [LV] 200 F5
Lauterecken [D] 44 H3
Lauterhofen [D] 46 H5
Lautiosaari [FIN] 198 C2
Lautrec [F] 106 B3
Lauvsnes [N] 190 C5
Lauvstad [N] 180 C4
Lauvuskylä [FIN] 198 G5
Lauvvik [N] 164 B3
Lauwersoog [NL] 16 G1
Lauzerte [F] 66 F5
Lauzun [F] 66 E4
Lavagna [I] 110 B3
Laval [F] 26 E6
la Vall d'Uixó [E] 98 F4
Lavamünd [A] 74 C3
Låvang [N] 190 D2
Lávara [GR] 130 H2
Lavardac [F] 66 E5
Lavardin [F] 42 C6
Lavarone [I] 72 D5
Lavaur [F] 106 B3
La Vecilla [E] 82 B3
Lavelanet [F] 106 A5
Lavello [I] 120 H3
Lavelsloh [D] 32 E2
Lavenham [GB] 14 F3
La Venta [E] 102 F4
la Veurdre [F] 56 D4
Lavia [FIN] 176 E1
Lavik [N] 170 B2
la Vila Joiosa / Villajoyosa [E] 104 E2
la Villa / Stern [I] 72 E3
Lavinio-Lido di Enea [I] 120 A1
La Virgen del Camino [E] 78 H5
Lavis [I] 72 C4
Lavit [F] 66 F6
Lavong [N] 190 D2
Lavos [P] 86 C2
La Voulte-sur-Rhône [F] 68 F5
Lavoûte-Chilhac [F] 68 D4
Lavoûte-sur-Loire [F] 68 D4
Lavre [P] 86 C6
Lávrion [GR] 136 H1
Lavry [RUS] 200 G4
La Wantzenau [F] 44 H6
Laxå [S] 166 G4
Laxe [E] 78 B2
Laxey [GBM] 10 C2
Laxo [GB] 6 G3
Laxsjö [S] 190 E6
Laxtjärn [S] 172 G5
Laxviken [S] 190 E6
Layer Marney [GB] 14 F4
La Yesa [E] 98 E3
Läyliäinen [FIN] 176 G4
La Yunta [E] 90 C5
Laza [E] 78 D6
Lazarevac [YU] 150 B1
Lazarovo [YU] 154 G1
Lazdijai [LT] 24 F2
Laži [LV] 200 C4
Lazise [I] 72 C6
Łaziska Górne [PL] 50 F3
Lazkao [E] 84 A3
Lázne Kynžvart [CZ] 48 C4
La Zubia [E] 102 E4
Łazy [PL] 22 A2
Leadenham [GB] 10 F5
Leaden Roding [GB] 14 F4
Leadhills [GB] 8 D4
Leamington Spa [GB] 14 D2
Leap [IRL] 4 B5
Leatherhead [GB] 14 E4
Łeba [PL] 22 C1
Lebach [D] 44 G3
Lebane [YU] 150 D4
Le Bar [F] 108 E4
Le Barp [F] 66 C4
Le Beausset [F] 108 C5
Lebesby [N] 196 D2
Le Blanc [F] 54 G4
Łebno [PL] 22 D2
Le Boréon [F] 108 F3
Lębork [PL] 22 C2
Le Boulou [F] 92 G1
Le Bourg d'Oisans [F] 68 H5
Le Bourget [F] 68 H3
le Bousquet-d'Orb [F] 106 D3
Lebrija [E] 100 G3
Le Bugue [F] 66 F3
Lebus [D] 34 G2
le Caloy [F] 66 C6
Le Cap-d'Agde [F] 106 E5
Le Cateau-Cambrésis [F] 28 G4
Le Catelet [F] 28 F5
Le Caylar [F] 106 E3
Lecce [I] 122 G4
Lecco [I] 70 G4
Lécera [E] 90 E5
Lech [A] 72 B1
Lechainá [GR] 136 B1

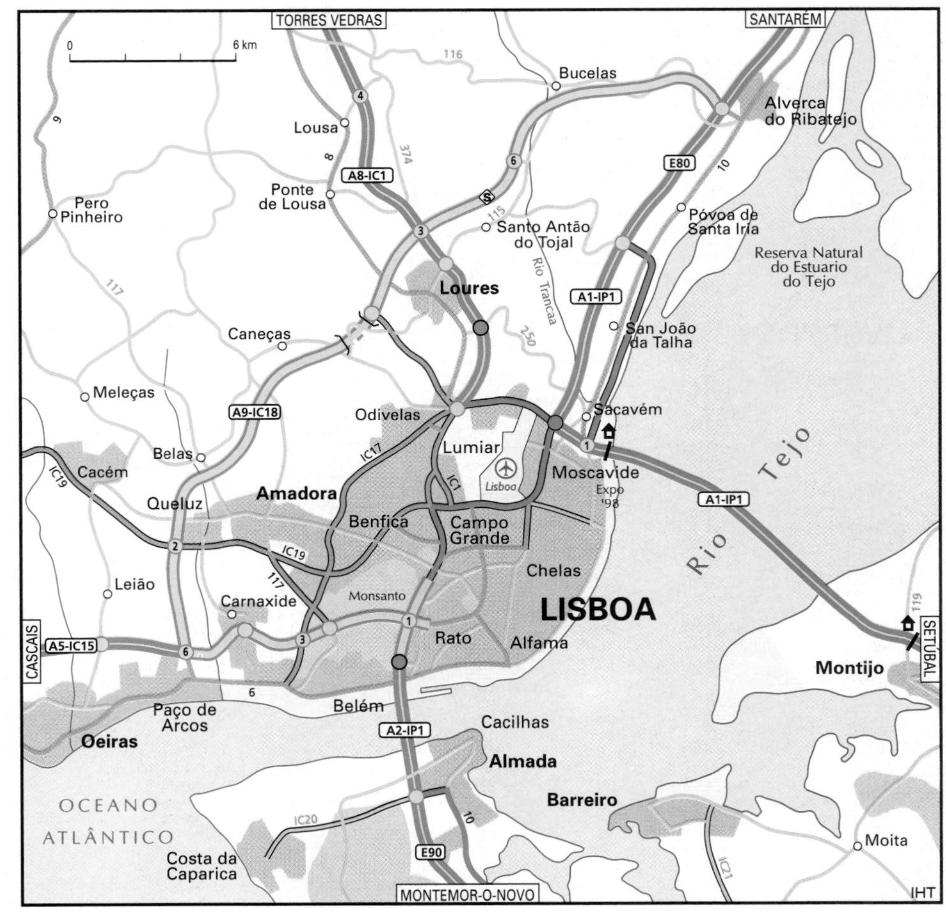
TORRES VEDRAS
SANTARÉM
0
6 km
Bucelas
Alverca do Ribatejo
Lousa
A8-IC1
E80
Ponte de Lousa
Pero Pinheiro
Santo Antão do Tojal
Póvoa de Santa Iria
Reserva Natural do Estuario do Tejo
Loures
Rio Trancão
A1-IP1
São João da Talha
Caneças
Meleças
A9-IC18
Odivelas
Sacavém
Belas
Cacém
Lumiar
Lisboa
Moscavide
Expo '98
Rio Tejo
Amadora
Queluz
Benfica
Campo Grande
IC19
Chelas
Leião
Monsanto
Carnaxide
LISBOA
Rato
Alfama
CASCAIS
A5-IC15
SETÚBAL
Montijo
Belém
Paço de Arcos
Cacilhas
Oeiras
A2-IP1
Almada
OCEANO ATLÂNTICO
Barreiro
Costa da Caparica
IC20
E90
Moita
MONTEMOR-O-NOVO
IHT

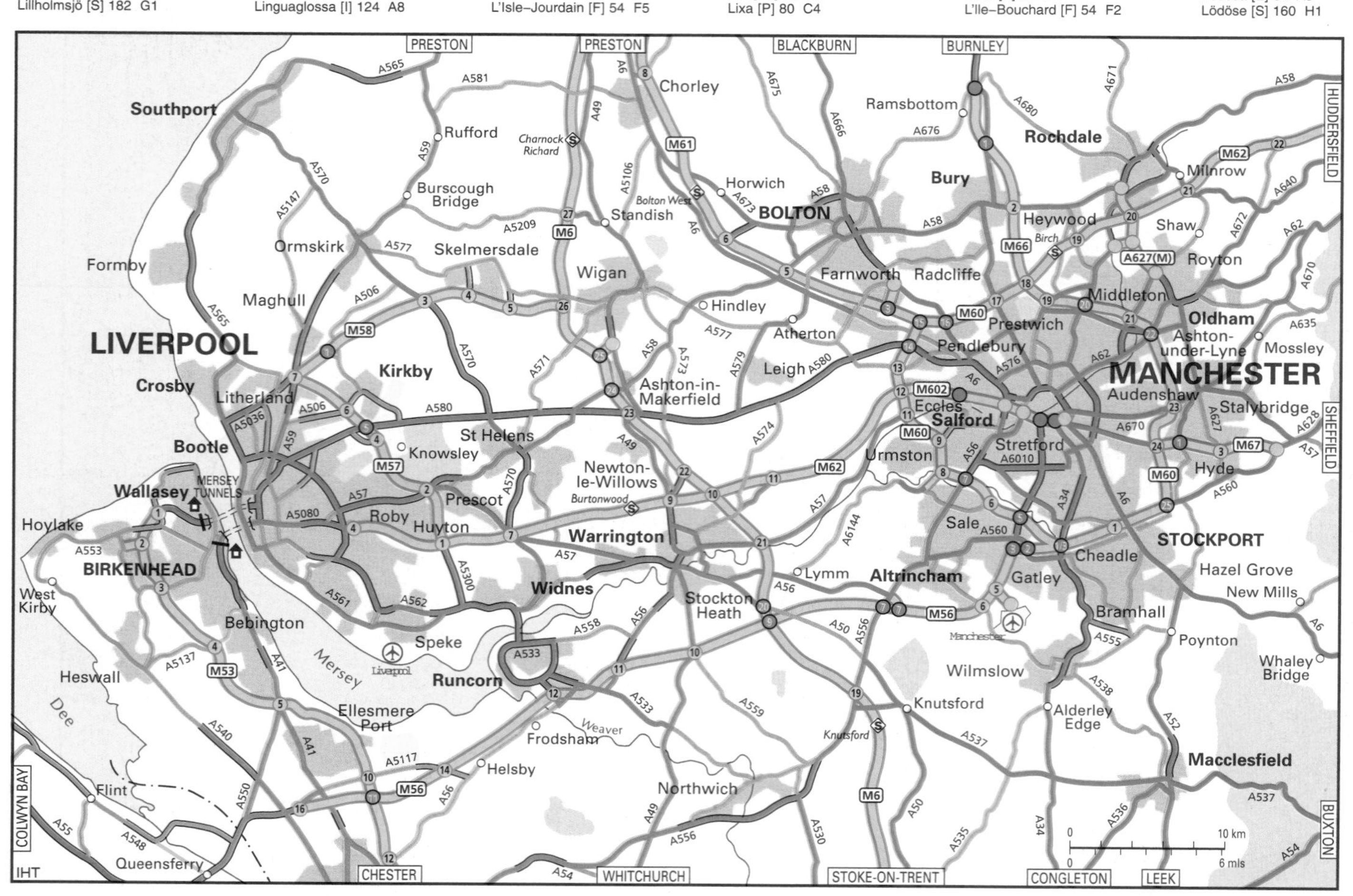

PRESTON
PRESTON
BLACKBURN
BURNLEY
HUDDERSFIELD
SHEFFIELD
BUXTON
LEEK
CONGLETON
STOKE-ON-TRENT
WHITCHURCH
CHESTER
COLWYN BAY
Southport
Rufford
Charnock Richard
Chorley
Ramsbottom
Rochdale
Milnrow
Burscough Bridge
Horwich
Bolton West
BOLTON
Bury
Heywood
Birch
Shaw
Royton
Standish
Ormskirk
Skelmersdale
Wigan
Formby
Farnworth
Radcliffe
Middleton
Oldham
Maghull
Hindley
Prestwich
Atherton
Ashton-under-Lyne
Mossley
LIVERPOOL
Kirkby
Pendlebury
MANCHESTER
Crosby
Litherland
Ashton-in-Makerfield
Leigh
Audenshaw
Stalybridge
Eccles
Salford
St Helens
Bootle
Knowsley
Newton-le-Willows
Burtonwood
Urmston
Stretford
Hyde
Wallasey
MERSEY TUNNELS
Prescot
Roby
Huyton
Hoylake
Warrington
Sale
BIRKENHEAD
Widnes
Lymm
Altrincham
STOCKPORT
Cheadle
Hazel Grove
Gatley
West Kirby
Stockton Heath
New Mills
Bramhall
Bebington
Speke
Liverpool
Manchester
Mersey
Runcorn
Poynton
Wilmslow
Whaley Bridge
Heswall
Dee
Ellesmere Port
Knutsford
Alderley Edge
Weaver
Frodsham
Helsby
Macclesfield
Flint
Northwich
Queensferry
IHT
M6
M61
M62
M60
M58
M57
M53
M56
M66
M602
M67
A627(M)
A533
A6010
10 km
6 mls

LONDON
IBB
LUTON
STEVENAGE
CAMBRIDGE
OXFORD
BASINGSTOKE
BRIGHTON
FOLKESTONE
HEMEL HEMPSTEAD
ST ALBANS
Hatfield
Hoddesdon
HARLOW
Berkhamsted
King's Langley
London Colney
Bovingdon
Chesham
Amersham
Chorleywood
WATFORD
Radlett
Shenley
Potters Bar
South Mimms
Cuffley
Cheshunt
Waltham Abbey
Epping
Theydon Bois
North Weald Bassett
Chipping Ongar
Borehamwood
Enfield
Abridge
Rickmansworth
Bushey
London Gateway
Whetstone
Southgate
Chingford
BRENTWOOD
Chalfont St Peter
Maple Cross
Barnet
Edgware
Finchley
Wood Green
Tottenham
Woodford Green
Chigwell
Northwood
Harefield
Pinner
Harrow
Hendon
Walthamstow
Romford
Gerrards Cross
Denham
Ruislip
Wembley
Hampstead
Hackney
Leytonstone
Ilford
Upminster
Willesden
Camden
Islington
Stratford
Barking
Iver Heath
Uxbridge
Euston
South Ockendon
SLOUGH
Iver
Greenford
City
Poplar
Rainham
Southall
Paddington
Hyde Park
Aveley
Hayes
Thamesmead
Langley
Ealing
Hammersmith
Westminster
Lambeth
Woolwich
Purfleet
Erith
Grays
Heston
Kensington
Greenwich
DARTFORD RIVER CROSSING
West Thurrock
Datchet
Hounslow
Kew
Battersea
Welling
Crayford
Windsor
Heathrow
Putney
Lewisham
Dartford
Wraysbury
Richmond
Wandsworth
Bexley
Greenhithe
Feltham
Twickenham
Richmond Park
Catford
Sidcup
Windsor Great Park
Egham
Streatham
Virginia Water
STAINES
Wimbledon
GRAVESEND
Sunbury
Hampton Court
KINGSTON UPON THAMES
Swanley
Mitcham
Beckenham
Bromley
Thames
Walton-on-Thames
Surbiton
Chertsey
Weybridge
West Wickham
Orpington
Carshalton
CROYDON
Eynsford
Ottershaw
Esher
Chobham
Hersham
Chessington
Sutton
West Kingsdown
Oxshott
Epsom
Purley
New Addington
Cobham
Banstead
Coulsdon
Warlingham
Biggin Hill
Otford
Wrotham
Woking
Ripley
East Horsley
Leatherhead
Sundridge
Borough Green
Lower Kingswood
Clacket Lane
Sevenoaks
Caterham
West Clandon
Effingham
Westerham
Limpsfield
Dorking
Redhill
Godstone
Oxted
Crockham Hill
Hadlow
GUILDFORD
Reigate
Hildenborough
Abinger Hammer
Four Elms
Edenbridge
Tonbridge
Shalford
South Holmwood
Salfords
0 8 km
0 5 mls

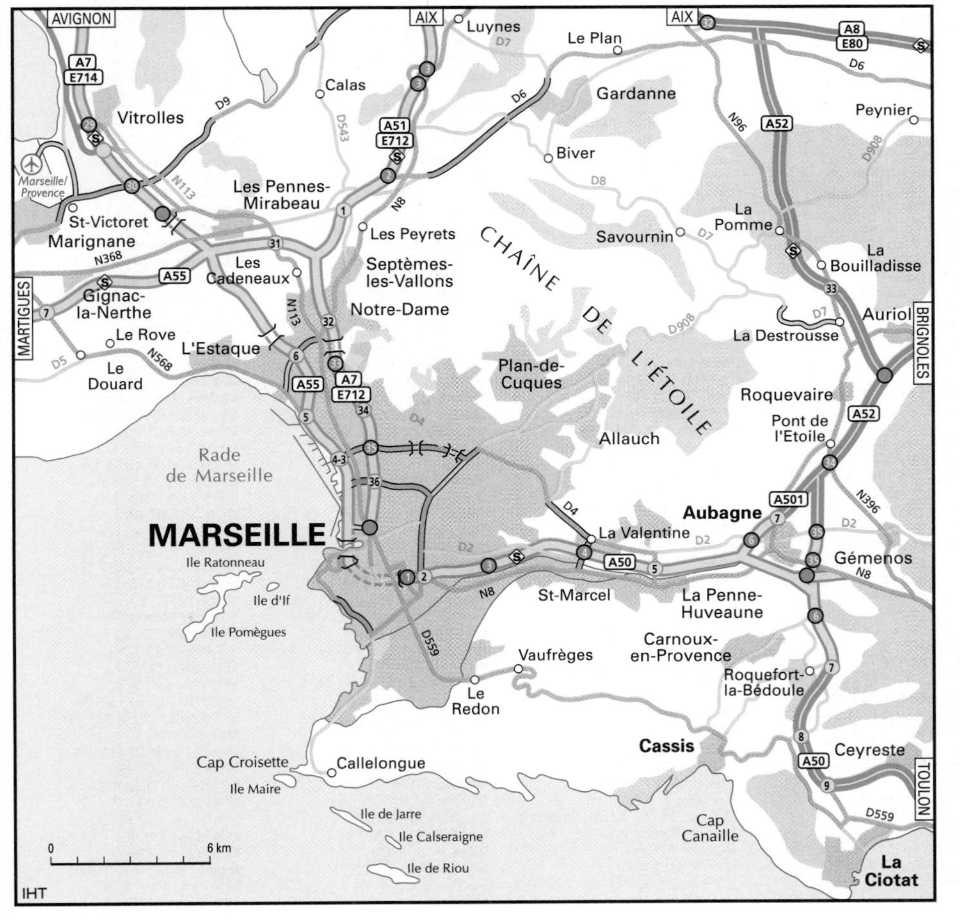
AVIGNON
AIX
AIX
Luynes
Le Plan
A8
E80
A7
E714
Calas
Gardanne
Vitrolles
Peynier
A51
E712
A52
Biver
Marseille/Provence
Les Pennes-Mirabeau
St-Victoret
Marignane
La Pomme
Les Peyrets
Savournin
La Bouilladisse
Les Cadeneaux
Septèmes-les-Vallons
CHAÎNE DE L'ÉTOILE
A55
Gignac-la-Nerthe
MARTIGUES
Notre-Dame
Auriol
BRIGNOLES
Le Rove
La Destrousse
L'Estaque
Le Douard
Plan-de-Cuques
Roquevaire
A55
A7
E712
Pont de l'Etoile
A52
Allauch
Rade de Marseille
A501
Aubagne
MARSEILLE
La Valentine
Ile Ratonneau
A50
Gémenos
Ile d'If
St-Marcel
La Penne-Huveaune
Ile Pomègues
Carnoux-en-Provence
Vaufrèges
Le Redon
Roquefort-la-Bédoule
Cassis
Cap Croisette
Callelongue
Ceyreste
A50
Ile Maire
TOULON
Ile de Jarre
Cap Canaille
Ile Calseraigne
Ile de Riou
La Ciotat
0
6 km
IHT

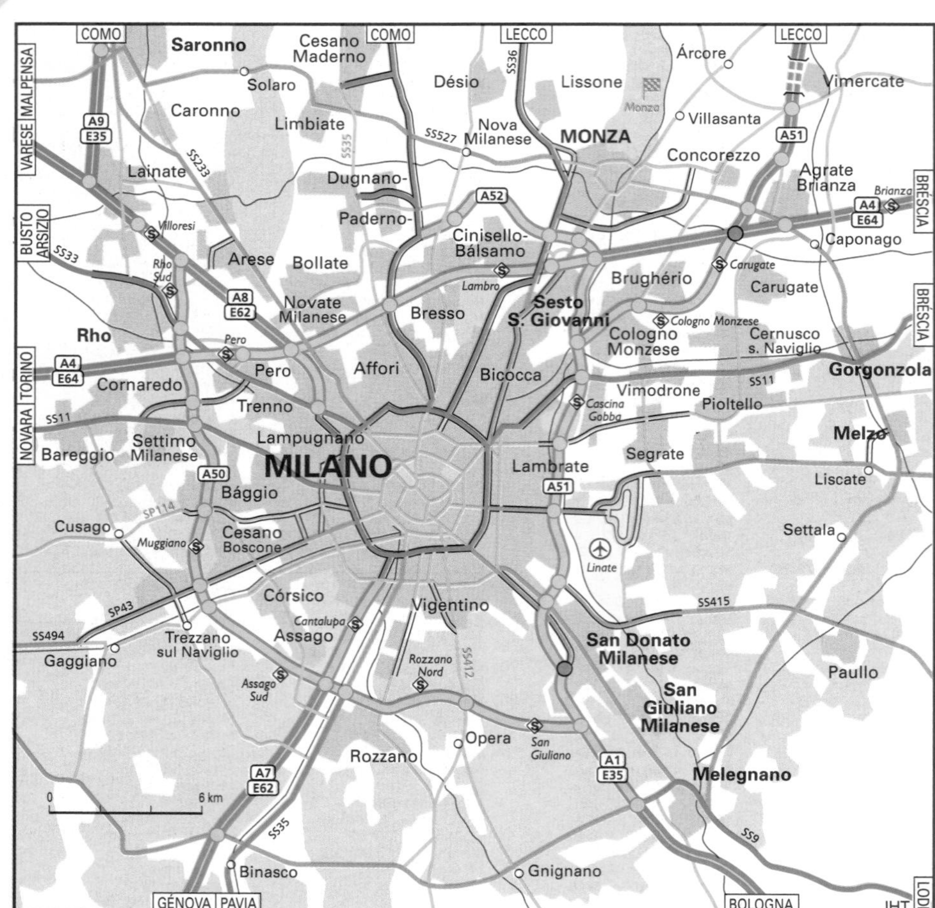
COMO
Saronno
Cesano Maderno
COMO
LECCO
LECCO
Árcore
Solaro
Désio
Lissone
Vimercate
VARESE MALPENSA
Caronno
Limbiate
Monza
Villasanta
A9
E35
SS35
SS527
Nova Milanese
MONZA
Concorezzo
A51
Lainate
SS233
Dugnano-
A52
Agrate Brianza
Brianza
BRESCIA
BUSTO ARSIZIO
Villoresi
Paderno-
A4
E64
SS33
Cinisello-Bálsamo
Caponago
Rho Sud
Arese
Bollate
Lambro
Carugate
Brughério
Carugate
A8
E62
Novate Milanese
Bresso
Sesto S. Giovanni
Cologno Monzese
BRESCIA
Rho
Pero
Cologno Monzese
Cernusco s. Naviglio
TORINO
A4
E64
Pero
Affori
Gorgonzola
Cornaredo
Bicocca
Vimodrone
SS11
Trenno
Cascina Gobba
Pioltello
NOVARA
SS11
Settimo Milanese
Lampugnano
Melzo
Bareggio
MILANO
Lambrate
Segrate
A50
A51
Liscate
Bággio
SP114
Cusago
Cesano Boscone
Settala
Muggiano
Linate
Córsico
SS415
SP43
Vigentino
Contalupa
San Donato Milanese
SS494
Trezzano sul Naviglio
Assago
Gaggiano
Rozzano Nord
SS412
Paullo
Assago Sud
San Giuliano Milanese
Opera
San Giuliano
Rozzano
A1
E35
Melegnano
A7
E62
0
6 km
SS35
SS9
Binasco
Gnignano
GÉNOVA
PAVIA
BOLOGNA
IHT
LODI

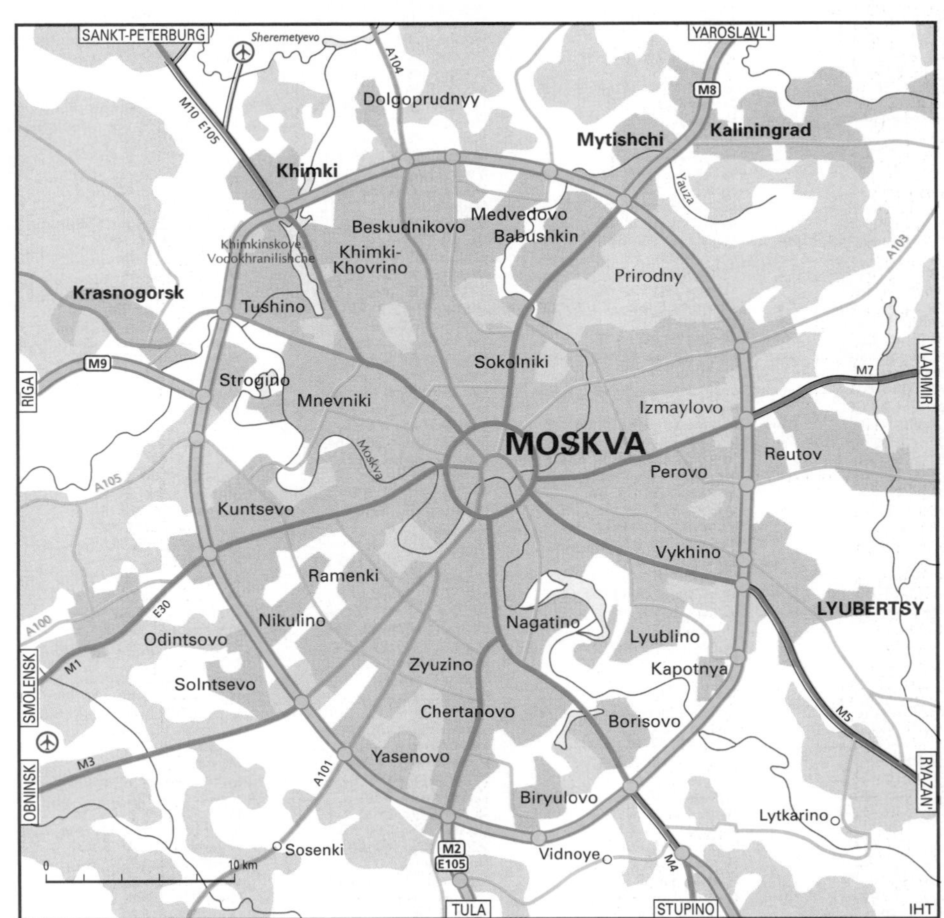

SANKT-PETERBURG
Sheremetyevo
YAROSLAVL'
M10 E105
A104
M8
Dolgoprudnyy
Mytishchi
Kaliningrad
Khimki
Yauza
Medvedkovo
Beskudnikovo
Babushkin
Khimkinskoye Vodokhranilishche
Khimki-Khovrino
A103
Prirodny
Krasnogorsk
Tushino
Sokolniki
M9
RIGA
Strogino
Mnevniki
VLADIMIR
M7
Izmaylovo
MOSKVA
Moskva
Reutov
Perovo
A105
Kuntsevo
Vykhino
Ramenki
E30
LYUBERTSY
A100
Nikulino
Nagatino
Odintsovo
Lyublino
M1
SMOLENSK
Kapotnya
Solntsevo
Zyuzino
Chertanovo
Borisovo
M5
M3
Yasenovo
OBNINSK
A101
RYAZAN'
Biryulovo
Lytkarino
Sosenki
M2
E105
Vidnoye
M4
0
10 km
TULA
STUPINO
IHT

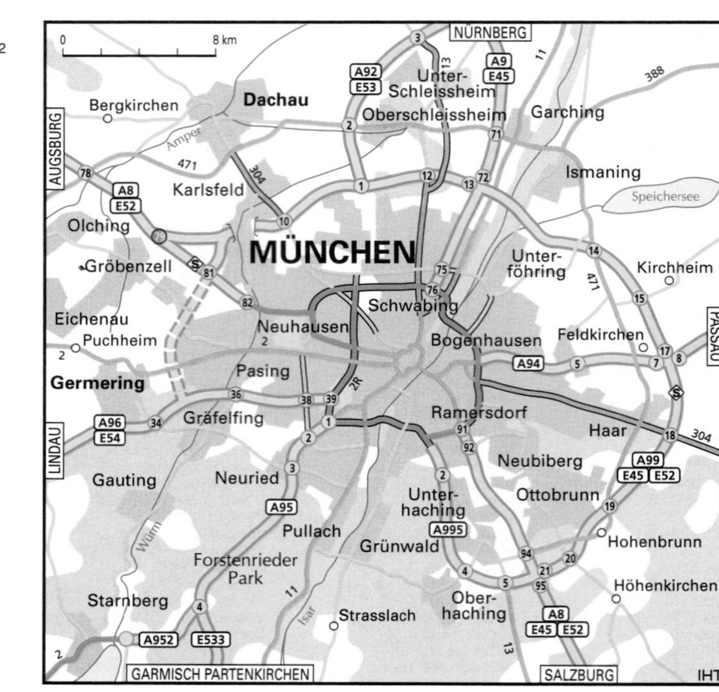

0
8 km
NÜRNBERG
A9
E45
A92
E53
Unter-
Schleissheim
Oberschleissheim
Dachau
Bergkirchen
Garching
AUGSBURG
Amper
Karlsfeld
Ismaning
Speichersee
A8
E52
Olching
MÜNCHEN
Gröbenzell
Unter-
föhring
Kirchheim
Eichenau
Puchheim
Neuhausen
Schwabing
Bogenhausen
Feldkirchen
PASSAU
A94
Germering
Pasing
A96
E54
Gräfelfing
Ramersdorf
Haar
LINDAU
Neubiberg
A99
E45
E52
Gauting
Neuried
Unter-
haching
Ottobrunn
A95
Pullach
A995
Grünwald
Hohenbrunn
Forstenrieder
Park
Würm
Starnberg
Isar
Höhenkirchen
Ober-
haching
Strasslach
A8
E45
E52
A952
E533
GARMISCH PARTENKIRCHEN
SALZBURG
IHT

N

Nagold [D] 58 G2
Nagu / Nauvo [FIN] 176 D5
Nagyatád [H] 74 H4
Nagybajom [H] 74 H4
Nagybaracska [H] 76 C5
Nagycenk [H] 62 F6
Nagycserkesz [H] 64 G5
Nagydorog [H] 76 B3
Nagygyimót [H] 74 H1
Nagyhalász [H] 64 H4
Nagyigmánd [H] 64 A6
Nagyiván [H] 64 F6
Nagykálló [H] 64 H5
Nagykanizsa [H] 74 G4
Nagykáta [H] 76 D1
Nagykónyi [H] 76 B3
Nagykőrös [H] 76 D2
Nagylak [H] 76 F4
Nagylóc [H] 64 D5
Nagymágocs [H] 76 F3
Nagymaros [H] 64 C5
Nagyoroszi [H] 64 C5
Nagyszénás [H] 76 F3
Nagyvázsony [H] 74 H2
Naharros [E] 98 B2
Nahe [D] 18 F3
Naila [D] 46 H3
Nailloux [F] 106 A4
Nailsea [GB] 12 F3
Nailsworth [GB] 12 G3
Naipu [RO] 148 C1
Nairn [GB] 6 E5
Najac [F] 66 H6
Nájera [E] 82 G6
Nakkila [FIN] 176 D2
Nakło nad Notecią [PL] 22 C6
Nakovo [YU] 76 F5
Nakskov [DK] 156 E5
Nälden [S] 182 G2
Nałęczów [PL] 38 D5
Nálepkovo [SK] 64 F2
Näljänkä [FIN] 198 F3
Nalzen [F] 106 A5
Nambroca [E] 96 F2
Namdalseid [N] 190 C5
Náměšť nad Oslavou [CZ] 50 B6
Námestovo [SK] 50 G5
Namsos [N] 190 C5
Namsskogan [N] 190 D4
Namur [B] 30 D5
Namysłów [PL] 36 D6
Nanclares de la Oca / Langraiz Oka [E] 82 G5
Nancy [F] 44 E5
Nangis [F] 42 G4
Nannestad [N] 172 B5
Nans-les-Pins [F] 108 C5
Nant [F] 106 E3
Nantes [F] 40 F6
Nanteuil-le-Haudouin [F] 42 G3
Nantiat [F] 54 G6
Nantua [F] 68 H2
Nantwich [GB] 10 D5
Náousa [GR] 138 E3
Náoussa [GR] 128 F4
Nápoli [I] 120 E3
Napp [N] 192 B4
Narach [BY] 202 H5
Narberth [GB] 12 D1
Narbolía [I] 118 C5
Narbonne [F] 106 D5
Narbonne-Plage [F] 106 D5
Narbuvollen [N] 182 C4
Narcao [I] 118 B7
Nardo [I] 122 G5
Narechenski Bani [BG] 148 B6
Narew [PL] 24 F6
Narila [FIN] 188 D5
Narkaus [FIN] 196 D8
Narlıca [TR] 146 F4
Narni [I] 116 A4
Naro [I] 126 D4
Naro-Fominsk [RUS] 204 F4
Narol [PL] 52 G2
Narón [E] 78 D4
Närpes / Närpiö [FIN] 186 A4
Närpiö / Närpes [FIN] 186 A4
Narta [HR] 74 G6
Narthákі [GR] 132 G3
Narva [EST] 200 G1
Narva-Jõesuu [EST] 200 G1
Narvik [N] 192 D4
Nås [S] 172 G5
Näsåker [S] 184 E1
Năsăud [RO] 206 C4
Nasbinals [F] 68 C5
Našice [HR] 154 D1
Nasielsk [PL] 38 B2
Näsinge [S] 166 C4
Naso [I] 124 B6
Nassau [D] 46 B2
Nassereith [A] 72 C1
Nässjö [S] 162 D2
Nasswald [A] 62 E6
Nästansjö [S] 190 F4
Nastazin [PL] 20 G5
Nästeln [S] 182 G4
Nastola [FIN] 178 B3
Näsviken [S] 174 E1
Näsviken [S] 190 E6
Natalinci [YU] 150 B1
Nattavaara [S] 198 A1
Nättraby [S] 158 F1
Naturno / Naturns [I] 72 C3
Naturns / Naturno [I] 72 C3
Nauders [A] 72 B2
Nauen [D] 34 D2
Naujoji Akmenė [LT] 200 C6
Naul [IRL] 2 F5
Naumburg [D] 34 B6
Naunhof [D] 34 D5
Naustbukta [N] 190 C4
Naustdal [N] 180 C6
Nauste [N] 180 F3
Nautsi [RUS] 196 E4
Nauvo / Nagu [FIN] 176 D5
Nava [E] 82 C2
Navacerrada [E] 88 F4
Nava de la Asunción [E] 88 E3
Nava del Rey [E] 88 D2
Navahermosa [E] 96 E2
Navahrudak [BY] 204 A5
Navalcán [E] 88 C6
Navalcarnero [E] 88 F6
Navaleno [E] 90 A2
Navalguijo [E] 88 C5
Navalmanzano [E] 88 F3
Navalmoral [E] 88 D5
Navalmoral de la Mata [E] 88 B6
Navalón [E] 98 D6
Navalperal de Pinares [E] 88 E5
Navalvillar de Pela [E] 96 B3
Navan / An Uaimh [IRL] 2 F5
Navarredonda de Gredos [E] 88 C5
Navarrenx [F] 84 D3
Navarrés [E] 98 E5
Navarrete [E] 82 G6
Navàs [E] 92 E3
Navascués / Nabaskoze [E] 84 C4
Navas del Madroño [E] 86 G4
Navas del Rey [E] 88 E5
Navas de Oro [E] 88 E3
Navas de San Juan [E] 102 F1
Navatalgordo [E] 88 D5
Navekvaren [S] 168 C5
Navelli [I] 116 C4
Nave Redonda [P] 94 B4
Naverstad [S] 166 C4
Navia [E] 78 F2
Navilly [F] 56 G5
Navlya [RUS] 204 E6
Náxos [GR] 138 E3
Nazaré [P] 86 C3
Nazilli [TR] 144 E5
N. Bystrica [SK] 50 G6
Ndroq [AL] 128 B3
Nea Anchiálos [GR] 132 H3
Néa Artáki [GR] 134 B5
Néa Epídavros [GR] 136 F2
Néa Fókaia [GR] 130 B6
Néa Kallikráteia [GR] 130 B5
Néa Karváli [GR] 130 D3
Néa Koróni [GR] 136 D4
Neale [IRL] 2 C4
Néa Mádytos [GR] 130 C4
Néa Mákri [GR] 134 C6
Néa Michanióna [GR] 128 H5
Néa Moudanía [GR] 130 B5
Néa Péramos [GR] 130 D3
Néa Plágia [GR] 130 B5
Neapoli [GR] 136 F5
Neápoli [GR] 140 F4
Neápoli [GR] 128 E5
Néa Poteídaia [GR] 130 B5
Néa Róda [GR] 130 C5
Néa Roúmata [GR] 140 B4
Néa Sánda [GR] 130 G2
Néa Skióni [GR] 130 C6
Néa Stýra [GR] 134 D5
Neath [GB] 12 E2
Néa Tríglia [GR] 130 B5
Neauvic [F] 66 E3
Néa Vissa [GR] 130 H1
Néa Zichni [GR] 130 C3
Nebiler [TR] 144 C2
Nebra [D] 34 B5
Nechanice [CZ] 50 A3
Neckarelz [D] 46 D5
Neckargemünd [D] 46 C5
Neckargerach [D] 46 D5
Neckarsteinach [D] 46 C5
Neckarsulm [D] 46 D5
Neda [E] 78 D1
Neded [SK] 64 A5
Nedelišće [HR] 74 F4
Nedervetil / Alaveteli [FIN] 198 C6
Neder Vindinge [DK] 156 F4
Nedre Soppero [S] 192 F4
Nedstrand [N] 164 B2
Nędza [PL] 50 E3
Neede [NL] 16 G5
Needham Market [GB] 14 G3
Neermoor [D] 18 B4
Negorci [MK] 128 G3
Negotin [YU] 150 E1
Negotino [MK] 128 F2
Negovanovci [BG] 150 E2
Negrar [I] 72 C6
Negreira [E] 78 B3
Negru Vodă [RO] 148 G1
Neheim-Hüsten [D] 32 C4
Nehoiu [RO] 206 C5
Neiden [N] 196 E3
Neittävä [FIN] 198 E4
Nejdek [CZ] 48 D3
Neksø [DK] 158 E4
Nelas [P] 80 C6
Nelidovo [RUS] 204 D4
Nellim [FIN] 196 E4
Nellimö [FIN] 196 E4
Nelson [GB] 10 E3
Neman [RUS] 202 D5
Nembro [I] 70 H4
Neméa [GR] 136 E1
Nemenčinė [LT] 202 G5
Nemesszalók [H] 74 G1
Németkér [H] 76 C3
Nemours [F] 42 G5
Nemšová [SK] 64 A2
Nemti [H] 64 D5
Nemyriv [UA] 206 E3
Nemyriv [UA] 52 G3
Nenagh [IRL] 2 D6
Nendeln [FL] 58 H5
Neochóri [GR] 136 B1
Neochori [GR] 132 E5
Neochóri [GR] 132 E3
Neohóri [GR] 134 A2
Neohóri [GR] 132 F2
Neohóri [GR] 134 C5
Néon Monastíri [GR] 132 G3
Néon Petrítsi [GR] 130 B2
Néos Marmarás [GR] 130 C6
Nepi [I] 114 H4
Nepomuk [CZ] 48 E5
Neptun [RO] 148 G1
Nérac [F] 66 E5
Neratovice [CZ] 48 G3
Neresheim [D] 60 C2
Nereta [LV] 200 E6
Nereto [I] 116 D3
Neretišća [HR] 152 A2
Neringa [LT] 202 D5
Neringa-Nida [LT] 202 D5
Néris-les-Bains [F] 56 C6
Nerja [E] 102 D5
Nérondes [F] 56 C4
Nerpio [E] 102 H2
Nersingen [D] 60 B3
Nerskogen [N] 180 H3
Nerva [E] 94 F5
Nervesa della Battaglia [I] 72 E5
Nervi [I] 110 B3
Nerviano [I] 70 G4
Nes [N] 170 H4
Nes [N] 170 D1
Nes [NL] 16 F1
Nesaseter [N] 190 D4
Nesbyen [N] 170 G4
Nesebŭr [BG] 148 F4
Nesflaten [N] 164 C1
Neskaupstaður [IS] 194 G5
Nesle [F] 28 F5
Nesna [N] 190 D2
Nesoddtangen [N] 166 B1
Nespereira [P] 80 C3
Nesseby [N] 196 E2
Nesselwang [D] 60 C5
Nestáni [GR] 136 E2
Nesterov [RUS] 24 D1
Nestório [GR] 128 D5
Nesttun [N] 170 B4
Nesvik [N] 164 A6
Netherwitton [GB] 8 F5
Netolice [CZ] 62 B2
Netretič [HR] 112 G1
Netta [PL] 24 E4
Nettancourt [F] 44 C4
Nettetal [D] 30 F3
Nettuno [I] 120 B1
Neubeckum [D] 32 D3
Neuberg an der Mürz [A] 62 D6
Neubrandenburg [D] 20 D4
Neubukow [D] 20 A3
Neubulach [D] 58 G1
Neuburg [D] 60 H3
Neuburg [D] 60 D2
Neuchâtel [CH] 58 C5
Neu Darchau [D] 18 G5
Neudorf [D] 46 C5
Neudorf-Platendorf [D] 32 H2
Neuenburg [D] 58 E3
Neuenbürg [D] 46 C6
Neuenburg [D] 18 C4
Neuenhaus [D] 16 G4
Neuenkirchen [D] 18 F5
Neuenwalde [D] 18 D3
Neufahrn [D] 60 F3
Neuf-Brisach [F] 58 E3
Neufchâteau [B] 44 D2
Neufchâteau [F] 44 D6
Neufchâtel [F] 44 B2
Neufchâtel-en-Bray [F] 28 C5
Neufelden [A] 62 B3
Neuffen [D] 58 H2
Neugersdorf [D] 48 G1
Neuhaus [D] 46 H4
Neuhaus [D] 46 G2
Neuhaus [D] 60 H3
Neuhaus [D] 18 E3
Neuhaus [D] 32 F4
Neuhaus [D] 18 H5
Neuhausen am Rheinfall [CH] 58 F4
Neuhof [D] 34 E3
Neuhofen an der Krems [A] 62 B4
Neuillé Port-Pierre [F] 54 F1
Neuilly-l'Évêque [F] 58 A3
Neuilly-St-Front [F] 42 H3
Neu-Isenburg [D] 46 C3
Neukalen [D] 20 C4
Neukirch [D] 34 F6
Neukirchen [A] 72 F1
Neukirchen [D] 156 B4
Neukloster [D] 20 A3
Neulengbach [A] 62 E4
Neu Lübbennau [D] 34 F3
Neum [BIH] 152 C3
Neumarkt [A] 74 B2
Neumarkt [A] 60 H5
Neumarkt [D] 46 H5
Neumarkt / Egna [I] 72 D4
Neumarkt-St Veit [D] 60 F4
Neu-Moresnet [B] 30 F5
Neumorschen [D] 32 F6
Neu Mukran [D] 20 D2
Neumünster [D] 18 F3
Neunagelberg [A] 62 C3
Neunburg [D] 48 C5
Neung-sur-Beuvron [F] 56 B2
Neunkirchen [A] 62 E6
Neunkirchen [D] 44 G3
Neuötting [D] 60 G4
Neupölla [A] 62 D3
Neuruppin [D] 20 C6
Neusiedl am See [A] 62 G5
Neuss [D] 30 G3
Neustadt [D] 32 E6
Neustadt [D] 60 E2
Neustadt [D] 46 G2
Neustadt [D] 48 B1
Neustadt [D] 58 F3
Neustadt [D] 34 F6
Neustadt [D] 18 H3
Neustadt [D] 34 C1
Neustadt am Rübenberge [D] 32 F2
Neustadt an der Aisch [D] 46 F5
Neustadt an der Waldnaab [D] 48 C4
Neustadt an der Weinstrasse [D] 46 B5
Neustadt-Glewe [D] 20 A5
Neustift [A] 72 D1
Neustrelitz [D] 20 C5
Neuves-Maisons [F] 44 E5
Neuvic [F] 68 B3
Neuville [F] 68 F2
Neuville [F] 54 E3
Neuville-aux-Bois [F] 42 E5
Neuvy [F] 54 H4
Neuvy-sur-Barangeon [F] 56 C3
Neuwied [D] 30 H6
Neuzelle [D] 34 G3
Neveklov [CZ] 48 G4
Nevel' [RUS] 204 C4
Nevers [F] 56 D4
Nevesinje [BIH] 152 C2
Nevlunghavn [N] 164 G3
Newark-on-Trent [GB] 10 F5
Newbiggin-by-the-Sea [GB] 8 G5
Newbliss [IRL] 2 F4
Newborough [GB] 10 B4
Newbridge / Droichead Nua [IRL] 2 E6
Newburgh [GB] 6 G6
Newburgh [GB] 8 E2
Newbury [GB] 12 H4
Newby Bridge [GB] 10 D2
Newcastle [GB] 2 G4
Newcastle Emlyn [GB] 10 A6
Newcastleton [GB] 8 E5
Newcastle-under-Lyme [GB] 10 E5
Newcastle upon Tyne [GB] 8 G6
Newcastle West [IRL] 4 C3
New Cumnock [GB] 8 D4
Newent [GB] 12 G2
New Galloway [GB] 8 D5
Newhaven [GB] 14 E6
Newinn [IRL] 4 D4
Newmarket [GB] 14 F3
Newmarket [IRL] 4 C4
Newmarket-on-Fergus [IRL] 2 C6
New Pitsligo [GB] 6 G5
Newport [GB] 4 H6
Newport [GB] 12 H5
Newport [GB] 10 D5
Newport [GB] 12 F3
Newport [IRL] 2 C3
Newport [IRL] 4 D3
Newport-on-Tay [GB] 8 F2
Newport Pagnell [GB] 14 E3
Newquay [GB] 12 C4
New Quay [GB] 10 B6
New Romney [GB] 14 F5
New Ross [IRL] 4 F4
Newry [GB] 2 F4
Newton Abbot [GB] 12 E5
Newtonferry / Port nan Long [GB] 6 A3
Newtonmore [GB] 6 D6
Newton Stewart [GB] 8 C5
Newtown [GB] 10 C6
Newtownabbey [GB] 2 G3
Newtownards [GB] 2 G3
Newtown Butler [GB] 2 E4
Newtownhamilton [GB] 2 F4
Newtownmountkennedy [IRL] 4 G3
Newtownstewart [GB] 2 F3
Nexon [F] 66 G2
Neyland [GB] 12 D2
Nežilovo [MK] 128 E2
Nibe [DK] 160 D4
Nicaj-Shalë [AL] 150 A6
Nicastro [I] 124 D5
Nice [F] 108 E4
Nickelsdorf [A] 62 G5
Nicknoret [S] 190 H4
Nicolosi [I] 126 G3
Nicosia [I] 126 F3
Nicotera [I] 124 C6
Nidderau [D] 46 D2
Nidzica [PL] 22 G5
Niebla [E] 94 F5
Nieborow [PL] 36 H3
Niebüll [D] 156 B4
Nieby [D] 156 C5
Niechorze [PL] 20 G3
Niedalino [PL] 20 H3
Niederalteich [D] 60 G3
Niederau [A] 60 F6
Niederaula [D] 46 E1
Niederbronn-les-Bains [F] 44 H5
Niederkrüchten [D] 30 F3
Niederoderwitz [D] 48 G1
Nieder Stotzingen [D] 60 C3
Niederwinkling [D] 60 G2
Nieder-Wöllstadt [D] 46 C2
Niedrzwica Duża [PL] 38 E6
Niemcza [PL] 50 C2
Niemegk [D] 34 D3
Niemisel [S] 198 B2
Niemisjärvi [FIN] 186 H4
Niemodlin [PL] 50 D2
Nienburg [D] 32 F1
Nienhagen [D] 20 B3
Niepołomice [PL] 52 B4
Nieppe [F] 28 F3
Nierstein [D] 46 C3
Niesky [D] 34 G5
Nieszawa [PL] 36 F1
Nieuil [F] 54 E6
Nieuweschans [NL] 16 H2
Nieuwpoort [B] 28 F1
Nigrán [E] 78 B5
Nigríta [GR] 130 B3
Niinimäki [FIN] 188 D3
Niinisalo [FIN] 186 C6
Niinivesi [FIN] 186 G2
Níjar [E] 102 G5
Nijkerk [NL] 16 E5
Nijmegen [NL] 16 E6
Nijverdal [NL] 16 G4
Níkaia [GR] 132 G2
Nikaranperä [FIN] 186 F3
Nikel' [RUS] 196 F3
Níki [GR] 128 E4
Nikiá [GR] 142 C4
Nikifóros [GR] 130 D3
Nikil [S] 166 H6
Nikíssiani [GR] 130 D3
Nikítas [GR] 130 C5
Nikkaluokta [S] 192 E5
Nikkaroinen [FIN] 178 A1
Nikkeby [N] 192 F1
Nikola Kozlevo [BG] 148 E2
Nikolayevo [RUS] 200 H2
Nikopol [BG] 148 B2
Nikopol' [UA] 206 G4
Nikšić [YU] 152 E3
Nilsiä [FIN] 188 D1
Nîmes [F] 106 F3
Nimféa [GR] 130 F2
Nin [HR] 112 G4
Ninove [B] 28 H3
Niort [F] 54 D4
Nirmiskylä [FIN] 198 G5
Nirou Khani [GR] 140 E4
Niš [YU] 150 D3
Nisa [P] 86 E4
Nisákio [GR] 132 B2
Niscemi [I] 126 F4
Niška Banja [YU] 150 D3
Niskakoski [RUS] 196 E4
Nisko [PL] 52 E2
Nissi [EST] 200 D2
Nissilä [FIN] 198 E5
Nītaure [LV] 200 E5
Nitlax [FIN] 176 F6
Nitra [SK] 64 A4
Nitrianske Pravno [SK] 64 B2
Nitrianske Rudno [SK] 64 B3
Nitry [F] 56 F2
Nittedal [N] 172 B5
Nittenau [D] 48 C6
Nittendorf [D] 60 F2
Nittkvarn [S] 166 G1
Nivå [DK] 156 G2
Niva [FIN] 198 G4
Nivala [FIN] 198 D5
Nivelles [B] 28 H3
Niversac [F] 66 F3
Nizhyn [UA] 204 D7
Nižná [SK] 50 H6
Nižná Boca [SK] 64 D2
Nižná Slaná [SK] 64 E3
Nizza Monferrato [I] 108 H2
Njegoševo [YU] 76 D6
Njurunda [S] 184 E5
Noailles [F] 28 D6
Noain (Elorz) [E] 84 B4
Noale [I] 72 E6
Noceda [E] 78 F5
Nocera [I] 120 E3
Nocera Umbra [I] 116 B2
Noceto [I] 110 D2
Noci [I] 122 E3
Nocito [E] 84 D6
Nodeland [N] 164 D5
Nods [F] 58 B5
Noé [F] 84 H4
Noépoli [I] 122 C5
Noeux [F] 28 E3
Nogales [E] 94 G2
Nogara [I] 110 F1
Nogaro [F] 84 F2
Nogent [F] 56 H2
Nogent-le-Roi [F] 42 E4
Nogent-le-Rotrou [F] 26 G6
Nogent-sur-Seine [F] 42 H5
Nogersund [S] 158 E2
Noginsk [RUS] 204 F4
Nohfelden [D] 44 G3
Noia [E] 78 B3
Noirétable [F] 68 E2
Noirmoutier-en-l'Ile [F] 54 A2
Noja [E] 82 F3
Nokia [FIN] 176 F1
Nol [S] 160 H1
Nola [I] 120 E3
Nol Alafors [S] 160 H1
Nolay [F] 56 F4
Noli [I] 108 H3
Nomeny [F] 44 E5
Nomexy [F] 44 E6
Nõmme [EST] 200 E2
Nonancourt [F] 26 H5
Nonant-le-Pin [F] 26 G5
Nonantola [I] 110 F3
Nonaspe [E] 90 G5
Nonnenhorn [D] 58 H4
Nontron [F] 66 F2
Nonza [F] 114 C2
Noordwijk aan Zee [NL] 16 C4
Noormarkku [FIN] 176 D1
Nora [S] 166 H2
Nora [S] 168 B6
Nørager [DK] 160 D4
Norberg [S] 168 B1
Norcia [I] 116 B3
Nordanas [S] 190 G5
Nordansjö [S] 190 F4
Nordausques [F] 14 H6
Nordberg [N] 180 F5
Nordborg [DK] 156 C4
Nordby [DK] 156 E1
Nordby [DK] 156 A3
Norddeich [D] 16 H1
Nordeide [N] 170 C1
Norden [D] 16 H1
Nordenham [D] 18 D4
Norderney [D] 18 B3
Norderstedt [D] 18 F4
Nordfjordeid [N] 180 C5
Nordfold [N] 192 C5
Nordhalben [D] 46 H2
Nordhausen [D] 32 H5
Nordhorn [D] 16 H4
Nordkapp [N] 196 C1
Nordkirchen [D] 32 C3
Nordkisa [N] 172 C5
Nordkjosbotn [N] 192 E3
Nordli [N] 190 D5
Nördlingen [D] 60 C2
Nordmaling [S] 184 H1
Nordmark [S] 166 F1
Nordmela [N] 192 C3
Nordre Osen [N] 172 D2
Nordsjö [S] 174 D1
Nordskot [N] 192 C5
Nordskov [DK] 156 E2
Nordwalde [D] 16 H5
Noresund [N] 170 G5
Norg [NL] 16 G2
Norheimsund [N] 170 C4
Norma [I] 116 B6
Norrahammar [S] 162 D2
Norraker [S] 190 E5
Norra Löten [S] 172 E3
Norra Mellby [S] 158 C1
Norra Tresund [S] 190 F4
Norrboda [S] 174 G5
Norrboda [S] 172 H3
Norrby [S] 190 G4
Nørre Åby [DK] 156 D3
Nørre Alslev [DK] 156 F5
Norre Bergnäss [S] 190 G2
Nørre Broby [DK] 156 D3
Nørre Lyndelse [DK] 156 D3
Nørre Nebel [DK] 156 A2
Nørre Snede [DK] 156 C1
Nørresundby [DK] 160 D3
Nørre Vejrup [DK] 156 B2
Nørre Vorupør [DK] 160 B4
Norr Hede [S] 182 F4
Norrhult [S] 162 E4
Norrköping [S] 168 B5
Norrnäs [FIN] 186 A4
Norrskedika [S] 174 G5
Norrsundet [S] 174 E3
Norrtälje [S] 168 E2
Norsholm [S] 168 B5
Norsjö [S] 190 H4
Norsjövallen [S] 190 H4
Nort [F] 40 F6
Nörten-Hardenberg [D] 32 G4
Northallerton [GB] 10 F2
Northam [GB] 12 D3
Northampton [GB] 14 D2
North Berwick [GB] 8 F3
Northeim [D] 32 G4
Northiam [GB] 14 F5
Northleach [GB] 12 H2
Northwall [GB] 6 G1
North Walsham [GB] 14 G2
Northwich [GB] 10 D4
Norton [GB] 10 G3
Nortorf [D] 18 F2
Norwich [GB] 14 G2
Nosivka [UA] 206 F1
Nossa Senhora do Cabo [P] 86 A6
Nossebro [S] 166 D6
Nössemark [S] 166 C3
Nossen [D] 34 E6
Nótia [GR] 128 G3
Nötö [FIN] 176 D6
Noto [I] 126 G5
Notodden [N] 164 F2
Nøtterøy [N] 164 H3

Orlik nad Vltavou [CZ] 48 F5
Orlovat [YU] 154 G1
Orly [F] 42 F4
Orlyak [BG] 148 F2
Ormanlı [TR] 146 D2
Ormea [I] 108 G3
Ormemyr [N] 164 F1
Órmos [GR] 138 D1
Órmos [GR] 128 H5
Órmos Panagías [GR] 130 C5
Órmos Prínou [GR] 130 E4
Ormož [SLO] 74 E4
Ormsjö [S] 190 F5
Ormskirk [GB] 10 D4
Ornans [F] 58 B5
Ornavasso [I] 70 F3
Ornes [N] 190 D4
Ørnes [N] 190 D1
Orneta [PL] 22 G3
ØrnhØj [DK] 160 B6
Örnsköldsvik [S] 184 G2
Orolik [HR] 154 E1
Oron–la–Ville [CH] 70 C1
Oropesa [E] 88 C6
Oropesa del Mar / Orpesa [E] 98 G3
Orosei [I] 118 E4
Orosháza [H] 76 F3
Oroso [E] 78 C3
Oroszlány [H] 64 B6
Oroszló [H] 76 B4
Orpesa / Oropesa del Mar [E] 98 G3
Orpington [GB] 14 E4
Orrefors [S] 162 F5
Orroli [I] 118 D6
Orsa [S] 172 G3
Orsara di Puglia [I] 120 G2
Orscholz [D] 44 F3
Örsebo [S] 162 E1
Orsha [BY] 204 C5
Orsières [CH] 70 C3
Örsjö [S] 162 F5
Ørslev [DK] 156 G4
Örslösa [S] 166 E5
Orsogna [I] 116 D5
Orsomarso [I] 120 H6
Orşova [RO] 206 A6
Orsoya [BG] 150 F2
Ørsta [N] 180 C4
Ørsted [DK] 160 E5
Örsundsbro [S] 168 D2
Ort [A] 60 H4
Ortaca [TR] 142 F3
Ortaca [TR] 146 B5
Ortakent [TR] 142 C2
Ortaklar [TR] 144 D5
Orta Nova [I] 120 G2
Ortaoba [TR] 146 C5
Orta San Giulio [I] 70 F4
Orte [I] 116 A4
Ortenberg [D] 46 D2
Ortenburg [D] 60 H3
Orth [A] 62 F4
Orthez [F] 84 D2
Orthovoúni [GR] 132 E1
Ortigueira [E] 78 E1
Ortisei / St Ulrich [I] 72 D3
Ortişoara [RO] 76 G5
Örtomta [S] 168 B5
Ortona [I] 116 E4
Ortrand [D] 34 E5
Örträsk [S] 190 H5
Ortueri [I] 118 C5
Ørum [DK] 160 E5
Ørum [DK] 160 D5
Orume [I] 118 D4
Orvalho [P] 86 E3
Ørvella [N] 164 F2
Orvieto [I] 114 H3
Orvinio [I] 116 B5
Oryakhovo [BG] 150 G2
Orzechowo [PL] 22 E6
Orzesze [PL] 50 F3
Orzinuovi [I] 70 H5
Orzola [E] 100 E4
Orzysz [PL] 24 C4
Os [N] 182 C4
Osby [S] 162 C6
Oschatz [D] 34 D5
Oschersleben [D] 34 B3
Öschiri [I] 118 D3
Ościłowo [PL] 38 A1
Ose [N] 164 D3
Osečina [YU] 154 F3
Oseja de Sajambre [E] 82 C3
Osen [N] 190 B5
Osenets [BG] 148 D2
Osera de Ebro [E] 90 F4
Osie [PL] 22 D4
Osieczna [PL] 36 C4
Osiek [PL] 22 E4
Osiek [PL] 52 D2
Osijek [HR] 76 C6
Osikovitsa [BG] 150 G4
Ösilo [I] 118 C3
Osimo [I] 116 C1
Osinja [BIH] 154 C2
Ósios Loukás [GR] 132 H5
Osipaonica [YU] 154 H3
Osječenica [YU] 152 D4
Oskar [S] 162 F5
Oskarshamn [S] 162 G3
Oskarström [S] 162 B5
Øskendalsøra [N] 180 F3
Oskowo [PL] 22 C2
Osl'any [SK] 64 B3
Oslo [N] 166 B1
Østøs [DK] 160 C3
Osmaneli [TR] 146 G4
Os'mino [RUS] 200 H1
Ösmo [S] 168 D4
Osnabrück [D] 32 D2
Ošno [PL] 34 G2
Osoblaha [CZ] 50 D3
Osor [HR] 112 E3
Osorno la Mayor [E] 82 D5
Osowo Leborskie [PL] 22 C2
Osowo Lešne [PL] 22 D4
Osøyro [N] 170 B4
Ospedaletti [I] 108 F4
Oss [NL] 16 E6
Óssa [GR] 130 B4
Ossa de Montiel [E] 96 H5
Ossiach [A] 74 B3
Ossjøen [N] 170 E4
Östansjö [S] 166 G4
Östansjö [S] 190 G3
Östanvik [S] 172 H3
Ostashkov [RUS] 204 D3
Östavall [S] 184 C4
Ostbevern [D] 32 C3
Østbirk [DK] 156 C1
Østby [N] 172 E2
Østed [DK] 156 G3
Ostellato [I] 110 G3
Østenå [N] 164 F2
Østerbø [N] 170 E3
Osterburg [D] 34 B1
Osterburken [D] 46 D5
Österbybruk [S] 174 F5
Østerby Havn [DK] 160 F3
Österbymo [S] 162 E2
Österfärnebo [S] 174 E5
Osterhofen [D] 60 G3
Osterholz–Scharmbeck [D] 18 D5
Øster Hurup [DK] 160 E4
Østerild [DK] 160 C3
Østerlars [DK] 158 E4
Østermarie [DK] 158 E4
Osterode [D] 32 G4
Östersund [S] 182 G2
Östersundom [FIN] 176 H5
Øster Ulslev [DK] 20 B1
Österunda [S] 168 C2
Östervåla [S] 174 E5
Östervallskog [S] 166 C2
Øster Vrå [DK] 160 E3
Östhammar [S] 174 G5
Ostheim [D] 46 F2
Osthofen [D] 46 B4
Ostiglia [I] 110 F2
Oštinski Pogost [RUS] 204 E1
Ostiz [E] 84 B3
Ostra [I] 112 C6
Östraby [S] 158 C2
Ostrach [D] 58 H3
Östra Ed [S] 162 G1
Östra Frölunda [S] 162 B3
Östra Kärne [S] 166 G2
Ostrava [CZ] 50 E4
Østre Kile [N] 164 E3
Oštrelj [BIH] 154 A3
Ostritz [D] 48 G1
Ostróda [PL] 22 G4
Ostrołęka [PL] 24 C6
Ostroróg [PL] 36 B2
Ostros [YU] 128 A1
Ostrov [CZ] 48 D3
Ostrov [RUS] 200 G4
Ostrovcy [RUS] 200 G2
Ostrowice [PL] 20 H4
Ostrowiec [PL] 22 B3
Ostrowiec Świętokrzyski [PL] 52 C1
Ostrowite [PL] 22 D5
Ostrów Mazowieka [PL] 38 D1
Ostrów Wielkopolski [PL] 36 E5
Ostrožac [BIH] 112 H3
Ostrožac [BIH] 152 C1
Ostrożany [PL] 38 E2
Ost Ryd [S] 168 B5
Ostrzeszów [PL] 36 E5
Ostuni [I] 122 F3
Østvika [N] 190 D4
Osuna [E] 102 B3
Oswestry [GB] 10 C5
Oświecim [PL] 50 G4
Osztopán [H] 74 H4
Otalampi [FIN] 176 G4
Otanmäki [FIN] 198 E5
Otanów [PL] 20 F6
Otava [FIN] 188 C6
Otepää [EST] 200 F3
Oterma [FIN] 198 E4
Otero de Bodas [E] 80 H3
Oteševo [MK] 128 D4
Othery [GB] 12 F4
Otivar [E] 102 D5
Otley [GB] 10 F3
Otmuchów [PL] 50 D3
Otnes [N] 182 C6
Otocac [HR] 112 G3
Otočec [SLO] 74 D5
Otok [HR] 154 E2
Otoka [BIH] 154 A2
Otorowo [PL] 36 C2
Otranto [I] 122 H5
Otrokovice [CZ] 50 D6
Otsagi / Ochagavía [E] 84 C4
Otta [N] 180 G6
Ottana [I] 118 D4
Ottaviano [I] 120 E3
Ottenby [S] 158 G1
Ottenschlag [A] 62 D4
Ottensheim [A] 62 B4
Otterbach [D] 44 H3
Otterburn [GB] 8 F5
Otter Ferry [GB] 8 C2
Otterlo [NL] 16 E5
Otterndorf [D] 18 E3
Ottersberg [D] 18 E5
Ottersøy [N] 190 C4
Otterup [DK] 156 D3
Ottery St Mary [GB] 12 E4
Öttevény [H] 62 H6
Ottobeuren [D] 60 C4
Ottone [I] 110 B3
Ottsjö [S] 182 E2
Ottweiler [D] 44 G3
Otwock [PL] 38 C3
Oucques [F] 42 D6
Oud Beijerland [NL] 16 C5
Ouddorp [NL] 16 B5
Oudenaarde [B] 28 G2
Oude–Pekela [NL] 16 H2
Oudewater [NL] 16 D5
Oughterard [IRL] 2 C4
Ouistreham [F] 26 F3
Oulainen [FIN] 198 D5
Oullins [F] 68 F3
Oulu / Uleåborg [FIN] 198 D4
Oulujoki [FIN] 198 D4
Oulunsalo [FIN] 198 D4
Oulx [I] 70 B5
Ounas [FIN] 198 E5
Oundle [GB] 14 E2
Oura [P] 80 E3
Ouranópoli [GR] 130 D5
Ourense / Orense [E] 78 C5
Ourique [P] 94 C4
Ourol [E] 78 E2
Oust [F] 84 G5
Outokumpu [FIN] 188 E2
Ouzouer–le–Marché [F] 42 D6
Ovada [I] 108 H2
Ovakent [TR] 144 E4
Ovar [P] 80 B4
Ovčar Banja [YU] 150 B2
Ovelgönne [D] 18 F4
Ovenstädt [D] 32 E2
Overåneset [N] 180 E4
Overath [D] 30 H4
Överbyn [S] 172 E5
Overgård [N] 192 E3
Overhalla [N] 190 C5
Over Jerstal [DK] 156 C3
Överkalix [S] 196 B8
Överlida [S] 162 B3
Övermark / Ylimarkku [FIN] 186 B4
Överö [FIN] 176 B5
Overscaig [GB] 6 D3
Övertänger [S] 174 C3
Overton [GB] 12 H4
Övertorneå [S] 196 B8
Överturingen [S] 182 H4
Överum [S] 162 G1
Oviedo [E] 78 H3
Ovindoli [I] 116 C5
Øvre Årdal [N] 170 E1
Øvre Espedal [N] 164 B3
Øvre Moen [N] 164 C2
Øvre Rendal [N] 182 C6
Övre Soppero [S] 192 F4
Øvrestøl [N] 180 E4
Ovruch [UA] 204 B7
Ovtrup [DK] 156 A2
Owschlag [D] 18 F2
Oxberg [S] 172 G3
Oxborough [GB] 14 F2
Oxelösund [S] 168 C5
Oxford [GB] 14 D3
Oxiá [GR] 132 E2
Oxie [S] 156 H3
Oxínia [GR] 132 E1
Oxwich [GB] 12 E2
Øy [N] 164 E4
Øyenkilen [N] 166 B3
Øyer [N] 172 B2
Øyermoen [N] 172 D5
Øyestad [N] 164 E5
Oyntdartfjørður [FR] 160 B1
Oyonnax [F] 68 H2
Øyslebø [N] 164 D5
Øystese [N] 170 C4
Oyten [D] 18 E5
Ozalj [HR] 74 D6
Ozarowo [AL] 52 D1
Ożarów Mazowiecki [PL] 38 B3
Ožbalt [SLO] 74 D3
Ózd [H] 64 E4
Ožďany [SK] 64 D4
Ozerki [RUS] 178 F4
Ozersk [RUS] 24 C2
Ozieri [I] 118 D3
Ozimek [PL] 50 E2
Ozora [H] 76 B3
Ozorkow [PL] 36 G4

P

Pääjärvi [FIN] 186 F3
Paakkila [FIN] 188 E2
Paatinen [FIN] 176 D4
Paavola [FIN] 198 D4
Pabianice [PL] 36 G4
Pabradė [LT] 202 G5
Paceco [I] 126 B2
Pachino [I] 126 G6
Paços de Ferreira [P] 80 C4
Pacov [CZ] 48 G5
Pacsa [H] 74 G3
Pacyna [PL] 36 H3
Pacy–sur–Eure [F] 42 E3
Paczków [PL] 50 C3
Padarosk [BY] 24 H6
Padasjoki [FIN] 176 H1
Padborg [DK] 156 C4
Padej [YU] 76 E5
Paderborn [D] 32 E4
Paderne [P] 94 C5
Padiham [GB] 10 E3
Padina [YU] 154 H2
Padjene [HR] 112 H5
Padova [I] 110 G1
Padrenda [E] 78 C5
Padrógão Grande [P] 86 E3
Padrón [E] 78 B3
Padru [I] 118 E3
Padstow [GB] 12 C4
Padul [E] 102 E4
Paesana [I] 108 F2
Paestum [I] 120 F4
Pag [HR] 112 F4
Pagani [I] 120 E3
Pagėgiai [LT] 202 D5
Pagny [F] 44 E4
Páhi [H] 76 D3
Pahiá [GR] 138 G5
Pahiá Ámos [GR] 140 G5
Pahranichny [BY] 24 G5
Paianía [GR] 134 C6
Paide [EST] 200 E2
Paignton [GB] 12 E5
Paijärvi [FIN] 178 D3
Pailhès [F] 84 H4
Paimboeuf [F] 40 E6
Paimio [FIN] 176 E4
Paimpol [F] 26 A3
Paisley [GB] 8 D3
Pajala [S] 192 G6
Pájara [E] 100 E5
Pajares, Puerto de– [E] 78 H4
Pajęczno [PL] 36 F6
Pajukoski [FIN] 198 F6
Pakość [PL] 36 E1
Pakoštane [HR] 112 G5
Pakosze [PL] 22 G3
Pakrac [HR] 154 B1
Pakruojis [LT] 202 F3
Paks [H] 76 C3
Palacios del Sil [E] 78 F4
Palacios de Sanabria [E] 80 G3
Paladru [F] 68 H4
Palafrugell [E] 92 G3
Palagianello [I] 122 E4
Palagiano [I] 122 E4
Palagonia [I] 126 F4
Palaía Epídavros [GR] 136 F2
Palaíkastro [GR] 140 H4
Palaiochóra [GR] 140 B5
Palaiochóri [GR] 130 C5
Palaiokastrítsa [GR] 132 A2
Palaiópoli [GR] 138 D1
Palaiópoli [GR] 130 G4
Pálairos [GR] 132 D4
Palaiseau [F] 42 F4
Palamás [GR] 132 F2
Palamós [E] 92 G3
Palamut [TR] 144 D3
Palanga [LT] 202 D4
Palas de Rei [E] 78 D3
Palasi [EST] 200 F1
Palatítsia [GR] 128 G5
Palatna [YU] 150 C4
Palau [I] 118 E2
Palavas–les–Flots [F] 106 F4
Palazzo Adriano [I] 126 C3
Palazzolo Acréide [I] 126 G5
Palazzolo sull'Oglio [I] 70 H4
Palazzo San Gervasio [I] 120 H3
Paldiski [EST] 200 D1
Pale [BIH] 152 D1
Pāle [LV] 200 E4
Palena [I] 116 D5
Palencia [E] 82 C6
Paleócastro [GR] 130 B3
Paleo Ginekokastro [GR] 128 H3
Paleohóri [GR] 132 E2
Paleohori [GR] 132 D3
Paleohóri [GR] 136 E3
Paleópirgos [GR] 132 F5
Palermo [AL] 128 B6
Palermo [I] 126 C2
Palestrina [I] 116 B5
Palič [YU] 76 D5
Palinuro [I] 120 G5
Paliomonastíri [GR] 132 E2
Paliópirgos [GR] 132 F2
Paliouriá [GR] 132 E1
Palioúrion [GR] 130 C6
Paliseul [B] 44 D1
Paljakka [FIN] 198 F4
Pälkäne [FIN] 176 G2
Palkino [RUS] 200 G4
Pallarés [E] 94 G4
Pallaruelo de Monegros [E] 90 F4
Pallasgreen [IRL] 4 D3
Pallastunturi [FIN] 192 H4
Pallíni [GR] 134 C6
Palma del Río [E] 102 B1
Palma de Mallorca [E] 104 E5
Palma di Montechiaro [I] 126 D4
Palmadula [I] 118 B3
Palma Nova [E] 104 D5
Palmanova [I] 72 G5
Palmela [P] 86 B6
Palmi [I] 124 C7
Palo del Colle [I] 122 D2
Páloi [GR] 142 C4
Palojärvi [FIN] 192 G4
Palojärvi [FIN] 196 C8
Palojoensuu [FIN] 192 G4
Palokastër [AL] 128 C6
Palokki [FIN] 188 E3
Palomaa [FIN] 196 D4
Palomäki [FIN] 198 F6
Palomares [E] 104 A5
Palomares del Campo [E] 98 A2
Palomas [E] 94 H2
Palombara Sabina [I] 116 B5
Palonurmi [FIN] 188 D1

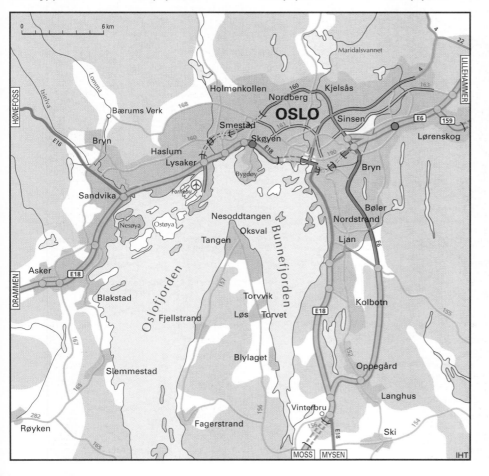

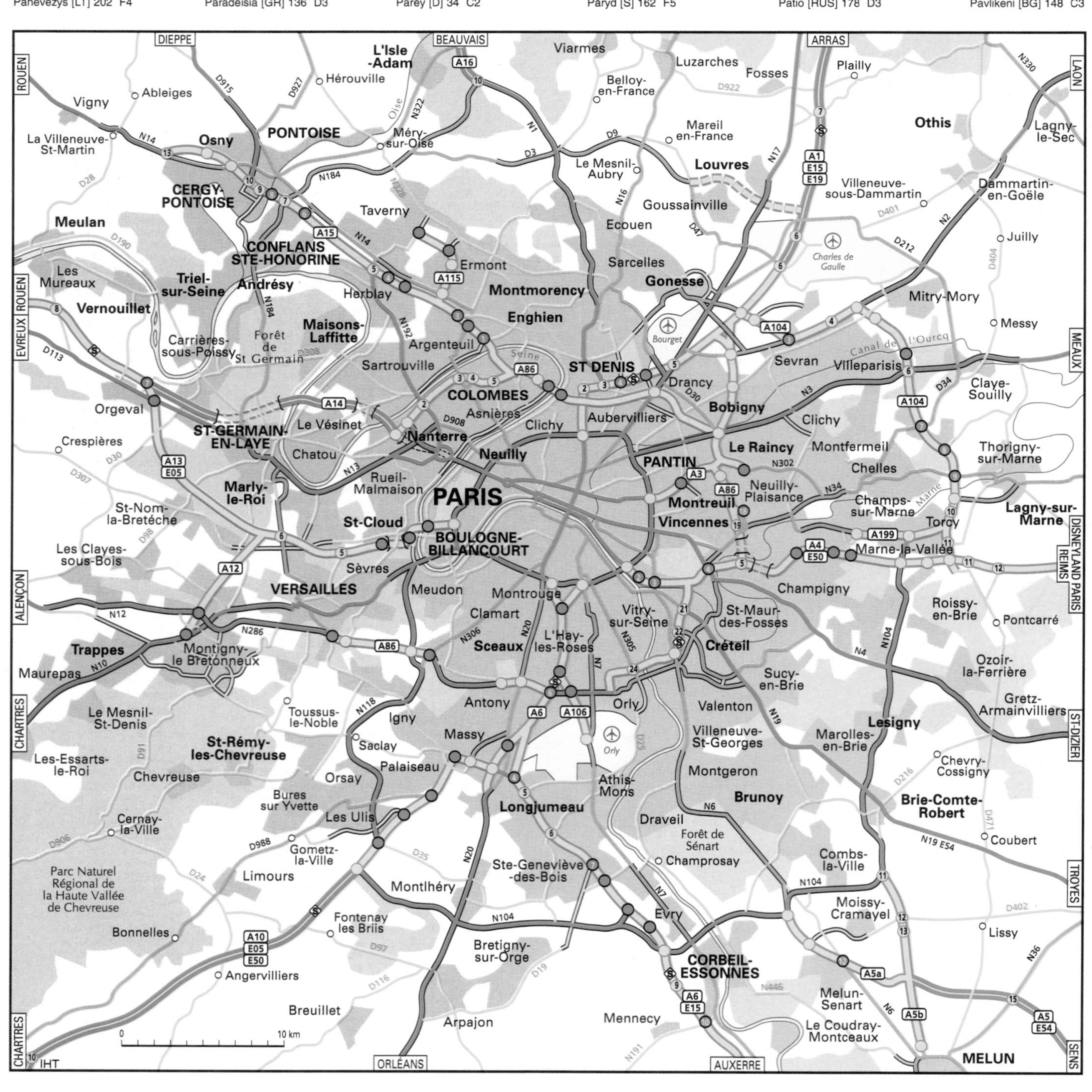
DIEPPE
BEAUVAIS
ARRAS
ROUEN
LAON
EVREUX ROUEN
MEAUX
ALENÇON
DISNEYLAND PARIS
REIMS
CHARTRES
ST-DIZIER
TROYES
SENS
ORLÉANS
AUXERRE
L'Isle -Adam
Viarmes
Luzarches
Fosses
Plailly
Hérouville
Ableiges
Vigny
Belloy-en-France
Othis
Lagny-le-Sec
La Villeneuve-St-Martin
Osny
PONTOISE
Méry-sur-Oise
Mareil en-France
Le Mesnil-Aubry
Louvres
CERGY-PONTOISE
Villeneuve-sous-Dammartin
Dammartin-en-Goële
Meulan
Taverny
Goussainville
Ecouen
Juilly
Charles de Gaulle
Les Mureaux
CONFLANS STE-HONORINE
Ermont
Sarcelles
Triel-sur-Seine
Andrésy
Montmorency
Gonesse
Vernouillet
Herblay
Mitry-Mory
Maisons-Laffitte
Enghien
Messy
Carrières-sous-Poissy
Forêt de St Germain
Argenteuil
Bourget
Sevran
Villeparisis
Canal de l'Ourcq
Sartrouville
ST DENIS
Drancy
Claye-Souilly
Orgeval
COLOMBES
Bobigny
Asnières
Le Vésinet
Clichy
Aubervilliers
Clichy
ST-GERMAIN-EN-LAYE
Nanterre
Crespières
Neuilly
Le Raincy
Montfermeil
Thorigny-sur-Marne
Chatou
PANTIN
Chelles
Marly-le-Roi
Rueil-Malmaison
PARIS
Neuilly-Plaisance
St-Nom-la-Bretèche
Montreuil
Champs-sur-Marne
Lagny-sur-Marne
St-Cloud
Vincennes
Torcy
BOULOGNE-BILLANCOURT
Les Clayes-sous-Bois
Marne-la-Vallée
Sèvres
VERSAILLES
Meudon
Champigny
Montrouge
Clamart
Vitry-sur-Seine
St-Maur-des-Fosses
Roissy-en-Brie
Pontcarré
Trappes
Montigny-le Bretonneux
Sceaux
L'Haÿ-les-Roses
Créteil
Maurepas
Sucy-en-Brie
Ozoir-la-Ferrière
Le Mesnil-St-Denis
Toussus-le-Noble
Antony
Orly
Valenton
Gretz-Armainvilliers
Igny
Lesigny
St-Rémy-les-Chevreuse
Massy
Villeneuve-St-Georges
Marolles-en-Brie
Les-Essarts-le-Roi
Saclay
Chevry-Cossigny
Palaiseau
Montgeron
Chevreuse
Orsay
Athis-Mons
Brunoy
Bures sur Yvette
Longjumeau
Brie-Comte-Robert
Cernay-la-Ville
Les Ulis
Draveil
Forêt de Sénart
Gometz-la-Ville
Coubert
Combs-la-Ville
Parc Naturel Régional de la Haute Vallée de Chevreuse
Limours
Ste-Geneviève-des-Bois
Champrosay
Montlhéry
Moissy-Cramayel
Evry
Bonnelles
Fontenay les Briis
Lissy
Bretigny-sur-Orge
CORBEIL-ESSONNES
Angervilliers
Melun-Senart
Breuillet
Mennecy
Le Coudray-Montceaux
Arpajon
MELUN
IHT
0
10 km

Pávlos [GR] 134 A5
Pavlovsk [RUS] 178 H5
Pavullo nel Frignano [I] 110 E4
Pavy [RUS] 200 H3
Pawłowiczki [PL] 50 E3
Paxoí [GR] 132 C3
Payerne [CH] 58 C6
Paymogo [E] 94 E4
Payrac [F] 66 G4
Pazardzhik [BG] 148 A6
Pazarköy [TR] 146 C6
Pazaryeri [TR] 146 G5
Pazin [HR] 112 D2
Pchelino [RUS] 178 F3
Peal de Becerro [E] 102 F2
Péaule [F] 40 E5
Peč [YU] 150 B5
Peccioli [I] 110 E6
Pechenga [RUS] 196 F3
Pechina [E] 102 G5
Pecica [RO] 76 G4
Pecineaga [RO] 148 G1
Pecka [YU] 154 F4
Peckelsheim [D] 32 E4
Pecorini a Mare [I] 124 A5
Pečory [RUS] 200 G3
Pec pod Sněžkou [CZ] 50 A2
Pécs [H] 76 B5
Pécsvárad [H] 76 B5
Pedaso [I] 116 D2
Pederobba [I] 72 E5
Pédio [GR] 142 D4
Pedráces / Pedratsches [I] 72 E3
Pedrafita do Cebreiro, Puerto– [E] 78 E4
Pedralba [E] 98 E4
Pedratsches / Pedráces [I] 72 E3
Pedraza [E] 88 G3
Pedreguer [E] 104 F1
Pedreira [E] 78 D2
Pedrera [E] 96 F3
Pedrizas, Puerto de las– [E] 102 C4
Pedro Abad [E] 102 D1
Pedro Andrés [E] 102 H2
Pedro Bernardo [E] 88 D5
Pedrógão [P] 86 C2
Pedrógão [P] 94 E3
Pedro Martínez [E] 102 F3
Pedro Muñoz [E] 96 G3
Pedrosillo el Ralo [E] 88 C3
Peebles [GB] 8 E4
Peel [GBM] 10 B1
Peenemünde [D] 20 E3
Peera [FIN] 192 F3
Péfkos [GR] 140 F5
Péfkos [GR] 128 D5
Pega [P] 86 G2
Pegau [D] 34 C6
Peggau [A] 74 D2
Pegli [I] 110 A3
Pegnitz [D] 46 H4
Pego [E] 104 F1
Pegões [P] 86 C6
Peguera [E] 104 D5
Pehčevo [MK] 128 H1
Pehlivanköy [TR] 146 B2
Peine [D] 32 G2
Peïra–Cava [F] 108 F4
Peiraías [GR] 134 C6
Peiss [D] 60 E5
Peissenberg [D] 60 D5
Peiting [D] 60 D5
Peitz [D] 34 F4
Pejo [I] 72 C3
Pekkala [FIN] 196 D8
Pelasgía [GR] 132 H4
Pełczyce [PL] 20 G6
Pelejaneta / La Pelechaneta [E] 98 F3
Pélekas [GR] 132 B2
Peletá [GR] 136 F4
Pelhřimov [CZ] 48 H5
Pelkosenniemi [FIN] 196 E7
Pélla [GR] 128 G4
Pellegrino Parmense [I] 110 C2
Pellegrue [F] 66 E4
Pellesmäki [FIN] 188 C2
Pellinge / Pellinki [FIN] 178 B5
Pellinki / Pellinge [FIN] 178 B5
Pello [FIN] 196 C7
Pello [S] 196 C7
Pellosniemi [FIN] 178 C1
Pelovo [BG] 148 A3
Pelplin [PL] 22 E4
Peltosalmi [FIN] 198 E6
Peltovuoma [FIN] 192 H4
Pélussin [F] 68 F3
Pembroke [GB] 12 D2
Peñacerrada [E] 82 G5
Penacova [P] 86 E2
Peñafiel [E] 88 F2
Penafiel [P] 80 C4
Peñaflor [E] 102 B1
Penaguiao [P] 80 D4
Peñalén [E] 90 B6
Peñalsordo [E] 96 C4
Penalva do Castelo [P] 80 D6
Penamacor [P] 86 G3
Peñaranda de Bracamonte [E] 88 D3
Peñaranda de Duero [E] 88 H2
Peñarroya–Pueblonuevo [E] 96 B5
Penarth [GB] 12 F3
Peñascosa [E] 96 H6
Peñas de San Pedro [E] 98 B6
Peñausende [E] 80 H5
Pendagí [GR] 132 F5
Pendálofo [GR] 132 E5
Pénde Vrísses [GR] 130 B4
Pendik [TR] 146 F3
Pendine [GB] 12 D2
Penedono [P] 80 E5
Penela [P] 86 D2
Penestin [F] 40 E5
Peniche [P] 86 B3
Penicuik [GB] 8 E3
Peñíscola / Peníscola [E] 98 G2
Peníscola / Peñíscola [E] 98 G2
Penkridge [GB] 10 D6
Penkum [D] 20 E5
Pennabilli [I] 110 H5
Penne [I] 116 D4
Penrith [GB] 8 E6
Penryn [GB] 12 C5
Pentálofos [GR] 128 E6
Pentrez–Plage [F] 40 B2
Penzance [GB] 12 B5
Penzberg [D] 60 D5
Penzlin [D] 20 D5
Pępowo [PL] 36 C4
Peqin [AL] 128 B3
Perachóra [GR] 134 A6
Perafita [P] 80 B3
Peraía [GR] 128 H5
Perälä [FIN] 186 B4
Peraleda del Zaucejo [E] 96 B4
Peralejos de las Truchas [E] 90 C6
Perales del Alfambra [E] 98 E1
Peralta [E] 84 B5
Pérama [GR] 140 D4
Pérama [GR] 132 D2
Peranka [FIN] 198 F3
Perä–Posio [FIN] 196 E8
Peräseinäjoki [FIN] 186 C4
Perast [YU] 152 D4
Perchauer Sattel [A] 74 B2
Perchtoldsdorf [A] 62 F5
Percy [F] 26 D4
Perdasdefogu [I] 118 D6
Perdifumo [I] 120 F5
Perdigão [P] 86 E4
Pérdika [GR] 132 D2
Pérdika [GR] 136 G2
Pérdika [GR] 132 C3
Pereda de Ancares [E] 78 F4
Peredo [P] 80 F4
Pereiaslav–Khmel'nyts'kyi [UA] 206 F2
Pereiro [P] 94 D5
Pereruela [E] 80 H5
Pereshchepyne [UA] 206 H3
Pereslavl' Zalesskiy [RUS] 204 F3
Peretu [RO] 148 B1
Perfugas [I] 118 C3
Perg [A] 62 C4
Pérgine Valsugana [I] 72 D4
Pergola [I] 112 B6
Perho [FIN] 186 E2
Periam [RO] 76 F5
Periana [E] 102 C4
Périers [F] 26 D3
Périgueux [F] 66 F3
Periš [YU] 150 E3
Perişoru [RO] 150 F1
Perissa [GR] 138 F5
Peristerá [GR] 130 B4
Perivóli [GR] 132 D1
Perjen Tunnel [A] 72 C1
Perkáta [H] 76 C2
Perkpolder [NL] 28 H1
Perleberg [D] 20 B6
Perlez [YU] 154 G1
Perly [PL] 24 C2
Përmet [AL] 128 C6
Pernå [FIN] 178 B4
Pernacha de Cima [P] 86 D5
Pernat [HR] 112 E2
Pernes [F] 106 H3
Pernes [P] 86 C4
Pernes–les–Fontaines [F] 106 H3
Pernik [BG] 150 F5
Perniö [FIN] 176 F5
Pernitz [A] 62 E5
Pernu [FIN] 196 E8
Péronne [F] 28 F5
Perosa Argentina [I] 70 C6
Pérouges [F] 68 G2
Perpignan [F] 92 G1
Perranporth [GB] 12 C4
Perros–Guirec [F] 40 D1
Persberg [S] 166 G2
Persenbeug [A] 62 D4
Pershagen [S] 168 D3
Pershore [GB] 12 H2
Perstorp [S] 158 C1
Perth [GB] 8 E2
Pertisau [A] 60 E6
Pertoča [SLO] 74 E3
Pertoúli [GR] 132 E2
Pertteli [FIN] 176 F4
Pertuis [F] 108 B4
Pertunmaa [FIN] 178 B1
Pertusa [E] 90 G3
Perúgia [I] 116 A2
Perushtica [BG] 148 B6
Perušić [HR] 112 G3
Péruwelz [B] 28 G3
Pervomais'k [UA] 206 E3
Pervomajskoje [RUS] 178 G3
Pesadas de Burgos [E] 82 F5
Pésaro [I] 112 B5
Pescaglia [I] 110 D5
Pescara [I] 116 D4
Pescasseroli [I] 116 C6
Péschici [I] 116 H5
Peschiera del Garda [I] 72 B6
Pescia [I] 110 E5
Pescina [I] 116 C5
Pescocostanzo [I] 116 D5
Pescolanciano [I] 116 D6
Pescopagano [I] 120 G3
Peshkëpija [AL] 128 B5
Peshkopi [AL] 128 C2
Peshtera [BG] 148 A6
Pesiökylä [FIN] 198 F3
Pesmes [F] 56 H4
Pesocani [MK] 128 D3
Pesochnyj [RUS] 178 H4
Peso da Régua [P] 80 D4
Pesoz [E] 78 F3
Pesqueza [E] 86 G4
Pessalompolo [FIN] 196 C8
Pessáni [GR] 130 G2
Pessin [D] 34 D2
Peštani [MK] 128 D4
Pestovo [RUS] 204 E2
Pešuriči [BIH] 152 E1
Peta [P] 86 C5
Petäiskylä [FIN] 198 G5
Petäjävesi [FIN] 186 F4
Petalídi [GR] 136 D4
Pétange [L] 44 E3
Peterborough [GB] 14 E2
Peterchurch [GB] 12 F2
Peterculter [GB] 6 F6
Peterhead [GB] 6 G5
Peterlee [GB] 10 F1
Petersdorf [D] 18 H2
Petersdorf [D] 20 B3
Petersfield [GB] 14 D5
Petershagen [D] 32 E2
Pétervására [H] 64 E5
Pethelinós [GR] 130 C3
Petikträsk [S] 190 H4
Petilia Policastro [I] 124 E5
Petkula [FIN] 196 D6
Petkus [D] 34 E3
Petlovača [YU] 154 F3
Petoússio [GR] 132 C2
Petra [E] 104 E5
Pétra [GR] 128 G6
Pétra [GR] 134 G2
Petralia Soprana [I] 126 E3
Petrálona [GR] 130 B5
Petraná [GR] 128 F5
Petrelë [AL] 128 B3
Petrella Tifernina [I] 116 E6
Petrer [E] 104 D2
Petreto–Bicchisano [F] 114 B5
Petrich [BG] 130 B2
Petrila [RO] 206 B5
Petrinja [HR] 154 A1
Petrodvorets [RUS] 178 G5
Pétrola [E] 98 C6
Petronell–Carnuntum [A] 62 G5
Petroşani [RO] 206 B5
Petrosino [I] 126 B3
Petrotá [GR] 146 A2
Petroússa [GR] 130 C2
Petrovac [YU] 152 E5
Petrovac [YU] 150 C1
Petrovaradin [YU] 154 F1
Petrovice [CZ] 48 F5
Petrovići [BIH] 152 B2
Petrovka [RUS] 178 F2
Petřvald [CZ] 50 E5
Petsákoi [GR] 132 F6
Petsikko [FIN] 196 D3
Pettenbach [A] 62 B5
Pettigo [GB] 2 E3
Petworth [GB] 14 D5
Peuerbach [A] 62 A4
Peura [FIN] 196 C8
Peurasuvanto [FIN] 196 D6
Pevensey [GB] 14 E6
Pewsey [GB] 12 H4
Peyrat–le–Chateaux [F] 66 H1
Peyrehorade [F] 84 D2
Peyrolles [F] 108 B4
Peyruis [F] 108 C3
Pézenas [F] 106 E4
Pezinok [SK] 62 G4
Pezoúla [GR] 130 E3
Pezuela de las Torres [E] 88 G6
Pfaffendorf [D] 46 G3
Pfaffenhausen [D] 60 C4
Pfaffenhofen [D] 60 E3
Pfäffikon [CH] 58 G5
Pfäffikon [CH] 58 G5
Pfafflar [A] 72 C1
Pfänder Tunnel [CH] 60 B6
Pfarrkirchen [D] 60 G3
Pfatter [D] 60 F2
Pfeffenhausen [D] 60 F3
Pforzheim [D] 46 C6
Pfreimd [D] 48 C5
Pfronten [D] 60 C6
Pfullendorf [D] 58 H3
Pfullingen [D] 58 H2
Pfundres / Fundres [I] 72 E2
Pfunds [A] 72 C2
Pfungstadt [D] 46 C4
Phalsbourg [F] 44 G5
Philippeville [B] 30 C6
Philippsreut [D] 62 A2
Philippsthal [D] 32 F6
Placenza [I] 70 H6
Piádena [I] 110 D1
Piaggine [I] 120 G4
Piana [F] 114 A4
Piana Crixia [I] 108 H2
Piana degli Albanesi [I] 126 C2
Pian Castagna [I] 108 H2
Pianella [I] 114 G1
Pianello Val Tidone [I] 70 G6
Piani Resinelli [I] 70 G4
Pianoro [I] 110 F4
Pias [P] 94 E3
Pias [P] 94 E2
Piaseczno [PL] 20 F6
Piaseczno [PL] 38 B3
Piaski [PL] 36 C4
Piaski [PL] 38 E6
Piastów [PL] 38 B3
Piaszczyna [PL] 22 C3
Piątek [PL] 36 G3
Piatra [RO] 148 B2
Piatra Neamţ [RO] 206 C4
Piatra Olt [RO] 150 G1
Piazza al Serchio [I] 110 D4
Piazza Armerina [I] 126 E4
Piazza Brembana [I] 70 H4
Piazzatorre [I] 70 H3
Piazzola sul Brenta [I] 72 D6
Pičan [HR] 112 E2
Picassent [E] 98 E5
Picerno [I] 120 G4
Pickering [GB] 10 G3
Pico [I] 120 C1
Picquigny [F] 28 D4
Piechowice [PL] 48 H1
Piecki [PL] 24 C4
Piedicavallo [I] 70 E4
Piedicroce [F] 114 C3
Piediluco [I] 116 B4
Piedimonte Etneo [I] 124 A8
Piedimonte Matese [I] 120 E2
Piedimulera [I] 70 E3
Piedrabuena [E] 96 E4
Piedrafita de Babia [E] 78 G4
Piedrahita [E] 88 C4
Piedralaves [E] 88 D5
Piedras Albas [E] 86 G4
Piekary Śląskie [PL] 50 F3
Pieksämäki [FIN] 188 C4
Pielavesi [FIN] 186 H1
Pieniężno [PL] 22 G3
Piennes [F] 44 E3
Pieńsk [PL] 34 G6
Pienza [I] 114 G2
Pierowall [GB] 6 G1
Pierre–Buffière [F] 66 G2
Pierre–de–Bresse [F] 56 H5
Pierrefitte [F] 44 D4
Pierrefitte–Nestalas [F] 84 E4
Pierrefonds [F] 42 G2
Pierrefort [F] 68 B4
Pierrelatte [F] 106 G2
Pierroton [F] 66 C3
Pieski [PL] 34 H2
Pieskowa Skala [PL] 50 H3
Piešťany [SK] 62 H3
Pieszyce [PL] 50 C2
Pietarsaari / Jakobstad [FIN] 198 B6
Pietragalla [I] 120 H3
Pietralba [F] 114 B3
Pietra Ligure [I] 108 G3
Pietralunga [I] 116 A1
Pietramelara [I] 120 D2
Pietraperzia [I] 126 E4
Pietrasanta [I] 110 D5
Pietrowice [PL] 50 D3
Pietrzwałd [PL] 22 G4
Pieve di Cadore [I] 72 F3
Pieve di Teco [I] 108 G4
Pievepelago [I] 110 E4
Pieve Santo Stéfano [I] 110 G6
Pigádi [GR] 132 H3
Pigés [GR] 132 E3
Pigi [GR] 132 F5
Pigna [I] 108 F4
Pihkala [FIN] 198 D5
Pihlajalahti [FIN] 188 E5
Pihlajavaarra [FIN] 188 H1
Pihlava [FIN] 176 C1
Pihtipudas [FIN] 186 F1
Piikkiö [FIN] 176 E4
Piipola [FIN] 198 D5
Piispa [FIN] 188 E1
Piispajärvi [FIN] 198 F3
Piittisjärvi [FIN] 196 D8
Pikalevo [RUS] 204 E1
Pila [I] 110 H2
Pila [I] 70 D4
Piła [PL] 22 B6
Pilar de la Mola [E] 104 C6
Pilas [E] 94 G6
Pilastri [I] 110 F2
Pilat–Plage [F] 66 B3
Pilés [GR] 140 H3
Pilgrimstad [S] 182 H3
Pili [GR] 134 B6
Pilica [PL] 50 H2
Pilio [GR] 134 B4
Pilis [H] 76 D1
Pilisvörösvár [H] 64 C6
Piliuona [LT] 202 F5
Pilviškiai [LT] 24 E1
Pilzno [PL] 52 C4
Pina de Ebro [E] 90 F4
Piñar [E] 102 E3
Pinarejos [E] 88 F3
Pinarellu [F] 114 B5
Pınarhisar [TR] 146 C2
Pınarköy [TR] 142 D2
Pınarlar [TR] 144 G6
Pincehely [H] 76 B3
Pińczów [PL] 52 B2
Pineda de la Sierta [E] 90 A1
Pineda de Mar [E] 92 F4
Pinerolo [I] 70 C6
Pineto [I] 116 D3
Piney [F] 44 B5
Pinhal Novo [P] 86 B5
Pinhel [P] 80 E6
Pinkafeld [A] 74 E1
Pinneberg [D] 18 F4
Pino [E] 78 H4
Pino [F] 114 C2
Pino do Val [E] 78 B2
Pinols [F] 68 D4
Piñor [E] 78 C4
Pinoso / el Pinós [E] 104 D2
Pinos Puente [E] 102 D3
Pinsk [BY] 204 A6
Pinsoro [E] 84 B6
Pintamo [FIN] 198 E3
Pinto [E] 88 F6
Pinwherry [GB] 8 C4
Pinzio [P] 80 E6
Pinzolo [I] 72 C4
Piòbbico [I] 110 H6
Piombino [I] 114 E2
Pionerskiy [RUS] 202 C5
Pionki [PL] 38 C5
Pionsat [F] 56 C6
Pióraco [I] 116 B2
Piossasco [I] 70 D6
Piotrkowice [PL] 52 B2
Piotrków Kujawski [PL] 36 F2
Piotrków Trybunalski [PL] 36 H5
Piotrovo [PL] 36 C2
Piotrów [PL] 38 E6
Piotrowice [PL] 38 C3
Piotta [CH] 70 F2
Piove di Sacco [I] 110 G1
Piovene–Rocchette [I] 72 D5
Pipriac [F] 40 F4
Piqeras [AL] 132 B1
Piqueras, Puerto de– [E] 90 B2
Piran [SLO] 72 H6
Piras [I] 118 E3
Pirdop [BG] 148 A4
Pirgadíkia [GR] 130 C5
Pirgí [GR] 134 G5
Piriac–sur–Mer [F] 40 D5
Pirin [BG] 130 B2
Pirkkala [FIN] 176 F1
Pirmasens [D] 44 H4
Pirna [D] 48 F1
Pirnmill [GB] 8 C3
Pirok [MK] 128 D1
Pirot [YU] 150 E4
Pirou–Plage [F] 26 D3
Pirovac [HR] 112 G6
Pirttikoski [FIN] 196 E8
Pirttikylä / Pörtom [FIN] 186 B3
Pirttiniemi [FIN] 198 C6
Pisa [I] 110 D5
Pisanets [BG] 148 D2
Pişchia [RO] 76 G5
Pisciotta [I] 120 F5
Písek [CZ] 48 F6
Pishcha [UA] 38 G4
Pisodéri [GR] 128 E4
Pisogne [I] 72 B5
Pisses [GR] 138 C2
Pissónas [GR] 134 C5
Pissos [F] 66 C4
Pistianá [GR] 132 D3
Pisticci [I] 122 D4
Pistóia [I] 110 E5
Pisz [PL] 24 C4
Pitäjänmäki [FIN] 198 D6
Piteå [S] 198 B3
Piteşti [RO] 206 C6
Pithiviers [F] 42 F5
Pitigliano [I] 114 G3
Pitkäjärvi [FIN] 176 F4
Pitkälahti [FIN] 188 C2
Pitlochry [GB] 8 E1
Pitomača [HR] 74 G5
Pitvaros [H] 76 F4
Pivka [SLO] 74 B6
Pivnica [HR] 74 H6
Piwniczna [PL] 52 C5
Pizarra [E] 102 B4
Pizzighettone [I] 70 H6
Pizzo [I] 124 D6
Pizzoli [I] 116 C4
Pjatihatki [UA] 206 G3
Pjätteryd [S] 162 C5
Plabennec [F] 40 B1
Plage de Pineto [F] 114 C3
Plagiá [GR] 130 G2
Plagiá [GR] 128 H3
Plaisance [F] 84 F2
Pláka [GR] 130 F6
Plakiás [GR] 140 D5
Plana [BIH] 152 D3
Planá [CZ] 48 D4
Planá nad Lužnicí [CZ] 48 G6
Plancios [I] 72 E3
Plancoët [F] 26 B4
Plandište [YU] 154 H1
Plan–du–Lac [F] 70 C2
Plánice [CZ] 48 E5
Planina [SLO] 74 B5
Planina [SLO] 74 D5
Planjane [HR] 154 A5
Plansee [A] 60 C6
Plasencia [E] 88 B5
Plasencia del Monte [E] 84 D6
Plaški [HR] 112 G2
Pláštóvce [SK] 64 C4
Plasy [CZ] 48 E4
Plataés [GR] 134 B6
Platamona Lido [I] 118 C3
Platamónas [GR] 128 H6
Platamónas [GR] 130 D3
Platanés [GR] 140 D4
Platánia [GR] 136 C3
Plataniá [GR] 134 B3
Plataniás [GR] 140 C4
Platanistós [GR] 134 D6
Plátanos [GR] 136 E3
Plátanos [GR] 140 B4
Plátanos [GR] 136 C2
Platariá [GR] 132 C2
Platerów [PL] 38 E2
Pláti [GR] 146 A2
Platì [I] 124 C7
Platiána [GR] 136 C2
Platígiali [GR] 132 D5
Platís [GR] 138 E2
Platja d'Aro [E] 92 G4
platja des Canar [E] 104 C5
Plátsa [GR] 136 E4
Plattling [D] 60 G3
Platýkampos [GR] 132 G2
Platýs Gialós [GR] 138 D3
Platystomo [GR] 132 F4
Plau [D] 20 B5
Plaue [D] 34 C2
Plauen [D] 48 C2
Plav [YU] 150 A5
Plavinas [LV] 200 E5
Plavna [YU] 150 E1
Plavsk [RUS] 204 F5
Playa Blanca [E] 100 E5
Playa de las Américas [E] 100 B5
Playa de San Juán [E] 104 E2
Pleaux [F] 68 A3
Plech [D] 46 H4
Pleinfeld [D] 46 G6
Plélan–le–Grand [F] 26 B6
Pleniţa [RO] 150 F1
Plentzia [E] 82 G3
Plépi [GR] 136 G2
Plešivec [SK] 64 E3
Plesse [F] 40 F5
Plestin–les–Grèves [F] 40 C1
Pleszew [PL] 36 E4
Pleternica [HR] 154 C1
Plettenberg [D] 32 C5
Pleumartin [F] 54 F4
Pleven [BG] 148 A3
Pleyben [F] 40 C2
Pliego [E] 104 B3
Plikáti [GR] 128 D6
Pliska [BG] 148 E2
Plitvice [HR] 112 G3
Plitvički Ljeskovac [HR] 112 G3
Pljevlja [YU] 152 E2
Ploaghe [I] 118 C3
Ploče [HR] 152 B3
Plochingen [D] 58 H1
Płock [PL] 36 H2
Ploërmel [F] 26 B6
Ploieşti [RO] 206 C6
Plomári [GR] 134 H3
Plombières–les–Bains [F] 58 C3
Plomin [HR] 112 E2
Plön [D] 18 G2
Plonéour Lanvern [F] 40 B3
Płońsk [PL] 38 A2
Plopii Slăviteşti [RO] 148 B2
Płoskinia [PL] 22 G2
Płoty [PL] 20 G4
Plouaret [F] 40 D2
Plouay [F] 40 C4
Ploubalay [F] 26 C4
Ploudalmézeau [F] 40 B1
Plouescat [F] 40 B1
Plougasnou [F] 40 C1
Plougastel–Daoulas [F] 40 B2
Plouguenast [F] 26 B5
Plouha [F] 26 A4
Plouigneau [F] 40 C2
Ploumanac'h [F] 40 D1
Plouray [F] 40 C3
Plovdiv [BG] 148 B6
Plozévet [F] 40 B3
Plumbridge [GB] 2 F2
Plungė [LT] 202 D4
Pluty [PL] 22 G2
Pluvigner [F] 40 D4
Plužine [BIH] 152 C2
Plužine [YU] 152 D2
Płużnica [PL] 22 E5
Plymouth [GB] 12 D5
Plympton [GB] 12 D5
Plytnica [PL] 22 B5
Plýtra [GR] 136 F5
Plyussa [RUS] 200 H2
Plzeň [CZ] 48 E4
Pnevo [RUS] 200 G3
Pniewo [PL] 38 C2
Pniewy [PL] 36 B2
Poarta de Fier a Transilvaniei [RO] 206 B5
Pobedino [RUS] 202 E5
Pobes [E] 82 G5
Pobiedziska [PL] 36 D2
Pobierowo [PL] 20 F3
Pobikry [PL] 38 E1
Pobladura de la Sierra [E] 78 F5
Pobra do Caramiñal / Puebla del Caramiñal [E] 78 B3
Počátky [CZ] 48 H6
Poceirão [P] 86 B6
Pochep [RUS] 204 D6

Pöchlarn [A] 62 D4
Počitelj [BIH] 152 C3
Pocking [D] 60 H4
Pocklington [GB] 10 G3
Pocrnje [BIH] 152 C3
Počuta [YU] 150 A2
Podari [RO] 150 G1
Podbořany [CZ] 48 E3
Podborovje [RUS] 200 G3
Poddębice [PL] 36 F4
Podd'sk [RUS] 204 F4
Poděbrady [CZ] 48 H3
Podence [P] 80 F4
Podensac [F] 66 D4
Podersdorf am See [A] 62 G5
Podgaje [PL] 22 B5
Podgarič [HR] 74 F6
Podgora [HR] 152 B2
Podgorač [HR] 154 D1
Podgorac [YU] 150 D2
Podgorica [YU] 152 E4
Podgorie [AL] 128 D4
Podgrad [SLO] 112 E1
Podgradec [AL] 128 D4
Podhalański [PL] 50 H4
Podivín [CZ] 62 G3
Podklasztorze [PL] 36 H5
Podkoren [SLO] 72 H3
Podkova [BG] 130 F2
Podkrepa [BG] 148 C6
Podkriváň [SK] 64 D3
Podnovlje [BIH] 154 D2
Podochóri [GR] 130 C4
Podogorá [GR] 132 E4
Podravska Slatina [HR] 74 H6
Podromanija [BIH] 152 D1
Podslon [BG] 148 D5
Podujevo [YU] 150 C4
Podunavci [YU] 150 B3
Podwilcze [PL] 20 H4
Poeldijk [NL] 16 C5
Poetto [I] 118 D7
Poggendorf [D] 20 D3
Poggibonsi [I] 110 E6
Póggio Rusco [I] 110 F2
Pöggstall [A] 62 D4
Pogonianí [GR] 132 C1
Pogoritsa [BG] 148 D3
Pogórze [PL] 50 D3
Pogrodzie [PL] 22 F2
Pohja [FIN] 176 G1
Pohja / Pojo [FIN] 176 F5
Pohja-Lankila [FIN] 188 F6
Pohjaslahti [FIN] 196 D8
Pohjaslahti [FIN] 186 E5
Pohjoislahti [FIN] 186 F4
Pohorelá [SK] 64 E2
Pohořelice [CZ] 62 F2
Poiana Braşov [RO] 206 C5
Poiana Mare [RO] 150 F2
Poibrene [BG] 148 A5
Pointe des Poulains [F] 40 C5
Poio / O Convento [E] 78 B4
Poirino [I] 70 D6
Poissons [F] 44 D6
Poitiers [F] 54 E4
Poix [F] 28 D5
Poix-Terron [F] 44 C2
Pojate [YU] 150 C2
Pojo / Pohja [FIN] 176 F5
Pokka [FIN] 196 C5
Pokój [PL] 50 E1
Pokrovs'ke [UA] 206 H3
Pokupsko [HR] 112 H1
Pol [E] 78 E3
Pola de Allande [E] 78 F3
Pola de Laviana [E] 82 B2
Pola de Lena [E] 78 H4
Pola de Siero [E] 78 H3
Pola de Somiedo [E] 78 G4
Połajewo [PL] 36 C1
Polán [E] 96 E2
Polanica-Zdrój [PL] 50 C3
Połaniec [PL] 52 C2
Polanów [PL] 22 B3
Polatsk [BY] 204 B4
Polcenigo [I] 72 F5
Połczno [PL] 22 C3
Połczyn-Zdrój [PL] 20 H4
Pölde [EST] 200 C3
Polegate [GB] 14 E6
Polesella [I] 110 G2
Polessk [RUS] 202 D5
Polgár [H] 64 G5
Polgárdi [H] 76 B2
Polianí [GR] 136 D3
Poliçan [AL] 128 C6
Poliçan [AL] 128 C5
Policastro Bussentino [I] 120 G5
Police [PL] 20 F5
Police nad Metují [CZ] 50 B2
Políchnitos [GR] 134 G2
Polička [CZ] 50 B5
Policoro [I] 122 D5
Polignano a Mare [I] 122 E3
Poligny [F] 58 A6
Polikárpi [GR] 128 F4
Polikástano [GR] 128 E5
Polikrayshte [BG] 148 C3
Polipótamo [GR] 128 E4
Políraho [GR] 128 F6
Polistena [I] 124 D7
Politiká [GR] 134 B4
Poljana [HR] 154 B1
Poljčane [SLO] 74 D4
Polkowice [PL] 36 B5
Pölläkkä [FIN] 188 E4
Pöllau [A] 74 E1
Polle [D] 32 F3
Pollença [E] 104 E4
Pollfoss [N] 180 E5
Polloch [GB] 6 B6
Polmak [N] 196 D2
Polná [CZ] 50 A5
Polohy [UA] 206 H4
Polomka [SK] 64 D2
Polop [E] 104 E2
Polperro [GB] 12 D5
Polski Gradets [BG] 148 D5
Polski Trŭmbesh [BG] 148 C3
Polsko Kosovo [BG] 148 C3
Poltava [UA] 206 G2
Põltsamaa [EST] 200 E2
Polusperä [FIN] 198 D5
Põlva [EST] 200 F3
Polvela [FIN] 188 E1
Polvijärvi [FIN] 188 F2
Polyany [RUS] 178 F4
Polýgyros [GR] 130 B5
Polýkastro [GR] 128 G3
Pomar [E] 90 G4
Pomarance [I] 114 F1
Pomarico [I] 122 D4
Pomarkku [FIN] 176 D1
Pombal [P] 86 D2
Pomellen [D] 20 E5
Pomeroy [GB] 2 F3
Pomézia [I] 116 A6
Pomezí nad Ohří [CZ] 48 C3
Pomigliano d'Arco [I] 120 E3
Pommersfelden [D] 46 G4
Pomorie [BG] 148 F4
Pompaples [CH] 70 B1
Pompei [I] 120 E3
Pompey [F] 44 E5
Pómpia [GR] 140 E5
Pomysk Mały [PL] 22 C3
Poncin [F] 68 H2
Ponferrada [E] 78 F5
Poniatowa [PL] 38 D6
Poniec [PL] 36 C4
Poniky [SK] 64 C3
Ponoarele [RO] 206 B6
Pons [F] 54 C6
Ponsa [FIN] 176 G1
Ponsacco [I] 110 E6
Pont [I] 70 C4
Pontacq [F] 84 E3
Ponta do Sol [P] 100 A3
Pontailler-sur-Saône [F] 56 H4
Pont-à-Mousson [F] 44 E4
Pontão [P] 86 D3
Pontarion [F] 54 H6
Pontarlier [F] 58 B6
Pontassieve [I] 110 F5
Pontaubault [F] 26 D4
Pont-Audemer [F] 26 G3
Pontaumur [F] 68 C2
Pont-Aven [F] 40 C3
Pont Canavese [I] 70 D4
Pont Cellier [F] 56 D5
Pontcharra [F] 70 A4
Pontchartrain [F] 42 E3
Pontchâteau [F] 40 E5
Pont-Croix [F] 40 B3
Pont-d'Ain [F] 68 G2
Pont-de-Briques [F] 28 D2
Pont-de-Dore [F] 68 D2
Pont-de-l'Arche [F] 28 B6
Pont-de-Roide [F] 58 C4
Pont-de-Salars [F] 68 B6
Pont-d'Espagne [F] 84 E4
Pont-de-Vaux [F] 56 G6
Ponte Arche [I] 72 C4
Ponteareas [E] 78 B5
Pontebba [I] 72 G3
Ponte-Caldelas [E] 78 B4
Ponteceso [E] 78 B2
Pontecesures / Enfesta [E] 78 B3
Pontechianale [I] 108 E2
Pontecorvo [I] 120 C1
Ponte da Barca [P] 78 B6
Pontedecimo [I] 110 B3
Ponte de Lima [P] 78 B6
Ponte della Venturina [I] 110 E4
Ponte dell'Olio [I] 110 C2
Pontedera [I] 110 E6
Ponte de Sôr [P] 86 D5
Pontedeume [E] 78 D2
Ponte di Legno [I] 72 B4
Ponte di Piave [I] 72 F5
Pontefract [GB] 10 F4
Ponteland [GB] 8 F6
Pontelandolfo [I] 120 E2
Ponte-Leccia [F] 114 B3
Pontelongo [I] 110 G1
Ponte nelle Alpi [I] 72 E4
Pont-en-Royans [F] 68 G5
Ponte Nuovo [F] 114 B3
Ponte Oliveras [E] 78 B2
Ponterwyd [GB] 10 B6
Ponte S. Pietro [I] 70 H4
Ponte Tresa [CH] 70 F3
Ponte Ulla [E] 78 C3
Pontevedra [E] 78 B4
Pontevico [I] 110 D1
Pontgibaud [F] 68 C2
Pontigny [F] 56 E1
Pontinia [I] 120 B1
Pontinvrea [I] 108 H3
Pontisméno [GR] 130 B3
Pontivy [F] 26 A5
Pont-l'Abbé [F] 40 B3
Pont-l'Evêque [F] 26 G3
Pontlevoy [F] 54 G2
Pontllanfraith [GB] 12 F2
Pontoise [F] 42 F3
Pontokómi [GR] 128 F5
Pontones [E] 102 G2
Pontoon [IRL] 2 C3
Pontorson [F] 26 D4
Pont-Réan [F] 26 C6
Pontremoli [I] 110 C3
Pontresina [CH] 72 A3
Pontrieux [F] 26 A3
Pontrilas [GB] 12 F2
Ponts [E] 92 C3
Pont-Scorff [F] 40 C4
Pont-St-Esprit [F] 106 G2
Pont-St-Martin [I] 70 D4
Pont-St-Vincent [F] 44 E5
Pont-sur-Yonne [F] 42 G5
Pontvallain [F] 42 B6
Pontypool [GB] 12 F2
Pontypridd [GB] 12 F2
Ponza [I] 120 B3
Poole [GB] 12 G5
Poperinge [B] 28 F2
Popina [BG] 148 E1
Popintsi [BG] 148 A5
Popoli [I] 116 D5
Popovaca [HR] 74 F6
Popovitsa [BG] 148 B6
Popovo [BG] 148 D3
Poppenhausen [D] 46 F3
Poppi [I] 110 G6
Poprad [SK] 64 E2
Popsko [BG] 130 G1
Populónia [I] 114 E2
Poraj [PL] 50 G2
Porasa [FIN] 176 G1
Porazava [BY] 24 G6
Porcuna [E] 102 D1
Porczyny [PL] 36 F4
Pordenone [I] 72 F5
Pordim [BG] 148 B3
Pordoi, Passo- [I] 72 E3
Poręba [PL] 50 G2
Poreč [HR] 112 D2
Porech'ye [BY] 24 G3
Pori [FIN] 176 D1
Porjus [S] 190 H1
Porkhov [RUS] 200 H3
Porkkala / Porkala [FIN] 176 G5
Porlock [GB] 12 E3
Pörnbach [D] 60 E3
Pornic [F] 54 B1
Pornichet [F] 40 E6
Porokylä [FIN] 198 F6
Poronin [PL] 52 A6
Póros [GR] 132 D5
Póros [GR] 136 G2
Póros [GR] 132 D6
Poroszló [H] 64 F6
Porozina [HR] 112 E2
Pórpi [GR] 130 F3
Porquerolles [F] 108 C6
Porrentruy [CH] 58 D4
Porretta Terme [I] 110 E4
Porsgrunn [N] 164 G3
Portacloy [IRL] 2 C2
Portadown [GB] 2 G4
Portaferry [GB] 2 H4
Portalegre [P] 86 E5
Portalrubio [E] 90 D6
Portardawe [GB] 12 E2
Portariá [GR] 132 H2
Portarlington [IRL] 2 E6
Port Askaig [GB] 8 B2
Portavogie [GB] 2 H4
Portbail [F] 26 D2
Port-Barcarès [F] 92 G1
Portbou [E] 92 G2
Port-Camargue [F] 106 F4
Port Charlotte [GB] 8 B2
Portchester [GB] 12 H5
Port-Cros [F] 108 D6
Port d'Adaia [E] 104 H4
Port-de-Bouc [F] 106 G5
Port de Pollença [E] 104 F4
Portel [P] 94 E2
Portela do Home [E] 78 B6
Port Ellen [GB] 2 H1
Portelo [P] 80 F3
Port-en-Bessin [F] 26 E3
Port Erin [GBM] 2 H5
Pórtes [GR] 136 G2
Port Eynon [GB] 12 E2
Portezuelo [E] 86 H4
Portglenone [GB] 2 G3
Port-Grimaud [F] 108 D5
Porth [GB] 12 F2
Porthcawl [GB] 12 E3
Port Henderson [GB] 6 C4
Porthmadog [GB] 10 B4
Porticcio [F] 114 A5
Portile de Fier [Eur.] 206 B6
Portilla de la Reina [E] 82 D3
Portillo [E] 88 E2
Portimão [P] 94 B5
Portimo [FIN] 196 D8
Portinatx [E] 104 C5
Portinho da Arrábida [P] 86 B6
Portishead [GB] 12 F3
Port-Joinville [F] 54 A2
Portlairge / Waterford [IRL] 4 E5
Port-la-Nouvelle [F] 106 D5
Port Laoise [IRL] 2 E6
Port-Leucate [F] 106 D6
Portloe [GB] 12 C5
Port-Louis [F] 40 C4
Portmahomack [GB] 6 E4
Portman [E] 104 C4
Port-Manech [F] 40 C4
Portmarnock [IRL] 2 F6
Port Mór [GB] 6 B5
Portnacroish [GB] 8 C1
Portnahaven [GB] 2 G1
Port nan Long / Newtonferry [GB] 6 A3
Port-Navalo [F] 40 D5
Port Nis / Port of Ness [GB] 6 C2
Porto [E] 78 E6
Porto [F] 114 A4
Porto [P] 80 B4
Porto Alto [P] 86 B5
Porto Azzurro [I] 114 E3
Portobello [I] 118 D2
Pórto Cárras [GR] 130 C6
Portocelo [E] 78 E1
Porto Ceresio [I] 70 F3
Porto Cervo [I] 118 E2
Porto Cesareo [I] 122 G5
Portochéli [GR] 136 F3
Porto Colom [E] 104 F5
Porto Corsini [I] 110 H3
Porto Covo [P] 94 B3
Porto Cristo [E] 104 F5
Porto da Cruz [P] 100 B3
Porto d'Áscoli [I] 116 D3
Porto de Mós [P] 86 C3
Porto di Levante [I] 124 A6
Porto do Son [E] 78 B3
Porto Empedocle [I] 126 D4
Porto Ércole [I] 114 F4
Portoferráio [I] 114 D2
Portofino [I] 110 B3
Port of Ness / Port Nis [GB] 6 C2
Porto Garibaldi [I] 110 H3
Pórto Germenó [GR] 134 B6
Portogruaro [I] 72 F5
Pórto Kágio [GR] 136 E5
Porto Levante [I] 110 H2
Pörtom / Pirttikylä [FIN] 186 B3
Portomaggiore [I] 110 G3
Portomarín [E] 78 D4
Porto Moniz [P] 100 A3
Portomouro [E] 78 C3
Porto Novo [P] 86 B4
Portopalo di Capo Passero [I] 126 G6
Porto-Pollo [F] 114 A5
Porto Potenza Picena [I] 116 C1
Portør [N] 164 F4
Pórto Ráfti [GR] 136 H1
Porto Recanati [I] 116 C1
Porto Rotondo [I] 118 E2
Portorož [SLO] 72 H6
Porto San Giorgio [I] 116 D2
Porto Sant'Elpidio [I] 116 C1
Porto Santo Stéfano [I] 114 F4
Portoscuso [I] 118 B7
Portos dos Fusos [P] 94 D5
Porto Tolle [I] 110 H2
Porto Tórres [I] 118 B3
Porto-Vecchio [F] 114 B6
Portovenere [I] 110 C4
Portpatrick [GB] 8 B5
Portreath [GB] 12 C5
Portree [GB] 6 B4
Portroe [IRL] 2 C6
Portrush [GB] 2 G2
Pörtschach [A] 74 B3
Portsmouth [GB] 12 H5
Port-Ste-Marie [F] 66 E5
Portstewart [GB] 2 G2
Port-St-Louis-du-Rhône [F] 106 G5
Port St. Mary [GB] 10 B2
Port-sur-Saône [F] 58 B3
Port Talbot [GB] 12 E2
Portuairk [GB] 6 B6
Portumna [IRL] 2 D6
Port-Vendres [F] 92 G2
Port William [GB] 8 C5
Porvoo / Borgå [FIN] 178 B4
Porządzie [PL] 38 C1
Porzuna [E] 96 E3
Posada [E] 78 H3
Posada [E] 82 D2
Posada [I] 118 E3
Posada de Valdeón [E] 82 C3
Posadas [E] 102 B1
Poschiavo [CH] 72 B3
Posedarje [HR] 112 G5
Poseidonía [GR] 138 D2
Poshnjë [AL] 128 B4
Posio [FIN] 196 E8
Positano [I] 120 E4
Possagno [I] 72 E5
Pössneck [D] 46 H2
Posta [I] 116 B4
Postbridge [GB] 12 D4
Postojna [SLO] 74 B6
Postoloprty [CZ] 48 E3
Postomino [PL] 22 B2
Posušje [BIH] 152 B1
Potamiá [GR] 130 E4
Potamiés [GR] 140 F4
Potamoí [GR] 130 D2
Potamós [GR] 136 F6
Potamós [GR] 140 A3
Potamoúla [GR] 132 E4
Potenza [I] 120 H4
Potenza Picena [I] 116 C1
Potes [E] 82 D3
Potoci [BIH] 152 C2
Potok [HR] 154 B1
Potok [PL] 52 D4
Potsdam [D] 34 D2
Pottenstein [A] 62 E5
Pottenstein [D] 46 H4
Potters Bar [GB] 14 E4
Pöttmes [D] 60 D3
Potworów [PL] 38 B5
Pouancé [F] 40 G5
Pougues-les-Eaux [F] 56 D4
Pouilly [F] 56 D3
Pouilly-en-Auxois [F] 56 F3
Pouilly-sous-Charlieu [F] 68 E1
Poulton-le-Fylde [GB] 10 D3
Poúnda [GR] 138 E3
Pourtalet, Col du- [Eur.] 84 D4
Poussu [FIN] 198 F2
Pouyastruc [F] 84 F3
Pouzauges [F] 54 C3
Považská Bystrica [SK] 64 B2
Poviglio [I] 110 E2
Povlja [HR] 152 A2
Póvoa [P] 94 E3
Póvoa de Lanhoso [P] 80 C3
Póvoa de Varzim [P] 80 B3
Powburn [GB] 8 F5
Powidz [PL] 36 E2
Powodow [PL] 36 G4
Poyatos [E] 98 C1
Poyntzpass [GB] 2 G4
Poyra [TR] 146 H5
Poyralı [TR] 146 C2
Poyrazdamları [TR] 144 E3
Poysdorf [A] 62 F3
Pöytyä [FIN] 176 E3
Poza de la Sal [E] 82 F5
Požarevac [YU] 206 A6
Pozazal, Puerto- [E] 82 E4
Požega [YU] 150 A2
Požeranje [YU] 150 C6
Poznań [PL] 36 C2
Pozo Alcón [E] 102 F3
Pozoblanco [E] 96 C5
Pozo-Cañada [E] 98 B6
Pozohondo [E] 98 B6
Pozondón [E] 98 D1
Poźrzadło [PL] 34 H3
Pozuel de Ariza [E] 90 C4
Pozuelo [E] 98 B5
Pozuelo de Zarzón [E] 86 H3
Pozzallo [I] 126 F6
Pozzomaggiore [I] 118 C4
Pozzuoli [I] 120 D3
Prabuty [PL] 22 F4
Prača [BIH] 152 D1
Prachatice [CZ] 62 B2
Pradelle [F] 68 G6
Pradelles [F] 68 D5
Prádena [E] 88 G4
Prades [F] 92 F1
Pradillo [E] 90 B1
Pradła [PL] 50 H2
Prado del Rey [E] 100 H4
Pradoluengo [E] 82 F6
Præstø [DK] 156 G4
Prägraten [A] 72 F2
Praha [CZ] 48 F3
Prahecq [F] 54 D4
Prahovo [YU] 150 E1
Praia a Mare [I] 120 G6
Praia da Barra [P] 80 B5
Praia da Vieira [P] 86 C2
Praia de Mira [P] 80 A5
Praia Grande [P] 86 A5
Praiano [I] 120 E4
Praias-Sado [P] 86 B6
Praisós [GR] 140 G5
Prakovce [SK] 64 F2
Prali [I] 70 C6
Pralognan-la-Vanoise [F] 70 B4
Prámanta [GR] 132 D2
Pranjani [YU] 150 B2
Prapatnica [HR] 116 H1
Prassiá [GR] 132 E3
Prassies [GR] 140 D4
Praszka [PL] 36 F6
Prat de Compte [E] 90 G6
Pratella [I] 120 D1
Prati di Tivo [I] 116 C4
Prato [I] 110 E5
Prats de Lluçanès [E] 92 E3
Prats-de-Mollo-la-Preste [F] 92 F2
Prauthoy [F] 56 H3
Pravdinsk [RUS] 22 H2
Pravets [BG] 150 G4
Pravia [E] 78 G3
Pravlov [CZ] 62 F2
Préchac [F] 66 D4
Prečno [HR] 74 F6
Précy-sous-Thil [F] 56 F3
Predappio [I] 110 G4
Predazzo [I] 72 D4
Preddvor [SLO] 74 B4
Predeal [RO] 206 C5
Predejane [YU] 150 E4
Predel [SLO] 72 H4
Predeşti [RO] 150 F1
Preding [A] 74 D3
Predlitz [A] 74 B2
Predoi / Prettau [I] 72 E2
Pré-en-Pail [F] 26 F5
Preesall [GB] 10 D3
Preetz [D] 18 G2
Pregarten [A] 62 C4
Preili [LV] 200 F6
Prekal [AL] 150 A6
Preko [HR] 112 G5
Prelog [HR] 74 F4
Přelouč [CZ] 48 H4
Prémery [F] 56 D3
Premià de Mar [E] 92 E4
Premnitz [D] 34 C2
Prenjas [AL] 128 C3
Prenzlau [D] 20 E5
Přerov [CZ] 50 D5
Prerow [D] 20 C2
Preselentsi [BG] 148 G2
Preševo [YU] 150 D6
Presicce [I] 122 G6
Prešov [SK] 64 G2
Pressac [F] 54 F5
Pressath [D] 48 B4
Pressbaum [A] 62 E4
Prestatyn [GB] 10 C4
Pré St-Didier [I] 70 C3
Presteigne [GB] 12 F1
Prestestranda [N] 164 F3
Prestfoss [N] 170 G5
Přeštice [CZ] 48 D5
Preston [GB] 10 D3
Prestwick [GB] 8 C4
Prettau / Predoi [I] 72 E2
Prettin [D] 34 D4
Pretzsch [D] 34 D4
Preuilly-sur-Claise [F] 54 G3
Préveranges [F] 56 B5
Préveza [GR] 132 D4
Priaranza del Bierzo [E] 78 F5
Pribeta [SK] 64 B5
Priboj [BIH] 154 E3
Priboj [YU] 152 E2
Příbor [CZ] 50 E5
Príbovce [SK] 64 C2
Příbram [CZ] 48 F5
Přibyslav [CZ] 50 A5
Prichsenstadt [D] 46 F4
Pridvorci [BIH] 152 C2
Pridvorica [YU] 150 B3
Priego [E] 90 B6
Priego de Córdoba [E] 102 D3
Priekulė [LT] 202 D4
Priekule [LV] 200 B6
Priekuli [LV] 200 E4
Prien [D] 60 F5
Prienai [LT] 24 F1
Prievidza [SK] 64 B3
Prignano Cilento [I] 120 F5
Prigrevica [YU] 76 C6
Prijeboj [HR] 112 G3
Prijedor [BIH] 154 B2
Prijepolje [YU] 150 A3
Prilep [MK] 128 E2
Prilike [YU] 150 A3
Priluka [BIH] 152 B1
Přimda [CZ] 48 C4
Primel-Trégastel [F] 40 C1
Primolano [I] 72 D5
Primorsk [RUS] 22 G1
Primorsk [RUS] 178 F4
Primorsko [BG] 148 F5
Primor'ye [RUS] 202 C5
Primošten [HR] 116 H1
Primstal [D] 44 G3
Princes Risborough [GB] 14 D3
Princetown [GB] 12 D4
Prínos [GR] 130 E4
Priolo Gargallo [I] 126 G4
Prioro [E] 82 C3
Priozersk [RUS] 178 G1
Prirečnyj [RUS] 196 F4
Priseltsi [BG] 148 F3
Prislop, Pasul- [RO] 206 C4
Prisoje [BIH] 152 B1
Prissac [F] 54 G4
Priština [YU] 150 C5
Pritzerbe [D] 34 C2
Pritzier [D] 18 H5
Pritzwalk [D] 20 B5
Privas [F] 68 F5
Priverno [I] 120 C1
Privlaka [HR] 112 F4
Privlaka [HR] 154 E2
Prizna [HR] 112 F3
Prizren [YU] 150 B6
Prizzi [I] 126 D3
Prnalija [MK] 128 G1
Prnjavor [BIH] 154 C2
Prnjavor [YU] 154 F3
Probištip [MK] 128 F1
Probstzella [D] 46 H2
Prochowice [PL] 36 B6
Prodromós [GR] 132 H5
Proença-a-Nova [P] 86 E3
Profítis [GR] 130 B4
Profondeville [B] 30 D5
Progled [BG] 130 E1
Prohor Pčinjski [YU] 150 D6
Prókhoma [GR] 128 H4
Prokópi [GR] 134 B4
Prokuplje [YU] 150 D4
Prolaz [BG] 148 D3
Promachónas [GR] 130 B2
Prómahi [GR] 128 F3
Promna [PL] 38 B4
Pronsfeld [D] 30 F6
Propriano [F] 114 A5
Prosenik [BG] 148 F4
Prosotsáni [GR] 130 C3
Prostějov [CZ] 50 C5
Prószków [PL] 50 E2
Proszowice [PL] 52 B3
Próti [GR] 130 C3
Protiči [BIH] 154 B4
Protivín [CZ] 48 F6
Protoklíssio [GR] 130 H2
Prötzel [D] 34 F2
Prousós [GR] 132 E4
Provadiya [BG] 148 F3

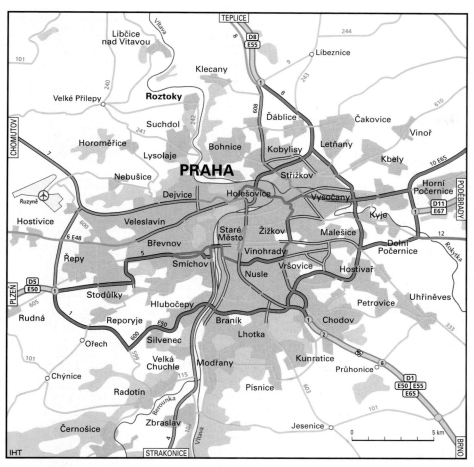

Provins [F] 42 H5
Prozor [BIH] 152 C1
Pruchnik [PL] 52 F4
Prudhoe [GB] 8 F6
Prudnik [PL] 50 D3
Prügy [H] 64 G4
Prüm [D] 30 F6
Pruna [E] 102 A3
Prundu [RO] 148 D1
Prunete [F] 114 C4
Prunetta [I] 110 E5
Prunn [D] 60 E2
Prusice [PL] 36 C5
Pruszcz [PL] 22 D5
Pruszcz Gdański [PL] 22 E3
Pruszków [PL] 38 B3
Pruzhany [BY] 38 H1
Pruzhicy [RUS] 178 F6
Pryluky [UA] 206 F2
Przasnysz [PL] 24 B6
Przechlewo [PL] 22 C4
Przedbórz [PL] 36 H6
Przedecz [PL] 36 F3
Przełęk [PL] 50 D3
Przemków [PL] 36 A5
Przemyšl [PL] 52 F4
Przewale [PL] 52 G2
Przeworsk [PL] 52 E3
Przezmark [PL] 22 F4
Przybiernów [PL] 20 F4
Przybychowo [PL] 36 C1
Przylesie [PL] 50 D2
Przysucha [PL] 38 B5
Przyszowa [PL] 52 B5
Przytoczna [PL] 36 A2
Przytoczno [PL] 38 D4
Przytyk [PL] 38 B5
Przywory [PL] 50 E2
Pšaca [MK] 150 E6
Psachná [GR] 134 B4
Psará [GR] 134 F4
Psarádes [GR] 128 D4
Psarshai [BY] 202 H6
Psáthi [GR] 138 D4
Psathópyrgos [GR] 132 F5
Psathotópi [GR] 132 D3
Psihikó [GR] 132 G2
Psihró [GR] 140 F5
Pskov [RUS] 200 G3
Pszczew [PL] 36 A2
Pszczyna [PL] 50 G4
Pteléa [GR] 130 D2
Ptolemáida [GR] 128 F5
Ptuj [SLO] 74 E4
Ptujska Gora [SLO] 74 E4
Puchberg [A] 62 E5
Púchov [SK] 50 F6
Pučišća [HR] 152 A2
Puck [PL] 22 D1
Puçol [E] 98 F4
Pudasjärvi [FIN] 198 E3
Puddletown [GB] 12 F5
Puebla de Alcocer [E] 96 C3
Puebla de Don Fadrique [E] 102 H2
Puebla de Don Rodrigo [E] 96 D3
Puebla de Guzmán [E] 94 E4
Puebla de la Calzada [E] 94 G1
Puebla de la Reina [E] 94 H2
Puebla del Brollón / A Pobra de Brollón [E] 78 D4
Puebla del Caramiñal / Pobra do Caramiñal [E] 78 B3
Puebla de Lillo [E] 82 C3
Puebla del Maestre [E] 94 H4
Puebla de Obando [E] 86 G6
Puebla de Sanabria [E] 80 G3
Puebla de Vallés [E] 88 G4
Pueblica de Valverde [E] 80 H4
Puente Almuhey [E] 82 C4
Puente de Domingo Flórez [E] 78 E5
Puente de Génave [E] 96 G6
Puente de Montañana [E] 92 B2
Puente Genil [E] 102 C2
Puente la Reina / Gares [E] 84 B4
Puente la Reina de Jaca [E] 84 D5
Puentelarra [E] 82 G5
Puentes de García Rodríguez / As Pontes de Garcá Rodríguez [E] 78 D2
Puente Viesgo [E] 82 E3
Puerto Banús [E] 102 A5
Puerto Castilla [E] 88 C5
Puerto de Bejar [E] 88 B4
Puerto de Itziar [E] 82 H4
Puerto de la Cruz [E] 100 B5
Puerto del Rosario [E] 100 E5
Puerto de Mazarrón [E] 104 C4
Puerto de Santa Cruz [E] 96 B2
Puerto de San Vicente [E] 96 C2
Puerto Lápice [E] 96 F3
Puertollano [E] 96 E5
Puerto Lumbreras [E] 104 A4
Puerto Real [E] 100 F4
Puerto Rey [E] 104 A5
Puertoserrano [E] 100 H3
Puffendorf [D] 30 F4
Puget-sur-Argens [F] 108 D5
Puget-Théniers [F] 108 E4
Puget-Ville [F] 108 C5
Pugnochiuso [I] 116 H6
Puhos [FIN] 188 F4
Puhos [FIN] 198 E3
Puig [E] 98 F4
Puigcerdà [E] 92 E1
Puig-reig [E] 92 E3
Puiseaux [F] 42 F5
Puivert [F] 106 B5
Pukavik [S] 158 E1
Pukë [AL] 128 B1
Pukiš [BIH] 154 E3
Pukkila [FIN] 178 B3
Pula [HR] 112 D3
Pula [I] 118 C7
Puławy [PL] 38 D5
Pulborough [GB] 14 D5
Pulgar [E] 96 E2
Pulju [FIN] 192 H4
Pulkau [A] 62 E3
Pulkkila [FIN] 198 D5
Pulkovo [RUS] 178 H5
Pulpí [E] 104 B4
Pulsa [FIN] 178 D2
Pulsnitz [D] 34 F6
Pułtusk [PL] 38 B1
Pumpėnai [LT] 202 F4
Punkalaidun [FIN] 176 E2
Punta Ala [I] 114 E2
Punta de Moraira [E] 104 F2
Puntagorda [E] 100 A5
Punta Križa [HR] 112 E3
Punta Marina [I] 110 H4
Punta Prima [E] 104 H5
Punta Umbría [E] 94 E6
Punxin [E] 78 C5
Puokio [FIN] 198 E4
Puolanka [FIN] 198 E4
Purbach [A] 62 F5
Purchena [E] 102 G4
Pürgg [A] 62 B6
Purgstall [A] 62 D5
Purkersdorf [A] 62 E4
Purmerend [NL] 16 D4
Purmojärvi [FIN] 186 D2
Purnumukka [FIN] 196 D5
Purullena [E] 102 F4
Pŭrvomay [BG] 148 C6
Puša [LV] 200 G6
Pushkinskiye Gory [RUS] 200 H4
Puškin [RUS] 178 H5
Puškino [RUS] 204 F4
Püspökladány [H] 76 G1
Pustevny [CZ] 50 E5
Pustków [PL] 52 D3
Pustoška [RUS] 204 C4
Pusula [FIN] 176 G4
Puszczykowo [PL] 36 C3
Pusztamonostor [H] 64 D6
Pusztaszemes [H] 76 A3
Putaja [FIN] 176 E1
Putanges-Pont-Ecrepin [F] 26 F5
Putbus [D] 20 D2
Putignano [I] 122 E3
Putikko [FIN] 188 F5
Putim [CZ] 48 F6
Putinci [YU] 154 G2
Putineiu [RO] 148 C1
Putineiu [RO] 148 B2
Putlitz [D] 20 B5
Putnok [H] 64 E4
Puttelange [F] 44 G4
Putten [NL] 16 E4
Puttgarden [D] 20 A2
Putyvl' [UA] 204 E7
Putzu Idu [I] 118 B5
Puumala [FIN] 188 E6
Puurmani [EST] 200 F2
Puy de Dôme [F] 68 C2
Puy-Guillaume [F] 68 D2
Puylaurens [F] 106 B3
Puy-l'Evêque [F] 66 F5
Puymorens, Col de- [F] 92 E1
Pvriatyn [UA] 206 F2
Pwllheli [GB] 10 B4
Pyhäjärvi [FIN] 178 E6
Pyhajärvi [FIN] 196 D7
Pyhäjoki [FIN] 198 C5
Pyhäkylä [FIN] 198 F3
Pyhältö [FIN] 178 D3
Pyhämaa [FIN] 176 C3
Pyhäntä [FIN] 198 E5
Pyhäntaka [FIN] 178 B2
Pyhäranta [FIN] 176 C3
Pyhäsalmi [FIN] 198 E6
Pyhäselkä [FIN] 188 F3
Pyhtää / Pyttis [FIN] 178 C4
Pyla-sur-Mer [F] 66 B3
Pylí [GR] 142 B3
Pýli [GR] 132 E2
Pylkönmäki [FIN] 186 F3
Pýlos [GR] 136 C4
Pyntäinen [FIN] 186 B6
Pyrgakia [GR] 138 F3
Pýrgoi [GR] 128 F4
Pýrgos [GR] 136 C2
Pýrgos [GR] 140 E5
Pýrgos [GR] 144 C5
Pýrgos Diroú [GR] 136 E5
Pyrsógianni [GR] 128 D6
Pyrzyce [PL] 20 F6
Pyšely [CZ] 48 G4
Pyskowice [PL] 50 F3
Pytalovo [RUS] 200 G4
Pythagóreon [GR] 142 B1
Pyttis / Pyhtää [FIN] 178 C4
Pyzdry [PL] 36 D3

Q

Quadri [I] 116 D5
Quakenbrück [D] 18 C6
Quarré-les-Tombes [F] 56 F3
Quarteira [P] 94 C5
Quartu Sant'Elena [I] 118 D7
Quebradas [P] 86 C4
Quedlinburg [D] 34 A4
Queluz [P] 86 B5
Quercamps [F] 28 E2
Quercianella [I] 110 D6
Querença [P] 94 C5
Querfurt [D] 34 B5
Quesada [E] 102 F2
Questembert [F] 40 E5
Quettehou [F] 26 E2
Quiberon [F] 40 C5
Quickborn [D] 18 F4
Quillan [F] 106 B5
Quimper [F] 40 B3
Quimperlé [F] 40 C4
Quinéville [F] 26 E2
Quingey [F] 58 B5
Quintana de la Serena [E] 96 B3
Quintana del Castillo [E] 78 G5
Quintana del Puente [E] 82 D6
Quintanaortuño [E] 82 E5
Quintanar de la Orden [E] 96 G3
Quintanar de la Sierra [E] 90 A2
Quintanar del Rey [E] 98 B4
Quintana Redonda [E] 90 B3
Quintanilha [P] 80 G4
Quintanilla de las Viñas [E] 88 H1
Quintanilla de Onésimo [E] 88 F2
Quintanilla-Sobresierra [E] 82 E5
Quintin [F] 26 A4
Quinto [E] 90 F4
Quiroga [E] 78 E5
Quissac [F] 106 F3
Qyteti Stalin [AL] 128 B4

R

Rââ [S] 156 H2
Raab [A] 62 A4
Raabs an der Thaya [A] 62 D2
Raahe [FIN] 198 C4
Rääkkylä [FIN] 188 F3
Raalte [NL] 16 F4
Raanujärvi [FIN] 196 C7
Raattama [FIN] 192 H4
Rab [HR] 112 F3
Rabac [HR] 112 E2
Rábade [E] 78 D3
Rábafüzes [H] 74 F2
Rabastens [F] 106 B2
Rabastens-de-Bigorre [F] 84 F3
Rabat [M] 126 C6
Rábatamasi [H] 62 G6
Rabbalshede [S] 166 C5
Rabí [CZ] 48 E6
Rabisha [BG] 150 E2
Rabka [PL] 50 H5
Rabsztyn [PL] 50 H3
Rača [SK] 62 G4
Rača [YU] 150 C1
Rača [YU] 150 C4
Racalmuto [I] 126 D4
Racconigi [I] 108 G2
Ráches [GR] 132 H4
Raciąż [PL] 36 H1
Raciażek [PL] 36 F1
Racibórz [PL] 50 E4
Ráckeve [H] 76 C2
Rackwick [GB] 6 F2
Racławice [PL] 52 B3
Rączki [PL] 22 G5
Raczki [PL] 24 E3
Råda [S] 166 F1
Radalj [YU] 154 E3
Radashkovichy [BY] 204 B5
Rădăuţi [RO] 206 C4
Radawnica [PL] 22 B5
Radcliffe-on-Trent [GB] 10 F5
Raddusa [I] 126 F3
Rade [D] 18 F4
Råde [N] 166 B3
Radeberg [D] 34 F6
Radebeul [D] 34 E6
Radeburg [D] 34 E6
Radeče [SLO] 74 D5
Radęcin [PL] 20 H6
Radegast [D] 34 C4
Radenci [SLO] 74 E3
Radenthein [A] 72 H3
Radevormwald [D] 30 H4
Radimlje [BIH] 152 C3
Radko Dimitrievo [BG] 148 E3
Radków [PL] 50 B2
Radlje ob Dravi [SLO] 74 D3
Radmirje [SLO] 74 C4
Radna [RO] 76 H4
Radnevo [BG] 148 D5
Radnica [PL] 34 H3
Radnice [CZ] 48 E4
Radolfzell [D] 58 G4
Radom [PL] 38 C5
Radomin [PL] 22 F6
Radomir [BG] 150 F5
Radomiru [RO] 150 G1
Radomsko [PL] 36 G6
Radomyšl Wielki [PL] 52 C3
Radošina [SK] 64 A3
Radošovce [SK] 62 G3
Radostowo [PL] 22 H3
Radoszyce [PL] 38 A6
Radotín [CZ] 48 F4
Radovanu [RO] 150 F1
Radovets [BG] 146 A1
Radoviš [MK] 128 G2
Radovljica [SLO] 74 B4
Radowo Wielkie [PL] 20 G4
Radstadt [A] 72 H1
Radstock [GB] 12 G3
Radujevac [YU] 150 E1
Radun' [BY] 24 H3
Radviliškis [LT] 202 F4
Radymno [PL] 52 F4
Radzanów [PL] 22 G6
Radziądz [PL] 36 C5
Radziejów [PL] 36 F2
Radziwie [PL] 36 G2
Radzymin [PL] 38 B2
Radzyn Chełmiński [PL] 22 E5
Radzyń Podlaski [PL] 38 E4
Raesfeld [D] 16 G6
Raffadali [I] 126 D4
Rafína [GR] 134 C6
Rafsbotn [N] 192 G1
Ragaciems [LV] 200 D5
Ragama [E] 88 D3
Ragana [LV] 200 E5
Rågeleje [DK] 156 G1
Raglan [GB] 12 F2
Råglanda [S] 166 E3
Ragusa [I] 126 F5
Raguva [LT] 202 F4
Rahachow [BY] 204 C6
Raharney [IRL] 2 E5
Rahden [D] 32 E2
Råholt [N] 172 C5
Rain [D] 60 D2
Raippaluoto / Replot [FIN] 186 A2
Räisälä [FIN] 196 E7
Raisio [FIN] 176 D4
Raistakka [FIN] 196 E8
Raivala [FIN] 186 C5
Raja-Jooseppi [FIN] 196 E5
Rajamäki [FIN] 176 G4
Rajë [AL] 150 A6
Rajec [SK] 64 B2
Rajecké Teplice [SK] 64 B2
Rajgród [PL] 24 E4
Rajka [H] 62 G5
Raka [SLO] 74 D5
Rakamaz [H] 64 G4
Rakhiv [UA] 206 C3
Rakitnica [BG] 148 C5
Rakitovo [BG] 148 A6
Rakkestad [N] 166 C2
Rákóczifalva [H] 76 E2
Rakoniewice [PL] 36 B3
Rákos [H] 76 F4
Rakoszyce [PL] 36 C6
Rakovica [HR] 112 G2
Rakovitsa [BG] 150 E2
Rakovník [CZ] 48 E3
Rakovski [BG] 148 B5
Raków [PL] 52 C2
Rakvere [EST] 200 F1
Ralja [YU] 154 G3
Ramacastañas [E] 88 D5
Ramacca [I] 126 F4
Ramales de la Victoria [E] 82 F3
Ramallosa [E] 78 B5
Ramallosa / Teo [E] 78 C3
Ramberg [N] 192 B4
Rambervillers [F] 44 F6
Rambin [D] 20 D2
Rambouillet [F] 42 E4
Ramirás [E] 78 C5
Ramkvilla [S] 162 E4
Ramljane [HR] 154 A5
Rammen [S] 166 F1
Ramnäs [S] 168 B2
Ramsau [A] 72 H1
Ramsberg [S] 166 H2
Ramsele [S] 184 D1
Ramsey [GB] 14 F2
Ramsey [GBM] 8 C6
Ramsgate [GB] 14 G5
Rämshyttan [S] 172 H5
Ramsjö [S] 184 C5
Ramstein [D] 44 H3
Ramsund [N] 192 D4
Ramvik [S] 184 F3
Ramygala [LT] 202 F4
Råna [N] 164 C5
Ranalt [A] 72 D2
Randaberg [N] 164 A3
Randalstown [GB] 2 G3
Randan [F] 68 D1
Randazzo [I] 124 A8
Randdalen [S] 182 F5
Randen [N] 180 G5
Randers [DK] 160 D5
Randín [E] 78 C6
Randsundet [S] 182 E5
Randsverk [N] 180 G6
Råneå [S] 198 B2
Rânes [F] 26 F5
Rangstrup [DK] 156 C3
Rankinen [FIN] 198 D4
Rankweil [A] 58 H5
Rannoch Station [GB] 8 D1
Ransta [S] 168 C2
Rantasalmi [FIN] 188 E4
Rantsila [FIN] 198 D4
Ranua [FIN] 198 D2
Ranum [DK] 160 D4
Raon-l'Etape [F] 44 F6
Rapallo [I] 110 B3
Räpina [EST] 200 G3
Rapla [EST] 200 D2
Rapness [GB] 6 G1
Rapolla [I] 120 G3
Raposa [P] 86 C5
Rapperswil [CH] 58 G5
Rappottenstein [A] 62 D3
Rapsáni [GR] 132 G1
Raron [CH] 70 E2
Raša [HR] 112 E2
Rascafría [E] 88 F4
Raseiniai [LT] 202 E4
Rasharkin [GB] 2 G2
Rasines [E] 82 F3

Rasivaara [FIN] 188 F3
Raška [YU] 150 B4
Rasktinkylä [FIN] 198 G5
Rasná [CZ] 48 H6
Rasovo [BG] 150 F2
Rasquera [E] 90 H6
Rast [RO] 150 F2
Rastatt [D] 46 B6
Råsted [DK] 160 D5
Rastede [D] 18 C5
Rastenfeld [A] 62 D3
Rasteš [MK] 128 D1
Rasti [FIN] 196 C6
Rastošnica [BIH] 154 E3
Rasueros [E] 88 D3
Raszków [PL] 36 D4
Rätansbyn [S] 182 G4
Rateče [SLO] 72 H3
Ratekau [D] 18 G3
Rathangen [IRL] 2 E6
Rathcoole [IRL] 2 F6
Rathcormack [IRL] 4 D5
Rathdrum [IRL] 4 G4
Rathenow [D] 34 C2
Rathfriland [GB] 2 G4
Rathkeale [IRL] 4 C3
Rath Luirc / Charleville [IRL] 4 C4
Rathmelton [IRL] 2 F2
Rathmolyon [IRL] 2 F5
Rathmullan / Rathmullen [IRL] 2 F2
Rathmullen / Rathmullan [IRL] 2 F2
Rathnew [IRL] 4 G4
Rathvilty [IRL] 4 F4
Ratingen [D] 30 G3
Ratne [UA] 38 H4
Ratten [A] 74 E1
Rattenberg [A] 60 E6
Rattersdorf [A] 74 F1
Rattosjärvi [FIN] 192 H6
Rättvik [S] 172 H3
Ratzeburg [D] 18 G4
Raubling [D] 60 F5
Raudaskylä [FIN] 198 D5
Raudeberg [N] 180 B4
Raufa [IS] 194 G3
Raufoss [N] 172 B3
Rauhala [FIN] 192 H5
Rauhaniemi [FIN] 188 E5
Rauland Høyfjellshotell [N] 164 E1
Rauma [FIN] 176 C2
Raumünzach [D] 58 F1
Rauna [LV] 200 E4
Rauris [A] 72 G1
Rautajärvi [FIN] 176 G1
Rautalampi [FIN] 186 H3
Rautaniemi [FIN] 176 E2
Rautas [S] 192 E5
Rautavaara [FIN] 198 F6
Rautila [FIN] 176 D4
Rautio [FIN] 198 C5
Rautjärvi [FIN] 178 F1
Rauvatn [N] 190 E2
Ravanusa [I] 126 E4
Rava-Rus'ka [UA] 52 G3
Ravatn [N] 190 D3
Ravattila [FIN] 178 E2
Ravda [BG] 148 F4
Ravello [I] 120 E4
Råvemåla [S] 162 E5
Ravenglass [GB] 10 D2
Ravenna [I] 110 H4
Ravensbrück [D] 20 D5
Ravensburg [D] 58 H4
Raversijde [B] 28 F1
Råvmarken [S] 166 C4
Ravna Dubrava [YU] 150 E4
Ravna Reka [YU] 150 D2
Ravno [BIH] 152 C3
Rawa Mazowiecka [PL] 38 A4
Rawicz [PL] 36 C5
Rawtenstall [GB] 10 E3
Rayleigh [GB] 14 F4
Rayol [F] 108 D6
Räyrinki [FIN] 186 D1
Razboj [BIH] 154 C2
Razbojna [YU] 150 C3
Razdrto [SLO] 74 B6
Razgrad [BG] 148 D2
Reading [GB] 14 D4
Réalmont [F] 106 B3
Realp [CH] 70 F1
Reanaclogheen [IRL] 4 D5
Reay [GB] 6 E2
Rebais [F] 42 H4
Rebolledo de la Torre [E] 82 D4
Reboly [RUS] 198 G5
Rebordelo [P] 80 E3
Rebŭrkovo [BG] 150 G4
Recanati [I] 116 C1
Recas [E] 96 F1
Recaş [RO] 76 H5
Recea [RO] 150 E1
Recey-sur-Ource [F] 56 G2
Rechnitz [A] 74 F1
Rechytsa [BY] 204 C6
Recke [D] 32 C2
Recklinghausen [D] 30 H2
Recoaro Terme [I] 72 C5
Recologne [F] 58 B4
Recsk [H] 64 E5
Recz [PL] 20 G5
Ręczno [PL] 36 H6
Reda [PL] 22 D2
Redalen [N] 172 B3
Redcar [GB] 10 G2
Redditch [GB] 12 H1
Redea [RO] 148 A1
Redefin [D] 18 H5
Rédics [H] 74 F3
Redon [F] 40 E5
Redondela [E] 78 B4
Redondo [P] 94 E1
Redruth [GB] 12 C5
Rees [D] 16 F6
Reeth [GB] 10 F2
Refnes [N] 192 C4
Refsnes [N] 192 C3
Reftele [S] 162 C4
Regalbuto [I] 126 F3
Regaly [H] 64 E4
Regéc [H] 64 G4
Regen [D] 60 H2
Regensburg [D] 48 B6
Regenstauf [D] 48 B6
Reggello [I] 110 F6
Réggio di Calábria [I] 124 C7
Reggiolo [I] 110 E2
Réggio nell'Emilia [I] 110 E3
Reghin [RO] 206 C4
Reguengos de Monsaraz [P] 94 E2
Rehau [D] 48 B3
Rehden [D] 32 E1
Rehna [D] 18 H4
Reichenau [D] 58 G4
Reichenau an der Rax [A] 62 E6
Reichenbach [D] 48 C2
Reichenbach [D] 34 G6
Reichenberg [D] 34 F2
Reichertshausen [D] 60 E3
Reichertshofen [D] 60 E3
Reiff [GB] 6 C3
Reigate [GB] 14 E5
Reignier [F] 70 B2
Reila [FIN] 176 C3
Reims [F] 44 B3
Reinach [CH] 58 E4
Reinach [CH] 58 F5
Reinberg [D] 20 D3
Reine [N] 192 B5
Reinfeld [D] 18 G3
Reinhardshagen [D] 32 F4
Reinheim [D] 46 C3
Reinosa [E] 82 E4
Reinsfeld [D] 44 G2
Reinsvoll [N] 172 B4
Reisbach [D] 60 G3
Reischach [D] 60 G4
Reischenhart [D] 60 F5
Reisjärvi [FIN] 198 D6
Reit im Winkl [D] 60 F5
Reitzehain [D] 48 D2
Rejmyre [S] 168 B4
Rejowiec Fabryczny [PL] 38 F6
Rejštejn [CZ] 48 E6
Reken [D] 16 G6
Remagen [D] 30 H5
Rémalard [F] 26 G6
Remels [D] 18 C4
Remeskylä [FIN] 198 E5
Remetea Mare [RO] 76 G5
Remich [L] 44 F3
Remiremont [F] 58 C3
Remnes [N] 190 D2
Remolinos [E] 90 E3
Remouchamps [B] 30 E5
Remoulins [F] 106 G3
Remscheid [D] 30 H4
Rémuzat [F] 108 B2
Rena [N] 172 C2
Renaison [F] 68 E2
Renaix (Ronse) [B] 28 G3
Renålandet [S] 190 E6
Rencēni [LV] 200 E4
Renchen [D] 58 F1
Renda [LV] 200 C5
Rendal [N] 180 G2
Rende [I] 124 D4
Rendsburg [D] 18 F2
Rengínio [GR] 132 H4
Reni [UA] 206 D5
Renko [FIN] 176 G3
Renkum [NL] 16 E5
Rennebu [N] 180 H3
Rennerod [D] 46 B1
Rennes [F] 26 C6
Rennweg [A] 72 H2
Renon / Ritten [I] 72 D3
Rens [DK] 156 B4
Rensjön [S] 192 E4
Rentería / Errenteria [E] 84 B2
Rentina [GR] 132 F3
Rentína [GR] 130 C4
Répáshuta [H] 64 F5
Répcelak [H] 74 G1
Repino [RUS] 178 G4
Replot / Raippaluoto [FIN] 186 A2
Repojoki [FIN] 196 C5
Reposaari [FIN] 176 C1
Reppen [N] 190 D1
République, Col de la- [F] 68 F4
Repvåg [N] 196 C2
Requena [E] 98 D4
Réquista [F] 106 C2
Rerik [D] 20 A3
Res [AL] 128 C1
Reşadiye [TR] 142 D3
Resana [I] 72 E6
Resen [MK] 128 D3
Reshety [RUS] 200 H4
Reshetylivka [UA] 206 G2
Reşiţa [RO] 206 A5
Resko [PL] 20 G4
Resmo [S] 162 G5
Ressons [F] 28 E6
Reszel [PL] 24 B3
Retama [E] 96 D3
Retamar [E] 102 G5
Retamosa [E] 96 C1
Retford [GB] 10 F5
Rethel [F] 44 C2
Rethem [D] 18 E6
Réthymno [GR] 140 D4
Retiers [F] 40 G4
Retortillo de Soria [E] 90 A3
Retournac [F] 68 E4
Rétság [H] 64 C5
Retuerta [E] 88 H1
Retuerta del Bullaque [E] 96 E2
Retz [A] 62 E3
Reuilly [F] 56 B3
Reus [E] 92 C5
Reusel [NL] 30 E3
Reuterstadt Stavenhagen [D] 20 C4
Reutlingen [D] 58 H2
Reutte [A] 60 C6
Revel [F] 106 B4
Revfülöp [H] 74 H3
Révigny [F] 44 C4
Révigny-sur-Ornain [F] 44 C4
Revin [F] 44 C1
Řevničov [CZ] 48 E3
Revonlahti [FIN] 198 D4
Revsnes [N] 170 D2
Revsnes [N] 190 B5
Revúca [SK] 64 E3
Rewal [PL] 20 F3
Rexbo [S] 172 H4
Reyðarfjörðer [IS] 194 G5
Reykhólar [IS] 194 C2
Reykholt [IS] 194 C4
Reykjahlið [IS] 194 F4
Reykjavík [IS] 194 B4
Rēzekne [LV] 200 G5
Rezovo [BG] 148 G5
Rgotina [YU] 150 E2
Rhayader [GB] 10 C6
Rheda [D] 32 D3
Rhede [D] 16 G6
Rheinau [D] 44 H6
Rheinbach [D] 30 G5
Rheinberg [D] 30 G2
Rheinböllen [D] 44 H2
Rheindahlen [D] 30 F3
Rheine [D] 16 H5
Rheinfelden [CH] 58 E4
Rheinfelden [D] 58 E4
Rheinsberg [D] 20 C6
Rheinzabern [D] 46 B5
Rhenen [NL] 16 E5
Rhens [D] 30 H6
Rheydt [D] 30 G3
Rhinau [F] 58 E2
Rhinow [D] 34 C1
Rho [I] 70 G5
Rhosneigr [GB] 10 B4
Rhuddlan [GB] 10 C4
Rhyl [GB] 10 C4
Rhymney [GB] 12 F2
Rhynern [D] 32 C4
Rhynie [GB] 6 F5
Riaillé [F] 40 G6
Riákia [GR] 128 G5
Riaño [E] 82 C3
Rians [F] 108 C4
Riaza [E] 88 G3
Ribadavia [E] 78 C5
Ribadelago [E] 78 E6
Ribadeo [E] 78 F2
Ribadesella [E] 82 C2
Ribaflecha [E] 90 C1
Ribaforada [E] 84 B6
Ribarci [YU] 150 E5
Ribariče [YU] 150 B4
Ribaritsa [BG] 148 A4
Riba-roja de Túria [E] 98 E4
Ribe [DK] 156 B3
Ribeauville [F] 58 D2
Ribécourt [F] 28 E6
Ribeira Brava [P] 100 A3
Ribeira de Pena [P] 80 D3
Ribemont [F] 28 F5
Ribera [I] 126 C3
Ribérac [F] 66 E2
Ribera de Cardós [E] 84 G6
Ribera del Fresno [E] 94 H3
Ribes de Freser [E] 92 E2
Ribnica [BIH] 154 D3
Ribnica [SLO] 74 C6
Rîbniţa [MD] 206 E4
Ribnitz-Damgarten [D] 20 C2
Ribolla [I] 114 F2
Ricadi [I] 124 C6
Říčany [CZ] 48 G4
Riccarton [GB] 8 E5
Riccia [I] 120 F1
Riccione [I] 112 B5
Richelieu [F] 54 F3
Richmond [GB] 10 F2
Richmond [GB] 14 E4
Richtenberg [D] 20 C3
Rickarum [S] 158 D2
Rickling [D] 18 G3
Ricla [E] 90 D4
Ricse [H] 64 H4
Riddarhyttan [S] 166 H2
Ridjica [YU] 76 C5
Ried [A] 72 C2
Riedenburg [D] 60 E2
Riedern [D] 58 F4
Ried im Innkreis [A] 60 H4
Riedlingen [D] 58 H3
Riegel [D] 58 E2
Riegersburg [A] 74 E2
Riello [E] 78 G5
Rieneck [D] 46 E3
Riesa [D] 34 E5
Riesi [I] 126 E4
Riestedt [D] 34 B5
Rietavas [LT] 202 D4
Rietberg [D] 32 D3
Rieti [I] 116 B4
Rieumes [F] 84 H3
Rieupeyroux [F] 66 H6
Rieux [F] 84 H4
Riez [F] 108 C4
Riezlern [A] 60 B6
Rīga [LV] 200 D5
Rigáni [GR] 132 F5
Rigeo [GR] 132 G2
Rignac [F] 68 A5
Rignano Flaminio [I] 116 A4
Rihéa [GR] 136 F4
Riihimäki [FIN] 176 G3
Riihivaara [FIN] 198 G5
Riihivalkama [FIN] 176 F3
Riistavesi [FIN] 188 D2
Rijeka [HR] 112 E1
Rijeka Crnojevića [YU] 152 E4
Rijssen [NL] 16 G5
Riksgränsen [S] 192 D4
Rila [BG] 150 F6
Rillé [F] 54 F1
Rillo [E] 90 D6
Rima [I] 70 E3
Rimavská Sobota [SK] 64 E4
Rimbo [S] 168 E2
Rimella [I] 70 E3
Rimforsa [S] 162 F1
Rímini [I] 110 H5
Rîmnicu Sărat [RO] 206 D5
Rîmnicu Vîlcea [RO] 206 B6
Rímnio [GR] 128 F6
Rimske Toplice [SLO] 74 D5
Rincón de la Victoria [E] 102 C5
Rincón de Soto [E] 84 A5
Rindal [N] 180 G2
Ring / An Rinn [IRL] 4 E5
Ringarum [S] 168 B6
Ringaskiddy [IRL] 4 D5
Ringe [DK] 156 D3
Ringebu [N] 170 H1
Ringkøbing [DK] 160 B6
Ringnes [N] 170 G5
Ringsted [DK] 156 F3
Ringwood [GB] 12 G5
Rinteln [D] 32 E2
Río [GR] 132 F5
Riobianco / Weissenbach [I] 72 D2
Ríofrio [E] 78 G5
Riola Sardo [I] 118 B5
Riolobos [E] 86 H4
Riolo Terme [I] 110 G4
Riom [F] 68 C2
Riomaggiore [I] 110 C4
Rio Maior [P] 86 C4
Riomar [E] 92 B6
Rio Mau [P] 80 B3
Riom-ès-Montagnes [F] 68 B3
Rion-des-Landes [F] 66 B5
Rionegro del Puente [E] 80 G3
Rionero in Vúlture [I] 120 G3
Riópar [E] 96 H6
Riós [E] 78 D6
Riosa [E] 78 H4
Rio Saliceto [I] 110 E2
Rio Torto [P] 80 D6
Rioz [F] 58 B4
Ripač [BIH] 112 H3
Ripacandida [I] 120 G3
Ripanj [YU] 154 G3
Riparbella [I] 114 E1
Ripatransone [I] 116 C2
Ripky [UA] 204 C7
Ripley [GB] 10 E5
Ripoll [E] 92 E2
Ripon [GB] 10 F3
Riposto [I] 124 B8
Ripponden [GB] 10 E4
Riquewihr [F] 58 D2
Risan [YU] 152 D4
Risbäck [S] 190 E4
Riscle [F] 84 E2
Rish [BG] 148 E3
Risliden [S] 190 H4
Risnes [N] 164 C4
Risnes [N] 170 B2
Risnovce [SK] 64 A4
Risør [N] 164 F4
Risøyhamn [N] 192 C3
Rissa [N] 190 B6
Risti [EST] 200 D2
Ristiina [FIN] 188 C6
Ristijärvi [FIN] 198 F4
Ristinge [DK] 156 E5
Ristna [EST] 200 C2
Ristovac [YU] 150 D5
Risum-Lindholm [D] 156 B5
Ritíni [GR] 128 G5
Rittmanshausen [D] 32 G6
Riva-Bella [F] 26 F3
Riva del Garda [I] 72 C5
Rivarolo Canavese [I] 70 D5
Rivarolo Mantovano [I] 110 E2
Rive-de-Gier [F] 68 F3
Rivergaro [I] 110 C2
Rivesaltes [F] 92 G1
Rivne [UA] 206 D2
Rivoli [I] 70 D5
Rizári [GR] 128 F4
Rízia [GR] 146 A2
Rízoma [GR] 132 E2
Rizómata [GR] 128 G5
Rizómylos [GR] 136 D4
Rizómylos [GR] 132 H2
Rjånes [N] 180 C4
Rjukan [N] 170 F6
Ro [I] 110 G2
Roa [E] 88 G2
Roa [N] 172 B5
Roanne [F] 68 E2

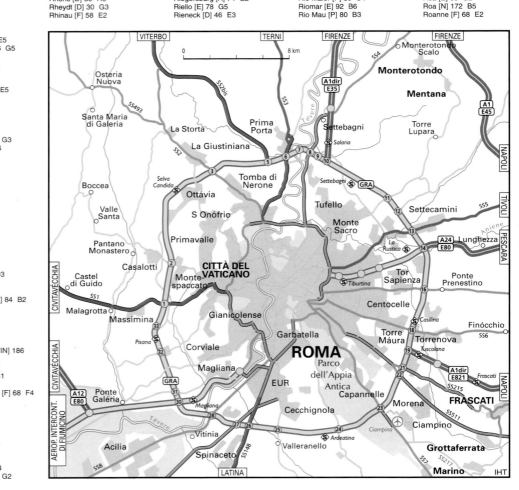

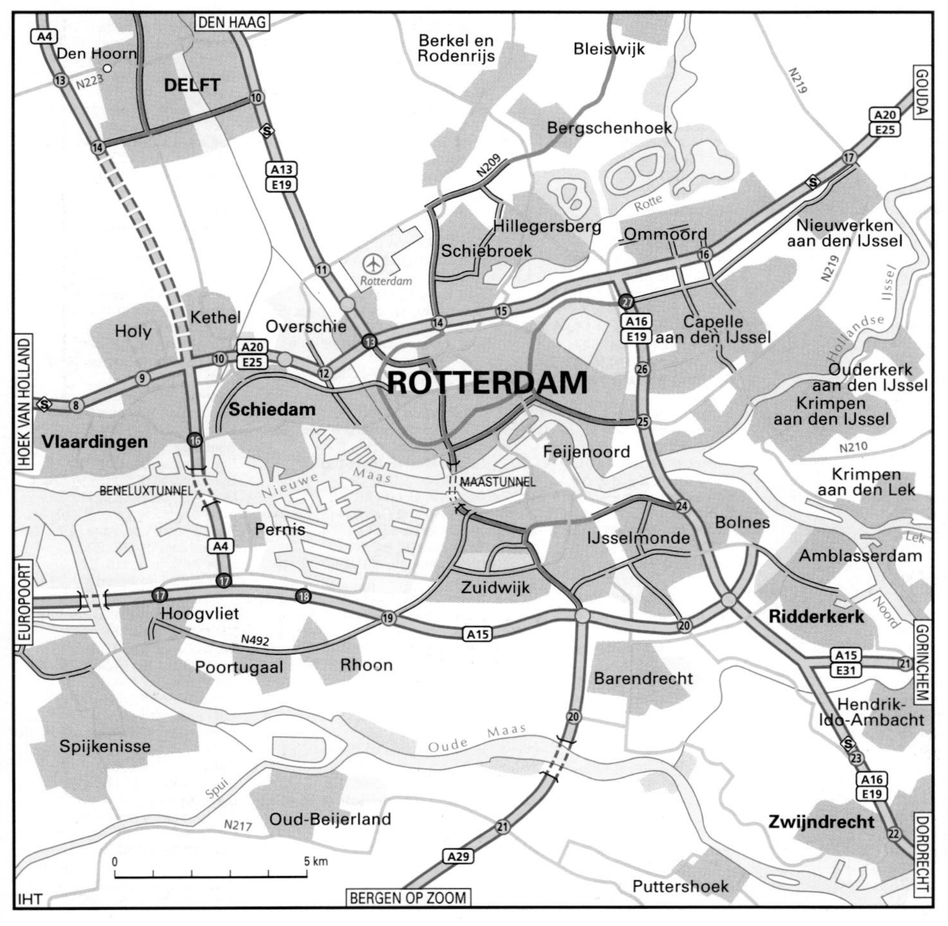
DEN HAAG
A4
Den Hoorn
DELFT
Berkel en Rodenrijs
Bleiswijk
GOUDA
A20
E25
Bergschenhoek
A13
E19
Hillegersberg
Schiebroek
Ommoord
Nieuwerken aan den IJssel
Rotterdam
Holy
Kethel
Overschie
A16
E19
Capelle aan den IJssel
A20
E25
ROTTERDAM
Schiedam
Ouderkerk aan den IJssel
Krimpen aan den IJssel
HOEK VAN HOLLAND
Vlaardingen
Feijenoord
BENELUXTUNNEL
MAASTUNNEL
Nieuwe Maas
Krimpen aan den Lek
Pernis
Bolnes
A4
IJsselmonde
Amblasserdam
EUROPOORT
Zuidwijk
Hoogvliet
A15
Ridderkerk
N492
Poortugaal
Rhoon
A15
E31
GORINCHEM
Barendrecht
Hendrik-Ido-Ambacht
Spijkenisse
Oude Maas
A16
E19
Oud-Beijerland
Zwijndrecht
DORDRECHT
0
5 km
A29
IHT
BERGEN OP ZOOM
Puttershoek

Sant Boi de Llobregat [E] 92 D4
Sant Carles de la Ràpita [E] 92 A6
Sant Celoni [E] 92 F4
Santed [E] 90 D5
Sant'Elia a Pianisi [I] 120 F1
Sant'Elia Fiumerapido [I] 120 D1
San Telmo [E] 94 F4
Santena [I] 70 D6
San Teodoro [I] 118 E3
Santéramo in Colle [I] 122 D3
Sant' Eufémia Lamézia [I] 124 D5
Sant Feliu de Codines [E] 92 E4
Sant Feliu de Guíxols [E] 92 G4
Sant Feliu de Llobregat [E] 92 E4
Sant Ferran de Ses Roquetes [E] 104 C6
Sant Francesc de Formentera [E] 104 C6
Santhià [I] 70 E5
Sant Hilari Sacalm [E] 92 F3
Sant Hipòlit de Voltregà [E] 92 E3
Santiago [P] 80 F5
Santiago de Alcántara [E] 86 F4
Santiago de Calatrava [E] 102 D2
Santiago de Compostela [E] 78 C3
Santiago de la Espada [E] 102 G2
Santiago de la Ribera [E] 104 D4
Santiago del Campo [E] 86 H5
Santiago do Cacém [P] 94 B2
Santiago do Escoural [P] 94 D1
Santibáñez [E] 82 D4
Santibáñez de la Sierra [E] 88 B4
Santibáñez de Vidriales [E] 80 H3
Santibañez Zarzaguda [E] 82 E5
Santi Kurutze Kanpezu / Santa Cruz de Campezo [E] 82 H6
Santillana del Mar [E] 82 E3
Santisteban del Puerto [E] 102 F1
Sant Jaume d'Enveja [E] 92 B6
Sant Joan d'Alacant / San Juan de Alicante [E] 104 E2
Sant Joan de les Abadesses [E] 92 E2
Sant Joan de Llabritja [E] 104 C5
Sant Joan de Vilatorrada [E] 92 D3
Sant Josep / San José [E] 104 C5
Sant Juliá de Lória [AND] 84 H6
Sant Llorenç de Morunys [E] 92 D2
Sant Lluís [E] 104 H5
Sant Martí Sarroca [E] 92 D4
Sant Miquel de Balansat [E] 104 C5
Santo Aleixo [P] 86 E6
Santo André [P] 94 B2
Santo Domingo de la Calzada [E] 82 G6
Santo Domingo de Silos [E] 88 H1
Santo Estevão [P] 86 G2
Santok [PL] 34 H2
Santoña [E] 82 F3
S. Antonio di Santadi [I] 118 B5
Santo Stefano Belbo [I] 108 H2
Santo Stefano di Cadore [I] 72 F3
Santo Stefano di Camastra [I] 126 F2
Santo Stefano Quisquina [I] 126 D3
Santo Stino di Livenza [I] 72 F5
Santo Tirso [P] 80 C3
Santo Tomé [E] 102 F2
Santo Tomé del Puerto [E] 88 G3
Sant Pau de Seguries [E] 92 F2
Sant Pere Pescador [E] 92 G3
Sant Pol de Mar [E] 92 F4
Sant Quirze de Besora [E] 92 E2
Sant Rafel [E] 104 C5
Sant Sadurní d'Anoia [E] 92 D4
Sant Tomàs [E] 104 G4
Santuário di Oropa [I] 70 E4
Santu Lussúrgiu [I] 118 C4
Santurce / Santurtzi [E] 82 G3
Santurtzi / Santurce [E] 82 G3
Sant Vicenç de Castellet [E] 92 D3
Sant Vicent del Raspeig / San Vicente del Raspeig [E] 104 E2
Sant Vicent de sa Cala [E] 104 C5
San Valentino alla Muta / Sankt Valentin auf der Maide [I] 72 B2
San Venanzo [I] 114 H3
San Vicente de Alcántara [E] 86 F5
San Vicente de la Barquera [E] 82 E3
San Vicente del Raspeig / Sant Vicent del Raspeig [E] 104 E2
San Vincenzo [I] 114 E2
San Vito [I] 118 D6
San Vito al Tagliamento [I] 72 F5
San Vito dei Normanni [I] 122 F4
San Vito di Cadore [I] 72 E3
San Vito lo Capo [I] 126 B1
San Vito Romano [I] 116 B5
San Vittore delle Chiuse [I] 116 B1
Sanxay [F] 54 E4
Sanxenxo [E] 78 B4
Sanza [I] 120 G5
São Barnabé [P] 94 C4
São Bartolomeu de Messines [P] 94 C5
São Brás de Alportel [P] 94 C5
São Cristóvão [P] 94 D1
São Domingos [P] 94 C3
São Francisco da Serra [P] 94 C2
São Gregório [P] 78 C5
São Jacinto [P] 80 B5
São João da Madeira [P] 80 B4
São João da Pesqueira [P] 80 E5
São João da Serra [P] 80 C5
São João dos Caldeireiros [P] 94 D4
São Luis [P] 94 B3
São Manços [P] 94 E2
São Marcos da Ataboeira [P] 94 D4
São Marcos da Serra [P] 94 C4
São Martinho [P] 86 E2
São Martinho das Amoreiras [P] 94 C4
São Martinho do Porto [P] 86 B3
São Miguel de Acha [P] 86 F3
São Miguel de Machede [P] 94 E1
São Miguel do Pinheiro [P] 94 D4
São Pedro da Cadeira [P] 86 B4
São Pedro de Muel [P] 86 C2
São Pedro de Solis [P] 94 D4
São Pedro do Sul [P] 80 C5
Saorge [F] 108 F4
São Romão [P] 94 C2
São Romão [P] 86 C6
São Teotónio [P] 94 B4
Saou [F] 68 F6
São Vicente [P] 100 A3
São Vicente da Beira [P] 86 F3
Sapakpınar [TR] 146 G3
Sapanca [TR] 146 G3
Sapareva Banya [BG] 150 F5
Sapernoye [RUS] 178 G2
Sápes [GR] 130 G3
Şaphane [TR] 144 F2
sa Pobla [E] 104 E4
Sapotskin [BY] 24 F3
Sappada [I] 72 F3
Sappee [FIN] 176 H1
Sappemeer [NL] 16 G2
Sapri [I] 120 G5
Saqués [E] 84 D5
Sarafovo [BG] 148 F4
Säräisniemi [FIN] 198 E4
Sarajevo [BIH] 152 D1
Sarakiní [GR] 128 F4
Sarakíniko [GR] 134 B4
Saramon [F] 84 G3
Sáránd [H] 76 H1
Saranda [AL] 132 B1
Saránti [GR] 132 H6
Sarantsi [BG] 150 G4
Sarata [UA] 206 E5
Saray [TR] 146 D2
Saraycık [TR] 144 E3
Sarayköy [TR] 144 F5
Šarbanovac [YU] 150 D2
Sarbia [PL] 36 C1
Sarbinowo [PL] 20 H3
Sarbinowo [PL] 34 G2
Sárbogárd [H] 76 B3
Sarceda [E] 82 E3
Sárdara [I] 118 C6
Sardínia [GR] 132 E4
Sardoal [P] 86 D4
S'Arenal [E] 104 E5
S'Arenal d'en Castell [E] 104 H4
Šarengrad [HR] 154 E1
Sarentino / Sarntheim [I] 72 D3
Sargans [CH] 58 H6
Sári [H] 76 C2
Sarıcakaya [TR] 146 H4
Sarıgöl [TR] 144 F4
Sarıkaya [TR] 144 E4
Sariñena [E] 90 G4
Sarısu [TR] 146 G3
Sarıyer [TR] 146 E2
Sarkad [H] 76 G3
Sarkadkeresztúr [H] 76 G3
Sárkeresztúr [H] 76 B2
Särkijärvi [FIN] 198 E4
Särkijärvi [FIN] 192 H5
Särkilahti [FIN] 186 G6
Särkilahti [FIN] 188 F6
Särkisalmi [FIN] 188 F5
Särkisalo / Finby [FIN] 176 E5
Şarköy [TR] 146 C4
Sarlat–la–Canéda [F] 66 G4
Sarmizegetuza [RO] 206 B5
Särna [S] 172 E1
Sarnaki [PL] 38 E2
Sarnano [I] 116 C2
Sarnen [CH] 58 F6
Sarnes [E] 82 C2
Sárnico [I] 72 A5
Sarno [I] 120 E3
Sarnowa [PL] 36 C5
Sarnówek [PL] 38 C6
Sarnthein / Sarentino [I] 72 D3
Sarny [UA] 204 A7
Särö [S] 160 G3
Saronída [GR] 136 H1
Saronno [I] 70 G4
Sárospatak [H] 64 G4
Šarovce [SK] 64 B5
Sarpsborg [N] 166 B3
Sarracín [E] 82 E6
Sarral [E] 92 C4
Sarralbe [F] 44 G4
Sarrebourg [F] 44 G5
Sarreguemines [F] 44 G4
Sárrétudvari [H] 76 G1
Sarre–Union [F] 44 G5
Sarria [E] 78 E4
Sarrión [E] 98 E2
Sarroch [I] 118 C7
Sarron [F] 84 E2
Sarsıla İskele [TR] 142 F3
Sársina [I] 110 G5
Sarstedt [D] 32 G2
Sarteano [I] 114 G2
Sartène [F] 114 B5
Sárti [GR] 130 D6
Sartilly [F] 26 D4
Sartmustafa [TR] 144 E4
Saruhanlı [TR] 144 D3
Sárvár [H] 74 G2
Sarvijoki [FIN] 186 B3
Sarvikumpu [FIN] 188 E3
Sarzana [I] 110 C4
Sarzeau [F] 40 D5
Sarzedas [P] 86 E3
Sasa [MK] 150 E6
Sa Savina [E] 104 C6
Sásd [H] 76 A4
Sassari [I] 118 C3
Sassello [I] 108 H3
Sassenage [F] 68 H4
Sassenberg [D] 32 D3
Sassenheim [NL] 16 D4
Sassnitz [D] 20 D2
Sassocorvaro [I] 110 H5
Sassoferrato [I] 116 B1
Sasso Marconi [I] 110 F4
Sassuolo [I] 110 E3
Šaštin–Stráže [SK] 62 G3
Šatalovo [RUS] 204 D5
Sátão [P] 80 D5
Såtenäs [S] 166 D5
Säter [S] 174 C5
Satırlar [TR] 144 D3
Sátoraljaújhely [H] 64 G3
Satovcha [BG] 130 C1
Satow [D] 20 B3
Satra brunn [S] 168 B1
Sátres [GR] 130 G2
Satrup [D] 18 F1
Sattanen [FIN] 196 D6
Satu Mare [RO] 206 B4
Saturn [RO] 148 G1
Saturnia [I] 114 G3
Saucats [F] 66 C4
Sauda [N] 164 C1
Sauðárkrókur [IS] 194 D3
Saudasjøen [N] 164 C1
Saue [EST] 200 D1
Sauerlach [D] 60 E5
Saugos [LT] 202 D4
Saugues [F] 68 D4
Saujon [F] 54 C6
Saukkola [FIN] 176 G4
Saukonkyla [FIN] 186 D2
Sauland [N] 164 F1
Saulgau [D] 58 H3
Saulieu [F] 56 F3
Saulkrasti [LV] 200 D4
Sault [F] 108 B3
Saulx [F] 58 B3
Saulxures [F] 58 C3
Saumur [F] 54 E2
Saundersfoot [GB] 12 D2
Sauvagnat [F] 68 B2
Sauve [F] 106 F3
Sauveterre–de–Béarn [F] 84 D2
Sauveterre–de–Guyenne [F] 66 D4
Sauvo [FIN] 176 E5
Sauxillanges [F] 68 D3
Sauze d'Oulx [I] 70 C5
Sauzé–Vaussais [F] 54 E5
Sauzon [F] 40 C5
Sava [I] 122 F4
Sävar [S] 198 A6
Savaştepe [TR] 144 D2
Säve [S] 160 G2
Savelletri [I] 122 F3
Savelli [I] 124 E4
Savenay [F] 40 E6
Saverdun [F] 84 H4
Saverne [F] 44 G5
Savi [FIN] 176 E1
Savigliano [I] 108 F2
Savignac–les–Eglises [F] 66 F3
Savignano Irpino [I] 120 F2
Savignano sul Rubicone [I] 110 H5
Savigny–sur–Braye [F] 42 C5
Savijärvi [FIN] 198 G5
Savikoski [FIN] 176 F2
Savikylä [FIN] 198 F6
Savines–le–Lac [F] 108 D2
Savino Selo [YU] 154 F1
Saviore dell'Adamello [I] 72 B4
Savitaipale [FIN] 178 D2
Šavnik [YU] 152 E3
Savognin [CH] 70 H2
Savona [I] 108 H3
Savonlinna [FIN] 188 E5
Savonranta [FIN] 188 F4
Sävsjö [S] 162 D3
Sävsjön [S] 166 G1
Sävsjöström [S] 162 E4
Savudrija [HR] 72 H6
Savukoski [FIN] 196 E6
Sävya [S] 168 D2
Sawston [GB] 14 F3
Sawtry [GB] 14 E2
Sax [E] 104 D2
Saxnäs [S] 190 E4
Säynätsalo [FIN] 186 G5
Säyneinen [FIN] 188 D1
Sázava [CZ] 48 G4
Sazonovo [RUS] 204 E2
S.Benito de la Contienda [E] 94 F2
Scaër [F] 40 C3
Scafa [I] 116 D4
Scalasaig [GB] 8 B2
Scalby [GB] 10 G3
Scalea [I] 120 H6
Scalloway [GB] 6 G4
Scandiano [I] 110 E3
Scanno [I] 116 D5
Scansano [I] 114 F3
Scanzano Jónico [I] 122 D5
Scarborough [GB] 10 G3
Scardovari [I] 110 H2
Scarinish [GB] 6 A6
Scarperia [I] 110 F5
Scarriff [IRL] 2 C6
Šćepan Polje [YU] 152 D2
Schaan [FL] 58 H6
Schachendorf [A] 74 F1
Schaffhausen [CH] 58 G4
Schafstädt [D] 34 B5
Schäftlarn [D] 60 E5
Schagen [NL] 16 D3
Schaprode [D] 20 D2
Scharbeutz [D] 18 G3
Schärding [A] 60 H3
Scharnitz [A] 60 D6
Scharnstein [A] 62 B5
Scheer [D] 58 H3
Scheessel [D] 18 E5
Schéggia [I] 116 A1
Scheibbs [A] 62 D5
Scheifling [A] 74 B2
Scheinfeld [D] 46 F4
Schenefeld [D] 18 F3
Scherfede [D] 32 E4
Schermbeck [D] 30 G2
Schesslitz [D] 46 G3
Scheveningen [NL] 16 C5
Scheyern [D] 60 E3
Schieder [D] 32 E3
Schierling [D] 60 F2
Schiermonnikoog [NL] 16 G1
Schifferstadt [D] 46 B5
Schilde [B] 30 D3
Schilpário [I] 72 B4
Schiltach [D] 58 F2
Schio [I] 72 D5
Schirmeck [F] 44 G6
Schirnding [D] 48 C3
Schitu [RO] 148 C1
Schkeuditz [D] 34 C5
Schladen [D] 32 H3
Schladming [A] 72 H1
Schlanders / Silandro [I] 72 C3
Schlangenbad [D] 46 B3
Schleching [D] 60 F5
Schleiden [D] 30 F5
Schleiz [D] 48 B2
Schleswig [D] 18 F1
Schleusingen [D] 46 G2
Schlieben [D] 34 E4
Schlierbach [A] 62 B5
Schliersee [D] 60 E5
Schlitz [D] 46 E1
Schlotheim [D] 32 H5
Schluchsee [D] 58 F3
Schlüchtern [D] 46 E2
Schluderbach / Carbonin [I] 72 E3
Schluderns / Sluderno [I] 72 C3
Schlüsselfeld [D] 46 F4
Schlutup [D] 18 H3
Schmalkalden [D] 46 F1
Schmallenberg [D] 32 D5
Schmidmühlen [D] 48 B6
Schmilka [D] 48 F1
Schmöllin [D] 48 C1
Schmölln [D] 20 E5
Schnackenburg [D] 20 A6
Schnaittenbach [D] 48 B5
Schneeberg [D] 48 D2
Schneverdingen [D] 18 F5
Schober Pass [A] 74 C1
Schöder [A] 74 B2
Schöllkrippen [D] 46 D3
Schönau [D] 58 E3
Schönbeck [D] 20 D4
Schönberg [A] 72 D1
Schönberg [D] 48 C3
Schönberg [D] 60 H2
Schönberg [D] 18 G2
Schönberg [D] 18 H3
Schönbergerstrand [D] 18 G2
Schönebeck [D] 20 B6
Schönebeck [D] 34 B3
Schönecken [D] 44 F1
Schongau [D] 60 D5
Schönhagen [D] 18 G1
Schöningen [D] 32 H3
Schönmünzach [D] 58 F1
Schönthal [D] 48 C5
Schönwald [D] 58 F3
Schönwalde [D] 18 H2
Schönwalde [D] 34 E2
Schoondijke [NL] 28 G1
Schoonebeek [NL] 16 G4
Schoonhoven [NL] 16 D5
Schoonoord [NL] 16 G3
Schopfheim [D] 58 E4
Schöppenstedt [D] 32 H3
Schoppernau [A] 60 B6
Schöppingen [D] 16 H5
Schorndorf [D] 60 B2
Schotten [D] 46 D2
Schramberg [D] 58 F2
Schrems [A] 62 D3
Schriesheim [D] 46 C4
Schrobenhausen [D] 60 D3
Schröcken [A] 72 B1
Schruns [A] 72 A1
Schull [IRL] 4 B5
Schüpfheim [CH] 58 E6
Schuttertal [D] 58 E2
Schüttorf [D] 16 H5
Schwaan [D] 20 B3
Schwabach [D] 46 G5
Schwabhausen [D] 60 D4
Schwäbisch Gmünd [D] 60 B2
Schwäbisch Hall [D] 46 E6
Schwabmünchen [D] 60 C4
Schwaigern [D] 46 D5
Schwalenberg [D] 32 E3
Schwalmstadt–Treysa [D] 32 E6
Schwalmstadt–Ziegenhain [D] 32 E6
Schwanbeck [D] 20 D4
Schwanden [CH] 58 G6
Schwandorf [D] 48 B5
Schwanebeck [D] 34 A3
Schwanenstadt [A] 62 A5
Schwanewede [D] 18 D5
Schwaney [D] 32 E4
Schwarmstedt [D] 32 F1
Schwarzach [A] 72 G1
Schwarzburg [D] 46 G2
Schwarzenau [A] 62 D3
Schwarzenbach [D] 48 B3
Schwarzenbek [D] 18 G4
Schwarzenberg [D] 48 D2
Schwarzenfeld [D] 48 B5
Schwarze Pumpe [D] 34 F5
Schwarzsee [CH] 70 D1
Schwaz [A] 72 E1
Schwechat [A] 62 F4
Schwedt [D] 20 E6
Schweich [D] 44 G2
Schweinfurt [D] 46 F3
Schwelm [D] 30 H3
Schwenningen [D] 58 F3
Schwerin [D] 20 A4
Schwerte [D] 32 C4
Schwetzingen [D] 46 C5
Schwyz [CH] 58 F6
Sciacca [I] 126 C3
Scicli [I] 126 F5
Scilla [I] 124 C7
Ścinawa [PL] 36 B5
Scoglitti [I] 126 F5
Scole [GB] 14 G3
S. Colombano al Lambro [I] 70 G6
Sconser [GB] 6 B4
Scopello [I] 70 E4
Scorzè [I] 72 E6
Scotch Corner [GB] 10 F2
Scourie [GB] 6 D2
Scrabster [GB] 6 F2
Screeb [IRL] 2 B4
Scritto [I] 116 A1
Scunthorpe [GB] 10 G4
Scuol [CH] 72 B2
Seaford [GB] 14 E6
Seaham [GB] 8 G6
Seatoller [GB] 10 D1
Seaton [GB] 12 F4
Sebbersund [DK] 160 D4
Sebečevo [YU] 150 B4
Sebeş [RO] 206 B5
Sebezh [RUS] 200 H5
Sebnitz [D] 48 F1
Seč [CZ] 48 E5
Seč [CZ] 50 A4
Sečanj [YU] 154 H1
Secemin [PL] 50 H2
Séchault [F] 44 C3
Seckau [A] 74 C1
Seclin [F] 28 F3
Secondigny [F] 54 D3
Sečovce [SK] 64 G3
Sedan [F] 44 D2
Sedbergh [GB] 10 E2
Séderon [F] 108 B2
Sedgefield [GB] 10 F2
Sédico [I] 72 E4
Sédilo [I] 118 C4
Sédini [I] 118 C3
Sedlčany [CZ] 48 F5
Sedlice [CZ] 48 E5
Sedrun [CH] 70 F1
Šeduva [LT] 202 F4
Sędziszów [PL] 52 D3
Sędziszów [PL] 52 A2
Seeboden [A] 72 H2
Seebruck [D] 60 F5
Seefeld in Tyrol [A] 72 D1
Seehausen [D] 34 B3
Seehausen [D] 20 A6
Seehausen [D] 34 D4
Seelbach [D] 58 E2
Seelisberg Tunnel [CH] 58 F6
Seelow [D] 34 F2
Seeon [D] 60 F5
Sées [F] 26 F5
Seesen [D] 32 G3
Seeshaupt [D] 60 D5
Seewalchen [A] 60 H5
Seewiesen [A] 62 D6
Seferihisar [TR] 144 C5
Segalstad bru [N] 172 B2
Segarcea [RO] 150 G1
Segerstad [S] 162 G6
Segesd [H] 74 G4
Seglinge [FIN] 176 B5
Segmon [S] 166 E3
Segonzac [F] 54 D6
Segorbe [E] 98 E3
Segovia [E] 88 F4
Segré [F] 40 G5
Segura [E] 102 G1
Segura [P] 86 G4
Segura de León [E] 94 G4
Segura de los Baños [E] 90 E6
Segurilla [E] 88 D6
Şehirlioğlu [TR] 144 F3
Sehnde [D] 32 G2
Seia [P] 86 F2
Seiches–sur–le–Loir [F] 40 H6
Seifhennersdorf [D] 48 G1
Seilhac [F] 66 H3
Seinäjoki [FIN] 186 C3
Seira [E] 84 F6
Seitenstetten Markt [A] 62 C5
Seixal [P] 86 B5
Seixo [P] 80 C6
Sejerby [DK] 156 E2
Sejny [PL] 24 E3
Sejs [DK] 156 C1
Seki [TR] 142 H2
Šeksna [RUS] 204 F1
Selanovtsi [BG] 150 G2
Selargius [I] 118 D7
Selaste [EST] 200 E1
Selb [D] 48 C3
Selbu [N] 182 C2
Selby [GB] 10 F4
Selce [HR] 112 F2
Selchow [D] 34 F3
Selçuk [TR] 144 D5
Selde [DK] 160 C4
Selendi [TR] 144 F3
Selenicë [AL] 128 B5
Selent [D] 18 G2
Sélestat [F] 58 E2
Seleuş [RO] 76 H4
Selevac [YU] 150 B1
Selfoss [IS] 194 B5
Séli [GR] 128 F5
Selianítika [GR] 132 F6
Seligenstadt [D] 46 D3
Selimiye [TR] 142 C1
Selínia [GR] 136 G1
Selishtë [AL] 128 C2
Selište [YU] 150 D2
Seližarovo [RUS] 204 D3
Selje [N] 180 B4
Seljestad [N] 170 C5
Seljord [N] 164 F2
Selkirk [GB] 8 E4
Sella [E] 104 E2
Sellasía [GR] 136 E3
Selles [F] 54 H2
Sellía [GR] 140 D5
Sellières [F] 56 H5
Sellin [D] 20 E2
Sellye [H] 76 A5
Selm [D] 32 C3
Selmsdorf [D] 18 H3
Selnes [N] 190 B5
Selongey [F] 56 H3
S.Elpidio a Mare [I] 116 C2
Selsey [GB] 14 D5
Selsingen [D] 18 E4
Seltz [F] 46 B6
Selva di Cadore [I] 72 E3
Selva di Val Gardena / Wolkenstein in Gardena [I] 72 E3
Selvik [N] 180 B6
Selvino [I] 70 H4
Sem [N] 164 H3
Semblana [P] 94 C4
Semily [CZ] 48 H2
Semizovac [BIH] 152 D1
Semmering [A] 62 E6
Semmering Pass [A] 62 E6
Semur–en–Auxois [F] 56 F3
Seňa [SK] 64 G3
Sena de Luna [E] 78 G4
Sénas [F] 106 H4
Senden [D] 16 H6
Sendenhorst [D] 32 C3
Sendim [P] 80 G5
Senec [SK] 62 H4
Senftenberg [D] 34 F5
Senica [SK] 62 G3
Senigállia [I] 112 C6
Senise [I] 122 C5
Senj [HR] 112 F2
Senjehopen [N] 192 D2
Senlis [F] 42 G3
Sennecey–le–Grand [F] 56 G5
Sennelager [D] 32 E3
Sennen [GB] 12 B5
Sennestadt [D] 32 D3
Sennik [BG] 148 B4
Sénnori [I] 118 C3

Sennybridge [GB] 12 F2
Senohrad [SK] 64 C4
Senokos [BG] 148 G2
Senonches [F] 26 H6
Senones [F] 44 G6
Senorbì [I] 118 D6
Senovo [SLO] 74 D5
Senožeče [SLO] 74 B6
Sens [F] 42 G6
Sens-de-Bretagne [F] 26 D5
Senta [YU] 76 E5
Senterada [E] 92 C1
Sentilj [SLO] 74 D3
Šentjur [SLO] 74 D4
Šentvid pri Zavodnju [SLO] 74 C4
Sepino [I] 120 E1
Sepólno Krajenskie [PL] 22 C5
Sępopol [PL] 22 H2
Septemvri [BG] 148 A6
Sept-Saulx [F] 44 B3
Sepúlveda [E] 88 G3
Sequeros [E] 88 B4
Seraincourt [F] 28 H6
Seraing [B] 30 E5
Seravezza [I] 110 D5
Sered' [SK] 62 H4
Seredka [RUS] 200 G3
Seredni Verets'kyi Pereval [UA] 206 B3
Seregélyes [H] 76 B2
Seregno [I] 70 G4
Sérent [F] 26 B6
Serfaus [A] 72 C2
Sergiyev Posad (Zagorsk) [RUS] 204 F3
Serhat [TR] 144 B1
Seriaji [LT] 24 F2
Seriate [I] 70 H4
Sérifos [GR] 138 D3
Serinhisar [TR] 144 G5
Serino [I] 120 F3
Sermaize-les-Bains [F] 44 C4
Sermide [I] 110 F2
Serock [PL] 38 B2
Serón [E] 102 G4
Serón de Nágima [E] 90 C3
Serós [E] 90 G5
Serpa [P] 94 E3
Serpins [P] 86 E2
Serpukhov [RUS] 204 F4
Serra [E] 98 E4
Serracapriola [I] 116 F6
Serrada [E] 88 E2
Serra de Agua [P] 100 B3
Serra de' Conti [I] 112 C6
Serradifalco [I] 126 D3
Serradilla [E] 88 A6
Serramazzoni [I] 110 E3
Serra Nova [E] 104 F5
Serra San Bruno [I] 124 D6
Serra San Quirico [I] 116 B1
Serrastretta [I] 124 D5
Serrenti [I] 118 C6
Serres [F] 108 C2
Sérres [GR] 130 C3
Serri [I] 118 D6
Serrières [F] 68 F4
Sersale [I] 124 E5
Sertã [P] 86 E3
Sérvia [GR] 128 F6
Serviana [GR] 132 D2
Servigliano [I] 116 C2
Sesa [E] 90 F3
Seseña Nuevo [E] 96 G1
Sesimbra [P] 86 B6
Seskinore [GB] 2 F3
Sésklo [GR] 132 H2
Sesma [E] 82 H6
Sessa Aurunca [I] 120 D2
Šestanovac [HR] 152 B2
Sestao [E] 82 G3
Sesto / Sexten [I] 72 F3
Sesto al Reghena [I] 72 F5
Sesto Calende [I] 70 F4
Sesto Fiorentino [I] 110 F5
Sestola [I] 110 E4
Sesto S. Giovanni [I] 70 G5
Sestriere [I] 70 C5
Sestri Levante [I] 110 B4
Sestroretsk [RUS] 178 G4
Sestu [I] 118 C7
Sesvete [HR] 74 E5
Séta [GR] 134 C4
Šeta [LT] 202 F4
Setcases [E] 92 F2
Sète [F] 106 E4
Seter [N] 182 D5
Setermoen [N] 192 D3
Setihovo [BIH] 152 E1
Settebagni [I] 116 A5
Settimo Torinese [I] 70 D5
Settle [GB] 10 E3
Setúbal [P] 86 B6
Seui [I] 118 D5
Seulo [I] 118 D5
Seurre [F] 56 G4
Sevaster [AL] 128 B5
Sevastopol' [UA] 206 G6
Sevel [DK] 160 C5
Sevenoaks [GB] 14 E5
Sever [P] 80 C5
Sévérac-le-Château [F] 68 C6
Severin [D] 20 B4
Severin [HR] 74 G5
Ševětín [CZ] 62 C2
Sevettijärvi [FIN] 196 E3
Sevilla [E] 94 G6
Sevilleja de la Jara [E] 96 D2
Şevketiye [TR] 146 B5
Şevketiye [TR] 146 D5
Sevlievo [BG] 148 B4
Sevnica [SLO] 74 D5
Sevojno [YU] 150 A2
Sevrier [F] 70 B3
Sexten / Sesto [I] 72 F3
Seyches [F] 66 E4
Seyda [D] 34 D4
Seydiköy [TR] 144 C4
Seyðisfjörður [IS] 194 G5
Seyitömer [TR] 146 G6
Seymen [TR] 146 D3
Seyne [F] 108 D2
Seyssel [F] 68 H2
Seysses [F] 84 H3
Sežana [SLO] 72 H6
Sézanne [F] 44 A4
Sezimovo Ústí [CZ] 48 G5
Sezze [I] 120 B1
Sfáka [GR] 140 G5
Sfákia [GR] 140 C5
S.Felices de los Gallegos [E] 80 F6
Sfîntu Gheorghe [RO] 206 C5
Sforzacosta [I] 116 C2
S. Geraldo [P] 86 D6
S. Giorgio della Richinvelda [I] 72 F5
S. Giorgio del Sannio [I] 120 F2
S. Giovanni Bianco [I] 70 H4
S. Gregorio Magno [I] 120 G4
Shabla [BG] 148 G2
Shaftesbury [GB] 12 G4
Shanagolden [IRL] 4 C3
Shanklin [GB] 12 H5
Shannonbridge [IRL] 2 D5
Sharnevo [BG] 148 D5
Shats'k [UA] 38 G4
Shawbury [GB] 10 D5
Shchekino [RUS] 204 F5
Shchors [UA] 204 D7
Shchuchin [BY] 24 H4
's Heerenberg [NL] 16 F6
Sheerness [GB] 14 F4
Sheffield [GB] 10 F4
Shefford [GB] 14 E3
Shëngjergj [AL] 128 B3
Shëngjin [AL] 128 A1
Shënmëri [AL] 150 B6
Shenval [GB] 6 E5
Shepetivka [UA] 206 D2
Shepshed [GB] 10 E6
Shepton Mallet [GB] 12 F4
Sherborne [GB] 12 F4
Shercock [IRL] 2 F4
Sheringham [GB] 14 G1
's-Hertogen-Bosch [NL] 16 E6
Shetaj [AL] 128 A2
Shiel Bridge [GB] 6 C5
Shieldaig [GB] 6 C4
Shifnal [GB] 10 D6
Shijak [AL] 128 A3
Shillelagh [IRL] 4 F4
Shinrone [IRL] 2 D6
Shipchenski Prokhad [BG] 148 C4
Shipka [BG] 148 C4
Shipkovo [BG] 148 B4
Shipley [GB] 10 E3
Shipston-on-Stour [GB] 12 H2
Shiroka Lŭka [BG] 130 D1
Shirokë [AL] 128 A1
Shivatsevo [BG] 148 D4
Shkodër [AL] 128 A1
Shkorpilovtsi [BG] 148 F3
Shmoylovo [RUS] 200 H3
Shoeburyness [GB] 14 F4
Shoreham-by-Sea [GB] 14 E5
Shostka [UA] 204 D7
Shotts [GB] 8 E3
Shranamanragh Bridge [IRL] 2 B3
Shrewsbury [GB] 10 D5
Shrewton [GB] 12 G4
Shrule [IRL] 2 C4
Shtërmen [AL] 128 B4
Shumen [BG] 148 E3
Shyshchytsy [BY] 204 B6
Siána [GR] 142 D5
Sianów [PL] 22 A3
Siare [EST] 200 D3
Siátista [GR] 128 E6
Šiauliai [LT] 202 E4
Šiabravas [LT] 202 F4
Sibari [I] 122 D6
Sibbhult [S] 158 D1
Sibbo / Sippo [FIN] 176 H4
Šibenik [HR] 112 H6
Sibiu [RO] 206 B5
Sičevo [YU] 150 D3
Sicignano degli Alburni [I] 120 G4
Šid [YU] 154 E2
Sidári [GR] 132 A2
Siddeburen [NL] 16 H2
Sideby / Siipyy [FIN] 186 A5
Sidensjö [S] 184 F2
Siderno [I] 124 D7
Sidiró [GR] 130 G3
Sidirókastro [GR] 130 B3
Sidirónero [GR] 130 D2
Sidmouth [GB] 12 E4
Sidra [PL] 24 F4
Sidzina [PL] 50 D2
Siecq [F] 54 D6
Siedlce [PL] 38 D3
Siedlinghausen [D] 32 D5
Siedlisko [PL] 22 A6
Siegburg [D] 30 H5
Siegen [D] 32 C6
Siegenburg [D] 60 E2
Sieggraben [A] 62 F6
Siegsdorf [D] 60 G5
Siekierki [PL] 34 F1
Siemiany [PL] 22 F4
Siemiatycze [PL] 38 E2
Siena [I] 114 F1
Sieniawa [PL] 52 F3
Sieniawka [PL] 48 G1
Siennica [PL] 38 C3
Sienno [PL] 38 C6
Sieppijärvi [FIN] 192 H6
Sieradz [PL] 36 F5
Sieraków [PL] 50 F2
Sieraków [PL] 36 B2
Sierakowice [PL] 22 D2
Sierck-les-Bains [F] 44 F3
Sierentz [F] 58 D4
Sierning [A] 62 B5
Sierpc [PL] 36 G1
Sierra de Fuentes [E] 86 H5
Sierra de Luna [E] 84 C6
Sierra de Yeguas [E] 102 B3
Sierra Nevada [E] 102 E4
Sierre [CH] 70 D2
Siete Aguas [E] 98 D4
Sievi [FIN] 198 D5
Siewierz [PL] 50 G2
Sifjord [N] 192 D3
Siğacik [TR] 144 C5
Sigean [F] 106 D5
Sigerfjord [N] 192 C4
Siggjarvåg [N] 170 A5
Sighetu Marmaţiei [RO] 206 B3
Sighişoara [RO] 206 C5
Siglufjörður [IS] 194 E2
Sigmaringen [D] 58 H3
Signes [F] 108 C5
Signy-l'Abbaye [F] 28 H6
Sígri [GR] 134 G2
Sigtuna [S] 168 D2
Sigüeiro [E] 78 C3
Sigüenza [E] 90 A4
Sigulda [LV] 200 E5
Sihtuuna [FIN] 196 C8
Siikainen [FIN] 186 B6
Siikajoki [FIN] 198 D4
Siilinjärvi [FIN] 188 C2
Siipyy / Sideby [FIN] 186 A5
Siivikko [FIN] 198 E3
Sijarinska Banja [YU] 150 D5
Sikaminiá [GR] 134 G2
Sikea [GR] 140 G5
Sikeå [S] 198 A5
Sikiá [GR] 132 F1
Síkinos [GR] 138 E4
Siklós [H] 76 B5
Sikórz [PL] 36 G2
Sikovuono [FIN] 196 D4
Šilale [LT] 202 D4
Silandro / Schlanders [I] 72 C3
Silánus [I] 118 C4
Silbaš [YU] 154 F1
Silberstedt [D] 18 F1
Şile [TR] 146 F2
Siles [E] 102 H1
Silíqua [I] 118 C7
Silistra [BG] 148 E1
Silivri [TR] 146 D3
Siljan [N] 164 G3
Siljansnäs [S] 172 G4
Silkås [S] 182 H1
Silkeborg [DK] 160 D6
Silla [E] 98 E5
Sillamäe [EST] 200 F1
Silleda [E] 78 C3
Sillé-le-Guillaume [F] 26 F6
Sillerud [S] 166 D3
Sillian [A] 72 F3
Silloth [GB] 8 D5
Silno [PL] 22 C4
Šilo [HR] 112 F2
Sils [E] 92 F3
Sils-Maria [CH] 70 H2
Šilutė [LT] 202 D5
Silva [E] 78 C2
Silvaplana [CH] 70 H2
Silvares [P] 86 F2
Silverdalen [S] 162 F3
Silvermines [IRL] 4 D3
Silves [P] 94 B5
Silvi [I] 116 D4
Silz [A] 72 C1
Simancas [E] 88 E2
Şimand [RO] 76 G4
Simaság [H] 74 G1
Simav [TR] 144 F2
Simaxis [I] 118 C5
Simbach [D] 60 G3
Simbach [D] 60 G4
Simeonovgrad [BG] 148 D6
Simferopol' [UA] 206 G6
Simitli [BG] 130 A1
Šimkaičiai [LT] 202 E5
Simlångsdalen [S] 162 B5
Şimleu Silvaniei [RO] 206 B4
Simmerath [D] 30 F5
Simmerberg [D] 60 B5
Simmern [D] 44 H2
Simo [FIN] 198 D3
Simonsbath [GB] 12 E3
Simonstorp [S] 168 B4
Simontornya [H] 76 B3
Simorre [F] 84 G3
Simpele [FIN] 188 F6
Simplon Dorf [CH] 70 E2
Simplonpass [CH] 70 E2
Simrishamn [S] 158 D3
Simuna [EST] 200 F2
Sinaia [RO] 206 C5
Sinalunga [I] 114 G2
Sinanaj [AL] 128 B5
Sinanpaşa [TR] 144 H2
Sinarcas [E] 98 D3
Sıncansarnıç [TR] 146 E5
Sindal [DK] 160 E2
Sindelfingen [D] 58 G1
Sindi [EST] 200 D3
Sındırgı [TR] 144 E2
Sinekçi [TR] 146 C5
Sinekli [TR] 146 D2
Sinemorets [BG] 148 G5
Sines [P] 94 B2
Sinettä [FIN] 196 C7
Sineu [E] 104 E5
Sinevo [RUS] 178 G2
Singen [D] 58 G4
Singleton [GB] 14 D5
Singsås [N] 182 B2
Singusdal [N] 164 F3
Siniscola [I] 118 E4
Sinj [HR] 152 A1
Sinnai [I] 118 D7
Sinnes [N] 164 C3
Sinópoli [I] 124 C7
Sinsheim [D] 46 C5
Sintea Mare [RO] 76 H3
Sintra [P] 86 A5
Sinzig [D] 30 H5
Siófok [H] 76 A2
Sion [CH] 70 D2
Sion Mills [GB] 2 F2
Siorac-en-Périgord [F] 66 F4
Šipovo [BIH] 154 B4
Sippo / Sibbo [FIN] 176 H4
Sippola [FIN] 178 C3
Sira [N] 164 C4
Siracusa [I] 126 G5
Siret [RO] 206 C4
Sirevåg [N] 164 B4
Şiria [RO] 76 H4
Sirig [YU] 154 F1
Sirkka [FIN] 192 H5
Sirma [N] 196 D2
Sirmione [I] 72 B6
Sirnach [CH] 58 G5
Sirok [H] 64 E5
Široké [SK] 64 F2
Sirolo [I] 116 C1
Siruela [E] 96 C3
Širvintos [LT] 202 G5
Sisak [HR] 154 A1
Sisamón [E] 90 C4
Sisante [E] 98 B4
Sissa [I] 110 D2
Sissach [CH] 58 E4
Sissonne [F] 28 G6
Şiştarovăţ [RO] 76 H5
Sisteron [F] 108 C3
Sistiana [I] 72 H5
Siteía [GR] 140 G4
Sitges [E] 92 D5
Sitrama de Tera [E] 80 H3
Sittard [NL] 30 F4
Sittensen [D] 18 E5
Sittersdorf [A] 74 C3
Sittingbourne [GB] 14 F5
Sitzendorf [A] 62 E3
Siurua [FIN] 198 E3
Siusi [I] 72 D3
Sivac [YU] 76 D6
Sivakka [FIN] 198 G5
Sivakka [FIN] 198 F5
Sivakkavaara [FIN] 188 E2
Sivaslı [TR] 144 G3
Siverskiy [RUS] 178 H6
Síviri [GR] 130 B6
Sivota [GR] 132 C2
Six-Fours-les-Plages [F] 108 C6
Sixmilebridge [IRL] 2 C6
Sixpenny Handley [GB] 12 G4
Sizun [F] 40 B2
Sjasstroj [RUS] 204 D1
Sjenica [YU] 150 A4
Sjoa [N] 180 G6
Sjøåsen [N] 190 C5
Sjöbo [S] 158 C3
Sjøholt [N] 180 D3
Sjørup [DK] 160 C5
Sjötofta [S] 162 B3
Sjötorp [S] 166 F4
Sjoutnäset [S] 190 E5
Sjøvegan [N] 192 D3
Sjövik [S] 160 H1
Sjuntorp [S] 166 D6
Sjusjøen [N] 172 B2
Skåbu [N] 170 G1
Skadovs'k [UA] 206 F5
Skælskør [DK] 156 F3
Skærbæk [DK] 156 B3
Skafidia [GR] 136 B2
Skaftafell [IS] 194 E6
Skaftung [FIN] 186 A5
Skagaströnd [IS] 194 D2
Skagen [DK] 160 F2
Skaidi [N] 196 B2
Skaistkalne [LV] 200 E6
Skála [GR] 136 E4
Skála [GR] 132 D6
Skála [GR] 138 H2
Skála [GR] 134 A4
Skála [GR] 134 G2
Skała [PL] 50 H3
Skála Eresoú [GR] 134 G2
Skála Kaliráhis [GR] 130 E4
Skålan [S] 182 G4
Skaland [N] 192 D2
Skála Oropoú [GR] 134 C5
Skálavík [FR] 160 B2
Skalbmierz [PL] 52 B3
Skåldö [FIN] 176 F6
Skalica [SK] 62 G3
Skalité [SK] 50 F5
Skalitsa [BG] 148 D5
Skallelv [N] 196 F2
Skallerup Klit [DK] 160 E2
Skallskog [S] 172 G4
Skalmoldal [S] 190 E3
Skalohóri [GR] 128 E5
Skalotí [GR] 140 C5
Skalotí [GR] 130 D2
Skals [DK] 160 D5
Skålsjön [S] 174 D3
Skalstugan [S] 182 E1
Skandáli [GR] 130 F6
Skanderborg [DK] 156 D1
Skanes Fagerhult [S] 162 C6
Skånevik [N] 170 B6
Skänninge [S] 166 H6
Skanör [S] 156 H3
Skansen [N] 190 C6
Skansholm [S] 190 F4
Skåpafors [S] 166 D4
Skąpe [PL] 34 H3
Skara [S] 166 E5
Skarberget [N] 192 C4
Skärblacka [S] 168 A5
Skarð [IS] 194 C5
Skåre [S] 166 E2
Skärhamn [S] 160 G1
Skarnes [N] 172 C5
Skarpengland [N] 164 D5
Skärplinge [S] 174 F4
Skarsvåg [N] 196 C1
Skarszewy [PL] 22 D3
Skårup [DK] 156 E4
Skarvsjö [S] 190 F4
Skaryszew [PL] 38 C5
Skarżysko-Kamienna [PL] 38 B6
Skata [FIN] 176 E6
Skattungbyn [S] 172 G2
Skaudvilė [LT] 202 E4
Skaulo [S] 192 F5
Skave [DK] 160 C5
Skavik [N] 196 B2
Skawina [PL] 50 H4
Skebobruk [S] 168 E1
Skedsmokorset [N] 172 B6
Skee [S] 166 C4
Skegness [GB] 10 H5
Skei [N] 180 D6
Skei [N] 180 G2
Skei [N] 190 C4
Skeiðflötur [IS] 194 C6
Skeie [N] 164 C5
Skela [YU] 154 G3
Skelde [DK] 156 C4
Skellefteå [S] 198 A4
Skellefteham [S] 198 A4
Skelleftehamn [S] 198 A4
Skelleftestrand [S] 198 A4
Skelmersdale [GB] 10 D4
Skelmorlie [GB] 8 C3
Skender Vakuf [BIH] 154 C3
Skene [S] 162 B3
Skepastó [GR] 130 B4
Skępe [PL] 36 G1
Skeppshult [S] 162 C4
Skerries [IRL] 2 F6
Ski [N] 166 B1
Skíathos [GR] 134 B3
Skibbereen [IRL] 4 B5
Skibby [DK] 156 G2
Skibniew-Podawce [PL] 38 D2
Skibotn [N] 192 E2
Skidal' [BY] 24 G4
Skien [N] 164 G3
Skierniewice [PL] 36 H4
Skiippagurra [N] 196 D2
Skillingaryd [S] 162 D3
Skillinge [S] 158 D3
Skiniás [GR] 140 F5
Skinnastaðir [IS] 194 F3
Skinnerup [DK] 160 C3
Skinnskatteberg [S] 168 A1
Skipness [GB] 8 C3
Skipton [GB] 10 E3
Skiptvet [N] 166 B2
Skive [DK] 160 C5
Skiveren [DK] 160 E2
Skivjane [YU] 150 B5
Skjærhalden [N] 166 B3
Skjeberg [N] 166 B3
Skjeggedal [N] 164 E4
Skjelten [N] 180 D3
Skjern [DK] 156 B1
Skjerstad [N] 192 C6
Skjervøy [N] 192 F1
Skjold [N] 164 B1
Skjold [N] 192 E3
Skjoldastraumen [N] 164 B1
Skjolden [N] 170 E1
Skjønhaug [N] 166 C2
Sklíthro [GR] 132 H2
Skoby [S] 168 D1
Skočivir [MK] 128 F3
Skoczów [PL] 50 F4
Skodje [N] 180 D3
Skødstrup [DK] 160 E6
Škofja Loka [SLO] 74 B4
Škofljica [SLO] 74 C5
Skog [S] 174 E3
Skoganvarre [N] 192 H1
Skoger [N] 164 H2
Skogly [N] 196 E3
Skogn [N] 190 C6
Skogsby [S] 162 G5
Skogstorp [S] 168 B3
Skoki [PL] 36 D2
Skokloster [S] 168 D2
Sköldinge [S] 168 B4
Skole [UA] 52 G6
Skollenberg [N] 164 G2
Sköllersta [S] 166 H3
Skomdal [N] 164 E3
Skomlin [PL] 36 F6
Skópelos [GR] 134 H2
Skópelos [GR] 134 B3
Skopí [GR] 140 G4
Skopiá [GR] 132 G3
Skopje [MK] 128 E1
Skopós [GR] 128 E4
Skopun [FR] 160 A2
Skórcz [PL] 22 E4
Skórka [PL] 22 B6
Skoroszów [PL] 36 D5
Skorovatn [N] 190 D4
Skørping [DK] 160 D4
Skórzec [PL] 38 D3
Skotoússa [GR] 130 B3
Skotselv [N] 164 G1
Skotterud [N] 166 D1
Skoulikariá [GR] 132 E3
Skoúra [GR] 136 E4
Skoútari [GR] 130 B3
Skovballe [DK] 156 D4
Skovby [DK] 156 D4
Skövde [S] 166 F6
Skrá [GR] 128 G3
Skrad [HR] 112 F1
Skradin [HR] 112 H6
Skråmestø [N] 170 A3
Skrea [S] 160 H4
Skreia [N] 172 B4
Skrīveri [LV] 200 E5
Skrunda [LV] 200 C5
Skudeneshavn [N] 164 A2
Skulgam [N] 192 E2
Skulsk [PL] 36 E2
Skulte [LV] 200 D4
Skultorp [S] 166 F6
Skultuna [S] 168 B2
Skuodas [LT] 200 B6
Skurup [S] 158 C3
Skušava [LV] 200 G5
Skuteč [CZ] 50 B4
Skutskär [S] 174 E4
Skutvik [N] 192 C5
Skvyra [UA] 206 E2
Skwierzyna [PL] 34 H2
Skýcov [SK] 64 B3
Skýdra [GR] 128 G4
Skýros [GR] 134 D3
Skyttmon [S] 184 C1
Skyttorp [S] 168 D1
Sládkovičovo [SK] 62 H4
Śladów [PL] 38 A2
Slagelse [DK] 156 F3
Slagnäs [S] 190 G3
Slaidburn [GB] 10 E3
Slane [IRL] 2 F5
Slangerup [DK] 156 G2
Slănic Moldova [RO] 206 C5
Slano [HR] 152 C3
Slantsy [RUS] 200 G1
Slaný [CZ] 48 F3
Slatina [HR] 74 E5
Slatina [RO] 206 B6
Slatina [YU] 150 B2
Slatiňany [CZ] 50 A4
Slatino [MK] 150 C6
Slåttevik [N] 164 A2
Slätthog [S] 162 D4
Slattum [N] 172 B6
Slavičín [CZ] 64 A2
Slavkovichi [RUS] 200 H3
Slavkov u Brna (Austerlitz) [CZ] 50 C6
Slavonice [CZ] 62 D2
Slavonska Požega [HR] 154 C1
Slavonski Brod [HR] 154 D2
Slavyanovo [BG] 148 B3
Sława [PL] 36 B4
Sławatycze [PL] 38 F4
Slawharad [BY] 204 C6
Sławków [PL] 50 G3
Sławno [PL] 22 B2
Sławoborze [PL] 20 H4
Sleaford [GB] 10 G6
Sledmere [GB] 10 G3
Slemmestad [N] 164 H1
Ślesin [PL] 22 C6
Ślesin [PL] 36 E3
Sletta [N] 190 D2
Slettestrand [DK] 160 D3
Sliedrecht [NL] 16 D5
Sliema [M] 126 C6
Sligachan [GB] 6 B4
Sligeach / Sligo [IRL] 2 D3
Sligo / Sligeach [IRL] 2 D3
Slite [S] 168 G4
Sliven [BG] 148 D4
Slivnitsa [BG] 150 F4
Slivno [HR] 152 B2
Slivo Pole [BG] 148 D1
Śliwice [PL] 22 D4
Slobozia [RO] 148 C2

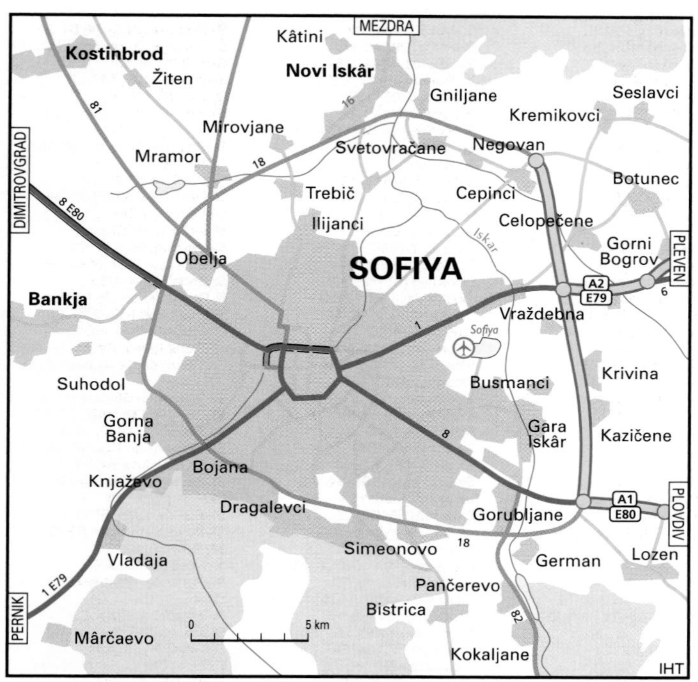
Kostinbrod
Žiten
Kâtini
MEZDRA
Novi Iskâr
Gniljane
Seslavci
Kremikovci
Mirovjane
Svetovračane
Negovan
Mramor
DIMITROVGRAD
8 E80
Trebič
Cepinci
Botunec
Ilijanci
Celopečene
Iskâr
Gorni
Bogrov
PLEVEN
Obelja
SOFIYA
A2
E79
Bankja
Vraždebna
Sofiya
Suhodol
Busmanci
Krivina
Gorna
Banja
Gara
Iskâr
Kazičene
Bojana
Knjaževo
Dragalevci
Gorubljane
A1
E80
PLOVDIV
Vladaja
Simeonovo
German
Lozen
Pančerevo
PERNIK
1 E79
Bistrica
Mârčaevo
0
5 km
Kokaljane
IHT

Slobozia [RO] 206 D6
Slobozia Mândra [RO] 148 B2
Słomniki [PL] 52 A3
Slonim [BY] 204 A6
Słońsk [PL] 34 G2
Sloten [NL] 16 F3
Slough [GB] 14 E4
Slovac [YU] 150 A1
Slovenj Gradec [SLO] 74 D4
Slovenska Bistrica [SLO] 74 D4
Slovenská L'upča [SK] 64 C3
Slovenske Konjice [SLO] 74 D4
Slovenské Nové Mesto [SK] 64 G3
Slovians'k [UA] 206 H3
Słubice [PL] 34 G3
Sluderno / Schluderns [I] 72 C3
Sluis [NL] 28 G1
Sluis [NL] 16 C6
Slŭnchev Bryag [BG] 148 F4
Slunj [HR] 112 G2
Słupca [PL] 36 E3
Słupia [PL] 52 C3
Słupiec [PL] 50 C2
Słupno [PL] 36 H2
Słupsk [PL] 22 B2
Slutsk [BY] 204 B6
Smålandsstenar [S] 162 C4
Smalåsen [N] 190 D4
Smalfjord [N] 196 D2
Smalininkai [LT] 202 E5
Smârdioasa [RO] 148 C2
Smarhon' [BY] 202 H5
S. Maria della Versa [I] 70 G6
S. Marina Salina [I] 124 A6
S.Martino in Pensilis [I] 116 F6
Smědeč [CZ] 62 B2
Smederevo [YU] 154 H3
Smederevska-Palanka [YU] 150 C1
Smedjebacken [S] 172 H5
Smeland [N] 164 E3
Smelror [N] 196 F2
Smidary [CZ] 48 H3
Śmigiel [PL] 36 C4
S.Miguel del Arroyo [E] 88 F2
Smila [UA] 206 F3
Smilde [NL] 16 G3
Śmiłowo [PL] 22 B6
Smiltene [LV] 200 F4
Smínthi [GR] 130 E2
Smögen [S] 166 B5
Smogulec [PL] 22 C6
Smołdzino [PL] 22 C1
Smolen [PL] 50 H3
Smolensk [RUS] 204 D5
Smolnica [PL] 34 G1
Smolník [SK] 64 F3
Smolyan [BG] 130 E1
Smolyanovtsi [BG] 150 F3
Smørfjord [N] 196 C2
Smørhamn [N] 180 B5
Smorten [N] 192 B4
Smyadovo [BG] 148 E3
Smyga [UA] 206 C2
Smygehamn [S] 158 C3
Snaptun [DK] 156 D2
Snarup [DK] 156 D4
Snåsa [N] 190 C5
Snavlunda [S] 166 G4
Snedsted [DK] 160 C4
Sneek [NL] 16 F2
Sneem [IRL] 4 B4
S. Nicola da Crissa [I] 124 D6
S. Nicolás del Puerto [E] 96 A5
Snihurivka [UA] 206 F4
Snina [SK] 64 H2
Snjatyn [UA] 206 C3
Šnjegotina Gornja [BIH] 154 C3
Snøde [DK] 156 E4
Snøfjord [N] 196 B2
Snogebaek [DK] 158 E4
Snössvallen [S] 182 F6
Snöstorp [S] 162 B5
Soajo [P] 78 B6
Soave [I] 72 C6
Söbbön [S] 166 C4
Sober [E] 78 D5
Soběslav [CZ] 48 G6
Sobibór [PL] 38 G5
Sobieszów [PL] 50 A1
Sobkow [PL] 52 B2
Sobotín [CZ] 50 C4
Sobotište [SK] 62 H3
Sobotka [CZ] 48 H2
Sobótka [PL] 50 C1
Sobowidz [PL] 22 E3
Sobra [HR] 152 C3
Sobrado [E] 78 D3
Sobral da Adiça [P] 94 E3
Sobral de Monte Agraço [P] 86 B4
Sobran [TR] 146 H5
Sobreira Formosa [P] 86 E3
Søby [DK] 156 D4
Sočanica [YU] 150 C4
Sochaczew [PL] 38 A3
Sochaux [F] 58 C4
Sochocin [PL] 38 A2
Sochós [GR] 130 B4
Socodor [RO] 76 G3
Socovos [E] 104 B2
Socuéllamos [E] 96 H4
Sodankylä [FIN] 196 D6
Sodderby Karl [S] 168 E1
Söderåkra [S] 162 F6
Söderbärke [S] 168 A1
Söderby [FIN] 178 C4
Söderfors [S] 174 E5
Söderhamn [S] 174 E2
Söderköping [S] 168 B5
Södertälje [S] 168 D3
Söderudden [FIN] 186 A2
Södra Vallgrund [FIN] 186 A2
Södra Vi [S] 162 F2
Sodražica [SLO] 74 C6
Sødring [DK] 160 E5
Soest [D] 32 D4
Soest [NL] 16 E5
Soestdijk [NL] 16 E5
Sofádes [GR] 132 F3
Sofikó [GR] 136 F1
Sofiya [BG] 150 F5
Sofó [GR] 132 G2
Sofporog [RUS] 198 G2
Sögel [D] 18 B6
Sogge bru [N] 180 E3
Sogndal [N] 170 D1
Sogndalstrand [N] 164 B5
Søgne [N] 164 D6
Soğuksu [TR] 146 H2
Söğüt [TR] 142 H2
Söğüt [TR] 146 H4
Söğütalan [TR] 146 E5
Soidinvaara [FIN] 198 F5
Soignies [B] 28 H3
Soini [FIN] 186 E3
Soinlahti [FIN] 198 E6
Soissons [F] 42 H2
Sokal' [UA] 52 H2
Söke [TR] 144 D5
Sokna [N] 170 H5
Soko Banja [YU] 150 D3
Sokolac [BIH] 154 E4
Sokółka [PL] 24 F5
Sokolniki [PL] 36 E5
Sokolov [CZ] 48 C3
Sokolovo [BG] 148 G2
Sokołów Malopolski [PL] 52 E3
Sokołów Podlaski [PL] 38 D2
Sola [N] 164 A3
Solana de los Barros [E] 94 G2
Solana del Pino [E] 96 E5
Solánas [I] 118 D7
Solares [E] 82 F3
Solberg [S] 190 G6
Solberga [S] 162 E2
Solbjerg [DK] 160 C4
Solčava [SLO] 74 C4
Solda / Sulden [I] 72 C3
Sölden [A] 72 C2
Soldeu [AND] 84 H6
Solec-Zdrój [PL] 52 C3
Solenzara [F] 114 B5
Solera del Gabaldón [E] 98 C3
Solesmes [F] 28 G4
Solevåg [N] 180 D3
Solf / Sulva [FIN] 186 B2
Solfonn [N] 170 C5
Solheim [N] 170 B2
Solignac [F] 66 G1
Solihull [GB] 12 H1
Solin [HR] 152 A2
Solingen [D] 30 H4
Söll [A] 60 F6
Sollana [E] 98 E5
Sollebrun [S] 162 B1
Sollefteå [S] 184 E2
Sollenau [A] 62 F5
Sollentuna [S] 168 D3
Sóller [E] 104 E4
Søllerød [DK] 156 G2
Sollerön [S] 172 G3
Søllested [DK] 156 E5
Solliès-Pont [F] 108 C5
Solmaz [TR] 144 F6
Solnechnogorsk [RUS] 204 F4
Solnhofen [D] 60 D2
Solosancho [E] 88 D4
Sološnica [SK] 62 G4
Solothurn [CH] 58 D5
Solovi [RUS] 200 G3
Sölöz [TR] 146 F4
Solrød Strand [DK] 156 G3
Sølsnes [N] 180 E3
Solsona [E] 92 D2
Solsvik [N] 170 A3
Solt [H] 76 C3
Soltau [D] 18 F6
Sol'tsy [RUS] 204 C2
Soltvadkert [H] 76 D3
Solund [N] 170 A2
Sölvesborg [S] 158 E1
Solvik [S] 166 D3
Solvorn [N] 170 D1
Soma [TR] 144 D2
Sombernon [F] 56 G3
Sombor [YU] 76 C6
Somerniemi [FIN] 176 F4
Somero [FIN] 176 F4
Somersham [GB] 14 F2
Somerton [GB] 12 F4
Somino [RUS] 204 E1
Sommariva del Bosco [I] 108 G2
Sommarset [N] 192 C5
Sommatino [I] 126 E4
Sommen [S] 162 E1
Sömmerda [D] 34 A6
Sommersted [DK] 156 C3
Sommesous [F] 44 B4
Sommières [F] 106 F3
Somo [E] 82 F3
Somogyszob [H] 74 G4
Somosierra [E] 88 G4
Somosierra, Puerto de- [E] 88 G4
Somovit [BG] 148 B2
Sompolno [PL] 36 F2
Son [N] 166 B2
Son Bou [E] 104 H4
Sonceboz [CH] 58 D5
Soncillo [E] 82 E4
Soncino [I] 70 H5
Sóndalo [I] 72 B3
Sondby [FIN] 178 B4
Søndeled [N] 164 F4
Sønder Balling [DK] 160 C5
Sønderborg [DK] 156 C4
Sønderby [DK] 156 C4
Sønderby [DK] 160 B6
Sønderby [DK] 156 F4
Sønder Dråby [DK] 160 C4
Sønder Felding [DK] 156 B1
Sønderho [DK] 156 A3
Sønder Omme [DK] 156 B1
Sondershausen [D] 32 H5
Søndersø [DK] 156 D3
Søndervig [DK] 160 B6
Søndervika [N] 182 D4
Sondrio [I] 70 H3
Söndrum [S] 162 B5
Songesand [N] 164 B3
Sonka [FIN] 196 C8
Sonkajärvi [FIN] 198 E6
Sonneberg [D] 46 G2
Sonogno [CH] 70 F2
Sonsbeck [D] 30 G2
Sonseca [E] 96 F2
Sonta [YU] 76 C6
Sonthofen [D] 60 B6
Sontra [D] 32 F6
Son Xoriguer [E] 104 G4
Sopeira [E] 84 F6
Sopela [E] 82 G3
Sopočani [YU] 150 B4
Sopot [BG] 148 B4
Sopot [PL] 22 E2
Sopot [YU] 150 B1
Sopron [H] 62 F6
Sora [I] 116 C6
Soragna [I] 110 D2
Söråker [S] 184 F4
Sorano [I] 114 G3
Sorbas [E] 102 H5
Sorbie [GB] 8 C5
Sørbø [N] 164 B2
Sore [F] 66 C4
Söréd [H] 76 B1
Søre Herefoss [N] 164 E5
Soresina [I] 70 H5
Sør-Flatanger [N] 190 B5
Sórgono [I] 118 D5
Sorgues [F] 106 G3
Sörgutvik [N] 190 C4
Soria [E] 90 B3
Soriano Calabro [I] 124 D6
Soriano nel Cimino [I] 114 H4
Sorica [SLO] 74 B4
Sorihuela del Guadalimar [E] 102 G1
Sorisdale [GB] 6 A6
Sorita [E] 98 G1
Sørli [N] 190 D5
Sorø [DK] 156 F3
Soroca [MD] 206 D3
Soroní [GR] 142 D4
Sorpe [E] 84 G5
Sørreisa [N] 192 D3
Sorrento [I] 120 E4
Sørrollnes [N] 192 D3
Sorsele [S] 190 G3
Sörsjön [S] 172 E2
Sorso [I] 118 C3
Sort [E] 84 G6
Sortavala [RUS] 188 H5
Sortino [I] 126 G4
Sortland [N] 192 C3
Sørumsand [N] 166 C1
Sorunda [S] 168 D4
Sörup [D] 156 C5
Sørup [DK] 160 D4
Sørvær [N] 196 A2
Sørvågen [N] 192 B5
Sørvágur [FR] 160 A1
Sörvattnet [S] 182 E5
Sörve [EST] 200 C4
Sørvik [N] 192 D3
Sösdala [S] 158 C2
Sos del Rey Católico [E] 84 C5
Soses [E] 90 H5
Sošice [HR] 74 D6
Sośnica [PL] 50 G2
Sośnicowice [PL] 50 F3
Sosnovo [RUS] 178 G3
Sosnovyy Bor [RUS] 178 F5
Sosnowica [PL] 38 F5
Sosnowiec [PL] 50 G3
Sospel [F] 108 F4
Sóstis [GR] 130 F2
Sotaseter [N] 180 E5
Søtholmen [N] 166 C4
Sotillo de la Adrada [E] 88 E5
Sotillo de las Palomas [E] 88 D6
Sotin [HR] 154 E1
Sotkamo [FIN] 198 F5
Sotkuma [FIN] 188 F2
Sotobañado y Priorato [E] 82 D5
Soto del Barco [E] 78 H3
Soto del Real [E] 88 F5
Sotos [E] 98 C2
Sotresgudo [E] 82 D5
Sotrondio / San Martín del Rey Aurelio [E] 78 H4
Sotta [F] 114 B6
Sottomarina [I] 110 H1
Sottrum [D] 18 E5
Sottunga [FIN] 176 B5
Sotuélamos [E] 96 H4
Soúda [GR] 140 C4
Souesmes [F] 56 C2
Soufflenheim [F] 46 B6
Souflí [GR] 130 H2
Soúgia [GR] 140 B5
Souillac [F] 66 G4
Souilly [F] 44 D4
Soulac-sur-Mer [F] 54 B6
Soulaines-Dhuys [F] 44 C6
Soulópoulo [GR] 132 C2
Soultz [F] 58 D3
Soultz [F] 44 H5
Soumoulou [F] 84 E3
Soúnio [GR] 136 H2
Souppes-sur-Loing [F] 42 G5
Sourdeval [F] 26 E4
Soure [P] 86 D2
Sournia [F] 92 F1
Souroti [GR] 130 B5
Soúrpi [GR] 132 H3
Sousceyrac [F] 66 H4
Sousel [P] 86 E6
Soustons [F] 66 A6
Soutelo [E] 78 C4
Southam [GB] 14 D2
Southampton [GB] 12 H5
South Balloch [GB] 8 C4
Southborough [GB] 14 E5
Southend [GB] 2 H2
Southend-on-Sea [GB] 14 F4
Southminster [GB] 14 F4
South Molton [GB] 12 E4
Southport [GB] 10 D3
South Queensferry [GB] 8 E3
Southsea [GB] 12 H5
South Shields [GB] 8 G6
Southwell [GB] 10 F5
Southwold [GB] 14 H3
Souvála [GR] 136 G1
Souvigny [F] 56 D5
Søvassli [N] 180 H1
Sovata [RO] 206 C5
Sover [I] 72 D4
Soverato [I] 124 E6
Soveria Mannelli [I] 124 D5
Sövestad [S] 158 D3
Sovetsk [RUS] 202 D5
Sovetskiy [RUS] 178 F3
Søvik [N] 180 D3
Sowia Góra [PL] 36 B2
Sowiniec [PL] 20 G6
Søyland [N] 164 A4
Sozopol [BG] 148 F4
Spa [B] 30 E5
Spaichingen [D] 58 G3
Spakenburg [NL] 16 E4
Spalding [GB] 10 G6
Spálené Poříčí [CZ] 48 E5
Spalt [D] 46 G6
Spandau [D] 34 E2
Spangenberg [D] 32 F5
Spangereid [N] 164 C6
S.Pantaleón de Losa [E] 82 F4
Sparanise [I] 120 D2
Spare [LV] 200 C5
Sparreholm [S] 168 C4
Spárta [GR] 134 B6
Spartà [I] 124 B7
Spárti [GR] 136 E4
Spárto [GR] 132 D4
Spasovo [BG] 148 G1
Spáta [GR] 134 C6
Spatharé [GR] 138 H1
Spean Bridge [GB] 6 C6
Spello [I] 116 A2
Spennymoor [GB] 10 F1
Spentrup [DK] 160 E5
Sperchеiáda [GR] 132 F4
Sperlonga [I] 120 C2
Spétses [GR] 136 F3
Speyer [D] 46 C5
Spezzano Albanese [I] 124 D3
Spicino [RUS] 200 G2
Spiddal / An Spidéal [IRL] 2 B5
Spiegelau [D] 60 H2
Spiekeroog [D] 18 C3
Spielfeld [A] 74 D3
Spiez [CH] 70 E1
Spijkenisse [NL] 16 C5
Spíli [GR] 140 D5
Spilimbergo [I] 72 F4
Spinazzola [I] 120 H3
Spincourt [F] 44 E3
Špindlerův-Mlýn [CZ] 50 A2
Spineta Nuova [I] 120 F4
Spionica Donja [BIH] 154 D3
Špišić Bukovica [HR] 74 G5
Spišská Belá [SK] 52 B6
Spišská Nová Ves [SK] 64 E2
Spišské Podhradie [SK] 64 F2
Spišský Štvrtok [SK] 64 E2
Spital am Pyhrn [A] 62 B6
Spittal an der Drau [A] 72 H3
Spittal of Glenshee [GB] 8 E1
Spitz [A] 62 D4
Spjald [DK] 160 B6
Spjelkavik [N] 180 D3
Spjutsund [FIN] 178 B4
Split [HR] 152 A2
Splügen [CH] 70 G2
Spodsbjerg [DK] 156 E4
Špogi [LV] 200 F6
Spoleto [I] 116 B3
Spoltore [I] 116 D4
Spotorno [I] 108 H3
Sprakensehl [D] 32 H1
Spręcowo [PL] 22 G4
Spremberg [D] 34 F5
Spresiano [I] 72 E5
Springe [D] 32 F2
Sproge [S] 168 F5
Spychowo [PL] 24 C4
Squillace [I] 124 E6
Squinzano [I] 122 G4
Srahmore [IRL] 2 C3
Srbac [BIH] 154 C2
Srbica [YU] 150 C5
Srbinje [BIH] 152 D2
Srbobran [YU] 76 E6
Srdeviči [BIH] 152 B1
Srebărna [BG] 148 E1
Srebrenica [BIH] 154 F4
Sredets [BG] 148 C5
Sredets [BG] 148 F5
Sredishte [BG] 148 F1
Srednogortsi [BG] 130 E1
Sredska [YU] 150 C6
Śrem [PL] 36 C3
Sremska Kamenica [YU] 154 F1
Sremska Mitrovica [YU] 154 F2
Sremska Rača [YU] 154 F2
Sremski Karlovci [YU] 154 F2
Sribne [UA] 206 F1
Środa Śląska [PL] 36 C6
Środa Wielkopolska [PL] 36 D3
Srokowo [PL] 24 C3
Srpska Crnja [YU] 76 F6
Srpski Miletić [YU] 76 C6
S. Silvestre de Guzmán [E] 94 E5
S. Stefano d'Aveto [I] 110 C3
Staaken [D] 34 E2
Staatz [A] 62 F3
Stabbestad [N] 164 F4
Stabbursnes [N] 192 H1
Stachy [CZ] 48 E6
Sta Comba Dão [P] 80 C6
Stade [D] 18 E4
Stadhampton [GB] 14 D3
Stadhlaigearraidh / Stilligarry [GB] 6 A4
Stadskanaal [NL] 16 H3
Stadt Allendorf [D] 32 E6
Stadthagen [D] 32 F2
Stadtilm [D] 46 G1
Stadtkyll [D] 30 F6
Stadtlauringen [D] 46 F3
Stadtlohn [D] 16 G5
Stadtoldendorf [D] 32 F3
Stadtroda [D] 48 B1
Stadtsteinach [D] 46 H3
St Aegyd [A] 62 D5
Staffelstein [D] 46 G3
Staffin [GB] 6 B4
Stafford [GB] 10 E5
St-Affrique [F] 106 D3
Stágira [GR] 130 C4
St-Agnant [F] 54 C5
St-Agrève [F] 68 E5
Stahle [D] 32 F3
Stai [N] 172 C1
Staicele [LV] 200 E4
St-Aignan [F] 40 G5
St-Aignan [F] 54 H2
Stainach [A] 62 B6
Staindrop [GB] 10 F2
Staines [GB] 14 E4
Stainville [F] 44 D5
Stainz [A] 74 D2
Stakčín [SK] 64 H2
Stalač [YU] 150 C3
St-Alban [F] 68 C5
St Albans [GB] 14 E3
Stalden [CH] 70 E2
Stalheim [N] 170 D3
Stalída [GR] 140 F4
Stall [A] 72 G2
Stallarholmen [S] 168 C3
Ställdalen [S] 166 G1
Stalon [S] 190 F4
Stalowa Wola [PL] 52 E2
St-Amand-en-Puisaye [F] 56 D2
St-Amand-les-Eaux [F] 28 G3
St-Amand-Longpré [F] 42 C6
St-Amand-Montrond [F] 56 C4
St-Amans [F] 68 C5
St-Amant-Roche-Savine [F] 68 D3
St-Ambroix [F] 106 F2
St-Amé [F] 58 C3
Stamford [GB] 14 E1
Stamná [GR] 132 E5
St-Amour [F] 56 H6
Stams [A] 72 C1
Stamsund [N] 192 B4
St Andrä [A] 74 C3
St-André [F] 42 D3
St Andreasberg [D] 32 G4
St-André-de-Cubzac [F] 66 D3
St-André-les-Alpes [F] 108 D3
St Andrews [GB] 8 F2
Stange [N] 172 C4
Stangerum [DK] 160 E5
Stanghelle [N] 170 B3
St. Angístis [GR] 130 C3
Stanhope [GB] 8 F6

Strelci [BG] 148 B5
Strel'na [RUS] 178 H5
St-Rémy-de-Provence [F] 106 G4
St-Renan [F] 40 B2
Strenči [LV] 200 E4
Strengberg [A] 62 C4
Stresa [I] 70 F3
S. Tresund [S] 190 F4
Strezimirovci [YU] 150 E4
Strib [DK] 156 C2
Stříbro [CZ] 48 D4
Strimasund [S] 190 E2
Strimonikó [GR] 130 B3
St-Riquier [F] 28 D4
Strizivojna [HR] 154 D1
Strmica [HR] 154 A4
Strmilov [CZ] 48 H6
Strobl [A] 60 H5
Strøby Egede [DK] 156 G3
Strofyliá [GR] 134 B4
Strokestown [IRL] 2 D4
Stromberg [D] 46 B3
Strómboli [I] 124 C5
St-Rome-de-Tarn [F] 106 D2
Strömfors [S] 198 A4
Strømmen [N] 166 B1
Strømmen [N] 190 C6
Strömnäs [S] 190 F4
Stromness [GB] 6 F2
Strompdalen [N] 190 D4
Strömsbruk [S] 184 E6
Stromsfors [S] 168 B5
Strömsnäsbruk [S] 162 C5
Strömstad [S] 166 B4
Strömsund [S] 190 E6
Stronachlacher [GB] 8 D2
Strongoli [I] 124 F4
Stronie Śląskie [PL] 50 C3
Strontian [GB] 6 B6
Stroove [IRL] 2 F2
Stropkov [SK] 52 D6
Stroppo [I] 108 E2
Stroud [GB] 12 G3
Strovlés [GR] 140 B5
Str. Pole [PL] 22 F3
Strub Pass [A] 60 G6
Strücklingen [D] 18 C5
Struer [DK] 160 B5
Struga [MK] 128 D3
Strugi-Krasnyye [RUS] 200 H2
Strumica [MK] 128 G2
Strumień [PL] 50 F4
Strupina [PL] 36 C5
Stryama [BG] 148 B5
Stryj [UA] 52 H5
Stryjów [PL] 52 F1
Stryków [PL] 36 G4
Stryn [N] 180 D5
Strzałkowo [PL] 36 E3
Strzegocin [PL] 38 B2
Strzegom [PL] 50 B1
Strzelce [PL] 36 G3
Strzelce Krajeńskie [PL] 36 A1
Strzelce Małe [PL] 36 H6
Strzelce Opolskie [PL] 50 E2
Strzelin [PL] 50 C2
Strzelno [PL] 36 E2
Strzyżów [PL] 52 D4
Strzyżów [PL] 38 G6
St-Saëns [F] 28 C5
St-Satur [F] 56 D3
St-Saturnin-lès-Apt [F] 108 B3
St-Saulge [F] 56 E4
St-Sauvant [F] 54 E4
St-Sauveur-en-Puisaye [F] 56 D2
St-Sauveur-le-Vicomte [F] 26 D2
St-Sauveur-sur-Tinée [F] 108 E3
St-Savin [F] 66 D2
St-Savin [F] 54 F4
St-Seine-l'Abbaye [F] 56 G3
St-Sernin-sur-Rance [F] 106 C3
St-Sever [F] 66 C6
St-Sever [F] 26 E4
St-Sulpice [F] 106 B3
St-Symphorien [F] 66 C4
St-Symphorien-de-Lay [F] 68 E2
St-Symphorien-d'Ozon [F] 68 F3
St-Symphorien-sur-Coise [F] 68 F3
St-Thégonnec [F] 40 C2
St-Thiébault [F] 58 A2
St-Trivier-de-Courtes [F] 56 G6
St-Tropez [F] 108 D5
St-Truiden [B] 30 D4
StubbekØbing [DK] 156 G5
Stuben [A] 72 B1
Štubik [YU] 150 E1
Stubline [YU] 154 G3
Studánky [CZ] 62 B3
Studena [BG] 150 F5
Studená [CZ] 48 H6
Studenec [CZ] 48 H2
Studenica [YU] 150 B3
Studland [GB] 12 G5
Studley [GB] 12 H1
Stugudal [N] 182 D3
Stugufläten [N] 180 F4
Stugun [S] 184 C2
Stühlingen [D] 58 F4
Stukenbrock [D] 32 E3
Stülpe [D] 34 E3
St Ulrich / Ortisei [I] 72 D3
Stupava [SK] 62 G4
Stupinigi [I] 70 D6
Stupino [RUS] 204 F4
Stupnik [HR] 74 E6
Sturminster Newton [GB] 12 G4
Štúrovo [SK] 64 B5
Sturry [GB] 14 G5
St-Ursanne [CH] 58 D4
Stuttgart [D] 58 H1
St-Vaast-la-Hougue [F] 26 E2
St Valentin [A] 62 C4
St-Valery-en-Caux [F] 26 H2
St-Valery-sur-Somme [F] 28 D4
St-Vallier-de-Thiey [F] 108 E4
St-Vallier-sur-Rhône [F] 68 F4
St-Vaury [F] 54 H5
St Veit [A] 74 B3
St-Véran [F] 108 E1
St. Vestec [CZ] 48 G3
St Vigil / Marebbe [I] 72 E3
St Vincent [I] 70 D4
St-Vincent-de-Tyrosse [F] 66 A6
St-Vincent-les-Forts [F] 108 D2
St Vith [B] 30 F6
St-Vivien-de-Médoc [F] 66 C1
St-Wandrille [F] 26 H3
St Wendel [D] 44 G3
St Wolfgang [A] 60 H5
St-Yan [F] 56 E6
Stykkishólmur [IS] 194 B3
Stylída [GR] 132 G4
St-Yorre [F] 68 D1
Stýra [GR] 134 D5
Styri [N] 172 C5
St-Yrieix-la-Perche [F] 66 G2
Styrsö [S] 160 G2
Suadiye [TR] 146 G3
Suances [E] 82 E3
Suaredda [I] 118 E3
Subačius [LT] 202 F4
Subaşi [TR] 146 D2
Subate [LV] 200 F6
Subbiano [I] 110 G6
Subiaco [I] 116 B5
Subotica [YU] 76 D5
Subotište [YU] 154 G2
Sučany [SK] 64 C2
Suceava [RO] 206 C4
Sučevici [HR] 112 H4
Sucha Beskidzka [PL] 50 H4
Suchań [PL] 20 G5
Suchdol nad Lužnicí [CZ] 62 C2
Suchedniów [PL] 38 B6
Suchorze [PL] 22 B3
Suchowola [PL] 24 E4
Suchożebry [PL] 38 D3
Süchteln [D] 30 G3
Sucina [E] 104 C3
Sućuraj [HR] 152 B3
Suda [RUS] 204 F2
Sudak [UA] 206 H6
Sudbø [N] 164 E1
Sudbury [GB] 14 F3
Süden [D] 18 E1
Süderbrarup [D] 18 F1
Süderende [D] 156 A4
Süderlugum [D] 156 B4
Sudova Vyshnia [UA] 52 G4
Suðureyri [IS] 194 C1
Sueca [E] 98 E5
Suelli [I] 118 D6
Sugères [F] 68 D3
Sügütlü [TR] 146 H2
Suhl [D] 46 G2
Suho Polje [BIH] 154 E3
Suhopolje [HR] 74 H6
Šuica [BIH] 152 B1
Suippes [F] 44 C3
Sukeva [FIN] 198 E5
Sukoły [PL] 24 E6
Sukošan [HR] 112 G5
Sükösd [H] 76 C4
Sul [N] 190 C6
Šula [YU] 152 E2
Sulåmo [N] 182 D1
Suldalseid [N] 164 C1
Suldalsosen [N] 164 C1
Sulden / Solda [I] 72 C3
Suldrup [DK] 160 D4
Sulechow [PL] 36 A3
Sulęczyno [PL] 22 C3
Sulejn [PL] 34 H2
Sulejów [PL] 36 H5
Sulejówek [PL] 38 C3
Sulesund [N] 180 C3
Sulina [RO] 206 E6
Sulingen [D] 32 E1
Sulitjelma [N] 192 C6
Sulkava [FIN] 188 E5
Sulkava [FIN] 198 E6
Sulkavanjärvi [FIN] 186 G1
Sulkavankylä [FIN] 186 D4
Sułkowice [PL] 50 H4
Süller [TR] 144 G4
Sully [F] 56 F4
Sully-sur-Loire [F] 56 C1
Sulmierzyce [PL] 36 G6
Sulmierzyce [PL] 36 D5
Sulmona [I] 116 D5
Suloğlu [TR] 146 B1
Sulów [PL] 36 D5
Sultanhisar [TR] 144 E5
Sultanköy [TR] 146 D3
Sülümenli [TR] 144 G4
Sulva / Solf [FIN] 186 B2
Sülysáp [H] 76 D1
Sulz [D] 58 G2
Sulzbach [D] 46 D6
Sulzbach-Rosenberg [D] 46 H5
Sumacarcer [E] 98 E5
Sumartin [HR] 152 A2
Sumba [FR] 160 A3
Sümeg [H] 74 G2
Sumiswald [CH] 58 E6
Summa [FIN] 178 D3
Šumperk [CZ] 50 C4
Sumsa [FIN] 198 G4
Šumvald [CZ] 50 D4
Sumy [UA] 206 G1
Sund [FIN] 176 B5
Sund [N] 192 B6
Sund [S] 166 C3
Sundborn [S] 174 C4
Sundbron [S] 184 F3
Sundbyberg [S] 168 D3
Sunde [N] 190 A6
Sunderland [GB] 8 G6
Sundern [D] 32 C5
Sundhultsbrunn [S] 162 E1
Sundö [S] 190 H5
Sundre [S] 168 F6
Sunds [DK] 160 C6
Sundsfjord [N] 190 E1
Sundsøre [DK] 160 C4
Sundsvall [S] 184 E4
Sundvollen [N] 170 H5
Sungurlare [BG] 148 E4
Suni [I] 118 C4
Sunion [GR] 130 E2
Sunja [HR] 154 B1
Sunnansjö [S] 172 G5
Sunndalsøra [N] 180 F3
Sunne [S] 166 E1
Sunnemo [S] 166 F1
Sunnersta [S] 168 D2
Suntaži [LV] 200 E5
Suodenniemi [FIN] 176 E1
Suolahti [FIN] 186 G3
Suolovuobme [N] 192 G2
Suomenniemi [FIN] 178 D1
Suomijärvi [FIN] 186 C5
Suomusjärvi [FIN] 176 F4
Suomussalmi [FIN] 198 F3
Suonenjoki [FIN] 188 C3
Suopelto [FIN] 176 H1
Suorva [S] 192 D5
Suosjavrre [N] 192 H2
Suovanlahti [FIN] 186 G2
Superespot [E] 92 E2
Supetar [HR] 152 A2
Supino [I] 116 B6
Supraśl [PL] 24 F5
Supru [FIN] 196 E3
Surahammar [S] 168 B2
Šurany [SK] 64 B5
Suraż [PL] 24 E6
Surazh [BY] 204 C4
Surčin [YU] 154 G2
Surduk [YU] 154 G2
Surdulica [YU] 150 E5
Surgères [F] 54 C5
Súria [E] 92 D3
Šurice [SK] 64 E4
Surju [EST] 200 E3
Surnadalsöra [N] 180 G2
Sŭrnitsa [BG] 130 C1
Sursee [CH] 58 E5
Surte [S] 160 H2
Survilliers [F] 42 G3
Susa [I] 70 C5
Sušara [YU] 154 H2
Susch [CH] 72 B2
Susek [YU] 154 F1
Sushitsa [BG] 148 C3
Sušice [CZ] 48 E6
Süssen [D] 60 B2
Susurluk [TR] 146 D5
Susz [PL] 22 F4
Sutivan [HR] 152 A2
Sutjeska [YU] 154 H1
Sutomore [YU] 152 E5
Sutri [I] 114 H4
Sutton Coldfield [GB] 10 E6
Suure-Jaani [EST] 200 E2
Suuremõisa [EST] 200 C2
Suva Reka [YU] 150 C6
Suvereto [I] 114 E2
Suvorovo [BG] 148 F2
Suwałki [PL] 24 E3
Suystamo [RUS] 188 H4
Suzzara [I] 110 E2
Svalöv [S] 158 C2
Svaneke [DK] 158 E4
Svanesund [S] 166 C6
Svängsta [S] 158 E1
Svaningen [S] 190 E5
Svanskog [S] 166 D3
Svanstein [S] 196 B8
Svanvik [N] 196 F3
Svappavaara [S] 192 F5
Svärdsjo [S] 174 D4
Svarstad [N] 164 G2
Svartå [S] 166 G3
Svärtinge [S] 168 B5
Svartisdalen [N] 190 E2
Svartlå [S] 198 A2
Svartnäs [S] 174 D3
Svartnes [N] 196 F2
Sväty Jur [SK] 62 G4
Svedala [S] 158 C3
Svedasai [LT] 202 G4
Svedje [S] 184 E5
Sveg [S] 182 G5
Sveindal [N] 164 D4
Švėkšna [LT] 202 D4
Svelgen [N] 180 B5
Svellingen [N] 190 A6
Svelvik [N] 164 H2
Svenarum [S] 162 D3
Švenčionėliaj [LT] 202 H4
Švenčionys [LT] 202 H5
Svendborg [DK] 156 E4
Svenes [N] 164 E4
Svenljunga [S] 162 B3
Svensby [N] 192 E2
Svenstavik [S] 182 G3
Svenstrup [DK] 160 D4
Švermov [CZ] 48 F3
S. Vero Milis [I] 118 C5
Sveti Naum [MK] 128 D4
Sveti Nikole [MK] 128 F1
Sveti Rok [HR] 112 G4
Sveti Stefan [YU] 152 E5
Světlá nad Sázavou [CZ] 48 H5
Svetlogorsk [RUS] 202 C5
Svetogorsk [RUS] 178 F2
Svetozarevo [YU] 150 C2
Svetozar Miletic [YU] 76 C5
Svetvinčenat [HR] 112 D2
S.Vicente de la Cabeza [E] 80 G4
Svidnik [SK] 52 D5
Švihov [CZ] 48 D5
Svilajnac [YU] 150 C1
Svilengrad [BG] 146 A2
Svinesund [S] 166 C3
Svingstad [N] 170 H3
Svingvoll [N] 170 H2
Svinhult [S] 162 E2
Svinninge [DK] 156 F2
Svir [BY] 202 H5
Svishtov [BG] 148 C2
Svislach [BY] 24 G5
Svitavy [CZ] 50 B4
Svitlovods'k [UA] 206 G3
Svodje [YU] 150 E4
Svoge [BG] 150 F4
Svolvær [N] 192 B4
Svorkmo [N] 180 H2
Svrčinovec [SK] 50 F5
Svrljig [YU] 150 D3
Svullrya [N] 172 D5
Swaffham [GB] 14 G2
Swalmen [NL] 30 F3
Swanage [GB] 12 G5
Swanlinbar [IRL] 2 E4
Swansea [GB] 12 E2
Swarożyn [PL] 22 E3
Swarzędz [PL] 36 C2
Swarzewo [PL] 22 D1
Swatragh [GB] 2 G2
Świdnica [PL] 50 B1
Świdnica [PL] 34 H4
Świdnik [PL] 38 E5
Świdwin [PL] 20 H4
Świebodzice [PL] 50 B1
Świebodzin [PL] 36 A3
Świecie [PL] 22 D5
Świecko [PL] 34 G3
Świeradów-Zdrój [PL] 48 H1
Świerczów [PL] 50 E1
Świerki [PL] 50 B2
Świerzawa [PL] 50 B1
Świerzno [PL] 20 F3
Święta Anna [PL] 50 G1
Swieta Lipka [PL] 24 B3
Święte [PL] 36 E3
Świętno [PL] 36 B4
Swindon [GB] 12 H3
Swinford [IRL] 2 C4
Świnoujście [PL] 20 E3
Swinton [GB] 8 F4
Swords [IRL] 2 F6
Sychevka [RUS] 204 E4
Syców [PL] 36 D6
Sykäräinen [FIN] 198 D6
Syke [D] 18 D6
Sykéa [GR] 136 F4
Sykeá [GR] 130 D6
Sykkylven [N] 180 D4
Sykoúri [GR] 132 G1
Sylling [N] 164 H1
Syltefjordfjellet [N] 196 E1
Symbister [GB] 6 H4
Sými [GR] 142 D4
Syötekylä [FIN] 198 E2
Syre [GB] 6 E3
Sysmä [FIN] 178 A1
Sysslebäck [S] 172 E4
Syston [GB] 10 F6
Syväjärvi [FIN] 196 D7
Syvänniemi [FIN] 188 C2
Syvde [N] 180 C4
Syvsten [DK] 160 E3
Syyspohja [FIN] 188 E6
Szabadszállás [H] 76 C3
Szabolcsbáka [H] 64 H4
Szadek [PL] 36 F4
Szakály [H] 76 B4
Szakcs [H] 76 B3
Szalkszentmárton [H] 76 C2
Szalonna [H] 64 F3
Szamocin [PL] 22 B6
Szamotuły [PL] 36 C2
Szany [H] 74 G1
Szarvas [H] 76 F2
Szarvaskő [H] 64 E5
Szczawnica [PL] 52 B5
Szczebrzeszyn [PL] 52 F1
Szczecin [PL] 20 F5
Szczecinek [PL] 22 B4
Szczekociny [PL] 50 H2
Szczerców [PL] 36 G5
Szczucin [PL] 52 C3
Szczuczyn [PL] 24 D4
Szczurowa [PL] 52 B3
Szczyrk [PL] 50 G5
Szczytna [PL] 50 B3
Szczytno [PL] 24 B4
Szécsény [H] 64 D5
Szederkény [H] 76 B5
Szeged [H] 76 E4
Szeghalom [H] 76 G2
Szegvár [H] 76 E3
Székely [H] 64 H4
Székesfehérvár [H] 76 B2
Székkutas [H] 76 F3
Szekszárd [H] 76 C4

Szendrő [H] 64 F4
Szentendre [H] 64 C6
Szentes [H] 76 E3
Szentlászló [H] 76 A5
Szentliszló [H] 74 G3
Szentlőrinc [H] 76 A5
Szerencs [H] 64 G4
Szestno [PL] 24 B3
Szetlew [PL] 36 E3
Szgliget [H] 74 H3
Szigetvár [H] 76 A5
Szikszó [H] 64 F4
Szil [H] 62 G6
Szilvásvárad [H] 64 E4
Szklarska Poreba [PL] 48 H1
Szklary [PL] 52 E4
Szklary Górne [PL] 36 B5
Szlichtyngowa [PL] 36 B4
Szob [H] 64 C5
Szolnok [H] 76 E2
Szombathely [H] 74 F2
Szonowice [PL] 50 E3
Szőny [H] 64 B6
Szprotawa [PL] 34 H5
Szreńsk [PL] 22 G6
Sztum [PL] 22 E4
Szubin [PL] 22 C6
Szulmierz [PL] 22 H6
Szumirad [PL] 50 E1
Szurdokpüspöki [H] 64 D5
Szwecja [PL] 22 B5
Szydłów [PL] 52 C2
Szydłów [PL] 36 G5
Szydłowiec [PL] 38 B6
Szydłowo [PL] 22 B6
Szymbark [PL] 22 F4
Szypliski [PL] 24 E2

T

Taalintehdas / Dalsbruk [FIN] 176 E6
Taapajärvi [FIN] 192 H6
Taavetti [FIN] 178 D2
Tab [H] 76 A3
Tabaja [BIH] 152 C3
Tábara [E] 80 H4
Tabernas [E] 102 G5
Tabiano Bagni [I] 110 D2
Taboada [E] 78 D4
Tábor [CZ] 48 G5
Tábua [P] 86 E2
Tabuaço [P] 80 D5
Tabuenca [E] 90 D3
Täby [S] 168 D2
Tachov [CZ] 48 C4
Tadcaster [GB] 10 F3
Tafalla [E] 84 B4
Tagaranna [EST] 200 C3
Taggia [I] 108 G4
Taghmon [IRL] 4 F5
Tagliacozzo [I] 116 B5
Táglio di Po [I] 110 H2
Tahal [E] 102 G4
Tahtaköprü [TR] 146 G5
Tai di Cadore [I] 72 F4
Tailfingen [D] 58 G2
Tain [GB] 6 E4
Tain-l'Hermitage [F] 68 F4
Taipadas [P] 86 C5
Taipaleenkyla [FIN] 186 D4
Taipalsaari [FIN] 178 D2
Tairbeart / Tarbert [GB] 6 B3
Taivalkoski [FIN] 198 F3
Taivassalo [FIN] 176 C4
Taizé [F] 56 F6
Tajcy [RUS] 178 H5
Takácsi [H] 74 H1
Talachyn [BY] 204 C5
Talamone [I] 114 F3
Talarrubias [E] 96 C3
Talaván [E] 86 H4
Talavera de la Reina [E] 88 D6
Talavera la Real [E] 94 G1
Talayuela [E] 88 B6
Talayuelas [E] 98 D3
Táliga [E] 94 F2
Tálkafjörður [IS] 194 B1
Talladale [GB] 6 C4
Tallaght [IRL] 2 F6
Tallard [F] 108 D2
Tällberg [S] 172 H3
Tallinn [EST] 200 D1
Talloires [F] 70 B3
Tallow [IRL] 4 D5
Talmont [F] 54 C6
Talmont-St-Hilaire [F] 54 B3
Talsi [LV] 200 C5
Talvik [N] 192 G1
Tamajón [E] 88 H4
Tamames [E] 88 B3
Tamarë [AL] 152 F4
Tamarino [BG] 148 E5
Tamarite de Litera [E] 90 H4
Tamási [H] 76 B3
Tambohuse [DK] 160 C4
Tammela [FIN] 176 F3
Tammensiel [D] 18 E1
Tammijärvi [FIN] 186 G5
Tammisaari / Ekenäs [FIN] 176 F6
Tamnič [YU] 150 E2
Tampere [FIN] 176 F1
Tamsalu [EST] 200 E1
Tamsweg [A] 72 H2
Tamworth [GB] 10 E6
Tana bru [N] 196 D2
Tanágra [GR] 134 B5
Tancarville [F] 26 G3
Tanda [YU] 150 D1
Tandragee [GB] 2 G4
Tandsjöborg [S] 172 G1
Tångaberg [S] 160 H3
Tangen [N] 166 B3
Tangen [N] 166 C1
Tangen [N] 172 C4
Tanger [Eur.] 100 F6
Tangerhütte [D] 34 B2
Tangermünde [D] 34 C2
Tanhua [FIN] 196 E6
Taninges [F] 70 B2
Tankavaara [FIN] 196 D5
Tanlay [F] 56 F2
Tann [D] 46 F1
Tannadice [GB] 8 F2
Tännäs [S] 182 E4
Tanne [D] 32 H4
Tannheim [A] 60 C6
Tannila [FIN] 198 D3
Tanum [S] 166 C4
Tanumshede [S] 166 C4
Tanvald [CZ] 48 H2
Taormina [I] 124 B8
Tapa [EST] 200 E1
Tapia de Casariego [E] 78 F2
Tapionkylä [FIN] 196 C7
Tapionniemi [FIN] 196 E7
Tápiószecső [H] 76 D1
Tápiószele [H] 76 D1
Tapolca [H] 74 H3
Tapolcafő [H] 74 H1
Taps [DK] 156 C3
Taraklı [TR] 146 H4
Taramundi [E] 78 F2
Tarancón [E] 96 H2
Táranto [I] 122 E4
Tarare [F] 68 F2
Tarascon [F] 106 G4
Tarascon-sur-Ariège [F] 84 H5
Tarasp [CH] 72 B2
Tarazona [E] 84 A6
Tarazona de la Mancha [E] 98 B4
Tårbæk [DK] 156 H2
Tarbert [GB] 8 C3
Tarbert [IRL] 2 B6
Tarbert / Tairbeart [GB] 6 B3
Tarbes [F] 84 F3
Tarbet [GB] 8 D2
Tarcento [I] 72 G4
Tarčin [BIH] 152 C1
Tarczyn [PL] 38 B4
Tardets-Sorholus [F] 84 D3
Tardienta [E] 90 F3
Tärendö [S] 192 G6
Tarhos [H] 76 G3
Tarifa [E] 100 G6
Tarleton [GB] 10 D3
Tarm [DK] 156 B1
Tarmstedt [D] 18 E5
Tärnaby [S] 190 E3
Tarnaméra [H] 64 E6
Tarnawałka [PL] 52 G2
Tarnobrzeg [PL] 52 D2
Tarnogród [PL] 52 F2
Tarnos [F] 66 A6
Târnova [RO] 76 H4
Tarnów [PL] 34 G1
Tarnów [PL] 52 C4
Tarnów [PL] 38 C4
Tarnowo Podgórne [PL] 36 C2
Tarnowskie Góry [PL] 50 F3
Tärnsjö [S] 174 E5
Tarouca [P] 80 D5
Tarp [D] 18 F1
Tarquínia [I] 114 G4
Tarquinia Lido [I] 114 G4
Tarragona [E] 92 C5
Tarrasa / Terrassa [E] 92 E4
Tàrrega [E] 92 C3
Tårs [DK] 156 E4
Tårs [DK] 160 E3
Tarsia [I] 124 D3
Tarskavaig [GB] 6 B5
Tartas [F] 66 B6
Tartu [EST] 200 F3
Tårup [DK] 156 E3
Tarutino [MD] 206 E5
Tarvasjoki [FIN] 176 E4
Tarvisio [I] 72 H3
Taşbükü [TR] 142 E2
Täsch [CH] 70 E3
Tåsjö [S] 190 F5
Taşköy [TR] 144 F3
Taşlıca [TR] 142 D3
Tassjö [S] 162 B6
Tåstrup [DK] 156 G2
Tata [H] 64 B6
Tatabánya [H] 64 B6
Tataháza [H] 76 D4
Tatarbunary [UA] 206 E5
Tatárszentgyörgy [H] 76 D2
Tatranská Kotlina [SK] 52 B6
Tau [N] 164 B3
Tauberbischofsheim [D] 46 E4
Taucha [D] 34 C5
Tauerntunnel [A] 72 G2
Tauern Tunnel [A] 72 H1
Taufers / Tubre [I] 72 B3
Taufkirchen [A] 60 H4
Taufkirchen [D] 60 F4
Taujėnai [LT] 202 G4
Taüll [E] 84 G6
Taunton [GB] 12 F4
Taunusstein [D] 46 B3
Tauplitz [A] 62 B6
Taurage [LT] 202 E5
Taurasi [I] 120 F3
Taurianova [I] 124 C7
Taurisano [I] 122 G6
Taurkains [LV] 200 E5
Tauste [E] 90 E3
Tauves [F] 68 B2
Tavannes [CH] 58 D5
Tavarnelle Val di Pesa [I] 110 F6
Tavas [TR] 144 G5
Tavascan [E] 84 G6
Tavastkenka [FIN] 198 E5
Tavaux [F] 56 H4
Taverna [I] 124 E5
Tavernelle [I] 114 H2
Tavernes [F] 108 C4
Tavernes de la Valldigna [E] 98 E6
Taviano [I] 122 G6
Tavira [P] 94 D5
Tavistock [GB] 12 D4
Tavşancıl [TR] 146 F3
Tavşanlı [TR] 144 G1
Taxenbach [A] 72 G1
Tayfur [TR] 146 B5
Tayinloan [GB] 2 H1
Tayport [GB] 8 F2
Tayvallich [GB] 8 C2
Tázlár [H] 76 D3
Tazones [E] 82 C1
Tczew [PL] 22 E3
Tczów [PL] 38 C5
Teano [I] 120 D2
Teascu [RO] 150 G1
Techendorf [A] 72 G3
Tecklenburg [D] 32 C2
Tecuci [RO] 206 D5
Teféli [GR] 140 E5
Tefenni [TR] 142 H1
Tegelen [NL] 30 F3
Tegernsee [D] 60 E5
Téglás [H] 64 H5
Teglio [I] 72 A4
Teguise [E] 100 E4
Teichel [D] 46 H1
Teignmouth [GB] 12 E5
Teillet [F] 106 C3
Teisendorf [D] 60 G5
Teisko [FIN] 186 E6
Teixeiro [E] 78 D2
Tejn [DK] 158 E4
Teke [TR] 146 F2
Tekeriš [YU] 154 F3
Tekirdağ [TR] 146 C3
Tekovské Lužany [SK] 64 B5
Telana [I] 118 E5
Telavåg [N] 170 A4
Telč [CZ] 48 H6
Telde [E] 100 C6
Telese Terme [I] 120 E2
Telford [GB] 10 D6
Telfs [A] 72 C1
Telgte [D] 32 C3
Telheiro [P] 94 B3
Telish [BG] 148 A3
Teljo [FIN] 198 G5
Tellingstedt [D] 18 E2
Telšiai [LT] 202 E4
Telti [I] 118 D3
Tembleque [E] 96 G2
Temerin [YU] 154 F1
Temmes [FIN] 198 D4
Témpio Pausánia [I] 118 D3
Temple Bar [GB] 10 B6
Templemore [IRL] 4 E3
Templepatrick [GB] 2 G3
Templetouhy [IRL] 4 E3
Templin [D] 20 D6
Temse [B] 28 H2
Temska [YU] 150 E3
Tenala / Tenhola [FIN] 176 F5
Tenbury Wells [GB] 12 G1
Tenby [GB] 12 D2
Tence [F] 68 E4
Tenda, Colle di- / Tende, Col de- [Eur.] 108 F3
Tende [F] 108 F3
Tendilla [E] 88 H6
Tenebrón [E] 88 A3
Tenevo [BG] 148 E5
Tenhola / Tenala [FIN] 176 F5
Tenhult [S] 162 D2
Tenja [HR] 154 E1
Tenk [H] 64 E6
Tennevik [N] 192 D4
Tennevoll [N] 192 D3
Tenterden [GB] 14 F5
Teo / Ramallosa [E] 78 C3
Teolo [I] 110 G1
Tepasto [FIN] 192 H4
Tepecik [TR] 144 G1
Tepecik [TR] 146 F3
Tepeköy [TR] 144 E4
Tepelenë [AL] 128 B6
Teplá [CZ] 48 D4
Teplice [CZ] 48 E2
Teplice nad Metují [CZ] 50 B2
Teploye [RUS] 204 F5
Tepsa [FIN] 196 C6
Téramo [I] 116 C3
Ter Apel [NL] 16 H3
Teratyn [PL] 38 G6
Terebiń [PL] 52 G1
Terebishche [RUS] 200 G3
Terebovlia [UA] 206 C3
Terehovo [RUS] 200 H4
Terespol [PL] 38 F3
Terezín [CZ] 48 F2
Terezino Polje [HR] 74 H5
Tergnier [F] 28 F6
Terkoz [TR] 146 E2
Terlizzi [I] 122 D2
Termal [TR] 146 F3
Termas de Monfortinho [P] 86 G3
Terme di Lurisia [I] 108 F3
Terme di Valdieri [I] 108 F3
Terme Luigiane [I] 124 C4
Terme S. Lucia [I] 116 C2
Terme Vigliatore [I] 126 D4
Términi Imerese [I] 126 D2
Terminillo [I] 116 B4
Terminón [E] 82 E5
Termís [GR] 134 H2
Térmoli [I] 116 F5
Termolovo [RUS] 178 G3
Termonfeckin [IRL] 2 F5
Terndrup [DK] 160 E4
Terneuzen [NL] 28 H1
Terni [I] 116 A3
Ternitz [A] 62 E6
Ternopil' [UA] 206 C2
Térovo [GR] 132 D2
Terpan [AL] 128 B5
Terpezita [RO] 150 F1
Terpní [GR] 130 B3
Terracina [I] 120 C2
Terradillos de los Templarios [E] 82 C5
Terråk [N] 190 D4
Terralba [I] 118 C5
Terranova di Pollino [I] 122 C6
Terrassa / Tarrasa [E] 92 E4
Terrasson-la-Villedieu [F] 66 G3
Terrateig [E] 98 E6
Terrazos [E] 82 F5
Terriente [E] 98 D2
Tertenía [I] 118 E6
Teruel [E] 98 E2
Tervakoski [FIN] 176 G3
Tervel [BG] 148 F1
Tervo [FIN] 186 H2
Tervola [FIN] 198 C2
Tervuren [B] 30 C4
Terz [A] 62 D5
Terzaga [E] 90 C6
Tesegerague [E] 100 E5
Teslič [BIH] 154 C3
Teslui [RO] 150 G1
Tessin [D] 20 C3
Tessy sur-Vire [F] 26 E4
Tét [H] 62 H6
Tetbury [GB] 12 G3
Teterow [D] 20 C4
Teteven [BG] 148 A4
Tetovo [BG] 148 D2
Tetovo [MK] 128 D1
Tetrálofo [GR] 128 F5
Tettnang [D] 58 H4
Teufen [CH] 58 H5
Teulada [E] 104 F2
Teulada [I] 118 C7
Teupitz [D] 34 E3
Teuro [FIN] 176 F3
Teuva [FIN] 186 B4
Tevaniemi [FIN] 186 D6
Tevfikiye [TR] 130 H5
Teviothead [GB] 8 E5
Tewkesbury [GB] 12 G2
Tewli [BY] 38 G2
Texeiro [E] 78 E3
Thale [D] 34 A4
Thalfang [D] 44 G2
Thalheim [D] 48 D2
Thalmässing [D] 46 G6
Thalwil [CH] 58 F5
Thame [GB] 14 D3
Thann [F] 58 D3
Thannhausen [D] 60 C3
Tharandt [D] 48 E1
Thásos [GR] 130 E4
Thatcham [GB] 12 H4
Thaumiers [F] 56 C4
Thaxted [GB] 14 F3
Them [DK] 156 C1
Themar [D] 46 F2
Thénezay [F] 54 E3
Thenon [F] 66 F3
Theodosiia [UA] 206 H6
Theológos [GR] 134 A4
Theológos [GR] 130 E4
Théoule [F] 108 E5
Thérma [GR] 138 G1
Thermá [GR] 130 G4
Thérmi [GR] 130 B4
Thermísia [GR] 136 G2
Thérmo [GR] 132 F5
Thermopíles [GR] 132 G4
Thérouanne [F] 28 E2
Thespies [GR] 134 A5
Thessaloníki [GR] 130 A4
Thetford [GB] 14 G2
Theux [B] 30 E5
Thevet-St-Julien [F] 56 B4
Theze [F] 84 E3
Thiaucourt-Regniéville [F] 44 E4
Thiberville [F] 26 G4
Thiélbemont-Farémont [F] 44 C5
Thiendorf [D] 34 E5
Thiene [I] 72 D5
Thiers [F] 68 D2
Thiersee [A] 60 F6
Thiesi [I] 118 C3
Thiessow [D] 20 E2
Thimariá [GR] 130 H3
Thimianá [GR] 134 G5
Thingeyri [IS] 194 C1
Thingvellir [IS] 194 C4
Thionville [F] 44 E3
Thíra / Fira [GR] 138 F5
Thirette [F] 68 H1
Thirsk [GB] 10 F3
Thisted [DK] 160 C4
Thísvi [GR] 132 H5
Thíva [GR] 134 B5
Thivars [F] 42 D4
Thiviers [F] 66 F2
Thizy [F] 68 F2
Thoissey [F] 68 G1
Tholey [D] 44 G3
Tholó [GR] 136 C3
Thomas Street [IRL] 2 D5
Thomastown [IRL] 4 E4
Thônes [F] 70 B3
Thonon [F] 70 B2
Thonon-les-Bains [F] 70 B2
Thorikó [GR] 136 H1
Thörl [A] 62 D6
Thorlákshöfn [IS] 194 B5
Thornbury [GB] 12 G3
Thorney [GB] 14 F2
Thornhill [GB] 8 D4
Thórshöfn [IS] 194 G3
Thouarcé [F] 54 D2
Thouars [F] 54 E2
Thouría [GR] 136 D4
Thourio [GR] 130 H1
Threshfield [GB] 10 E3
Thueyts [F] 68 E5
Thuin [B] 28 H4
Thuir [F] 92 G1
Thum [D] 48 D2
Thun [CH] 70 D1
Thürkow [D] 20 C4
Thurles / Durlas [IRL] 4 E3
Thurnau [D] 46 H3
Thurn Pass [A] 72 F1
Thurso [GB] 6 F2
Thury-Harcourt [F] 26 F4
Thusis [CH] 70 H1
Thyborøn [DK] 160 B4
Thyregod [DK] 156 C1
Tiana [I] 118 D5
Tibava [SK] 64 H2
Tibro [S] 166 F5
Ticha [BG] 148 D3
Tidaholm [S] 166 F6
Tidan [S] 166 F5
Tiefenbronn [D] 58 G1
Tiefencastel [CH] 70 H2
Tiefensee [D] 34 F2
Tiel [NL] 16 E5
Tielt [B] 28 G2
Tiemassaari [FIN] 188 D4
Tienen [B] 30 D4
Tiengen [D] 58 F4
Tiercé [F] 40 H6
Tierga [E] 90 D3
Tiermas [E] 88 H3
Tierp [S] 174 F5
Tigharry / Tigh Ghearraidh [GB] 6 A3
Tigh Ghearraidh / Tigharry [GB] 6 A3
Tighina [MD] 206 E4
Tighnabruaich [GB] 8 C2
Tigkáki [GR] 142 C3
Tignes [F] 70 C4
Tihany [H] 76 A2
Tihío [GR] 128 E5
Tihuța, Pasul- [RO] 206 C4
Tiistenjoki [FIN] 186 D3
Tikhvin [RUS] 204 D1
Tikkakoski [FIN] 186 G4
Tikkala [FIN] 186 F5
Tilberga [S] 168 C2
Tilburg [NL] 30 E2
Tilbury [GB] 14 F4
Til-Châtel [F] 56 H3
Tílisos [GR] 140 E4
Tillicoultry [GB] 8 E2
Tiltagals [LV] 200 F5
Tiltrem [N] 190 B5
Tilži [LV] 200 G5
Timahoe [IRL] 4 F3
Timișoara [RO] 76 G5
Timmel [D] 18 B4
Timmele [S] 162 C2
Timmendorfer Strand [D] 18 H3
Timmernabben [S] 162 G4
Timmersdala [S] 166 F5
Timoleague [IRL] 4 C5
Timrå [S] 184 E4
Tinahely [IRL] 4 F4
Tinajo [E] 100 E4
Tinca [RO] 76 H3
Tinchebray [F] 26 E4
Tineo [E] 78 G3
Tingelstad [N] 170 H4
Tinglev [DK] 156 B4
Tingsryd [S] 162 E5
Tingstäde [S] 168 G4
Tingvoll [N] 180 F2
Tínos [GR] 138 E2
Tiñosillos [E] 88 E4
Tintagel [GB] 12 C4
Tinuži [LV] 200 E5
Tiobraid Arann / Tipperary [IRL] 4 D4
Tione di Trento [I] 72 C4
Tipasjoki [FIN] 198 F5
Tipperary / Tiobraid Arann [IRL] 4 D4
Tiranë [AL] 128 B3
Tirano [I] 72 B4
Tiraspol [MD] 206 E4
Tire [TR] 144 D5
Tirgo [E] 82 G6
Tîrgoviște [RO] 206 C6
Tîrgu Frumos [RO] 206 D4
Tîrgu Jiu [RO] 206 B6
Tîrgu Lăpuș [RO] 206 B4
Tîrgu Mureș [RO] 206 C5
Tîrgu Neamț [RO] 206 C4
Tîrgu Secuiesc [RO] 206 C5
Tiriolo [I] 124 E5
Tirmo [FIN] 178 B4
Tîrnăveni [RO] 206 B5
Tírnavos [GR] 132 G1
Tirol / Tirolo [I] 72 C3
Tirolo / Tirol [I] 72 C3
Tirós [GR] 136 F3
Tirrénia [I] 110 D6
Tirschenreuth [D] 48 C4
Tirstrup [DK] 160 E6
Tišča [BIH] 154 E4
Tiscar-Don Pedro [E] 102 F2
Tisno [HR] 112 G6
Tišnov [CZ] 50 B6
Tisovec [SK] 64 D3
Tistrup [DK] 156 B2
Tisvilde [DK] 156 G1
Tiszaalpár [H] 76 E3
Tiszabábolna [H] 64 F6
Tiszacsege [H] 64 F6
Tiszaföldvár [H] 76 E2
Tiszafüred [H] 64 F6
Tiszakécske [H] 76 E2
Tiszalök [H] 64 G5
Tiszalúc [H] 64 F5
Tiszaörs [H] 64 F6
Tiszaroff [H] 76 E1
Tiszaszőlős [H] 64 F6
Tiszaújváros [H] 64 F5
Tiszavasvári [H] 64 G5
Titel [YU] 154 G1
Titisee [D] 58 F3
Titov Veles [MK] 128 F1
Titran [N] 190 A6
Tittling [D] 60 H3
Tittmoning [D] 60 G4
Titz [D] 30 F4
Tiuccia [F] 114 A4
Tiukka / Tjöck [FIN] 186 B4
Tivat [YU] 152 D4
Tived [S] 166 G4
Tiverton [GB] 12 E4
Tivoli [I] 116 B5
Tizzano [F] 114 A6
Tjæreborg [DK] 156 B2
Tjällmo [S] 166 H5
Tjåmotis [S] 190 G1
Tjentište [BIH] 152 D2
Tjöck / Tiukka [FIN] 186 B4
Tjolmen [N] 190 E3
Tjøme [N] 164 H3
Tjong [N] 190 D1
Tjønnefoss [N] 164 E3
Tjørhom [N] 164 C3
Tjørnhom [N] 164 C5
Tjørnuvik [FR] 160 A1
Tjøtta [N] 190 D3
Tkon [HR] 112 G5
Tleń [PL] 22 D4
Tlmače [SK] 64 B4
Tłuchowo [PL] 36 G1
Tłuszcz [PL] 38 C2
Tobarra [E] 98 B6
Tobercurry [IRL] 2 D3
Tobermore [GB] 2 F3
Tobermory [GB] 6 B6
Toblach / Dobbiaco [I] 72 E3
Tocha [P] 80 A6
Tocina [E] 94 H5
Töcksfors [S] 166 C2
Todi [I] 116 A3
Todoriči [BIH] 154 B4
Todtmoos [D] 58 E4
Todtnau [D] 58 E3
Tofte [N] 164 H2
Toftir [FR] 160 B2
Toftlund [DK] 156 B3
Togher [IRL] 2 D5
Tohmajärvi [FIN] 188 G3
Toholampi [FIN] 198 C6
Tohvri [EST] 200 E3
Toijala [FIN] 176 F2
Toivakka [FIN] 186 G5
Toivola [FIN] 178 C1
Töjby [FIN] 186 A4
Tojšiči [BIH] 154 E3
Tokaj [H] 64 G4
Tokari [PL] 36 F4
Tokarnia [PL] 50 H4
Tokarnia [PL] 52 B2
Tokmak [UA] 206 H4
Toksovo [RUS] 178 H4
Tolastadh / Tolsta [GB] 6 C2
Tolcsva [H] 64 G4
Toledo [E] 96 F1
Tolentino [I] 116 C2
Tolfa [I] 114 G4
Tolg [S] 162 E4
Tolga [N] 182 C4
Tolkis / Tolkkinen [FIN] 178 B4
Tolkkinen / Tolkis [FIN] 178 B4
Tolkmicko [PL] 22 F2
Tollarp [S] 158 D2

Tølløse [DK] 156 F3
Tolmachevo [RUS] 200 H1
Tolmezzo [I] 72 G4
Tolmin [SLO] 72 H4
Tolna [H] 76 C4
Tolne [DK] 160 E2
Toló [GR] 136 F2
Tolob [GB] 6 G4
Tolosa [E] 84 B3
Tolosa [P] 86 E4
Tolox [E] 102 B4
Tolsta / Tolastadh [GB] 6 C2
Tolva [FIN] 196 F8
Tolve [I] 120 H4
Tomar [P] 86 D3
Tomaševo [YU] 150 A4
Tomaszów Lubelski [PL] 52 G2
Tomaszów Mazowiecki [PL] 36 H5
Tomatin [GB] 6 E5
Tombebœuf [F] 66 E4
Tomdoun [GB] 6 C5
Tomelilla [S] 158 D3
Tomelloso [E] 96 G4
Tomintoul [GB] 6 E5
Tømmernes [N] 192 C5
Tommerup [DK] 156 D3
Tømmervåg [N] 180 F2
Tompa [H] 76 D4
Tomra [N] 180 D3
Tomter [N] 166 B2
Tona [E] 92 E3
Tonara [I] 118 D5
Tonbridge [GB] 14 E5
Tondela [P] 80 C6
Tønder [DK] 156 B4
Tongeren (Tongres) [B] 30 E4
Tongres (Tongeren) [B] 30 E4
Tongue [GB] 6 E2
Tonnay–Boutonne [F] 54 C5
Tonnay–Charente [F] 54 C5
Tonneins [F] 66 E5
Tonnerre [F] 56 F2
Tönning [D] 18 E2
Tønsberg [N] 164 H3
Tonstad [N] 164 C4
Tonypandy [GB] 12 F2
Toomyvara [IRL] 2 D6
Toourmakeady [IRL] 2 C4
Topares [E] 102 H3
Topchii [BG] 148 D2
Töpchin [D] 34 E3
Toplița [RO] 206 C4
Toplou [GR] 140 G4
Topola [YU] 150 B1
Topolcani [MK] 128 E3
Topol'čany [SK] 64 B3
Topólia [GR] 140 B4
Topolovățu Mare [RO] 76 H5
Topolovgrad [BG] 146 A1
Topolovo [BG] 148 B6
Toporu [RO] 148 C1
Toques [E] 78 D3
Torà [E] 92 D3
Toral de los Vados [E] 78 F5
Torbalı [TR] 144 D4
Torbole [I] 72 C5
Torcello [I] 72 F6
Torcross [GB] 12 E5
Tordera [E] 92 F4
Tordesillas [E] 88 E2
Tordesilos [E] 90 C6
Töre [S] 198 B2
Töreboda [S] 166 F5
Torekov [S] 160 H6
Torelló [E] 92 E3
Toreno [E] 78 F5
Torfyanovka [RUS] 178 E3
Torgau [D] 34 D5
Torgelow [D] 20 E4
Torgiano [I] 116 A2
Torhamn [S] 158 G1
Torhout [B] 28 F2
Tori [EST] 200 E3
Torigni–sur–Vire [F] 26 E3
Torija [E] 88 H5
Toril [E] 98 D2
Torino [I] 70 D5
Torino di Sangro [I] 116 E5
Torino di Sangro Marina [I] 116 E5
Torla [E] 84 E5
Torma [EST] 200 F2
Tormac [RO] 76 H6
Törmänen [FIN] 196 D5
Törmänmäki [FIN] 198 E4
Törmäsjärvi [FIN] 196 C8
Tormos [E] 84 D6
Tornal'a [SK] 64 E4
Tornavacas [E] 88 B5
Torneträsk [S] 192 E4
Tornio [FIN] 198 C2
Tornjoš [YU] 76 E5
Toro [E] 88 D1
Törökszentmiklós [H] 76 E2
Toróni [GR] 130 C6
Torony [H] 74 F2
Torpa [S] 162 C5
Torpo [N] 170 F3
Torpoint [GB] 12 D5
Torpsbruk [S] 162 D4
Torquay [GB] 12 E5
Torquemada [E] 82 D6
Torralba [E] 90 B4
Torralba [E] 96 F4
Torrão [P] 94 D2
Torre [E] 102 D5
Torre Annunziata [I] 120 E3
Torre Beretti [I] 70 F6
Torreblanca [E] 98 G3
Torrecaballeros [E] 88 F4
Torrecampo [E] 96 D5
Torre Canne [I] 122 F3
Torrecilla [E] 98 C1
Torrecillas de la Tiesa [E] 96 B1
Torre de D. Chama [P] 80 F3
Torre de Juan Abad [E] 96 G5
Torre de la Higuera [E] 100 F2
Torre del Bierzo [E] 78 F5
Torre del Compte [E] 102 E2
Torre del Greco [I] 120 E3
Torre del Lago Puccini [I] 110 D5
Torre del Mar [E] 102 C5
Torredembarra [E] 92 C5
Torre de Moncorvo [P] 80 E5
Torre de' Pàsseri [I] 116 D4
Torre de Santa María [E] 86 H6
Torredonjimeno [E] 102 D2
Torre Faro [I] 124 C7
Torrefarrera [E] 90 H4
Torregamones [E] 80 G4
Torre Grande [I] 118 B5
Torreguadiaro [E] 100 H5
Torreira [P] 80 B5
Torrejoncillo [E] 86 H4
Torrejón de Ardoz [E] 88 G6
Torrejón de la Calzada [E] 88 F6
Torrejón del Rey [E] 88 G5
Torrejón el Rubio [E] 88 A6
Torrelaguna [E] 88 G4
Torrelapaja [E] 90 C3
Torrelavega [E] 82 E3
Torrelobatón [E] 88 E1
Torrelodones [E] 88 F5
Torremaggiore [I] 116 F6
Torremejia [E] 94 H2
Torre Melissa [I] 124 F4
Torremocha [E] 86 H6
Torremolinos [E] 102 B5
Torremormojón [E] 82 C6
Torrenostra [E] 98 G3
Torrent [E] 98 E5
Torrente de Cinca [E] 90 G5
Torrenueva [E] 102 E5
Torre Orsaia [I] 120 G5
Torre–Pacheco [E] 104 C4
Torre Pellice [I] 70 C6
Torreperogil [E] 102 F2
Torrequemada [E] 86 H5
Torre Santa Susanna [I] 122 F4
Torres Cabrera [E] 102 C1
Torres Novas [P] 86 C4
Torre S. Sabina [I] 122 F3
Torres Vedras [P] 86 B4
Torretta [I] 124 F4
Torrette di Fano [I] 112 C6
Torre Vă [P] 94 C3
Torrevieja [E] 104 D3
Torricella [I] 122 F5
Torri del Benaco [I] 72 C6
Torríglia [I] 110 B3
Torrijas [E] 98 E3
Torrijos [E] 96 E1
Tørring [DK] 156 C2
Torrita di Siena [I] 114 G2
Torroella de Montgrí [E] 92 G3
Torrox [E] 102 D5
Torsåker [S] 174 D4
Torsås [S] 162 F6
Torsborg [S] 182 F3
Torsby [S] 172 E5
Torshälla [S] 168 B3
Tórshavn [FR] 160 B2
Torsken [N] 192 D2
Torslanda [S] 160 G2
Torsminde [DK] 160 B5
Tortinmäki [FIN] 176 E4
Tórtola de Henares [E] 88 H5
Tórtoles de Esgueva [E] 88 G2
Tortolì [I] 118 E5
Tortona [I] 110 B2
Tortoreto [I] 116 D3
Tortoreto Lido [I] 116 D3
Tortorici [I] 126 F2
Tortosa [E] 92 A5
Tortosendo [P] 86 F2
Toruń [PL] 22 E6
Torup [S] 162 B4
Torup Strand [DK] 160 C3
Tõrva [EST] 200 E3
Tor Vaiánica [I] 116 A6
Torvikbukt [N] 180 F2
Torvikbygd [N] 170 C4
Torvinen [FIN] 196 D7
Torvsjö [S] 190 F5
Torzhok [RUS] 204 E3
Torzym [PL] 34 H3
Tosbotn [N] 190 D3
Toscaig [GB] 6 C4
Toscolano Maderno [I] 72 B5
Toses, Collado de– [E] 92 E2
Tosno [RUS] 204 C1
Tossa de Mar [E] 92 F4
Tösse [S] 166 D4
Tostedt [D] 18 F5
Tószeg [H] 76 E2
Toszek [PL] 50 F3
Totana [E] 104 B3
Totebo [S] 162 F2
Tôtes [F] 28 B5
Tótkomlós [H] 76 F4
Tøtlandsvik [N] 164 C2
Totnes [GB] 12 E5
Tottijärvi [FIN] 176 F2
Totton [GB] 12 H5
Toucy [F] 56 E2
Toul [F] 44 E5
Toulon [F] 108 C6
Toulon–sur–Arroux [F] 56 F5
Toulouse [F] 84 H3
Tourcoing [F] 28 F3
Tourmalet, Col du– [F] 84 E4
Tournai (Doornik) [B] 28 G3
Tournan [F] 42 G4
Tournay [F] 84 F4
Tournon [F] 68 F5
Tournon–d'Agenais [F] 66 F5
Tournon–St–Martin [F] 54 G4
Tournus [F] 56 G6
Tours [F] 54 F2
Tourves [F] 108 C5
Toury [F] 42 E5
Toutes Aures, Col de– [F] 108 D4
Toužim [CZ] 48 D3
Tovarnik [HR] 154 E2
Tøvik [N] 180 E2
Tovste [UA] 206 C3
Towcester [GB] 14 D2
Töysä [FIN] 186 D3
Trabada [E] 78 F2
Trabadelo [E] 78 E5
Trabanca [E] 80 G5
Traben–Trarbach [D] 44 G2
Trabía [I] 126 D2
Trabotivište [MK] 128 H1
Tracheiá [GR] 136 F2
Tracino [I] 126 A5
Trädet [S] 162 C1
Trafaria [P] 86 A5
Trafoi [I] 72 B3
Tragacete [E] 98 C1
Trahíli [GR] 134 C5
Traian [RO] 148 B2
Traiguera [E] 92 A6
Traisen [A] 62 D5
Traiskirchen [A] 62 F5
Traismauer [A] 62 E4
Trakai [LT] 24 H1
Trakoščan [HR] 74 E4
Tralee / Trá Lí [IRL] 4 B3
Trá Lí / Tralee [IRL] 4 B3
Tramaríglio [I] 118 B3
Tramelan [CH] 58 D5
Tramonti di Sopra [I] 72 F4
Tramore [IRL] 4 E5
Tranås [S] 158 D3
Tranås [S] 162 E1
Tranby [N] 164 H1
Trancoso [P] 80 D6
Tranderup [DK] 156 D4
Tranekær [DK] 156 E4
Tranemo [S] 162 C3
Tranent [GB] 8 F3
Trångsviken [S] 182 G2
Tranhult [S] 162 C3
Trani [I] 122 D2
Tranóvalto [GR] 128 F6
Transtrand [S] 172 F3
Tranum Strand [DK] 160 D3
Tranvik [S] 168 E3
Trápani [I] 126 B2
Trapishte [BG] 148 D3
Trappes [F] 42 F4
Traryd [S] 162 C5
Träskvik [FIN] 186 B5
Träslövsläge [S] 160 H4
Trasmiras [E] 78 D6
Trassem [D] 44 F3
Trăstenik [BG] 148 A3
Traun [A] 62 B4
Traunkirchen [A] 62 A5
Traunreut [D] 60 G5
Traunstein [D] 60 G5
Travemünde [D] 18 H3
Travers [CH] 58 C6
Travnik [BIH] 154 C4
Travo [F] 114 B5
Trazo [E] 78 C2
Trbovlje [SLO] 74 C5
Trebatsch [D] 34 F3
Trebbin [D] 34 E3
Třebechovice pod Orebem [CZ] 50 B3
Třebenice [CZ] 48 F2
Trébeurden [F] 40 D1
Třebíč [CZ] 50 A6
Trebinje [BIH] 152 D3
Trebisacce [I] 122 D6
Trebišov [SK] 64 G3
Trebnje [SLO] 74 C5
Třeboň [CZ] 62 C2
Tréboul [F] 40 B3
Třebovice [CZ] 50 B4
Trebujena [E] 100 F3
Trecastagni [I] 126 G3
Trecate [I] 70 F5
Trecenta [I] 110 F2
Treffurt [D] 32 G5
Tregaron [GB] 10 B6
Trégastel [F] 40 D1
Tréguier [F] 26 A3
Treherbert [GB] 12 F2
Treia [D] 18 E1
Treignac [F] 66 H2
Treis [D] 44 H1
Trekanten [S] 162 F5
Trelleborg [S] 158 C3
Tremês [P] 86 C4
Tremestieri [I] 124 B7
Tremezzo [I] 70 G3
Třemošná [CZ] 48 E4
Tremp [E] 92 C2
Trenčianska Turná [SK] 64 A2
Trenčín [SK] 64 A2
Trend [DK] 160 C4
Trendelburg [D] 32 F4
Trengereid [N] 170 B4
Trent [CH] 70 C3
Trento [I] 72 C4
Treppeln [D] 34 G3
Trescore Balneario [I] 70 H4
Tresenda [I] 72 B4
Tresfjord [N] 180 E3
Tresigallo [I] 110 G2
Treski [EST] 200 G3
Trespaderne [E] 82 F5
Tresta [GB] 6 H3
Třeštice [CZ] 48 H6
Trets [F] 108 B5
Tretten [N] 170 H2
Treuchtlingen [D] 60 D2
Treuenbrietzen [D] 34 D3
Treveles [E] 102 E4
Trevi [I] 116 B3
Treviglio [I] 70 H5
Trevignano Romano [I] 114 H4
Treviso [I] 72 E6
Trévoux [F] 68 F2
Trezzo sull'Adda [I] 70 G4
Trgovište [YU] 150 E5
Trhové Sviny [CZ] 62 C2
Triaize [F] 54 C4
Triánta [GR] 142 E4
Triaucourt–en–Argonne [F] 44 D4
Tribanj Kruščica [HR] 112 G4
Triberg [D] 58 F3
Tribsees [D] 20 C3
Tricárico [I] 120 H4
Tricesimo [I] 72 G4
Trichiana [I] 72 E4
Trie [F] 84 F3
Trieben [A] 62 C6
Trier [D] 44 F2
Trieste [I] 72 H6
Trígono [GR] 128 E4
Trigueros [E] 94 F5
Tríkala [GR] 128 G4
Tríkala [GR] 132 F2
Tríkalón [GR] 136 E1
Tríkeri [GR] 134 A3
Trilj [HR] 152 A1
Trillo [E] 90 A5
Trílofo [GR] 132 G3
Trim [IRL] 2 F5
Trindade [P] 80 E4
Trindade [P] 94 D3
Třinec [CZ] 50 F5
Trinita d'Agultu [I] 118 D2
Trinitápoli [I] 120 H2
Trino [I] 70 E5
Triollo [E] 82 D4
Triora [I] 108 F4
Trípoli [GR] 136 E2
Triponzo [I] 116 B3
Tripótama [GR] 136 D1
Trittau [D] 18 G4
Trittenheim [D] 44 G2
Trivento [I] 116 E6
Trnava [SK] 62 H4
Trnovo [BIH] 152 D1
Troarn [F] 26 F3
Trocnov [CZ] 62 C2
Trodje [S] 174 E3
Troense [DK] 156 E4
Trofaiach [A] 74 C1
Trofors [N] 190 D3
Trogir [HR] 116 H1
Troia [I] 120 G2
Tróia [P] 86 B6
Troina [I] 126 F3
Trois–Ponts [B] 30 E5
Troïts'ke [UA] 206 E4
Trojane [SLO] 74 C4
Trollhattan [S] 166 D6
Tromello [I] 70 F5
Tromsø [N] 192 E2
Tronco [P] 80 E3
Trondheim [N] 182 B1
Trönninge [S] 162 B5
Trôo [F] 42 C6
Troon [GB] 8 C3
Tropea [I] 124 C6
Tropojë [AL] 150 B5
Trosa [S] 168 D4
Troškūnai [LT] 202 G4
Trossachs [GB] 8 D2
Trossingen [D] 58 G3
Tröstau [D] 48 B3
Trostberg [D] 60 F4
Trosterud [N] 166 C2
Trostianets' [UA] 206 G2
Trouville [F] 26 G3
Trowbridge [GB] 12 G3
Troyan [BG] 148 B4
Troyanovo [BG] 148 E4
Troyanski Pateka [BG] 148 B4
Troyes [F] 44 B6
Trpanj [HR] 152 B3
Tršić [YU] 154 F3
Trstená [SK] 50 H6
Trstena [YU] 150 D5
Trstenik [YU] 150 C3
Trsteno [HR] 152 C3
Trstín [SK] 62 H3
Truchas [E] 78 F6
Truchtersheim [F] 44 H5
Trud [BG] 148 B5
Trujillo [E] 96 B1
Trŭn [BG] 150 E4
Trun [F] 26 F4
Truro [GB] 12 C5
Truskavets' [UA] 52 G5
Trustrup [DK] 160 F6
Trutnov [CZ] 50 B2
Trutnowy [PL] 22 E3
Tryavna [BG] 148 C4
Tryggelev [DK] 156 E5
Tryńcza [PL] 52 E3
Trýpi [GR] 136 E4
Trypití [GR] 130 C5
Tryszczyn [PL] 22 D5
Trzcianka [PL] 22 A6
Trzciel [PL] 36 B3
Trzcinna [PL] 34 H1
Trzcińsko Zdrój [PL] 20 F6
Trzebiatów [PL] 20 G3
Trzebiel [PL] 34 G5
Trzebież [PL] 20 F4
Trzebinia [PL] 50 G3
Trzebnica [PL] 36 C6
Trzemeszno [PL] 36 E2
Trzepowo [PL] 22 D3
Tržič [SLO] 74 B4
Tsagkaráda [GR] 134 A2
Tsamandás [GR] 132 C1
Tsangário [GR] 132 C3
Tsapel'ka [RUS] 200 H3
Tsarevets [BG] 148 C2
Tsarevo [BG] 148 G5
Tsarítsani [GR] 132 G1
Tschernitz [D] 34 G5
Tsenovo [BG] 148 C2
Tsiurupyns'k [UA] 206 F4
Tsotíli [GR] 128 E6
Tsoútsouros [GR] 140 F5
Tua [P] 80 E4
Tuaim / Tuam [IRL] 2 C4
Tuam / Tuaim [IRL] 2 C4
Tubilla del Agua [E] 82 E5
Tübingen [D] 58 G2
Tubre / Taufers [I] 72 B3
Tučepi [HR] 152 B2
Tuchan [F] 106 C5
Tüchen [D] 20 B6
Tuchola [PL] 22 D4
Tuchomie [PL] 22 C3
Tuchów [PL] 52 C4
Tuczno [PL] 20 H6
Tuddal [N] 164 F1
Tudela [E] 84 B6
Tudela de Duero [E] 88 E2
Tudulinna [EST] 200 F2
Tuffé [F] 42 C5
Tuhkakylä [FIN] 198 F5
Tui [E] 78 B5
Tuin [MK] 128 D2
Tuixén [E] 92 D2
Tūja [LV] 200 D4
Tukums [LV] 200 D5
Tula [RUS] 204 F5
Tulare [YU] 150 D5
Tuławki [PL] 22 H3
Tulca [RO] 76 H3
Tulcea [RO] 206 E6
Tul'chyn [UA] 206 E3
Tulla [IRL] 2 C6
Tullamore [IRL] 2 E6
Tulle [F] 66 H3
Tullebolle [DK] 156 E4
Tullinge [S] 168 D3
Tullins [F] 68 G4
Tulln [A] 62 E4
Tullow [IRL] 4 F4
Tułowice [PL] 50 D2
Tulppio [FIN] 196 F6
Tulsk [IRL] 2 D4
Tum [PL] 36 G3
Tumba [S] 168 D3
Tummel Bridge [GB] 8 E1
Tun [S] 166 D5
Tuna [S] 162 F3
Tunaberg [S] 168 C5
Tuna Hästberg [S] 172 H5
Tunbridge Wells [GB] 14 E5
Tunçbilek [TR] 146 G6
Tune [DK] 156 G3
Túnel del Cadí [E] 92 E2
Túnel de Viella [E] 84 F5
Tungelsta [S] 168 E4
Tungozero [RUS] 198 G2
Tunhovd [N] 170 F4
Tunnerstad [S] 162 D1
Tuohikotti [FIN] 178 C2
Tuohittu [FIN] 176 F5
Tuolluvaara [S] 192 F5
Tuorila [FIN] 186 B6
Tupadły [PL] 36 E2
Tuplice [PL] 34 G4
Tura [H] 64 D6
Turalići [BIH] 154 E4
Turan [TR] 146 F4
Turanlı [TR] 144 C2
Turany [SK] 50 G6
Türas [TR] 146 G2
Turbe [BIH] 154 C4
Turčianske Teplice [SK] 64 C2
Turckheim [F] 58 D3
Turda [RO] 206 B4
Turégano [E] 88 F3
Turek [PL] 36 F4
Turenki [FIN] 176 G3
Turenne [F] 66 G3
Turgeliai [LT] 202 G6
Tŭrgovishte [BG] 148 D3
Turgut [TR] 142 D1
Turgutbey [TR] 146 C2
Turgutlu [TR] 144 D4
Turgutreis [TR] 142 C3
Türi [EST] 200 E2
Turi [I] 122 E3
Turiis'k [UA] 38 H5
Turís / Torís [E] 98 E5
Turka [UA] 52 F6
Türkeli [TR] 146 C4
Túrkeve [H] 76 F2
Türkheim [D] 60 C4
Türkmen [TR] 144 C3
Turku / Åbo [FIN] 176 D4
Turleque [E] 96 F2
Turlough [IRL] 2 C4
Turmantas [LT] 202 H4
Turňa nad Bodvou [SK] 64 F3
Turnberry [GB] 8 C4
Turnhout [B] 30 D3
Türnitz [A] 62 D5
Turnov [CZ] 48 H2
Turnu Măgurele [RO] 148 B2
Turnu Roşu, Pasul– [RO] 206 B5
Turobin [PL] 52 F1
Túrony [H] 76 B5
Turoši [PL] 24 C5
Turów [PL] 38 E4
Turrach [A] 74 A2
Turre [E] 102 H5
Turriff [GB] 6 F5
TurtagrØ [N] 170 E1
Turtola [FIN] 196 C8
Turunç [TR] 142 E3
Turzovka [PL] 50 F5
Tuscánia [I] 114 G4
Tushielaw Inn [GB] 8 E4
Tušilovic [HR] 112 G1
Tuszyn [PL] 36 G5
Tutin [YU] 150 B4
Tutjunniemi [FIN] 188 F3
Tutrakan [BG] 148 D1
Tutrakan [BG] 206 D6
Tuttlingen [D] 58 G3
Tutzing [D] 60 D5
Tuukkala [FIN] 186 H6
Tuulos [FIN] 176 G2
Tuupovaara [FIN] 188 G3
Tuusjärvi [FIN] 188 D2
Tuuski [FIN] 178 C4
Tuusniemi [FIN] 188 E2
Tuusula [FIN] 176 H4
Tuv [N] 170 F3
Tuzi [YU] 152 E4
Tuzla [BIH] 154 E3
Tuzla [TR] 146 F3
Tuzla [TR] 134 G1
Tuzlata [BG] 148 G2
Tvååker [S] 160 H4
Tvärålund [S] 190 H5
Tväråträsk [S] 190 G4
Tvedestrand [N] 164 F4
Tveita [N] 170 B4
Tveitsund [N] 164 E3
Tver' (Kalinin) [RUS] 204 E3
Tverai [LT] 202 D4
Tversted [DK] 160 E2
Tving [S] 158 F1
Tvis [DK] 160 C5
Tvøroyri [FR] 160 A3
Tvorozhkovo [RUS] 200 G2
Tvrdošovce [SK] 64 A5
Tvŭrditsa [BG] 148 D4
Twardogóra [PL] 36 D5
Tweedsmuir [GB] 8 E4
Twimberg [A] 74 C2
Twist [D] 16 H4
Twistringen [D] 18 D6
Tworków [PL] 50 E4
Tworóg [PL] 50 F2
Twyford [GB] 14 D4
Tychowo [PL] 22 A4
Tychy [PL] 50 G3
Tyczyn [PL] 52 E4
Tyfors [S] 172 G5
Tyholland [GB] 2 F4
Tyin [N] 170 F2
Tykocin [PL] 24 E5
Tylawa [PL] 52 D5
Tylldal [N] 182 B5
Tylösand [S] 162 B5
Tylstrup [DK] 160 E3
Tymfristós [GR] 132 F4
Tympáki [GR] 140 D5
Tyndrum [GB] 8 D2
Tynemouth [GB] 8 G6
Tyniec [PL] 50 H4
Týniště nad Orlicí [CZ] 50 B3
Tynkä [FIN] 198 C5
Týn nad Vltavou [CZ] 48 F6
Tynset [N] 182 B4
Typpö [FIN] 198 C5
Tyrävaara [FIN] 198 F3
Tyresö [S] 168 E3
Tyringe [S] 158 C1
Tyrislöt [S] 168 C6
Tyristrand [N] 170 H5
Tyrjänsaari [FIN] 188 G1
Tyrnävä [FIN] 198 D4
Tyrrellspass [IRL] 2 E5
Tysse [N] 170 B4
Tyssedal [N] 170 C5
Tystberga [S] 168 C4
Tyszki–Nadbory [PL] 24 D6
Tytuvėnai [LT] 202 E4
Tyulenovo [BG] 148 G2
Tyvsen [DK] 156 B4
Tywyn [GB] 10 B5
Tzermiádo [GR] 140 F5
Tzummarum [NL] 16 F2

U

Ub [YU] 150 A1
Úbeda [E] 102 F2
Ubergsmoen [N] 164 F4
Überlingen [D] 58 G4
Ubrique [E] 100 H4
Uchanie [PL] 38 G6
Uchte [D] 32 E1
Uckange [F] 44 E3
Uckfield [GB] 14 E5
Ucria [I] 124 A7
Udbina [HR] 112 H4
Udbyhøj [DK] 160 E5
Udbyhøj Vasehuse [DK] 160 E5
Udden [S] 166 D5
Uddevalla [S] 166 C5
Uddheden [S] 166 E1
Uden [NL] 16 E6
Udine [I] 72 G5
Udovo [MK] 128 G2
Ūdrupij [LV] 200 F4
Udvar [H] 76 B5
Ueckermünde [D] 20 E4
Uelsen [D] 16 G4
Uelzen [D] 18 G6
Uetersen [D] 18 F4
Uetze [D] 32 G2
Uffenheim [D] 46 F5
Ugāle [LV] 200 C5
Ugao [YU] 150 A4
Ugao-Miraballes [E] 82 G4
Ugento [I] 122 G6
Ugerløse [DK] 156 F3
Ugíjar [E] 102 F5
Ugine [F] 70 B3
Uglich [RUS] 204 F3
Ugljan [HR] 112 F5
Ugljane [HR] 152 A2
Ugrinovci [YU] 150 B2
Ugŭrchin [BG] 148 A4
Uğurlutepe [TR] 130 G5
Uherse Mineralne [PL] 52 E5
Uherské Hradiště [CZ] 62 H2
Uherský Brod [CZ] 62 H2
Uhlířské Janovice [CZ] 48 G4
Uh. Ostroh [CZ] 62 H2
Uhříněves [CZ] 48 G4
Uhyst [D] 34 G5
Uig [GB] 6 B4
Uimaharju [FIN] 188 G1
Uithoorn [NL] 16 D4
Uithuizen [NL] 16 G1
Ujazd [PL] 50 E3
Ujazd [PL] 36 H5
Ujazd [PL] 52 C2
Újfehértó [H] 64 H5
Ujšcie [PL] 22 B6
Újszász [H] 76 E1
Ujué [E] 84 B5
Ukkola [FIN] 188 F1
Ukmerge [LT] 202 G5
Ukonjärvi [FIN] 196 D4
Ula [BY] 204 C4
Ula [TR] 142 E2
Ul'anka [SK] 64 C3
Ulan Majorat [PL] 38 E4
Ulanów [PL] 52 E2
Ulbjerg [DK] 160 D5
Ulceby Cross [GB] 10 G5
Ulcinj [YU] 152 E5
Uldum [DK] 156 C2
Uleåborg / Oulu [FIN] 190 D4
Ulefoss [N] 164 F2
Uleila del Campo [E] 102 H5
Ulëzë [AL] 128 B2
Ulfborg [DK] 160 B5
Ulinia [PL] 22 C1
Uljma [YU] 154 H2
Ullapool [GB] 6 D3
Ullared [S] 162 B4
Ullatti [S] 192 F6
Ullava [FIN] 198 C6
Ulldecona [E] 92 A6
Ulldemolins [E] 90 H5
Ullerslev [DK] 156 E3
Üllés [H] 76 E4
Ullisjaur [S] 190 F4
Üllő [H] 76 D1
Ullock [GB] 8 D6
Ulm [D] 60 B3
Ulme [P] 86 D4
Ulmen [D] 44 G1
Ulmeni [RO] 148 D1
Ulnes [N] 170 G2
Ulog [BIH] 152 D2
Ulricehamn [S] 162 C2
Ulrika [S] 162 E1
Ulriksfors [S] 190 E6
Ulsberg [N] 180 H3
Ulsta [GB] 6 H3
Ulsted [DK] 160 E4
Ulsteinvik [N] 180 C4
Ulstrup [DK] 156 E2
Ulstrup [DK] 160 D5
Uluabat [TR] 146 E5
Ulubey [TR] 144 G3
Uludağ [TR] 146 F5
Ulvåila [N] 172 D3
Ulverston [GB] 10 D2
Ulvestad [N] 170 D1
Ulvik [N] 170 D3
Ulvila [FIN] 176 D2
Ulvsjön [S] 172 G1
Ulvsvåg [S] 192 C4
Umag [HR] 112 D1
Uman' [UA] 206 E3
Umbertide [I] 116 A1
Umbukta [N] 190 E2
Umčari [YU] 154 H3
Umeå [S] 198 A6
Umfors [S] 190 E2
Umhausen [A] 72 C1
Umka [YU] 154 G3
Umurbey [TR] 146 B5
Umurbey [TR] 146 F4
Umurlu [TR] 144 E5
Uña [E] 98 C2
Unaðsdalur [IS] 194 C1
Unari [FIN] 196 D7
Uncastillo [E] 84 C5
Undenäs [S] 166 G5
Undersåker [S] 182 F2
Úněšov [CZ] 48 D4
Ungheni [MD] 206 D4
Unhošť [CZ] 48 F3
Unichowo [PL] 22 C3
Uničov [CZ] 50 C4
Uniejow [PL] 36 F4
Unirea [RO] 150 F1
Unisław [PL] 22 D6
Unna [D] 32 C4
Unnaryd [S] 162 C4
Unserfrau / Madonna di Senales [I] 72 C2
Unterach [A] 60 H5
Unterlüss [D] 18 G6
Unter Pfaffenhofen [D] 60 D4
Unter-Schleissheim [D] 60 E4
Unteruhldingen [D] 58 H4
Unterwasser [CH] 58 H5
Unterweissenbach [A] 62 C4
Unterwössen [D] 60 F5
Upavon [GB] 12 G4
Úpice [CZ] 50 B2
Uppad [S] 166 D6
Upper Chapel [GB] 12 F1
Upper Ruskoe [GB] 8 C5
Uppingham [GB] 14 E1
Upplands Väsby [S] 168 D2
Uppsala [S] 168 D1
Upyna [LT] 202 E4
Úras [I] 118 C6
Ura Vajgurore [AL] 128 B4
Urbánia [I] 110 H6
Urbino [I] 112 B6
Urçay [F] 56 C5
Urda [E] 96 F3
Urdos [F] 84 D4
Uriage-les-Bains [F] 68 H5
Uriz / Arze-Arce [E] 84 C4
Urjala [FIN] 176 F2
Urk [NL] 16 E3
Urla [TR] 144 C4
Urlingford [IRL] 4 E3
Urnäsch [CH] 58 H5
Urnes [N] 170 D1
Uroševac [YU] 150 C6
Urroz [E] 84 B4
Ursus [PL] 38 B3
Ururi [I] 116 F6
Ury [F] 42 F5
Urziceni [RO] 206 D6
Urzicuța [RO] 150 F2
Usagre [E] 94 H3
Uşak [TR] 144 G3
Ušće [YU] 150 B3
Uście Gorlickie [PL] 52 C5
Usedom [D] 20 E4
Ushakovo [RUS] 22 G2
Uši [MK] 128 F2
Usingen [D] 46 C2
Usk [GB] 12 F2
Uskedal [N] 170 B5
Uskudar [TR] 146 E3
Üsküp [TR] 146 C1
Uslar [D] 32 F4
Usmate Velate [I] 70 G4
Úsov [CZ] 50 C4
Usseglio [I] 70 C5
Ussel [F] 68 B2
Usseln [D] 32 D5
Usson-du-Poitou [F] 54 F5
Usson-les-Bains [F] 106 B6
Ustaoset [N] 170 E4
Ustaritz [F] 84 C2
Úštěk [CZ] 48 F2
Uster [CH] 58 G5
Ustibar [BIH] 152 E2
Ústí nad Labem [CZ] 48 F2
Ústí nad Orlicí [CZ] 50 B4
Ustiprača [BIH] 152 E1
Ustka [PL] 22 B2
Ust'-Luga [RUS] 178 E6
Ustrem [BG] 146 A1
Ustroń [PL] 50 F5
Ustronie Morskie [PL] 20 H3
Ustrzyki Dolne [PL] 52 F5
Ustrzyki Górne [PL] 52 F6
Ustye [RUS] 200 H1
Ustyluh [UA] 38 G6
Ustyuzha [RUS] 204 E2
Ususău [RO] 76 H5
Utajärvi [FIN] 198 E4
Utåker [N] 170 B5
Utbjoa [N] 164 B1
Utebo [E] 90 E3
Utena [LT] 202 G4
Uthlede [D] 18 D4
Utiel [E] 98 D4
Utne [N] 170 C4
Utrecht [NL] 16 D5
Utrera [E] 100 G2
Utrillas [E] 90 E6
Utrine [YU] 76 E5
Utsjoki [FIN] 196 D3
Uttendorf [A] 72 F1
Uttendorf [A] 60 G4
Utti [FIN] 178 C3
Utting [D] 60 D4
Uttoxeter [GB] 10 E5
Utvalnäs [S] 174 E4
Utvängstorp [S] 162 C1
Utvik [N] 180 D5
Utvorda [N] 190 C4
Uukuniemi [FIN] 188 G5
Uurainen [FIN] 186 F4
Uusikaarlepyy / Nykarleby [FIN] 186 C1
Uusikaupunki / Nystad [FIN] 176 C3
Uusikylä [FIN] 178 B3
Uusi-Värtsilä [FIN] 188 G3
Uva [FIN] 198 F4
Uvac [BIH] 152 E1
Úvaly [CZ] 48 G4
Uvanå [S] 172 F5
Uyeasound [GB] 6 H3
Uzdowo [PL] 22 G5
Uzel [F] 26 A5
Uzerche [F] 66 G2
Uzès [F] 106 G3
Uzeste [F] 66 D4
Uzhorod [UA] 206 B3
Užice [YU] 150 A2
Užokski, pereval- [UA] 52 F6
Üzümlü [TR] 142 G3
Uzunköprü [TR] 146 B3
Uzunkuyu [TR] 144 B4
Uzuntarla [TR] 146 G3
Užventis [LT] 202 E4

V

Vå [N] 164 E1
Vaajakoski [FIN] 186 G4
Vääkiö [FIN] 198 F3
Vääksy [FIN] 178 A2
Vaala [FIN] 198 E4
Vaalajärvi [FIN] 196 D6
Vaalimaa [FIN] 178 D3
Väärinmaja [FIN] 186 E5
Vaas [F] 42 B6
Vaasa / Vasa [FIN] 186 B2
Vaassen [NL] 16 F4
Väätäiskylä [FIN] 186 E3
Vabalninkas [LT] 202 F3
Vác [H] 64 C5
Vacha [D] 46 F1
Váchartyán [H] 64 C6
Väckelsång [S] 162 E5
Väderstad [S] 166 G6
Vadheim [N] 170 C1
Vado Ligure [I] 108 H3
Vadsø [N] 196 E2
Vadstena [S] 166 G5
Vaduz [FL] 58 H6
Væggerløse [DK] 20 B1
Vafáika [GR] 130 E3
Vafiohóri [GR] 128 G3
Vågaholmen [N] 190 D1
Vågåmo [N] 180 G5
Vågan [N] 192 C6
Våge [N] 164 C6
Våge [N] 170 B5
Våge [N] 164 A1
Vägeva [EST] 200 E2
Vaggeryd [S] 162 D3
Vaggsvik [N] 192 D3
Vágia [GR] 134 B5
Vagioniá [GR] 140 E5
Vaglio Basilicata [I] 120 H4
Vagnhärad [S] 168 D4
Vagos [P] 80 B5
Vågsbygd [N] 164 D6
Vägsele [S] 190 G5
Vägsjöfors [S] 172 E5
Vågslid [N] 164 D1
Vágur [FR] 160 A3
Vahanka [FIN] 186 E3
Vái [GR] 140 H4
Vaiano [I] 110 F5
Vaiges [F] 40 H5
Vaiguva [LT] 202 E4
Vaihingen [D] 46 C6
Väike-Maarja [EST] 200 F1
Vailly [F] 56 C2
Vailly [F] 44 A2
Vainikkala [FIN] 178 E2
Vainutas [LT] 202 D5
Vaison-la-Romaine [F] 106 H3
Vajszló [H] 76 A5
Vajza [AL] 128 B5
Vakarel [BG] 150 G5
Vakern [S] 172 F5
Vakıfköy [TR] 144 F5
Vakiflar [TR] 146 C2
Vakijaur [S] 190 H1
Vaksdal [N] 170 B3
Valaajärvi [FIN] 196 D6
Vålådalen [S] 182 E2
Valandovo [MK] 128 G2
Valanída [GR] 132 F1
Valareña [E] 84 B6
Valašská Polanka [CZ] 50 E6
Valašske Klobouky [CZ] 50 E6
Valašské Meziříčí [CZ] 50 E5
Valbella [CH] 70 H1
Valberg [F] 108 E3
Vålberg [S] 166 E3
Valbiska [HR] 112 E2
Valbondione [I] 72 A4
Valbonë [AL] 150 A5
Valbonnais [F] 68 H5
Valcarlos / Luzaide [E] 84 C3
Val-Claret [F] 70 C4
Valdagno [I] 72 D6
Valdahon [F] 58 B5
Valdaj [RUS] 204 D3
Valdalen [N] 182 D5
Valdecaballeros [E] 96 C2
Valdecabras [E] 98 C2
Valdecarros [E] 88 C3
Valdeganga [E] 98 C5
Valdeltormo [E] 90 G6
Valdemärpils [LV] 200 C4
Valdemarsvik [S] 168 C6
Valdemorillo [E] 88 F5
Valdemoro [E] 88 F6
Valdemoro Sierra [E] 98 C2
Valdenoceda [E] 82 F4
Valdepeñas [E] 96 F5
Valdepeñas de Jaén [E] 102 E3
Valdepolo [E] 82 C4
Valderas [E] 82 B5
Valderice [I] 126 B2
Valderöy [N] 180 C3
Valderrobres [E] 98 G1
Val d'Esquières [F] 108 D5
Valdeverdeja [E] 96 C1
Val d'Isère [F] 70 C4
Val-d'Izé [F] 26 D6
Valdobbiádene [I] 72 E5
Valdoviño [E] 78 D1
Vale [GBG] 18 C2
Valea lui Mihai [RO] 206 B4
Valebø [N] 164 F2
Vale de Açor [P] 94 D3
Vale de Cambra [P] 80 C5
Vale de Lobos [P] 94 C5
Vale do Arco [P] 86 D4
Vale do Poço [P] 94 D4
Válega [P] 80 B5
Váleggio sul Míncio [I] 110 E1
Valença do Minho [P] 78 B5
Valençay [F] 54 H3
Valence [F] 66 E6
Valence [F] 66 F6
Valence [F] 68 F5
Valence d'Albigeois [F] 106 C2
Valencia [E] 98 E4
Valencia de Alcántara [E] 86 F5
Valencia de Don Juan [E] 82 B5
Valencia de las Torres [E] 94 H3
Valencia del Ventoso [E] 94 G3
Valencia de Mombuey [E] 94 F3
Valenciennes [F] 28 G4
Văleni [RO] 148 B1
Vălenii de Munte [RO] 206 C6
Valensole [F] 108 C4
Valentano [I] 114 G3
Valentigney [F] 58 C4
Valenza [I] 70 F6
Våler [N] 166 B2
Våler [N] 172 D4
Valeria [E] 98 B3
Valevåg [N] 170 B6
Valfàbbrica [I] 116 A2
Valga [EST] 200 F4
Valgeristi [EST] 200 D2
Valgrisenche [I] 70 C4
Valguarnera Caropepe [I] 126 F3
Välikyla [FIN] 198 C6
Valimítika [GR] 132 G6
Valjevo [YU] 150 A1
Valjok [N] 196 C3
Valka [LV] 200 F4
Valkeakoski [FIN] 176 F2
Valkeala [FIN] 178 C2
Valkenburg [NL] 30 F4
Valkenswaard [NL] 30 E3
Valkininkai [LT] 24 H2
Valko / Valkom [FIN] 178 B4
Valkom / Valko [FIN] 178 B4
Vallada [E] 78 F4
Valladolid [E] 88 E2
Vallåkra [S] 156 H2
Vallata [I] 120 F3
Valldal [N] 180 E4
Valldemossa [E] 104 E4
Valle [LV] 200 E6
Valle [N] 164 D2
Valle de Abdalajís [E] 102 B4
Valle de Cabuérniga [E] 82 E3
Valle de la Serena [E] 96 A3
Valle de Matamoros [E] 94 F3
Valledoria [I] 118 C2
Vallehermoso [E] 100 B5
Vallelunga Pratameno [I] 126 D3
Vallen [S] 184 D1
Vallentuna [S] 168 E2
Valleraugue [F] 106 E2
Vallet [F] 54 C2
Valletta [M] 126 C6
Vallfogona de Ripollès [E] 92 E2
Vallo di Lucania [I] 120 F5
Valloire [F] 70 B5
Vallombrosa [I] 110 F5
Vallon-en-Sully [F] 56 C5
Vallon-Pont-d'Arc [F] 68 E6
Vallorbe [CH] 58 B6
Vallorcine [F] 70 C3
Vallouise [F] 70 B6
Valls [E] 92 C4
Vallset [N] 172 C4
Vallsta [S] 174 D1
Vallter 20 [E] 92 E2
Valmadrid [E] 90 E4
Valmiera [LV] 200 E4
Valmojado [E] 88 E6
Valmontone [I] 116 B6
Valmorel [F] 70 B4
Valognes [F] 26 D2
Valongo [P] 80 C4
Valoria la Buena [E] 88 F1
Valøy [N] 190 C4
Valozhyn [BY] 202 H6
Valpaços [P] 80 E3
Valporquero de Torío [E] 78 H5
Valpovo [HR] 76 B6
Valras-Plage [F] 106 D5
Valréas [F] 106 H2
Vals [CH] 70 G2
Valset [N] 190 B6
Valsjöbyn [S] 190 E5
Vals-les-Bains [F] 68 E6
Valsøybotn [N] 180 G2
Val-Suzon [F] 56 G3
Valtessiníko [GR] 136 D2
Val Thorens [F] 70 B5
Valtiendas [E] 88 G3
Valtierra [E] 84 B5
Valtimo [FIN] 198 F5
Váltos [GR] 130 H1
Valtournenche [I] 70 D3
Valverde [E] 100 A6
Valverde de Cervera [E] 84 A6
Valverde de Júcar [E] 98 B3
Valverde del Camino [E] 94 F5
Valverde de Leganés [E] 94 F2
Valverde del Fresno [E] 86 G3
Vama Veche [RO] 148 G1
Vamberk [CZ] 50 B3
Vamdrup [DK] 156 C3
Våmhus [S] 172 G3
Vammala [FIN] 176 E2
Vámos [GR] 140 C4
Vámosmikola [H] 64 C5
Vámospércs [H] 64 H6
Vámosszabadi [H] 62 H6
Vampula [FIN] 176 E3
Vamvakoú [GR] 132 G2
Vanda / Vantaa [FIN] 176 H4
Vandel [DK] 156 C2
Vandellòs [E] 90 H6
Vandenesse [F] 56 E4
Vandoies / Vintl [I] 72 E2
Vändra [EST] 200 E2
Vāne [LV] 200 C5
Vänersborg [S] 166 D5
Vånga [S] 158 D1
Vängel [S] 190 F6
Vangshylla [N] 190 C6
Vangsnes [N] 170 D2
Vangsvik [N] 192 D3
Vanhakylä [FIN] 186 B5
Vanhamäki [FIN] 188 C5
Vänjaurfräsk [S] 190 G5
Vânju Mare [RO] 150 E1
Vännacka [S] 166 D2
Vännäs [S] 190 H6
Vannes [F] 40 D5
Vansbro [S] 172 G4
Vanse [N] 164 C5
Vantaa / Vanda [FIN] 176 H4
Vanttauskoski [FIN] 196 D8
Vanvik [N] 164 C1
Vanvikan [N] 190 B6
Vanyarc [H] 64 D5
Vara [S] 166 E6
Varabla [EST] 200 D3
Varades [F] 40 G6
Varaklāni [LV] 200 F5
Varallo [I] 70 E4
Varanava [BY] 202 G6
Varangerbotn [N] 196 E2
Varaždin [HR] 74 F4
Varaždinske Toplice [HR] 74 F4
Varazze [I] 108 H3
Varberg [S] 160 H4
Varbola [EST] 200 D2
Varces [F] 68 H5
Várda [GR] 136 B1
Varde [DK] 156 B2
Vardim [BG] 148 C2
Vårdö [FIN] 176 B5
Vardø [N] 196 F2
Várdomb [H] 76 C4
Varduva [LT] 202 D3
Varel [D] 18 C4
Vareleí [GR] 134 D5
Varena [LT] 24 G2
Varengeville-sur-Mer [F] 28 C4
Varenna [I] 70 G3
Varennes-en-Argonne [F] 44 D3
Varennes-sur-Allier [F] 56 D6
Vareš [BIH] 154 D4
Varese [I] 70 F4
Varese Ligure [I] 110 C3
Vårgårda [S] 162 B1
Vargön [S] 166 D5
Varhaug [N] 164 A4
Várí [GR] 138 D2
Varilhes [F] 84 H5
Váris [GR] 128 F6
Varkaus [FIN] 188 D4
Várkiza [GR] 136 H1
Varmahlið [IS] 194 D3
Värmdö [S] 168 E3
Värmlandsbro [S] 166 E3
Värmskog [S] 166 E2
Varna [BG] 148 F3
Varna [YU] 154 F3
Värnamo [S] 162 D4
Varnany [BY] 202 H5
Varnhem [S] 166 F5
Varniai [LT] 202 E4
Varnja [EST] 200 F2
Varnsdorf [CZ] 48 G1
Városföld [H] 76 D3
Varovnik [BG] 148 F5
Varpaisjärvi [FIN] 198 F6
Várpalota [H] 76 B2
Varpanen [FIN] 178 C1
Varparanta [FIN] 188 E4
Várpslőd [H] 74 H2
Värriö [FIN] 196 E6
Vars [F] 108 E2
Vârşand [RO] 76 G3
Varsi [I] 110 C3
Varsseveld [NL] 16 F6
Vartdal [N] 180 C4
Vartius [FIN] 198 G4
Vârtoapele [RO] 148 B1
Vârtopu [RO] 150 F1
Värtsilä [FIN] 188 G3
Varvara [BG] 148 A6
Varvara [BG] 148 G5
Varvará [GR] 130 C4
Varzi [I] 110 B2
Varzy [F] 56 E3
Vasa / Vaasa [FIN] 186 B2
Vasalemma [EST] 200 D1
Vasankari [FIN] 198 C5
Vasarapera [FIN] 196 F8
Vásárosnamény [H] 206 B3
Väse [S] 166 F3
Vasiláki [GR] 136 C2
Vasiliká [GR] 134 B3
Vasiliká [GR] 130 B5
Vasilikí [GR] 132 C5
Vasilikó [GR] 134 B5
Vasilikós [GR] 136 B2
Vasilishki [BY] 24 H3
Vaskelovo [RUS] 178 H3
Vaskelovo [RUS] 200 H6
Vaskio [FIN] 176 E4
Vaskivesi [FIN] 186 D5
Vasknarva [EST] 200 G2
Vasles [F] 54 E4
Vaslui [RO] 206 D5
Vassarás [GR] 136 E3
Vassbø [N] 164 B4
Vassbotten [S] 166 C4
Vassenden [N] 180 C6
Vassiliká [GR] 134 G2
Vassilítsi [GR] 136 D5
Vassmolösa [S] 162 F5
Vassy [F] 26 E4
Västansfors [S] 168 A1
Västemyrriset [S] 190 G5
Västerås [S] 168 B2
Västergärn [S] 168 F5
Västerhaninge [S] 168 E3
Västerrottna [S] 166 E1
Västervik [S] 162 G2
Vastila [FIN] 178 C3
Västland [S] 174 F5
Vasto [I] 116 E5
Vasvár [H] 74 G2
Vasylivka [UA] 206 H4
Vasyl'kiv [UA] 206 E2
Vát [H] 74 G1
Vatan [F] 54 H3
Vaterá [GR] 134 G3
Vathí [GR] 144 C6
Váthi [GR] 128 H3
Vathí [GR] 138 H4
Vathílakos [GR] 130 D2
Vathílakos [GR] 128 F5
Vathiý [GR] 134 B5
Vathýpetrou [GR] 140 E5
Vatland [N] 164 C5
Vatne [N] 164 D4
Vatne [N] 180 D3
Vatne [N] 164 B3
Vatnstraum [N] 164 E5
Vatólakkos [GR] 128 E6
Vatoúsa [GR] 134 G2
Vatra Dornei [RO] 206 C4
Vau [P] 94 B5
Vauclaix [F] 56 E3
Vaucouleurs [F] 44 D5
Vau i Dejës [AL] 128 B1
Vauldalen [N] 182 D3
Vauvenargues [F] 108 B4
Vauvert [F] 106 F4
Vauville [F] 26 D1
Vauvillers [F] 58 B3
Vawkavysk [BY] 24 G5
Vaxholm [S] 168 E3
Växjö [S] 162 E4
Våxtorp [S] 162 B6
Väylä [FIN] 196 D4
Vayrac [F] 66 H4
V. Bodarna [S] 160 H1
Veberöd [S] 158 C3
Veblungsnes [N] 180 E3
Vechta [D] 18 C6
Vecilla de Valderaduey [E] 82 C4
Vecinos [E] 88 B3
Vecpiebalga [LV] 200 F5
Vecsés [H] 76 C1
Vecumnieki [LV] 200 E5
Vedavågen [N] 164 A2
Vedbaek [DK] 156 G2
Veddige [S] 160 H3
Vedea [RO] 148 C2
Vedelago [I] 72 E5
Vedersø Klit [DK] 160 B5
Vedum [S] 166 E6
Veendam [NL] 16 H2
Veenendaal [NL] 16 E5

Veere [NL] 16 B6
Vegacervera [E] 78 H5
Vega de Espinareda [E] 78 F4
Vega de los Árboles [E] 96 G4
Vegadeo [E] 78 F2
Vega de Pas [E] 82 F3
Vega de Valcarce [E] 78 E4
Vegårshei [N] 164 F4
Vegas de Coria [E] 88 B4
Vegas del Condado [E] 78 H5
Vegger [DK] 160 D4
Veggli [N] 170 F5
Veghel [NL] 16 E6
Veglie [I] 122 G5
Vegusdal [N] 164 E4
Vehkajärvi [FIN] 176 G1
Vehmaa [FIN] 176 D4
Vehmasmäki [FIN] 188 C3
Vehu [FIN] 186 E3
Veidnesklubben [N] 196 C2
Veinge [S] 162 B5
Veiros [P] 86 E6
Veitshöchheim [D] 46 E4
Veiviržėnai [LT] 202 D4
Vejano [I] 114 H4
Vejbystrand [S] 162 B6
Vejen [DK] 156 B2
Vejer de la Frontera [E] 100 F5
Vejers Strand [DK] 156 A2
Vejle [DK] 156 C2
Vejprty [CZ] 48 D2
Velada [E] 88 D6
Velagići [BIH] 154 B3
Vela Luka [HR] 152 A3
Velanídia [GR] 136 F5
Velaská Belá [SK] 64 B2
Velbert [D] 30 H3
Velburg [D] 46 H6
Velbuzhdki Prolaz (Velbuzhdki Pateka) [Eur.] 150 E6
Veldemelen [N] 190 C5
Velden [A] 74 B3
Velden [D] 60 F4
Velden [D] 46 H4
Veldhoven [NL] 30 E2
Velebit [YU] 76 E5
Velefique [E] 102 G4
Velēna [LV] 200 F4
Velenje [SLO] 74 D4
Velešin [CZ] 62 C2
Velešta [MK] 128 D3
Velestínon [GR] 132 H2
Vélez-Blanco [E] 102 H3
Vélez-Málaga [E] 102 C5
Vélez-Rubio [E] 102 H3
Vel. Grđevac [HR] 74 G6
Veličani [BIH] 152 C3
Velika [HR] 154 C1
Velika Brusnica [BIH] 154 D2
Velika Drenova [YU] 150 C3
Velika Gorica [HR] 74 E6
Velika Kladuša [HR] 112 H2
Velika Kruša [YU] 150 B6
Velika Plana [YU] 150 C1
Velike Lašče [SLO] 74 C5
Veliki Preslav [BG] 148 E3
Veliki Šiljegovac [YU] 150 D3
Velikiye Luki [RUS] 204 C4
Veliki Zdenci [HR] 74 G6
Veliko Orašje [YU] 150 C1
Veliko Tŭrnovo [BG] 148 C3
Veli Losinj [HR] 112 E4
Velingrad [BG] 150 G6
Velipojë [AL] 128 A1
Velizh [RUS] 204 C4
Veljun [HR] 112 G2
Velká Bíteš [CZ] 50 B6
Velká Hled'sebe [CZ] 48 C4
Velká nad Veličkou [CZ] 62 H2
Velké Březno [CZ] 48 F2
Velké Kapušany [SK] 64 H3
Velké Karlovice [CZ] 50 E6
Vel'ké Leváre [SK] 62 G3
Velké Losiny [CZ] 50 C4
Velké Meziříčí [CZ] 50 B6
Velké Němčice [CZ] 62 F2
Vel'ke Ripňany [SK] 64 A3
Vel'ké Uherce [SK] 64 B3
Velkua [FIN] 176 D4
Velký Folkmar [SK] 64 F2
Vel'ký Krtíš [SK] 64 D4
Vel'ký Meder [SK] 64 A5
Velký Újezd [CZ] 50 D5
Velletri [I] 116 A6
Vellinge [S] 158 B3
Velp [NL] 16 F5
Velpke [D] 34 A2
Vel. Trnovac [YU] 150 D5
Veltrusy [CZ] 48 F3
Velušina [MK] 128 E4
Velvary [CZ] 48 F3
Velvendós [GR] 128 F5
Velyka Lepetykha [UA] 206 G4
Velykyi Bereznyi [UA] 206 B3
Vemb [DK] 160 B5
Vemdalen [S] 182 F4
Vemhån [S] 182 G5
Vemmelv [DK] 156 F3
Vemmenaes [DK] 156 E4
Véna [GR] 130 F3
Vena [S] 162 F3
Venabu [N] 170 H1
Venaco [F] 114 B4
Venafro [I] 120 D1
Venaria Reale [I] 70 D5
Venčane [YU] 150 B1
Vence [F] 108 E4
Venda Nova [P] 80 D3
Vendargues [F] 106 F4
Vendas de Galizes [P] 86 E2
Vendas Novas [P] 86 C6
Vendays-Montalivet [F] 66 C1
Vendel [S] 174 F5
Vendelsö [S] 168 E3
Vendeuvre [F] 44 B6
Vendôme [F] 42 D6
Veneheitto [FIN] 198 E4
Veneskoski [FIN] 186 C3
Venetpalo [FIN] 198 D5
Venets [BG] 148 E2
Venets [BG] 148 E4
Venevere [EST] 200 F2
Venézia [I] 72 E6
Venlo [NL] 30 F3
Vennesla [N] 164 D5
Vennesund [N] 190 C4
Venosa [I] 120 H3
Venray [NL] 30 F2
Vent [A] 72 C2
Venta de Arraco [E] 84 D4
Venta del Moro [E] 98 D4
Venta de los Santos [E] 96 G6
Venta del Pobre [E] 102 H5
Venta El Alto [E] 94 G5
Venta Nueva [E] 78 F4
Ventas de Huelma [E] 102 D4
Ventas de Zefarraya [E] 102 C4
Ventė [LT] 202 D5
Ventimíglia [I] 108 F4
Ventnor [GB] 12 H5
Ventosa de Pisuerga [E] 82 D5
Ventspils [LV] 200 B4
Venus [RO] 148 G1
Venzone [I] 72 G4
Vepsä [FIN] 198 D4
Vera [E] 102 H5
Vera [N] 190 C6
Vera de Bidasoa / Bera [E] 84 B2
Verbania-Pallanza [I] 70 F3
Verberie [F] 42 G2
Verbicaro [I] 120 H6
Verbier [CH] 70 D3
Vercelli [I] 70 E5
Verch. Oselki [RUS] 178 H4
Verdalsøra [N] 190 C6
Verden [D] 18 E6
Verdens Ende [N] 164 H3
Verdikoússa [GR] 132 F1
Verdun [F] 44 D4
Verea [E] 78 C5
Verest [RUS] 200 H1
Verfeil [F] 106 A3
Vergato [I] 110 F4
Vérgi [GR] 130 B3
Vergiate [I] 70 F4
Vergína [GR] 128 G5
Vergt [F] 66 F3
Verín [E] 78 D6
Verket [N] 164 H2
Verkhn'odniprovs'k [UA] 206 G3
Verkhnyaya Tulivaara [RUS] 198 G5
Verl [D] 32 D3
Verma [N] 180 F4
Vermenton [F] 56 E2
Vermeş [RO] 76 H6
Vermiglio [I] 72 C4
Vermosh [AL] 150 A5
Vermuntila [FIN] 176 C3
Vernazza [I] 110 C4
Vernet [F] 84 H3
Vernet-les-Bains [F] 92 F1
Verneuil [F] 26 H5
Vernio [I] 110 F5
Vernon [F] 42 E2
Verny [F] 44 E4
Véroia [GR] 128 G5
Verolanuova [I] 72 A6
Veroli [I] 116 C6
Verona [I] 72 C6
Verrabotn [N] 190 B6
Verrès [I] 70 D4
Verrières-de-Joux [F] 58 B6
Versailles [F] 42 F3
Versmold [D] 32 D3
Versoix [CH] 70 B2
Vertaala [FIN] 186 G4
Verteillac [F] 66 E2
Vertou [F] 54 C1
Vertus [F] 44 B4
Verucchio [I] 110 H5
Verviers [B] 30 E5
Vervins [F] 28 G5
Verwood [GB] 12 G5
Verzuolo [I] 108 F2
Verzy [F] 44 B3
Vesanka [FIN] 186 G4
Vesanto [FIN] 186 G2
Vescovato [F] 114 C3
Vescovato [I] 110 D1
Vése [H] 74 G4
Veselí nad Lužnicí [CZ] 48 G6
Veselí nad Moravou [CZ] 62 H2
Veselinovo [BG] 148 E3
Veselynove [UA] 206 F4
Veshchevo [RUS] 178 F3
Vesivehmaa [FIN] 178 A2
Veskoniemi [FIN] 196 D4
Vesoul [F] 58 B3
Véssa [GR] 134 G5
Vessingebro [S] 162 B4
Vestbjerg [DK] 160 E3
Vestby [N] 166 B2
Vestbygd [N] 164 B5
Vesterby [DK] 156 F4
Vester Egense [DK] 156 D2
Vester Egesborg [DK] 156 F4
Vesterø Havn [DK] 160 F3
Vestervig [DK] 160 B4
Vestfossen [N] 164 G1
Vestmanna [DK] 160 A1
Vestmarka [N] 166 D1
Vestnes [N] 180 E3
Vestone [I] 72 B5
Vestre Gausdal [N] 170 H2
Vestre Jakobselv [N] 196 E2
Ves'yegonsk [RUS] 204 F2
Veszprém [H] 76 A2
Veszprémvarsány [H] 76 A1
Vésztő [H] 76 G2
Veteli [FIN] 186 D1
Vetlanda [S] 162 E3
Vetovo [BG] 148 D2
Vetovo [HR] 154 C1
Vetralla [I] 114 H4
Vetren [BG] 148 C4
Vetren [BG] 148 F4
Vetrino [BG] 148 F2
Vetriolo Terme [I] 72 D4
Vetschau [D] 34 F4
Vetsikko [FIN] 196 D3
Vettasjärvi [S] 192 F6
Veules-les-Roses [F] 28 B4
Veulettes-sur-Mer [F] 26 H2
Veurne (Furnes) [B] 28 F1
Vevey [CH] 70 C1
Vévi [GR] 128 E4
Veynes [F] 108 C2
Veyrier [F] 70 B3
Vezdemarbán [E] 88 D1
Vézelay [F] 56 E3
Vézelise [F] 44 E6
Vézénobres [F] 106 F3
Vezirhan [TR] 146 G4
Vezzano [I] 72 C4
Viadana [I] 110 E2
Viais [F] 54 B2
Viana [E] 82 H6
Viana do Alentejo [P] 94 D2
Viana do Bolo [E] 78 E6
Viana do Castelo [P] 78 A6
Vianden [L] 44 F2
Viane [F] 106 C3
Vianen [NL] 16 D5
Vianne [F] 66 E5
Viaréggio [I] 110 D5
Vias [F] 106 E4
Viator [E] 102 G5
Viborg [DK] 160 D5
Vibo Valentia [I] 124 D6
Vibraye [F] 42 C5
Viby [DK] 156 G3
Vic [F] 68 D2
Vič [SLO] 74 C3
Vic / Vich [E] 92 E3
Viča [YU] 150 B3
Vicchio [I] 110 F5
Vicdessos [F] 84 H5
Vicedo [E] 78 E1
Vic-en-Bigorre [F] 84 F3
Vicenza [I] 72 D6
Vic-Fezensac [F] 84 F2
Vich / Vic [E] 92 E3
Vichy [F] 68 D1
Vickan [S] 160 G3
Vico [F] 114 A4
Vico del Gargano [I] 116 H6
Vico Equense [I] 120 E4
Vicovaro [I] 116 B5
Vic-sur-Aisne [F] 28 F6
Vic-sur-Cère [F] 68 B4
Victoria [M] 126 C5
Vidago [P] 80 E3
Vidamlya [BY] 38 G2
Viðareiði [FR] 160 B1
Vidauban [F] 108 D5
Viddalba [I] 118 D2
Vide [P] 86 F2
Videbæk [DK] 156 B1
Videle [RO] 206 C6
Videseter [N] 180 E5
Vidigueira [P] 94 D2
Vidin [BG] 150 E2
Vidlin [GB] 6 H3
Vidnava [CZ] 50 D3
Vidsel [S] 198 A3
Vidzy [BY] 202 H4
Viechtach [D] 48 D6
Vieira [P] 86 C2
Vieki [FIN] 198 G6
Viekšniai [LT] 200 C6
Viella [E] 84 G5
Vielsalm [B] 30 E6
Vienenburg [D] 32 H3
Vienne [F] 68 F3
Vieremä [FIN] 198 E6
Viersen [D] 30 G3
Vieru [RO] 148 C2
Vierumäki [FIN] 178 B2
Vierzehnheiligen [D] 46 G3
Vierzon [F] 56 B3
Viesīte [LV] 200 E6
Viesites [LV] 200 E6
Vieste [I] 116 H6
Vietasbygget [S] 192 E5
Vietri di Potenza [I] 120 G4
Vietri sul Mare [I] 120 E4
Vietsiluoto [FIN] 198 C3
Vieux-Boucau-les-Bains [F] 66 A6
Vievis [LT] 202 G5
Vif [F] 68 H5
Vig [DK] 156 F2
Vigeland [N] 164 C6
Vigévano [I] 70 F5
Viggiano [I] 120 H5
Vígla [GR] 132 D3
Vignale Monferrato [I] 70 E6
Vignanello [I] 114 H4
Vigneulles [F] 44 E4
Vignola [I] 110 E3
Vignory [F] 44 C6
Vigo [E] 78 B4
Vigo di Fassa [I] 72 D3
Vigrestad [N] 164 A4
Viguera [E] 90 B1
Vihantasalmi [FIN] 178 C1
Vihanti [FIN] 198 D4
Vihiers [F] 54 D2
Vihren [BG] 130 B1
Vihtari [FIN] 188 E3
Vihtasuo [FIN] 198 G6
Vihti [FIN] 176 G4
Vihtijärvi [FIN] 176 G4
Vihtiläjärvi [FIN] 186 C6
Viiala [FIN] 176 F2
Viiksimo [FIN] 198 G4
Viinijärvi [FIN] 188 E2
Viinikoski [FIN] 198 E3
Viinistu [EST] 178 B6
Viitajärvi [FIN] 186 F2
Viitaniemi [FIN] 188 D1
Viitasaari [FIN] 186 G2
Viitna [EST] 200 E1
Vijküla [EST] 200 D3
Vijterna [EST] 200 C2
Vík [IS] 194 C6
Vik [N] 164 E5
Vik [N] 170 C2
Vik [N] 190 C3
Vik [S] 158 D3
Vika [S] 174 C4
Vikajärvi [FIN] 196 D7
Vikane [N] 166 B3
Vikanes [N] 170 B3
Vikarbyn [S] 172 H3
Vikastin [S] 172 G3
Vikebukt [N] 180 E3
Vikedal [N] 164 B1
Viken [S] 156 H1
Vikersund [N] 170 G5
Vikeså [N] 164 B4
Vikmanshyttan [S] 174 C5
Vikran [N] 192 E2
Viktring [A] 74 B3
Viladamat [E] 92 G3
Vila de Rei [P] 86 D3
Vila do Bispo [P] 94 A5
Vila do Conde [P] 80 B3
Vilafamés [E] 98 F3
Vila Fernando [P] 86 G2
Vila Flor [P] 80 E4
Vilafranca de Bonany [E] 104 E5
Vilafranca del Maestrat / Villafranca del Cid [E] 98 F2
Vilafranca del Penedès [E] 92 D4
Vila Franca de Xira [P] 86 B5
Vila Fresca de Azeitão [P] 86 B6
Vilagarcía de Arousa [E] 78 B3
Vilaka [LV] 200 G4
Vila Mea [P] 80 E3
Vilamor [E] 84 G6
Vilamoura [P] 94 C5
Vilāni [LV] 200 F5
Vila Nogueira de Azeitão [P] 86 B6
Vilanova d'Alcolea [E] 98 G3
Vilanova de Arousa [E] 78 B3
Vila Nova de Cerveira [P] 78 A5
Vila Nova de Famalicão [P] 80 C3
Vila Nova de Foz Côa [P] 80 E5
Vila Nova de Gaia [P] 80 B4
Vilanova de la Barca [E] 90 H4
Vila Nova de Milfontes [P] 94 B3
Vila Nova de Ourém [P] 86 D3
Vila Nova de Paiva [P] 80 D5
Vila Nova de São Bento [P] 94 E3
Vilanova i la Geltrú [E] 92 D5
Vila Pouca de Aguiar [P] 80 D3
Vila Praia de Âncora [P] 78 A5
Vilarandelo [P] 80 E3
Vilar de Barrio [E] 78 D5
Vilardevós [E] 78 D6
Vila Real [P] 80 D4
Vila Real de Santo António [P] 94 D5
Vilar Formoso [P] 86 H2
Vila-rodona [E] 92 C4
Vilarouco [P] 80 E5
Vila-seca [E] 92 C5
Vilassar de Mar [E] 92 E4
Vila Velha de Ródão [P] 86 E4
Vila Verde [P] 78 B6
Vila Verde da Raia [P] 80 E3
Vila Verde de Ficalho [P] 94 E3
Vila Viçosa [P] 86 E6
Vilches [E] 102 F1
Vildbjerg [DK] 160 C6
Vilémov [CZ] 48 H4
Vilhelmina [S] 190 F5
Vília [GR] 134 B6
Viljakkala [FIN] 186 D6
Viljandi [EST] 200 E3
Viljolahti [FIN] 188 E4
Vilkaviškis [LT] 24 E1
Vilkija [LT] 202 F5
Villablino [E] 78 G4
Villabona [E] 84 B2
Villacañas [E] 96 G2
Villacarrillo [E] 102 F1
Villa Castelli [I] 122 F4
Villacastín [E] 88 E4
Villach [A] 74 A3
Villacidro [I] 118 C6
Villada [E] 82 C5
Villadangos del Páramo [E] 78 G6
Villa del Prado [E] 88 E6
Villa del Río [E] 102 D1
Villa de Ves [E] 98 D5
Villadiego [E] 82 E5
Villadossola [I] 70 E3
Villa Estense [I] 110 G2
Villafranca del Bierzo [E] 78 F5
Villafranca del Cid / Vilafranca del Maestrat [E] 98 F2
Villafranca de los Barros [E] 94 G3
Villafranca de los Caballeros [E] 96 G3
Villafranca di Verona [I] 110 E1
Villafranca Montes de Oca [E] 82 F6
Villafranca Piemonte [I] 70 D6
Villafranca Tirrena [I] 124 B7
Villafranco del Guadalquivir [E] 100 G2
Villafrati [I] 126 D2
Villafrechós [E] 82 B6
Villafruela [E] 88 G1
Villafuerte [E] 88 F2
Villaggio Mancuso [I] 124 E5
Villagordo [E] 102 E2
Villagrains [F] 66 C4
Villagrande Strisaili [I] 118 E5
Villaharta [E] 96 C6
Villahermosa [E] 96 G5
Villahoz [E] 88 G1
Villaines-la-Juhel [F] 26 F6
Villajoyosa / la Vila Joiosa [E] 104 E2
Villala [FIN] 188 F4
Villalba Alta [E] 78 E2
Villalba Baja [E] 88 F5
Villalba de Guardo [E] 82 C4
Villalba de la Sierra [E] 98 C2
Villalba de los Barros [E] 94 G2
Villalcázar de Sirga [E] 82 D5
Villalgordo del Marquesado [E] 98 A3
Villa Literno [I] 120 D3
Villalón de Campos [E] 82 C6
Villalpando [E] 82 B6
Villalpardo [E] 98 C4
Villamalea [E] 98 C4
Villamañán [E] 82 B5
Villamanín de la Tercia [E] 78 H5
Villamanrique [E] 96 G6
Villamanrique de la Condesa [E] 94 F6
Villamar [I] 118 C6
Villamartín [E] 100 G3
Villamartín de Campos [E] 82 C6
Villamassargia [I] 118 B7
Villamayor de Santiago [E] 96 H2
Villamediana de Iregua [E] 82 H6
Villamesias [E] 96 B2
Villa Minozzo [I] 110 D3
Villandraut [F] 66 D4
Villandry [F] 54 F2
Villanova d'Asti [I] 70 D6
Villanova Monteleone [I] 118 B3
Villanova Tulo [I] 118 D5
Villanúa [E] 84 D5
Villanubla [E] 88 E1
Villanueva de Alcardete [E] 96 H3
Villanueva de Argaño [E] 82 E5
Villanueva de Cañedo [E] 80 H6
Villanueva de Córdoba [E] 96 C5
Villanueva de Gállego [E] 90 E3
Villanueva de Huerva [E] 90 E4
Villanueva del Aceral [E] 88 E3
Villanueva de la Fuente [E] 96 H5
Villanueva de la Jara [E] 98 B4
Villanueva de la Reina [E] 102 E1
Villanueva del Arzobispo [E] 102 G1
Villanueva de las Cruces [E] 94 E5
Villanueva de la Serena [E] 96 B3
Villanueva de la Sierra [E] 88 A4
Villanueva de las Torres [E] 102 F3
Villanueva de la Vera [E] 88 C5
Villanueva del Campo [E] 82 B6
Villanueva del Duque [E] 96 C5
Villanueva del Fresno [E] 94 F2
Villanueva de los Castillejos [E] 94 E5
Villanueva de los Infantes [E] 96 G5
Villanueva de los Infantes [E] 98 F3
Villanueva del Rey [E] 96 B5
Villanueva del Río y Minas [E] 94 H5
Villanueva de San Carlos [E] 104 H5
Villanueva de Sigena [E] 90 G4
Villány [H] 76 B5
Villa Opicina [I] 72 H6
Villapalacios [E] 96 H6
Villapiana Scalo [I] 122 D6
Villa Potenza [I] 116 C1
Villaputzu [I] 118 E6
Villaquejida [E] 82 B5
Villaquilambre [E] 78 H5
Villarcayo [E] 82 F4
Villard-de-Lans [F] 68 G5
Villardebelle [F] 106 B5
Villar de Cantos [E] 98 B3
Villar de Ciervo [E] 80 E6
Villardeciervos [E] 80 G3
Villar de Domingo García [E] 98 B1
Villardefrades [E] 88 D1
Villar del Arzobispo [E] 98 E3
Villar del Pedroso [E] 96 C1
Villar del Pozo [E] 98 B5
Villar del Rey [E] 86 F6
Villar de Olalla [E] 98 B2
Villar de Rena [E] 96 B3
Villarejo de Fuentes [E] 96 H2
Villarejo de Salvanés [E] 96 G1
Villares del Saz [E] 98 B2
Villargordo del Cabriel [E] 98 C4
Villaricos [E] 104 A5
Villariño de Conso [E] 78 D6
Villarluengo [E] 98 F1
Villarmayor [E] 80 G6
Villarquemado [E] 98 D1
Villarramiel [E] 82 C6
Villarreal de San Carlos [E] 88 A6
Villarrobledo [E] 96 H4
Villarroga de los Pinares [E] 98 F1
Villarroja [E] 84 A5
Villarroya de la Sierra [E] 90 C4
Villarrubia de los Ojos [E] 96 F3
Villars [CH] 70 C2
Villars [F] 108 E4
Villars-les-Dombes [F] 68 G2
Villars-sur-Var [F] 108 E4
Villarta [E] 98 C4
Villarta de los Montes [E] 96 D3
Villarta de San Juan [E] 96 F3
Villarubia de Santiago [E] 96 G1
Villasalto [I] 118 D6
Villasana de Mena [E] 82 F4
Villa San Giovanni [I] 124 C7
Villa Santa Maria [I] 116 D5
Villa Santina [I] 72 G4
Villaseco de los Gamitos [E] 80 G6
Villaseco de los Reyes [E] 80 G5
Villasimíus [I] 118 D7
Villasor [I] 118 C6
Villasrubias [E] 86 H3
Villastar [E] 98 D2
Villatobas [E] 96 G2
Villatoro [E] 82 E6
Villatoya [E] 98 C4
Villavelayo [E] 90 A1
Villaverde del Río [E] 94 H5
Villaviciosa [E] 96 C6
Villaviciosa [E] 82 C2
Villavieja [E] 80 F6
Villa Vomano [I] 116 C3
Villé [F] 58 D2
Villebois-Lavalette [F] 66 E2
Villedieu-les-Poêles [F] 26 D4
Ville-en-Tardenois [F] 44 B3
Villefagnan [F] 54 E5
Villefontaine [F] 68 G3
Villefort [F] 68 D6
Villefranche [F] 108 F4
Villefranche-d'Albigeois [F] 106 C2
Villefranche-de-Conflent [F] 92 F1
Villefranche-de-Lauragais [F] 106 A4
Villefranche-de-Lonchat [F] 66 E3
Villefranche-de-Panat [F] 106 D2
Villefranche-de-Rouergue [F] 66 H5
Villefranche-du-Périgord [F] 66 F4
Villefranche-sur-Cher [F] 54 H2
Villefranche-sur-Saône [F] 68 F2
Villel [E] 98 D2
Villemur [F] 106 A2
Villena [E] 104 D1
Villenauxe-la-Grande [F] 42 H5
Villeneuve [F] 66 H5
Villeneuve [F] 106 G3
Villeneuve-de-Berg [F] 68 E6
Villeneuve-de-Marsan [F] 66 C6
Villeneuve-l'Archevêque [F] 42 H6
Villeneuve-Loubet [F] 108 E4
Villeneuve-sur-Allier [F] 56 D5
Villeneuve-sur-Lot [F] 66 E5
Villeneuve-sur-Yonne [F] 42 G6
Villeréal [F] 66 F4
Villers [F] 26 G3
Villers-Bocage [F] 26 E3
Villers-Bretonneux [F] 28 E5
Villers-Cotterêts [F] 42 H3
Villersexel [F] 58 C4
Villers-le-Lac [F] 58 C5
Villers-St-Georges [F] 42 H4
Villerville [F] 26 G3
Villeta Barrea [I] 116 D6
Villingen [D] 58 F3
Villoldo [E] 82 C5
Villorba [I] 72 E5
Villoria [E] 88 D3
Vilnius [LT] 202 G5

Vilppula [FIN] 186 E5
Vils [D] 60 H3
Vilsbiburg [D] 60 F3
Vilseck [D] 46 H5
Vilshofen [D] 60 H3
Vilsund [DK] 160 C4
Vilunai [LT] 24 G1
Vilusi [YU] 152 D3
Viluste [EST] 200 F3
Vilyeyka [BY] 204 B5
Vilyki Mosty [UA] 52 H3
Vimianzo [E] 78 B2
Vimieiro [P] 86 D6
Vimioso [P] 80 G4
Vimmerby [S] 162 F2
Vimoutiers [F] 26 G4
Vimpeli [FIN] 186 D2
Vimperk [CZ] 62 A2
Vina [YU] 150 D4
Vinac [BIH] 154 C4
Vinádio [I] 108 E3
Vinaixa [E] 92 C4
Vinaròs [E] 92 A6
Vinay [F] 68 G4
Vinça [F] 92 F1
Vinchiaturo [I] 120 E1
Vinci [I] 110 E5
Vindbyholt [DK] 156 G4
Vindelgransele [S] 190 G4
Vindeln [S] 190 H5
Vinderup [DK] 160 C5
Vindsvik [N] 164 C2
Vinga [RO] 76 G5
Vingåker [S] 168 B4
Vingnes [N] 172 B2
Vinhais [P] 80 F3
Vinica [MK] 128 G1
Viničani [MK] 128 F2
Viniegra de Abajo [E] 90 B1
Vinishte [BG] 150 F3
Vinje [N] 164 E1
Vinje [N] 170 C3
Vinjeøra [N] 180 G2
Vinkovci [HR] 154 E1
Vinliden [S] 190 G5
Vinnytsia [UA] 206 D3
Vinon–sur–Verdon [F] 108 C4
Vinslöv [S] 158 D1
Vinsternes [N] 180 F1
Vinstra [N] 170 H1
Vintjärn [S] 174 D3
Vintrosa [S] 166 G3
Viñuelas [E] 88 G5
Vinuesa [E] 90 B2
Vinzelberg [D] 34 B2
Vipiteno / Sterzing [I] 72 D2
Vira [HR] 152 A2
Vire [F] 26 E4
Vireši [LV] 200 F4
Virgen [A] 72 F2
Virgen de la Cabeza [E] 96 E6
Virginia [IRL] 2 E5
Virieu [F] 68 G4
Virieu–le–Grand [F] 68 H3
Virkby / Virkkala [FIN] 176 G5
Virkkala / Virkby [FIN] 176 G5
Virklund [DK] 156 C1
Virmutjoki [FIN] 178 E1
Virojoki [FIN] 178 D3
Virolahti [FIN] 178 D3
Virónia [GR] 130 B2
Virovitica [HR] 74 H5
Virpazar [YU] 152 E5
Virrat [FIN] 186 D4
Virsbo [S] 168 B1
Virsbo bruk [S] 168 B1
Virserum [S] 162 F3
Virtaniemi [FIN] 196 E4
Virtasalmi [FIN] 188 D4
Virton [B] 44 E2
Virtsu [EST] 200 D3
Virttaa [FIN] 176 E3
Viru–Jaagupi [EST] 200 F1
Virvoru [RO] 150 F1
Visaginas [LT] 202 H4
Visbek [D] 18 C6
Visby [DK] 156 B4
Visby [S] 168 G4
Visé [B] 30 E4
Višegrad [BIH] 152 E1
Visegrád [H] 64 C5
Viseu [P] 80 C6
Vishnyeva [BY] 202 H6
Vishovgrad [BG] 148 C3
Visiedo [E] 90 D6
Vişina Veche [RO] 148 A2
Viskafors [S] 162 B2
Viskinge [DK] 156 F2
Vislanda [S] 162 D5
Visočka Ržana [YU] 150 E4
Viso del Marqués [E] 96 F5
Visoka [YU] 150 A3
Visoko [BIH] 154 D4
Visp [CH] 70 E2
Vissefjärda [S] 162 F5
Visselhövede [D] 18 E6
Vissenbjerg [DK] 156 D3
Vissiniá [GR] 128 E5
Visso [I] 116 B2
Vistheden [S] 198 A3
Vištytis [LT] 24 D2
Visuvesi [FIN] 186 E5
Visz [H] 76 A3
Vităneşti [RO] 148 C1
Vitanovac [YU] 150 B3
Vitemölla [S] 158 D2
Viterbo [I] 114 H4
Vithkuq [AL] 128 C5
Vitigudino [E] 80 F6
Vitina [BIH] 152 B2
Vitina [YU] 150 C6
Vitis [A] 62 D3
Vitkovo [YU] 150 C3
Vitolište [MK] 128 F3
Vitomirica [YU] 150 B5
Vitoria–Gasteiz [E] 82 G5
Vitré [F] 26 D6
Vitry–le–François [F] 44 C5
Vitsand [S] 172 E5
Vitsyebsk [BY] 204 C4
Vittangi [S] 192 F5
Vitteaux [F] 56 G3
Vittel [F] 58 B2
Vittjärn [S] 172 D5
Vittória [I] 126 F5
Vittoriosa [M] 126 C6
Vittório Véneto [I] 72 E5
Vitträsk [S] 196 A8
Vittsjö [S] 162 C6
Viù [I] 70 D5
Vivario [F] 114 B4
Viveiro [E] 78 E1
Vivel del Río Martín [E] 90 E6
Viver [E] 98 E3
Viverone [I] 70 E5
Viveros [E] 96 H5
Viviers [F] 68 F6
Vivikonna [EST] 200 F1
Vivonne [F] 54 E4
Vize [TR] 146 C2
Vizille [F] 68 H5
Vižinada [HR] 112 D1
Vizovice [CZ] 50 E6
Vizsoly [H] 64 G4
Vizzavona [F] 114 B4
Vizzini [I] 126 F4
Vlaardingen [NL] 16 C5
Vlachiótis [GR] 136 E4
Vlachokerasiá [GR] 136 E3
Vlachovo Březí [CZ] 48 E6
Vladičin Han [YU] 150 D5
Vlădila [RO] 148 A1
Vladimirescu [RO] 76 G4
Vlagan [BIH] 154 B4
Vlagtweed [NL] 16 H3
Vlaháva [GR] 132 E1
Vlas [BG] 148 F4
Vlasenica [BIH] 154 E4
Vlašim [CZ] 48 G5
Vlaşin [RO] 148 C1
Vlasina Okruglica [YU] 150 E5
Vlasotince [YU] 150 D4
Vlissingen [NL] 16 B6
Vlochós [GR] 132 F2
Vlorë [AL] 128 A5
Vlotho [D] 32 E2
Vlychó [GR] 132 D5
Vočin [HR] 74 H6
Vöcklabruck [A] 62 A5
Vodice [HR] 112 H6
Voditsa [BG] 148 D3
Vodňany [CZ] 48 F6
Vodnjan [HR] 112 D2
Vodskov [DK] 160 E3
Voe [GB] 6 G3
Voerså [DK] 160 E3
Vogatsikó [GR] 128 E5
Voghera [I] 70 F6
Vohburg [D] 60 E2
Vohenstrauss [D] 48 C5
Vohma [EST] 200 C3
Võhma [EST] 200 E2
Vöhringen [D] 60 B4
Void [F] 44 D5
Voikoski [FIN] 178 C2
Voïnka [UA] 206 G5
Voiron [F] 68 H4
Voise [F] 42 E4
Vöiske [EST] 200 D3
Voitsberg [A] 74 D2
Voix [F] 108 C3
Vojakkala [FIN] 176 G3
Vojčice [SK] 64 G3
Vojens [DK] 156 C3
Vojlovica [YU] 154 H2
Vojnić [HR] 112 H1
Vojnik [SLO] 74 D4
Vojtanov [CZ] 48 C3
Voknavolok [RUS] 198 G3
Voláda [GR] 140 H2
Vólakas [GR] 130 C2
Volary [CZ] 62 B2
Volda [N] 180 C4
Volders [A] 72 D1
Volendam [NL] 16 E4
Volimés [GR] 136 A2
Volissós [GR] 134 G4
Volkach [D] 46 F4
Völkermarkt [A] 74 C3
Volkhov [RUS] 204 D1
Völklingen [D] 44 G4
Volkmarsen [D] 32 E5
Volkovija [MK] 128 D2
Volochys'k [UA] 206 C2
Volodymyr–Volyns'kyi [UA] 38 H6
Volokolamsk [RUS] 204 E4
Vólos [GR] 132 H2
Volosovo [RUS] 178 G6
Volosovo [RUS] 200 G2
Volovo [BG] 148 C2
Volpiano [I] 70 D5
Volterra [I] 114 F1
Voltri [I] 110 A3
Voltti [FIN] 186 C2
Volturara Appula [I] 120 F1
Volvic [F] 68 C2
Volyně [CZ] 48 E6
Vónitsa [GR] 132 D4
Võnnu [EST] 200 F3
Voorschoten [NL] 16 C4
Voorst [NL] 16 F5
Vopnafjörður [IS] 194 G4
Vörå / Vöyri [FIN] 186 B2
Vorau [A] 74 E1
Vorbasse [DK] 156 B2
Vorchdorf [A] 62 B5
Vörden [D] 32 D1
Vordernberg [A] 62 C6
Vorderriss [D] 60 D6
Vordingborg [DK] 156 F4
Vorë [AL] 128 B3
Voreppe [F] 68 H4
Vorey [F] 68 E4
Vorinó [GR] 128 F3
Vormsund [N] 172 C5
Vorozhba [UA] 204 E7
Vorsfelde [D] 32 H2
Võru [EST] 200 F3
Voskopojë [AL] 128 C5
Voss [N] 170 C3
Vossijatskoje [UA] 206 F4
Votice [CZ] 48 G5
Votonósi [GR] 132 D1
Vouillé [F] 54 E4
Voukoliés [GR] 140 B4
Voúla [GR] 136 G1
Vouliagméni [GR] 136 G1
Voúlpi [GR] 132 E3
Vourkári [GR] 138 C2
Vourvouroú [GR] 130 C5
Voutás [GR] 134 A4
Vouvant [F] 54 C3
Vouvray [F] 54 G2
Vouzela [P] 80 C5
Vouziers [F] 44 C3
Voves [F] 42 E5
Vovoússa [GR] 132 D1
Voxna [S] 174 C2
Voynitsa [RUS] 198 G3
Vöyri / Vörå [FIN] 186 B2
Voz [HR] 112 F2
Vozarci [MK] 128 F2
Voznesens'k [UA] 206 F4
Vrå [DK] 160 E3
Vrå [S] 162 C5
Vráble [SK] 64 B4
Vračevšnica [YU] 150 B2
Vrådal [N] 164 E2
Vrahnéika [GR] 132 F6
Vråliosen [N] 164 E2
Vrana [HR] 112 E3
Vrana [HR] 112 G5
Vranduk [BIH] 154 D4
Vranino [BG] 148 G2
Vranja [HR] 112 E1
Vranje [YU] 150 D5
Vranjska Banja [YU] 150 D5
Vranov [SK] 64 G2
Vranov nad Dyjí [CZ] 62 E2
Vransko [SLO] 74 C4
Vrástama [GR] 130 C5
Vratarnica [YU] 150 E2
Vratnica [MK] 150 C6
Vratno [HR] 74 E4
Vratsa [BG] 150 G3
Vražogrnac [YU] 150 E2
Vrbanja [HR] 154 E2
Vrbas [YU] 76 D6
Vrbaška [BIH] 154 C2
Vrbnica [YU] 150 B6
Vrbnik [HR] 112 F2
Vrbno pod Pradědem [CZ] 50 D3
Vrboska [HR] 152 A2
Vrbové [SK] 62 H3
Vrbovec [HR] 74 F5
Vrbovsko [HR] 112 F1
Vrchlabí [CZ] 50 A2
Vrčin [YU] 154 G3
Vreden [D] 16 G5
Vrees [D] 18 C5
Vrelo [HR] 112 G3
Vrena [S] 168 C4
Vreoci [YU] 150 B1
Vresse [B] 44 D1
Vretstorp [S] 166 G4
Vrgorac [HR] 152 B2
Vrhnika [SLO] 74 B5
Vrhpolje [BIH] 154 B3
Vrigstad [S] 162 D3
Vrin [CH] 70 G1
Vrínena [GR] 132 H3
Vrissoúla [GR] 132 C3
Vrlika [HR] 154 A4
Vrnjačka Banja [YU] 150 C3
Vron [F] 28 D3
Vrondoú [GR] 128 G6
Vrontádos [GR] 134 G4
Vroomshoop [NL] 16 G4
Vrosína [GR] 132 C2
Vrouhás [GR] 140 F4
Vroutek [CZ] 48 E3
Vrpolje [HR] 112 H6
Vršac [YU] 206 A5
Vršani [BIH] 154 E2
Vrsar [HR] 112 D2
Vrska Cuka [YU] 150 E2
Vrtoče [BIH] 154 A3
Vrútky [SK] 50 F6
Vrŭv [BG] 150 E1
Vrýses [GR] 140 C4
Vsetín [CZ] 50 E6
V. Torsas [S] 162 D5
Vučitrn [YU] 150 C5
Vučkovci [BIH] 154 D2
Vuckovica [YU] 150 B2
Vught [NL] 16 E6
Vŭglevtsi [BG] 148 C4
Vukovar [HR] 154 E1
Vukovec [HR] 74 F5
Vulcăneşti [MD] 206 D5
Vŭlchedrŭm [BG] 150 F2
Vŭlchidol [BG] 148 F2
Vuojärvi [FIN] 196 D7
Vuokatti [FIN] 198 F5
Vuolenkoski [FIN] 178 B2
Vuolijoki [FIN] 198 E5
Vuollerim [S] 198 A2
Vuonislahti [FIN] 188 F1
Vuontisjärvi [FIN] 192 G4
Vuoriniemi [FIN] 188 F5
Vuostimo [FIN] 196 E7
Vuotner [S] 190 H3
Vuotsino [FIN] 196 E7
Vuotso [FIN] 196 D5
Vuottolahti [FIN] 198 E5
Vŭrbitsa [BG] 148 E3
Vŭrshets [BG] 150 F3
Vyartsilya [RUS] 188 G3
Vyaz'ma [RUS] 204 E4
Vybor [RUS] 200 H4
Vyborg [RUS] 178 F3
Vyerkhnyadzvinsk [BY] 204 B4
Vynohradiv [UA] 206 B3
Vyra [RUS] 178 H6
Vyritsa [RUS] 178 H6
Vyshgorodok [RUS] 200 G4
Vyshniy Volochek [RUS] 204 E3
Vyskatka [RUS] 200 G1
Vyškov [CZ] 50 C6
Vyšná Revúca [SK] 64 C2
Vyšné Raslavice [SK] 52 D6
Vysokaye [BY] 38 F2
Vysoké Mýto [CZ] 50 B4
Vyšší Brod [CZ] 62 B3
Vytína [GR] 136 D2

W

Waabs [D] 18 F1
Waalwijk [NL] 16 D6
Wabern [D] 32 E5
Wąbrzeżno [PL] 22 E5
Wąchock [PL] 38 B6
Wachow [D] 34 D2
Wächtersbach [D] 46 D2
Wackersdorf [D] 48 C5
Waddington [GB] 10 G5
Wadebridge [GB] 12 C4
Wädenswil [CH] 58 F5
Wadlew [PL] 36 G5
Wadowice [PL] 50 G4
Wagenfeld [D] 32 E1
Wageningen [NL] 16 E5
Waging [D] 60 G5
Wagrain [A] 72 G1
Wągrowiec [PL] 36 D1
Wahlwies [D] 58 G4
Wahrenholz [D] 32 H1
Waiblingen [D] 58 H1
Waidhaus [D] 48 C5
Waidhofen an der Thaya [A] 62 D3
Waidhofen an der Ybbs [A] 62 C5
Waidring [A] 60 F6
Wainfleet all Saints [GB] 10 G6
Waischenfeld [D] 46 G4
Wakefield [GB] 10 F4
Walbeck [D] 34 A2
Walberswick [GB] 14 H3
Wałbrzych [PL] 50 B2
Walchensee [D] 60 D6
Walchsee [A] 60 F5
Walcourt [B] 28 H4
Wałcz [PL] 22 A5
Wald [CH] 58 G5
Wald–angelloch [D] 46 C5
Waldbröl [D] 32 C6
Waldeck [D] 32 E5
Waldenbuch [D] 58 H1
Waldenburg [D] 48 C1
Waldfischbach [D] 44 H4
Waldheim [D] 34 D6
Waldkirch [D] 58 E3
Waldkirchen [D] 62 A3
Waldkraiburg [D] 60 F4
Waldmünchen [D] 48 C5
Waldowice [PL] 34 H2
Waldsassen [D] 48 C4
Waldshut [D] 58 F4
Walenstadt [CH] 58 H6
Wallasey [GB] 10 D4
Walldorf [D] 46 C5
Walldürn [D] 46 D4
Wallenfels [D] 46 H3
Wallersdorf [D] 60 G3
Wallerstein [D] 60 C2
Wallingford [GB] 14 D3
Walls [GB] 6 G4
Wallsbüll [D] 156 B4
Walsall [GB] 10 E6
Walsrode [D] 18 E6
Walten [GB] 6 F3
Walton–on–the–Naze [GB] 14 G4
Waltrop [D] 30 H2
Wambierzyce [PL] 50 B2
Wanderup [D] 18 E1
Wanfried [D] 32 G5
Wangen [D] 60 B5
Wangenbourg [F] 44 G6
Wangerooge [D] 18 C3
Wängi [CH] 58 G5
Wankendorf [D] 18 G2
Wantage [GB] 12 H3
Wanzleben [D] 34 B3
Warburg [D] 32 E4
Wardenburg [D] 18 C5
Ware [GB] 14 E3
Waregem [B] 28 G2
Wareham [GB] 12 G5
Waremme [B] 30 E4
Waren [D] 20 C4
Warendorf [D] 32 D3
Warin [D] 20 A4
Warka [PL] 38 C4
Warkworth [GB] 8 G5
Warlubie [PL] 22 E4
Warmbad Villach [A] 72 H3
Warmensteinach [D] 46 H4
Warminster [GB] 12 G4
Warnemünde [D] 20 B3
Warnice [PL] 34 G1
Warnice [PL] 20 F5
Warnsveld [NL] 16 F5
Warrenpoint [GB] 2 G4
Warrington [GB] 10 D4
Warsop [GB] 10 F5
Warstein [D] 32 D4
Warszawa [PL] 38 B3
Warta [PL] 36 F4
Warta Bolesławiecka [PL] 36 A6
Warth [A] 72 B1
Wartha [D] 32 G6
Warwick [GB] 12 H2
Wasbister [GB] 6 G1
Wasdale Head [GB] 10 D1
Washington [GB] 8 G6
Wasilków [PL] 24 E5
Wąsosz [PL] 36 C5
Wasselonne [F] 44 G6
Wassen [CH] 70 F1
Wassenaar [NL] 16 C4
Wassenberg [D] 30 F4
Wasseralfingen [D] 60 C2
Wasserbillig [L] 44 F2
Wasserburg [D] 60 F4
Wassertrüdingen [D] 46 F6
Wassy [F] 44 C5
Wasungen [D] 46 F1
Watchet [GB] 12 E3
Waterford / Portlairge [IRL] 4 E5
Watergrasshill [IRL] 4 D5
Waterloo [B] 30 C4
Waterlooville [GB] 12 H5
Waterville [IRL] 4 A4
Watford [GB] 14 E4
Watten [F] 14 H6
Wattens [A] 72 D1
Watton [GB] 14 G2
Wattwil [CH] 58 G5
Waulsort [B] 30 D6
Wavre [B] 30 D4
Waxweiler [D] 44 F1
Ważne Młyny [PL] 36 G6
Wda [PL] 22 D4
Wdzydze Kiszewskie [PL] 22 D3
Węchadłów [PL] 52 B2
Wedel [D] 18 F4
Weener [D] 18 B5
Weert [NL] 30 E3
Weesen [CH] 58 G6
Weeze [D] 30 F2
Wegberg [D] 30 F3
Wegeleben [D] 34 A4
Weggis [CH] 58 F6
Węgliniec [PL] 34 H6
Węgorzewo [PL] 24 C2
Węgorzyno [PL] 20 G5
Węgrów [PL] 38 D2
Węgrzynice [PL] 34 H3
Wegscheid [D] 62 A3
Wehr [D] 58 E4
Wehr [D] 30 H6
Weichshofen [D] 60 F3
Weida [D] 48 C1
Weiden [D] 48 C4
Weidenberg [D] 46 H4
Weigetschlag [A] 62 B3
Weikersheim [D] 46 E5
Weil [D] 58 G1
Weilburg [D] 46 C2
Weilheim [D] 60 D5
Weimar [D] 32 D6
Weimar [D] 34 A6
Weinfelden [CH] 58 G4
Weingarten [D] 60 B5
Weinheim [D] 46 C4
Weinsberg [D] 46 D5
Weismain [D] 46 G3
Weissbriach [A] 72 G3
Weissenbach [A] 60 C6
Weissenbach / Riobianco [I] 72 D2
Weissenburg [D] 46 G6
Weissenfels [D] 34 C6
Weissenhorn [D] 60 B3
Weissenkirchen [A] 62 D4
Weissensee [D] 32 H5
Weissenstadt [D] 48 B3
Weisskirchen [A] 74 C2
Weisswasser [D] 34 G5

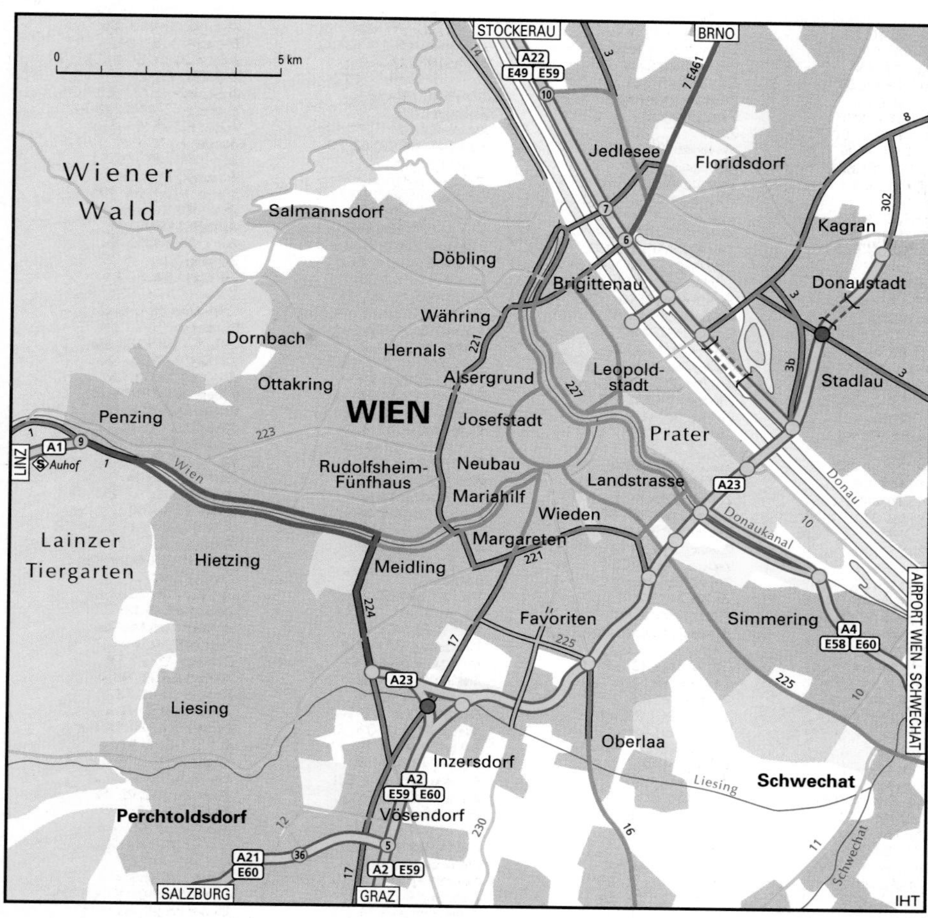

Yeşilyurt [TR] 144 F4
Yeşlköy [TR] 146 E3
Yeste [E] 102 H1
Yetholm [GB] 8 F4
Yevpatoria [UA] 206 G5
Yezyaryshcha [BY] 204 C4
Yiğitler [TR] 144 B1
Ylakiai [LT] 200 C6
Ylämaa [FIN] 178 E3
Yläne [FIN] 176 D3
Ylihärmä [FIN] 186 C2
Yli-Ii [FIN] 198 D3
Yli-Kärppä [FIN] 198 D2
Ylikiiminki [FIN] 198 D4
Yli-Lesti [FIN] 186 E1
Yli-Ii [FIN] 198 D3
Ylimarkku / Övermark [FIN] 186 B4
Yli-Muonio [FIN] 192 G4
Yli-Nampa [FIN] 196 D7
Ylistaro [FIN] 186 C3
Ylitornio [FIN] 196 B8
Ylivieska [FIN] 198 D5
Ylöjärvi [FIN] 176 F1
Yngsjö [S] 158 D2
Yockenthwaite [GB] 10 E2
Yoğuntas [TR] 146 B1
Yolüstü [TR] 144 F5
Yordankino [BG] 150 G4
York [GB] 10 F3
Youghal [IRL] 4 D5
Youlgreave [GB] 10 E5
Yport [F] 26 G2
Yppäri [FIN] 198 C5
Ypres (Ieper) [B] 28 F2
Ýpso [GR] 132 B2
Ypsous [GR] 136 D2
Yset [N] 182 B4
Yssingeaux [F] 68 E4
Ystad [S] 158 D3
Yste brød [N] 164 B4
Ystradgynlais [GB] 12 E2
Ytre Arna [N] 170 B3
Ytre Enebakk [N] 166 B1
Ytterby [S] 160 G1
Ytterbyn [S] 198 C3
Ytterhogdal [S] 182 H5
Yttermalung [S] 172 F4
Yukhavichy [BY] 200 H6
Yukhnov [RUS] 204 E5
Yulga Urpala / Torf'anovka [RUS] 178 E3
Yuncos [E] 96 F1
Yundola [BG] 150 G6
Yunquera [E] 102 B4
Yunquera de Henares [E] 88 H5
Yuntdağ [TR] 144 C3
Yunuseli [TR] 146 F4
Yuratsishki [BY] 202 H6
Yürücekler [TR] 146 F5
Yushkozero [RUS] 198 H3
Yverdon-les-Bains [CH] 58 C6
Yvetot [F] 26 H3
Yvoir [B] 30 D5
Yvoire [F] 70 B2
Yxnerum [S] 168 B6

Z

Zaandam [NL] 16 D4
Žabalj [YU] 154 G1
Zăbalt [RO] 76 H5
Zabar [H] 64 E4
Žabari [YU] 150 C1
Žabice [PL] 36 B5
Zabierzów [PL] 50 H3
Zabki [PL] 38 B3
Zabkowice Śląskie [PL] 50 C2
Zablače [HR] 112 H6
Žabljak [YU] 152 E2
Zabłudów [PL] 24 F6
Žabno [HR] 74 F5
Žabno [PL] 52 C3
Zabok [HR] 74 E5
Zabolottia [UA] 38 G4
Zabór [PL] 36 A4
Zăbrani [RO] 76 H5
Zábřeh [CZ] 50 C4
Zabrodzie [PL] 38 C2
Zabrze [PL] 50 F3
Zabrzeż [PL] 52 B5
Zacháro [GR] 136 C3
Zadar [HR] 112 G5
Zadvarje [HR] 152 A2
Zadzyezhzha [BY] 200 H6
Zafferana Etnea [I] 126 G3
Zafirovo [BG] 148 E1
Zafra [E] 94 G3
Žaga [SLO] 72 H4
Zagań [PL] 34 H5
Zagare [LT] 200 D6
Zaglav [HR] 112 F5
Zaglavak [YU] 150 A2
Zagorá [GR] 132 H2
Zagorje [SLO] 74 C5
Zagórów [PL] 36 E3
Zagorye [RUS] 200 G1
Zagórz [PL] 52 E5
Zagreb [HR] 74 E6
Žagubica [YU] 150 D1
Zagvozd [HR] 152 B2
Zagwiździe [PL] 50 E1
Zahara [E] 100 H3
Zahara de los Atunes [E] 100 G5
Zahinos [E] 94 F3
Zahlorou [GR] 132 G6
Zahna [D] 34 D4
Zaiceva [LV] 200 G4
Zaidin [E] 90 G4
Zajas [MK] 128 D2
Zaječar [YU] 150 E2
Zakliczyn [PL] 52 C4
Zaklików [PL] 52 E1
Zakopane [PL] 50 H6
Zakroczym [PL] 38 B2
Zákros [GR] 140 H5
Zakrzewo [PL] 36 F1
Zákupy [CZ] 48 G2
Zákynthos [GR] 136 B2
Zalaapáti [H] 74 G3
Zalabaksa [H] 74 F3
Zalabér [H] 74 G2
Zalaegerszeg [H] 74 G3
Zalakomár [H] 74 G4
Zalalövő [H] 74 F3
Zalamea de la Serena [E] 96 B4
Zalamea la Real [E] 94 F5
Zalaszántó [H] 74 G3
Zalaszentbalázs [H] 74 G3
Zălau [RO] 206 B4
Žalec [SLO] 74 D4
Zalewo [PL] 22 F4
Zalishchyky [UA] 206 C3
Zalla [E] 82 G4
Zaltbommel [NL] 16 E6
Załuski [PL] 38 A2
Załuż [PL] 52 E5
Zalužnica [HR] 112 G3
Zamárdi [H] 76 A3
Zamarte [PL] 22 C4
Žamberk [CZ] 50 B4
Zambrana [E] 82 G5
Zambrów [PL] 24 D6
Zambujeira do Mar [P] 94 B4
Zamora [E] 80 H5
Zamość [PL] 52 F1
Zamość [PL] 24 C6
Zamostne [PL] 22 D2
Zandvoort [NL] 16 D4
Zanglivéri [GR] 130 B4
Zangoza / Sangüesa [E] 84 C5
Zaniemyśl [PL] 36 D3
Zante [LV] 200 C5
Zaorejas [E] 90 B5
Zaostrog [HR] 152 B3
Zapałów [PL] 52 F3
Zapfendorf [D] 46 G3
Zapolyarnyy [RUS] 196 F3
Zaporizhzhia [UA] 206 H3
Zaporozhskoye [RUS] 178 H3
Záppeio [GR] 132 G2
Zapponeta [I] 120 H1
Zaprešić [HR] 74 E5
Zaprudy [BY] 38 H2
Zapyškis [LT] 202 F5
Zaragoza [E] 90 E4
Zárakes [GR] 134 D5
Zărand [RO] 76 H4
Zarańsko [PL] 20 H5
Zarasai [LT] 202 H4
Zarautz [E] 84 A2
Zaręby-Warchoły [PL] 38 D1
Żarki [PL] 50 G2
Zárkos [GR] 132 F2
Zărnești [RO] 206 C5
Žarnovica [SK] 64 B3
Żarnów [PL] 38 A6
Żarnowiec [PL] 50 H2
Zarós [GR] 140 E5
Zarošice [CZ] 62 G2
Żarów [PL] 50 B1
Zarrentin [D] 18 H4
Zarszyn [PL] 52 E5
Żary [PL] 34 H5
Zarza de Alange [E] 94 H2
Zarzadilla de Totana [E] 104 B3
Zarza la Mayor [E] 86 G4
Zás [E] 78 B2
Zasa [LV] 200 F6
Zasieki [PL] 34 G4
Žatec [CZ] 48 E3
Zator [PL] 50 G4
Zauchwitz [D] 34 D3
Zauczyn Poduchowny [PL] 38 D3
Zavala [BIH] 152 C3
Zavet [BG] 148 D2
Zavidoviči [BIH] 154 D3
Zavlaka [YU] 154 F3
Zawada [PL] 36 A4
Zawada [PL] 50 E2
Zawady [PL] 50 F1
Zawadzkie [PL] 50 F2
Zawichost [PL] 52 D1
Zawidów [PL] 48 G1
Zawiercie [PL] 50 G2
Zawoja [PL] 50 H5
Žažina [HR] 154 A1
Zázrivá [SK] 50 G6
Zbaszyń [PL] 36 B3
Zbąszynek [PL] 36 A3
Zblewo [PL] 22 D4
Zbojno [PL] 22 F6
Zborov [SK] 52 D5
Zborowice [PL] 52 C4
Zbraslav [CZ] 48 F4
Zbraslavice [CZ] 48 H4
Ždár [CZ] 48 E3
Žd'ár nad Sázavou [CZ] 50 B5
Zdiby [CZ] 48 F3
Zdice [CZ] 48 F4
Ždírec nad Doubrava [CZ] 50 A5
Zdounky [CZ] 50 D6
Zdunje [MK] 128 D1
Zduńska Wola [PL] 36 F5
Zduny [PL] 36 D5
Zdziechowice [PL] 52 E1
Zdzieszowice [PL] 50 E3
Žebrák [CZ] 48 E4
Zebreira [P] 86 G4
Zebrzydowa [PL] 34 H6
Zeddiani [I] 118 C5
Žednik [YU] 76 D5
Zeebrugge [B] 28 G1
Zefýria [GR] 138 D4
Żegiestów [PL] 52 C5
Zehdenick [D] 20 D6
Zeist [NL] 16 E5
Zeitz [D] 34 C6
Zelazno [PL] 22 D1
Zelechów [PL] 38 D4
Zelenika [YU] 152 D4
Zelenogorsk [RUS] 178 G4
Zelenogradsk [RUS] 202 C5
Želetava [CZ] 50 A6
Železná Ruda [CZ] 48 D6
Železnik [YU] 154 G3
Železniki [SLO] 74 B4
Železný Brod [CZ] 48 H2
Želiezovce [SK] 64 B5
Želin [SLO] 74 A5
Zelina [HR] 74 F5
Zèlio [GR] 132 H4
Želiv [CZ] 48 H5
Želizna [PL] 38 E4
Żelkowo [PL] 22 C2
Zell [A] 62 A4
Zell [D] 44 G2
Zell [D] 58 E4
Zella-Mehlis [D] 46 G2
Zell am See [A] 72 F1
Zell am Ziller [A] 72 E1
Želnava [CZ] 62 B2
Zelów [PL] 36 G5
Zeltini [LV] 200 F4
Zeltweg [A] 74 C2
Zel'va [BY] 24 H5
Zelwa [PL] 24 F3
Zelzate [B] 28 H1
Žemaičiu Naumiestis [LT] 202 D5
Žemberovce [SK] 64 C4
Zemblak [AL] 128 D4
Zeme [I] 70 F5
Zemen [BG] 150 F5
Zemite [LV] 200 C5
Zenica [BIH] 154 D4
Žepa [BIH] 154 E4
Zepče [BIH] 154 D3
Zerbst [D] 34 C3
Zerevna [BG] 148 D4
Zerf [D] 44 F3
Zeri [I] 110 C3
Zerind [RO] 76 G3
Zermatt [CH] 70 D3
Zernez [CH] 72 B2
Zernien [D] 18 H6
Zerniki [PL] 36 C6
Zerqan [AL] 128 C2
Zestoa / Cestona [E] 84 A2
Zetel [D] 18 C4
Zeulenroda [D] 48 B2
Zeven [D] 18 E5
Zevenaar [NL] 16 F5
Zevenbergen [NL] 16 C6
Zevgaráki [GR] 132 E5
Zeybekçayırı [TR] 146 C6
Zeytinbaği [TR] 146 E4
Zeytindağ [TR] 144 C3
Zgierz [PL] 36 G4
Zgniłocha [PL] 22 H4
Zgórsko [PL] 52 C3
Zgorzelec [PL] 34 G6
Zhaludok [BY] 24 H4
Zhashkiv [UA] 206 E3
Zhelenodorozhnyy [RUS] 24 B2
Zheleznitsa [BG] 150 F5
Zheleznogorsk [RUS] 204 E6
Zhlobin [BY] 204 C6
Zhmerynka [UA] 206 D3
Zhodzina [BY] 204 B5
Zhovkva [UA] 52 H3
Zhovten' [UA] 206 E4
Zhuprany [BY] 202 H6
Zhydachiv [UA] 52 H5
Zhytkavichy [BY] 204 B6
Zhytomyr [UA] 206 E2
Ziákas [GR] 132 E1
Žiar nad Hronom [SK] 64 C3
Zicavo [F] 114 B5
Zickhusen [D] 20 A4
Zidani Most [SLO] 74 D5
Židlochovice [CZ] 62 F2
Ziębice [PL] 50 C2
Ziegenrück [D] 46 H2
Zielona Chocina [PL] 22 C4
Zielona Góra [PL] 34 H4
Zielonka [PL] 38 B3
Zieluń-Osada [PL] 22 G6
Zierikzee [NL] 16 B6
Ziersdorf [A] 62 E3
Zierzow [D] 20 A5
Ziesar [D] 34 C3
Ziethen [D] 20 D4
Žiežmariai [LT] 202 F5
Zijpe [NL] 16 C6
Žilina [SK] 50 F6
Zilupe [LV] 200 G5
Zimandu Nou [RO] 76 G4
Zimnicea [RO] 148 C2
Zimnitsa [BG] 148 E4
Zinal [CH] 70 D3
Zingst [D] 20 C2
Zinnowitz [D] 20 E3
Zinnwald-Georgenfeld [D] 48 E2
Zipári [GR] 142 C3
Zirc [H] 76 A2
Zirchow [D] 20 E4
Žiri [SLO] 74 B5
Zirl [A] 72 D1
Zíros [GR] 140 G5
Žirovnice [CZ] 48 G6
Zistersdorf [A] 62 F3
Žitište [YU] 154 G1
Zitomislići [BIH] 152 C2
Žitoradja [YU] 150 D4
Zitsa [GR] 132 C2
Zittau [D] 48 G1
Živaja [HR] 154 B1
Zivinice [BIH] 154 E3
Živogošće [HR] 152 B2
Zizers [CH] 70 H1
Zlatá Koruna [CZ] 62 B2
Zlatar [BG] 148 E3
Zlatar Bistrica [HR] 74 E5
Zlatarevo [GR] 128 H2
Zlatari [YU] 150 C3
Zlaté Hory [CZ] 50 D3
Zlaté Klasy [SK] 62 H4
Zlaté Moravce [SK] 64 B4
Zlatitsa [BG] 148 A4
Zlatna Panega [BG] 148 A4
Zlatni Pyasŭtsi [BG] 148 G2
Zlatograd [BG] 130 E2
Žleby [CZ] 48 H4
Zliechov [SK] 64 B2
Zlín [CZ] 50 D6
Žljebovi [BIH] 154 E4
Złocieniec [PL] 20 H5
Złoczew [PL] 36 F5
Zlonice [CZ] 48 F3
Zlot [YU] 150 D2
Złotniki [PL] 36 E1
Złotoryja [PL] 36 B6
Złotów [PL] 22 B5
Złoty Stok [PL] 50 C3
Žlutice [CZ] 48 D3
Zlynka [RUS] 204 D6
Żmigród [PL] 36 C5
Žminj [HR] 112 D2
Znamenka [RUS] 204 E5
Znamensk [RUS] 24 B1
Znamianka [UA] 206 F3
Żnin [PL] 36 D1
Znojmo [CZ] 62 E3
Zoetermeer [NL] 16 C5
Zofingen [CH] 58 E5
Zogaj [AL] 150 B6
Zolder [B] 30 E4
Żółki [PL] 24 E5
Żołkiewka [PL] 38 E6
Zolotonosha [UA] 206 F2
Żółtki [PL] 24 E5
Zomba [H] 76 B4
Zóni [GR] 130 G1
Zonza [F] 114 B5
Zörbig [D] 34 C4
Zorge [D] 32 H4
Zorita [E] 96 B2
Zorneding [D] 60 E4
Zornitsa [BG] 148 E5
Żory [PL] 50 F4
Zossen [D] 34 E3
Zoutkamp [NL] 16 G2
Zoutleeuw [B] 30 D4
Zoúzouli [GR] 128 D6
Zovka [RUS] 200 G2
Zreče [SLO] 74 D4
Zrenjanin [YU] 154 G1
Zrinski Topolovac [HR] 74 F5
Zrze [YU] 150 B6
Zsadány [H] 76 G2
Zsana [H] 76 D4
Zschopau [D] 48 D2
Zubin Potok [YU] 150 B4
Zubiri [E] 84 B3
Zubrzyca Górna [PL] 50 H5
Zubtsov [RUS] 204 E4
Zudar [D] 20 D2
Zuera [E] 90 E3
Zug [CH] 58 F5
Zuidhorn [NL] 16 G2
Zuidlaren [NL] 16 G2
Zújar [E] 102 F3
Żukowo [PL] 22 D2
Zülpich [D] 30 G5
Zumaia [E] 84 A2
Zumarraga [E] 82 H4
Zundert [NL] 30 D2
Zuoz [CH] 72 A3
Županja [HR] 154 E2
Žur [YU] 150 B6
Żurawica [PL] 52 F4
Zürich [CH] 58 F5
Żuromin [PL] 22 G6
Żurrieq [M] 126 C6
Zürs [A] 72 B1
Zurzach [CH] 58 F4
Zusmarshausen [D] 60 C3
Züsow [D] 20 A3
Žuta Lokva [HR] 112 F2
Zutphen [NL] 16 F5
Žužemberk [SLO] 74 C5
Zvarisht [AL] 128 C4
Zvezdel [BG] 130 F1
Zvezdets [BG] 148 F5
Zvolen [SK] 64 C3
Zvonce [YU] 150 E4
Zvornik [BIH] 154 E3
Zweibrücken [D] 44 G4
Zweisimmen [CH] 70 D1
Zwettl [A] 62 D3
Zwettl an der Rodl [A] 62 B3
Zwickau [D] 48 C2
Zwiefalten [D] 58 H3
Zwierzno [PL] 22 F3
Zwierzyniec [PL] 52 F2
Zwiesel [D] 60 H2
Zwijndrecht [NL] 16 D5
Zwingenberg [D] 46 D5
Zwoleń [PL] 38 C5
Zwolle [NL] 16 F4
Zychlin [PL] 36 G3
Żydowo [PL] 36 D2
Zyel'va [LT] 202 G5
Zyrardow [PL] 38 A3
Żywiec [PL] 50 G5
Żywocice [PL] 50 E3

2nd edition January 2001

Published by Istituto Geografico De Agostini S.P.A.
and Automobile Association Developments Limited whose registered office is Nortfolk House, Priestly Road, Basingstoke, Hampshire RG24 9NY. Registered number 1878835.

ISBN 07495 2977 6
ISBN 07495 2978 4

A CIP catalogue record for this book is available from the British Library.

Printed in Italy by Rotolito Lombarda S.P.A., Milan